Page Numbers of Some Important Tables and Charts

D0023327

Names, Formulas, and Charges of Some Common Ions

Positive Ions (Cations)

aluminum	Al^{3+}
ammonium	NH_4^+
barium	Ba^{2+}
cadmium	Cd^{2+}
calcium	Ca^{2+}
chromium(II)	Cr^{2+}
chromium(III)	Cr^{3+}
cobalt	Co^{2+}
copper(I)	Cu^+
copper(II)	Cu^{2+}
hydrogen, hydronium	H^+, H_3O^+
iron(II)	Fe^{2+}
iron(III)	Fe^{3+}
lead(II)	Pb^{2+}
lithium	Li^+
magnesium	Mg^{2+}
manganese(II)	Mn^{2+}
mercury(I)	Hg_2^{2+}
mercury(II)	Hg^{2+}
nickel	Ni^{2+}
potassium	K^+
scandium	Sc^{3+}
silver	Ag^+
sodium	Na^+
strontium	Sr^{2+}
tin(II)	Sn^{2+}
tin(IV)	Sn^{4+}
zinc	Zn^{2+}

Negative Ions (Anions)

acetate	CH_3COO^- or $C_2H_3O_2^-$
bromide	Br^-
carbonate	CO_3^{2-}
hydrogen carbonate, bicarbonate	HCO_3^-
chlorate	ClO_3^-
chloride	Cl^-
chlorite	ClO_2^-
chromate	CrO_4^{2-}
dichromate	$Cr_2O_7^{2-}$
fluoride	F^-
hydride	H^-
hydroxide	OH^-
hypochlorite	ClO^-
iodide	I^-
nitrate	NO_3^-
nitrite	NO_2^-
oxalate	$C_2O_4^{2-}$
oxide	O^{2-}
perchlorate	ClO_4^-
permanganate	MnO_4^-
phosphate	PO_4^{3-}
monohydrogen phosphate	HPO_4^{2-}
dihydrogen phosphate	$H_2PO_4^-$
sulfate	SO_4^{2-}
hydrogen sulfate, bisulfate	HSO_4^-
sulfide	S^{2-}
hydrogen sulfide, bisulfide	HS^-
sulfite	SO_3^{2-}
hydrogen sulfite, bisulfite	HSO_3^-

HEATH
CHEMISTRY
TEACHER'S EDITION

AUTHORS

J. Dudley Herron, Ph.D.
Professor of Chemistry and
   Education
Purdue University
West Lafayette, IN

David V. Frank, Ph.D.
Associate Professor of Chemistry
Ferris State University
Big Rapids, MI

Jerry L. Sarquis, Ph.D.
Associate Professor of Chemistry
Miami University
Middleton, OH

Mickey Sarquis, M.S.
Chemistry Professor
Miami University
Middletown, OH

Clifford L. Schrader, Ph.D.
Science Supervisor
Summit County Board of
   Education
Akron, OH

David A. Kukla, M.Ed.
Science Department Chair
North Hollywood High School
North Hollywood, CA

CONTRIBUTING AUTHORS

Chapter 23—
The Chemistry of Life
Ricki Lewis, Ph.D.
Adjunct Professor of Biology
State University of New York
   at Albany
Albany, NY

In-Text Investigations
Darrel H. Beach, Ed.D.
Eppley Chairholder of Chemistry
The Culver Academies
Culver, IN

Otto Phansteil, M.Ed.
Chemistry Teacher
Stanton College Preparatory
   School
Jacksonville, FL

Marie C. Sherman, M.Ed.
Science Teacher
Ursuline Academy
St. Louis, MO

CONTENT CONSULTANTS

Assa Auerbach, Ph.D.
Assistant Professor of Physics
Boston University
Boston, MA

David W. Brooks, Ph.D.
Professor of Chemistry Education
University of Nebraska
Lincoln, NE

Doris K. Kolb, Ph.D.
Professor of Chemistry
Bradley University
Peoria, IL

Ross Latham, Ph.D.
Professor of Chemistry
Adrian College
Adrian, MI

Joe Peterson, Ph.D.
Professor of Chemistry
University of Tennessee
Knoxville, TN

Neil M. Wolfman, Ph.D.
Principal Scientist
Genetics Institute
Cambridge, MA

SOLUTIONS TO PROBLEMS
Margaret G. Kimble
Instructor of Chemistry
Indiana-Purdue Universities
Fort Wayne, IN

MULTICULTURAL REVIEWER
Derrick Arnelle, Ph.D.
Brandeis University
Waltham, MA

HEATH

D.C. Heath and Company
Lexington, Massachusetts
Toronto, Ontario

HEATH
CHEMISTRY

Cover Photograph: By showing colored water being heated, this retouched photograph illustrates the interaction of matter and energy. The photograph is for artistic purposes only.

CAUTION: When heating an aqueous solution in a test tube, use a test tube holder, and wear safety goggles and a lab apron. Slowly move the tube back and forth across the flame of a Bunsen burner. Point the open end of the test tube away from yourself and anyone else in the laboratory. It is not safe to heat flammable liquids directly with a Bunsen burner or other source of ignition.

Copyright © 1993
D.C. Heath and Company.
All rights reserved.
No part of this publication
may be transmitted in any
form by any means, electronic
or mechanical, including
photocopy, recording, or any
information storage or retrieval
system, without permission in
writing from the publisher.

Published simultaneously
in Canada
Printed in the
United States of America
International Standard Book
Code Number: 20368-8
1 2 3 4 5 6 7 8 9 0-RRD-96 95 94 93 92

Heath Chemistry Program
Student Text
Teacher's Edition
Laboratory Manual
Laboratory Manual,
    Teacher's Edition
Study Guide
Computer Test Bank
Computer Test Bank,
    Teacher's Guide
Transparencies
    with Worksheets

Executive Editor:
Ceanne Pelletier
Supervising Editor:
Christine H. Wang
Project Editor:
Rosemary E. Previte
Editorial Development:
Ann E. Bekebrede
Fran Needham
M. Frances Boyle
Anne G. Jones
Development Assistance:
Learning Design Associates, Inc.
Teacher's Edition Design:
Reynolds Design and Management
Professional Pages Design:
Lynda Fishbourne
Production Coordinator:
Donna Lee Porter

Writing Assistance:
Concept Mapping—
'Laine Gurley-Dilger, Ph.D.
Science, Technology, and Society—
Mary Jo Diem
Women and Minorities in Science—
Stephanie J. Bird, Ph.D.
Laboratory Safety Consultant:
Jay A. Young, Ph.D.
Readability Testing:
J & F Readability Service
Cover Design:
Lisa Fowler
Cover Photography:
Francisco Chanes/
Custom Medical Stock Photo

Teacher Reviewers
Evelyn Barrett
Science Department Chair/
Chemistry Teacher
San Marcos High School
San Marcos, TX

Hugh J. Carr
Chemistry Teacher
Mount Lebanon High School
Pittsburgh, PA

Robert S. Claxton
Chemistry Instructor
Brainerd High School
Brainerd, MN

Michael Connolly
Science Department Chair
S. Tahoe High School
S. Lake Tahoe, CA

Dana M. Dunnan
Chemistry Teacher
Masconomet Regional High School
Topsfield, MA

Michael H. Farmer
Professor of Physics
Physical Science Department
Greenville Technical College
Greenville, SC

Mary Gromko
Science Consultant
Colorado Department of Education
Denver, CO

Jerry R. Kent
Science Coordinator, Renton
Chemistry Teacher
Hazen High School
Renton, WA

Kenneth Lyle
High School Teacher
Robert E. Lee High School
President, Associated Chemistry
  Teachers of Texas
Houston, TX

Lee Marek
Chemistry Teacher
Naperville North High School
Naperville, IL

Donald R. Parkhurst
Chemistry Teacher
Fayette County High School
Fayetteville, GA

William N. Schmidt
Chemistry Teacher
Princeton High School
Cincinnati, OH

Harriet Spinn
Chemistry Teacher
Waco High School
Waco, TX

Kathee Gerde Terry
Chemistry Teacher
Lake Washington High School
Kirkland, WA

Bertha I. Tomiyasu
Chemist/Petroleum Inspector
SGS Hawaii, Inc.
Former Chemistry Teacher
Iolani School
Honolulu, HI

Chemistry Review Board
Janice H. Arceneaux
Milby High School
Houston, TX

Jeanette DeLuca
M. Evans High School
Orlando, FL

David K. Drown
Bowie High School
Bowie, MD

David Fawcett
Alternative High School
Columbus, OH

James Max Hollon
Evansville North High School
Evansville, IN

Nancy Motsinger
West Mesquite High School
Mesquite, TX

Patricia G. Sharpton
Meadow Creek High School
Norcross, GA

Barbara Sitzman
Chatsworth High School
Chatsworth, CA

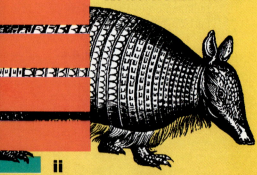

Delivering the Future:

*Helping students recognize the lifelong value –
and excitement – of chemistry*

by Christine Wang

High school chemistry has long been seen as a filter for aspiring science students: Only those who could pass it were encouraged to pursue science further. Today *all* of us need to be scientifically literate in order to succeed in a high-technology, information-based workplace. We need to find ways for all students to learn, appreciate, and succeed in the sciences.

Heath Chemistry makes chemistry understandable and accessible to all students—through careful concept development that recognizes different learning styles, hands-on laboratory activities, and a thorough grounding in problem-solving strategies.

Providing for varied learning styles

To help students move comfortably from concrete to abstract thinking, *Heath Chemistry* links students' prior knowledge to the concepts of chemistry. Theory is introduced only after a concrete basis has been developed. Once this is linked to what students already know, it becomes more meaningful.

Every chapter in *Heath Chemistry* explains why students are learning a particular concept and how it relates to what they have already learned and will be learning. Concept mapping helps all learners understand concepts and solve problems.

Motivating activities

Heath Chemistry gets students into the lab early to do creative chemistry. This concrete groundwork helps students understand the submicroscopic reasons for their observations. Plus, real-world applications to science—such as Do You Know?; Science, Technology, and Society; Careers; Consumer Chemistry; and History of Science—give students a sense of the vitality and everyday usefulness of chemistry.

Strategies—the master key

Heath Chemistry encourages students to turn to problem-solving strategies when they feel they have reached a "dead end" in their thinking. Eleven problem-solving strategies are described in detail. Then, Problem-Solving Strategy reminders throughout the text prod students to recall those strategies and use them. *Heath Chemistry* also urges students to use math as a problem-solving tool. Rather than review math in an early chapter, the text covers math skills right at point of use.

Heath Chemistry sets new standards for chemistry instruction in high schools—standards that promote habits of lifelong learning, inquiry, and independence of spirit.

Christine Wang is Supervising Editor of *Heath Chemistry.*

Contents for Teacher's Edition

The Case for Chemistry Literacy

by Jerry L. Sarquis

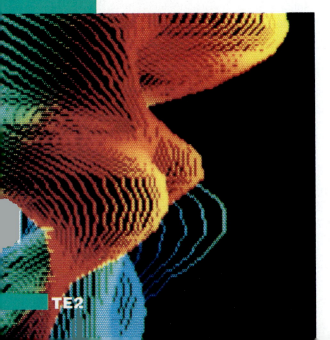

Healthy Disagreement

Science does not provide unambiguous answers to questions. Often, very respected and competent chemists disagree on the interpretation of a set of facts.

In March 1989, for instance, two chemists at the University of Utah, Stanley Pons and Martin Fleischmann, announced that they had achieved cold fusion for the first time. Their report was received with much skepticism. Today, three years later, the controversy remains unresolved, as numerous other researchers continue to try to replicate the Pons and Fleischmann experiments.

People who are chemically literate appreciate uncertainty and strive to develop experiments that will resolve disagreements. — **J.L.S.**

By far the strongest argument for chemistry literacy is the need for scientifically literate citizenry, in which all people—scientists and non-scientists alike—have a working knowledge of chemistry and recognize the crucial role it plays in everyday life.

The scientific and technological issues that dominate today's headlines directly affect our lives. All of us must have a general working knowledge of the principles of science to help us make informed, reasoned decisions on those issues. We need to be conversant in the language of science. We must be able to evaluate where facts end and speculation begins.

The need to make chemistry interesting and accessible to all is a driving force behind the new *Heath Chemistry*.

Learning to think logically

Studying chemistry is valuable because it helps students learn to think logically—and to take the skills of analysis and logical thinking with them when they leave the chemistry classroom.

Chemists are skeptical people; they want to understand, and insist that proposed ideas be defensible. In making observations, careful methods are used; reasoning in chemistry is logical.

Heath Chemistry encourages students to analyze, to question, and to reason—in the lab; when solving problems; when debating issues raised in Science, Technology, and Society features; and when making concept maps.

The value of creativity

To fully appreciate chemistry, students must also be creative, so we must continually look for ways to encourage their creativity. We also want to provide students with additional information, then challenge them to test their hypotheses against that information. To become chemically literate, students need to keep an open mind and consider alternate explanations. At the same time, we must insist on accuracy and respect for scientific methods.

Sometimes it seems that for every question answered, new questions are generated. This is the nature of science. People who are scientifically literate are curious: They ask questions and seek answers. *Heath Chemistry* encourages healthy curiosity in students— in the lab and in its creative approach to problem solving.

Speaking the language

Finally, to fully enjoy chemistry literacy, it's important to understand the language of chemistry. *Heath Chemistry* helps students learn to use the language of chemistry with confidence.

In many ways, learning chemistry is like learning a second language. A language is learned by actively communicating with others who use the language seriously. We should give students lots of opportunities to communicate with us, and encourage them to use the language of chemistry.

In the end, there is one overriding reason why chemistry literacy is important: A real, working knowledge of the concepts and principles of chemistry will give students the power to make informed decisions on issues that directly affect them and their world.

Jerry L. Sarquis, an author of *Heath Chemistry*, js Associate Professor of Chemistry at Miami University (Ohio).

Sequence with a History of Success

Heath Chemistry starts with concrete fundamentals—chemistry in the real world, problem-solving techniques and hands-on lab experience—and builds to abstract concepts like atomic structure and bonding.

Chapters 1 through 7
*Heath Chemistry introduces **problem-solving strategies** as they are needed and develops students' problem-solving skills over time. Students learn eleven strategies in Chapters 1-7; throughout the rest of the text, Problem-Solving Strategy reminders encourage students to recall and use those strategies.*

Chapters 1 through 5
*These chapters build students' **understanding of basic concepts** before introducing atomic theory.*

Chapter 5
*Because **stoichiometry** is such a complex topic, Heath Chemistry introduces in this chapter a useful **problem-solving technique** that keeps students feeling confident: They learn to break problems into manageable parts.*

Chapter 1
*Chapter 1 **develops significant chemistry concepts,** and is not simply a review of math and measurement. Math is taught and reinforced at point of use throughout the text. Chapter 1 also shows students various ways to handle laboratory data.*

Chapters 2 and 3
Students learn to use the language of chemistry and work effectively in the lab. They are also introduced to the periodic table and descriptive chemistry.

Chapter 4
*This chapter features **chemistry problems with real-world background** to keep students motivated. Students are encouraged to use the problem-solving strategies they have learned and to think about the processes they're using to solve problems.*
*   In Section 4.6 students learn about **concentrations** from a real-world perspective.*
*   In Section 4.12 students learn about **significant digits** in calculations and data only after they fully understand basic chemistry concepts and how to solve problems.*

eath Chemistry

Chapters 11 through 13
*These chapters provide a macroscopic to sub-micro-scopic **presentation of the elements,** beginning with their organization on the periodic table.*

Chapter 12
***Descriptive chemistry** is presented with a real-world emphasis.*

Chapter 13
*Students learn to **represent sub-microscopic concepts** with diagrams.*

Chapters 14 and 15
*These chapters present the **sub-microscopic properties of solids and liquids.***

Heath Chemistry

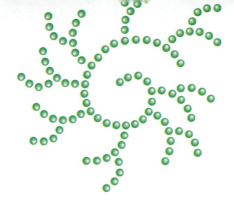

Chapter 21
This chapter presents concepts that can be developed further in the lab or worked into previous chapters on precipitation reactions or solutions.

Chapter 22
This chapter presents the vast number and **uses of organic chemicals** in our world.

Chapter 23
Chemistry concepts as applied to plants and human physiology are explored and developed.

Problem-Solving Reinforcements—reminders to students to apply the eleven different problem-solving strategies they have learned—appear on the pages listed:

The Factor-Label Method **12**
pages 13, 22, 122, 123, 126, 135, 141, 163, 241, 517, 570, 650

Using What You Know **58**
pages 60, 62, 69, 94, 96, 110, 139, 144, 176, 199, 210, 212, 218, 243, 255, 269, 280, 300, 301, 310, 352, 377, 435, 448, 456, 461, 469, 476, 511, 517, 519, 541, 542, 572, 587, 616, 617, 638, 640, 647, 651, 652, 655, 662, 663, 667, 682, 685, 713

Using Similar Problems **65**
pages 64, 69, 122, 130, 131, 147, 149, 168, 170, 172, 176, 178, 212, 241, 297, 308, 461, 517, 570, 684, 686, 696, 794

Using Patterns **100**
pages 06, 110, 111, 168, 176, 212, 301, 351, 371, 375, 400, 625, 639, 647, 684, 716, 719, 720, 744, 762

Making an Estimate **125**
pages 126, 131, 140, 301

Using Calculators **134**
pages 135, 139, 140, 144, 145, 147, 149, 153, 163, 167, 169, 171, 176, 178, 181, 199, 210, 212, 218, 231, 234, 236, 243, 245, 254, 299, 301, 517, 519, 520, 522, 536, 538, 541, 550, 570, 612, 615, 617, 650, 658, 659, 667

Verifying Your Answer **154**
pages 14, 23, 60, 62, 64, 67, 70, 94, 106, 110, 126, 129, 131, 132, 140, 141, 144, 145, 148, 150, 163, 170, 173, 177, 179, 182, 200, 204, 210, 212, 218, 232, 234, 237, 243, 246, 255, 274, 297, 300, 301, 352, 375, 435, 436, 442, 445, 446, 448, 456, 461, 511, 517, 519, 520, 522, 536, 539, 542, 551, 570, 612, 616, 618, 651, 658, 659, 682, 684, 697, 713, 716, 720, 730, 747

Breaking Problems into Manageable Parts **166**
pages 170, 171, 172, 179, 238, 304, 511, 520, 605, 607, 612, 650, 652, 726, 747

Rereading the Problem **201**
pages 203, 346, 602, 696

Making Diagrams **216**
pages 29, 36, 76, 96, 116, 189, 218, 221, 226, 238, 247, 255, 270, 274, 287, 288, 352, 353, 358, 385, 390, 411, 425, 450, 461, 465, 466, 467, 487, 512, 527, 593, 631, 698, 707, 736, 752, 762, 767, 768, 769, 770, 803

Writing Chemical Equations **244**
pages 247, 398, 601, 645, 682, 789

Correlation to Texas Essential Elements

■ Process Skills

Chemistry I textbooks shall provide for laboratory and field-oriented learning in the following:

1. Manipulative laboratory materials and equipment

1.1 demonstrating the safe use of chemical laboratory equipment and supplies
2: 72–73; 3: 112–113; 4: 154–155; 5: 184–185; 7: 256–257, 261; 9: 318–319, 326–327; 12: 422–423; 14: 492–493; 15: 524–525; 16: 560–561; 17: 588–589; 18: 626–627; 19: 668–669; 20: 704–705; 21: 713, 720–721, 732–733, 737; 23: 798–799

1.2 demonstrating basic chemistry laboratory techniques
1: 30–31; 2: 72–73; 3: 112–113; 4: 154–155; 5: 184–185; 6: 222–223; 7: 256–257; 8: 284–285; 9: 318–319; 10: 354–355; 11: 386–387; 12: 422–423; 13: 462–463; 14: 492–493; 15: 524–525; 16: 560–561; 17: 588–589; 18: 626–627; 19: 668–669; 20: 704–705; 21: 732–733; 22: 764–765; 23: 798–799

1.3 practicing safe and proper disposal of chemicals
3: 112–113; 4: 154–155; 5: 184–185; 9: 318–319; 14: 492–493; 15: 524–525; 16: 560–561; 17: 588–589; 18: 626–627; 19: 668–669; 20: 704–705; 21: 713, 720–721, 732–733, 737; 23: 798–799

2. Acquiring data through the senses

2.1 observing chemical reactions
2: 72–73; 3: 112–113, 119; 5: 184–185; 12: 422–423; 14: 492–493; 15: 524–525; 19: 646, 668–669; 20: 680, 704–705; 21: 712–713, 715, 732–733; 23: 798–799

2.2 exploring chemical reaction rates
3: 101; 12: 422–423; 17: 574, 588–589

3. Classifying, ordering, and sequencing of data

3.1 classifying chemical reactions of substances according to similarities and differences
2: 72–73; 3: 117; 19: 668–669; 21: 732–733; 22: 762, 769–770; 23: 798–799

3.2 arranging chemistry related events and activities in a sequential order
10: 354–355, 357–358; 11: 386–387; 12: 400; 19: 650–652; 20: 707; 21: 725–730, 736–737; 22: 761; 23: 791, 801

4. Communicating orally and in writing data and information in appropriate form

4.1 describing chemical processes and interactions
2: 72–73; 3: 96, 111, 115–116; 6: 221; 7: 232, 238, 258–259; 8: 270–274, 287–288; 15: 512, 524–525, 527; 16: 540; 18: 631; 20: 698, 704–705, 707–708; 23: 785

4.2 explaining meaningful arrangements of chemistry related information and materials
1: 32; 2: 74; 3: 114; 4: 133, 156; 5: 168–173, 186; 6: 224; 7: 258; 8: 287, 290; 9: 321; 10: 356; 11: 362, 368, 380, 385, 388; 12: 424; 13: 464; 14: 494; 15: 526; 16: 562; 17: 590; 18: 628, 631; 19: 670; 20: 698, 706–708; 21: 718, 726, 734; 22: 746–748, 751, 753, 762, 764–769; 23: 785, 800–801, 803

4.3 recording and interpreting data on graphs, tables, and other displays
1: 20–21, 23, 30–31, 35; 2: 42–43, 45, 64, 71–73, 76–77; 3: 112–113, 119; 4: 129, 131–132, 135, 141, 148, 150, 153–155, 157–159; 5: 184–185; 6: 210, 222–223; 7: 256–257; 8: 284–285, 289–291; 9: 318–319, 323, 325; 10: 354–355; 11: 363–365, 370–372, 375, 377, 379–380, 382–391; 12: 422–423, 427; 13: 440–442, 444–

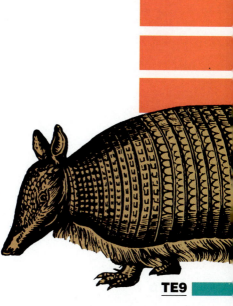

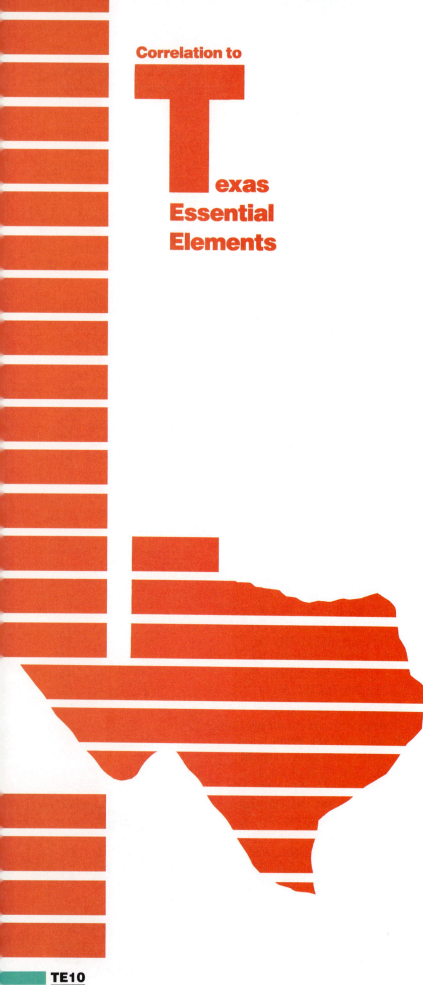

Correlation to
Texas Essential Elements

■ Content Requirements

Chemistry I textbooks shall present content in sufficient depth appropriate for high school instruction. Textbooks shall include content on:

1. Measurements

1.1 units of measurements/SI (Systéme Internationale) units
1: 10–11, 30–31; 806

1.2 significant figures
1: 19; 4: 151–152

1.3 factor label method-metrics
1: 12–13

1.4 density/graphical representation
1: 20–21

1.5 exponential notation
4: 122; 806

1.6 percent error
4: 151

2. Matter and energy

2.1 classification: homogeneous, heterogeneous, mixtures, elements, compounds
2: 42, 45–49

2.2 states: gases, liquids, solids, plasma
1: 7, 27–29; 3: 86; 14: 469–470

2.3 phase changes/graphical representation
2: 41–43; 14: 476–480; 16: 537–540

2.4 change in matter: physical and chemical
1: 25–26; 2: 72–73; 3: 81–82, 104, 112–113; 18: 606–607

2.5 classes of energy
3: 83–84

2.6 forms of energy: heat, electrical, chemical, electromagnetic radiation
3: 82–83; 10: 342; 13: 451; 16: 533, 542; 20: 687

2.7 exothermic and endothermic reactions
3: 88–89; 16: 546–555, 560–561

3. Atomic structure

3.1 subatomic particles and their properties
2: 68; 8: 265–270, 276–278, 284–285

3.2 concepts of atomic mass and mass number
2: 51; 8: 278–280, 284–285

3.3 nature of light and radiation/electromagnetic radiation
10: 331–336, 348

3.4 historical development of atomic theory: Bohr, Rutherford, Heisenberg, Schrodinger
8: 263–265, 272–275; 10: 337–338, 343–344

3.5 present model of atomic structure
10: 343–347

3.6 atomic mass unit and atomic weight
4: 123

3.7 electronic configuration
10: 343–347, 349–352, 354–355; 11: 370–377

3.8 orbital diagrams
10: 346, 350–353

3.9 electron dot diagrams
13: 434–436, 438, 443–457, 462–463

3.10 valence electrons
11: 371–372; 13: 434–436

4. Periodicity

4.1 periodic law
11: 362

4.2 arrangement of periodic table
2: 51–53; 11: 363–368, 370–377, 386–387

4.3 periodic trends: radii of ions and atoms, boiling point, electronegativity, ionization energy/graphical representation
11: 378–387

4.4 properties of specific metals and nonmetals
2: 51–53; 11: 373, 386–387; 12: 395–405, 411–423

Boost Your Students' Problem-Solving Power with *Heath Chemistry.*

by David V. Frank

If you took a poll of high school chemistry teachers and asked what aspect of chemistry was most difficult to teach, it wouldn't be surprising to see problem solving high on the list. Undoubtedly, many students would concur.

What makes problem solving so difficult? For some students, it is a lack of good math skills: It's not easy to solve problems involving gas laws without a firm handle on proportions. Other students seem to have mastered basic mathematics but just don't do well on word problems. And, of course, there's always going to be some degree of struggle when students first approach problems in an unfamiliar subject.

Poor problem solvers can be difficult to teach. What they have learned about solving density problems doesn't transfer very readily to concentration problems, even though the mathematics underlying both concepts is similar.

How can we teach students more effectively so we don't have to start from the beginning each time?

"What you do when you don't know what to do"

One way of presenting problem solving to your students is that it's "what you do when you don't know what to do." This approaches the subject in a broader sense rather than narrowing in on solution methods that apply only to specific problems.

The approach in *Heath Chemistry* helps you teach general problem solving in two ways. First, students learn strategies that can be applied to a wide range of problems:

- rereading the problem
- using what you already know
- looking for patterns
- applying the solution to a similar problem
- making a picture or diagram.

In the first half of the text, eleven strategies are taught. Throughout the rest of the text, Problem-Solving Strategy sidebars demonstrate how these strategies are applied.

Second, each example problem in the text is set up in a four-part framework. Students are shown how to analyze the problem, apply a strategy, work a solution, and verify their answer. By seeing these steps over and over, students are encouraged to think through a problem first.

Your role as problem solver

Of course, the textbook should not be the only model of good problem solving. Your role as teacher is critical. It's easy to forget that steps that are "apparent" to you may not be apparent to your students. When covering problems in class, try to communicate all the reasoning behind the solution. Don't just show a step; explain why a problem solver would want to use that step.

Better yet, keep your students actively involved in solving a variety of problems. Ask them to provide the details of their solutions. Assign novel problems to solve in class, with students working in pairs. Have one partner solve a problem out loud while the other follows the reasoning. After they have worked on a series of problems, ask students to compare their approaches.

Together with the strategies outlined in *Heath Chemistry*, these hints should give your students the confidence they need to be successful problem solvers in chemistry class.

David V. Frank is Associate Professor of Chemistry, Ferris State University and an author of *Heath Chemistry*.

> "It's easy to forget that steps that are 'apparent' to you may not be apparent to your students."
>
> — D.V.F.

Heath Chemistry teaches students 11 useful problem-solving strategies:

- The Factor-Label Method
- Using What You Know
- Using Similar Problems
- Using Patterns
- Making an Estimate
- Using a Calculator
- Verifying Your Answer
- Breaking Problems into Manageable Parts
- Rereading the Problem
- Making Diagrams
- Writing Chemical Equations

EXAMPLE 4-1

How many moles of carbon are in 26 g of carbon?

■ **Analyze the Problem** Write out what you are asked to find.

? moles correspond to 26 g of carbon

Determine what you need to know in order to convert from grams to moles. In this case, you need to know the mass in grams of 1 mole of carbon—the molar mass.

■ **Apply a Strategy** Find the molar mass of carbon from the periodic table and write the information as a ratio. When you do problems, round off the atomic masses from the periodic table to the tenths place. You can write the ratio two ways.

$$\frac{1 \text{ mol C}}{12.0 \text{ g C}} \quad \text{or} \quad \frac{12.0 \text{ g C}}{1 \text{ mol C}}$$

Use the ratio on the left because it will allow you to cancel the units of grams, leaving moles in the answer.

■ **Work a Solution** Calculate the answer from the mathematical statement and cancel units as necessary.

$$? \text{ mol C} = 26 \text{ g C} \times \frac{1 \text{ mol C}}{12.0 \text{ g C}} = \frac{26}{12.0} \text{ mol C} = 2.2 \text{ mol C}$$

■ **Verify Your Answer** Work the problem in reverse, starting from the answer. If 1 mole of carbon has a mass of 12 g, then 2.2 moles of carbon has a mass of (2.2)(12) or 26 g. Check the size of your answer. Is it reasonable? You should have a little more than 2 moles because 26 g is just a little more than double the mass of 1 mole of carbon.

Practice Problems

1. How many moles of nickel are in 25 g of nickel?
   Ans. 0.43 mol
2. How many grams of copper are in 2.50 moles of copper?
   Ans. 159 g

In Example 4-1 you found that 26 g of carbon contains 2.2 moles of carbon atoms. Can you calculate the number of carbon atoms in 26 g? If one mole contains 6.02×10^{23} atoms, you can apply the f...

PROBLEM-SOLVING STRATEGY

*Use the **factor-label method** to help you solve this problem. (See Strategy, page 12.)*

PROBLEM-SOLVING STRATEGY

*Working backwards to the number you started with and **making an estimate** are two reliable verification strategies. (See Strategy, page 125.)*

Example problems show students how to approach problems in chemistry— and encourage them to think a problem through before trying to solve it. Problem-solving strategy reminders in the margins urge students to apply strategies they learned earlier to the problems at hand. After each Example, **Practice Problems** reinforce what students have just learned, with worked-out solutions in the Appendix.

Chapter Reviews give students even more practice with problem-solving techniques. The Questions and Problems section is organized by learning objective, so students can easily see the connection between the questions and what they learned in the chapter.

What to look for in *Heath Chemistry:*

A problem-solving approach that …

… presents problem-solving strategies as they are needed, and develops and reinforces students' problem-solving skills throughout the text.

… develops problem solving as a process that requires thought and reflection, not just rote application of prescribed steps.

… helps students begin to solve a chemistry problem when they don't quite know where to begin.

… provides problem-solving strategies students will find useful not just in chemistry class, but in real-world decision making as well.

CHAPTER *Review*

Questions and Problems

APPLYING A SCIENTIFIC METHOD

A. Objective: **Recognize** *how knowledge obtained from the study of chemistry can be applied in your life.*

1. Name at least ten things that you use on a daily basis that you would not have if chemists had not learned how to change substances into new substances.
2. Give at least two examples of situations when it was important for you to know how much of a chemical was safe and healthy to put into your body.
3. Give an example of some chemical change that you would like to go very fast. Give an example of one that you would like to go very slowly.
4. What is likely to be the first question emergency crews will want answered when they respond to an overturned chemical transport truck?

6. Recall when you disagreed with a friend, parent, or teacher about something both of you observed. What can account for such disagreements?
7. Would you expect disagreements like those suggested by question 6 to occur more often between people of the same age or people of different ages? From similar or dissimilar home environments? From the same or different countries? Explain the reasoning you used in answering these questions.
8. Why do scientists insist that observations be made by at least two independent observers before they accept the observation as valid?

C. Objective: **Describe** *the functions of a hypothesis and a theory in the scientific method.*

9. Describe some regularity that you have observed about chemicals in your home and propose a hypothesis to explain that regularity. (For example, what have you observed to be true of all kinds of soap? What could explain the regularity you identified?)
10. What is the difference between the hypothesis that you made in answering question 9

When a Chemistry Lab Really Works . . . Students Get Actively Involved.

by Clifford L. Schrader

> *"A challenging task for an author is to write experiments that are clear, unambiguous, and safe—without 'giving away the store.' There should be some mystery in the outcome, after all, or there may be no real need to do the experiment! However, though the outcome may be in doubt, the aim of the experiment must, of course, be clearly understood. — C.L.S.*

"Is this what is supposed to happen, teacher?" This is a question you hear all too often in the chemistry laboratory. It is a symptom of the student's desire to get the experiment done, record the answers, and earn a good grade.

It is an attitude encouraged by "cookbook" experiments that are designed to have students verify an existing "recipe" rather than investigate an idea, to confirm a product rather than discover something fresh. These highly structured experiments tend to be results-oriented rather than open-ended explorations.

Structure *does* belong in the laboratory—particularly since most chemical experiments involve some risk. The educational benefits must always be weighed carefully against the risks and the hazards minimized. Ensuring the safety of an experiment requires a carefully thought-out procedure in which exploration is carefully guided.

Freedom within constraints

However, while experiments must be carefully controlled for safety, they can be unstructured in several ways. In an unstructured experiment, students are required to design the procedure, interpret the results, devise a data table, or invent a method for calculating a result—a process as important as the final results themselves. All of these activities demand the active involvement of students and require them to think for themselves. In the *Heath Chemistry* laboratory program, chapters in which students identify a chemical reaction (Chapter 3) or discover trends in a chemical family (Chapter 12) exemplify this kind of active involvement.

To design an experiment, students must first understand its purpose. Predicted outcomes are compared to the experimental results, and the students modify their concepts as required. When the purpose of the experiment is clear from the start, students are far more successful in analyzing, synthesizing, and evaluating data, and in developing their problem-solving skills.

A vital, active chemistry lab has many extended benefits. Involved students develop self-confidence, strengthen problem-solving skills, and develop real understanding of research procedures. Moreover, the interest and enjoyment these students find in the lab carry over to homework and class discussions.

Drawings clarify concepts

One important technique to practice in science—one used consistently in *Heath Chemistry* —is to have students describe their understanding by making two sets of drawings. One set shows the macroscopic changes observed in the experiment, and a corresponding set represents what the student imagines is occurring on a submicroscopic level. This technique is essential for helping students—particularly those who are not comfortable with abstractions—understand key concepts. The drawings also help teachers to recognize and correct student misconceptions.

Dr. Schrader, Science Supervisor of the Summit County (Ohio) Board of Education, is an author of *Heath Chemistry*.

In-text labs in *Heath Chemistry*, which appear at the end of each chapter, are directly related to concepts discussed in the chapter.

In-text labs that are
- *related to text content*
- *classroom-tested*
- *safety-approved*
- *designed to encourage students to analyze and make predictions*
- *focused on real-world topics*
- *performed with easily accessible or inexpensive material*
- *easy to setup and dismantle*
- *designed to provide experience in microscale techniques*

Heath Chemistry labs always provide clearly stated objectives, so that students are better equipped to design and analyze an experiment.

A separate Laboratory Manual that
- *contains all the in-text labs*
- *provides additional structured and inquiry labs*
- *includes microscale labs*
- *includes computer-interfaced labs*

L a b o r a t o r y
Investigation

Household Substances and Chemical Change

Many common substances used in the home are taken for granted. Only rarely do you stop to investigate them or even read the label on their packages. For example, you might have noticed baking soda and baking powder in the kitchen cabinet. Both of these products are used to cause cakes, cookies, and other baked products to rise during the baking process. Are these products the same? Do they give the same results?

In this investigation, you will perform experiments using common household products. Then you will determine the composition of a third common product, Alka-Seltzer.

L a b o r a t o r y
Investigation

Indicators

You learned that acid-base indicators are molecules that can be found in a weak-acid form or a weak-base form. Each of these forms usually has a different color. For example, the acidic form of bromthymol blue is yellow, while the basic form is blue. Because of these colors, indicators can be used to identify the pH of a solution and determine the point at which a neutralization reaction has occurred.

In this activity, you will investigate the colors of three indicators: bromthymol blue, phenolphthalein, and Universal Indicator (a mixture of several indicators). Then you will use that information to determine the pH of an unknown solution.

Objectives

Compare the colors of bromthymol blue, phenolphthalein, and Universal Indicator in a series of different pH solutions.

Estimate the pH of an unknown solution.

Materials

Apparatus
- □ 10-mL graduated cylinder
- □ 24-well plate
- □ 24 toothpicks
- □ wax marking pencil

Reagents
- □ dropper bottles containing:
- □ vinegar
- □ seltzer water
- □ household ammonia
- □ 0.1M NaHCO$_3$
- □ pH 7 solution
- □ solution of unknown pH
- □ Indicators:
  Universal Indicator
  bromthymol blue
  phenolphthalein

Procedure

1. Put on your lab apron and safety goggles.
2. Obtain a well plate and one bottle of each solution listed under reageants.
3. Using a wax pencil, label your well plate to match the data table for Part 1. Notice that each box on the data table corresponds to a well on the plate. The solutions with various pH values and unknown pH value are listed across the top, and the indicators are listed along the side.

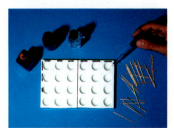

Where Science, Technology, and Society Intersect, Responsible Citizenship Begins.

by Mickey Sarquis

Classrooms that include a Science, Technology, and Society (STS) focus allow learners to see how science relates to them as individuals as well as to the larger world. STS issues represent the social, ethical, and moral side of science. Examining them not only fosters positive attitudes toward science and technology, but also gives students the confidence they need to make judgments for themselves when dealing with scientific and technological information.

An STS focus makes it possible for students to see that science is not a body of value-free facts. Gradually these young people come to realize that the social and cultural values they adopt as they become adults influence the funding of scientific projects and help shape the policies, laws, and regulations that affect the course of scientific development.

Chemistry and current events

An STS program usually takes advantage of local and national newspapers and magazines, television documentaries, field trips, and guest speakers to investigate such topics as energy use, medical break-throughs, waste management, use of natural resources, national defense and space issues, environmental quality issues, and risk benefit issues.

Heath Chemistry challenges students—through special magazine-like features on nine different STS issues and ten Consumer Chemistry topics —to become involved in decision-making about the real world of science.

Mickey Sarquis is professor of chemistry, Miami University (Ohio), and an author of *Heath Chemistry*.

CHEMICAL PERSPECTIVES

Science
Technology &
Society

Food Additives—Food for Thought

If you walked down the food aisles in any supermarket today, you would find many people examining cans and boxes closely. Some would simply be comparison-shopping. But many more would be reading the content labels, trying to find what type of additives may have been put into the food they are about to purchase. The presence of many of these food additives is offensive to some people. They regard food additives as unnecessary and, in some cases, even harmful. Other people consider additives essential for an abundant, safe, nutritious, and available food supply.

Food additives are any ingredients intentionally added to food products by the food manufacturers. As people become more aware of the harmful nature of some chemicals, they increasingly question the need for putting them into food. Over 2,800 additives are used. Some additives increase the nutritional value of foods. Others improve color, texture, or flavor. Still others are food preservatives.

Food preservation is a broad term for any process that slows the normal spoilage rate of food. Two main causes of spoilage are oxidation and decay due to microorganisms. Oxidation is the reaction of natural components in food with oxygen in the air. The browning of fresh fruit and the development of rancid fats and oils are some examples of oxidation. Microorganisms such as bacteria, molds, and yeast cause another type of food spoilage that alters the color, odor, and appearance of food.

Antioxidants and antimicrobials are two general types of additives used for food preservation. Antioxidants prevent or slow down the oxidation of foods. Antimicrobials prevent spoilage by inhibiting the

Science, Technology, and Society (STS) features in *Heath Chemistry* provide students with opportunities to discuss issues related to their lives and to take action on these issues.

CONSUMER CHEMISTRY

Why Popcorn Pops

Americans eat ten billion liters of popcorn each year. How does something as unappetizing as a kernel of corn become so delectable? Part of the answer lies in the starchy composition of corn and part in the physical behavior of gases.

A kernel of corn has three parts. The outer shell is called the hull, or pericarp. The inside of the kernel is composed of starch, or the endosperm and an embryo plant. The endosperm acts as food for the embryo as it germinates.

When kernels of corn are placed into heated oil or a hot-air popper, water inside the kernel becomes superheated, which means it is hot enough to vaporize but does not have the room to do so. These rapidly moving water molecules cause a tremendous increase in pressure on the hull. The superheated water penetrates the endosperm structure under high pressure, and the hull ruptures. When the hull ruptures, the pressure surrounding the starch is then greatly reduced. The water now vaporizes and expands as described by Boyle's law. This change also causes the starch to expand to

The addition of heat sets in motion a series of reactions that change hard kernels of corn into fluffy popcorn.

about 30 times its original size. The expansion is so rapid that the kernel explodes, or pops, and the endosperm bursts out. A fluffy white piece of popcorn is the result.

Consumer Chemistry features motivate students by showing them how chemistry concepts are related to everyday life.

What to look for in *Heath Chemistry:*

Science, Technology, and Society Issues

- *Everyday Chemical Risk— What Can You Do?*
- *Global Warming— A Heated Debate*
- *Radioactivity— Harmful or Helpful?*
- *Strategic Metals*
- *Polluted Waters*
- *Food Additives— Food for Thought*
- *Chlorofluorcarbons— Wonder Chemicals?*
- *Air Pollution and Acid Rain*
- *A Test You Cannot Afford to Fail (drug testing)*

Consumer Chemistry

- *Breath Analyzers*
- *Why Popcorn Pops*
- *Compact Disks*
- *Essential Element— The Chemistry of Life*
- *Colored Gemstones*
- *Practical Uses of Microwaves*
- *Paints*
- *Lost Memories— Deteriorating Paper Treasures*
- *Nylon—Fabric from a Beaker*
- *How Sweet It Is!*

Concepts Versus Factoids:* How Should We Teach Chemistry?

Which is the more valuable currency in chemistry—concepts or isolated facts?

by David Kukla

Students learn chemistry best when they are able to relate their everyday experiences with matter and energy to molecules, atoms, and ions. They use their macroscopic experiences to think submicroscopically.

Think about water, for instance. Water is familiar to everyone. We wash in it, drink it, swim in it. When students understand water chemically, however, they discover important concepts. Water is made up of atoms of oxygen and hydrogen joined together in molecules, and these molecules interact with each other and with many substances that enter water. The submicroscopic understanding of water becomes the springboard for interpreting concepts, like solutions and bonding, and investigating issues such as water purification and water pollution. Delving beneath the surface of chemistry means gaining the ability to interpret and make judgments about real-life issues.

Yet we all know that high school chemistry has long had a reputation for being an "impossible" course. Perhaps it is the emphasis on memorization in chemistry that has turned some students away from it. All too often students memorize the symbols for all the elements, the charges and formulas for the ions, and even formulas for hundreds of compounds—with the result that they barely have time to see the proverbial forest for the trees (in this case, the nature of chemical bonding).

Of course, some memorization of facts is necessary. Students may need to know the formulas and charges for some common ions, for instance. Yet, which students should we be proud of in June—those who have memorized that 3s follows 2p, or those who have seen and understood that chemistry is all around them? The point is, we need to go beyond memorization.

The goal—seeing relationships

Discovering that they can count and keep track of atoms by massing them (the mole concept) is far more interesting to students than memorizing the formulas of compounds. Investigating how they can "train" electrons to pass through a wire to do useful work (an electrochemical cell) is more absorbing than committing to memory the symbols and charges of ions. By the same token, students are better prepared for more advanced courses in chemistry if they understand some of the relationships in the Periodic Table rather than mindlessly memorizing the sequence of energy levels (1s, 2s, 2p, and so on).

In short, there is too much important chemistry to learn and discover for students to be spending so much energy on mental exercises that are already well organized in books and tables. The new *Heath Chemistry* recognizes this, and allows students more opportunities to view, draw, and interpret the microscopic world of atoms, ions, and molecules. By providing a meaningful context for facts, *Heath Chemistry* makes the science both relevant and interesting to all students, not just to a select few.

The word "factoid" is used here to mean a fact that stands isolated from context.

David A. Kukla, an author of *Heath Chemistry*, is chair of the Science Department at North Hollywood (CA) High School.

PART **1** ***Identifying Chemical Reactions***

Have you ever thought about the tremendous variety of matter that makes up your world? Look around at all the different substances in your view. From what you learned in Chapter 2, you should be able to tell whether some are elements or compounds, pure substances or mixtures. This great variety arises from all the many combinations that matter can enter into as well as the tendency of matter to change, sometimes quickly, sometimes very slowly. Matter can combine or break apart to produce new kinds of matter with different properties. When this occurs, it is said that matter has undergone a **chemical reaction.** In this chapter, you will learn how macroscopic observations can help you recognize that a chemical reaction has occurred. You can then put to use what you learned about chemical formulas in Chapter 2 and find out how to represent accurately what happens.

Objectives

Part 1

A. ***Recognize*** the occurrence of chemical reactions by macroscopic observations.
B. ***Define*** energy and ***differentiate*** between its two kinds, kinetic and potential.
C. ***Interpret*** the meaning of symbols in chemical equations.
D. ***Describe*** chemical reactions by writing balanced chemical equations.
E. ***Explain*** the difference between exothermic and endothermic reactions and ***recognize*** equations that represent them.

3.1 Evidence for Chemical Reactions

Studying chemistry can be just like solving a mystery. To determine whether or not a chemical reaction has occurred, you need to look for observable clues.

Release of a gas If you have ever had a cake come out of the oven flat and heavy, you may have figured out that it was because you forgot to add baking powder or baking soda. In the baking process, these substances generate bubbles of gas that cause the cake to rise and become light. You can observe the generation of these bubbles by adding a spoonful of vinegar to a small amount

Conceptual development is an integral part of the text narrative in *Heath Chemistry*. Frequent **Concept Checks** help students evaluate their learning at regular intervals throughout the text. Answers are provided in the Appendix.

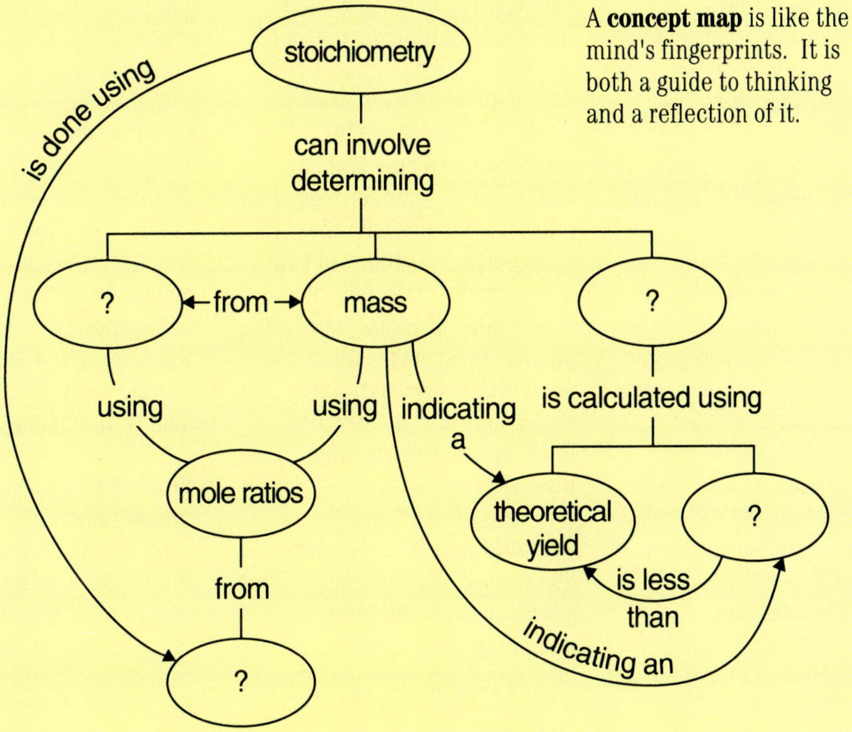

A **concept map** is like the mind's fingerprints. It is both a guide to thinking and a reflection of it.

What to look for in *Heath Chemistry:*

Concept Mapping

Concept mapping *is part of every chapter review. It helps students see how concepts are interrelated. Making a concept map—a visual representation of the relationships among ideas—encourages students to deal with information in meaningful ways. They must think through their own understanding and transfer that cognition to a more concrete form with paper and pencil.*

Making a Concept Map

1. Identify the concepts to be mapped.
2. Decide which one is the main idea. Then classify the remaining ones, from the most general to the most specific.
3. Pick linking words—words that connect concept words but are not concepts themselves.
4. Begin mapping by branching one or two general concepts from the main concept. Use more and more specific concepts as your branching progresses.
5. Look for ways to draw cross-linkages to connect concepts from different branches of the map.

Women and Minorities in Science

by Stephanie J. Bird

*Ellen Joy Kapinos
Patent Attorney*

*Miriam Santana
Electrical Engineer*

*Dave Goodwin
Environmental
Technologist*

Women and many ethnic and racial minorities are seriously underrepresented in science and engineering majors in United States colleges, as well as in science and technology careers. There is no biological basis for this underrepresentation. For example, there is no evidence that the biological differences between males and females make any difference when it comes to interest in and capacity to "do" science. Girls start out with comparable interest and skills in science, and in other countries this continues into college and professional life. The factors that result in a paucity of women and minorities in science are cultural. Science teachers can address these factors through teaching techniques.

Be aware of language and its implications.

Language, images, and references to experiences that portray science as a white male endeavor can cause women and minorities to feel excluded from science. Language used in teaching and in teaching materials can perpetuate sexist and racist stereotypes. The use of masculine pronouns—as in "The doctor tells his patients" or "The nurse helps her patients"— are examples of expressions that contribute to these stereotypes. In addition to the use of pronouns, there are other ways for teachers to counteract these stereotypes.

For example, when you discuss the work and achievement of scientists, make students aware of the contributions of women and minorities.

Provide hands-on science.

It is the excitement that comes with the firsthand experience of the wonder of science that keeps students persevering, even when some concepts are not immediately obvious. Female and minority students' enthusiasm for science can be dampened by the misconception that they are less capable of understanding scientific concepts. When they do encounter difficulty, it is important to emphasize that this does not indicate a lack of ability.

Providing hands-on experiences and extra time for students to become familiar with materials and devices, their relationships to each other, and mechanism of action will help to overcome limitations in experience. It is also helpful to provide experiences related to students' own backgrounds, such as offering open-ended inquiry activities on a topic of their choice.

Promote equity in the lab.

Sue Rosser, a leading science educator, has suggested a number of ways to teach laboratory science to counteract misconceptions about females and minorities as science students. Among her many excellent suggestions are: (1) increasing the time for observa-tion in lab work to compensate for less experience and familiarity with equipment; (2) encouraging both female-female lab teams as well as male-female lab teams since, in the latter, the boys often use the equipment while the girls record the data; or fostering cooperative learning techniques and monitoring the allocation of responsibilities within the team to assure that all team members have equal opportunity to carry out all activities; (3) being aware of how gender might be a part of the experiment, such as in the use of male and female animals or students in experiments; (4) emphasizing qualitative as well as quantitative aspects of experimental findings to counteract the perception that the questions asked in science are narrow and uninteresting; (5) discussing the context of the experiments, that is, how they relate to other activities, other classes, and to society as a whole; (6) emphasizing applications of chemistry and science to technology that include positive contributions to society and humanity.

Be aware of questioning techniques.

In addition to engaging students' interest and excitement about science, teachers should be aware that young women and minority students need the confidence that they can and should pursue their interest in science. Teachers have the ability to either counteract or perpetuate lowered expecta-

tions and negative stereotypes, since they play a critical role in the direction and development of students. As all teachers know, success breeds success!

But, teachers can unknowingly bring societal expectations and values into the classroom through their behaviors toward students. Classroom teachers trained to monitor their own behavior notice what Myra and David Sadker and other researchers have found: that they call on boys more often and generally give them more reinforcement and attention. Teachers tend to ask boys more abstract questions (for example, "Why did the litmus paper change color?"), and tend to ask girls more factual, less challenging questions, which can discourage females from reflective thinking and risk taking. Classroom studies also show that teachers tend to interrupt girls more frequently and allow boys to interrupt them as well. Similar behaviors are seen with minority students. All these behaviors reinforce the unconscious message that only some students can and should do better in science.

Address different learning styles.

All students benefit from teaching that recognizes individual differences in learning style. Cooperative rather than competetive approaches to learning are more effective for females and minority students. In fact, it is valuable for all students to participate in interactive group efforts and to feel that they are able to contribute to such efforts.

Present career choices.

Students often become more interested in science as a career when they are able to see its wider applications and implications. Therefore, it is important to focus on women and minorities not only as science professionals and educators, but also as purveyors and users of science at every level. There is an extraordinary range of career choices that build on scientific concepts and training beyond the laboratory and combine other skills and interests. Examples include art, photography, journalism, and law as well as architecture, engineering, environmental science, and the health care professions. Students need to see that perseverance in science will expand their career choices and opportunities in ways they find appealing. It may be surprising to learn that for students without a solid foundation in high school math and science, the majority of choices of college majors will be unavailable.

Address society's needs.

All students, but especially women and minorities, need to feel qualified to participate in the political and social discussions that affect their lives. The contributions of all citizens to discussions will enrich the evaluation, appreciation, and regulation of the role of science and technology in our lives. Their ability to contribute and to make informed decisions depends upon their science literacy, for which we as educators are responsible.

Explore new resources.

There are many national and local programs, places, and people that can serve as resources both to generate excitement about science and to highlight various careers in science. Science museums and zoos, Science-By-Mail, and science professionals in local communities—such as health care workers, research scientists, environmentalists, and engineers—are all potential resources. *Changing America*, from the Task Force on Women, Minorities, and the Handicapped in Science and Technology in Washington, D.C., includes a listing of several national and regional programs. In addition, the Association for Women in Science, Society of Women Engineers, the American Chemical Society, the National Society of Professional Engineers, and other professional societies can help identify women and minority professionals who could be a resource for your class.

Dr. Bird is a lecturer at the Massachusetts Institute of Technology and president of the Association for Women in Science, 1990-92.

What to look for in *Heath Chemistry:*

Role Models

Having significant role models to emulate can make all the difference to students who are just beginning to think seriously of a career in chemistry. This is especially important for women and minority students.

Heath Chemistry helps you increase students' awareness of past achievements of women and minorities in the field. In addition, several chapter openers illustrate that various civilizations, not just Western European ones, contribute to the creation of knowledge.

History of Science features give interesting historical sketches of women and minority scientists' contributions to the exciting history of science. Careers in Chemistry present portraits of successful individuals at work and help you focus on some of the opportunities available. These features also help you emphasize that a strong background in chemistry is not just for students wanting to pursue careers that focus primarily on chemistry, but for all students who want to increase their career choices. Emergency Response Coordinator and Patent Attorney are only two examples of increasingly novel careers open now to today's students prepared in science.

A Rich Variety of Assessment Options—
to help you fully evaluate your students' understanding of chemistry concepts.

Heath Chemistry provides a rich variety of assessment materials that can be tailored to meet your specific evaluation needs and your students' ability levels and individual learning styles.

1. Core Assessment

The core assessment strategy—Practice Problems, Part Reviews, and Chapter Reviews—guides students to become more independent and take greater responsibility for their own learning and self-evaluation.

Practice Problems

More than 75 Example Problems—worked-out examples of common chemistry problems—are included in lessons throughout the text where they are needed to more fully explain concepts. Each Example leads students through a four-step problem-solving process—Analyze the Problem, Apply a Strategy, Work a Solution, and Verify Your Answer—with complete explanations of the reasoning, processes, and calculations involved.

Each set of Example Problems concludes with Practice Problems that ask students to apply the four-step process on their own. To ensure student mastery—and to build student confidence—quantitative answers are given immediately following the problems, and fully worked solutions are provided in the Appendix.

Students can not only verify their final answers but also evaluate the process they used.

Part Reviews

Each Part within a chapter concludes with a Part Review that assesses students' understanding of the major concepts taught in that Part. Because these concepts are identified in the objectives listed at the beginning of the Part, students get a greater sense of purpose in their learning—and feel more involved.

Part Reviews emphasize student understanding of concepts and processes, not rote learning of factual details and vocabulary. Question numbers that are boxed in the Teacher's Edition identify questions involving higher-order thinking skills—interpretation, application, and analysis. Many Part Review questions also give students the chance to relate chemistry principles to their own everyday experiences.

Some Part Review problems draw on material developed in the Examples and Practice Problems. Quantitative answers are given for immediate feedback and verification, but worked-out solutions are not provided, to encourage students to apply the four-step process on their own. As additional support, Part Reviews include margin notes cuing students to apply strategies developed in the Problem-Solving Strategy features in Chapters 1–7. These reminders prepare students for fully independent evaluation in the Chapter Reviews.

Chapter Reviews

Each Chapter Review begins with a summary, a concise part-by-part synopsis of the chapter's major concepts, followed by Chemically Speaking, a list of the chapter vocabulary with section references.

The remaining sections—Concept Mapping, Questions and Problems, Critical Thinking, Projects, and Research and Writing—are described below. They emphasize conceptual understanding, not fact-recall or simple comprehension. There are no multiple-choice, fill-in-the-blank, or other rote exercises.

■ *Concept Mapping*

Concept mapping (described on pages TE14 and TE15) gives students a chance to demonstrate their overall grasp of the chapter material by relating chemistry terms and ideas in a meaningful way. Because students' maps may vary widely and still be correct, and because maps may be as simple or complex as students wish, students of all ability levels can succeed. To develop students' confidence, the Concept Mapping sections for Chapters 1, 3, 4, and 5 provide partial maps for students to complete. For all other chapters, students generate their own maps.

■ *Questions and Problems*

Unlike conventional reviews, the questions and problems are organized by the instructional objectives they assess, not by "difficulty level." With questions

keyed to learning objectives, students can readily grasp the link between the questions and problems and the material they learned in the chapter. They can also see which concepts, processes, or principles are causing them difficulty and which chapter material to study further.

For each objective, different levels of questions and problems are provided—from explaining terms and calculating quantities, to writing and balancing equations and predicting results, to making inferences and relating chemistry principles to everyday life. Science process skills and chemistry content are assessed as well. Boxed numbers in the Teacher's Edition indicate questions that involve interpretation, application, and analysis.

■ *Critical Thinking*

Critical Thinking questions and problems require students to synthesize information—to form meaningful relationships between concepts presented in different sections of the textbook. Synthesis Within Chapters draws on concepts in different parts of one chapter; Synthesis Across Chapters draws on concepts presented in earlier chapters as well. Again, boxed numbers indicate questions involving interpretation, application, and analysis.

■ *Projects*

Projects provide an excellent opportunity to tailor assessment according to students' individual learning styles. Projects may range from activities such as using a scientific device, building a model, and performing an experiment, to making observations and creating visual displays (such as graphs, tables, models, and classroom presentations); from interviewing a scientist or people in industry, to more open-ended tasks involving student creativity such as inventing a new measurement system, designing an experiment, and developing a plan to address an environmental problem.

■ *Research and Writing*

In addition to extension and enrichment for all students, these activities are useful when assessing students who enjoy reading and writing activities as a way of demonstrating what they've learned.

2.Computer Test Bank

The *Heath Chemistry* Computer Test Bank—available in IBM, Apple, and Macintosh versions—is a test-construction program complete with graphics capability. Over 1,600 items are included, correlated to the instructional objectives listed for each chapter Part. With the test bank, you can construct customized tests to meet your evaluation needs.

3.Other Assessment Options

Concept Checks

The Concept Check feature—found periodically within lessons—lets students check their own understanding. Using Concept Checks as the basis for class discussion will give you insight into students' thinking and can help guide your instruction.

Science, Technology, and Society

The "Discussing the Issues and Taking Action" sections at the end of each Science, Technology, and Society feature may be used to evaluate both students' understanding of the issue as well as their ability to apply factual information to their reasoning. As students answer the questions and participate in the activities, they exercise their critical-thinking skills. Because there are no "right" answers to the questions and problems, all students can feel free to participate.

Cooperative Learning

Many of the projects, research and writing activities, and Science, Technology, and Society questions and activities provide excellent opportunities for students to work cooperatively—each student assuming a different role in the activity and all students contributing to the final product. Make sure students understand that the success of the final product depends on each student's contribution and on teamwork. Emphasize the *total* group effort and result, not the quality of each student's contribution.

What to look for in *Heath Chemistry:*

Heath Chemistry provides a wide range of flexible assessment materials.

1. *Core Assessment*
   • *Practice Problems*
   • *Part Reviews*
   • *Chapter Reviews*

2. *Computer Test Bank*

3. *Other Assessment Options*
   • *Concept Checks*
   • *Science, Technology, and Society*
   • *Cooperative Learning*

Safety During Activities

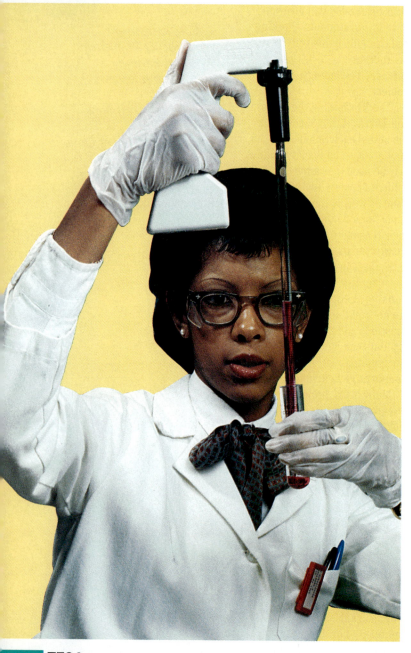

The activities in **Heath Chemistry** are designed to give students an active involvement in the processes of science. Each activity has been developed with safety as a major concern. The activities use readily accessible materials and can easily be performed by high-school chemistry students.

Laboratory safety can only be achieved by constant vigilance on the part of both teachers and students. Be alert to potential danger. Chemicals, sharp instruments, glassware, electric circuits, and fire are often used. By your continuous insistence on the use of precautions, you can prevent mishaps.

■ General Safety Procedures

Safety Rules General safety rules are summarized for you and your students on pages xiv–1. Additional safety information can be found in the teacher's edition of the Laboratory Manual for **Heath Chemistry**.

Each activity should begin with a review of appropriate safety procedures. Pay special attention to the safety symbols used to flag specific caution statements necessary for each activity. Each caution statement provides a brief explanation of the specific danger present and signals you and your students to take appropriate safety precautions. These safety symbols are listed on page 1. Also, be sure to read the safety information provided in the margins of the teacher's edition. Here you will find additional precautions and potential hazards for the activity.

Facilities It is your responsibility to provide a safe environment for laboratory work. Check your work area on a regular basis to ensure that all possible safety precautions are being taken. Equipment and materials should be properly stored. Hazardous materials should never be left exposed. Never keep food or drink in the classroom or laboratory, or in a refrigerator that is used for chemicals or biological samples. Your laboratory, classroom, and storage facilities should be locked at all times when not under your direct supervision.

Safety Equipment Check smoke detectors, safety showers, and eyewash facilities before each activity. Know the location of and how to operate all master shutoffs for any utilities used.

Activity Preparation Before handling equipment and materials, thoroughly familiarize yourself with necessary precautions. Read and follow the instructions in equipment manuals and material safety data sheets, and on labels for chemicals. You should always perform each activity before assigning it to your students. Always wear required safety equipment when performing demonstrations for your students and when showing them the proper use of equipment and materials.

Time Allotment The size of the group working on an activity should be limited to a number that you can safely supervise without causing confusion and accidents. Be sure to allow sufficient time for students to perform each activity and to clean up afterward. Students hurrying to finish their work often become careless and inattentive to safety procedures.

Waste Disposal Dispose of dangerous waste chemicals and materials as prescribed by appropriate standards and the laws of your community. Provide separate labeled waste receptacles for certain chemicals as called for in the margins of this Teacher's edition; also provide labeled receptacles for broken glass, waste paper, and used matches.

Accident Policies In case of accidents, know your school's policy and procedures. Make accident reports promptly, accurately, and completely.

Using Chemicals Safely

Review the safety rules listed on page 1 regarding chemical use. Both you and your students should wear plastic gloves when working with poisonous, corrosive, or irritating chemicals. Instruct students never to smell a chemical directly. Vapor should be wafted toward the nose by fanning with the hand. When diluting acid with water, always add acid *TO* water.

Once a chemical has been removed from its stock bottle, discard properly. Do not return any unused chemical to its stock bottle for future use. Equip chemical storage shelves with ledges to prevent slipping or sliding of stock bottles.

Using Glassware Safely

Broken Glass Examine all glassware for chips or cracks before dispensing to your students. Avoid glass breakage by directing your students to keep flasks, bottles, beakers, and other equipment away from the edges of tables or lab benches. If glass breakage does occur, use a dustpan and brush, not your fingers, to pick up broken glass.

Inserting Glass Tubing The ends of glass tubing are very sharp and should always be polished before use. Warn students to allow glass tubing that has just been bent or polished to cool before handling.

Protect hands with leather gloves or several layers of cloth toweling when inserting glass tubing into stopper holes. Lubricate the glass and stopper with water or with glycerine. Do not force the glass into the stopper. Use these same precautions when removing glass tubing from stoppers.

Storage Make sure all glassware is clean before returning it to its storage location. Shelves in your classroom used for glassware storage should also be equipped with ledges.

Using Heat and Fire Safely

Be especially cautious when dealing with fire hazards. Review the cautions listed on page 1 regarding heat and fire safety. Familiarize your students with the school's fire regulations, drills, and evacuation procedures. You should know the location and use of first-aid supplies and of fire-fighting equipment such as fire extinguishers and fire blankets.

Demonstrate the correct procedure for lighting a Bunsen burner; instructions can be found in the Laboratory Manual for *Heath Chemistry*. When lighting a Bunsen burner, students should wear safety goggles and a lab apron; long hair should be confined; and long, floppy sleeves should be rolled up. Instruct students to immediately turn off the gas outlet if the burner does not light or if the flame goes out. Instruct your students never to reach over an open flame or other heat source. Remind students to keep books and papers as far away from a source of flame as possible.

Give your students only Pyrex glassware to use when heating substances. When students are heating test tubes, always supervise closely to ensure that students point the test tube opening away from themselves and their classmates. Before using any flammable chemical, be sure there are no ignition sources in the room.

Using Electrical Equipment Safely

All devices using 110-115 volt AC power should be equipped with three-wire cords and three-prong plugs. Each socket should be three-hole, be protected with a ground fault interrupter (GFI), and be checked for correct polarity (polarity testing devices display a coded sequence of red and green lights). Instruct students to switch *off* equipment before plugging it into the socket and to turn equip-

ment off and unplug it after an activity is completed. Use 1.5 volt or 9 volt "dry-cell" batteries as direct current sources; do not use 6 or 12 volt automobile storage batteries. Wiring hookups should not be made, or altered, except when both the power switch is off and the apparatus has been disconnected from its AC or DC power supply. Cover battery terminals with insulating tape when stored.

Student Safety Contract

The following student safety contract was adapted from one that was developed by the National Science Teachers' Association. Before being allowed to work on activities, students should sign the safety contract. However, they must be thoroughly familiar with the rules for proper laboratory behavior and safety precautions before signing.

I will
- follow all instructions given by the teacher
- protect eyes, face, hands, and body while conducting class and laboratory activities
- carry out good housekeeping practices
- know the location of first-aid and fire-fighting equipment
- conduct myself in a responsible manner at all times.

I, _____ , have read and agree to abide by the safety regulations set forth above and also any additional printed instructions provided by the teacher and/or the district. I further agree to follow all other written and oral instructions given to me by the teacher in charge.

SIGNATURE _____ DATE _____

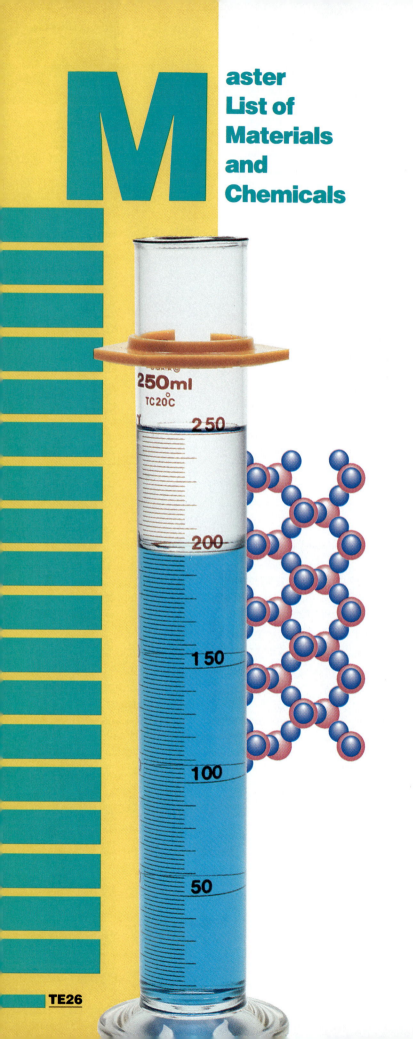

Master List of Materials and Chemicals

GLASSWARE	Quantity	Experiment Number
beakers, 100-mL	24	18
beakers, 150-mL	12	4, 5
beakers, 250-mL	24	2, 4, 12
beakers, 400-mL	12	4, 6, 20, 23
Beral pipets	120	18, 19, 21, 23
bottles, dropper, 30-mL	22	12, 19
bottles, thick-walled with lid	12	5
droppers, medicine	12	6
evaporating dishes, 75-mm	12	4
flasks, Erlenmeyer, 125-mL	12	3, 6, 17
flasks, Florence, 250-mL	24	14
funnels	12	4
graduated cylinders, 10-mL	12	5, 14, 17, 18, 23
graduated cylinders, 25-mL	12	6
graduated cylinders, 50-mL	12	17
graduated cylinders, 100-mL	12	6
graduated cylinders, 250-mL	12	7
Petri dishes, 10-cm diameter	12	15, 20
pipets, delivery, 5-mL	12	17
plates, square	12	7
stirring rods	36	2, 4
test tubes, 13x100-mm	108	1, 2, 5, 18, 21
test tubes, 18x150-mm	80	5, 12, 16, 20, 23
tubing, glass, 6-mm diameter	0.5 m	14
watch glasses	12	4, 7

HARDWARE	Quantity	Experiment Number
alligator clips, with wire leads	12	20
balances, centigram	12	1, 4, 5, 7, 18
batteries, 9-volt	6	20
Bunsen burners	12	4, 6, 16, 18
clamps, buret	6	14
clay, modeling	1/2 kg	13
fume hood	1	2, 17
Geiger counter tubes	12	9
Geiger counters	12	9
hot plates	12	2, 4
Isogenerator	1	9
paper clips, #1	12	20
ring stands	12	4, 6, 14, 16
rings, iron	24	4, 6, 16
Scoopulas	24	15, 16
small light bulbs and sockets (1.5–2 volts)	12	20
spatulas	36	2
test tube holders	12	18
test tube racks	12	2, 3, 18
tongs, beaker	12	3, 6
troughs, pneumatic	12	3, 6, 7
voltmeters	6	20
wire gauzes	12	4, 6

GENERAL SUPPLIES	Quantity	Experiment Number
bottles, wash	12	4
buckets	12	3
cheesecloth	12 pc.	6
CRC handbook	1-2	11
4- or 6-sided die	6	10
6-sided die	6	8
filter paper	24 pc	4
fishing line (nylon)	1 pkg	16
lab aprons	24	2, 3, 4, 5, 6, 7, 9, 12, 14, 15, 16, 17, 18, 19, 20, 21, 22, 23
lids, jar	12	9
markers	24	8
matches	12 pkg	2
meterstick	6	14
molecular model kits	6	22
mortar and pestle	12	2
oranges	6	20
paper or boats for massing	1 box	4, 5
paper, graph, 1-cm ruled	74	1, 6, 9, 17
paper, white	24	13
pencils, marking	24	2, 4, 6, 17, 18, 19, 21, 23
pennies	6	10
periodic tables, blank	24	11
plastic gloves, disposable	24 pr	9
poster board	2 large	1
protractors	6	22
rubber bands	24	10, 16
rulers, metric 30-cm	24	1, 16
safety goggles	24	2, 3, 4, 5, 6, 7, 9, 12, 14, 15, 16, 17, 18, 19, 20, 21, 22, 23
sandpaper, fine	12 pc	12
spot well plates	24	19
stoppers, 1-hole, for 125-mL flasks	12	3, 6
stoppers, 1-hole, for Florence flasks	6	14
stoppers for 13x100-mm test tube	24	1, 5
stoppers for 18x150-mm test tube	12	5
table of radioactive particles or rays	24	8
tape, masking	1 roll	5, 21
thermometers, Celsius	12	3, 7, 16
thread, polyester	1 spool	16
thread, silk	1 spool	16
toothpicks	2 boxes	13, 19
tubing, rubber	6 m	14
watches, with second hand	12	9, 17
weights, steel, 10 oz	12	16
well strips	24	18
wood splints	48	2

CHEMICALS	Quantity	Experiment Number
acetic acid, CH_3COOH, glacial	52 mL	21, 23
acetone	200 mL	14
Alka-Seltzer tablets	15	2
aluminum foil	0.5 m	3
ammonia, household	400 mL	2, 3, 19
baking powder	200 g	2
baking soda	300 g	2, 3
barium chloride, $BaCl_2 \cdot 2H_2O$	25 g	5
Benedict's solution	280 mL	23
bleach, household	20 mL	21
bromthymol blue	150 mL	19, 20
butane lighters	12	7
calcium, small chunks	24 pc	12
calcium chloride, $CaCl_2 \cdot 6H_2O$	5 g	15
candles, birthday	12	3
copper acetate, $Cu(CH_3COO)_2 \cdot H_2O$	15 g	23
copper(I) chloride, $CuCl$	5 g	15
copper(II) chloride, $CuCl_2 \cdot 2H_2O$	25.6 g	18
copper(II) sulfate, $CuSO_4 \cdot 5H_2O$	120 g	3, 20
copper strips	18 cm	20
ethanol	200 mL	14
glucose	1 g	23
glycerin	20 mL	14
hydrochloric acid, $1M$	1.4 L	12, 17
hydrochloric acid, $0.1M$	200 mL	19
hydrochloric acid, $0.5M$	120 mL	5
hypo solution, photographic	4 L	17
ice cubes	100	6, 18
iodine	10 g	23
lactose	1 g	23
lead strips	18 cm	20
magnesium, ribbon	75 cm	12
magnesium carbonate, $MgCO_3$	12 g	5
magnesium hydroxide, $Mg(OH)_2$	5 g	15
magnesium sulfate, $MgSO_4 \cdot 10H_2O$	15 g	19
methanol	100 mL	14
oil, vegetable	100 mL	3
potassium iodide, KI	35 g	15, 21, 23
silver nitrate, $AgNO_3$	0.5 g	18
sodium acetate, $CH_3COONa \cdot 3H_2O$	200 g	16
sodium bicarbonate, $NaHCO_3$	8.4 g	19
sodium carbonate, $NaCO_3 \cdot H_2O$	50 g	4
sodium chloride, $NaCl$	14 g	18
sodium hydroxide, $NaOH$, pellets	30 g	3, 19
sodium nitrate, $NaNO_3$	60 g	5
sodium sulfate, $Na_2SO_4 \cdot 10H_2O$	180 g	5, 15, 20
sodium thiosulfate, $Na_2S_2O_3$	2.5 g	21
starch, soluble	2 g	21, 23
strontium chloride, $SrCl_2 \cdot 6H_2O$	100 g	4
sucrose	1 g	23
Tes-tape paper	1 roll	23
Universal Indicator	50 mL	19
vinegar, household, white	400 mL	2, 3, 19
water, carbonated	100 mL	19
zinc, mossy	100 g	20
zinc strips	18 cm	20

Skills Chart

Developing Skills in Chemistry

A student can more effectively learn and understand the body of knowledge in chemistry by developing and applying process skills as well as problem-solving skills. Process skills are those skills necessary to conduct investigations of the natural world. Problem-solving skills involve cognitive skills of analysis and logic including the application of strategies and verification techniques.

Skills can be developed by having students conduct laboratory investigations and solve problems. However, they can also be practiced and developed when reading the text, when participating in group discussion, when answering questions posed by the teacher, and when developing complete answers to part and chapter review questions and problems.

The following chart provides you with a summary of where skills are developed and applied in *Heath Chemistry*. By emphasizing and reinforcing these skills in your classroom, you can help students be successful in learning and understanding chemistry.

Chapter 1

Category	Skill	Part 1	Part 2	Part 3	Part 4	Ch. Rev.	Lab
Making Observations	Observing	5			27-29	37	
Communicating	Describing	5, 8			27-29	33, 37	30
	Summarizing				29	37	
Comparing	Measuring					34-35	30
	Comparing/Contrasting				28		
Organizing Information	Classifying	8	15		29	34, 36	
	Constructing tables and graphs			17, 23		34-36	30-31
Proposing Explanations or Testing Explanations	Forming hypotheses	8				33	
	Designing and performing experiments				29		
	Identifying and controlling variables						
	Determining main ideas	8					
	Determining sources of error					35	
Making Inferences	Predicting		11, 15				
	Forming models				29	36	
	Interpreting diagrams						
	Determining cause and effect					37	
	Stating a conclusion	8	15	23		36, 37	31
Applying Knowledge for Problem-Solving	Analyzing data		13-15	20-23	29	34-37	31
	Applying a strategy		13-15	22-23		34-37	30-31
	Calculating		13-15	22-23		34-37	31
	Verifying results		13-15	22-23	29	34-37	31

Chapters 6, 7, 8

Category	Skill	Ch6 Part 1	Ch6 Part 2	Ch6 Ch. Rev.	Ch6 Lab	Ch7 Part 1	Ch7 Part 2	Ch7 Part 3	Ch7 Ch. Rev.	Ch7 Lab	Ch8 Part 1	Ch8 Part 2	Ch8 Part 3	Ch8 Ch. Rev.	Ch8 Lab
Making Observations	Observing				222-223				261	256-257				291	285
Communicating	Describing			224-227	223				261					291	
	Summarizing			225-227					261					291	
Comparing	Measuring				222-223				261	256-257					
	Comparing/Contrasting	204		224-227		235, 238	246	249-251, 255	260, 261	256-257	269-270		282	287-290	285
Organizing Information	Classifying											272		288	
	Constructing tables and graphs			226	223				257					289-291	
Proposing Explanations or Testing Explanations	Forming hypotheses		206		223										
	Designing and performing experiments				222-223				261	257	267			291	
	Identifying and controlling variables			225-226	222-223				258, 259, 261	256-257	267				
	Determining main ideas	204	221	224-227			246	255	259-260			274	282	287, 289	
	Determining sources of error							255	260	257				290	
Making Inferences	Predicting			224, 226-227	223			240, 246	254-255	259, 261	257	270			
	Forming models	204	221	224		238	247				270	272, 274		287, 288	
	Interpreting diagrams	197						252	259-261						
	Determining cause and effect			224-227	223	235, 238			259-261	257	270				285
	Stating a conclusion			225-227	223				261	257				287, 288, 291	285
Applying Knowledge for Problem-Solving	Analyzing data	199-200, 203-204	210-212, 218, 221	224-227	222-223	231-232, 234-238	241, 243, 245-247	254-255	258-261	257	270		281	288-291	
	Applying a strategy	199-200, 203-204	210-212, 218, 221	224-227	222-223	231-232, 234-238	241, 243, 245-247	254-255	258-261	257			281		
	Calculating	199-200, 203-204	210-212, 218, 221	225-227	222-223	231-232, 234-238	241, 243, 245-247	254-255	258-261	257			281, 282	288-291	
	Verifying results	199-200, 203-204	210-212, 218, 221	225-227	222-223	231-232, 234-238	241, 243, 245-247	254-255	258-261	257					

Chapter 2

Part 1	Part 2	Part 3	Ch. Rev.	Lab	STS	Part 1	Part 2	Ch. Rev.	Lab	Part 1	Part 2	Part 3	Ch. Rev.	Lab	STS	Part 1	Part 2	Ch. Rev.	Lab	STS
				72-73		91	97-99	115, 119	113		138			154-155			178		184-185	
		77	73			91, 96		115, 119	113	135	138		158, 159				178	189		
		76, 77			79			115, 117, 119		135			156-159			163		189		191
									113	124, 127, 135		151	159	154-155				184-185		
44, 49			73			91	101, 102, 107, 111	115, 117, 118	113	133, 135	141		157-158	155				189	185	
40-41	50, 60	75	76	73	79		97-99	117												
			73						113		141		159						185	
			73			91	97-101													
49			72-73						113					154-155				184-185		
														154-155						
								115, 116, 119		133, 135	140-141		156-159					188-189		
								116						155			181-182	188-189	185	
	50, 60	62, 63, 64	77	73	79		98, 107, 109-111	117, 118						154			178	188-189		191
		76				96	116										178	189		
						91, 92	116, 119									162				
		75	73		79			113						155				188-189	185	191
49		75	73		79		108		113					155		23		185		191
	60		73		78-79	93-95, 96	106-107, 109-111	116-118	113	126, 129-132, 134	139-141	144-150, 153	156-159	154-155		163, 167-170, 171-173	173, 176-179, 181-182	186-189	184-185	
	56, 60	62-71				93-95, 96	106-107, 109-111	116-118		126, 129-132, 134	139-141	144-150, 153	156-159	154-155		163, 167-170, 171-173	176-179, 181-182	186-189	184-185	
						93-95, 96	106-107, 109-111	116-118		126, 129-132, 134	139-141	144-150, 153	156-159	154-155		163, 167-170, 171-173	176-179, 181-182	186-189	184-185	
	60	62-71				93-95, 96	106-107, 109-111	116-118		126, 129-132, 134	139-141	144-150, 153	156-159	154-155		163, 167-170, 171-173	176-179, 181-182	186-189	184-185	

Column groups above: **Chapter 2** (Part 1–STS), **Chapter 3** (Part 1–Lab), **Chapter 4** (Part 1–STS), **Chapter 5** (Part 1–STS).

Chapter 9 · Chapter 10 · Chapter 11 · Chapter 12

Part 1	Part 2	Part 3	Ch. Rev.	Lab	STS	Part 1	Part 2	Part 3	Ch. Rev.	Lab	Part 1	Part 2	Part 3	Ch. Rev.	Lab	Part 1	Part 2	Part 3	Part 4	Ch. Rev.	Lab	STS
				319	327				354-355									410			423	429
	310		323, 325	319	327	336		352, 353	356-359					388-391			405		421	425-427	423	429
		317	325		327				357-358					391	387	400				425, 427	423	429
				319	327															422-423		
301		314, 317	321-325		327	330-331, 336	347	352, 353	357-359	354-355	362, 366-367	370-371	379	389-391	386-387	396-397, 400	405	410	421	425-427	422-423	
304			321			336			357-358		368			389	386-387				421	425-427		
			319						359						386-387				427	423		
						330-331					363						404-405					
			318-319																	422-423		
																				422-423		
304	310		321-325	319		336	347	353	356-359		368		385	388-391	387	400	405	410	421	424-427		429
	310								357						387							
297-298, 304	309		322-323	319			344		357		365	375	385	389-391	387	400			421	427	422-423	
								358-359	355		378-380	370	378-381	390		393-394, 400	401-403	410	421	425		
									355													
	310		322-325	319	327				359	355				388		400	405	410	421	425-427	423	429
		317	323-325	319	327		347		359	355			385	390	387					427	423	429
297, 299-301, 304	310		321-325	319	327	332	337	352, 353	356-359		363, 366-367, 368	375, 377			386-387	400				426-427	423	429
297, 299-301, 304	310		321-325	319				352, 353	357-359	354-355		375, 377		388-391	386-387	400			421	426-427	423	429
297, 299-301, 304	310		321-325	319					357						387	400				426-427	423	
297, 299-301, 304	310		321-325	319				352, 353	357-359			375, 377		388-391	386-387	400				426-427	423	

Column groups above: **Chapter 9** (Part 1–STS), **Chapter 10** (Part 1–Lab), **Chapter 11** (Part 1–Lab), **Chapter 12** (Part 1–STS).

Skills Chart
(continued)

Chapter 13 / Chapter 14

Category	Skill	Ch.13 Part 1	Part 2	Part 3	Ch. Rev.	Lab	Ch.14 Part 1	Part 2	Part 3	Part 4	Ch. Rev.	Lab
Making Observations	Observing					462					497	492-493
Communicating	Describing			461	466, 467	462-463					495-497	492-493
	Summarizing		450		465, 467	463			487		497	
Comparing	Measuring											492-493
	Comparing/Contrasting	442	444-447	457, 461	464-466		469-470, 475	478, 482	486-487	491	495-497	
Organizing Information	Classifying	441-442			465-467					489-490, 491	495-497	
	Constructing tables and graphs					463						492-493
Proposing Explanations or Testing Explanations	Forming hypotheses										497	
	Designing and performing experiments											492-493
	Identifying and controlling variables											492-493
	Determining main ideas	442	448-450	461	464-467	463	475	482	487		494-497	493
	Determining sources of error											
Making Inferences	Predicting	442		445-446, 460-461	465, 466		469-470	482			495-497	
	Forming models	435-436, 442	444-447, 450-451	457, 461	465-467	462-463	469-470	476-480	484-486, 487	489-490		
	Interpreting diagrams						474	481			497	
	Determining cause and effect			461	464, 467	463	475	482	487	491	495-497	493
	Stating a conclusion				464, 467	463					495-497	493
Applying Knowledge for Problem-Solving	Analyzing data	435-436, 441-442	444-447, 450-451	455-456, 460-461	465-467	462		481			495-497	493
	Applying a strategy	435-436, 441-442	444-447, 450-451	455-456, 460-461	465-467	462					497	493
	Calculating										497	493
	Verifying results	435-436, 441-442	444-447, 450-451	455-456, 460-461	465-467	462					497	493

Chapter 19 / Chapter 20

Category	Skill	Ch.19 Part 1	Part 2	Part 3	Ch. Rev.	Lab	STS	Ch.20 Part 1	Part 2	Part 3	Ch. Rev.	Lab
Making Observations	Observing				669			680		703		704-705
Communicating	Describing	645			672-673, 675	669	677		698	703	708-709	704-705
	Summarizing				671, 673, 675		677				707-709	
Comparing	Measuring					669						704-705
	Comparing/Contrasting	638, 645			672, 674-675	669			698		706, 708-709	705
Organizing Information	Classifying	645			670-675			679-682, 686		701-702		
	Constructing tables and graphs					669			698			705
Proposing Explanations or Testing Explanations	Forming hypotheses					669						705
	Designing and performing experiments				672-673, 675	669						705
	Identifying and controlling variables				672-673, 675	669						704-705
	Determining main ideas	645	652		670-675	669	677	686			706-709	
	Determining sources of error		652		678							
Making Inferences	Predicting				672, 674			686	690, 698		708-709	705
	Forming models							681-682	698		707	
	Interpreting diagrams	636	646	662, 666	675			680				
	Determining cause and effect				671-675	669	677		698	703	707-708	705
	Stating a conclusion				672-673, 675		677				706-707	705
Applying Knowledge for Problem-Solving	Analyzing data		650-652	658-659, 667	671-675	669		681-686	696-698	703	707-709	705
	Applying a strategy	645	650-652	658-659, 667	671-675	669		681-686	696-698	700, 703	707-709	705
	Calculating		650-652	658-659, 667	671-675			681-686	696-698	701, 703	707-709	705
	Verifying results		650-652	658-659, 667	671-675	669		681-686	696-698	703	707-709	705

Chapter 15 – Chapter 18

| Chapter 15 | | | | | | Chapter 16 | | | | | Chapter 17 | | | | | | Chapter 18 | | | | | |
Part 1	Part 2	Part 3	Ch. Rev.	Lab	STS	Part 1	Part 2	Part 3	Ch. Rev.	Lab	Part 1	Part 2	Part 3	Ch. Rev.	Lab	STS	Part 1	Part 2	Part 3	Ch. Rev.	Lab	STS
				524-525						560-561				595	589						626-627	
		527, 529	524-525		531					560-561				591-593, 595			607			629, 631	627	
		523	528-529		531									595		597				631		633
						534-535				560-561				595	589						626-627	
		515, 523	526-527	524-525	531	533-534, 542	546-547, 553	554-555, 559				582-583		590, 592-595	589		599					
499-500, 508	509						553													629		
			529								572			595				609-611				
	512-513	523	527, 529	525							575			592, 595	589						626-627	
			529							561	575			591-595	589						627	
			526-529	525	531						575	583	587	590-594	589	597	602-603, 604	612		628-631		633
										561												
508	509, 512, 513		527-529		531					561	560	582		591-593, 595	589	597	607		625	630-631	626-627	
501-503	512-513		527	525		553	558						586-587	590, 592						631		
						534					569, 572, 575	580	586						622	631		633
		523	527-529	525		542		559				582-583	587	590-595	589	597			625	628, 630-631	626-627	633
508	513		527	525	531									591	589	597				631	627	633
505, 508	511-513	517-520, 522-523	527-529	525		538-539, 541-542	550-551, 553			561	569, 570, 572, 575	580	586	591-592, 594-595	589		611-612, 615-618	620-621, 625		628-631	627	
	511-513	517-520, 522-523	527-529	525	531	538-539, 541-542	550-551, 553			561	572, 575			591, 594-595			611-612, 615-618			629-631	627	
		517-520, 522-523	527-529	525		538-539, 541-542	550-551, 553	558			572, 575			591-595			611-612, 615-618			629-631		
511-513	511-513	517-520, 522-523	527-529	525		538-539, 541-542	550-551, 553			561	572, 575			591, 594-595	589		611-612, 615-618			629-631	627	

Chapter 21 – Chapter 23

| Chapter 21 | | | | Chapter 22 | | | | Chapter 23 | | | | | |
Part 1	Part 2	Ch. Rev.	Lab	Part 1	Part 2	Ch. Rev.	Lab	Part 1	Part 2	Part 3	Ch. Rev.	Lab	STS
720-721		737	732-733				765				798-799		805
720-721	730	736-737	732-733			767, 770-771	765				801-803	798-799	805
721		734, 737				767, 770-771			791		801-803	799	805
			732-733				764-765				798-799		
720-721	729-730	734-736	733	741-742	762	767-770	765	774-775	788-789	796	801-803	799	
720-721	730	735		741-742, 752	762	768, 770	765	785		793-794	801-803	799	
719, 720-721		736	733								799		
											801		
		737	732-733								799		
	729-730		733								798-799		
721	730	734-736		752	762	766-771		785	791	796	800-803		805
													805
		735-737				769		782-785		793-794	801		805
				746-748, 752	755-762	767-771	764-765				803		
715	730			741-742, 747	755, 762	767-770	764-765	774-775					
721	729-730	735-737	733	752		767-771	765	785	791		800-803	799	805
	729-730	736				770-771	765			796	801-803	799	805
713, 715-716, 719-721	729-730	734-737	733	746-748, 752		767-771					801-803	799	805
713, 715-716, 719-721	729-730	734-737	733	746-748, 752		767-771	765					799	
		737	733								803		
713, 715-716, 719-721	729-730	734-737	733	746-748, 752		767-771							

Science Technology & Society:

Thinking Critically about Issues

At the end of selected chapters in the text, the feature entitled **Science, Technology, and Society–Chemical Perspectives** informs students about the social and ethical implications of various aspects of chemical technology. For each of the issues presented in the textbook, students are encouraged to gather further information and evaluate alternative viewpoints. In so doing, students find that scientific discoveries and technological advances often have a complex impact on society, and that members of our society are faced with difficult decisions about the use of technology.

Critical-Thinking Skills

In order to form an opinion about an issue, individuals need to call upon their critical-thinking skills as well as their own values. At the end of each STS feature, there are exercises entitled **Discussing the Issues** and **Take Action.** As students answer the questions and participate in these activities, they will gain practice in the following critical-thinking skills:

Distinguishing between Fact and Opinion A fact is a statement that can be proved true by objective criteria. An opinion, in contrast, cannot be proved or disproved; it is a subjective judgment based on a person's values. As students discuss the issues, help them distinguish between the factual statements they make and the opinions they express. When students do additional reading, encourage them to distinguish between the writer's opinions and the facts that he or she uses to support those opinions. Tell them to beware of opinions that are not supported soundly by facts. Also emphasize that a well-reasoned opinion considers all the relevant facts, not just those that are favorable to the argument.

Evaluating the Relevance of Information When people advocate a cause, they may sometimes present information or arguments that are not really relevant to the issue–as, for example, when political campaigns focus on candidates' personalities rather than their experience or voting records. Encourage students to evaluate the relevance of their own and others' arguments.

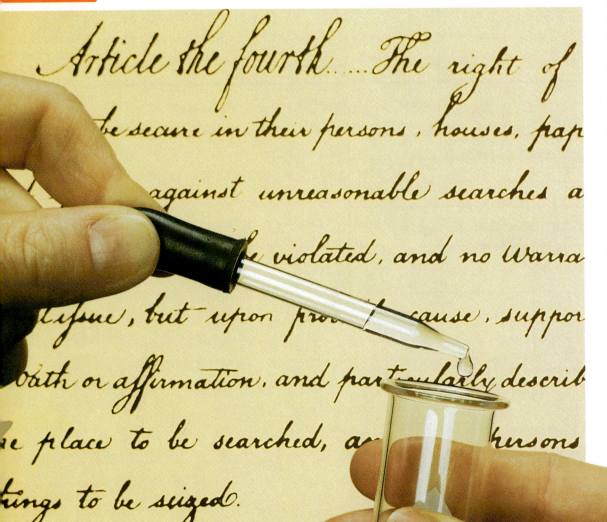

Devising Multiple Solutions/Interpretations

Students learn that many problems and questions lend themselves to a variety of solutions and answers. Emphasize that complex problems usually require many different approaches.

Identifying Valid/Invalid Interpretations

When students are presented with an interpretation of data, ask them to decide whether that interpretation is valid. To do this, they must examine the data carefully and think about the implications.

Identifying Illogical Thinking

Students will sometimes encounter arguments based on emotionalism rather than logical thinking. Ask students to point out the fallacies in such arguments.

Evaluating an Opinion or Point of View

A reasonable opinion is supported by facts and logical arguments. Encourage students to use these criteria to evaluate a point of view.

Making an Informed Decision

Encourage students to take a stand on the issues presented in the STS features. To reach their decisions, students should read and listen to various points of view.

Using Library Resources (and Other Sources of Information)

Students can use diverse sources of information, including library materials, computer data banks, videotapes, interviews, and opinion polls to learn more about an issue. Arrange for professionals who know about the technology and the issues, such as chemists, drug counselors, and environmental scientists, to visit classes and inform students about the scientific background and societal ramifications of these topics. Also encourage students to seek out experts to learn more about the chemical technology featured.

Dealing with Controversy

Before beginning a discussion of controversial issues, consider how your class will react. Some issues may be especially sensitive for your community or particular students. Consider all possible risks and benefits before you approach these topics. Also be alert to students' reactions during a discussion. If a student seems especially uncomfortable, consider changing the focus of the discussion. Avoid violating students' privacy; do not require them to explain why a topic is disturbing.

It is important that students realize that people can and do differ in their opinions on these issues. Use the following guidelines to foster intelligent discussion and respect for different viewpoints:

1. Before discussing the societal and ethical aspects of an issue, students need to understand the science that underlies it.

2. The more information that students have about an issue, the greater their understanding of it will be.

3. Emphasize that students should keep an open mind, listen to different points of view, and be willing to change opinions if new information makes their previous attitude seem unreasonable.

4. Encourage all students to participate but do not single out those who fail to do so or insist that they voice an opinion.

5. Keep your own views out of the discussion. Respond to all opinions in a neutral manner.

6. Allow students to express their opinions freely. Ask them to explain the reasoning behind their opinions. Get students to support their opinions with facts.

7. Insist on moderate, temperate, and rational language. Do not allow students to use emotionally charged or judgmental expressions when they voice their own opinions or respond to someone else's.

8. Encourage students to regard these social-ethical issues as problems that are best solved by a cooperative effort rather than by hostile individuals battling for their own doctrinaire points of view.

9. In general, cultivate a climate of respect, tolerance, and interest in learning and understanding diverse ideas.

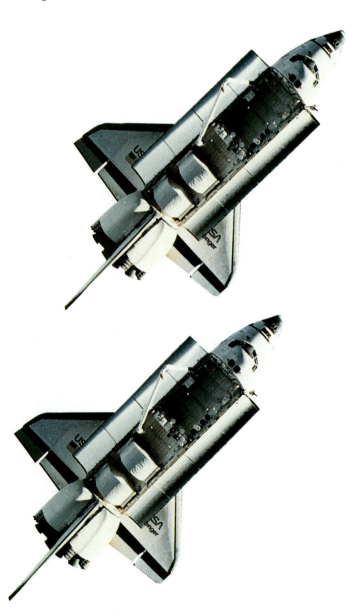

Multimedia Resources

■ Printed Materials

Books

(Individual page numbers of books and journal articles will be noted in the Teacher's Edition at point of use.)

Alyea, Hubert N., and Frederic B. Dutton, eds., *Tested Demonstrations in Chemistry,* 6th ed., Ann Arbor, MI: Books on Demand

Ebbing, Darrell D., *General Chemistry,* Boston: Houghton Mifflin Company, 1990

Ege, Seyhan, *Organic Chemistry,* Lexington, MA: D. C. Heath and Company, 1990

Herron, J. Dudley, *Understanding Chemistry: A Preparatory Course,* New York: Random House, 1985

Holtzclaw, Henry F., Jr. et al, *College Chemistry with Qualitative Analysis,* Lexington, MA: D. C. Heath and Company, 1988

Kotz, J. and K. Purcell, *Chemistry and Chemical Reactivity,* Saunders Publishing, 1987

McQuarrie, Donald A., and Peter A. Rock, *General Chemistry,* NY: W. H. Freeman and Company, 1986

Morrison, R. and R. Boyd, *Organic Chemistry,* Allyn and Bacon, Inc., 1987

Shakhashiri, Bassam Z., *Chemical Demonstrations: A Handbook for Teachers of Chemistry,* 3 vols., Madison: University of Wisconsin Press, 1983, 1989

Zumdahl, Steven S., *Chemistry,* Lexington, MA: D. C. Heath and Company, 1990

Periodicals

Business Week

Chemecology

Chemical and Engineering News

CHEM Matters

Discover

FDA Consumer

Journal of Chemical Education

National Geographic

OMNI

Physics Today

Popular Science

Science

Science Digest

Science News

The Science Teacher

Scientific American

Technology Review

■ Audiovisual Resources

The materials below can be obtained from the following sources:

Videodiscs

Heath Chemistry is correlated to Optical Data Corporation's *Cosmic Chemistry* (sides 1–6). Bar codes for specific selections are included on the appropriate pages of the *Heath Chemistry Teacher's Edition.*

Optical Data Corporation
30 Technology Drive
Warren, NJ 07059
(800) 534-2481

Videodiscovery: *Chemistry at Work; Doing Chemistry*
Videodiscovery, Inc.
1700 Westlake Ave N. Suite 600
Seattle, WA 98109
(800) 548-3472

Videotapes

American Chemical Society
P. O. Box 57136
Washington, D. C. 20037

The World of Chemistry
Videotapes for High School
Wings for Learning
1600 Green Hills Road
P. O. Box 66002
Scotts Valley, CA 95067
(800) 321-7511

Films

Carolina Biological Supply
2700 York Road
Burlington, NC 27215

CHEM STUDY video/film series
Ward's Natural Science
Establishment, Inc.
Modern Learning Aids Division
P. O. Box 1712
Rochester, NY 14692
(800) 962-2660

Coronet Films
65 E. South Water St.
Chicago, IL 60601

Encyclopaedia Britannica
Educ. Corp.
425 W. Michigan Ave.
Chicago, IL 60611

Fisher Scientific Co.
Educational Materials Division
4901 West LeMoyne Street
Chicago, IL 60651

Modern Talking Pictures
5000 Park Street, North
St. Petersburg, FL 33709

The Search for Solutions
Booking Center
708 Third Ave.
New York, NY 10017
(800) 223-1928

Shell Oil Film Library
433 Sadlier Creek, W. Drive
Indianapolis, IN 46232

Time-Life Video
Time & Life Building
New York, NY 10020

■ Software

Andromeda Software Inc.
P. O. Box 605
Amherst, NY 14226

Compress
P. O. Box 102
Wentworth, NH 32282

IBM Personal Science Laboratory
P.O. Box 2150
Atlanta, GA 30301
(404) 238-3000

KC? Discoverer: Exploring the Properties of the Chemical Elements
This and other software programs are available from:
Journal of Chemical Education: Software
Project Seraphim
Dept. of Chemistry
Univ. of Wisconsin–Madison
1101 University Avenue
Madison, WI 53706
(608) 262-5153

Programs for Learning
30 Elm St.
(P.O. Box 954)
New Milford, CT 06776

Queue, Inc.
338 Commerce Drive
Fairfield, CT 06430
(800) 232-2224

Snowbird Software
71A Leland St.
Hamilton, Ontario,
Canada L8S 3A1
(416) 521-9667

Vernier Software
2920 S.W. 89th Street
Portland, OR 97225

■ Other Resources

Chemistry of Toys
Flinn Scientific Inc.
P.O. Box 219
Batavia, IL 60510
(708) 879-6900

Pacing Chart

This text was developed for a variety of students across the United States. You are in the best position to judge what your students are capable of mastering and what content serves their educational needs. In the final analysis, pacing must be an individual decision. The outline that follows is primarily for inexperienced teachers (both new teachers and older ones with little experience in chemistry). It is based on the experience of the authors who have over 40 years of experience teaching chemistry at the secondary level and 20 years of experience teaching at the university level. It represents our estimate of the class time required to teach each chapter and the priority we would give to various sections in the text.

■ Content Levels

We recommend **core topics** for all first year regular chemistry classes. **Optional topics** are appropriate for regular level chemistry classes that have sufficient time to cover the material. **Advanced topics** are appropriate for upper level or honors classes that can handle more complex topics.

■ Time

The time required to teach a topic depends on so many factors that it is impossible to provide firm guidelines. We provide a range of class periods that should be devoted to a chapter.

While teaching the first chapter or two, you can learn what pace seems best for you and your students. By comparing the time you actually need with the estimates we made for those chapters, you can make more refined estimates for the rest of the school year.

Core topics should be covered in the first year of regular chemistry. **Optional** topics are appropriate for regular level chemistry classes that have sufficient time to cover the material. **Advanced** topics are appropriate for upper level or honors classes that can handle more complex topics.

Chapter 1: Activities of Science

Time: 4–5 Class Days

Core: Part 1: 1.1; **Part 2:** 1.3, 1.4; **Part 3:** 1.5, 1.6, 1.7; **Part 4:** 1.8, 1.9

Optional: Part 1: 1.2

Special Features:
Part 1: Connecting Concepts;
Part 2: Problem-Solving Strategy, Careers in Chemistry; Part 4: Laboratory Investigation

Chapter 2: Describing Matter

Time: 7–9 Class Days

Core: Part 1: 2.1, 2.2, 2.3, 2.4, 2.5; **Part 2:** 2.6, 2.7, 2.8, 2.9; **Part 3:** 2.10, 2.11, 2.12, 2.13

Special Features:
Part 2: Problem-Solving Strategy;
Part 3: Problem-Solving Strategy, Research and Technology, Laboratory Investigation, STS

Chapter 3: Chemical Reactions and Equations

Time: 3–6 Class Days

Core: Part 1: 3.1, 3.2, 3.3, 3.4, 3.5, 3.6

Advanced: Part 2: 3.12

Optional: Part 2: 3.7, 3.8, 3.9, 3.10, 3.11

Special Features: Part 2:
Problem-Solving Strategy, Consumer Chemistry, Laboratory Investigation

Chapter 4: Molar Relationships

Time: 6–8 Class Days

Core: Part 1: 4.1, 4.2, 4.3, 4.4, 4.5; **Part 2:** 4.7; **Part 3:** 4.12

Optional: Part 2: 4.6, 4.8; **Part 3:** 4.9, 4.10, 4.11

Special Features:
Part 1: Problem-Solving Strategy, Problem-Solving Strategy;
Part 2: Careers in Science;
Part 3: Laboratory Investigation

Chapter 5: Stoichiometry

Time: 6–10 Class Days

Core: Part 1: 5.1, 5.2, 5.3, 5.4

Advanced: Part 2: 5.5, 5.6

Special Features:
Part 1: Problem-Solving Strategy, Problem-Solving Strategy;
Part 2: Careers in Chemistry, Laboratory Investigation, STS

Chapter 6: Gases and Their Properties

Time: 4–6 Class Days

Core: Part 1: 6.1, 6.2, 6.3; **Part 2:** 6.4, 6.5, 6.6

Special Features:
Part 1: Problem-Solving Strategy;
Part 2: Problem-Solving Strategy, History of Science, Laboratory Investigation

Chapter 7: Predicting Gas Behavior

Time: 4–6 Class Days

Core: Part 1: 7.1, 7.2; **Part 3:** 7.5, 7.6

Advanced: Part 3: 7.7

Optional: Part 2: 7.3, 7.4

Special Features:
Part 1: Careers in Chemistry;
Part 2: Problem-Solving Strategy, Consumer Chemistry; **Part 3:** Laboratory Investigation

Pacing Chart
(continued)

Chapter 8: Composition of the Atom

Time: 3–5 Class Days

Core: **Part 1:** 8.1, 8.2, 8.3; **Part 2:** 8.5, 8.6, 8.7; **Part 3:** 8.8, 8.9, 8.10

Optional: **Part 1:** 8.4

Special Features:
Part 2: History of Science; **Part 3:** Research and Technology, Laboratory Investigation

Chapter 9: Nuclear Chemistry

Time: 4–7 Class Days

Core: **Part 1:** 9.1, 9.2, 9.3, 9.4, 9.5; **Part 2:** 9.6, 9.7, 9.8; **Part 3:** 9.9, 9.10, 9.11, 9.12

Special Features: **Part 2:** Research and Technology; **Part 3:** Laboratory Investigation, STS

Chapter 10: Electrons in Atoms

Time: 4–6 Class Days

Core: **Part 1:** 10.1, 10.2, 10.3, 10.4; **Part 2:** 10.5, 10.6, 10.7; **Part 3:** 10.9

Advanced: **Part 2:** 10.8

Optional: **Part 3:** 10.10

Special Features: **Part 2:** Consumer Chemistry, History of Science; **Part 3:** Laboratory Investigation

Chapter 11: The Periodic Table

Time: 4–7 Class Days

Core: **Part 1:** 11.1, 11.2; **Part 2:** 11.3, 11.4, 11.5; **Part 3:** 11.6, 11.7

Special Features: **Part 1:** Careers in Chemistry; **Part 2:** Research and Technology; **Part 3:** Consumer Chemistry, Laboratory Investigation

Chapter 12: Elements: A Closer Look

Time: 2–4 Class Days

Optional: **Part 1:** 12.1, 12.2, 12.3, 12.4; **Part 2:** 12.5, 12.6; **Part 3:** 12.7, 12.8; **Part 4:** 12.9, 12.10, 12.11, 12.12, 12.13

Special Features: **Part 2:** Research and Technology; **Part 4:** Consumer Chemistry, Laboratory Investigation, STS

Chapter 13: Chemical Bonding

Time: 4–7 Class Days

Core: **Part 1:** 13.1, 13.2, 13.3; **Part 2:** 13.5; **Part 3:** 13.7

Advanced: **Part 2:** 13.6; **Part 3:** 13.8

Optional: **Part 1:** 13.4

Special Features:
Part 2: Consumer Chemistry; **Part 3:** Research and Technology, Laboratory Investigation

Chapter 14: Condensed States of Matter

Time: 2–5 Class Days

Core: **Part 1:** 14.1, 14.2; **Part 2:** 14.3, 14.4; **Part 3:** 14.5, 14.6

Optional: **Part 4:** 14.7, 14.8

Special Features: **Part 2:** History of Science, Research and Technology, Laboratory Investigation

Chapter 15: Solutions

Time: 5–7 Class Days

Core: **Part 1:** 15.1, 15.2, 15.3, 15.4; **Part 2:** 15.5, 15.6; **Part 3:** 15.7

Advanced: **Part 3:** 15.8, 15.9, 15.10

Special Features: **Part 1:** Consumer Chemistry; **Part 3:** Laboratory Investigation, STS

Chapter 16: Thermodynamics

Time: 4–8 Class Days

Core: **Part 1:** 16.1, 16.2, 16.3, 16.4; **Part 2:** 16.6, 16.7, 16.8, 16.9

Advanced: **Part 3:** 16.11, 16.12

Optional: **Part 2:** 16.10

Special Features:
Part 1: Careers in Chemistry; **Part 3:** Laboratory Investigation

Chapter 17: Reaction Rates

Time: 3–5 Class Days

Core: **Part 1:** 17.1, 17.2, 17.3; **Part 2:** 17.4, 17.5, 17.6, 17.7, 17.8

Advanced: **Part 3:** 17.9, 17.10

Special Features: **Part 2:** Research and Technology; **Part 3:** Laboratory Investigation, STS

Chapter 18: Reaction Equilibrium

Time: 3–6 Class Days

Core: **Part 1:** 18.1, 18.2, 18.3; **Part 2:** 18.4, 18.5

Advanced: **Part 2:** 18.6, 18.7; **Part 3:** 18.8, 18.9

Special Features: **Part 1:** Careers in Chemistry; **Part 3:** Laboratory Investigation, STS

Chapter 19: Acids and Bases

Time: 5–7 Class Days

Core: **Part 1:** 19.1, 19.2, 19.3; **Part 2:** 19.4, 19.5; **Part 3:** 19.6

Advanced: **Part 3:** 19.7, 19.8

Special Features:
Part 1: History of Science; **Part 3:** Consumer Chemistry, Laboratory Investigation, STS

Chapter 20: Electrochemistry

Time: 8–10 Class Days

Core: **Part 1:** 20.1, 20.2; **Part 2:** 20.4, 20.5; **Part 3:** 20.7, 20.8, 20.9

Advanced: **Part 1:** 20.3; **Part 2:** 20.6

Special Features: **Part 1:** Research and Technology; **Part 3:** Laboratory Investigation

Chapter 21: Chemical Analysis

Time: 9–10 Class Days

Core: **Part 1:** 21.1, 21.2, 21.3; **Part 2:** 21.4

Advanced: **Part 2:** 21.5

Special Features:
Part 1: Careers in Chemistry; **Part 2:** Research and Technology, Laboratory Investigation

Chapter 22: Organic Chemistry

Time: 5–8 Class Days

Core: **Part 1:** 22.1, 22.2

Advanced: **Part 2:** 22.8, 22.9, 22.10, 22.11

Optional: **Part 1:** 22.3, 22.4, 22.5, 22.6, 22.7

Special Features:
Part 1: Consumer Chemistry, History of Science; **Part 2:** Careers in Chemistry, Laboratory Investigation

Chapter 23: The Chemistry of Life

Time: 3–5 Class Days

Core: **Part 1:** 23.4, 23.5; **Part 3:** 23.8, 23.9, 23.10

Optional: **Part 1:** 23.1, 23.2, 23.3; **Part 2:** 23.6, 23.7

Special Features:
Part 1: Consumer Chemistry, Research and Technology; **Part 3:** Careers in Chemistry; Laboratory Investigation

HEATH
CHEMISTRY

J. Dudley Herron, Ph.D.
Professor of Chemistry and Education
Purdue University
West Lafayette, IN

Jerry L. Sarquis, Ph.D.
Associate Professor of Chemistry
Miami University
Oxford, OH

Clifford L. Schrader, Ph.D.
Science Supervisor
Summit County Board of Education
Akron, OH

David V. Frank, Ph.D.
Associate Professor of Chemistry
Ferris State University
Big Rapids, MI

Mickey Sarquis, M.S.
Chemistry Professor
Miami University
Middletown, OH

David A. Kukla, M.Ed.
Science Department Chair
North Hollywood High School
North Hollywood, CA

Contributing Authors

Chapter 23   The Chemistry of Life
Ricki Lewis, Ph.D.
Adjunct Professor of Biology
State University of New York at Albany
Albany, NY

In-Text   Investigations
Otto Phansteil, M.Ed.
Chemistry Teacher
Stanton College Preparatory School
Jacksonville, FL

In-Text   Investigations
Darrel H. Beach, Ed.D.
Eppley Chairholder of Chemistry
The Culver Academies
Culver, IN

Marie C. Sherman, M.Ed.
Science Teacher
Ursuline Academy
St. Louis, MO

 D.C. Heath and Company
Lexington, Massachusetts/Toronto, Ontario

The Heath Chemistry Program

Pupil's Edition
Teacher's Edition
Laboratory Manual
Laboratory Manual, Teacher's Edition
Study Guide

Study Guide, Teacher's Edition
Computer Test Bank
Computer Test Bank, Teacher's Guide
Transparencies with Worksheets

Executive Editor: Ceanne Pelletier
Supervising Editor: Christine H. Wang
Editorial Development: Ann E. Bekebrede,
    Fran Needham, Judith Mabel, Ruth Nadel,
    Edwin M. Scheile, M. Frances Boyle,
    Margaret Auerbach, Virginia A. Flook
Design Management: Jane Miron
Program Design: Bonny Pope
Design Development: Lisa Fowler, Kathy
    Meisl, Nancy Smith-Evers, L. Camille Venti

Cover Design: Lisa Fowler
Cover Photography: Francisco Chanes/Custom
    Medical Stock Photo

Production Coordinator: Donna Lee Porter
Editorial Services: Marianna Frew Palmer
Writing Assistance:
    Concept Mapping—'Laine Gurley-Dilger
    Science, Technology, and Society—Mary Jo
    Diem
Laboratory Safety Consultant: Jay A. Young,
    Ph.D.
Readability Testing: J & F Readability Service

Cover Photograph: By showing colored water being heated, this retouched photograph illustrates the interaction of matter and energy. The photograph is for artistic purposes only. ⚠️ **CAUTION:** When heating an aqueous liquid in a test tube, use a test tube holder, and wear safety goggles and a lab apron. Slowly move the tube back and forth across the flame of a Bunsen burner. Point the open end of the test tube away from yourself and anyone else in the laboratory. It is not safe to heat flammable liquids directly with a Bunsen burner or other source of ignition.

Content Consultants

Assa Auerbach, Ph.D.
Assistant Professor of Physics
Boston University
Boston, MA

David W. Brooks, Ph.D.
Professor of Chemistry Education
University of Nebraska
Lincoln, NE

Doris K. Kolb, Ph.D.
Professor of Chemistry
Bradley University
Peoria, IL

Ross Latham, Ph.D.
Professor of Chemistry
Adrian College
Adrian, MI

Joe Peterson, Ph.D.
Professor of Chemistry
University of Tennessee
Knoxville, TN

Neil M. Wolfman, Ph.D.
Principal Scientist
Genetics Institute
Cambridge, MA

Solutions to Problems

Margaret G. Kimble
Columbia City, IN

Multicultural Reviewer

Derrick Arnelle, Ph.D.
Brandeis University
Waltham, MA

Copyright © 1993 D.C. Heath and Company. All rights reserved. No part of this publication may be transmitted in any form by any means, electronic or mechanical, including photocopy, recording, or any information storage or retrieval system, without permission in writing from the publisher.

Published simultaneously in Canada
Printed in the United States of America
International Standard Book Code Number: 0-669-20367-X
1 2 3 4 5 6 7 8 9 10 -RRD- 96 95 94 93 92

Contents

To the Student

CHAPTER **1**

Activities of Science   2

CHAPTER **2**

Describing Matter   38

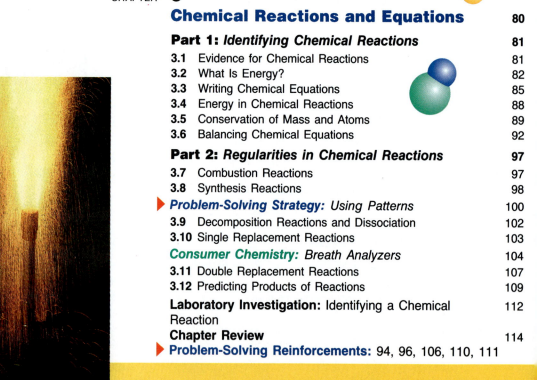

CHAPTER **3**

Chemical Reactions and Equations   80

H_2

N_2

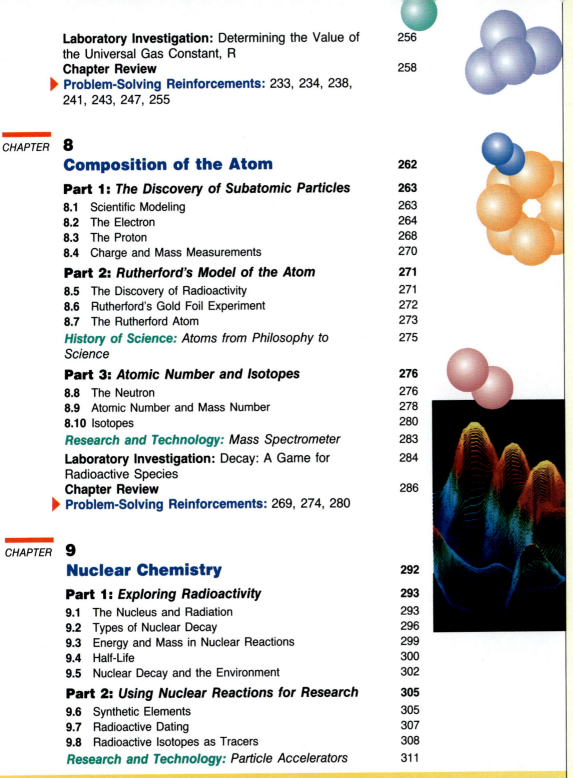

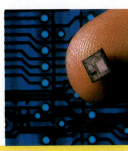

Tix

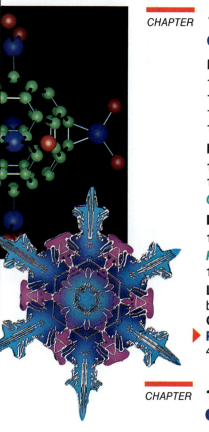

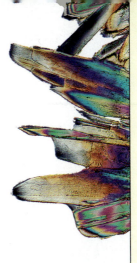

Special Features

In-Text Laboratory Investigations

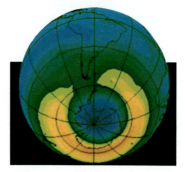

Science, Technology, and Society/ Chemical Perspectives

How to Become a Better Problem Solver

Welcome to your study of chemistry! During the time you spend in this class, you will begin to learn the fundamentals of chemistry. For many of you, this subject will provide a foundation for further studies in science or in science-related fields. Engineers, nurses, dental hygienists, biologists, environmental scientists, and—yes—even chemists are just a few of the professionals who must have a basic knowledge of chemistry in order to perform their jobs. Even if you are planning a career that does not require chemistry, you will find that learning about matter will help you understand better what is happening in the world around you.

Glance through the pages of this book. It would be hard to miss the emphasis on problem solving. Example problems and practice problems appear throughout the chapters; review problems follow each of the chapter parts; the Chapter Review sections contain multiple questions and problems for you to solve. Clearly, problem solving will be an important part of your chemistry course. But there is no need to worry; this book offers ample assistance in helping you become a better problem solver.

▶ Problem Solving in Chemistry

It has been said that "problem solving is what you do when you don't know what to do." This is certainly true when you encounter a problem unlike any you have solved before. This book includes the resources you will need to learn how to solve chemistry problems. As you learn new concepts, you will find that this book provides more than simple definitions. Background information will help you understand how a new concept fits in with other ideas you already have. You will see several examples, often coming from everyday life, to illustrate the new concepts. You also will learn how to view concepts from a chemist's standpoint, by imagining on a submicroscopic level the behavior of atoms and molecules. Making drawings to represent the submicroscopic level will become a useful problem-solving tool for you. Pay attention to these resources throughout the book. When you can make chemistry concepts seem as familiar to you as everyday objects, you will find that problem solving has been simplified for you.

The example problems throughout the book will help you learn to solve chemistry problems. The examples have been written with the understanding that you are not yet an expert in chemistry. Detailed solutions are provided to help you understand the problem one step at a time. When you study the example problems, try to understand the

xviii

strategies that are used. You may pick up some ideas from these examples of "what to do when you don't know what to do" in later problems.

▶ Problem-Solving Features

There are several special features in this book to help you become a better problem solver. Look at an Example Problem on page 13. The solution is divided into four sections. The first section, **Analyze the Problem,** helps you find the relevant information in the problem. What exactly is the problem asking? What information is provided that will help you find an answer to the problem? In **Apply a Strategy,** you will be given some hints about how you can use the information. What relationships do you need to use to transform the given information into the information asked for in the problem? How can you go about making these transformations? **Work a Solution** gives you step-by-step help in finding the solution by using the strategy that was just developed. Finally, **Verify Your Answer** helps you take another look at your solution. How do you know that your answer to a problem is correct? What steps can you take to check your answer?

▶ Problem-Solving Strategies

The example problems within the chapters will give you practice in solving specific problems. However, in order to become a truly successful problem solver, you will need to employ some general problem-solving strategies. This book contains a series of special features that can be applied to a wide range of problems. In the first seven chapters of this book, you will find a special feature, **Problem-Solving Strategies.** Each feature will help you focus on one general strategy—for example, breaking a problem into simpler parts or writing a chemical equation to help solve a problem. These strategies are introduced near an example that makes use of them. You can see how the strategy is applied by working the accompanying example.

> ### PROBLEM-SOLVING
> # STRATEGY
>
> *You can **identify patterns** by organizing your work as you solve Question 22. Compare your solutions with those of a classmate. How are your solutions similar? How do they differ? (See Strategy, page 100.)*

These problem-solving strategies are meant to be general ones, that is, they can be applied over and over again as you encounter problems throughout the book. To highlight where to apply a strategy, a sidebar feature labeled **Problem-Solving Strategy** can be found in the margin next to many of the worked-out examples in the book. Most of these sidebars refer directly to a strategy that was described in more detail in previous chapters. Not only do

xix

they point out where a general strategy is being applied in a specific problem, but they also include a page reference if you want more information about that strategy. Some of the problem-solving strategies that you will learn are so general that you may also make use of them when you carry out investigations and devise models to interpret their results.

▶ Developing Your Own Problem-Solving Skills

All the information in a textbook won't help you solve problems unless you put in your own effort. You cannot become a better problem solver just by reading and watching your teacher solve examples. Here are some steps that you can take to improve your problem-solving skills.

1. Become actively involved in the solution of example problems. Don't just read a sample. Pull out a piece of paper and a pencil and work through the example after you read it. If your teacher is working a problem in class, be constantly thinking about the steps that you would use to solve it. Be ready to volunteer your ideas if you are asked!

2. Work all the problems that you are assigned. You will become a better problem solver as you practice. On the other hand, don't be afraid to abandon a problem temporarily if it is taking you an extraordinary amount of time. Sometimes a bit of a rest can help you to refocus your thoughts, and you may be better prepared to complete a solution.

3. Work problems with a partner. There are a variety of ways to do this. You could work together on a given problem so that each partner contributes to the overall solution. Or you could work together so that one

partner is the solver and the other is the listener. If you are the listener, ask your partner to say aloud everything that he or she does to solve the problem. Thinking aloud will help your partner pay closer attention to each of the steps in the solution. When your partner has finished solving the problem or cannot finish it, you might want to volunteer your ideas about the solution. Exchange roles, so that each person can be the solver and the listener.

4. When you are stuck on a problem, ask for specific help. Don't just go to your teacher or to a classmate, asking, "Can you show me how to work this problem?" You will learn very little about problem solving by using this approach. Instead, work as far as you can and explain what you know about the problem. Then see if your teacher or your classmate can provide you with a hint to complete the solution yourself.

If you use these suggestions in conjunction with what you already know, you will be well on your way to becoming a good problem solver. Good luck to you as you embark on your chemistry adventure!

Concept Mapping

A Study Technique for Success

How do you study? Do you reread a chapter over and over the night before a test, hoping you will remember all the information the next day? Do you take notes and try to memorize them? Or do you perhaps make flash cards of the information and quiz yourself? If your study method is one of the methods described, you are learning by rote memorization. When you learn by rote memorization, information is stored in your short-term memory. Often this kind of learning lasts only a short time.

Learning information so that you can remember it longer and use it to solve problems involves getting that information into your long-term memory. Does your method of studying help you transfer information from short-term memory to long-term memory? Does your method of studying help you find relationships between ideas you are learning? Most methods do not. Making a concept, or idea, map does.

Processing Information

Making a concept map is based on how you process or remember information. Quickly read the sentences below. Then cover up the sentences and take the miniquiz that immediately follows.

1. Nick walked on the roof.
2. George chopped down the tree.
3. Chris sailed the boat.
4. Ben flew the kite.

Miniquiz:

1. Who chopped down the tree?
2. Who walked on the roof?
3. Who flew the kite?
4. Who sailed the boat?

You probably did fairly well on the quiz because deep in your long-term memory you know about Santa "St. Nick" Claus, George Washington, Christopher Columbus, and Benjamin Franklin. Now look at this list of words. Read it over slowly for about 20 seconds and then cover up the words. Recall as many as you can.

black	sweater	brown	shirt
cinnamon	dove	gloves	green
canary	garlic	parrot	pepper

Look at this second list of words and again memorize as many as you can in 20 seconds.

vanilla	yellow	horse	desk
chocolate	red	camel	table
strawberry	green	elephant	chair

Which list was easier to remember? The second list was easier to remember because the words are grouped. The grouping, or categories, linked words together and helped you remember them. For example, the category *flavors* helped you remember *vanilla, chocolate,* and *straw-*

xxi

berry. Grouping words also reduces how much information you must memorize. For example, by using what's in your long-term memory and recognizing 4 groups in the list, you could more easily memorize 12 concepts.

You can also look at groups of terms and give them a name that represents their main idea. For example, math, science, English, history, and art are all school subjects. The main idea for that group of items is *school subjects*. Try to find the main idea for these terms.

Canada, Germany, Mexico, United States, and France are _____.

The banjo, guitar, violin, piano, and drum are _____.

Soccer, basketball, baseball, track, gymnastics, and swimming are _____.

Concept Mapping

Concept mapping helps you figure out the main ideas in a piece of reading material. A concept map can also help you understand that ideas have meanings because they are connected to other ideas. For example, when you define a pencil as a writing utensil, you have linked the idea, or concept, of *pencil* to the ideas of *writing* and *utensil*.

Look at the following words.

car	tree	raining	thundering
dog	cloud	playing	thinking

All of these words are concepts because they cause a picture to form in your mind. Are the following words concept words?

are	when	the	with
where	then	is	to

No. These are linkage words. They connect, or link, concept words together. In a concept map, words that are concepts go in circles or boxes, and words that link the concepts go on a line connecting the circles or boxes.

How is making a concept map different from note-taking or making an outline? If you outlined pages 39–46 it might look like this.

Outline

I. Matter
  A. Mixtures
    1. Some are solutions
    2. Separated by distillation
    3. Separation represents a physical change
  B. Pure Substances
    1. Separated by decomposition
    2. Can be compounds or elements
    3. Separation represents a chemical change

Now look back at pages 39–46. Would you want to reread those pages over again, trying to learn all of that information for a test? Would you prefer the slightly shorter outline? Or would you rather study a concept map like the one shown especially if you had made it yourself? If you made the map, your long-term memory would already *know* parts of that map. Reviewing the map would make studying easier.

How to Make a Concept Map

First identify the main concepts by writing them in a list. Then put each separate concept from your list on a small piece of paper. You will not have to use this paper technique once you make a few maps, but it is helpful at first. Remember, your list shows how the concepts appeared in the reading, but this need not represent how *you* link the concepts. The next step is to put the concepts in order from most general to most specific. Examples are "most specific" and will go at the bottom.

Now begin to rearrange the concepts you have written on the pieces of paper on a table or desktop. Start with the most general main idea. If that main idea can be broken down into two or more equal concepts, place those concepts on the same line. Continue to do this until all the concepts have been laid out.

Use lines to connect the concepts. Write a statement on the line that tells why the concepts are connected. Do this for all the lines connecting the concepts.

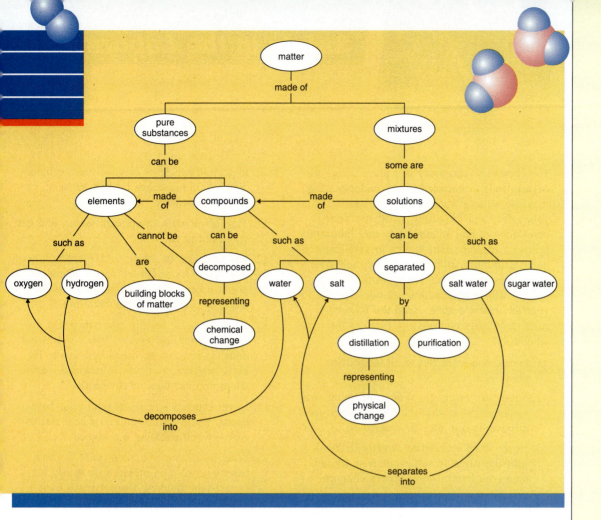

Do not expect your map to be exactly like anyone else's map. Everyone thinks a little differently and will see different relationships between certain concepts. Practice is the key to good concept mapping. Here are some points to remember as you get started.

1. A concept map does not have to be symmetrical. It can be lopsided or have more concepts on the right side than on the left.

2. Remember that a concept map is a shortcut for representing information. Do not add anything but concepts and links.

3. There is no one perfect or correct map for a set of concepts. Errors in a concept map occur only if links between concepts are incorrect.

Getting Started

Even by concept mapping old and familiar material, you can recognize new relationships and meanings. The best thing you can do is to choose a topic you know a lot about—stereos, baseball cards, music, or sports, for example. Use one of these or some other topic as your main idea at the top of a concept map and branch out into subtopics. Begin to break it down from more general to more specific ideas. Follow the guidelines given in this feature to help you as you start to map. You'll probably be quite successful with this, and it will give you encouragement and confidence to concept map new material in your text.

xxiii

The chemistry laboratory is a place where discovery leads to knowledge and understanding. It is also a place where caution is essential for your safety and the safety of others. Your knowledge of and adherence to safe laboratory practices are important factors in avoiding accidents. The information below describes some basic rules for safe laboratory work. Your teacher will provide additional rules specific to your laboratory setting. Read the following rules thoroughly and observe them in the laboratory.

1. Locate and learn to use all laboratory safety equipment.

2. Never eat, drink, chew gum, or apply cosmetics in the laboratory. Do not store food or beverages in the lab area.

3. Never smell a chemical directly; instead waft the vapor toward your nose by fanning your hand. Never taste a chemical.

4. Never force or twist glass tubing into a stopper. Protect both hands with cloth pads when inserting or removing glass tubing.

5. Never reach over a flame or heat source. Keep hair and clothing away from flames.

6. Never do an investigation without your teacher's supervision.

7. Read all parts of an investigation before you begin work. Follow your teacher's directions completely.

8. Never run, push, play, or fool around in the laboratory.

9. Keep your work area clean and uncluttered. Store items such as books and purses in designated areas. Keep glassware and containers of chemicals away from the edges of your lab bench.

10. Report all accidents to your teacher immediately. Do not touch broken, cracked, or chipped glassware.

11. Turn off electric equipment, water, and gas when not in use.

12. Pay attention to safety **CAUTIONS.** Wear safety goggles and a lab apron whenever you use heat, chemicals, solutions, glassware, or other dangerous materials.

13. Dress properly for the laboratory. Do not wear loose-fitting sleeves, bulky outerwear, dangling jewelry, or open-toed shoes. Tie back long hair and tuck in ties and scarves when you use heat or chemicals.

14. Never touch a hot object with your bare hands. Use a clamp, tongs, or heat-resistant gloves when handling hot objects.

15. When heating a test tube, point it away from yourself and others. Use sturdy tongs or test-tube holders. Do not reach over a flame.

16. Use care in handling electrical equipment. Do not touch electrical equipment with wet hands or use it near water. Check for frayed cords, loose connections, or broken wires. Use only equipment with three-pronged plugs. Make sure cords do not dangle from work tables. Disconnect appliances from outlets by pulling on the plug, not on the cord.

17. Use flammable chemicals only after ensuring that there are no flames anywhere in the laboratory.

18. Use care when working with chemicals. Keep all chemicals away from your face and off your skin. Keep your hands away from your face while working with chemi-

cals. If a chemical gets in your eyes or on your skin or clothing, wash it off immediately with plenty of water. Tell your teacher what happened.

19. Do not return any unused chemical to its bottle. Follow your teacher's directions for disposal of chemicals, used matches, filter papers, and other materials. Do not discard solid chemicals, chemical solutions, matches, papers, or any such substances in the sink.

20. Always clean your equipment and work space after you finish an investigation. Always wash your hands with soap and water before leaving the laboratory.

Safety in the Laboratory

Throughout the investigations in *Heath Chemistry,* you will see a variety of symbols relating to safe laboratory procedures. These symbols and their meanings are shown below. Study the information and become familiar with all **CAUTIONS** in an investigation before you begin your work.

Wear safety goggles and lab aprons. Investigation involves chemicals, hot materials, lab burners, or possibility of broken glass.

Danger of chemical splashes exists. Wear a face shield to protect face in addition to safety goggles to protect eyes.

Danger of cuts exists. Investigation involves scissors, wire cutters, pins, or other sharp instruments. Handle with care.

Investigation involves hot plates, lab burners, lighted matches, or flammable liquids with explosive vapors.

Investigation involves chemicals that are very poisonous. Avoid spills. Avoid touching chemicals directly.

Investigation involves handling irritating or corrosive chemicals. Use plastic gloves to handle corrosive chemicals.

Investigation involves use of corrosive or irritating chemicals. In case of a spill, wash skin and clothes thoroughly with plenty of water and call your teacher.

Investigation involves reagents that have dangerous fumes. Do your work under a fume hood.

Investigation involves use of electrical equipment, such as electric lamps and hot plates.

Investigation involves using radioactive materials. Use tongs to handle samples. Follow directions of your teacher.

The triangle alerts you to additional, specific safety procedures in an investi- gation. Always discuss safety CAUTIONS with your teacher before you begin work.

1

Activities of Science

Investigations	Demonstrations	Texas Essential Elements★
Laboratory Manual 1–1 S		**Process:** 10.1
		Content: 1.1, 1.3, 2.2, 13.4 **Process:** 10.1, 10.2, 10.4
Laboratory Manual 1–3 S In-text Investigation, page T30		**Content:** 1.2, 1.4 **Process:** 4.3, 5.2
Laboratory Manual 1–2 M Laboratory Manual 1–4 IM Laboratory Manual 1–5 I	Chemical Changes, page T25 Gases, page T27	**Content:** 2.2, 2.4, 8.1 **Process:** 7.2, 9.1, 9.2, 10.1, 10.2
		Content: 1.1 **Process:** 1.2, 4.3, 5.1, 5.2, 6.1
		Process: 4.2, 4.3, 5.2, 7.1, 7.2, 10.1, 10.2, 10.3, 10.4
KEY: **M**–Microscale **S**–Structured **I**–Inquiry **IM**–Inquiry Microscale		★See pages T8–T11 for complete listing of Texas Essential Elements.

Activities of Science

1

Chapter Rationale

Chapter 1 introduces students to the nature of chemistry and the processes of science. Measurement and graphing are included in this chapter in order to develop some basic skills students need for working in the laboratory. Scientific notation appears in the Appendix and significant digits are integrated into a later chapter. If you prefer to teach these topics with this chapter, refer to Appendix A (scientific notation) and Section 4.12 (significant digits).

About the Photograph

Lobsters turn red as a result of a simple chemical reaction. A carotenoid pigment known as *astaxanthin* ($C_{40}H_{52}O_4$) in the shells of lobsters and other crustaceans changes from blue or green to red when heated.

Chapter Planning Hints

Plan to complete the chapter, including the Laboratory Investigation and the Chapter Review, in four to five class sessions. Some students may need individual tutoring for Part 3. To introduce measuring in Part 1, you may wish to obtain the videotape *Measurement* from the series The World of Chemistry. The address is listed at the front of the Teacher's Edition. You may also wish to obtain the article "Physical Versus Chemical Change" in the *Journal of Chemical Education*, February, 1970, for use when introducing Part 4. You will find two optional demonstrations suggested for this chapter on pages T25 and T27. You may wish to preview them at this time.

Overview

A knowledge of chemistry can help you answer the question—What causes a lobster to turn red when it is heated?

PART **1** Applying a Scientific Method

Science is a way of gaining knowledge, but it is only one way of knowing. Religion and philosophy are other ways of knowing—ways that contributed much to civilization before science was developed. These fields continue to contribute to today's body of knowledge. Science, religion, philosophy, literature, art, and other fields of study contribute different kinds of knowledge and use different techniques. Today you need to know the problem-solving techniques that are used in science, in order to make informed decisions about how science will affect your life.

1.1 Questions Chemistry Tries to Answer

Most chemical knowledge revolves around answering just a few questions. In this course, you will learn scientific problem-solving techniques to try to answer these questions.

What is this matter that I have? How can you tell whether a clear, colorless liquid is water that you need to survive, alcohol that can dull your senses to the point that you do not care to survive, or sulfuric acid that can injure you to the point of not surviving? How can you determine whether there is mercury or asbestos in the water you drink, enough protein in your food for good health, or enough phosphorus in the soil to grow corn?

Chemists use a variety of techniques to answer such questions, but they all boil down to looking at properties. If the properties of an unknown substance are identical to the properties of a known substance, the substances are the same. In this course, you will learn about many properties that you can use to identify matter, and you will learn how to measure those properties.

How much do I have? It is not always enough to know what you have; you often need to know how much. The water you drink, the air you breathe, and the food you eat contain many chemicals. Some of these chemicals are needed by your body in specific amounts to keep you healthy. There are daily requirements for iodine to prevent goiter, for vitamin C to prevent scurvy, and for iron to prevent anemia, just to name a few. In some concentrations, chemicals may be poisonous, or can cause birth defects or cancer. It is clearly important to know how much and what chemicals are present in food and water.

Objectives

Part 1

A. *Recognize* how knowledge obtained from the study of chemistry can be applied in your life.

B. *Explain* why communication is an important aspect of obtaining scientific knowledge.

C. *Describe* the functions of a hypothesis and a theory in the scientific method.

Developing Skills

Students may apply these skills in their study of Part 1.

Observing and describing: Have students examine Figure 1–3 on page 5 and describe what is in the photograph.

Forming a hypothesis: Have students examine Figure 1–4 on page 8 and suggest a reason why the paper does not burn.

≡ FOCUS

Activate Prior Knowledge

Students make observations in their everyday lives. After your introduction, engage the class in observation activities. Ask them to describe what they observed. Be alert for statements of inference rather than observation. Focus on the distinction between the two, and discuss the importance in science of reporting observations before drawing inferences.

≡ TEACH

Teaching Strategy

Questions Chemistry Tries to Answer

The first day of class can set the tone for the entire year. Encourage students to recognize the importance of chemistry in their lives and the environment. Remind them that everything is made of chemicals: the air they breathe, the foods they eat, the clothes they wear, and so on.

(continued on page T4)

(continued from page T3)
Point out that while the study of chemistry is challenging, it can also be fun. Perform some of your favorite demonstrations to generate anticipation in your students for their study of chemistry.

Figure 1-1 *In this course, you will be learning scientific problem-solving techniques to answer questions about matter.*

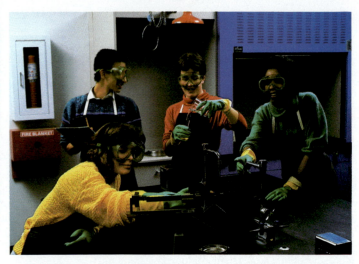

How can I change it? Never satisfied with what they have, people search for something new and different. They not only want to know what they have and how much but how to turn what they have into something more useful.

Most early efforts to make new materials were trial and error, and good fortune still plays a role in discovery. However, the more you understand about matter, the less you must rely on chance to change matter into more useful forms. Your study of chemistry will furnish a foundation for understanding changes in matter so that it can be changed into useful products.

How much can I get and how fast? If you can get a 12 percent yield for the same cost that a chemist gets a 10 percent yield, you have a new line of work, while the chemist may be looking for another job! If you know what affects the speed of a chemical change, you can speed up reactions that produce desired products and slow down those that do not. The implications of such control are vast—from regulating body metabolism, to preventing corrosion, to growing crops, to eliminating wastes, to killing bacteria, to curing cancer, to living for 500 years. The more you know about equilibrium and reaction kinetics, the closer you come to solving such problems.

The legacy of matter The particles making most of the matter around you—from your own body, the clothes you wear, the food you eat, the house you live in, and the book you are reading—are the same particles that have existed on Earth since it first formed. They are the same particles that will exist for generations of people to follow. By understanding what matter is, how much you have of what kinds, how it can be changed from one form to another, and how fast those changes occur, you have the power to leave the world better than you found it. The alternative is to remain ignorant of matter, to allow changes to occur without considering their effect on your life, or to allow others to decide what changes will be made in the matter that makes up your world and that of future generations. This book provides the tools you will need to understand matter and its changes, to learn what you must know to be a good steward of your resources. The choice of what to do with that knowledge is yours.

Figure 1-2 *Some giant red-woods have existed for 4000 years. Decisions made in your lifetime concerning toxic waste, air pollution, and chemical use will affect the rate of their survival as well as your own.*

1.2 Searching for Regularities among Facts

What do people really mean when they say, "Let's take a look at this problem scientifically?" They mean you should begin by taking a close look at the facts involved in the problem. Facts that can be analyzed to solve problems come from careful observations. Observations are the basis for all science.

Obtaining facts The first technique you need to learn for problem solving in chemistry is to make careful observations. That may seem to be an easy task to you. But look at Figure 1-3. What do you observe? If you said a dog sniffing a curb, your response could be considered a wrong interpretation. You actually observe a pattern of black dots. Because you are familiar with a dog and a curb, you inferred that the dots represented a dog. An **inference** is an interpretation of an observation. How might someone who had never seen a dog or a curb interpret the picture?

One way to make sure your observations are accurate is to have other people verify them. That is why communication in science is

Figure 1-3 *When you first look at this picture, you probably see nothing but black dots. After a while, you should see an animal sniffing at the ground.*

Cooperative Learning

Classification

Teams of 4; **Time:** 25 minutes
Objective: Students will classify laboratory equipment into groups of correctly named items.
Task: Before students begin doing laboratory investigations, get them acquainted with the equipment they will be using. Have students wear safety goggles. Have each group classify 12 different pieces of laboratory equipment. Make sure each group is classifying the same 12 items. Possible classification groupings could be breakable and nonbreakable items, low and high temperature materials, metallic and nonmetallic equipment, or calibrated and non-calibrated equipment. Each group should compile complete lists for each classification grouping with each piece of equipment correctly named. Then the groups can compare their lists.
Team responsibility: Compile complete lists with correct names for each classification grouping.
Evaluation: After groups have compared their lists, compile consensus lists. Have each group compare their lists with the consensus lists.

Teaching Strategy

Connecting Concepts

The Connecting Concepts features that appear in the margins of the pupil book highlight broad relationships among concepts in chemistry. Use the Connecting Concepts features as opportunities to remind students of connections that can be made among topics discussed in the text. By making links between ideas, students will better understand and remember what they study.

CONNECTING CONCEPTS

Organizing Information

Chemistry is more than just a collection of facts and ideas to be memorized. It is an analysis of information in an attempt to solve problems and answer questions about the world around you. To help you see how ideas can be organized and interrelated, five *Connecting Concepts* features will be highlighted in the margins.

Connecting Concepts will provide you with a basis for organizing and managing a large volume of new information. They will make it easier to remember what you are learning and to use that information for problem solving.

Processes of science Scientists use many techniques for obtaining and analyzing information when trying to solve problems. Those techniques include making observations, taking measurements, classifying and interpreting data, making predictions, explaining regularities, and communicating results with others.

Models Problems involving substances and interactions that cannot be seen are studied by using models. A model is a description, picture, or idea about something that cannot be viewed directly. It is used to explain current data and predicts new data.

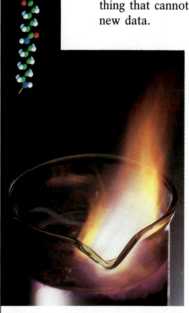

Change and interaction Matter constantly undergoes change. The food you eat combines with oxygen to give you energy. Ozone in the atmosphere is destroyed as a result of interactions with certain air pollutants. One aspect of problem solving in chemistry is to study chemical reactions in an attempt to explain how these interactions and changes occur.

Structure and properties of matter How matter changes and interacts with other matter (its properties) is a function of its structure and forces acting upon that structure. The composition of matter and how it is held together can determine whether or not it will undergo a certain kind of chemical or physical change.

Energy Changes in matter are usually related to energy in some way. Energy can be absorbed or released during a chemical reaction. It can be used as a means of predicting whether or not a chemical reaction will occur.

so important. Scientists communicate their experiments and observations to others for confirmation. As observations are repeated and confidence in them grows, that knowledge then can be accepted as factual.

Classification As you gather facts about a given problem, techniques can be used to manage and organize them. One way to manage large amounts of information is to categorize and deal with the category rather than with the individual facts. This is the process you go through when you make a statement like "Birds lay eggs." You do not need to say that chickens lay eggs and ducks lay eggs and robins lay eggs. You categorize all those animals as birds so you can economize with words and say "Birds lay eggs." This process of placing similar things into categories is **classification.**

Classification would be impossible if you did not see regularity in diversity. Just think about birds and the regularity summarized by "Birds lay eggs." People noticed that wrens and chickens and turkeys and emus and many other animals lay eggs, but cows and dogs and people and goats do not. In other words, they noticed a regularity—something that was common to a large group of animals.

Noticing regularities across observed events helps in communicating, just as classification does. These regularities take many forms. Statements like "Metals conduct electricity" or "Foods that taste sour contain acids" describe regularities in observed events. These statements summarize and describe many separate observations.

Using a scientific method Sometimes the regularity in many observations is the knowledge you are looking for. But in scientific problem solving, great advances are usually made when people try to explain the regularity.

A scientific **hypothesis** is a temporary explanation for an observed regularity. However, *explanation* can be a misleading word. By providing an explanation, you may think that people are talking about things as they really are, when in fact they are talking about things only as they might be. Science says something has been explained when over time the explanation or hypothesis accounts for past events and accurately predicts future ones. When the hypothesis or explanation can do this, it is then called a **theory** in science.

Developing theories Theories often take the form of models. You probably think of a model as a physical object, such as a model train or model airplane. Although a model may be a physical object, **model** in science refers to any representation intended to convey information about another object or event. A model airplane is a physical representation that conveys information

CONNECTING CONCEPTS

Processes of Science—Classifying "What is it?" is a question frequently asked in chemistry. The answer always results in having to classify. Solid, liquid, gas, or plasma are answers that tell you something about the physical state of matter.

PART **1**

Section 1.2 *continued*

Science Background

Developing Theories

The student text presents an inductive approach to science in describing hypotheses and theories. In science, the term *theory* may also have a deductive meaning. As such, a theory may be a conceptual framework that explains observations about the natural world and leads us to make predictions (hypotheses) about what we might observe under given circumstances. Theories are evaluated through the testing of these hypotheses.

Guided Practice

Ask students how knowledge obtained from the study of chemistry has been applied in producing mechanical and electronic watches. Ask students what questions related to chemistry might have been asked in developing the watch band, the crystal, the display, and the power source. (Accept all reasonable answers.)

PART 1
Section 1.2 *continued*

Reteaching Idea

If students need practice in seeing patterns and making predictions, use the following data for discussion. Distribute five sizes of nails along with the number of each size of nails in a pound. (*3d* is read "3 penny." A pound of 3d nails once cost only 3 pennies.)

Designation	Approximate Number in a Pound
3d	880
4d	630
6d	290
8d	195

Ask students what pattern they see and what could account for it. Accept reasonable answers such as increasing length, diameter, size of head, and so on. Ask students to predict how many nails might be in a pound of 10d nails. Ask how there could be a pound of nails made up of 380 nails.

≡ CLOSE

Summing Up Main Ideas

Have student groups list ways in which they use the scientific method in their daily lives.

PART 1 REVIEW

Assign the Part Review questions.

Evaluating Skills

These skills are evaluated in the Part Review questions indicated. **Determining main ideas: 1; Stating a conclusion: 2; Classifying: 3; Forming a hypothesis: 4; Describing: 5**

CONNECTING CONCEPTS

Models Models take many forms. The most important model in chemistry is the *mental model* of atoms, the basic building blocks of all matter.

Figure 1-4 **Left:** *Water is being boiled in a paper container. What is your hypothesis as to why the paper does not burn?* **Right:** *The illustration shows a physical model of DNA. Not all models are physical representations, some are mental models.*

Boxed numbers indicate questions that involve skills in interpretation, application, and analysis.

about a real airplane. Some models, however, are just mental pictures. These mental models allow scientists to work on problems involving processes that cannot be seen.

Developing a good theory or model usually requires a great deal of experimentation and careful analysis of the results. Some important theories in science have developed over hundreds of years with the help of many scientists. In this course, you may not have time to develop any new theories, but you will be using theories or models to help you understand facts and information as you solve problems.

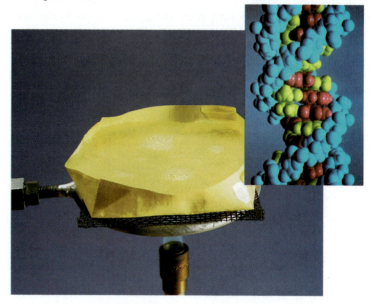

PART 1 REVIEW

1. Name four basic questions in chemistry and give an example for each (other than those used in the book) to illustrate why answers to those questions may be important in your life.

2. Scientific journals are essential to the development of scientific theories. Explain why.

3. Name three classes of foods and give three examples of each class. What properties led you to classify them as you did?

4. A teacher assigned seats on the first day of class but did not describe the basis for the assignment. Write a hypothesis to explain how seat assignments were made. How could your hypothesis be elevated to a theory?

5. Use your knowledge of science to describe three problems that scientists are currently trying to solve. State each problem clearly in a sentence.

PART 1 REVIEW

ANSWERS

■ Keyed to Objectives

A 1. What is this matter that I have?— the development and use of new light-weight plastics to build safer, more fuel-efficient cars.
How much do I have?—determining the amount and kind of fat in your diet.

How can I change it?— recycling plastics, metals, and paper products to preserve the environment.
How much can I get and how fast?—obtaining new chemical treatments for an illness.

B 2. Scientific journals facilitate communication in science so that research data can be verified to strengthen a hypothesis.

C 3. One possible answer is vegetables, meat, and dairy products. Potatoes, beets, and cabbage are classified as vegetables because they come from non-reproductive plant parts. Beef, pork, and chicken are meats because they come from land animals. Ice cream, cheese, and yogurt are dairy products because they are made from cows' milk.

PART 2 Using Mathematical Knowledge

Facts used to solve problems in science can be more than just observations of physical objects or phenomena. Facts can also be measurements that contain numbers, and working with numbers means using knowledge from the field of mathematics.

Measurements describe quantities such as length, mass, or temperature. All measurements are comparisons to some standard. If you are five feet ten inches tall, your height is five times the length of a standard called a foot plus ten times the length of a standard called an inch. Standard measures, like those shown in Figure 1-5, are kept in the United States at the National Institute of Standards and Technology.

A **quantity** is a property that can be measured and described by a number and a unit that names the standard used. For example, 165 and 75 name *numbers;* 165 pounds and 75 kilograms name *quantities.* This distinction between numbers and quantities is very important when you use mathematics in science. As you will learn in this part of the chapter, mathematics deals with relationships among numbers; science deals with relationships among quantities.

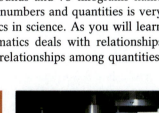

Figure 1-5 *These photos show standard weights that are carefully preserved by the National Institute of Science and Technology. These weights are made of durable materials that resist corrosion, and are never handled directly. Why?*

1.3 Mathematics as a Tool

A number can refer to anything. When you say that two plus two is equal to four, it does not matter whether you are adding chickens, people, or peanuts. You could even be adding a mixture of all three; the mathematical statement would still be valid, and the idea can be expressed in the language of mathematics as this:

$$2 + 2 = 4$$

A **4.** If the teacher uses the alphabet to seat students, then the last names of the students will determine the seating arrangement in class. Find out the order in which students were seated in past classes. Predict how students will be seated in future classes. If your hypothesis is correct for past events and predicts future events, its validity is strengthened.

A **5.** Answers will vary. Check that students have cited valid problems and described them clearly.

PART 2
Using Mathematical Knowledge

Section 1.3

Developing Skills

Students may apply these skills in their study of Part 2.
Predicting: In Section 1.4, have students predict what units of measurement would be most useful in measuring the textbook.
Analyzing data: In Section 1.4 on page 14, have students interpret the measurements given for the pages to decide which page has a larger area.
Calculating: In Section 1.4, have students compute the number of mm^2 in $1\ m^2$.

☰ FOCUS

Activate Prior Knowledge

Students are well acquainted with many measuring instruments. Distribute meter sticks, centimeter rulers, and calipers to students and ask them to make the following measurements: their height, the thickness of a piece of paper, and the volume of a box. Discuss the need to choose appropriate tools for measurement based on the object to be measured and the dimension needed.

Objectives

Part 2

D. *Differentiate* between quantities and numbers.
E. *Recognize* the meaning of base SI units, including their abbreviations and the quantities those units describe.
F. *Apply* problem-solving strategies to convert SI units and to *calculate* derived quantities from base SI units.

PART **2**
Section 1.4

TEACH

Teaching Strategy

Mathematics As a Tool

Be sure students understand the distinction between numbers and quantities. Emphasize the importance of using the appropriate units every time they write quantities, and help them make the practice a habit.

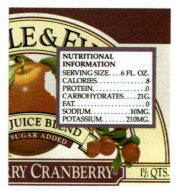

NUTRITIONAL
INFORMATION
SERVING SIZE....6 FL. OZ.
CALORIES..............8
PROTEIN..............0
CARBOHYDRATES....21G.
FAT...................0
SODIUM...........10MG.
POTASSIUM.......210MG.

Figure 1-6 *How many measurement units appear on this fruit juice label?*

In science, the rules of mathematics must be adapted to handle quantities. New language is required, and care must be taken to ensure that the rules that apply to pure numbers still make sense when you apply them to quantities. Imagine you have two yard-sticks and two standard rulers. These four measuring devices reach from one wall of a room to the other when they are laid end to end. How wide is the room? You can see that it will not make sense simply to add two plus two to get four. Two yards plus two feet are not equal to four of anything!

"First change the yards to feet," you say? Of course! In doing so, you are applying one of the first rules of mathematics to quantities: **Only like quantities can be added or subtracted.**

Units are important because they name the quantity measured. A bottle of diet cola boasts less than 1 *Calorie* per bottle, a bottle of vitamin C might contain 250-*milligram* tablets, and a bottle of cough syrup may contain 8 *ounces*. Paper is purchased by the *ream*, pencils by the *gross*, eggs by the *dozen*, and diamonds—if you can afford them—by the *carat*. Figure 1-6 shows that units are an important part of everyday life.

1.4 SI Units in Measurements

If scientists did not limit the kinds of units used, communication among scientists throughout the world could become confusing. For that reason, scientists use the *Système Internationale d'Unités*, more commonly referred to as "SI." SI is a modification of the older metric system that was developed by the French.

The popularity of SI is the result of two characteristics. First, SI has the same numerical base as the decimal number system. That is, every unit in the system is ten times the size of the next smaller

TABLE 1-1

SI Base Units		
Quantity	**Name**	**SI Unit Abbreviation**
length	meter	m
mass	kilogram	kg*
time	second	s
temperature	kelvin	K
amount of substance	mole	mol
electric current	ampere	A
luminous intensity	candela	cd

* Kilogram is the base unit in the system, but "gram" is the name modified by prefixes to obtain all other units of mass. The quantities in bold type will be used in this course.

unit, just as every place in a multidigit number is ten times the value of any place directly to its right. Second, units for various quantities are defined in terms of units for simpler quantities.

Every quantity that people presently know how to measure can be expressed in terms of only seven fundamental units, the **SI base units.** These units are listed in Table 1-1 along with the quantity that the unit describes and the symbol for the unit.

Science Background

SI Units in Measurements

The standard kilogram is used not more than once a year to minimize any changes that would be caused by handling. When other masses are calibrated, the temperature, humidity, and elevation must be controlled precisely. Even the slightest variation in these conditions can change the buoyancy of air and thus the mass of the standard by several millionths of a gram.

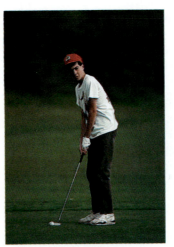

Figure 1-7 *A golf club is about one meter long.*

Length As shown in Table 1-1, the basic unit of length is the meter. As you can see in Figure 1-7, the meter is approximately the length of a golf club. You will want to talk about lengths that are as small as the diameter of an atom (about 0.000 000 000 100 m)** and as large as the distance to the sun (about 150 000 000 000 m). It is convenient to define larger and smaller units so as not to use such large numbers. All SI units are derived from the base unit by using prefixes that stand for some multiple of ten. Table 1-2 lists some common prefixes and their meaning.

Conversions between units Table 1-2 indicates that *centi-* is the prefix meaning "one one-hundredth." Then one centimeter is one one-hundredth of a meter. Applying mathematics to quantities and using the correct abbreviations, you can say

$$1 \text{ cm} = 0.01 \text{ m}$$
or
$$100 \text{ cm} = 1 \text{ m}$$

These mathlike statements simply say that the length described in one unit is the same length as described in another unit. These equalities can be used to change from one unit to another as shown in the following *Problem-Solving Strategy.*

** Various styles are used to group digits in large and small numbers to make them easier to read. In this book, a space is used in place of a comma to group digits. Thus, 10,000 appears as 10 000.

TABLE 1-2

Some SI Prefixes*		
Factor	**Prefix**	**Abbrev.**
10^6	mega	M
10^3	kilo	k
10^2	hecto	h
10^1	deka	da
10^{-1}	deci	d
10^{-2}	centi	c
10^{-3}	milli	m
10^{-6}	micro	μ
10^{-9}	nano	n
10^{-12}	pico	p

* See Appendix A for information about numbers written in scientific notation.

► FOCUS ON
PROBLEM SOLVING

Activate Prior Knowledge

Have each student or student groups make a list of familiar expressions that are labeled ratios involving two types of units. After about five minutes, begin writing expressions that students give you on the chalkboard. Select two of these expressions that involve units for the same physical quantities. For example, km/h and m/s both involve units for length and time. Give students a measurement in one expression and ask them to convert the same measurement to the other expression. Request that students show you their work, then collect their papers. This will not be a graded assignment, but it will show you how your students do conversion problems before you introduce them to the factor-label method.

► TEACH
THE STRATEGY

Guided Practice

Before doing a conversion problem, ask students what label will be used in the answer. Analyze each step when you do conversions using the factor-label method. Show students how certain units will cancel to leave an answer with the label they were expecting.

The Factor-Label Method

The factor-label method is an approach to problem solving that is useful in a wide variety of science problems. To use the factor-label method, there are two important points you need to learn. First, you must routinely *carry along the units with any measurement that you use*. Even the name *factor-label* implies that every quantity should include units. For example, the length of a line must be written as "15.0 cm," not "15."

Second, you need to learn how to form appropriate labeled ratios. You may not realize it, but you have already worked with labeled ratios. For example, you may have traveled in an automobile at 100 kilometers per hour, $\left(\dfrac{100 \text{ kilometers}}{\text{hour}}\right)$, or about 65 miles per hour $\left(\dfrac{65 \text{ miles}}{\text{hour}}\right)$. You may have a friend who purchased tickets for a basketball game for $5 a seat $\left(\dfrac{5 \text{ dollars}}{\text{seat}}\right)$ or babysat for young children for $4 an hour $\left(\dfrac{4 \text{ dollars}}{\text{hour}}\right)$. Each one of these familiar expressions represents a labeled ratio involving two types of units.

► Using Factor Labels to Solve Problems

To learn how the factor-label method works, suppose your teacher announced that you would be given a quiz with five questions, and that each question would be worth four points. By multiplying 4×5, you can easily determine that the entire quiz is worth twenty points. In order to use the factor-label method, you must first translate the information that each question is worth four points into a labeled ratio:

$$\frac{4 \text{ points}}{\text{question}}$$

To find the point value of 5 questions, you may now write

$$5 \text{ questions} \times \frac{4 \text{ points}}{\text{question}}$$
$$= 20 \text{ points}$$

Notice how the same rules that apply to numbers in equations also apply to the units. The word "question" that appears first in this equation is cancelled by the "question" that appears in the denominator of the ratio. The only unit that is left is the unit "points."

► Conversion Problems

The factor-label method helps organize your work when you must convert from one set of units to another. Try this problem. How many kilometers are there in 475 meters? The relationship between kilometers and meters can be expressed as two ratios:

$$\frac{1000 \text{ meters}}{\text{kilometer}} \quad \text{or} \quad \frac{1 \text{ kilometer}}{1000 \text{ meters}}$$

Which ratio should you use? Think about the unit cancellation from the last example. In order to cancel the unit in the distance 475 meters you must choose the ratio that has the word *meters* in the denominator. You can now finish the problem this way:

$$475 \text{ meters} \times \frac{1 \text{ kilometer}}{1000 \text{ meters}}$$
$$= 0.475 \text{ kilometer}$$

If all the calculations in science were as simple as the ones shown here, there would be no need to learn how to use the factor-label method. However, many of the problems you will encounter can be so complex that a systematic procedure helps you to keep track of your work. By handling units carefully now, you will soon master a good habit that will make it easier for you to solve more complex problems later. To get started, work through the following Example.

EXAMPLE 1-1

Assume your mass is 73 kilograms. What is your mass expressed in grams?

■ *Analyze the Problem* You are to find the number of grams that is equivalent to 73 kilograms. This equivalence can be expressed by the following statement.

$$? \text{ g} = 73 \text{ kg}$$

■ *Apply a Strategy* Knowing how many grams there are in one kilogram enables you to answer the question. Table 1-2 shows that *kilo* means "1000." Then

1 kg corresponds to 1000 g

Write this information as a labeled ratio.

$$\frac{1000 \text{ g}}{1 \text{ kg}} \quad \text{or} \quad \frac{1 \text{ kg}}{1000 \text{ g}}$$

Use the ratio that will give you grams in the answer.

■ *Work a Solution* Multiply 73 kilograms by the number of grams in each kilogram.

$$? \text{ g} = 73 \text{ kg} \times \frac{1000 \text{ g}}{1 \text{ kg}} = 73\ 000 \text{ g}$$

Notice that the units in the numerator and denominator cancel.

PROBLEM-SOLVING

S T R A T E G Y

*Use the **factor label method** to set up the problem, and verify your answer by obtaining the correct units in your answer. (See Strategy, page 12.)*

Reteaching Idea

For students experiencing difficulty with Example 1–1, provide additional practice using problems that employ familiar ratios, such as minutes per class period, school days per week, or chairs per row in the classroom. Emphasize that "per" means "divided by" when you are generating conversion factors. How many school days in 30 weeks of school? How many chairs in a classroom having 5 rows of 6 chairs per row? How many chairs are there per school if there are 12 rooms per school with 5 rows per room and 6 chairs per row?

PROBLEM SOLVING

▶ Point out to students that a labeled ratio does not always have to have a whole number in the numerator. Work out an example such as determining how many grams are in 50 mg. Show students that from Table 1–2 on page 11 they can find *milli* means 1/1000th, or 1000 times smaller than the unit it precedes. Then 1 mg = 0.001 g, and the labeled ratio is 0.001 g/1 mg. Some students are uncomfortable using decimals in a fraction. If they remember that 1 g corresponds to 1000 mg, they may write 1000 mg/1 g and then use the reciprocal (1 g/1000 mg) to solve the problem. Show them, by dividing the numerator and denominator by 1000, that this expression is the same in a fraction or a decimal.

PART 2

Section 1.4 continued

Practice Problems

Assign the Practice Problems.

Guided Practice

Have students do the following conversion problems: 1000 cm to mm, 1000 cm² to mm², and 1000 cm³ to mm³. Point out that length is one dimension, area is two dimensions, and volume is three dimensions.

Reteaching Idea

Students will feel more comfortable if they become familiar with SI prefixes. Give them the responsibility of becoming familiar with Table 1–2. Then divide the class into two teams. Each member of Team A challenges a student on Team B to interpret an SI prefix for mass, volume, length, time, and so on. For example, a student might say "one deciliter." Her opposite on Team B should reply one-tenth liter, 10^{-1} liter, or 100 mL. A second round might involve any number other than 1. For example, 3 picoseconds or 5 kilograms should be answered with 3×10^{-12} seconds and 5000 grams. For the second round, students may use paper and pencil. This would provide a review of scientific notation (see Appendix A).

PROBLEM-SOLVING

S T R A T E G Y

Complete solutions to the Practice Problems can be found in the Appendix at the back of the book.

■ **Verify Your Answer** The units are grams, which is what you are asked to calculate. Also, the number of grams is much larger than the number of kilograms. Since a gram is smaller than a kilogram, it should take far more gram masses to balance your mass than kilogram masses.

Practice Problems

6. How many millimeters are there in 2 meters?

   Ans. 2000 mm

7. A piece of wire is 1.30 meters long. How many 10-cm sections can be cut from this wire? **Ans.** 13 sections

Derived quantities If the base units shown in Table 1-1 were the only SI units, you would be limited in describing all the quantities you observe. Take, for example, the size of this page. How big is it? You could measure its length and width, but just knowing the length and width of a page does not tell you how much space there is for writing. On which page could you write more, one that is 18 centimeters wide and 22 centimeters long or one that is 4 centimeters wide and 1 meter long?

Area To answer this question, you need to know how much surface the page covers—its area. **Area** is usually described in terms of the number of squares of some given size needed to cover a surface.

If this page were covered with squares that measure one centimeter on each side, its area could be found in square centimeters by counting the squares. You do not usually determine area this

Figure 1-8 The surface of a football field is described by an area. The gymnasium shown on the right can be described by measuring its volume.

way because you have probably learned the mathematical equation that describes area—length in centimeters times width in centimeters. The numerical answer is followed by the unit *centimeters squared*, since units are multiplied just like numbers: (cm × cm) = cm².

Volume Area multiplied by height gives you **volume**. What is the volume of the object in Figure 1-9? To obtain the answer of 1000 cm³, first the numbers were multiplied to get 1000, and then the units were multiplied. The exponent *three* indicates the number of times the unit was a factor. However, you also should see that *cm³* has a very sensible physical interpretation. The volume of the object contains 1000 cubes that measure one centimeter on a side. The new unit, cubic centimeter, can be interpreted as the name for one of those cubes.

SI units for all quantities that you may wish to measure can be derived from the base units in Table 1-1. Some derived quantities discussed in this course are shown in Appendix B.

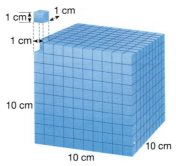

Figure 1-9 *There are 1000 cubes one centimeter on a side or 1000 cubic centimeters making up the volume of this object.*

PART 2 REVIEW

8. In the field of nutrition, research is done on how the intake of food can affect a person's weight. How would that research be affected if there were no measurement standards?

9. Identify the number and the quantity in each example:
   a. 750 grams   **b.** 62 kilometers

10. Complete the following equivalence statement:
$$1 \text{ m} = \underline{\ ?\ } \text{ dm} = \underline{\ ?\ } \text{ cm} = \underline{\ ?\ } \text{ mm}$$
   What characteristic of the SI system does this statement represent?

11. Calculate the following equalities:
   a. 70 kg = ? g   **d.** ? cm² = 1 m²
   b. ? mm = 63 cm   **e.** 1 km³ = ? m³
   c. 2.5 L = ? mL   **f.** ? mm² = 1 cm²

12. Calculate the following equalities:
   a. 5 mg = ? g   **d.** 80 μg = ? g
   b. 150 mL = ? L   **e.** ? m = 50 cm
   c. ? g = 42 μg   **f.** ? g = 64 mg

13. Convert the area represented by 15.50 cm² into mm² in two ways:
   a. by changing the equality 100 mm² = 1 cm² into an appropriate ratio of quantities.
   b. by changing the equality 1 mm² = 0.01 cm² into an appropriate ratio of quantities.

14. Explain why the two different methods of solution in Question 13 should result in the same answer.

DO YOU KNOW?

The SI unit of volume, 1 m³, is too large to be practical for use in chemistry laboratories.

Most equipment in a laboratory will be marked in milliliters (mL). By definition, 1 mL equals 1 cm³.

PART 2
Section 1.4 *continued*

≡CLOSE

Summing Up Main Ideas

Tables 1–1 and 1–2 on pages 10 and 11 are useful references for each chapter in this book. Have students prepare an index card with the units and prefixes from these tables, which they can use throughout the year.

PART 2 REVIEW

Assign the Part Review questions.

Evaluating Skills

These skills are evaluated in the Part Review questions indicated. **Stating a conclusion:** 8, 14; **Classifying:** 9; **Applying a strategy:** 10, 11, 12, 13; **Calculating:** 10, 11, 12, 13; **Verifying results:** 10, 11, 12, 13

PART 2 REVIEW

ANSWERS

■ Keyed to Objectives

D **8.** Data would be useless and comparisons among studies would be difficult (perhaps impossible) if different measurements were used in each study.

D **9.** numbers: 750, 62; quantities: 750 g, 62 km

E **10.** 1 m = 10 dm = 100 cm = 1000 mm; every unit is ten times the size of the next smaller unit.

F **11.** **a.** 0.005 g   **d.** 10 000 cm²
   b. 630 mm   **e.** 1 000 000 000 m³
   c. 2500 mL   **f.** 100 mm²

F **12.** **a.** 0.005 g   **d.** 0.000 08 g
   b. 0.150 L   **e.** 0.59 m
   c. 0.000 042 g **f.** 0.064 g

F **13.** Encourage students to use the factor-label method to solve this problem.

   a. $\dfrac{15.50 \text{ cm}^2 \times 100 \text{ mm}^2}{1 \text{ cm}^2} = 1550 \text{ mm}$

   b. $\dfrac{15.50 \text{ cm}^2 \times 1 \text{ mm}^2}{0.01 \text{ cm}^2} = 1550 \text{ mm}^2$

F **14.** The two ratios, 100 mm²/1 cm² and 1 mm²/0.01 cm², are equivalent ratios.

CAREERS IN CHEMISTRY

Teaching Strategies

1. Have students discuss differences in job requirements for a dentist versus a laboratory technician. Compare educational preparation, daily work environment, and work location (for example, self-employment versus a large research institution or laboratory).

2. In addition to atomic weapons testing, nuclear power plants and nuclear medicine generate radioactive waste. Have students discuss the problems of disposing of nuclear waste, variations in the degree of radioactivity of different types of waste, and its reactivity with other substances.

Look Ahead

Tie in a discussion of this career with the **Science Technology & Society** feature on radioactivity on pages 326–327. Have students discuss the responsibility of those who use radioactive substances to their co-workers, family, community, and to society.

Related Careers

Contact the American Chemical Society; the Nuclear Regulatory Commission, 1717 H St., N.W., Washington, DC 20555; or the American Nuclear Society, 555 North Kensington Ave., LaGrange Park, IL 60525, for additional information on careers and to identify local society members who could speak to your class.

Resources

Members of your community who might be contacted to speak to your class about the use of radioactive isotopes in their professions include radiologists and X-ray technicians, as well as dental hygienists and dentists.

Chemical Laboratory Technician

Michael Cisneros' path to his career in isotope chemistry was anything but planned. In high school, he hoped for a career in athletics. However, his father urged him to work toward becoming a dentist, and that meant building a good foundation in math and science.

■ *Many students are afraid of tough subjects, but the keys to success are hard work and setting reachable goals.*

Michael Cisneros Laboratory Technician in Isotope and Nuclear Chemistry

Changing career choices Michael accepted an athletic scholarship from a state university, but a knee injury put an end to his athletic career. Consequently, he decided to follow his father's advice and become a dentist. After earning his bachelor of science degree in biology, Michael was ready to enter dental school, but he found himself questioning whether this was what he really wanted to do. He decided to delay making a career choice and took a job as a chemical laboratory technician dealing with radioactive materials. Two years later he joined the Isotope and Nuclear Chemistry Group of the Los Alamos National Laboratory, where he is working today.

Finding a place for nuclear waste As a chemical laboratory technician, Michael uses a variety of techniques for the analysis of the radioactive elements of the actinide series (atomic numbers 90–103). His work is part of the United States weapons test program. Recently he worked on the Yucca Mountain Project, which investigated the interaction of radioactive materials with rocks and sought to find a suitable place to bury the nation's nuclear waste.

Setting reachable goals Michael believes that education is a continuing process that leads to success. He is active in the newly created Division of Chemical Technicians of the American Chemical Society and travels to scientific meetings and training sessions. He is involved in an outreach program that encourages young people to study science and math. He says that many students are afraid of these these "tough" subjects just as he was, but he uses his story to show that hard work and setting reachable goals are the keys to success.

PART **3** Developing Tools for Analysis

PART 3
Developing Tools for Analysis

Once observations and facts have been collected in science, they are referred to as **data.** In this course, you will be asked to analyze data. By analyzing data you will find regularities in observations. The following techniques used in science not only organize information but also make sense out of observations by revealing relationships that are not obvious.

1.5 Making Tables and Graphs

Table 1-3 shows numbers of rice grains and their corresponding masses. There is no order to the data. It is difficult to see that the mass increases as the number of grains increases. Table 1-4 shows the data ordered from the smallest to the largest number of grains, and the corresponding order in the mass is more evident.

TABLE 1-3

Number of Rice Grains and Their Mass	
Number of Grains	**Corresponding Mass**
400	7.00 g
200	3.50 g
100	1.75 g
800	14.00 g
1300	22.75 g

TABLE 1-4

Number of Rice Grains and Their Mass	
Number of Grains	**Corresponding Mass**
100	1.75 g
200	3.50 g
400	7.00 g
800	14.00 g
1300	22.75 g

It is not always clear how data should be recorded to make interpretation easy. As you make observations, you should try various ways of presenting the data and select the one that reveals relationships that seem important.

Graphing Pictures, histograms, graphs, and physical models often reveal things that tables do not. Graphs are particularly useful when you suspect a proportional relationship like the one shown in Table 1-4. Figure 1-10 on the next page represents the data from Table 1-4 in graphical form. A graph can reveal many things if it is carefully prepared and the reader knows how to interpret it. A few measurements are recorded on the graph, and these points are used to predict what may be seen if more measurements were made. The line drawn in Figure 1-10 *(Left)* predicts where data points would be if more rice were counted and its mass found. The more points plotted to predict the line, the better the prediction. Once you are confident that enough points are plotted to locate the line,

Objectives

Part 3

G. *Construct tables and graphs* to organize data.
H. *Determine* density by *interpreting* data on a graph.
I. *Calculate* density by using problem-solving strategies.

Developing Skills

Students may apply these skills in their study of Part 3.
Constructing graphs and tables: Have students graph data in Tables 1–3 and 1–4 on page 17.
Analyzing data: Have students examine Figure 1–12 on page 20, and recognize the difference in the masses of the pennies.
Analyzing data: Have students identify the relationship between mass and volume indicated on the graph in Figure 1–13 on page 21.

≡ FOCUS

Activate Prior Knowledge

Give students visual proof that a 1000-cm^3 container can hold 1000 mL. Milk cartons are very close to 10 cm by 10 cm. Cut the container to precisely 10 cm high, and fill it with water using a 100-mL beaker or graduated cylinder. The container will just be filled when 1000 mL are added. Volume, expressed in cm^3 or mL, will be one measurement used in graphing data in Part 3.

PART 3
Section 1.6

≡TEACH

Teaching Strategy

Making Tables and Graphs

One way of demonstrating the importance of the rules for good graphing is to pass out sample graphs that omit titles, labels, marked points, and so on, and ask students what would make it easier for them to interpret the graphs. Later, give students practice in graphing. Double all the numbers in Table 1–4 and have students graph the data.

you can use the graph to predict what a measurement would be without bothering to measure it. The upward slope of the line in Figure 1-10 *(Left)* indicates that the more grains you have, the greater the mass of the rice. This interpretation certainly makes sense.

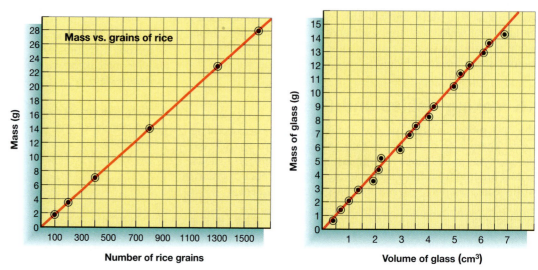

Figure 1-10 **Left:** *This graph shows the mass of rice as a function of the number of grains. The data used to locate the line appear to have no uncertainty since all points fall on the line.* **Right:** *This graph shows the mass of glass as a function of its volume. The line is not drawn through all data points because it is assumed that there was uncertainty in the measurements used to locate the points.*

1.6 Graphing Real Data

Figure 1-10 *(Left)* contradicts experience in that it is too good to be true. All data points fall on the curve. This happens when data are artificial; it seldom happens with real data. Real data come from measurements that are a little greater or less than the actual value.

Figure 1-10 *(Right)* shows a graph of real data. The mass and volume of 18 pieces of glass were measured and used to plot the graph. A straight line was drawn to predict where data points should be, even though the line does not pass through all points representing actual measurements. The line was drawn to represent best what the data would look like if there were no uncertainty in the measurements. However, measurements are uncertain.

Uncertainty in measurement The most common reason for uncertainty in measurements is that measuring tools are limited. Figure 1-11 shows the beams on a balance. If you use such a balance to measure the mass of something, the best you can do is estimate

CHEMICAL UPDATE

Uncertainty in Measurement

Meteorologists use a complex computer model and current measurements to forecast the weather. Slight uncertainties in the measurements lead to chaotic variations in the long-term predictions. It is unlikely that accurate forecasts for a period longer than a month can be achieved. For more information read *Chaos,* by James Gleick (Viking, 1987).

the mass at the 0.01 gram position, since the last rider does not fall on a line. It is common practice to imagine that the space between lines is divided into tenths and estimate the last digit. You could estimate the mass of the marbles in Figure 1-11 as 459.11 grams, while a classmate might estimate it as 459.14 grams. The last digit recorded in a measurement in science is an estimate of this kind, and it is uncertain. Although the last digit is uncertain, it is still considered *significant*. In Chapter 4 you will learn more about significant digits and their usefulness in science.

Best-fit line You have no way of knowing whether a measurement recorded is larger or smaller than the true value. However, in making many measurements, you assume that there will be as many measurements that are too large as there are measurements too small. The chance of error in either direction is the same. Consequently, when the line is drawn to represent where points would be if there were no uncertainty in them, it is drawn so there are as many points above the line as below it. The line is also drawn so points that do not fall on the line are scattered along it.

The line described is called the *best fit* for the data. In careful scientific work, mathematical equations are used to locate this best-fit line. In this course, you will do it by eye.

PART 3

Section 1.6 *continued*

Look Ahead

If you wish to teach significant digits at this point, you can use Section 4.8 on page 150 as a reference.

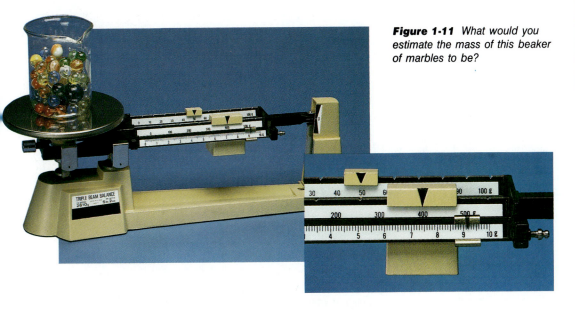

Figure 1-11 *What would you estimate the mass of this beaker of marbles to be?*

Concept ✔ Check

If you were given two sets of data, how could you determine whether they were data from measurements or data that have no uncertainty?

PART 3
Section 1.7

Teaching Strategy

Density

Discuss why objects like a foam ball, a lead sinker, and a block of clay have different densities. Shape clay into a 10 cm × 10 cm × 10 cm block, and have students find its mass. Use wire to cut the block into ten slices that are 1 cm thick. Further cut one of the slices into 100 1-cm³ cubes. Have students compare the mass of one slice and one cube with the mass of the whole block.

CONNECTING CONCEPTS

Processes of Science—Observation "What is it?"—one of the persistent questions chemists ask,—is answered by examining characteristic properties. If the characteristic properties of matter are the same as the properties of something you already know, you can say you have some of the familiar substance. If the properties are different from anything previously known, you can say you have discovered something new and give it a name.

1.7 Using Graphs to Find Density

You may think, based on casual observations, that all United States pennies are the same. But if you explore further by finding the mass of pennies made in 1980 and those made in 1984, you will discover a difference. The graph in Figure 1-12 compares the mass of pennies made in 1984 with the mass of pennies made in 1980. As you can see, the points do not fall on the same line. Both lines pass through the origin, which makes sense. You would expect 0 pennies to have no mass, whether the pennies were made in 1980 or 1984.

The line for the 1980 pennies climbs faster—that is, it has a greater slope. If you think about the graph, you realize that it climbs because the mass of pennies increases as the number of pennies increases. Then the line for the 1980 pennies must climb faster because more mass is added when the number of 1980 pennies increases than when the number of 1984 pennies increases. In other words, 1980 pennies must have more mass than the same number of 1984 pennies!

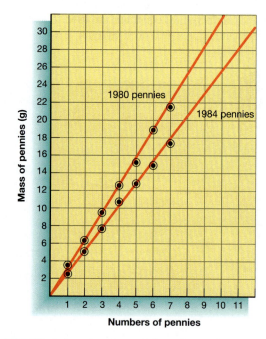

Figure 1-12 *What does the slope of these lines tell you about the mass of 1980 pennies versus 1984 pennies?*

Density Pennies made in 1980 are the same size as those made in 1984, but they have more mass. Prior to 1982, pennies were made of copper; pennies made during and after that date have been made of zinc with a thin copper coating. The newer pennies look like the older ones, but you can tell them apart because they have different masses. Density can be used to describe this difference in mass. **Density** is defined as mass per unit volume or the ratio of mass to volume. Mathematically this can be written as

$$D = \frac{m}{V}$$

In SI units, density is expressed as the mass in kilograms of one cubic meter (1 m^3) of material. A cubic meter is a very large piece of matter, so more commonly used metric units for density are grams per cubic centimeter (g/cm^3).

If the copper in a 1980 penny has a density of 8.92 g/cm^3, then each cubic centimeter of copper has a mass of 8.92 grams. Density is a ratio indicating how much the mass of some material increases each time the volume is increased by one cubic centimeter.

Graphing density On a graph, a ratio such as density can be found from the slope of the line. The **slope** of the line shows how much the quantity plotted along the y-axis increases when the quantity plotted along the x-axis increases by one unit. As you can see from the graph in Figure 1-13, the slope of the line shows that the mass of copper increases by 8.92 grams each time the volume increases by one cubic centimeter. Mass and volume are said to be directly proportional.

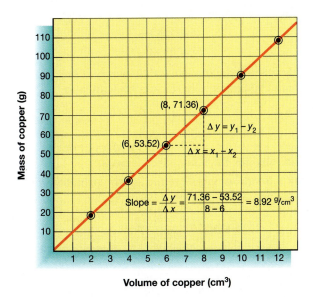

Figure 1·13 *By finding the slope, you know that for every cm^3, the mass of copper increases by 8.92 grams.*

Concept ✓ Check

The line on the graph in Figure 1-13 passes through the origin. Why is this reasonable?

PART 3
Section 1.7 continued

PROBLEM SOLVING

▶ Graphing data is a useful method of finding a relationship between two variables. Another method is to multiply each pair of numbers to find if the product is constant or to divide each pair to see if the ratio is constant. Have students try both multiplying and dividing the data in Table 1–4 to determine if either shows a relationship. They will get a constant for the ratio of mass to number of grains.

Teaching Strategy

Ex. 1–2 Expected Solution

Before students read the solution to the problem, ask them to think about the amount of mass they *expect* the object to have. A density of 13.60 g/cm³ indicates a large ratio of mass to unit volume. Students should reason that the mass of the object will be much greater than 825 g.

Guided Practice

Review the Concept Check questions on pages 19 and 21 with students, and have students demonstrate their understanding of Example 1–2 by telling you, in their own words, how to solve it.

Constants derived from proportional relationships If any two points are chosen on the line in Figure 1-13, the slope that is found representing the ratio of mass to volume, $\left(\dfrac{m}{V}\right)$, will always equal the density of 8.92 grams/centimeters³. The slope of the line is a **constant**.

Any two quantities that are directly proportional produce a constant number when one of the quantities is divided by the other. This is often expressed mathematically by the equation

$$\frac{A}{B} = k$$

The letters A and B represent the two quantities, and k represents the constant number produced when one quantity is divided by the other. The expression is read as "A divided by B is equal to a constant." Just what the constant number turns out to be depends entirely on what quantities are divided.

EXAMPLE 1-2

An object has a volume of 825 cm³ and a density of 13.60 g/cm³. What is the mass of the object?

■ *Analyze the Problem* You are asked to find mass, knowing values for density and volume. Write down what you know.

$$V = 825 \text{ cm}^3$$
$$D = 13.60 \text{ g/cm}^3$$

■ *Apply a Strategy* You know that density is the ratio of mass to volume. Mathematically this can be written as

$$D = \frac{m}{V}$$

Since you know two of the three variables in this relationship, you can solve for the third, which is mass.

■ *Work a Solution* Substitute the known quantities into the relationship and solve for mass.

$$13.60 \text{ g/cm}^3 = \frac{m}{825 \text{ cm}^3}$$
$$m = (13.60 \text{ g/cm}^3)(825 \text{ cm}^3)$$
$$= 11\,220 \text{ g}$$

PROBLEM-SOLVING

STRATEGY

Using the factor-label method allows you to cancel units to get the answer you need. (See Strategy, page 12.)

If you did not remember the mathematical formula for density, you could have solved the problem by using the *factor-label method*. Use density as a labeled ratio and multiply by the volume.

$$?\,\text{g} = \frac{13.60 \text{ g}}{1 \text{ cm}^3} \times 825 \text{ cm}^3 = 11\,220 \text{ g}$$

PART 3 REVIEW

ANSWERS

■ **Keyed to Objectives**

G **17.**

Mass	Volume
8.0 g	10 mL
15.8 g	20 mL
24.3 g	30 mL

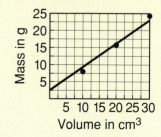

■ **Verify Your Answer** The unit for mass is grams. The answer has the correct unit. Check your answer by using the value for mass in the relationship $D = m/V$. $D = 11\,220$ g$/825$ cm^3. $D = 13.60$ g/cm^3. This answer should agree with what you found in the problem, and it does.

Practice Problems

15. Find the volume of a container needed by a chemical company in order to ship 760.00 grams of benzene at room temperature. At room, temperature the density of benzene equals 0.8787 g/cm^3.   **Ans.** 864.9 cm^3

16. You have a sample of material with a mass of 620 grams and a volume of 753.00 cm^3. Another sample of material has a density of 0.70 g/cm^3. Are the two samples the same material? Explain your answer.

◄ **PROBLEM·SOLVING STRATEGY**

Complete solutions to the Practice Problems can be found in the Appendix at the back of the book.

PART 3 REVIEW

17. Organize the following data by constructing a table and a graph:
    24.3 g of rubbing alcohol has a volume of 30 mL
    8.0 g of rubbing alcohol has a volume of 10 mL
    15.8 g of rubbing alcohol has a volume of 20 mL

18. Determine the density of rubbing alcohol from the slope of the graph in question 17.   **Ans.** 0.85 g/mL

19. Do you think the data used to make your graph were actual laboratory data or data that have no uncertainty? Explain your answer.

20. Find the density of a piece of wood that has a mass of 50 g and a volume of 210 cm^3.   **Ans.** 0.24 g/cm^3

21. A piece of copper has a volume of 28.6 cm^3. The density of copper is 8.92 g/cm^3. What is the mass of the copper?
        Ans. 255 g

22. A student was trying to find the density of a piece of plastic. She measured the volume of the plastic to be 3.2 cm^3. The mass of the plastic was 4.2 g. What is the density of the plastic?   **Ans.** 1.3 g/cm^3

23. If you and a classmate collected data and plotted graphs of mass versus volume for two different kinds of pure metals, how could you tell from the graph which metal had the greater density?

24. In Figure 1-12, would you expect straight line graphs if a variety of 1980 and 1984 foreign copper coins were used? Explain your answer.

Boxed numbers indicate questions that involve skills in interpretation, application, and analysis.

H **18.** The slope of the graph from a best-fit line is $\Delta y/\Delta x = 8.5$ g$/10$ mL $= 0.85$ g/mL.

I **19.** Actual laboratory data, since the data is rounded off

I **20.** 50 g$/210$ cm$^3 = 0.24$ g/cm^3

I **21.** 28.6 cm$^3 \times 8.92$ g/cm$^3 = 255$ g

I **22.** 4.2 g$/3.2$ cm$^3 = 1.3$ g/cm^3

H **23.** Density would be the slope of the graph for either metal. The graph with the steepest slope would represent the largest density.

H **24.** The graph would be a straight line if each coin were 100 percent copper. The slope of the graph would represent the density of copper.

PART 3
Section 1.7 *continued*

Practice Problems

Assign the Practice Problems.

Reteaching Idea

If students need more practice in interpreting graphs, divide the class into groups of three or four and have students make graphs of the following data relating numbers of gizmos and the boxes they occupy. Students should plot gizmos on the *y*-axis and boxes on the *x*-axis. (36 gizmos, 1.5 boxes; 48 gizmos, 2.0 boxes; 60 gizmos, 2.5 boxes; 96 gizmos, 4.0 boxes)

Ask students to explain how the number of boxes changes as the number of gizmos increases. Have them find how many boxes would be needed to provide 132 gizmos. Ask students how they could determine this from the graph. Ask students to find the slope of the line and to write an equation for it using *G* for gizmos and *B* for boxes. Finally, ask if the data have uncertainty.

≡ **CLOSE**

Summing Up Main Ideas

Give a table of data to students that includes the mass and volume measurements for five samples of aluminum. Sample mass and volume measurements are (54 g, 20 mL), (41 g, 15 mL), (27 g, 10 mL), (14 g, 5 mL), and (19 g, 7 mL). Ask students to graph the data and determine the density of aluminum from the graph.

PART 3 REVIEW

Assign the Part Review questions.

Evaluating Skills

These skills are evaluated in the Part Review questions indicated. **Constructing graphs and tables:** 17; **Analyzing data:** 18, 19, 20, 21, 22, 23, 24; **Applying a strategy:** 20, 21, 22; **Calculating:** 20, 21, 22; **Verifying results:** 20, 21, 22

PART **4**
Exploring Matter
Section 1.8

Developing Skills

Students may apply these skills in their study of Part 4.

Observing and describing: Have students name characteristics of common forms of matter as described in Section 1.9.

Comparing/Contrasting: Have students recognize the submicroscopic differences among solids, liquid, and gases as illustrated in Figures 1–17, 1–18, and 1–19 on page 28.

≡FOCUS

Activate Prior Knowledge

Copper and aluminum are substances that students will recognize. Have students record observations as you do the following demonstration. Then analyze the observations in a class discussion.

⚠ **CAUTION: Everyone must wear goggles and a lab apron.**

1. Put about 5 g of crushed $CuCl_2 \cdot 2H_2O$ crystals into a dry 400-mL beaker. Add 100-mL of water but do not stir. After students have a chance to make observations, stir the solution. Ask them to observe the contents of the beaker again and record their observations.

2. Hold up a 4-cm^2 piece of aluminum foil for the class to observe. Then drop it into the $CuCl_2$ solution. Ask students to continue to observe the contents of the beaker for a few minutes and record their observations.

3. To dispose of the solutions, dilute them with double the volume of water and pour down the drain. Wrap any solids in old newspaper and put into the wastebasket.

(continued on page T25)

O b j e c t i v e s

Part 4

J. *Discuss* how properties of matter can be used for identification of matter.

K. *Distinguish* between chemical and physical changes.

L. *Use models* to explain different properties of solids, liquids, and gases.

PART
4 *Exploring Matter*

Having learned some basic skills of scientific problem solving, you are now ready to take a closer look at matter. By observing matter around you, you begin the task of trying to answer one of the basic questions that chemistry addresses—what is matter?

1.8 Properties of Matter

You may have learned about matter in previous science courses—that matter is defined as anything that has mass and takes up space, and that matter can be changed by energy. Through experimentation, it is known that matter is neither created nor destroyed when it is changed by energy—it is conserved.

Even without studying science, you know a great deal about matter because you have made observations about what you see, feel, and smell in a world made up of matter. Such observations are **macroscopic observations** (*macro* means "large"; *scopic* means "viewing or observing"). You know that water commonly exists as a liquid that pours freely to fill any container and that water will change to a solid when cooled, or to a gas when heated. You know that iron, aluminum, salt, and sugar normally exist as solids that keep their shape, and that salt and sugar will dissolve in water but that iron and aluminum will not. You know that solids like iron and aluminum will flatten when hit by a hammer but that they normally do not shatter. By contrast, you know that cubes of sugar and salt will shatter when struck by a hammer. Look at Figure 1-14. Can you describe additional characteristics of these examples of matter?

Figure 1-14 *What properties could be used to distinguish the different kinds of matter in this photograph?*

Chemical and physical changes Characteristics that allow you to distinguish one kind of matter from another are called properties. Table 1-5 lists properties of some common substances. Notice that melting points and boiling points are not shown for sugar or baking soda. When sugar is heated, it bubbles and turns black, as shown in Figure 1-15. If the mouth of the test tube is cool, a colorless liquid forms on the walls of the test tube as sugar is heated. The sugar does not melt. When cooled, a black solid and colorless liquid remain. If the solid and liquid are mixed together, it becomes a wet mess that is not at all like sugar. There is no way to get the original sugar back. Instead of melting, the sugar changes into new substances with new properties. The black solid does not taste like sugar, look like sugar, or have the same density as sugar. The colorless liquid does not have the same properties as sugar either. Because the properties have changed, it is said that the sugar has changed to a new substance or substances.

TABLE 1-5

Representative Properties of Some Common Substances			
Name	Melting Point (°C)	Boiling Point (°C)	Density (g/cm³)
sucrose (table sugar)	—	—	1.58
sodium bicarbonate (baking soda)	—	—	2.16
sodium chloride (table salt)	801	1413	2.16
water	0	100	1.00
iron	1535	3000	7.87
carbon (graphite)	3550	4827	1.9–2.3
copper	1083	2595	8.96

Similarly, when baking soda is heated, a colorless gas is driven away, leaving behind a white solid that looks like the original baking soda, but with different properties. Baking soda has a density of 2.159 g/cm³; the white solid that remains after heating has a density of 2.532 g/cm³. Baking soda can be added to cake batter to make the cake rise; the white solid that forms after the baking soda is heated will not make cake batter rise. Other properties of the two substances differ. Again, when baking soda is heated, some new kind of matter is formed. Changes that produce a new kind of matter with different properties are called **chemical changes.**

Physical changes Compare what happens when moth flakes are heated to what happens when sugar is heated. When moth flakes are heated, the solid material disappears and a liquid appears in its place. If the liquid is allowed to cool, the liquid turns back to a solid that has the same properties as the original moth

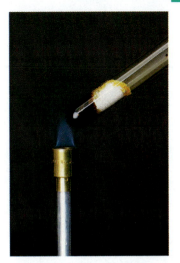

Figure 1-15 When sugar is heated, it decomposes to form a black solid and gaseous products. Some of the gaseous products condense to form a clear liquid.

PART **4**

Section 1.8 continued

(continued from page T24)

Students will first see physical changes. (The solution starts to turn blue-green as the solid dissolves slowly; the solution becomes more blue as the Cu^{2+} ions become surrounded by more water molecules; the physical changes accelerate when more energy is added in the form of stirring.) Then they will see chemical changes. (The aluminum foil disappears as it reacts with the Cl^- ion. Copper metal appears as it precipitates, and heat is given off.)

≡TEACH

Resources

The discussion here implies that there is a clear distinction between chemical and physical changes, which is not necessarily true. Read "Physical Versus Chemical Change" by Walter J. Gansler, *Journal of Chemical Education*, Vol. 47, No. 2 (February, 1970), pp. 154–155, for an interesting discussion of the subtle issues involved.

Science Background

Physical Changes

The vapors from moth flakes are toxic. If you decide to demonstrate changes in state with moth flakes, do it under a hood.

Videodisc Connections

25788 to 27044, side 2
Crystal growth under microscope (movie)

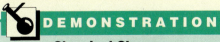

DEMONSTRATION

Chemical Changes

To demonstrate a chemical change, put a 1-cm × 1-cm piece of aluminum foil into a 100-mL Pyrex beaker containing 10 mL of 3.0*M* sodium hydroxide. Cover the beaker with a wire screen and place it on the overhead projector. Place a shield between the beaker and the students. Aluminum hydroxide will precipitate in the beaker. The chemical changes will be magnified by the overhead projector.

⚠ **CAUTION: Wear a lab apron, safety goggles, gloves, and a face shield. Position a shield between the demonstration and your students. All students should wear safety goggles.** For disposal, neutralize the solution with 1*M* (or less concentrated) acid and pour the solution down the drain.

PART 4

Section 1.8 continued

Videodisc Connections

2140 to 3263, side 3
Hubert Alyea: color changes
(movie)

10584 to 12844, side 1
Chemiluminescent NH₃ fountain
(movie)

38409 to 38946, side 3
Cooking an egg (movie)

Figure 1-16 *The reaction of vinegar and baking soda result in the formation of a gas indicating a chemical change has taken place.*

flakes. The new solid has the same smell as the original one, has the same density as the original solid, melts at the same temperature as the original solid, and so forth. Every observation indicates that the two solids are, in fact, the same kind of matter. Because of these observations, you infer that the moth flakes melt when they are heated. **Melting** is the term used to describe the change of a solid to a liquid without the formation of any new kind of matter. Melting and other changes that are easily reversed to get the original material back again are described as physical changes. They do not produce new kinds of matter.

The chemical change taking place in sugar when it is heated differs from the melting of moth flakes in two ways: First, the change in sugar is not reversible. Second, the black solid and the liquid formed when sugar is heated are nothing like sugar used at the start.

Everyday chemical changes An interesting part of chemistry is seeing the many chemical changes that matter undergoes. It can also be interesting to try to figure out what is actually happening when those changes take place. You have probably mixed baking soda with vinegar and seen the bubbles of gas produced, as shown in Figure 1-16. Where do the bubbles come from and what are they? What happens to the baking soda and vinegar? Virtually every home contains laundry bleach. How does liquid bleach act on stains to remove them? Is the action of liquid bleach the same as solid bleach? These are the kinds of questions chemistry can answer.

Chemicals make people's lives more convenient. In your home you may find ammonia, toilet-bowl cleaners, paint removers, gasoline, oven cleaners, fertilizers, herbicides, and pesticides. All are helpful in their particular ways, but some of these chemicals can undergo chemical changes that are extremely hazardous. They should always be used with care. Also when some household products are washed down the drain or into the ground, they can produce dangerous and toxic effects in the environment. It is clear that understanding how chemical changes take place and how to avoid hazardous chemical reactions is important for everyone. In order to control chemical changes so that your lives are made better rather than worse, you need to understand the properties of matter.

Concept ✔ Check

In your own words, describe the difference between a chemical change and a physical change. Make a list of chemical changes and physical changes that occur around you every day.

Myths and Misconceptions

Some students believe that a particle of a substance exhibits the same properties as the substance. For example, students often express the belief that a single particle of a solid substance is also solid, a liquid is made of liquid particles, and a gas is made up of gas particles. This mis-conception may hinder understanding of the interactive nature of chemistry. You might ask questions such as: What would a single particle of copper look like? Given a small enough mallet, could you bend a copper particle the way you could bend a copper tube?

1.9 Comparing Solids, Liquids, and Gases

One of the properties of matter is the physical state it exists in—either solid, liquid, or gas at a given temperature. It may be helpful to summarize some of the things you may already know about these three states. Solids, liquids, and gases are states that you have seen, handled, worn, eaten, and breathed. A **solid** is generally rigid. Solids have their own shapes, and their volumes change only slightly in response to changes in temperature or pressure. Examples of solids are wood, metal coins, crystals of table salt, and ice. A **liquid** is a substance that takes the shape of its container. Liquids like water, oil, alcohol, and mercury metal at room temperature have volumes that change very little in response to changes in temperature or pressure. Unlike a solid or a liquid, a **gas** not only takes the shape of its container but completely fills its container. Its volume is drastically changed by temperature and pressure changes. Examples of gases at room temperature are those found in Earth's atmosphere—such as nitrogen, oxygen, argon, helium, and carbon dioxide—as well as nitrogen dioxide and chlorine.

Particle model for matter   How can these differences between the three states of matter be explained? Using a particle theory or a model may be helpful. Since scientists cannot easily magnify matter enough to see its smallest parts, they have developed a theory stating that matter is made up of tiny particles. Figures 1-17–1-19 on the next page show a simple model for particles in the solid, liquid, and gaseous states.

The properties of matter visible on the macroscopic level can now be understood on an invisible, or **submicroscopic,** level by imagining that all matter is composed of particles.

Solids   Figure 1-17 shows that the particles of a solid are, for all practical purposes, arranged in an orderly manner. The particles can be compared to people sitting in stadium seats at a baseball game. Does this suggest why solids are rigid and have constant volume? A solid is composed of particles packed closely together with little space between them. The particles that compose a solid do not move from place to place to any noticeable extent. As a result, a solid maintains a specific shape. The volume of the solid is composed almost entirely of the volume of the particles themselves. Therefore, compressing the solid to any great extent is not possible.

Liquids   On a particle scale, liquids resemble people in the stadium aisles, who move more freely than when sitting in their seats. A liquid is an example of a **fluid,** which is any substance that flows. Flowing occurs when particles are free to slide past one

PART 4
Section 1.9

Teaching Strategy

Particle Model for Matter

Students can observe that ice melts and water evaporates, but they have difficulty in imagining what is taking place on a submicroscopic level. Have students make drawings to represent the arrangement of particles (atoms) in aluminum as a solid, liquid, and a gas. Points to emphasize: The size and shape of the particles should be the same. (Some students may think that the particles swell up to fill the container.) The particles are just slightly farther apart in a liquid than in a solid and very far apart (about 10 diameters) in a gas. Use student drawings to diagnose misconceptions about matter. Ask students to evaluate the drawings to determine which is the best model.

 **Videodisc Connections**

22328 to 23515, side 2
States of matter (movie)

DEMONSTRATION

Gases

Demonstrate the increase in space occupied by a gas. Use a funnel to add 1 to 2 cm of finely crushed dry ice into the neck of a transparent balloon. Clamp the balloon closed, and watch the balloon inflate. Note the change in volume from solid to gas.

⚠️ **CAUTION: Wear safety goggles. Do not touch the crushed dry ice; handle it with a spoon or spatula, or wear thick gloves.**

Teaching Strategy

Gases

Have students make drawings of only the dry ice molecules in the balloon before and after evaporation. Points to emphasize: the molecules of CO_2 should be the same size and shape in both drawings; the number of molecules of CO_2 should be the same in both drawings; and the molecules should be orderly in the solid and randomly oriented in the gaseous state.

Guided Practice

Review the Concept Check question on page 26 with students. Answers can be found in Appendix E on page 808.

Reteaching Idea

If students have difficulty visualizing the states of matter at the submicroscopic level, develop class discussion around observations like the following. Ask students to come up with others. (a) A pail of water can hold only so much water, but the amount of air you can pump into a tire depends only on the strength of the tire. (b) A golf ball is hard and heavy for its size; a balloon is light and soft. (c) Molten lava flows down a volcanic mountain and stops when it cools enough to harden into rock. (d) You can smell the cake baking in the kitchen even though you are upstairs.

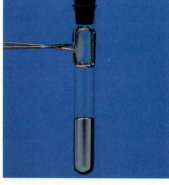
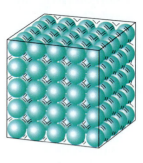

Figure 1-17 *Compare the structured shape of the solid in this figure with the shapes of the liquid and the gas shown in the next two figures. Only the solid has a definite shape and volume.*

Particles in a solid

Figure 1-18 *Molecules in a liquid have greater freedom of movement than in a solid. They easily tumble around each other, yet they are essentially in contact with each other at all times.*

Particles in a liquid

Figure 1-19 *Gas molecules move with greater freedom than those of solids and liquids. Spaces between gas molecules are large in comparison to the spaces between molecules of the other two states.*

Particles in a gas

another and continually change their relative positions. The particles are in constant motion. They are free to flow under, over, and around their neighboring particles, as shown in Figure 1-18. They are confined only by the borders of their container. As a result, liquids conform to the shape of their containers. Like a solid, most of the volume of the liquid is taken up by the volume of the particles themselves. In general, compressing a liquid does not change its volume significantly.

PART 4 REVIEW

A N S W E R S

■ **Keyed to Objectives**

L 25.

a.   b.

Gases Gases, like liquids, are fluids and are composed of particles in constant, random motion. However, one of the most surprising characteristics of a gas is that its particles have a much different environment from that of either a solid or a liquid. As illustrated in Figure 1-19, gas particles are not neatly "packaged" or arranged, nor are they touching each other most of the time. The gas particles resemble somewhat the crowd leaving the baseball stadium. Gas particles will move throughout their container, but without a container, they disperse freely.

As you can see from the previous passages, the particle model for matter is very useful in describing and explaining some properties of different states of matter. But it is much more useful than that. In the following chapters, you will discover how this model can explain what different kinds of matter have in common, how matter differs, how it can be changed, and even how it can be kept the same.

PART 4 REVIEW

25. The drawing represents a side view of a closed container that contains sixteen particles of lead. Each lead particle is represented by a circle.
   a. Draw the particles after the lead is melted.
   b. Draw the particles after the liquid lead has all evaporated.

26. Of the following properties—mass, density, and temperature—which one(s) must have the same value in order to allow you to conclude that the two substances are the same? Explain your answer.

27. Make a list of *all* the properties of matter that were mentioned in Part 4. Then choose three of the properties in the list and name an instrument that can measure that property.

28. Design an experiment that distinguishes between a piece of aluminum and a piece of silver. What property or properties would you use to distinguish between them?

29. Is breaking an egg a physical or a chemical change? Is frying an egg a physical or chemical change? Explain each answer.

30. Briefly explain how a gas differs on the particle level from a liquid or a solid.

Boxed numbers indicate questions that involve skills in interpretation, application, and analysis.

PART 4
Section 1.9 *continued*

☰CLOSE

Summing Up Main Ideas

Have students describe the changes of an ice cube and a stick of margarine when each is placed in a separate pan and heated. In their descriptions they should mention whether the change is physical or chemical. If the change is physical, they should use the particle model to describe the new physical state. For each chemical change, students should include how the properties of the substance changed.

PART 4 REVIEW

Assign the Part Review questions.

Evaluating Skills

These skills are evaluated in the Part Review questions indicated. **Classifying:** 26, 27, 29; **Predicting:** 28; **Designing and performing experiments:** 28; **Forming models:** 25

The models should conserve particles, show the correct spacing and location, and show a constant size and shape of particles.

J **26.** Density is a characteristic property; 10 g of aluminum are different from 10 g of salt.

K **27.** melting point—thermometer; boiling point—thermometer; density—graduated cylinder and balanced chemical reactions

J,K **28.** Measure the mass and volume and calculate the density. Al = 2.7 g/mL, Ag = 10 g/mL density. Place in 3.0M sodium hydroxide. Al reacts vigorously while Ag does not react.

K **29.** Breaking an egg is a physical change. The shell has the same properties, such as density and hardness, before and after breaking. Frying an egg causes a chemical change. The melting point of a fried egg is higher.

L **30.** In a gas, the particles are randomly oriented, relatively far apart (10 diameters), and are moving quite rapidly.

Using a Graph to Find Area

Estimated time: 45 minutes (Procedural Hints #1 and #2) or 2 45-minute periods (#3)

Process Skills

Measuring
Calculating
Constructing tables and graphs
Analyzing
Determining

Preparation

■ Materials

(for a class of 24, working in pairs)
Apparatus
(12 of each unless noted)
centigram balances, poster board rectangles (36 pieces for Procedural Hint #1, 12 pieces for #2 or #3), irregularly shaped samples of poster board (6) (Cut into free-form shapes; at least one should weigh more than the heaviest rectangle), graph paper (5 squares per inch is suitable), rulers, pencils

■ Preparation Hints

Use a paper cutter to make rectangles of poster board. Samples should vary from about 2" × 3" to 6" × 9". For these sizes the masses will vary from approximately 1.6 g to 13 g. It requires about 15 minutes to cut the set of 12 rectangles and 6 irregular samples. Label the rectangles 1–12 and the irregulars A–F.

Guiding the Investigation

■ Procedural Hints

There are several strategies for handling this activity:
1. Each pair finds mass of 3 rectangular and 1 irregular sample. Each pair plots graph and determines area of 1 irregular sample.
2. Each pair finds mass of 1 rectangular sample and 1 irregular
(continued on page T31)

L a b o r a t o r y
Investigation

Using a Graph to Find Area

Modern technology makes it possible for paper and cardboard mills to produce products of extremely uniform thickness. Many of these paper products are used in your everyday life—for example, notebook paper, cereal boxes, or tissues. In this activity, you will be using a sample of ordinary poster board with uniform thickness to study area. Since the thickness is constant, you can measure the mass and area of rectangular poster board samples and graph the data to find a relationship between mass and area (mass/area). Using the graph, you will then be able to find the unknown area of an irregularly shaped sample of poster board.

O b j e c t i v e s

Measure the mass (g) and **calculate** the area (cm^2) of rectangular samples of poster board.

Graph mass and area data, drawing a "best-fit" line through the origin.

Interpret a graph to find the area of an irregularly shaped sample of poster board.

■ MATERIALS

Apparatus
□ centigram balance
□ 4 rectangles of poster board
□ 1 irregular sample of poster board
□ graph paper
□ ruler
□ pencil

■ PROCEDURE

1. Obtain four rectangles of poster board from your teacher.
2. Find the mass of each sample of poster board and record the sample number and mass in the data table.

3. Measure the length and width of each sample to the nearest 0.1 cm. Record the measurements under length and width in the data table.
4. Calculate the area of each sample of poster board.
5. Obtain an irregularly shaped sample of poster board. Find the mass and record the mass and sample letter in the data table.

■ DATA ANALYSIS   Data Table

Rectangle code	Mass	Length	Width	Area

Irregular sample	Mass	Area

Data Table

Rectangle	Mass	Length	Width	Area
1	2.16 g	6.1 cm	8.7 cm	53 cm^2
2	4.97 g	11.65 cm	11.35 cm	132.0 cm^2
3	7.70 g	18.3 cm	11.3 cm	207 cm^2
4	13.12 g	22.5 cm	15.6 cm	351 cm^2
Irregular sample				
A	7.27 g			196 cm^2

1. Plot a graph of mass versus area for your rectangular samples. Use the instructions for graphing provided at the bottom of this page. Place mass on the y-axis and area on the x-axis.

2. Using your ruler, draw a "best-fit" line for your data points. Why should the line on your graph go through the origin?

3. Locate the mass of your irregular sample on the line and determine its area by moving down vertically to the x-axis. Record the area in the data table.

4. To verify the answer, compare your value for the area of this sample with a classmate's value.

■ CONCLUSIONS

1. Use your graph to find the mass of a poster board sample with an area of 300 cm^2.

2. What is the mass of 1 cm^2 of poster board?

3. Find the mass of a whole sheet of poster board measuring 71.2 cm by 56.4 cm.

4. If you had an unknown sample with a mass greater than the heaviest rectangle, what could you do to the line on the graph to help you find its area?

5. a. Could you have measured the size of the irregular sheet of poster board with a ruler and calculated its area? Explain.
   b. How would the calculated value compare with the value from the graph?

Rules for Good Graphing

1. *Give your graph a descriptive title.* The purpose of a graph is to communicate information in a concise manner. A graph conveys little information if it is not labeled properly.

2. *Indent the axes from the edge of the graph paper* and draw them with a straightedge.

3. *Label each axis and indicate the units used.* Numbers along each axis are useless if you do not show what they represent. Numbers representing variables, which you change throughout an experiment, are called independent variables. Independent variables are labeled on the horizontal (x) axis. Variables that change because of changes in the independent variable are called dependent variables. Dependent variables are labeled on the vertical (y) axis.

4. *Choose an appropriate scale* that allows you to get all data on the graph. Check the largest and smallest values to determine the range for each axis. For most graphs, there is no need to begin the scale

at zero. Just be sure you begin with a number lower than your lowest data point.

5. *Choose a convenient scale.* A graph is easier to read (and plot) when each square represents a value of 1, 2, 5, or a multiple of ten times these numbers: 10, 20, 50, or 0.2, 0.5. Maintain the same scale for the length of the graph.

6. *Locate points with an X or a dot with a small circle around it.* An X or a dot with a circle around it can be located after the graph line is drawn.

7. *Draw a smooth curve or straight line to represent the general tendency of the data points.* Graphs drawn in math classes represent absolute numbers, and each data point falls on the curve being plotted. This situation is seldom the case in science, where the data points represent experimental measurements. Data points based on experimental measurements have uncertainty associated with them.

(continued from page T30)
sample. Pair records their mass and area values in a class data table. Each pair uses class data to plot graph and determine area of irregular sample. Compare value with other pairs.

3. a. First period: Put 1 rectangular sample beside each balance and have students move from station to station. Each pair plots graph for all rectangles.
   b. Second period: Each pair finds mass of an irregular sample, determines its area, and compares values with other pairs.

For all strategies, discuss these concepts: proper method for drawing graphs; interpolation and extrapolation; errors in determining mass and measurements; and determination of a "standard," g/cm^2, which is the slope of the line.

If you wish to discuss significant digits and rounding off of numbers, refer to Chapter 4.

Data Analysis
■ Sample Data
(See table and graph below.)

Conclusions
1. According to the sample data given, a poster board with an area of 300 cm^2 would have a mass of about 11.5 g.

2. According to the sample data given, a poster board with an area of 1 cm^2 would have a mass of about 0.038 g. This would also be the slope of the graph.

3. According to the sample data given, a poster board measuring 71.2 cm by 56.4 cm (4015.68 cm^2) would have a mass of about 153g.

4. You must extrapolate (extend) the line, using a dotted line.

5. a. No. The irregular piece of poster board contains curves and holes. Only a rough "guess" could be made.
   b. The calculated value would be much less accurate than the one on the graph.

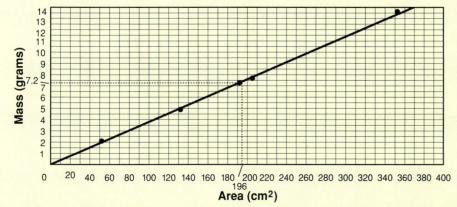

Chapter 1
Review
ANSWERS
begin on page
T37a.

Summary

Applying a Scientific Method

■ Science is a way of knowing based on careful observation. Scientists look for and summarize regularities through classifying, testing hypotheses, and developing theories.

Using Mathematical Knowledge

■ Matter is measured by comparing an unknown quantity with a standard. Measurements result in a number and a unit that identifies the standard.

■ Many units are in common use, but scientists use SI units. SI units are defined so that all quantities can be expressed in terms of seven fundamental quantities, or base units.

■ Prefixes are used with base units to name units larger or smaller than the base unit. Units for area and volume are derived from the base unit for length. Units for other quantities are derived by combining base units.

■ The mathematics for measured quantities is similar to any mathematics, but units are included in calculations.

Developing Tools for Analysis

■ Data from observations are organized in tables and graphs to reveal trends and relationships among two or more quantities. The slope of a straight-line graph is a ratio that describes how much one variable changes as the other variable increases by one unit.

■ Density is a ratio that indicates how much mass there will be in each cubic centimeter (or other unit volume) of matter.

Exploring Matter

■ Properties of matter can be used to identify matter. Density is one of those properties.

■ Changes that produce new kinds of matter are chemical changes. Changes that do not produce new kinds of matter are physical changes.

■ Solids, liquids, and gases are states of matter. Each state has its own properties, based on the arrangement and energy of its particles.

Chemically Speaking

area *1.4*
chemical changes *1.8*
classification *1.2*
constant *1.7*
data *1.5*
density *1.7*
fluid *1.9*
gas *1.9*
hypothesis *1.2*
inference *1.2*
liquid *1.9*

macroscopic
    observations *1.8*
melting *1.8*
model *1.2*
quantity *1.3*
SI base units *1.4*
slope *1.7*
solid *1.9*
submicroscopic *1.9*
theory *1.2*
volume *1.4*

Concept Mapping

Using the method of concept mapping described at the front of this book, complete the concept map for the term *chemistry*.

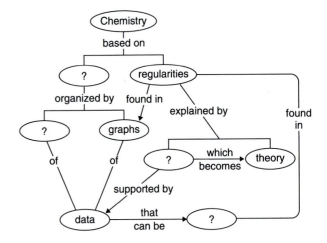

PROBLEM-SOLVING STRATEGIES

Students apply these strategies in the following questions.

■ **Factor-label method:** 22, 25, 26, 32, 34, 35, 36, 37, 38, 52, 53, 54, 55

■ **Using what you know:** 22, 24, 25,

26, 27, 28, 53, 55

■ **Verifying your answer:** 27, 28

Questions and Problems

APPLYING A SCIENTIFIC METHOD

A. Objective: **Recognize** *how knowledge obtained from the study of chemistry can be applied in your life.*

1. Name at least ten things that you use on a daily basis that you would not have if chemists had not learned how to change substances into new substances.
2. Give at least two examples of situations when it was important for you to know how much of a chemical was safe and healthy to put into your body.
3. Give an example of some chemical change that you would like to go very fast. Give an example of one that you would like to go very slowly.
4. What is likely to be the first question emergency crews will want answered when they respond to an overturned chemical transport truck?

B. Objective: **Explain** *why communication is an important aspect of obtaining scientific knowledge.*

5. Which of the following statements appear to describe observations and which describe inferences?
   a. The sky is cloudy today.
   b. It is going to rain.
   c. Joan is 6 feet, 4 inches tall.
   d. Bill is clumsy.
   e. Manuel is in love with Maria.
   f. Smoke from that smokestack is polluting the air.
   g. Our drinking water contains 1.0 ppm of fluoride ion.
   h. Drinking water that contains more than 1 ppm of fluoride ion significantly reduces tooth decay.

6. Recall when you disagreed with a friend, parent, or teacher about something both of you observed. What can account for such disagreements?
7. Would you expect disagreements like those suggested by question 6 to occur more often between people of the same age or people of different ages? From similar or dissimilar home environments? From the same or different countries? Explain the reasoning you used in answering these questions.
8. Why do scientists insist that observations be made by at least two independent observers before they accept the observation as valid?

C. Objective: **Describe** *the functions of a hypothesis and a theory in the scientific method.*

9. Describe some regularity that you have observed about chemicals in your home and propose a hypothesis to explain that regularity. (For example, what have you observed to be true of all kinds of soap? What could explain the regularity you identified?)
10. What is the difference between the hypothesis that you made in answering question 9 and a scientific theory related to the same observations?
11. Hypotheses are usually written in the form of an *if . . . then . . .* statement. For example: If white powder is added to water, then it will dissolve. Explain why the *if . . . then . . .* statement exemplifies the function of a hypothesis in any scientific method.

USING MATHEMATICAL KNOWLEDGE

D. Objective: **Differentiate** *between quantities and numbers.*

12. What is the difference between a quantity and a number?
13. What is wrong with adding 2 yd + 2 ft?
14. Why is "Your mass is 165" meaningless?

Boxed numbers indicate questions that involve skills in interpretation, application, and analysis.

15. State your age. Does the statement represent a number or a quantity? Why?

16. Change each of the following numbers into a *quantity*. Then briefly describe the physical reality that the quantity could express. For example, *8* can be *8 cm*, the length of your index finger.
    a. 28   c. 1
    b. 1050   d. 0.010

E. Objective: **Recognize** *the meaning of base SI units, including their abbreviations and the quantities those units describe.*

17. Write the names for the following units.
    a. mm   g. mg
    b. Mm   h. dm
    c. km   i. m^3
    d. kg   j. cm^3
    e. μg k. mm^2
    f. Mg   l. km^2

18. Identify which units in item 17 could be used to describe the width of this book.

19. Identify which units in item 17 could be used to describe the mass of this book.

20. Which units in item 17 could be used to describe the surface covered by this page?

21. Which units in item 17 could be used to describe the amount of water you drank today?

22. Write two equivalents between the units listed in item 17 and the base unit. For example:

    $$1000 \text{ mm} = 1 \text{ m}$$
    $$1 \text{ mm} = 0.001 \text{ m}$$

23. Match the following quantities with the measurements they describe:
    a. 6 dm   d. 20 g
    b. 2 m^3 e. 20 kg
    c. 300 cm^2
       1. Total surface of a paperback book.
       2. Mass of a sack of concrete.
       3. Volume of a refrigerator.
       4. Mass of a pencil.
       5. Length of a beagle.

F. Objective: **Apply** *problem-solving strategies to convert SI units and to* **calculate** *derived quantities from base SI units.*

24. Complete the indicated conversions.
    a. ? mg = 37 g
    b. ? g = 4.7 kg
    c. ? km = 138 m
    d. ? m = 4 021 mm

25. Complete the indicated conversions.
    a. ? mm^2 = 1 m^2 e. ? cm^3 = 1 mm^3
    b. ? km^2 = 1 m^2 f. ? m^3 = 1 cm^3
    c. ? cm^2 = 1 mm^2 g. ? km^3 = 1 m^3
    d. ? μm^2 = 1 mm^2 h. ? dm^3 = 1 m^3

26. Complete the following conversions.
    a. ? m^2 = 5 280 mm^2
    b. ? m^2 = 2.5 km^2
    c. ? mm^2 = 453 cm^2
    d. ? mm^2 = 9 055 033 μm^2

27. John converted his mass from kilograms to grams and got an answer of 0.072 g. How do you know that this answer is unreasonable?

28. Alice calculated the volume of a box and got an answer of 256 cm^2. Can this be correct? How do you know?

DEVELOPING TOOLS FOR ANALYSIS

G. Objective: **Construct** tables and graphs *to organize data.*

29. Make the following measurements and organize your data in a table.
    a. Using a measuring cup and a watch with a second hand, collect data that show the volume of water that drips from a faucet over a period of time. Make at least ten readings of time and volume.
    b. If you have a kitchen scale, take several readings for one, two, three, etc., objects of uniform size. You could use spoons, forks, cups, candy, beans, or any convenient objects around the house.

c. Make a chain of paper clips or other objects of uniform length and measure the length containing one, two, etc., objects.

30. Use the data collected in one item of number 29 to plot a graph.

31. When you plotted a graph of your data, did all your data points fall on the line (or curve) that you drew to represent the points? Do you think they should have? Explain.

H. Objective: Determine *density by interpreting data on a graph.*

32. a. On the same graph, plot both sets of data given below for Object A and Object B.
   b. Look at the graph. How do the densities of the two objects compare?
   c. Use the graph to calculate the density of each object. How do they compare?
   d. Verify the densities you found from the graph by calculating the density.

Object A		Object B	
Volume	**Mass**	**Volume**	**Mass**
20 cm^3	4.8 g	20 cm^3	14 g
40 cm^3	9.6 g	40 cm^3	28 g
80 cm^3	19.2 g	80 cm^3	56 g
100 cm^3	24.0 g	100 cm^3	70 g

33. a. Use the following data to make a graph (mass on the y-axis) that contains two lines, one for aluminum and one for lead.

Aluminum		Lead	
mass	volume	mass	volume
15 g	5.5 cm^3	20 g	1.7 cm^3
42 g	15.5 cm^3	35 g	2.9 cm^3
70 g	25.9 cm^3	63 g	5.3 cm^3

b. Do both lines pass through the origin? Explain why or why not.
c. Use the graph to determine the mass of 20 cm^3 of aluminum.
d. Use the graph to determine the volume of 50 g of lead.
e. What is the relationship between the mass and volume of aluminum? What is the relationship between the mass and volume of lead? What is the common name given to this relationship?

I. Objective: Calculate *density by using problem-solving strategies.*

34. What is the density of 19.2 g of oak that has a volume of 25.7 cm^3?

35. In an experiment used to find the density of an aluminum block by water displacement, a student gathered the following data:

Volume of water in graduated cylinder without the aluminum block	14.6 mL
Volume of water plus aluminum block in graduated cylinder	21.9 mL
Mass of the aluminum block	19.73 g

Using these data, find the density of the aluminum.

36. A chemist wants to confirm whether a piece of metal is pure gold or an alloy of gold and less dense metals. She determines the volume by water displacement to be 6.35 mL and the mass of the object to be 101.6 g. Is the object pure gold? (The density of gold is 19.3 g/cm^3.)

37. A 1980 penny has a mass of about 3.5 g. What is its volume?

38. The following table lists the mass, volume, and density of several objects. Supply the missing values.

Mass	Volume	Density
a. 45.2 g	8.4 cm^3	____
b. ____	13.3 cm^3	4.30 g/cm^3
c. 2 356 g	____	4.30 g/cm^3

EXPLORING MATTER

J. Objective: Discuss *how properties of matter can be used for identification of matter.*

39. List all of the objects that you can see right now and classify those objects into groups with similar properties. What characteristics did you use as a basis for classification?

40. Why did you use certain properties of the things you saw to classify the objects in item 39 but did not use other properties for the classification?

41. What properties of matter can be used to distinguish between a cube of copper and a sugar cube?

42. Measuring the mass or volume of an object gives no clue to its identity. What could you do with mass and volume to produce a quantity describing a characteristic property?

43. Some students obtain a solid as a result of an experiment. They find that the solid has a fixed melting point and boiling point and that it has a uniform density. They conclude that they have discovered a new substance. Is the conclusion justified?

K. Objective: Distinguish *between chemical and physical changes.*

44. Indicate whether each of the following changes is chemical or physical. Explain why you answered as you did.
   a. leaves changing color in autumn
   b. crushing a dry leaf in your hand
   c. an aspirin dissolving in your mouth or stomach
   d. an aspirin acting on the body to relieve a headache
   e. water boiling
   f. beans cooking
   g. grass growing
   h. cutting grass
   i. bleaching clothes

L. Objective: Use models *to explain different properties of solids, liquids, and gases.*

45. Make a drawing that represents 15 particles of mercury doing the following:
   a. changing from a liquid to a solid
   b. changing from a gas to a liquid

46. Make a drawing of ten particles of water (H_2O) changing from a liquid to a gas.

47. List two properties that are characteristic of all liquids and two properties that are not characteristic of all liquids.

48. Using the particle model, explain a characteristic you listed in item 47.

49. Explain what gives a solid its property of rigidity.

50. Draw a particle model to explain why a gas is compressible, whereas a solid and a liquid are not.

51. Devise a model to explain why ten different potassium alum crystals may be of different sizes but all have the same angular shape.

Critical Thinking

SYNTHESIS WITHIN THE CHAPTER

52. Cement has a density of about 3 g/cm^3 once it has set. What is the mass of a cubic meter of cement? How many cubic centimeters of cement would you be able to lift?

53. A rock has a volume of 3.4 m^3 and a mass of 1.09 kg. Could the rock be diamond? (What information do you need to look up?)

54. Pollutants in air and water are frequently measured in parts per million (ppm) or parts per billion (ppb). One part per million would mean that there is one gram of the pollutant in one million grams of air or water. At ordinary temperature and pressure, air has a density of 1.2×10^{-3} g/cm^3. What volume of air would contain one gram of sulfur dioxide, a pollutant that causes acid rain, if the sulfur dioxide concentration is 2 ppm?

55. In the decomposition of water, 1 g of hydrogen gas occupies twice the volume of 8 g of oxygen gas. Which gas has the greater density? How do you know?

Using these data, complete the following statement to describe the facts given: "The density of (hydrogen, oxygen) is ____ times the density of (hydrogen, oxygen)."

Projects

56. Invent a new system of measurement. To be useful and reliable, the system should have these characteristics:
   a. All standards should be ones that can be kept for centuries without change.
   b. It should be easy to copy the standard to make practical measuring devices.
   c. It should be possible to express all quantities in terms of a few standards.
   d. Conversion from one unit to another should be simple.

57. Identify a pollution problem in your community. Find out causes of the problem and steps that can reduce it.

58. Make arrangements to tour a municipal water-treatment plant. Find out what procedures are used to ensure that the treated water is safe.

59. Attention to toxic substances in food, water, and air has increased in recent years. For a toxic substance that is in the news, find out how it is detected and how much must be present to be detected.

60. Choose a partner and do the following. One of you should build something with blocks or similar construction material and then write a description of what has been built so that the other partner can reproduce it without looking at the original construction. Compare the two constructions and talk about what was said that helped describe the construction process and what was said that seemed to hinder it.

Research and Writing

61. Although science can contribute to the solution of many social problems, it cannot solve those problems, because the methods of science do not apply. Select a social problem that interests you (pollution, nuclear war, drug abuse) and outline aspects of the problem. After outlining the problem, write a paper on how science might be applied to some aspect of the problem. Identify those aspects of the problem that cannot be addressed by science and explain why.

62. Many laws controlling toxic substances are written to require elimination of the substance. Interview individuals who work in industries affected by these laws or interview environmentalists who have worked to enact the laws. Write a paper about the implications and alternatives that are available to protect life without adversely affecting the economy.

63. Go to your school or public library and obtain a scientific journal. (*Scientific American* or *Science News* are most commonly found.) Write to the editors of the journal you chose and inquire how an article gets accepted for publication, including the reviewing process. Choose an article in the journal in which you are interested. Do additional reading on the topic and then write a review of the article.

☐ Boxed numbers indicate questions that involve skills in interpretation, application, and analysis.

Chapter 1 Review Concept Map

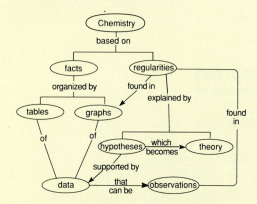

1. Any object made of plastic; any object made of metal other than gold; any paper product; paint or varnish; most dyes; most food flavorings; food that has a long shelf life; most clothes that you wear; any rubber product; carpeting and other floor coverings; gasoline and other petroleum products; drugs of all kinds.

2. When taking painkillers or cold medications; if on a diet, what you eat; when taking insulin if one is diabetic.

3. Speed up: Decomposition of waste in a landfill; cooking food. Slow down: Rusting of iron; aging process

4. What kind of matter do we have?

5. a. observation
   b. inference
   c. observation
   d. inference (This might be debated. However, what is observed is that Bill knocks things over, spills things, stumbles, and so on. We infer that he is poorly coordinated and describe it as "clumsy." Another possibility is that Bill has poor eyesight.)
   e. inference
   f. inference ("Smoke" seen coming from stacks is often harmless water vapor.)
   g. inference (This may also be debated. The statement is assumed to be based on some observation and measurement. However, what was observed was almost certainly how much light of a particular wavelength was absorbed by the sample or how much precipitate formed when a certain reagent was added to a sample.)
   h. inference

6. Teachers and parents are normally older, and they have experienced different things in their lives than you have experienced in yours. Whether they are actually wiser as well as older is open to debate, but the differences in experience account for many disagreements.

7. People of different ages, people from dissimilar home environments, and people from different countries are more likely to disagree. The reasoning is that they are more likely to have different experiences, and the experiences we have determine how we interpret events.

8. What we observe and how we interpret it is influenced by what we already know and believe. Since no two people are likely to know and believe exactly the same things, the more people who agree about what happened, the more likely it actually happened.

9. Answers will vary, but the reasons for regularity (such as the slipperiness of soaps and detergents and their ability to dissolve grease) stem from the similarities in chemical structure and chemical properties of the substance.

10. A hypothesis is a proposed explanation, whereas a theory is a hypothesis that has been tested many times and found to be valid in every test.

11. The function of a hypothesis is to explain events or reactions that have already occurred and to predict the outcome of similar events or reactions in the future, so the if…then… approach is an example of using one set of observations to predict other events.

12. A quantity is something that can be measured and described with a number and a unit, which refers to a standard; a number merely states "how many" and is not useful in measuring unless we know the units also.

13. 2 yd and 2 ft have different units and cannot be added until the units of one are converted to the same units as the other.

14. No units are given.

15. If you state your age in years or years and months, it is a quantity, because it has a number and units associated with it.

16. Answers will vary.
    a. 28 could be 28 days, the number of days in 4 weeks
    b. 1050 could be 1050 grams, the mass of a large rock
    c. 1 could be 1 mile, the distance you walk to school
    d. 0.010 could be 0.010 L, the amount of cough medicine you take

17. a. millimeter
    b. megameter
    c. kilometer
    d. kilogram
    e. microgram
    f. megagram
    g. milligram
    h. decimeter
    i. cubic meter
    j. cubic centimeter
    k. square millimeter
    l. square kilometer

18. a, b, c, and h

19. d, e, f, and g

20. k and l

21. i and j could be used to describe the volume of water and d, e, f, and g could be used to describe its mass.

22. a. $1000 \text{ mm} = 1 \text{ m}$, $1 \text{ mm} = 0.001 \text{ m}$
    b. $0.000\ 001 \text{ Mm} = 1 \text{ m}$, $1 \text{ Mm} = 1\ 000\ 000 \text{ m}$
    c. $0.001 \text{ km} = 1 \text{ m}$, $1 \text{ km} = 1000 \text{ m}$
    d. $0.001 \text{ kg} = 1 \text{ g}$, $1 \text{ kg} = 1000 \text{ g}$
    e. $1\ 000\ 000 \text{ μg} = 1 \text{ g}$, $1 \text{ μg} = 0.000\ 001 \text{ g}$
    f. $0.000\ 001 \text{ Mg} = 1 \text{ g}$, $1 \text{ Mg} = 1\ 000\ 000 \text{ g}$
    g. $1000 \text{ mg} = 1 \text{ g}$, $1 \text{ mg} = 0.001 \text{ g}$
    h. $10 \text{ dm} = 1 \text{ m}$, $1 \text{ dm} = 0.1 \text{ m}$
    i. m^3 is the base unit for volume
    j. $1\ 000\ 000 \text{ cm}^3 = 1 \text{ m}^3$, $1 \text{ cm}^3 = 0.000\ 001 \text{ m}^3$
    k. $1\ 000\ 000 \text{ mm}^2 = 1 \text{ m}^2$, $1 \text{ mm}^2 = 0.000\ 001 \text{ m}^2$
    l. $0.000\ 001 \text{ km}^2 = 1 \text{ m}^2$, $1 \text{ km}^2 = 1\ 000\ 000 \text{ m}^2$

23. 1. c
    2. e
    3. b
    4. d
    5. a

24. a. $? \text{ mg} = 37 \text{ g} \times 1000 \text{ mg}/1 \text{ g}$
       $= 37\ 000 \text{ mg}$
    b. $? \text{ g} = 4.7 \text{ kg} \times 1000 \text{ g}/1 \text{ kg}$
       $= 4700 \text{ g}$
    c. $? \text{ km} = 138 \text{ m} \times 1 \text{ km}/1000 \text{ m}$
       $= 0.138 \text{ km}$
    d. $? \text{ m} = 4021 \text{ mm} \times 1 \text{ m}/1000 \text{ mm}$
       $= 4.021 \text{ m}$

25. a. $10^6 \text{ mm}^2 = 1 \text{ m}^2$
    b. $10^{-6} \text{ km}^2 = 1 \text{ m}^2$
    c. $10^{-2} \text{ cm}^2 = 1 \text{ mm}^2$
    d. $10^6 \text{ μm}^2 = 1 \text{ mm}^2$

e. 10^{-3} cm^3 = 1 mm^3

f. 10^{-6} m^3 = 1 cm^3

g. 10^{-9} km^3 = 1 m^3

h. 10^{-3} dm^3 = 1 m^3

26. a. ? m^2 = 5280 m̶m̶^{2} × 1 m^2/10^6 m̶m̶^{2} = 0.005280 m^2

b. ? m^2 = 2.5 k̶m̶^{2} × 1 m^2/10^{-6} k̶m̶^{2} = 2.5 × 10^6 m^2

c. ? mm^2 = 453 c̶m̶^{2} × 1 mm^2/10^{-2} c̶m̶^{2} = 4.53 × 10^4 mm^2

d. ? mm^2 = 9 055 033 μ̶m̶^{2} × 1 mm^2/10^6 μ̶m̶^{2} = 9.055 033 mm^2

27. Grams are a small unit of measurement, so the answer should be a large number of grams.

28. No; cm^2 is a unit for area not volume.

29. Answers will vary.

30. Answers will vary.

31. All the data points were not on the line because of variation in the objects measured and uncertainty in the data and plotting the points.

32. a.

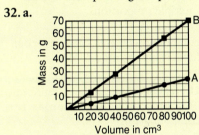

b. B is more dense because the slope of the line is greater.

c. The densities can be calculated from the slope of each line, 0.24 g/cm^3 for A and 0.70 g/cm^3 for B.

d. 0.24 g/cm^3 for A and 0.70 g/cm^3 for B

33. a.

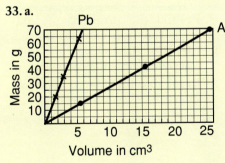

b. Yes; In both cases when the volume is zero, the mass will be zero.

c. 54 g

d. 4.2 cm^3

e. 2.70 g/cm^3, 11.2 g/cm^3, density

34. 19.2 g/25.7 cm^3 = 0.747 g/cm^3

35. 21.9 mL − 14.6 mL = 7.3 mL
19.73 g/7.3 mL = 2.7 g/mL

36. 101.6 g/6.35 mL = 16.0 g/mL
This is not gold. The density is too low.

37. 3.5 g̶ × 1 cm^3/8.96 g̶ = 0.39 cm^3

38. a. 45.2 g/8.4 cm^3 = 5.4 g/cm^3

b. 13.3 c̶m̶^{3} × 4.30 g/c̶m̶^{3} = 57.2 g

c. 2356 g̶ × 1 cm^3/4.30 g̶ = 548 cm^3

39. Answers will vary.

40. Answers will vary.

41. Density, color, malleability, solubility in water, melting point, hardness

42. The ratio of mass to volume is a characteristic property called density.

43. No; They have found a pure substance but for it to be a new substance they must show that it has properties different from any known substance.

44. a, d, f, g, i are chemical changes. All involve changes in the composition of the substances—each produced a new kind of matter with different properties.

45. a.

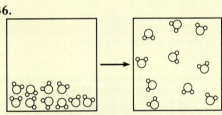

b.

46.

47. The particles in a liquid can move around freely within the substance and the substance takes the shape of the container. Two properties not characteristic of all liquids are being colored and having an odor.

48. The particles in a liquid are not bonded with directional forces; therefore, a liquid is shapeless.

49. In every crystal the atoms are arranged the same way in space; therefore, no matter what size the crystal is, the shape is the same.

50.

solid   liquid   gas

51. The amount of matter is different in each crystal, but the spatial arrangement of particles is the same in each, so all have the same shape.

52. 1 m̶^{3} × 10^6 cm^3/m̶^{3} × 3 g/c̶m̶^{3} = 3 × 10^6 g
Answers will vary, for example:
48 k̶g̶ × 1000 g̶/k̶g̶ × 1 cm^3/3 g̶ = 12 000 cm^3

53. $$\dfrac{1.09 \text{ k̶g̶} \times \frac{10^3 \text{ g̶}}{1 \text{ k̶g̶}}}{3.4 \text{ m̶}^3 \times \frac{10^6 \text{ c̶m̶}^3}{1 \text{ m̶}^3}} = 3.2 \times 10^{-4} \text{ g/cm}^3$$

This is too small for the density of diamond given in the Handbook of Chemistry as 3.52 g/cm^3

54. 1 g̶ S̶O̶$_2$ × $\dfrac{10^6 \text{ g̶ a̶i̶r̶}}{2 \text{ g̶ S̶O̶}_2}$

× $\dfrac{1 \text{ cm}^3}{1.2 \times 10^{-3} \text{ g̶ a̶i̶r̶}}$ = 4.2 × 10^8 cm^3

55. Oxygen has the greater density since a smaller volume has a larger mass. "The density of oxygen is 16 times the density of hydrogen."

Describing Matter

Investigations	Demonstrations	Texas Essential Elements★
Laboratory Manual 2–1 M Laboratory Manual 2–2 S In-text Investigation, page T72	Electrolysis, page T44	**Content:** 2.1, 2.3 **Process:** 4.3, 7.2
Laboratory Manual 2–3 IM		**Content:** 3.2, 4.2, 4.4, 6.1
		Content: 6.1 **Process:** 4.3, 10.3, 10.4
		Content: 2.4 **Process:** 1.1, 1.2, 2.1, 3.1, 4.1, 4.3, 7.2, 10.1
		Process: 4.2, 4.3, 7.1, 10.4
		Content: 8.9 **Process:** 10.1, 10.2, 10.4

KEY:
M–Microscale **S**–Structured
I–Inquiry **IM**–Inquiry Microscale

★*See pages T8–T11 for complete listing of Texas Essential Elements.*

2

Describing Matter

Chapter Rationale

Chapter 2 introduces students to the symbols used for elements and the rules for writing formulas and names for compounds. The differences in bonding between molecular compounds, such as water and carbon dioxide, and ionic compounds, such as calcium carbonate and potassium chloride, are explained in a later chapter.

About the Photograph

As students study the composition of matter, they may observe the color, texture, and uniformity of a substance. The purity of a substance can sometimes be determined by simple observation.

Chapter Planning Hints

Plan to spend seven to nine class sessions to complete the chapter, including the Laboratory Investigation and the Chapter Review. You may wish to obtain the KC? Discoverer program *Exploring the Properties of the Chemical Elements* in Part 2. You will find one optional demonstration suggested for this chapter on page T44. You may wish to preview it at this time.

The macroscopic observation of color indicates that this crystal is a mixture. The crystal contains colorless calcite and green malachite.

PART **Defining Mixtures**
1 **and Pure Substances**

You know after studying Chapter 1 that macroscopic observations such as boiling point, melting point, and physical state can be used for identifying matter. Explaining macroscopic observations is the essence of chemistry because it contributes to an understanding of what matter is like at the particle, or submicroscopic, level.

For example, if muddy water is left standing in a glass for hours or days, it will separate into layers of dirt and clear water. This observation can be explained by saying that the water sample is not a single type of matter. It is a mixture—two (or more) kinds of matter that have separate identities because of different properties. Matter that can be physically separated into component parts is a **mixture.**

When the component parts of a mixture can no longer be separated into simpler substances, each component can be classified as a pure substance. Classifying matter into pure substances and mixtures is one step toward understanding matter at the submicroscopic level and developing a language to describe that understanding.

2.1 Separating Mixtures

If you compare the water from which dirt has settled with water from your kitchen tap, you can probably tell them apart by the property of taste and possibly by appearance. If you shine a strong light through the samples, as shown in Figure 2-1 on the next page, the light is hardly scattered at all by the settled muddy water, but it is not scattered by most tap water. (Some tap water contains impurities that scatter light.) Is the scattered light due to some kind of matter mixed with the water? If so, you should be able to separate the mixture. But how?

Purifying water If you have visited a water-purification plant or purified water yourself, you know the answer. By adding alum and lime to the water, a gelatinous (jellylike) material is produced, as shown in Figure 2-2 on the next page. Small particles suspended in the water stick to the gelatinous material and are removed as the gelatinous material settles out or is removed by filtering through beds of sand. These processes leave water that does not scatter light. The mixture has been separated into components. But is the water now pure?

Objectives

Part 1

A. *Discuss* properties and techniques that can be used to determine whether matter is a mixture or a pure substance.

B. *Summarize* how decomposition of a pure substance can be used to differentiate between elements and compounds.

C. *Compare and contrast* compounds and mixtures, using the law of definite composition and the law of multiple proportions.

D. *Distinguish* between elements and compounds on the submicroscopic level using the atomic model.

Developing Skills

Students may apply these skills in their study of Part 1.

Classifying: Have students examine the substances in Figures 2–2 and 2–3 and classify them as elements or compounds.

Comparing and contrasting: Have students compare the properties of the compounds with the elements that compose them in Figures 2–7 and 2–8, including physical state, color, odor, and toxicity.

Forming models: Have students make submicroscopic drawings of the substances in Figure 2–11 that distinguish between elements and compounds.

☰ FOCUS

Activate Prior Knowledge

Lead a discussion about mixtures and pure substances from everyday life. Have students think of examples and ask them to what degree the components of these mixtures can be separated. Ask students at what point the substances would be classified as pure substances.

☰ TEACH

Teaching Strategy

Separating Mixtures

Display several nails in a beaker containing sugar. After students identify components of the mixture, ask for suggestions of how to separate the mixture. If the nails are fragmented into dust, which of the methods could still be used?

Figure 2-1 *When a beam of light passes through pure water or a solution, the light is not scattered and is barely visible when viewed from the side. When light passes through a liquid with minute particles mixed in it, the light is scattered and is visible when viewed from the side.*

Solutions By adding things to pure water you can make mixtures that do not scatter light. For example, if table salt or sugar is added to water, it disappears. Taste suggests that the salt or sugar is still there, but it cannot be seen; neither will the mixture scatter light. Thus light scattering cannot be used as a test of whether a material is pure. Mixtures like salt water or sugar water which look uniform throughout and do not scatter light, are called **solutions.** If solutions such as salt water and sugar water are mixtures, how can they be separated into component parts?

Techniques for separation If you ever have let a pan of salt water boil dry on the stove, you have a clue about how solutions can be separated. When the pan boils dry, you see a white solid that remains and conclude that it is the salt that was dissolved in the water. If this procedure is carried out so that the water that boils away is recovered, solutions like salt water and sugar water can be separated into their component parts by using a procedure

Figure 2-2 *By adding alum and lime to muddy water (left), a gelatinous substance is formed, removing impurities (right).*

PART 1
Section 2.1 continued

Science Background

Purifying Water

The water you drink contains small amounts of dozens of chemicals. Local water authorities test for a few substances daily. Water samples are sent regularly to a laboratory where the water is analyzed for the minute amounts of many chemicals.

Teaching Strategy

Representing Mixtures

Make microscopic drawings showing 10 particles of each of the following mixtures using the symbols indicated.
1. powdered iron and powdered sugar
2. alcohol dissolved in water

Points of emphasis:
a. particles on bottom
b. constant size and shape of symbols
c. random orientation

Teaching Strategy

Techniques for Separation

Call the local water department. Ask the chemist or water treatment engineer to give a talk to your chemistry class or to arrange a field trip to the water treatment plant.

T40

 D E M O N S T R A T I O N

Defining Mixtures and Pure Substances

In a beaker, add 5.0 g of $CuCl_2 \cdot 2H_2O$ and add 10.0 g of it to 100 mL of boiled, distilled water in another.

⚠ **CAUTION: Wear a lab apron and safety goggles. Put a shield in front of the demonstration.** Weigh two nails; put one in each beaker. Have students identify the elements (Fe), compounds (H_2O, copper(II) chloride), mixtures ($CuCl_2(aq)$), and pure substances (H_2O, $CuCl_2 \cdot 2H_2O$, Fe). The next day classify again (elements: Fe, Cu; compounds: H_2O, $FeCl_2$; mixtures: $FeCl_2(aq)$). Remove nails, rinse copper off into the beaker, and dry them. The color of solution shows all the $CuCl_2$ reacted and iron is left over. Ask students if the weight of the nail will change.

(continued on page T41)

called **distillation.** Figure 2-3 shows a simple apparatus for separating mixtures by distillation.

Although most mixtures containing water can be separated by distillation, some cannot. For example, household ammonia is a solution of ammonia and water that cannot be separated totally by distillation.

Many mixtures are extremely difficult to separate. Such mixtures may be considered pure for many years—until someone invents a new procedure or a better instrument for analysis and separation. Much of the recent awareness of air pollution, water pollution, carcinogens in foods, and similar environmental concerns has come about because new and better techniques have been found to detect those impurities.

2.2 Characteristics of Pure Substances

After a mixture is separated, how can you tell if the component parts are pure substances? You can answer this question if you examine some physical properties of the components. For example, you learned in Chapter 1 that density is a property that can be used to identify matter. Comparing the density of a component of a mixture to the density of a known pure substance may help confirm its purity.

DO YOU KNOW?

One of the gases produced when wood is heated in the absence of air can be condensed, thus forming an alcohol. This alcohol, methanol, is also known as wood alcohol.

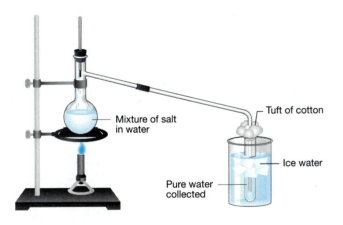

Mixture of salt in water

Tuft of cotton

Ice water

Pure water collected

Figure 2-3 Salt can be removed from a mixture of table salt and water and from ocean water or salt water by placing the mixture in a flask and boiling it. The water in the mixture will change to a gas, then move through the tube where it cools to become liquid once more. Because the boiling point of pure salt is well over 1000°C, it remains in the original flask after all the water has boiled off.

Boiling point If you measured the temperature of a boiling liquid while it was being distilled, as shown in Figure 2-3, you would detect an important difference between mixtures and pure substances that could also be used to verify the purity of the separated components. As a solution of salt water is boiled, the temperature gradually rises as the water boils away. However, if you boil the water collected in this way, you will find that the temperature will remain constant from the time the water first boils until it all disappears. You can identify a pure substance because it has

DEMONSTRATION

(continued from page T40)
The amount of iron that reacts is proportional to the amount of $CuCl_2 \cdot 2H_2O$ used, showing compounds have a definite composition. For disposal, the nails may be rinsed with water and saved, or disposed of by rinsing, wrapping in newspaper, and placing in the waste basket. Save the solid $CuCl_2$ for reuse in this demonstration. The copper-containing solution may be diluted with water and poured down the drain.

Figure 2-4 As pure methanol is heated, the temperature gradually rises to 68°C, where it begins to boil and releases methanol vapor. The temperature remains constant throughout the boiling. By contrast, a mixture containing 75% water and 25% methanol begins boiling at about 86°C, but the temperature continues to rise as the mixture boils.

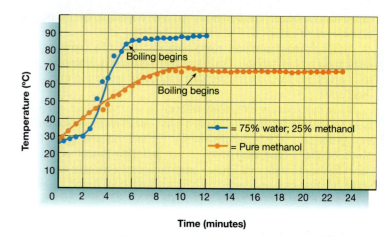

a constant boiling point; mixtures ordinarily do not. Figure 2-4 contrasts the constant temperature at which pure methanol (wood alcohol) boils, with the gradually increasing temperature observed when a mixture of methanol and water boils.

Unfortunately nature seems to defy simple description. It would be easy to say that mixtures *never* have a constant boiling point, but a few do. Water and grain alcohol cannot be separated completely by distillation because a mixture of 95.6 percent ethanol and 4.4 percent water has a constant boiling point of 78.2°C. Any other mixture of ethanol and water changes temperature as it boils.

Freezing and melting point Figure 2-5 shows the difference between mixtures and pure substances when they freeze. The curves in Figure 2-5 contrast the behavior of pure paradichlorobenzene, a compound sold as a moth repellent, with a mixture of

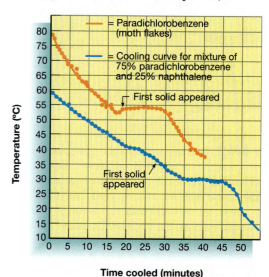

Figure 2-5 The graph shows cooling curves for paradichlorobenzene and for a mixture of paradichlorobenzene and naphthalene. What is the difference between the freezing point of paradichlorobenzene and naphthalene?

paradichlorobenzene and naphthalene, another moth repellent. The temperature at which a liquid changes to a solid is called its freezing point. The freezing point is the same as the melting point, the temperature at which a solid becomes a liquid. Looking at the two curves on the graph can you see the difference between the freezing point of pure substances and the freezing point of mixtures?

Concept ✓ Check

Compare the temperature of a liquid mixture after it starts boiling with the temperature of a pure substance after it starts boiling. Are there any exceptions?

2.3 Decomposing Pure Substances

If the separation of a mixture leads to obtaining pure substances, can pure substances ever be separated into any other kind of matter? To answer that question, the properties of pure substances can be studied using another experimental technique.

Figure 2-6 Left: *When dry salt (sodium chloride) is used to connect the electrodes the bulb on the conductivity tester does not light. This indicates that dry salt does not conduct electricity.* Right: *When melted salt is used to connect the wires, however, the bulb does light. Salt dissolved in water will also conduct electricity.*

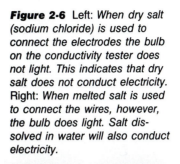

Electrical conductivity Figure 2-6 shows a simple apparatus that can be used to test the property of electrical conductivity. When that apparatus is used to test the electrical conductivity of dry sodium chloride (table salt), a pure substance, the bulb does not light, as shown on the left in Figure 2-6. However, if the salt is melted before it is tested, it conducts electricity as shown on the right. Something else happens too.

PART 1
Section 2.3 continued

Videodisc Connections

48928 to 50116, side 3
Electrolysis of water (movie)

Figure 2-7 *When salt is melted and an electric current is passed through the melt, the salt decomposes to form sodium metal at the negative electrode and chlorine gas at the positive electrode.* ▲CAUTION: *Do not do an electrolysis of sodium chloride in your school laboratory. The salt's melting point is too high, and the chlorine gas produced is too toxic. Sodium metal is also very dangerous.*

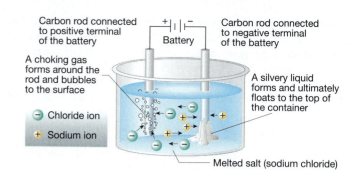

Electrolysis

Figure 2-7 shows a diagram of a container with two carbon rods immersed in melted salt and connected to a battery. Because melted salt conducts electricity, electricity will flow from the negative terminal of the battery to the carbon rod labeled *minus* (−), through the melted salt to the carbon rod labeled *plus* (+), and back to the positive terminal of the battery. If the battery is left connected, a silver liquid will form on the negative rod and rise to the top of the liquid NaCl. Simultaneously, a choking gas forms around the positive rod and bubbles out of the liquid salt. If these new substances are collected and their properties checked, it is found that the silvery liquid is sodium metal and the choking gas is chlorine.

The process just described is called electrolysis. **Electrolysis** involves passing an electric current through a substance, causing it to decompose into new kinds of matter.

Figure 2-8 *Apparatus used for the electrolysis of water. The apparatus is designed to collect the two gases formed by the decomposition of water. The center tube of the apparatus is filled with water. The clamps on the outer tubes are open. When the apparatus is full, the clamps are closed and the two electrodes are connected to the battery. Oxygen gas is produced at the positive electrode and bubbles to the top of the tube. Hydrogen gas is produced at the negative electrode.*

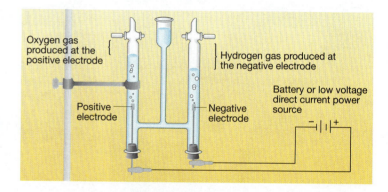

Electrolysis of water

Another pure substance, water, can be decomposed by electrolysis, using the apparatus shown in Figure 2-8. Since water is a very poor conductor of electricity, the reaction is too slow to see unless something that conducts electricity is dissolved in the water. Sulfuric acid is normally added because it does not interfere with the decomposition of water. Other conducting substances can also be used, but many of them will react before the water does.

DEMONSTRATION

Electrolysis

Add 10 grams of sodium sulfate to 250 mL of distilled water. The water can then be electrolyzed using a Hoffman apparatus as shown in Figure 2–8. If no Hoffman apparatus is available, test tubes can be filled with the sodium sulfate solution and clamped in a beaker.

 CAUTION: Everyone should wear safety goggles.

A 9-volt transistor radio battery with copper electrodes will decompose the water into hydrogen and oxygen. For disposal, dilute the solution with double its volume of water and pour down the drain. Worn-out batteries should be wrapped in newspaper and taken to a recycling center.

If the electrolysis of water is allowed to continue for a long time, the water will eventually change into two new substances, hydrogen gas and oxygen gas, leaving behind nothing but the substance added to make the water conduct.

The products of the electrolysis of sodium chloride and of water have none of the properties of the original material. Consequently electrolysis represents a chemical change in which a pure substance decomposes to form different kinds of matter.

Decomposition versus distillation Decomposition of a pure substance and distillation of a mixture are both processes in which matter is broken down into components, but they are fundamentally different processes. In decomposition, a single, pure substance with constant, characteristic properties is somehow changed into new substances with different properties. Decomposition represents a chemical change. In distillation, the separated components exist in the original mixture as individual substances. The properties of the mixture are a blend of the properties of these components of the mixture. Distillation is a physical change that separates two or more things that are present in the mixture. No new substances are formed.

Describing pure substances Can all pure substances be decomposed? In Chapter 1, you learned that sugar and baking soda can be decomposed by heat. Sugar and baking soda are pure substances—so are iron and copper. However, iron and copper cannot be decomposed by heat or electrolysis. No means has been found to separate copper or iron into new kinds of matter. This property represents an important difference between pure substances such as iron and copper and pure substances such as sugar, baking soda, salt, and water. To describe these different kinds of pure substances, chemists use the terms *compounds* and *elements*. Pure substances that can be decomposed into new kinds of matter are called **compounds.** They appear to be "compounded," or put together, from simpler substances. The substances that they are composed of— sodium and chlorine in the case of salt, hydrogen and oxygen in the case of water—are like iron, carbon, and copper. These pure substances cannot be decomposed into new kinds of matter. They are the elemental building blocks of all kinds of matter and are called **elements.**

Elements There are now 109 known elements. Some of these elements are listed in alphabetical order in Table 2-1, and they are listed in a table on the inside back cover of this book. Several of these elements have been made in atomic reactors and do not exist in nature. Virtually all matter on Earth is made of only 85 elements, and just eight of these account for 99 percent of Earth's crust, as shown in Figure 2-9. All other elements in Earth's crust make up only 1 percent of its mass!

CONNECTING CONCEPTS

Processes of Science— Classifying Science searches for *regularities.* Regularities in characteristic properties for all samples of a substance lead scientists to say it is *pure.*

PART 1
Section 2.3 *continued*

Videodisc Connections

852-902, side 6
Elements, (50-frame seq.)

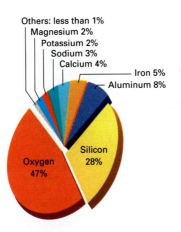

Others: less than 1%
Magnesium 2%
Potassium 2%
Sodium 3%
Calcium 4%
Iron 5%
Aluminum 8%
Silicon 28%
Oxygen 47%

Figure 2-9 *Percent abundance of elements in Earth's crust. What eight elements account for 99% of Earth's crust?*

2.4 Compounds Have a Definite Composition

You now know that elements are pure substances that cannot be decomposed into new kinds of matter, and that compounds are pure substances put together by chemically combining elements. You also know that not all combinations of elements are compounds, some are mixtures.

The hydrogen and oxygen gases produced when water is decomposed can be mixed together in any proportion. One liter of hydrogen can be mixed with 100 liters of oxygen, with 50 liters of oxygen, or any other amount. The result will be a colorless, odorless gas like air. However, if the mixture is ignited, specific amounts of the hydrogen and oxygen combine to form water again. If that water (or any other water) is decomposed by electrolysis, the volume of hydrogen gas produced will always be twice the volume of oxygen gas produced, as shown in Figure 2-8.

Law of definite composition An important difference between mixtures of elements and compounds of elements is that the mixtures can have almost any composition that is desired, but the compounds will have a definite composition. This regularity is called the **law of definite composition.**

The definite composition of water was described in terms of volume: The volume of hydrogen gas obtained from water is always twice the volume of oxygen gas obtained. The definite composition also could be described in terms of mass. In the case of water, every nine grams of water contains one gram of hydrogen and eight grams of oxygen.

Law of multiple proportions It is possible to make several different compounds containing the same elements, but each of them has a definite composition different from the others. For example, a compound can be made from 100 grams of copper and 25 grams of oxygen. Under different conditions, a different compound containing 200 grams of copper and 25 grams of oxygen can be made. The fact that two or more compounds with different proportions of the same elements can be made is known as the **law of multiple proportions.** A *particular* compound does not have multiple proportions like a mixture; rather, the same elements can form *different* compounds, each with a definite composition, but each having a composition that differs from the others.

Concept ✔ Check

Explain how the law of definite composition applies to both volume and mass. Give an example.

CONNECTING CONCEPTS

Models Matter has been classified as pure and impure by observing the regularity that some matter has constant properties and other matter does not. Another regularity has been observed: Some pure substances can be broken down into simpler forms of matter while others cannot. This regularity was used to classify substances as compounds and elements. The atomic model was developed to explain these regularities.

2.5 Atoms in Elements and Compounds

If you take a piece of matter such as an iron nail and break it again and again, it seems reasonable that you will eventually obtain some "smallest possible piece" that can still be called iron. The word **atom** means this smallest possible piece of something.

Since you cannot see real atoms and it is easier to describe things that can be seen, chemists normally represent atoms by spheres of various sizes and colors, as seen in Figure 2-10. The size for the spheres is usually selected to suggest the relative size of the actual atom. It is difficult to keep everything to scale, and you should not assume that the spherical models are exact representations of real atoms. Chemists use the spheres as models of atoms to help them imagine what is happening in the submicroscopic world.

An element contains only one kind of atom, and there are as many kinds of atoms as there are elements, 109. Numbers can be assigned to each kind of atom, beginning with 1 and ending with 109; that number is called the **atomic number.** (A more complete description of atomic number appears in Chapter 8.) The table on the inside back cover of this book shows the atomic number for each element at the top of the rectangle representing the element.

Helium and polyatomic molecules

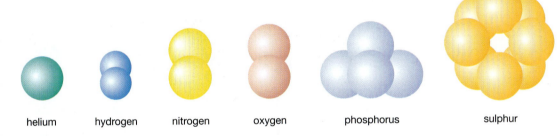

| helium | hydrogen | nitrogen | oxygen | phosphorus | sulphur |

Figure 2-10 *Some elements exist in molecules composed of two or more atoms in various combinations.*

Molecules In gaseous form, most elements seem to exist as individual atoms. Elements that exist as two atoms are called **diatomic elements.** Figure 2-10 illustrates gaseous particles of several elements. These are called **molecules.** A molecule is the smallest particle of a substance that retains all the properties of the substance and is composed of two or more atoms. There is no simple way to tell which elements exist as individual atoms in a gas and which exist as molecules.

Elements have different melting points and boiling points. How can this observation be explained? Atoms vary in size and in mass. You know that it takes more energy to move a massive object than a light one, so one explanation for differences in melting points and

PART 1
Section 2.5

Teaching Strategy

Atoms in Elements and Compounds

Have students make a submicroscopic drawing of an iron nail in a beaker of sodium chloride. Compare the drawings and discuss which best represents the difference between an element and a compound.

PART 1

Section 2.5 *continued*

Guided Practice

Review the Concept Check questions on pages 43 and 46 with students. Answers can be found in Appendix E on page 808.

Reteaching Idea

Reinforce student understanding of molecular structure by having students make drawings. Use student drawings as a basis for class discussion.

Solid iodine evaporates to form diatomic molecules (molecules with two atoms each). Picture a closed container containing iodine crystals. Make a drawing of the iodine after evaporation.

As students become familiar with the process of drawing models of microscopic events, succeeding questions will consider additional facets of the model. Points of emphasis:

a. The particle size stays the same.

b. The container is filled.

c. The molecules are diatomic.

d. The molecules are randomly oriented.

DO YOU KNOW?

It has been said that early Greek philosophers believed all matter to be made up of only four elements—air, earth, fire, and water. Scholars of ancient Greek civilization and philosophy point out that the Greeks may have actually been referring to "states of matter." Earth would represent a solid, water a liquid, and air a gas. Fire would represent energy that can change matter.

boiling points of elements is that more energy is required to get large atoms moving with enough energy to break away from their neighbors. As you will learn later, other factors are involved as well.

Compounds You learned in Section 2-4 that compounds are made by combining elements in definite proportions. Then all molecules of compounds must be made up of two or more kinds of atoms. Molecules have definite shapes as well as definite composition, but you do not have to worry about why until later.

You can now begin to understand what happens when a compound decomposes into its elements. Since the molecules of compounds are made up of two or more kinds of atoms, the different atoms can be separated if enough energy is supplied to break the molecules up. Heat and electricity are forms of energy, and both heating and electrolysis can supply the energy needed to decompose the compound.

Compounds can exist as solids, liquids, and gases. Figure 2-11 shows water in these three states. Just keep in mind that the basic particle of water is a molecule rather than an atom. When ice melts or water boils, the molecules have more freedom to move, but the atoms do not. If the atoms within a water molecule came apart, there would be new substances (hydrogen and oxygen) with new properties.

 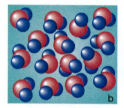 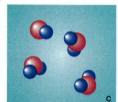

Figure 2-11 (a) *Solid water is composed of molecules bonded together in an ordered array. More energy is required to break the bonds holding atoms together in a molecule than to break the bonds holding molecules together in the solid. (b) When the solid melts, the molecules can now slip past each other. (c) When water boils, the molecules move far apart to form gaseous water. The atoms making the water molecules are still joined together. Some compounds, such as sugar and baking soda, decompose before they melt or boil.*

Ionic compounds Not all compounds are made up of molecules. Sodium chloride exists as positively charged sodium ions and negatively charged chloride ions. **Ions** are particles that have an electrical charge. The difference between ions and atoms is described in Chapter 8. For the present, it is enough to say that compounds that melt, or dissolve, to form ions conduct an electric current, and compounds that do not form ions do not conduct an electric current. One way to know which compounds are ionic (form

PART 1 REVIEW

ANSWERS

■ Keyed to Objectives

A 1. Let the dirt settle. Filter out the water and measure its freezing point and density. Examine the solid with a microscope.

A 2. Cool it until it freezes and graph the temperature versus time to see if a freezing plateau is obtained.

ions) and which compounds are molecular (form molecules) is to check them for conductivity.

Substances such as water, ammonia, sugar, and moth flakes are molecular compounds. Salt, lye, and baking soda are compounds containing ions. It is not possible simply to look at a compound and know whether it is composed of molecules or ions. As you learn more chemistry, you will become familiar with examples of both types of compounds.

PART 1 REVIEW

1. Observations are often misleading. You can gain confidence in ideas when several independent observations lead you to the same conclusion. Suggest something you could do to increase your confidence that the muddy water from a river is a mixture of dirt in water.

2. If sawdust is heated in an apparatus like the one shown in Figure 2-3, the sawdust will turn black, and brown liquid will collect in the test tube. A gas with a bad odor will escape into the room. How could you test the brown liquid to see if the liquid is pure?

3. Gold jewelry is not pure gold. It is made by combining less expensive metals with gold. The amount of gold used in jewelry can vary from 10 karats to 22 karats. Do you think that your gold jewelry is a compound or a mixture? Why?

4. How could you test your gold jewelry to determine whether it is a pure compound or a mixture?

   Is an element or a compound represented in Figure 2-13a?

   Figure 2-13b shows two kinds of atoms. Does it represent a compound? Explain your answer.

7. Which diagrams in Figure 2-13 show only molecules? What is different about the molecules represented by the diagrams?

8. Which diagrams in Figure 2-13 represent mixtures? Compare the mixtures and tell what is different about the mixtures represented.

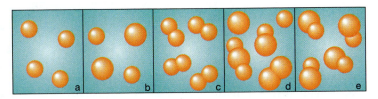

Figure 2-13

9. Water has a definite composition; there are eight grams of oxygen for each gram of hydrogen in water. Use the idea of atoms to explain why water has a definite composition.

Figure 2-12 *Sodium chloride crystals can melt, or dissolve, releasing ions.*

Boxed numbers indicate questions that involve skills in interpretation, application, and analysis.

☰CLOSE

Summing Up Main Ideas

Deciding whether matter is composed of a mixture or is a pure substance can be done by taking into account a variety of properties. Ask students to determine if something given to them in a beaker is a pure substance or a mixture. Permit them to heat, filter, freeze, weigh, and test the conductivity (using a 9-volt transistor battery) and magnetic properties of the substance. Using their data, they can decide whether the substance is a pure substance or a mixture.

⚠ **CAUTION: Make sure students wear safety goggles and a lab apron.**

PART 1 REVIEW

Assign the Part Review questions.

Evaluating Skills

These skills are evaluated in t¹e Part Review questions indicated.
Designing experiments: 1, 2, 4;
Stating a conclusion: 3, 9;
Comparing/contrasting: 5, 6, 7, 8

 **Videodisc Connections**

23516 to 23915, side 2
Salt crystal dissolving in water (movie)

C 3. Jewelry is probably a mixture because pure gold is too soft. Adding an alloying element improves the properties and reduces the cost.

C 4. Measure the density of the jewelry. Pure gold has a density of 19.3 g/mL, and alloys of silver and copper are less dense.

D 5. An element

D 6. No. The atoms are separate. In a compound two or more atoms are bonded together.

D 7. Diagrams c and e are only molecules. The molecules in c are made up of like atoms, and the molecules in e are made up of two different atoms.

D 8. Diagrams b and d are mixtures. Diagram b is a mixture of elements, and d is a mixture of two different elements and two different com- pounds. If only two elements are represented, the diagram contains a diatomic element, a diatomic compound, and a triatomic compound.

C 9. The mass ratio of eight grams of oxygen to one gram of hydrogen can be explained if the ratio of oxygen to hydrogen atoms is constant.

PART 2
Symbols and Names of
Molecular Compounds
Section 2.6

Developing Skills

Students may apply these skills in their study of Part 2.
Predicting: Have students predict which of the 109 elements are most commonly used.
Applying a strategy: Have students summarize the rules for naming the common compounds of carbon and oxygen.
Classifying: Have students classify the elements in Table 2–1 as metals or nonmetals.
Applying a strategy: Have students identify the formula of a binary compound, given the name.

≡ FOCUS

Activate Prior Knowledge

The discussion in Part 1 introduced the students to the concept of a pure substance. Elements are pure substances that cannot be broken down into new kinds of matter. Elements that students may already be able to recognize include carbon, magnesium, aluminum, silicon, sulfur, iron, nickel, copper, zinc, silver, tin, iodine, gold, and lead. Display as many of these elements as possible in numbered, sealed test tubes. See how many elements students can correctly identify.

≡ TEACH

Teaching Strategy

Chemical Symbols

Ask students to memorize the names and symbols of the elements in Table 2–1. Elemental symbols are part of the language of chemistry needed for easy communication. When you call the roll ask each student to respond with the name and symbol

(continued on page T51)

PART 2 Symbols and Names of Molecular Compounds

O b j e c t i v e s

Part 2

E. *Use chemical symbols* to represent elements and the formulas for compounds.

F. *Summarize* information about the elements and their properties from the periodic table.

G. *Identify* the names of binary molecular compounds from their formulas.

Diagrams of atoms and molecules like those in Figure 2-10 are useful, but they can be awkward. It takes a long time to draw diagrams. Chemists have developed an easier and faster way to represent atoms and molecules. In this part of the chapter, you will learn how to use chemical language to describe matter and its changes at the submicroscopic level.

2.6 Chemical Symbols

The language of chemistry is based on abbreviations for the names of the elements. Such abbreviations are called chemical symbols. The simplest way to abbreviate is to use the first letter of the name of the element as its symbol. Since the names of several elements begin with the same letter, two letters are used for many abbreviations. Only the first letter of the symbol is capitalized.

Table 2-1 lists the names and symbols for some of the elements. You should note that not all symbols are letters taken from the English name of the element. Many elements were first named in Latin or Greek, and some elements were named by people who spoke languages other than English.

TABLE 2-1

Elements to Learn					
Name	**Symbol**	**Name**	**Symbol**	**Name**	**Symbol**
aluminum	Al	helium	He	plutonium	Pu
antimony	Sb	hydrogen	H	potassium	K
argon	Ar	iodine	I	radium	Ra
arsenic	As	iron	Fe	radon	Rn
barium	Ba	krypton	Kr	selenium	Se
beryllium	Be	lead	Pb	silicon	Si
boron	B	lithium	Li	silver	Ag
bromine	Br	magnesium	Mg	sodium	Na
calcium	Ca	manganese	Mn	strontium	Sr
carbon	C	mercury	Hg	sulfur	S
cesium	Cs	neon	Ne	tin	Sn
chlorine	Cl	nickel	Ni	tungsten	W
chromium	Cr	nitrogen	N	uranium	U
cobalt	Co	oxygen	O	xenon	Xe
copper	Cu	palladium	Pd	zinc	Zn
fluorine	F	phosphorus	P	zirconium	Zr
gold	Au	platinum	Pt		

Since symbols are used in place of the name of an element, you should learn to recognize an element by its symbol. Those in Table 2-1 are most important because they are the elements you will see most often. Your teacher may ask you to memorize others.

2.7 Periodic Table and Properties of Elements

Table 2-2 on the next two pages and on the inside back cover is known as the periodic table. It shows the symbol, the atomic number, and the atomic mass for each element. The **atomic number** indicates the number of protons in the nucleus of an atom of the element, and the **atomic mass** is the mass of an atom of the element in atomic mass units (amu's). The atomic mass unit is simply defined as one twelfth the mass of a carbon-12* atom. These terms will be discussed in more detail in later chapters. For now it is important to learn that the periodic table is arranged to show similarities and trends in the properties of elements.

Metallic character The periodic table shows metallic elements in yellow. As you can see, most elements are metals. **Metals** are silver-gray in color, with the exceptions of copper and gold. All metals are solids at room temperature, except for mercury, which is a liquid. Metals reflect light when they are polished, can be bent or hammered flat, generally have high melting points (many above 800°C), and are good conductors of heat and electricity. However, some metals reflect light better, can be flattened easier, and conduct heat and electricity better than other metals. You might say that some metals show more metallic properties than others.

Figure 2-14 *The greatest advantage of building cars mostly out of steel is for strength and durability. However, steel also has the advantage of being malleable. This allows cars to be compacted in a junk yard.*

* Carbon-12 denotes a particular type of carbon atom. This notation will be discussed further in Chapter 9.

PART **2**

Section 2.7

(continued from page T50)
of an element. Student A names an element, student B gives the symbol and then names a new element for student C, and so on. Repetition and practice are the keys to memorizing the elements and symbols.

Resources

The KC? Discoverer program *Exploring the Properties of the Chemical Elements* has data on the properties of the elements and will graph elements according to properties, such as density and melting point, versus another characteristic, such as atomic number.

PART 2

Section 2.7 continued

Science Background

Periodic Table and Properties of Elements

All the elements past uranium on the periodic table (called trans-uranium elements) are synthetic. The process requires large, complicated devices and enormous amounts of energy. When element 109 was produced, only one atom was detected, and the amount of energy used would have lit a city of ten thousand for one month.

Videodisc Connections

718-723, side 6
Periodic Table: group identification (6-frame seq.)

red phosphorus

bromine   chlorine

sulfur

Figure 2-15 *How are the nonmetals in this figure different from the metals?*

Position on the periodic table Elements at the bottom of a column in the periodic table generally are more metallic than those at the top. For example, consider the elements in column 5A: Nitrogen is a gas with no metallic characteristics; phosphorus is a solid at room temperature; arsenic is a gray, brittle solid but does not conduct electricity well; antimony is brittle and does not conduct electricity or heat well but has a metallic luster; and bismuth, because of its appearance, was confused with the metals tin and lead in earlier times.

In general, the more-metallic elements can be found at the left and bottom of the periodic table. The less-metallic elements can be found at the upper right of the table. An important exception to this rule is hydrogen. Hydrogen is a nonmetal with very few of the properties normally associated with metals.

Nonmetals The elements shown in blue on the periodic table are **nonmetals.** They do not reflect light, are poor conductors of heat and electricity, and generally have low melting points. Many nonmetals are brittle and therefore cannot be hammered or rolled into sheets. At room temperature, nonmetals can exist as solids—like carbon—and as gases—like nitrogen and oxygen. One nonmetal, bromine, exists as a liquid.

TABLE 2-2

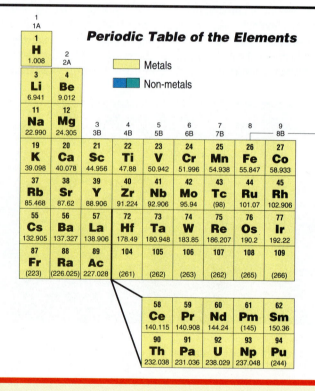

Metalloids Metals and nonmetals are separated by the zigzag line on the periodic table. Elements found along the zigzag line are called **metalloids.** (Aluminum is an exception. Although it can be found along the zigzag line, it is considered a metal.) Metalloids have properties of both metals and nonmetals. While metalloids are typically dull, gray solids that can be hammered, they are not good conductors of electricity at room temperature. When metalloids are mixed with small amounts of other elements, their conductivity increases dramatically. Therefore, they are often called semiconductors.

Noble gases Another group of elements that are nonmetals, is shown in green on the periodic table. They are known as the **noble gases.** Noble gases get their name from their unique property of not generally combining with other elements. Using special equipment and procedures, compounds of xenon, krypton, and radon have been made, but no compounds of helium, neon, or argon have been made to date.

In future chapters, you will learn more about the periodic table and properties of the elements. You will need to describe how elements combine to form compounds and how compounds react. To communicate this information in chemistry, you need to first learn the language of chemical formulas.

Figure 2-16 *Noble gases are used to produce colored signs. Neon is red, helium is lavender and argon is purple.*

						18 8A
13 3A	14 4A	15 5A	16 6A	17 7A		2 **He** 4.003
5 **B** 10.811	6 **C** 12.011	7 **N** 14.007	8 **O** 15.999	9 **F** 18.998		10 **Ne** 20.180
13 **Al** 26.982	14 **Si** 28.086	15 **P** 30.974	16 **S** 32.066	17 **Cl** 35.453		18 **Ar** 39.948

10	11 1B	12 2B						
28 **Ni** 58.693	29 **Cu** 63.546	30 **Zn** 65.39	31 **Ga** 69.723	32 **Ge** 72.61	33 **As** 74.922	34 **Se** 78.96	35 **Br** 79.904	36 **Kr** 83.80
46 **Pd** 106.42	47 **Ag** 107.868	48 **Cd** 112.411	49 **In** 114.82	50 **Sn** 118.710	51 **Sb** 121.757	52 **Te** 127.60	53 **I** 126.904	54 **Xe** 131.29
78 **Pt** 195.08	79 **Au** 196.967	80 **Hg** 200.59	81 **Tl** 204.383	82 **Pb** 207.2	83 **Bi** 208.980	84 **Po** (209)	85 **At** (210)	86 **Rn** (222)

63 **Eu** 151.965	64 **Gd** 157.25	65 **Tb** 158.925	66 **Dy** 162.50	67 **Ho** 164.930	68 **Er** 167.26	69 **Tm** 168.934	70 **Yb** 173.04	71 **Lu** 174.967
95 **Am** (243)	96 **Cm** (247)	97 **Bk** (247)	98 **Cf** (251)	99 **Es** (252)	100 **Fm** (257)	101 **Md** (258)	102 **No** (259)	103 **Lr** (260)

PART **2**
Section 2.8

Teaching Strategy

Formulas of Compounds

Make a point to connect this section with the law of definite composition in Section 2.4. Also, make sure students understand why this law is not contradicted by the law of multiple proportions, also in Section 2.4.

2.8 Chemical Formulas

A chemical formula tells you what kinds of atoms and how many of each kind are combined together. A chemical formula consists of the symbols of the elements accompanied by subscripts (small lowered numbers) to the right of the symbols. In a compound or molecule, the **subscript** indicates the number of atoms of the element to its left. For example, the formula H_2 tells you that there are two hydrogen atoms that compose one hydrogen molecule. Table 2-3 lists the formulas for elements such as hydrogen that exist in nature as diatomic molecules.

Figure 2-17 *Solid table salt (sodium chloride) is made of crystals. A crystal contains equal numbers of sodium and chlorine ions. Like all compounds, salt has a definite composition. However, there is no unit that can be accurately described as a molecule. Each sodium atom is attracted to all the chlorine atoms around it, and each chlorine atom is attracted to all the sodium atoms around it.*

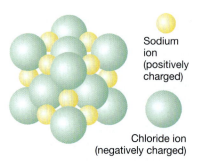

Sodium ion (positively charged)

Chloride ion (negatively charged)

Formulas of compounds Every compound is represented by a specific formula. The formula for water, H_2O, indicates that one molecule of water is made up of two atoms of hydrogen and one atom of oxygen. As Figure 2-17 shows, ionic compounds such as salt (sodium chloride) exist as extended networks of ions. Since these networks vary in size, the formula indicates the smallest whole-number ratio of each element in the compound and is called a **formula unit.** For example, CuO and Cu_2O are the chemical formulas for two compounds of copper and oxygen. The first formula indicates that there is one atom of copper for each atom of oxygen in the ionic network. The second formula shown indicates that there are two atoms of copper for each atom of oxygen in the ionic network.

TABLE 2-3

Elements That Exist as Diatomic Molecules			
Name	Formula	Name	Formula
hydrogen	H_2	chlorine	Cl_2
oxygen	O_2	bromine	Br_2
nitrogen	N_2	iodine	I_2
fluorine	F_2		

Rules for writing formulas The first two rules for writing formulas are:

Rule 1: *Represent each kind of element in a compound with the correct symbol for that element.*

Rule 2: *Use subscripts to indicate the number of atoms of each element in the compound. If there is only one atom of a particular element, no subscript is used.*

Applying these rules for a molecule composed of one atom of oxygen, O, and two atoms of hydrogen, H, the formula could be written OH_2. You probably would not recognize this formula as water but would recognize H_2O. To avoid confusion, the symbols are written in a particular order, which is expressed in Rule 3.

Rule 3: *Write the symbol for the more metallic element first.*

Neither hydrogen nor oxygen is a metal. However, the location of hydrogen with the metallic elements in the periodic table suggests that it should appear before oxygen in the formula. Similarly, for a compound containing oxygen and sulfur, the location of sulfur below oxygen in the periodic table suggests that it is more metallic than oxygen and should be written first in the formula. For example, SO_2 is the compound formed when sulfur burns. Figure 2-18 illustrates the three rules for writing formulas.

CONNECTING CONCEPTS

Processes of Science—

Communication A systematic approach to representing elements and formulas of compounds avoids confusion when people communicate chemical information.

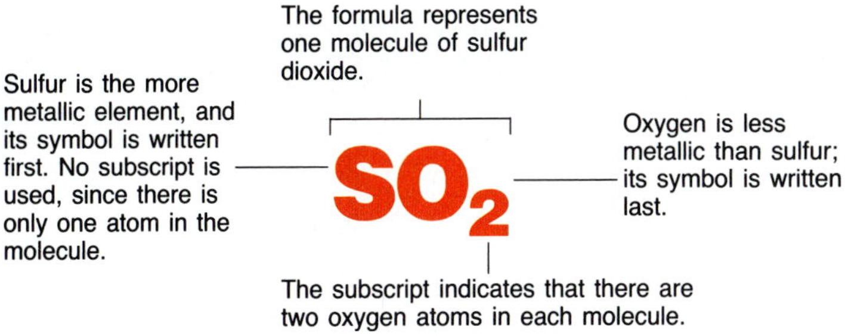

The formula represents one molecule of sulfur dioxide.

Sulfur is the more metallic element, and its symbol is written first. No subscript is used, since there is only one atom in the molecule.

Oxygen is less metallic than sulfur; its symbol is written last.

SO₂

The subscript indicates that there are two oxygen atoms in each molecule.

Figure 2-18 *The formula for sulfur dioxide illustrates the information conveyed by a chemical formula.*

Using these three rules, you can write the correct formula for almost any compound if you know the elements it contains and the number of atoms of each element in one molecule (or formula unit) of that compound. However, the only way chemists can get that information is by experimental analysis.

Formulas are a convenient way to represent compounds, but compounds have names as well. There are millions of compounds, and it is impossible for you to memorize millions of names. Learning rules for naming will help you

Unfortunately many common compounds were named before it became obvious that a systematic method would be needed. H_2O is called water by everyone (including chemists), even though its systematic name is dihydrogen monoxide. To add to the confusion, the system for naming compounds has changed over the years. People who learned obsolete systems continue to use them through

Teaching Strategy

Naming Binary Molecular Compounds

Have students make up names of binary compounds (sulfur heptachloride) to use in practicing the rules for writing formulas. Make no restrictions except that both must be nonmetals. In a later chapter they will learn common compounds and why they exist. At this point the goal is to gain familiarity in classifying elements as metals or nonmetals and learning the prefixes.

habit. Books printed years ago but still in use also help to perpetuate the use of old names.

Therefore, you will probably encounter chemical names other than those you learn to write in this chapter. Two current systems of nomenclature will be presented here.

2.9 Naming Binary Molecular Compounds

The first system is used to name binary compounds that exist as distinct molecules rather than as ionic compounds. (*Bi-* is a Latin prefix meaning "twice." **Binary compounds** are compounds made up of two elements.) There is no way to look at the formula of a compound and know whether it is molecular or ionic. However, binary compounds containing two nonmetals are always molecular, whereas binary compounds containing a metal and a nonmetal are usually ionic. If you are not sure whether a compound is ionic or molecular, look to see if it contains a metal. If it does not, use the following system to name it.

TABLE 2-4

Greek Prefixes			
Prefix	**Number**	**Prefix**	**Number**
mono-	1	penta-	5
di-	2	hexa-	6
tri-	3	hepta-	7
tetra-	4	octa-	8

The name tells what elements are in the molecule and includes Greek prefixes (Table 2-4) to indicate the number of atoms of each element present. The system involves these steps:

1. *Name the elements in the same order that they appear in the formula.*

2. *Drop the last syllable (two syllables in some cases) in the name of the final element and add -ide.*

3. *Add prefixes to the name of each element to indicate the number of atoms of that element in the molecule. In practice, the mono- prefix is frequently omitted, particularly for the first element in the name.*

Figure 2-19 shows how these steps are used to name CO_2. Notice how each step in the naming process reduces ambiguity about what compound is being named. The first step clarifies what elements are involved, but the resulting name does not make clear that the elements are in a compound. Changing the ending of the second element in step two signals that you are talking about a compound rather than isolated elements. Step three adds prefixes to indicate the number of atoms of each element present.

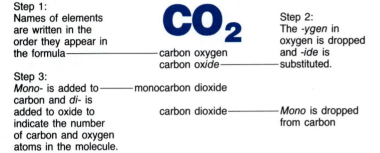

Step 1:
Names of elements are written in the order they appear in the formula ———— carbon oxygen
carbon ox*ide*

Step 2:
The -*ygen* in oxygen is dropped and -*ide* is substituted.

Step 3:
Mono- is added to ———— monocarbon dioxide
carbon and *di*- is
added to oxide to
indicate the number
of carbon and oxygen
atoms in the molecule.

carbon dioxide ———— *Mono* is dropped from carbon

Figure 2-19

There are two oxides of carbon. The systematic names of the compounds make perfectly clear that carbon dioxide is CO_2 and carbon monoxide is CO. As is the normal practice, the prefix "mono" is omitted from carbon.

You should also notice how the general term *oxide* is used in the preceding discussion. Remember that the ending -*ide* indicates a binary compound. Used here to modify the name of the element *oxygen,* the ending indicates that in this binary compound, oxygen is the less metallic element. Similarly, chlorides are binary compounds containing chlorine as the less metallic element, sulfides are binary compounds containing sulfur as the less metallic element, and nitrides are binary compounds containing nitrogen as the less metallic element.

*mono*carbon   *mono*xide

A molecule of
*mono*carbon
monoxide
contains *one*
carbon atom.

A molecule of
monocarbon
*mono*xide
contains one
oxygen atom.

Figure 2-20

Concept ✔ **Check**

Why is it important to have a systematic method of naming compounds?

▶ **FOCUS ON**
PROBLEM SOLVING

Activate Prior Knowledge

An example of a use of the problem-solving strategy described here is using a dictionary. Without knowing how to spell a word, a student still uses prior knowledge to find the word. Ask students to use a dictionary to correctly spell and define the word *precipitate*. Listing what they know may be the next step when they make an approximation of how the word might be spelled in order to find it. Finally, they will be finding information when they examine the definitions.

▶ **TEACH**
THE STRATEGY

Guided Practice

Have students use what they know to name the compounds $MgCl_2$ and HF. Accept magnesium chloride and magnesium dichloride as names for $MgCl_2$. Accept hydrogen fluoride, hydrogen monofluoride, and hydrofluoric acid for HF.

PROBLEM-SOLVING
▶ STRATEGY

Using What You Know

When you are working on problems, whether in a chemistry course or elsewhere, you may not be given all of the information or all of the relationships that you need for the solution. In those cases, you must rely on what you already know or can look up to finish your work.

For example, one of these two problems provides more information than the other. What differences do you notice?

Problem A. A small amount of a white powder has a mass of 0.279 g. What is its mass in milligrams?

Problem B. A sheet of paper has a length of 0.279 m. One meter is equivalent to 1000 mm. What is the length of this sheet expressed in millimeters?

One difference between these two problems is that Problem A deals with mass, while Problem B deals with length. Otherwise the solutions resemble each other. In fact, the numbers used in the solution are identical; only the units are different.

Problem A.

$$0.279 \text{ g} \times \frac{1000 \text{ mg}}{\text{g}} = 279 \text{ mg}$$

Problem B.

$$0.279 \text{ m} \times \frac{1000 \text{ mm}}{\text{m}} = 279 \text{ mm}$$

Did you notice that one problem contained more information than the other? In Problem B, if you knew how to set up an answer in the form of factor-labels, you could make use of what the problem told you to find the answer. However, in Problem A you had to determine what the relationship was between grams and milligrams. From your prior knowledge that the prefix *milli* means "0.001," it is not hard to determine that a millimeter means one thousandth of a meter. At this point, you can set up the factor-label needed for the solution.

▶ **List What You Know**

In these examples, it was not hard to see when you needed extra information to finish the problem. In fact, you probably knew how to solve Problem A as soon as you read it! In other problems, there may be so much information that you will not be certain if the difficulty in solving the problem is because of missing information or something else. One strategy that many good problem solvers use in this situation is to list all the information given in the problem. For example, the first thing you might do in Problem B is to write 0.279 m and 1 m = 1000 *mm*. Looking at these data, you realize that it would be helpful to turn the equality into a properly labeled fraction. When solving Problem A, you could write only 0.279 g. In this problem, you need additional information to form the proper factor-label before finishing the problem.

▶ Finding Information

The kind of information that you may need to supply in a problem is limited only by the extent of your knowledge of chemistry. For example, if you read about a process taking place in ice water, you might need to make use of the fact that the temperature of freezing water is 0°C, even though this number may not be explicitly stated. You should be alert to situations in which you need to examine a problem carefully to take advantage of everything it tells you.

There are certainly times when you will *not* know all the information needed to solve a problem. This is true for everyday problems as well as for textbook or laboratory problems. For example, suppose you would like to buy a new compact disk player.

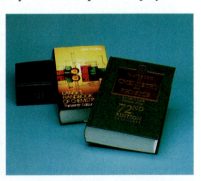

Certainly you want to get the best value for your dollar. You might start your search by scanning recent issues of a consumer magazine to see what kinds of ratings the various players have received. Then you might look in the Sunday edition of your local newspaper to find out how much they cost at different stores. Armed with this information, you are now ready to shop intelligently for the best deal.

Just as in the case of making an informed decision, practical problem solving is often a matter of finding the information that you need. For a chemistry problem, you may find that your textbook supplies what you need. For example, the periodic table in this book contains organized data about each element. In some chapters, you will also find helpful tables giving densities, solubility rules, and values for equilibrium constants.

But complete as it is, this textbook cannot contain everything you need for all of your problems. Your teacher will help you become familiar with other reference materials that are available for your use, including specialized college-level textbooks, the CRC (Chemical Rubber Company) Handbook of Chemistry and Physics, and the Merck Index. Take some time to scan these materials so that you will have an idea of where to find what you need for complex laboratory or research problems.

PART **2**
Section 2.9 *continued*

Reteaching Idea

Reinforce student understanding of binary molecular compounds by having students make drawings, then using them for class discussion. Have them draw six molecules of each of the following gases in a closed container:
1. sulfur dioxide
2. dichlorine monoxide
3. sulfur trioxide

Points of emphasis:
a. The container is filled.
b. The molecules are randomly oriented.
c. different symbols used for each element: O = sulfur, o = oxygen
d. The symbols are used consistently. Note that the geometry of the molecules will be considered in Chapter 10. For sulfur dioxide a linear shape is incorrect and a bent shape is correct. For now, either representation should be accepted.

Guided Practice

Review the Concept Check question on page 57 with students. Answers can be found in Appendix E on page 808.

Reteaching Idea

If students need practice in naming binary compounds, make a list of ionic and covalent binary compounds and challenge pairs of students to name them. As students report their results, write the correct names on the chalkboard. Then challenge your students to write the formulas from the names.

PART 2
Section 2.9 continued

Practice Problems

Assign the Practice Problems.

☰CLOSE

Summing Up Main Ideas

Have students list the three kinds of information they learned in Part 2 that will enable them to write formulas and name compounds. Their lists should include the following:

1. Metals versus nonmetallic elements
2. Chemical symbols
3. Greek prefixes

Also ask students to list two kinds of information that are represented in a chemical formula. Their lists should include the following:

1. The kinds of atoms in the compound
2. The number of each kind of atom represented

PART 2 REVIEW

Assign the Part Review questions.

Evaluating Skills

These skills are evaluated in the Part Review questions indicated. **Predicting:** 13, 14; **Classifying:** 15, 16; **Applying a strategy:** 17, 18

PROBLEM·SOLVING

S T R A T E G Y

In this example, *use what you know*. Recall the rules for naming compounds and then apply those rules. (See Strategy, page 58.)

Complete solutions to the Practice Problems can be found in the Appendix at the back of the book.

Boxed numbers indicate questions that involve skills in interpretation, application, and analysis.

PROBLEM·SOLVING

S T R A T E G Y

By *using what you know* about the prefixes, you should be able to write formulas even if the names are not familiar to you. (See Strategy, page 58.)

EXAMPLE 2-1

What is the name of the compound N_2O_4?

■ *Analyze the Problem* The formula tells you the two elements are *nitrogen* and *oxygen*. This is a binary compound, so the compound is *nitrogen oxide*. From the subscripts, you know there are *two* atoms of nitrogen and *four* atoms of oxygen, so the complete name is *dinitrogen tetroxide*.

■ *Verify Your Answer* Checking the name, you see that it says there are two nitrogen atoms and four oxygen atoms, which is what the formula shows.

Practice Problems

Name the following compounds.
10. SiC   11. CS_2 12. SF_6

PART 2 REVIEW

13. Write the chemical symbol for each of the following elements *without* referring to the tables in the text.
    a. nickel   f. fluorine
    b. iron   g. sulfur
    c. aluminum   h. phosphorus
    d. sodium   i. tin
    e. silver   j. magnesium

14. Write the name for each of the following elements *without* referring to the tables in the text.
    a. Mn   f. He
    b. Ne   g. Ca
    c. Cr   h. Cl
    d. Co   i. K
    e. Si   j. Sb

15. In which columns of the periodic table do you find each of the elements listed in question 13?

16. Which of the elements in question 14 are *not* metals?

17. Name each of the following molecular compounds.
    a. SiO_2 b. CSe_2 c. S_4N_2

18. If you remember the meaning of the Greek prefixes, you should be able to write formulas for the following compounds. Try to do it without referring to Table 2-3.
    a. chlorine dioxide
    b. dichlorine monoxide
    c. diphosphorus tetroxide

PART 2 REVIEW

ANSWERS

■ **Keyed to Objectives**

E **13. a.** Ni   **f.** F
      b. Fe   **g.** S
      c. Al   **h.** P
      d. Na   **i.** Sn
      e. Ag   **j.** Mg

E **14. a.** manganese   **f.** helium
      b. neon   **g.** calcium
      c. chromium   **h.** chlorine
      d. cobalt   **i.** potassium
      e. silicon   **j.** antimony

F **15.** Ni–10(8B)   F–17(7A)
      Fe–8   S–16(6A)
      Al–13(3A)   P–15(5A)
      Na–1(1A)   Sn–14(4A)
      Ag–11(1B)   Mg–2(2A)

F **16.** neon, silicon, helium, chlorine

G **17. a.** silicon dioxide
      b. carbon diselenide
      c. tetrasulfur dinitride

G **18. a.** ClO_2
      b. Cl_2O
      c. P_2O_4

PART 3 Formulas and Names of Ionic Compounds

You have learned to name molecular compounds given their formulas and vice versa. The smallest unit of a molecular compound capable of retaining the chemical characteristics of the compound is a molecule. In ionic compounds, however, because the ions exist in an extended network, there is no single unit. Consequently using Greek prefixes to indicate the number of atoms in a molecule of the compound does not make sense when applied to ionic compounds.

Ionic compounds can form from metals and nonmetals. The metallic elements in these compounds have a positive (+) charge and the nonmetallic elements have a negative (−) charge. In Chapter 13, you will learn more about how ionic networks form. For now, it is only important to know that the charges on each ion are necessary for determining the formula and the name of ionic compounds.

Objectives

Part 3

H. *Predict* the formulas of ionic compounds from ionic charge.

I. *Identify* the names of ionic compounds from their formulas.

J. *Recognize* the charge of an ion from a chemical formula.

Developing Skills

Students may apply these skills in their study of Part 3.
Predicting: Have students predict the formulas for magnesium fluoride, barium fluoride, and radium fluoride.
Applying a strategy: Have students identify the charge of the ions of magnesium, barium, and radium.
Applying a strategy: Have students use the formula to identify the charge of the metal ion in: $FeCl_2$, $FeCl_3$, Cr_2O_3, Cu_2CO_3, $CuCO_3$.

2.10 Using Ion Charge to Predict Formulas

Before you can write the formulas for ionic compounds, you must learn how to predict the charge on ions. Fortunately the charge on many ions can be predicted from the periodic table, and the charge on other ions can be calculated.

Predicting ion charge from the periodic table The following rules for finding the charge on an ion are based on regularities discovered by analyzing ionic compounds.

Rule 1: *Ions formed from elements in Group 1A of the periodic table have a 1+ charge.*

Rule 2: *Ions formed from elements in Group 2A of the periodic table have a 2+ charge.*

Rule 3: *Aluminum ions have a 3+ charge. Other elements in Group 3A normally form ions with a 3+ charge, but there are exceptions.*

Rule 4: *Elements in all other groups form ions with various charges.* However, the following rules concerning a few of the elements will enable you to write formulas and assign names for most binary ionic compounds.

≡FOCUS

Activate Prior Knowledge

Trying to maintain an average number of hours of sleep per day involves mathematical thinking similar to the kind required to write correct chemical formulas. Have students solve the following problem involving an irregular sleeper.

Lisa tries to average 8 hours of sleep every 24 hours. Suppose she sleeps from 11 P.M. to 6 A.M. on the first night and from 9 P.M. to 7 A.M. on the second night of a three-day weekend. What time would she need to go to sleep on the third evening if she plans to awaken at 7 A.M. and average 8 hours of sleep for the three nights?

Using a clock will help students count the hours of sleep. They will also need to determine the total hours of sleep for the three nights (24). Subtracting the total of the first two nights (17) from the total for all three nights will give the hours of sleep on the third night (7). Go counterclockwise from 7 a.m. for this number of hours to get the final answer of 12 A.M. Note that this problem actually involves more math than they will need to write chemical formulas.

PART **3**

Section **2.10** continued

☰ TEACH

Teaching Strategy

Predicting Ion Change From the Periodic Table

The periodic table has been called the ideal memory aid (cheat sheet). Encourage students to use the periodic table by allowing them to see the wall periodic table during quizzes.

PROBLEM SOLVING

▶ Tacit knowledge is that information which must be known to answer a question or to solve a problem. Identifying the tacit knowledge in a question is often the key to assembling enough information to solve the problem. List the tacit knowledge needed to write the name for Cu_2SO_4.

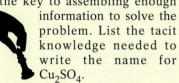

PROBLEM-SOLVING

S T R A T E G Y

Use what you know about the charges on Ca and Cl to figure out the subscripts in the formula. (See Strategy, page 58.)

---

a. *The nitride ion has a 3− charge.* (Nitrides are binary compounds of metals and nitrogen.)

b. *The sulfide ion has a 2− charge.* (Sulfides are binary compounds of metals and sulfur.)

c. *The oxide ion has a 2− charge.* (Oxides are binary compounds of metals and oxygen.)

d. *All halogens (elements in Group 7A) form halide ions with a 1− charge.* (Halides are binary compounds of a metal and a halogen.)

Rule 5: *The algebraic sum of the charges in a compound is zero.*

You can now use these rules to predict the formulas for some binary ionic compounds.

EXAMPLE 2-2

Predict the formula for a compound of calcium and chlorine.

■ *Analyze the Problem* Since calcium is in Group 2A of the periodic table, you know that the charge on the calcium ion will be 2+ (Rule 2). Chlorine is in Group 7A so the charge on the chloride ion will be 1− (Rule 4d).

■ *Apply a Strategy* In order to balance the charge on the compound, there must be two chloride ions for each calcium ion (Rule 5).

■ *Work a Solution*

Calcium is in Group 2A of the periodic table. These ions have a charge of 2+ (Rule 2).

Chlorine is in Group 7A of the periodic table. Halogens form ions with a 1− charge (Rule 4d).

$$\overset{2+}{}\overset{1-}{}$$

$CaCl_2$

Calcium chloride

There must be 2 chloride ions for each calcium ion in order for the algebraic sum of the charges to be zero. $(2+) + 2(-1) = 0$ (Rule 5).

■ *Verify Your Answer* Check your answer to be sure the sum of the charges in the formula equals zero. A 2+ charge on the one calcium ion balances the 1− charges on each of the two chloride ions. After you have checked your answer, you can erase the charges you may have written over the ions while you were figuring out the formula.

Practice Problems

Write the formula for the ionic compounds of the elements listed.

19. magnesium and oxygen
20. aluminum and bromine
21. sodium and sulfur
22. potassium and nitrogen

Complete solutions to the Practice Problems can be found in an Appendix at the back of the book.

Practice Problems

Assign the Practice Problems.

The formulas for ionic compounds such as those in the problems above look just like the formulas for molecular compounds, such as CO_2. However, there is an important difference in ionic and molecular compounds that does not show in the formulas. Ions that compose ionic compounds can **dissociate** or separate from the ionic network. For example, when calcium chloride dissolves in water, the compound comes apart (dissociates) to form separate calcium ions and chloride ions. These ions are represented by Ca^{2+} and Cl^-. (The number *1* is not usually written.) Notice the difference between the symbol for an atom of calcium, Ca, and a calcium ion, Ca^{2+}. A detailed discussion of the difference between atoms of an element and ions of that element will follow after atomic structure is presented in Chapter 10 and Chapter 13. For now, keep in mind that *when a chemical symbol is written alone and without a charge, it stands for the neutral atom. When a symbol is written with a charge, it stands for an ion of that element.* Since the properties of neutral atoms and ions are very different, this difference in the way they are represented is very important.

In the formulas you have written so far, the subscript of only one element had to be adjusted to balance the charges in the compound. What if both subscripts must be adjusted? The following example will help answer that question.

EXAMPLE 2-3

What is the formula for aluminum oxide?

▪ *Analyze the Problem* The name tells you that aluminum oxide is a binary compound containing aluminum and oxygen and that oxygen is the less metallic element in the compound.

▪ *Apply a Strategy* Organize your work by writing the charge over the symbols for the elements just as before.

Aluminum always has a 3+ charge (Rule 3) ——— **3+ 2−** ——— Since this is a binary compound of a metal and oxygen, the charge on oxygen is 2− (Rule 4)

AlO

PART **3**

Section 2.10 *continued*

Practice Problems

Assign the Practice Problems.

PROBLEM·SOLVING

S T R A T E G Y

Check your understanding by solving a similar problem. (See Strategy, page 65.)

PROBLEM·SOLVING

S T R A T E G Y

You may see other ways to solve this problem. Most problems can be solved in several ways. Remember that the best solution is the one that makes the most sense to you and results in a correct answer. See Strategy, page 58.)

Complete solutions to the Practice Problems can be found in the Appendix at the back of the book.

The only problem is how to figure out the subscripts. Begin by trying some different combinations.

Trial 1	Trial 2	Trial 3	Trial 4	Trial 5
3+ 2−	3+ 2−	3+ 2−	3+ 2−	3+ 2−
Al_1O_1	Al_1O_2	Al_2O_1	Al_2O_2	Al_2O_3

Begin by assuming that there is one aluminum ion in the formula. Try to balance the charge. You will find that one oxide ion does not provide enough negative charge to balance the positive charge on the aluminum ion, and in trial 2, two oxide ions provide too much negative charge. Since it seems that you cannot balance the charge using a single aluminum ion, try two aluminum ions next.

Two aluminum ions produce a total charge of 6+. In trials 3 and 4, the sum of the charges was 4+ and 2+, so increasing the number of oxide ions clearly gets you closer to the zero sum needed. On trial 5, the algebraic sum of the charge is zero, so the formula must be correct.

■ **Verify Your Answer** Although this trial-and-error procedure worked, it isn't very efficient. Looking back at what was done may suggest a more efficient way to arrive at a formula. Notice that the *subscript* for aluminum was numerically the same as the *charge* on oxygen and vice versa. Would this always work? To find out, look at the examples you did in the Practice Problems after Example 2-2:

$$2+ \; 2− \qquad 3+1− \qquad 1+2− \qquad 1+3−$$
$$Mg_2O_2 \qquad Al_1Br_3 \qquad Na_2S_1 \qquad K_3N_1$$

It works! At least it always produces a formula with zero charge. You know that the subscript 1 is never written, so you could rewrite the last three formulas as $AlBr_3$, Na_2S, and K_3N. Look at the first example. The formula would normally be written MgO. You should realize that the formula for an ionic compound shows the *ratio* of ions. The ratios—such as of 1:1, 2:2, 3:3—all represent the same ratio. Generally, ionic compounds are written using the simplest formula. The simplest formula, MgO, is obtained from the formula Mg_2O_2 by dividing all subscripts by 2.

Practice Problems

Use the periodic table to predict the formula for these ionic compounds.

23. potassium bromide

24. calcium oxide

25. magnesium nitride

PROBLEM-SOLVING
S T R A T E G Y

Using Similar Problems

It is easier to solve an unfamiliar problem if you can relate it to a problem whose solution you already understand. For example, the chemical problem of naming CoCl$_2$ in Example 2-6 will compare the reverse process of writing formulas from names. By recognizing that a new problem can be seen as the reverse of one you already understand, you have a basis from which to begin solving that problem.

▶ Simplify the Problem

Besides finding a problem that appears to be opposite of the one you are solving, you can make changes. That is, make the problem simpler to solve. Suppose you want to know how long it takes a car to travel 280 km when its average speed is 95 km/h. If you substitute the simpler numbers 300 km at 100 km/h, you may find that you can see what operations are needed to solve the easier problem.

▶ Relate the Problem to Real-Life Experiences

Some of the best similar problems are related to real-life experiences that you already know how to handle. If you know that one notebook costs $2, how much would 4 notebooks cost? From this question, you can see you are already an expert at problems involving the total cost of a given number of articles purchased.

When solving density problems, it may be easier to tell yourself that density is similar to the cost per item, volume is similar to the number of items, and mass is similar to the total cost someone has to pay. To find the mass of an object, given its volume and density, compare it to finding out what total amount you have to pay if you know the cost per item and the number of items you wish to buy.

▶ Use Analogies

In this textbook, be alert for everyday analogies that help clarify concepts you are trying to learn. In future chapters, you will be taught how to solve problems in chemistry dealing with quantities by using the analogy of following a road map. These comparisons will also help you understand concepts better.

▶ Your Own Knowledge

Finding a similar problem with which to compare a new problem is a very personalized strategy. You may find a particular problem is similar to mixing the ingredients for a cake. A friend may find that the problem seems similar to the selection of the right kind of people to make up a sports team. One of the best ways for learning this strategy is to get involved in identifying similar problems. Share your ideas and see how problem solving can become easier.

DESCRIBING MATTER **65**

▶FOCUS ON
PROBLEM SOLVING

Activate Prior Knowledge

In the Problem-Solving Strategy in Section 2.9, students were given concrete steps to use in working on a problem. Ask students to describe these three steps. They are (a) using what students know, (b) listing what they know, and (c) finding information. This Problem-Solving Strategy section will continue in that same manner, giving students more tools to consciously use as they work on chemistry problems.

▶TEACH
THE STRATEGY

Guided Practice

Present the following problems for students to solve. (1) How many grams of water would yield 2 grams of hydrogen and 16 grams of oxygen? Refer to a similar problem in Question 9 of the Part 1 Review. That problem explains that water decomposes to 1 gram of hydrogen and 8 grams of oxygen. (2) Is the freezing point of a substance raised or lowered when a second material is added? Students may have real-life experience with salt being spread on roads in winter to melt ice. From this knowledge students will reason that salt must lower the freezing point of water.

Reteaching Idea

If students have difficulty figuring out formulas, try another approach—finding the total charge which must be on each element in a formula. This approach is like the process of finding a common denominator in math. For aluminum oxide, students can find the smallest possible number into which the charge on aluminum (3) and the

(continued on page T66)

(continued from page T65)

charge on oxygen (2) will divide evenly. This number (6) becomes the total charge on each atom. It follows that there must be two aluminums and three oxygens. Have students try this approach on K_2O, CaF_2, and B_2O_3.

Teaching Strategy

Predicting Formulas Containing Polyatomic Ions

Have students classify the common polyatomic ions in Table 2–5 according to charge. Noticing that only one has a charge of 3−, one is 1+, six are 2−, and all the rest are 1− will help them learn the correct charge for each. Noting the pattern for nitrate/nitrite, sulfate/sulfite, and phosphate/phosphite will also help them manage the information.

2.11 Predicting Formulas Containing Polyatomic Ions

Vinegar is a water solution of a compound with the formula $HC_2H_3O_2$. Vinegar conducts an electric current so you know that it must contain ions. Experiments show that one of the ions is H^+. The other is $C_2H_3O_2^-$, which is composed of several atoms joined together with a 1− charge on the ion as a whole. Such ions are often called **polyatomic ions** (*poly* means "many").

Sulfuric acid, the substance added to water to increase its conductivity in an electrolysis experiment, has the formula H_2SO_4. It breaks apart in water to give H^+ and HSO_4^-, another polyatomic ion with a 1− charge. Under certain conditions, this HSO_4^- ion breaks apart to form H^+ and SO_4^{2-}.

It is difficult to predict what compounds will break apart into ions or what ions they will form until you have learned more about chemistry. For now, Table 2-5 lists the names, formulas, and charges of several common polyatomic ions. The table also lists common compounds containing polyatomic ions and their formula.

TABLE 2-5

Common Polyatomic Ions and Representative Compounds			
Ion Name	**Ion Formula**	**Compound Name**	**Compound Formula**
acetate	$C_2H_3O_2^-$	hydrogen acetate (acetic acid, vinegar)	$HC_2H_3O_2$
ammonium	NH_4^+	ammonium nitrate (in fertilizer)	NH_4NO_3
carbonate	CO_3^{2-}	calcium carbonate (limestone)	$CaCO_3$
hydrogen carbonate (bicarbonate)	HCO_3^-	sodium hydrogen carbonate (sodium bicarbonate, baking soda)	$NaHCO_3$
hypochlorite	ClO^-	sodium hypochlorite (bleach, Clorox)	$NaClO$
chlorate	ClO_3^-	potassium chlorate	$KClO_3$
chromate	CrO_4^{2-}	potassium chromate	K_2CrO_4
hydroxide	OH^-	sodium hydroxide (lye, Drano)	$NaOH$
nitrate	NO_3^-	hydrogen nitrate (nitric acid)	HNO_3
nitrite	NO_2^-	calcium nitrite	$Ca(NO_2)_2$
oxalate	$C_2O_4^{2-}$	dihydrogen oxalate (oxalic acid)	$H_2C_2O_4$
phosphate	PO_4^{3-}	sodium phosphate	Na_3PO_4
sulfate	SO_4^{2-}	calcium sulfate (in plaster of Paris)	$CaSO_4$
sulfite	SO_3^{2-}	sodium sulfite	Na_2SO_3

The formulas for compounds containing polyatomic ions are predicted in exactly the same ways that you predicted formulas for other compounds containing ions. The positive (metallic) ion is written first, followed by the negative ion. Remember that the algebraic sum of the charges must be zero. The only thing new is that the charge on the polyatomic ion pertains to the ion as a whole, so parentheses must be placed around the ion as a whole before a subscript is written.

Practice Problems

Assign the Practice Problems.

EXAMPLE 2-4

What is the formula for a compound containing calcium ions and hydroxide ions?

■ *Analyze the Problem* The compound contains calcium ions and hydroxide ions. The metal ion is written first.

CaOH

This formula represents the ions, but it is incorrect, because the charges are not balanced. Calcium is in Group 2A of the periodic table, so its ion will have a 2+ charge. The hydroxide ion has a 1− charge (Table 2-4).

$Ca^{2+}OH^{1-}$

■ *Work a Solution*

Number of calcium ions	Charge on each ion	Total charge
?	× 2+ =	2+

Number of hydroxide ions	Charge on each ion	Total charge
?	× 1− =	2−

Using 1 calcium ion and 2 hydroxide ions gives a total charge that would algebraically equal zero.

Number of calcium ions	Charge on each ion	Total charge
1	× 2+ =	2+

Number of hydroxide ions	Charge on each ion	Total charge
2	× 1− =	2−

In order to indicate two hydroxide ions, parentheses are used around the ion before writing the subscript.

$Ca(OH)_2$

■ *Verify Your Answer* Use the strategy developed while doing Example 2-3 to check your formula. The charge on the hydroxide ion, 1−, becomes the subscript for the calcium ion; and the charge on the calcium ion, 2+, becomes the subscript for the hydroxide ion. The formula is $Ca(OH)_2$. This agrees with your answer.

Be sure you understand why the formula is written with parentheses rather than as "CaOH₂." If you do not understand, take a few minutes to draw pictures like those in Figure 2-23 to represent $Ca(OH)_2$ and to represent $CaOH_2$. Which picture shows two hydroxide ions for each calcium ion?

Practice Problems

Write the formula for the following compounds.

26. calcium acetate
28. aluminum hydroxide
27. sodium phosphate
29. ammonium phosphate

PROBLEM-SOLVING STRATEGY

Use what you know to help you verify your answer. The strategy used in Example 2-3 can be applied here. (See Strategy, page 58.)

Complete solutions to the Practice Problems can be found in the Appendix at the back of the book.

■ CHEMICAL UPDATE

A major success of chemistry was the analysis of complex substances. Frederick Sanger was able to determine the formula and structure of the insulin molecule. As a result, insulin can be synthesized chemically in large amounts and at a reasonable price. Many other complex substances have also been analyzed. The Human Genome Project has the complete analysis of the entire nucleotide sequence of human DNA as its aim.

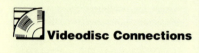

Videodisc Connections

23916 to 24846, side 2
Silicon surface (movie)

Scanning Tunneling Microscope

What would atoms look like if you could actually see them? Ordinary optical microscopes can only distinguish objects that are several thousand times bigger than atoms. Electron microscopes, developed in 1931, achieve higher resolution, using beams of high-energy electrons focused by magnetic fields instead of light focused by lenses. A scanning electron microscope produces images with a three-dimensional quality, but its resolution is still 50 to 100 times larger than an atom. Transmission electron microscopes have slightly better resolution but produce only two-dimensional images and require elaborate specimen preparation.

Because high-energy electrons are deeply penetrating, electron microscopes provide information only about the internal structure of the material being examined and reveal nothing about its surface. In 1981, two scientists at IBM's Zurich Research Laboratory developed a scanning tunneling microscope (STM) that can resolve details as small as 0.1 nm in width and 0.01 nm in depth. With this resolution, an STM can actually "see" the atoms on a material's surface as shown below.

An STM works by applying a small voltage between a tiny probe and the surface of a sample. This voltage produces a "tunneling" current that is very sensitive to the width of the gap between the probe and sample. As the probe scans the surface, its tip is moved up and down in order to keep the current constant. By measuring this up-and-down motion, a computer can produce a three-dimensional map of the atoms on the sample's surface.

STM's are used to look at the surface structure of metals and semiconductors. Biologists use STM's to study viruses and diagram the helix structure of DNA, while chemists research reactions that occur on the surfaces of materials.

The advantages of STM's include high-resolving power and no elaborate sample preparation. However, the picture produced by an STM can be difficult to interpret if several types of atoms are present on the sample's surface. Also, they do not work extremely well on nonconducting materials. The limitations of STM's have led researchers to develop different types of scanning microscopes. Many function similarly to STM's but depend on different interactions between the probe and the tip, such as friction or magnetic force.

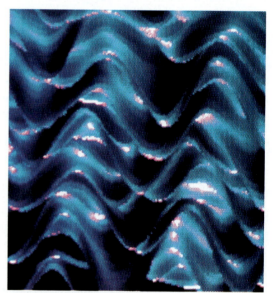

2.12 Naming Ionic Compounds

In Section 2-9, you learned to name molecular compounds. The common system for naming ionic compounds is a little different because Greek prefixes are not used. If the compound is composed of ions whose charge can be predicted from the rules in Section 2-10, you simply name the ions in the compound. The name of the negative ion in binary compounds always ends in *ide*, just as the name of binary molecular compounds ends in *ide*. If the compound contains a polyatomic ion, use the name of the ion as it is written in Table 2-4. Use Table 2-4 and the periodic table as guides in assigning names to ionic compounds.

EXAMPLE 2-5

What is the name of $(NH_4)_2SO_4$?

The compound contains ammonium ions and sulfate ions. The name is ammonium sulfate. If you can recognize the name of the ions, you can name any ionic compound for which the charge on the ion can be predicted. Notice that the name is not "diammonium" sulfate, as it would be if this compound were made up of molecules, not ions.

Practice Problems
Name these ionic compounds.

30. Na_2O
31. $Mg(OH)_2$
32. $Al(NO_3)_3$
33. NH_4Cl

2.13 Predicting Ion Charge from a Chemical Formula

So far you have seen how to name compounds containing polyatomic ions and elements whose charges can be predicted. However, there are many elements that form more than one ionic compound, and the charge on the metal ion varies from one compound to another. For example, iron and chlorine form two ionic compounds, $FeCl_2$ and $FeCl_3$. If both compounds were called iron chloride, you would not know which compound was meant. The name must indicate which compound is described. In Section 2-9, you learned that this problem is solved when naming molecular compounds by using Greek prefixes to indicate the number of atoms of each element in the compound. Using that system, the two chlorides of iron would be named iron *di*chloride and iron *tri*chloride. Although these names would be understood, ionic compounds are named instead

PROBLEM-SOLVING STRATEGY

Comparing this problem to *a problem you have already encountered,* will make this problem easier to understand. (See Strategy, page 65.)

Complete solutions to the Practice Problems can be found in the Appendix at the back of the book.

PART 3
Section 2.12

Teaching Strategy

Naming Ionic Compounds

Learning how to write formulas and name compounds is a vital part of learning the language of chemistry. All communication is facilitated or impeded by the level of students' proficiency. Have students work in cooperative groups of 3 or 4 to practice writing formulas and naming compounds. Students need to determine the type of compound, understand the process of formula writing to balance the charge, recognize the use of parentheses, and finally memorize symbols for elements, names of prefixes, and the formula and charge of the complex ions. Group practice will allow students to share memory aids. Offer bonus points to everyone in the group if all group members score 80 percent or above to provide incentive for the students to help each other.

Practice Problems

Assign the Practice Problems.

PART 3

Section 2.13 *continued*

Cooperative Learning

Teams of 4; **Time:** 15 minutes
Objective: All students will be able to write formulas correctly and, given the formula, name the compound.
Task: Provide students with a worksheet of chemical names with blanks for the formulas. Each student writes a formula and then the students confer until they agree. Provide a second sheet of formulas with blanks for the names, which has the same compounds in the same order. When students notice this correspondence they can check their work and realize they know the formulas forward and backward.
Team responsibility: Have students keep track of the tacit knowledge required, the classification used, and the mathematical skills used.
Evaluation: Have a brief class discussion in which teams share their strategies, insights, and memory aids.

Guided Practice

Have students write the formula for the compound of strontium and bromine. Repeat for cesium and chlorine. [$SrBr_2$; $CsCl$] Also have students write the formulas for the following compounds: sodium sulfide, strontium oxide, hydrogen nitride. [Na_2S; SrO; H_3N]

by indicating the charge on the metal ion by a Roman numeral. $FeCl_2$ is iron(II) chloride and $FeCl_3$ is iron(III) chloride. There is no space between the name of the metal and the parentheses indicating the charge on the ion. Also keep in mind that the Roman numeral does *not* indicate the number of atoms of an element in the formula. For example, FeO is the formula for iron(II) oxide. The formula indicates one iron ion and one oxide ion. The Roman numeral *II* indicates that the charge on the iron ion is $2+$.

EXAMPLE 2-6

How would you name the ionic compound $CoCl_2$?

■ *Analyze the Problem* Recognize that you can name the compound by determining the charge on the cobalt ion. This problem is similar to the problems you faced when you knew the ionic charges and had to predict the formula. In this case, you know the formula and need to predict the charge.

■ *Apply a Strategy* Rewrite the information to include the charge on the chloride ion and the subscript *1* for cobalt.

$$? \quad 1-$$
$$Co_1Cl_2$$

The subscript for the cobalt ion is the same as the charge on the chloride ion. Use the subscript for the chloride ion as the charge on the cobalt ion to produce a neutral compound.

$$2+ \quad 2(1-)$$
$$Co_1Cl_2$$

If one cobalt ion has a positive charge of $2+$, then that combined with the two chloride ions (with a $1-$ charge each) give an algebraic sum of zero. The charge on the cobalt ion must be $2+$.

■ *Work a Solution* Reread the problem before going on. You are asked to *name* the compound, not just find the charge on the cobalt ion. Given that you now know the charge on the cobalt ion, you can name the ions by using a Roman numeral to indicate the charge on the cobalt ion. The name is cobalt(II) chloride.

■ *Verify Your Answer* Check your answer by using a table.

Name of ion	Number of ions in the formula	Charge on one ion		Total charges
cobalt	1	(?)	=	+2
chloride	2	(−1)	=	−2
		Overall charge		0

The charge on one cobalt ion in this problem must be $2+$, to get the charges to add to zero.

Practice Problems

Name the following ionic compounds.

34. $Sn(NO_3)_2$

35. Cu_2CO_3

36. NiC_2O_4

37. Cr_2O_3

◄ *Complete solutions to the Practice Problems can be found in the Appendix at the back of the book.*

Practice Problems

Assign the Practice Problems.

Reteaching Idea

Reinforce student understanding of formulas and polyatomic ions by having students make drawings to represent a solid containing 3 particles of the following:

1. sodium sulfate
2. aluminum hydroxide
3. calcium nitrate

Points of emphasis:

a. Particles are stacked on bottom.

b. Different symbols for each kind of atom

c. The particles in perfect solid crystals are oriented alike.

Count the number of each kind of atom in drawings.

1. sodium 6, sulfur 3, oxygen 12
2. aluminum 3, oxygen 6, hydrogen 6
3. calcium 3, nitrogen 3, oxygen 6

PART 3 REVIEW

38. The following compounds contain ions whose charges can be predicted from the periodic table or the rules in Section 2-10. Write the formula of each compound.
    a. potassium iodide
    b. magnesium chloride
    c. calcium nitride
    d. aluminum iodide
    e. barium fluoride

39. The metals in the following compounds form ions with different charges, so the charge cannot be predicted from the periodic table. Determine the charge on the metal ion and write the name for each compound.
    a. SnO
    b. $SnBr_4$
    c. FeS
    d. $CuSO_4$

◄ **PROBLEM-SOLVING**

STRATEGY

By using what you know about the charge of the nonmetal ion, you should be able to determine the charge of the metal ion. (See Strategy, page 58.)

40. Write the formula for each of the following compounds.
    a. tin(IV) chloride
    b. iron(III) sulfide
    c. mercury(II) oxide
    d. cobalt(III) oxide
    e. copper(II) sulfate

41. Write the formulas for the following compounds containing polyatomic ions.
    a. calcium nitrate   c. aluminum acetate
    b. potassium phosphate d. ammonium sulfate

42. Write the name of the following compounds containing polyatomic ions.
    a. $Al(OH)_3$
    b. Cu_2SO_4
    c. $NH_4C_2H_3O_2$

Boxed numbers indicate questions that involve skills in interpretation, application, and analysis.

☰ CLOSE

Summing Up Main Ideas

Ask students to list the information they use when they name ionic compounds and predict their formulas. Answers could include predicting ion charge from the element's placement in the periodic table, knowing that the sum of the charges of the elements in a compound is zero, recognizing polyatomic ions and their charges, and recognizing that metal ions can have more than one charge.

PART 3 REVIEW

Assign the Part Review questions.

Evaluating Skills

These skills are evaluated in the Part Review questions indicated. **Predicting:** 38; **Applying a strategy:** 39, 40, 41, 42; **Verifying results:** 39, 40, 41, 42

PART 3 REVIEW

A N S W E R S

■ **Keyed to Objectives**

H 38. a. KI   d. AlI_3
      b. $MgCl_2$ e. BaF_2
      c. Ca_3N_2

J 39. a. tin(II) oxide
      b. tin(IV) bromide
      c. iron(II) sulfide
      d. copper(II) sulfate

H 40. a. $SnCl_4$ d. Co_2O_3
      b. Fe_2S_3 e. $CuSO_4$
      c. HgO

H 41. a. $Ca(NO_3)_2$
      b. K_3PO_4
      c. $Al(C_2H_3O_2)_2$
      d. $(NH_4)_2SO_4$

I,J 42. a. aluminum hydroxide
        b. copper(I) sulfate
        c. ammonium acetate

**Household Substances
and Chemical Change**
Estimated Time: (50 minutes)

■ **Process Skills**

Analyzing data
Comparing/Contrasting

■ *Preparation*

■ **Materials**

(for 24 students, working in pairs)
Apparatus
(12 of each unless noted)
13 × 100-mm test tubes (108),
250-mL beakers, test-tube racks,
hot plates or Bunsen burners,
wooden splints, matches, marking pencils, stirring rods (36),
mortars and pestles, scoops or
spatulas (36)
Reagents
■ baking soda
■ baking powder
■ vinegar
■ household ammonia solution
■ Alka-Seltzer tablets
■ distilled or deionized water

■ **Preparation Hints**

Use Alka-Seltzer tablets or a
brand with a close equivalent of
the ingredients. Alka-Seltzer has
citric acid, which will partially
neutralize the ammonia, but
Alka-Seltzer will still react similarly to baking soda. Either
Calumet or Davis brands of baking powder work well.

■ **Safety**

Use ammonia under the
hood. Avoid breathing
fumes. Remind students that
although a hot plate may look
cool, it can burn, so avoid touching it.

L a b o r a t o r y

Investigation

Household Substances and Chemical Change

Many common substances used in the home are taken for
granted. Only rarely do you stop to investigate them or even
read the label on their packages. For example, you might have
noticed baking soda and baking powder in the kitchen cabinet.
Both of these products are used to cause cakes, cookies, and
other baked products to rise during the baking process. Are these
products the same? Do they give the same results?

In this investigation, you will perform experiments using common household products. Then you will determine the composition of a third common product, Alka-Seltzer.

O b j e c t i v e s

Identify the evidence of chemical change.

Identify the differences between two substances,
based on evidence from your observations.

Classify some substances as pure substances or
mixtures, based on your data.

■ Materials

Apparatus
□ 9 13 × 100 mm
  test tubes
□ 1 250-mL beaker
□ test-tube rack
□ hot plate or Bunsen
  burner
□ wooden splints
□ matches
□ marking pencil
□ stirring rods
□ mortar and pestle
□ scoops or spatulas

Reagents
□ baking soda
□ baking powder
□ vinegar
□ household ammonia
  solution
□ Alka-Seltzer tablets
□ distilled or
  deionized water

■ Procedure

1. Put on your lab apron and safety goggles.

2. Fill a beaker about one-third full of water
   and heat it until it comes to a boil.

3. Mark 2 lines on each of 9 test tubes—one
   at 1 cm from the bottom and one at 4 cm
   from the bottom.

4. Put baking soda into each of 3 test tubes,
   up to the lower line. Label the tubes *A-1*,
   A-2, and *A-3*.

5. Put baking powder into each of 3 test
   tubes, up to the lower line. Label the
   tubes *B-1*, *B-2*, and *B-3*.

6. To test tubes A-1 and B-1, add distilled
   water to the upper line. Stir with separate
   glass rods. Test the gas given off in each
   tube immediately, using a glowing splint.
   Recall from previous science classes that a
   glowing splint bursts into flame in the
   presence of oxygen and is extinguished in
   the presence of carbon dioxide. Record all
   your observations on the data table.

72 *CHAPTER 2*

7. To test tubes A-2 and B-2, add vinegar to the upper line. Stir with separate glass rods. Test the gas given off in each tube immediately, using a glowing splint. Record your observations on the data table.

8. To test tubes A-3 and B-3, add ammonia to the upper line. Stir with separate glass rods. Test the gas given off in each tube immediately, using a glowing splint. Record your observations in the data table.

   CAUTION: Irritant. Do in hood. Do not inhale fumes of ammonia.

9. Heat test tubes A-1 and B-1 in the beaker with the boiling water. Has any additional fizzing occurred? Has any additional dissolving occurred? Record these observations in the data table.

10. Heat test tubes A-2 and B-2 in the beaker with the boiling water. Make observations as before. Again record your observations in the data table.

11. Crush one or two Alka-Seltzer tablets with a mortar and pestle. Put the powder into each of 3 test tubes to the lower mark. Label the tubes *C-1*, *C-2*, and *C-3*.

12. Test the Alka-Seltzer in the same way as the baking soda and baking powder. Add water to tube C-1, vinegar to C-2, and ammonia to C-3. Remember to add ammonia in the hood. Record your results in the data table. Heat the tubes in the beaker of boiling water, and record your observations again.

Data Analysis

1. What happened when you added the glowing splint to the gases?

2. Which conditions were best for the fizzing of baking soda? The fizzing of baking powder? Can you identify the gas given off?

3. List the ingredients labeled on the packages of baking soda and baking powder.

Conclusions

1. Which tests gave evidence of a chemical change?

2. a. Basing your conclusions on the results shown in the data table, which baking product would you say Alka-Seltzer most resembles? Explain your answer.
   b. Obtain the ingredient label for Alka-Seltzer. Was your conclusion correct?

3. Can you determine if baking soda and baking powder are mixtures or pure substances? Why or why not? Recall from Chapter 1 that dissolving is a physical change that can be used to distinguish among substances.

4. Write a hypothesis based on your data to explain how you could differentiate between baking soda and baking powder if you were given an unknown sample.

Data Table

	A—Baking Soda	B—Baking Powder	C—Alka-Seltzer
Water without heat			
with heat			
Vinegar without heat			
with heat			
Ammonia			

■ **Procedural Hints**

To test for the presence of CO_2, you can also bubble CO_2 into limewater to produce calcium carbonate, if you wish. The splint tests should be done as soon as the gas forms.

Data Analysis

■ **Sample Data**
(See table below.)

■ **Analysis**
1. The glowing splint went out.
2. The fizzing is best in vinegar for both baking soda and baking powder. The gas given off is carbon dioxide.
3. Baking soda is $NaHCO_3$. Baking powder varies, depending on the type used.

Conclusions
1. Chemical change occurred any time that a gas was given off. See data table for a complete set of results.
2. a. Alka-Seltzer most resembles baking soda.
   b. Answers will vary.
3. Baking soda reacts uniformly at different temperatures and to acid. This is supporting evidence, but not proof, that it is a pure substance. Baking powder is not a pure substance because it does two different things—it fizzes in water at room temperature and again when the water is heated.
4. I would do the same experiments on unknown as I did on the known samples. If the unknown followed the results pattern I got with baking soda, it would be baking soda. If it followed the pattern of results that I got with baking powder, it would be baking powder.

Data Table

		A. Baking Soda	B. Baking Powder	C. Alka-Seltzer
Water	without heat	NR	NR	fizzed
	with heat	NR	fizzed—splint goes out	fizzed
Vinegar	without heat	fizzed—splint goes out	fizzed—splint goes out	fizzed
	with heat	NR	fizzed	fizzed
Ammonia		NR	NR	fizzed

Chapter 2
Review
ANSWERS
begin on page
T77a.

Summary

Defining Mixtures and Pure Substances

- Matter can be pure or mixed with other kinds of matter. Mixtures often can be separated by filtration or distillation.

- Pure substances have constant boiling points and constant melting points; mixtures usually do not.

- Pure substances that can be decomposed into simpler substances are called compounds. Pure substances that cannot be decomposed into simpler substances are called elements.

- There are 109 known elements, but some of these are artificial elements that do not exist in nature. All matter on Earth is composed of about 85 elements; 99% of Earth is composed of only eight elements.

- Compounds are made of elements in definite proportions; mixtures of elements can be made using any proportions.

- The same elements can be combined in different proportions to make many different compounds.

- All matter is made up of atoms. Elements contain only one kind of atom. Compounds contain two or more kinds of atoms joined together.

Symbols and Names of Molecular Compounds

- The periodic table is an arrangement of the elements that reveals trends in their properties.

- Chemical symbols are used to represent elements.

- Chemical symbols are combined to write formulas for chemical compounds.

- Chemical formulas indicate the proportion of each element in a compound.

- Compounds are named systematically. Several systems for naming compounds are in use.

- The names for molecular compounds contain Greek prefixes to indicate the number of atoms of each element in a molecule.

Formulas and Names of Ionic Compounds

- The charge on many ions in ionic compounds can be predicted from the periodic table.

- Ionic charges can be used to predict formulas for ionic compounds.

- Many ionic compounds contain polyatomic ions whose names and charges must be memorized.

- Names of some ionic compounds use Roman numerals to indicate the charge on metal ions when those charges cannot be predicted from the periodic table.

Chemically Speaking

atom *2.5*
atomic mass *2.7*
atomic number *2.5*
binary compounds *2.9*
compounds *2.3*
diatomic elements *2.5*
dissociate *2.10*
distillation *2.1*
electrolysis *2.3*
elements *2.3*
formula unit *2.8*
ions *2.5*

law of definite composition *2.4*
law of multiple proportions *2.4*
metalloids *2.7*
metals *2.7*
mixture *2.1*
molecules *2.5*
noble gases *2.7*
nonmetals *2.7*
polyatomic ion *2.11*
solutions *2.1*
subscript *2.8*

Concept Mapping

Using the method of concept mapping described at the front of this book, construct a concept map for the term *chemical formulas*. Use the concepts listed below and additional concepts from this chapter or the previous chapter as necessary.

chemical symbol   atom(s)
subscript   molecule(s)

PROBLEM-SOLVING STRATEGIES

Students apply these strategies in the following questions.

- Using what you know: 3, 12, 14, 15, 18, 19, 20, 21, 22, 23, 24, 25, 26
- Verifying your answer: 27, 28

Questions and Problems

DEFINING MIXTURES AND PURE SUBSTANCES

A. Objective: **Discuss** *properties and techniques that can be used to determine whether matter is a mixture or a pure substance.*

1. How could you demonstrate that a bottle of a soft drink is a mixture rather than a single, pure substance?

2. Suggest a way to separate these mixtures:
   a. salt dissolved in water
   b. alcohol dissolved in water
   c. pieces of iron and wood
   d. sugar and powdered glass

3. The following excerpt is taken from a laboratory report for an experiment in which students were given samples of substances and asked to decide whether the samples were pure and whether they were the same or different substances. Decide whether the student's conclusion was correct and whether there was sufficient information to make a decision. Explain the reason for *your* conclusions.

   > The two samples were dull, gray solids. Neither sample was soluble in water and neither could be melted using the Bunsen burner. One sample had a mass of 2.6 g and a volume of 1.2 cm^3. The other sample had a volume of 2.5 cm^3 and a mass of 5.4 g. The two samples were not pure and were also not the same substance.

B. Objective: **Summarize** *how decomposition of a pure substance can be used to differentiate between elements and compounds.*

4. From the following observations, explain whether the change is more likely to represent (1) an element combining to form a compound or (2) a compound decomposing.

   a. When a white solid is heated in a closed container, a gas appears to be produced, and the solid that remains after heating has less mass than the original solid.
   b. When a metal is heated in air, it changes color and gains mass.
   c. The mass of a log is found, and then the log is left to rot. The rotted log has less mass than it did before rotting.

5. What tests would you perform on an unknown substance to decide whether it is an element or a compound?

C. Objective: **Compare** **and** **contrast** *compounds and mixtures using the law of definite composition and the law of multiple proportions.*

6. Students came back from a field trip with rock samples that appeared to be identical. The rocks contained only iron and oxygen, but one was 70% iron by mass, another was 72% iron, and a third was 78% iron.
   a. Could the three rocks be samples of the same compound of iron and oxygen? Why?
   b. Could the three rocks be different mixtures of iron and oxygen? Why?
   c. Could the three rocks be different compounds of iron and oxygen? Why?

7. A compound of carbon and sulfur has a definite composition of 16% carbon and 84% sulfur by mass. It is certainly possible to make a mixture of carbon and sulfur with that same composition. How could you decide which is the compound and which is the mixture?

8. Two pure solids are analyzed for copper. One contains 32% copper by mass, and the other contains 43% copper by mass. Could these solids be samples of the same compound? Explain your answer.

9. Two solids are analyzed and found to contain only copper and chlorine. Could the two solid samples be the same compound? Explain your answer.

Boxed numbers indicate questions that involve skills in interpretation, application, and analysis.

D. Objective: **Distinguish** *between elements and compounds on the submicroscopic level, using the atomic model.*

10. Draw pictures (or make models) to represent the submicroscopic nature of the following.
    a. a mixture of hydrogen and oxygen gas
    b. a compound of hydrogen and oxygen
    c. two oxygen atoms
11. Draw a picture to represent a single molecule of each of the following compounds.
    a. nitrogen monoxide and nitrogen dioxide (two common air pollutants)
    b. ammonia, NH_3 (a fertilizer, household cleaner, and industrial chemical)

SYMBOLS AND NAMES OF MOLECULAR COMPOUNDS

E. Objective: **Use chemical symbols** *to represent elements and formulas for compounds.*

12. Answer the questions in each set *without referring to the text*. Then check your answers. If you miss *any* item in the first set, review the material and then try the next set.

    Set I
    a. What element is represented by *K*?
    b. What is the symbol for mercury?
    c. What is the formula for a compound containing one atom of zinc and two atoms of iodine?

    Set II
    d. What element is represented by *Br*?
    e. What is the symbol for copper?
    f. What is the formula of a molecule containing one atom of phosphorus and five atoms of chlorine?

    Set III
    g. What element is represented by *Au*?
    h. What is the symbol for lead?
    i. What is the formula for a molecule containing one atom of boron and one atom of nickel?

13. Determine how many of each kind of atom is represented in each formula.
    a. H_2O_2
    b. $CuSO_4$
    c. $(NH_4)_2CO_3$
    d. $CH_3(CH_2)_5OH$

F. Objective: **Summarize** *information about the elements and their properties from the periodic table.*

14. Identify which elements mentioned in question 12, Sets I–III, are metals and which are nonmetals.
15. Do any of the elements mentioned in question 12, Sets I–III, appear in the same column of the periodic table? If so, which ones?
16. What characteristics distinguish metals from nonmetals?
17. What information about the metallic properties of elements can you obtain by looking at the positions in the periodic table?
18. For each of the following pairs of elements, choose the one that is more metallic in character.
    a. potassium or sulfur
    b. vanadium or iodine
    c. argon or molybdenum

G. Objective: **Identify** *the names of binary molecular compounds from their formulas.*

19. Write the name for each of the following compounds formed from two nonmetals.
    a. SiO_2 d. PCl_5
    b. BF_3 e. N_2O_5
    c. SO_2 f. NO
20. If you remember the meaning of the Greek prefixes, you should be able to write formulas for the following compounds. Try to do it without referring to Table 2-4.
    a. sulfur hexafluoride
    b. tetraphosphorus hexoxide
    c. iodine tribromide
    d. tetraphosphorous heptoxide
    e. carbon tetrachloride
    f. arsenic pentachloride

FORMULAS AND NAMES OF IONIC COMPOUNDS

H. Objective: **Predict** *the formulas of ionic compounds from ionic charge.*

21. The following compounds contain ions whose charges can be predicted from the periodic table. Use the periodic table to predict the formula of each compound.
  a. cesium bromide
  b. magnesium fluoride
  c. calcium oxide
  d. potassium iodide

22. Write formulas for the following compounds containing polyatomic ions.
  a. calcium hydrogen carbonate
  b. magnesium sulfite
  c. sodium hydroxide
  d. ammonium carbonate

I. Objective: **Identify** *the names of ionic compounds from their formulas.*

23. Name the following ionic compounds. Identify those that do not contain polyatomic ions.

  a. NaI e. $MgCO_3$ i. $CrCl_3$
  b. $K_2Cr_2O_7$ f. $Na_2C_2O_4$ j. $FeSO_3$
  c. $CoBr_2$ g. $CaCl_2$ k. $KHCO_3$
  d. $Cu_3(PO_4)_2$ h. H_2SO_3 l. $Ca(NO_3)_2$

J. Objective: **Recognize** *the charge of an ion from a chemical formula.*

24. Write the formulas for these compounds.
  a. tin(II) chloride   d. lead(II) chromate
  b. tin(IV) oxide   e. copper(II) sulfate
  c. iron(II) fluoride   f. iron(II) phosphate

25. The metals in the following compounds can form ions with different charges, so the charge cannot be predicted from the periodic table. Predict the charge on the metal ion and write the name for the compound.
  a. $FeCl_3$ c. $NiCl_2$ e. $CuSO_4$
  b. $CuBr_2$ d. $Fe_2(SO_4)_3$ f. Cu_2O

Critical Thinking

SYNTHESIS WITHIN THE CHAPTER

26. Write the name of each of the following formulas and indicate whether it represents a molecule or an ion.
  a. SO_3^{2-} c. CS_2 e. PO_4^{3-} g. CO_3^{2-}
  b. SO_3 d. P_4O_{10} f. CO h. NO_2

SYNTHESIS ACROSS CHAPTERS

27. Look up values for melting points, boiling points, densities, or other properties of the elements. Enter the values on a periodic table. Identify any trends in the properties as you go across or down a column of the table.

Projects

28. Many types of matter can be found as mixtures. Find out how mixtures of chemicals are separated so that valuable materials can be separated in a pure form or toxic materials can be separated and disposed of safely. If there is an industry in your community, you may be able to find out how the problem is solved in that industry. If not, you can read about it in the library.

Research and Writing

29. Pick an element and learn as much about it as you can. Write an advertising brochure for the element. Include information such as the following: Where is it found in nature? In what form is it found? How is it obtained in pure form? What commercial value does it have? What dangers are associated with its use? What are some of its properties? Become the class authority on this element and share your knowledge with your teacher and classmates.

☐ Boxed numbers indicate questions that involve skills in interpretation, application, and analysis.

1. Separate some of the components. Dissolved carbon dioxide can be removed by shaking or heating. Distilling the soft drink will reveal flavors, sweeteners, and coloring agents. Look at the label. The ingredients listed on a soft drink may include: carbonated water, orange juice, citric acid, aspartame, potassium benzoate, citrus pectin, potassium citrate, caffeine, maltodextrin, gum arabic, brominated vegetable oil, yellow 5 dye, and erythorbic acid.

2. a. distillation
   b. distillation
   c. magnetism
   d. Mix with water, filter out the glass and evaporate the water to recover the sugar.

3. The conclusion is incorrect. There is not enough information to determine if the samples were pure substances and, since they had four properties alike, they are more probably the same than different substances.

4. a. This change is most likely a compound decomposing because a gas was given off and the mass decreased.
   b. This change is most likely an element combining with oxygen or nitrogen from air resulting in a compound with a larger mass.
   c. The decrease in mass would most likely be the result of a compound decomposing.

5. Heat it or use electricity to try to decompose it into elements.

6. a. No. If the rocks are only iron and oxygen, they must have the same percent composition to be the same compound. They could be three different compounds or two different compounds and a mixture of the two compounds.
   b. The rocks cannot be mixtures of iron and oxygen. Oxygen is a gas if it is not combined chemically.
   c. Yes. The three rocks could be three compounds. Most probably there are two compounds, Fe_2O_3 and FeO, and a mixture of the two compounds.

7. The compound will have one melting point and boiling point. The mixture will react when heated to form a compound.

8. No. A given compound always has the same percent composition by mass.

9. Yes, but they could also be different. Quantitative analysis must be done. If the percent composition is the same for both solids they are the same compound.

10. a.   b.   c.

11. a.   b.

12. a. potassium
    b. Hg
    c. ZnI_2
    d. bromine
    e. Cu
    f. PCl_5
    g. gold
    h. Pb
    i. NiB

13. a. hydrogen, 2 atoms
       oxygen, 2 atoms
    b. copper, 1 atom
       sulfur, 1 atom
       oxygen, 4 atoms
    c. nitrogen, 2 atoms
       hydrogen, 8 atoms
       carbon, 1 atom
       oxygen, 3 atoms
    d. carbon, 6 atoms
       hydrogen, 14 atoms
       oxygen, 1 atom

14. metals: potassium, mercury, zinc, copper, gold, lead, nickel
    nonmetals: iodine, bromine, phosphorus, chlorine, boron

15. Yes. Column 11: gold, copper
    Column 12: zinc, mercury
    Column 17: iodine, bromine, chlorine

16. Metals are solid at room temperature except Hg, silvery in color except Cu and Au, reflect light when polished, can be bent or hammered, and are good conductors of heat and electricity.

17. The more metallic elements are to the left and toward the bottom of the periodic table.

18. a. potassium
    b. vanadium
    c. molybdenum

19. a. silicon dioxide
    b. boron trifluoride
    c. sulfur dioxide
    d. phosphorus pentachloride
    e. dinitrogen pentoxide
    f. nitrogen monoxide

20. a. SF_6
    b. $P4O_6$
    c. IBr_3
    d. P_4O_7
    e. CCl_4
    f. $AsCl_5$

21. a. CsBr
    b. MgF_2
    c. CaO
    d. KI

22. a. $Ca(HCO_3)_2$
    b. $MgSO_3$
    c. NaOH
    d. $(NH_4)_2 CO_3$

23. a. sodium iodide
    b. potassium dichromate
    c. cobalt(II) bromide
    d. copper(II) phosphate
    e. magnesium carbonate
    f. sodium oxalate
    g. calcium chloride
    h. hydrogen sulfite
    i. chromium(III) chloride
    j. iron(II) sulfite
    k. potassium hydrogen carbonate
    l. calcium nitrate
       a, c, g, and i do not contain polyatomic ions.

24. a. $SnCl_2$
    b. SnO_2
    c. FeF_2
    d. $PbCrO_4$
    e. $CuSO_4$
    f. $Fe_3(PO_4)_2$

25. a. iron(III) chloride
    b. copper(II) bromide
    c. nickel(II) chloride
    d. iron(III) sulfate
    e. copper(II) sulfate
    f. copper(I) oxide

26. a. sulfite, ion
    b. sulfur trioxide, molecule
    c. carbon disulfide, molecule
    d. tetraphosphorus decoxide, molecule
    e. phosphate, ion
    f. carbon monoxide, molecule
    g. carbonate, ion
    h. nitrogen dioxide, molecule

27. In general, for metals the melting point and boiling point decrease and density increases as you go down the periodic table. In general, for non-

metals the melting point, boiling point, and density increase as you go down the periodic table.

C HEMICAL PERSPECTIVES

Critical Thinking Skills

These skills are applied in the feature.

Evaluating the relevance of information

Making an informed decision

Devising multiple solutions/ interpretations

FOCUS

Activate Prior Knowledge

Remind students of all the products in their homes that carry "Caution" or "Warning" statements or state "Keep out of the reach of children." Such advice suggests the spectrum from safe use of beneficial products to inappropriate or careless use to overuse or abuse.

TEACH

Science Background

The Environmental Protection Agency updates its list of hazardous chemicals every few years. Some environmental groups suggest that this time frame needs to be shortened to minimize the risk of exposure once a chemical has been identified as hazardous.

Teaching Strategy

Before students read the discussion, have them make individual lists of hazardous materials they think can be found in their own homes. Then make a collective list on the board. Ask students to describe the criteria they used to identify specific items as hazardous. Have students find out what labels are found on each of the chemicals listed. After students read the text material, ask them how they would revise their criteria.

Everyday Chemical Risk— What Can You Do?

Chemicals have a great effect on how you live, especially in your home. Consider all the different types of chemicals that you may use in a day. Some are used without a thought as to their ingredients, their degree of usefulness, or their influence on safety or the environment. While chemicals are hazardous, many chemicals can be used safely. The overuse and abuse of some substances can pose a significant risk.

The average household in the U.S. uses about 25 gallons of hazardous products each year! These products contain over 55 000 chemicals. Even household cleaning products—such as scouring powders, laundry bleach, tub and tile cleaners, drain and oven cleaners, and polishes—contain hazardous chemicals.

Think back to the last time you walked into a freshly painted room. Do you remember that strong smell of fresh paint? What you smelled were the fumes from chemicals in the paint. Some of these fumes can be poisonous, or toxic. It is becoming apparent that some of these household products can pose a threat to your health.

The concern with indoor air pollution has been recently publicized by the Environmen-

 Videodisc Connections

47489 to 49088, side 5
Sulfite substitutes in food
preservation (movie)

The EPA found that the presence of poisonous pollutants was 5 to 40 times greater inside certain homes than outside.

tal Protection Agency, which stresses the significance of the risks being faced by people today, who live in a society with so many chemical products. Citing a recent environmental study, the EPA found that the presence of poisonous pollutants was from 5 to 40 times greater inside certain homes than outside. These homes were located throughout the country—in rural areas as well as in big industrial areas.

Because the list of ingredients on many household products reads like a chemistry dictionary, labels on products that pose a hazard must include one of three signal words to indicate the degree of potential harm that can result. **DANGER,** the severest signal word, alerts the product user that death or serious bodily injury can occur. **CAUTION** informs the public that minor, reversible bodily harm can occur. **WARNING** is used when the potential bodily harm is between those included in **DANGER** and **CAUTION.** Emphasizing the need to protect a product-user from harm, the label also includes a precautionary statement, a statement of hazard, and first aid treatment.

Ignoring the warning labels on products can be even more

hazardous than the chemicals themselves. For example, when cleaning products containing ammonia are accidentally mixed with bleach, deadly chlorine gas is produced.

As you learn more about each chemical group and its characteristics, you will become aware of the risks and benefits involved in using certain products. By assessing both the risks and benefits of these products, you will be able to make informed decisions regarding their use.

A dilute solution of soapy water can act as a mild insecticide.

Chemical Alternatives

Household product	Alternative
Air freshener	Set vinegar out in an open dish.
All-purpose cleaner	Use soap and water.
Plant insecticide	Spray plant with soapy water, then rinse.
Oil-based paint	Use water-based paint.
Aerosol cans	Substitute spray-pumps or regular liquids.
Ant and roach poison	Place a line of cream of tartar, bay leaves, or red pepper at entry points.

Discussing the Issues

1. Make a list of cleaning, automobile, and wood-finishing products and paints and insecticides that you find in your home. Which of these could be considered hazardous? Why?
2. Is it better to subsidize the cost of producing a less harmful product than to pay to clean up a hazardous one? Would you use a less effective product if it was less harmful?

Take Action

1. Can the use of hazardous products be eliminated? Explain specific steps that could be taken to eliminate the harm from a hazardous product.
2. Select a household chemical you feel is hazardous. Write to the chemical firm and ask what research is in progress to make the chemical less harmful to use.

79

Discussing the Issues

Several of the discussion questions provide excellent opportunities for class debates or debates within cooperative learning groups. Help students use facts, not emotions, to present or defend their positions. Give students practice in building their communication skills by assigning them to the side they agree with in one debate and the side they disagree with in another.

1. In their answers, students should provide logical arguments, using the facts they have learned from the text material or from their research.
2. Answers will vary. Students may consider manufacturers whose prices subsidize product development, governments that underwrite research and cleanups, or efforts by industrialized countries to protect—and exploit—the resources of less developed countries. They can address these questions as a cost-benefit analysis more easily with a list on the board.

Take Action

1. Encourage students to consider possible substitutes for a hazardous product, replacements for harmful ingredients, safer disposal methods for products they believe cannot be eliminated, and ways to disseminate information about the product, its risks, and how to use and discard it safely.
2. Provide an opportunity for interested students to report orally on responses they receive. Ask the students to evaluate how well companies' replies and plans address the hazards involved.

Chemical Reactions and Equations

Investigations	Demonstrations	Texas Essential Elements★
Laboratory Manual 3–2 S Laboratory Manual 3–4 IM In-text Investigation, page T112	Evidence for Chemical Reactions, page T81 Evidence for Chemical Reactions, page T82 Symbols Indicate State, page T86 Exothermic Reactions, page T88 Endothermic Reactions, page T90	**Content:** 2.2, 2.4, 2.5, 2.6, 2.7, 6.4, 10.5 **Process:** 4.1, 10.1, 10.2
Laboratory Manual 3–1 M Laboratory Manual 3–3 IM	Decomposition Reactions and Dissociation, page T103	**Content:** 2.4, 6.5, 6.6 **Process:** 2.2, 4.1, 10.1, 10.4
		Content: 2.4 **Process:** 1.1, 1.2, 1.3, 2.1, 4.3, 5.1, 7.2
		Process: 2.1, 3.1, 4.1, 4.2, 4.3, 7.1, 10.1, 10.2

KEY:
M–*Microscale* **S**–*Structured*
I–*Inquiry* **IM**–*Inquiry Microscale*

★*See pages T8–T11 for complete listing of Texas Essential Elements.*

Chapter Rationale

Chapter 3 extends the use of symbolic language (equations for reactions) to represent the submicroscopic events that occur in chemical reactions. Students can observe macroscopic events that signal chemical change. The reactions selected for this chapter illustrate several simple types of reactions that can be generalized. Some chemical reactions, such as the color change in leaves or the decomposition of a rotting apple, are too complex to be represented by a simple chemical equation.

Many first-year chemistry students have difficulty understanding the abstractions of atoms and molecules. It is vital to help them understand the connection between what is observed, what we imagine is happening on the atomic level, and the symbolic language used to summarize those changes.

About the Photograph

Copper metal is relatively inactive, but it can react with concentrated nitric acid to produce the red-brown gas, nitrogen dioxide (NO_2). The solution turns green because of the presence of Cu^{2+} ions. Since NO_2 combines with water and air to form nitric acid, it is toxic when inhaled. NO_2 is also emitted from automotive exhaust systems and contributes to smog.

Chapter Planning Hints

Plan to use three to six class sessions to complete both Parts, the Chapter Review, and the Laboratory Investigation. You may wish to obtain The World of Chemistry videotape, *The Driving Forces*, for use in Part 2 of this chapter. You will find optional demonstrations for this chapter on pages T81, T82, T86, T88, T90, and T103. You may wish to preview them at this time.

3
Chemical Reactions and Equations

Overview

Part 1: *Identifying Chemical Reactions*

3.1 Evidence for Chemical Reactions
3.2 What Is Energy?
3.3 Writing Chemical Equations
3.4 Energy in Chemical Reactions
3.5 Conservation of Mass and Atoms
3.6 Balancing Chemical Equations

Part 2: *Regularities in Chemical Reactions*

3.7 Combustion Reactions
3.8 Synthesis Reactions
3.9 Decomposition Reactions and Dissociation
3.10 Single Replacement Reactions
3.11 Double Replacement Reactions
3.12 Predicting Products of Reactions

A copper penny placed in colorless nitric acid provides dramatic evidence of a chemical reaction. ▲ CAUTION: *Because nitric acid is corrosive, and the red-brown gas is very toxic, this reaction should only be performed in a hood by an experienced chemist.*

Myths and Misconceptions

Students should not misinterpret the change in the color of leaves as a change from green chlorophyll to red or yellow chlorophyll. The chemical reaction involves the degradation of chlorophyll through the breaking open of the porphyrin ring structure. With the decay of the green pigment, red and yellow compounds already present in the leaves are unmasked. You may want to discuss this with your students and note that later they will encounter chemical changes—for example, with indicators—that actually do involve changes in color.

PART 1 Identifying Chemical Reactions

Have you ever thought about the tremendous variety of matter that makes up your world? Look around at all the different substances in your view. From what you learned in Chapter 2, you should be able to tell whether some are elements or compounds, pure substances or mixtures. This great variety arises from all the many combinations that matter can enter into as well as the tendency of matter to change, sometimes quickly, sometimes very slowly. Matter can combine or break apart to produce new kinds of matter with different properties. When this occurs, it is said that matter has undergone a **chemical reaction.** In this chapter, you will learn how macroscopic observations can help you recognize that a chemical reaction has occurred. You can then put to use what you learned about chemical formulas in Chapter 2 and find out how to represent accurately what happens.

3.1 Evidence for Chemical Reactions

Studying chemistry can be just like solving a mystery. To determine whether or not a chemical reaction has occurred, you need to look for observable clues.

Release of a gas If you have ever had a cake come out of the oven flat and heavy, you may have figured out that it was because you forgot to add baking powder or baking soda. In the baking process, these substances generate bubbles of gas that cause the cake to rise and become light. You can observe the generation of these bubbles by adding a spoonful of vinegar to a small amount of baking soda in your kitchen. The release of gas bubbles can also be seen when a solid Alka-Seltzer tablet is dropped into water. In both cases, the appearance of bubbles is evidence of a gas being released, a macroscopic observation that tells you a chemical reaction has occurred.

Color changes Color changes are also clues that a chemical reaction has occurred. Each fall you can see the leaves turn red and yellow. A compound called chlorophyll is responsible for the green color in leaves. Chlorophyll absorbs light from the sun and initiates the processes of plant growth, which continue throughout the summer. The disappearance of chlorophyll in the fall is the result of a chemical reaction. Similarly, when a peeled apple is left

Objectives

Part 1

A. *Recognize* the occurrence of chemical reactions by macroscopic observations.

B. *Define* energy and **differentiate** between its two kinds, kinetic and potential.

C. *Interpret* the meaning of symbols in chemical equations.

D. *Describe* chemical reactions by writing balanced chemical equations.

E. *Explain* the difference between exothermic and endothermic reactions and **recognize** equations that represent them.

Developing Skills

Students may apply these skills in their study of Part 1.

Observing and describing: Have students examine the molecules in Figure 3–7, and write the chemical formula and symbol for each.

Forming models: Figure 3–9 shows two hydrogen molecules reacting with one oxygen molecule to form two molecules of water. Suppose an additional molecule of oxygen were present. Have students make a drawing of the reaction to show what products will be formed.

Comparing/Contrasting: Have students compare the physical properties of the reactants in Figure 3–10 with the products.

Observing and describing: Have students identify the reactants and products in Figure 3–11.

≡ FOCUS

Activate Prior Knowledge

The concept of formula writing learned in Chapter 2 will be needed when writing and balancing chemical reactions. Have students review ions, polyatomic ions, and compounds formed from two ions as they work on this section.

DEMONSTRATION

Evidence for Chemical Reactions

Show 20 mL of concentrated sulfuric acid and 100 mL of distilled water at room temperature. Pour the acid into the water in a pyrex flask and use a thermometer to show the increase in temperature of about 50°C that results.

⚠ **CAUTION: Handle concentrated sulfuric acid carefully. Wear goggles, face shield, lab apron, and rubber** gloves. Students should wear goggles and lab aprons. Place the reaction behind a plexiglass shield to protect students. Students must not handle the concentrated acid or the flask. For disposal, dilute the acid further to 1 M or less and use as a laboratory reagent, or neutralize with 1 M or less concentrated base and pour down the drain.

≣ T E A C H

Teaching Strategy

Evidence for Chemical Reactions

Begin a discussion of chemical reactions by demonstrating simple reactions. Recall the reaction of aluminum with a solution of copper(II) chloride. Contrast physical and chemical changes. Copper(II) chloride dissociating in water is a physical change, and the element aluminum reacts to produce the element copper and hydrogen gas.

uncovered, it reacts with the oxygen in the air and soon turns brown. What happens when white bread is left in a toaster too long? All of these changes in color provide macroscopic evidence of chemical reactions.

Formation of a precipitate If the water in your bathtub is hard water, you know that adding soap causes an unwanted solid substance to form, something referred to as soap scum. The appearance of a new solid is evidence that something in hard water is changed by soap. Solid substances formed from solutions are called **precipitates** and can often be observed as a result of a chemical reaction, as shown in Figure 3-1.

Figure 3-1 *Macroscopic evidence for chemical reactions includes* Left: *a color change,* Middle: *the formation of a solid when two clear liquids are mixed, and* Right: *the release of bubbles.*

Changes in heat and light If you think about a lighted candle, charcoal burning in your grill, or fuel oil providing heat for your home, you realize that in each case heat and light are produced. The production of heat or light is another familiar observation that provides evidence of a chemical reaction.

It is important to recognize, however, that in some chemical reactions heat or light must be absorbed for the reaction to occur. Green plants use sunlight to combine water and carbon dioxide into sugar, and in the process give off oxygen. Similarly, baking soda dissolving in water takes in heat from its surroundings. Whenever a change in heat or light is detected, it is additional evidence that a chemical reaction has occurred.

3.2 What Is Energy?

Light and heat are forms of energy, and energy plays a fundamental role in chemical reactions. When individual atoms combine to form a compound, energy is *released* often in the form of light or heat or both. The opposite is true when a compound breaks apart into individual atoms. Energy is *required* to decompose a compound. Therefore, to understand chemistry, it is important to ask the question "What is energy?"

D E M O N S T R A T I O N

Evidence for Chemical Reactions

Show an example of each of the changes described in Section 3.1 as follows:

Release of a gas: Add 50 mL of 0.80*M* HCl to 2.0 grams of sodium carbonate.

Color change: Add 20 mL of 0.80*M* NaOH to a 150-mL beaker containing 50 mL of water and 5 drops of 1% phenolphthalein dissolved in alcohol.

Formation of precipitate: Add 50 mL of

0.50*M* sodium carbonate to 50 mL of 0.50*M* calcium chloride.

Changes in heat and light: Light a candle or a bunsen burner. In each case, have students record a description of the substances before and after the reaction and give evidence for the reaction. Ask which symbols in Table 3–1 can be used.

(continued on page T83)

Energy causes changes in matter One useful definition of energy is anything that is not matter and can cause a change in matter. Light from the sun certainly changes matter as it plays a key role in plant growth and the production of food in green plants. Exposure to sunlight causes your skin to darken as the pigment melanin is formed. Sunlight can fade rugs and draperies and make them deteriorate. Heat can also change matter. It can burn toast, cook eggs, or ignite paper. Lightning can split a tree, kill a cow, burn out a TV, or cause your house to catch fire. Lightning is just a gigantic electric spark. More usable forms of energy come in batteries or from electric generators in a power station.

Kinetic and potential energy Although energy may exhibit many different *forms*—heat, light, electricity—there are only two *kinds* of energy. These are **kinetic energy** and **potential energy**. Kinetic energy is energy of motion. Potential energy is energy stored in an object because of its position relative to other objects. An object, macroscopic or submicroscopic, acquires either of these kinds of energy when work is done on it. Work can be equated with a force (a push or a pull) acting through a distance. Work always results in movement in the direction of the force.

Kinetic energy When a hockey stick starts a puck sliding across the ice, it does work on the puck. The puck gains kinetic energy—a small amount if it receives only a gentle tap, a larger amount if it is slammed. As Figure 3-2 suggests, the puck (and any moving object) has energy. That's why goalies wear masks! The amount of kinetic energy depends on the velocity of the object and its mass. The following equation shows how these variables are related.

$$\text{kinetic energy} = \frac{1}{2}(\text{mass})(\text{velocity})^2$$

The equation states that the kinetic energy of an object is equal to one half of its mass multiplied by its velocity squared. To understand the meaning of the equation, ask yourself whether a sports car or a loaded truck, each traveling at 50 miles per hour, would do more damage in a crash. Or if the same amount of kinetic energy was given to each vehicle, which would attain the greater velocity?

Potential energy Motion is an obvious indication of kinetic energy, but potential energy can be present when no apparent evidence of energy can be observed. Suppose you lift a book over your head. In doing so, you are doing work on the book; the book acquires potential energy. But how does the raised book differ from a similar one lying on the floor? If you let go, the book falls with increasing velocity and kinetic energy as it does so. The instant before it hits the floor, its kinetic energy is essentially equal to the

DO YOU KNOW?

To burn 38 liters (10 gallons) of gasoline in an internal combustion engine requires 77 000 liters of oxygen or 390 000 liters of air. This is the amount of air breathed by 30 people in one day.

Figure 3-2 *The moving hockey puck has kinetic energy as a result of the work done by the player's stick. How can a player control the kinetic energy of the puck to make a play?*

DEMONSTRATION

(continued from page T82)

⚠️ **CAUTION: Wear goggles, a lab apron, and a face shield.**
For disposal, combine the liquids and solids, decant or filter if necessary, and pour the liquid down the drain. Wrap the solid in newspaper and place it in the wastebasket.

Figure 3-3 *The conversion of energy back and forth between kinetic and potential is evident in a basketball game. What evidence do you see that the ball and the players are experiencing energy conversions?*

potential energy it possessed while you held it aloft. But is this energy destroyed when the book hits the floor? The answer is no. The energy is changed to heat and sound, which disperse into the air, the book, and the floor. The potential energy you gave to the book by lifting it was converted to kinetic energy in its fall; the kinetic energy was changed to heat and sound on striking the floor. What energy conversions are indicated in Figure 3-3?

Atoms and molecules have energy Books and hockey pucks are macroscopic objects. You can observe how work done on them is converted to energy. But do submicroscopic atoms and molecules possess kinetic and potential energy? Consider a bowl of water left on your kitchen counter for a week. You know that it will disappear into the air by evaporation. This could not happen if the water molecules did not have kinetic energy, the energy of motion. Later in your study of chemistry, you will realize that the water molecules in the air have potential energy because of their separation from one another. This potential energy will be released when the water molecules return to liquid again by condensing on a cold window, or forming drops of rain. Just as the lifted book gave up its potential energy in its fall to the floor, so the molecules release theirs as they return to liquid.

Conservation of energy These illustrations point up the importance of energy in all the interactions of matter. They also suggest that energy is neither created nor destroyed. The form that energy takes may change, but the total amount remains constant. Countless investigations support this important conclusion, which is called the **law of conservation of energy.** Later in your study of chemistry, you will learn more about the role of energy in chemical reactions.

Energy measurement Energy changes are measured using the SI standard the **joule.** A joule (J) is the amount of energy produced when the force of 1 newton acts over a distance of 1 meter. It is a small amount of energy. An ordinary match, burned completely, liberates about 1050 joules. A joule is also the amount of energy used by a 100-watt light bulb in 0.01 second. Throughout this course, energy values will be expressed in either joules or kilojoules (1000 J).

Concept ✔ Check

What is meant by the law of conservation of energy? Define kinetic and potential energy and give examples of conversions of kinetic energy to potential energy that were not mentioned in the text.

3.3 Writing Chemical Equations

Many chemical reactions are important principally for the energy they release. Figure 3-4 shows the popular fuel propane being used for cooking food on a gas grill. Propane is one of a group of compounds called **hydrocarbons.** All hydrocarbons contain only carbon and hydrogen atoms, and they combine with oxygen in chemical reactions to form carbon dioxide and water. The reaction that occurs when propane is burned can be represented by the following word equation.

$$\text{propane} + \text{oxygen} \rightarrow \text{carbon dioxide} + \text{water} + \text{energy}$$

By convention, an arrow is used in chemistry to signify a change. The substances that existed before the change, the **reactants,** are written to the left of the arrow, and the substances that are produced by the change, the **products,** are written to the right. If there is more than one reactant, the different reactants are separated by plus signs. The same is true when there is more than one product.

Using chemical formulas Although word equations provide useful descriptions of chemical reactions, additional information can be provided if chemical formulas are substituted for the words in equations. For example, the word equation for the reaction of propane and oxygen can be rewritten as follows.

$$C_3H_8 + O_2 \rightarrow CO_2 + H_2O + \text{energy}$$

What additional information do you now have about the reaction? From this **chemical equation** you can see that propane exists as molecules containing three carbon atoms and eight hydrogen atoms. The formulas show the reactant, oxygen, as a diatomic molecule, O_2, and the products, carbon dioxide and water, as CO_2 and H_2O. Since energy is a useful product of this reaction, an energy term on the product side is also included.

CONNECTING CONCEPTS

Change and Interaction A chemical is identified by its characteristic properties. When a chemical reaction takes place, new chemicals with different properties are formed.

Figure 3-4 *Hydrocarbons like propane are important for the energy they produce in chemical reactions. Here propane gas is being used for cooking food in a gas grill. Where else have you seen propane used?*

Teaching Strategy

Writing Chemical Equations

To demonstrate writing an equation for a chemical reaction, ignite a 3.0-cm strip of magnesium held with tongs behind a dark glass mask.

⚠ **CAUTION: Wear safety goggles and leather gloves. Protect students with a shield.** The element magnesium clearly has different properties from the compound produced. Pass a strip of magnesium around so students can observe its flexibility. Write:

Mg(?) + ?(?) → ?

Students will be able to tell the state of magnesium (solid) and suggest it reacts with something from air (oxygen) and use their problem-solving skills to predict the formula for the product (MgO). Follow this by having students make drawings of ten atoms of magnesium reacting with oxygen to form magnesium oxide. Check the drawings to determine if magnesium is represented as a solid, oxygen as a gas, and magnesium oxide as a solid. Require them to conserve atoms. Have them make notes of the macroscopic changes observed before, during, and after the reaction. When students can see the connection between the macroscopic changes observed, the symbolic language used to summarize the changes (equations for reactions), and the models they draw to represent what is happening on a submicroscopic level, they truly understand chemistry. Use students' drawings to analyze their misconceptions. For each drawing exercise focus on only one or two important aspects at a time, rather than trying to make sure each drawing is correct in every aspect.

TABLE 3-1

Symbols Used in Equations	
Symbol Used	**Meaning**
+	Read *plus* or *and*. Used between two formulas to indicate reactants combined or products formed.
→	Read *yields* or *produces*. Used to separate reactants (on the left) from products (on the right). The arrow points in the direction of change.
(s)	Read *solid*. Written after a symbol or formula to indicate that the physical state of the substance is solid.
(l)	Read *liquid*. Written after a symbol or formula to indicate that the physical state of the substance is liquid.
(g)	Read *gas*. Written after a symbol or formula to indicate that the physical state of the substance is gaseous.
(aq)	Read *aqueous*. Written after a symbol or formula to indicate that the substance is dissolved in water.
$\xrightarrow{\text{(acetone)}}$	Indicates the reaction takes place in acetone.
$\xrightarrow{\triangle}$	Indicates reactants must be heated.
⇌	Indicates that the reaction is reversible.
N.R.	Read *no reaction*. Indicates that the given reactants do not react with each other.

Symbols indicate state Equations can also be written to indicate the physical state of the reactants and products. In fact, sometimes an equation cannot be fully understood unless that information is shown. For example, if you tried adding vinegar to baking soda, you know that the two substances react vigorously to produce bubbles of gas.

The equation for this reaction is as follows.

$$HC_2H_3O_2 + NaHCO_3 \rightarrow CO_2 + NaC_2H_3O_2 + H_2O$$

Although much information is provided by this equation, it does not tell you that acetic acid, $HC_2H_3O_2$, is in a water solution, nor that sodium monohydrogen carbonate, $NaHCO_3$, is a solid. Do you know that the carbon dioxide is a gas, that the sodium acetate, $NaC_2H_3O_2$, is in water solution, or that the water formed is in the liquid state? That information should be included in the chemical equation.

$$HC_2H_3O_2(aq) + NaHCO_3(s) \rightarrow$$
$$CO_2(g) + NaC_2H_3O_2(aq) + H_2O(l)$$

The symbols (g), (l), (s), and (aq) indicate whether the substance is a gas, a liquid, a solid, or one dissolved in water. Table 3-1 shows these and other conventions used in writing chemical equations.

DEMONSTRATION

Symbols Indicate State

Add 30 mL of concentrated sulfuric acid to 30 mL of sucrose in a 150-mL Pyrex beaker in a hood. Concentrated sulfuric acid is a powerful dehydrating agent and removes water from the sugar, leaving carbon as the obvious product.

$$C_{12}H_{22}O_{11}(s) + H_2SO_4(l) \rightarrow$$
$$12C(s) + 12H_2O(g) + energy$$

The reaction is very exothermic and much of the water is given off as steam while some is trapped and expands, causing a cylinder of porous black carbon foam to rise.

⚠️ **CAUTION: When handling concentrated sulfuric acid, wear goggles, face shield, lab apron, and rubber gloves. Students should wear goggles and lab aprons. Conduct the reaction** *(continued on page T87)*

Concept ✔ Check

Solid zinc metal reacts with oxygen gas to form solid zinc oxide. Express this information in a chemical equation.

Reversible reactions While the arrow in an equation shows the direction of change, it implies that reactions occur in only one direction. This is not always the case. Under suitable conditions, some chemical reactions can be reversed. Consider the reaction that powers the main stage of the space shuttle. Liquid hydrogen and oxygen, H_2 and O_2, are the fuels. When mixed, they combine vigorously to form a most common and stable compound, water, as well as sufficient energy to lift an enormous payload above Earth's atmosphere, as shown in Figure 3-5. The same reaction occurs when gaseous hydrogen combines with oxygen in the air. The reaction is over in an instant with a loud bang!

$$H_2(g) + O_2(g) \rightarrow H_2O(l) + energy$$

But you have already learned that water can be separated into its elements. The reaction can be written as follows.

$$energy + H_2O(l) \rightarrow H_2(g) + O_2(g)$$

Notice that the second equation is the reverse of the first. A chemical reaction that is reversible can be described by a single equation in which a double arrow shows that the reaction is possible in both directions.

$$H_2(g) + O_2(g) \rightleftharpoons H_2O(l) + energy$$

The equation says that hydrogen and oxygen combine to form water, releasing energy in the process. It also says that with the addition of energy to water, under suitable conditions, hydrogen and oxygen will be formed.

The reversible car battery Another familiar example of a reversible reaction is the one that takes place in a car battery, like that shown in Figure 3-6. The battery is made of two kinds of plates, one lead, Pb, and the other lead(IV) oxide, PbO_2. The plates are placed in a solution of sulfuric acid, H_2SO_4. When the battery discharges, lead, lead(IV) oxide and sulfuric acid react to form lead(II) sulfate, $PbSO_4$ and water. The equation is

$$Pb(s) + PbO_2(s) + H_2SO_4(aq) \rightarrow$$
$$PbSO_4(s) + H_2O(l) + energy$$

Figure 3-5 *The space shuttle's three main rocket engines are fueled by liquid hydrogen and oxygen. The enormous energy released as hydrogen and oxygen react is obvious in this photograph of lift-off.*

PART **1**

Section 3.3 *continued*

Teaching Strategy

Reversible Reactions

If the reaction of hydrogen gas combining with oxygen is done as a demonstration, have students list forms of energy observed, for example, light, heat, and sound.

DEMONSTRATION

(continued from page T86)
behind a plexiglass shield to protect students. Students must not touch the beaker. Some SO_2 and CO may also be formed as by-products of the reaction; so ventilation is desirable. For disposal, still wearing protective gear, put the 150-mL beaker, blackened sugar, and acid into a 500-mL beaker half full of water. Swish it around, then neutralize with $1M$ or less

concentrated base; pour the liquid down the drain. Then refill the big beaker half full with water, with the little beaker still inside. Let it stand overnight, check the pH and if acid, neutralize and pour down the drain. Repeat one or more times as necessary . Clean up the big and little beakers and wrap the solids in newspaper and put into the wastebasket.

PART **1**

Section 3.4

Teaching Strategy

Exothermic Reactions

Ask students to explain why an exothermic reaction may not always be detected by touching. If the reaction takes place slowly, the energy is lost to the surroundings before it can accumulate and raise the temperature. Even if the temperature rises it will not be felt by touch until it is at least a few degrees above body temperature, 37°C. If room temperature is 20°C, an increase to 45°C may be required to be noticed.

Resources

The World of Chemistry videotape, *The Driving Forces*, explains how the energy released from one exothermic reaction in an industrial plant is used to increase the speed of a subsequent reaction.

Videodisc Connections

23547 to 25287, side 3
Thermite reaction (movie)

3264 to 5632, side 3
Sodium chloride (movie)

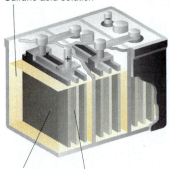

Sulfuric acid solution

Lead plates   Lead (IV) oxide plates

Figure 3-6 *Lead, lead(IV) oxide, and sulfuric acid are reactants in the car battery. When the battery is connected in an electric circuit, a reaction takes place releasing energy in the form of electricity. The reverse reaction occurs when electricity from an outside source is fed into the circuit.*

DO YOU KNOW?

Some hand warmers contain iron powder. When a bag containing the iron is removed from an outer plastic bag, oxygen and iron react to give enough heat to keep your hands warm.

When the battery is charged, the reverse reaction takes place.

$$\text{energy} + \text{PbSO}_4(\text{s}) + \text{H}_2\text{O}(\text{l}) \rightarrow \text{Pb}(\text{s}) + \text{PbO}_2(\text{s}) + \text{H}_2\text{SO}_4(\text{aq})$$

This reversible reaction can be represented by a single equation using double arrows.

$$\text{Pb}(\text{s}) + \text{PbO}_2(\text{s}) + \text{H}_2\text{SO}_4(\text{aq}) \rightleftharpoons \text{PbSO}_4(\text{s}) + \text{H}_2\text{O}(\text{l}) + \text{energy}$$

Notice that when the reaction moves in the forward direction (to the right), electrical energy is released to start the car and power the lights and radio when the car engine is not running. Operating in the forward direction, the battery is said to discharge. It will eventually run down, or die, because all the reactants have been used up. However, when the car engine runs, an electrical generator powered by the engine feeds electrical energy into the battery causing the reaction to move in the opposite direction (to the left). The battery becomes charged once again by regenerating the reactants on the left.

3.4 Energy in Chemical Reactions

The equations for reversible reactions make it clear that some reactions release energy as they occur, while others require energy in order to proceed. When oxygen and hydrogen combine to form water, there is a noticeable release of energy. For the reverse reaction, the separation of water into its elements, an equal amount of electrical energy must be supplied. Look again at the equation for the reversible reaction in the car battery. In which direction is energy released? Notice that when the reaction moves to the left, energy is absorbed. Most chemical reactions either release or absorb energy.

Exothermic reactions When a chemical reaction releases energy, it is called **exothermic.** The prefix *exo* means "outside," and *therm* refers to "heat." Sometimes the release of heat is obvious, as in the burning of hydrocarbons like propane; at other times, careful measurements are needed to detect it. The slow rusting of iron is an example of such a reaction.

Endothermic reactions Chemical reactions that absorb energy are called **endothermic.** *Endo* is a prefix meaning "inside" and is used with *therm* for "heat." You may have thought of the cooling effect of the cold pack used in first aid for athletes as a macroscopic observation identifying a chemical reaction. The cold pack is an obvious example of an endothermic reaction. The pack contains ammonium nitrate and water separated by a barrier, as

DEMONSTRATION

Exothermic Reactions

Slaking of lime: Add about 100 g of fresh calcium oxide lumps to an aluminum pie plate resting in a glass plate. Pour 25 mL of distilled water over the lumps and crack a fresh egg in a second aluminum pie plate and place it on top of the lumps of calcium oxide. The temperature will rise to about 90°C in less than a minute and to 115°C in about 5 minutes, hot enough to fry the egg.

CAUTION: The calcium oxide, calcium hydroxide, and water mixture in the aluminum pie plate is extremely corrosive to human eyes and skin and to aluminum. Do not allow students to handle. Discard the cooked egg and rinse all pie plates with water. Neutralize the solid residue with 0.5*M*, or less

(continued on page T89)

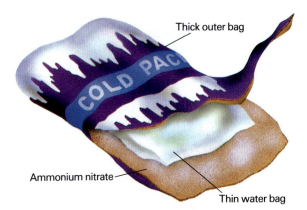

Thick outer bag

Ammonium nitrate

Thin water bag

Figure 3-7 *Water and solid ammonium nitrate are separated by a thin barrier in this cold pack used by athletes. When the barrier is broken, the two substances interact in a process which absorbs energy, lowering the temperature of the cold pack.*

Teaching Strategy

Conservation of Mass and Atoms

After you have reviewed techniques for writing and balancing equations, ask students to analyze each to determine why it works. Analyzing an algorithm is a higher order thinking process that will be generally useful to students. In addition, as students learn to analyze algorithms to learn how they work, they will learn to formulate or construct algorithms themselves.

shown in Figure 3-7. When the barrier is broken and ammonium nitrate is mixed with water, energy is absorbed from the water, and the temperature of the bag goes down.

$$NH_4NO_3(s) + H_2O(l) + energy \rightarrow NH_4NO_3(aq)$$

When the cold pack is placed on an injured area, as shown in Figure 3-8, heat transfers from the athlete to the cold pack as the reaction proceeds. This causes the injury to cool, thus reducing swelling, pain, and tissue damage.

3.5 Conservation of Mass and Atoms

In Section 3.2, you learned that the law of conservation of energy says that energy is conserved in all its interactions. It should not surprise you that a similar law governs what happens to matter in chemical reactions. The **law of conservation of mass** states that mass is neither created nor destroyed in chemical reactions. This appears to contradict everyday observations, for example that a burning candle consumes its wax or an automobile gas tank becomes empty. Such observations also confused early chemists because it was not obvious that sometimes substances from the air participated in a reaction, and at other times, gaseous products were unrecognized because they disappeared into the atmosphere. It was the French chemist Antoine Laurent Lavoisier [ləv wäz′ ē ā], (1743–1794), who was able to state this fundamental law as a result of the many careful experiments he carried out using a *closed system*. A closed system is a sealed reaction vessel, which does not allow matter to enter or leave after a reaction has started. Lavoisier showed that when a closed system is used, no change in mass is observed. The mass of the reaction vessel and reactants before reaction is the same as the mass of the vessel and products after the reaction. Many experiments by other chemists since Lavoisier's time have added a considerable amount of data that supports the law of conservation of mass. Another way of stating the law is that in a chemical reaction, the numbers and kinds of atoms present in the products are the same as those present in the reactants. Why is that so?

Figure 3-8 *Swelling and tissue damage are lessened when an activated cold pack is placed on an injured area. The cooling effect continues as the temperature of the pack becomes equal to its surroundings.*

DEMONSTRATION

(continued from page T88)
concentrated, acid and then pour down the drain. Discard the aluminum pie plates; do not use the glass pie plate for the preparation of food to be eaten.

Calcium oxide, also called quicklime, is prepared by heating calcium carbonate (limestone). The equation is

$$CaCO_3 (s) + energy \rightarrow CaO(s) + CO_2(g)$$

Slaked lime, $Ca(OH)_2$, is formed by the reaction of quicklime and water. This reaction is accompanied by a threefold increase in volume, so masonry workers are required to keep their lime supplies dry. The equation for the reaction is

$$CaO(s) + H_2O(l) \rightarrow Ca(OH)_2(aq) + 82 \text{ kJ}$$

Look Ahead

Moles will be covered in Chapter 4 when equation balancing is introduced.

***

CONNECTING CONCEPTS

Processes of Science—Communicating Chemical equations summarize submicroscopic events that explain macroscopic observations.

***

Conservation of mass and chemical equations A chemical equation that accurately represents a chemical reaction obeys the law of conservation of mass. The mass of all the reactants must equal the mass of all the products. Consider the equation for the burning of carbon.

$$C(s) + O_2(g) \rightarrow CO_2(g)$$

Notice that there is 1 carbon atom on the left as the reactant and 1 carbon atom on the right as part of the carbon dioxide molecule. There are 2 oxygen atoms in the reactant oxygen molecule and 2 in the product, carbon dioxide. Since the equation shows that the same number and kind of atoms are present after the reaction as were present before, you can conclude that mass is conserved.

Making reactant and product masses equal But look at the equation for the formation of water from Section 3.3.

$$H_2(g) + O_2(g) \rightarrow H_2O(l)$$

There are 2 atoms of hydrogen in the reactant molecule, H_2, and 2 in the product molecule, H_2O. Hydrogen atoms are conserved. But notice that although there are 2 atoms of oxygen in the reactant molecule, O_2, there is only 1 in the product. In its present form, the equation does not reflect the requirement that all atoms are conserved. If the number 2 is placed in front of the symbol for water, H_2O—saying in effect that 2 molecules of water are produced—then the number of oxygen atoms on each side of the equation becomes equal.

$$H_2(g) + O_2(g) \rightarrow 2H_2O(l)$$

However, the equation no longer shows that hydrogen atoms are conserved. There are 4 hydrogen atoms in the 2 water molecules on the right and only 2 in the hydrogen molecule on the left. To make the number of hydrogen atoms on each side of the equation equal, a 2 must also be placed in front of the hydrogen molecule on the left.

$$2H_2(g) + O_2(g) \rightarrow 2H_2O(l)$$

The number 2 placed in front of the hydrogen molecule and the water molecule is called a **coefficient.** When there is no number before a term of an equation, it is understood to have the coefficient *1.* The equation says that 2 molecules of hydrogen gas (4 hydrogen atoms) react with 1 molecule of oxygen gas (2 oxygen atoms) to form 2 molecules of water (4 atoms of hydrogen and 2 atoms of oxygen). The equation shows that all the atoms in the reactants are now accounted for in the products. Atoms and mass are conserved, and the equation is said to be balanced.

***

DEMONSTRATION

Endothermic Reactions

Add 32 g of barium hydroxide octahydrate to a 250-mL pyrex Erlenmeyer flask. Pour 11 g of ammonium chloride from a beaker into the flask, stopper and swirl until the solids mix thoroughly and form a slush. Put a few drops of water on a board 30 cm × 30 cm and 1 cm thick and place the flask on the water. In a few minutes the endothermic reaction will freeze the water and the flask can be used to pick up the board. The equation for the reaction can be written as a problem-solving project:

$Ba(OH)_2 \cdot 8H_2O(s) + 2NH_4Cl(s) \rightarrow$
$BaCl_2 \cdot 2H_2O(s) + 2NH_3(aq) + 8H_2O(l)$

CAUTION: Except for BaSO_4, commonly available barium compounds are very toxic. Wear gloves in addition to safety goggles and lab apron.

(continued on page T91)

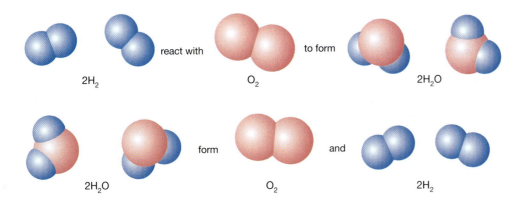

Figure 3-9 shows models for the reactants and products to help you visualize what the equation is saying. Count the numbers of both kinds of atoms on each side and convince yourself that atoms are conserved.

Knowing what you do about reversible reactions, you should not be surprised that the equation for the separation of water into its elements is balanced in the same way but written in the reverse direction. Use Figure 3-10 to convince yourself that this is true.

Figure 3-9 *Two diatomic hydrogen molecules (four atoms) react with one diatomic oxygen molecule (two atoms) to produce two molecules of water.*

Videodisc Connections

19979 to 23546, side 3
Loud explosion (movie)

1174 to 2134, side 3
Hindenburg (movie)

Balanced equations show proportions The equation for the formation of water is balanced in terms of individual atoms and molecules. The proportions of reactant molecules to product molecules is given by the coefficients. One oxygen molecule produces 2 water molecules. Two hydrogen molecules produce 2 water molecules. Two hydrogen molecules react with 1 oxygen molecule. In reality, however, every reaction involves not 1 or 2 but very large numbers of atoms and molecules. Nevertheless, the balanced equation is valid because the coefficients tell the proportion of reactants to each other and to the products. The equation could be read this way: Two billion hydrogen molecules react with 1 billion oxygen molecules to produce 2 billion water molecules. Any other numbers could be used, provided that the number of hydrogen and water molecules is twice the number of oxygen molecules.

Figure 3-10 *The formation of water from hydrogen and oxygen is the reverse of the decomposition of water to form hydrogen and oxygen.*

Concept ✔ Check

What must be equal on the two sides of any chemical equation?

DEMONSTRATION

(continued from page T90)
Wash your hands thoroughly when finished with this demonstration. Do not allow students to touch or handle the flask or board. Barium compounds should never be poured down the drain. Treat the contents of the flask with sufficient 1M NaSO$_4$ solution to precipitate all the barium as the sulfate. The decantate
may be poured down the drain; the precipitate should be saved in a labeled container for disposal by a waste disposal contractor.

Add 50 grams of ammonium chloride to 100 mL of distilled water at room temperature in a pyrex Erlenmeyer flask. Use a thermometer to show that the temperature decreases, indicating an endothermic process.

Teaching Strategy

Balancing Chemical Equations

After you have demonstrated each of the balancing techniques, ask students to analyze each to determine why it works.

3.6 Balancing Chemical Equations

When sodium metal, Na, and chlorine gas, Cl_2, react, the product is the ionic compound NaCl. The first step in writing the balanced equation for this reaction is to write the correct formulas for the reactants and products on the appropriate sides of the arrow.

$$Na(s) + Cl_2(g) \rightarrow NaCl(s)$$

In balancing the equation, these formulas *may not be changed.* Changing coefficients is the only way to make the number of each kind of atom the same on both sides of the equation. Placing the coefficient 2 in front of NaCl says that 2 sodium chloride units are formed. Figure 3-11 gives a visual representation; it also shows that the equation is not yet balanced. Two atoms of sodium are needed on the left. By placing the coefficient 2 in front of the sodium, the equation is balanced, as shown below and in Figure 3-12.

$$2Na(s) + Cl_2(g) \rightarrow 2NaCl(s)$$

Figure 3-11 *Two formula units of sodium chloride are formed when one molecule of chlorine reacts. What additional change is needed to balance the equation?*

Figure 3-12 *Compare the visual models with the balanced equation. How do the models help you recognize the difference between coefficients and subscripts?*

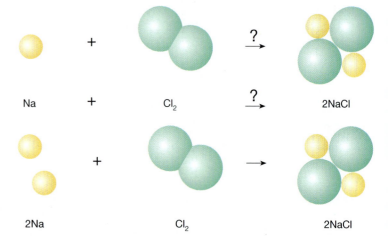

Na   + Cl_2 $\overset{?}{\rightarrow}$ 2NaCl

2Na Cl_2 2NaCl

Counting atoms Although it is helpful to have models like those in Figure 3-12 to visualize submicroscopic events, it is necessary for you to learn to balance equations without having to rely on pictures. Is the following equation for the burning of propane balanced?

$$C_3H_8(g) + 5O_2(g) \rightarrow 3CO_2(g) + 4H_2O(g)$$

Check to see if atoms are conserved. Starting with carbon, note that there are 3 atoms of carbon in the 1 molecule of propane, C_3H_8. There are also 3 carbon atoms on the product side of the equation, 1 in each of the 3 molecules of CO_2 that are formed. Therefore, atoms of carbon are conserved.

One molecule of propane on the left contains 8 atoms of hydrogen. On the right, 4 molecules of water also contain 8 hydrogen atoms. You can quickly determine the number of hydrogen atoms in 4 molecules of water by multiplying the coefficient *4* by the subscript *2* on hydrogen in the term $4H_2O$. The four molecules each contain 2 atoms of hydrogen—a total of eight hydrogen atoms.

Oxygen is found in both products. Multiply the coefficients by the subscripts on oxygen in each of the terms on the right containing oxygen. There are 6 oxygens in the carbon dioxide and 4 in the water, a total of 10 in the products. Ten oxygen atoms are found in the 5 oxygen molecules on the left. You have verified that atoms are conserved and that the equation is balanced. Table 3-2 summarizes steps you can follow in writing and balancing equations.

TABLE 3-2

Writing and Balancing Chemical Equations

1. Write the formulas for all reactants to the left of an arrow and all products to the right. Be sure that the formulas correctly represent the species that exist in the reaction.

2. Once formulas are correctly written, do not change them. Use coefficients in front of the formulas to balance the equation.

3. Begin balancing with an element that occurs only once on each side of the arrow.

4. To determine the number of atoms of a given element in a term of the equation, multiply the coefficient by the subscript of the element.

Just as in the case of learning to write chemical formulas, writing chemical equations becomes easier when you practice it. The method of balancing equations used here is a "trial and error" process; if you make a mistake, try again. Example 3-1 will help you learn how to write and balance a chemical equation.

EXAMPLE 3-1

Write and balance the equation for the burning, or combustion of ethylene, C_2H_4.

■ *Analyze the Problem* In order to solve the problem, you need to know what a combustion reaction is and that ethylene is a reactant. You must also recognize that in order for the equation to be balanced, there must be the same numbers of each kind of atom on the reactant and product sides.

■ *Apply a Strategy* Since ethylene is a hydrocarbon like propane, the equation for the combustion of propane can serve as a model. Begin by writing a word equation for the combustion

PART 1
Section 3.6 continued

PROBLEM SOLVING

▶ Encourage students to look for general principles that will help them balance equations. Examples are even/odd, intact polyatomic ions, and in the combustion of hydrocarbons the number of hydrogen atoms in the reactants must be divisible by four. To illustrate each:

In the reaction
$$Fe + O_2 \rightarrow Fe_2O_3$$
the number of oxygen atoms on the left must be even. Begin by making the number of oxygen atoms on the right even, then balance the iron atoms.
In the reaction
$$Fe + Pb(C_2H_3O_2)_2 \rightarrow$$
$$Fe(C_2H_3O_2)_3 + Pb$$
the atoms in the polyatomic ion, acetate, can be balanced as a group.
In the reaction
$$C_2H_2 + O_2 \rightarrow CO_2 + H_2O$$
begin by making the number of hydrogen atoms on the left 4 by choosing a coefficient of 2 for C_2H_2. The equation then balances easily. When the number of atoms of hydrogen is already divisible by 4 this technique is not needed, as in
$$C_5H_{12} + O_2 \rightarrow CO_2 + H_2O$$

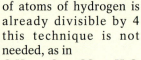

PROBLEM·SOLVING

S T R A T E G Y

Use what you know about writing formulas to help you with the equation. (See Strategy, page 58.)

PROBLEM·SOLVING

S T R A T E G Y

Making a table to check your answer is one way to organize your work. (See Strategy, page 100.)

of ethylene. Then substitute for the words the correct formulas for all reactants and products.

■ **Work a Solution** The equations for the combustion of ethylene are these.

$$\text{ethylene} + \text{oxygen} \rightarrow \text{carbon dioxide} + \text{water}$$
$$C_2H_4 + O_2 \rightarrow CO_2 + H_2O$$

Since both carbon and hydrogen occur only once on each side of the arrow, you can begin with either element. If you start with hydrogen, the equation can be balanced by placing a 2 in front of the water on the right.

$$C_2H_4 + O_2 \rightarrow CO_2 + 2H_2O$$

Now the number of hydrogen atoms is balanced, but the number of carbon and oxygen atoms is not. Balance the carbons next. Notice that if you change the coefficient of C_2H_4, you also change the number of hydrogens.

$$C_2H_4 + O_2 \rightarrow 2CO_2 + 2H_2O$$

Now both the carbon and hydrogen are balanced, but there are six oxygen atoms indicated on the right and only two on the left. Placing a three in front of the oxygen in the equation will complete the process.

$$C_2H_4 + 3O_2 \rightarrow 2CO_2 + 2H_2O$$

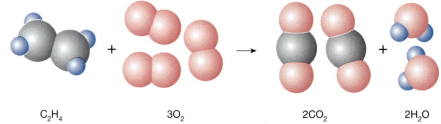

C_2H_4 $3O_2$ $2CO_2$ $2H_2O$

Figure 3-13 *As you can see from these molecular models for the combustion of ethylene, the same number of each kind of atom appears in the reactants as in the products.*

■ **Verify Your Answer** At first, you may want to draw models of the reactants and products in your balanced equation, as in Figure 3-13, and count the number of each kind of atom on each side. However, as you become more confident, you can use a table like the one below as you apply step 4 of Table 3-2.

Reactants	→	Products
2	C	2
4	H	4
6	O	6

Practice Problems

1. Write and balance the equation for the reaction of sodium and water to produce sodium hydroxide and hydrogen gas.

2. Write and balance the equation for the formation of magnesium nitride from its elements.

Coefficients are whole numbers Sometimes, in balancing equations, you will find that a fractional coefficient seems necessary. For example, consider how you balance this equation.

$$NH_3 + O_2 \rightarrow NO_2 + H_2O$$

The hydrogen can be balanced by placing a 2 in front of NH_3 and a 3 in front of H_2O.

$$2NH_3 + O_2 \rightarrow NO_2 + 3H_2O$$

Placing a 2 in front of NO_2 balances the nitrogen.

$$2NH_3 + O_2 \rightarrow 2NO_2 + 3H_2O$$

Now everything is balanced except the oxygen, but do you see a problem? The only source of oxygen on the left is O_2. Any whole number coefficient that you place in front of O_2 will result in an *even* number of oxygen atoms, and there are 7 oxygen atoms shown on the right. Only the fractional coefficient $\frac{7}{2}$ for O_2 will balance the equation as it now stands.

$$2NH_3 + \frac{7}{2}O_2 \rightarrow 2NO_2 + 3H_2O$$

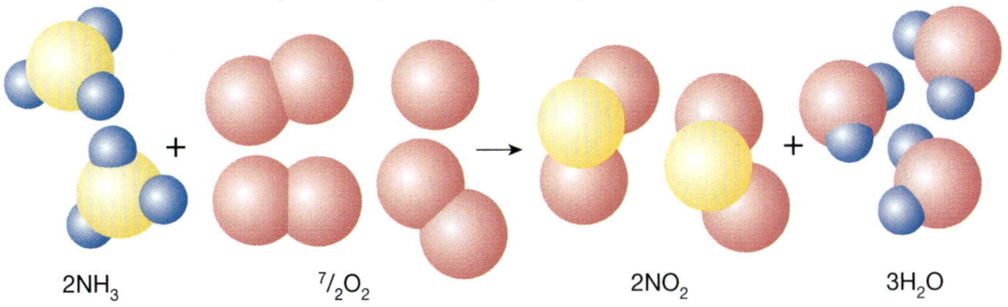

2NH₃   ⁷/₂O₂   2NO₂   3H₂O

Although this equation is balanced, it makes no sense at the molecular level. You cannot have one half of an oxygen molecule. To avoid this problem, all the coefficients are multiplied by 2.

$$4NH_3 + 7O_2 \rightarrow 4NO_2 + 6H_2O$$

Is this equation balanced?

$$8NH_3 + 14O_2 \rightarrow 8NO_2 + 12H_2O$$

The answer is yes. On both the reactant and product sides, there are 8 nitrogen, 24 hydrogen, and 28 oxygen atoms. However it is standard practice to use the set of smallest whole number coefficients. Since all the coefficients are divisible by 2, the properly balanced equation is as previously obtained.

$$4NH_3 + 7O_2 \rightarrow 4NO_2 + 6H_2O$$

Figure 3-14 *Three and one half molecules of oxygen implies incorrectly that there are two different kinds of oxygen reacting.*

Practice Problems

Assign the Practice Problems.

Guided Practice

Review the Concept Check questions on pages 84, 87, and 91 with students. Answers can be found in Appendix E on page 808.

Reteaching Idea

Reinforce student understanding of balanced equations by having them make drawings to show the decomposition of 6 molecules of ammonia gas to hydrogen and nitrogen. How many molecules of nitrogen are produced? How many molecules of hydrogen are produced? (3 molecules of nitrogen, 9 molecules of hydrogen) Points of emphasis:

a. conservation of atoms

b. diatomic molecules of nitrogen and hydrogen

c. same size and shape used for a given atom

d. random orientation of all molecules

e. homogeneous mixture of hydrogen and nitrogen gas

PART 1

Section 3.6 *continued*

⊟ CLOSE

Summing Up Main Ideas

Have students put into their own words how a balanced chemical reaction illustrates the law of conservation of mass. Possible answer: A balanced equation shows that atoms are neither created nor destroyed in a chemical reaction, only rearranged. The same atoms compose the reactants and the products.

PART 1 REVIEW

Assign the Part Review questions.

Evaluating Skills

These skills are evaluated in the Part Review questions indicated.
Describing: 3; **Analyzing data:** 3, 5, 6, 7, 8, 9, 10; **Applying a strategy:** 3, 6, 7, 8, 9; **Calculating:** 3, 6, 7, 8, 9; **Verifing results:** 3, 6, 7, 8, 9; **Forming models:** 3

Boxed numbers indicate questions that involve skills in interpretation, application, and analysis.

PROBLEM-SOLVING

STRATEGY

Use what you know about naming compounds to translate these words into symbols. (See Strategy, page 58.)

PART 1 REVIEW

3. Answer the following for the reaction of solid carbon with oxygen gas to produce carbon dioxide gas.
   a. Name the reactants.
   b. List some macroscopic properties of the reactants and products.
   c. Draw models that represent the reaction of the atoms and molecules.
   d. Write the equation for the reaction.
   e. Balance the equation.

4. Represent the following substances using the symbols found in chemical equations.
   a. solid aluminum   f. liquid ammonia
   b. nitrogen gas   g. crystals of sodium sulfate
   c. zinc sheet   h. oxygen gas
   d. liquid mercury   i. ice
   e. gaseous sulfur dioxide j. solid aluminum bromide

5. Write the following equations in words.
   a. $Fe(s) + H_2O(l) + O_2(g) \rightarrow Fe(OH)_2(s)$
   b. $HC_2H_3O_2(aq) + NaHCO_3(s) \rightarrow$
      $CO_2(g) + NaC_2H_3O_2(aq) + H_2O(l)$

6. Using formulas rewrite the following word equations and balance them.
   a. lithium + water → lithium hydroxide + hydrogen
   b. barium + water → barium hydroxide + hydrogen
   c. ammonium nitrate + sodium hydroxide →
      ammonia + water + sodium nitrate

7. Balance the following equations.
   a. $K + F_2 \rightarrow KF$
   b. $Ca + H_2O \rightarrow Ca(OH)_2 + H_2$
   c. $NH_4Cl + Ca(OH)_2 \rightarrow NH_3 + H_2O + CaCl_2$
   d. $ZnO + HCl \rightarrow ZnCl_2 + H_2O$
   e. $CuSO_4 + Fe \rightarrow Fe_2(SO_4)_3 + Cu$
   f. $Cu_2S + O_2 \rightarrow Cu_2O + SO_2$

8. Balance these equations and classify the reactions as exothermic or endothermic.
   a. $Cl_2(aq) + KI(aq) \rightarrow KCl(aq) + I_2(aq) + energy$
   b. $Mg(s) + O_2(g) \rightarrow MgO(s) + energy$
   c. $energy + NaClO_3(s) \rightarrow NaCl(s) + O_2(g)$
   d. $C_8H_{18}(l) + O_2(g) \rightarrow CO_2(g) + H_2O(g) + energy$

9. Write and balance the equation for the burning of butane, C_4H_{10}, to form carbon dioxide and water. Include energy in your equation.

10. Write the words represented by each symbol in this equation.

    $energy + 2Sb(s) + 3I_2(s) \rightarrow 2SbI_3(s)$

PART 1 REVIEW

ANSWERS

■ **Keyed to Objectives**

A **3. a.** carbon, oxygen
   b. Carbon is a black solid, but oxygen and carbon dioxide are colorless, odorless gases.
   c.

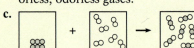

   d. $C(s) + O_2(g) \rightarrow CO_2(g)$
   e. $C(s) + O_2(g) \rightarrow CO_2(g)$

C **4. a.** $Al(s)$ **f.** $NH_3(l)$
   b. $N_2(g)$ **g.** $NaSO_4(s)$
   c. $Zn(s)$ **h.** $O_2(g)$
   d. $Hg(l)$ **i.** $H_2O(s)$
   e. $SO_2(g)$ **j.** $AlBr_3(s)$

B **5. a.** solid iron + liquid water + oxygen gas produce solid iron(II) hydroxide
   b. acetic acid in solution + solid

sodium monohydrogen carbonate produce carbon dioxide gas + sodium acetate in solution + liquid water

C **6. a.** $2Li(s) + 2H_2O(l) \rightarrow 2LiOH(aq) + H_2(g)$
   b. $Ba(s) + 2H_2O(l) \rightarrow Ba(OH)_2(s) + H_2(g)$
   c. $NH_4NO_3(aq) + NaOH(aq) \rightarrow$
      $NH_3(g) + H_2O(l) + NaNO_3(aq)$

PART 2 Regularities in Chemical Reactions

In most of the equations you have seen so far, you were given the reactants and products. Where does such information come from? For you, it came from this textbook, but how did the authors of the book know? The products of a chemical reaction are identified by doing experiments. Over the years, chemists have collected data from many such experiments. As a result, often it is possible to predict the products of a reaction from knowledge of other reactions.

In the equations that follow, you see the complete combustion of octane, methane, and acetylene. Octane is a component of gasoline, methane is the major component of natural gas, and acetylene is used in welding torches, as shown in Figure 3-15.

octane combustion: $2C_8H_{18} + 25O_2 \rightarrow 16CO_2 + 18H_2O$
methane combustion: $CH_4 + 2O_2 \rightarrow CO_2 + 2H_2O$
acetylene combustion: $2C_2H_2 + 5O_2 \rightarrow 4CO_2 + 2H_2O$

What regularities do you observe in these chemical reactions? All three equations describe the combustion of hydrocarbons. In each case, the products are carbon dioxide and water. Rather than memorize every equation, you can study regularities in how substances react. These regularities can be used to classify reactions into general categories. Recognizing types of reactions will enable you to predict the products in many equations.

Objectives

Part 2

F. *Classify* reactions as belonging to one of five general types of chemical reactions.

G. *Predict* the products of a reaction from the reactants.

H. *Differentiate* between decomposition reactions and dissociation.

I. *Determine* by using an activity series whether a single replacement reaction will occur.

3.7 Combustion Reactions

Combustion is an exothermic reaction in which a substance combines with oxygen forming products in which all elements are combined with oxygen. It is the process we commonly call burning. Usually energy is released in the form of heat and light. The general form of combustion equations for hydrocarbons is this.

$$C_xH_y + O_2 \rightarrow CO_2 + H_2O$$

The **combustion,** or burning, of a variety of hydrocarbons—such as propane, gasoline, fuel oil, and natural gas—provides most of the energy for people's homes, factories, and cars. The combustion of octane in gasoline produces carbon dioxide and water.

$$2C_8H_{18}(l) + 25O_2(g) \rightarrow 16CO_2(g) + 18H_2O(g)$$

The combustion of heptane is similar.

$$C_7H_{16}(g) + 11O_2(g) \rightarrow 7CO_2(g) + 8H_2O(g)$$

Figure 3-15 *The combustion of acetylene in a welding torch generates intense heat needed to fuse metals.*

Developing Skills

Students may apply these skills in their study of Part 2.

Observing and classifying: Have students study the photographs of reactions in Figures 3–15, 3–16, and 3–17 and classify each reaction.

Predicting: Both magnesium oxide and magnesium nitride are formed when magnesium burns in air. Have students predict the formulas of the two magnesium compounds being formed in Figure 3–16.

Classifying: Have students describe the reactions in Figures 3–15 and 3–16 as exothermic or endothermic.

Predicting: Have students hypothesize which types of reactions are likely to be exothermic.

Comparing/Contrasting: Have students differentiate between the products for equations A and B in Section 3.9.

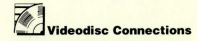 Videodisc Connections

11593 to 12553, side 3
Ethanol explosion (movie)

36377 to 38314, side 2
Firefighting breathing system (movie)

C 7. a. $2K(s) + F_2(g) \rightarrow 2KF(s)$
   b. $Ca(s) + 2H_2O(l) \rightarrow Ca(OH)_2(s) + H_2(g)$
   c. $2NH_4Cl(s) + Ca(OH)_2(s) \rightarrow 2NH_3(g) + 2H_2O(l) + CaCl_2(s)$
   d. $ZnO(s) + 2HCl(l) \rightarrow ZnCl_2(aq) + H_2O(l)$
   e. $3CuSO_4(aq) + 2Fe(s) \rightarrow Fe_2(SO_4)_3(aq) + 3Cu(s)$
   f. $2Cu_2S(s) + 3O_2(g) \rightarrow 2Cu_2O(s) + 2SO_2(g)$

C 8. a. $Cl_2(aq) + 2KI(aq) \rightarrow 2KCl(aq) + I_2(aq) + energy$ (exothermic)
   b. $2Mg(s) + O_2(g) \rightarrow 2MgO(s) + energy$ (exothermic)
   c. $energy + 2NaClO_3(s) \rightarrow 2NaCl(s) + 3O_2(g)$ (endothermic)
   d. $2C_8H_{18}(l) + 25O_2(g) \rightarrow 16CO_2(g) + 18H_2O(g) + energy$ (exothermic)

C 9. $2C_4H_{10}(l) + 13O_2(g) \rightarrow 8CO_2(g) + 10H_2O(g) + energy$

C 10. Heat plus solid antimony and solid iodine yield solid antimony(III) iodide.

PART **2**
Section 3.8

≡ FOCUS

Activate Prior Knowledge

Students are acquainted in their everyday lives with many substances that burn as well as substances that do not burn. Have students predict the products of a combustion reaction involving water or alcohol. Then place 5 mL of water and 5 mL of ethyl alcohol in separate evaporating dishes that are under a hood. Place a lighted match in each evaporating dish. Explain that adding the match to water can be written as

$$H_2O + O_2 \rightarrow N.R.$$

and adding a match to ethyl alcohol can be written as

$$C_2H_5OH(l) + 3O_2(g) \rightarrow 2CO_2(g) + 3H_2O(g)$$

 CAUTION: Wear safety goggles and work under a hood. Make sure that the alcohol container is closed and that it is not sitting under the hood.

≡ TEACH

Teaching Strategy

Reaction Types

If students see many examples of each type of reaction, they are more likely to understand how to classify reactions. Write two equations of the same type on the chalkboard such as:

$$2Fe + O_2 \rightarrow 2FeO$$
$$2K + I_2 \rightarrow 2KI$$

Ask students to copy and balance both equations. Challenge students to write and balance an equation similar to these. As you check their equations, have some students put their equations on the chalkboard. Ask a student to identify the type of equation. Look for errors in writing formulas for diatomic elements and known compounds. Ask students to identify the tacit knowledge needed to write equations. Then repeat the process for a different type of reaction.

Figure 3-16 *Solid magnesium metal reacts with oxygen from the air to form white, solid magnesium oxide.* CAUTION: *The intense, bright light produced by the reaction is harmful to your eyes.*

CONNECTING CONCEPTS

Processes of Science—Classifying and Interpreting Data

By finding regularities in chemical reactions, you can summarize and describe many separate observations through classification.

Substances other than hydrocarbons will burn in oxygen. For example, combustion may refer to burning wood, charcoal, paper, sugar, or even metals such as iron or magnesium. Figure 3-16 shows the combustion of magnesium. Write the equation for the reaction.

3.8 Synthesis Reactions

What regularities do you see in the following chemical reactions?

$$C + O_2 \rightarrow CO_2$$
$$2H_2 + O_2 \rightarrow 2H_2O$$
$$4Fe + 3O_2 \rightarrow 2Fe_2O_3$$
$$2Sb + 3I_2 \rightarrow 2SbI_3$$
$$2Na + Cl_2 \rightarrow 2NaCl$$

The reactants in these equations are all elements, and in each case the elements combine to form a compound. Such reactions are called combination reactions or **synthesis** reactions. The latter is the term normally used in chemistry.

Synthesis is the combination of two or more substances to form a compound. The equation for synthesis reactions has this general form.

$$A + B \rightarrow AB$$

Two different substances, represented by the letters A and B, combine to form a compound represented by AB. The product, AB, has properties different from either of the reactants that formed it. For example, Figure 3-17 shows the elements sodium and chlorine. Sodium is a soft, shiny metal that reacts quickly with air. It is kept under oil to maintain its purity. The element chlorine is a pale yellow-green gas and is poisonous. When the sodium is quickly transferred to the bottle of chlorine and the mixture is warmed, the reaction shown in Figure 3-17 takes place. A new substance is formed that is a combination of sodium and chlorine. Sodium chloride has properties very different from those of the two elements that combined to form it. While sodium and chlorine are both toxic,

 **Videodisc Connections**

3264 to 5632, side 3
Sodium chloride (movie)

12845 to 14468, side 1
Chlorine and hydrogen gas reaction (movie)

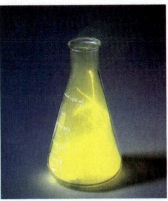

the compound sodium chloride is common table salt that is sold in the grocery store. It is a white crystalline solid that is soluble in water. Oceans contain 3 percent sodium chloride. You can shake it on your hamburgers!

What would you expect for a product if aluminum metal reacts with chlorine gas? Based on the observed regularity, the following reaction seems likely.

$$2Al(s) + 3Cl_2(g) \rightarrow 2AlCl_3(s)$$

Keep in mind that this is not a prediction that aluminum metal *will* react with chlorine. Whether a reaction occurs depends on many factors. At the moment, you have no basis for concluding that a reaction between aluminum and chlorine will occur. However, you can predict that *if* a reaction occurs, it will be the one described by the equation shown above. The reaction does, in fact, occur.

Predicting synthesis reactions You can predict an equation for the reaction between aluminum and chlorine because of the observed regularity that elements react to form compounds. You can write the formula for the product because of regularities concerning chemical formulas. In Chapter 2, you learned that aluminum *always* has a 3+ charge in compounds and that chlorine *always* has a 1– charge when it forms binary compounds with metals. You would not be able to predict the product of the reaction between iron and oxygen in the same way because the charge on iron varies. You could predict that *some* oxide of iron would be produced, but you have no way of knowing whether the product would be FeO, Fe_2O_3, or Fe_3O_4. In fact, powdered iron burns readily in oxygen to form both FeO and Fe_2O_3 as shown in Figure 3-18. The two reactions are represented by these equations.

$$2Fe(s) + O_2(g) \rightarrow 2FeO(s)$$
$$4Fe(s) + 3O_2(g) \rightarrow 2Fe_2O_3(s)$$

Figure 3-17 ▲ Left: *The bottle contains chlorine, a pale yellow-green, poisonous gas.* Middle: *Sodium metal is kept under oil to prevent its reacting with substances in the air.* Right: *A vigorous reaction occurs when sodium and chlorine are mixed. White, solid sodium chloride, NaCl, is formed.*

Figure 3-18 *Iron(III) oxide, Fe_2O_3, is one product of the exothermic combustion of iron in oxygen. Iron(II) oxide, FeO, is also formed.*

Teaching Strategy

Synthesis Reactions

Ask students to describe the appearance of the reactants and products for the reactions they write. This will remind them that all metals are shiny and silvery except copper and gold. They will learn that they do not know the appearance of most non-metals or the compounds that are formed. Show the students how to use a handbook to find the color and state of unknown substances.

▶ FOCUS ON
PROBLEM SOLVING

Activate Prior Knowledge

Students have had previous experience using patterns in math. For example, one way to write the equation of a straight line is y = mx + b, where *x* and *y* are variables, *m* is the slope of the line, and *b* is the y-intercept. Have students graph the following values for *x* and *y*: (0,3), (1,6), (2,9), and (3,12). Then, ask students to predict the next value for *y* if *x* = 4, and to write an equation that describes the relationship between *x* and *y*. Students will realize that the values for *x* and *y* show a pattern described by the equation, y = 3x + 3. Patterns in chemistry often lead to predictions and sometimes an equation that describes the pattern.

▶ TEACH
THE STRATEGY

Guided Practice

Have students use the periodic table to determine if the following elements are metals or nonmetals; Na, F, O, Mg, Fe, and I. They should also explain the pattern among the elements in the periodic table that enables them to predict whether an element is a metal or a nonmetal. Since Na, Mg, and Fe are located in the left side of the periodic table, and F, O, and I are found in the upper right part, the pattern is metals on the left and nonmetals on the right.

Reteaching Idea

Refer students to these equations:
a. $Cl_2(aq) + KI(aq) \rightarrow KCl(aq) + I_2(aq) + energy$
b. $Mg(s) + O_2(g) \rightarrow MgO(s) + energy$
c. $energy + NaClO_3(s) \rightarrow NaCl(s) + O_2(g)$

(continued on page T101)

Using Patterns

Many subjects are easier to learn if you understand the patterns on which they are based. For example, try to supply the next number in these sequences.

1,4,9,16,25,36,___

2,3,5,7,11,13,17,19,23,___

How did you complete the sequences? You could have looked for a series of even or odd numbers, a sequence of squares, or one having a common difference or multiplier. Your guess is correct if you could generate each number in the sequence and fill in the missing number. Notice how you used your knowledge of mathematics.

▶ Patterns in Science

Searching for patterns in science also begins with what you already know. To predict the product of a chemical reaction, you may find it useful to compare the reactants with those in reactions that are familiar to you. For example, in this chapter you learn that oxygen is always a reactant in combustion reactions, and that the products of combustion are compounds containing oxygen. You can apply this information to any unknown reaction in which oxygen is a reactant as a first step in predicting the products. This kind of reasoning from the known to the unknown,

will also help you with numerical problems in chemistry.

▶ Discovering Patterns

In this course, you will discover patterns for yourself using data provided to you, or obtained through laboratory experiments. Sometimes a pattern will not be obvious by simply examining the data. You will need to organize it in a logical way. For example, you could make a table listing your data according to some property—mass, length, or density. A plot of the data would also help to expose the pattern.

If your first attempt to organize your data is unsuccessful, you may need to try another way.

▶ Patterns and the Periodic Table

The periodic table is one of the first attempts of scientists to arrange the elements in a way that is based on patterns. As you continue your study of chemistry, you will find many properties of elements that can be related to the periodic table. You will also see examples of how scientists "look for patterns" in their work. Practice this strategy yourself in solving your chemistry problems.

Overlapping categories How do these reactions of iron compare to the reaction of magnesium and oxygen?

$$2Mg(s) + O_2(g) \rightarrow 2MgO(s)$$

Although the reaction of magnesium and oxygen has been classified earlier as a combustion reaction, it can also be classified as a synthesis reaction. Do you see why? Compare it with the general equation for synthesis reactions.

In fact, all three reactions can be described as either synthesis or combustion. Many of the reactions you will encounter can be classified in several ways. Describing the reaction of magnesium and oxygen as combustion calls attention to the large amount of heat and light it produces. It is just as accurate, though, to call it a synthesis reaction, since two reactants are combining to form a product. It may seem less accurate to categorize as combustion the very slow reaction of iron with oxygen in the air to form brown iron(III) oxide (rust), as shown in Figure 3-19. However, it would be correct to do so. Even the reaction of hydrogen and oxygen to form water can be considered as either a combustion reaction or as a synthesis reaction. These categories of reactions can overlap, just as you can be classified both as a student and, at the same time, as a human being.

Figure 3-19 Iron(III) oxide, rust, is the product of the slow process shown in this photograph. Compare it with Figure 3-18. What factors do you think account for the difference in rate of reaction?

DO YOU KNOW?

Exothermic reactions power rockets. The reaction of hydrazine, N_2H_4, and hydrogen peroxide, H_2O_2, is highly exothermic. The reactants are liquids, and their flow rates can be controlled easily. The reaction products, N_2 and H_2O, are gases. Gaseous products provide the maximum thrust for the rocket because the molecules are moving at very high speeds.

PART 2

Section 3.8 *continued*

(continued from page T100)

d. $C_6H_{12}(l) + O_2(g) \rightarrow CO_2(g)$
$\qquad + H_2O(g) + energy$

Ask them what pattern they could use to tell whether a reaction is endothermic or exothermic.

Science Background

Overlapping Categories

A balanced equation for a reaction does not indicate how fast a reaction occurs. For example, iron reacts with oxygen from air so slowly that days may be required to produce a noticeable amount of product. On the other hand, potassium reacts noticeably with oxygen from air in a fraction of a second. In addition, the equation for a reaction does not indicate if the reaction takes place in steps or how the atoms in the products are bonded together.

PART 2
Section 3.9

Teaching Strategy

Decomposition Reactions and Dissociation

Ask students to classify the reaction as either exothermic or endothermic and to provide evidence to support their conclusion. Through discussion explore the reversibility of the reaction. Help students recognize that the reverse reaction is endothermic as shown by the need to boil the pad to restore its original condition.

Look Ahead

The generalization that the reverse of an exothermic reaction is always endothermic will be revisited in Chapter 16.

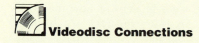

Videodisc Connections

23516 to 23915, side 2
Salt crystal dissolving in water (movie)

48928 to 50116, side 3
Electrolysis of water (movie)

3.9 Decomposition Reactions and Dissociation

Decomposition is the opposite of synthesis. In a decomposition reaction, a compound breaks down to form two or more simpler substances.

The equation for **decomposition** reactions has this general form.

$$AB \rightarrow A + B$$

The decomposition of the ionic compound ammonium nitrate is shown in Figure 3-20. What is the equation for the decomposition of water, H_2O? Since water contains only two elements, the decomposition products can be predicted as the individual elements.

$$2H_2O(l) \rightarrow 2H_2(g) + O_2(g)$$

Decomposition versus dissociation The equation that describes a chemical reaction tells you much of what you need to know to understand the process. All of the information given provides clues to what happens in the reaction. For example, look at the following equations.

A. $2NaCl(l) \xrightarrow{\text{elec}} 2Na(l) + Cl_2(g)$

B. $NaCl(s) \xrightarrow{\text{water}} Na^+(aq) + Cl^-(aq)$

Although these equations at first glance may *look* very much alike, they describe very different reactions. Read all the information contained in an equation and use it to visualize what is happening at the submicroscopic level.

The "elec", written over the arrow in equation A indicates that this equation describes electrolysis, a process in which electricity is used to decompose compounds into their elements, as shown in Figure 3-21. The "(l)" after NaCl shows that the reaction takes place at a temperature high enough to melt salt. Both pieces of information suggest that a considerable amount of energy is required to cause this reaction. Most decomposition reactions are endothermic—that is, they require energy. Are the products of equation A what you would predict for the decomposition of sodium chloride? Sodium chloride contains only the elements sodium and chlorine. There are no other possible products.

Equation B is *not* a decomposition. It describes what happens when you dissolve ordinary table salt in water and it is called dissociation. What information in the equation tells you that this process is different from the previous one? The "(s)" written after NaCl indicates that the salt is a solid, as it is at ordinary temperatures. *Water* written over the arrow indicates that water is present as a solvent. Notice that the products are *ions* rather than neutral elements. These ions are dissolved in water and are shown by the symbol (aq).

Figure 3-20 ▲ *Under suitable conditions, ammonium nitrate, NH_4NO_3, decomposes explosively into the simpler substances, N_2O and H_2O. Try to write the equation that describes the reaction.*

Although equation B looks like equation A, the macroscopic conditions are very different: The chemical change described in equation A takes place when salt is melted and an electric current passes through it. The change described in equation B takes place when salt is dissolved in water. The submicroscopic changes are also very different: The chemical change described in equation A produces sodium metal and chlorine gas, substances with properties very different from those of salt. The change described in equation B produces no new substances. The sodium *ions* and chloride *ions*, shown as products in equation B, are present in solid sodium chloride. They have very different properties from those of the neutral elements shown as products in equation A. Reactions such as those described by equation A are called decomposition reactions; changes like those in equation B are called **dissociation.** Other dissociations are described by the following equations.

$$KBr(s) \xrightarrow{\text{water}} K^+(aq) + Br^-(aq)$$
$$CaI_2(s) \xrightarrow{\text{water}} Ca^{2+}(aq) + 2I^-(aq)$$

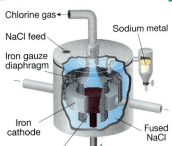

Figure 3-21 *In this electrolytic cell, electrical energy is supplied to decompose melted sodium chloride. The products, sodium metal and chlorine gas, are drawn from the cell as the reaction proceeds.*

Concept ✓ Check

Write an equation for the decomposition of lithium chloride, LiCl, and one for its dissociation.

3.10 Single Replacement Reactions

Synthesis reactions occur between two or more different elements. But elements may also react with compounds. A reaction in which one element takes the place of another element as part of a compound, is called a **single replacement reaction.** In this type of reaction, a metal *always* replaces another metal and a nonmetal replaces another nonmetal. The general equation for a single replacement reaction is this.

$$A + BC \rightarrow AB + C$$

Notice that element A replaces C in the compound BC. Is the product, C, an element or a compound?

If chlorine gas is bubbled through a solution of potassium bromide, chlorine replaces bromine in the compound and elemental bromine is produced. The reaction is described by the following equation.

$$Cl_2(aq) + 2KBr(aq) \rightarrow 2KCl(aq) + Br_2(aq)$$

Notice that before reacting, chlorine is uncombined. It is a *free* (uncombined) element. Bromine, however, is combined with potassium in the compound potassium bromide. After reacting, the opposite is true. The chlorine is now combined with potassium in the compound potassium chloride, and bromine exists as a free

PART 2
Section 3.10

Teaching Strategy

Reaction Types

To help students learn the types of reactions, have them invent different names. Examples: combustion—burning up; single replacement—rejection and heartbreak; double replacement—double divorce.

Videodisc Connections

390 to 1173, side 3
Cinnabar (movie)

DEMONSTRATION
Decomposition Reactions and Dissociation

A hot pack that can be recharged and reused is available from many department and sporting goods stores. It consists of sodium acetate trihydrate, which is heated until it dissolves in its own water of hydration. When cooled slowly the system does not crystallize until disturbed. A clicker is used by the consumer to produce a shock wave and initiate crystallization. The entire crystallization process takes place in a few minutes, and the pad remains warm for nearly an hour. The original condition can be restored by immersing the pad in gently boiling water for 15 to 20 minutes.

C O N S U M E R   C H E M I S T R Y

Breath Analyzers

Since the amount of alcohol in the breath is directly proportional to the amount of alcohol in the blood, law officers using breath analyzers can determine objectively and quickly if a driver is intoxicated.

People who drive under the influence of alcohol are a major factor in traffic accidents. In fact, a large percent of all vehicular fatalities are caused by drunk drivers. Breath analyzers were developed to give the police an objective measuring tool to determine, in a matter of seconds, if a driver is intoxicated.

The simplest and most common type of breath analyzer consists of an inflatable bag attached to a tube containing a solution of sulfuric acid and potassium dichromate. When someone blows into the mouthpiece of the tube, any alcohol in that person's breath reacts with this mixture, producing a color change from reddish-orange to blue-green. The amount of blue-green color produced is proportional to the amount of alcohol in the breath. The color change is compared to a standard that is the color of the unreacted mixture.

Breathalyzer results have been questioned in recent years. However, law enforcement agencies are expected to continue using them while newer techniques are being developed and refined. The Breathalyzer is still considered a reliable, noninvasive instrument for forensic alcohol analysis.

element. The reaction is usually described with the words, *chlorine has replaced bromine,* and the reaction is called a single replacement reaction.

Replacement reactions are not reversible. In other words, the following reaction will *not* take place.

$$Br_2(aq) + 2KCl(aq) \rightarrow 2KBr(aq) + Cl_2(aq)$$

The fact that a particular reaction will not take place is often indicated by writing *N.R.*, for "no reaction", in place of products.

$$Br_2(aq) + KCl(aq) \rightarrow N.R.$$

Activity series: halogens There is an interesting regularity observed in replacement reactions involving the halogens: fluorine, chlorine, bromine, and iodine. Each halogen will react to replace any of the halogens below it in the periodic table, but will

PART 2
Section 3.10 *continued*

Videodisc Connections

594 -596, side 6
Iron in copper sulfate
(3-frame seq.)

not replace those above. For example, chlorine will replace bromine and iodine, but it will not replace fluorine.

Activity series: metals Metals also undergo replacement reactions, and regularities similar to those described for the halogens are observed. Metals can be listed in a series in which each metal will replace all the metals below it on the list, but none of the metals above it. Such a list is commonly called an **activity series.** The activity series for the halogens follows the order of the elements in Group 7A of the periodic table, but no simple regularity exists for most groups of metals. The activity series for metals is determined by experiments in which pairs of metals are compared for reactivity.

Suppose you made solutions of magnesium sulfate and copper(II) sulfate and placed a small clean iron nail in each. You would observe that the nail in the magnesium sulfate solution does not change, as shown in Figure 3-22. The experimental result can be represented by this expression.

$$Fe(s) + MgSO_4(aq) \rightarrow N.R.$$

Figure 3-22 *On the left, an iron nail placed in magnesium sulfate solution gives no evidence of reaction, while one placed in copper(II) sulfate solution turns black. When reaction is complete, note the disappearance of the blue color of the copper solution. The nail has dissolved and red-brown copper metal covers the bottom of the test tube.*

You would also observe that the nail placed in the solution of copper(II) sulfate soon turns dark. If the nail is left in long enough, it reacts completely, the original blue copper(II) sulfate solution becomes colorless, and there is a red-brown substance at the bottom of the container, as shown in Figure 3-22. The red-brown substance is finely divided copper. Iron has replaced copper in copper(II) sulfate and solid copper has formed.

$$Fe(s) + CuSO_4(aq) \rightarrow Cu(s) + FeSO_4(aq)$$

The results of these two tests can be used to place iron, magnesium, and copper in an activity series like the one shown in Table 3-3. Because iron replaces copper in copper(II) sulfate, iron is said to be *more active* than copper. Because iron *does not* replace magnesium from magnesium sulfate, iron is said to be *less active* than magnesium. Listed in order of activity, magnesium is more active than iron and iron is more active than copper. A series of similar tests can be done to list all the metals from the most active to the least active. The activity series can, then, be used to predict whether single replacement reactions involving certain metals can take place, as shown in Example 3-2.

CHEMICAL UPDATE

Some reactions once thought to be impossible have been achieved. For example, elemental fluorine has recently been formed in a chemical reaction without using electrolysis.

TABLE 3-3

Two Activity Series		
Metals	**Decreasing Activity**	**Halogens**
lithium		fluorine
potassium		chlorine
calcium		bromine
sodium		iodine
magnesium		
aluminum		
zinc		
chromium		
iron		
nickel		
tin		
lead		
HYDROGEN*		
copper		
mercury		
silver		
platinum		
gold		

* Hydrogen is in capital letters because the activities of the metals are often de-termined in relation to the activity of hydrogen.

EXAMPLE 3-2

Use the activity series to predict whether the following re-action can occur under normal conditions.

$$Mg(s) + CuSO_4(aq) \rightarrow Cu(s) + MgSO_4(aq)$$

■ **Analyze the Problem** You need to identify the type of reaction you are given as a single replacement reaction, with magnesium replacing copper in the compound copper(II) sulfate, $CuSO_4(aq)$.

■ **Apply a Strategy** Look up the relative positions of copper and magnesium on the activity series. Determine which metal is more active.

■ **Work a Solution** Since magnesium is above copper on the activity series, magnesium is more active and will replace copper in the compound $CuSO_4$. This reaction will occur.

$$Mg(s) + CuSO_4(aq) \rightarrow MgSO_4(aq) + Cu(s)$$

■ **Verify Your Answer** Compare your answer to what happens in another reaction. You know from the text that Fe replaces Cu

CONNECTING CONCEPTS

Processes of Science—Making Predictions An important part of the study of chemistry is the ability to predict the outcome of a chemical reaction before it occurs. Regularities enable sci-entists to make predictions.

in $CuSO_4$ and that it is also above copper on the activity series. Thus you can conclude that your answer is correct, since magnesium is above copper on the activity series also.

Practice Problems

11. Predict whether copper will replace silver in silver nitrate, $AgNO_3$, to form copper(II) nitrate. If it will, write the equation. Indicate N.R. if no reaction will occur.

12. Complete the following equation: $Ni(s) + MgCl_2(aq) \rightarrow$

Practice Problems

Assign the Practice Problems.

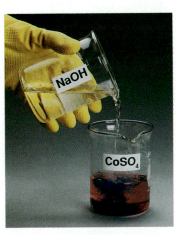
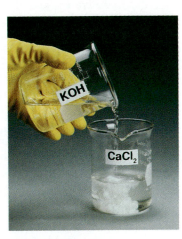

Figure 3-23 *This chemical magic is the result of combining colorless solutions to form solid precipitates. The "secret" to the magic lies in the differing solubilities of the reactants and product.*

3.11 Double Replacement Reactions

As Figure 3-23 shows, the production of purple, red, or white solids from test tubes of clear solution seems like magic, but it's really science that you can easily understand. The chemical "trick" is that each pair of test tubes contains two soluble ionic compounds that will react when mixed to form a compound that is insoluble in water. For example, lead nitrate is soluble in water as Table 3-4 shows, and it forms a colorless solution. Potassium iodide also forms a colorless solution in water. When test tubes of these two solutions are poured together, brilliant yellow lead iodide forms because it is insoluble in water. You can see it in Figure 3-24. The equation for the reaction is this.

$$Pb(NO_3)_2(aq) + 2KI(aq) \rightarrow PbI_2(s) + 2KNO_3(aq)$$

Reactions of this kind are often described as **double replacement,** or metathesis, reactions. *Metathesis* is a Greek term meaning "*changing partners*" and accurately describes what happens. The positive metal ion in one of the compounds combines with the negative ion in the other, and vice versa. The general equation for a double replacement reaction is this.

$$AB + XY \rightarrow AY + XB$$

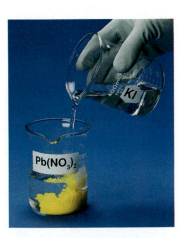

Figure 3-24 *When colorless ionic solutions of lead nitrate, $Pb(NO_3)_2$, and potassium iodide, KI, are mixed, the lead ions from one solution combine with the iodide ions from the other to form insoluble, yellow lead iodide, PbI_2.* ▲ CAUTION: *Lead compounds are toxic. Do not perform this chemical magic.*

TABLE 3-4

Solubility of Some Ionic Compounds in Water			
Negative Ion	**Plus**	**Positive Ion**	**Form a Compound Which Is**
Any negative ion	+	Alkali metal ions (Li^+, Na^+, K^+, Rb^+, or Cs^+)	Soluble, i.e., >0.1 mol/L
Any negative ion	+	Ammonium ion, NH_4^+	Soluble
Nitrate, NO_3^-	+	Any positive ion	Soluble
Acetate, CH_3COO^-	+	Any positive ion except Ag^+ or Hg^{2+}	Soluble
Chlorine, Cl^-, or Bromide, Br^-, or Iodide, I^-	+ +	Ag^+, Pb^{2+}, Hg_2^{2+}, or Cu^+ Any other positive ion	Not soluble Soluble
Sulfate, SO_4^{2-}	+ +	Ca^{2+}, Sr^{2+}, Ba^{2+}, Ra^{2+}, Ag^+, or Pb^{2+} Any other positive ion	Not soluble Soluble
Sulfide, S^{2-}	+ + +	Alkali ions or NH_4^+, Be^{2+}, Mg^{2+}, Ca^{2+}, Sr^{2+}, Ba^{2+}, or Ra^{2+} Any other positive ion	Soluble Soluble Not soluble
Hydroxide, OH^-	+ +	Alkali ions or NH_4^+ Any other positive ion	Soluble Not soluble
Phosphate, PO_4^{3-}, or Carbonate, CO_3^{2-}, or Sulfite, SO_3^{2-}	+ +	Alkali ions or NH_4^+ Any other positive ion	Soluble Not soluble

NaOH   Ca(OH)$_2$ Fe(OH)$_3$ Ni(OH)$_2$

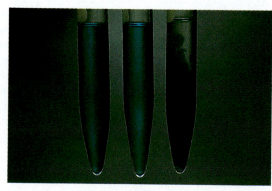

Cu(NO$_3$)$_2$ CuSO$_4$ Cu(OH)$_2$

Figure 3-25 *These photographs can help you visualize some of the regularities found in Table 3-4. Note that compounds of the positive ions Na^+ (an alkali metal), and NH_4^+ are always soluble, as are those of the negative ion NO_3^-. Most hydroxides are insoluble, and only metals of Groups 1 and 2 form soluble sulfides. What conclusion can you draw about the solubility of silver compounds?*

Predicting double replacement reactions Deciding whether a double replacement reaction will occur is a matter of predicting whether an insoluble product can form. If sodium nitrate is substituted for lead nitrate, you will see no reaction when the solutions in the two test tubes are mixed. Why not? If you write out all the possible combinations of metal and nonmetal ions and check Table 3-4 you will see that none of them is insoluble. Figure 3-25 shows the combinations of a number of different positive and negative ions to form precipitates and soluble compounds. Compare the photographic information with the data in Table 3-4. Reactions of ionic compounds in solution will be discussed in more detail in Chapter 15.

Concept ✔ Check

Will a double replacement reaction occur if solutions of silver nitrate and sodium bromide are mixed?

3.12 Predicting Products of Reactions

Chemical changes are influenced by temperature, pressure, physical state, and other conditions. Predicting the products of a chemical reaction without experimentation is no more than an educated guess. Such guesses are useful, however, because they indicate what products to expect if the reaction does take place. Example 3-3 suggests how to use the regularities described in the previous sections to predict the products of reactions.

EXAMPLE 3-3

Predict the products of the following reactions and write balanced equations to describe them.

    a. magnesium metal reacts with iodine vapor
    b. naphthalene, $C_{10}H_8(s)$, burns in air
    c. $H_2SO_4(aq) + BaCl_2(aq)$

■ **Analyze the Problem** You have been given the reactants in three chemical reactions. You must use what you know about the five general types of reactions to predict the products and write the balanced equation which represents each.

■ **Apply a Strategy** Write out the reactant side of each equation using correct formulas. Look at each set of reactants to help identify the type of reaction to which each belongs. Once you have identified the type of reaction you can use the regularities you know to predict the products. Complete the equation and balance it.

Cooperative Learning

Teams of 3; **Time:** 30 minutes
Objective: Students will learn to predict products of reactions.
Task: One student writes the reactants of a reaction. The two other students predict the products and write the balanced equation to describe it. The process continues as students take turns writing the reactants of the first reaction.
Team responsibility: Keep track of which reactions were difficult to predict products of and to balance.
Evaluation: Have a brief class discussion in which teams present a few of their examples, challenge others to predict their products and describe any insights which were helpful in this task.

Guided Practice

Review the Concept Check questions on pages 103 and 109 with students. Answers can be found in Appendix E on page 808.

■ **Work a Solution** The reactant sides of the equations written using formulas are these.

$$
\text{a. } Mg(s) + I_2(g) \rightarrow
$$
$$
\text{b. } C_{10}H_8(s) + O_2(g) \rightarrow
$$
$$
\text{c. } H_2SO_4(aq) + BaCl_2(aq) \rightarrow
$$

In equation **a,** notice that both magnesium and iodine are elements. The only possible reaction would be a synthesis reaction in which the elements combine to form a compound. By checking the periodic table, you will find that magnesium is in Group 2 and forms 2+ ions when combining with nonmetals like iodine. Since iodine always forms 1− ions, there is only one product possible, MgI_2. The equation is this.

$$
Mg(s) + I_2(g) \rightarrow MgI_2(s)
$$

By counting the number of atoms on both sides of the equation, you find that the equation is already balanced.

In equation **b,** notice that naphthalene is a hydrocarbon. Since burning is indicated, this is a combustion reaction.

$$
C_{10}H_8(s) + O_2(g) \rightarrow CO_2(g) + H_2O(g)
$$

A balanced equation looks like this.

$$
C_{10}H_8(s) + 12O_2(g) \rightarrow 10CO_2(g) + 4H_2O(g)
$$

Because equation **c** involves two compounds, there may be several possibilities for products. Of the reaction types you are familiar with, this is likely to be a double replacement reaction, in which barium and hydrogen *change partners.* A double replacement reaction would be this.

$$
H_2SO_4(aq) + BaCl_2(aq) \rightarrow HCl(aq) + BaSO_4(s)
$$

As you can see the equation is not balanced. It is balanced by showing 2 molecules of HCl.

$$
H_2SO_4(aq) + BaCl_2(aq) \rightarrow 2HCl(aq) + BaSO_4(s)
$$

By checking the solubility of barium sulfate in Table 3-4, you can determine that it is not soluble in water.

■ **Verify Your Answer** Compare your answers to examples given in the text for each type of reaction. If your equations exhibit the same regularities, they are likely to have the correct products. In equation *a*, a compound is formed from two simpler substances as in a synthesis reaction. The products of equation *b* are compounds of oxygen as in combustion reactions. Equation *c* shows that a solid precipitate forms as in a double replacement reaction.

PART 2 REVIEW

ANSWERS

■ **Keyed to Objectives**

G **15. a.** $C_2H_4(g) + 3O_2(g) \rightarrow 2CO_2(g) + 2H_2O(g)$
b. $C_6H_{12}O_6(s) + 6O_2(g) \rightarrow 6CO_2(g) + 6H_2O(l)$
c. $C_2H_5OH(l) + 3O_2(g) \rightarrow 2CO_2(g) + 3H_2O(g)$
d. $C_5H_{12}(l) + 8O_2(g) \rightarrow 5CO_2(g) + 6H_2O(l)$
e. $2Sr(s) + O_2(g) \rightarrow 2SrO(s)$
f. $4Na(s) + O_2(g) \rightarrow 2Na_2O(s)$
g. $2K(s) + Cl_2(g) \rightarrow 2KCl(s)$
h. $Ca(s) + F_2(g) \rightarrow CaF_2(s)$
i. $MgBr_2(l) \rightarrow Mg(l) + Br_2(g)$
j. $2AlCl_3(l) \rightarrow 2Al(l) + 3Cl_2(g)$
k. $2H_2O(l) \rightarrow 2H_2(g) + O_2(g)$
l. $2KI(l) \rightarrow 2K(l) + I_2(l)$
m. $Zn(s) + CuSO_4(aq) \rightarrow ZnSO_4(aq) + Cu(s)$
n. $Cl_2(g) + 2KI(aq) \rightarrow 2KCl(aq) + I_2(aq)$
o. $Ni(s) + MgSO_4(aq) \rightarrow N.R.$
p. $Br_2(aq) + CaCl_2(aq) \rightarrow N.R.$
q. $FeCl_2(aq) + K_2S(aq) \rightarrow FeS(s) + 2KCl(aq)$
r. $ZnSO_4(aq) + SrCl_2(aq) \rightarrow SrSO_4(s) + ZnCl_2(aq)$

Practice Problems

13. Write a balanced equation for the synthesis of sodium oxide from sodium and oxygen.

14. The first two containers in Figure 3-26 represent sodium and oxygen before reaction. Draw a representation of the product, solid sodium oxide.

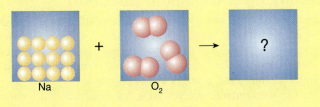

Figure 3-26 *Models are shown for the reactants in the synthesis of sodium oxide. Complete the equation by drawing a model of the product.*

PART 2 REVIEW

Boxed numbers indicate questions that involve skills in interpretation, application, and analysis.

15. Predict the products and write the balanced equation for each of these reactions.

Combustion
   a. $C_2H_4(g) + O_2(g) \rightarrow$
   b. $C_6H_{12}O_6(s) + O_2(g) \rightarrow$
   c. $C_2H_5OH(l) + O_2(g) \rightarrow$
   d. $C_5H_{12}(l) + O_2(g) \rightarrow$

Synthesis
   e. $Sr(s) + O_2(g) \rightarrow$
   f. $Na(s) + O_2(g) \rightarrow$
   g. $K(s) + Cl_2(g) \rightarrow$
   h. $Ca(s) + F_2(g) \rightarrow$

Decomposition
   i. $MgBr_2(l) \rightarrow$
   j. $AlCl_3(l) \rightarrow$
   k. $H_2O(l) \rightarrow$
   l. $KI(l) \rightarrow$

Single replacement
   m. $Zn(s) + CuSO_4(aq) \rightarrow$
   n. $Cl_2(g) + KI(aq) \rightarrow$
   o. $Ni(s) + MgSO_4(aq) \rightarrow$
   p. $Br_2(aq) + CaCl_2(aq) \rightarrow$

Double replacement
   q. $FeCl_2(aq) + K_2S(aq) \rightarrow$
   r. $ZnSO_4(aq) + SrCl_2(aq) \rightarrow$
   s. $AlCl_3(aq) + Na_2CO_3(aq) \rightarrow$
   t. $(NH_4)_2SO_4(aq) + BaCl_2(aq) \rightarrow$

16. Predict the product and write a balanced equation for each of the following. Write N.R. if no reaction occurs.

   a. $MgCl_2(l) \xrightarrow{(elec)}$
   b. $Zn(s) + MgSO_4(aq) \rightarrow$
   c. $Zn(s) + Ni(NO_3)_2(aq) \rightarrow$
   d. $KCl(aq) + AgNO_3(aq) \rightarrow$

17. Complete the equation for these dissociation reactions.
   a. $NaCl(s) \rightarrow$
   b. $K_2SO_4(s) \rightarrow$
   c. $Hg(NO_3)_2(s) \rightarrow$
   d. $ZnCl_2(s) \rightarrow$

18. Predict whether the following reactions will occur.
   a. $3Mg(s) + 2AlCl_3(aq) \rightarrow 3MgCl_2(aq) + 2Al(s)$
   b. $Cl_2(g) + 2KBr(aq) \rightarrow 2KCl(aq) + Br_2(aq)$

PART 2

Section 3.12 *continued*

Practice Problems

Assign the Practice Problems.

Reteaching Idea

If students need more practice in understanding the implications of the balanced equation, use the following reaction and models. Write a balanced equation for the synthesis of solid sodium oxide from oxygen and sodium. Draw the product, sodium oxide, as a solid.
Points of emphasis:
   a. particles on bottom
   b. conservation of atoms
   c. same size and shape
   d. regular arrangement in crystal
   e. ratio of 2 sodium atoms to 1 oxygen atom

Make up your own representations for other classes of reactions—for example, the decomposition of K_2O or the combustion of zinc.

≡CLOSE

Summing Up Main Ideas

Have students summarize how predicting the products of a chemical reaction contributes to their understanding of atoms, ions, and molecules. Students should mention the references used in predicting a chemical reaction. References such as an activity series or a table of solubilities include information on atoms becoming ions, ions becoming atoms, or ions forming new molecules.

PART 2 REVIEW

Assign the Part Review questions.

Evaluating Skills

These skills are evaluated in the Part Review questions indicated.
Predicting: 15, 16, 17, 18;
Comparing/Contrasting: 15

s. $2AlCl_3(aq) + 3Na_2CO_3(aq) \rightarrow$
   $Al_2(CO_3)_3(s) + 6NaCl(aq)$
t. $(NH_4)_2SO_4(aq) + BaCl_2(aq) \rightarrow$
   $2NH_4Cl(aq) + BaSO_4(s)$

G 16. a. $MgCl_2(l) \xrightarrow{elec} Mg(l) + Cl_2(g)$
   b. $Zn(s) + MgSO_4(aq) \rightarrow N.R.$
   c. $Zn(s) + Ni(NO_3)_2(aq) \rightarrow$
      $Zn(NO_3)_2(aq) + Ni(s)$
   d. $KCl(aq) + AgNO_3(aq) \rightarrow$
      $KNO_3(aq) + AgCl(s)$

H 17. a. $NaCl(s) \rightarrow Na^+(aq) + Cl^-(aq)$
   b. $K_2SO_4(s) \rightarrow 2K^+(aq)$
      $+ SO_4^{2-}(aq)$
   c. $Hg(NO_3)_2(s) \rightarrow Hg^{2+}(aq)$
      $+ 2NO_3^-(aq)$
   d. $ZnCl_2(s) \rightarrow Zn^{2+}(aq)$
      $+ 2Cl^-(aq)$

I 18. a. yes
   b. yes

Identifying a Chemical Reaction

Estimated Time: (45 minutes)

Process Skills

Comparing/Contrasting
Analyzing data
Constructing tables and graphs

Preparation

■ Materials

(for a class of 24, working in pairs)

Apparatus

(12 of each unless noted)
10-mL graduated cylinders, lab buckets, 125-mL Erlenmeyer flasks, one-hole stoppers, test tubes (72), solid stoppers for test tubes, test-tube racks, lab aprons (24), safety goggles (24), thermometers, troughs, tongs, boxes of matches, plastic bags, wooden splints, birthday candles

Reagents

- sodium hydroxide pellets
- small box of baking soda
- 250 mL of 1.0M copper(II) sulfate
- 2 ft. of aluminum foil
- 1 pint bottle ammonia water
- 1 pint white vinegar
- vegetable oil

■ Preparation Hints

Try to use many items with which students are familiar. For example, show a can of commercial lye (sodium hydroxide) to students, and perhaps they will recognize the can as one their families use as a drain cleaner. Any garden store will sell root killer with copper(II) sulfate. To make 1M $CuSO_4 \cdot 5H_2O$, use 62.5 g per 250 mL total volume.

■ Safety

 Ammonia should be used under the hood.

Laboratory
Investigation

Identifying a Chemical Reaction

Chemical reactions are constantly occurring all around you. You have learned that to identify whether or not a chemical reaction has occurred, you can look for observable evidence. Observable evidence includes the formation of a precipitate, release of a gas, changes in color, and changes in temperature.

In this experiment, you will look for evidence that a chemical reaction has taken place. Remember that mixing substances does not necessarily mean that a chemical reaction has occurred. A change in state, such as from a solid to a liquid or from a liquid to a gas, may look like a chemical reaction, but you still have the same substance—just in a different form.

O b j e c t i v e s

Observe several possible chemical reactions.

Identify observations that indicate that a chemical reaction has taken place.

Distinguish between mixing, a change of state, and a chemical reaction.

■ Materials

Apparatus
- lab apron and safety goggles
- 125-mL Erlenmeyer flask with one-hole stopper
- thermometer
- trough
- 6 test tubes
- solid stopper for test tube
- spatula or tongs
- candles
- matches
- wooden splints
- Ziploc plastic bag

Reagents
- aluminum foil
- NaOH pellets or lye
- vinegar
- distilled water
- baking soda
- 1.0M copper(II) sulfate solution
- vegetable oil
- ammonia water

■ Procedure

1. Put on your lab apron and safety goggles.
2. Roll a 10 cm × 10 cm piece of aluminum foil into a ball and place it in a 125-mL Erlenmeyer flask. Using your spatula or

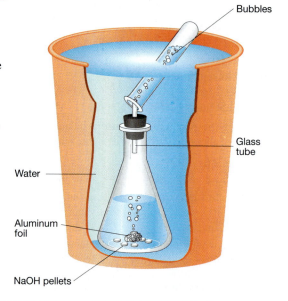

Bubbles

Glass tube

Water

Aluminum foil

NaOH pellets

tongs, add one or two pellets of sodium hydroxide or a few crystals of lye.

🛑 **CAUTION: Sodium hydroxide pellets are very corrosive to eyes, skin, and clothing. If any sodium hydroxide gets in your eyes, use the eyewash fountain immediately. Do not try to pick up or move spilled pellets. Immediately wash spilled pellets and residues off your skin or clothing.**

3. Add a few drops of water to the aluminum and sodium hydroxide mixture and put the one-hole stopper on the flask. Fill a trough with water and place the flask completely under water. Collect the gas in a test tube by placing the test tube under water and inverting it so that the opening is over the flask. Stopper the test tube when filled with gas and remove it from the trough.

4. Test the gas by placing a glowing splint inside the tube and observing the splint. Record your observations on the data table.

5. Add 5 mL of vegetable oil to 5 mL of water in a test tube. Shake well. Place a thermometer in the test tube. Record your observations and the initial temperature in the data table. Wait a minute and record the temperature again.

6. Record the temperature of 10 mL of vinegar in a test tube. Add 10 mL of ammonia water. Observe the temperature again and record your data.

7. Add 5 mL of a 1.0M copper(II) sulfate solution to 5 mL of ammonia water in a test tube. Record the initial temperature. Wait a minute and record the temperature again.

8. Light a candle and make observations. Record your observations on the data table.

9. Place 10 mL of vinegar in a Ziploc plastic bag and add a scoop of baking soda. Close the bag until the reaction subsides. Open the bag and immediately test the gas by placing a glowing splint inside the bag and observing the splint. Record your observations on the data table.

■ Data Analysis

Data Table

Step	Observations		
		Temp. 1	Temp. 2
4			
5			
6			
7			
8			
9			
10			

■ Conclusions

1. In which steps were you simply mixing substances? In each case, how could you have separated the substances in the mixtures?

2. In which steps did you observe a physical change (change of state)?

3. Basing your answer on your observations, which trials do you think were chemical reactions? What observations led you to your conclusions?

4. In which steps was a gas produced? Can you name the gases? Explain why some of the gases were not the result of chemical change.

5. What chemical change occurred in step 8? What physical change occurred?

6. What gas do you think causes a glowing splint to burn?

Guiding the Investigation

■ Procedural Hints

The reaction of aluminum and sodium hydroxide will work well if the sodium hydroxide solution is the right concentration. Note that if too much water is added or leaks in from the top, the reaction will stop.

Disposal

Add 25 mL of water to each flask and to each plastic bag. Combine all liquids and solids, and neutralize with acid or base of 0.1M or less, and decant the liquid down the drain. Filter out residual solids, wrap the filter paper in newspaper, and dispose in wastebasket.

Data Analysis

Some students may think the presence of a vapor (such as steam) means the same as the production of a gas, which indicates a chemical reaction. This misconception can be clarified in a postlab discussion.

■ Sample Data
(See table below.)

Conclusions

1. In step 5, substances were mixed. They then separated due to the different densities of oil and water.

2. In step 8, the wax melted before it underwent a chemical reaction.

3. Step 4—a gas was produced; Step 6—heat was given off; Step 7—a color change occurred; Step 8—a gas evolved, heat was given off; Step 9—a gas was produced.

4. In step 4, the pop indicated hydrogen gas was present. In step 8, CO_2 and H_2O are produced but not tested, so the student cannot identify them. In step 9, CO_2 is produced, which puts out the glowing splint.

5. The chemical change is the conversion of paraffin to carbon dioxide and water through combustion. The physical change is the melting of the paraffin.

6. oxygen

Data Table

Step	Observations	Temp. 1	Temp. 2
4	gas pops (H_2)	NA	temperature increases
5	forms two layers	21°C	21°C
6	no change	21°C	22.5°C
7	deep blue color	21°C	temperature increases
8	wax turns to liquid and disappears	NA	temperature increases
9	bubbles of gas form, bag expands, splint goes out	NA	temperature increases

Chapter 3
Review
ANSWERS
begin on page
T119a.

Summary

Identifying Chemical Reactions

- Chemical changes occur constantly in everyday life. Many of these changes can be identified by such macroscopic observations as energy changes, color changes, the generation of gas bubbles, or the formation of a precipitate.

- Chemical equations are written using the symbols and formulas for elements and compounds. These symbols represent the substances present and summarize the macroscopic changes you observe. Once the formulas of elements and compounds are correctly written, only coefficients can be changed to balance an equation.

- The physical state of the reactants and products is indicated by a symbol in parentheses after each formula. The common symbols are (s) for *solid*, (l) for *liquid*, (g) for *gas*, and (aq) for *dissolved in water*.

- The law of conservation of mass states that the total mass of reactants equals the total mass of products when a chemical reaction takes place. A balanced equation is a natural consequence of the law of conservation of mass.

- The law of conservation of energy states that energy is neither created nor destroyed in a chemical reaction. When a chemical change results in a release of energy, the reaction is exothermic, and this is indicated by writing *energy* as a product. When energy is required for the reaction to occur, the reaction is endothermic, and this is indicated by writing *energy* as a reactant. There are two kinds of energy, kinetic energy and potential energy.

Regularities in Chemical Reactions

- Similar reactions can be classified using a generalized equation. Five representative types of reactions were mentioned, and their general equations are as follows.

Synthesis	$A + B \rightarrow AB$
Decomposition	$AB \rightarrow A + B$
Combustion	$C_xH_y + O_2 \rightarrow CO_2 + H_2O$
Single replacement	$A + BC \rightarrow AC + B$
Double replacement	$AB + XY \rightarrow AY + XB$

Recognizing the type of reaction will help you to predict the products that will occur if you know the reactants.

- Decomposition reactions result in the formation of different substances, while in a dissociation ions are released in solution.

- In a replacement reaction, an element will be replaced only by a more active element. If the replacing element is less active, no reaction will occur, and this is represented by *N.R.*

Chemically Speaking

activity series *3.10*
chemical equation *3.3*
chemical reaction *3.1*
coefficient *3.5*
combustion *3.7*
decomposition *3.9*
dissociation *3.9*
double replacement *3.11*
endothermic *3.4*
exothermic *3.4*
hydrocarbon *3.3*

joule *3.2*
kinetic energy *3.2*
law of conservation of mass *3.5*
law of conservation of energy *3.2*
potential energy *3.2*
products *3.3*
reactants *3.3*
single replacement *3.10*
synthesis *3.8*

Concept Mapping

Using the concept mapping method described at the front of this book, complete the concept map for the term *chemical reactions*. Copy the incomplete map shown at the top of the next page. Then fill in the missing terms to complete the map.

PROBLEM-SOLVING
▶ **S T R A T E G I E S**
Students apply these strategies in the following questions.

- Factor-label method: 38
- Using what you know: 6, 8, 9, 10, 12, 13, 14, 16, 17, 18, 19, 21, 22, 23, 25, 26, 27, 28, 29, 30, 31, 32, 33, 34, 35, 36, 37, 38, 39, 40, 41

- Using similar problems: 25, 26, 27, 28, 29, 30, 31, 33, 37
- Using patterns: 21, 22, 23, 25, 26, 27, 28, 29, 30, 31, 32, 33, 34, 35, 36, 37, 40

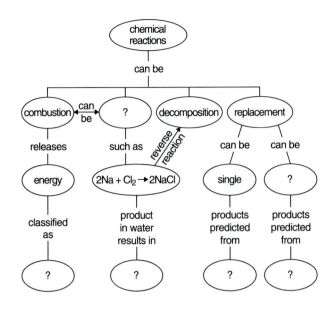

Questions and Problems

IDENTIFYING CHEMICAL REACTIONS

A. Objective: **Recognize** *the occurrence of chemical reactions by macroscopic observations.*

1. **a.** List macroscopic observations you have made that suggest that a chemical reaction is taking place.
   b. List color changes you may have observed recently. Propose a reasonable explanation for them, based on your knowledge of chemistry.
2. Give one piece of evidence that a chemical reaction is taking place in each of the following situations:
   a. digestion of protein by a 15-year-old boy
   b. activating a light stick for your little sister on Halloween
   c. striking a match
   d. starting the car in the morning
   e. making a piece of toast
   f. frying an egg
   g. having your hair permanented or straightened

B. Objective: **Define** *energy and* **differentiate** *between its two kinds, kinetic and potential.*

3. Explain the difference between kinetic energy and potential energy.
4. Describe two instances where potential energy is changed to kinetic energy.

C. Objective: **Interpret** *the meaning of symbols in chemical equations.*

5. **a.** In an equation, what are the substances on the right side of the arrow called?
   b. What are the substances on the left side of the arrow called?
6. A term in an equation might be $2Ga_2O_3(s)$.
   a. What is the subscript of oxygen?
   b. What is the ratio of gallium atoms to oxygen atoms?
   c. What is the coefficient?
   d. What is the physical state of the substance?
7. What symbol in an equation is read *yields* or *produces*?
8. Consider this equation.

$$4Al(s) + 3O_2(g) \rightarrow 2Al_2O_3(s)$$

   a. Name the reactants and products.
   b. Is the equation balanced?
   c. What is the physical state of Al_2O_3?
9. Change these equations to word equations.
   a. $MgCl_2(s) \rightarrow Mg(s) + Cl_2(g)$
   b. $Pb(NO_3)_2(aq) + K_2CrO_4(aq) \rightarrow$
   $$PbCrO_4(s) + 2KNO_3(aq)$$
10. Change these word equations to balanced equations using symbols.
    a. On heating, solid calcium carbonate yields solid calcium oxide and carbon dioxide.
    b. Solid lithium metal reacts with oxygen gas to form solid lithium oxide.
    c. Magnesium metal burns in oxygen to form solid magnesium oxide.
11. How do you show, in a chemical equation, that the reaction is reversible?

Boxed numbers indicate questions that involve skills in interpretation, application, and analysis.

D. Objective: Describe *chemical reactions by writing balanced chemical equations.*

12. Figure 3-27 is a representation of the reaction of methane gas burning in the presence of air. Copy the drawing and determine which represents carbon dioxide, water, oxygen and methane.

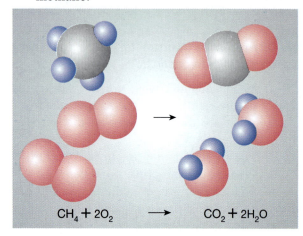

$$CH_4 + 2O_2 \longrightarrow CO_2 + 2H_2O$$

13. Use pictures of molecules to represent the following reactions.
    a. The decomposition of phosphorus pentachloride to produce phosphorus trichloride and chlorine gas.
    b. The decomposition of mercury(II) oxide to produce mercury and oxygen gas.

14. Change these word equations to symbols.
    a. Barium chlorate, when heated, produces barium chloride and oxygen.
    b. Methane combines with oxygen to produce carbon dioxide and water.
    c. Chlorine replaces iodine in calcium iodide.
    d. Chromium reacts with oxygen to produce chromium(VI) oxide.
    e. Aqueous solutions of hydrogen chloride and barium hydroxide react to form barium chloride and water.
    f. Lime, which is the common name for calcium oxide, reacts with gaseous sulfur dioxide to form solid calcium sulfite.
    g. Calcium metal reacts with chlorine gas to produce solid calcium chloride.

15. For an equation to be balanced, what must be the same on both sides?
16. a. Hydrogen peroxide, H_2O_2, used as an antiseptic, decomposes rapidly to give gaseous oxygen and liquid water. Write and balance the equation.
    b. Make drawings that represent the balanced equation.
17. a. Hydrogen gas reacts with nitrogen gas to produce ammonia. Write and balance the equation.
    b. Make drawings showing the decomposition of six molecules of ammonia gas to form hydrogen and nitrogen.
    c. How many molecules of nitrogen are produced? How many molecules of hydrogen are produced?
18. Balance these equations.
    a. $Fe(s) + H_2O(g) \rightarrow Fe_3O_4(s) + H_2(g)$
    b. $Al(s) + NaOH(s) + H_2O(l) \rightarrow$
       $$NaAl(OH)_4(aq) + H_2(g)$$
    c. $Ni(s) + I_2(s) \rightarrow NiI_2(s)$
    d. $C(s) + H_2O(g) \rightarrow CO(g) + H_2(g)$
    e. $AlBr_3(aq) + Cl_2(g) \rightarrow$
       $$AlCl_3(aq) + Br_2(l)$$
    f. $HNO_3(aq) + Ba(OH)_2(aq) \rightarrow$
       $$Ba(NO_3)_2(aq) + H_2O(l)$$
    g. $Al(s) + Pb(NO_3)_2(aq) \rightarrow$
       $$Al(NO_3)_3(aq) + Pb(s)$$
    h. $C_3H_8(g) + O_2(g) \rightarrow CO_2(g) + H_2O(g)$
    i. $Na_2CO_3(s) + HCl(aq) \rightarrow$
       $$NaCl(aq) + H_2O(l) + CO_2(g)$$
    j. $PbCO_3(s) + HNO_3(aq) \rightarrow$
       $$Pb(NO_3)_2(aq) + H_2O(l) + CO_2(g)$$
    k. $CaCO_3(s) + HC_2H_3O_2(aq) \rightarrow$
       $$Ca(C_2H_3O_2)_2(aq) + H_2O(l) + CO_2(g)$$
    l. $K_2CO_3(s) + H_3PO_4(aq) \rightarrow$
       $$K_3PO_4(aq) + H_2O(l) + CO_2(g)$$
19. A student wrote the following equation.
    $$2P(s) + \frac{5}{2}O_2(g) \rightarrow P_2O_5(s)$$
    a. What is incorrect about the equation as written?
    b. How would you change it?

E. Objective: Explain *the difference between exothermic and endothermic reactions* and **recognize** *equations that represent them.*

20. **a.** Define an exothermic reaction.
    b. How does an exothermic reaction differ from an endothermic reaction?

21. Is the reaction in Figure 3-15 endothermic or exothermic? Explain your answer.

22. Classify each of these reactions as exothermic or endothermic.
    a. energy + $SO_2(g) \rightarrow S(g) + O_2(g)$
    b. $2C_8H_{18}(g) + 25O_2(g) \rightarrow$
         $16CO_2(g) + 18H_2O(g) + energy$
    c. energy + $P_4O_{10}(s) \rightarrow P_4(s) + 5O_2(g)$
    d. $Mg(s) + H_2SO_4(aq) \rightarrow$
         $MgSO_4(aq) + H_2(g) + energy$

23. Classify each of the reactions in question 22 as exothermic or endothermic.

REGULARITIES IN CHEMICAL REACTIONS

F. Objective: Classify *reactions as belonging to one of five general types of chemical reactions.*

24. Name five general types of reactions.

25. For each of the following equations, state the general type of reaction that identifies the equation.
    a. $Cu + Cl_2 \rightarrow CuCl_2$
    b. $2H_2O \rightarrow 2H_2 + O_2$
    c. $KBr + AgNO_3 \rightarrow KNO_3 + AgBr$
    d. $CH_4 + 2O_2 \rightarrow CO_2 + 2H_2O$
    e. $Zn + CuBr_2 \rightarrow ZnBr_2 + Cu$

26. Classify each of these reactions as one of the five general types of reactions.
    a. $2Ba(s) + O_2(g) \rightarrow 2BaO(s) + energy$
    b. $PCl_3(l) + Cl_2(g) \rightarrow PCl_5(s) + energy$
    c. $2Sb(s) + 3I_2(g) + energy \rightarrow 2SbI_3(s)$
    d. $C_3H_8(g) + 5O_2(g) \rightarrow$
         $3CO_2(g) + 4H_2O(g) + energy$
    e. $Fe(s) + CuSO_4(aq) \rightarrow$
         $FeSO_4(aq) + Cu(s) + energy$

f. $CS_2(g) + 3O_2(g) \rightarrow$
     $CO_2(g) + 2SO_2(g) + energy$
g. $NH_3(g) + HCl(g) \rightarrow NH_4Cl(s) + energy$
h. $3Mg(s) + 2CrCl_3(aq) \rightarrow$
     $3MgCl_2(aq) + 2Cr(s) + energy$
i. $2KNO_3(s) + energy \rightarrow$
     $2KNO_2(s) + O_2(g)$
j. $Pb(NO_3)_2(aq) + Na_2SO_4(aq) \rightarrow$
     $PbSO_4(s) + 2NaNO_3(aq) + energy$
k. $KBr(aq) + AgNO_3(aq) \rightarrow$
     $AgBr(s) + KNO_3(aq) + energy$

27. Note this reaction.

$$S(g) + O_2(g) \rightarrow SO_2(g)$$

   a. It can be classified as one of two different reaction types. What are they?
   b. Explain how the reaction fits both classifications.

G. Objective: Predict *the products of a reaction from the reactants.*

28. For each of the following reactions, predict the products and balance the equation.
    a. $C_6H_6(l) + O_2(g) \rightarrow$
    b. $Cu(s) + AgNO_3(aq) \rightarrow$
    c. $Pb(ClO_3)_2(aq) + KI(aq) \rightarrow$
    d. $BaCO_3(l) \overset{\triangle}{\rightarrow}$
    e. $Br_2(aq) + FeI_3(aq) \rightarrow$
    f. $BaCl_2(aq) + H_2SO_4(aq) \rightarrow$
    g. $C_4H_{10}(g) + O_2(g) \rightarrow$
    h. $Ca(s) + O_2(g) \rightarrow$
    i. $HgO(l) \overset{\triangle}{\rightarrow}$
    j. $Li_2SO_4(aq) + BaCl_2(aq) \rightarrow$
    k. $F_2(g) + KCl(aq) \rightarrow$
    l. $NH_4Cl(aq) + Pb(NO_3)_2(aq) \rightarrow$

29. Complete and balance each equation.
    a. $Ni(s) + FeSO_4(aq) \rightarrow$
    b. $Sr(s) + N_2(g) \rightarrow$
    c. $C_4H_8(g) + O_2(g) \rightarrow$
    d. $CoBr_2(l) \overset{\triangle}{\rightarrow}$
    e. $Na_2S(aq) + Ni(NO_3)_2(aq) \rightarrow$
    f. $Pb(NO_3)_2(aq) + NaCl(aq) \rightarrow$
    g. $Zn(s) + CuCl_2(aq) \rightarrow$
    h. $AlCl_3(aq) + Pb(NO_3)_2(aq) \rightarrow$

i. $CH_3OH(l) + O_2(g) \rightarrow$

j. $Li(s) + N_2(g) \rightarrow$

k. $Al(s) + O_2(g) \rightarrow$

l. $Zn(s) + AgCl(aq) \rightarrow$

30. Aqueous solutions of the following compounds are mixed. Complete and balance the equations.

a. aluminum + nickel(II) sulfate →

b. ammonium chloride + silver nitrate →

31. Complete and balance these equations.

a. zinc + iodine →

b. lead(II) carbonate $\overset{\triangle}{\rightarrow}$

H. Objective: **Differentiate** *between decomposition reactions and dissociation.*

32. Identify the following reactions as decomposition reactions or dissociations.

a. $CuCl_2(l) \rightarrow Cu(l) + Cl_2(g)$

b. $CaCl_2(s) \rightarrow Ca^{2+}(aq) + 2Cl^-(aq)$

c. $2NaCl(l) \rightarrow 2Na(l) + Cl_2(g)$

d. $CuCl_2(s) \rightarrow Cu^{2+}(aq) + 2Cl^-(aq)$

33. Write equations for the following reactions.

a. Solid lithium hydroxide dissolves in water.

b. Solid ammonium iodide dissolves in water.

c. Sodium bromide dissolves in water.

d. Sodium bromide decomposes to yield the elements from which it is made.

e. Zinc nitrate dissolves in water.

I. Objective: **Determine** *by using an activity series whether a single replacement reaction will occur.*

34. Explain why the following reaction will not take place.

$$Zn + Mg(NO_3)_2 \rightarrow N.R.$$

35. A student does an experiment to determine the correct position of titanium metal on the activity series of Table 3-3. She places newly polished pieces of titanium in solutions of nickel(II) nitrate, lead nitrate and magnesium

nitrate. She finds that the titanium corrodes in the nickel(II) and lead nitrate solutions but not in the magnesium nitrate solution. From this information, place titanium in the activity series.

36. Predict whether each of the following reactions will occur under normal conditions. If it will not occur, explain why not.

a. $Cu(s) + Pb(NO_3)_2(aq) \rightarrow$
$$Cu(NO_3)_2(aq) + Pb(s)$$

b. $Cl_2(aq) + 2NaBr(aq) \rightarrow$
$$Br_2(aq) + 2NaCl(aq)$$

c. $Mg(s) + Zn(NO_3)_2(aq) \rightarrow$
$$Mg(NO_3)_2(aq) + Zn(s)$$

d. $Cu(s) + Mg(NO_3)_2(aq) \rightarrow$
$$Mg(s) + Cu(NO_3)_2(aq)$$

Critical Thinking

SYNTHESIS WITHIN THE CHAPTER

37. Write a balanced equation for each of the chemical reactions described below. Include a heat term in the equation if you can determine whether the reaction is endothermic or exothermic.

a. Powdered aluminum will react with crystals of iodine when moistened with dish washing detergent. The reaction produces violet sparks, flaming aluminum and much heat. The major product is aluminum iodide. The detergent is not a reactant.

b. A form of rust, iron(III) oxide, reacts with powdered aluminum to produce molten iron and aluminum oxide in a spectacular reaction.

c. Lithium hydroxide is used in spacecraft to cleanse the air of excess carbon dioxide. The products are lithium carbonate and water.

d. The main engines of the space shuttle burn 1 457 000 liters of liquid hydrogen with 534 000 liters of liquid oxygen. The product is water in the gaseous state.

e. When a silver spoon tarnishes it combines with sulfur, found in egg products. The product is silver sulfide.

f. Methane, CH_4, the gas used in many homes to heat the house and cook food reacts with oxygen gas in the air to produce the gases carbon dioxide and water.

g. Copper(II) oxide, a black powder, can be decomposed to produce pure copper by heating the powder in the presence of methane gas. The products are copper, and the gases carbon dioxide and water.

38. Figure 3-28 shows the relationship between grams of methane, CH_4, burned and heat produced in kJ.

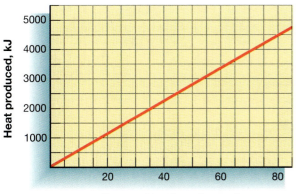

Grams of methane burned

Use the graph to answer the following questions.

a. How much heat can be obtained from burning 53 g of methane? (53 g is the mass of methane in one cubic foot, the unit often used by gas companies to measure household usage.)

b. Determine the kJ of heat produced for each gram of methane burned.

c. Explain why it makes sense that the origin of the graph is 0.0 g and 0.0 kJ.

SYNTHESIS ACROSS CHAPTERS

39. What information would be lost in the description of a chemical reaction if chemical formulas were not used in chemical equations?

40. How can the ability to predict formulas from ionic charge be helpful in predicting the products of a chemical reaction?

41. Explain how you can tell without seeing the chemical equation which of these two compounds, CO_2 or CsCl, can undergo dissociation and which cannot.

Projects

42. Over a period of two weeks, make a record of 10 chemical reactions that you see happening around you. Identify the macroscopic observations that helped you realize that a reaction was occurring.

43. Contact local industries in or near your community. Try to find out what type of chemical reactions are used in the production of products in each type of industry.

Research and Writing

44. Some reactions are considered beneficial, while others are considered harmful. Choose a reaction considered beneficial and a reaction considered harmful. After doing research on each reaction, explain why they are considered either beneficial or harmful. Are there ways in which the harmful reaction you chose could be beneficial? Could your beneficial reaction, under certain circumstances, be harmful? Include any information on how a harmful reaction can be made less harmful.

45. The accomplishments of Antoine Lavoisier were cut short because of the political environment of his time. Research the life and times of Lavoisier and write a paper on the impact of social change on science during his lifetime. Compare what you find to the impact of social change and politics on science today.

☐ Boxed numbers indicate questions that involve skills in interpretation, application, and analysis.

Chapter 3 Review Concept Map

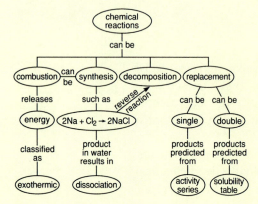

1. **a.** Plants get larger, suggesting that photosynthesis and other chemical reactions are taking place. A raw egg in a pan changes in color and texture as it is heated and cannot be changed back again, suggesting that cooking causes chemical changes.
   b. Sugar browns as it caramelizes, apples turn brown when oxidized, egg albumin whitens as it is heated (due to denaturation), hot tea gets lighter when lemon juice is added; lemon juice is an acid and something in tea is an acid-base indicator.

2. **a.** The protein changes form and the boy grows bigger.
   b. Light is given off.
   c. Heat, light, and gases are given off and the color changes.
   d. The energy stored in the battery is used to start the car. After a time, the battery wears out.
   e. The color, texture, and odor of the bread change.
   f. The egg solidifies. Colorless "white" becomes opaque.
   g. Straight hair becomes curled; curled hair straightened.

3. Kinetic energy is energy of motion. Potential energy is stored energy or energy of position.

4. water falling and striking a match

5. **a.** products   **b.** reactants

6. **a.** 3   **c.** 2
   b. 2 to 3   **d.** solid

7. the arrow

8. **a.** reactants—aluminum and oxygen
       product—aluminum oxide
   b. yes
   c. solid

9. **a.** Solid magnesium chloride decomposes to form magnesium metal and chlorine gas.
   b. Aqueous solutions of lead(II) nitrate and potassium chromate react to form a precipitate of lead(II) chromate and a solution of potassium nitrate.

10. **a.** $CaCO_3(s) + heat \rightarrow$
       $CaO(s) + CO_2(g)$
    b. $4Li(s) + O_2(g) \rightarrow 2Li_2O(s)$
    c. $2Mg(s) + O_2(g) \rightarrow 2MgO(s)$

11. Use a double arrow.

12.

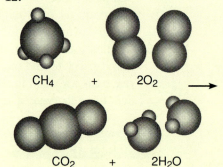

CH_4 + $2O_2$

CO_2 + $2H_2O$

13. **a.**

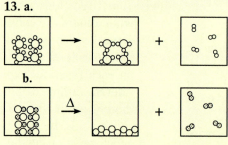

b.

14. **a.** $Ba(ClO_3)_2 + energy \rightarrow BaCl_2$
       $+ 3O_2$
    b. $CH_4 + 2O_2 \rightarrow CO_2 + 2H_2O$
    c. $Cl_2 + CaI_2 \rightarrow CaCl_2 + I_2$
    d. $2Cr + 3O_2 \rightarrow 2CrO_3$
    e. $2HCl(aq) + Ba(OH)_2(aq) \rightarrow$
       $BaCl_2(aq) + 2H_2O(l)$
    f. $CaO(s) + SO_2(g) \rightarrow CaSO_3(s)$
    g. $Ca(s) + Cl_2(g) \rightarrow CaCl_2(s)$

15. The number of atoms of each element

16. **a.** $2H_2O_2(l) \rightarrow 2H_2O(l) + O_2(g)$
    b.

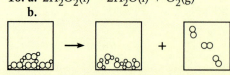

17. **a.** $3H_2(g) + N_2(g) \rightarrow 2NH_3(g)$
    b.

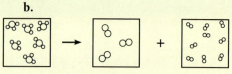

    c. 3 molecules of nitrogen
       9 molecules of hydrogen

18. **a.** $3Fe(s) + 4H_2O(g) \rightarrow Fe_3O_4(s)$
       $+ 4H_2(g)$
    b. $2Al(s) + 2NaOH(s) + 6H_2O(l) \rightarrow$
       $2NaAl(OH)_4(aq) + 3H_2(g)$
    c. $Ni(s) + I_2(s) \rightarrow NiI_2(s)$
    d. $C(s) + H_2O(g) \rightarrow CO(g) + H_2(g)$
    e. $2AlBr_3(aq) + 3Cl_2(g) \rightarrow$
       $2AlCl_3(aq) + 3Br_2(l)$
    f. $2HNO_3(aq) + Ba(OH)_2(aq) \rightarrow$
       $Ba(NO_3)_2(aq) + 2H_2O(l)$
    g. $2Al(s) + 3Pb(NO_3)_2(aq) \rightarrow$
       $2Al(NO_3)_3(aq) + 3Pb(s)$
    h. $C_3H_8(g) + 5O_2(g) \rightarrow 3CO_2(g)$
       $+ 4H_2O(g)$
    i. $Na_2CO_3(s) + 2HCl(aq) \rightarrow$
       $2NaCl(aq) + H_2O(l) + CO_2(g)$
    j. $PbCO_3(s) + 2HNO_3(aq) \rightarrow$
       $Pb(NO_3)_2(aq) + H_2O(l) + CO_2(g)$
    k. $CaCO_3(s) + 2HC_2H_3O_2(aq) \rightarrow$
       $Ca(C_2H_3O_2)_2(aq) + H_2O(l)$
       $+ CO_2(g)$
    l. $3K_2CO_3(s) + 2H_3PO_4(aq) \rightarrow$
       $2K_3PO_4(aq) + 3H_2O(l) + 3CO_2(g)$

19. **a.** A fractional coefficient is used.
    b. Multiply all coefficients by 2 to make them whole numbers.

20. **a.** a reaction in which heat or another form of energy is given off.
    b. In an endothermic reaction, energy is absorbed.

21. The reaction is exothermic. Light and heat energy are given off.

22. **a.** endothermic
    b. exothermic
    c. endothermic
    d. exothermic

23. **a.** exothermic
    b. exothermic
    c. endothermic
    d. exothermic
    e. exothermic
    f. exothermic
    g. exothermic
    h. exothermic
    i. endothermic
    j. exothermic
    k. exothermic

24. synthesis, decomposition, single replacement, double replacement, combustion

25. **a.** synthesis
    b. decomposition
    c. double replacement
    d. combustion
    e. single replacement

26. a. synthesis
b. synthesis
c. synthesis
d. combustion
e. single replacement
f. combustion
g. synthesis
h. single replacement
i. decomposition
j. double replacement
k. double replacement

27. a. combustion or synthesis
b. combustion—because an element combines with oxygen and releases energy

synthesis—because a compound is formed from combining elements

28. a. $2C_6H_6(l) + 15O_2(g) \rightarrow 12CO_2(g) + 6H_2O(g) +$ energy
b. $Cu(s) + 2AgNO_3(aq) \rightarrow Cu(NO_3)_2(aq) + 2Ag(s)$
c. $Pb(ClO_3)_2(aq) + 2KI(aq) \rightarrow PbI_2(s) + 2KClO_3(aq)$
d. $BaCO_3(l) \rightarrow BaO(s) + CO_2(g)$
e. $3Br_2(aq) + 2FeI_3(aq) \rightarrow 2FeBr_3(aq) + 3I_2(aq)$
f. $BaCl_2(aq) + H_2SO_4(aq) \rightarrow BaSO_4(s) + 2HCl(aq)$
g. $2C_4H_{10}(g) + 13O_2(g) \rightarrow 8CO_2(g) + 10H_2O(g) +$ energy
h. $2Ca(s) + O_2(g) \rightarrow 2CaO(s)$
i. $2HgO(l) \rightarrow 2Hg(l) + O_2(g)$
j. $Li_2SO_4(aq) + BaCl_2(aq) \rightarrow BaSO_4(s) + 2LiCl(aq)$
k. $F_2(g) + 2KCl(aq) \rightarrow 2KF(aq) + Cl_2(aq)$
l. $2NH_4Cl(aq) + Pb(NO_3)_2(aq) \rightarrow PbCl_2(s) + 2NH_4NO_3(aq)$

29. a. $Ni(s) + FeSO_4(aq) \rightarrow$ NR
b. $3Sr(s) + N_2(g) \rightarrow Sr_3N_2(s)$
c. $C_4H_8(g) + 6O_2(g) \rightarrow 4CO_2(g) + 4H_2O(g) +$ energy
d. $CoBr_2(l) \rightarrow Co(l) + Br_2(l)$
e. $Na_2S(aq) + Ni(NO_3)_2(aq) \rightarrow NiS(s) + 2NaNO_3(aq)$
f. $Pb(NO_3)_2(aq) + 2NaCl(aq) \rightarrow PbCl_2(s) + 2NaNO_3(aq)$
g. $Zn(s) + CuCl_2(aq) \rightarrow ZnCl_2(aq) + Cu(s)$
h. $2AlCl_3(aq) + 3Pb(NO_3)_2(aq) \rightarrow 3PbCl_2(s) + 2Al(NO_3)_3(aq)$
i. $2CH_3OH(l) + 3O_2(g) \rightarrow 2CO_2(g) + 4H_2O$
j. $6Li(s) + N_2(g) \rightarrow 2Li_3N(s)$
k. $4Al(s) + 3O_2(g) \rightarrow 2Al_2O_3(s)$
l. $Zn(s) + 2AgCl(aq) \rightarrow ZnCl_2(aq) + 2Ag(s)$

Note: AgCl is insoluble in water. However, this equilibrium is set up:
$AgCl(s) \rightleftharpoons Ag^+(aq) + Cl^-(aq)$
If zinc is placed in an equilibrium solution of silver ions, Zn will be oxidized and Ag^+ will be reduced. The equilibrium will shift to the right to produce more $Ag^+(aq)$ to react further.

30. a. $2Al(s) + 3NiSO_4(aq) \rightarrow Al_2(SO_4)_3(aq) + 3Ni(s)$
b. $NH_4Cl(aq) + AgNO_3(aq) \rightarrow AgCl(s) + NH_4NO_3(aq)$

31. a. $Zn(s) + I_2(s) \rightarrow ZnI_2(s)$
b. $PbCO_3(l) \overset{\Delta}{\rightarrow} PbO(s) + CO_2(g)$

32. a. decomposition
b. dissociation
c. decomposition
d. dissociation

33. a. $LiOH(s) \rightarrow Li^+(aq) + OH^-(aq)$
b. $NH_4I(s) \rightarrow NH_4^+(aq) + I^-(aq)$
c. $NaBr(s) \rightarrow Na^+(aq) + Br^-(aq)$
d. $2NaBr(l) \rightarrow 2Na(l) + Br_2(l)$
e. $Zn(NO_3)_2(s) \rightarrow Zn^{2+}(aq) + 2NO_3^-(aq)$

34. Zinc is less active than magnesium.

35. Mg > Ti > Ni > Pb

36. a. NR: Copper is less active than lead.
b. yes
c. yes
d. NR: Copper is less active than Mg.

37. a. $2Al(s) + 3I_2(s) \rightarrow 2AlI_3(s) +$ heat
b. $Fe_2O_3(s) + 2Al(s) \rightarrow 2Fe(l) + Al_2O_3(s) +$ heat
c. $2LiOH(s) + CO_2(g) \rightarrow Li_2CO_3(s) + H_2O(l)$
d. $2H_2(l) + O_2(l) \rightarrow 2H_2O(g) +$ energy
e. $2Ag(s) + S(s) \rightarrow Ag_2S(s)$
f. $CH_4(g) + 2O_2(g) \rightarrow CO_2(g) + 2H_2O(g) +$ energy
g. $4CuO(s) + CH_4(g) +$ heat $\rightarrow 4Cu(s) + CO_2(g) + 2H_2O(g)$

38. a. 3000 kJ
b. 57 kJ
c. If no methane is burned, then no heat is produced.

39. The ratios of combining atoms, the identity of reactants and products

40. If you know ionic charges, you can write reasonable formulas of the products and then verify them experimentally.

41. CsCl is an ionic compound that dissociates in water. Carbon dioxide is composed of two nonmetals and is not ionic, so it cannot undergo dissociation.

Molar Relationships

Investigations	Demonstrations	Texas Essential Elements★
Laboratory Manual 4–1 M Laboratory Manual 4–2 M Laboratory Manual 4–5 IM	The Mole, page T122	**Content:** 1.5, 3.6, 6.3, 7.1, 7.2 **Process:** 4.2, 4.3
	"ppm" for Dilute Solutions, page T136	**Content:** 8.9, 9.7 **Process:** 4.3, 10.1, 10.2
Laboratory Manual 4–3 S Laboratory Manual 4–4 S In-text Investigation, page T154	Percent Composition, page T143	**Content:** 1.2, 1.6, 6.2 **Process:** 4.3
		Content: 6.3, 6.4, 6.6 **Process:** 1.1, 1.2, 1.3, 4.3, 5.1, 6.1, 7.3
		Process: 4.2, 4.3, 5.1, 5.2, 7.1, 8.2
KEY: **M**–*Microscale* **S**–*Structured* **I**–*Inquiry* **IM**–*Inquiry Microscale*		★*See pages T8–T11 for complete listing of Texas Essential Elements.*

4 Molar Relationships

How could you go about counting the individual grains of sand needed to make this Navajo Sandpainting? One method that you will study in this chapter is counting by mass

Chapter Rationale

Chapter 4 introduces the fundamental unit of measurement in chemistry—the mole. An explanation of scientific notation and exponential rules accompanies this section. A separate discussion of significant digits and scientific notation may give students the feeling they are studying mathematics, and they may wonder, "Where is the chemistry?" Show students examples of one mole of chemicals they will be using in experiments.

Introduction of each mathematical skill as it is needed shows that math is an important tool. As students learn and practice the math skills, they relate this information to chemistry. Knowledge of the mole is essential for an understanding of how much of one chemical reacts with another.

About the Photograph

Navajo artists have made sandpaintings for centuries to use in ceremonies. Sandpaintings consist of a background of clean, smooth sand. Colored sandstone, charcoal, and pollen are among the substances used to paint designs on the sand background. Many Navajos believe that the purpose of the sandpainting is only accomplished if the painting is destroyed after the ceremony.

Chapter Planning Hints

Completing Chapter 4, including the Chapter Review and Laboratory Investigation, will require six to eight class sessions. You will find three optional demonstrations suggested for this chapter. They appear on pages T122, T136, and T143. You may wish to obtain The World of Chemistry videotape *The Mole.*

(continued on page T121)

Myths and Misconceptions

The mole is one of the most basic concepts in chemistry, yet students often have difficulty understanding it. When introducing the mole, add numerous examples from everyday life. Emphasize that the mole can be used as a unit for counting *numbers* of particles. In developing the mole concept, pose questions that guide students through the reasoning process. For example, a ream of paper has 500 sheets. How many sheets are in a carton of paper if there are 12 reams per carton? How many sheets of paper are in a dozen cartons? How many sheets of paper in a mole of cartons? How many Cl atoms are in one molecule of CCl_4? In one mole of CCl_4 molecules? In four moles of CCl_4 molecules? Ask students to compare the number of atoms in one mole of hydrogen atoms and one mole of lead atoms. Stress that one mole of different substances may vary in mass and volume, but not in the number of particles present.

PART

1 Counting Atoms

As you learned in Chapter 3, predicting the products of a chemical reaction is easier when you can recognize regularities in reactions. Many times, however, it is important to know not only *what* will be produced but also *how much*. Predicting the amount of product that will result from a reaction requires that you first learn how to count atoms. You know that atoms, however, are much too small to count individually, so counting them requires some other approach.

Many familiar items are counted in groups rather than individually. Shoes come in pairs, eggs are counted by the dozen, and paper is packed in reams (500 sheets). Small items especially are frequently counted in bulk rather than one by one. Rubber bands, paper clips, and marbles all are examples of things you can buy in specific numbers or by weight. Finding a similar way to count atoms would help you answer the question *how much?*.

4.1 How Many Is a Mole?

A dozen is a convenient unit for expressing a frequently used quantity. However, one or two dozen atoms are too small to be seen, let alone counted. In the case of atoms, a much larger counting unit would be more useful. Chemists use the term *mole* to talk about a number of atoms, molecules, ions, or electrons, just as shoppers use *dozen* to talk about eggs, oranges, or doughnuts. A **mole** (abbreviation: mol) is simply the amount of a substance that contains 6.02×10^{23} particles*. The particles may be anything—atoms, molecules, green peas, or baseballs.

Avogadro's number The number 6.02×10^{23} is called **Avogadro's number** in honor of Amadeo Avogadro, the Italian scientist from whose work the concept was developed. Because atoms are very small, Avogadro's number is very large, so large that it is difficult to imagine unless you relate it to something more familiar than atoms.

Suppose the average mass of a grain of rice is 1.75×10^{-5} kg. What would the mass of one mole, 6.02×10^{23}, grains of rice be? You can multiply the mass of one grain of rice by the number of grains in a mole to get the answer.

* See Appendix A for information about writing and using numbers in scientific notation.

Objectives

Part 1

A. *Define* the term *mole* and *describe* how it is used in chemistry.

B. *Explain* and *calculate* molar mass.

C. *Calculate* equivalents among grams, moles, and numbers of particles.

PART **1**
Counting Atoms
Section 4.1

(continued from page T120)

Make plans to celebrate MOLE Day at 6:02 A.M. or 6:02 P.M. on October 23rd (10/23). Outside the chemistry lab, propose a toast to Avogadro as you raise your cups containing 18 mL (a mole) of water. Use paper cups at a drinking fountain in the hall. Have students write an 18 mL capacity mark on the outside of their cups. (Determine this beforehand.) Discard cups after the toast.

Developing Skills

Students may apply these skills in their study of Part 1.
Calculating: Given the thickness of aluminum foil is 0.0025 cm, the width 30.5 cm, and the density 2.70 g/cm^3, have students calculate the length needed for 0.10 mol.
Describing: Have students observe the substances in Figure 3–11 and describe one mole each.
Measuring: Have students measure 1.0 mol of water and 0.10 mol of aluminum foil.

FOCUS

Activate Prior Knowledge

By observing one mole of familiar substances students can relate the mole concept to something concrete. Put one mole of each of the following substances into sealed bottles: Al, Sn, Cu, Mg, Zn, I_2, C (charcoal), H_2O, NaCl (salt), CH_3OH (wood alcohol), K_2SO_4, $Ca(OH)_2$ (antacid), $MgSO_4 \cdot 7H_2O$ (Epsom Salts), $CuCl_2 \cdot 2H_2O$, $Pb(NO_3)_2$, KI, $(CH_3)_2CO$ (acetone), $CuSO_4 \cdot 5H_2O$ (Blue Vitriol), $C_{12}H_{22}O_{11}$ (sucrose), H_3BO_3 (roach killer), and NaOH (drain cleaner). Provide either the name or the formula and assign students to construct a table with the correct names and formulas.

(continued on page T122)

(continued from page T121)

Instruct students to observe, but not to handle the containers. In their table, students should classify these substances as elements or compounds, metals or nonmetals, and liquids or solids. Review naming and formula writing. Explain the formula for hydrates and how they are named. Discuss household uses such as copper wire (Cu), zinc-coated garbage cans (Zn), charcoal briquettes (C), alcohol burners (CH_3OH), nail polish remover (($CH_3)_2O$), algicide ($CuSO_4 \cdot 5H_2O$), and so on.

≣ TEACH

Science Background

How Many Is a Mole?

One of the first estimates of Avogadro's number made use of measurements on Brownian motion by A. Perrin combined with the theoretical calculations of Albert Einstein.

Teaching Strategy

Avogadro's Number

Help students gain some sense of the size of Avogadro's number, and have them practice problem solving using the factor-label method, metrics, estimation, and scientific notation. Significant digits will be used later in this chapter. Assign students to count the number of drops of water in 5.00 mL. The number of drops will be 100 ± 10. Calculate the number of drops in 1 mL and the number of mL in 1 drop. Use these unit factors to calculate the number of drops of water in:

a. 50 mL

b. 50 cm^3

c. A tank of water 15 m long, 10 m wide, and 1 m deep

d. a layer of water 10 cm deep covering the school parking lot

(continued on page T123)

> When **multiplying exponential numbers,** the exponents are added. Find the product of the decimal numbers and multiply it by the product of the exponential numbers. See Appendix A.

> When **dividing exponential numbers,** the exponents are subtracted. Find the quotient for the decimal numbers and multiply it by the quotient of the exponential numbers. See Appendix A.

Figure 4-1 *The vast number of cars on this parking lot represents a small fraction of 5.9 × 10^{15} cars. You would need 7.4 × 10^{12} lots of cars to equal that number.*

$$? \text{ kg} = 1.75 \times 10^{-5} \frac{\text{kg}}{1 \text{ grain}} \times 6.02 \times 10^{23} \frac{\text{grains}}{\text{mol}}$$

$$= 1.05 \times 10^{19} \frac{\text{kg}}{\text{mol}}$$

This answer probably means little to you. Perhaps if you compared the mass of 6.02×10^{23} grains of rice to something familiar, it would help. You already have a concept of how massive an automobile is. A typical car has a mass of about 1.8×10^3 kg. How many cars would have the same mass as all that rice?

$$? \text{ cars} = 1.05 \times 10^{19} \text{ kg} \times \frac{1 \text{ car}}{1.8 \times 10^3 \text{ kg}} = 5.9 \times 10^{15} \text{ cars}$$

Again, you have an answer that probably means little to you. If the cars are divided among all the people on Earth, would there be enough to go around? There are about 5 billion (5×10^9) people on Earth, so if the cars are distributed to everyone on Earth, each person would get

$$\frac{5.9 \times 10^{15} \text{ cars}}{5 \times 10^9 \text{ people}} = 1 \times 10^6 \text{ cars/person}$$

That's about a million cars for every person on Earth! In other words, 6.02×10^{23} grains of rice would have the same mass as almost a million cars for every man, woman, and child on Earth!

Perhaps now you are beginning to have an idea of the size of Avogadro's number. Problems in the Part 1 Review and Chapter Review will give you additional experience in grasping the concept of the magnitude of a mole. Answers to these problems have been rounded off from calculator answers. The reason for rounding off the answers and how to round them will be discussed in Section 4.12. First, however, you need to be sure you understand the problems and the strategies used to get the answers.

 DEMONSTRATION

The Mole

Measure one mole of aluminum foil and tape it to the bulletin board for reference. Regular aluminum foil is 30.5 cm wide and 0.0025 cm thick, and the density is 2.70 g/cm^3.

27.0 g Al × 1 cm^3/2.70 g = 10.0 cm^3
length × width × height = volume
length × 30.5 cm × 0.0025 cm = 10.0 cm^3
length = 131 cm

4.2 Mass of a Mole of Atoms

Because 6.02×10^{23} is too large to count one by one, this number of atoms is determined by measuring the mass of the substance. This idea will make more sense if you think about a familiar example of counting by mass. If you have ever collected aluminum cans for recycling, you know that the cans are not counted individually at the recycling center; however, payment is often made on a per-can basis. The cans are actually "counted" by weight. Counting in this way involves using the mass, or weight, of one aluminum can to determine the number of cans in a given weight, or mass. For example, if one can has a mass of 10 grams and a group of cans has a mass of 1000 g, then there are

$$1000 \text{ grams} \times \frac{1 \text{ can}}{10 \text{ grams}} = 100 \text{ cans}$$

Molar mass Counting by mass can be applied to large quantities of atoms. From the periodic table, you can find the atomic mass of an atom in atomic mass units (amu). For example, the mass of one atom of aluminum is 26.98 amu. However, because it is more convenient to measure mass with a balance, it is helpful to know how amu's compare with grams. By definition,

$$1 \text{ amu} = 1.66 \times 10^{-24} \text{ g}$$

Therefore, the mass of one atom of aluminum *in grams* is

$$26.98 \text{ amu} \times \frac{1.66 \times 10^{-24} \text{ g}}{1 \text{ amu}} = 4.48 \times 10^{-23} \text{ g}$$

Suppose you have a sample of aluminum with a mass of 26.98 g. To determine how many atoms you have, apply the method just used with the aluminum cans.

$$26.98 \text{ g Al} \times \frac{1 \text{ atom Al}}{4.48 \times 10^{-23} \text{ g Al}} = 6.02 \times 10^{23} \text{ atoms Al}$$

Did you recognize the answer as Avogadro's number? The answer tells you that the mass of 1 mole (6.02×10^{23}) of aluminum atoms is 26.98 g. *The mass of one mole of any element is the* **molar mass** *of that element.*

The mass of an atom and molar mass The molar mass of aluminum is 26.98 g while the mass of one atom is 26.98 amu. You should notice that the *numbers* are the same. This relationship is valid for all elements. The mass in grams of one mole of atoms is *numerically* the same as the mass in atomic mass units of one of those atoms. Because of this relationship, you can use the periodic table to obtain not only the mass of one atom of an element (in amu's) but also the mass of one mole of atoms (in grams).

Figure 4-2 *How many dollars would you have if you had a mole of pennies?*

Figure 4-3 *The cost of recycling is lowered by "counting" the cans by weight rather than individually.*

PART 1
Section 4.2

(continued from page T122)
Assign one problem each day and write the solution on the chalkboard each day. For example:
a. 50 mL H_2O × 20 drops H_2O/1 mL H_2O = 1.0×10^3 drops H_2O
b. 50 cm³ H_2O × 1 mL/1 cm³ × 20 drops H_2O/1 mL H_2O = 1.0×10^3 drops
c. Volume of water
15 m × 10 m × 1 m = 150 m³
150 m³ H_2O × 10^6 cm³/1 m³ × 20 drops H_2O/1 cm³ H_2O = 3.0×10^9 drops H_2O
d. Have students estimate the size of the school parking lot. This is a good opportunity to discuss uncertainty in measurements, estimated uncertainty, and how you can determine when two measured or derived quantities are the same within experimental uncertainty.

Look Ahead

Significant digits are covered in Section 4.12. After completing Section 4.12, have students go back to Practice Problems 1–8 and determine the significant digits for each answer.

Teaching Strategy

Mass of a Mole of Atoms

Have students calculate the **mass** of one mole of each substance in the mole display described in **Activate Prior Knowledge.** Example: sucrose $C_{12}H_{22}O_{11}$ 12(12.0) + 22(1.0) + 11(16.0) = 342.0
Have students calculate the **volume** of one mole of each substance in the mole display described in **Activate Prior Knowledge.** Example: sucrose 342.0 g/mol × 1 mL/1.59 g = 215.1 mL

PART 1
Section 4.3

Teaching Strategy

Comparing Molar Masses

A knowledge of moles is necessary in medicine and in many industrial and agricultural processes. Examples are the amount of each substance used in preparing intravenous solutions and the amount of each reactant when extracting a valuable metal, such as silver from a compound, or in calculating the amount of an insecticide that should be applied to crops.

Videodisc Connections

902, side 6
Element and compound: mole samples (1 frame)

DO YOU KNOW?

One can count the number of oranges in six dozen in a few minutes. However, six moles of oranges would have a mass as large as the entire Earth. The mole is a manageable unit for very small particles like atoms or molecules.

Figure 4-4 Left: *You see the same number of grapes as grapefruit—one dozen of each. Even though there is a dozen of each, the masses are quite different.* Right: *A mole of aluminum and a mole of lead have the same number of atoms but different masses.*

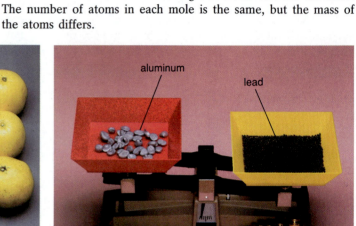

Comparing molar masses If you compare the molar mass of lead with the molar mass of aluminum, you find that a mole of lead has a mass of 207.2 g, while a mole of aluminum has a mass of 26.98 g. Is this reasonable if one mole of any element contains the same number of atoms, 6.02×10^{23}? Figure 4-4 shows one dozen grapefruit and one dozen grapes. Remember, a dozen always represents the same number of particles, 12, but all dozens do not have the same mass. This reasoning also holds true for the mole. The number of atoms in each mole is the same, but the mass of the atoms differs.

4.3 Molar Conversions for Elements

Relationships involving the mole, such as molar mass or Avogadro's number, are used constantly to measure amounts involved in chemical changes. Examples in this section will help you learn some of these relationships and how they are used. As you study the Examples, notice how the logic used in the problems is similar to the logic you use in solving everyday problems. For example, if you are given 36 oranges and asked how many dozen this amount represents, you would have little difficulty in answering 3 dozen. This problem is simple because you are very familiar with oranges and dozens. If you are asked to find the mass of 36 oranges if 1 dozen has a mass of 2160 g, you can easily determine the answer using the ratio of grams per dozen.

$$3 \text{ doz} \times 2160 \text{ g/doz} = 6480 \text{ g}$$

If similar questions are asked about moles, molecules, or atoms, the answers may not occur to you as readily because you are not as familiar with these objects and concepts. Working through the Examples and doing the Practice Problems will help you to become more familiar with the concepts as well as to learn the relationships.

PROBLEM-SOLVING

STRATEGY

Making an Estimate

One day a student was working on a problem that involved finding the number of people who were traveling in a minivan. When she first obtained her answer, she exclaimed, "Forty-eight people! I know I made a mistake—you just can't fit that many people into a van."

There may be times when you too will obtain an answer that you just cannot believe. The answer is so unlikely that you return to your figures to check your work. For situations or objects that you know quite well, you can often catch these so-called silly mistakes by refusing to believe every answer that you obtain.

Although you may not describe it quite this way, you are really making use of an estimate in your work. As you study chemistry, you will become more aware of how large certain answers should be. For example, if you look at the smallest atomic mass given on the periodic table, you should not expect to calculate a molar mass of 0.001 g/mol for a substance since the smallest possible value is 1 g/mol for a hydrogen atom.

▶ Estimation Strategies

One good way to estimate is to think about whether an answer should be larger or smaller than the starting value. For example, if you are carrying out metric system conversions, you may want to try to visualize the size of the units involved. If you are given a distance of 25 km, think of that as the distance a car might travel on a short trip. A meterstick is no longer than the distance between your outstretched hands. Therefore, if you are converting the distance of 25 km into meters, your number in meters must be larger than 25. You could apply this same strategy to problems involving masses and moles. If 1.0 mole of calcium has a mass of 40 g, should 5.0 moles of calcium have a mass *more* than 40 g or *less* than 40 g?

Always estimate the size of any answer when you use a calculator. It is quite easy to make a mistake by pushing a wrong button or forgetting to enter a decimal point. Estimate what your answer should be by rounding off your numbers to the closest easy numbers. Solve the problem in your head or with paper and pencil using the simpler values. Is your calculated value close to your estimate? The process of making an estimate can be extremely helpful in judging the correctness of your answers especially when you are working with new and unfamiliar concepts.

▶ FOCUS ON
PROBLEM SOLVING

Activate Prior Knowledge

Submitting cost estimates to prospective customers is the responsibility of many businesses. Have students discuss why a cost estimate is necessary (cost comparisons; information on which to base a decision about a service purchase).

Continue the discussion by asking on what factors an estimate for car repairs might be based (hourly cost of labor; previous experience with a repair to know about how long it will take; price of replacement parts).

▶ TEACH
THE STRATEGY

Guided Practice

Help students practice making estimates by solving the following problem:

Lynn is planning to buy her first car. She works part time for $4.76/hour, 3.25 hours per day, five days a week. The down payment will be $807. Estimate how many weeks Lynn will have to work before she can purchase the car. Assume taxes are withheld at a rate of 28 percent. (Estimate a take-home pay of two-thirds of $4.50, which is $3 per hour. Estimate 15-hour work weeks, at $3 an hour, $45 per week. $800 divided by $45/week equals approximately 18 weeks.)

PART 1

Section 4.3 *continued*

Practice Problems

Assign the Practice Problems.

EXAMPLE 4-1

How many moles of carbon are in 26 g of carbon?

■ *Analyze the Problem* Write out what you are asked to find.

? moles correspond to 26 g of carbon

Determine what you need to know in order to convert from grams to moles. In this case, you need to know the mass in grams of 1 mole of carbon—the molar mass.

■ *Apply a Strategy* Find the molar mass of carbon from the periodic table and write the information as a ratio. When you do problems, round off the atomic masses from the periodic table to the tenths place. You can write the ratio two ways.

$$\frac{1 \text{ mol C}}{12.0 \text{ g C}} \quad \text{or} \quad \frac{12.0 \text{ g C}}{1 \text{ mol C}}$$

Use the ratio on the left because it will allow you to cancel the units of grams, leaving moles in the answer.

■ *Work a Solution* Calculate the answer from the mathematical statement and cancel units as necessary.

$$? \text{ mol C} = 26 \text{ g C} \times \frac{1 \text{ mol C}}{12.0 \text{ g C}} = \frac{26}{12.0} \text{ mol C} = 2.2 \text{ mol C}$$

■ *Verify Your Answer* Work the problem in reverse, starting from the answer. If 1 mole of carbon has a mass of 12 g, then 2.2 moles of carbon has a mass of (2.2)(12) or 26 g. Check the size of your answer. Is it reasonable? You should have a little more than 2 moles because 26 g is just a little more than double the mass of 1 mole of carbon.

Practice Problems

1. How many moles of nickel are in 25 g of nickel?

    Ans. 0.43 mol

2. How many grams of copper are in 2.50 moles of copper?

    Ans. 159 g

> ### PROBLEM-SOLVING
> ## S T R A T E G Y
> Use the **factor-label method** to help you solve this problem. (See Strategy, page 12.)

> ### PROBLEM-SOLVING
> ## S T R A T E G Y
> Working backwards to the number you started with and **making an estimate** are two reliable verification strategies. (See Strategy, page 125.)

In Example 4-1 you found that 26 g of carbon contains 2.2 moles of carbon atoms. Can you calculate the number of carbon atoms in 26 g? If one mole contains 6.02×10^{23} atoms, you can apply the factor-label method this way.

$$\text{atoms carbon} = 2.2 \text{ mol C} \times \frac{6.02 \times 10^{23} \text{ atoms}}{1 \text{ mol C}}$$

$$= 1.3 \times 10^{24} \text{ C atoms}$$

4.4 Molar Conversions for Compounds

How would you solve the problem that asks you to find the number of CO_2 molecules in 0.75 mole of carbon dioxide gas? Since a mole is defined as the amount of *any substance* that contains 6.02×10^{23} parts, then there are 6.02×10^{23} molecules of carbon dioxide in one mole of the gas. To calculate the number of molecules in 0.75 mole, write a ratio using the factor-label method and multiply.

? molecules $CO_2(g)$

$$= 0.75 \text{ mol CO}_2 \times \frac{6.02 \times 10^{23} \text{ molecules CO}_2}{1 \text{ mol CO}_2}$$

$$= 4.5 \times 10^{23} \text{ molecules CO}_2$$

What if you were asked how many oxygen atoms are in 0.75 moles of carbon dioxide? To solve this problem, you must account for the fact that there are 2 oxygen atoms in every carbon dioxide molecule. You would know this information from looking at the formula for carbon dioxide.

? atoms oxygen =

$$0.75 \text{ mol CO}_2 \times \frac{6.02 \times 10^{23} \text{ molecules CO}_2}{1 \text{ mol CO}_2} \times \frac{2 \text{ atoms O}}{1 \text{ molecule CO}_2} = 9.0 \times 10^{23} \text{ atoms O}$$

Ratios of atoms versus ratios of moles This problem illustrates an important point about compounds that you first learned in Chapter 2—the law of definite proportions. Recall that elements combine in constant ratios to form compounds; that is, every molecule (or formula unit) of a specific compound has the same composition. You could reason, then, that the ratio of atoms in a single molecule (or formula unit) is the same as the ratio of moles of atoms in a mole of molecules (or formula unit). For example, if a molecule of carbon dioxide contains 1 carbon atom for every 2 oxygen atoms, a mole of carbon dioxide molecules contains 1 mole of carbon atoms for every 2 moles of oxygen atoms.

Knowing this relationship, you could approach the question about oxygen and carbon dioxide in a different way. If you have 0.75 mole of carbon dioxide, you would have 2×0.75 moles of oxygen atoms. The equation to solve the question would be

$$? \text{ atoms O} = 0.75 \text{ mol CO}_2 \times \frac{2 \text{ mol O}}{1 \text{ mol CO}_2} \times \frac{6.023 \times 10^{23} \text{ atoms O}}{1 \text{ mol O}}$$

$$= 9.0 \times 10^{23} \text{ atoms O}$$

Mathematically the result is the same.

Concept ✔ Check

How many atoms of chlorine are there in 0.20 mole of phosphorus trichloride, PCl_3?

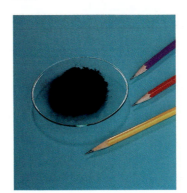

Figure 4-5 *One mole of carbon in the form of graphite is shown here.*

Teaching Strategy

Molar Conversions for Compounds

Students need not correctly distinguish between molecular and ionic substances. At this time the term *molecule* can be used to mean formula unit. The problem will always be stated correctly in the text. Requiring students to manage the terminology may overload their working memory and interfere with their ability to solve the problems. Similarly, the answers can be rounded to the correct number of significant digits after completing the solution.

PROBLEM-SOLVING
STRATEGY

*Several different approaches to solving a problem can help you **see patterns** that will make problem solving easier. (See Strategy, page 100.)*

Molar mass of a compound If you want to answer the question *How much do I have?* about substances other than elements, you need to be able to count molecules, ions, or formula units just as you count atoms. In other words, you need to have a convenient way to measure how many particles you have. The concept of counting by mass that you learned in Section 4.2 also applies in these instances. The definition of molar mass can be expanded to mean the mass in grams of one mole of atoms, molecules, formula units, or ions.

Figure 4-6 *One mole of each compound is shown. That mass is the molar mass of the compound.* ⚠ CAUTION: *Nickel chloride, potassium chromate and potassium dichromate are suspected of causing cancer.*

To find the molar mass of a compound, simply add the molar masses of the elements in the compound. Be sure to account for the proportions of the elements in the compound. For example, the formula for nitrogen dioxide is NO_2. It represents one part nitrogen and two parts oxygen. Using the periodic table, you see that the molar masses (rounded to one-tenth gram) are 14.0 grams per mole for nitrogen and 16.0 grams per mole for oxygen. The molar mass of nitrogen dioxide is found this way.

$$\underset{\text{nitrogen}}{\left(\frac{14.0\text{ g}}{\text{mol}}\right)} + 2\underset{\text{oxygen}}{\left(\frac{16.0\text{ g}}{\text{mol}}\right)} =$$

$$\left(\frac{14.0\text{ g}}{\text{mol}}\right) + \left(\frac{32.0\text{ g}}{\text{mol}}\right) = 46.0\ \frac{\text{g}}{\text{mol}}\ NO_2$$

Notice that one mole of nitrogen dioxide contains one mole of nitrogen atoms and two moles of oxygen atoms. Finding the molar mass of a compound is a matter of adding the molar masses of each element multiplied by its subscript. The molar mass of any compound or ion may be found in this manner.

EXAMPLE 4-2

What is the molar mass of sucrose, $C_{12}H_{22}O_{11}$?

■ *Analyze the Problem* Note from the formula for sucrose, that 1 mole of sucrose consists of 12 moles of carbon, 22 moles of hydrogen, and 11 moles of oxygen. To find the molar mass of sucrose, you need the molar mass of each of these elements.

■ *Apply a Strategy* Obtain the molar mass of each element from the periodic table and multiply it by the mole ratio for that element. Organize the information in a table to make your calculations easier.

■ *Work a Solution*

	molar mass	×	mole ratio	=	mass in 1 mole of sucrose
C	12.0 g	×	12	=	144.0 g
H	1.0 g	×	22	=	22.0 g
O	16.0 g	×	11	=	176.0 g
			total	=	342.0 g

■ *Verify Your Answer* Check your math to be sure you did not introduce any errors. One method is to work the problem backwards to verify the molar masses of the elements. You can use carbon as an example.

$$144.0 \text{ g}/12 \text{ mol} = 12.0 \text{ g/mol}$$

PROBLEM-SOLVING
STRATEGY

When you are dealing with a lot of information, organizing it in a table will help you keep track of your calculations and avoid errors.

Practice Problems

3. What is the molar mass of sodium carbonate, Na_2CO_3?
   Ans. 106.0 g/mol

4. What is the molar mass of aluminum sulfate, $Al_2(SO_4)_3$?
   Ans. 342.0 g/mol

Grams, moles, and compounds It is not necessary to learn any new relationships when solving molar conversion problems that involve compounds. A molar conversion problem involving the compound carbon dioxide with a molar mass of 44.0 g could involve the following ratios.

$$\frac{1 \text{ mol } CO_2}{6.02 \times 10^{23} \text{ molecules } CO_2}$$

$$\frac{1 \text{ mol } CO_2}{44.0 \text{ g } CO_2}$$

$$\frac{44.0 \text{ g } CO_2}{6.02 \times 10^{23} \text{ molecules } CO_2}$$

Ratios also can be written for substances that are not molecular.

Practice Problems

Assign the Practice Problems.

Figure 4-7 *Sucrose is one of the naturally occurring sugars.*

For sodium carbonate, an ionic compound, the ratios are

$$\frac{1 \text{ mol Na}_2\text{CO}_3}{6.02 \times 10^{23} \text{ formula units Na}_2\text{CO}_3}$$

$$\frac{1 \text{ mol Na}_2\text{CO}_3}{106.0 \text{ g Na}_2\text{CO}_3}$$

$$\frac{106.0 \text{ g Na}_2\text{CO}_3}{6.02 \times 10^{23} \text{ formula units Na}_2\text{CO}_3}$$

From the factor-label method, you have learned to invert ratios.

$$\frac{1 \text{ mol Na}_2\text{CO}_3}{106.0 \text{ g Na}_2\text{CO}_3} \quad \text{can also be} \quad \frac{106.0 \text{ g Na}_2\text{CO}_3}{1 \text{ mol Na}_2\text{CO}_3}$$
written as

The following Examples show how to apply what you already know about molar conversion problems to conversions involving compounds.

EXAMPLE 4-3

The odor of bananas is due to the compound isopentyl acetate, $C_7H_{14}O_2$. How many moles of isopentyl acetate are present in a 1.0-gram sample of the compound?

PROBLEM·SOLVING

S T R A T E G Y

When working on a new problem, **look for similarities** with problems you have solved previously. (See Strategy, page 65.)

■ *Analyze the Problem* Write out what you are asked to find.

? moles correspond to 1.0 g of $C_7H_{14}O_2$

Determine what you need to know to convert from grams to moles. In this case, you need to find the mass in grams of 1 mole of the compound isopentyl acetate—its molar mass. This is the same type of calculation that you did in Example 4-2.

■ *Apply a Strategy* Find the molar mass of each element from the periodic table, and use the information to compute the molar mass of isopentyl acetate. Then determine the ratio needed to convert from grams to moles.

■ *Work a Solution*

	molar mass		moles		
C	12.0 g/mol	×	7	=	84.0 g/mol
H	1.0 g/mol	×	14	=	14.0 g/mol
O	16.0 g/mol	×	2	=	32.0 g/mol
			total	=	130.0 g/mol
					= the molar mass of $C_7H_{14}O_2$

To find the number of moles in 1.0 g, multiply by the form of the molar mass ratio that gives you moles.

$$? \text{ mol C}_7\text{H}_{14}\text{O}_2 = 1.0 \text{ g C}_7\text{H}_{14}\text{O}_2 \times \frac{1 \text{ mol C}_7\text{H}_{14}\text{O}_2}{130.0 \text{ g C}_7\text{H}_{14}\text{O}_2}$$

$$= 0.0077 \text{ mol C}_7\text{H}_{14}\text{O}_2$$

- **Verify Your Answer** Check to see if your answer seems reasonable. If the molar mass of isopentyl acetate is 130.0 g, and you have only 1 g, you have less than one hundredth of the molar mass. You then should have less than one hundredth of a mole. The answer *0.0077 moles* is reasonable.

Practice Problems

5. What is the mass in grams of 1.25 moles of sulfur trioxide?
   Ans. 100. g

6. How many moles of calcium carbonate, $CaCO_3$, are present in a 350-gram sample of $CaCO_3$? ***Ans.*** 3.5 mol

PROBLEM-SOLVING
S T R A T E G Y

Making an estimate will help you to determine if your answer is reasonable. (See Strategy, page 125.)

Practice Problems

Assign the Practice Problems.

EXAMPLE 4-4

When bees sting, they also release the compound isopentyl acetate, $C_7H_{14}O_2$. How many molecules of isopentyl acetate are there in 2.00 grams of $C_7H_{14}O_2$?

- **Analyze the Problem** Write out what you are being asked to find.

    ? molecules correspond to 2.00 g of $C_7H_{14}O_2$

In this problem, you need to convert from grams of a compound to number of moles and number of moles to number of molecules. Identify the relationships necessary to make these conversions. They are

$$\frac{1 \text{ mol } C_7H_{14}O_2}{\text{molar mass in g } C_7H_{14}O_2} \quad \text{and} \quad \frac{6.02 \times 10^{23} \text{ molecules}}{1 \text{ mol } C_7H_{14}O_2}$$

- **Apply a Strategy** Compute the molar mass of isopentyl acetate in a column format, as shown in Example 4-3. Then write a one-step mathematical statement converting grams to molecules, using the ratios above.

- **Work a Solution** Calculate the molar mass of $C_7H_{14}O_2$.

C 7 × 12.0 g/mol = 84.0 g
H 14 × 1.0 g/mol = 14.0 g
O 2 × 16.0 g/mol = 32.0 g
                total = 130.0 g = the molar mass of $C_7H_{14}O_2$

The mathematical statement would be

$$2.00 \text{ g } C_7H_{14}O_2 \times \frac{1 \text{ mol } C_7H_{14}O_2}{130.0 \text{ g } C_7H_{14}O_2} \times \frac{6.02 \times 10^{23} \text{ molecules}}{1 \text{ mol } C_7H_{14}O_2}$$
$$= 9.26 \times 10^{21} \text{ molecules}$$

PROBLEM-SOLVING
S T R A T E G Y

*By comparing the steps in this problem to those in Example 4-3, you can **see similarities.** Except for converting moles to molecules, the same steps are followed. (See Strategy, page 65.)*

PART **2**

Section 4.5

Practice Problems

Assign the Practice Problems.

> ## DO YOU KNOW?
>
> Avogadro's number is so large that if you could count 100 particles every minute and counted twelve hours every day and had every person on Earth also counting, it would still take more than four million years to count a mole of anything.

■ **Verify Your Answer** Work the problem another way, using the relationship that there are 6.02×10^{23} molecules in 130.0 g of $C_7H_{14}O_2$.

$$2.00 \text{ g } C_7H_{14}O_2 \times \frac{6.02 \times 10^{23} \text{ molecules}}{130.0 \text{ g } C_7H_{14}O_2} = 9.26 \times 10^{21}$$

The answers agree.

Practice Problems

7. Dioxin, $C_{12}H_4Cl_4O_2$, is a powerful poison. How many moles of dioxin are there in 700.0 g of dioxin? How many molecules are there? **Ans.** 2.17 mol, 1.31×10^{24} molecules

8. One type of antibiotic, penicillin F, has the formula $C_{14}H_{20}N_2SO_4$. How many molecules of penicillin are there in a 250.0-mg dose of penicillin?

Ans. 4.82×10^{20} molecules

Figure 4-8 One compound is responsible for both the characteristic odor of bananas and the sting of bees—isopentyl acetate, $C_7H_{14}O_2$.

4.5 A Mnemonic for Molar Relationships

In this chapter, you have expressed amounts of substances in three ways.

1. in terms of the number of atoms, molecules, or formula units

2. in terms of the number of moles

3. in terms of mass

To express amounts in these different ways, you applied the relationships summarized in Table 4-1. As you have seen, the solutions to the Example problems in the chapter involved using the relationships as ratios.

TABLE 4-1

Conversion Relationships
1 mole contains 6.02×10^{23} particles.
1 mole has a mass that corresponds to: ■ the molar mass of an atom of a given element.   ■ the molar mass of a compound.
6.02×10^{23} atoms has a mass that corresponds to: ■ the molar mass of an atom of a given element.   ■ the molar mass of a compound.

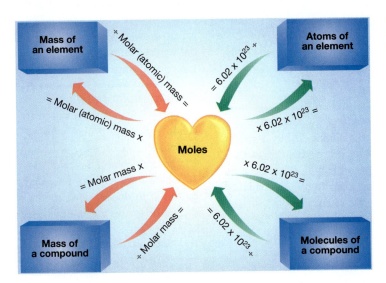

Figure 4-9 *Use this diagram to help you remember all the relationships based on the mole.*

It has been said that "the mole is at the heart of chemistry." This statement reflects how significant the concept of the mole is to understanding chemistry. A diagram of how to use the information in Table 4-1, with the mole at the heart, is shown in Figure 4-9.

Look back at the Example problems in this part of the chapter to see how Figure 4-9 applies to each. For instance, it you are working a problem similar to Example 4.1, in which you are given the mass of an element and have to determine the number of moles, you can do the calculation shown by arrow 2. Review the Practice Problems you have done so far. Which paths of the diagram did you follow in each case?

You may find Figure 4-9 helpful and copy it on a card to use as you work problems. While this diagram may help you remember the relationships based on the mole, it will not teach you the strategies you need to use in order to solve a given problem. Always try to solve each problem without the card first. After some practice, you will find that you do not need the card.

PART 1
Section 4.5 *continued*

Teaching Strategy

A Mnemonic for Molar Relationships

Have students make cards containing the mole ratios shown in Section 4.4 and in Table 4–1. The cards can be used to help them solve practice problems until they are no longer needed.

Begin class by asking each student to give a unit factor for some substance. When you call the roll, the students could answer with a unit factor.

Teacher: "Robyn."

Robyn: "1 mol $C_{12}H_{22}O_{11}$ per 342 g $C_{12}H_{22}O_{11}$."

Teacher: "Anne."

Anne: "6.02×10^{23} molecules K_2SO_4 per 1 mole K_2SO_4."

Teacher: "Carl."

Carl: "98 g H_3PO_4 per 6.02×10^{23} molecules H_3PO_4."

Teacher: "George."

George: "1 mol $C_{254}H_{377}N_{65}O_{75}S_6$ per 5.73×10^3 g." (This compound is one of the known enzymes.)

FOCUS ON PROBLEM SOLVING

Activate Prior Knowledge

Students already have experience using calculators. Have them bring calculators to class. These calculators may be used for balancing checkbooks, performing bookkeeping functions, or doing scientific and engineering calculations.

Draw attention to calculators with functions that would meet the needs of the chemistry class.

TEACH THE STRATEGY

Guided Practice

Have students use calculators for Practice Problems 7 and 8 on page 132. Both problems require the use of scientific notation.

Reteaching Idea

Use this cooperative learning activity to reinforce problem solving with the mole concept.
Teams of 3; **Time:** 30 minutes
Objective: Students will practice problem-solving skills and compare the strategies used.
Task: Students will solve problems similar to the Practice Problems 1–8 in small groups. One student will think aloud, another will record the strategies used, and the third student will encourage the problem solver and offer suggestions.
Team responsibility: After the problem is solved, each person will take a new role. Each team will list their techniques.
Evaluation: Have students solve problems similar to the Part 1 Review problems. Offer a bonus to groups scoring 80% or higher.

Guided Practice

Review the Concept Check question on page 127 with students. Answers can be found in Appendix E on page 808.

Using Calculators

You have set up a solution to a problem as follows:

9.5×10^{23} C atoms

$$\times \frac{1 \text{ mol C}}{6.02 \times 10^{23} \text{ C atoms}}$$

$$\times \frac{12.0 \text{ g}}{1 \text{ mol}} \text{ C} = ?$$

Now a calculator can help you get the answer quickly. A calculator is a useful tool, but you still need to supply the thinking.

▶ Selecting a Calculator

If you are planning to buy a calculator, look for a scientific calculator that can handle scientific notation and logarithms. A calculator that handles scientific notation usually has either an EXP button (*exponent*) or an EE button (*enter exponent*). A calculator that can do logarithms usually has buttons marked LOG and LN. If you also plan to use your calculator in trigonometry or in physics, you will want your calculator to be able to handle sines, cosines, and tangents.

▶ Arithmetic Functions

Before you use your calculator, see if it follows the same order of operations as the rules of arithmetic. For example, you know from your math classes that when you solve the expression

$$25 + 4 \times 5 = ?$$

you should first find the product of 4 times 5 and then add 25 to it. Most scientific calculators will automatically do this same grouping for you. That is, if you want to solve the expression, you only need to enter it into your calculator as shown. When you hit the final *equals* button, you will obtain the correct answer.

▶ Scientific Notation

To enter 9.5×10^{23} in your calculator, you will probably press buttons in this order: 9.5, EXP, 23. Your calculator assumes the 10 when you press the EXP or EE button. You do not need to enter the 10 or to use the multiplication key ($\times$).

▶ Checking Calculated Answers

Because it is easy to press a wrong button on a calculator, it is important that you monitor your work for errors by estimating the size of your answers. For example, with the problem shown at the beginning of this feature, you can reason that 9.5×10^{23} is about 1.5 times as large as 6.02×10^{23}, and 1.5 times 12 is 18. The calculator answer should be close to this number. If not, you should recheck your calculations.

PART 1 REVIEW

ANSWERS

■ **Keyed to Objectives**

A **9. a.** Find out how many apples are in a bag or a basket and use that as a factor to calculate the number of bags or baskets of apples needed.

b. In chemistry we calculate the number of grams in one mole (molar mass) and use that in a factor to measure the mass of a compound.

C **10.** $\dfrac{1.80 \times 10^3 \text{ kg}}{\text{auto}} \times \dfrac{6.02 \times 10^{23} \text{ auto/mol}}{1}$

$\times \dfrac{\text{Earth}}{5.977 \times 10^{24} \text{ kg}} = 181 \text{ Earths}$

C **11.** $2.45 \text{ mol} \times \dfrac{40.1 \text{ g}}{\text{mol}} = 98.2 \text{ g}$

C **12.** $1.75 \text{ mol} \times \dfrac{6.02 \times 10^{23} \text{ formula units}}{\text{mol}}$

$= 1.05 \times 10^{24} \text{ formula units}$

PART 1 REVIEW

9. Suppose you need to buy apples to supply all the students in your school with one apple each.
   a. Explain how you would ensure that you have enough apples without taking time at the store to count them.
   b. Explain how your answer to Part **a** compares with the way moles are used in chemistry.

10. The mass of an automobile is about 1.80×10^3 kg. How would the mass of 1 mole of automobiles compare to the mass of Earth (5.977×10^{24} kg)?
    Ans. Equal to 181 Earths

11. What is the mass, in grams, of 2.45 moles of calcium atoms?
    Ans. 98.2 grams

12. How many Na_2SO_4 formula units are in 1.75 moles of Na_2SO_4?   ***Ans.*** 1.05×10^{24} formula units

13. How many moles of HCl do you have when you have 1.81×10^{25} HCl molecules?   ***Ans.*** 30.1 mol

14. How many oxygen atoms are in 1.25 moles of sulfur trioxide?   ***Ans.*** 2.26×10^{24} atoms

15. How many oxygen atoms are there in 3.15 moles of manganese(IV) oxide, MnO_2?   ***Ans.*** 3.79×10^{24} atoms

16. Use the periodic table to determine the mass of 1.0000 mole of sodium sulfate, Na_2SO_4.   ***Ans.*** 142.10 g

17. How many moles of sodium carbonate, Na_2CO_3, are in 53 grams?   ***Ans.*** 0.50 mol

18. Which has a greater mass, 1 mole of lead atoms or 10 moles of water molecules?   ***Ans.*** 1 mol Pb

19. What is the mass of 1.31 moles of silver nitrate, $AgNO_3$?   ***Ans.*** 223 g

20. Find the molar mass for each of the following molecules to the nearest tenth of a gram.
    a. carbon monoxide   ***Ans.*** 28.0 g
    b. C_8H_{18} ***Ans.*** 114.0 g
    c. H_2SO_4 ***Ans.*** 98.1 g
    d. carbon disulfide   ***Ans.*** 76.2 g

21. Find the molar mass of the following:
    a. $KMnO_4$ ***Ans.*** 158.0 g
    b. manganese(IV) oxide   ***Ans.*** 86.9 g
    c. $Ca_3(PO_4)_2$ ***Ans.*** 310.3 g

22. How many moles are in a 56-gram sample of carbon disulfide?   ***Ans.*** 0.73 mol

23. Explain the fact that a mass equal to the molar mass of an element contains Avogadro's number of atoms.

Boxed numbers indicate questions that involve skills in interpretation, application, and analysis.

PROBLEM·SOLVING
S T R A T E G Y

*Use the **factor-label method** to keep track of your work. (See Strategy, page 12.)*

PROBLEM·SOLVING
S T R A T E G Y

*Simplify your work by **using a calculator**, especially when you are dealing with large numbers such as these. (See Strategy, page 134.)*

PROBLEM·SOLVING
S T R A T E G Y

*You can **identify patterns** by organizing your work as you solve Question 22. Compare your solutions with those of a classmate. How are your solutions similar? How do they differ? (See Strategy, page 100.)*

Reteaching Idea

To reinforce the concept of the mole and the calculations involved, have students create posters, mobiles, or a display on the mole. Students can work individually or in pairs to "brainstorm" and create visuals to illustrate the mole. For example, a mole of M&M candies has a mass of _____, and would cost $ _____. It would last the average student _____(× time) if consumed at the rate of _____ per day.

≡CLOSE

Summing Up Main Ideas

Help students to appreciate the significance of the concepts in Part 1 of Chapter 4 to laboratory work. To sum up these concepts, have students decide which of each pair of terms is more useful, explaining why.
a. a dozen molecules, a mole of molecules (A mole of molecules is more easily massed.)
b. the atomic mass of an atom, the molar mass of that element (The molar mass is easily massed.)
c. a gram, an atomic mass unit (A gram is easily massed.)
d. the molar mass of an element, the molar mass of a compound (Molar mass of an element. The atomic mass can be more easily determined.)

PART 1 REVIEW

Assign the Part Review questions.

Evaluating Skills

These skills are evaluated in the Part Review questions indicated.
Determining main ideas: 9, 23;
Comparing/Contrasting: 10;
Analyzing data: 10–22;
Calculating: 10–15, 17–22;
Applying a strategy: 11–15, 17–22; **Verifying results:** 11–15, 17–22

C 13. $\dfrac{1.81 \times 10^{25} \text{ molecules}}{6.02 \times 10^{23} \text{ molecules/mol}} = 30.1$ mol

C 14. $1.25 \text{ mol} \times \dfrac{6.02 \times 10^{23} \text{ molecules}}{\text{mol}}$
$\times \dfrac{3 \text{ atoms of O}}{\text{molecule}} = 2.26 \times 10^{24}$ atoms

C 15. $3.15 \text{ mol} \times \dfrac{6.02 \times 10^{23} \text{ molecules}}{\text{mol}}$
$\times \dfrac{2 \text{ atoms of O}}{\text{molecule}} = 3.79 \times 10^{24}$ atoms

B 16. $2(22.990) + 32.070 + 4(15.999)$
$= 142.10$ g

C 17. $\dfrac{53 \text{ g}}{106 \text{ g}}$ of Na_2CO_3 per mol
$= 0.50$ mol

B 18. 1 mol Pb $= \dfrac{207 \text{ g}}{\text{mol}}$,
10 mol $H_2O = \dfrac{180 \text{ g}}{\text{mol}}$

C 19. 170 g of $AgNO_3$ per mol
$\times 1.31 \text{ mol} = 223$ g

B 20. a. $12.0 \text{ g} + 16.0 \text{ g} = 28.0$ g
b. $8(12.0 \text{ g}) + 18(1.0 \text{ g}) = 114.0$ g

(answers are continued on page T841)

PART 2
Concentration
Section 4.6

Developing Skills

Students may apply these skills in their study of Part 2.

Observing and Describing: Have students describe the appearance of 1.67 mol of sodium chloride and water before and after mixing to prepare a 1.5 molar solution.

Calculating: Have students calculate how much water is used to prepare 750 mL of a 1.5 molar solution of NaCl.

≡ FOCUS

Activate Prior Knowledge

This activity will help students to see why it is important to know the concentration of a solution. Suggest students write down common household products that might be used in various concentrations and describe how the concentration affects its use.

Some examples might include salt water for a fish tank (dilute) vs. warm, concentrated salt water to soothe a sore throat; laundry detergent diluted for general use as opposed to a concentrated paste used as a prewash treatment for stains.

Point out that some ingredients of food products are safe at very low concentrations, but toxic at higher concentrations. For example, phosphoric acid is an ingredient present in low concentration in soft drinks. However, concentrated phosphoric acid is toxic.

PART
2 Concentration

Objectives

Part 2

D. *Calculate* the amount of a compound in a given volume of solution, using the concept of molarity.

E. *Explain* how to prepare molar solutions.

Many chemical compounds are stored, measured, and used as solutions. Medicines are commonly prepared by dissolving them in water so they may enter the bloodstream more quickly. Household cleaners like bleach, ammonia, and vinegar contain compounds dissolved in water so they can be used and measured more easily.

Solutions can range from very dilute to very concentrated. Therefore, in using a solution a chemist needs to know how much of a certain substance the solution contains. This is a measure of its **concentration.** There are various ways you can express concentration. The way that is chosen depends upon how the concentration is being used, on convenience, and on clarity.

4.6 ppm and the Real World

When you make grape juice from frozen concentrate, you mix 3 containers of water with 1 container of concentrate. How could you describe this mixture? You might say that it is 1 part grape juice concentrate in 4 parts of ready-to-drink grape juice. Putting concentration in terms of the number of parts of a component contained in the total is a convenient way to describe how concentrated a mixture or a solution is. One part concentrate in 4 parts mixture is the same as 25 parts in 100, or 25 percent (parts per hundred). The grape juice is therefore 25 percent grape juice concentrate.

"ppm" for dilute solutions While it may be convenient to talk about the concentration of juice as parts per hundred, the concentrations of other solutions are best expressed in parts per million, ppm. You may ask yourself if such a dilute concentration can be significant. Remember that an atom is very small, so even a very dilute solution contains a very large number of atoms.

As you might expect, often you cannot detect the presence of either harmful or beneficial substances because they are so dilute. You can demonstrate this for yourself by diluting grape juice. Set up 6 juice glasses, and use a new juice glass for each dilution. By taking 1 drop of grape juice and diluting it with 9 drops of water, you have a solution that is 1 part grape juice per 10 parts of solution. If you take a drop of this first solution and mix it with 9 drops of water, your second solution becomes 1 part per hundred (or percent). A further dilution of this solution, 1 drop to 9 drops of water, gives a third solution that is 1 part per thousand. Make three more dilutions, continuing 1 drop to 9 drops of water, to produce a sixth and final solution having 1 part grape juice per million parts of solution. Do you think you could detect any purple color? The answer is no. Does it taste like juice? No. You will find that even before your solution reaches a dilution of 1 ppm, you will be unable

---

DEMONSTRATION

"ppm" for Dilute Solutions

You may wish to perform the demonstration in the pupil text on page 136. You may use beakers instead of juice glasses. You may choose to vary the demonstration by using different concentrations of solutions of food coloring and water.

⚠️ **CAUTION: Remind students not to drink anything in the chemistry lab or classroom.**

to detect the presence of any purple color or the taste of the grape juice.

You may be surprised to learn that solutions with concentrations in the range of 1 ppm, like the dilution of grape juice described here, do affect your daily life.

Drinking water additives Many people who get their water from public water systems receive beneficial additives daily. The water contains substances that are vital to good health, but in very small concentrations. Many communities add from 0.7 to 1.0 ppm of sodium fluoride to the water supply as a means of preventing tooth decay. Maintaining a concentration this small is essential because larger concentrations of fluoride can cause mottling of the tooth enamel. Iodine is also added in some localities in concentrations of 5 to 20 ppm, depending upon the deficiency of this element in the food or water in the area. Iodine in very small quantities prevents the formation of goiter, an enlargement of the thyroid gland visible as a swelling of the neck. Another element, chlorine, is added to drinking water to kill harmful bacteria. The concentration needed for chlorine is even smaller than that for fluoride. Typically, 0.5 ppm of chlorine is required to make drinking water safe. To chlorinate a swimming pool, however, 2–3 ppm is required. You may have experienced the difference between these concentrations when the water in a pool has irritated your eyes.

Figure 4-10 *A concentration of 2–3 ppm of chlorine is usually sufficient to make swimming pool water safe from harmful bacteria.*

Atmospheric carbon dioxide When you read about the greenhouse effect on pages 190–191, you will learn that increasing concentrations of CO_2 and other gases in the atmosphere could cause the Earth's temperature to rise. During the period of rapid industrial growth in the second half of the twentieth century, the concentration of carbon dioxide rose from 315 ppm to 355 ppm. The expectation is that this figure could reach 600 ppm by the twenty-first century. The ability of scientists to detect and record these and even smaller concentrations of environmental components is crucial in making wise decisions regarding the future. You should not be surprised to learn that the unit parts per billion (ppb) is also often used. How does ppb compare with ppm?

4.7 Molarity

Percentage, ppm, and ppb have many applications in science, but chemists find it most useful to describe the concentration of solutions used in the lab by indicating the number of moles of a substance dissolved in each liter of solution. The amount of solution is commonly described in liters or cubic decimeters and is measured in a graduated cylinder.

Moles in a given volume Now look at the mole and volume relationships for a solution of sodium chloride, NaCl. Table 4-2 gives the number of grams of sodium chloride that are contained in a given volume of solution. These masses were obtained by boiling the water off and determining the mass of the resulting residue (which is NaCl). The mass in each case was converted to moles by using the procedure you learned in Section 4-4. Make the conversions yourself to be sure you understand how the values were obtained.

TABLE 4-2

Moles of Sodium Chloride in a Solution		
Volume of Solution (in L)	Mass NaCl (in g)	Moles NaCl
0.130	37.1	0.634
0.340	97.5	1.67
0.460	131.4	2.25
0.580	166.4	2.84
0.820	234.3	4.01

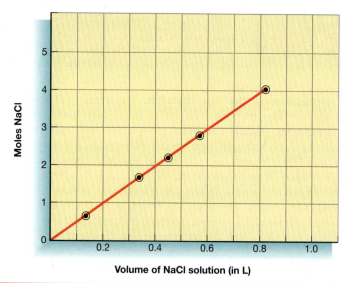

Figure 4-11 *The graph shows the moles of salt present at each volume for a salt solution. The best fit line passes through the origin and represents a direct proportion. The slope of the line is moles per liter, which is molarity.*

Moles NaCl

Volume of NaCl solution (in L)

Myths and Misconceptions

Students often have misconceptions about concentration that can interfere with their understanding of molarity. Concentration—the amount of a substance dissolved in a solution—can be expressed in different ways. General terms such as *strong, weak, dilute,* or *concentrated* do not describe the amount of a substance dissolved in a solution. Explain why more quantitative ways of measuring concentration are sometimes needed.

The terms *percentage, ppm,* or *molarity* are more precise measures of concentration. In chemical reactions, the number of reacting particles (atoms, ions, or molecules) is important, and many reactions take place in solution. Since a mole of a substance contains the same number of particles, chemists find molarity an accurate and convenient way to measure the concentration of solutions.

Figure 4-11 is a graph of the data in Table 4-2 and shows the relationship between moles and volume of solution. Note that the graph shows a straight line that passes through the origin. Therefore, the relationship between moles of NaCl and volume of the solution is a direct proportion. If the moles of NaCl are divided by the volume of the solution for the data points listed in Table 4-2, a constant is obtained. This constant is the same as the slope of the line, and represents molarity. **Molarity** is the concentration of a solution in moles per liter.

Think about the significance of the data in Table 4-2 again. The moles per volume is a constant. Thus, for a given solution, you can select any volume and still have the same concentration in moles per liter. The NaCl solution described here has a molarity of 4.90. The symbol for molarity is *M*. A 4.90*M* solution of NaCl means that there are 4.90 moles of NaCl in 1 liter of the solution.

Moles in a given volume of solution Do not confuse the molarity of the solution with the number of moles of a substance in a particular sample of the solution. For example, if you have 250 mL of a 4.90*M* NaCl solution, the molarity is 4.90, but the number of moles of NaCl in the solution is not 4.90. You can use the graph in Figure 4-12 to find the number of moles in the solution, or you can calculate the number. To use the graph, find the point for 250 mL (0.250 L) on the dotted line. You should see that the corresponding number of moles is about 1.2. To calculate the number of moles, multiply the molarity in moles per liter by the volume of the sample in liters.

$$4.90M = \frac{4.90 \text{ mol}}{\text{L}}$$

$$\frac{4.90 \text{ mol}}{\cancel{\text{L}}} \times 0.250 \, \cancel{\text{L}} = 1.23 \text{ mol}$$

The following Example shows how molarity can be used to determine the amount of the dissolved substance contained in a given volume of a solution.

EXAMPLE 4-5

How many moles of HCl are contained in 1.45 L of a 2.25*M* solution?

PROBLEM·SOLVING STRATEGY

Use what you know about the symbol M *and translate it as moles per liter. (See Strategy, page 58.)*

■ *Analyze the Problem* Recognize that a 2.25*M* solution has a concentration of 2.25 moles per 1 liter. You have 1.45 L of this solution.

■ *Apply a Strategy* Write the concentration as a ratio.

$$2.25M = \frac{2.25 \text{ mol of solution}}{1 \text{ L}}$$

≡ T E A C H

Practice Problems

Assign the Practice Problems.

Teaching Strategy

Preparing Solutions

Actually preparing molar solutions will help students understand this concept.

Cooperative Learning

Preparing Solutions

Teams of 2; **Time:** 30 minutes
Objective: Students will learn to prepare molar solutions.
Task: Each student will independently calculate the amount of substance required to prepare the assigned solution.
Team responsibility: Team members compare answers, resolve any differences, and as a team check their calculations with the teacher. The mass of the beaker, the mass of the beaker and dissolved substance, and the final volume are measured by one person and checked by the other team member.
Evaluation: Have team A prepare 100 mL of 0.55*M* sodium carbonate and team B prepare 100 mL of 0.55*M* calcium chloride.

⚠ **CAUTION: Students must wear lab aprons and safety goggles.** The solutions can be reacted, filtered, and the mass of the calcium carbonate predicted and measured. The lines on a graduated beaker are precise enough for this experiment. For disposal, decant and pour the decantate down the drain. Wrap solids in newspaper and discard in the wastebasket.

PROBLEM-SOLVING
S T R A T E G Y

*Check your answer by **making an estimate**.
(See Strategy, page 125.)*

Multiply the ratio by the volume in liters to get an answer in moles.

■ **Work a Solution**

$$1.45\ \cancel{L} \times \frac{2.25\ \text{mol HCl}}{1\ \cancel{L}} = 3.26\ \text{mol HCl}$$

■ **Verify Your Answer** Check to see if your answer is reasonable. Since 1 liter of solution contains 2.25 moles of HCl, you would expect 1.45 liter to have a larger number of moles.

Practice Problems

24. How many moles of H_2SO_4 are contained in 3.5 L of a 6.5*M* solution? **Ans.** 23 moles

25. How many moles of NaCl are contained in 2.5 L of a 1.5*M* solution? **Ans.** 3.8 moles

Figure 4-12 *One liter of a 1 M sugar solution requires 342 grams of sugar and a volumetric flask. The flask is used in diluting the sugar with water to a volume of 1 liter. About 790 mL of water is required to make the solution, but it is not necessary to measure this volume exactly. It is only necessary that the final volume of the solution be one liter.*

4.8 Preparing Solutions

In the previous section, the molarity of a solution of sodium chloride was found by plotting experimental data, but it is certainly not necessary to plot a graph in order to know the molarity of a solution. All you need to know is the number of moles of solute contained in each liter of solution.

The preparation of one liter of a 1.00*M* sugar solution involves the same process anywhere in the world. Molar solutions contain a known amount of the dissolved substance in a given volume of solution. For example, a 1.00*M* solution of sugar, $C_{12}H_{22}O_{11}$, is prepared by measuring 342 grams of sugar (one mole) and then adding enough water so that the volume of the solution is 1.00 liter when the sugar is completely dissolved.

EXAMPLE 4-6

Give directions for the preparation of 2.50 L of a 1.34*M* sodium chloride solution.

■ *Analyze the Problem* Write what you need to find.

? g NaCl needed to make 2.50 liters of 1.34*M* NaCl

■ *Apply a Strategy* One way to solve the problem would be to calculate the number of moles of salt needed to make the solution. The number of moles is then converted to grams by using the molar mass of NaCl.

■ *Work a Solution* The number of moles is found by multiplying the molarity by the volume of the solution.

$$2.50 \cancel{L} \times \frac{1.34 \text{ mol NaCl}}{\cancel{L}} = 3.35 \text{ mol NaCl}$$

The molar mass of NaCl is 58.5 grams per mole.

$$3.35 \cancel{\text{mol}} \times \frac{58.5 \text{ g}}{\cancel{\text{mol}}} = 196 \text{ grams NaCl}$$

So the instructions for making the solution would be: Measure 196 grams of NaCl and add enough water so that the final volume of the solution is 2.50 liters when the solution process is complete.

■ **Verify Your Answer** Check to see if your answer is reasonable. Since the molarity of your solution is 1.34M, you know that you have 1.34 moles per liter of solution. If you have over 2 liters of solution, you would expect to have more than two times the number of moles. The calculation shows 3.35 moles. Also 196 grams of NaCl is more than three times the mass of 1 mole of NaCl, so the answer is reasonable.

Practice Problems

26. Give directions for the preparation of 3.00 L of a 1.50M CuSO$_4$ solution.   ***Ans.*** Measure 718 g of CuSO$_4$ and add enough water so the final solution is 3.00 L.

27. Give directions for the preparation of 2.0 L of a 1.0M NaOH solution.   ***Ans.*** Measure 80. g of NaOH and add enough water so that the final solution is 2.0 L.

PART 2 REVIEW

28. Use the data in Table 4-2 to prove to yourself that molarity is a constant, regardless of the volume of the solution sample.

29. How many moles of H$_2$SO$_4$ are in 1.00 liter of a 1.55M H$_2$SO$_4$ solution?   ***Ans.*** 1.55 mol

30. How many grams of H$_2$SO$_4$ are in 1.00 liter of a 1.55M H$_2$SO$_4$ solution?   ***Ans.*** 152 g

31. Use your knowledge of molarity of water solutions to fill in the blanks in the table below:

Formula	Grams dissolved	Moles dissolved	Volume of solution	Molarity
KBr	5.00 g		2.50 L	
NiSO$_4$		3.4 × 10^{-3}	1.90 L	
NaOH	8.40 g		200. mL	

Boxed numbers indicate questions that involve skills in interpretation, application, and analysis.

PROBLEM-SOLVING STRATEGY

*Use the **factor-label** method as you do these calculations. (See Strategy, page 12.)*

PART 2

Section 4.8 *continued*

Practice Problems

Assign the Practice Problems.

Guided Practice

Chlorine bleach is a 0.57M solution of sodium hypochlorite (NaOCl) in water. Calculate how many grams of NaOCl are needed to prepare 4 liters of chlorine bleach. (Formula mass of NaOCl is 74.5 g. 74.5 g/mol × 0.57 mol/liter = 42.5 g/L; 42.5 g/L × 4 liters = 170 g of NaOCl.

Reteaching Idea

Have students determine how to make the following concentrations of sodium chloride in 100 mL of water:

a. 0.5 percent (0.5 grams in 100 mL H$_2$O)
b. 500 ppm (0.05 grams)
c. 0.5M (2.9 grams)

Ask students to predict which solution would have the highest salt concentration—0.5 percent, 500 ppm, or 0.5M? Have students justify their predictions.

☰CLOSE

Summing Up Main Ideas

The concentrations of most solutions found in everyday life are given in percentage by volume. However, molarity is more useful to chemists because it tells how many moles are in a given volume, and every mole contains the same number of units.

PART 2 REVIEW

Assign the Part Review questions.

Evaluating Skills

These skills are evaluated in the Part Review questions indicated.
Comparing/Contrasting: 28;
Analyzing data: 28, 29, 30, 31;
Verifying results: 28, 29, 30, 31;
Applying a strategy: 29, 30, 31;
Calculating: 29, 30, 31; **Constructing tables and graphs:** 31

PART 2 REVIEW
ANSWERS
■ **Keyed to Objectives**

E **28.** The straight line of the graph indicates the molarity is constant.

D **29.** $1.00 \cancel{L} \times \frac{1.55 \text{ mol}}{\cancel{L}} = 1.55$ mol

D **30.** $1.00 \cancel{L} \times \frac{1.55 \cancel{\text{mol}}}{\cancel{L}} \times \frac{98.0 \text{ g}}{\cancel{\text{mol}}} = 152$ g

D **31.** KBr: 39.1 + 79.9 = 119.0 g/mol

$5.00 \cancel{g} \times \frac{1 \text{ mol}}{119.0 \cancel{g}} = 4.22 \times 10^{-2}$ mol

$\frac{0.0420 \text{ mol}}{2.50 \text{ L}} = 0.0168M$

NiSO$_4$: 58.7 + 32.0 + 64.0
= 155 g/mol

$3.4 \times 10^{-3} \cancel{\text{mol}} \times \frac{155 \text{ g}}{\cancel{\text{mol}}} = 0.51$ g

$\frac{3.4 \times 10^{-3} \text{ mol}}{1.90 \text{ L}} = 0.0018M$

NaOH: 23.0 + 16.0 + 1.0
= 40.0 g/mol

$8.40 \cancel{g} \times \frac{1 \text{ mol}}{40.0 \cancel{g}} = 2.10 \times 10^{-1}$ mol

$\frac{0.210 \text{ mol}}{0.200 \text{ L}} = 1.05M$

CAREERS IN CHEMISTRY

PART 2

Section 4.8 *continued*

CAREERS IN CHEMISTRY

Teaching Strategies

1. Discuss the differences between basic and applied research. (While basic research works to understand basic functions, applied research utilizes the understanding of basic research to develop products.)

2. Sometimes research findings are used to develop destructive technologies such as weapons. Have students debate the pros and cons of the use of research in this way. Have students also consider whether researchers are responsible for the uses to which their research is put.

Related Careers

Have students identify related careers. Some examples include the development of pharmaceuticals, ceramics, and dyes. For additional career opportunities, write to the Manufacturing Chemists Association, 1825 Connecticut Ave., NW, Washington, DC 20415, or the American Pharmaceutical Association, 2215 Constitution Ave., NW, Washington, DC 20037.

Resources

Contact the American Chemical Society or the Association for Women in Science for additional information and to identify Society members in your area who might be invited to speak to your class.

Research Chemist

Some people do not follow a direct path to a specific career, but rather arrive at a particular career after a series of different experiences.

■ *Luck happens when opportunity meets preparedness.*

A career via a detour Dave Dellar didn't intend to become a research scientist. He had his sights set early on becoming a pharmacist. After high school, he worked for three years as a pharmacy technician and then traveled the country to see what there was beyond his hometown. He found lots of jobs, but none that offered him more than a minimal lifestyle. He came home and began a demanding program to realize his ambition. It turned out that pharmacy was not what he wanted after all. Fortunately all the courses in chemistry, biology, and math that he had taken to meet the requirements to become a pharmacist could be applied to an associate's degree in industrial chemical technology and to a bachelor's degree in applied biology. He had little difficulty finding his present job with a major chemical company.

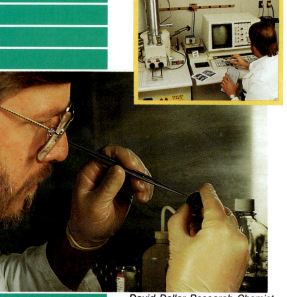

David Dellar Research Chemist

The excitement of invention Dave enjoys his job because his work is so varied and interesting. He has a great deal of independence and the opportunity to exercise his creativity. He designs and carries out experiments on consumer products, analyzes data, and makes suggestions for future work. His research resulted in three inventions for which U.S. patents have been awarded. He finds excitement in discovering new things and satisfaction in being able to understand how science shapes the world.

Creative minds and computers Jobs in chemical and biological research will continue to need people with backgrounds in math and science like Dave's, but knowledge of computers is also a must. Dave believes that the combination of the creative human mind with the efficiency of the computer can speed the solution of many of life's pressing problems.

Getting lucky means being prepared Dave believes in asking questions about everything and trying to understand what you are doing and why. He thinks that to get lucky in life, you need to be prepared to recognize an opportunity when it is presented to you. "Luck happens," he says, "when opportunity meets preparedness."

PART

3 *Formula Calculations*

If you mixed two solutions together and got a solid, how could you identify the solid? In Chapter 3, you learned that by knowing the reactants, you could predict the type of reaction that occurs and what the products would be. By using tables showing ion charges, you could even apply rules that allowed you to write the formula for products you predicted.

While predictions based on regularities are useful in science, those regularities are the result of experimentation and constant verification. Even after predicting what the product could be, it is important to verify your answer. One verification strategy is to determine the percentage by mass of each element in the compound, the **percent composition,** and compare the results to a known sample.

4.9 Percent Composition

Determining the percent of elements in a compound is accomplished in the same way that grades are determined. If you score 25 points out of a possible 50 points on one test and 45 out of a possible 60 points on another test, which score is better? You would not know unless you establish a basis, such as percent, for the comparison.

Percent means "parts per hundred." In this case, *percent* indicates the score you would have gotten if the test had been graded on a 100-point basis. In the first test, you earned 25 points out of 50. How many would you have earned out of 100? In the second test, you scored 45 out of 60. How many would you have scored out of 100? To find parts per hundred or percent, divide the part by the total and multiply by 100.

$$25/50 = 0.50 \times 100 = 50\%, \text{ or } 50/100$$
$$45/60 = 0.75 \times 100 = 75\%, \text{ or } 75/100$$

One way to interpret these results is to say that you got 50 hundredths of the items on the first test right and 75 hundredths of the items on the second test right. If each test had been worth 100 points, your scores would be 50 and 75 respectively.

In a similar fashion, if a 36-g sample of iron oxide produces 28 g of iron and 8 g of oxygen, while a 160-g sample of iron oxide produces 112 g of iron and 48 g of oxygen, you can determine whether the two samples are the same compound or different oxides of iron by using percent of iron and oxygen as a basis of comparison. Example 4-7 shows how a **percent composition** analysis by mass can be done.

O b j e c t i v e s

Part 3

F. *Calculate* percent composition by mass and use it to compare compounds.

G. *Determine* empirical and molecular formulas for compounds.

H. *Recognize* significant digits in a recorded measurement and *determine* the number of significant digits in a calculated value.

Developing Skills

Students may apply this skill in their study of Part 3.
Calculating: Have students calculate the percentage of students in your chemistry class who are (a) juniors, (b) girls. Have students calculate the percentage of substances in the mole display that are (a) elements, (b) colored, (c) metals, (d) ionic.

☰ FOCUS

Activate Prior Knowledge

Students have had practice calculating percentages. Ask students to count the total number of answers in the Part 1 Review on page 135. Then ask them to determine the percent of the total represented by the answers for question 20. (4 answers/21 total = 19%)

D E M O N S T R A T I O N

Percent Composition

Determine the mass of a 1983 or newer penny. File off the copper edge 7 or 8 mm and put it in a beaker containing 30 mL of 3.0*M* HCl placed on an overhead projector. ⚠ **CAUTION: Teacher and students must wear safety goggles and lab aprons. Protect students with a shield.** The following day, wearing rubber gloves, remove copper shells from acid with tongs, and rinse them three times as follows: Insert a narrow strip of filter paper into the hollowed out portion to blot up the liquid inside. Fill the hollowed out space with tap water and repeat two more times. Dry the coin and determine the mass. Have students calculate the percentage of Cu in the penny. For disposal, neutralize the acid and pour down the drain.

PART **3**
Section 4.10

≡ **TEACH**

Practice Problems

Assign the Practice Problems.

PROBLEM-SOLVING
STRATEGY

Use what you know about the meaning of percent to start the solution to this problem. (See Strategy, page 58.)

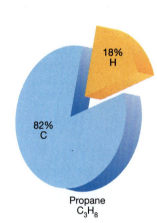

Propane
C_3H_8

18%
H

82%
C

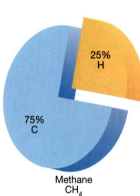

Methane
CH_4

25%
H

75%
C

Figure 4-13 *Two hydrocarbons—methane and propane—have different percent compositions.*

EXAMPLE 4-7

The following data are obtained from analyzing two iron oxide samples. Are the samples the same compound?

A 36-g sample contains 28 g Fe and 8 g O.
A 160-g sample contains 112 g Fe and 48 g O.

■ **Apply a Strategy** Using the definition of *percent*, set up the equation that you need in order to find the percentages of iron or oxygen in each sample. Begin by finding the percent by mass of iron in each sample.

$$\frac{\text{mass of Fe in sample}}{\text{total mass of sample}} \times 100\% = \% \text{ Fe}$$

■ **Work a Solution** Substitute the data into the equation and solve for the percentage of iron in each sample.

Sample 1 $\dfrac{28 \text{ g Fe}}{36\text{-g sample}} \times 100\% = 78\%$ Fe

Sample 2 $\dfrac{112 \text{ g Fe}}{160\text{-g sample}} \times 100\% = 70\%$ Fe

The percentages indicate that the two samples are different compounds.

■ **Verify Your Answer** Check that each percent calculated does indeed represent that amount of the sample. For example, if 78% of a 36-g sample is iron, then 78% of 36 should equal 28 g and it does—(0.78)(36 g) = 28 g. You can also calculate the percent composition of oxygen in each sample to verify that those percentages are different in each sample.

Practice Problems

Determine if the following samples are the same compound.

32. 45.0-g sample containing 35.1 g Fe and 9.9 g O
215.0-g sample containing 167.7 g Fe and 47.3 g O
Ans. Yes, 78% Fe in each

33. 75.0-g sample containing 20.5 g C and 54.5 g O
135.0-g sample containing 67.5 g C and 90.0 g O
Ans. No, % C differs in each, 27.3% versus 50.0%

4.10 Determining Empirical Formulas

You learned in Chapter 2 that every compound can be represented by a chemical formula. The formula that represents the smallest whole-number ratio of the various types of atoms in a compound is called the **empirical formula**.

To determine the empirical formula for an unknown compound, the compound is analyzed to find the mass of each element in the compound. Using this information, the percent composition by mass of each element in the sample is determined. Example 4-8 illustrates how the empirical formula can be calculated.

EXAMPLE 4-8

What is the empirical formula for an iron oxide compound having the following composition?

a 36-g sample that is 78% iron

■ **Analyze the Problem** Recognize that the name of the compound, iron oxide, tells you that iron and oxygen are present in the compound. Since the ratio of atoms given in a formula is the same as the ratio of moles, you can reason that you need to determine the number of moles of each element from the given data. To find the number of moles, begin by finding the number of grams.

■ **Apply a Strategy** When finding the formula of a compound from percentage data, use the fact that *percent* means "per hundred parts" to determine how many grams of iron and oxygen there are in each sample. In a 100-g sample, there would be 78 parts out of 100, or 78 g of iron. There would be 22 g of oxygen (100 − 78). Using the molar masses of each element, calculate the number of moles present to determine the mole ratio in the compound.

■ **Work a Solution** Using 78 g of iron and 22 g of oxygen, calculate the moles of iron and oxygen.

$$78\ \text{g Fe} \times \frac{1\ \text{mol}}{55.8\ \text{g}} = 1.4\ \text{mol Fe}$$

$$22\ \text{g O} \times \frac{1\ \text{mol}}{16.0\ \text{g}} = 1.4\ \text{mol O}$$

The mole ratio is 1 to 1 which means the formula must be FeO for the first sample.

■ **Verify Your Answer** Work the problem another way. If there is 78% iron in a 36-g sample, then there is (.78)(36 g) = 28 g Fe and (36 g) − (28) = 8 g O. Finding the number of moles of Fe and O, you get

$$28\ \text{g Fe} \times \frac{1\ \text{mol Fe}}{55.8\ \text{g Fe}} = 0.50\ \text{mol Fe}$$

and

$$8\ \text{g O} \times \frac{1\ \text{mol O}}{16.0\ \text{g O}} = 0.5\ \text{mol O}.$$

CONNECTING CONCEPTS

Process of Science—Measurement The mole concept is a measurement that answers the question "How much do I have?" It is particularly useful, since it provides a basis of comparison among compounds in terms of mass, numbers of particles, and concentration.

Teaching Strategy

Determining Empirical Formulas

Use the data in the following example to explore the question of whole numbers in empirical formulas. A 4.3 g sample of graphite (C) is burned in pure oxygen. The gas formed is collected and massed at 15.9 g. The mass of oxygen (11.6 g) would be found by subtracting the mass of the carbon from the mass of the compound. The calculations are:

$$4.3\ \text{g C} \times \frac{1\ \text{mol C}}{12.0\ \text{g C}} = 0.36\ \text{mol C}$$

$$11.6\ \text{g O} \times \frac{1\ \text{mol O}}{16.0\ \text{g O}} = 0.72\ \text{mol C}$$

Divide both by 0.36 to get a ratio of 1C:2O (CO_2). Have students verify the answer by determining the percent of carbon in the compound using the formula and comparing it to the percent of carbon determined from the data.

$$\frac{12.0\ \text{g C}}{44.0\ \text{g CO}_2} \times 100 = 27.3\%$$

$$\frac{4.3\ \text{g C}}{15.9\ \text{g gas}} \times 100 = 27.0\%$$

The value deviates due to experimental error.

PART **3**

Section 4.10 continued

Practice Problems

Assign the Practice Problems.

PROBLEM·SOLVING
S T R A T E G Y

Several different approaches
to solving a problem can
help you **see patterns**.
Compare notes with
a friend. (See Strategy,
page 100.)

This is also a ratio of 1:1 and agrees with the answer in the problem.

Practice Problems

What are the formulas for two sulfur oxide compounds having the following compositions?

34. a 27.0-g sample that is 50% sulfur by mass   **Ans.** SO_2

35. a 78.0-g sample that is 60% oxygen   **Ans.** SO_3

To determine the empirical formula for a compound, it is not always necessary to know the percent composition. If you know the mass of each element in the compound you can find the number of moles and determine the empirical formula. You are interested in finding the ratios of moles of elements in a compound. It does not matter if the total mass of the compound is 100 g—as in a percent composition problem—or some other total mass of the compound. You can also find the empirical formula of a binary compound if you know the mass of the compound and the mass of one element.

Table 4-3 summarizes the steps for finding the empirical formula of a compound. These steps can be used to find the formula of any compound for which at least one element is present as a single atom per molecule or formula unit. Refer to the table and follow the steps in solving problems until you become familiar with the calculations. An additional step is required for compounds like N_2O_5, in which all atoms occur in multiples. Example 4.9 illustrates this additional step as well as how you can use masses which are not derived from percent composition in solving empirical formula problems. The reaction that occurs in the Example is the same reaction used in industry to obtain large amounts of iron from iron ore. In the example you will be determining the formula for the principle oxide of iron in iron ore and the formula for rust. Scrap iron and steel are effectively recycled through this process.

TABLE 4-3

Finding Empirical Formulas
1. The mass (or mass percent) of each element in a sample of the compound is determined.
2. The mass (or mass percent) of each element is divided by its molar mass to determine the number of moles of each element in the sample of the compound.
3. The number of moles of each element is divided by the smallest number of moles to give the ratio of atoms in the compound.

EXAMPLE 4-9

Charcoal is mixed with 15.53 g of rust (an oxide of iron) and heated in a covered crucible to keep out air until all of the oxygen atoms in the rust combine with carbon. When this process is complete, a pellet of pure iron with a mass of 10.87 g remains. What is the empirical formula for rust?

■ *Analyze the Problem* Begin by writing an equation that summarizes what you know about the reaction.

$$C(s) + Fe_?O_?(s) \rightarrow Fe(s) + CO_?(g)$$
$$15.53 \text{ g} 10.87 \text{ g}$$

■ *Apply a Strategy* Since you know the mass of the iron oxide $(Fe_?O_?)$ and the mass of the iron (Fe), the mass of the oxygen can be found by subtraction. Using the molar masses of iron and oxygen atoms, calculate the number of moles of each element, as you did in Example 4-8. Organize the data in a table.

Substance	Mass
iron oxide analyzed	15.53 g (stated in the problem)
pure iron	10.87 g (stated in the problem)
oxygen in rust	4.66 g (found by subtraction of given values)

■ *Work a Solution*

$$10.87 \text{ g Fe} \times \frac{1 \text{ mol Fe}}{55.8 \text{ g Fe}} = 0.195 \text{ mol Fe}$$

$$4.66 \text{ g O} \times \frac{1 \text{ mol O}}{16.0 \text{ g O}} = 0.291 \text{ mol O}$$

The ratio of Fe moles to O moles can be written as

$$\frac{Fe}{O} = \frac{0.195 \text{ mol}}{0.291 \text{ mol}}$$

Divide by the smallest number of moles to get the simplest ratio of atoms.

$$Fe = \frac{0.195}{0.195} = 1$$

$$O = \frac{0.291}{0.195} = 1.49$$

There are 1.49 moles of oxygen atoms for every mole of iron atoms in the compound. The formula could be written as $Fe_1O_{1.49}$. However, because atoms combine in whole-number ratios, multiply both numbers by some whole number. Multiplying by 2 gives 2.00 moles of iron and 2.98 moles of oxygen. Because of

PROBLEM-SOLVING
S T R A T E G Y

Look for similarities between problems. Many steps in this problem are the same as those in Example 4-8. (See Strategy, page 65.)

PROBLEM-SOLVING
S T R A T E G Y

When ratios give numbers such as 1.49, 2.33, 1.67, 1.25, and 1.72, they should not be rounded; they should be multiplied by a whole number like 2, 3, or 4 so that the result for each atom is a whole number.

PART **3**

Section 4.11

Practice Problems

Assign the Practice Problems.

the uncertainty involved in the experimental measurements, you can assume that 2.98 is the same as 3. The ratio expressed in whole numbers becomes Fe_2O_3 for rust.

■ **Verify Your Answer** Check that the percent composition of iron in the empirical formula is the same as the percent iron in the compound.

$$Fe_2O_3: \frac{Fe}{Fe_2O_3} \frac{(2)(55.8 \text{ g})}{(2)(55.8 \text{ g}) + 3(16.0 \text{ g})} \times 100\% = 69.9\% \text{ Fe}$$

$$Data: \frac{10.87 \text{ g Fe}}{10.87 \text{ g Fe} + 4.66 \text{ g O}} \times 100\% = 70.0\% \text{ Fe}$$

The comparison of the empirical formula agrees with the experimental data.

Practice Problems

36. When iron oxide, Fe_2O_3, reacts with 18.94 g of aluminum metal, iron is produced along with 35.74 g of aluminum oxide. What is the empirical formula for aluminum oxide?

Ans. Al_2O_3

37. Propane is a gas commonly used for cooking and heating. It contains the elements carbon and hydrogen. When 72.06 g of carbon reacts with hydrogen gas, 88.06 g of propane is produced. What is the empirical formula of propane?

Ans. C_3H_8

DO YOU KNOW?

To obtain Avogadro's number of grains of sand, it would be necessary to dig up the entire surface of the Sahara (desert whose area of 8×10^6 km^2 is slightly less than that of the United States) to a depth of 200 m.

4.11 Determining Molecular Formulas

Rust, Fe_2O_3, is an ionic compound that forms crystals of various sizes rather than molecules. In ionic compounds, the empirical formula indicates the proportions of elements in the compound. As you know from Chapter 2, this is the *formula unit* of the ionic compound.

The formula for a molecular compound is the **molecular formula.** The molecular formula of ethylene is C_2H_4. The empirical formula of ethylene is CH_2. Remember, the empirical formula gives only the *simplest* whole number ratio of atoms. In the case of ethylene, the empirical formula tells you only that there are twice as many hydrogen atoms as carbon atoms in the molecule so CH_2 is the empirical formula.

In general,

molecular formula = (empirical formula)$_n$

To find n, or the multiple of the empirical formula, compare the molecular formula mass to the empirical formula mass. The empirical formula and molecular formula masses are the sum of the molar masses of the atoms in the formulas.

$$n = \frac{\text{molecular formula mass}}{\text{empirical formula mass}}$$

This ratio tells you how many empirical formula units are in the actual molecule. From this information, you can determine the molecular formula of the compound, as shown in Example 4-10.

EXAMPLE 4-10

A compound composed of hydrogen and oxygen is analyzed and a sample of the compound yields 0.59 g of hydrogen and 9.40 g of oxygen. The molecular mass of this compound is 34.0 g/mole. Find the empirical formula and the molecular formula for the compound.

PROBLEM-SOLVING

S T R A T E G Y

*Because the first part of this problem is finding an empirical formula, you can apply the same strategies you have used in **similar problems.** (See Strategy, page 65.)*

■ **Apply a Strategy** Determine the empirical formula by finding the number of moles of each element and the ratio of atoms in the compound, as you did in previous problems. Then compare each empirical formula mass to the molecular formula mass to find the molecular formula.

■ **Work a Solution** Determine the number of moles of each element.

$$0.59 \text{ g H} \times \frac{1 \text{ mol H}}{1.01 \text{ g H}} = 0.58 \text{ mol H}$$

$$9.40 \text{ g O} \times \frac{1 \text{ mol O}}{16.0 \text{ g O}} = 0.588 \text{ mol O}$$

The ratio of hydrogen atoms to oxygen atoms is 1:1. The empirical formula is HO. The empirical formula mass is

$$1.0 \text{ g H} + 16.0 \text{ g O} = 17.0 \text{ g}$$

Solve for n.

$$n = \frac{\text{molecular formula mass}}{\text{empirical formula mass}} = \frac{34.0 \text{ g/mol}}{17.0 \text{ g/mol}} = 2.00$$

The molecular formula for the compound is $(HO)_2$, which is commonly written as H_2O_2.

■ **Verify Your Answer** Using the molecular formula, calculate the molar mass of H_2O_2.

$$2(1.0 \text{ g/mol}) + 2(16.0 \text{ g/mol}) = 34.0 \text{ g/mol}$$
$$\text{H} \qquad\qquad \text{O}$$

The molecular formula has a molar mass of 34.0 g/mol which agrees with the data in the problem.

PART 3
Section 4.12

Practice Problems

Assign the Practice Problems.

Teaching Strategy

Significant Digits

A store sells a watch that will give the time to the hundredth of a second when a button is pushed. Example: 11:42; 12:02. But the watch is 5 minutes slow. The time given is precise but not accurate. Students can use the rule for rounding: we round off after each step in a calculation.

Practice Problems

38. The empirical formula for a common drying agent is P_2O_5. The molecule has a molar mass of 283.88 g/mol. Find the molecular formula of the compound. **Ans.** P_4O_{10}

39. Hydrazine is a widely used compound. It can be used to treat waste water from chemical plants removing ions that may be hazardous to the environment; it can be used in rocket fuels; and it can help prevent corrosion in the pipes of electric plants. In a 32.0-g sample of hydrazine, there are 28.0 g of nitrogen and 4.0 g of hydrogen. The molar mass of the molecule is 32.0 g/mol. What is the empirical formula and the molecular formula of hydrazine?

Ans. empirical formula: NH_2
molecular formula: N_2H_4

Figure 4-14 *A three percent solution of hydrogen peroxide is used as an antiseptic for minor cuts and abrasions. A six percent solution is used for bleaching purposes. More concentrated solutions should not be used.*

Figure 4-15 *A micrometer can be used to measure small thicknesses. The object to be measured is placed between the jaws, and the movable jaw is rotated down until the jaws touch the object on both sides.*

4.12 Significant Digits

The terms *precision* and *accuracy* are often used interchangeably in everyday conversation. However, in science, they have different, but related meanings. **Precision** represents the agreement between several measurements of the same quantity. If all values are close to one another—that is reproducible—the measurement has a high degree of precision. **Accuracy** represents the agreement between a measured value and the true value. If there is close agreement, the measured value is accurate.

Precision is often used as an indicator of accuracy. However, precise measurements are not always accurate. The micrometer shown in Figure 4-15 is capable of giving very reproducible measurements when measuring small thicknesses. However, a damaged micrometer—one that does not read zero when the jaws are closed—will give precise, but inaccurate results. Figure 4-16 illustrates the difference between precision and accuracy in another way.

Percent error In recording experimental measurements, scientists often record the percent error along with their measurements. Percent error is calculated by dividing the difference between the true value and the measured value by the true value and multiplying by 100.

Recording measured results If you worked Example 4-10 using a calculator, you noticed that 0.59 divided by 1.01 does not equal 0.58. The answer actually is 0.584158415. Also, 9.40 divided by 16 equals 0.5875, not 0.59. Why, then, were the answers written with fewer digits? The reason has to do with how experimental measurements are recorded.

You know from Chapter 1 that when a measurement is made, such as mass, you record the measurement by estimating the last digit which is uncertain. The total number of digits you record, however, is determined by the precision of the instrument you use to make the measurement. For example, a micrometer can be used to estimate a thickness to the nearest thousandth of a centimeter. Using a micrometer, the estimate for the thickness of a book was 2.878 cm. Using a metric ruler, the measurement was 2.88 cm. The measurement made with the micrometer is said to be more precise than the measurement made with the ruler. However, the last digit in each case is assumed to be uncertain. The certain digits in a measurement—plus one uncertain digit which you have estimated—are called **significant digits.**

Significant digits are easy to determine when you are recording a measurement that you have made. You are unlikely to record more than one uncertain digit. However, if you make a calculation, you need to be able to determine the proper number of digits to be recorded in the answer so that you do not indicate more precision than is actually correct. Table 4-4 provides a summary of how to determine the significant digits in a measurement.

Multiplying and dividing with significant digits If you look at the measurements again in Example 4-10, 0.59 g has 2 significant digits, while 1.01 g has 3 significant digits. When 0.59 g is divided by 1.01 g, the number of significant digits in the answer is determined by the following rule. *When multiplying or dividing measurements recorded with significant digits, the measurement with the fewest significant digits determines the number of significant digits in the answer.* Since 0.59 g has only 2 significant digits, the answer, 0.584158415 g should be recorded with only 2 significant digits—that is, as 0.58 g.

Exact numbers It is important to remember that significant digits have meaning only in relation to uncertain values. There are numbers that have no uncertainty. How many eggs are in a dozen?

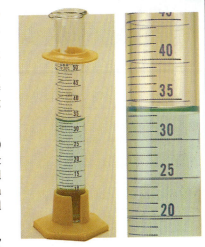

Figure 4-16 *Can you see that the volume of the liquid—read from the bottom—is between 33 and 34 mL? If you estimate to the nearest 0.1 mL, you might read 33.5 or 33.6 mL. The tenths place is uncertain.*

PROBLEM-SOLVING STRATEGY

Your calculator will not tell you how many significant digits are justified from your work. You must **know how many digits** *you are justified in using in your answer.*

Guided Practice

Have students determine the empirical and molecular formulas for acetylene and benzene, both of which have a composition of 92.3 percent carbon and 7.7 percent hydrogen. The molecular mass of acetylene is 26 g/mol, and for benzene it is 78 g/mol.

Solution: In a 100-gram sample, there would be 92.3 grams of C and 7.7 g of H.

$$\frac{92.3 \text{ g C}}{12 \text{ g C/mol}} = 7.7 \text{ mol}$$

$$\frac{7.7 \text{ g H}}{1 \text{ g H/mol}} = 7.7 \text{ mol}$$

The mole ratio is 1 to 1. Therefore, the empirical formula is CH. The total mass of one C and one H is 13. Thirteen divides into 26 two times, and into 78 six times. Therefore, the molecular formula of acetylene is $(CH)_2$, or C_2H_2. The molecular formula of benzene is $(CH)_6$, or C_6H_6.

Reteaching Idea

For a concrete example to help students better understand empirical and molecular formulas, use the following idea, which has been adapted from "Gleel— A Substance of Substance," Erhardt, W., *The Science Teacher*, LVIII, (September, 1991) pp. 36–40.

Divide students into groups of 3 to 4. Distribute boxes containing steel and glass marbles. Each box should have different numbers of marbles, but always in a ratio of 2 glass to 1 steel. The marbles represent individual atoms. Using balances to obtain masses, students fill in data tables that show the mass of the sample, the mass of steel, the mass of glass, the mass ratio of steel to glass, and the mass ratio by percent. In comparing data from different groups, students should conclude that atoms combine in whole number ratios. Additional sets of data tables can be completed using information such as a 54.0 g sample of H_2O has 6.1 g H and 48.0 g O, or 46.0 g Na are in a 117.0 g sample of NaCl. Lead discussions by posing questions relating to the ratio of atoms, the smallest mass of a sample, i.e., molecular mass, empirical formulas, and molecular formulas. Ask students to compare and contrast the data in the tables.

TABLE 4-4

Number	Digits to Count	Example*	Number of Significant Digits
Nonzero digits	All	3279	4
Leading zeros (zeros before an integer)	None	0.0045	2 (4 and 5 only)
Captive zeros (zeros between two integers)	All	5.007	4
Trailing zeros (zeros after the last integer)	Counted only if the number contains a decimal point	100 100. 100.0 0.0100	1 3 4 3 (1 and zero's following 1)
Scientific notation	All	1.7×10^{-4} 1.30×10^{-2}	2 3

* Significant digits are shaded.

About 12? No, exactly 12. Similarly, there is no uncertainty in the number *1*, as in *1 mole*. These are called exact numbers. They do not limit the number of significant digits in a calculation.

Addition and subtraction with significant digits

When doing addition and subtraction, the measurement with the digit having the lowest decimal value determines the correct number of significant digits in your answer. For example, when adding the values 3.75 and 4.1, since 4.1 has the lower decimal value, the answer will have only two significant digits.

$$3.75$$
$$+4.1 \leftarrow \text{determines significant digit place in answer}$$
$$\overline{7.85} \rightarrow \text{becomes 7.8}$$

Notice that extra digits are carried along in the calculation until your final answer is obtained. The answer is then rounded off to the correct number of significant digits.

Rounding fives

The value 7.85 is halfway between 7.80 and 7.90, so when the answer is rounded, how do you determine what the nearer tenth is? The following rule is frequently used because it is convenient and it causes you to round to the larger number as often as you round to the smaller number. *Round down if the digit before the 5 is even. Round up if the digit before the five is odd.*

PART 3 REVIEW

ANSWERS

■ Keyed to Objectives

H 40. 21.3 cm × 1.3 cm = 27.69 cm^2
= 28 cm^2

D 41. 12.0 + 2(32.0) = 76.0

percent C = $\frac{12.0}{76.0}$ = 15.7%

percent S = $\frac{64.0}{76.0}$ = 84.3%

D 42. Percent C = $\frac{24}{54}$ = 44%. No. The percent C is not 15.8.

E 43. 4.20 g N × $\frac{1 \text{ mol N}}{14.0 \text{ g N}}$ = 0.300 mol N

12.0 g O × $\frac{1 \text{ mol O}}{16.0 \text{ g O}}$ = 0.75 mol O

The ratio is 1.00 mol N to 2.50 mol O. Multiplying by 2 gives the ratio of 2.00 mol N to 5.00 mol O. The empirical formula is N_2O_5.

E 44. In a 100 gram sample:

40 g C × $\frac{1 \text{ mol C}}{12.0 \text{ g C}}$ = 3.33 mol C

6.7 g H × $\frac{1 \text{ mol H}}{1.0 \text{ g H}}$ = 6.67 mol H

53.3 g O × $\frac{1 \text{ mol O}}{16.0 \text{ g O}}$ = 3.33 mol O

The ratio is 1.00 mol C to 2.00 mol H to 1.00 mol O. The formula is CH_2O.

E 45. 4.80 g C × $\frac{1 \text{ mol C}}{12.0 \text{ g C}}$ = 0.400 mol C

0.40 g H × $\frac{1 \text{ mol H}}{1.00 \text{ g H}}$ = 0.40 mol H

PART 3 REVIEW

Boxed numbers indicate questions that involve skills in interpretation, application, and analysis.

40. The length and width of a piece of paper is measured to the nearest tenth of a centimeter. The length is 21.3 cm and the width is 1.3 cm. Calculate the area and record an answer that has one and only one uncertain digit.   *Ans.* 28 cm

41. Calculate the percent carbon and the percent sulfur in carbon disulfide.   *Ans.* 15.7% C, 84.3% S

42. A 54-g sample of an unknown compound contains 24 g of carbon and 30 g of sulfur. Is the compound carbon disulfide? How do you know?

43. A compound of nitrogen and oxygen is found to contain 4.20 g of nitrogen and 12.0 g of oxygen. Find the empirical formula for this compound.   *Ans.* N_2O_5

44. A 43-g sample of a compound contains 40% by mass carbon, 6.7% by mass hydrogen, and 53.3% by mass oxygen. What is the compound's empirical formula?   *Ans.* CH_2O

45. A compound is composed of 4.80 g of carbon and 0.40 g of hydrogen. Calculate the empirical formula.   *Ans.* CH

46. The molar mass of the compound in item 45 is 78 g. What is the molecular formula?   *Ans.* C_6H_6

47. When 20.16 g of magnesium oxide reacts with carbon, carbon monoxide and 12.16 g of magnesium are produced. What is the empirical formula for magnesium oxide?
   Ans. MgO

48. Look back at the number of moles calculated to determine the mole ratios in Examples 4-8 and 4-9. How many significant digits are there in the number of moles calculated? Which measurement in each example determines the number of significant digits in each answer?

49. The following measurements were properly recorded so that the final digit is the uncertain digit. How many significant digits are represented by each measurement?

a. 21.35 cm   **d.** 0.000823 kg
b. 8.705 g   **e.** 0.0910 m
c. 121.2000 g   **f.** 38 002 cm

50. Determine the answer to **a** through **f**. Use the correct number of significant digits in your answers.

a. 7.2 mm × 1.56 mm =   **d.** 288 g/16.9 cm^3 =
b. 99.5 cm^2 × 0.0084 cm = **e.** 0.001 g + 5.3 g + 162 g =
c. 63.6 g/2.7 cm^3 =   **f.** 32.58 cm^3 − 5.2 cm^3 =

51. Round each of the following measurements to two places after the decimal.

a. 0.03466 g   **c.** 6.2477 kg   **e.** 87.465 g   **g.** 63.9972 kJ
b. 94.117 km   **d.** 0.035 cm   **f.** 4.2853 cm^3

◄ **PROBLEM-SOLVING STRATEGY**

Use your calculator first to determine what the numerical answer is, and then round it off to the proper number of significant digits. (See Strategy, page 134.)

PART 3
Section 4.12 *continued*

☰CLOSE

Summing Up Main Ideas

Have students describe the steps they would use to determine a compound's empirical and molecular formulas if they knew its percent composition. Their answers should resemble Table 4–3 (p. 146). After determining the empirical formula, the molecular formula can be determined by dividing the molecular formula mass by the empirical formula mass.

Have students summarize the rules for significant digits. Assign teams to go back to earlier Practice Problems and Part Review problems to see if their answers conform to the rules.

PART 3 REVIEW

Assign the Part Review questions.

Evaluating Skills

These skills are evaluated in the Part Review questions indicated.
Analyzing data: 40, 41, 42, 43, 44, 45, 46, 47, 48, 49;
Calculating: 40, 41, 42, 43, 44, 45, 46, 47; **Verifying results:** 40, 41, 42, 43, 44, 45, 46, 47;
Applying a strategy: 41, 42, 43, 44, 45, 46, 47, 48, 49, 50, 51;
Determining main ideas: 42, 48, 49, 50, 51; **Classifying:** 42

The ratio is 1.00 mol C to 1.00 mol H. The empirical formula is CH.

E **46.** $n = \dfrac{78\ \cancel{g/mol}}{13\ \cancel{g/mol}} = 6$

The molecular formula is C_6H_6.

E **47.** $12.16\ \cancel{g\ Mg} \times \dfrac{1\ mol\ Mg}{24.3\ \cancel{g\ Mg}}$
$= 0.500\ mol\ Mg$

$8.00\ \cancel{g\ O} \times \dfrac{1\ mol\ O}{16.0\ \cancel{g\ O}} = 0.500\ mol\ O$

The ratio is 1.00 mol Mg to 1.00 mol O. The formula is MgO.

F **48.** 4.8: 2 significant digits, mass of O
4–9: 3 significant digits, mass of O

F **49. a.** 4   **d.** 3
b. 4   **e.** 3
c. 7   **f.** 5

F **50. a.** 11 mm^2 **d.** 17.0 g/cm^3
b. 0.84 cm^3 **e.** 167 g
c. 24 g/cm^3 **f.** 27 cm^3

F **51. a.** 0.03 g   **e.** 87.46 g
b. 94.12 km   **f.** 4.29 cm^3
c. 6.25 kg   **g.** 64.00 kJ
d. 0.04 cm

Chemical Calculations and Measurement

Estimated time: (30 minutes prelab, 1 or 2 lab periods, 15 minutes postlab)

Process Skills

Measuring
Predicting
Analyzing data
Calculating
Determining sources of error

Preparation

■ Materials

(for a class of 24, working in pairs)

Apparatus

(12 of each unless noted)
centigram balance (preferably 24), ring stands, ring clamps, filter paper, funnels, stirring rods, wash bottles, massing boats, 150-mL beakers (24), 400-mL beakers, evaporating dishes, marking pencils, hot plates (2)

Reagents

■ 100 g of strontium chloride hexahydrate solid, $SrCl_2 \cdot 6H_2O$

■ 50 g of sodium carbonate monohydrate solid, $Na_2CO_3 \cdot H_2O$

■ distilled or deionized water

■ Preparation Hints

Spend a few minutes of class time to explain what is required for prelab calculations. Provide students with a blank copy of the prelab data table. Provide a means to dry the contents of the evaporating dishes and the 400-mL beakers.

■ Safety

Remind students that although a hot plate may look cool, it may be hot and can burn, so avoid touching it.

Laboratory

Investigation

Chemical Calculations and Measurement

Measurement is one of the hallmarks of every science. Of all the measurements made in chemistry, those made when substances react are the most important.

In this experiment, you will use a balanced chemical equation and known amounts of reactants to predict the masses of the products. You will then experimentally check your prediction by measuring the actual mass of the products. In this way, you will obtain a working, practical understanding of molar relationships and an appreciation of the importance of chemical equations.

■ Objectives

Balance the equation for a given reaction and **calculate** the mass of each product.

Measure the actual masses of the product and compare them with the predicted masses.

■ Materials

Apparatus
□ balance
□ stirring rods
□ ring stand
□ ring clamp
□ filter paper
□ funnel

□ wash bottle
□ massing boats
□ 2 150-mL beakers
□ 400-mL beaker
□ evaporating dish
□ marking pencil
□ hot plate

Reagents
□ strontium chloride hexahydrate, $SrCl_2 \cdot 6H_2O$
□ sodium carbonate monohydrate, $Na_2CO_3 \cdot H_2O$
□ distilled or deionized water

■ Procedure

Part 1

1. A strontium chloride solution(aq) mixed with a sodium carbonate solution(aq) yields strontium carbonate(s) and sodium chloride(aq). Write and balance the equation for this reaction.

2. Calculate and record the masses of 0.010 mol of $SrCl_2 \cdot 6H_2O$ and $Na_2CO_3 \cdot H_2O$.

3. Using the balanced equation and assuming the complete conversion of 0.010 mol of reactants to products, calculate and record your mass predictions for $SrCO_3(s)$ and NaCl(s).

Part 2

4. 👓 🧴 Put on your lab apron and safety goggles.

5. Mass a clean, dry evaporating dish to the nearest 0.01 g and record this mass.

6. Using clean, dry massing boats, separately mass 0.010 mol of $SrCl_2 \cdot 6H_2O$ and 0.010 mol of $Na_2CO_3 \cdot H_2O$.

7. Transfer the mass of each solid from step 6 into separate 150-mL beakers. Add

Prelab Data Table

Balanced equation from procedure (before lab) 1.

$SrCl_2 + Na_2CO_3 \rightarrow SrCO_3 + 2NaCl$

Calculated molar mass of $SrCl_2 \cdot 6H_2O$	266.6 g/mol
Calculated molar mass of $Na_2CO_3 \cdot H_2O$	124.0 g/mol
Required mass of $SrCl_2(s) \cdot 6H_2O$ needed for a 0.010 mol	2.67 g
Required mass of $Na_2CO_3(s) \cdot H_2O$ needed for a 0.010 mol	1.24 g
Calculated molar mass of $SrCO_3$	147.6 g/mol

50 mL deionized or distilled water. Stir with separate stirring rods until the solids dissolve.

8. Determine the mass of a piece of filter paper. Record this mass on the data table.

9. Pour the SrCl₂ solution into the beaker containing the Na₂CO₃ solution. Stir. Place your massed filter paper into a funnel on a ring stand. Under the funnel, place a clean, dry, massed (to the nearest 0.01 g) 400-mL beaker that has been marked "SrCO₃." Record this mass.

10. Filter the mixture of SrCO₃(s) and NaCl(aq).

11. Wash the SrCO₃(s) three times with deionized water from a wash bottle.

12. Place the marked 400-mL beaker with the NaCl(aq) on a hot plate in the hood until the water has evaporated. Finish the drying process at room temperature. After this solid has cooled, record the mass of the beaker and the solid sodium chloride.

⚠ **CAUTION: Beakers heated to dryness may crack when reused.**

13. Transfer the filter paper and the solid SrCO₃(s) into the massed evaporating dish.

14. Place the dish with the filter paper and strontium carbonate in a drying oven. When it is dry, record the total mass.

■ Data Analysis

Data Table

Mass (g)		Calculated Mass		Percentage Error	
☐ clean dry evaporating dish	___ g	SrCO₃(s)	___ g	SrCO₃(s)	___ %
☐ dry piece of filter paper	___ g	NaCl(s)	___ g	NaCl(s)	___ %
☐ 400-mL beaker	___ g	**Actual Mass**			
☐ 400-mL beaker and solid NaCl	___ g				
☐ evaporating dish, filter paper(s), and strontium carbonate	___ g	SrCO₃(s)	___ g		
		NaCl(s)	___ g		

1. From your data, calculate the actual mass of SrCO₃(s) produced. Record this mass on the data table.

2. From your data, calculate the actual mass of NaCl(s) produced. Record this mass on the data table.

3. Determine the percentage error of SrCO₃(s) and NaCl(s). To do this, find the difference between each of your predicted masses and the actual mass of that substance produced. Divide each difference by the predicted mass and multiply by 100.

■ Conclusions

1. Look at your completed data and consult with the other members of your class. Do your experimental data support your predictions?

2. How can you account for the differences between the results you obtained and those of other classmates?

MOLAR RELATIONSHIPS **155**

■ **Procedural Hints**

Have students clearly label all beakers and evaporating dishes before their contents are dried. A second piece of filter paper may be used, if needed. Add its mass to the final mass of the evaporating dish, filter paper(s), and strontium carbonate.

Disposal

Combine all mixtures. Let settle and decant. Pour the decantate down the drain. Wrap the solids in newspaper and put in the wastebasket

Data Analysis

(See Prelab Data Table below.)

■ **Sample Data**

1. Sample data are shown in the table below.

2. Sample data are shown in the table below.

3. $\dfrac{(\text{predicted mass} - \text{actual mass})}{\text{predicted mass}}$

$\times 100 = \%$ of error

For SrCO₃:

$\dfrac{(1.48 - 1.43)}{1.48} \times 100 = 3.38\%$

For NaCl:

$\dfrac{(1.17 - 1.15)}{1.17} \times 100 = 1.71\%$

Conclusions

1. yes

2. Some reasons for differences are not washing all material into filter paper, error in measuring, and rounding errors.

Data Table

Mass		Calculated Mass		Percentage Error	
clean, dry evaporating dish	38.69 g	SrCO₃(s)	1.48 g	SrCO₃(s)	3.38%
dry piece of filter paper	0.69 g	NaCl(s)	1.17 g	NaCl(s)	1.71%
400-mL beaker	141.74 g				
400-mL beaker and solid NaCl	142.8 g	**Actual Mass**			
evaporating dish, filter paper(s), and strontium carbonate	40.81 g	SrCO₃(s)	1.43 g		
		NaCl(s)	1.15 g		

CHAPTER 4
Review

Chapter 4
Review
ANSWERS
begin on page
T159a.

4 CHAPTER Review

Summary

Counting Atoms

- Avogadro's number represents the number of atoms, ions, molecules, or other particles in one mole. The mass of Avogadro's number of any of these is called the molar mass.

- The molar mass of a compound is found by adding the masses of the atoms in that compound.

Concentration

- Concentration is often described by ppm (parts per million) or molarity. Molarity is the number of moles of a substance per liter of solution.

Formula Calculations

- Percent composition data can be used to compare the composition of compounds having the same elements and also to determine the empirical formula for a compound.

- The empirical formula for a compound represents the simplest whole number ratio of the atoms in a compound. It can represent the formula unit of an ionic compound. The formulas for molecular compounds can be the same as the empirical formula or some multiple of it.

- The uncertainty in a measurement is indicated by the number of digits recorded for that measurement. When making calculations using experimentally measured quantities, the result must be rounded to the correct number of digits.

Chemically Speaking

Avogadro's number *4.1*

accuracy *4.12*

concentration *4.7*

empirical formula *4.10*

mole *4.1*

molarity *4.7*

molar mass *4.2*

molecular formula *4.11*

percent composition *4.9*

ppm *4.12*

precision *4.6*

significant digits *4.12*

Concept Mapping

Using the method of concept mapping described at the front of this book, complete the following concept map for the term *moles*.

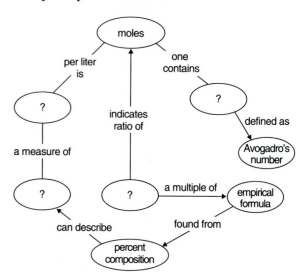

Questions and Problems

COUNTING ATOMS

A. Objective: **Define** *the term mole and* **describe** *how it is used in chemistry.*

1. What are moles and how are they used in chemistry?
2. Why does the mole have to be such a large number?
3. How many years is a mole of seconds?
4. The human heart beats an average of 65 beats per minute, and the average human life span is 75 years.
   a. How many moles of heartbeats occur in one person's lifetime?
   b. How long would a person have to live in order for their heart to beat a mole of heartbeats?

PROBLEM-SOLVING
► STRATEGIES

Students apply these strategies in the following questions.

■ Factor-label method: 3, 4, 5, 6, 7, 8, 9, 10, 11, 12, 13, 14, 18, 19, 20, 21, 22, 23, 24, 25, 26, 27, 28, 29, 30, 31, 32, 33, 35, 36, 37, 38, 42, 43, 44, 45

■ Making an estimate: 12, 13, 14, 15, 16, 17, 18, 19, 20, 21, 22

■ Using calculators: 3, 4, 5, 6, 7, 8, 9, 10, 11, 12, 13, 14, 18, 19, 20,

B. Objective: **Explain** *and* **calculate** *molar mass.*

5. Calculate the molar mass of each of the following compounds.
   a. K_2SO_4 f. iron(II) sulfate
   b. H_3PO_4 g. iron(III) sulfate
   c. NH_4Cl h. copper(I) carbonate
   d. Na_3PO_4 i. copper(II) carbonate
   e. $Ni(CN)_2$ j. dinitrogen trioxide
6. What is the mass of one mole of each of the following compounds?
   a. AgCl   d. $CuSO_4$
   b. $MgCrO_4$ e. chromium(VI) oxide
   c. K_2CrO_4 f. sodium sulfide
7. Calculate the molar mass of each compound.
   a. 2 moles of compound A have a mass of 80 grams.
   b. 1.57×10^{23} molecules of compound B have a mass of 7.56 g.
   c. 1.35 g of compound C contain 4.55×10^{22} molecules.
8. What is the molar mass of fluorine gas?
9. What is the molar mass of cobalt(II) chloride?
10. What is the molar mass of sulfuric acid, H_2SO_4?
11. What is the molar mass of juglone, $C_{10}H_6O_3$, a dye made from the husks of black walnuts?

C. Objective: **Calculate** *equivalents among grams, moles, and numbers of particles.*

12. How many carbon atoms contain the same amount of mass as one molybdenum atom?
13. How many iron atoms are there in 5.33 moles of iron(III) chloride?
14. How many moles of oxygen atoms are in 1.2×10^{25} molecules of diphosphorous pentoxide?
15. How many atoms are in one mole of neon atoms?
16. How many molecules are there in one mole of silver cyanide molecules?
17. How many atoms are in one molecule of a diatomic element?

18. If 2.5 moles of hydrogen gas (H_2) react in an experiment, how many grams of hydrogen react?
19. How many atoms are in a copper penny if the penny has a mass of 2.5 grams? Assume the penny is pure copper.
20. For each of the following, find the number of atoms represented or the number of molecules represented.
    a. 28 g of sodium   d. 2.4 g of calcium
    b. 28 g of iron   e. 150 g of chlorine gas
    c. 150 g of zinc   f. 21 g of fluorine gas
21. a. How many moles are in a 22-g sample of manganese?
    b. How many molecules are in 14.0 g of nitrogen gas?
    c. How many atoms of aluminum are in 17.1 g of aluminum sulfate?
    d. What is the mass of one atom of aluminum?
    e. How many atoms of carbon are in 17.1 g of sucrose, $C_{12}H_{22}O_{11}$?
22. Dioxin, $C_{12}H_4Cl_4O_2$, is a powerful poison. How many moles of dioxin are there in 700. g of dioxin? How many molecules are there?

CONCENTRATION

D. Objective: **Calculate** *the amount of a compound in a given volume of solution, using the concept of molarity.*

23. A $0.050M$ solution of glycerine, $C_3H_8O_3$, and a $0.050M$ solution of lysine, $C_5H_{11}NO_2$, are prepared. Which solution contains the most dissolved molecules per liter?
24. Determine the number of moles of zinc sulfate, $ZnSO_4$, in each solution.

Moles of $ZnSO_4$	Volume of solution	Molarity
	3.44 L	1.71 M
	0.400 L	7.8×10^{-1} M
	650 mL	0.725 M

Boxed numbers indicate questions that involve skills in interpretation, application, and analysis.

MOLAR RELATIONSHIPS **157**

21, 22, 23, 24, 25, 26, 27, 28, 29, 30, 31, 32, 33, 35, 36, 37, 38, 41, 42, 43, 44, 45

7, 8, 9, 10, 11, 12, 13, 14, 18, 19, 20, 21, 22, 23, 24, 25, 26, 27, 28, 29, 30, 31, 32, 33, 35, 36, 37, 38, 42, 43, 44, 45

■ Verifying your answer: 3, 4, 5, 6,

T157

25. How many grams of sodium sulfate, Na_2SO_4, are contained in 1.50 L of $0.25M$ solution?
26. How many grams of silver nitrate, $AgNO_3$, are contained in 500. mL of $0.200M$ solution?

E. Objective: Explain *how to prepare molar solutions.*

27. Describe how you would prepare 1.50 L of a $0.25M$ solution of sodium sulfate.
28. How many grams of ammonium sulfate, $(NH_4)_2SO_4$, are required to prepare 3.50 L of a $1.55M$ solution?
29. A student needs to prepare 100. mL of a $0.50M$ ammonium chloride, NH_4Cl, solution. Describe how it should be done.
30. How many grams of manganese nitrate, $Mn(NO_3)_2$, are needed to prepare 500. mL of a $0.750M$ solution?

FORMULA CALCULATIONS

F. Objective: Calculate *percent composition by mass and use it to compare compounds.*

31. Calculate the percent by mass of each element in limestone, $CaCO_3$.
32. A sample of the oxide of sodium has a mass of 4.55 g. Of this mass, 1.17 g is oxygen. Find the percent composition of each element in sodium oxide.
33. It is known that two compounds contain only tungsten and carbon. Analysis of the two compounds gives 1.82 g of tungsten per 0.12 g of carbon for the first compound, and 3.70 g of tungsten per 0.12 g of carbon for the second compound. Compare the percent composition of the two compounds.

G. Objective: Determine *empirical and molecular formulas for compounds.*

34. The compound benzene has two formulas, CH and C_6H_6. Which is the empirical formula and which is the molecular formula?

35. There are two common oxides of sulfur. One contains 32 g of sulfur for each 32 g of oxygen. The other oxide contains 32 g of sulfur for each 48 g of oxygen. What are the empirical formulas for the two oxides?
36. A form of phosphorus called red phosphorus is used in match heads. When 0.062 g of red phosphorus burns, 0.142 g of phosphorus oxide is formed. What is the empirical formula of this oxide?
37. A compound is composed of 7.20 g of carbon, 1.20 g of hydrogen, and 9.60 g of oxygen. The molar mass of the compound is 180 g. Find the empirical and molecular formulas for this compound.
38. Oxalic acid is a compound used in cosmetics and paints. A 0.725-g sample of oxalic acid was found to contain 0.194 g of carbon, 0.016 g of hydrogen, and 0.516 g of oxygen. If the molar mass of oxalic acid is 90.04 g/mol, what is the molecular formula?

H. Objective: Recognize *significant digits in a recorded measurement and* determine *the number of significant digits in a calculated value.*

39. The following problems have been solved using a calculator. Express the answer in the proper units and significant digits.
  a. $\dfrac{21.3 \text{ cm}}{1.3 \text{ cm}} = 16.384\ 615$
  b. $\dfrac{6.34 \text{ cm}^2 \times 1.2 \text{ cm}}{1.217 \text{ cm}^2} = 6.251\ 437\ 9$
  c. $13.21 \text{ m} \times 61.5 \text{ m} = 812.415$
  d. $\dfrac{21.50 \text{ cm}}{8.50 \text{ in}} = 2.529\ 411\ 765$
  e. $63.43 + 34.5 = 97.93$
  f. $124 - 87.2 = 36.8$
  g. $27.35 - 21.2 = 6.15$
40. Determine the number of significant digits in each measurement listed below.
  a. 1.005 kg   d. 0.00380 mol
  b. 35440.002 m   e. 100 m
  c. 0.005 g   f. 7.8×10^{-3} kJ

41. Perform the following operations on these measurements. Express your answer with the correct number of significant digits.
  a. 14.58 m + 33.1 m + 0.095 m
  b. 9.55 g/8.8 mL
  c. 8.13 g/10.00 mL
  d. 34.3 g − 30.0001 g

Critical Thinking

SYNTHESIS WITHIN THE CHAPTER

42. Use the graph to answer the questions.
  a. Find the molarity of the solution.
  b. What are the units of molarity?
  c. What is the mass of zinc chloride dissolved in 2.00 L of the solution?
  d. What volume of this solution would contain 3.0 moles of zinc chloride?

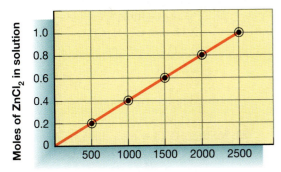

Volume of ZnCl₂ (in mL)

43. Use your knowledge of molarity to fill in the blank spaces in the table below.

SYNTHESIS ACROSS CHAPTERS

44. Determine the simplest formula for the following compounds and write their name.
  a. 63.6% iron and 36.4% sulfur
  b. 79.9% copper and 20.1% sulfur
45. Describe how you would prepare 2.00 liters of a 3.00M solution of HCl by using a 100-mL graduated cylinder, a 2-L volumetric flask, and a stock solution of HCl, which is 37% HCl by volume (the rest is water) and has a density of 1.37 g/mL.

Projects

46. Measure your classroom and find its volume. Record the correct number of significant digits in your measurements and your answer.
47. Think of something you can count by measuring the mass. Measure the mass of known amounts of this thing. Make a graph that shows the relationship between the mass of a known number and the number of your item.

Research and Writing

48. The kind of careful analysis needed in determining experimental uncertainty led to the discovery of argon and a Nobel Prize for Baron Rayleigh and William Ramsey. Research how this discovery came about and write a paper about the role of experimental uncertainty in this discovery.

Formula of substance dissolved	Grams dissolved	Moles dissolved	Volume of solution	Molarity
CaCl₂	15.00 g		0.200 L	
Fe(NO₃)₃			1.00 L	1.00M
Na₂CO₃		0.035 mol		1.50M
MgSO₄			300 mL	2.4×10^{-2} M

☐ Boxed numbers indicate questions that involve skills in interpretation, application, and analysis.

Chapter 4 Review Concept Map

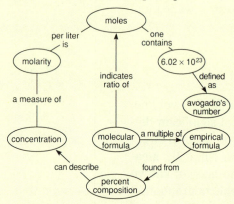

1. Moles are the basic counting unit in chemistry. All moles contain the same number of particles, 6.02×10^{23}. Using the atomic masses given in the periodic table, the masses of equal numbers of particles can be calculated and then measured.

2. Since atoms are too small to be counted, a large counting unit, Avogadro's number, is needed. Thus, the number of atoms in 1 mole, or 12 grams, of carbon is large because atoms are so small.

3. $6.02 \times 10^{23} \, s \times \dfrac{1 \text{ year}}{365.25 \text{ days}}$

$\times \dfrac{1 \text{ day}}{24 \text{ hrs.}} \times \dfrac{1 \text{ hr.}}{60 \text{ min}} \times \dfrac{1 \text{ min}}{60 \, s}$

$= 1.91 \times 10^{16}$ years
This is one million times the age of the universe.

4. a. $75 \text{ years} \times \dfrac{365.25 \text{ days}}{1 \text{ year}} \times \dfrac{24 \text{ hrs.}}{1 \text{ day}}$

$\times \dfrac{60 \text{ min}}{1 \text{ hr.}} \times \dfrac{65 \text{ beats}}{\text{min}}$

$= 2.6 \times 10^{9}$ beats / lifetime

$2.6 \times 10^{9} \text{ beats} \times \dfrac{1 \text{ mole beats}}{6.02 \times 10^{23} \text{ beats}}$

$= 4.3 \times 10^{-15}$ moles of beats

b. $6.02 \times 10^{23} \text{ beats} \times \dfrac{1 \text{ year}}{3.4 \times 10^{7} \text{ beats}}$

$= 1.8 \times 10^{16}$ years

5. a. $2(39.1) + 32.1 + 4(16.0) = 174.3$ g
   b. $3(1.0) + 31.0 + 4(16.0) = 98.0$ g
   c. $14.0 + 4(1.0) + 35.5 = 53.5$ g
   d. $3(23.0) + 31.0 + 4(16.0) = 164.0$ g
   e. $58.7 + 2(12.0) + 2(14.0) = 110.7$ g

f. $55.8 + 32.1 + 4(16.0) = 151.9$ g
g. $2(55.8) + 3(32.1) + 12(16.0)$
   $= 399.9$ g
h. $2(63.6) + 12.0 + 3(16.0) = 187.2$ g
i. $63.6 + 12.0 + 3(16.0) = 123.6$ g
j. $2(14.0) + 3(16.0) = 76.0$ g

6. a. $107.9 + 35.5 = 143.4$ g
   b. $24.3 + 52.0 + 4(16.0) = 140.3$ g
   c. $2(39.1) + 52.0 + 4(16.0) = 194.2$ g
   d. $63.6 + 32.1 + 4(16.0) = 159.7$ g
   e. $52.0 + 3(16.0) = 100.0$ g
   f. $2(23.0) + 32.1 = 78.1$ g

7. a. $\dfrac{80 \text{ g A}}{2 \text{ mol A}} = \dfrac{40 \text{ g A}}{1 \text{ mol A}}$

b. $\dfrac{7.56 \text{ g B}}{1.57 \times 10^{23} \text{ molecules B}}$
$\times \dfrac{6.02 \times 10^{23} \text{ molecules B}}{1 \text{ mol B}} = \dfrac{29.0 \text{ g}}{\text{mol B}}$

c. $\dfrac{1.35 \text{ g C}}{4.55 \times 10^{22} \text{ molecules C}}$
$\times \dfrac{6.02 \times 10^{23} \text{ molecules C}}{1 \text{ mol C}} = \dfrac{17.9 \text{ g}}{\text{mol C}}$

8. $2(19.0) = 38.0$ g
9. $58.9 + 2(35.5) = 130.0$ g
10. $2(1.0) + 32.0 + 4(16.0) = 98.0$ g
11. $10(12.0) + 6(1.0) + 3(16.0) = 174$ g
12. $\dfrac{95.9 \text{ g/mol Mo}}{12.0 \text{ g/mol C}} = 7.95$ mol C / mol Mo
One molybdenum atom has slightly more mass than 8 carbon atoms.

13. $5.33 \text{ mol FeCl}_3 \times \dfrac{6.02 \times 10^{23} \text{ atoms Fe}}{1 \text{ mol FeCl}_3}$

$= 3.21 \times 10^{24}$ atoms Fe

14. $1.2 \times 10^{25} \text{ molecules P}_2\text{O}_5$
$\times \dfrac{5 \text{ mol O}}{6.02 \times 10^{23} \text{ molecules P}_2\text{O}_5}$

$= 1.0 \times 10^{2}$ mol O

15. 6.02×10^{23} atoms of Ne
16. 6.02×10^{23} formula units of Ag(CN)_2
17. 2 atoms
18. $2.5 \text{ mol H}_2 \times \dfrac{2.0 \text{ g H}_2}{1 \text{ mol H}_2} = 5.0 \text{ g H}_2$

19. $2.5 \text{ g Cu} \times \dfrac{6.02 \times 10^{23} \text{ atoms}}{63.6 \text{ g Cu}}$

$= 2.4 \times 10^{22}$ atoms Cu

20. a. $28 \text{ g Na} \times \dfrac{6.02 \times 10^{23} \text{ atoms Na}}{23 \text{ g Na}}$

$= 7.3 \times 10^{23}$ atoms Na

b. $28 \text{ g Fe} \times \dfrac{6.02 \times 10^{23} \text{ atoms Fe}}{55.8 \text{ g Fe}}$

$= 3.0 \times 10^{23}$ atoms Fe

c. $150 \text{ g Zn} \times \dfrac{6.02 \times 10^{23} \text{ atoms Zn}}{65.4 \text{ g Zn}}$

$= 1.4 \times 10^{24}$ atoms Zn

d. $2.4 \text{ g Ca} \times \dfrac{6.02 \times 10^{23} \text{ atoms Ca}}{40.1 \text{ g Ca}}$

$= 3.6 \times 10^{22}$ atoms Ca

e. $150 \text{ g Cl}_2 \times \dfrac{6.02 \times 10^{23} \text{ molecules Cl}_2}{71 \text{ g Cl}_2}$

$= 1.3 \times 10^{24}$ molecules Cl_2

f. $21 \text{ g F}_2 \times \dfrac{6.02 \times 10^{23} \text{ molecules F}_2}{38.0 \text{ g F}_2}$

$= 3.3 \times 10^{23}$ molecules F_2

21. a. $22 \text{ g Mn} \times \dfrac{1 \text{ mol Mn}}{54.9 \text{ g Mn}} = 0.40$ mol Mn

b. $14.0 \text{ g N}_2 \times \dfrac{6.02 \times 10^{23} \text{ molecules N}_2}{28.0 \text{ g N}_2}$

$= 3.01 \times 10^{23}$ molecules N_2

c. $17.1 \text{ g Al}_2(\text{SO}_4)_3$

$\times \dfrac{6.02 \times 10^{23} \text{ formula units Al}_2(\text{SO}_4)_3}{342.0 \text{ g Al}_2(\text{SO}_4)_3}$

$\times \dfrac{2 \text{ atoms Al}}{1 \text{ formula unit Al}_2(\text{SO}_4)_3}$

$= 6.02 \times 10^{22}$ atoms Al

d. $\dfrac{27.0 \text{ g Al}}{6.02 \times 10^{23} \text{ atoms Al}}$

$= 4.48 \times 10^{-23}$ g / atom Al

e. $17.1 \text{ g C}_{12}\text{H}_{22}\text{O}_{11}$

$\times \dfrac{6.02 \times 10^{23} \text{ molecules C}_{12}\text{H}_{22}\text{O}_{11}}{342.0 \text{ g C}_{12}\text{H}_{22}\text{O}_{11}}$

$\times \dfrac{12 \text{ atoms C}}{1 \text{ molecule C}_{12}\text{H}_{22}\text{O}_{11}}$

$= 3.61 \times 10^{23}$ atoms C

22. a. $700 \text{ g C}_{12}\text{H}_4\text{Cl}_4\text{O}_2$

$\times \dfrac{1 \text{ mol C}_{12}\text{H}_4\text{Cl}_4\text{O}_2}{322.0 \text{ g C}_{12}\text{H}_4\text{Cl}_4\text{O}_2}$

$= 2.17 \text{ mol C}_{12}\text{H}_4\text{Cl}_4\text{O}_2$

b. $700 \text{ g C}_{12}\text{H}_4\text{Cl}_4\text{O}_2$

$\times \dfrac{6.02 \times 10^{23} \text{ molecules C}_{12}\text{H}_4\text{Cl}_4\text{O}_2}{322.0 \text{ g C}_{12}\text{H}_4\text{Cl}_4\text{O}_2}$

$= 1.31 \times 10^{24}$ molecules
$\text{C}_{12}\text{H}_4\text{Cl}_4\text{O}_2$

23. Neither. Both contain the same number of molecules (3.01×10^{23}) per liter.

24. Moles ZnSO_4:
5.88 mol
0.31 mol
0.471 mol

25. $1.50 \, L \times 0.25 \text{ mol}/L \times 142.0 \text{ g/mol}$
$= 53 \text{ g Na}_2\text{SO}_4$

26. $0.500 \, L \times 0.200 \text{ mol}/L$
$\times 170.0 \text{ g/mol} = 17.0 \text{ g AgNO}_3$

27. $1.50 \, L \times 0.25 \text{ mol}/L \times 142.0 \text{ g/mol}$
$= 53 \text{ g Na}_2\text{SO}_4$
Measure 53 g Na_2SO_4 and add enough water so that when the solution process is complete the volume is 1.50 L.

28. $3.50 \, L \times 1.55 \text{ mol}/L \times 132.0 \text{ g/mol}$
$= 716 \text{ g (NH}_4)_2\text{SO}_4$

29. $100 \text{ mL} \times 1 \, L/1000 \text{ mL} \times 0.50$
$\text{mol}/L \times 53.50 \text{ g/mol} = 2.7 \text{ g NH}_4\text{Cl}$
Measure 2.7 g of NH_4Cl and add enough water to yield 100 mL of solution.

30. $500 \text{ mL} \times 1 \, L/1000 \text{ mL}$
$\times 0.750 \text{ mol}/L \times 178.9 \text{ g/mol}$
$= 67.1 \text{ g Mn(NO}_3)_2$

31. $CaCO_3$: $40.1 + 12.0 + 3(16.0)$
$= 100.1$

Percent $Ca = \frac{40.1 \text{ g}}{100.1 \text{ g}} \times 100\%$

$= 40.06\%$

Percent $C = \frac{12.00 \text{ g}}{100.1 \text{ g}} \times 100\%$

$= 11.99\%$

Percent $O = \frac{48.00 \text{ g}}{100.1 \text{ g}} \times 100\%$

$= 47.95\%$

32. $4.55 \text{ g} - 1.17 \text{ g} = 3.38 \text{ g Na}$

Percent $Na = \frac{3.38 \text{ g}}{4.55 \text{ g}} \times 100\%$

$= 74.3\%$

Percent $O = \frac{1.17 \text{ g}}{4.55 \text{ g}} \times 100\%$

$= 25.7\%$

33. Compound A: $1.82 \text{ g} + 0.12 \text{ g}$
$= 1.94 \text{ g}$

Percent $W = \frac{1.82 \text{ g}}{1.94 \text{ g}} \times 100\%$

$= 93.8\%$

Percent $C = \frac{0.12 \text{ g}}{1.94 \text{ g}} \times 100\%$

$= 6.2\%$

Compound B: $3.70 \text{ g} + 0.12 \text{ g}$
$= 3.82 \text{ g}$

Percent $W = \frac{3.70 \text{ g}}{3.82 \text{ g}} \times 100\%$

$= 96.9\%$

Percent $C = \frac{0.12 \text{ g}}{3.82 \text{ g}} \times 100\%$

$= 3.1\%$

34. CH is the empirical formula.
C_6H_6 is the molecular formula.

35. $32 \text{ g S} \times \frac{1 \text{ mol S}}{32.0 \text{ g S}} = 1.0 \text{ mol S}$

$32 \text{ g O} \times \frac{1 \text{ mol O}}{16.0 \text{ g O}} = 2.0 \text{ mol O}$

Empirical formula: SO_2

$32 \text{ g S} \times \frac{1 \text{ mol S}}{32.0 \text{ g S}} = 1.0 \text{ mol S}$

$48 \text{ g O} \times \frac{1 \text{ mol O}}{16.0 \text{ g O}} = 3.0 \text{ mol O}$

Empirical formula: SO_3

36. $0.142 \text{ g} - 0.062 \text{ g} = 0.080 \text{ g O}$

$0.062 \text{ g P} \times \frac{1 \text{ mol P}}{31.0 \text{ g P}} = 0.0020 \text{ mol P}$

$0.080 \text{ g O} \times \frac{1 \text{ mol O}}{16.0 \text{ g O}}$

$= 0.00500 \text{ mol O}$

Empirical formula: P_2O_5

37. $7.20 \text{ g C} \times \frac{1 \text{ mol C}}{12.0 \text{ g C}} = 0.600 \text{ mol C}$

$1.20 \text{ g H} \times \frac{1 \text{ mol H}}{1.0 \text{ g H}} = 1.2 \text{ mol H}$

$9.60 \text{ g O} \times \frac{1 \text{ mol O}}{16.0 \text{ g O}} = 0.600 \text{ mol O}$

Divide all by 0.600;

$\frac{0.600 \text{ mol C}}{0.600} = 1.00 \text{ C}$

$\frac{1.2 \text{ mol H}}{0.600} = 2.0 \text{ H}$

$\frac{0.600 \text{ mol O}}{0.600} = 1.00 \text{ O}$

Empirical formula: CH_2O
Empirical formula mass $= 12.0$
$+ 2(1.0) + 16.0 = 30.0$

$\frac{180}{30} = 6$

Molecular formula: $C_6H_{12}O_6$

38. $0.194 \text{ g C} \times \frac{1 \text{ mol C}}{12.0 \text{ g C}} = 0.0162 \text{ mol C}$

$0.016 \text{ g H} \times \frac{1 \text{ mol H}}{1.0 \text{ g H}} = 0.016 \text{ mol H}$

$0.516 \text{ g O} \times \frac{1 \text{ mol O}}{16.0 \text{ g O}} = 0.0322 \text{ mol O}$

Divide all by 0.016;

$\frac{0.0162 \text{ mol C}}{0.016} = 1.0 \text{ C}$

$\frac{0.016 \text{ mol H}}{0.016} = 1.0 \text{ H}$

$\frac{0.0322 \text{ mol O}}{0.016} = 2.0 \text{ O}$

Empirical formula: CHO_2
Empirical formula mass $= 12.0$
$+ 1.0 + 2(16.00) = 45.0$

$\frac{90.04}{45.0} = 2$

Molecular formula: $C_2H_2O_4$

39. a. 16
b. 6.3 cm
c. 812 m^2
d. 2.53 cm/in.
e. 97.9
f. 36.8
g. 6.15

40. a. 4
b. 8
c. 1
d. 3
e. 1
f. 2

41. a. 47.8 m
b. 1.1 g/mL
c. 0.813 g/mL
d. 4.3 g

42. a. 0.40M
b. moles per liter
c. 109 g
d. 7.5 L

43. Formula
$CaCl_2$ 111.1
$Fe(NO_3)_3$ 241.8
Na_2CO_3 106.0
$MgSO_4$ 120.3
Grams
242 g $Fe(NO_3)_3$
3.7 g Na_2CO_3
0.87 g $MgSO_4$
Moles
0.135 mol $CaCl_2$
1.00 mol $Fe(NO_3)_3$
0.0072 mol $MgSO_4$
Volume
0.023 L Na_2CO_3
Molarity
0.675M $CaCl_2$

44. Assume 100.0 g of the compound
a. $63.6 \text{ g Fe} \times \frac{1 \text{ mol Fe}}{55.8 \text{ g Fe}}$

$= 1.14 \text{ mol Fe}$

$36.4 \text{ g S} \times \frac{1 \text{ mol S}}{32.1 \text{ g S}} = 1.13 \text{ mol S}$

Empirical formula: FeS
(iron(II)sulfide)

b. $79.9 \text{ g Cu} \times \frac{1 \text{ mol Cu}}{63.6 \text{ g Cu}} = 1.26 \text{ mol Cu}$

$20.1 \text{ g S} \times \frac{1 \text{ mol S}}{32.0 \text{ g S}} = 0.628 \text{ mol S}$

Empirical formula: Cu_2S
(copper(II) sulfide)

45. $2.00 \text{ L} \times \frac{3.00 \text{ mol HCl}}{\text{L solution}} \times \frac{36.5 \text{ g HCl}}{\text{mol HCl}}$

$\times \frac{1 \text{ mL solution}}{1.37 \text{ g solution}} \times \frac{100 \text{ g solution}}{37 \text{ g HCl}}$

$= 432 \text{ mL of the } 37\% \text{ HCl solution}$
Wearing safety goggles, face shield, lab apron, and rubber gloves, measure 432 mL of the concentrated HCl stock solution with the graduate and pour it into the 2-L volumetric flask, which contains 1 L of distilled water. Rinse the graduate with 50 mL of distilled water three times, and pour this into the 2-L volumetric flask. Finally, add enough water so that the final volume is 2.00 L when the solution process is complete.

Stoichiometry

Investigations	Demonstrations	Texas Essential Elements★
Laboratory Manual 5–1 S Laboratory Manual 5–2 M Laboratory Manual 5–3 M In-text Investigation, page T184		**Content:** 7.3 **Process:** 4.2
Laboratory Manual 5–4 M Laboratory Manual 5–5 I Laboratory Manual 5–6 I	Determining Product Amounts, page T178	**Content:** 7.3 **Process:** 10.1
		Content: 7.3 **Process:** 1.1, 1.2, 1.3, 2.1, 5.1, 6.3, 9.1, 9.2
		Process: 4.2, 7.1, 10.1, 10.2
		Content: 8.9 **Process:** 10.1, 10.2, 10.3, 10.4

KEY:
M–Microscale   **S**–Structured
I–Inquiry   **IM**–Inquiry Microscale

★*See pages T8–T11 for complete
listing of Texas Essential Elements.*

5

Stoichiometry

Chapter Rationale

Chapter 5 focuses on problem-solving skills and introduces several problem-solving strategies.

The use of verification strategies is an important part of problem solving. Stoichiometry problems can be verified experimentally. The experiments presented in this chapter will reinforce the problem-solving skills developed. Students can verify their calculated values by comparing them with experimental data. Stoichiometry involves extensive use of calculators. Since calculators commonly display eight or more digits, this is an opportunity to practice using significant digits. An understanding of stoichiometric calculations depends on an understanding of the underlying chemical processes: atoms and molecules combine in the ratio of small whole numbers.

About the Photograph

Recipes are more than lists of ingredients. They provide information about what conditions must be met to form the desired product.

In this chapter students will begin to see that chemical reactions involve more than balancing moles on both sides of a chemical equation. Just as in a recipe, reaction conditions must be met before a final product can be formed.

Chapter Planning Hints

Plan to spend six to ten class sessions to complete the chapter, including the Laboratory Investigation and Chapter Review. You may wish to obtain The World of Chemistry videotapes *The Mole* and *Metals* for use with this chapter. One optional demonstration is suggested for this chapter on page T178. You may wish to preview it at this time.

A recipe tells you how much of each ingredient you need in order to make a certain quantity of food, just as a balanced chemical equation tells you the amount of each reactant needed to produce a specific amount of product.

PART **1** **Quantitative Meaning of Equations**

Many products of chemical reactions are used every day. When a mixture of lard and lye is heated, the lard and lye are transformed into soap. Medications, such as penicillin, as well as plastics and synthetic fibers are also products of chemical reactions. It is through chemical reactions that important building materials such as aluminum and steel are obtained.

To avoid waste and obtain these products economically, a chemist needs to know exactly how much of each reactant is consumed to yield a desired amount of product. By applying the chemistry you already know—writing formulas, balancing equations, finding molar mass, doing molar conversions—you will be able to answer the questions *How much can I get?* or *How much do I need?*

5.1 Proportional Relationships

Determining the amounts of reactants needed to produce a specific amount of product is easier to do if you keep in mind that cooking and chemistry are similar. Cooking involves mixing the ingredients (reactants) given in a recipe (equation) to make a desired quantity of food (product).

The cook as chemist The recipe below gives the specific amount of each ingredient that is necessary to produce 24 brownies.

Brownies

$\frac{1}{2}$ cup butter
2 squares unsweetened chocolate (2 oz)
1 cup sugar
2 eggs

1 teaspoon vanilla
$\frac{2}{3}$ cup flour
$\frac{1}{2}$ teaspoon baking powder
$\frac{1}{4}$ teaspoon salt

Bake at 350°F for 30 minutes. Makes 24 brownies.

You could write this recipe to make it look more like a chemical equation.

$\frac{1}{2}$ cup butter + 2 squares chocolate +
1 cup sugar + 2 eggs +
1 teaspoon vanilla + $\frac{2}{3}$ cup flour + $\xrightarrow{\text{350°F}}$ 24 brownies
$\frac{1}{2}$ teaspoon baking powder +
$\frac{1}{4}$ teaspoon salt

Objectives

Part 1

A. *Determine* the number of moles of reactants or products involved in a chemical reaction, using mole ratios.

B. *Calculate* the masses of reactants or products in a reaction, given data in either moles or mass.

C. *Interpret data* to determine the amounts of reactants or products involved in replacement reactions, using molarity.

Developing Skills

Students may apply these skills in their study of Part 1.

Calculating: Have students determine the metric equivalent of each measurement in the recipe in Section 5.1 using 1 cup = 236 mL and 1 teaspoon = 4.9 mL or 1 teaspoon = 11 g.

Have students calculate the mass of 2 mol of magnesium atoms, 1 mol of oxygen molecules, and 2 mol of magnesium oxide. Add the mass of magnesium and oxygen and compare it to the mass of magnesium oxide.

Summarizing: Have students summarize the comparison of the mass of the reactants and products.

Applying a strategy: Have students interpret the correct number of significant digits for each measurement.

≡ FOCUS

Activate Prior Knowledge

Make arrangements to use the Home Economics department or school kitchen. Use the recipe given in Section 5.1 to prepare brownies for the class. Proportionality is at the center of converting recipes and applies to the stoichiometry of chemical reactions. Have students work in pairs to calculate the amount of each ingredient for a number of servings other than 24.

While waiting for the brownies to bake, discuss standards of measurement. Recipe measurements are usually given in cups, teaspoons, and so on. Display several different sizes of cups and spoons and ask students to describe the problems in having one cook use the recipe of another. Ask the students to convert the recipe into metric

(continued on page T162)

PART **1**

Section 5.1 *continued*

(continued from page T161)

units using the factors 1 cup = 236 mL and 1 teaspoon = 4.9 mL or 1 teaspoon = 11 g. Use only kitchen measuring devices such as a kitchen measuring cup marked in mL, and a kitchen balance for measuring. Do not use a balance from the chemistry lab! The question "Do eggs come in quantum units?" is an opportunity to introduce the concept of an indivisible amount.

≡TEACH

Science Background

The Chemist As Cook

Even though we cannot see individual atoms, they are the fundamental unit in chemistry. The existence of atoms, although proposed by Dalton in 1800, was not generally accepted until this century. Stoichiometry experiments provided the most convincing evidence for atoms.

Teaching Strategy

The Chemist As Cook

Making drawings of atoms and molecules before and after a reaction in which the number of atoms is shown to be conserved helps students understand the connection between macroscopic observations, the submicroscopic events, and the symbolic language (balanced equation) used to summarize the changes taking place. The drawings also help students develop an understanding for the underlying mathematical proportions.

Make drawings of the reaction of nitrogen with oxygen to form nitrogen dioxide. Write the balanced equation and use the drawings to explore the proportional ratios.

(continued on page T163)

DO YOU KNOW?

When magnesium rapidly combines with oxygen, a great deal of energy is produced in the form of light. Old-fashioned camera flashbulbs contained very fine magnesium wires that were surrounded by oxygen. They produced a flash of light when sparked by the camera battery. Harmful ultraviolet rays were filtered out by a coating on the bulb.

This recipe shows the ratios among the various ingredients used to make a specific number of brownies. The information in the recipe can be used proportionally. You can use twice as much of each ingredient if you want 48 brownies. You can cut the recipe in half if you want only 12 brownies.

Recipes are based on observations and on trial and error that have occurred over a long period of time. You can write any recipe you like, but it does not mean that the desired food will be the result. If the proportions used to make brownies are not correct, the product can be more like rocks than brownies!

The chemist as cook You know from Chapter 4 that an equation is like a recipe in that it also shows the ratios or proportions of reactants and products. Consider, for example, the equation for the combustion of magnesium in oxygen.

$$2 \text{ atoms Mg} + 1 \text{ molecule O}_2 \rightarrow 2 \text{ formula units of MgO}$$

Suppose you double the amounts of magnesium and oxygen used. Just like doubling the amounts of ingredients in the recipe to get more brownies, you should expect to get twice as much magnesium oxide.

$$4 \text{ atoms Mg} + 2 \text{ molecules O}_2 \rightarrow 4 \text{ formula units of MgO}$$

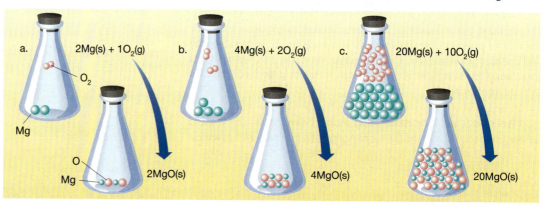

Figure 5-1 *The equation for the combustion of magnesium in oxygen to form magnesium oxide is represented here on the submicroscopic level. Notice how the proportions of reactants and products are the same.*

If you used ten times the original amount, how much magnesium oxide would you expect to get? As Figure 5-1 shows

$$20 \text{ atoms Mg} + 10 \text{ molecules O}_2 \rightarrow 20 \text{ formula units MgO}$$

You can continue to increase the amounts of magnesium and oxygen as long as the proportions are kept the same.

$$2 \times 10^{12} \text{ atoms Mg} + 1 \times 10^{12} \text{ molecules O}_2 \rightarrow$$
$$2 \times 10^{12} \text{ formula units MgO}$$
$$2(6 \times 10^{23}) \text{ atoms Mg} + 1(6 \times 10^{23}) \text{ molecules O}_2 \rightarrow$$
$$2(6 \times 10^{23}) \text{ formula units MgO}$$
$$2 \text{ (moles) atoms Mg} + 1 \text{ (mole) molecules O}_2 \rightarrow$$
$$2 \text{ (moles) formula units MgO}$$

The balanced equation describes the ratio in which the substances combine. The ratio is obtained from the coefficients of the balanced equation. That ratio is the **mole ratio** of the combining substances. In the example of magnesium oxide, the mole ratio of magnesium to oxygen is two to one. The mole ratio can be used to predict the amount of any reactant or product involved in a reaction if the amount of another reactant or product is known.

EXAMPLE 5-1

How many moles of potassium chlorate, $KClO_3(s)$, must decompose in order to produce 9 moles of oxygen gas? The other product is potassium chloride, KCl.

■ *Analyze the Problem* Since you are comparing numbers of moles (? moles $KClO_3$: 9 moles O_2), recognize that you may use a mole ratio to solve this problem. That ratio is obtained from a balanced equation, which you must write for this reaction.

$$2KClO_3(s) \rightarrow 2KCl(s) + 3O_2(g)$$

■ *Apply a Strategy* From the balanced equation, determine a mole ratio of potassium chlorate to oxygen. The ratios can be

$$\frac{2 \text{ mol } KClO_3}{3 \text{ mol } O_2} \quad \text{or} \quad \frac{3 \text{ mol } O_2}{2 \text{ mol } KClO_3}$$

Choose the mole ratio that gives you moles of potassium chlorate, $KClO_3$, in your answer.

■ *Work a Solution* Multiply moles of oxygen, O_2, given in the problem by the mole ratio.

$$? \text{ mol} = 9 \text{ mol } O_2 \times \frac{2 \text{ mol } KClO_3}{3 \text{ mol } O_2} = 6 \text{ mol } KClO_3$$

■ *Verify Your Answer* Look back at the balanced equation. If three times as much potassium chlorate, $KClO_3$, decomposes $(3 \times 2 \text{ mol} = 6 \text{ mol})$, then, since this is a proportional relationship, three times as much oxygen, O_2, will be produced, $(3 \times 3 \text{ mol} = 9 \text{ mol})$ which agrees with the data.

Practice Problems

1. Calculate the number of moles of sodium oxide, $Na_2O(s)$, that will be produced when 5.00 moles of solid sodium completely react with oxygen gas. **Ans.** 2.50 mol

2. Calculate the number of moles of oxygen gas needed to burn 1.22 moles of ammonia, $NH_3(g)$, and then find the number of moles of nitrogen dioxide, $NO_2(g)$, and gaseous water produced. **Ans.** 2.14 mol O_2; 1.22 mol NO_2; 1.83 mol H_2O

Figure 5-2 *Manufacturing everyday items, such as those shown here, requires an understanding of how to determine the amount of reactants needed to yield a specific amount of product.*

▶ **PROBLEM-SOLVING**

S T R A T E G Y

*You can use the **factor-label method** to help you choose the ratio. Moles of O_2 must cancel to leave moles of $KClO_3$ in the answer. (See Strategy, page 12.)*

(continued from page T162)
Have students complete the table at the bottom of this page. Emphasize that the ratio of molecules and of moles is identical, because all moles contain the same number of molecules. The masses, however, vary widely depending on the relative masses of the atoms.

Practice Problems

Assign the Practice Problems.

N_2 (g)	+	$2O_2$ (g)	→	$2NO_2$ (g)
1 molecule N_2	+	_____ molecules O_2	→	_____ molecules NO_2
10 molecules N_2	+	_____ molecules O_2	→	_____ molecules NO_2
1×10^{12} molecules N_2	+	_____ molecules O_2	→	_____ molecules NO_2
6.02×10^{23} molecules N_2	+	_____ molecules O_2	→	_____ molecules NO_2
_____ moles N_2	+	_____ moles O_2	→	_____ moles NO_2
_____ grams N_2	+	_____ grams O_2	→	_____ grams NO_2

▶ FOCUS ON
PROBLEM SOLVING

Activate Prior Knowledge

Remind students that they have probably used at least one of the verification methods mentioned in the strategy. In Chapter 4, students learned to make estimates. Estimating an answer is one way to verify an answer to a problem.

▶ TEACH
THE STRATEGY

Guided Practice

Students can apply this strategy when working any stoichiometry problem in this chapter, as well as any other problems they may encounter. In Practice Problem 1 on page 163, students can verify their result by estimating their answer from the balanced equation or by working the problem backwards from the answer to the mole ratio to the balanced equation.

Reteaching Idea

If students need some extra grounding in verifying problem-solving results, try having them solve the following problem, which involves nonthreatening data. The first- through fifth-grade classes of a school each have an equal number of boys and girls. The five classes have 18, 24, 30, 20, and 22 students. The average mass (weight) of girls in the school is 58 lbs. The average mass of boys is 65 lbs. From the data given, determine the total mass difference between the girls and the boys. Have students work in pairs, and when they have an answer, ask some pairs to outline on the chalkboard the steps in their solution, but *without revealing the answer*. Do not be concerned if some methods are not efficient. You should have at

(continued on page T165)

Verifying Your Answer

Beginning with the first worked example in this book, you have seen the phrase "verify your answer" as a part of the problem solution. There is good reason for this reminder. Good problem solvers tend to effectively look back at the work they have done in a problem before they proceed. They do this not only at the end of a problem, but depending upon the complexity of a problem, they may check their work throughout. Good problem solvers seem to know when they are likely to make mistakes, and they take steps to prevent those mistakes.

As you solve problems, begin to practice verification strategies until you discover the ones that work best for you. Some ideas for you to try include:

- **If you have done any calculations as you solved a problem, do them all a second time.** Redo each calculation immediately, rather than saving all of the work for the end. This strategy will increase your chances of reporting the correct number.

- **If a problem has been difficult for you to set up, you might want to review the logic of your work.** Does each step make sense? If you catch an error in your reasoning, then no amount of recalculating will salvage your work. You need to find another way to solve the problem.

- **One good way to check your work is to estimate the size of the answer.** You can do this either before or after you have done the actual calculations. When you are making an estimate, change difficult numbers into more simple ones that you can handle more easily. For example, in order to estimate the answer to 19×31, you might change the problem into 20×30, which you can easily see has the value of 600. Is the answer that you obtain to a problem close to the estimate?

- **Working the problem by another method is a good way to check your work.** Not only does this method let you check to see if your calculations are correct, but if you obtain the same answer with two different methods, your logic is probably true, also.

- **One way to find another method is to work a problem backwards.** That is, once you have obtained the answer to the problem, see if you can use it to come up with one of the original values given in the problem.

Certainly you do not have the time on each problem to apply all of these methods for verification. However, it will improve your own trouble-shooting ability if you try at least one or two of these ideas for each problem.

5.2 Mole-Mass Calculations

You are going to a party! There will be 12 people coming, and at the last minute, you have been asked to help out by making a vegetable dip. At home that afternoon, the only recipe you can find is the one below.

Vegetable Dip

sour cream
2 times as much mayonnaise as sour cream
$\frac{1}{4}$ as much fresh parsley as mayonnaise
$\frac{1}{4}$ as much onion as parsley
$\frac{1}{12}$ as much salt as onion

Could you make this recipe into something that is edible?

What makes this recipe different from the one in Section 5.1? You should see that it only provides information about the proportions of ingredients to use and does not include the specific amounts of each one. A recipe that gives just proportions is not as easy to use as one that gives actual measurements.

Like the recipe above, a balanced chemical equation also gives information about the proportions of reactants and products. It does not specify the amount of each substance that you would use if you were trying to perform the reaction in the lab.

Specifying actual amounts The study of the amount of substances consumed and produced in chemical reactions is called **stoichiometry** (stoi kē om′ i trē). The word is formed from a Greek word, *stoicheion*, meaning "element," and the suffix *metry*, which means "to measure." Stoichiometry involves measuring or calculating the amounts of elements or compounds involved in a chemical change. The calculations in stoichiometry problems are not difficult once you recognize what you need to know in order to do the calculation. By using a balanced chemical equation, the mole ratios represented in the equation, and the mathematical relationships you learned in Chapter 4, you can specify the amounts of each substance needed in a reaction. However, as the following *Problem-Solving Strategy* illustrates, stoichiometric problems may require several steps before you find the answer you want. Furthermore, a problem may not give all the information that you need. In order to solve the problem, you must realize what necessary information is missing and either recall it from memory or look it up.

Concept ✔ Check

To prepare yourself for solving stoichiometric problems, review the molar relationships presented in Chapter 4.

(continued from page T164)

least two different approaches. Now ask students to use a method different from their own to rework the problem and verify their answer. If their two answers do not correspond, have them check all their calculations. Have students save their calculations for further discussion in connection with the Problem-Solving Strategy **Breaking Problems into Manageable Parts** (Section 5.2).

Teaching Strategy

Mole-Mass Calculations

Review frequently with students the fundamental chemical principles of stoichiometry:

1. Balancing the equation conserves atoms.
2. The balanced equation gives the mole ratios.
3. The mass ratio depends on the molar masses.

FOCUS ON
PROBLEM SOLVING

Activate Prior Knowledge

This activity will demonstrate how to break a problem into manageable parts and how to follow through to complete the problem successfully. Have students divide into committees of four. Their job is to arrange a school-wide recycling effort. Suggest that they break up the responsibilities into manageable parts. Ask how they could formulate a specific plan that includes all waste materials in the school that should be recycled. Finally, discuss how they could make sure that all tasks are accomplished.

TEACH
THE STRATEGY

Guided Practice

Students will use this strategy to solve all stoichiometry problems in this chapter. Use Example 5–2 to illustrate the steps needed to solve the problem.

Breaking Problems into Manageable Parts

As you work through the examples in this chapter, you will encounter many problems like this one: What mass of magnesium oxide can be produced from the complete combustion of 10 g of magnesium? Your initial reaction may be: "I can't solve this problem! I know how to write formulas from names, I know how to write balanced chemical equations for reactions, and I even know how to convert between moles and mass of a substance by using the molar mass. But I don't know a way to solve this problem in one step."

Your concern is certainly a valid one. In fact, it gets at the heart of a method for unlocking a wide variety of problems, including stoichiometry problems. You have already mastered the individual steps required for solving the magnesium problem. Your main task is to determine how to put together what you already know how to do. You need to break down the problem into more manageable parts that you already know how to handle and then put the parts together to solve the problem completely.

▶ Using the Strategy

Because this strategy is one that can be used in a large number of settings, you may have already broken other problems down into simpler parts in other contexts. For example, in English classes, you may be regularly asked to write themes or term papers. You probably do not start with a blank piece of paper and compose a well-organized final product. Instead, you may begin by outlining the points you want to make and gradually change your outline to prose. In a computer class, people seldom write programs from beginning to end. Usually a good programmer will outline the tasks a computer must sequentially perform in a flowchart, which is then translated into a program. Even shoppers who visit the grocery store for their weekly supplies usually break this task into parts. Most people do not arrive at the store without an idea of what to purchase; instead, they prepare for the trip at home by jotting down the most important purchases in the form of a grocery list.

▶ Formulate a Plan

Once you have learned the individual steps involved in a problem, how do you go about breaking the problem apart into smaller tasks? You could try writing down all of the information that is given in the problem, along with a short description of the goal. For example, in the problem at the beginning of this feature, the information given is: 10 g of magnesium, a combustion reaction involving magnesium, and the identity of the product (magnesium oxide). The goal is the mass (number of grams) of the product.

By writing down all the information, you might realize that a balanced chemical equation would be necessary in solving this problem. It would be one of the early steps in the problem solution. If you could determine how many moles of magnesium oxide were formed (by using the balanced chemical equation), you could then use its molar mass to obtain the mass of the product in grams. This would be the last step. By working through the problem like this, you can systematically construct an overall plan.

▶ **Keep Track of Your Steps**
As you are going through the thought process involved, you need to have some way of keeping track of your overall plan. Jot down a short description of the steps you intend to follow. You might want to list all of the units used. In this chapter, you will notice an emphasis on making road maps. These road maps can also be used to provide a record of your overall plan. Whichever method you choose, once you have decided on an overall plan, you can then go back and fill in the missing steps. In this chapter, you will be able to see several examples that make use of breaking problems into manageable parts in their solution. Study these examples carefully until you understand how this method applies to stoichiometry problems. When you think you have succeeded, practice the skill by solving the problem stated at the beginning of this feature.

Reteaching Idea

To help students realize the effectiveness of the Problem-Solving Strategy **Breaking Problems into Manageable Parts,** revisit the problem given on page T164 concerning the mass difference between girls and boys. Ask students to verbalize the steps they used to solve the problem. Then pose the following chemical problem and have pairs of students develop a plan for solution. The purpose is not to calculate but to learn to break a problem into parts that lead logically to the answer.

You have a mixture of powdered iron and sugar having a known mass. Seventy-five percent of the mass is iron. What is the difference between the number of iron atoms and the number of sugar molecules in the mixture?

Videodisc Connections

7390 to 11592, side 3
Production of acetylene (movie)

EXAMPLE 5-2

A camping lantern uses the reaction of calcium carbide, $CaC_2(s)$, and water to produce acetylene gas, $C_2H_2(g)$, and calcium hydroxide, $Ca(OH)_2(s)$. How many grams of water are required to produce 1.55 moles of acetylene gas?

■ *Analyze the Problem* The question asks about a relationship between reactants and products in a chemical reaction. Write a balanced equation for the reaction.

$$CaC_2(s) + 2H_2O(l) \rightarrow C_2H_2(g) + Ca(OH)_2(s)$$

Write down what you are given and what you are being asked to find.

$$1.55 \text{ mol } C_2H_2 \rightarrow ? \text{ g } H_2O$$

Recognize that the balanced equation is written in terms of moles but you are asked to find the answer in grams.

Figure 5-3 The study of chemical reactions has led to the development of new products. In this lantern, the combustion of gasoline keeps the lamp burning.

PART 1

Section 5.2 *continued*

Practice Problems

Assign the Practice Problems.

PROBLEM·SOLVING

S T R A T E G Y ▶

To help you **look for patterns**, or **similarities between problems**, colored arrows have been used. As you compare problems, notice that arrows of the same color indicate similar steps. (See Strategy, page 100.)

PROBLEM·SOLVING

S T R A T E G Y ▶

By **looking for similarities** with problems you know how to solve, new problems become easier. Finding the mole ratio is done just as you learned in Example 5-1. In Chapter 4, you learned to find the number of grams of a compound from the number of moles. (See Strategy, page 65.)

■ **Apply a Strategy** A good strategy to help you solve this problem is to draw a kind of "road map" to help organize your thinking. There is no direct route to go from moles of C_2H_2 to grams of H_2O so you must find an alternative route. Keeping in mind that "the mole is at the heart of chemistry," the road map becomes:

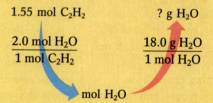

Write down the relationships that can be used to calculate what you want to find. You can obtain a mole ratio from the balanced equation. To convert from moles of water to grams of water, you need to write a ratio by using its molar mass. Add these relationships to your road map.

$$1.55 \text{ mol } C_2H_2 \qquad\qquad ? \text{ g } H_2O$$

$$\frac{2.0 \text{ mol } H_2O}{1 \text{ mol } C_2H_2} \qquad\qquad \frac{18.0 \text{ g } H_2O}{1 \text{ mol } H_2O}$$

$$\text{mol } H_2O$$

■ **Work a Solution** First, calculate the moles of water.

$$1.55 \text{ mol } C_2H_2 \times \frac{2 \text{ mol } H_2O}{1 \text{ mol } C_2H_2} = 3.10 \text{ mol } H_2O$$

Next, convert the moles of water to grams of water.

$$3.10 \text{ mol } H_2O \times \frac{18.0 \text{ g } H_2O}{1 \text{ mol } H_2O} = 55.8 \text{ g } H_2O$$

You can get the same answer by combining these two steps and solving a single mathematical statement.

$$1.55 \text{ mol } C_2H_2 \times \frac{2 \text{ mol } H_2O}{1 \text{ mol } C_2H_2} \times \frac{18.0 \text{ g } H_2O}{1 \text{ mol } H_2O} = 55.8 \text{ g}$$

■ **Verify Your Answer** Check that your setup results in the units of grams. Also check your math by working the problem from the answer back to the given data to be sure you have no errors.

Practice Problems

3. How many grams of potassium chlorate, $KClO_3(s)$ must decompose to produce potassium chloride, $KCl(s)$, and 1.45 moles of oxygen gas? **Ans.** 119 g $KClO_3$

4. How many moles of solid copper must react with silver nitrate, $AgNO_3(aq)$, to produce 5.5 g of solid silver and copper(II) nitrate, $Cu(NO_3)_2(aq)$? **Ans.** 0.025 mol Cu

5.3 Mass-Mass Calculations

In the lab, substances are not measured in moles but in units of mass, such as grams. For example, when working in the lab, there may be times when you will be asked to calculate the number of grams of product yielded by a certain mass of reactant. You might also have a limited amount of one reactant and must calculate how many grams will be needed to complete a reaction.

Although this type of calculation may seem more complex than the calculations you have done so far, it involves no new skills. The only difference is an additional step to convert the grams of reactant given in the problem to moles. As you will see in Example 5-3, using a road map will again serve as a problem-solving strategy.

EXAMPLE 5-3

How many grams of oxygen gas are required to react completely with 14.6 g of solid sodium to form sodium oxide, $Na_2O(s)$?

■ **Analyze the Problem** Begin by showing the relationship between reactants and products in the balanced equation for the reaction.

$$4Na(s) + O_2(g) \rightarrow 2Na_2O(s)$$

Write down what you are given and what you are asked to find.

$$14.6 \text{ g Na} \rightarrow ? \text{ g } O_2$$

■ **Apply a Strategy** Diagram a road map and look for relationships that can be used to calculate what you want to find.

$$14.6 \text{ g Na} \qquad ? \text{ g } O_2$$
$$\text{mol Na} \longrightarrow \text{mol } O_2$$

Obtain the mole ratio between sodium and oxygen from the balanced equation. Find the molar masses of sodium and oxygen using the periodic table. Construct a complete road map with this information.

$$14.6 \text{ g Na} \qquad\qquad ? \text{ g } O_2$$
$$\frac{1 \text{ mol Na}}{23.0 \text{ g Na}} \qquad\qquad \frac{32.0 \text{ g } O_2}{1 \text{ mol } O_2}$$
$$\text{mol Na} \xrightarrow{\dfrac{1 \text{ mol } O_2}{4 \text{ mol Na}}} \text{mol } O_2$$

PART **1**
Section 5.4

Practice Problems

Have students use the cooperative learning strategy described below to solve these problems.

Cooperative Learning

Teams of 2; **Time:** 30 minutes
Objective: Students will practice the problem-solving skills described in Chapter 5.
Task: One team member solves a practice problem while thinking aloud. The second student encourages, makes suggestions, looks for errors, and makes notes on the techniques used. Watching someone else think through a problem helps one learn how to avoid errors, and produces a model of the problem-solving process.
Team responsibility: Partners switch roles for the next practice problem. Both team members then list the most useful ideas and the greatest difficulties they encounter.
Evaluation: Have a class discussion in which teams share their ideas. Then give a quiz from the Chapter Review Questions and Problems and have students solve the problems as teams.

Teaching Strategy

Molarity and Replacement Reactions

Most solutions look like water. Help students visualize the makeup of solutions by asking them to make drawings of the ions in solution. They should note that most solutions are 90 percent water and that although water molecules do not react, they are needed to facilitate the reaction. Review the concepts needed to calculate the number of moles in a given amount of solution.

PROBLEM·SOLVING

S T R A T E G Y

Remember that molar relationships can be written in their reciprocal form. Using the **factor-label method** *will help you choose the form that will give you the units you need. (See Strategy, page 12.)*

PROBLEM·SOLVING

S T R A T E G Y

When **breaking this problem into manageable parts,** *notice that working with the units of kilograms adds another step to the solution. (See Strategy, page 166.)*

■ *Work a Solution* The calculations indicated on the road map can be done in three steps.
Convert grams of sodium to moles of sodium.

$$14.6 \text{ g Na} \times \frac{1 \text{ mol Na}}{23.0 \text{ g Na}} = 0.635 \text{ mol Na}$$

Calculate moles of oxygen from the mole ratio of oxygen to sodium.

$$0.635 \text{ mol Na} \times \frac{1 \text{ mol O}_2}{4 \text{ mol Na}} = 0.159 \text{ mol O}_2$$

Convert moles of oxygen to grams of oxygen.

$$0.159 \text{ mol O}_2 \times \frac{32.0 \text{ g O}_2}{1 \text{ mol O}_2} = 5.09 \text{ g O}_2$$

You can get the same answer by combining these three steps and solving a single mathematical statement.

$$14.6 \text{ g Na} \times \frac{1 \text{ mol Na}}{23.0 \text{ g Na}} \times \frac{1 \text{ mol O}_2}{4 \text{ mol Na}} \times \frac{32.0 \text{ g O}_2}{1 \text{ mol O}_2} = 5.08 \text{ g O}_2$$

Notice that the answers differ in the last digit. This difference is due to rounding uncertain digits. Both answers are correct.

■ *Verify Your Answer* Check that your setup results in the units of grams. Then check your math to be sure that you have not introduced any errors.

Practice Problems

5. When 20.4 g of sodium metal are mixed with chlorine gas, are 52.0 g of sodium chloride, $NaCl(s)$, produced? Explain your answer.

6. Limestone, calcium carbonate, $CaCO_3(s)$, is heated to produce lime, calcium oxide, $CaO(s)$, and carbon dioxide gas. How much limestone is required to produce 10.0 kg of lime?
   Ans. 17.8 kg

5.4 Molarity and Replacement Reactions

Figure 5-4, on the left, shows a piece of copper wire that has been placed in a solution of silver nitrate. Figure 5-4, on the right, shows the copper and silver nitrate reaction one day later. The blue solution is characteristic of copper(II) ions. The assumption is made that copper ions have replaced silver ions in the solution. The metallic silver atoms are attached to the remaining copper wire.

How could you predict how much silver forms when you are dealing with a reactant that is a solution? To find the answer, go back to what you know from Chapter 4 about the concentration of a solution. If you know the molarity of the original silver nitrate solution, you can deal with the solution in terms of the number of moles of silver nitrate it contains. The following example shows how this problem could be solved.

 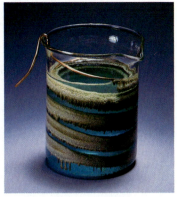

Figure 5-4 On the left, the copper wire is just beginning to react. The solution is still colorless, but some silver crystals have been produced on the copper wire. On the right, the reaction is complete. Silver crystals have covered the wire, and the blue color shows that copper(II) nitrate is in solution.

Videodisc Connections

591-593, side 6
Copper strip in silver nitrate
(3-frame seq.)

EXAMPLE 5-4

How many grams of copper will be required to completely replace silver from 208 mL of a 0.100M solution of silver nitrate, AgNO₃?

■ **Analyze the Problem** Write the balanced equation for the reaction.

$$Cu(s) + 2AgNO_3(aq) \rightarrow Cu(NO_3)_2(aq) + 2Ag(s)$$

Write down what you are being asked to find.

$$208 \text{ mL of } 0.100M \text{ AgNO}_3 \rightarrow \text{? g Cu}$$

Recognize that if you convert the molarity of the solution into moles of silver nitrate, AgNO₃, this problem becomes similar to problems you have already solved—converting moles to grams.

■ **Apply a Strategy** Diagram a road map and look for relationships that can be used to calculate what you want to find.

208 mL of 0.100M AgNO₃   ? g Cu

mol AgNO₃ ⟶ mol Cu

Notice that the volume is given in milliliters but that molarity is expressed in moles per liter. You will have to change the volume from milliliters to liters.

PROBLEM·SOLVING
STRATEGY

Remember that "the mole is at the heart of chemistry" whenever you are **breaking stoichiometric problems into manageable parts.**
(See Strategy, page 166.)

Guided Practice

Review the Concept Check question on page 165 with students. Answers can be found in Appendix E on page 808.

Reteaching Idea

If your students are having difficulty understanding molar relationships, let them act out a chemical reaction such as the combustion of magnesium. Assign eight students to represent eight moles of magnesium atoms. Have the remainder of the class link arms in pairs to represent moles of oxygen molecules. There should be at least five pairs representing oxygen so that one or more pairs will not be able to react. Have students make signs to tape to their clothing showing they are Mg (24.3 g/mol) or O (16.0 g/mol). When the activity begins, let students choreograph the event. (Four moles of oxygen molecules break apart and each oxygen atom links arms with one of the eight moles of magnesium. Leftover oxygens remain as unreacted oxygen molecules.) Have students count and record on the chalkboard the moles of magnesium and oxygen that reacted and the moles of magnesium oxide that formed. From this data, have another student write the ratios of moles of the reactants to each other and to the product. When these are reduced to ratios of the smallest whole numbers, students can see how they relate to

(continued on page T173)

PROBLEM·SOLVING
S T R A T E G Y

Look back at similar problems in Chapter 4 if you need to review how to do calculations involving molarity. (See Strategy, page 65.)

PROBLEM·SOLVING
S T R A T E G Y

In this Example, you not only need to **break the problem into manageable steps,** but also solve one of those steps in order to **make the problem similar to problems you have already solved.**

■ **Apply a Strategy** Begin by converting molarity to number of moles. Change the volume given in milliliters to liters.

$$208 \text{ mL AgNO}_3 \times \frac{1 \text{ L}}{1000 \text{ mL}} = 0.208 \text{ L AgNO}_3$$

Now calculate the number of moles of silver nitrate, $AgNO_3$ by multiplying the volume in liters by molarity, just as you did in Chapter 4.

$$0.208 \text{ L AgNO}_3 \times \frac{0.100 \text{ mol}}{1 \text{ L}} = 0.0208 \text{ mol AgNO}_3$$

The problem is now one you should be familiar with, that of converting moles of reactant to grams of product.

$$0.0208 \text{ mol AgNO}_3 \rightarrow \text{? g Cu}$$

Complete your road map with the information you need to carry out the conversions.

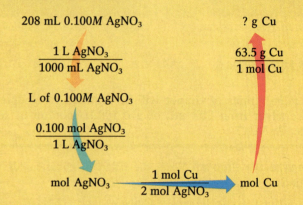

■ **Work a Solution** The calculations necessary to complete the problem can be done in the following steps.

Calculate moles of copper using the mole ratio of copper to silver nitrate.

$$0.0208 \text{ mol AgNO}_3 \times \frac{1 \text{ mol Cu}}{2 \text{ mol AgNO}_3} = 0.0104 \text{ mol Cu}$$

Convert moles of copper to grams of copper.

$$0.0104 \text{ mol Cu} \times \frac{63.5 \text{ g Cu}}{1 \text{ mol Cu}} = 0.660 \text{ g Cu}$$

You can get the same answer by combining these three steps and solving a single mathematical statement.

$$208 \text{ mL AgNO}_3 \times \frac{0.100 \text{ mol AgNO}_3}{1000 \text{ mL AgNO}_3}$$
$$\times \frac{1 \text{ mol Cu}}{2 \text{ mol AgNO}_3} \times \frac{63.5 \text{ g Cu}}{1 \text{ mol Cu}} = 0.660 \text{ g Cu}$$

PART 1 REVIEW

A N S W E R S

■ **Keyed to Objectives**

A 9. $CH_4(g) + 2O_2(g) \rightarrow$
$\quad\quad CO_2(g) + 2H_2O(g) + \text{energy}$

$$1.06 \text{ mol CH}_4 \times \frac{2 \text{ mol O}_2}{1 \text{ mol CH}_4}$$

$$= 2.12 \text{ mol O}_2$$

A 10. a. $4Na(s) + O_2(g) \rightarrow 2Na_2O(s)$

$$92 \text{ g Na} \times \frac{1 \text{ mol Na}}{23.0 \text{ g Na}} \times \frac{1 \text{ mol O}_2}{4 \text{ mol Na}}$$

$$\times \frac{32.0 \text{ g O}_2}{1 \text{ mol O}_2} = 32.0 \text{ g O}_2$$

b. $92 \text{ g Na} \times \frac{1 \text{ mol Na}}{23.0 \text{ g Na}} \times \frac{2 \text{ mol Na}_2\text{O}}{4 \text{ mol Na}}$

$$\times \frac{62.0 \text{ g Na}_2\text{O}}{1 \text{ mol Na}_2\text{O}} = 124 \text{ g Na}_2\text{O}$$

c. $9.2 \text{ g Na} \times \frac{1 \text{ mol Na}}{23.0 \text{ g Na}} \times \frac{1 \text{ mol O}_2}{4 \text{ mol Na}}$

$$\times \frac{32.0 \text{ g O}_2}{1 \text{ mol O}_2} = 3.20 \text{ g O}_2$$

d. $9.2 \text{ g Na} \times \frac{1 \text{ mol Na}}{23.0 \text{ g Na}} \times \frac{2 \text{ mol Na}_2\text{O}}{4 \text{ mol Na}}$

$$\times \frac{62.0 \text{ g Na}_2\text{O}}{1 \text{ mol Na}_2\text{O}} = 12.4 \text{ g Na}_2\text{O}$$

B 11. $4Na(s) + O_2(g) \rightarrow 2Na_2O(s)$

$$5.00 \text{ mol Na} \times \frac{2 \text{ mol Na}_2\text{O}}{4 \text{ mol Na}}$$

$$\times \frac{62.0 \text{ g Na}_2\text{O}}{1 \text{ mol Na}_2\text{O}} = 155 \text{ g Na}_2\text{O}$$

B 12. $4Na(s) + O_2(g) \rightarrow 2Na_2O(s)$

■ **Verify Your Answer** Check that the setup of your solution results in the units you want. Then check your math to be sure that you have not introduced any errors.

Practice Problems

7. When copper ions replace silver ions in 208 mL of 0.100M silver nitrate, $AgNO_3$(aq), how many grams of silver will be produced?   **Ans.** 2.24 g Ag

8. When an excess of lead(II) carbonate, $PbCO_3$(s), reacts with 27.5 mL of 3.00M nitric acid, HNO_3(aq), what mass of lead(II) nitrate, $Pb(NO_3)_2$(aq), will be formed?   **Ans.** 13.7 g

PART 1 REVIEW

9. Calculate the number of moles of oxygen gas that will be required to completely burn 1.06 moles of methane, CH_4, to form carbon dioxide and water.   **Ans.** 2.12 mol

10. **a.** How many grams of oxygen gas will be required to react completely with 92.0 g of solid sodium to form solid sodium oxide?   **Ans.** 32.0 g O_2

    b. How many grams of sodium oxide will be produced by the reaction in **a**?   **Ans.** 124 g Na_2O

    c. How many grams of oxygen will be required to react completely with 9.20 g of sodium?   **Ans.** 3.20 g O_2

    d. How many grams of sodium oxide will be produced by the reaction in **c**?   **Ans.** 12.4 g Na_2O

11. Calculate the number of grams of sodium oxide, Na_2O(s), that will be produced when 5.00 moles of solid sodium react with oxygen gas.   **Ans.** 155 g Na_2O

12. Calculate the number of grams of solid sodium oxide that will be produced when 115 g of solid sodium react with oxygen gas.   **Ans.** 155 g Na_2O

13. For this reaction, answer the questions that follow.

$$Cu(s) + 2AgNO_3(aq) \rightarrow Cu(NO_3)_2(aq) + 2Ag(s)$$

   a. How many grams of copper are required to displace 9.35 g of silver from the solution of silver nitrate?
                                                  Ans. 2.75 g Cu

   b. If 5.50 g of silver are produced in the above reaction, how many moles of copper were reacted?
                                                  Ans. 0.0255 mol Cu

14. How much Zn metal will react with 24.5 mL of 2.0M hydrochloric acid?   **Ans.** 1.60 g Zn

Boxed numbers indicate questions that involve skills in interpretation, application, and analysis.

(continued from page T172)
the balanced equation. Have students add up the masses labeled on all students representing magnesium. Do the same for those representing the oxygens that reacted. Verify that the sum of the masses of the reacting substances equals the mass of the product. Have students calculate the number of moles of oxygen required to form that mass of magnesium oxide. Emphasize that reactants combine according to molar ratios given in the chemical equation and that extra reactants are left over. Students will deal later in this chapter with limiting reactants.

Practice Problems

Assign the Practice Problems.

☰ CLOSE

Summing Up Main Ideas

Have students make a flow chart describing the steps needed to solve problems involving (a) mole-mass calculations and (b) mass-mass calculations.

PART 1 REVIEW

Assign the Part Review questions.

Evaluating Skills

These skills are evaluated in the Part Review questions indicated. **Analyzing data:** 9, 10, 11, 12, 13, 14; **Applying a strategy:** 9, 10, 11, 12, 13, 14; **Calculating:** 9, 10, 11, 12, 13, 14; **Verifying results:** 9, 10, 11, 12, 13, 14

$$115 \text{ g Na} \times \frac{1 \text{ mol Na}}{23.0 \text{ g Na}} \times \frac{2 \text{ mol Na}_2\text{O}}{4 \text{ mol Na}}$$

$$\times \frac{62.0 \text{ g Na}_2\text{O}}{1 \text{ mol Na}_2\text{O}} = 155 \text{ g Na}_2\text{O}$$

C 13. **a.** $9.35 \text{ g Ag} \times \frac{1 \text{ mol Ag}}{108 \text{ g Ag}} \times \frac{1 \text{ mol Cu}}{2 \text{ mol Ag}}$

$$\times \frac{63.65 \text{ g Cu}}{1 \text{ mol Cu}} = 2.75 \text{ g Cu}$$

b. $5.50 \text{ g Ag} \times \frac{1 \text{ mol Ag}}{108 \text{ g Ag}} \times \frac{1 \text{ mol Cu}}{2 \text{ mol Ag}}$

$$= 0.0255 \text{ mol Cu}$$

C 14. $24.5 \text{ mL} \times \frac{1 \text{ L}}{1000 \text{ mL}} \times \frac{2.00 \text{ mol HCl}}{1 \text{ L}}$

$$\times \frac{1 \text{ mol Zn}}{2 \text{ mol HCl}} \times \frac{65.4 \text{ g Zn}}{1 \text{ mol Zn}} = 1.60 \text{ g Zn}$$

Developing Skills

Students may apply these skills in their study of Part 2.

Observing and describing: Have students describe the contents of the reaction flask in Example 5–6 before the reaction starts and again when the reaction is complete.

Forming models: Have students make a submicroscopic drawing of the reaction in Example 5–6.

Determining sources of error: In Example 5–7 the percent yield of potassium chloride is 93.5 percent. Have students suggest several reasons for the loss of potassium chloride.

Predicting: Have students predict the appearance at the end of the reaction when a 2.05 g coil of copper is placed in 115 mL of a 0.125M solution of silver nitrate.

Applying a strategy and Calculating: Have students calculate the amount of reactant in excess when a 4.53 g iron nail is placed in 125 mL of a 2.45M solution of copper(II) chloride.

≡ FOCUS

Activate Prior Knowledge

Students know from their observations of combustion reactions that merely having compounds and elements in contact with each other in ratios specified by a balanced equation does not ensure that the reaction takes place or goes to completion.

Ask students to write a balanced equation for the combustion of carbon. Then show a piece of charcoal to the class and ask why the carbon in the charcoal is not combining with oxygen in the air. Students will tell you that the charcoal must become very hot. Then point to the balanced equation for the combustion of carbon.

$$C(s) + O_2(g) \rightarrow CO_2(g)$$

(continued on page T175)

PART
2 Adjusting to Reality

Objectives

Part 2

D. Determine the limiting reactant in a chemical reaction to **predict** the amount of product that can be formed.

E. Calculate the percent yield of a product using the ratio of experimental mass produced to theoretical mass predicted.

It is important to remember that a balanced equation can be used to make many predictions. However, there are a number of factors associated with reactions that are not described by the equation. The equation describes what might happen. Balanced equations can be written for reactions that do not occur. For example, consider the following equation for the production of sugar from carbon and water.

$$12C(s) + 11H_2O(l) \rightarrow C_{12}H_{22}O_{11}(s)$$

At the present time, no one knows how to make sugar using only carbon and water.

An equation does not describe the exact conditions needed to make a reaction occur. If a specific temperature must be maintained, if constant mixing is required, or if a solvent like water or alcohol must be used, this information is determined through experimentation. Equations also do not describe the behavior of atoms during a reaction. Electrons may be exchanged, collisions occur, and intermediate products may be formed. All these things are important in understanding how a chemical reaction occurs, but the equation for the reaction does not provide this information.

Have you ever attempted a reaction that failed to occur in the lab? Missing or implied information may be responsible for your unsuccessful experiment. Have you ever tried a recipe that was not successful? Often there is some hidden condition or cooking technique necessary that may not be mentioned in the recipe.

To represent the actual results obtained in a reaction accurately, specific types of calculations are used.

5.5 Reactants in Excess

The equation for the combustion of magnesium shows atoms of magnesium and oxygen combining in a 1-to-1 ratio in the product, magnesium oxide.

$$2Mg(s) + O_2(g) \rightarrow 2MgO(s)$$

If magnesium atoms contact an oxygen molecule under the right conditions, the atoms will react to form magnesium oxide.

However, it is virtually impossible to have every atom or molecule of the reactants come together so that they will combine. Consequently it is a common practice to add more than is necessary of one reactant—that is, an excess of one reactant. It is usually the cheaper one or the one that can be easily separated from the desired product. In this way, one reactant will be completely used up and what is left of the other reactant can be recovered to be used again.

Limiting reactants Figure 5-5 shows a reaction in which there is an excess of oxygen reacting with magnesium. How much magnesium oxide can be produced? By examining Figure 5-5, you can see that there are 6 atoms of magnesium and 14 atoms (7 molecules) of oxygen present. Since magnesium and oxygen are in a 1-to-1 ratio in magnesium oxide, there are 8 atoms of oxygen (4 molecules) in excess. The amount of magnesium oxide formed is determined by the number of magnesium atoms present. Once all the magnesium atoms are reacted, no more magnesium oxide is produced. Since magnesium is the reactant that limits the amount of product obtained, magnesium is called the **limiting reactant.**

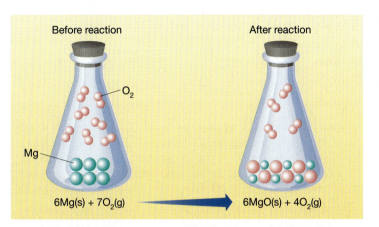

Before reaction

After reaction

O_2

Mg

$6Mg(s) + 7O_2(g) \longrightarrow 6MgO(s) + 4O_2(g)$

Figure 5-5 *The drawing shows 6 atoms of magnesium and 7 molecules of oxygen reacting to produce 6 formula units of magnesium oxide. Which reactant is in excess and by how much?*

Determining product amounts Go back to the brownie recipe. Suppose you were intent on making brownies for dessert but discovered that you had only one square of chocolate instead of the two squares called for in the recipe. Could you still make the brownies? Of course, but you would need to cut the amount of each ingredient in the recipe by $\frac{1}{2}$ (and you would get half the number of brownies). In this example, you could think of the chocolate as the limiting reactant.

When two reactants are not present in the exact mole ratio given in the balanced equation, one reactant will be the limiting reactant. The reactant that is in excess, the amount of excess, and the amount of product can all be determined. For example, according to the balanced equation oxygen and hydrogen react in a ratio of 1 to 2 to produce water.

$$O_2 + 2H_2 \rightarrow 2H_2O$$

If 1 mole of oxygen reacts with 3 moles of hydrogen, it is not difficult to reason that one mole of hydrogen is in excess, making oxygen the limiting reactant. You still obtain 2 moles of water. Example 5-5 shows you how to apply this type of reasoning using typical laboratory data to determine the amounts of products actually obtained in a reaction.

(continued from page T174)
Ask students to explain why there is solid residue left after burning a piece of charcoal. Two possible explanations are incomplete combustion and that there are other substances in addition to carbon in the charcoal.

≡TEACH

Resources

The World of Chemistry video *Metals* shows the production of iron from iron(III) oxide by reduction with hydrogen. This is followed by an attempt to remove oxygen from aluminum oxide, also using hydrogen. The video shows that no reaction takes place even though the following balanced equation can be written:

$$Al_2O_3(s) + 3H_2(g) \rightarrow 2Al(s) + 3H_2O(g)$$

Teaching Strategy

Determining Product Amounts
Making drawings of the submicroscopic processes helps students connect macroscopic observations (a strip of magnesium reacts with hydrochloric acid to produce bubbles of hydrogen gas) with the symbolic representation:

$$Mg(s) + 2HCl(aq) \rightarrow MgCl_2(aq) + H_2(g)$$

and with what is occurring on an atomic level. Conservation of atoms is an important part of the process in which reactants change to products. Use relatively small numbers of atoms and molecules (10–12) so the drawing process does not become tedious.

EXAMPLE 5-5

If 1.21 moles of solid zinc are added to 2.65 moles of hydrochloric acid, HCl, then zinc chloride, $ZnCl_2(aq)$, and hydrogen gas, $H_2(g)$, are formed. Determine which reactant is in excess and by what amount and calculate the number of moles of each product.

■ *Analyze the Problem* Begin by writing the balanced equation for the reaction.

$$Zn(s) + 2HCl(aq) \rightarrow ZnCl_2(aq) + H_2(g)$$

List what you know and what you are being asked to find.

$$1.21 \text{ mol Zn} + 2.65 \text{ mol HCl} \rightarrow \text{? reactant in excess}$$
$$\rightarrow \text{? amount of excess}$$
$$\rightarrow \text{? mol } ZnCl_2$$
$$\rightarrow \text{? mol } H_2$$

PROBLEM-SOLVING
S T R A T E G Y

Since the mole is central to many kinds of calculations, **use what you know** *about the coefficients of a balanced equation to help you solve a new problem. (See Strategy, page 58.)*

■ *Apply a Strategy* Compare the moles of each reactant to the mole ratio from the balanced equation. This will tell you which reactant is in excess. Once you know which reactant is in excess, you can then reason that the amount of the other reactant (which is the limiting reactant) will determine how many moles of each product can be produced.

■ *Work a Solution* The mole ratio of Zn to HCl in the equation is 1:2. The given ratio of moles of Zn to moles of HCl can be written and reduced by dividing both numerator and denominator by 1.21, as follows.

$$\frac{1.21 \text{ mol Zn}}{2.65 \text{ mol HCl}} = \frac{1 \text{ mol Zn}}{2.19 \text{ mol HCl}}$$

Compare this to the mole ratio from the balanced equation.

$$\frac{1 \text{ mol Zn}}{2 \text{ mol HCl}} : \frac{1 \text{ mol Zn}}{2.19 \text{ mol HCl}}$$

PROBLEM-SOLVING
S T R A T E G Y

Look for regularities *that will help you solve the problem. The ratio from the balanced equation is a comparison to 1 mole of Zn (1 mol Zn: 2 mol HCl) so change the ratio obtained from the data into a comparison to 1 mole of Zn also. (See Strategy, page 100.)*

Since you have more HCl than the reaction requires, 2.19 moles for each mole of Zn as compared to 2 moles, you can assume HCl is in excess.

Next, work with the moles of the limiting reactant, zinc. Calculate, in moles, the amount of hydrochloric acid necessary to react with 1.21 moles of zinc, using the mole ratio from the balanced equation.

$$1.21 \text{ mol Zn} \rightarrow \text{? mol HCl}$$

$$\text{? mol HCl} = 1.21 \text{ mol Zn} \times \frac{2 \text{ mol HCl}}{1 \text{ mol Zn}} = 2.42 \text{ mol HCl required}$$

Myths and Misconceptions

Although Chapters 2 and 3 covered chemical formulas and balancing equations, students often still confuse subscripts and coefficients in analyzing stoichiometry problems. This can lead to difficulty in determining the number of atoms or ions in the reactants and products in chemical reactions. To clarify this misconception or to reinforce what they learned in previous chapters, present an equation to your students such as $4Na + O_2 \rightarrow 2Na_2O$. Ask students to make a drawing of the reactants and products of the reaction (such as in Figure 5–5). Another method that can be used to help students visualize the number of atoms is to use objects such as nuts and bolts to represent the atoms. Students can quickly see that the same number of each kind of atom is on both sides of the equation. To help students avoid confusion in solving stoichiometry problems, suggest they make drawings of balanced equations with their solutions.

There are 2.65 moles of HCl available, so the amount of excess can be found by subtraction.

2.65 mol HCl − 2.42 mol HCl = 0.23 mol HCl in excess.

Since HCl is in excess, then Zn is the limiting reactant. Determine how many moles of each product are obtained with the limiting reactant, 1.21 moles of zinc, using the mole ratios from the balanced equation.

$$1.21 \text{ mol Zn} \rightarrow ? \text{ mol ZnCl}_2$$

$$1.21 \text{ mol Zn} \times \frac{1 \text{ mol ZnCl}_2}{1 \text{ mol Zn}} = 1.21 \text{ mol ZnCl}_2$$

$$1.21 \text{ mol Zn} \rightarrow ? \text{ mol H}_2$$

$$1.21 \text{ mol Zn} \times \frac{1 \text{ mol H}_2}{1 \text{ mol Zn}} = 1.21 \text{ mol H}_2$$

■ *Verify Your Answer* Verify that Zn is the limiting reactant by calculating the moles of Zn needed to react with 2.65 moles of HCl.

$$2.65 \text{ mol HCl} \rightarrow ? \text{ mol Zn}$$

$$? \text{ mol Zn} = 2.65 \text{ mol HCl} \times \frac{1 \text{ mol Zn}}{2 \text{ mol HCl}} = 1.33 \text{ mol Zn required}$$

Since 1.33 moles of zinc are required and only 1.21 moles of Zn are available, zinc is the limiting reactant.

You should also be able to reason that the moles of products are correct. Since the mole ratios are 1:1 for both Zn and $ZnCl_2$, as well as Zn and H_2, then the number of moles of Zn will determine the number of moles of each product.

Practice Problems

15. When 7.24 moles of magnesium, Mg(s), and 3.86 moles of oxygen gas, O_2(g), react to form magnesium oxide, MgO(s), which reactant will be left over? How much of the excess reactant will remain?   *Ans.* 0.24 mol O_2

16. When 0.50 mole of aluminum reacts with 0.72 mole of iodine, to form aluminum iodide, AlI_3(s), how much of the excess reactant will remain?   *Ans.* 0.02 mol Al

Figure 5-6 *On the left, zinc and hydrochloric acid are just beginning to react. The bubbles of hydrogen can be seen forming at the surface of the zinc and escaping into the air. When the reaction is complete, no zinc remains in the test tube. What substances will be present in the test tube?*

When the experiment outlined in Example 5-5 is done in the laboratory, the amount of zinc is measured in grams and the amount of hydrochloric acid is measured using the molarity and volume of the solution. As Example 5-6 will show you, solving a problem with the amount of reactants given in grams or liters involves one additional step of converting grams and molarity of a given volume of solution to moles.

EXAMPLE 5-6

When 79.1 g of solid zinc react with 1.05 L of 2.00M hydrochloric acid, HCl(aq), to produce zinc chloride, $ZnCl_2$(aq), and hydrogen gas, H_2(g), which reactant will be in excess and by how much? Calculate the number of grams of each product.

■ *Analyze the Problem* First, write the balanced equation.

$$Zn(s) + 2HCl(aq) \rightarrow ZnCl_2(aq) + H_2(g)$$

Next, write down what you are asked to find.

79.1 g Zn + 1.05 L of 2.00M HCl → ? reactant in excess
→ ? amount of excess
→ ? g ZnCl
→ ? g H_2

■ *Apply a Strategy* Follow the same steps that you used in Example 5-5. Draw a road map to help you find the relationships you need in order to solve the problem.

PROBLEM-SOLVING
STRATEGY

*Recognize that this problem is **similar to the problem** solved in Example 5-5 so the strategy to solve it will be the same. All you must do differently is to begin by converting the given data to moles and calculate the answer in grams. (See Strategy, page 65.)*

■ *Work a Solution* Convert grams of zinc and liters of 2.00M hydrochloric acid to moles.

$$79.1 \text{ g Zn} \times \frac{1 \text{ mol Zn}}{64.5 \text{ g Zn}} = 1.21 \text{ mol Zn}$$

$$1.05 \text{ L HCl} \times \frac{2.00 \text{ mol HCl}}{1.00 \text{ L HCl}} = 2.10 \text{ mol HCl}$$

The ratio in moles of the reactants in the problem may be written and reduced as follows:

$$\frac{1.21 \text{ mol Zn}}{2.10 \text{ mol HCl}} = \frac{1 \text{ mol Zn}}{1.74 \text{ mol HCl}}$$

The mole ratio from the balanced equation tells you that 1 mole of zinc must react with 2 moles of hydrochloric acid. Since there are only 1.74 moles of HCl in the actual amounts given, HCl is the limiting reactant and Zn is in excess.

$$\frac{1 \text{ mol Zn}}{2 \text{ mol HCl}} : \frac{1 \text{ mol Zn}}{1.74 \text{ mol HCl}}$$

Find the amount of excess zinc by calculating the number of moles needed to react with 2.10 moles of hydrochloric acid present.

$$? \text{ mol Zn} \rightarrow 2.10 \text{ mol HCl}$$

$$2.10 \text{ mol HCl} \times \frac{1 \text{ mol Zn}}{2 \text{ mol HCl}} = 1.05 \text{ mol Zn required}$$

Subtract to find the moles of Zn in excess.

$$1.21 \text{ mol Zn} - 1.05 \text{ mol Zn} = 0.16 \text{ mol Zn in excess.}$$

DEMONSTRATION

Determining Product Amounts

Measure 3 pieces of magnesium ribbon, each with a mass of 1.22 g (0.0500 mol). Cut each into 0.5-cm segments and place in 3 separate balloons of equal size. Label 3 250-mL pyrex flasks A, B, and C. Add 200 mL of 1.00M HCl to A, 200 mL of 0.50M HCl to B, and 200 mL of 0.25M HCl to C.

⚠️ **CAUTION: Wear a lab apron and goggles.**

Put the mouth of each balloon over the neck of a flask and droop the balloon over the side. Ask students to calculate which reactant is in excess and to predict what will happen. Shake all of the Mg pieces into the flasks.

$$Mg(s) + 2HCl(aq) \rightarrow MgCl_2(aq) + H_2(g)$$

(continued on page T179)

Use the number of moles of the limiting reactant, hydrochloric acid, HCl, to calculate the number of moles of zinc chloride, $ZnCl_2$, and hydrogen gas, H_2, produced. Then convert moles of each product into grams. The relationships needed are shown in the road map.

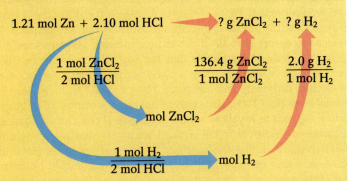

$$1.21 \text{ mol Zn} + 2.10 \text{ mol HCl} \longrightarrow ? \text{ g ZnCl}_2 + ? \text{ g H}_2$$

$$\frac{1 \text{ mol ZnCl}_2}{2 \text{ mol HCl}} \qquad \frac{136.4 \text{ g ZnCl}_2}{1 \text{ mol ZnCl}_2} \qquad \frac{2.0 \text{ g H}_2}{1 \text{ mol H}_2}$$

$$\text{mol ZnCl}_2$$

$$\frac{1 \text{ mol H}_2}{2 \text{ mol HCl}} \quad \text{mol H}_2$$

Practice Problems

Assign the Practice Problems.

> **PROBLEM-SOLVING**
> **S T R A T E G Y**
>
> When you **break a problem into manageable parts,** you see that you already know how to solve many of the steps. (See Strategy, page 166.)

Calculate the number of grams of zinc chloride, $ZnCl_2$, produced.

$$2.10 \text{ mol HCl} \rightarrow ? \text{ g ZnCl}_2$$

$$2.10 \text{ mol HCl} \times \frac{1 \text{ mol ZnCl}_2}{2 \text{ mol HCl}} \times \frac{136.4 \text{ g ZnCl}_2}{1 \text{ mol ZnCl}_2} = 143 \text{ g ZnCl}_2$$

Calculate the number of grams of hydrogen gas, H_2, produced.

$$2.10 \text{ mol HCl} \rightarrow ? \text{ H}_2$$

$$2.10 \text{ mol HCl} \times \frac{1 \text{ mol H}_2}{2 \text{ mol HCl}} \times \frac{2.0 \text{ g H}_2}{1 \text{ mol H}_2} = 2.12 \text{ g H}_2$$

■ **Verify Your Answer** Check that the setups of your solution result in the units you want. Then check your math to be sure that you have not introduced any errors.

Practice Problems

17. When 1.00 g of zinc metal is placed in 25 mL of a 0.250M lead nitrate solution, $Pb(NO_3)_2$(aq), crystals of lead form on the corroding zinc. The other product is zinc nitrate, $Zn(NO_3)_2$(aq). Which reactant is in excess? How many grams of lead will be formed? ***Ans.*** Zn excess, 1.3 g Pb

18. If 7.56 g of iron metal are placed in 100. mL of a 1.00M hydrochloric acid, HCl, solution, hydrogen gas, H_2, and iron(II) chloride, $FeCl_2$(aq), are obtained. Which reactant will be in excess and by how much? Calculate the number of grams of each product.
    Ans. .0855 mol Fe excess, 0.100 g H_2, 6.34 g $FeCl_2$

DEMONSTRATION

(continued from page T178)
Results: The balloon over flask C is inflated least; half the Mg remains unreacted. The balloons over A and B are inflated equally and contain twice as much H_2 as flask C. In flasks A and B all the magnesium reacts.

The reaction in A will be fastest and half of the HCl will be in excess.

For disposal, neutralize with 0.1M or less concentrated base, decant, and pour the decantate down the drain. Wrap the solids in newspaper and put in the wastebasket.

CONNECTING CONCEPTS

Processes of Science—Predicting A study of many reactions allows you to see patterns that can be generalized to represent similar reactions. Once these patterns are known and can be expressed as balanced equations, they can be used to predict the amount of each substance involved.

5.6 Percent Yield

A balanced chemical equation indicates the mole *ratios* among reactants and products in a reaction. The actual *measured amounts* of material that react and form, however, may not be exactly what you would predict. There are several reasons for this. One is that in reactions it is advantageous to add an excess of an inexpensive reagent to ensure that all of the more expensive reagents react to form the product. Another is that the reactants may not be 100 percent pure. If you are using a piece of yellow chalk as a source of calcium carbonate and measured 100 g of $CaCO_3$, then there is actually less than 100 g since part of the chalk is composed of other materials, such as a yellow substance to give it color and a coating to make it "dustless." Still a third reason is that materials are inevitably lost during the reaction. If the reaction takes place in solution, it may be impossible to get all of the reactants or products out of the solution. If the reaction takes place at a high temperature, materials may be vaporized and escape into the air. In still other cases, it may be possible for side reactions to occur so that products other than those described by the equation are formed. For example, when magnesium ribbon is burned in air to get magnesium oxide, MgO, some of the magnesium reacts with the nitrogen in the air, reducing the amount of magnesium oxide formed.

Predicting yields The amount of product predicted to form on the basis of the balanced chemical equation is called the **theoretical yield.** The amount of product actually obtained in a reaction, the **actual yield,** can be less than the theoretical yield. The theoretical yield for a given reaction is always the same, but the actual yield will depend on a number of variables, such as the temperature and pressure at which the reaction takes place, the purity of the reactants and the occurrence of side reactions. It is customary to describe the efficiency of the reaction in terms of the **percent yield.** As Example 5-7 shows, the percent yield is found by dividing the actual yield by the theoretical yield and expressing that ratio as a percent.

Figure 5-7 *Why do manufacturers of chalk need to take into consideration the percent yield of their product as well as the theoretical yield?*

 CHEMICAL UPDATE

Percent Yield

Car, truck, and airplane engines operate by reacting hydrocarbon fuels with oxygen to produce energy. Increasing the efficiency of the reaction can save millions of dollars in fuel costs. Chemists are constantly searching for ways to make sure all of the fuel is reacted. Techniques include compressors to force air into the engine faster, improved carburetion, better mixing within the engine, and improved sparking of the reaction.

EXAMPLE 5-7

Potassium chloride, KCl(s), can be prepared from potassium carbonate, K_2CO_3(s), by treating the carbonate with hydrochloric acid, HCl(aq). When 45.8 g of K_2CO_3(s) are added to an excess of HCl(aq), 46.3 g of KCl(s) are recovered from the reaction mixture. Water, and carbon dioxide (g) are also formed. Calculate the theoretical yield and the percent yield of potassium chloride.

- **Analyze the Problem** Write the balanced equation for the reaction.

$$K_2CO_3(s) + 2HCl(aq) \rightarrow 2KCl(s) + H_2O(l) + CO_2(g)$$

Recognize that the theoretical yield is a calculation of how much potassium chloride could be made from 45.8 g of potassium carbonate under ideal conditions: ? g KCl = 45.8 g K_2CO_3(s) Solving this part of the problem becomes a familiar mass-mass calculation. (Although the problem does not directly tell you to find the yield in grams, you should see that grams of product are more useful as a measurement to calculate than moles of product because the actual yield is given in grams.)

- **Apply a Strategy** Diagram a road map to calculate the amount of potassium chloride, KCl, produced.

- **Work a Solution**

$$45.8 \text{ g } K_2CO_3 \qquad\qquad ? \text{ g KCl}$$

$$\frac{1 \text{ mol } K_2CO_3}{138 \text{ g } K_2CO_3} \qquad\qquad \frac{74.5 \text{ g KCl}}{1 \text{ mol KCl}}$$

$$\text{mol } K_2CO_3 \quad \xrightarrow{\dfrac{2 \text{ mol KCl}}{1 \text{ mol } K_2CO_3}} \quad \text{mol KCl}$$

The calculation to find the theoretical yield may be combined in one step.

$$45.8 \text{ g } K_2CO_3 \times \frac{1 \text{ mol } K_2CO_3}{138.2 \text{ g } K_2CO_3} \times \frac{2 \text{ mol KCl}}{1 \text{ mol } K_2CO_3} \times \frac{74.5 \text{ g KCl}}{1 \text{ mol KCl}}$$
$$= 49.5 \text{ g KCl}$$

Calculate the percent yield by dividing the actual yield given in the problem to the theoretical yield and multiplying by 100 to change into a percent.

$$\text{percent yield} = \frac{\text{actual yield}}{\text{theoretical yield}} \times 100\%$$

$$\text{percent yield} = \frac{46.3 \text{ g KCl}}{49.5 \text{ g KCl}} \times 100\% = 93.5\%$$

PROBLEM·SOLVING STRATEGY

*This problem is **similar** to other mass-mass stoichiometry problems you have solved. At the end of this problem, you will have the additional step of determining percent yield. (See Strategy, page 65.)*

Guided Practice

If 49.0 g of phosphoric acid react completely with 1 mole of zinc, how many grams of zinc phosphate would be produced? [96.5 g of $Zn_3(PO_4)_2$] Which reactant, zinc or phosphoric acid, is the limiting reactant? (phosphoric acid) If the reaction is not complete and only 77.4 grams of zinc phosphate are produced, what is the percent yield? (80%)

Reteaching Idea

To reinforce the ideas of this and previous chapters, have students make drawings to represent 12 atoms of magnesium reacting with 10 molecules of nitrogen to form solid magnesium nitride. Points of emphasis:

a. consistent size and shape for each atom

b. conservation of atoms

c. location of reactant particles (solid and gas)

d. magnesium nitride as a solid regular crystalline arrangement

e. excess nitrogen as a diatomic gas randomly oriented

f. ratio of three magnesium atoms to two nitrogen atoms in magnesium nitride

g. all magnesium reacts

h. 6 molecules of nitrogen in excess

PART **2**
Section 5.6 *continued*

Practice Problems

Assign the Practice Problems.

☰ CLOSE

Summing Up Main Ideas

Write a balanced equation for zinc replacing copper from a solution of copper sulfate and yielding zinc sulfate and copper. Suppose the reaction begins with 5.0 g of zinc placed in a solution that contains 10 g of copper sulfate. Make a table including the following information.

a. limiting reactant ($CuSO_4$, 0.06 mol)

b. reactant in excess (Zn, 0.08 mol)

c. mass of product 1 (Cu, 3.8 g, 0.06 mol)

d. mass of product 2 ($ZnSO_4$, 9.5 g, 0.06 mol)

e. moles of reactants and products

$$Zn(s) + CuSO_4(aq) \rightarrow$$
$$Cu(s) + ZnSO_4(aq)$$

PART 2 REVIEW

Assign the Part Review questions.

Evaluating Skills

These skills are evaluated in the Part Review questions indicated. **Predicting:** 23; **Analyzing data:** 24, 25, 26; **Applying a strategy:** 24, 25, 26; **Calculating:** 24, 25, 26; **Verifying results:** 24, 25, 26

PROBLEM·SOLVING

S T R A T E G Y

*By answering these questions in the order given, you will **break this problem into simpler parts.** See Strategy, page 65.)*

Boxed numbers indicate questions that involve skills in interpretation, application, and analysis.

■ **Verify Your Answer** Determine if your answer seems reasonable. Since 46.3 g is only slightly less than 49.5 g, the percent yield should be high, and it is.

Practice Problems

19. If 12.5 g of copper are reacted with an excess of chlorine gas, then 25.4 g of copper(II) chloride, $CuCl_2(s)$, are obtained. Calculate the theoretical yield and the percent yield.

Ans. 26.5 g; 95.8%

20. In the reaction of Zn with HCl, 140.15 g of $ZnCl_2$ was actually formed, although the theoretical yield was 143 g. What was the percent yield? *Ans.* 98.0%

PART 2 REVIEW

21. Give three pieces of information that the following equation does *not* give about the reaction.

$$Zn(s) + MgCl_2(aq) \rightarrow ZnCl_2(aq) + Mg(s)$$

22. a. If 20 molecules of hydrogen are added to 20 molecules of oxygen to form water, which reactant will be in excess?

  b. How many molecules of water can be produced?

23. A mixture of zinc metal and hydrochloric acid is placed in a beaker. After several days, what substances are likely to be present in the beaker?

24. If 10.45 g of aluminum metal are reacted with 66.55 g of copper(II) sulfate, $CuSO_4(aq)$, then aluminum sulfate, $Al_2(SO_4)_3(aq)$, and copper are formed.

  a. Which reactant is in excess?

  b. Calculate the mass of the excess. *Ans.* 2.94 g

  c. Calculate the mass of each product.

  Ans. 47.5 g $Al_2(SO_4)_3$; 26.5 g Cu

25. If 15.50 g of lead(II) nitrate, $Pb(NO_3)_2(aq)$ are reacted with 3.81 g of sodium chloride, $NaCl(aq)$ then sodium nitrate, $NaNO_3(aq)$ and lead(II) chloride, $PbCl_2(s)$ are formed.

  a. Which reactant will be in excess?

  b. Calculate the mass of the excess. *Ans.* 4.7 g

  c. Calculate the mass of lead(II) chloride produced.

  Ans. 9.06 g $PbCl_2$

26. If 6.57 g of iron are reacted with an excess of hydrochloric acid, HCl, then hydrogen gas and 14.63 g of iron(II) chloride are obtained. Calculate the theoretical yield and the percent yield. *Ans.* 14.93 g, 98.0 %

PART 2 REVIEW

A N S W E R S

■ **Keyed to Objectives**

D 21. The behavior of the atoms as they react, the temperature of the reaction, the speed of the reaction, and the extent to which the reaction will occur. This reaction does not take place because zinc is less active than magnesium.

D 22. a. oxygen (10 molecules in excess)

  b. 20 molecules of water

D 23. Zinc chloride, water, and either excess zinc or excess hydrochloric acid. The hydrogen gas produced will diffuse out of the beaker.

D 24. $2Al + 3CuSO_4 \rightarrow 3Cu + Al_2(SO_4)_3$

  a. $10.45 \text{ g Al} \times \dfrac{1 \text{ mol Al}}{27.0 \text{ g Al}}$

  $\times \dfrac{3 \text{ mol } CuSO_4}{2 \text{ mol Al}} \times \dfrac{159.6 \text{ g } CuSO_4}{1 \text{ mol } CuSO_4}$

  $= 92.66 \text{ g } CuSO_4$

required to react with 10.45 g Cu. There are 66.55 g $CuSO_4$ present, so Al is in excess.

  b. $66.55 \text{ g } CuSO_4 \times \dfrac{1 \text{ mol } CuSO_4}{159.6 \text{ g } CuSO_4}$

  $\times \dfrac{2 \text{ mol Al}}{3 \text{ mol } CuSO_4} \times \dfrac{27.0 \text{ g Al}}{1 \text{ mol Al}}$

  $= 7.50 \text{ g Al}$

required to react with 66.55 g $CuSO_4$. The amount of excess is $10.45 - 7.50 = 2.95$ g Al.

Plastics Engineer

Experiments performed on a small chemistry set in her basement sparked Michelle Gauthier's interest in chemistry. She looked forward to taking chemistry in high school and had no difficulty deciding to major in it in college. Eventually she earned a Ph.D. in chemistry, with emphasis on polymer science and plastics engineering.

An early interest explodes into a career Now, in her work for a technological manufacturing company, Michelle deals with all types of plastics and polymers, including adhesives and paints. In the laboratory, she performs material testing; on the production floor, she solves problems related to the materials being used.

A look to the future Michelle sees the field of advanced engineering materials, which include polymers, as a growing one. For example, efforts are underway to reduce the weight of conventional materials, such as metals, without loss of strength. One important application of strong, light materials is in the growing aerospace industry. Advanced ceramic materials will also receive more emphasis in the future.

A goal through hard work To have a career like hers, Michelle says you will need a background similar to hers and some familiarity with computers. As a high school student, you should elect science courses and persevere. No matter how difficult a course may be, the willingness to work hard and not quit will bring you success. "You do not need to be a genius in order to pursue a career in chemistry or engineering." She is involved in the continuing education program for a state college, where she teaches general chemistry and a course in materials and processes.

Michelle feels rewarded by her work because the technology that she is a part of contributes to making a better life for people. Beyond that, she's glad she studied chemistry because it has helped her to be analytical and organized in her daily life, to look at problems from all sides and make good decisions, and oddly enough to appreciate even more the non-science areas of life, like art and music.

> No matter how difficult a course may be, the willingness to work hard and not quit will bring you success.

Michelle M. Gauthier
Plastics Engineer

CAREERS IN CHEMISTRY

Teaching Strategies

1. Some plastics can be recycled. Have students research differences between plastics, which can be recycled, and why.

2. Have students identify other uses of strong, light materials. Examples include bicycles and other sports equipment and automobiles, especially as fuel becomes increasingly costly, both economically and environmentally.

3. Discuss the teamwork associated with research. Research scientists are not isolated, individual workers but are part of a team effort. The value of the team is enhanced by each individual's unique experience and contribution to the joint effort.

Look Ahead

Chlorofluorocarbons are used in some plastics and insulation. Tie discussion of this career with the **Science Technology & Society** features on global warming and chlorofluorocarbons on pages 190–191 and 632–633, and consider the role of engineers in developing environmentally safe alternatives.

Related Careers

Have students identify other related careers in metallurgy and chemical engineering. Diverse opportunities in food processing, agricultural chemical development, plastics, drug development, and cosmetics are grounded in studies of chemical engineering. For further information on careers, write to Society of Plastics Engineers, 14 Fairfield Dr., Brookfield, CT 06804; Mining and Metallurgical Society of America, 9 Escalle Lane, Larkspur, CA 94939; or the American Institute of Chemical Engineers, 345 E. 47th St., New York, NY 10017.

c. The limiting reactant, $CuSO_4$, is used to determine the mass of all products.

$$66.55 \text{ g } CuSO_4 \times \frac{1 \text{ mol } CuSO_4}{159.6 \text{ g } CuSO_4}$$

$$\times \frac{1 \text{ mol } Al_2(SO_4)_3}{3 \text{ mol } CuSO_4} \times \frac{342 \text{ g } Al_2(SO_4)_3}{1 \text{ mol } Al_2(SO_4)_3}$$

$$= 47.5 \text{ g } Al_2(SO_4)_3$$

$$66.55 \text{ g } CuSO_4 \times \frac{1 \text{ mol } CuSO_4}{159.6 \text{ g } CuSO_4}$$

$$\times \frac{3 \text{ mol } Cu}{3 \text{ mol } CuSO_4} \times \frac{63.5 \text{ g } Cu}{1 \text{ mol } Cu} = 26.5 \text{ g } Cu$$

(answers are continued on page T841)

Resources

Contact the American Chemical Society or the Society of Women Engineers, 345 E. 47th St., New York, NY 10017 for additional information and to identify individuals in your area who might be invited to speak to your class.

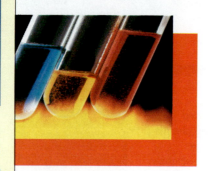

Conservation of Mass

Estimated Time: (35–40 minutes)

Measuring

Calculating

Analyzing data

Determining sources of error

Preparation

■ Materials

(for a class of 24, working in pairs)

Apparatus

(12 of each unless noted)
150-mL beakers, 10-mL graduated cylinders, Erlenmeyer flasks, 13 × 100-mm test tubes (24), corks to fit test tubes (24), No. 2 rubber stoppers, large test tubes (18 × 150 mm), small watch glasses, centigram balances (electronic will be best), papers for massing

Reagents

- 100 mL 0.10M sodium sulfate
- 100 mL 0.10M strontium chloride
- 500 mL 0.05M hydrochloric acid
- 25 g magnesium carbonate
- 100 g sodium nitrate

■ Preparation Hints

- 0.10M sodium sulfate solution; 32.22 g $Na_2SO_4 \cdot 10H_2O$ to 100 mL total volume
- 0.10M strontium chloride solution; 26.73 g $SrCl_2 \cdot 6H_2O$ to 100 mL total volume
- 0.05M hydrochloric acid solution; purchase as is or dilute 1:1 from 1.0M HCl

Laboratory
Investigation

Conservation of Mass

The law of conservation of mass states that in a chemical reaction, matter is neither created nor destroyed. Stating the law another way, the total mass of the reactants is the same as the total mass of the products. In this laboratory investigation, you will perform three reactions and observe how this law is valid under ordinary laboratory conditions. You will do this by comparing the masses present before the reaction with the masses present after the reaction.

Objectives

Measure the mass of reactants before a reaction and the mass of products after a reaction.

Calculate the percent difference of mass before and after the reaction.

Evaluate the validity of the law of conservation of mass under ordinary laboratory conditions.

■ Materials

Apparatus
- □ balance
- □ 150-mL beaker
- □ Erlenmeyer flask
- □ 10-mL graduated cylinder
- □ 2 13 × 100 mm test tubes
- □ 2 corks to fit test tubes
- □ 18 × 150 mm test tube
- □ No. 2 rubber stopper for large test tube
- □ small watch glass
- □ paper for massing

Reagents
- □ 0.1M sodium sulfate solution
- □ 0.1M strontium chloride solution
- □ 0.5M hydrochloric acid
- □ magnesium carbonate, $MgCO_3(s)$
- □ sodium nitrate, $NaNO_3(s)$

Procedure

Part 1

1. Put on your safety goggles and laboratory apron.

2. Place 2.0 mL of 0.1M sodium sulfate solution, Na_2SO_4(aq), in a 13 × 100 mm test tube. Place 2.0 mL of 0.1M strontium chloride solution, $SrCl_2$(aq), in another test tube. Cork and label each test tube.

3. Place the corked test tubes with their contents in a 150-mL beaker. Determine the total mass of the solutions, test tubes, beaker, and corks. Record the total mass in your data table.

4. Pour the strontium chloride solution into the test tube containing the sodium sulfate solution. Observe the chemical reaction.

5. Place the product test tube with cork and the empty test tube with cork in the 150-mL beaker. Mass the two test tubes, the beaker, the two corks, and the reacted solution. Record this combined product mass in your data table.

Part 2

6. Place 10 mL of water in the large test tube and stopper it.

7. Place approximately 5 g of sodium nitrate solid, $NaNO_3(s)$, on paper.

8. Find the total mass of the test tube, water, stopper, sodium nitrate solid, and paper. Record this total mass on the data table.

9. Transfer the sodium nitrate solid to the water, recork the test tube, and shake the mixture until the sodium nitrate dissolves.

10. Find the total mass of the test tube, sodium nitrate solution, stopper, and paper. Record this total mass on the table.

Part 3

11. Mass 1 g of magnesium carbonate, $MgCO_3(s)$, on a small square of paper.
    ⚠ **CAUTION: Hydrochloric acid is corrosive to skin and eyes. Wash off spills and splashes. If hydrochloric acid gets in your eyes, use the eyewash fountain immediately.**

12. Place 10 mL of 0.5M hydrochloric acid in a 125-mL Erlenmeyer flask and cover with a small watch glass. Find the total mass of the flask, watch glass, hydrochloric acid, and the magnesium carbonate on the paper. Record this total mass on the data table.

13. Carefully transfer the solid magnesium carbonate from the paper to the hydrochloric acid and place the watch glass on top.

14. After the reaction has subsided, find the total mass of the flask, watch glass, product contents of the flask, and the paper. Record this total mass.

Data Analysis

Data Table

Experiment	Total Mass Before Reaction	Total Mass After Reaction
Part 1		
Part 2		
Part 3		

1. Calculate the change in mass for each part of the experiment. Record your results on the table below.

2. Calculate the percent change in mass and record your results in the table below.
$$\frac{(\text{mass after} - \text{mass before})}{\text{mass before}} \times 100 = \% \text{ change}$$

Experiment	Change in Mass	Percent Change in Mass
Part 1		
Part 2		
Part 3		

3. How could you revise the experiment to improve the result?

4. Calculate how many grams of gas must have been produced in the third part.

5. What effect does the leftover strontium chloride in the test tube have on your results in Part 1?

Conclusions

1. Basing your answer on the data and calculations, did you find the law of conservation of mass to be valid in all three parts?

2. If your data did not confirm the law in every part, can you suggest a reason?

■ **Procedural Hints**

Explain to students that all reactants must be accurately massed.

Disposal

Combine all liquids and solids. Neutralize with 0.1M or less concentrated base, decant, and pour the decantate down the drain. Wrap the solids in newspaper and put in the wastebasket.

Data Analysis

■ **Sample Data**

1. (Sample data are given in the tables below.)

2. (See table below).

3. depends on what went wrong for student

4. $MgCO_3 + 2HCl \rightarrow$
   $\quad MgCl_2 + H_2O + CO_2$
   Moles $MgCO_3$ = 1 g × 1 mol/84.3 g = 0.012 mol
   Moles HCl = 0.010 L × 0.05 moles/liter × 36.5 g/mole = 0.018 mol
   Therefore $MgCO_3$ is the limiting reagent.
   g CO_2 = 0.012 mol × 44.0 g/mol × 1 mol $MgCO_3$/1 mol CO_2 = 0.53 g CO_2

5. The mass of final products will be decreased.

Conclusions

1. yes

2. various types of experimental errors

Data Table

Experiment	Total Mass Before Reaction (g)	Total Mass After Reaction (g)
Part 1	183.88	183.88
Part 2	37.24	37.24
Part 3	186.08	186.08

Experiment	Change in Mass	Percent Change in Mass
Part 1	0.0 g	0.0 %
Part 2	0.0 g	0.0 %
Part 3	0.0 g	0.0 %

Chapter 5
Review
ANSWERS
begin on page
T189a.

Summary

Quantitative Meaning of Equations

- The coefficients in a balanced equation give the ratio in which atoms, molecules, or formula units combine and form the products during a reaction. That combining ratio is the mole ratio. The mole ratio described by the equation is proportional. Mole ratios can be used to predict the mass of one chemical needed to react with another.

- *Stoichiometry* is a general term used to describe all the quantitative relationships given in the equation. Stoichiometric calculations can be used to predict the amount of reactant or product involved in a reaction.

- Relationships between mass and moles can be used to convert the mole ratios of the balanced equation into specific masses. Molarity can be used to measure the moles of a substance dissolved in a solution.

Adjusting to Reality

- In many experiments, the reactants usually are not combined in the exact amounts given in the equation, so one of the reactants is in excess. The reactant that is completely used up determines how much of the products will form and is called the limiting reactant.

- The amount of product predicted under ideal reaction conditions is called the theoretical yield. The actual amount measured experimentally can be less than or equal to the theoretical amount. The actual yield divided by the theoretical yield gives the percent yield.

Chemically Speaking

actual yield *5.6*   percent yield *5.6*
limiting reactant *5.5*   stoichiometry *5.2*
mole ratio *5.1*   theoretical yield *5.6*

Concept Mapping

Using the method of concept mapping described at the front of this book, complete the following concept map for the term *stoichiometry*.

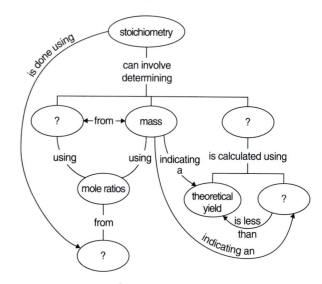

Questions and Problems

QUANTITATIVE MEANING OF EQUATIONS

A. Objective: **Determine** *the number of moles of reactants or products involved in a chemical reaction using mole ratios.*

1. If 2 molecules of oxygen react with 1 molecule of methane gas, CH_4, how many moles of oxygen gas will react with 1 mole of methane gas?

2. Write the balanced equation for hydrogen peroxide, H_2O_2, decomposing to form water and oxygen.
   a. What is the ratio of moles of hydrogen peroxide decomposed to moles of water produced?

- **Factor-label method:** 3, 8, 9, 10, 11, 12, 13, 14, 15, 16, 17, 18, 19, 22, 23, 24, 25, 27, 28, 30, 31, 32, 33
- **Using similar problems:** 6, 8, 9,

10, 11, 12, 13, 14, 16, 17, 18, 19, 22, 23, 24, 25, 27, 28, 31, 32, 33
- **Using calculators:** 3, 8, 9, 10, 11, 12, 13, 14, 15, 16, 17, 18, 19, 22,

b. What is the ratio of moles of hydrogen peroxide decomposed to moles of oxygen produced?

3. For the following reaction, determine how many moles of oxygen gas, O_2, are needed to react with each of the given moles of glucose, $C_6H_{12}O_6$, listed below:

$C_6H_{12}O_6(s) + 6 O_2(g) \rightarrow 6 CO_2(g) + 6 H_2O(l)$

   a. 5 moles $C_6H_{12}O_6$
   b. 0.05 moles $C_6H_{12}O_6$
   c. 2.5×10^{-6} moles $C_6H_{12}O_6$

4. How many moles of hydrogen gas would be needed to form 8.0 moles of water from the reaction of hydrogen and oxygen gases?

5. A mass of 46.0 g of solid sodium reacts with 38.0 g of fluorine gas to produce 84.0 g of sodium fluoride, NaF(s).
   a. Write a balanced equation for this reaction.
   b. Calculate the number of moles of each substance.

B. Objective: **Calculate** *the masses of reactants or products in a reaction given data in either moles or mass.*

6. Calculate the number of moles of potassium chlorate, $KClO_3(s)$, that must decompose to produce potassium chloride, KCl(s), and 1.80 moles of oxygen gas.

7. When 111.7 g of iron and 212.7 g of chlorine gas completely react, iron(III) chloride, $FeCl_3(s)$, is formed.
   a. Write the balanced equation for the reaction.
   b. Calculate the number of moles of each reactant.
   c. How many grams of the product are formed?

8. Calculate the number of grams of nitrogen dioxide gas formed when 1.22 moles of ammonia, $NH_3(g)$, react with 2.14 moles of oxygen gas to produce nitrogen dioxide gas and water.

9. Calculate the number of grams of potassium chloride, KCl(s), that will be formed by the decomposition of 6.45 g of potassium chlorate, $KClO_3(s)$.

10. Hydrazine, $N_2H_4(l)$, and hydrogen peroxide, $H_2O_2(l)$, react exothermically to produce nitrogen gas and water. When these are used as rocket fuel, how many grams of hydrogen peroxide are needed to react with 100.0 grams of hydrazine?

11. In a car battery, lead, lead(IV) oxide, $PbO_2(s)$, and sulfuric acid, $H_2SO_4(aq)$, are reacted to produce lead(II) sulfate, $PbSO_4(s)$, and water.
   a. Write the balanced equation for the reaction.
   b. When 10.45 g of lead, 15.66 g of lead(IV) oxide, and 25.55 g of sulfuric acid are mixed, which is the limiting reactant?
   c. How many grams of lead(II) sulfate will be produced?

12. The methyl alcohol, $CH_3OH(l)$, used in alcohol burners combines with oxygen gas to form carbon dioxide and water. How many moles of oxygen are required to burn 34.2 g of methyl alcohol?

13. Silver reacts with nitric acid, $HNO_3(aq)$, to form nitrogen monoxide, NO(g), silver nitrate, $AgNO_3(aq)$, and water.
   a. How many grams of nitric acid are required to react with 5.00 g of silver?
   b. How many grams of silver nitrate will be formed?
   c. How many moles of nitrogen monoxide will be produced?

14. If 17.5 g of zinc metal are reacted with phosphoric acid, $H_3PO_4(aq)$, then zinc phosphate, $Zn_3(PO_4)_2(aq)$, and hydrogen are produced.
   a. How many moles of phosphoric acid are required?
   b. If the phosphoric acid is a 3.00 molar solution, how many liters are needed?
   c. What mass of zinc phosphate will be produced?
   d. How many moles of hydrogen will be given off?

Boxed numbers indicate questions that involve skills in interpretation, application, and analysis.

23, 24, 25, 26, 27, 28, 30, 31, 32, 33
■ **Verifying your answer:** 8, 9, 10, 11, 12, 13, 14, 16, 17, 18, 19, 22, 23, 24, 25, 27, 28, 30, 31, 32, 33

■ **Breaking problems into manageable parts:** 16, 17, 18, 19, 22, 23, 24, 25, 27, 28, 32, 33
■ **Making diagrams:** 29, 33

■ **Writing chemical equations:** 4, 6, 7, 8, 9, 10, 11, 12, 13, 14, 16, 17, 18, 19, 22, 23, 24, 27, 28, 30, 31, 32, 33

C. Objective: **Interpret data** *to determine the amounts of reactants or products involved in replacement reactions using molarity.*

15. For this reaction, answer the questions that follow.

$$Zn(s) + 2HCl\ (aq) \rightarrow ZnCl_2(aq) + H_2(g)$$

   a. How many moles of hydrogen chloride are needed to completely react with 12.35 g of zinc?
   b. What volume of 3.00 molar hydrochloric acid is required to react with 12.35 g of zinc?

16. If 75.0 mL of $0.100M$ mercury(II) nitrate, $Hg(NO_3)_2(aq)$, are reacted with 150.0 mL of $0.100M$ sodium iodide, $NaI(aq)$, then orange, solid mercury(II) iodide, HgI_2, and sodium nitrate, $NaNO_3(aq)$, are formed. Calculate the mass in grams of the mercury(II) iodide that is formed.

17. What volume of $0.55M$ nickel(II) nitrate, $Ni(NO_3)_2(aq)$, will react with 85 mL of $0.25M$ potassium carbonate, $K_2CO_3(aq)$, to form nickel(II) carbonate, $NiCO_3(s)$, and potassium nitrate, $KNO_3(aq)$?

18. What volume of $0.60M$ copper(II) sulfate, $CuSO_4(aq)$, will react with 45 mL of $1.50M$ sodium hydroxide, $NaOH(aq)$, to form copper(II) hydroxide, $Cu(OH)_2(s)$, and sodium sulfate, $Na_2SO_4(aq)$?

19. What volume of $0.45M$ sodium carbonate, $Na_2CO_3(aq)$ will react with 82 mL of $0.25M$ iron(III) chloride, $FeCl_3(aq)$, to form iron(III) carbonate, $Fe_2(CO_3)_3(s)$, and sodium chloride, $NaCl(aq)$?

ADJUSTING TO REALITY

D. Objective: **Determine** *the limiting reactant in a chemical reaction to* **predict** *the amount of product that can be formed.*

20. What is the reason for using an excess of one reactant during a chemical reaction?

21. Explain why the percent yield of a product in a reaction is usually less than 100.

22. a. When an excess of copper is reacted with 208 mL of $0.100M$ silver nitrate solution, what is the theoretical yield of silver in grams?
   b. The silver crystals produced in **a.** are shaken off the copper wire, washed, dried, and weighed. They are found to have a mass of 2.07 g. Suggest two circumstances that could explain the loss of silver.

23. If 15.5 g of aluminum are reacted with 46.7 g of chlorine gas, then aluminum chloride, $AlCl_3(s)$, is formed.
   a. Which reactant is in excess?
   b. Calculate the number of grams of excess.
   c. Calculate the mass of aluminum chloride produced.

24. How many grams of $FeI_2(s)$ can be formed when 25.7 g of $Fe(s)$ reacts with 105 g of $I_2(s)$?

25. When 50.0 mL of 2.00 M $H_2SO_4(aq)$ react with 75.0 mL of $2.00M$ $NaOH(aq)$, find the reactant in excess. How many grams of Na_2SO_4 will be formed? The *unbalanced* equation for the reaction is this.

$$H_2SO_4(aq) + NaOH(aq) \rightarrow$$
$$Na_2SO_4(aq) + H_2O(l)$$

E. Objective: **Calculate** *the percent yield of a product using the ratio of experimental mass produced to theoretical mass predicted.*

26. Calculate percent yield for each of the following situations:

Actual yield	Theoretical yield	Percent yield
4.62 g	5.02 g	
9.31 g	10.67 g	
6.9×10^5 kg	8.2×10^6 kg	

27. A chemist burns 160. g of Al(s) in excess air to produce aluminum oxide, Al_2O_3(s). She produces 260. g of solid aluminum oxide.
    a. Write a balanced equation for the reaction.
    b. Determine the theoretical yield.
    c. Determine the percent yield.
28. If 5.45 g of potassium chlorate, $KClO_3$(s), are decomposed to form potassium chloride, KCl(s), then 1.95 g of oxygen(g) also are given off.
    a. Calculate the theoretical yield of oxygen.
    b. Calculate the percent yield of oxygen.
    c. Explain why the percent yield of oxygen is less than 100.

Critical Thinking

SYNTHESIS WITHIN THE CHAPTER

29. The equation for the reaction of nitrogen and hydrogen to produce ammonia, NH_3, is

$$N_2(g) + 3H_2(g) \rightarrow 2NH_3(g)$$

    a. Given 6 molecules of nitrogen and 12 molecules of hydrogen, make a drawing that represents the reaction container before the reaction.
    b. Make a drawing that represents the same reaction container after the reaction.
    c. How many molecules of ammonia are formed?
    d. Which reactant is in excess?
    e. How many molecules are in excess?
30. When 14.97 g of iron metal react with chlorine gas, 43.47 g of product are formed. Write the balanced equation for this reaction.

SYNTHESIS ACROSS CHAPTERS

31. The charcoal briquettes used to cook in an outdoor grill are composed of 99-percent carbon. How many grams of oxygen are required when a 100.0-g briquette is burned to produce carbon dioxide and energy?

32. When 26.42 g of molybdenum metal are reacted with an excess of oxygen gas, a black compound with a mass of 33.04 g is formed.
    a. Write the balanced equation for the reaction.
    b. What is the name of the compound formed?
33. A strip of zinc with a mass of 19.43 g is placed in a beaker containing 425 cm^3 of 0.25M chromium(III) nitrate.
    a. Which reactant is in excess?
    b. Make a labeled drawing of the beaker and contents when the reaction is complete.
    c. Calculate the mass of chromium metal produced.

Projects

34. Call an industry in your area. Find out what chemical reactions they use to produce their products? How much product is produced daily? What is their percent yield?
35. Interview a chemical engineer. Find out what the engineer does. Try to discover how the engineer controls the reactions taking place in the plant.

Research and Writing

36. Find out about air pollution in your community. List the sources, the pollutants they produce, and the number of metric tons each source produces. Find out the reactions that occur in the air to produce the pollutants. Write an article for your school paper based on your information. Include ways you and your fellow students can help reduce air pollution.
37. Write a paper discussing the advantages of recycling aluminum. Include how aluminum is made from its ore, bauxite, how much energy is needed, and what the percent yield is. Compare your findings with the energy needed to recycle aluminum and what the percent yield is when aluminum is recycled.

☐ Boxed numbers indicate questions that involve skills in interpretation, application, and analysis.

Chapter 5 Review Concept Map

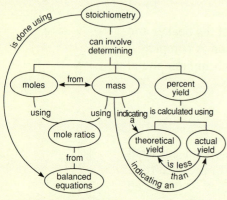

1. 2 mol oxygen

2. $2H_2O_2(l) \rightarrow 2H_2O(l) + O_2(g)$
   a. 1 mol H_2O_2 to 1 mol H_2O
   b. 2 mol H_2O_2 to 1 mol O_2

3. a. $5 \text{ mol } C_6H_{12}O_6 \times \dfrac{6 \text{ mol } O_2}{1 \text{ mol } C_6H_{12}O_6}$
   $= 30 \text{ mol } O_2$
   b. $0.05 \text{ mol } C_6H_{12}O_6$
   $\times \dfrac{6 \text{ mol } O_2}{1 \text{ mol } C_6H_{12}O_6} = 0.3 \text{ mol } O_2$
   c. $2.5 \times 10^{-6} \text{ mol } C_6H_{12}O_6$
   $\times \dfrac{6 \text{ mol } O_2}{1 \text{ mol } C_6H_{12}O_6}$
   $= 1.5 \times 10^{-5} \text{ mol } O_2$

4. 8 mol hydrogen gas

5. a. $2Na(s) + F_2(g) \rightarrow 2NaF(s)$
   b. $46.0 \text{ g Na} \times \dfrac{1 \text{ mol Na}}{23.0 \text{ g Na}}$
   $= 2.00 \text{ mol Na}$
   $38.0 \text{ g F}_2 \times \dfrac{1 \text{ mol F}_2}{38.0 \text{ g F}_2}$
   $= 1.00 \text{ mol F}_2$
   $84.0 \text{ g NaF} \times \dfrac{1 \text{ mol NaF}}{42.0 \text{ g NaF}}$
   $= 2.00 \text{ mol NaF}$
   $2.00 \text{ mol Na} + 1.00 \text{ mol F}_2 \rightarrow$
   $\qquad\qquad\qquad 2.00 \text{ mol NaF}$

6. $2KClO_3 \rightarrow 2KCl + 3O_2$
   $1.80 \text{ mol O}_2 \times \dfrac{2 \text{ mol KClO}_3}{3 \text{ mol O}_2}$
   $= 1.20 \text{ mol KClO}_3$

7. a. $2Fe + 3Cl_2 \rightarrow 2FeCl_3$

b. $111.7 \text{ g Fe} \times \dfrac{1 \text{ mol Fe}}{55.85 \text{ g Fe}}$
   $= 2.000 \text{ mol Fe}$
   $212.7 \text{ g Cl}_2 \times \dfrac{1 \text{ mol Cl}_2}{70.90 \text{ g Cl}_2}$
   $= 3.000 \text{ mol Cl}_2$

c. $2.000 \text{ mol Fe} \times \dfrac{2 \text{ mol FeCl}_3}{2 \text{ mol Fe}}$
   $\times \dfrac{162.2 \text{ g FeCl}_3}{1 \text{ mol FeCl}_3} = 324.4 \text{ g FeCl}_3$

8. $4NH_3 + 7O_2 \rightarrow 4NO_2 + 6H_2O$
   $1.22 \text{ mol NH}_3 \times \dfrac{4 \text{ mol NO}_2}{4 \text{ mol NH}_3}$
   $\times \dfrac{46.0 \text{ g NO}_2}{1 \text{ mol NO}_2} = 56.1 \text{ g NO}_2$

9. $2KClO_3 \rightarrow 2KCl + 3O_2$
   $6.45 \text{ g KClO}_3 \times \dfrac{1 \text{ mol KClO}_3}{122.5 \text{ g KClO}_3}$
   $\times \dfrac{2 \text{ mol KCl}}{2 \text{ mol KClO}_3} \times \dfrac{74.6 \text{ g KCl}}{1 \text{ mol KCl}}$
   $= 3.93 \text{ g KCl}$

10. $N_2H_4 + 2H_2O_2 \rightarrow N_2 + 4H_2O$
    $100.0 \text{ g N}_2H_4 \times \dfrac{1 \text{ mol N}_2H_4}{32.06 \text{ g N}_2H_4}$
    $\times \dfrac{2 \text{ mol H}_2O_2}{1 \text{ mol N}_2H_4} \times \dfrac{34.02 \text{ g H}_2O_2}{1 \text{ mol H}_2O_2}$
    $= 212.3 \text{ g H}_2O_2$

11. a. $Pb + PbO_2 + 2H_2SO_4 \rightarrow$
    $\qquad\qquad 2PbSO_4 + 2H_2O$
    b. $10.45 \text{ g Pb} \times \dfrac{1 \text{ mol Pb}}{207.2 \text{ g Pb}}$
    $= 0.0504 \text{ mol Pb}$
    $15.66 \text{ g PbO}_2 \times \dfrac{1 \text{ mol PbO}_2}{239.2 \text{ g PbO}_2}$
    $= 0.0655 \text{ mol PbO}_2$
    $25.55 \text{ g H}_2SO_4 \times \dfrac{1 \text{ mol H}_2SO_4}{98.08 \text{ g H}_2SO_4}$
    $= 0.260 \text{ mol H}_2SO_4$
    Dividing all the moles by the smallest amount (0.0504) gives 1 mol Pb, 1.3 mol PbO_2, and 5.16 mol H_2SO_4. The limiting reactant is Pb.
    c. The limiting reactant is used to calculate the mass of a product.
    $10.45 \text{ g Pb} \times \dfrac{1 \text{ mol Pb}}{207.2 \text{ g Pb}}$
    $\times \dfrac{2 \text{ mol PbSO}_4}{1 \text{ mol Pb}} \times \dfrac{303.3 \text{ g PbSO}_4}{1 \text{ mol PbSO}_4}$
    $= 30.59 \text{ g PbSO}_4$

12. $2CH_3OH + 3O_2 \rightarrow 2CO_2 + 4H_2O$
    $34.2 \text{ g CH}_3OH \times \dfrac{1 \text{ mol CH}_3OH}{32.0 \text{ g CH}_3OH}$
    $\times \dfrac{3 \text{ mol O}_2}{2 \text{ mol CH}_3OH} = 1.60 \text{ mol O}_2$

13. $3Ag + 4HNO_3 \rightarrow NO + 3AgNO_3$
    $\qquad\qquad\qquad\qquad + 2H_2O$
    a. $5.00 \text{ g Ag} \times \dfrac{1 \text{ mol Ag}}{107.9 \text{ g Ag}}$
    $\times \dfrac{4 \text{ mol HNO}_3}{3 \text{ mol Ag}} \times \dfrac{63.02 \text{ g HNO}_3}{1 \text{ mol HNO}_3}$
    $= 3.89 \text{ g HNO}_3$

b. $5.00 \text{ g Ag} \times \dfrac{1 \text{ mol Ag}}{107.9 \text{ g Ag}}$
   $\times \dfrac{3 \text{ mol AgNO}_3}{3 \text{ mol Ag}} \times \dfrac{169.9 \text{ g AgNO}_3}{1 \text{ mol AgNO}_3}$
   $= 7.87 \text{ g AgNO}_3$

c. $5.00 \text{ g Ag} \times \dfrac{1 \text{ mol Ag}}{107.9 \text{ g Ag}} \times \dfrac{1 \text{ mol NO}}{3 \text{ mol Ag}}$
   $= 0.0154 \text{ mol NO}$

14. $3Zn + 2H_3PO_4 \rightarrow Zn_3(PO_4)_2 + 3H_2$
    a. $17.5 \text{ g Zn} \times \dfrac{1 \text{ mol Zn}}{65.4 \text{ g Zn}} \times \dfrac{2 \text{ mol H}_3PO_4}{3 \text{ mol Zn}}$
    $= 0.178 \text{ mol H}_3PO_4$
    b. $0.178 \text{ mol H}_3PO_4 \times \dfrac{1 \text{ L H}_3PO_4}{3.00 \text{ mol H}_3PO_4}$
    $= 0.0593 \text{ L H}_3PO_4$
    c. $17.5 \text{ g Zn} \times \dfrac{1 \text{ mol Zn}}{65.4 \text{ g Zn}}$
    $\times \dfrac{1 \text{ mol Zn}_3(PO_4)_2}{3 \text{ mol Zn}} \times \dfrac{386.2 \text{ g Zn}_3(PO_4)_2}{1 \text{ mol Zn}_3(PO_4)_2}$
    $= 34.4 \text{ g Zn}_3(PO_4)_2$
    d. $17.5 \text{ g Zn} \times \dfrac{1 \text{ mol Zn}}{65.4 \text{ g Zn}}$
    $\times \dfrac{3 \text{ mol H}_2}{3 \text{ mol Zn}} = 0.268 \text{ mol H}_2$

15. $Zn + 2HCl \rightarrow ZnCl_2 + H_2$
    a. $12.35 \text{ g Zn} \times \dfrac{1 \text{ mol Zn}}{65.38 \text{ g Zn}}$
    $\times \dfrac{2 \text{ mol HCl}}{1 \text{ mol Zn}} = 0.3778 \text{ mol HCl}$
    b. $0.3778 \text{ mol HCl} \times \dfrac{1000 \text{ mL HCl}}{3 \text{ mol HCl}}$
    $= 125.9 \text{ mL HCl}$

16. $Hg(NO_3)_2(aq) + 2NaI(aq) \rightarrow HgI_2$
    $\qquad\qquad\qquad\qquad + 2NaNO_3(aq)$
    $75.0 \text{ mL Hg(NO}_3)_2$
    $\times \dfrac{0.100 \text{ mol Hg(NO}_3)_2}{1000 \text{ mL Hg(NO}_3)_2}$
    $= 0.00750 \text{ mol Hg(NO}_3)_2$
    $150.0 \text{ mL NaI} \times \dfrac{0.100 \text{ mol NaI}}{1000 \text{ mL NaI}}$
    $= 0.0150 \text{ mol NaI}$
    Dividing both by the smaller number of moles:
    $\dfrac{0.00750}{0.00750} = 1 \text{ mol Hg(NO}_3)_2$
    $\dfrac{0.0150}{0.00750} = 2 \text{ mol NaI}$
    This is the correct mole ratio. Neither reactant is in excess and either can be used to calculate the product.
    $150.0 \text{ mL NaI} \times \dfrac{0.100 \text{ mol NaI}}{1000 \text{ mL NaI}}$
    $\times \dfrac{1 \text{ mol HgI}_2}{2 \text{ mol NaI}} \times \dfrac{454.4 \text{ g HgI}_2}{1 \text{ mol HgI}_2}$
    $= 3.41 \text{ g HgI}_2$

17. $Ni(NO_3)_2(aq) + K_2CO_3(aq) \rightarrow$
    $\qquad NiCO_3(s) + 2KNO_3(aq)$
    $85.0 \text{ mL K}_2CO_3 \times \dfrac{0.25 \text{ mol K}_2CO_3}{1000 \text{ mL K}_2CO_3}$
    $\times \dfrac{1 \text{ mol Ni(NO}_3)_2}{1 \text{ mol K}_2CO_3} \times \dfrac{1000 \text{ mL Ni(NO}_3)_2}{0.55 \text{ mol Ni(NO}_3)_2}$
    $= 39 \text{ mL Ni(NO}_3)_2$

18. $CuSO_4(aq) + 2NaOH(aq) \rightarrow$
$$Cu(OH)_2(s) + Na_2SO_4(aq)$$

$45 \text{ mL NaOH} \times \dfrac{1.50 \text{ mol NaOH}}{1000 \text{ mL NaOH}}$

$\times \dfrac{1 \text{ mol } CuSO_4}{2 \text{ mol NaOH}} \times \dfrac{1000 \text{ mL } CuSO_4}{0.60 \text{ mol } CuSO_4}$

$= 56 \text{ mL } CuSO_4$

19. $3Na_2CO_3(aq) + 2FeCl_3(aq) \rightarrow$
$$Fe_2(CO_3)_3(s) + 6NaCl(aq)$$

$45 \text{ mL NaOH} \times \dfrac{1.50 \text{ mol NaOH}}{1000 \text{ mL NaOH}}$

$\times \dfrac{1 \text{ mol } CuSO_4}{2 \text{ mol NaOH}} \times \dfrac{1000 \text{ mL } CuSO_4}{0.60 \text{ mol } CuSO_4}$

$= 56 \text{ mL } CuSO_4$

20. To make sure that all of the more expensive reactant is consumed; to increase the percent yield

21. If all chemicals are 100% pure, and all react with no atoms lost, the yield is 100%. Usually some atoms are lost or impurities are present. Therefore the yield is frequently less than 100%. If the apparent yield is more than 100%, there must be some impurity present in the product.

22. a. $Cu(s) + 2AgNO_3(aq) \rightarrow$
$$Cu(NO_3)_2(aq) + 2Ag(s)$$

$208 \text{ mL} \times \dfrac{0.100 \text{ mol } AgNO_3}{1000 \text{ mL}}$

$\times \dfrac{1 \text{ mol } Ag}{1 \text{ mol } AgNO_3} \times \dfrac{107.9 \text{ g } Ag}{1 \text{ mol } Ag}$

$= 2.24 \text{ g } Ag$

b. The $AgNO_3(aq)$ concentration may have been slightly less than $0.100M$, not enough to react, or the 208 mL was not accurately measured, or some of the $Ag(s)$ was not washed off the Cu wire.

23. $2Al + 3Cl_2 \rightarrow 2AlCl_3$

a. $15.5 \text{ g } Al \times \dfrac{1 \text{ mol } Al}{27.0 \text{ g } Al} \times \dfrac{3 \text{ mol } Cl_2}{2 \text{ mol } Al}$

$\times \dfrac{70.9 \text{ g } Cl_2}{1 \text{ mol } Cl_2} = 61.1 \text{ g } Cl_2$ required

This means that since there are 46.7 g Cl_2 present, Al is in excess.

b. $46.7 \text{ g } Cl_2 \times \dfrac{1 \text{ mol } Cl_2}{70.9 \text{ g } Cl_2} \times \dfrac{2 \text{ mol } Al}{3 \text{ mol } Cl_2}$

$\times \dfrac{27.0 \text{ g } Al}{1 \text{ mol } Al} = 11.9 \text{ g } Al$

$15.5 \text{ g} - 11.9 \text{ g} = 3.6 \text{ g } Al$ in excess

c. $46.7 \text{ g } Cl_2 \times \dfrac{1 \text{ mol } Cl_2}{70.9 \text{ g } Cl_2}$

$\times \dfrac{2 \text{ mol } AlCl_3}{3 \text{ mol } Cl_2} \times \dfrac{133.3 \text{ g } AlCl_3}{1 \text{ mol } AlCl_3}$

$= 58.5 \text{ g } AlCl_3$

24. $Fe(s) + I_2(s) \rightarrow FeI_2(s)$

$25.7 \text{ g } Fe \times \dfrac{1 \text{ mol } Fe}{55.8 \text{ g } Fe} = 0.461 \text{ mol } Fe$

$105 \text{ g } I_2 \times \dfrac{1 \text{ mol } I_2}{253.8 \text{ g } I_2} = 0.414 \text{ mol } I_2$

Fe is in excess and I_2 is the limiting reactant.

$105 \text{ g } I_2 \times \dfrac{1 \text{ mol } I_2}{253.8 \text{ g } I_2} \times \dfrac{1 \text{ mol } FeI_2}{1 \text{ mol } I_2}$

$\times \dfrac{309.6 \text{ g } FeI_2}{1 \text{ mol } FeI_2} = 128 \text{ g } FeI_2$

25. $H_2SO_4(aq) + 2NaOH(aq) \rightarrow$
$$Na_2SO_4(aq) + 2H_2O(l)$$

$50.0 \text{ mL} \times \dfrac{2.00 \text{ mol } H_2SO_4}{1000 \text{ mL}}$

$= 0.100 \text{ mol } H_2SO_4$

$75.0 \text{ mL} \times \dfrac{2.00 \text{ mol NaOH}}{1000 \text{ mL}}$

$= 0.150 \text{ mol NaOH}$

Dividing both by 0.100 gives a ratio of 1 mol H_2SO_4 to 1.5 mol NaOH. H_2SO_4 is in excess.

$0.150 \text{ mol NaOH} \times \dfrac{1 \text{ mol } Na_2SO_4}{2 \text{ mol NaOH}}$

$\times \dfrac{142.1 \text{ g } Na_2SO_4}{1 \text{ mol } Na_2SO_4} = 10.7 \text{ g } Na_2SO_4$

26. $\dfrac{4.62 \text{ g}}{5.02 \text{ g}} \times 100 = 92.0\%$ yield

$\dfrac{9.31 \text{ g}}{10.67 \text{ g}} \times 100 = 87.3\%$ yield

$\dfrac{6.9 \times 10^5 \text{ kg}}{8.2 \times 10^6 \text{ kg}} \times 100 = 8.4\%$ yield

27. a. $4Al(s) + 3O_2(g) \rightarrow 2Al_2O_3(s)$

b. $160.0 \text{ g } Al \times \dfrac{1 \text{ mol } Al}{27.0 \text{ g } Al}$

$\times \dfrac{2 \text{ mol } Al_2O_3}{4 \text{ mol } Al} \times \dfrac{102.0 \text{ g } Al_2O_3}{1 \text{ mol } Al_2O_3}$

$= 302 \text{ g } Al_2O_3$ theoretical yield

c. $\dfrac{260 \text{ g}}{302 \text{ g}} \times 100 = 86.1\%$

28. $2KClO_3 \rightarrow 2KCl + 3O_2$

a. $5.45 \text{ g } KClO_3 \times \dfrac{1 \text{ mol } KClO_3}{122.5 \text{ g } KClO_3}$

$\times \dfrac{3 \text{ mol } O_2}{2 \text{ mol } KClO_3} \times \dfrac{32.0 \text{ g } O_2}{1 \text{ mol } O_2}$

$= 2.14 \text{ g } O_2$

b. % yield $= \dfrac{\text{actual yield}}{\text{theoretical yield}}$

$= \dfrac{1.95}{2.14} = 91.1\%$

c. Some oxygen may have escaped or dissolved in the water, or the $KClO_3$ may not have reacted completely.

29. a. before reaction

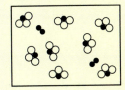

$6N_2 + 12H_2$

b. after reaction

$8NH_3 + 2N_2$

c. 8
d. N_2
e. 2 molecules N_2

30. $Fe + Cl_2 \rightarrow FeCl_2$

$Fe = 14.97 \text{ g}$

$Cl = 43.47 \text{ g} - 14.97 \text{ g} = 28.50 \text{ g}$

$14.97 \text{ g } Fe \times \dfrac{1 \text{ mol } Fe}{55.85 \text{ g } Fe}$

$= 0.2680 \text{ mol } Fe$

$28.50 \text{ g } Cl \times \dfrac{1 \text{ mol } Cl}{35.45 \text{ g } Cl}$

$= 0.8039 \text{ mol } Cl$

Divide both by the smaller number of moles

$\dfrac{0.2680}{0.2680} = 1.000 \text{ mol } Fe$

$\dfrac{0.8039}{0.2680} = 3.000 \text{ mol } Cl$

Therefore the formula is $FeCl_3$

$2Fe + 3Cl_2 \rightarrow 2FeCl_3$

31. $C + O_2 \rightarrow CO_2$

$C + O_2 \rightarrow CO_2$

$99 \text{ g } C \times \dfrac{1 \text{ mol } C}{12.0 \text{ g } C} \times \dfrac{1 \text{ mol } O_2}{1 \text{ mol } C}$

$\times \dfrac{32.0 \text{ g } O_2}{1 \text{ mol } O_2} = 264 \text{ g } O_2$

32. a. mass of Mo = 26.42 g
mass of O = 33.04 g − 26.42 g
$= 6.62 \text{ g}$

$26.42 \text{ g } Mo \times \dfrac{1 \text{ mol } Mo}{95.94 \text{ g } Mo}$

$= 0.2754 \text{ mol } Mo$

$6.62 \text{ g } O \times \dfrac{1 \text{ mol } O}{16.0 \text{ g } O}$

$= 0.414 \text{ mol } O$

Dividing both by 0.275 equals 1 mol Mo and 1.50 mol O
Multiply both by 2 to keep the ratio the same.
2 mol Mo to 3 mol O
4 mol Mo to 3 mol O_2
$4Mo + 3O_2 \rightarrow 2Mo_2O_3$

b. molybdenum(III) oxide

33. $3Zn(s) + 2Cr(NO_3)_3(aq) \rightarrow$
$$3Zn(NO_3)_2(aq) + 2Cr(s)$$

$425 \text{ cm}^3 \text{ } Cr(NO_3)_3$

$\times \dfrac{0.25 \text{ mol } Cr(NO_3)_3}{1000 \text{ cm}^3 \text{ } Cr(NO_3)_3}$

$\times \dfrac{3 \text{ mol } Zn}{2 \text{ mol } Cr(NO_3)_3} \times \dfrac{65.4 \text{ g } Zn}{1 \text{ mol } Zn}$

$= 10.42 \text{ g } Zn$

a. Zinc is in excess since 10.42 g are required to react with 425 cm³ of $Cr(NO_3)_3$ and 19.43 g are present.
Mass of zinc in excess
$= 19.43 \text{ g} - 10.42 \text{ g} = 9.01 \text{ g}$

(answers are continued on page T841)

Critical Thinking Skills

These skills are applied in the feature.

- Evaluating the relevance of information
- Making an informed decision
- Evaluating an opinion or point of view
- Devising multiple solutions

Focus

Activate Prior Knowledge

Have students search for aerosol cans around their homes. Ask them to examine the label to see if chlorofluorocarbons (CFCs) are used in the cans. Some cans may have CFCs because the cans may be old or used legally to hold refrigerants. Ask students why CFCs have been banned from many products.

Teach

Science Background

Like any environmental threat, the greenhouse effect is controversial. Some scientists predict that the average global temperature will rise as much as 3°C in the next 50 years. Many organisms on Earth can survive only within a narrow temperature range. Earth's temperature has not varied more than 2°C since the end of the last ice age, some 18 000 years ago. This temperature change occurred over thousands of years. The 3°C temperature rise as a result of the greenhouse effect is predicted to occur in less than one human generation.

Teaching Strategy

Ask students if they can remember the summers of 1987, 1988, and 1991. Point out that these are three of the hottest years on

(continued on page T191)

CHEMICAL PERSPECTIVES

Global Warming—A Heated Debate

How would you like to take part in a science experiment that might have an adverse effect on your well-being? Some people suggest that everyone is already taking part in a gigantic global experiment. Many scientists agree that a trend of global warming is occurring; however, there is some debate as to the cause and the extent. In addition, many scientists claim that global warming, if not halted or reversed, will ultimately yield catastrophic effects, destroying nature and civilization.

Gases in Earth's atmosphere allow radiation from the sun to pass through. While some of this radiation escapes, the rest is absorbed by the gases, heating the atmosphere. Since atmospheric gases trap heated air much as glass in a greenhouse does, this phenomenon is called the greenhouse effect. It is this natural warming process that controls the global thermostat.

Some scientists say global warming is caused by an increased greenhouse effect. One chemical reaction is generally being blamed for this— the combustion of fossil fuels and wood, increasing the emission of greenhouse gases, such as carbon dioxide, methane, nitrous oxide, and chlorofluorocarbons (CFC's). Levels of carbon dioxide are increasing, not

If global warming increases, will disasters like this become common events?

only due to the burning of fuels and wood but also due to deforestation, resulting in fewer trees to absorb carbon dioxide. It is predicted that by the year 2000, global temperatures could increase from 0.7 to 3 degrees Celsius.

Scientists use computer models to predict what events might occur if global warming continued. Some examples include the melting of the edges of the Arctic and Antarctic ice sheets, rising sea levels, and the flooding of coastal areas, which would trigger the widespread loss of farmland and the contamination of drinking water. Other parts of the globe would experience changes in weather patterns. Some forests would change to grasslands and grasslands to deserts, lowering crop yields. Strong winds, hurricanes, and other storms, caused by shifting ocean currents and coastal flooding, would intensify, destroying cities and populations.

Shifting ocean currents and coastal flooding would increase, destroying cities and populations.

Some scientists say that global warming is not caused by the increased levels of greenhouse gases. For example, despite the rapid increase in the levels of these gases from 1940 through 1970, Earth did cool. While debate over the cause of global warming continues, many scientists fear that the time needed to find solutions will be lost. Governments and corporations as well as scientists, politicians, and citizens are frustrated by the disagreements and the subsequent delays in critical decisions and actions.

Discussing the Issues

1. Do you agree with those who think you are taking part in a gigantic global experiment? Defend your position.
2. Do you think taking action now to reduce greenhouse gases could be beneficial? What are the risks you foresee if action is not taken to change the course of global warming? Explain.

Take Action

1. Find out if any steps are being taken by your local community or government to reduce the emission of greenhouse gases. What steps can you take to reduce greenhouse gases?
2. A "strategic environment initiative" has been proposed in Congress. Explore the objectives. Also, find out what you can do to help achieve the goals of Congress.

191

(continued from page T190) record. What impact did these higher-than-normal temperatures have? Have them study the photograph of the parched field on page 190. Point out that even if they don't live near these fields, they would be affected by the reduced availability of food. Then ask if they think that they should be concerned about rising temperatures.

Chemical Update
The Clean Air Act of 1990 set new, stricter guidelines for the burning of fossil fuels. The new law affects automobile, power plant, and industrial emissions. Because of the stricter guidelines, the operating expenses of businesses will increase, and individuals may have to pay more for automobiles and electricity.

*C*lose

Discussing the Issues
1. Students should focus on the definition of global warming in defending their position. If the definition includes every location on the globe, few students will deny their involvement in a huge global experiment.
2. Most students will say yes. Risks may include changes in weather patterns, food and water shortages, and widespread extinction of plants and animals.

Take Action
1. Students may contact a local environmental organization or the state EPA office for information about local efforts to reduce the emission of greenhouse gases. For their own part, students may suggest biking or walking instead of driving, using home heating and cooling wisely, planting trees, and so on.
2. Have students contact their U.S. representative or senator for information on national efforts to clean up the environment.

Gases and Their Properties

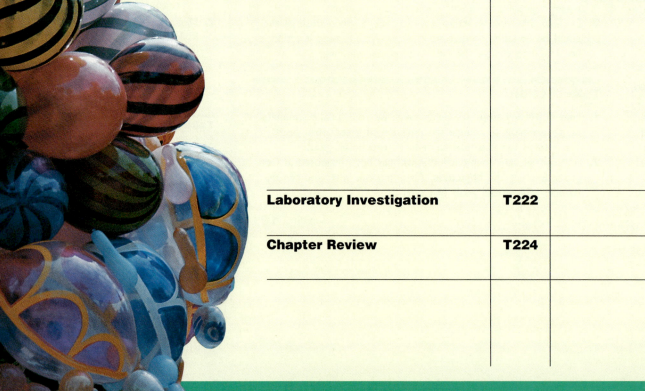

Part and Section Title	Page	Objectives
■ PART 1 Physical Properties of Gases	**T193**	A. **Describe** a gas on the submicroscopic level, using the variables of volume, temperature, and pressure.
6.1 Describing Gases	T193	
6.2 Measuring Gas Pressure	T197	B. **Explain** what gas pressure is and **describe** how it can be measured.
6.3 Dalton's Law of Partial Pressures	T202	C. **Apply** Dalton's law of partial pressures to determine the total pressure of a mixture of gases or the partial pressure of an individual gas in the mixture.
■ PART 2 Relationships among Gas Properties	**T205**	D. **Apply** Charles's law to **describe** how the volume of a gas is related to its temperature.
6.4 Charles's Law: The Temperature-Volume Relationship	T206	E. **Apply** Boyle's law to **describe** how the volume of a gas is related to pressure.
6.5 Boyle's Law: The Pressure-Volume Relationship	T213	F. **Explain** how the law of combining volumes can be used to **describe** volume relationships and show how Avogadro's principle can explain this law.
6.6 Avogadro's Principle	T219	
Laboratory Investigation	**T222**	
Chapter Review	**T224**	

Investigations	Demonstrations	Texas Essential Elements★
Laboratory Manual 6–1 S	Volume, page T193 Gas Pressure, page T196	**Content:** 8.5, 8.9 **Process:** 10.1
Laboratory Manual 6–2 IM In-text Investigation, page T222	Charles's Law, page T207 Boyle's Law, page T214	**Content:** 8.3, 8.4 **Process:** 4.1, 5.2, 10.4
		Content: 8.4 **Process:** 1.2, 4.3, 5.1, 5.2, 6.3
		Process: 4.2, 5.2, 7.1, 10.2

KEY:
M–*Microscale*   **S**–*Structured*
I–*Inquiry*   **IM**–*Inquiry Microscale*

★*See pages T8–T11 for complete
listing of Texas Essential Elements.*

6

Gases and Their Properties

Chapter Rationale

This chapter is the first of a two-chapter sequence covering gases and gas laws. These chapters are placed in this section of the text to allow students a chance to integrate what they have already learned about stoichiometry with the study of gases.

Following these two chapters, material on subatomic structure and bonding is introduced. However, some instructors may prefer to cover chapters on atomic structure and bonding first since the material for these chapters does not depend on the gas law chapters.

The material in the latter half of this chapter is designed to teach not only the gas laws, but also the mathematical relationships behind the gas laws. Here is a chance to help your students with the direct and inverse proportions that they will encounter several times in their quantitative study of science.

About the Photograph

Air is more than 70 percent nitrogen with a density nearly equal to the density of nitrogen. Balloons filled with helium easily float in air since helium has a density much less than the density of the air displaced by the helium-filled balloons.

Chapter Planning Hints

Plan to complete the chapter, including the Laboratory Investigation and Chapter Review, within four to six class sessions. Optional demonstrations can be found on pages T193, T196, T207, T213, and T214. You may wish to preview them at this time.

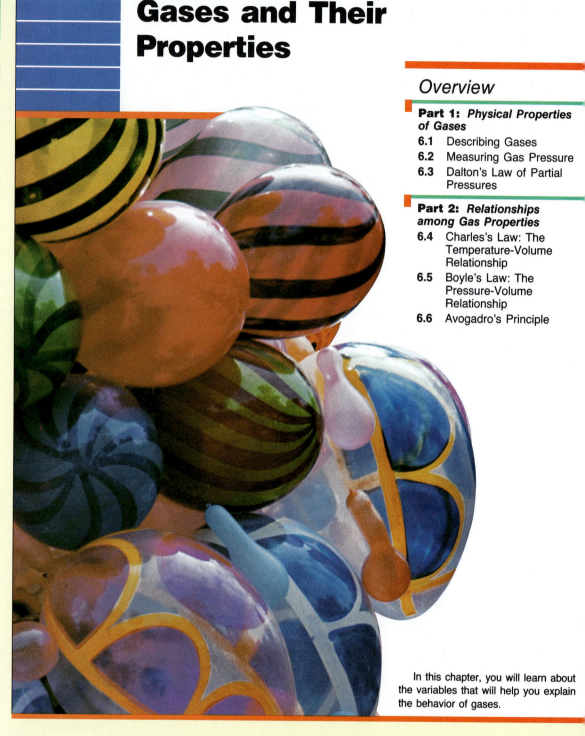

In this chapter, you will learn about the variables that will help you explain the behavior of gases.

PART 1 Physical Properties of Gases

Gases are easily the most overlooked form of matter. When you consider chemical reactions, you may think about dramatic color changes as two liquids are mixed or the formation of a new solid when a shiny metal is dipped into a solution. Since many gases are both colorless and odorless, it is easy to forget that gases may also play a role in chemical reactions.

Even though people may overlook gases more readily than other states of matter, gases are extremely important from a chemist's standpoint. A few simple variables, including pressure, volume, and temperature, can be used to determine the amount of a gas available for a reaction. Neither liquids nor solids have such a simple description. In this chapter, you will learn the interrelationships among the important gas variables. Then, in the next chapter, you will learn how to apply these relationships, and solve problems involving gaseous reactants and products.

O b j e c t i v e s

Part 1

A. *Describe* a gas on the submicroscopic level, using the variables of volume, temperature, and pressure.

B. *Explain* what gas pressure is and *describe* how it can be measured.

C. *Apply* Dalton's law of partial pressures to determine the total pressure of a mixture of gases or the partial pressure of an individual gas in the mixture.

6.1 Describing Gases

In Chapter 1, you learned that macroscopic properties can be understood by imagining matter to be composed of particles. Unlike the closely packed particles in solids or liquids, particles in a gas are farther apart and moving more rapidly in a random fashion. To describe such gas particles, measurements of three macroscopic variables of a given quantity of gas are needed—volume, temperature, and pressure.

Volume As you have already learned, volume refers to the space matter occupies. The volume of 1 mole of solid carbon dioxide (dry ice) is 28 cm^3, a space not much bigger than a large ice cube. Almost all of the volume of that solid is taken up by the carbon dioxide molecules themselves. Yet, as a gas at room temperature, the same number of carbon dioxide molecules occupies 25 000 cm^3, a volume almost 1000 times greater! Only a small fraction of the total volume of the gas is occupied by the molecules themselves. The rest of the volume is empty space.

From another point of view, there is also a lot of room for the molecules to move closer together—for instance, when the gas is compressed. When a gas is compressed, the same number of particles can now occupy a different volume.

Developing Skills

Students may apply this skill in their study of Part 1.
Interpreting diagrams: Discuss the barometers shown in Figure 6–4 and ask students to explain how they work.

≡ FOCUS

Activate Prior Knowledge

Help students preview this chapter by making use of the analogy developed in Part 1 before they begin reading the chapter. Find two boxes of different sizes and some small balls (Ping-Pong balls, golf balls, Styrofoam balls, or some other type). Put some balls into a box and shake it. The sound of the balls will give the students some idea of the frequency of collisions with the walls of the box. (You might ask students to shake the box themselves, so that they can follow this variable with the sense of touch.) Ask students what can be done to increase the frequency of collisions. They may suggest these factors which can be related to gas behavior:

1. Put the balls in a smaller box. (A decrease in volume corresponds to an increase in pressure.)

2. Shake the box harder. (An increase in temperature corresponds to an increase in pressure.)

3. Put more balls into the box. (More gas increases pressure.)

≡ TEACH

Teaching Strategy

Describing Gases

Students should have a clear mental picture of a gas on the molecular level. The molecules
(continued on page T194)

🔧 D E M O N S T R A T I O N

Volume

NOTE: You may have used this demonstration with Chapter 1, Section 1.9 (Comparing Solids, Liquids, and Gases). If so, it would be helpful to remind students of the concepts introduced then, and to reinforce them again here.

Demonstrate the difference in the amount of space occupied by a solid versus the same amount of substance in the

gaseous state. Put some finely crushed dry ice through a funnel into a balloon.

⚠️ **CAUTION: Do not allow the dry ice to come into contact with your skin.** Dry off the balloon and it will inflate. Call attention to the fact that you added a very small amount of solid carbon dioxide to the balloon, and now it has increased tremendously in size.

(continued from page T193)

are in constant and random motion. Oxygen molecules move at about 1000 miles per hour. A tremendous amount of empty space exists between the molecules.

Use an analogy to help students more fully understand the chaos in the movement of gas molecules. Increasing the scale by a factor of one billion changes the size of the oxygen atoms from 10^{-8} cm^3 to the size of an average student and changes the speed from 1000 miles per hour to one trillion miles per hour. On this scale, only three gas molecules would occupy a space as large as a lab classroom.

Figure 6-1 You may have seen the result of dry ice (solid carbon dioxide) in the special effects of a rock concert or a video. ⚠ CAUTION: Dry ice is extremely cold. Do not pick it up or even touch it with your bare hands.

You may have seen tanks of compressed helium gas that are used to fill balloons at amusement parks, parades, sporting events, or fairs. A typical 44-liter tank is able to fill roughly 500 balloons that are each 25 cm in diameter for a total volume of over 6500 liters! The compressibility of gases is a property that is applied to such diverse purposes as filling scuba tanks, inflating tires, and pressurizing airplanes.

Temperature You hear about gas temperature every day when the weather forecaster tells you what the previous day's high temperature has been and predicts what the evening low will be. To understand the effect of temperature on a gas, consider this analogy. Imagine some Ping-Pong balls confined to a box. This box has a volume much larger than that of the balls themselves. Then imagine that you shake the box. Shaking the box slowly results in the balls moving around slowly. This corresponds to a low temperature. Shaking the box vigorously results in a rapid motion of the balls. This corresponds to a high temperature. Similarly, the motion of molecules of a gas increases as the temperature increases.

Pressure Have you ever experienced a popping sensation in your ears as you quickly traveled up or down an elevator in a tall building or flew in an airplane? Or have you noticed how a balloon responds when you poke it with a sharp object? Both of these experiences are related to the effects of pressure.

To understand the concept of pressure, imagine a wood block resting on a tabletop, as shown in Figure 6-2. This wood block has dimensions of 5 cm by 9 cm by 20 cm. Its mass is 450 grams. Due to gravity, the block exerts a force on the tabletop. You can also say that it exerts pressure on the table. What exactly is the difference between force and pressure?

DO YOU KNOW?

"Dry ice" gets its name from the fact that solid carbon dioxide resembles frozen water. It is "dry" because at typical pressures found outside (at a picnic, for instance), the CO_2 passes directly from the solid state to the gaseous state without becoming a liquid. This process is referred to as sublimation.

The force that the block exerts on the tabletop is proportional to the mass of the block. As long as the block is resting on the table at the same altitude (that is, as long as all of the measurements are performed in the same locale, without a move from sea level for one measurement to the top of Mount McKinley for another), the block exerts the same force on the table.

The same is not true for **pressure.** Pressure is a force exerted over a given area. Since the block has three distinctly different sides, there are three different areas of contact it can have with the table. Since the force of the block may be distributed over different areas, the pressure depends upon which side of the block is face down.

In Figure 6-2 you can see that the value of *mass per unit area* has been calculated for each of the three different faces of the wood block. This value is proportional to the pressure corresponding to each face. The block exerts the greatest pressure when it rests on the side having the smallest area. It exerts the least pressure when on the side having the largest area.

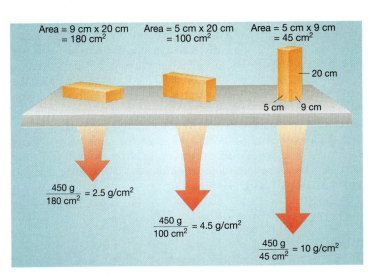

Figure 6-2 *The pressure exerted by a wood block when it stands on its smallest face is nearly four times the pressure exerted when it stands on its widest face.*

Force versus pressure The difference between force and pressure is very clear if a woman wearing high-heeled shoes accidentally steps on your toes with the heel. You feel the pressure, and, unfortunately, the pain too! The weight of the woman is concentrated over a small area producing a huge amount of pressure. The same woman in a pair of sneakers would exert much less pressure (although your foot might still hurt). Remember that pressure is measured in *force per area.* The high heel transmits the force to a much smaller area than that covered by the sneaker; therefore the resulting pressure is greater.

Some people who live in northern latitudes wear snowshoes to walk in deep snow. These shoes resemble oversized tennis rackets that can be lashed onto your feet. The idea behind snowshoes is simply an extension of the analogy between high-heeled shoes and sneakers. By spreading the force of your body upon the ground over an even larger area provided by the snowshoes, the pressure exerted upon the snow becomes less than what it would be in regular shoes. By wearing snowshoes, you can remain on top of the snow whereas you might sink to your knees if you wore ordinary boots.

Gas pressure The concept of pressure can be applied to gases because moving molecules of a gas exert pressure on their container. Again the analogy of the Ping-Pong balls in a box is useful. As the box is put into motion, the balls fly around randomly in all directions. If you put your hands on the outside of the box, you will feel the balls as they bounce off the sides. Each time one ball rebounds, there is a force exerted on the box.

If this force is measured for a given unit of area on the wall of the box, the *pressure* of the moving Ping-Pong balls is obtained. In Figure 6-3 (left), there are a small number of Ping-Pong balls in the box, so only a few collisions per second occur within the target area. The pressure exerted by the Ping-Pong balls is relatively low. On the other hand, the box in Figure 6-4 (right) contains many Ping-Pong balls. More collisions within the target area occur per second because there are more balls moving in the same volume. In this situation, the pressure of the Ping-Pong balls against the container walls at any one instant is greater than before. Can you think of a way of increasing the number of collisions within the target area in Figure 6-3 (left) without adding more balls to the box? Molecules of a gas behave in much the same way as Ping-Pong balls in a box. When gas molecules strike the walls of their container, they also exert a force on the walls. This force per unit area is known as gas pressure.

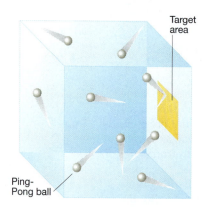
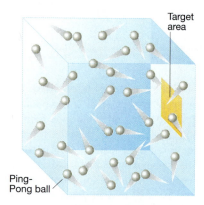

Target area

Ping-Pong ball

Target area

Ping-Pong ball

Figure 6-3 Left: *Each time the box is shaken, the Ping-Pong balls bounce in every direction. Collisions with the walls and the other balls occur constantly. The force of the collisions on the target area represents the overall pressure that the balls exert in the box.* Right: *The pressure on the target area is greater in this box. The pressure has increased because more Ping-Pong balls hit the target area at any instant.*

D E M O N S T R A T I O N

Gas Pressure

Demonstrate the surprising force of air pressure. Rinse out an empty metal can (such as a duplicator fluid can). Place about 200 cm³ of water into it. Heat the can with the cap off until the water boils. Remove the can from the heat, cap it tightly, and place it in a pan of cold water. As the water vapor inside the can condenses,

the inside air pressure decreases, and the can will be crushed by the greater pressure of the air on the outside.

⚠ **CAUTION: Wear safety goggles. Do not reheat the sealed can. It may rupture, and the escaping steam may burn the skin.**

Concept ✓ Check

Explain how the analogy of Ping-Pong balls in a box can be used to understand the concepts of volume, temperature, and pressure of a gas.

6.2 Measuring Gas Pressure

Why would it be useful to know the pressure of a gas? When working with gases, you need to know how much gas you have, but measuring the mass of a gas can be difficult. Measuring the volume is much easier. You will soon learn in this chapter that volume can be calculated if you know the pressure and temperature of a given quantity of gas. A value for pressure can be obtained through measurement.

Figure 6-4 *Weather forecasters, scientists, airplane pilots, and sailors are examples of people who need to know atmospheric pressure. Barometers are made in a variety of shapes and sizes. Are any of these barometers familiar to you?*

Barometers You have already encountered measurements of pressure. Your bicycle tire may be somewhat flat if its pressure is only 25 pounds per square inch. The weather reporter may state that the evening's air pressure is 29.95 inches. You know a gauge can be used to measure the pressure of your bicycle tire, but how can someone measure the pressure of a gas that is not confined?

A device that is used to measure atmospheric pressure is called a **barometer.** The simplest barometer consists of a long tube containing a column of mercury. It measures pressure by allowing the air to exert a force against something else (mercury), which exerts

DO YOU KNOW?

When you use a gauge to measure the pressure of your car tire, you are actually measuring the difference between your tire's pressure and the air pressure. If the air pressure is 14.5 pounds per square inch and the gauge reads 30 pounds per square inch, then the pressure inside your tire is actually 44.5 pounds per square inch.

Science Background

Measuring Gas Pressure

Although the pascal is the officially accepted unit of pressure in the SI system, it may not be as familiar as the older units of atmosphere (atm) or torr. The pascal is a unit of pressure equal to one newton per square meter. The pressure in pascals of a volume of mercury 1 m^2 × 760 mm high is calculated as follows. The volume of the column is 0.760 m^3, or 7.60×10^5 cm^3. The density of mercury is 13.596 g/cm^3. Using the formula, density = mass/volume, the mass of the mercury column is 1.033×10^4 kg. Since force is m × a, the force exerted by the column is $(1.033 \times 10^4$ kg$) \times (9.806$ m/s$^2)$, or 1.013×10^5 kg m/s^2, which is 1.013×10^5 newtons. The pressure (force per unit area) of the column of mercury is 1.013 × 10^5 N/1 m^2 = 101 300 pascals, or 101.3 kPa.

Science Background

Measuring Gas Pressure

If you live at an elevation above sea level, your students may notice that air pressures reported by meteorologists are higher than those in the classroom. Point out to students that for the purposes of comparability, all of the pressures that are reported have been converted to sea-level equivalents. Otherwise, Denver would always appear to be in a low pressure zone when compared to San Francisco.

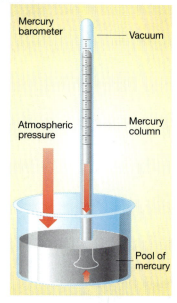

Mercury barometer

Vacuum

Atmospheric pressure

Mercury column

Pool of mercury

Figure 6-5 *The atmospheric pressure supports the column of mercury at a specific height inside the tube. Atmospheric pressure balances the pressure exerted by the mercury column. When atmospheric pressure decreases, the column falls. When atmospheric pressure increases, the column rises.* ⚠ *CAUTION: Liquid mercury evaporates, and the vapor is toxic.*

DO YOU KNOW?

Scuba divers have experienced the effects of increased pressure. For every 10 meters in water depth, the pressure is increased by 100 kPa. A 4-liter balloon would be reduced to a volume of 2 liters at a depth of 10 meters and a volume of 1 liter at a depth of 30 meters.

a force back. Although any liquid could be used inside this column, mercury makes a convenient choice. It has a high density for a liquid so a relatively small amount of mercury can be used to balance common atmospheric pressures. Mercury does not readily react with other substances. Mercury is a liquid between −39°C and 357°C, and can therefore be used over a wide range of temperatures, including some temperatures well below the freezing point of water.

A barometer can be constructed by using a meter-long glass tube that is sealed at one end. Enough mercury is poured in to fill the tube and while the open end of the tube is plugged, the tube is inverted into a pool of more mercury. When the plug is removed, what do you think will happen to the column of mercury in the tube? Remember that the upper end of the tube is sealed. Figure 6-5 depicts the result of the procedure. Some of the mercury will run out of the tube and into the mercury pool. Since no air has been able to get into the tube above the column of mercury, air is not exerting a force on the mercury. Yet the mercury column in the tube must be supported by some force; otherwise all of the mercury in the tube would run out into the pool. The force is Earth's atmosphere, which is pushing down on the pool. The pressure of the atmosphere is exactly balanced by the pressure exerted by the column of mercury pushing against this pool. Because the mercury runs out of the full tube until it is exactly counterbalanced by the atmosphere, the level of mercury inside the barometer can be used as a measure of air pressure. The level of mercury rises or falls as the air pressure increases or decreases.

Units of pressure When you use a barometer, the height of the mercury column above the pool of mercury at the bottom can be read as an indication of air pressure. When pressure is recorded from a barometer, the units used may be *mm Hg* (read as "millimeters of mercury"). In honor of Evangelista Torricelli—the Italian mathematician and physicist who invented the barometer in the 1640's—the unit *torr* is synonymous with *mm Hg*.

In SI units, pressure is measured in **pascals** (Pa)—named for Blaise Pascal, a French mathematician who studied air pressure. A pascal is so small, however, that the unit kilopascal (kPa) is more commonly used. By applying what you already know about metric prefixes, you should be able to calculate that 1 kPa is equal to 1000 Pa.

$$1 \text{ kPa} = 1000 \text{ Pa}$$

Gases have a tremendously wide range of pressures. The pressure of Earth's atmosphere on your body is about 10^5 pascals (or 100 kPa). This pressure is more accurately reported as 101.325 kilopascals. The pressure in a full tank of compressed helium gas is 10^7 pascals (or 10 000 kPa). By contrast, the pressure of hydrogen gas in deep space is about 10^{-23} pascals. This pressure is equivalent to 1 molecule of hydrogen gas per 400 cubic meters. For all practical purposes, deep space is a **vacuum**, a system in which the pressure is zero pascals.

Myths and Misconceptions

Students often have a misconception about normal atmospheric pressure (at sea level, 1 atm at 25°C), because they cannot actually feel or observe the effects of this air pressure in their everyday lives. The effects of air pressure are only apparent in certain situations, such as a decrease in pressure at higher elevations, or the "popping" of ears when one yawns. To help students grasp the concept of air pressure, focus on several concrete examples and demonstrations that illustrate the effects of air pressure.

Pressure also can be measured in **atmospheres.** One atmosphere is equivalent to 101.325 kilopascals. Both values are called **standard pressure,** the average pressure of air at sea level.

$$1 \text{ atm} = 101.325 \text{ kPa}$$

Table 6-1 lists several of the different units of pressure. You should learn to interchange pascals, kilopascals, and atmospheres because you will work with all of these units in chemistry.

TABLE 6-1

Units of Pressure	
Unit	Equivalence of 1 kPa
Pascal (Pa)	1 kPa = 1000 Pa
Atmosphere (atm)	1 kPa = 0.009 869 atm
Bar	1 kPa = 0.01 bar
Torr	1 kPa = 7.501 torr
Millimeter of mercury (mm Hg)	1 kPa = 7.501 mm Hg
Pounds per square inch (psi)	1 kPa = 0.145 psi

EXAMPLE 6-1

When reading a classroom barometer, you find that the mercury has risen to a height of 72.9 cm. What is this value expressed in kilopascals and atmospheres?

■ **Analyze the Problem** Write down what you are being asked to find.

$$? \text{ kPa} = 72.9 \text{ cm Hg}$$
$$? \text{ atm} = 72.9 \text{ cm Hg}$$

■ **Apply a Strategy** List the relationships that you will need in order to complete the conversions. From Table 6-1 you can see that there is no conversion given between cm Hg and kPa. A relationship that is listed, however, is

$$1 \text{ kPa} = 7.501 \text{ mm Hg}$$

To use this relationship, first change cm Hg to mm Hg. You can write the relationship as

$$1 \text{ cm Hg} = 10 \text{ mm Hg}$$

These two relationships will allow you to convert 72.9 cm Hg to kPa. Once you have the value in kPa, you can change kPa to atm, using the relationship

$$101.325 \text{ kPa} = 1.00 \text{ atm}$$

DO YOU KNOW?

A pressure of 1 Pa is approximately equivalent to the weight of one apple, finely ground, spread over the area of 1 m^2 (near sea level). Needless to say, compared to atmospheric pressure (approximately 100 000 Pa), this is quite a small unit of pressure!

PROBLEM·SOLVING

S T R A T E G Y

***Use what you know** to help solve this problem. In this case, you have to draw on your knowledge of metric prefixes. (See Strategy, page 58.)*

Teaching Strategy

Apply Example 6–1 to your own classroom setting. Show students how to read a mercury barometer, and ask them to convert the reading in mm Hg into torr, cm Hg, atm, and kPa.

PART 1

Section 6.2 *continued*

Practice Problems

Assign the Practice Problems.

**Videodisc Connections**

569, side 6
Underwater pressure gradient
(1 frame)

■ *Work a Solution* First, convert cm Hg to kPa.

$$72.9 \ \cancel{cm \ Hg} \times \frac{10 \ \cancel{mm \ Hg}}{1 \ \cancel{cm \ Hg}} \times \frac{1 \ kPa}{7.501 \ \cancel{mm \ Hg}} = 97.2 \ kPa$$

Next, convert kPa to atm.

$$97.2 \ \cancel{kPa} \times \frac{1 \ atm}{101.325 \ \cancel{kPa}} = 0.959 \ atm$$

■ *Verify Your Answer* From the text, you know that standard pressure is 101.325 kPa. Your answer in kilopascals should be close to that value to be correct, and it is. Also, the answer in atmospheres should have a smaller numerical value than the pressure in pascals because there are more kilopascals per atmosphere. Again, the answer illustrates this.

Practice Problems

1. Change the pressure of 74.5 cm Hg into atmospheres.
   Ans. 0.980 atm

2. What is the pressure of 97.5 kPa in atmospheres?
   Ans. 0.962 atm

Figure 6-6 *Gas molecules push against the mercury surface, exerting a pressure that can be measured by finding the difference in the height of the mercury columns. This value can be converted into SI units.*

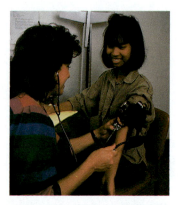

Figure 6-7 *Have you had your blood pressure measured when giving blood? The blood pressure cuff that doctors and nurses use is a type of manometer.*

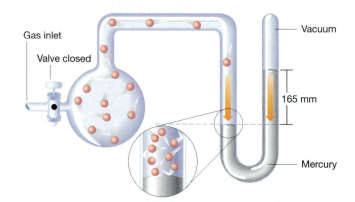

Close-ended manometer A device similar to a barometer can be used to measure the pressure of gases other than the atmosphere. Such an apparatus is called a **manometer.** In Figure 6-6 above, you can see how a close-ended manometer operates. (It is called a close-ended manometer because the tube is sealed off at one end, creating a vacuum in this portion of the manometer.) The U-tube containing mercury is connected to a flask containing the gas in question. Gas molecules moving within the flask rebound against the walls of the flask and the surface of the mercury. As the molecules push against the mercury, they exert a force that supports the column at a specific height. The difference in height of the mercury in the two sides of the U-tube can be used to find the gas pressure.

Rereading the Problem

One of the easiest mistakes to make when solving problems is to stop working before you have arrived at the final goal of the program. For example, the sales tag on a black-and-gold sweatshirt at a local discount store reads $30.00. The sales tax in your state is 5 percent. What is the total price that the cashier will charge you for this sweater? To solve the problem, you must remember to change 5 percent to 0.05. You can then determine the sales tax that you will pay by multiplying.

$$0.05 \times \$30.00 = \$1.50$$

Are you done? If you think that this is the final answer, take a closer look at the problem statement. It asks for the *total price* of the sweatshirt (including sales tax), not just the amount of sales tax that you will pay. In order to finish this problem, you must add the sales tax of $1.50 to the $30.00 cost, obtaining an answer of $31.50.

▶ When to Reread

Rereading a problem when you are finished will help you avoid such mistakes. By referring back to the statement you can make sure that you have all of the information you need. In addition, try rereading a problem at these points as well.

■ Reread the problem just after you first read it, before you be-

gin to work, especially if the problem is long. The first time you read the problem, become oriented to its setting. On the second reading, you should take a more interactive approach. Try to determine which information in the problem is important, and jot it down on a sheet of paper. Pay close attention to the question.

■ All problem solvers find that they hit a blind alley every once in a while. When this happens you may be tempted to look for the mistake in your work. But do not forget to look back at the problem. You may have misinterpreted a phrase in the problem when you read it.

■ One good strategy for solving complex problems is to set subgoals. This lets you work with smaller, more manageable pieces of the problem. However, if you spend a long time working on a particular subgoal, it is easy to lose sight of the ultimate question posed by the problem. For example, when you are solving a stoichiometry problem involving the masses of a reactant and a product, you may set as a subgoal finding the number of moles of reactant that you have available. After you have completed this step, it is useful to reread the problem to remind yourself what you are ultimately trying to determine.

▶ FOCUS ON
PROBLEM SOLVING

Activate Prior Knowledge

Students are well acquainted with various units used for measuring time. Ask students to find how many seconds are in a year and to identity information from the problem that is given and that is asked for. Then ask students to write the relationships that link seconds and years, such as 60 seconds equals 1 minute, 60 minutes equals 1 hour, and so on. Show students how to write the problem using the factor-label method. After students solve the problem, have them reread their work to verify their answers.

▶ TEACH
THE STRATEGY

Guided Practice

Use the strategy of rereading for Practice Problems 1, 2, 3, and 4 on pages 200 and 204.

Reteaching Idea

If you need to emphasize the importance of rereading problems, read some problems to your students without explanation of your objective. You might use Part 1 Review problem 13 on page 204 or Chapter Review problems 14a and 15 on page 223. Any stoichiometry problem in Chapter 5 could also be used. Make the exercise more challenging by rephrasing some problems to put what must be calculated into the middle of the problem. For example, in reading problem 13 in Part 1 Review, you might reverse the order of the second and third sentences.

After reading each problem, have students write down what must be calculated. If they ask for a second reading, your point is made.

Teaching Strategy

Dalton's Law of Partial Pressures

Use the Ping-Pong ball analogy to help illustrate Dalton's law. Suppose you place blue balls and red balls into a box. The total number of hits against the sides of the box is the sum of the hits of blue balls and red balls.

6.3 Dalton's Law of Partial Pressures

When you do experiments involving gases, you may need to collect a sample of gas and measure the volume that it occupies. This task seems easy to do; just find an empty bottle and let the gas fill it. However, any bottle or flask open to the atmosphere is not really empty; it is filled with air. If you try to collect another gas in a bottle that already has air in it, the new gas simply mixes with the air already present.

How can you collect a gas without its mixing with air? The common solution is to use water displacement. First fill the collecting bottle with water to get rid of the air. Then invert the bottle in a tank of water and bubble the gas into the bottle to displace the water. The setup is shown in Figure 6-8. In cases where the gas is not very soluble in water, this arrangement works well. However, a small amount of water evaporates and mixes with the gas being collected. An adjustment must be made to account for the part of the total pressure that is due to the water vapor.

Figure 6-8 As the gas bubbles through the water in the inverted bottle, most of the water is forced out, leaving the sample of the desired gas. However, some water molecules remain in vapor form and contribute to the total gas pressure in the bottle.

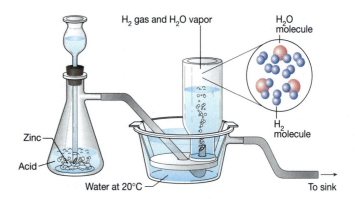

Adjusting for water vapor In Figure 6-9, there are three 1-liter bulbs at 25°C. The first bulb contains 0.0050 mole of oxygen at a pressure of 12.4 kPa. There is 0.0011 mole of water vapor in the second bulb, and the pressure is 2.7 kPa. What happens when the oxygen and water vapor are combined in the same bulb? The third bulb shows that the pressure is 15.1 kPa, the sum of the two previous pressures.

The individual pressure of each gas is called the **partial pressure.** The partial pressure of a gas is the pressure that the gas would exert if it were the only gas in the container. There is so much space between molecules in a gas that molecules of another gas can readily share the space. Each gas behaves independently of the other and makes its own contribution to the total pressure.

The same addition technique can be applied to successfully predict the total pressure when several gases are mixed together. In 1801, John Dalton, an English scientist, was the first to suggest that the total pressure of a mixture of gases is the sum of the partial

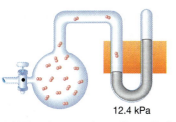

12.4 kPa

0.0050 mole oxygen in one liter at 25°C

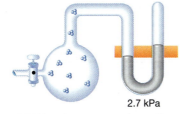

2.7 kPa

0.0011 mole water vapor in one liter at 25°C

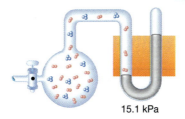

15.1 kPa

0.0050 mole oxygen + 0.0011 mole water vapor in one liter at 25°C

pressures of the individual gases in the mixture. **Dalton's law of partial pressures** can be expressed in the form of an equation.

$$P_{Total} = P_a + P_b + P_c$$

P_{Total} is the total pressure; and P_a, P_b, and P_c symbolize the partial pressure of the individual gases in the mixture. If there are more than three gases in the mixture, then the right-hand side of this equation would contain a partial-pressure value for each gas.

In the laboratory, you can subtract the partial pressure of water vapor when you collect a gas over water, using the law of partial pressures. Example 6-2 shows how to make such a correction.

Figure 6-9 *The total pressure of a mixture of gases equals the sum of the partial pressures of all the gases in the container.*

EXAMPLE 6-2

What is the pressure of hydrogen gas collected over water at 24°C? The water levels inside and outside the collecting bottle are equal at the end of the experiment. The atmospheric pressure is 94.4 kPa. At this temperature, the vapor pressure of water is 3.0 kPa.

■ *Analyze the Problem* You are told that the water levels inside and outside the bottle are the same. From this information, you can conclude that the total pressure inside the bottle is exactly balanced by the total atmospheric pressure outside the bottle.

$$P_{Total} = P_{atm} = 94.4 \text{ kPa}$$

The problem also gives you the value for the vapor pressure of water. Since the pressure of a gas collected over water is due to two gases, you know that you have the value for at least one of those gases and must now find the value for the other—hydrogen.

■ *Apply a Strategy* Apply the law of partial pressures to the information given in the example. Write out the equation.

$$P_{Total} = P_{H_2} + P_{H_2O}$$

Substitute into the equation the values you know.

$$94.4 \text{ kPa} = P_{H_2} + 3.0 \text{ kPa}$$

■ *Work a Solution* Rearrange the equation and solve for P_{H_2}.

$$P_{H_2} = 94.4 \text{ kPa} - 3.0 \text{ kPa} = 91.4 \text{ kPa}$$

PROBLEM-SOLVING STRATEGY

Reread the problem to look for all of the relevant information in a problem. (See Strategy, page 201.)

Guided Practice

Review the Concept Check question on page 197 with students. Answers can be found in Appendix E on page 808.

Reteaching Idea

You can reinforce Dalton's law and the behavior of gases in general by revisiting the electrolysis of water discussed in Chapter 2. If you have an electrolytic apparatus, you may want to repeat the demonstration, this time collecting both gases in one large test tube. An alternative is to discuss the process as a thought experiment.

A test tube of the gases has been collected and the level of water inside the test tube has been made equal to the level outside. Ask students what gases are present (H_2, O_2, H_2O). Ask them if they know how to find the pressure of the gas mixture (atmospheric pressure). Read the barometer or assume a typical value; then ask if they can determine the pressure of each gas in the mixture. Elicit that the vapor pressure of water is a known value for the temperature of the room and can be subtracted from the total pressure.

To determine the partial pressures of H_2 and O_2, students may need to have you refer them to the equation for the decomposition of water and the ratio of moles of H_2 to O_2. Recall the Ping-Pong ball model in Section 6.1 and note that it applies to all gases regardless of composition. Try to get students to conclude that after the vapor pressure of water is subtracted, $2/3$ of the remaining pressure is due to H_2 and $1/3$ to O_2. If you use actual data for atmospheric pressure and the vapor pressure of water, the partial pressures of H_2 and O_2 can be calculated. To go further, ask what would happen to the volume of the collected gas if the temperature in the room drops during the night or if atmospheric pressure rises.

PART 1
Section 6.3 *continued*

Practice Problems

Assign the Practice Problems.

☰ CLOSE

Summing Up Main Ideas

Ask students to explain how volume, temperature, and pressure affect the air in an automobile tire. Also ask students to convert a tire pressure of 35 psi into kPa, torr, and atm. (A tire has a fixed volume, so temperature changes will most affect tire pressure. During cold weather, tire pressure will decrease. 35 psi = 241 kPa = 1808 torr = 2.4 atm)

PART 1 REVIEW

Assign the Part Review questions.

Evaluating Skills

These skills are evaluated in the Part Review questions indicated. **Forming models:** 5; **Determining main ideas:** 6, 8, 9, 11, 12; **Comparing/Contrasting:** 7; **Analyzing data:** 8, 9, 10, 13; **Applying a strategy:** 10, 13; **Calculating:** 10, 13; **Verifying results:** 10, 13

Boxed numbers indicate questions that involve skills in interpretation, application, and analysis.

PROBLEM-SOLVING

S T R A T E G Y

Reread the problem carefully so that you can identify which information is important and which is not. (See Strategy, page 201.)

■ **Verify Your Answer** Check your answer by substituting the values for P_{H_2} and P_{H_2O} into the equation and solve for P_{Total}. You get 91.4 kPa + 3.0 kPa = 94.4 kPa, which is what you expect if your answer for P_{H_2} is correct.

Practice Problems

3. You collect a sample of oxygen gas by the water-displacement method described in the example. If the atmospheric pressure is 99.4 kPa and the water-vapor pressure is 4.5 kPa, then what is the partial pressure of the oxygen gas?

Ans. 94.9 kPa

4. A balloon contains a mixture of helium and nitrogen. The partial pressure of the helium is 93 kPa. If the total pressure inside the balloon is 101 kPa, then what is the partial pressure of the nitrogen gas? *Ans.* 8 kPa

PART 1 REVIEW

5. Using the Ping-Pong balls analogy given in this section as a model, develop your own model to
   a. explain why gases exert a pressure.
   b. explain what is meant by the temperature of a gas.

6. When you talk about the volume of a gas, are you referring to the volume of the molecules themselves? Explain.

7. What is the difference between a pressure and a force?

8. Due to gravity, does a 50-kilogram woman exert more or less force on the ground than a 70-kilogram man? Explain.

9. Is it possible for a 50-kilogram woman to exert greater pressure on the ground than a 70-kilogram man? Explain.

10. A gas is put into a closed-end manometer. The mercury that separates the flask from the vacuum is found to be 165 mm higher on the side with the vacuum.
    a. What is the pressure of this gas in torr?
    Ans. 165 torr
    b. What is the pressure of this gas in kPa?
    Ans. 22.0 kPa

11. What is meant by the term *partial pressure of a gas*?

12. State the law of partial pressures in words and in the form of an equation.

13. A sample of nitrogen is collected over water at 21.5°C. The vapor pressure of water at 21.5°C is 2.6 kPa. What is the partial pressure of the nitrogen if the total pressure in the flask is 99.4 kPa? *Ans.* 96.8 kPa

---

PART 1 REVIEW

ANSWERS

■ **Keyed to Objectives**

A 5. a. Gas molecules strike the sides of their container.
   b. As the molecular velocity increases, so does the temperature of a gas.

A 6. No; you are referring to the volume of the container.

B 7. A pressure is a force per unit area.

B 8. There is a greater gravitational attraction for the 70-kg man, so, this is a greater force.

B 9. Yes; if she wears shoes with a much smaller surface area than he does.

B 10. a. 165 mm Hg × 1 torr/1 mm Hg = 165 torr
   b. 165 torr × 1 atm/760 torr × 101.3 kPa/atm = 22.0 kPa

C 11. The pressure that one component of a gas mixture exerts individually is its partial pressure.

C 12. The total pressure of a gas mixture is equal to the sum of the partial pressures of its components.
$P_{tot} = P_a + P_b + P_c \ldots$

C 13. 99.4 kPa − 2.6 kPa = 96.8 kPa

PART 2 Relationships among Gas Properties

At the beginning of the nineteenth century, science took to the air. Ballooning was the rage. Two French scientists who had a thirst for adventure made great strides in the art and science of ballooning. They were Jacques Charles and Joseph Gay-Lussac. Both men developed hydrogen-filled balloons. In 1804, Joseph Gay-Lussac used a hydrogen-filled balloon to ascend 7000 meters. This record stood unmatched for nearly 40 years.

A modern hot-air balloon, like the one shown in Figure 6-10, does not contain hydrogen. It is open at the bottom so that a heat source can increase the temperature of the air inside. As the air in the balloon gets warmer, it becomes less dense than the surrounding atmosphere. The balloon rises for the same reason that a piece of wood floats on water—the balloon, like the wood, is less dense than its surroundings. The question in the case of the hot-air balloon is "Why does the air inside the balloon become less dense than the air outside the balloon?" What is happening when the air is heated that causes a change in the density of the gas?

To answer questions such as these, you need to consider possible relationships among volume, temperature, and pressure of a gas. In the process of learning about these relationships, you will acquire the knowledge and tools not only to predict *how* gases will behave but also to explain on the submicroscopic level *why* gases behave as they do—including the gas in a hot-air balloon.

Objectives

Part 2

D. **Apply** Charles's law to **describe** how the volume of a gas is related to its temperature.

E. **Apply** Boyle's law to **describe** how the volume of a gas is related to pressure.

F. **Explain** how the law of combining volumes can be used to **describe** volume relationships and show how Avogadro's principle can explain this law.

Developing Skills

Students may apply this skill in their study of Part 2.

Forming hypotheses: Ask students to hypothesize what would happen to the volume of an inflated balloon if the balloon were put in a refrigerator.

☰ FOCUS

Activate Prior Knowledge

Some students may have used a tire gauge and know that it measures air pressure. Use a manual tire pump, tire gauge, and an inner tube from a bicycle tire to demonstrate relationships between temperature, volume, and pressure. Try to expel as much air as possible from the tube before using the gauge to measure the air pressure. Have a student pump some air into the tube. Measure the air pressure, and then try to squeeze the air into a smaller volume by stepping on the tube. Measure the air pressure for the compressed tube. Try to inflate the tube to the recommended pressure. Measure this air pressure with the gauge, and place the tube in ice water for about 15 minutes. Measure the air pressure after the tube has cooled. Have students explain any differences in the measurements.

Figure 6-10 *A modern balloon is open at the bottom so the temperature of the air inside can be increased by a heat source.*

≡ TEACH

Cooperative Learning

Teams of 2; **Time:** 20 minutes
Objective: Students will use familiar objects to study the concept of direct proportion.

Task: Using a compass, one student will draw a circle on a sheet of paper. A partner will determine the diameter and the circumference using a string and a ruler. Partners will trade roles until data are obtained for at least four circles of varying sizes.

Team responsibility: After gathering their data, teams will be asked to describe the relationships that they find in their data. Ask them how the circumference and diameter are related and to express this relationship in as many ways as possible.

Evaluation: Lead a class discussion so that teams can compare their results. Some may say that as the diameter increases, so does the circumference. Others may express an algebraic relationship that they found. Use this discussion as a springboard for asking if they can think of any other variables that have a relationship similar to the one they have been describing.

Extension: Ask students to plot their data, using circumference as the *y*-axis and diameter as the *x*-axis. What is the value of the slope of their line? What significance does this number have? Hopefully, some students will recognize that the slope is the familiar value of pi.

Videodisc Connections

568, side 6
Charles' Law; computer graphic
(1 frame)

6.4 Charles's Law: The Temperature-Volume Relationship

Jacques Charles is given credit for correctly describing a fundamental relationship between the volume of a gas and its temperature. This temperature-volume relationship, or **Charles's law,** can be demonstrated with the apparatus shown in Figure 6-11.

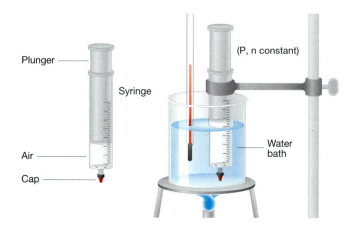

Figure 6-11 *Air is at room temperature in the syringe on the left. On the right, air is being heated as the water is heated. The plunger moves up as the volume of the gas increases.*

A calibrated syringe is partially filled with air at room temperature, and the volume is read. The syringe is then placed in a beaker of heated water. The plunger of the syringe may move up or down to allow a constant pressure to be maintained. As the water warms up, the gas expands. The new volume is measured at increments of 10°C. The number of moles of gas in the syringe does not change. Table 6-2 shows the data from this experiment.

TABLE 6-2

Volume of a Sample of Air at a Constant Pressure	
Temperature (°C)	Volume (cm³)
20.0	65.2
30.0	67.4
40.0	69.2
50.0	71.6
60.0	73.1
70.0	75.7
80.0	78.0
90.0	80.2
100.0	82.4

Look closely at the data. Do you notice a regularity? As the temperature of the trapped air increases, the volume of the trapped gas also increases. This relationship holds true for most gases at moderate temperatures when the pressure and the number of moles remain constant.

The Kelvin scale A graph of the data in Table 6-2 appears in Figure 6-12 (top). Recall from your earlier study of graphs that this graph resembles that of a direct proportion. If that is so, then the line should pass through the origin. However, the bottom graph of Figure 6-12 shows that the point of intercept with the *x*-axis is at −273°C rather than at the origin.

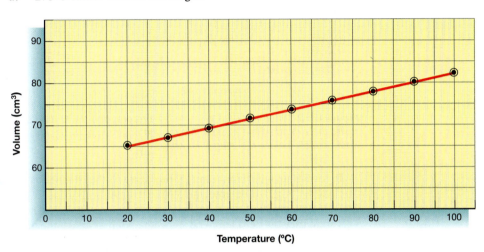

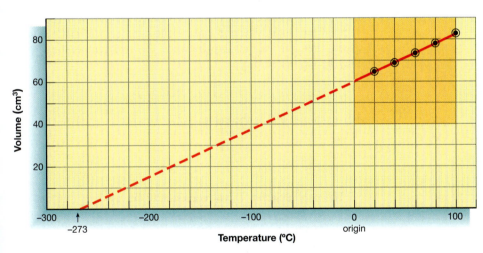

Figure 6-12 Top: *A graph of the data in Table 6-2 indicates that the volume of the air increases with increasing temperature.* Bottom: *If the line is extended, however, it does not pass through the origin, as it would for a direct proportion.*

DEMONSTRATION

Charles's Law

Demonstrate to students how gas volume varies with temperature.

⚠ **CAUTION: Wear safety goggles.**
Use two 1000-mL beakers and blow up two balloons so that each balloon can barely fit into a beaker. Partially fill one beaker with ice water, and put boiling water into the other beaker. Show how the balloon in ice water is easy to remove as it shrinks, while the balloon in hot water becomes difficult to remove from the beaker as it expands.

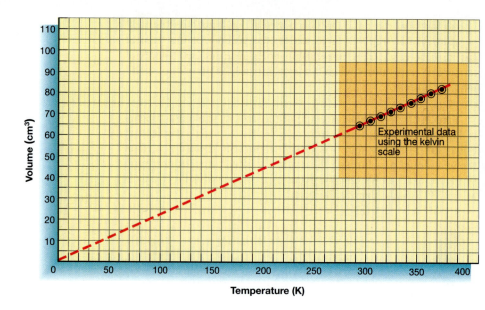

Figure 6-13 *When the data in Table 6-2 are graphed using the kelvin scale, the extended line passes through the origin. In actuality, the gas would liquefy before reaching 0 kelvins.*

If you set up a different temperature scale so that the line passes through the origin, then you would have a direct proportion. Figure 6-13 shows a graph of the same data using such a temperature scale. This scale uses the zero temperature as the point at which the graph crosses the *x*-axis (in Figure 6-12). This new temperature scale varies from the Celsius scale by 273 units. The scale is called the **kelvin scale** and is divided into increments called **kelvins.** If *T* represents temperature in kelvins and *t* represents temperature in Celsius degrees, then the relationship between the two temperature scales may be expressed as

$$T = t + 273$$

For example, 0°C is the same as 273 kelvins.

$$T = 0°C + 273$$
$$T = 273 \text{ K}$$

The capital letter *T* will consistently be used in this book to represent temperatures reported in the kelvin scale. Note that temperatures on this scale are read as "273 kelvins," and not "273 degrees kelvin." Neither the degree symbol (°) nor the word *degree* is used with kelvin temperatures. Table 6-3 shows the data plotted in Figure 6-14, using the kelvin temperature scale. This table reveals another property that is characteristic of a direct proportion: the quotient of *V/T* consistently gives close values.

TABLE 6-3

Volume of a Sample of Air at a Constant Pressure		
Temperature (K)	Volume (cm³)	V/T (cm³/K)
293	65.2	0.223
303	66.2	0.218
313	69.2	0.221
323	71.6	0.222
333	73.1	0.220
343	75.7	0.221
353	78.0	0.221
363	80.2	0.221
373	82.4	0.221

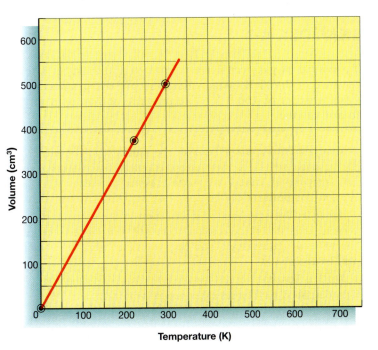

Figure 6-14 *A graph of the data in Table 6-3 shows that V/T is a direct proportion.*

PART 2
Section 6.4 *continued*

Teaching Strategy

Expressing a Direct Proportion
As students learn different ways to solve problems, you will find that they try different approaches in their solutions. Remind students that their answers may vary slightly depending on the methods they use. Rounding to significant digits during calculations will affect answers slightly. When several calculations are done in succession to arrive at a final answer, it is good practice to carry at least one digit more than will show when the final answer is properly rounded. If this is done, the rounding errors will be minimized.

Expressing a direct proportion Why go to all this trouble of changing temperature scales? Remember that you are looking for a way to express a proportionality between the volume of a gas and its temperature. You have learned that if the line of a graph passes through the origin, you can express the relationship as

$$\frac{A}{B} = k \text{ (where k is a constant)}$$

In this case, *A* is volume and *B* is temperature, so $\frac{V}{T} = k$ (where T is in kelvins; the amount of gas and its pressure are held constant).

PART **2**

Section 6.4 continued

The constant k tells you how much the volume changes for every change in temperature of 1 K. Note the value of k for these data is about 0.221 cm³/K. Therefore, the volume of the gas changes by 0.221 cm³ per kelvin.

Recall that a constant can also be determined by finding the slope of a line which is Δy/Δx. Prove to yourself that 0.221 cm³/K is correct by calculating the slope of the line shown in Figure 6-14.

This example is typical of any gas at moderate temperatures. Charles's law states that **when the pressure and amount of a gas are held constant, the volume of the gas is directly proportional to its kelvin temperature.** For any sample of gas, a constant may be calculated for the V/T ratio. This constant can be used to find the volume of that particular sample at any other temperature, as shown in the following example problems.

PROBLEM·SOLVING

S T R A T E G Y

Remember, when using experimental data to find Δy/Δx, it is best to choose points from the best-fit line rather than adjacent data points on the table. The actual data points have some amount of uncertainty. The uncertainty is reduced by drawing the best-fit line when making the graph.

EXAMPLE 6-3

If a sample of gas occupies a volume of 100.0 cm³ at a temperature of 200.0 K, what volume would the gas occupy at a temperature of 150.0 K? The pressure and amount of gas do not change.

■ **Analyze the Problem** Look at the numbers in the problem that change and those that remain constant. Since the volume and temperature change while the pressure and amount of gas do not, this problem can be solved by applying Charles's law.

■ **Apply a Strategy** Use the information in the problem to determine the value of the constant from $V/T = k$. Once you know the value of the constant, you can determine what the volume will be at 150.0 K.

■ **Work a Solution** Substitute what you know into the relationship described by Charles's law and solve for k.

$$\frac{V}{T} = k = \frac{100.0 \text{ cm}^3}{200.0 \text{ K}} = \frac{0.5000 \text{ cm}^3}{K}$$

Using k, solve for the volume at 150.0 K.

$$? \text{ cm}^3 = 150.0 \text{ K} \times 0.5000 \frac{\text{cm}^3}{\text{K}} = 75.00 \text{ cm}^3$$

■ **Verify Your Answer** Check that your answer is reasonable. The temperature as stated in the problem has decreased from 200.0 K to 150.0 K, so you would expect the volume to decrease. The new volume is indeed smaller than the original volume. The units also work out correctly, increasing your confidence that the answer is correct.

PROBLEM·SOLVING

S T R A T E G Y

Use what you know. If you had a graph of the volume versus temperature for this gas, you should recognize that k is the slope that is constant for all values of volume and temperature if the pressure and number of moles remain the same. (See Strategy, page 58.)

Practice Problems

14. A sample of air has a volume of 2.25 dm³ when its temperature is 298 K. If the temperature is increased to 373 K without changing the pressure, what is the new volume of the sample of air?   ***Ans.*** 2.82 dm³

15. As the temperature of a sample of nitrogen increases from 273 K, the volume of the sample changes from 275 cm³ to 325 cm³. Assuming that the pressure does not change, what is the final temperature of the gas?   ***Ans.*** 323 K

Practice Problems

Assign the Practice Problems.

In chemistry, as in many other subjects, there is more than one way to solve a problem. Look back at the work in the previous exercise. Notice that the value of the constant k was first calculated this way:

$$k = \frac{100.0 \text{ cm}^3}{200.0 \text{ K}}$$

After you completed this calculation, you used the *value* of k in the next equation. Let's look at this equation a second way, using the *expression* for k rather than its value:

$$? \text{ cm}^3 = 150.0 \text{ K} \times \frac{100.0 \text{ cm}^3}{200.0 \text{ K}}$$

$$= 75.0 \text{ cm}^3$$

By applying the properties of mathematics, this expression may be rearranged this way:

$$? \text{ cm}^3 = \frac{150.0 \text{ K}}{200.0 \text{ K}} \times 100.0 \text{ cm}^3$$

Notice that all of the steps shown come from the work done in the solution to the example. Do you see how this work has been rewritten to show a temperature ratio, $\frac{150.0 \text{ K}}{200.0 \text{ K}}$, as a part of the solution? Since 150.0 K is smaller than 200.0 K, this temperature ratio is smaller than one. When the ratio is applied to the original volume of 100.0 cm³ through multiplication, the resulting volume is also smaller.

These observations suggest another method for working temperature-volume problems. As you read through the next example, look for both the similarities and differences between the solution to Example 6-3 and the solution to Example 6-4.

Practice Problems

Assign the Practice Problems.

EXAMPLE 6-4

A gas occupies a volume of 473 cm³ at 36.0°C. What will be the volume of the gas when the temperature is raised to 94.0°C? Assume pressure and number of moles are constant.

■ *Analyze the Problem* You are interested in the new volume of a gas after a change in temperature. Notice that the temperature increases. Therefore, by using Charles's law, you can reason that the volume must also increase.

■ *Apply a Strategy* First, notice that temperature is recorded in °C in this problem. Recalling that Charles's law can be used only when the temperature is expressed on an absolute scale, convert the temperatures to kelvins before you use them.

To use the method of temperature ratios here, you need to find an appropriate ratio. You have already determined that the volume will go up. You must form your temperature ratio by dividing the larger temperature by the smaller temperature; this will give a ratio that is larger than one.

■ *Work a Solution* Convert the temperatures into K:

$$T = t + 273 = 36.0°C + 273 = 309 \text{ K}$$
$$T = t + 273 = 94.0°C + 273 = 367 \text{ K}$$

Now you are ready to formulate the temperature ratio. Based on the expected increase in volume, put the larger temperature over the smaller temperature:

$$\frac{367 \text{ K}}{309 \text{ K}}$$

Apply the temperature ratio to the initial volume:

$$? \text{ cm}^3 = 473 \text{ cm}^3 \times \frac{367 \cancel{K}}{309 \cancel{K}} = 562 \text{ cm}^3$$

■ *Verify Your Answer* Work the problem the same way you did in Example 6-3. Find the value of the constant k for the gas at the given volume and temperature; then multiply it by the new temperature. The answers should be the same.

PROBLEM-SOLVING
S T R A T E G Y

Look for regularities when solving problems. You should recognize that this equation represents exactly what was done in Example 6-3. If 473 cm³ was divided by 309, you would have the value for k. (See Strategy, page 100.)

PROBLEM-SOLVING
S T R A T E G Y

*The point 0, 0 comes from **using what you know** about Charles's law. The volume of any gas is zero at a temperature of 0 K. (See Strategy, page 58.)*

Practice Problems

16. Verify the answer in Example 6-4, using a graph. Place temperature on the *x*-axis and volume on the *y*-axis. Plot the point given in the example and the point (0, 0). Draw a straight line through the points and determine the volume at 94.0°C.   ***Ans.*** 560 cm³

17. A gas occupies a volume of 500 cm³ at 27°C. What will be the volume of the gas when the temperature is −48°C? Assume pressure and moles are constant.   ***Ans.*** 375 cm³

Now consider the question about the hot-air balloon. Can you explain why the air becomes less dense when it is heated? Using Charles's law, you can reason that as the air inside the balloon is heated, it expands. As a result of the increase in air volume, some of the air escapes from the opening at the bottom. This means the mass of air inside the balloon is less. Since the volume of the balloon is the same, the mass/volume ratio (the density) is less than that of the surrounding atmosphere, and the balloon rises.

6.5 Boyle's Law: The Pressure-Volume Relationship

In 1660, Robert Boyle, a British scientist, performed an experiment that measured the volume of a gas as the pressure on the gas changed. The relationship that Boyle discovered may be demonstrated by a simple experiment such as the one shown in Figure 6-15.

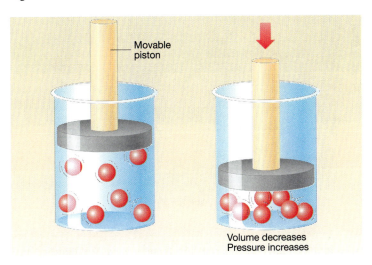

Volume decreases
Pressure increases

Figure 6-15 *As the piston is lowered (right), the space available to the moving balls decreases. The number of collisions with the walls of the container increases, and pressure goes up.*

A calibrated syringe is filled with air, and the volume is read. A weight placed on top of the plunger increases the pressure on the air in the syringe. As the temperature is held constant, even more weight is added to the plunger. The volume is measured for several different pressures.

Table 6-4 on the next page shows the data that have been collected from such an experiment. When you look at these numbers, you see that as the pressure increases from 66.7 kPa to 222.3 kPa, the volume of the gas decreases from 50 cm³ to 15 cm³. If the data are graphed, as in Figure 6-16 on the next page, the result is a curve. Note that this graph is different from the graph illustrating Charles's law. That law describes a direct proportionality, in which volume increases with increasing temperature. In the case of pres-

Videodisc Connections

567, side 6
Boyle's Law; computer graphic
(1 frame)

Teaching Strategy

Boyle's Law Demonstration

Use a Boyle's Law apparatus and books to demonstrate the "spring" in air (as Boyle called it), or how changing the pressure on a gas changes its volume. Record the volume of the syringe each time you increase the number of textbooks you place on it. The number of textbooks corresponds to pressure. Have students graph the results using the number of books on the y-axis and the volume of air in mL on the x-axis. The resulting graph will be a curve, characteristic of an inverse relationship.

Have students replot the number of books versus the reciprocal of the volume ($1/V$) on the x-axis. The result should be a straight line with the general equation $y = mx + b$ where y is the number of books (P_b) and x is $1/V$. The equation becomes $P_b = m(1/V) + b$. The intercept, b, corresponds to atmospheric pressure—that is, the pressure on the gas when no books have been added. The intercept will have a negative value since zero books does not correspond to actual zero pressure. Advise students to set up their coordinates with space below the x-axis for extrapolation of the line to the y-intercept.

Rearrange the equation: $P_b - b = m(1/V)$. Since $P_b - b$ is the total pressure of the books and the atmosphere, the equation becomes $P_{Total} = m(1/V)$. Since the slope of the line, m, is a constant, the expression of Boyle's law becomes $PV = c$. Point out to students that the value of c is different from the value of the constant k used for Charles's law. If your class is ready for more math, have them determine the value of b in terms of numbers of books and then relabel the y-axis of their graphs starting with zero at the y-intercept.

PART **2**

Section 6.5 continued

TABLE 6-4

Compression of a Sample of Air*		
Volume (cm³)	Pressure (kPa)	V × P (cm³ · kPa)
50.0	66.7	3340
31.0	107.5	3330
21.0	158.6	3330
15.0	222.3	3330

* Temperature and moles are constant.

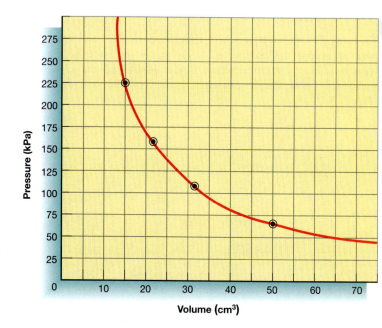

Figure 6-16 *A plot of the data in Table 6-4 indicates a relationship different from Charles's law. The pressure and volume of a gas are inversely related. When one increases, the other decreases.*

sure and volume, the relationship is an *inverse* (or indirect) proportionality: Volume decreases with increasing pressure. Mathematically, an inverse proportionality may be expressed as

$$AB = c \text{ (where } c \text{ is a constant)}$$

In this case, A is pressure and B is volume so that the equation may be rewritten as

$$PV = c \text{ (when temperature and moles are held constant)}$$

The product of the pressure and the volume of any one gas sample is constant. You can see from the third column of Table 6-4 that $P \times V$ for the air in the syringe at any one instant is constant within the range of experimental uncertainty. According to the pressure-volume law, **Boyle's law,** *when the temperature and the number of moles of a sample of gas are held constant, its volume is inversely proportional to the pressure applied.*

DEMONSTRATION

Boyle's Law

If you have a vacuum pump and a bell jar, it is easy to demonstrate the relationship between pressure and volume. Put an inflated balloon inside the bell jar, and turn on the pump.

The balloon expands as the pressure inside the bell jar drops.

⚠ **CAUTION: Wear safety goggles. Use a shield to protect students.**

The Ping-Pong model that was described in Part 1 can be used to understand why there is an inverse relationship between pressure and volume. Suppose you have a gas-containing syringe with a movable plunger, as shown in Figure 6-17. You can think of the gas particles as Ping-Pong balls, continuously moving around, hitting each other and the walls of the syringe. If the plunger is lowered so that the available space is decreased, the number of collisions will increase in a given period of time. As you have already learned, if the number of collisions with the container walls increases, the pressure will increase.

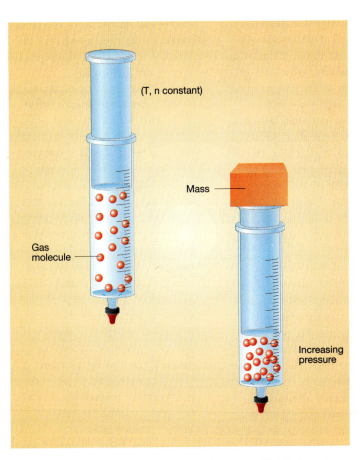

Figure 6-17 *As the pressure on a gas increases (right), the volume of the gas decreases.*

Concept ✓ Check

Explain in your own words how Figure 6-17 illustrates an inverse relationship.

CONNECTING CONCEPTS

Processes of Science—Predicting Discovering and stating laws (as Charles and Boyle did) is an important step in the advancement of science. A law is based on several observations (or experiments) on different substances. A law provides a summary statement or equation that lets you predict the results of other similar experiments. After a law has been stated and verified, other scientists will look for an explanation or theory for why that law works.

Myths and Misconceptions

Air is referred to throughout this chapter—in reference to atmospheric pressure, Dalton's law of partial pressures, "hot air" balloons, and air compression. Students sometimes have the misconception that there are "air molecules." Stress that air is a mixture composed of molecules of oxygen, nitrogen, water vapor, argon, hydrogen, carbon dioxide, and other gases.

▶ # F O C U S O N
PROBLEM SOLVING

Activate Prior Knowledge

The parts and operation of the internal combustion engine are familiar to many students. Have students draw a diagram to show how the gas molecules are spaced when the piston is relaxed and when it is pushed into the cylinder. Remind students that making diagrams is a useful way of visualizing microscopic events.

Making Diagrams

After initially reading a new problem, you may feel that you have just gone through a confusing mass of words. Perhaps you do not understand the problem or are unable to visualize all of the relationships that are specified. Using a variety of pictures—in your mind or on paper—can help you deal with such problems. After all, when drawing or thinking about a problem, you are providing your own translation of the words into another kind of image. This image is more likely to be meaningful to you, since you are the architect of the image.

The strategy of making diagrams is probably not entirely new to you. Many people make diagrams to solve problems in everyday settings. Suppose you ask a friend for directions to a new shopping mall. Her reply is this: "Just take Greenville Road south from school about eight miles, going past the airport and over the county line. Make a right turn at the stop sign when the road ends. Drive into town, go over the bridge, and about six blocks later you will see a water tower on the left. Turn left, and the mall is on the right, just a couple of blocks down the road." Many people would feel over-

whelmed by all this information and ask for written directions. Drawing a diagram—in this case a map—that shows all of the landmarks mentioned, along with the distance information, would make finding the mall easier.

▶ ### Translating Information into a Picture

When solving problems in chemistry, a drawing should show your interpretation of the problem as well as indicate the conditions set up by the problem. For example, if you are solving a problem that involves pressure changes inside a piston as the volume changes, you can begin by sketching two pistons with the same number of gas particles on a piece of paper as shown in Figure 6-18. Beside each piston, put labels showing the conditions of pressure and volume that are given in the problem. This diagram would be helpful in clarifying the mathematical relationships you need in order to solve a given problem.

Follow these additional suggestions for using and drawing diagrams. They will provide some helpful hints when solving chemistry problems.

■ Do not worry about trying to make a perfect drawing. Your reason for making a drawing is

PROBLEM-SOLVING

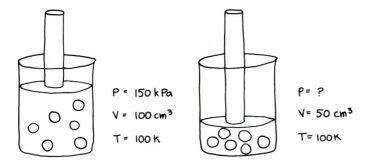

P = 150 kPa
V = 100 cm³
T = 100 K

P = ?
V = 50 cm³
T = 100 K

►TEACH
THE STRATEGY

Guided Practice

Have students make diagrams to help them solve Practice Problems 18 and 19 on page 218 in Part 2. Also, **making diagrams** is a useful strategy for solving Part 2 Review problems 20–25 on page 221.

to help you decide how to solve the problem. All you need to do is put down on paper an aid that will help you get started.

■ When you are making a diagram, try to put down only those elements of the problem that seem to have a direct bearing on its solution. Of course, this may not be easy to do if your purpose is to gain a better understanding of the problem. You simply may not be certain which information is relevant and which is not. In this case, sketch anything that seems important. When you look over all of the information, you will be in a better position to decide what is truly important.

■ Since chemistry often depends on your ability to understand what is happening at the submicroscopic level, it can be helpful to draw a picture that helps you visualize what is happening to the atoms and molecules in the situation described.

■ A graph can be an excellent drawing to make because it helps you quickly grasp the relationship between variables. Drawing a graph can lead you directly to the solution of a problem.

■ If necessary, use real, three-dimensional objects to help solve a problem. Some people have difficulty using two-dimensional paper-and-pencil pictures that are supposed to represent objects or actions in three dimensions. If you have this difficulty, just use real objects and arrange them according to the conditions that are specified.

As with any problem-solving strategy, making a diagram may not always lead directly to the solution of a problem, but it can certainly help you get started. Just remember to be resourceful when solving any problem. By using diagrams, you have one more resource upon which to draw!

GASES AND THEIR PROPERTIES **217**

Practice Problems

Assign the Practice Problems.

PROBLEM·SOLVING
S T R A T E G Y

Use what you know to solve the problem. Just as in Charles's law, you can solve for the constant first and use it to get the missing variable. (See Strategy, page 58.)

EXAMPLE 6-5

If a sample of gas has a volume of 100.0 cm³ when the pressure is 150.0 kPa, what is its volume when the pressure is increased to 200.0 kPa? Temperature and amount of gas remain constant.

■ **Analyze the Problem** Examine the problem to see which variables remain constant and which change. Since the volume and pressure change while the temperature and amount of gas remain constant, you may apply Boyle's law to solve this problem.

■ **Apply a Strategy** Find the value of the constant from the information in the problem. Knowing the constant, you can find the volume of the gas at the new pressure.

■ **Work a Solution** Substitute the data into Boyle's law using the relationship $PV = c$ and solve for c.

$$150.0 \text{ kPa} \times 100.0 \text{ cm}^3 = c = 15\ 000 \text{ kPa} \cdot \text{cm}^3$$

Next use the value of c to find the volume at 200.0 kPa.

$$200.0 \text{ kPa} \times ? \text{ cm}^3 = 15\ 000 \text{ kPa} \cdot \text{cm}^3$$

Rearranging the equation to solve for volume, you get the following mathematical statement.

$$? \text{ cm}^3 = \frac{15\ 000 \text{ kPa} \cdot \text{cm}^3}{200.0 \text{ kPa}} = 75.00 \text{ cm}^3$$

■ **Verify Your Answer** Check the answer to this problem by solving it a different way. Try the strategy used in Example 6-4. According to Boyle's law, when the pressure increases, the volume should decrease. Form a pressure ratio that will cause the volume to become smaller (that is, the pressures should be arranged so that the smaller pressure is on top and the larger pressure is on the bottom) and apply this ratio to the initial volume of 100.0 cm³. You should obtain the same answer.

Practice Problems

18. If a sample of gas has a volume of 25 dm³ when the pressure is 100.0 kPa, what is its volume when the pressure falls to 75.0 kPa, providing that the temperature and amount of gas do not change?   *Ans.* 33 dm³

19. What pressure is required to reduce the volume of a sample of air from 1.00 L to 0.250 L? The original pressure on the sample is 98.0 kPa; the amount and temperature of the sample remain fixed.   *Ans.* 392 kPa

6.6 Avogadro's Principle

Through Charles's law and Boyle's law, you have learned that temperature and pressure affect the volume of a gas. Another variable can also affect volume. As you add air while blowing up a balloon, it is easy to see that the volume increases. The relationship between volume and quantity of a gas can be understood by looking at the works of Joseph Gay-Lussac and Amadeo Avogadro.

Gay-Lussac Joseph Louis Gay-Lussac was a French chemist who lived from 1778 to 1850. He investigated how elements that are gases combine to form compounds that also are gases. Much of his work was done on a series of different gaseous compounds formed from the same two elements, nitrogen and oxygen. He noted that for all compounds formed, the ratios of the volumes of gases used were simple, whole-number ratios. His analysis of data for various oxides of nitrogen are shown in Table 6-5. Notice that the volume ratios are not precisely whole numbers. For Compound 1, 100 to 49.5 is not exactly a 2 to 1 ratio. However, when more accurate measurements are made, the volume ratios are whole numbers within experimental uncertainty.

When gases other than nitrogen and oxygen are studied, the volume ratios of the reactants involved are also simple whole numbers. This result can be summarized as the **law of combining volumes.** The law states that whenever gases react under the same conditions of temperature and pressure, the volume ratios of the reactants can be expressed as simple whole numbers (integers).

TABLE 6-5

Combining Volumes of Gases				
Compound	Volume of Nitrogen (in cm³ or mL)	Volume of Oxygen (in cm³ or mL)	Approximate Volume Ratio of Nitrogen to Oxygen	Accepted Formula
Compound 1	100	49.5	2 to 1	N_2O
Compound 2	100	108.9	1 to 1	NO
Compound 3	100	204.7	1 to 2	NO_2

Amadeo Avogadro The importance of the law of combining volumes was recognized by Amadeo Avogadro, an Italian scientist and contemporary of Gay-Lussac. In 1811, Avogadro wrote a paper in which he suggested that Gay-Lussac's data on combining volumes of gases could be explained very simply. He hypothesized that *equal volumes of gases (at the same temperature and pressure) contain equal numbers of particles.* This explanation of combining volumes was not accepted until several years after Avogadro's death. It is now known as **Avogadro's principle.**

PART 2
Section 6.6

Science Background

Avogadro's Principle

A law is sometimes defined as a generalization that summarizes the results from a series of experiments. Boyle's law summarizes pressure-volume behavior of a gas, while Charles's law summarizes the temperature-volume behavior of a gas. Avogadro's statement concerning equal volumes of gases does not summarize observable gas behavior; rather, it provides an explanation for the observable behavior summarized by Gay-Lussac's law of combining volumes. For that reason, we refer to Avogadro's principle in this text, rather than Avogadro's law.

Guided Practice

Review the Concept Check question on page 215 with students. Answers can be found in Appendix E on page 808.

Reteaching Idea

If students need more grounding in Boyle's, Charles's, and Dalton's laws, and Avogadro's principle, have a contest between teams in which students are expected to demonstrate their understanding of these regularities.

(continued on page T220)

Myths and Misconceptions

Students might have misconceptions about the characteristics of gases that can hinder their understanding of Avogadro's principle. For example, students may think that the volume of a gas equals the volume of the actual gas molecules, rather than the volume in which the molecules are contained. Ask students to predict the relative volumes of oxygen and hydrogen gas, given equal numbers of both gas molecules. Remind students that gas molecules are very far apart, so the volume of the molecules is negligible compared to the volume of the gas.

(continued from page T219)

Divide your class into two or four teams. Have each pair of teams compete against each other. You present a situation involving gases. The first teams must describe what is happening. The second teams must put the happening in terms of a law or principle. Reverse the procedure for the second situation, and so on. If you want to keep score, give one point for a correct answer, and give the opposing team the point if a team is unsuccessful. Here are some situations and some models of situations; you can add more.

- The pressure shown on a tire gauge doubles as twice the volume of air is added at the same temperature. (Avogadro's principle)

- A balloon over the mouth of a bottle containing air begins to inflate as it stands in the sunlight. (Charles's law)

- An automobile piston compresses gases. (Boyle's law)

- An inflated raft gets softer when some of the gas is allowed to escape. (Avogadro's principle)

- A balloon placed in the freezer decreases in size. (Charles's law)

- A hot air balloon takes off when burners heat the air under its open end. (Charles's law)

- When you squeeze an inflated balloon, it seems to push back harder. (Boyle's law)

- A tank of helium gas will fill hundreds of balloons. (Boyle's law)

- Model: When red, blue, and white Ping-Pong balls are shaken in a box, the effect is the same as if an equal number of red balls were in the box. (Dalton's Law)

- Model: When the number of Ping-Pong balls is doubled, the effect (as far as can be ascertained) is doubled. (Avogadro's principle)

H I S T O R Y   O F   S C I E N C E

Contributions beyond the Gas Laws

Robert Boyle and Joseph Gay-Lussac are associated with the gas laws, but each made many other important contributions to physics and chemistry. Robert Boyle, a British scientist, discovered that air is needed for combustion and respiration. He is also credited for discovering that sound does not travel in a vacuum. In 1661, the primary particles existed that could combine to form "corpuscles" and the motion and organizations of these particles could explain all natural phenomena. Boyle's experiments in chemistry distinguishing between acids and bases introduced the use of chemical indicators. He also instituted new methods to discover the identity and chemical composition of substances. Boyle's ideas and work separated chemistry from alchemy.

Joseph Gay-Lussac, a French chemist, also made notable scientific contributions. Charles had not published his results on temperature-volume relationships, they were unknown to Gay-Lussac when he published the same relationships in 1802. These relationships became known as Charles's law. In 1804, Gay-Lussac reached a height of 7 016 m (23 018 ft.) in a balloon in order to learn that the chemical composition of the atmosphere remained constant, at least to that altitude. In the following year, Gay-Lussac discovered the law of combining volumes. During the same time, British chemist John Dalton based his laws of chemical composition on combining weights. Eventually their works were reconciled through explanations by Avogadro.

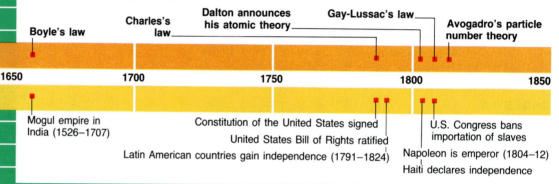

Relating volume and gas quantity A graph of the relationship between volume and the numbers of particles (moles) present is a straight line passing through the origin, as shown in Figure 6-19. You should reason that the volume of a gas is directly proportional to the number of moles of a gas if temperature and pressure remain constant. This means that as the number of moles of a gas increases (at constant temperature and pressure), the volume increases. Mathematically, the relationship can be expressed as

$$V = an \text{ (at constant temperature and pressure)}$$

where V is volume of a gas, n is the number of moles of a gas, and a is another proportionality constant. While Avogadro's principle does not directly address the issue of volume changes, the mathematical statement is consistent with Avogadro's principle.

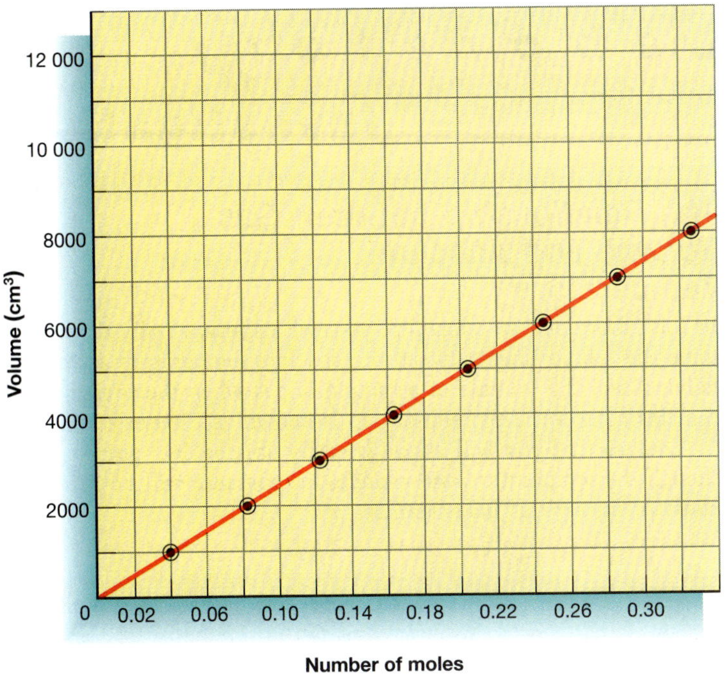

Figure 6-19 *What type of relationship does this graph of volume versus number of moles represent?*

PART 2 REVIEW

20. How can the relationship between gas pressure and volume be described?

21. How can the relationship between gas temperature and volume be described?

22. How can the relationship between moles of gas and gas volume be described?

23. **a.** If a sample of gas has a volume of 3.00 dm^3 (or liters) at a temperature of 52.3°C, what will the volume be if the temperature of the gas system is lowered to -27.0°C? Assume that the pressure and number of moles are held constant. *Ans.* 2.27 dm^3
    b. Make two drawings of the container before and after the temperature change. Compare the spaces between the particles.

24. A gas has a volume of 1.0 dm^3 at a pressure of 1.1 kPa. What will the volume be when the pressure is increased to 315 kPa? Assume that the temperature and number of moles remain constant. *Ans.* 0.0035 dm^3

25. The pressure of a 5.71-L sample of neon gas is 23.4 kPa. Calculate the new pressure when the volume becomes 3.40 L. Assume that the temperature and amount of gas remain unchanged. *Ans.* 39.3 kPa

PROBLEM-SOLVING
STRATEGY

Check your answer by *making a drawing* at the submicroscopic level. Use your drawing to determine whether the pressure should increase or decrease. (See Strategy, page 216.)

Boxed numbers indicate questions that involve skills in interpretation, application, and analysis.

≡CLOSE

Summing Up Main Ideas

Tell students that a gas contained in a stretchable container has a volume of 6.0 dm^3. Have students find how the volume will change if conditions are altered in the following ways.

a. Pressure is tripled
$$(6.0 \text{ dm}^3 \times \tfrac{1}{3} = 2.0 \text{ dm}^3)$$

b. temperature is doubled
$$(6.0 \text{ dm}^3 \times 2 = 12 \text{ dm}^3)$$

c. pressure and temperature are both tripled
$$(6.0 \text{ dm}^3 \times \tfrac{1}{3} \times 3 = 6.0 \text{ dm}^3)$$

d. pressure is tripled and temperature is halved
$$(6.0 \text{ dm}^3 \times \tfrac{1}{3} \times \tfrac{1}{2} = 1.0 \text{ dm}^3)$$

e. pressure and temperature are both halved
$$(6.0 \text{ dm}^3 \times \tfrac{1}{2} \times 2 = 6.0 \text{ dm}^3)$$

PART 2 REVIEW

Assign the Part Review questions.

Evaluating Skills

These skills are evaluated in the Part Review questions indicated.
Determining main ideas: 20, 21, 22; **Forming models:** 23; **Analyzing data:** 23, 24, 25; **Applying a strategy:** 23, 24, 25; **Calculating:** 23, 24, 25; **Verifying results:** 23, 24, 25

PART 2 REVIEW

ANSWERS

■ **Keyed to Objectives**

E 20. The relationship between gas pressure and gas volume is an inverse proportion.

D 21. The relationship between gas temperature and gas volume is a direct proportion, provided that the gas temperature is expressed in kelvins.

F 22. The relationship between moles of gas and gas volume is a direct proportion.

D 23. a. $3.00 \text{ dm}^3 \times \dfrac{(273 - 27)\text{K}}{(273 + 52.3)\text{K}}$

$= 2.27 \text{ dm}^3$

b. After students make their drawings, they should note that the spaces between molecules are smaller when the volume is

smaller, since the volumes of the individual gas molecules do not change.

E 24. $1.0 \text{ dm}^3 \times \dfrac{1.1 \text{ kPa}}{315 \text{ kPa}} = 0.0035 \text{ dm}^3$

E 25. $23.4 \text{ kPa} \times \dfrac{5.71 \text{ L}}{3.4 \text{ L}} = 39.3 \text{ kPa}$

The Relationship between Gas Volume and Absolute Temperature

Estimated Time: (50 minutes)

Process Skills

Measuring
Constructing tables and graphs
Identifying and controlling variables
Applying a strategy

Preparation

■ Materials

(for a class of 24, working in pairs)
Apparatus
(12 of each unless noted)
125-mL Erlenmeyer flasks with #5 stoppers and the glass part of eye droppers, pairs of goggles (24), laboratory aprons (24), 400-mL beakers, pneumatic troughs or similar devices, marking pencils, Bunsen burners, graph paper (24), 100-mL graduated cylinders, ring stands and wire gauze, rings to support the beaker, larger rings to hold the beaker securely, buret clamps, barometers, tongs

■ Preparation Hints

Put the #5 stoppers and the glass part of the eye droppers together before the students arrive. Be certain to put the restricted part so it protrudes out the top of the stopper.

■

⚠ Care must be taken when handling hot items. Use tongs. The large ring around the 400-mL beaker will serve as an extra protection against burns.

L a b o r a t o r y

Investigation

The Relationship between Gas Volume and Absolute Temperature

In this laboratory investigation, you will experimentally determine the relationship between the absolute temperature scale (in kelvins) and the volume of a sample of gas when the pressure remains constant. This relationship is known as Charles's law.

The gas that you will utilize is easily obtainable—air. Although the temperature will change, the pressure will be held constant during this investigation.

Objectives

Determine the effect of temperature on the volume of a gas at constant pressure.

Graph your data to see what kind of relationship exists between gas volume and kelvin temperature at constant pressure.

Materials

- □ 125-mL Erlenmeyer flask with stopper-glass attachment
- □ 400-mL beaker
- □ pneumatic trough
- □ Bunsen burner
- □ graph paper
- □ 100-mL graduated cylinder
- □ ring stand with wire gauze and 2 rings
- □ buret clamp
- □ barometer
- □ hot pad or tongs

Procedure

1. Put on your safety goggles and lab apron.
2. Record the barometric reading for the room in Data Table A.
3. Fill a 400-mL beaker approximately one-third full with water. Place a large ring

around the beaker as an extra precaution against burns. Set up the apparatus as shown in the figure.

4. Clamp the flask assembly to the ring stand so that it is suspended in the water. Make sure that the flask has some space between it and the walls of the beaker so that steam is free to leave the beaker.

5. Boil the water for three minutes and record its temperature in Data Table A. Remove the thermometer.

Data Table A

Measurements and Collected Data	
Barometric reading	735 kPa or torr
Temperature boiling water	90.0 °C
Temperature water in trough	13.0 °C
Final volume water in flask	30 mL
Total volume of flask	130 mL

6. Fill the pneumatic trough with water. Carefully remove the flask and assembly from the beaker.

   ⚠️ **CAUTION: Use tongs or a hot pad to protect your hand.**

   Place your index finger firmly over the narrow end of the eyedropper and turn the assembly upside down. Quickly plunge the flask into the trough. Try not to allow air to enter the flask during the transferring process.

7. Water will enter the flask through the dropper tube. After no more water has entered, raise the flask *still upside down* until the water level *inside* the flask is *equal to the water level* in the trough. This will make the pressure inside the flask equal to the pressure outside the flask. Record the temperature of the water in the trough in Data Table A.

8. Once again put your index finger over the end of the eyedropper in the flask. Place the flask assembly right side up on your bench before removing your finger.

9. Dry the flask assembly with a paper towel and carefully make a mark at the bottom of the rubber stopper.

10. Remove the stopper and measure the volume of water left in the flask. Record this in Data Table A.

11. Fill the flask with water so the meniscus matches the mark in step 9. Measure and record the total volume of the water now in the flask.

Data Analysis

Data Table A

Measurements and Collected Data	
Barometric reading	_____ kPa or torr
Temperature of boiling water	_____ °C
Temperature of water in trough	_____ °C
Final volume of water in flask	_____ mL
Total volume of flask	_____ mL

Data Table B

Calculations	
Temperature of boiling water	_____ K
Temperature of water in trough	_____ K
Final volume of gas	_____ mL
Final vapor pressure H$_2$O	_____ kPa or torr
Volume of Drygas	_____ kPa or torr

1. Convert the water temperatures from °C to kelvin and record in Data Table B.

2. Calculate the final volume of the gas in the flask by subtracting the volume of the water left in the flask from the total volume in the flask. Record in Data Table B.

3. Use a vapor pressure table and record the vapor pressure of the water at the lower temperature in Data Table B.

4. Calculate the volume of Drygas as follows, and record it in Data Table B.

$$\frac{\text{(barometric pressure} - \text{vapor pressure of water)} \times \text{(final volume of gas)}}{\text{barometric pressure}}$$

5. Plot the kelvin temperature on the *x*-axis and the volume of gas in milliliters on the *y*-axis. Draw a best-fit line.

Conclusions

1. What was the relationship between the temperature and the gas volume you measured?

2. On your graph, where did the line cross the *x*-axis?

3. At what temperature (in kelvins) will the volume of the gas be zero?

Guiding the Investigation

■ Explain to students why the liquid levels in the 125-mL flask must be the same to make the pressure in the flask equal to the barometric pressure.

Data Analysis

■ **Sample Data**
(See table below.)

■
1 through 4: Sample data are given in the table below.
5. See graph below.

Conclusions

1. direct proportional relationship (straight line)
2. 27 K
3. zero

Data Table B
Calculations	
Temperature boiling water	363 K
Temperature water in trough	286 K
Final volume of gas	100 mL
Vapor pressure of water	11.2 kPa or torr
Final volume of dry gas	98.5 kPa or torr

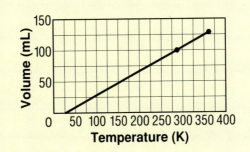

Chapter 6
Review
ANSWERS
begin on
page T227a.

Summary

Physical Properties of Gases

- Gases are compressible because the molecules are far apart. They can be forced closer together by increasing the pressure of the gas.

- Gas molecules move faster as their temperature increases.

- The pressure of a gas is caused by the collisions of the gas molecules with the sides of their container.

- Gas pressure can be measured with a barometer and with a manometer. A typical value for air pressure is about 1 atm.

- In a mixture of gases, the total pressure of the gas is equal to the sum of the partial pressures of each gas in the mixture.

Relationships among Gas Properties

- The volume of a gas increases as its temperature increases (no matter what scale is used to measure the temperature). Only when the temperature is measured in kelvins is the relationship between volume and temperature a direct proportion.

- The volume of a gas is inversely proportional to its pressure.

- When gases react with each other, the ratios of their combining volumes are small whole numbers, provided that the gases are being measured under the same conditions of temperature and pressure.

- Avogadro's principle, which states that equal volumes of gases contain the same number of particles under the same conditions of temperature and pressure, can be used to explain the law of combining volumes.

Chemically Speaking

atmosphere 6.2
Avogadro's principle 6.6
barometer 6.2
Boyle's law 6.5
Charles's law 6.4
Gay-Lussac's law 6.6
kelvins 6.4
kelvin scale 6.4
law of combining volumes 6.6

law of partial pressures 6.3
manometer 6.2
partial pressure 6.3
pascal 6.2
pressure 6.1
standard pressure 6.2
vacuum 6.2

Concept Mapping

Using the method of concept mapping described at the front of this book, draw a concept map for the term *variable*.

Questions and Problems

PHYSICAL PROPERTIES OF GASES

A. Objective: Describe *a gas on the submicroscopic level, using the variables of volume, temperature, and pressure.*

1. Using a molecular model of matter, explain what the difference is between a gas that exerts a pressure of 1.0 atm and one that exerts a pressure of 1.5 atm.

2. Using a molecular model, explain why a gas can be easily compressed, while a liquid and a solid cannot.

3. If you collect a gas so that it completely fills a 250 cm^3 Erlenmeyer flask, the volume of the gas is actually *greater* than 250 cm^3.
   a. Explain why this is true.
   b. How could you determine what the volume of the gas is?

PROBLEM-SOLVING
▶ **STRATEGIES**
Students apply these strategies in the following questions.

- Factor-label method: 10, 11, 19, 20, 23, 29, 30, 31, 32, 37, 38, 39
- Using similar problems: 19, 20, 23, 28, 29, 30, 31, 32, 37

- Using calculators: 10, 11, 14, 15, 19, 20, 21, 23, 28, 29, 30, 31, 32, 37, 38, 39
- Verify your answer: 10, 11, 19, 20, 23, 28, 29, 30 , 31, 32, 37, 38, 39

T224

4. The volume of a gas is often referred to as one of the properties that can be measured. Is this volume simply the sum of all of the individual molecular volumes? Explain your answer.

B. Objective: **Explain** *what gas pressure is* and **describe** *how it can be measured.*

5. A brick, like a wood block, has three distinctly different sides that can be placed face-down. How does the force exerted by a brick change as you put it on its three different faces? How does the pressure applied by the brick change?

6. Is there a difference in the force exerted by the same brick if it is moved from San Francisco to Denver? Is there a difference in the pressure even if the same side is placed facedown?

7. Explain how a barometer works.

8. Explain why the air pressure is greater on Waikiki Beach (on the Pacific Ocean) than it is on top of Mauna Kea, one of Hawaii's volcanoes.

9. Give two examples of units used to measure pressure.

10. Carbon dioxide does not exist in the liquid state unless the pressure is at least 5.1 atm. Convert this pressure into:
  a. torr   **b.** kPa

11. If air pressure is reduced from normal sea level values (this happens at higher elevations), the boiling point of a liquid falls. For instance, water boils at only 95°C if the atmospheric pressure is 634 mm Hg. Convert this pressure into:
  a. atm
  b. Pa

C. Objective: **Apply** *Dalton's law of partial pressures to determine the total pressure of a mixture of gases or the partial pressure of an individual gas in the mixture.*

Boxed numbers indicate questions that involve skills in interpretation, application, and analysis.

12. What is partial pressure?

13. You have a mixture of gases consisting of oxygen, nitrogen, and carbon dioxide. State in words how the partial pressures of these gases is related to the total pressure of the gas mixture.

14. Hydrogen gas is collected by bubbling it through water. Calculate the partial pressure of the hydrogen gas if
  a. the total pressure is 94 000 Pa, and the partial pressure of water is 1200 Pa.
  b. the total pressure is 100.3 kPa, and the partial pressure of water is 2600 Pa.

15. In a flask that has a volume of 273 dm^3, you have a sample of two noble gases: neon and xenon. The partial pressure of the neon is 96 950 Pa, and the partial pressure of the xenon is 1.025 atm. What is the total pressure (in kPa) exerted by these two gases?

RELATIONSHIPS AMONG PROPERTIES

D. Objective: **Apply** *Charles's law to* **describe** *how the volume of a gas is related to its temperature.*

16. Describe in words how the temperature of a gas is related to its volume.

17. State a mathematical equation that shows the relationship between the temperature and volume of a gas. In order for this relationship to hold true, what other gas variables should remain constant?

18. Explain why you must convert the temperature to an absolute temperature scale (such as the Kelvin scale) when you wish to use the direct proportionality of the temperature-volume law.

19. Change the following volumes of gases from the conditions given to the new conditions. Assume that the pressure and amount of gas is constant.
  a. 85 cm^3 at 61°C to 35°C
  b. 7.3 dm^3 from 228°C to −48°C

GASES AND THEIR PROPERTIES **225**

■ Breaking problems into manageable parts: 38, 39
■ Making diagrams: 21

20. An anaesthesiologist is about to administer gas to a patient. The gas has a temperature of 22.4°C. When the gas enters the patient's body, it is warmed to a temperature of 37.2°C. Assuming that the gas does not undergo a change in pressure, what percentage increase in volume does the gas experience as it reaches the new temperature?

21. Given the following data:

Volume of Nitrogen Gas (L)	Temperature (K)
4.28 L	303 K
5.79 L	410 K

a. Draw a graph of the relationship between volume and temperature.
b. Determine the slope of the line.
c. Find the slope of a line in relationship to the temperature-volume law expressed as $V/T = k$.
d. Calculate the expected volume of the gas when the temperature reaches 1200 K.

22. It would be impossible for a gas to have one of these temperatures: 50°C, 50 K, −50°C, −50 K. Which is the impossible one? Why?

23. A sample of carbon dioxide has a volume of 2.0 dm^3 at a temperature of −10°C. What volume will this sample have when the temperature is increased to 110°C? Assume that the pressure does not change and that no carbon dioxide leaks from the sample.

24. Why would a 1 mol sample of water have a much greater increase in volume than a 1 mol sample of carbon dioxide when its temperature rises from −10°C to 110°C?

E. Objective: Apply *Boyle's law to de-scribe how the volume of a gas is related to pressure.*

25. Describe in words how the pressure of a gas is related to its volume.
26. Give a mathematical equation that shows the relationship between the temperature and volume of a gas. In order for this relationship to hold true, what other gas variables should remain constant?

27. When you apply the temperature-volume law, you must always use temperature expressed on an absolute scale. Do you have to use any particular set of units for pressure when you use the pressure-volume law?

28. Change the following volumes of gases from the conditions given to the new conditions. Assume that the temperature and amount of gas is constant.
   a. 1.15×10^3 cm^3 at 75.2 kPa to 14.0 kPa
   b. 94.7 dm^3 at 1.00 kPa to 100.0 kPa

29. At a depth of 30 meters, the combined pressure of air and water on a diver is about four times the normal atmospheric pressure (400 kPa rather than 100 kPa). Suppose a diver exhales into the water, and one of the air bubbles has a volume of 10.0 mL. What will be the volume of this bubble when it reaches the surface of the water, assuming that it does not break apart and that its temperature does not change?

30. A 12.7-L sample of gas is under a pressure of 9.3 kPa. What will be the pressure of the gas when the volume increases to 20.1 L (assuming the temperature is held constant)?

31. What is the volume occupied by 10.0 dm^3 of gas at 100.2 kPa after it has been compressed at a constant temperature to 325.5 kPa?

32. A sample of nitrogen gas having a volume of 2.55 dm^3 is collected at a temperature of 67.4 kPa. What volume will the gas occupy when its pressure is changed to 145.1 kPa if the temperature is held constant?

F. Objective: Explain *how the law of combining volumes can be used to describe volume relationships and show how Avogadro's principle can explain this law.*

33. State in words Gay-Lussac's law of combining volumes.
34. Would you expect a scientist to discover that 1.72859 liters of one gas reacts with exactly

1.00000 liters of another gas (assuming that both gases are measured at the same temperature and pressure)? Why or why not?

35. What did Avogadro assume to be true about equal volumes of gases? What conditions must be met for his assumption to be true?

36. Give a mathematical equation that expresses how the volume of a gas changes as the number of moles of gas changes, assuming that the pressure and temperature of the gas do not change.

37. Calculate the number of moles of gas required to produce the new volumes given below. Assume that the temperature and pressures of the two samples are the same.
   a. Sample 1: 5.0 moles of O_2, 85 L
      Sample 2: 45 L
   b. Sample 1: 0.225 moles of N_2, 9.0 L
      Sample 2: 15.0 L

38. Which of the following samples of gases occupies the largest volume, assuming that each sample is at the same temperature and pressure—50.0 g of neon, 50.0 g of argon, or 50.0 g of xenon?

39. What volume of carbon dioxide gas contains the same number of oxygen atoms as 250.0 cm^3 of carbon monoxide gas, if each gas sample is measured at the same temperature and pressure?

Critical Thinking

SYNTHESIS WITHIN THE CHAPTER

40. As you read this chapter, you encountered some examples which illustrate gas properties. For instance, the increasing difficulty you have inflating a bicycle tire as it becomes more and more inflated illustrates Boyle's law. Think of an example you could cite to illustrate the following.
   a. The relationship between partial pressure and total pressure.
   b. The relationship between pressure of a gas and its temperature.

SYNTHESIS ACROSS CHAPTERS

41. In an experiment to find the molarity of an unknown sample of hydrochloric acid, the acid reacted with calcium carbonate, $CaCO_3$, to produce carbon dioxide, water, and a solution of calcium chloride. Use the following data to determine the molarity of the acid:

   Volume of dry CO_2 collected = 345 mL
   Barometric Pressure = 0.955 atm
   Temperature of the gas = 22.3°C
   Volume of HCl used = 50.00 mL

42. Carbon dioxide is a major contributor to the greenhouse effect. A gallon of gasoline has a mass of about 2700 g. Presume that the gasoline is composed of octane, C_8H_{18}, and the only emission products are carbon dioxide and water. How much carbon dioxide is produced by the average car in a year? The average car uses 1 gallon of gas in 20 miles and travels about 12,000 miles in a year.

Projects

43. What is the SCTP (Standard Classroom Temperature and Pressure) in your chemistry classroom? Over a two-week period, monitor the temperature and pressure at the same time of day. The average values you obtain will define the SCTP for your room. What is the molar volume of a gas under SCTP?

Research and Writing

44. Explore the universe! Find out the nature and conditions under which gases exist on the planets of the solar system. What conditions of temperature and pressure make Earth unique in the solar system?

☐ Boxed numbers indicate questions that involve skills in interpretation, application, and analysis.

1. The molecules of the gas at the higher pressure strike the walls of their container more often and/or with more force.

2. There is a large amount of space between molecules of a gas, but not for a liquid or solid.

3. a. An Erlenmeyer flask has a volume larger than 250 cm³. A flask marked "250 cm³" holds that volume when filled with a liquid to its highest mark, but a gas fills the (greater) volume of the entire flask.

   b. Fill the entire flask with water, and pour it into a graduated cylinder to measure the volume. (Or fill the flask by measuring how much water you pour into it from a graduated cylinder.)

4. No, because the molecules of a gas are much smaller than their entire container. The volume of the gas is the volume a given amount occupies at a given temperature and pressure.

5. The force remains constant because the brick's weight doesn't change. The pressure is greatest when the brick is placed on the side with the smallest surface area.

6. Yes. In San Francisco, the brick has a greater weight than in Denver. Its pressure will also be greater on the same side.

7. When a long, closed tube of mercury is inverted in a dish of mercury, the column of mercury falls until the pressure it exerts at the surface equals the pressure exerted by the atmosphere. The height of the column of mercury inside the barometer is proportional to the pressure of the air.

8. The amount of air above Waikiki Beach is greater than the amount of air above Maunea Kea, so the air pressure is greater on the beach.

9. Some choices: mm Hg, torr, atm, Pa, kPa

10. a. $5.1 \text{ atm} \times \frac{760 \text{ torr}}{1 \text{ atm}} = 3900 \text{ torr}$

    b. $5.1 \text{ atm} \times \frac{101.325 \text{ kPa}}{1 \text{ atm}} = 520 \text{ kPa}$

11. a. $634 \text{ mm Hg} \times \frac{1 \text{ atm}}{760 \text{ mm Hg}}$

    $= 0.834 \text{ atm}$

    b. $634 \text{ mm Hg} \times \frac{1 \text{ atm}}{760 \text{ mm Hg}}$

    $\times \frac{101\ 325 \text{ Pa}}{\text{atm}} = 84\ 500 \text{ Pa}$

12. Partial pressure is the pressure that one component of a mixture of gases would exert in the absence of all the other gases in that mixture.

13. The sum of the partial pressures of oxygen, nitrogen, and carbon dioxide is the total pressure of this gas mixture.

14. a. $94\ 000 \text{ Pa} - 1200 \text{ Pa} = 92\ 800 \text{ Pa}$
    b. $100\ 300 \text{ Pa} - 2600 \text{ Pa} = 97\ 700 \text{ Pa}$

15. $1.025 \text{ atm} \times \frac{101.325 \text{ kPa}}{\text{atm}} = 103.9 \text{ kPa}$

    $103.9 \text{ kPa} + 96.950 \text{ kPa}$

    $= 200.8 \text{ kPa}$

16. The volume of a gas is directly proportional to its absolute temperature.

17. $\frac{T}{V} = \text{constant or } \frac{T_1}{V_1} = \frac{T_2}{V_2}$,

    provided pressure and moles of gas are constant.

18. The volume of an ideal gas goes to zero when the temperature is 0 K (–273°C), not when the temperature is 0°C.

19. a. $85 \text{ cm}^3 \times \frac{(35 + 273)}{(61 + 273)} = 78 \text{ cm}^3$

    b. $7.3 \text{ dm}^3 \times \frac{(-48 + 273)}{(228 + 273)} = 3.3 \text{ dm}^3$

20. $1.00 \text{ L} \times \frac{(37.2 + 273.1)}{(22.4 + 273.1)} = 1.05 \text{ L}$

    This is a 5.0% increase.

21. a. Plot of $V (y\text{-axis})$ vs. $T (x\text{-axis})$

    b. $\text{Slope} = \frac{\Delta V}{\Delta T} = \frac{(5.79 \text{ L} - 4.28 \text{ L})}{(410 \text{ K} - 303 \text{ K})}$

    $= 0.0141 \text{ L/K}$

    c. $\frac{V}{T} = 0.0141 \text{ L/K}$

    d. $\frac{V}{T} = k$

    $V = kT = (0.0141 \text{ L/K})(1200 \text{ K})$

    $= 16.9 \text{ L}$

22. –50 K, because 0 K (absolute zero) is the lowest temperature a substance can reach.

23. $2.0 \text{ dm}^3 \times \frac{(110 + 273) \text{ K}}{(-10 + 273) \text{ K}} = 2.9 \text{ dm}^3$

24. Water changes from solid to liquid to gas over this temperature range, whereas carbon dioxide remains a gas throughout.

25. The pressure of a gas is inversely proportional to its volume.

26. $PV = \text{constant or } P_1V_1 = P_2V_2$, provided that temperature and number of moles remain constant.

27. No special set of units is required.

28. a. $1.15 \times 10^3 \text{ cm}^3 \times \frac{75.2 \text{ kPa}}{14.0 \text{ kPa}}$

    $= 6.18 \times 10^3 \text{ cm}^3$

    b. $94.7 \text{ dm}^3 \times \frac{1.00 \text{ kPa}}{100.0 \text{ kPa}}$

    $= 0.947 \text{ dm}^3$

29. $10.0 \text{ mL} \times \frac{400 \text{ kPa}}{100 \text{ kPa}} = 40.0 \text{ mL}$

30. $9.3 \text{ kPa} \times \frac{12.7 \text{ L}}{20.1 \text{ L}} = 5.9 \text{ kPa}$

31. $10.0 \text{ dm}^3 \times \frac{100.2 \text{ kPa}}{325.5 \text{ kPa}} = 3.08 \text{ dm}^3$

32. $2.55 \text{ dm}^3 \times \frac{67.4 \text{ kPa}}{145.1 \text{ kPa}} = 1.18 \text{ dm}^3$

33. When measured at the same temperature and pressure, the volumes of reacting gases are in small whole number ratios.

34. No, because this non-whole number ratio violates Gay-Lussac's law.

35. Under the same conditions of temperature and pressure, equal volumes of gases have equal numbers of molecules.

36. $\frac{V}{n} = \text{constant or } \frac{V_1}{n_1} = \frac{V_2}{n_2}$

37. a. $5.0 \text{ mol} \times \frac{45 \text{ L}}{85 \text{ L}} = 2.6 \text{ mol}$

    b. $0.225 \text{ mol} \times \frac{15.0 \text{ L}}{9.0 \text{ L}} = 0.38 \text{ mol}$

38. Since neon has the smallest molar mass, 50.0 g of neon has the largest number of atoms and therefore the largest volume.

39. Since CO_2 has twice as many O atoms as CO, 250.0 cm³ of CO_2 has twice as many O atoms as 250.0 cm³ of CO. Therefore, 125.0 cm³ of CO_2 has the same number of O atoms as 250.0 cm³ of CO.

40. Answers will vary.

    a. The measured pressure of a gas collected over water is the sum of the partial pressure of the gas itself and the partial pressure of the water vapor.

    b. Spray cans warn "do not incinerate" because heating the can would increase the pressure of the gas inside so much that the can could explode.

41. $CaCO_3 + 2HCl \rightarrow$

    $\qquad\qquad CaCl_2 + H_2O + CO_2$

    $\text{moles of } CO_2 = \frac{PV}{RT}$

    $= \frac{(0.955 \text{ atm})(0.345 \text{ L})}{(\frac{0.0821 \text{ L atm}}{\text{mol} \cdot \text{K}})(273 + 22.3) \text{ K}}$

    $= 0.0136 \text{ mol}$

    $\text{mol of HCl} = 0.0136 \text{ mol } CO_2$

    $\times \frac{2 \text{ mol HCl}}{1 \text{ mol } CO_2} = 0.0272 \text{ mol HCl}$

    $\frac{0.0272 \text{ mol HCl}}{0.0500 \text{ L}} = 0.544 \text{ mol/L}$

    $= 0.544 M$

42. $2C_8H_{18} + 25O_2 \rightarrow$
$$16CO_2 + 18H_2O$$

$12\ 000 \ \text{miles} \times \dfrac{1 \ \text{gal}}{20 \ \text{miles}}$

$\times \dfrac{2700 \ \text{g } C_8H_{18}}{1 \ \text{gal}} \times \dfrac{1 \ \text{mol } C_8H_{18}}{114 \ \text{g } C_8H_{18}}$

$\times \dfrac{16 \ \text{mol } CO_2}{2 \ \text{mol } C_8H_{18}} \times \dfrac{44.0 \ \text{g } CO_2}{1 \ \text{mol } CO_2}$

$= 5.0 \times 10^6 \ \text{g } CO_2$

Predicting Gas Behavior

Investigations	Demonstrations	Texas Essential Elements★
In-text Investigation, page T256	Behavior of Gases, page T231	**Content:** 8.6 **Process:** 4.1, 10.1, 10.4
Laboratory Manual 7–1 M		**Content:** 7.3 **Process:** 10.1
	Graham's Law and Diffusion, page T252	**Content:** 8.7, 8.8
		Content: 8.6 **Process:** 1.1, 1.2, 4.3, 5.1, 6.3, 7.3
		Process: 1.1, 1.2, 4.1, 4.2, 7.1, 9.1, 9.2

KEY:
M–Microscale **S**–Structured
I–Inquiry **IM**–Inquiry Microscale

★See pages T8–T11 for complete
listing of Texas Essential Elements.

7

Predicting Gas Behavior

Chapter Rationale

This chapter completes the introduction to gases. The first topic covered is the ideal gas law. This law is presented as a natural extension of the relationships students learned in the last chapter. The ideal gas law is immediately used to solve several types of problems, including stoichiometry problems involving gases.

In the middle of the chapter, students will look at gas stoichiometry from another viewpoint: using the molar volume of gases at STP and applying the law of combining volumes. Finally, at the end of the chapter, students will learn the kinetic molecular theory and how it explains gas behavior.

About the Photograph

A gas (carbon dioxide) is dissolved in a sweetened, flavored liquid solvent to make a carbonated soft drink. Lowering the temperature and raising the pressure are ways to keep the gas dissolved in the liquid. The photograph shows how depressurizing the can results in a decreased solubility of the gas in the liquid. Some liquid is pushed out of the can with the escaping carbon dioxide.

Chapter Planning Hints

Plan to complete the chapter, including the Laboratory Investigation and the Chapter Review, in four to six class sessions. Optional demonstrations appear on pages T231 and T252. You may wish to preview them at this time.

The macroscopic behavior of a gas in the real world is often predictable. In this chapter, you will learn about a theory that will help you explain gas behavior. ▲ CAUTION: When opening a can of carbonated beverage that has been shaken, always point it away from others and yourself.

Myths and Misconceptions

Before students study the ideal gas law, clarify any misconceptions they may have about the gas laws covered in Chapter 6. Unless these laws are reinforced, students often confuse the relationships described by each law, as well as the distinction between inverse and direct proportions.

Ask students to state each law in their own words. Review the relationship between the volume of a gas and pressure, temperature, and the number of moles of gas, as stated by Boyle's and Charles's laws and by Avogadro's principle, respectively.

PART

1 *Ideal Gas Law*

Consider all of the common gases around you. For example, oxygen (a gas that accounts for more than 20% of the atmosphere) is one of the most reactive gases. You may have already seen a demonstration of the explosive reaction that takes place when a spark ignites a mixture of hydrogen and oxygen to form water. But there are many more commonplace reactions involving oxygen, too. When you burn wood in a fireplace, oxygen is consumed. If you use a propane stove on a camping trip, you use the reaction between propane and oxygen to provide heat for your food. Your body needs a constant supply of oxygen because oxygen is involved in a complex set of reactions producing energy for your cells.

A firm knowledge of the behavior of gases is essential to understanding how gases react. In Chapter 6 you studied several important gas properties, including pressure, volume, temperature, and amount of gas (number of moles). You know how these properties are related. Pressure and volume, for example, are inversely proportional, while kelvin temperature and volume are directly proportional. Once you have mastered these relationships, you are ready to increase your understanding of gas behavior by extending and applying what you know.

You will extend what you already know by learning the ideal gas law, which summarizes the other gas laws by combining them into a single statement. You will see how to use the ideal gas law in problems involving changes in several gas variables, similar to the problems you solved in Chapter 6. Since the ideal gas law contains all of the important gas properties, you can apply this law to more complex problems than before, involving changes in more than one variable at a time. As you read this chapter, be sure to pay attention to the use of the ideal gas law in stoichiometry problems involving gaseous reactants and products.

7.1 Defining the Ideal Gas Law

Figure 7-1 on the next page represents the three laws you have learned that describe gas behavior. As Table 7-1 on the next page illustrates, these three laws can be rewritten to show how the volume of a gas is related to pressure, temperature, and number of moles of a gas.

Objectives

Part 1

A. **Summarize** the gas laws using the ideal gas law.

B. **Determine** changes in pressure, volume, temperature, and moles of a gas sample.

Developing Skills

Students may apply this skill in their study of Part 1.

Calculating: Ask students to look at some of the review problems involving Boyle's law, Charles's law, and Avogadro's principle from the previous chapter, resolving them with the ideal gas law method introduced in this part.

≡ FOCUS

Activate Prior Knowledge

Students know that some chemical reactions produce a gas. Demonstrate a reaction involving a gas product. Put 1*M* HCl into a flask, and turn it upside down in a container of water. Slip a small piece of magnesium into the flask.

⚠ **CAUTION: Protect students with a shield. Wear safety goggles and a lab apron.**

Ask students to determine how much hydrogen gas would be produced if 0.1 g of Mg reacted. How could they verify their answers? At this point, their only suggestion may be to obtain the mass of the gas. Explain to students that in this chapter they will use the easily-measured variables of volume, temperature, and pressure to determine how much gas they have. (Note: you might also point out to students that water vapor is collected in the flask, as well as hydrogen gas.) For disposal, neutralize with 0.1*M* or less concentrated acid and pour down the drain. Wrap any solid residue in newspaper and put in the wastebasket.

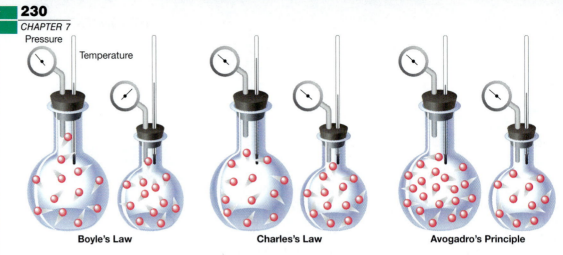

Boyle's Law   Charles's Law   Avogadro's Principle

Figure 7-1 Left: *According to Boyle's law, at a constant temperature, the pressure exerted by a given quantity of gas increases as the volume of the gas decreases.* Center: *According to Charles's law, at a constant pressure, the volume occupied by a given quantity of gas decreases as the temperature of the gas decreases.* Right: *According to Avogadro's principle, at a constant temperature and pressure, the volume occupied by a gas depends directly on the number of gas particles.*

TABLE 7-1

Gas Laws				
Charles's law	$\dfrac{V}{T} = k$	or	$V = kT$	(constant P and n)
Boyle's law	$PV = c$	or	$V = \dfrac{c}{P}$	(constant T and n)
Avogadro's principle	$\dfrac{V}{n} = a$	or	$V = an$	(constant T and P)

If all three laws are combined, the result is

$$V = kca\,\frac{(nT)}{P} \quad \text{or} \quad V = R\,\frac{(nT)}{P}$$

where R is a proportionality constant replacing kca and is called the **universal gas constant.** By multiplying both sides of the equation by P, the equation becomes

$$PV = nRT$$

and is known as the **ideal gas law.** While Charles's law and Boyle's law relate two properties of gases (volume and temperature—pressure and volume), the ideal gas law relates four properties; the amount of gas, the volume, the temperature, and the pressure.

The universal gas constant Before you can use the ideal gas law, you need a value for its constant, R. This value can be found experimentally under carefully controlled conditions. By convention, many chemists report gas volumes at standard temperature

---

PART **1**

Section 7.1 continued

≡ **TEACH**

Teaching Strategy

The Universal Gas Constant

In order to help your students focus on the ideal gas law itself, you many wish to provide them with the values of R given in this text instead of requiring them to memorize several constants.

and pressure conditions, or **STP** for short. Standard temperature and pressure have been arbitrarily defined as a temperature of 0°C and a pressure of 1 atm. Under these conditions, measurements performed on several different gases show that one mole of any gas occupies a volume of 22.4 liters. This information may be used to calculate the value of R, as shown here:

$$R = \frac{PV}{nT} = \frac{1.00 \text{ atm} \times 22.4 \text{ L}}{1.00 \text{ mol} \times 273 \text{ K}} = 0.0821 \text{ L} \cdot \text{atm/mol K}$$

More precise measurements reveal that the value of R to four significant figures is 0.08206 L · atm/mol K. Although the units for R may look confusing, you shouldn't worry about what they mean. R is simply the gas law constant; it does not stand for a variable, such as V (volume) or T (temperature). The units look complex only because of the way R is calculated.

As you have learned earlier in this text, chemists are gradually converting to the use of SI units. For this reason, you may prefer to use this alternative value of R. If you remember that a volume of 1 liter is the same as 1 dm³ and that there are 101.325 kPa in 1 atm, you can see that the units of R may be converted into SI units this way:

$$R = 0.08206 \cancel{L} \cdot \cancel{\text{atm}}/\text{mol} \cdot K \times \frac{1 \text{ dm}^3}{1 \cancel{L}} \times \frac{101.325 \text{ kPa}}{1 \cancel{\text{atm}}}$$
$$= 8.315 \text{ dm}^3 \cdot \text{kPa/K} \cdot \text{mol}$$

While it is possible to convert the units of R in this way, in practice you will find it easier to change the units of the gas variables you are using to match the units of the gas constant you choose to use. If you want to use the SI version shown here, you must make sure that you convert your volumes to dm³, your pressures to kPa, and your temperatures to K when you solve gas problems.

> **PROBLEM-SOLVING STRATEGY**
>
> *Use what you have already **learned** about converting to SI units to understand this expression.*

EXAMPLE 7-1

Calculate the pressure of 1.65 g of helium gas at 16.0°C and occupying a volume of 3.25 L.

■ ***Analyze the Problem*** Determine which gas law might apply to this problem. The problem provides data on volume and temperature. The number of moles can be calculated from the mass that is given. All of the variables are accounted for except pressure. The ideal gas law can be used to solve the problem.

■ ***Apply a Strategy*** Rearrange the ideal gas law by dividing both sides by V to solve for P.

$$P = \frac{nRT}{V}$$

DEMONSTRATION

Behavior of Gases

For a change of pace, open a bottle of perfume in the room. Have students raise their hands as soon as they detect the scent. Keep a record of how long it takes the odor to travel across the room. Elicit students' reactions to the demonstration and involve them in a discussion of what they already know about gases from Chapter 6. Point out that they will learn about the diffusion of gases in Section 7.7.

PART **1**
Section 7.1 *continued*

Practice Problems

Assign the Practice Problems.

PROBLEM-SOLVING

S T R A T E G Y

*This solution is easier to obtain if you **break the problem into parts.** (See Strategy, page 166.)*

Make a data table of the variables so you can organize your work and determine what must be calculated.

Variable	Given	Need to Calculate
P	unknown	from ideal gas law
n	1.65 g	number of moles
T	16.0°C	value in K
R	constant	
	8.315 dm$^3 \cdot$ kPa/K $\cdot$ mol	no
V	3.25 L	becomes 3.25 dm^3

■ *Work a Solution* The molar mass of helium is 4.00 g/mol so the number of moles is

$$1.65 \ \cancel{g} \times \frac{1 \text{ mol}}{4.00 \ \cancel{g}} = 0.412 \text{ mol}$$

Convert the temperature from Celsius to kelvin.

$$T = 16.0°C + 273 = 289 \text{ K}$$

Substitute all the known values into the ideal gas equation to solve for P.

$$P = \frac{0.412 \text{ mol} \times 8.315 \ \cancel{dm^3} \cdot \text{kPa/K} \cdot \text{mol} \times 289 \text{ K}}{3.25 \ \cancel{dm^3}} = 305 \text{ kPa}$$

■ *Verify Your Answer* Check that the setup will yield an answer in units of pressure. Work the problem again by substituting the value for P into the ideal gas law and solve for R. If your answer is correct, you should get the universal gas constant as 8.315 dm^3 kPa/K mol.

Practice Problems

1. Work the previous problem, using the value of 0.08206 L $\cdot$ atm/K $\cdot$ mol. Demonstrate that the answer you get is equivalent to the answer in kPa.   ***Ans.*** 3.01 atm or 305 kPa

2. What is the volume in dm^3 of 2.5 moles of oxygen gas measured at 25°C and a pressure of 104.5 kPa?   ***Ans.*** 59 dm^3

3. At what temperature will 0.0100 mole of argon gas have a volume of 275 mL at a pressure of 100 kPa?
      Ans. 331 K or 58°C

7-2 Applying the Ideal Gas Law

One advantage of knowing the ideal gas law is that it can be applied to many types of gas problems, including Charles's law and Boyle's law problems. Suppose that you are working a problem in which the temperature and number of moles of gas do not change; only the pressure and volume are allowed to vary. From this information,

Boyle's law can be applied. However, if you have forgotten the mathematical form of Boyle's law, you may use the ideal gas law to obtain it.

Here is how to rearrange the ideal gas law. At some initial conditions of pressure and volume, P_1 and V_1, the ideal gas law says that this is true:

$$P_1V_1 = nRT$$

Similarly, this relationship is true for the final conditions of pressure and volume, P_2 and V_2:

$$P_2V_2 = nRT$$

Since the number of moles and the temperature do not change, and since the value of R also remains constant, the product nRT represents the same value in both equations. Using the constant k to represent this constant (nRT), these expressions may be rewritten this way:

$$P_1V_1 = k = P_2V_2$$

The form of this expression shows that pressure and volume are inversely related.

In the same way, if the pressure and number of moles are held constant, the ideal gas law can be rearranged to give this form:

$$\frac{V_1}{T_1} = \frac{nR}{P} = \frac{V_2}{T_2} \quad \text{or} \quad \frac{V_1}{T_1} = k = \frac{V_2}{T_2}$$

Concept ✔ Check

Why is it often necessary to rearrange the equation for the ideal gas law?

PROBLEM-SOLVING STRATEGY

In mathematics, when two different expressions are equal to each other, you can substitute one expression for the other in an equation. This is often helpful when it comes to deriving new equations.

Teaching Strategy

Applying the Ideal Gas Law

Have students rearrange the ideal gas law so that they can obtain the expressions for Boyle's law, Charles's law, and Avogadro's principle that they have already learned. Explain to students that if they memorize one gas law (the ideal gas law) and know how to rearrange it, they will not need to memorize the mathematical forms of these other three laws.

This is the same form predicted by Charles's law, showing a direct relationship between the two variables, volume and temperature.

The expressions you have seen here suggest another way of working a gas law problem. One of the ways you have previously solved Boyle's law problems is by calculating the value of the constant using one set of conditions, and then solving for the unknown variable using the known value for the pressure or the volume. Notice from the equations shown above, both P_1V_1 and P_2V_2 are equal to the same constant, so they are equal to each other:

$$P_1V_1 = P_2V_2$$

This equation suggests that you can eliminate the intermediate step of calculating the value of the constant, k. Simply substitute the three known values into this equation and solve for the fourth value.

The next example is a problem in which the number of moles of a gas is held constant, while the pressure, volume, and temperature are allowed to change. Notice two features in the solution: the use of the ideal gas law to determine an appropriate relationship among the three relevant variables, and the use of a derived equation which does not require the calculation of a constant.

EXAMPLE 7-2

A sample of oxygen gas has a volume of 7.84 cm³ at a pressure of 71.8 kPa and a temperature of 25°C. What will be the volume of the gas if the pressure is changed to 101 kPa and the temperature is changed to 0°C?

■ **Analyze the Problem** Identify the variables used in the problem—volume, temperature, and pressure. Recognize that you are going from an initial set of conditions to a final set of conditions. Since no gas is being added to the system and no gas removed, you can assume n is constant as well as R. Using the ideal gas law you can divide both sides by T and write

$$\frac{P_1 V_1}{T_1} = \underset{\text{constant}}{nR} = \frac{P_2 V_2}{T_2}$$

Therefore,

$$\frac{P_1 V_1}{T_1} = \frac{P_2 V_2}{T_2}$$

■ **Apply a Strategy** Record what you know from the problem.

$$P_1 = 71.8 \text{ kPa} \qquad P_2 = 101 \text{ kPa}$$
$$V_1 = 7.84 \text{ cm}^3 \qquad V_2 = ?$$
$$T_1 = 25°C \qquad T_2 = 0°C$$

Recognize that you must convert °C to K.

■ **Work a Solution** Convert the temperatures to Kelvin.

$$T = 25°C + 273 = 298 \text{ K}$$
$$T = 0°C + 273 = 273 \text{ K}$$

Substitute the values given in the problem into the equation and solve for V_2.

$$\frac{71.8 \text{ kPa} \times 7.84 \text{ cm}^3}{298 \text{ K}} =$$

$$\frac{101 \text{ kPa} \times V_2}{273 \text{ K}}$$

$$V_2 = 5.11 \text{ cm}^3$$

■ **Verify Your Answer** Work the problem another way to check your answer. Since $\frac{P_1 V_1}{T_1}$ = a constant and $\frac{P_2 V_2}{T_2}$ = a constant, you can solve for the constant, given the data for P_1, V_1, and T_1. With this constant, you can now solve for V_2, using the fact that $\frac{P_2 V_2}{T_2}$ equals that same constant.
The answers should agree.

PROBLEM-SOLVING

S T R A T E G Y

*Since **R** is not part of the equation, you do not need to convert volume to dm³. All units except those for volume will cancel out of the equation.*

Practice Problems

4a. A sample of nitrogen gas has a pressure of 2.5 atm at a temperature of 25°C. What temperature is required to increase the pressure to 4.0 atm, assuming that the volume is fixed and the amount of gas does not change?

Ans. 204°C

4b. What happens to the pressure inside a rigid container if the amount of nitrogen gas increases from 0.50 mole to 0.75 mole? The original pressure is 98.0 kPa, and the temperature remains constant.

Ans. 147 kPa

Practice Problems

Assign the Practice Problems.

The equation you obtained in Example 7-2 is called the **combined gas law.** As you have seen, it is a convenient equation to use when solving gas problems. However, you should remember that all the equations you learned in Part 2 of Chapter 6 can be similarly derived from the ideal gas law. If you know the ideal gas law, you do not have to memorize the combined gas law or any other gas law equation.

The ideal gas law and stoichiometry Not only can the ideal gas law be used to solve problems similar to those in Chapter 6, but it can also be applied to stoichiometry problems involving gases. As you have seen, one of the variables in the ideal gas law is the amount of gas (or number of moles). Of course, you know that one of the keys to solving any stoichiometry problem is using a balanced chemical equation to provide information about the moles of reactants and products. It is easy to weigh solids and liquids, so for these states of matter you are likely to use the molecular mass to calculate the number of moles. But gases can be conveniently described in terms of their pressure, temperature, and volume, which you can use to compute the number of moles.

One type of reaction which produces a gas is the reaction between an ionic solid containing the carbonate ion, CO_3^{2-}, or the bicarbonate ion, HCO_3^-, to produce carbon dioxide. When calcium carbonate or sodium bicarbonate is mixed with hydrochloric acid, these reactions take place:

$$CaCO_3(s) + 2HCl(aq) \rightarrow CO_2(g) + H_2O(g) + CaCl_2(aq)$$
$$NaHCO_3(aq) + HCl(aq) \rightarrow CO_2(g) + H_2O(g) + NaCl(aq)$$

Your stomach contains hydrochloric acid. When people complain of indigestion, there is an excessive amount of this acid. Remedies involve reacting the acid with antacids. As you see from these equations, both calcium carbonate and sodium bicarbonate can serve as antacids. Sodium bicarbonate is the active ingredient in baking soda, and calcium carbonate is found in some commercial antacid preparations.

In this next example, you will learn how much carbon dioxide forms when calcium carbonate reacts with hydrochloric acid.

Figure 7-2 *Sodium bicarbonate ($NaHCO_3$), also known as baking soda, has the ability to absorb gases. It is therefore often used in refrigerators to absorb unpleasant odors.*

DO YOU KNOW?

Geologists often use hydrochloric acid to test soil samples for the presence of calcium carbonate. If calcium carbonate is present, a visible reaction will occur.

EXAMPLE 7-3

What volume of carbon dioxide forms when 525 mg of calcium carbonate completely reacts with hydrochloric acid? Assume that the carbon dioxide is formed at a pressure of 101 kPa and a temperature of 25°C.

■ *Analyze the Problem* Since this is a stoichiometry problem, you know that you will need the balanced chemical equation to solve it:

$$CaCO_3(s) + 2HCl(aq) \rightarrow CO_2(g) + H_2O(g) + CaCl_2(aq)$$

The equation reminds you that you will need to calculate the number of moles of calcium carbonate that you start with, and that you may determine the number of moles of carbon dioxide that can be produced.

■ *Apply a Strategy* Although this problem will involve several steps, you have already worked problems involving each one of these steps. You can outline what you need to do this way:

1. In order to find the number of moles of calcium carbonate, you need to convert the milligrams into grams and then convert into moles by using its molecular mass (100 g/mol).

2. The balanced chemical equation provides the mole-to-mole relationship you need to convert moles of calcium carbonate into moles of carbon dioxide (1 mol $CaCO_3$ = 1 mol CO_2). Draw these two steps as a roadmap.

mg $CaCO_3$? mol CO_2

$$\dfrac{1\ g}{1000\ mg} \qquad\qquad \dfrac{1\ mol\ CO_2}{1\ mol\ CaCO_3}$$

g $CaCO_3$ $\dfrac{1\ mol\ CaCO_3}{100\ g\ CaCO_3}$ mol $CaCO_3$

3. When you have the moles of CO_2, you can combine that with the pressure and temperature information already given to solve for volume with the ideal gas law. Don't forget that the temperature must be expressed in kelvins before you can use it.

■ *Work a Solution* Follow the plan that was just developed. First, calculate the number of moles of calcium carbonate involved:

$$525\ mg\ CaCO_3 \times \frac{1\ g}{1000\ mg} \times \frac{1\ mole\ CaCO_3}{100\ g\ CaCO_3}$$
$$= 0.00525\ mol\ CaCO_3$$

Next, use the mole-mole relationship from the balanced chemical equation to calculate the number of moles of carbon dioxide produced:

$$0.00525 \text{ mol } \cancel{CaCO_3} \times \frac{1 \text{ mole } CO_2}{1 \text{ mole } \cancel{CaCO_3}}$$

$$= 0.00525 \text{ mol } CO_2$$

Finally, you are ready to apply the ideal gas law. Change the temperature to the kelvin scale:

$$25°C + 273 = 298 \text{ K}$$

Now, rearrange the ideal gas law to solve for volume, and substitute the known values in the equation:

$$PV = nRT$$

$$V = \frac{nRT}{P} = \frac{0.00525 \cancel{\text{mol}} \times 8.314 \text{ L} \cdot kPa/\cancel{\text{mol}} \cdot \cancel{K} \times 298 \text{ K}}{101 \cancel{kPa}}$$

$$= 0.129 \text{ L (or 129 mL)}$$

■ *Verify Your Answer* Since this problem involved several steps, you should review your work carefully. In this case, it would be easy to rework the entire problem backwards. Ask yourself this question: What mass (in milligrams) of calcium carbonate is required to produce 0.129 L of carbon dioxide at a temperature of 25°C and a pressure of 101 kPa? How would you set up the ideal gas law equation to answer this question. If the problem has been worked correctly, you should obtain 525 mg.

Practice Problems

Use the equation for the ideal gas law to calculate each of the following volumes.

5a. What volume of carbon dioxide forms at 10°C and 99 kPa pressure when 0.50 g of sodium bicarbonate reacts completely with hydrochloric acid?   *Ans.* 0.14 L

b. Unlike oxygen, nitrogen (the other major component of air) is generally unreactive. Magnesium is one metal that can react with nitrogen directly. What volume of nitrogen, measured at a pressure of 102 kPa and a temperature of 27°C, will react with 5.0 g of magnesium?   *Ans.* 1.7 L

Figure 7-3 *Most seashells are made of calcium carbonate $CaCO_3$. They will therefore react with hydrochloric acid HCl producing the products shown in the reaction in Example 7-3.*

PART 1
Section 7.2 *continued*

Practice Problems

Assign the Practice Problems.

Guided Practice

Review the Concept Check question on page 233 with students. Answers can be found in Appendix E on page 808.

Reteaching Idea

Note: this activity can also be used in Section 7.6, Kinetic Molecular Theory. To aid students in understanding the concept of the ideal gas law and the kinetic molecular theory, the following analogy may be used. Compare gases in a container to a dance in the school gym. Each student at the dance represents a gas molecule. The size of the gym is compared to the volume of the container. The tempo of the music corresponds to the temperature of the gas—the faster the music, the higher the temperature. The pressure of the gas is represented by the number of collisions or bumpings occurring. The situation can be varied by changing the music (Charles's Law), the number of students (Avogadro's principle), or by partitioning off the gym (Boyle's Law). Students will probably want to try out this activity!

☰ CLOSE

Summing Up Main Ideas

Assign students to calculate how much each of the four properties included in the ideal gas law change in the following problem. A basketball is inflated to 2.0 atm in a garage that is at 20°C. The basketball is then taken outside to a playground where the temperature is −5.0°C, where it feels flat. (The volume does not change since the space occupied by the air inside the basketball does not change. The amount of gas also remains the same. The temperature decreases by 25°C. The pressure also decreases.

$$P_2 = T_2 \times \frac{P_1}{T_1}, \; P_2 = 268 \text{ K}$$

$$\times \frac{2.0 \text{ atm}}{293 \text{ K}} = 1.8 \text{ atm.}$$

PART 1 REVIEW

Assign the Part Review questions.

Evaluating Skills

These skills are evaluated in the Part Review questions indicated. **Comparing/Contrasting:** 6, 9, 10; **Forming models:** 6; **Determining cause and effect:** 6; **Analyzing data:** 6, 7, 8, 9, 10; **Applying a strategy:** 6, 7, 8, 10; **Calculating:** 6, 7, 8, 10; **Verifying results:** 6, 7, 8, 10

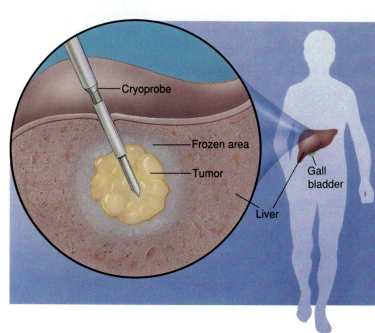

Figure 7-4 *In order to convert nitrogen gas, N_2, into a liquid, the nitrogen must be cooled to 126.1 K (−146.9°C). Liquid nitrogen is made commercially by taking compressed nitrogen gas and allowing it to expand to a lower pressure. This is done repeatedly until the gas is cold enough that it condenses. Applications for liquid nitrogen include cryogenic research (the study of extremely cold temperatures) and some surgical procedures.*

Cryoprobe
Frozen area
Tumor
Gall bladder
Liver

PROBLEM·SOLVING STRATEGY

*You may want to **break this problem into parts:** choose a value for R, convert the data to correct units, and then apply the appropriate gas law. (See Strategy, page 166.)*

Boxed numbers indicate questions that involve skills in interpretation, application, and analysis.

PART 1 REVIEW

6. a. The volume of a sample of gas is 200 mL at 275 K and 92.1 kPa. What will the new volume of the gas be at 350 K and 98.5 kPa?   ***Ans.*** 238 mL

    b. Make two drawings of the container before and after the changes showing the same number of particles in each. Explain the effect of the change in pressure on the space between the particles. What effect does the change in temperature have?

7. How many moles of chloroform, $CHCl_3$, are required to fill a flask with a volume of 273 cm^3 at a temperature of 100°C and a pressure of 940 torr?   ***Ans.*** 0.0110 mol

8. What is the volume occupied by 36.0 g of water vapor at a temperature of 125°C and a pressure of 102 kPa?   ***Ans.*** 64.9 L

9. A particular sample of sulfur dioxide occupies a volume of 10.0 L. What would be the volume of a sample of neon gas that has the same number of moles under the same temperature and pressure conditions?

10. A helium balloon containing 0.25 mole of helium has a volume of 6.25 L. How many moles of helium would be required to fill a 15.0 L balloon under the same conditions of temperature and pressure?   ***Ans.*** 0.60 mol

---

PART 1 REVIEW

ANSWERS

■ Keyed to Objectives

B 6. a. $\dfrac{P_1 V_1}{T_1} = \dfrac{P_2 V_2}{T_2}$

$V_2 = \dfrac{P_1}{P_2} \times \dfrac{T_2}{T_1} \times V_1 = \dfrac{92.1 \text{ kPa}}{98.5 \text{ kPa}}$

$\times \dfrac{350 \text{ K}}{275 \text{ K}} \times 200 \text{ mL} = 238 \text{ mL}$

b.

The pressure change tends to decrease the space between the particles. The relative increase in the temperature, however, is greater, so that overall the space between particles increases.

B 7. $n = \dfrac{PV}{RT} =$

$\dfrac{\left(\frac{940}{760} \text{ atm}\right)(0.273 \text{ L})}{\left(\frac{0.08206 \text{ L} \cdot \text{atm}}{\text{mol} \cdot \text{K}}\right)(373 \text{ K})} = 0.0110 \text{ mol}$

B 8. $V = \dfrac{nRT}{P} = \left(\dfrac{36.0 \text{ g} \times 1 \text{ mol}}{18 \text{ g}}\right)$

$\left(8.314 \dfrac{\text{dm}^3 \cdot \text{kPa}}{\text{mol} \cdot \text{K}}\right)\left(\dfrac{398 \text{ K}}{102 \text{ kPa}}\right)$

$= 64.9 \text{ dm}^3 \text{ or L}$

CAREERS IN CHEMISTRY

Senior Engineering Technician

To indulge her interest in science and to make a contribution to the world are two goals that have combined nicely for Elizabeth (Liz) Crawford-Harrison in her career as a Senior Engineering Technician in the Safety Research Laboratory of a major chemical company.

Preventing hazards Liz assesses the hazards of chemical substances and is responsible for writing the Fire and Explosion Hazards section of her company's material safety data sheets. The data she provides allow quick, correct response in the case of an accident that could pose a danger to people's health and safety or cause damage to the environment. Her responsibility is to see to it that hazardous chemicals are handled according to safety guidelines.

Personal perspective Working as she does with hazardous chemicals, you might expect that Liz would view chemistry in a negative light. But that's not the case. She is tremendously appreciative of the benefits that have flowed from chemical research in the past and optimistic about the role that chemistry will play in solving the pressing problems of hunger, disease, and the environment.

Nothing worthwhile comes easy.

Elizabeth Crawford-Harrison
Senior Engineering Technician

Keeping up and contributing Liz prepared for her career by earning a bachelor of science degree in medical laboratory technology. However, as technology advances, more education may be needed to qualify for positions in the field. As an established professional, Liz must also continue to learn. Staying involved with the scientific community through her participation in the American Chemical Society helps Liz keep up with what's happening, and she also helps others do the same. She founded and still edits *Technicians Today*, the only professional and technical publication for chemical technicians.

Liz's career satisfies her desire to make a contribution through science to improve humankind. She expects that there will continue to be job opportunities in her field in the future. She finds her career so rewarding that she urges students to study science and work with diligence and determination. "Nothing worthwhile comes easy," she says. Liz also encourages students to set goals and to persevere to reach them.

CAREERS IN CHEMISTRY

Teaching Strategies

1. Have students identify other fields that have safety guidelines. These might include nuclear energy, radioactive materials, household cleaners and other chemicals, pesticides and herbicides, biological toxins, pathogens, and disease vectors in a hospital or other health care setting.

2. Have students find out uses of chemicals in food processing and preservation (for example, decaffeinating coffee, freeze-drying, pasteurization, and so on) and discuss the pros and cons of food additives in the preparation or improvement of processed foods.

Look Ahead

Tie in your discussion of chemicals used in food processing and preservation with the **Science Technology & Society** feature on food additives on page 596.

Related Careers

This profession combines writing skills with an understanding of science. Discuss other professions that combine communication skills and science (for example, print and electronic journalism, editing, teaching, writing technical manuals, sales of pharmaceuticals and biomedical devices). For information on careers, contact the National Institute for Certification in Engineering Technologies, 2029 K St., NW, Washington, DC 20008; the National Association of Science Writers, Inc., P.O. Box 294, Greenlawn, NY 11740; or your local or state institution of higher education.

Resources

Contact the American Chemical Society or the Association for Women in Science for additional information.

B **9.** Based on Avogadro's principle, this sample also has a volume of 10.0 L.

B **10.** $\dfrac{V_1}{n_1} = \dfrac{V_2}{n_2}$

$n_2 = \dfrac{V_2}{V_1} \times n_1 = \dfrac{15.0\,L}{6.25\,L}$

$\times 0.25 \text{ mol} = 0.60 \text{ mol}$

PART **2**
Gas Stoichiometry

Section 7.3

Developing Skills

Students may apply these skills in their study of Part 2.

Predicting: Ask students to predict what would happen to the molar volume at STP if (a) the temperature was increased or decreased, or (b) the pressure was increased or decreased.

Comparing/Contrasting: After students have solved several gas stoichiometry problems, ask them when they used volume ratios and when they had to use the ideal gas law or some other method.

Analyzing data and Applying a strategy: Have students plan a roadmap for the Practice Problems on page 241 before they start their calculations.

☰FOCUS

Activate Prior Knowledge

This activity will review students' concept of the mole. Ask students how much volume a mole of CO_2 should occupy as a solid and as a gas.

⚠ **CAUTON: Wear safety goggles. Do not touch dry ice with bare skin; use leather gloves or a scoop.**
Mass out 1 mole of crushed dry ice, determine its volume, and place it in a large plastic garbage bag. Seal the bag and allow the CO_2 to sublime and fill the bag with gaseous CO_2. Measure the approximate volume of the bag. (about 22.4 L)

Objectives

Part 2

C. *Calculate* how much gas is produced in a reaction by using standard molar volume at STP.

D. *Apply* stoichiometric principles to *calculate* the amount of gas produced in a chemical reaction.

Figure 7-5 *Weather balloons are used to gather weather data in the upper atmosphere. How can you use the ideal gas law to explain the ability to monitor weather conditions at high altitude?*

PART
2 Gas Stoichiometry

You learned in Chapter 5 that it is important in chemistry to know not only *what* is produced in a chemical reaction but also *how much* is produced. For chemical reactions involving gases, one way of dealing with the quantity of a gas is by measuring its volume. Using that volume and the ideal gas law, the number of moles of a gas can be determined if you have values for pressure, temperature, and R. However, if you first use the ideal gas law to find the volume of 1 mole of a gas at standard conditions, you can solve problems involving the quantity of a gas from a different perspective.

7.3 STP and Molar Volume

Earlier you saw how the value of the ideal gas law constant, R, can be determined using the values of the other variables in the ideal gas law. The set of variables used to calculate R include the volume of one mole of gas measured under standard conditions, that is, under a pressure of 1 atm (101.325 kPa) and 0°C (273 K). You might recall that this volume was 22.4 L (or 22.4 dm³). The volume of one mole of a gas is often called a **molar volume.** But unlike molar masses, which depend on the substance being measured, the molar volume of every gas is the same, regardless of identity—provided that they are under the same conditions. For example, the molar mass of carbon dioxide (44.0 g/mole) is different from the molar mass of oxygen (32.0 g/mole). At 1 atm and 0°C, the molar volumes of both CO_2 and O_2 are 22.4 dm³/mole.

The molar volumes of gases do change as the conditions of temperature and pressure change. Here is where the ideal gas law can be helpful. Suppose you are measuring gases at a pressure of 100 kPa and a temperature of 22°C (or 295 K). The molar volume of 22.4 dm³ no longer applies, because the conditions are no longer at STP. Recalling that molar volume refers to the volume of one mole of a gas, you can calculate the molar volume by rearranging the ideal gas law to solve for V, as follows:

$$V = \frac{nRT}{P} = \frac{1.00 \text{ mole} \times 8.315 \frac{dm^3 \cdot kPa}{K \cdot mol} \times 295 \text{ K}}{100 \text{ kPa}} = 24.5 \text{ dm}^3$$

Molar volumes such as these can be useful in solving gas law problems, especially in repeated problems in which you are dealing with several different gases measured under the same set of temperature and pressure conditions. In the next example, you will find the number of moles of a gas sample present from its molar volume, which is 22.4 dm³ at STP. Using this fact, you can avoid doing the longer calculations of the ideal gas law.

EXAMPLE 7-4

A sample of oxygen gas occupies 5.6 dm³ at STP. How many moles of oxygen are present? What is the mass of the gas sample?

■ **Analyze the Problem** Write down what you are asked to find.

$$5.6 \text{ dm}^3 \text{ at STP} = ? \text{ mole} = ? \text{ grams at STP}$$

Recognize that since you are being asked to find the number of moles, you can use the relationship that 1 mole of a gas has a specific molar volume. Once you know the number of moles you then can use the molar mass of oxygen gas to calculate the mass of the sample in grams.

■ **Apply a Strategy** The volume of 1 mole of a gas at STP is 22.4 dm³ (22.4 L) which can be written as

$$\frac{1 \text{ mol}}{22.4 \text{ dm}^3} \quad \text{or} \quad \frac{22.4 \text{ dm}^3}{1 \text{ mol}}$$

Diagram a road map to help you organize the relationships you will need to solve the problem.

5.6 dm³ (volume)	grams in sample
$\dfrac{1 \text{ mol}}{22.4 \text{ dm}^3}$	$\dfrac{32 \text{ g O}_2}{1 \text{ mol O}_2}$

moles in sample

■ **Work a Solution** Multiply the given volume by the ratio representing the standard molar volume and solve for the number of moles of oxygen.

$$5.6 \text{ dm}^3 \text{ O}_2 \times \frac{1 \text{ mol}}{22.4 \text{ dm}^3} = 0.25 \text{ mol O}_2$$

Next convert the number of moles to grams, using the molar mass of oxygen gas.

$$0.25 \text{ mol O}_2 \times \frac{32 \text{ g O}_2}{1 \text{ mol O}_2} = 8.0 \text{ g O}_2$$

■ **Verify Your Answer** Since the volume given in the problem is less than the molar volume, you would expect your answer for the number of moles to be less than one, and it is. Also check that your final answer has the correct units, which it does.

Practice Problems

11. How many moles of ammonia gas are required to fill a volume of 50 dm³ at STP? **Ans.** 2.2 mol

12. What is the mass of 1.00 dm³ of nitrogen at STP? **Ans.** 1.25 g

PROBLEM·SOLVING STRATEGY

This problem is similar to the mole-mass calculations done in Chapter 5. You have only added the step of converting volume to moles before finding the number of grams.

PROBLEM·SOLVING STRATEGY

*Use what you know about **factor-label analysis** to determine how to write the ratio. In this instance, you need dm³ to cancel to leave moles. (See Strategy, page 12.)*

PROBLEM·SOLVING STRATEGY

Good problem solvers realize that you can solve problems in more than one way. In this example, you can get the same answer by substituting the given volume and the values for pressure and temperature at STP into the ideal gas law and solve for n, the number of moles. Prove to yourself that the answer will be the same.

≣ TEACH

Teaching Strategy

STP and Molar Volume
In the lab, students will encounter room temperature more commonly than STP (0°C). Students need to learn to work with varying conditions. Provide opportunities for them to become proficient in using a wide variety of temperature-pressure situations.

Practice Problems

Assign the Practice Problems.

PART **2**
Section 7.4

Teaching Strategy

Determining Volume Ratios

Ask students to solve one or more of the problems they encounter in this section by using the ideal gas law method developed in Part 1.

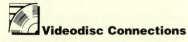

Videodisc Connections

17620 to 19978, side 3
Fairly noiseless explosion
(movie)

7.4 Determining Volume Ratios

In Chapter 5, you studied chemical reactions in a quantitative sense. You learned that the coefficients in a balanced chemical equation give you information about the number of molecules, (or formula units), and moles that react. Table 7-2 lists the ratios that can be derived from the coefficients of a balanced chemical equation describing the reaction of hydrogen gas and nitrogen gas to produce ammonia gas.

TABLE 7-2

Coefficient Ratios in the Production of Ammonia (T, P Constant)				
balanced equation	$3H_2(g)$	$+$ $N_2(g)$	$\rightarrow$	$2NH_3(g)$
molecule ratio	3	1		2
mole ratio	3	1		2
volume ratio	3	1		2

The volume ratio can be more easily understood if you consider an example where 1 mole of a gas occupies 22.4 L. The volume ratios can then be written as

$$3(22.4\ L)\ H_2(g)\ +\ 1(22.4\ L)\ N_2(g) \rightarrow 2(22.4\ L)\ NH_3(g)$$

giving a ratio of 67.2 L:22.4 L:44.8 L, which reduces to 3:1:2. This means that the coefficients in a balanced chemical equation not only indicate the ratio of reacting molecules and moles yielding a product but also the ratio of reacting volumes.

The fact that the coefficients may represent the ratio of reacting volumes can be explained if you remember that according to Avogadro's principle, equal volumes of gases at the same temperature and pressure contain equal numbers of particles. In this reaction, a given volume of hydrogen gas will have the same number of molecules as the same volume of nitrogen gas. If the molecules of hydrogen gas react in a ratio of 3 molecules of hydrogen to 1 molecule of nitrogen, then you must have 3 volumes of hydrogen (containing 3 times as many molecules) available to react with 1 volume of nitrogen to get 2 volumes of ammonia.

Predicting volumes Consider the equation in Table 7-2 again. If you have 6 dm³ of hydrogen gas reacting with 2 dm³ of nitrogen gas, how much ammonia will be produced? Using the coefficients of the balanced equation, you can predict the volume of a product. The ratio of hydrogen to nitrogen to ammonia is 3:1:2, indicating that for every mole of nitrogen that reacts, 2 moles of ammonia are formed. Therefore, 4 dm³ of ammonia are produced.

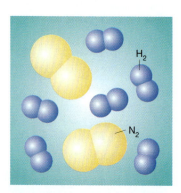

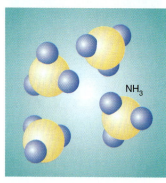

Figure 7-6 Top: *Hydrogen gas (H₂) and nitrogen gas (N₂) react to form ammonia gas (bottom). The molecule ratio of H₂ to N₂ is 3 to 1. During this reaction the number of molecules decreases such that there are one-half as many gas molecules (NH₃) after the reaction as there are gas molecules (H₂ and N₂) before the reaction. As a result, the volume of the product is one-half the total volume of the reactants. Therefore, the total volume ratios for reactants and products is 3H₂:1N₂:2NH₃.*

EXAMPLE 7-5

How many dm^3 of carbon dioxide gas are formed when 4.0 dm^3 of methane gas (CH_4) react with 0.50 dm^3 of oxygen gas to form carbon dioxide and water vapor? All gases are measured at the same temperature and pressure.

■ *Analyze the Problem* Write the balanced equation for the reaction.

$$CH_4(g) + 2O_2(g) \rightarrow CO_2(g) + 2H_2O(g)$$

List what you are being asked to find.

$$4.0 \text{ } dm^3 \text{ } CH_4(g) + 0.50 \text{ } dm^3 \text{ } O_2(g) \rightarrow ? \text{ } dm^3 \text{ } CO_2$$

■ *Apply a Strategy* Compare the ratio of reacting volumes for $CH_4(g)$ and $O_2(g)$ to the volumes of reactants given in the problem. The volume ratio is obtained from the coefficients of the balanced equation and is 1:2. The ratio of the volumes given in the problem can be written and reduced by dividing both the numerator and denominator by 4.0 as follows:

$$\frac{4.0 \text{ } dm^3 \text{ } CH_4}{0.50 \text{ } dm^3 \text{ } O_2} = \frac{1 \text{ } dm^3 \text{ } CH_4}{0.125 \text{ } dm^3 \text{ } O_2}$$

Since you have less O_2 than the problem requires, CH_4 is in excess and O_2 is the limiting reactant. Determine how much CO_2 will be produced in the reaction with 0.50 dm^3 O_2.

■ *Work a Solution* Use the ratio of volumes for CO_2 and O_2 from the balanced equation to solve for the amount of CO_2 produced.

$$? \text{ } dm^3 \text{ } CO_2 = 0.50 \text{ } \cancel{dm^3 \text{ } O_2} \times \frac{1 \text{ } dm^3 \text{ } CO_2}{2 \text{ } \cancel{dm^3 \text{ } O_2}} = 0.25 \text{ } dm^3 \text{ } CO_2$$

■ *Verify Your Answer* The ratio of volumes for O_2 to CO_2 from the balanced equation is 2:1. The problem states that 0.050 dm^3 of O_2 is present. According to the ratio, this volume must be twice the volume of the CO_2 produced, so you can reason that the volume of CO_2 will be half the volume of the O_2 or 0.25 dm^3, which agrees with your answer.

> **PROBLEM-SOLVING**
>
> **STRATEGY**
>
> *Use what you have already learned from Chapter 5 involving problems with excess reactants to solve this problem. Refer back to Example 5-5.*

Practice Problems

13. What volume of carbon dioxide gas forms when 350 cm^3 of methane reacts with oxygen? Assume temperature and pressure remain constant.   ***Ans.*** 350 cm^3

14. Propane, C_3H_8, burns in oxygen to form CO_2 and H_2O. If 22.5 dm^3 of propane burns, what volume of CO_2 forms at the same temperature and pressure?   ***Ans.*** 67.5 dm^3

Practice Problems

Assign the Practice Problems.

► **FOCUS ON**
PROBLEM SOLVING

Activate Prior Knowledge

Review students' knowledge of writing chemical equations by assigning them to write an equation for the following reaction: methane gas is burned in the presence of oxygen gas to form carbon dioxide and water vapor. [$CH_4(g) + 2O_2(g) \rightarrow CO_2(g) + 2H_2O(g)$]

Writing Chemical Equations

In an earlier feature, you have read about using mathematical symbols and equations to solve problems. For example, in solving certain gas law problems, you find it helpful to use the equation $PV = nRT$. This equation expresses a quantitative relationship among four of the variables related to gases.

Chemists certainly make use of mathematical equations to solve many problems. In addition, since chemists work with matter, they often need to express what happens to the matter they are using when they solve a problem. For this reason, when you are solving a chemistry problem, you may find that writing a chemical equation is a useful strategy.

► Solving Stoichiometric Problems

When you studied stoichiometry, you learned that writing a chemical equation is necessary for solving certain types of problems. For example, if you need to predict the mass of ammonia, NH_3, that can be produced from 15.0 g of nitrogen gas, one of the first things you do is to write a balanced chemical equation representing the reaction between nitrogen and hydrogen to produce ammonia. If a problem is clearly a stoichiometry problem, you will probably find that writing a chemical equation comes to mind almost automatically, since you practiced so many problems in which this was a key step.

► Reactions Involving Gases

You should be alert to other situations where it might be helpful to write a chemical equation. When you study gases, one of the topics you learn about is reactions involving gases. For example, you might be asked to solve a problem that asks you to determine the volume of oxygen gas that will react with 2.5 liters of sulfur dioxide gas to form sulfur trioxide, with all gases being measured under the same conditions of temperature and pressure. This problem does not talk about the number of moles or the number of grams of the gases involved. However, when you see that a chemical reaction is involved, you should recognize that this problem, too, is a stoichiometry problem. One of the steps you might take to solve this problem is to write this balanced chemical equation:

$$2SO_2(g) + O_2(g) \rightarrow 2SO_3(g)$$

Of course, this chemical equation shows the relationships among the number of moles of reactants and products involved. After studying the gas laws, you should also recognize another interpretation for

this equation: under certain conditions (what are these conditions?), it also represents the volumes of the gases that react. This equation makes the rest of the solution to this problem easier. As you study chemistry, you should be alert to the situations where a chemical equation is a necessary part of solving a problem, and learn how to interpret chemical equations in a variety of ways.

▶ **When to Write an Equation**

Under what circumstance should you think about writing a chemical equation? You should look for a chemical change. You should ask yourself if one substance is changing into a different substance in the problem. If the answer to this question is yes, and you find that you have run out of other ideas about how to solve the problem, you should do your best to write a chemical equation. Be sure you take care that your equation conveys no more information than the problem itself lets you infer. Even if you do not make direct use of this equation in your solution, you may find that you get an idea from the equation about how to proceed with the rest of the problem.

▶ **TEACH**
THE STRATEGY

Guided Practice

Have students use this problem-solving strategy when doing Practice Problems 15–16 and problems 20–22 in the Part 2 Review. You may also want to use this technique to solve Practice Problems 13–14 in Part 2.

As you have seen, chemical reactions involve substances in the solid, liquid, or gaseous state. In Chapter 5, you dealt with amounts of solids, liquids, and gases in terms of numbers of particles, moles, and grams. You now know how to deal with gases in terms of volume. In the following Example, you will see how to combine what you learned about stoichiometry in Chapter 5 with what you have learned about gases in this chapter.

EXAMPLE 7-6

When $CaCO_3$ decomposes, how many grams of $CaCO_3$ are needed to produce 9.00 dm^3 of CO_2 measured at STP?

■ *Analyze the Problem* Write the balanced equation for the reaction.

$$CaCO_3(s) \rightarrow CO_2(g) + CaO(s)$$

Write down what you are being asked to find.

? grams of $CaCO_3$ = 9.00 dm^3 of CO_2

Recognize that the problem is being carried out under specific conditions, at STP. This means that you can use the standard molar volume. From this you can determine how many moles of CO_2 are produced. The balanced equation tells you the ratio between the number of moles of $CaCO_3$ reacted and CO_2 gen-

PART **2**

Section 7.4 *continued*

Practice Problems

Assign the Practice Problems.

Guided Practice

Ethane burns completely to form carbon dioxide and water. If all substances are gases measured at the same temperature and pressure, how many liters of ethane will produce 12.0 liters of carbon dioxide?

$(2C_2H_6 + 7O_2 \rightarrow 4CO_2 + 6H_2O$

$12.0 \text{ L } CO_2 \times \dfrac{2 \text{ L } C_2H_6}{4 \text{ L } CO_2}$

$= 6.0 \text{ L } C_2H_6)$

Reteaching Idea

To enable students to visualize molar volume of a gas, have them identify items from the real world that are of 22.4 L. For example, collect 23 1-L soda or water bottles, marking off 4/10ths on one bottle; or using cardboard, create a cube containing 22.4 dm^3. Other variations could include creating a cube containing 24.5 dm^3 ·(25°C). In addition, have students draw diagrams representing 1 mole of a gas at STP and an illustration of the volume ratios of the reactants and products using a balanced equation for a reaction of gases.

☰CLOSE

Summing Up Main Ideas

Two equal volume containers, X and Y, contain the same gas. At 25°C the pressure in container X is three times that of container Y. Ask students to explain how the contents of the two containers differ. (Container X has three times as many molecules as container Y.)

PROBLEM-SOLVING STRATEGY

Use what you know about making road maps to solve this problem.

Boxed numbers indicate questions that involve skills in interpretation, application, and analysis.

---

erated. The value you find for the number of moles of CO_2 produced will also be the number of moles of $CaCO_3$ needed.

- **Apply a Strategy** Diagram a road map to help you organize the relationships you need to solve the problem.

$9.0 \text{ dm}^3 CO_2 \qquad\qquad ? \text{ g } CaCO_3$

$\dfrac{1 \text{ mol } CO_2}{22.4 \text{ dm}^3} \qquad\qquad \dfrac{100.1 \text{ g } CaCO_3}{1 \text{ mol } CaCO_3}$

$\text{moles } CO_2 = \text{moles } CaCO_3$

- **Work a Solution** Determine the number of moles of CO_2 produced.

$? \text{ mol } CO_2 = 9.00 \text{ dm}^3 CO_2 \times \dfrac{1 \text{ mol}}{22.4 \text{ dm}^3}$

$= 0.40 \text{ mol } CO_2$

From the balanced equation you know that

$1 \text{ mole } CaCO_3 = 1 \text{ mole } CO_2$

Therefore, moles $CaCO_3 = 0.40 \text{ mol}$
Using the molar mass of $CaCO_3$, convert moles to grams.

$? \text{ g } CaCO_3 = 0.40 \text{ mol} \times \dfrac{100.1 \text{ g } CaCO_3}{1 \text{ mol } CaCO_3}$

$= 40.0 \text{ g } CaCO_3$

- **Verify Your Answer** Check the steps of the solution by following the units used in each step. They should cancel out in each case to give you the units desired, and they do.

Practice Problems

15. What mass of $CaCO_3$ must decompose to produce 250 cm^3 of CO_2 at STP? **Ans.** 1.1 g

16. How many moles of mercury(II) oxide must decompose to produce 2.00 dm^3 of oxygen at STP? **Ans.** 0.179 mol

PART 2 REVIEW

17. What volume does 1 mole of nitrogen gas occupy at STP?

18. Is the typical classroom colder or warmer than 0°C? In your classroom, would you expect the molar volume of nitrogen to be larger or smaller than the value reported in question 17? Explain your answer.

19. What is the volume at STP of 150.0 g of $H_2S(g)$?
Ans. 98.53 L

PART 2 REVIEW

ANSWERS

■ **Keyed to Objectives**

C 17. 1 mole of any gas occupies 22.4 dm^3.

C 18. A classroom is warmer than 0°C. Because Charles's law states that gas volumes expand as the temperature increases, molar volumes at classroom temperatures will be larger than 22.4 dm^3.

C 19. $150.0 \text{ g } H_2S \times \dfrac{1 \text{ mol}}{34.10 \text{ g}} \times \dfrac{22.4 \text{ dm}^3}{1 \text{ mol}}$

$= 98.53 \text{ dm}^3$

D 20. $PCl_5 \rightarrow PCl_3 + Cl_2$

$23.2 \text{ g } PCl_5 \times \dfrac{1 \text{ mol } PCl_5}{208.5 \text{ g } PCl_5}$

$\times \dfrac{1 \text{ mol } Cl_2}{1 \text{ mol } PCl_5} \times \dfrac{22.4 \text{ dm}^3 Cl_2}{1 \text{ mol } Cl_2}$

$= 2.50 \text{ dm}^3 Cl_2$

20. When phosphorus pentachloride gas, $PCl_5(g)$, is heated, it decomposes into phosphorus trichloride gas, $PCl_3(g)$, and chlorine gas $Cl_2(g)$. If 23.2 g of PCl_5 decomposes, what is the volume of Cl_2 produced at STP? **Ans.** 2.50 L

21. a. How many liters of phosphorus pentachloride gas, PCl_5, are formed when 7.0 liters of phosphorus trichloride gas, PCl_3, react with 9.0 liters of chlorine gas, Cl_2? All gases are at equal temperature and pressure. **Ans.** 7.0 L

b. Complete a drawing for the reaction in **a.** Explain why particles can be used to symbolize a volume.

22. How many liters of gaseous water, $H_2O(g)$, can be produced from the combustion of 8.0 liters of hydrogen with 5.0 liters of oxygen? Assume that the $H_2O(g)$ produced is measured at the same temperature and pressure as the reactants. **Ans.** 8.0 L

PROBLEM·SOLVING

S T R A T E G Y

*You should **write a chemical equation** as a part of your solution to this problem (See Strategy, page 244.)*

PART 2

Section 7.4 *continued*

PART 2 REVIEW

Assign the Part Review questions.

Evaluating Skills

These skills are evaluated in the Part Review questions indicated. **Determining main ideas:** 17; **Predicting:** 18; **Analyzing data:** 19, 20, 21, 22; **Applying a strategy:** 19, 20, 21, 22; **Calculating:** 19, 20, 21, 22; **Verifying results:** 19, 20, 21, 22; **Forming models:** 21

C O N S U M E R   C H E M I S T R Y

Why Popcorn Pops

Americans eat ten billion liters of popcorn each year. How does something as unappetizing as a kernel of corn become so delectable? Part of the answer lies in the starchy composition of corn and part in the physical behavior of gases.

A kernel of corn has three parts. The outer shell is called the hull, or pericarp. The inside of the kernel is composed of starch, or the endosperm and an embryo plant. The endosperm acts as food for the embryo as it germinates.

When kernels of corn are placed into heated oil or a hot-air popper, water inside the kernel becomes superheated, which means it is hot enough to vaporize but does not have the room to do so. These rapidly moving water molecules cause a tremendous increase in pressure on the hull. The superheated water penetrates the endosperm structure under high pressure, and the hull ruptures. When the hull ruptures, the pressure surrounding the starch is then greatly reduced. The water now vaporizes and expands as described by Boyle's law. This change also causes the starch to expand to

The addition of heat sets in motion a series of reactions that change hard kernels of corn into fluffy popcorn.

about 30 times its original size. The expansion is so rapid that the kernel explodes, or pops, and the endosperm bursts out. A fluffy white piece of popcorn is the result.

D 21. a. Limiting reactant is PCl_3

$$7.0 \text{ L PCl}_3 \times \frac{1 \text{ L PCl}_5}{1 \text{ L PCl}_3}$$

$$= 7.0 \text{ L PCl}_5$$

b.

PCl_3 + Cl_2 → PCl_5

When gases are measured at the same temperature and pressure, their volumes are proportional to their number of moles.

D 22. $2H_2 + O_2 \rightarrow 2H_2O$.

Limiting reactant is H_2

$$8.0 \text{ L H}_2 \times \frac{2 \text{ L H}_2O}{2 \text{ L H}_2}$$

$$= 8.0 \text{ L H}_2O(g)$$

PART 3
Explaining Gas Behavior

Developing Skills

Students may apply these skills in their study of Part 3.

Comparing/Contrasting: Have students compare the Ping-Pong ball analogy developed in the last chapter with the kinetic molecular theory described in this part.

Comparing/Contrasting: Have students compare the behavior of an ideal gas with that of real gases.

Predicting: Have students identify gas molecules that should travel more quickly than oxygen molecules.

☰ FOCUS

Activate Prior Knowledge

Students may have had previous experience compressing gases in air pumps or syringes. Ask students to explain what happens when a gas is put into a cylinder and compressed using a piston. According to the ideal gas law, the piston can compress the gas until there is no volume. Have students try to compress the gas in a blocked syringe.

⚠️ **CAUTION:** **Students should wear safety goggles.** Then ask them to describe how reality differs from the ideal gas law. Differences that students will mention include the impossibility of reducing a volume to nothing and increased air pressure causing a gas to rupture its container.

Objectives

Part 3

E. **Differentiate** ideal gas behavior from real gas behavior.

F. **Explain** gas behavior using the kinetic molecular theory.

G. **Apply** Graham's law to **calculate** the molar mass of a gas.

Figure 7-7 *This graph shows the change in volume of a substance as its temperature changes (blue line) and the change in volume predicted by Charles's law (red line).*

In your study of gases, you have been learning about the properties of gases and the laws that describe their behavior. These laws are useful because in one statement they summarize generalizations that can be applied to a wide variety of specific problems. Equations such as the ideal gas law help you determine *what happens* as the pressure, temperature, or volume of a gas changes.

Scientists are interested not only in summarizing observable behavior through laws, but they are also interested in explaining *why* such behavior takes place. Why, for example, should the pressure of a gas be inversely proportional to its volume? In order to answer the "why" questions, scientists propose a model of gases called the **kinetic molecular theory.** This theory has two fundamental assumptions about gases: they are composed of small particles (atoms or molecules) and these particles are constantly moving.

Although the kinetic molecular theory is useful in predicting properties of gases, it does have some limitations. The simple assumption that the properties of water vapor can be described by molecules in rapid motion does not readily explain why gaseous water should condense to a liquid under certain conditions. To answer questions such as these, you will need to study even more about water, including the structures of the atoms making up the water molecules, the forces holding these atoms together, and the forces of attraction that water molecules have for each other. For now, in explaining the properties of the gaseous state alone, you can ignore these realities about the submicroscopic model of water. In the next chapter, you will start to fill in the details of the atomic-level model of matter, after you see how a less detailed model is adequate for the gaseous state.

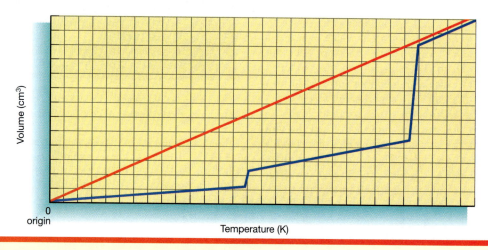

7.5 Deviations from Ideal Behavior

The kinetic molecular model of a gas is often said to provide a description of an ideal gas. In order to understand how the actual (or real) behavior of gases differs from that of an ideal gas, you should look at Figure 7-7.

The red line on the graph resembles the graph you saw when you first learned about the temperature-volume law. Notice that the straight line goes directly to the origin. This means that when the temperature of the gas becomes 0 K, the gas occupies no volume. Is this really possible? Of course not. You have learned that all matter has mass and occupies space (volume). The point 0, 0 on the graph seems to violate a basic definition of matter.

Real-world substance The blue line on the graph lets you compare a *typical* substance as the temperature of the gas drops. Notice that at higher temperatures (on the right of the graph), the line seems to resemble that of the red-lined graph. But there are two points indicating a change in volume not predicted by the red-lined graph. The sudden drop in volume at the higher temperature shows what happens to the gas as it liquefies; the drop at the lower temperature shows what happens as the liquid solidifies. The red-lined graph does not reflect the fact that in the real world, when gases cool, they become liquids and solids. It only represents what would happen ideally if the gas continued to behave consistently all the way down to absolute zero. Because *every* substance can solidify when the temperature is low enough, no substance can follow the red-lined graph at every temperature. For this reason, the ideal gas equation $PV = nRT$ does not hold true for every possible combination of temperature, volume, and pressure when it comes to real-world gases. It does, however, hold true for gases at pressures of 1 atmosphere or lower near room temperature and therefore is valuable for making useful and accurate predictions.

An ideal gas is one that perfectly meets the criteria of the ideal gas law, under all conditions. Although no such gas actually exists, a model can be formed of what such an ideal gas must be. Such a model is the kinetic molecular theory, which is described in the next section. As you study the next few chapters, you will have the opportunity to improve your submicroscopic model of matter, because you will be adding detail not provided by the kinetic molecular theory. Keep in mind as you read about all of these theories that scientists form models to explain observations they have made concerning the behavior of matter. Try to relate the theories to the knowledge you already have about gases.

Concept ✔ Check

Can you use the ideal gas law to predict the volume of a substance as it cools to 0K? Explain.

CONNECTING CONCEPTS

Process of Science — Predicting Many times, scientists will utilize laws such as the ideal gas to make predictions even when these laws are not entirely accurate. For example, the behavior of ideal gases as predicted by the ideal gas law, differs in several important ways from the behavior of real gases. Despite this, the ideal gas law is still extremely useful for studying the behavior of gases and making rough predictions. However, it is essential to fully understand its limitations.

Science Background

Deviations from Ideal Behavior

The kinetic molecular theory is valid only for ideal gases. Most gases at room temperature and 1 atm of pressure behave as if they are ideal. However, under conditions of very low temperature and very high pressure, gases deviate from the ideal and are said to be real gases. Real gas molecules have a volume that is part of the total volume of the gas. As a gas cools, attractive forces between molecules lower the pressure below what it would be ideally and also cause the molecules to liquify. The volume of the gas as it cools will become constant and is determined by the density of the liquid. Johannes van der Waals developed an equation (there are others) that compensates for these two factors:

$$(P + an^2/V^2)(V - nb) = nRT$$

The expression an^2/V^2 compensates for the reduced pressure due to attractive forces and nb compensates for the increased volume due to the volume of the molecules themselves. Terms a and b are coefficients that vary from gas to gas.

7.6 Kinetic Molecular Theory

You can begin to understand the ideas that make up the kinetic molecular theory based on the name alone. The *molecular* portion implies that gases consist of molecules (or, in the case of noble gases, individual atoms). This is not surprising, since you already have used a molecular model to learn about other concepts in chemistry, such as stoichiometry. The word *kinetic* suggests that the molecules are in motion.

The major conditions of the kinetic molecular theory were first proposed around 1860. Two scientists from different countries, Ludwig Boltzmann from Germany and James Clerk Maxwell from Scotland, proposed the theory to describe the behavior of an ideal gas. The five major conditions that describe the behavior of gas molecules are shown in Table 7-3.

TABLE 7-3

Kinetic Molecular Theory

1. *The molecules of an ideal gas are dimensionless points.* If you have already studied geometry, remember how a point was described. It has no length, width, or height and therefore no volume. Since the volume of gas molecules is very small in comparison to the total volume of the gas in its container, the molecular volume can be ignored in most gas calculations.

2. *The molecules of an ideal gas are in constant, random, straight-line motion.* This motion is interrupted only by the collision of the molecules with the walls of the container and with each other. Think about the Ping-Pong ball analogy introduced in Chapter 6 to explain gas pressure. The balls travel in a straight line until they hit the container or another ball.

3. *The average kinetic energy of the ideal gas molecules is proportional to the absolute temperature of the molecules.* Mathematically, this condition can be expressed in this form: K.E. (average) $= k\, T$, an equation in which K.E. stands for kinetic energy—the energy associated with motion of a particle, T stands for Kelvin temperature, and k is a constant that relates the two variables. As stated in this condition, if a gas is heated to a higher temperature, the average speed of the particle will increase.

4. *When molecules collide with each other, the collisions are elastic.* In an elastic collision, there is no gain or loss in total kinetic energy.

5. *The molecules of an ideal gas do not exert any attractive or repulsive forces on each other.*

Teaching Stategy

Kinetic Molecular Theory

A high bounce ball dropped (not bounced) from shoulder height will not return to your hand because its elasticity is not perfect. Demonstrate elasticity using several kinds of balls.

Myths and Misconceptions

Students may have misconceptions about pressure that can interfere with their understanding of the gas laws. Many students think that the pressure on a surface is exerted directly above the surface, and not on the sides. Refer back to the "crushed can" demonstration in Chapter 6, Section 6.2. When the gas inside the can condensed to a liquid, there were fewer gas molecules in the can, resulting in a decrease in pressure. The higher atmospheric pressure on the outside of the can crushed the can in all directions, including the sides.

Gas laws and the kinetic molecular theory How does the kinetic molecular theory help explain the gas laws you learned? Use the conditions of this theory to predict what should happen to the pressure of an ideal gas when you change its temperature. Since there are two other gas variables, amount and volume, you need to hold these constant to study only temperature and pressure. You can keep the volume of the gas constant if you use a rigid container for the gas, such as a steel box rather than a balloon.

Temperature changes First, increase the temperature. According to the kinetic molecular theory, what will happen to the gas molecules? One of the conditions of this theory says that temperature is proportional to the average kinetic energy of the molecules. Since kinetic energy is the energy of motion, as the temperature increases, you should expect the speed of the molecules to increase also. If you go back to the Ping-Pong balls analogy, you can increase the speed of the bouncing balls inside the box by shaking the box harder.

Pressure changes Consider what causes pressure at the submicroscopic level. You have learned that pressure is due to a force applied over a given area. In this example, the box is rigid, so neither its volume nor its surface area changes. There can be no change in pressure due to the total area that the molecules are bumping into. However, there is certainly a change in the force applied to the walls of the container! The increased energy of motion of the gas molecules results in an increased force. (Again, think about the Ping-Pong balls inside a box that is being shaken harder than before.) Therefore, the pressure will also increase. According to the kinetic molecular theory, then, as the temperature of a gas increases, the pressure of the gas will also increase.

This idea is consistent with the ideal gas law that you have learned. Since the volume and number of moles are constant, from the ideal gas law, you can derive this relationship:

$$\frac{P}{T} = \text{constant} \quad \text{or} \quad P = \text{constant} \times T$$

This mathematical statement shows the direct proportionality between these two variables.

You can test your understanding of the kinetic molecular theory by seeing if you can use it to predict how other gas laws are related. What does this theory predict will happen to the pressure if you decrease the volume without changing the temperature? (Will the kinetic energy of the molecules change?) What will happen to volume if you increase temperature without changing pressure?

Concept ✔ Check

Explain why increasing the temperature of a gas increases pressure.

CONNECTING CONCEPTS

Models Using Ping-Pong balls to describe the behavior of gases is a very useful method for helping us understand a complex process. Scientists often use such models that can be easily visualized when explaining abstract concepts.

Science Background

Temperature Changes

The velocities of molecules determine the temperature of a gas. Temperature is a measure of kinetic energy. An increase in kinetic energy causes both temperature and velocity to increase. Kinetic energy is the cause, rise in temperature and velocity are effects. There is no cause-and-effect relationship between increased temperature and increased velocity, but both are based on increases in kinetic energy.

This section relates average kinetic energy of molecules to temperature. A more rigorous treatment, which is derived from the kinetic molecular theory, yields the following equation:

velocity = $(3RT/\text{mol. mass})^{1/2}$

For a given sample of gas, R and molar mass are constants. Temperature and velocity are related; as the average velocity of gas molecules increases, so does the absolute temperature of the gas.

Science Background

Graham's Law and Diffusion

Effusion is the term that describes the dispersion of a gas in a vacuum, while diffusion applies to a gas dispersing into another gas.

7.7 Graham's Law and Diffusion

If gas molecules are constantly in rapid motion, does this mean that one gas can instantly mix with another gas? A moment's thought will convince you that the answer is no. Suppose you set out a bottle of perfume and open it. Someone within 1 meter of the bottle will notice its odor before someone 3 meters away. Although the molecules of the perfume are moving very rapidly, it takes a while for them to "bump" through the maze of the air molecules that are already there. This ability of a gas to move from one place to another is called **diffusion.**

Not only is a certain amount of time required for one gas to travel through another, but different gases travel at different rates. This fact is demonstrated by the apparatus in Figure 7-8. One small cotton ball was soaked in a dilute solution of ammonia, and another was soaked in dilute hydrochloric acid. The cotton balls were simultaneously placed into opposite ends of a long glass tube. Ammonia, NH_3, vaporizes and mixes with the air on one side, while hydrochloric acid, HCl, vaporizes on the other side. When the two gases meet, they react to form a white cloud consisting of the suspended solid, ammonium chloride.

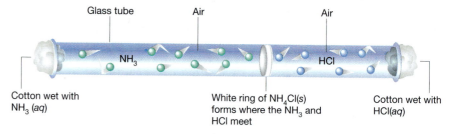

Glass tube   Air   Air

NH_3 HCl

Cotton wet with NH_3 (aq)

White ring of $NH_4Cl(s)$ forms where the NH_3 and HCl meet

Cotton wet with HCl(aq)

Figure 7-8 *Two cotton plugs, one dipped in HCl(aq), and one dipped in NH_3(aq), are simultaneously inserted into the ends of the tube. Gaseous NH_3 and HCl vaporizing from the cotton plugs diffuse toward each other. Where do they meet to form NH_4Cl(s)?*

Where does the white cloud form inside the tube? The diagram shows that the cloud appears closer to the cotton ball soaked in hydrochloric acid. Although both gases mixed with the air as soon as they were placed into the tube, the molecules of ammonia must have been moving at a greater speed. Both gases were under the same conditions of temperature and pressure, so this could not explain the differing speeds. The relevant factor is the mass of the particles involved: Ammonia, NH_3, has a molar mass of 17 g/mol, while hydrogen chloride, HCl, has a molar mass of 36.5 g/mol. The heavier molecule was traveling more slowly.

DEMONSTRATION

Graham's Law and Diffusion

On a ring stand, horizontally support a glass tube that has an inside diameter of 1 cm and is 0.75 meter long. Place two drops of concentrated HCl on one ball of cotton and two drops of concentrated ammonium hydroxide on another.

⚠️ **CAUTION: Wear safety goggles, face shield, lab apron, and gloves.** Handle the cotton balls with tongs.

Protect students with a shield.
Simultaneously place the balls of cotton in opposite ends of the glass tube. In time, a white ring of NH_4Cl will form inside the tube. Measure the distance from each end of the tube to the ring. Since both gases traveled different distances in the same amount of time, the distances can be used *(continued on page T253)*

Graham's Law Thomas Graham, a Scottish scientist, developed a mathematical relationship for this phenomenon in 1829. **Graham's law** has this form:

$$\frac{v_A}{v_B} = \sqrt{\frac{m_B}{m_A}}$$

In this formula, v_A stands for the velocity of molecules of substance A and m_A stands for the molar mass of this substance. You can apply this law to determine the relative rates of travel of HCl and NH_3. Let substance A be ammonia to get

$$\frac{v(NH_3)}{v(HCl)} = \sqrt{\frac{m(HCl)}{m(NH_3)}} = \sqrt{\frac{36.5 \text{ g/mol}}{17.0 \text{ g/mol}}} = 1.47$$

This calculation shows that NH_3 travels 1.47 times as fast as HCl.

Is this equation consistent with the kinetic molecular theory? One of its conditions is that gas molecules at the same temperature have the same average kinetic energy. This condition is helpful, but it doesn't directly apply, since you are interested in the velocity of the molecules, not their kinetic energy.

There is a relationship between kinetic energy, velocity, and mass. The kinetic energy of a particle increases as its velocity increases. This idea makes sense if you consider a marble thrown at a slow speed and then at a high speed. Which impact would cause

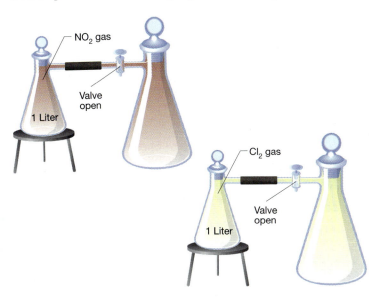

Figure 7-9 *Will two different gases at identical temperature and pressure disperse at the same rate? Nitrogen dioxide has a molecular mass of 17.0 g/mol whereas chlorine gas has a molecular mass of 36.5 g/mol. The two gases have the same kinetic energy because the temperature is the same yet have different molecular masses. According to Graham's law, the lighter gas (NO_2) has a greater velocity than the heavier gas (Cl_2). Therefore, NO_2 will disperse faster.*

DEMONSTRATION

(continued from page T252)
as the rate of diffusion.

Find the ratio of the distances traveled by the gases, and compare the square of this ratio to the ratio of the molar masses of the gases. When finished, put the cot-

ton balls in a beaker containing 50 mL of water. Swirl the beaker. Neutralize the solution if necessary. Discard the cotton in the wastebasket; the liquid may be poured down the drain.

PART **3**
Section 7.7 continued

Cooperative Learning

Determining Molar Mass

Teams of 2; **Time:** 20 minutes
Objective: Students will look for similar problems by sorting them into problems of similar types.
Task: Give students a list of problems from the end of the chapter or write at least eight to ten problems on the board. Students should only classify the problems in three to five categories.
Team responsibility: Partners will decide which of their assigned problems belong in similar categories. They will also come up with names for their problem categories.
Evaluation: Ask students to discuss their categories and the reasoning behind them. After students solve the problems as homework, have them relate whether looking for similarities helped them on the solutions.

Guided Practice

Review the Concept Check questions on pages 249 and 251. Answers can be found in Appendix E on page 808.

Reteaching Idea

To reinforce the concept of diffusion, review the demonstration on page T252 and speculate with students what would happen if the experiment were changed. For example, if NH_3 and phenolphthalein were used and both ends of the tube were stoppered, *(continued on page T255)*

more damage? The kinetic energy of a particle also increases as its mass increases. A baseball would create a bigger impact when it hit another object than a marble traveling at the same speed.

In this case, you want two objects that have different masses to possess the same kinetic energy. How is this possible? The lighter object will have to be traveling faster than the heavier one. This is exactly what the mathematical equation proposed by Graham predicts.

Determining molar mass One use of Graham's law is the determination of the molar mass of an unknown gas. Suppose you have a colorless, odorless gas and do not know what it is. How might you find out? Knowing the molar mass might help. Determine the rate at which a gas of known molar mass travels and compare this rate with that of a sample of the unknown gas. One way to measure these rates is to time how long it takes for an equal-sized sample of each gas to escape through a small hole. As Example 7-6 illustrates, once you have these rates, you can determine the molar mass of the unknown.

EXAMPLE 7-7

The rate of diffusion of an unknown gas is four times faster than the rate of oxygen gas. Calculate the molar mass of the unknown gas and identify it.

■ *Analyze the Problem* You are given the rate of diffusion for an unknown gas in comparison with the rate of diffusion for oxygen gas. Since you can find the molar mass of oxygen gas from the periodic table, you have the values you need to apply Graham's law.

■ *Apply a Strategy* Use *A* to represent oxygen and *B* to represent the unknown gas. Since the unknown gas travels four times as fast as oxygen gas, the ratio of their rates is

$$\frac{\text{Rate } (O_2)}{\text{Rate unknown}} = \frac{1}{4}$$

Using this rate and the molar mass of oxygen gas as 32.0 g/mol, substitute the values into Graham's law and solve for the molar mass of the unknown.

■ *Work a Solution* Substituting into the equation representing Graham's law, you get

$$\frac{v_A}{v_B} = \sqrt{\frac{m_B}{m_A}}$$

$$\frac{1}{4.0} = \sqrt{\frac{\text{molar mass of unknown}}{32.0 \text{ g/mol}}}$$

PART 3 REVIEW

ANSWERS

■ **Keyed to Objectives**

E **25.** According to the ideal gas law, the volume of a gas decreases to 0 at −273°C. No substance shows such behavior; in fact, no substance is a gas at such a low temperature. Liquids and solids occupy a definite volume.

E **26.** The model for the ideal gas does not allow for a gas to become a liquid.

F **27.** The kinetic molecular theory is a model of a gas based on molecular motion. Its conditions are: (1) the molecules of an ideal gas are dimensionless points, (2) the molecules of an ideal gas are in constant, straight-line motion, (3) the average kinetic energy of ideal gas molecules is proportional to the

absolute temperature of the molecules, (4) collisions between ideal gas molecules are elastic, and (5) the molecules of an ideal gas do not exert any attractive or repulsive forces on each other.

F **28.** $PV = nRT$

$$\frac{P}{T} \quad \frac{nR}{V} = \text{constant}$$

$$\frac{P_1}{T_1} = \frac{P_2}{T_2}$$

$$0.25 = \sqrt{\frac{\text{molar mass of unknown}}{32.0 \text{ g/mol}}}$$

Square both sides of this equation to get

$$0.0625 = \frac{\text{molar mass of unknown}}{32.0 \text{ g/mol}}$$

Now multiply both sides of this equation by 32.0 g/mol to find the molar mass.

$$\text{molar mass of unknown} = 2.0 \text{ g/mol}$$

The unknown gas is hydrogen.

■ **Verify Your Answer** The problem states that the unknown gas travels 4 times as fast as oxygen. This answer is consistent with the fact that a gas with a smaller molar mass should travel faster than one with a larger molar mass.

Practice Problems

23. What is the molar mass of a gas that diffuses 0.71 times as fast as oxygen, O_2?   *Ans.* 63 g/mol

24. What is the molar mass of a gas that diffuses 0.34 times as fast as hydrogen?   *Ans.* 17 g/mol

PART 3 REVIEW

25. What does the ideal gas law predict about the volume of an ideal gas at −273°C? Does any real substance actually have this predicted volume? Explain your answer.

26. Oxygen gas liquefies at a temperature of −183°C. Explain why this fact is inconsistent with the model of an ideal gas.

27. What is the kinetic molecular theory? What five conditions does it use to describe an ideal gas?

28. Starting with the ideal gas law, derive an expression that shows the relationship between the pressure and temperature of a gas that occupies a fixed volume. Is this mathematical expression consistent with the prediction you would make using the kinetic molecular theory?

29. Using the conditions of the kinetic molecular theory, show that it is reasonable to expect the pressure of an ideal gas to increase when its volume decreases.

30. State in words the law that relates the rates of diffusion of two gases with their molar masses.

31. Which gas travels faster, carbon monoxide or carbon dioxide? Explain.

32. What is the molar mass of an unknown gas if it diffuses 0.906 times as fast as argon gas?   *Ans.* 49.0 g/mol

Boxed numbers indicate questions that involve skills in interpretation, application, and analysis.

◄ **PROBLEM·SOLVING**

S T R A T E G Y

*You might want to **make a diagram** as you answer the last part of this problem. (See Strategy, page 216.)*

PROBLEM·SOLVING

S T R A T E G Y

*In order to check your answer, **use what you know** about diffusion rates and molar masses. Should the molar mass of the unknown be larger or smaller than that of argon? (See Strategy, page 58.)*

(continued from page T254)
the phenolphthalein-treated cotton turns pink in about one minute. If the glass tube were warmed or cooled ahead of time, the volume or concentration of NH_3 were varied, or the diameter or length of the glass tube were changed, how would the results be affected? Have students predict outcomes of other variations of this experiment.

Practice Problems

Assign the Practice Problems.

☰CLOSE

Summing Up Main Ideas

Ask students to use Graham's Law to determine the velocity of helium when the velocity of hydrogen is 10 m/s.

$$\frac{V_{He}}{V_{H_2}} = \sqrt{\frac{m_{H_2}}{m_{He}}} = \sqrt{\frac{2.02 \text{ g}}{4.00 \text{ g}}}$$
$$= \sqrt{0.50} = 0.71$$
$$0.71 \times 10 \text{ m/s} = 7.1 \text{ m/s}$$

PART 3 REVIEW

Assign the Part Review questions.

Evaluating Skills

These skills are evaluated in the Part Review questions indicated. **Determining sources of error:** 25, 26; **Determining main ideas:** 27, 30; **Applying a strategy:** 28, 32; **Comparing/Contrasting:** 31; **Analyzing data:** 32; **Calculating:** 32; **Verifying results:** 32

According to this expression, pressure is directly proportional to temperature. As temperature increases, molecular velocity also increases. When the molecules collide with the container more often, the pressure also increases.

F 29. When the volume decreases, there is less space between the walls of the container. Molecules collide more often with the container, so the pressure increases.

G 30. The ratio of the rates of diffusion of two gases is equal to the square root of the inverse ratio of their molar masses.

G 31. Carbon monoxide travels faster because it has a smaller molar mass.

G 32.
$$\frac{V_{Ar}}{V_x} = \sqrt{\frac{m_x}{m_{Ar}}}$$
$$m_x = \frac{V_{Ar}^2}{V_x^2} = \frac{(1)^2}{(0.906)^2}$$
$$\times 39.9 \text{ g/mol} = 49.0 \text{ g/mol}$$

Determining the Value of the Universal Gas Constant, R

Estimated Time: (45 minutes)

Process Skills

Identifying and controlling variables
Calculating
Determining cause and effect

Preparation

■ Materials

(for a class of 24, working in pairs)
Apparatus
(12 of each)
pneumatic troughs, 250-mL graduated cylinders, centigram balances (electronic or triple beam), glass plates, thermometers, barometers
Reagents
■*modified butane flint-sparking lighters (12)

■ Preparation Hints

*Remove the cylindrical, serrated surface wheels from the lighters, or cover the wheels with tape so they cannot be moved. Do not use piezoelectric or battery-powered lighters. The water temperature must equilibrate to room temperature. For best results, let the water stand in the pneumatic troughs overnight. Cover the trough so the water does not evaporate. Also, fill the graduated cylinder with water and instruct the students not to add water or pour water out of the system for the entire lab period.

■ Safety

Butane is flammable, and mixtures with air can explode. Be sure that there are no flames, hot plates, or other ignition sources in the laboratory.

Laboratory

Investigation

Determining the Value of the Universal Gas Constant, R

When Charles's law, Boyle's law, and Avogadro's principle are combined, the result is the *ideal gas law*, $PV = nRT$. In this equation, pressure (P), volume (V), temperature (T), and n are variables; R is a constant called the *universal gas constant*. You can use the ideal gas law to calculate the value of R if you know the values of P, V, T, and n for a sample of gas.

Objectives

Measure the volume, pressure, and temperature of a sample of wet butane gas, $C_4H_{10}(g)$.

Determine the pressure of dry butane gas by correcting for the partial pressure of water.

Calculate the experimental value of the universal gas constant, R, and **compare** it with the accepted value.

Materials

Apparatus
☐ centigram balance
☐ thermometer
☐ pneumatic trough
☐ barometer

☐ 250-mL graduated cylinder
☐ glass plate

Reagent
☐ butane lighter

Procedure

1. Put on your lab apron and safety goggles.
2. Fill a pneumatic trough with room-temperature tap water. Record the water temperature in the data table.
3. Fill a 250-mL graduated cylinder to the top with room-temperature tap water. Displace all air bubbles.

4. Obtain a new butane lighter from your instructor. Mass the lighter to the nearest 0.01 gram. Record your data.

   CAUTION: At no time should you light the lighter. Be sure there are no flames in the lab.

5. While holding a glass plate on top of the filled graduated cylinder, invert the cylinder into the pneumatic trough over an opening in the rack.

6. As one partner holds the cylinder in place, the other should hold the butane lighter under the water, just below the opening in the rack of the pneumatic trough. Without trying to light the butane, open the trigger of the lighter and displace 200–250 mL water from the graduated cylinder.

7. Remove the lighter from the water and dry it. When it is completely dry, mass it, and record its new mass. Record the volume of butane gas on your data table.

8. Record the difference in mm between the level of the water remaining in the graduated cylinder and the level of water in the pneumatic trough. Keep the graduated cylinder inverted in the pneumatic trough, with the open end under water, until you complete step 9.

9. Record the barometric pressure of the room in your data table.

10. Remove the graduated cylinder from the pneumatic trough, turning it upright as you do so. Take the butane to an operating fume hood and pour the gas out.

Data Analysis

Data Table

Observations	
Initial mass of butane lighter	_____ g
Final mass of butane lighter	_____ g
Barometric pressure of room	_____ kPa or Torr
Height difference between water levels	_____ mm
Temperature of water	_____ °C
Volume of gas collected	_____ mL

Calculations	
Mass difference of butane lighter	_____ g
Vapor pressure of water at room temperature	_____ kPa or Torr
Partial pressure of dry butane gas	_____ kPa or Torr
Your value of R	_____ $dm^3 \cdot kPa/K \cdot mol$
Accepted value of R	_____ $dm^3 \cdot kPa/K \cdot mol$
Percent error in your value of R	_____ %

1. Subtract the final mass from the initial mass of the butane lighter. Record your answer.

2. Look up the vapor pressure of water at the temperature of the water in the pneumatic trough. Record this value in kPa or Torr in your data table. Subtract this number from the room pressure reading.

3. The pressure of the collected gas will equal atmospheric pressure only if the levels of water inside the graduated cylinder and in the pneumatic trough are the same. Convert the height difference, if any, between these levels to Pa and subtract from barometric pressure.

$$13.6 \text{ mm water} = 1 \text{ torr}$$
$$760 \text{ torr} = 101.3 \text{ kPa}$$

After making these corrections, calculate and record the partial pressure of *dry* butane.

4. Calculate your experimental value of R by rearranging the ideal gas law expression, $PV = nRT$, in this manner: $R = PV/nT$. P is equal to the partial pressure of the dry butane in kPa; V is equal to the volume of gas collected in dm^3 (recall that 1.00 L is equal to 1.00 dm^3); n is equal to the number of moles of butane; and T is the absolute temperature in degrees kelvin (the Celsius temperature plus 273.15).

5. Calculate the percent error for your experimental value of R. This is done by first finding the difference between the accepted value and the experimental value. Then the difference is divided by the accepted value and multiplied by 100.

Conclusion

1. If your percent error is large, what factors do you think account for the error?

2. Would the value of R go up or down if you had not corrected the gas for partial pressure of water? Why?

■ Procedural Hints

Instruct students to displace more than 200 mL but *less* than 250 mL of water in the graduated cylinder. Have students place a mark on the graduated cylinder indicating the level of the water remaining in the cylinder. The volume of gas collected is measured from the bottom of the graduated cylinder to this mark. Be sure that students measure the water level from the meniscus. A mercury equivalent should be explained to students.

Disposal

Have students place the graduated cylinder upright under the fume hood until the butane is completely drawn out.

Data Analysis

■ Sample Data

1. through 5. Sample data and calculations have been provided in the table below. Note that a 500-mL graduated cylinder was used to obtain this data. For more detail see *Chem 13 News*, December 1984, Number 154, pages 7–8, D. Beach and C. Coldin, "Determining the Value of R in *PV = nRT*."

Conclusions

1. Possible error factors include incorrect temperature or pressure recordings, the introduction of air into the graduated cylinder as it is inverted in the trough, and inaccurate measurement of water levels.

2. It would go up.

Data Table

Observations		Calculations	
Initial mass of butane lighter	19.54 g	Mass difference of butane lighter	0.70 g
Final mass of butane lighter	18.84 g	Vapor pressure of water at room temperature	23.8 torr
Room barometric pressure	748 torr	Partial pressure of dry butane gas	724.2 torr
Height differences between water levels	150 mm	Experimental value of R 8.336 dm^3 kPa/K•mol	
Temperature of the water	25.2°C	Accepted value of R 8.315 dm^3 kPa/K•mol	
Volume of gas collected	325 mL	Percent error in your value of R	0.25%

Chapter 7
Review
ANSWERS
begin on page
T261a.

Summary

Ideal Gas Law

- The ideal gas law, $PV = nRT$, summarizes the relationships among the four important gas variables. R is the universal gas constant.

Gas Stoichiometry

- Measured at standard conditions (pressure = 1 atm, temperature = 0°C), 1 mole of an ideal gas occupies a volume of 22.4 dm^3 (or 22.4 L).

- Some reactions involve two or more gases as reactants or products. If all the gases in a chemical reaction are measured under the same conditions of temperature and pressure, then the coefficients in the balanced chemical equation give not only mole ratios but also the volume ratios *for the gases involved*.

Explaining Gas Behavior

- Under certain conditions, real substances do not behave according to the ideal gas law.

- The kinetic molecular theory states the assumptions that are made about an ideal gas, such as constantly moving molecules that collide elastically with each other.

- At the same conditions of temperature and pressure, lower molecular mass gas particles move faster than higher molecular mass ones. Graham's law provides a quantitative statement of this principle, permitting a scientist to determine the relative molecular masses of two gases based on their relative rates of diffusion.

Chemically Speaking

combined gas law 7.2
diffusion 7.7
Graham's law 7.7
ideal gas law 7.1
kinetic molecular
  theory 7.5

molar volume 7.3
STP 7.1
universal gas constant
  7.1

Concept Mapping

Using the method of concept mapping described at the front of this book, draw a concept map for the term *gas law*.

Questions and Problems

IDEAL GAS LAW

A. Objective: **Summarize** *the gas laws using the ideal gas law.*

1. Mathematically, the ideal gas law may be expressed as $PV = nRT$. What do each of the letters in this equation represent? Identify the variables and constants.

B. Objective: **Determine** *changes in pressure, volume, temperature, and moles of a gas sample.*

2. What is the volume in dm^3 of 12.0 g of nitrogen gas if the gas is measured at a pressure of 125 kPa and a temperature of 45°C?

3. What mass of carbon dioxide will occupy a volume of 5.5 L at a temperature of 5°C and a pressure of 75 kPa?

4. If you carry out a series of experiments in which you will measure pressure in torr and volume in mL, you may find it convenient to derive a value for the gas law constant (R) which has units of $mL \cdot torr/K \cdot mol$. Using any other value for R given in this chapter, calculate the value of R with these units.

5. What is the temperature of a 0.00893 mol sample of neon gas that has a volume of 302 mL and a pressure of 715 torr?

6. Suppose you are working a problem in which the number of moles, the pressure, and the volume of the gas may change but the temperature remains constant. Using the ideal

PROBLEM-SOLVING
STRATEGIES
Students apply these strategies in the following questions.

- **Factor-label method:** 2, 3, 4, 5, 7, 9, 10, 13, 14, 15, 18, 19, 20, 21, 47, 49, 50
- **Using what you know:** 6, 9, 25,

31, 33, 42, 43
- **Using similar problems:** 2, 3, 5, 7, 9, 10, 14, 15, 18, 19, 20, 21, 38, 39, 40, 44, 47, 49, 50

T258

gas law, derive an equation that you can use to help solve this problem.

7. A sample of propane has a volume of 250.0 L at a pressure of 125 kPa and a temperature of 38°C. What volume will this sample have at a reduced pressure of 100.0 kPa and increased temperature of 95°C?

8. One of the pairs of variables you can work with in the ideal gas law is pressure and volume. All together, there are six possible pairs of variables. Which pair is *least* likely to appear when you are solving a problem?

9. A balloon is filled with helium to a volume of 12.5 liters. If the temperature of the gas is 25°C and the pressure is 101 kPa, how many moles of helium are in the balloon? How many helium atoms are in it?

10. What is the volume (in dm^3) of 2.5 moles of a gas that has a pressure of 5.25 atm and a temperature of 450 K?

GAS STOICHIOMETRY

C. Objective: **Calculate** *how much gas is produced in a reaction by using standard molar volume at STP.*

11. What is the significance of the number 22.4 dm^3?

12. What is the value of standard temperature expressed in °C? In K?

13. What volume will 25.0 g of ammonia, NH_3, occupy at STP?

14. Gaseous hydrogen chloride may be produced by the direct reaction of elemental hydrogen and elemental chlorine.
   a. Write a balanced chemical equation for this reaction.
   b. Determine the volume of HCl produced at STP if 142 g of chlorine gas is converted into hydrogen chloride.

15. One of the most important industrial reactions is the production of sulfuric acid. One of the steps in this process is the catalyzed conversion of SO_2 into SO_3, as shown here:
$$2SO_2 + O_2 \rightarrow 2SO_3$$

What volume of sulfur dioxide and what volume of oxygen is required to produce 1000.0 g of sulfur trioxide? Assume that these gaseous volumes are measured at STP.

D. Objective: **Apply** *stoichiometric principles to* **calculate** *the amount of gas produced in a chemical reaction.*

16. What conditions must be met in order to say that the mole ratio of gases in a chemical reaction is equal to the volume ratio?

17. Why is it *incorrect* to say that 1 dm^3 $CaCO_3$ = 1 dm^3 CO_2 in the following reaction?
$$CaCO_3(s) \rightarrow CO_2(g) + CaO(s)$$

18. Cooks sometimes use the fermentation of glucose to produce the gas required to make bread rise, as shown by the following chemical equation:
$$C_6H_{12}O_6(s) + 2O_2(g) \rightarrow$$
$$2CH_3COOH(l) + 2CO_2(g) + 2H_2O(l)$$
What mass of glucose is required to produce 150 cm^3 of carbon dioxide gas measured at STP?

19. Another substance used to make baking foods rise is baking soda. When baking soda (sodium bicarbonate) decomposes, it produces carbon dioxide gas, as shown here:
$$2NaHCO_3(s) \rightarrow$$
$$Na_2O(s) + H_2O(l) + 2CO_2(g)$$
What mass of sodium bicarbonate is needed to produce 2.4 dm^3 of carbon dioxide at STP?

20. When coke (almost pure carbon) is burned in the presence of air, the product is carbon dioxide in the following equation:
$$C(s) + O_2(g) \rightarrow CO_2(g)$$
How many liters of carbon dioxide are produced from burning 750 g of coke with an excess supply of oxygen? Assume that the carbon dioxide is measured at STP.

21. During the metabolic process called respiration, your body obtains energy from the breakdown of glucose as shown below.
$$C_6H_{12}O_6(aq) + 6O_2(g) \rightarrow$$
$$6H_2O(l) + 6CO_2(g)$$

Boxed numbers indicate questions that involve skills in interpretation, application, and analysis.

■ Using calculators: 2, 3, 4, 5, 7, 9, 10, 13, 14, 15, 18, 19, 20, 21, 38, 39, 40, 44, 47, 49, 50
■ Verifying your answer: 2, 3, 4, 5,

7, 9, 10, 13, 14, 15, 18, 19, 20, 21, 38, 39, 40, 44, 47, 49, 50
■ Breaking problems into manageable parts: 4, 49, 50

■ **Making diagrams:** 37, 48
■ **Writing chemical equations:** 14, 49, 50

What volume of O_2, measured at 37°C and 1.00 atm pressure, is required to react with 1.00 g of glucose, $C_6H_{12}O_6$?

EXPLAINING GAS BEHAVIOR

E. Objective: Differentiate *ideal gas behavior from real gas behavior.*

22. What is meant by the term *ideal gas*? What is a *real gas*?
23. Dry ice is carbon dioxide in the solid state. Explain how dry ice shows that CO_2 does not always act like an ideal gas.
24. At what temperature does water better obey the ideal gas law, at −10°C or at 250°C? Explain.
25. Based on the relative volumes of the two gases, which gas do you suppose would better follow the ideal gas law at 25°C—butane, C_4H_{10}, or hydrogen, H_2? Explain your answer.
26. Gases tend to follow the ideal gas law more closely when their pressure is low than when it is high. Considering what happens to gas volumes under high pressure, why do you suppose this trend is true?
27. Charles's law predicts that the volume of a gas is 0 mL when its temperature is 0 K. Is this literally possible for any gas? What does this tell you about all gases at low temperatures?

F. Objective: Explain *gas behavior using the kinetic molecular theory.*

28. What does the word *kinetic* imply about the molecules of a gas?
29. According to the kinetic molecular theory, what is different about a sample of xenon gas at 25°C and another sample at 100°C?
30. Later in this course, you will learn that ammonia molecules have strong attractions for each other. Does ammonia meet all of the criteria for an ideal gas? Explain.

31. According to the kinetic molecular theory, what is the relationship between the average kinetic energy of a sample of gas molecules and their temperature? Does it matter what scale is used to express this temperature?
32. What do you think should happen to the pressure inside a fixed volume container as more gas is added to the container, assuming that the temperature does not change? Support your response with details from the kinetic molecular theory.
33. Suppose you have two balloons filled with air. The smaller balloon has a volume of 500 mL, while the larger balloon has a volume of 1500 mL. Both balloons have the same temperature and pressure. In which balloon (if either) are the nitrogen molecules moving faster, the larger balloon or the smaller? How do you know?
34. The collision of two oxygen molecules more closely resembles which of these collisions, the collision of two sticky pieces of gum or the collision of two billard balls.
35. Bromine molecules, Br_2, have stronger attractions for each other than fluorine molecules, F_2. Which substance is more likely to behave as an ideal gas? Explain your answer.

G. Objective: Apply *Graham's law to* calculate *the molar mass of a gas.*

36. What is meant by the term *diffusion*?
37. If you place a cotton ball soaked in dilute HCl in one end of a sealed-off glass tube and another cotton ball soaked in dilute NH_3 in the other end, will the white cloud of ammonium chloride appear closer to the ammonia end or to the hydrogen chloride end of the tube? Explain.
38. At the same temperature and pressure, which gas moves faster: oxygen or nitrogen? How many times is the speed of the faster gas greater than that of the slower gas?
39. What is the ratio of the rates of diffusion of hydrogen gas to ethane gas, C_2H_6?

40. In an experiment, it takes an unknown gas 1.5 times longer to diffuse than the same amount of oxygen gas, O_2. Find the molar mass of the unknown gas.

41. Suppose you have a sample of Gas A, with a molar mass of 75 g/mol, and another sample of Gas B, with a molar mass of 150 g/mol. Assuming that each gas has a distinctive odor, if you are seated 10 meters away when these gases are released into the air, which gas will you smell first? Why?

42. What can you conclude about the molar mass of a gas that diffuses *faster* than chloroform, $CHCl_3$?

43. Explain why a helium balloon usually deflates faster than a balloon filled with air.

44. Suppose a gas diffuses 1.41 times as fast as sulfur dioxide at the same temperature and pressure. What is the molar mass of the unknown gas?

Critical Thinking

SYNTHESIS WITHIN THE CHAPTER

45. Use the kinetic molecular theory to explain Avogadro's principle.

46. Use the kinetic molecular theory to explain why an increase in the temperature of a gas will increase the pressure of the gas.

47. What is the molar volume of air at $-180°C$, just above the boiling point of liquid air?

48. Using a molecular model of gases, explain why the pressure of a mixture of gases confined to a container at a specific temperature must be greater than the pressure of any single gas in that mixture confined to the same container at the same temperature.

SYNTHESIS ACROSS CHAPTERS

49. Write the equation for the displacement reaction that takes place when magnesium is placed into hydrochloric acid. What volume of hydrogen, measured at 1.00 atm pressure and 23°C can be theoretically produced from the complete reaction of 0.243 g of magnesium?

50. NO_2 is a toxic gas that forms acid rain when mixed with water in the air. The major source of NO_2 is the combustion of $N_2(g)$ in the cylinders of automobile engines. How many metric tons (1×10^6 grams) of NO_2 are produced when 5.0×10^8 dm^3 of N_2 react with excess oxygen in the auto engines in a city? Assume 25°C and 1.00 atm pressure.

Projects

51. Scientists have determined the value of R, the gas law constant, through experimental methods. One reaction that can be safely employed to determine this value is:

$$Mg(s) + 2HCl(ag) \rightarrow MgCl_2(ag) + H_2(g)$$

Devise an experiment to carry out this reaction, collecting the gas produced in a gas-collecting bottle or a eudiometer. Be sure to plan for all the variables you need to measure. You may wish to consult with your teacher for helpful hints, including reference materials on setting up an apparatus for a gas experiment. Describe the steps of your planned procedure in writing; be sure to include the safety precautions you will follow.

CAUTION: You *must* have the permission of your teacher before conducting any experiment!

Research and Writing

52. Cryogenics is the study of the "supercold"—temperatures near absolute zero. Find out how the characteristics of common materials change at temperatures near absolute zero. What can be said about helium under these conditions?

Review ANSWERS

☐ Boxed numbers indicate questions that involve skills in interpretation, application, and analysis.

1. Variables: P—pressure T—absolute temperature, V—volume, n—moles Constant: R—ideal gas law constant

2. $12.0 \text{ g } N_2 \times \frac{1 \text{ mol } N_2}{28.0 \text{ g } N_2} = 0.429 \text{ mol}$

   $V = \frac{nRT}{P} = (0.429 \text{ mol})$

   $\times \left(\frac{8.315 \text{ dm}^3 \cdot \text{kPa}}{\text{mol} \cdot \text{K}} \right)(45 + 273)$

   $\times \left(\frac{\text{K}}{125 \text{ kPa}} \right) = 9.07 \text{ dm}^3$

3. $n = \frac{PV}{RT} = (75 \text{ kPa}) \times$

   $\left(\frac{5.5 \text{ dm}^3}{8.315 \text{ dm}^3 \cdot \text{kPa/mol} \cdot \text{K}} \right)(5+273)\text{ K}$

   $= 0.18 \text{ mol}$

   $0.18 \text{ mol } CO_2 \times 44.0 \text{ g/mol}$

   $= 7.9 \text{ g } CO_2$

4. $\frac{0.0821 \text{ L} \cdot \text{atm}}{\text{mol} \cdot \text{K}} \times \frac{760 \text{ torr}}{1 \text{ atm}} \times \frac{1000 \text{ mL}}{1 \text{ L}}$

   $= 62\ 400 \text{ mL} \cdot \text{torr/mol} \cdot \text{K}$

5. $T = \frac{PV}{nR} = (715 \text{ torr})$

   $\times \left(\frac{302 \text{ mL}}{0.00893 \text{ mol}} \right) \left(\frac{\text{mol} \cdot \text{K}}{62\ 400 \text{ mL} \cdot \text{torr}} \right)$

   $= 388 \text{ K} = 115°\text{C}$

6. $PV = nRT$

   $\frac{PV}{n} = RT;$ where RT is constant

   $\frac{P_1 V_1}{n_1} = \frac{P_2 V_2}{n_2}$

7. $\frac{P_1 V_1}{T_1} = \frac{P_2 V_2}{T_2}$

   $V_2 = \frac{T_2}{T_1} \times \frac{P_1}{P_2} \times V_1 = \frac{(95+273)\text{ K}}{(38+273)\text{ K}}$

   $\times \frac{125 \text{ kPa}}{100 \text{ kPa}} \times 250.0 \text{ L} = 370 \text{ L}$

8. Number of moles and temperature—it is unlikely that changing the number of moles of a gas will affect its temperature. It is more likely that its pressure or volume will change instead.

9. $n = \frac{PV}{RT} = (101 \text{ kPa})$

   $\times \left(\frac{12.5 \text{ dm}^3}{8.315 \text{ dm}^3 \cdot \text{kPa/mol} \cdot \text{K}} \right)(251\ 273)\text{ K}$

   $= 0.510 \text{ mol}$

   $\times 6.02 \times 10^{23} \text{ atoms/mol}$

   $= 3.07 \times 10^{23} \text{ atoms}$

10. $V = \frac{nRT}{P} = (2.5 \text{ mol})$

    $\times \left(\frac{0.0821 \text{ dm}^3 \cdot \text{atm}}{\text{mol} \cdot \text{K}} \right) \left(\frac{450 \text{ K}}{5.25 \text{ atm}} \right)$

    $= 18 \text{ dm}^3$

11. 22.4 dm^3 is the volume of one mole of any gas when the temperature is 0°C and the pressure is 1 atm.

12. 0°C, 273 K

13. $25.0 \text{ g } NH_3 \times \frac{1 \text{ mol}}{17.0 \text{ g}} \times \frac{22.4 \text{ dm}^3}{\text{mol}}$

    $= 32.9 \text{ dm}^3$

14. a. $H_2(g) + Cl_2(g) \rightarrow 2HCl(g)$

    b. $142 \text{ g } Cl_2 \times \frac{1 \text{ mol } Cl_2}{71.0 \text{ g } Cl_2}$

    $\times \frac{2 \text{ mol HCl}}{1 \text{ mol } Cl_2} \times \frac{22.4 \text{ dm}^3}{\text{mol}}$

    $= 89.6 \text{ dm}^3$

15. $1000.0 \text{ g } SO_3 \times \frac{1 \text{ mol } SO_3}{80.1 \text{ g } SO_3}$

    $= 12.5 \text{ mol } SO_3$

    $12.5 \text{ mol } SO_3 \times \frac{2 \text{ mol } SO_2}{2 \text{ mol } SO_3} \times \frac{22.4 \text{ dm}^3}{\text{mol}}$

    $= 280 \text{ dm}^3 \text{ } SO_2$

    $12.5 \text{ mol } SO_3 \times \frac{1 \text{ mol } O_2}{2 \text{ mol } SO_3} \times \frac{22.4 \text{ dm}^3}{\text{mol}}$

    $= 140 \text{ dm}^3 \text{ } O_2$

16. The volumes of all the gases involved must be measured under the same conditions of temperature and pressure.

17. Because $CaCO_3$ is a solid, not a gas.

18. $150 \text{ cm}^3 \text{ } CO_2 \times \frac{1 \text{ dm}^3}{1000 \text{ cm}^3} \times \frac{1 \text{ mol } CO_2}{22.4 \text{ dm}^3}$

    $\times \frac{1 \text{ mol } C_6H_{12}O_6}{2 \text{ mol } CO_2} \times \frac{180 \text{ g } C_6H_{12}O_6}{1 \text{ mol } C_6H_{12}O_6}$

    $= 0.60 \text{ g } C_6H_{12}O_6$

19. $2.4 \text{ dm}^3 \text{ } CO_2 \times \frac{1 \text{ mol } CO_2}{22.4 \text{ dm}^3}$

    $\times \frac{2 \text{ mol NaHCO}_3}{2 \text{ mol } CO_2} \times \frac{84.0 \text{ g NaHCO}_3}{1 \text{ mol NaHCO}_3}$

    $= 9.0 \text{ g NaHCO}_3$

20. $750 \text{ g } C \times \frac{1 \text{ mol C}}{12.0 \text{ g } C} \times \frac{1 \text{ mol } CO_2}{1 \text{ mol C}}$

    $\times \frac{22.4 \text{ dm}^3 \text{ } CO_2}{1 \text{ mol } CO_2} = 1400 \text{ dm}^3 \text{ } CO_2$

21. $1.00 \text{ g } C_6H_{12}O_6 \times \frac{1 \text{ mol } C_6H_{12}O_6}{180 \text{ g } C_6H_{12}O_6}$

    $\times \frac{6 \text{ mol } O_2}{1 \text{ mol } C_6H_{12}O_6} \times \frac{22.4 \text{ dm}^3}{1 \text{ mol}}$

    $= 0.747 \text{ dm}^3$

22. An **ideal** gas obeys the five conditions of the kinetic molecular gases, while a **real** gas is a real-world substance that does not obey all of these conditions.

23. Ideal gases do not solidify as the temperature drops.

24. At 250°C, because it is a gas at this temperature, while it is a solid at −10°C.

25. Since an ideal gas has essentially no volume, the smaller molecule, H_2, will follow the ideal gas law better than C_4H_{10}.

26. The volume of a gas decreases when the pressure increases, so the relative volume occupied by the gas molecules themselves increases. Under these conditions, a gas violates one of the basic postulates of the ideal gas law (relating to molecular volume).

27. A volume of 0 mL is impossible because gas molecules occupy a finite volume. For this reason, gases do not follow the ideal gas law very well when the temperature is sufficiently low.

28. Kinetic means that the gas molecules are in motion.

29. The atoms are moving faster and have more kinetic energy at 100°C.

30. No, because ideal gas molecules neither attract nor repel each other.

31. The average kinetic energy of a sample of gas molecules is directly proportional to its temperature, provided that the temperature is measured on an absolute scale.

32. The pressure will increase, because as more molecules are added to the container, there will be more frequent collisions between molecules and the container.

33. On average, the nitrogen molecules are moving with the same velocity in both balloons because they are at the same temperature.

34. The collision of two billiard balls, which is the more elastic of these two collisions

35. Fluorine, because an ideal gas has no forces of attraction

36. The ability of a gas to move from one place to another through another gas

37. The cloud appears closer to the HCl end; molecules of HCl move more slowly than NH_3 because they have a greater mass.

38. The lighter nitrogen molecules move faster.

    $\frac{v_{N_2}}{v_{O_2}} = \sqrt{\frac{m_{O_2}}{m_{N_2}}} = \sqrt{\frac{32.0 \text{ g/mol}}{28 \text{ g/mol}}} = 1.07$

39. $\frac{v_{H_2}}{v_{C_2H_6}} = \sqrt{\frac{m_{C_2H_6}}{m_{H_2}}} = \sqrt{\frac{30.0 \text{ g/mol}}{20 \text{ g/mol}}}$

    $= 3.87$

40. $1.5 = \sqrt{\frac{x}{32 \text{ g/mol}}}$

    $(1.5)^2 = \sqrt{\frac{x}{32.0 \text{ g/mol}}}$

    $x = 72 \text{ g/mol}$

41. Gas A, because the lighter gas diffuses faster

42. Its molar mass must be less than the molar mass of chloroform.

43. Helium diffuses faster than nitrogen or oxygen (the major constituents of air) because it is lighter than these two gases.

44. $1.41 = \sqrt{\dfrac{64.2 \text{ g/mol}}{x}}$

$x = \dfrac{64.2 \text{ g/mol}}{1.41^2} = 32.3 \text{ g/mol}$

45. As more molecules are added to a container, its volume must also expand if the same pressure is to be maintained. Otherwise, molecules will strike the container more frequently when there are more of them.

46. When the kinetic energy of molecules is increased, their greater velocity results in more frequent and more forceful collisions with the container.

47. $22.4 \text{ dm}^3 \times \dfrac{(273-180)\,\cancel{K}}{273\,\cancel{K}} = 7.63 \text{ dm}^3$

48. The entire mixture has more collisions with the container than any single component of the mixture.

49. $Mg(s) + 2HCl(aq) \rightarrow H_2(g) + MgCl_2(aq)$

$0.243\ \cancel{\text{g Mg}} \times \dfrac{1\ \cancel{\text{mol Mg}}}{24.3\ \cancel{\text{g Mg}}} \times \dfrac{1\ \cancel{\text{mol H}_2}}{1\ \cancel{\text{mol Mg}}}$

$\times \dfrac{22.4 \text{ dm}^3\ H_2}{1\ \cancel{\text{mol H}_2}} = 0.224 \text{ dm}^3\ H_2 \text{ at STP}$

$0.224 \text{ dm}^3 \times \dfrac{296\ \cancel{K}}{273\ \cancel{K}} = 0.243 \text{ dm}^3\ H_2$

50. $N_2(g) + 2O_2(g) \rightarrow 2\ NO_2(g)$

$\dfrac{22.4 \text{ dm}^3}{1 \text{ mol}} \times \dfrac{298\ \cancel{K}}{273\ \cancel{K}} = 24.5 \text{ dm}^3\text{/mol at } 25°C$

The number of moles of N_2 reacted

is: $\dfrac{5.0 \times 10^8\ \cancel{\text{dm}^3}}{24.5\ \cancel{\text{dm}^3}\text{/mol}} = 2.04 \times 10^7 \text{ mol } N_2$

$2.04 \times 10^7\ \cancel{\text{mol N}_2} \times \dfrac{2\ \cancel{\text{mol NO}_2}}{1\ \cancel{\text{mol N}_2}}$

$\times \dfrac{46.0\ \cancel{\text{g NO}_2}}{1\ \cancel{\text{mol NO}_2}} \times \dfrac{1 \text{ metric ton } NO_2}{1 \times 10^6\ \cancel{\text{g NO}_2}}$

$= 1900 \text{ metric tons } NO_2$

Composition of the Atom

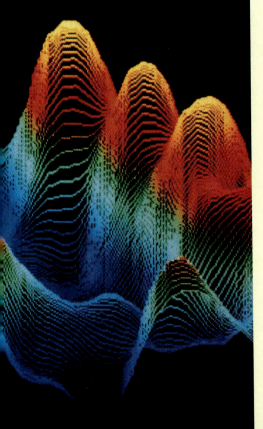

Investigations	Demonstrations	Texas Essential Elements★
Laboratory Manual 8–1 S	The Electron, page T266 Deflection of a Charged Particle, page T267	**Content:** 3.1, 3.4 **Process:** 4.1, 6.3, 7.1, 10.1
Laboratory Manual 8–2 I	The Discovery of Radioactivity, page T271 Rutherford's Gold Foil Experiment, page T272	**Content:** 3.4, 7.1, 13.1, 13.2 **Process:** 4.1, 6.3, 7.1
In-text Investigation, page T284		**Content:** 3.1, 3.2 **Process:** 6.3, 7.1, 10.1, 10.4
		Content: 3.1, 3.2, 13.1 **Process:** 4.3
		Process: 4.1, 4.2, 4.3, 5.2, 6.3, 7.1, 10.1, 10.4

KEY:
M–Microscale **S**–Structured
I–Inquiry   **IM**–Inquiry Microscale

★*See pages T8–T11 for complete listing of Texas Essential Elements.*

Chapter Rationale

To study chemistry is to study the changes in atoms. Because atoms are submicroscopic and cannot be seen directly, scientists create models based upon experimental results. We have learned much about the atom in this century. However, only the most basic facts will be presented in this text. Through an historical approach, Chapter 8 develops a model of the atom and explores the characteristics of atomic particles and the nucleus.

Chapter 8 also introduces isotopes and discusses how their existence helps explain why the atomic masses of the elements are not whole numbers.

About the Photograph

The structure of the DNA molecule was proposed in 1953 by James D. Watson and Francis Crick. They used X-ray diffraction patterns, data on the distances between bonded atoms, the angles between bonds, and the sizes of atoms to create their model.

Recently, a scanning tunneling microscope (STM) has been used to produce images of DNA molecules. The STM uses electric current to "feel" atoms on the surface of a molecule. A sample of DNA is attached to a sheet of mica to improve electrical conductivity. A needle from the STM moves up and down as it scans the surface of a DNA molecule. A computer translates the motions of the needle into a picture. STM images of specific elements and compounds are greatly advancing knowledge in the field of atomic and molecular structure.

Chapter Planning Hints

To complete Chapter 8, including the Laboratory Investigation
(continued on page T263)

8

Composition of the Atom

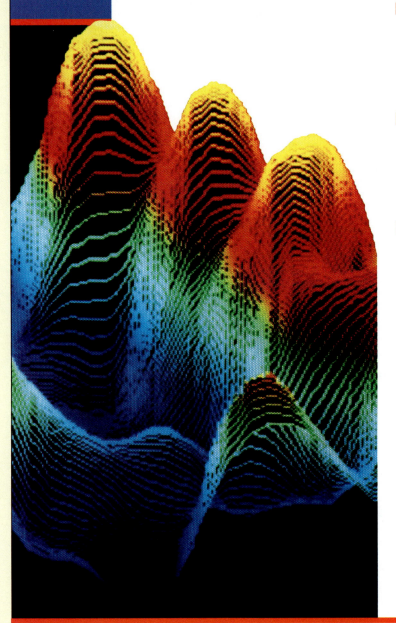

In this photograph, the DNA molecule is magnified 1 500 000 times through the technique of electron tunneling micrography. Although individual atoms cannot be distinguished, such techniques bring you as close to viewing atoms on the submicroscopic level as is currently possible.

PART
1 # The Discovery of Subatomic Particles

Imagine that you were given a sealed box with an unknown object inside. How would you describe the object if you were unable to open the box and look at it? Your first step might be to perform some experiments to gather information about the object. For example, you could guess its shape by tilting the box to see whether the object rolls or slides. By judging how far the object rolls or slides inside the box, you could estimate its size. Can you think of a way to estimate the object's mass? Are there any characteristics that could not be determined without opening the box?

After gathering as much information as possible, you could then form a mental picture, or model, to represent the object in the box. The scientists who worked to determine the nature of the atom had similar difficulties to those that would arise in determining the details about an unknown object in a sealed box. Atoms are so small that they cannot be observed directly. Scientists have had to use the experimental data available at the time to construct a model that describes the atom.

The evolution of the atomic model is a fascinating example of the application of several scientific processes—experimental observation, theoretical modeling, and subsequent experimental verification. Modern atomic theory was developed through a series of discoveries that began in the late 1800's.

8.1 Scientific Modeling

Perhaps when you were younger, you devised models to explain phenomena that you could not understand. For example, to explain how thunder is produced, children may form a simple model of two huge, rain-laden clouds crashing into each other with great force. Models allow you to form concrete pictures of abstract concepts. Models also help communicate knowledge to others.

Scientists develop models to explain things that they cannot observe directly. Scientific models are based on a large quantity of experimental data. Scientists constantly check their models by making predictions, proposing experiments, and, if necessary, revising their models as new experimental data are obtained.

Dalton's atomic theory In the early 1800's, a British schoolteacher named John Dalton applied the idea of the atom to chemistry. Experimental data indicated that whenever a given compound was formed, the elements combined in the same percentage

O b j e c t i v e s

Part 1

A. *Evaluate* the factors that influence the deflection of a charged particle.
B. *Compare* and *contrast* the atomic models of Dalton and Thomson.
C. *Differentiate* between atoms and ions.

(continued from page T262)
and the Chapter Review will require three to five class sessions. There are four optional demonstrations for this chapter. They appear on pages T266, T267, T271, and T272. You may wish to preview them at this time. You may wish to obtain The World of Chemistry videotape *The Atom*

Developing Skills

Students may apply these skills in their study of Part 1.
Comparing/Contrasting: Have students compare the models of the atom shown in Figures 8–6, 8–7, and 8–10. List similarities and differences.
Designing experiments: A beam of unknown particles is visible inside a glass vacuum tube. Have students design an experiment to determine if the particles are positive, negative, or neutral.
Identifying and controlling variables: Figure 8–4 shows the deflection of a beam. Have students list variables that must be controlled when comparing the deflection of two different beams.

☰ FOCUS

Activate Prior Knowledge

This activity will help students understand the kinetic theory involving submicroscopic particles moving in random motion. Create a dust cloud by clapping two erasers together. Darken the room and project a beam of light through the cloud. Ask students to propose an explanation. This is an example of Brownian motion, named for Robert Brown, the Scottish scientist who first described it in detail.

Albert Einstein used the kinetic theory of James Clerk Maxwell and Ludwig Boltzman to show that the motion of the
(continued on page T264)

(continued from page T263)

dust particles can be explained by a model of submicroscopic air particles randomly bombarding the dust particles.

TEACH

Teaching Strategy

Scientific Modeling

The concept of scientific modeling is an important part of Chapters 9, 11, 12, and 13. The historical development of atomic theory will help students appreciate how scientific models develop. A model is an attempt to explain reality. Each new or revised model improves the understanding of reality by integrating newly discovered phenomena into the previous model. For example, Thomson incorporated the results of his experiments with electrons and protons into Dalton's model of the atom.

Teaching Strategy

Scientific Modeling

Ask students to recall childhood explanations they formed for natural events such as the bubbles forming in boiling water, a car rusting, day turning into night, a helium-filled balloon shrinking, summer changing into winter, water changing to ice, and so on. Ask them for their present models and determine why they have changed their models.

by mass. For example, carbon dioxide was always 27.3 percent carbon and 72.7 percent oxygen, which means that 100 g of carbon dioxide has 27.3 g of carbon and 72.7 g of oxygen. You learned in Chapter 2 that this experimental fact is called the law of definite proportions. Dalton showed that this law could be explained by assuming that matter is composed of atoms.

In Dalton's model, illustrated in Figure 8-1, an atom is an indivisible sphere with a uniform density throughout. All atoms of the same element have the same mass and the same chemical behavior, while atoms of different elements have different masses and different chemical behaviors. Dalton theorized that atoms of different elements always combine in fixed number ratios to produce specific compounds. He also showed how the concept of relative atomic mass could be used as a guide to determining the composition of a compound.

Dalton's model

1807

Figure 8-1 *John Dalton theorized that an atom was an indivisible, uniformly dense, solid sphere that participated in, but was unchanged by chemical reactions.*

Fixed ratios of atoms By assuming that compounds have a fixed ratio by number of atoms, Dalton could explain why they always have the same percentage composition by mass. Look at the example of carbon dioxide. You learned in Chapter 4 that the relative atomic mass of carbon is 12.0 and the relative atomic mass of oxygen is 16.0. If one atom of carbon combines with two atoms of oxygen, the total relative atomic mass is 12.0 + 2(16.0), or 44.0. To find the percentage composition by mass of carbon, divide the mass of carbon by the total mass—that is, 12.0 ÷ 44.0 = 0.273, or 27.3 percent. Similarly, the percent composition by mass of oxygen is 32.0 ÷ 44.0 = 0.727, or 72.7 percent. These percentages agree with the percentages obtained from experiments.

Dalton's introduction of the concept of atomic mass gave chemists a quantitative way to differentiate the atoms of different elements. As a result, chemists in the early 1800's analyzed many compounds to determine their percentage composition by mass. Then they used the relative atomic masses to calculate formulas for the compounds, as described in Chapter 4. Although Dalton's atomic model helped explain some aspects of chemical compound formation, problems remained. For example, measurements of the relative atomic mass of the same element were often contradictory. Some chemists thought that the atomic model should be discarded. However, by 1860, most of the discrepancies were resolved, and Dalton was credited with founding modern atomic theory.

Further support for atomic theory The development of the kinetic molecular theory during the period of 1850 to 1900 further advanced the acceptance of the atomic model. Remember from Chapter 7 that the kinetic molecular theory explains the behavior of gases by assuming that a gas consists of atoms or molecules in rapid motion. Several experimentally determined properties of gases, including Charles's law and Boyle's law, were explained by applying the laws of motion to these molecules. Yet further discoveries in the late 1800's indicated that Dalton's model of the atom as an indivisible unit of matter needed to be modified.

8.2 The Electron

After Benjamin Franklin's famous (and very dangerous) experiment with a kite and key, the passage of electricity through gases became a very active field of study. In the 1870's, a British scientist, Sir William Crookes, was investigating the flow of electric current in gases. His work laid the foundation for further discoveries, which provided evidence for a new atomic model.

Crookes' experiments Crookes experimented with a partially evacuated tube containing gas at low pressure. Such a tube is illustrated in Figure 8-2 *(left)*. Inside the tube were two electrodes. An **electrode** is a conductor used to establish electrical contact with

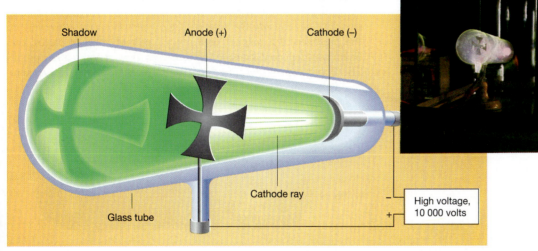

Figure 8-2 *Crookes' glass tube contained gas at very low pressure. A disk-shaped cathode was at the narrow end of the tube, and a cross-shaped anode was at the wide end of the tube. When a high voltage was applied to the electrodes, a greenish glow appeared, caused by negative particles coming from the cathode. Some particles in the beam struck the anode, forming a shadow on the wide end of the tube.*

PART 1

Section 8.2

Science Background

Scientific Modeling

The model of the atom continues to change as more knowledge is gained from experiments. Accurate models of the atom present difficulties for many students. First, the principles of quantum mechanics are different from those of classical mechanics in the macroscopic world. Making measurements and calculating the path of an orbiting satellite with great accuracy is possible; however, these methods do not apply to subatomic particles. The Heisenberg Uncertainty Principle tells us that the act of determining the position of a subatomic particle changes its trajectory. Only the probable location of an electron over a given period of time can be found. The current models of the atom are highly mathematical models that seem to violate common sense. For this reason, a full understanding is not accessible to students.

Cooperative Learning

Scientific Modeling

Teams of 3; **Time:** 20 minutes
Objective: Students will describe a model of an unseen object.
Task: The first student puts an object in a paper bag without letting the other students see it. The second student, without opening the bag or looking inside (although reaching inside to feel it is permitted), describes the object to the third student. The third student tries to draw or otherwise identify the object. Have students note the difference between the object and the third student's model.
Team responsibility: Have students use a new object and change roles. Each team then lists information that was most effective in helping the third student to identify the object.
Evaluation: Have teams pool their findings and make a class list of effective strategies.

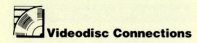

PART 1

Section 8.2 *continued*

Videodisc Connections

27960 to 28164, side 1
Cathode ray tube (movie)

DO YOU KNOW?

Until recently, most information was processed and transmitted through electronic media, such as telephones, televisions, radios, and computers, which depend on the flow of electrons. In recent decades, the development of fiber optics has enabled information to be processed and transmitted optically rather than electronically.

DO YOU KNOW?

Laundry additives that reduce static cling have a large molecule that can absorb the electrons in a thin layer. This thin layer of charge causes the fibers to repel each other and gives softness to the cloth.

Figure 8-3 *In Thomson's cathode-ray tube, only a narrow cathode-ray beam passes through the hole in the anode. This beam travels in a straight line, striking the center of the fluorescent screen.*

a nonmetallic part of a circuit—in this case, the gas. One electrode was shaped like a broad, flat cross and was connected to the positive terminal of an electric power source. The other, disk-shaped electrode was connected to the negative terminal. In this experiment, the positive electrode is called an **anode,** and the negative electrode is called a **cathode.**

When Crookes applied a voltage to the electrodes, he noticed a glowing greenish beam coming from the disk-shaped cathode. Was this beam composed of particles with an electric charge or was it a beam of light? In order to answer this question, he placed a magnet close to the tube and noted that the beam was deflected from its straight-line course. Since light has no electric charge, it should not be influenced by a magnet. Therefore, Crookes concluded that the beam was composed of charged particles.

Crookes also noticed that the beam produced a shadow of the cross on the large end of the tube as shown in Figure 8-2 *(right)*. The location of the shadow meant that the beam was coming from the disk-shaped cathode. Therefore, Crookes called the beam a cathode ray. Because the charged particles in the beam moved toward the positive anode, he concluded that the charge of the particles must be negative. This type of tube is now known as a **cathode-ray tube,** or CRT. CRT's are currently used in most television screens and computer terminal displays.

Thomson's experiments In 1897, another British scientist, J. J. Thomson, devised an experiment to determine the nature of cathode rays. He constructed a CRT similar to the one shown in Figure 8-3. At the far end of the tube, he placed a screen coated with a **fluorescent** material that glowed when struck by a beam of charged particles. Normally the beam of cathode rays moved in a straight line, causing the screen to glow at its center. However, in the presence of a magnet or a second pair of charged plates, the beam was deflected, causing the screen to glow at some other point. The fluorescent screen provided Thomson with a way to measure the deflection of the beam.

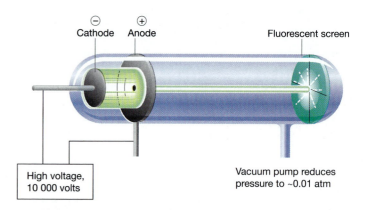

⊖ Cathode   ⊕ Anode   Fluorescent screen

High voltage, 10 000 volts

Vacuum pump reduces pressure to ~0.01 atm

DEMONSTRATION

The Electron

If you have not done so already, now is a good time to demonstrate the nature of electrical charges. Use pith balls, a glass rod rubbed with pure silk, and a rubber rod rubbed with fur. Touch two pith balls hanging together with the charged glass rod. The pith balls should separate since they both have acquired the same charge. Charge the rubber rod and bring it close to one of the pith balls. The ball will be attracted to the rubber rod. However, after touching the rod, the ball will be repelled. This demonstration works best in dry weather.

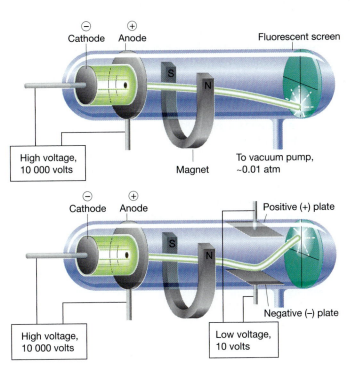

Figure 8-4 Top: *Since the cathode rays are deflected by a magnetic field, they must be charged particles rather than light.* Bottom: *An electric field is located between the positive and negative plates. Since the cathode ray is deflected by the negative plate toward the positive plate, it must be composed of negatively charged particles.*

Figure 8-4 illustrates the setup of Thomson's experiment. Like Crookes, Thomson positioned a magnet close to the tube in order to deflect the cathode ray. Next he added a set of charged plates above and below the beam. The cathode-ray beam was first deflected downward by the magnetic field and then deflected back upward as it passed between the charged plates. Look at the positions of the positive and negative plates. The upward deflection of the beam as it passed between the charged plates proved that cathode rays were made up of negatively charged particles.

Deflection of a charged particle In order to understand Thomson's experiment, you need to examine the factors that affect the deflection of a moving, charged particle. The deflection caused by a magnet or by charged plates depends on the following.

1. the mass of the particle
2. the velocity of the particle
3. the electric charge of the particle
4. the strength of the magnet
5. the amount of charge on the plates

To discuss the effect of each of these factors on the deflection of a particle, assume that all the other factors are kept constant.

The path of a heavier, more massive particle is bent less than the path of a lighter particle. The path of faster particles is bent less than that of slower particles. More highly charged particles

DEMONSTRATION

Deflection of a Charged Particle

Roll a ball bearing down a ramp onto an overhead projector and past a magnet strong enough to deflect the path. Ask students how they could affect the path of the ball bearing. Examples: replace the ball bearing with an aluminum ball, use different ramp heights, use stronger or weaker magnets, use a smaller or larger ball bearing.

have their path bent more. Stronger magnets or more highly charged plates bend the path of the charged particle more. The direction of the deflection depends on the sign of the electric charge. Positively charged particles are deflected in one direction, while negatively charged particles are deflected in the opposite direction.

Charge to mass ratio By measuring the amount and direction of the deflection of the beam, Thomson was able to calculate the ratio of the charge to mass of the particles that composed the cathode rays. He used many different cathode-ray tubes in his experiments, changing both the metal of the electrodes and the type of gas in the tube. When the strength of the magnet and the amount of charge on the plate were both kept constant, the deflection of the beam was always the same. This indicated that the particles composing the cathode rays always had the same ratio of charge and mass, regardless of the type of gas or metal used in the cathode-ray tube.

Based on this result, Thomson concluded that the particles in the cathode rays were identical to one another. He further concluded that these particles were actually subatomic particles found in all atoms. As a result of his experiments, Thomson is credited with discovering the first type of subatomic particle—the electron. An **electron** is a negatively charged particle found in atoms.

Concept ✔ Check

How did Thomson know that electrons are negatively charged subatomic particles?

8.3 The Proton

Atoms usually have no apparent charge—that is, they are electrically neutral. Therefore, once it became apparent that negative particles could be separated from atoms, researchers assumed there must also be positive particles in atoms. A beam of such positive particles was discovered in 1885.

J. J. Thomson conducted further experiments with a cathode-ray tube containing hydrogen gas at very low pressure. When a very high voltage was applied to the electrodes, the expected negative beam of electrons moved to the positive anode. But careful observations showed that a second beam of particles was moving in the opposite direction toward the cathode! The tube was modified to contain a cathode that was perforated with a hole, similar to the one shown in Figure 8-5. Some of the particles passed through the hole of the cathode to the end of the tube. Thomson realized that this new beam had to be composed of positive particles since they moved toward the negative cathode.

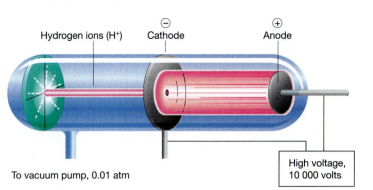

Hydrogen ions (H⁺) Cathode ⊖ Anode ⊕

To vacuum pump, 0.01 atm

High voltage, 10 000 volts

PART 1
Section 8.3 *continued*

Thomson reasoned that when a very large voltage is applied to the electrodes, hydrogen atoms are broken down into two oppositely charged particles—negatively charged electrons and positively charged hydrogen ions. Recall that an ion is a charged atom or group of atoms. Since a hydrogen atom is electrically neutral, the charge of the ion must be equal to, but opposite that of the electron.

Comparing deflection patterns Unlike the deflection of electrons, which was the same for all gases, Thomson found that the deflection of positive ions varied with different gases in the tube. Since the deflection of hydrogen ions was larger than the deflection of any other positive ions, Thomson concluded that hydrogen ions had the smallest mass. He theorized that the positive ion formed from a hydrogen atom was, in fact, a single particle with a charge equal to, but opposite that of an electron. By 1920, the positive hydrogen ion was identified as a **proton**—a positively charged particle found in all atoms.

As a result of Thomson's further studies, another piece of the atomic puzzle had been revealed. Revising Dalton's atomic model, Thomson imagined an atom to be like plum pudding—a common dessert of that era. As illustrated in Figure 8-6, the pudding, representing the positive charge and most of the mass of the atom, was uniformly distributed throughout a sphere of radius 10^{-10} meter. (This value of the radius was based on other experimental evidence available at the time.) The plums were the electrons scattered throughout the pudding in order to make the atom electrically neutral.

The formation of ions In order to explain exactly how an atom differs from an ion, look again at Thomson's atomic model. Normally an atom is neutral. However, if an atom loses one or more electrons, it becomes positively charged. If an atom gains one or more electrons, it becomes negatively charged. Thus an ion can be simply an atom that has either lost or gained electrons. A positive ion is called a **cation,** and a negative ion is called an **anion.** Ions can be symbolized by writing the chemical symbol for the atom, followed by a superscript indicating the ion's charge. For example,

Figure 8-5 *When a large voltage was applied to the cathode-ray tube, Thomson found that positive particles were attracted to the negative cathode. He concluded that hydrogen atoms were separated into negative electrons and positive hydrogen ions.*

Thomson's model

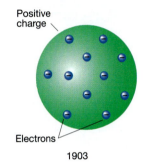

Positive charge

Electrons

1903

Figure 8-6 *Thomson's plum-pudding model of the atom was the first major modification of atomic theory since Dalton's.*

PROBLEM·SOLVING
S T R A T E G Y

*By **using what you know** so far about atoms—they contain negatively charged electrons, yet are themselves neutral in charge—you can hypothesize that atoms contain positively charged particles also. (See Strategy, page 58.)*

Science Background

Comparing Deflection Patterns

Electrons are the same in charge and mass for all atoms. Therefore, the charge-to-mass ratio for an electron is constant. Protons also have a constant charge and mass. However, charge-to-mass ratios do vary for the positive ions of gaseous atoms stripped of at least one electron. The charges of these ions are usually the integers, 1+ or 2+. The greater the mass of the ion, the less it is deflected by the electric field. For example, an Ar⁺ ion (atomic weight of 40 amu) is deflected less than a Ne⁺ ion (atomic weight of 20 amu).

The positive beam produced from H_2 gas has the highest charge-to-mass ratio because the H⁺ ion (a single proton) has the smallest mass. This knowledge, along with Thompson's cathode ray tube experiments, was the basis for the mass spectrometer.

Guided Practice

Review the Concept Check question on page 268 with students. Answers can be found in Appendix E on page 808.

Reteaching Idea

To make the concept of charged particles more concrete for students, give each of them two pieces of plastic tape about six inches long. Have them fold over about a half inch on each and stick them smoothly to their desk tops. Then have them pull up both tapes simultaneously and slowly move the nonsticky sides of the tapes toward each other, without allowing them to touch. Ask students to describe what happens in terms of electrons. (The tapes repel each other because each lost or gained electrons to/from the desk.) Next, have students stick one tape on the desk and the other on top of the first. Have them pull the tapes up together (continued on page T270)

(continued from page T269)
and separate them. Ask them to describe what happens when they bring the nonsticky sides of the tapes toward each other. (The tapes attract each other because when they were pulled apart, one tape lost and the other gained electrons.) Ask if they can tell whether a tape is positive or negative. (No) When a tape is pulled from the desk, how could it acquire a positive charge? (By leaving some of its electrons on the desk.) How could it acquire a negative charge? (By taking some electrons from the desk.) Emphasize that it is the electrons that move, and ask how this relates to the findings of J.J. Thomson and the Thomson model of the atom.

☰ CLOSE

Summing Up Main Ideas

Draw a time line from the year 1800 to 1920 that summarizes the major steps in the development of a model of the atom. For each major development on the time line, have students write a paragraph explaining the significance of that particular discovery or theory.

PART 1 REVIEW

Assign the Part Review questions.

Evaluating Skills

These skills are evaluated in the Part Review questions indicated.
Analyzing data: 1; **Predicting:** 2;
Determining cause and effect: 2;
Forming models: 4, 5

PART 1 REVIEW

ANSWERS

■ Keyed to Objectives

A **1.** The beam was deflected away from the negative plate and attracted toward the positive plate.

A **2.** The beams will bend in opposite directions. The beam of electrons will bend toward the positive plate and the beam of protons will bend

N
Nitrogen atom

7 electrons
Net charge = 0

N³⁻
Nitrogen ion

10 electrons
Net charge = 3–

Figure 8-7 *In the Thomson model of a neutral nitrogen atom, 7 electrons are imbedded in a sphere of positive charge. If a nitrogen atom gains 3 electrons, it becomes a nitrogen ion with a net charge of 3⁻.*

Boxed numbers indicate questions that involve skills in interpretation, application, and analysis.

the ion formed when calcium loses two electrons is written as Ca^{2+}. If a nitrogen atom gains three electrons, the ion is symbolized as N^{3-}, as indicated in Figure 8-7.

8.4 Charge and Mass Measurements

Once the existence of electrons and protons was established, scientists wanted to know more about the characteristics of these particles. What were their masses? What was the value of their electric charges?

Thomson found that the path of an electron was bent much more than the path of a hydrogen ion—or proton. Since the magnitude of an electron's charge equaled that of a proton, the only explanation for this observation was that the mass of an electron must be very small compared to the mass of a proton.

A few years after Thomson's discoveries, an American physicist, Robert Millikan successfully measured the charge of an electron to be 1.602×10^{-19} coulombs. (A coulomb is the SI unit for electric charge.) He combined this information with the results obtained by Thomson to calculate the value of the mass of an electron. Millikan received the Nobel Prize in 1923 for his determination of this fundamental constant of nature. Eventually the mass of an electron was found to be 9.10953×10^{-28} gram.*

Since the magnitude of a proton's charge is equal to an electron's charge, the mass of a proton could be similarly calculated. The mass of a proton is 1.67265×10^{-24} gram, which is 1836 times larger than the mass of an electron. As Thomson had predicted, the mass of an electron was indeed very small compared to the mass of a proton!

PART 1 REVIEW

1. What evidence showed that the particles in the beam of Crookes' tube were negatively charged?

2. Suppose that two beams pass between a pair of oppositely charged plates. One of the beams is composed of electrons, and the other is composed of protons. Will the two beams bend in the same direction or in opposite directions? Why?

3. What main feature of Dalton's atomic model was abandoned after Thomson's discoveries?

4. Make a diagram of a lithium atom, based on Thomson's atomic model.

5. Suppose that a lithium atom lost one electron, forming a positive ion. How would the diagram drawn in question 4 be changed?

* If you need to review the use of scientific notation, refer to the Appendix.

toward the negative plate. Opposite charges attract.

B **3.** The atom was no longer the smallest indivisible particle; it contained smaller particles called electrons.

B **4.**

B **5.** It would contain one less electron.

PART 2 Rutherford's Model of the Atom

The concept of the atom was firmly established at the turn of this century. All atoms were known to contain electrons, and all electrons had the same mass and charge. Atoms of different elements were known to have different masses. Scientists continued to look for other differences between atoms as well.

The discovery of radioactivity during this period gave birth to a new branch of science—nuclear science. Experiments performed on radioactivity, particularly by the English physicist Ernest Rutherford, greatly advanced scientists' understanding of the atom. The atomic model previously suggested by Thomson had to be modified in order to account for Rutherford's findings.

8.5 The Discovery of Radioactivity

Radioactivity was accidentally discovered by the French scientist Henri Becquerel in 1896. Becquerel was intrigued by the earlier discovery that the fluorescent screens used in cathode-ray tubes not only glowed when struck by electrons but also emitted X rays. He knew that certain minerals, including a uranium mineral, would glow, or fluoresce, when illuminated by sunlight. Becquerel speculated that these materials would also emit X rays when fluorescing.

To investigate his idea, Becquerel first wrapped a photographic plate with black paper to prevent sunlight from exposing it. Then he put a fluorescent uranium mineral on the plate and placed it in sunlight. When developed, the photographic plate showed the image of the uranium mineral, even though the plate had been wrapped in black paper. Becquerel incorrectly assumed that X rays produced by the fluorescing uranium had exposed the photographic plate.

Since he was unable to repeat the experiment because of cloudy weather, Becquerel put the uranium and the photographic plates away in a closed drawer for several days. By chance, he decided to develop the plates before continuing the experiment. Since the uranium had not been exposed to sunlight, he did not expect to see anything. Imagine Becquerel's surprise when instead of blank plates, he found strong images of the uranium mineral.

Radiation   After conducting many more experiments, Becquerel determined that radiation was coming from the uranium itself and had nothing to do with fluorescence. **Radiation** is a general term for energy that is emitted from a source and travels through space. Becquerel found that the radiation was emitted steadily in all directions. Furthermore, he did not detect any chemical reactions or change in mass. As a result of his experiments, Becquerel concluded that the radiation emitted by uranium was a new phenomenon—radioactivity. **Radioactivity** is the spontaneous emission of

Objectives

Part 2

D. *Identify* the characteristics of alpha, beta, and gamma radiation.

E. *Analyze* how Rutherford's atomic model explains the results of his gold foil experiment.

DO YOU KNOW?

Some radioactive compounds glow continuously in the dark. The hands and numerals of clocks and watches were often painted with such radioactive compounds until it was discovered that many of the workers who applied the radioactive compounds became ill from radiation poisoning.

Developing Skills

Students may apply these skills in their study of Part 2.

Forming models: Have students develop a model for the interaction of alpha, beta, and gamma radiation and charged plates.

Classifying: Have students classify alpha, beta, and gamma radiation by penetrating power and according to deflection by charged plates.

≡ FOCUS

Activate Prior Knowledge

The day before you begin Part 2 of Chapter 8, ask students to make a list of scientific models in other fields of science. Discuss these in class the next day. Emphasize that models are still in the process of development and revision as new experimental data accumulate.

Examples may include models of our universe, evolution, the human brain, weather phenomena, or the events leading to an earthquake. How many of the models had a religious or philosophical basis before the advent of modern science?

DEMONSTRATION

The Discovery of Radioactivity

Dip a water color brush in a 0.05*M* solution of $AgNO_3$ and flick the solution several times on two pieces of white paper.

⚠ **CAUTION: Silver nitrate is poisonous and corrosive to skin and eyes. Wash any spills or splashes with plenty of water. Everyone must wear safety goggles, lab aprons, and gloves.** Place a large irregular flat rock on one sheet

and put it by the window sill. Place the other in a closed drawer. Have students compare and explain the differences they observe the next day. If both papers had been put in the drawer with a piece of uranium ore, how would the results differ? For disposal, rinse the $AgNO_3$ onto a piece of paper. Dry the paper. Give the contaminated sheets of paper to a waste disposal contractor.

PART 2
Section 8.6

TEACH

Teaching Strategy

Radiation

Radioactivity is mentioned very briefly here because it was directly involved in Rutherford's gold foil experiment (Section 8.6). Chapter 9 deals with radioactivity in more detail. If you choose to skip Chapter 9, you may want to introduce nuclear decay at this time. Nuclear equations can be introduced with Sections 8–9 and 8–10, when students have a better understanding of the structure of the atom.

Videodisc Connections

37247 to 38383, side 1
Alpha, beta, and gamma rays
(movie)

8714 to 10582, side 1
Rutherford's gold foil experiment
(movie)

DO YOU KNOW?

Many problems in science are interrelated. Rutherford's work required a way to detect alpha radiation. Detecting radiation became extremely important after it was recognized as potentially hazardous. Rutherford's assistant, Hans Geiger, invented the Geiger counter—one of many instruments that detect and measure amounts of radiation.

radiation from the nucleus of an atom. (You will learn about the nucleus in Section 8.7.)

Becquerel's discoveries immediately sparked a search for other radioactive elements. As a result of much painstaking effort, the French scientists Marie and Pierre Curie discovered two new radioactive elements—radium and polonium. By 1900, three different types of radiation emitted by radioactive elements were identified— alpha, beta, and gamma—named after the first three letters of the Greek alphabet.

Types of radiation **Alpha radiation** consists of rapidly moving helium ions that have no electrons and are positively charged. Such helium ions are called alpha particles. Most alpha particles are emitted at about one tenth the speed of light. (The speed of light is 3×10^8 meters per second.) **Beta radiation** consists of electrons emitted at very high speeds, often approaching the speed of light. Because of their tremendous speed, these electrons have much higher kinetic energy than the electrons produced in cathode-ray tubes. **Gamma radiation** is a form of electromagnetic radiation similar to, but more energetic than, X rays. All electromagnetic radiation, including gamma radiation, travels through empty space at the speed of light, has no mass, and has no electric charge. You will learn more about electromagnetic radiation in Chapter 10.

These three types of radiation can be distinguished by their ability to penetrate matter. Alpha particles have limited penetrating ability; they can be stopped by a thin sheet of paper or clothing. Beta radiation is stopped by a few millimeters of aluminum. Gamma radiation penetrates the farthest; several centimeters of lead, or an even greater thickness of concrete, will stop most gamma rays.

Concept ✔ Check

Briefly explain the experiment that led to the discovery of radioactive materials.

8.6 Rutherford's Gold Foil Experiment

Ernest Rutherford recognized that alpha particles could be used to probe the atom. In 1909, Rutherford and his colleagues designed an experiment to test Thomson's model of the atom. Their experimental setup is illustrated in Figure 8-8. Rutherford used alpha particles to bombard targets made of thin sheets of gold, platinum, copper, and tin foil. A source of alpha particles—such as radioactive radium or polonium—was placed in a cavity inside a lead block. Since lead absorbs alpha particles, only those particles emitted in the direction of the small opening escaped. In this way, a narrow beam of alpha particles was directed at the foil target. A fluorescent screen was placed around the target in order to detect the alpha

DEMONSTRATION
Rutherford's Gold Foil Experiment

Hold up a tissue a few meters in front of the chalkboard and ask students to imagine several sheets of tissue there. If a bb gun shoots toward the chalkboard, the tissue would not deflect the pellets. Crumple the tissue into a small sphere and ask students to imagine the sphere a thousand times smaller. (The other pieces of tissue would be crumpled similarly.) If the bb gun shoots at the tissue now, most of the pellets would pass right by. But it is now possible that a pellet could strike a tissue wad and bounce back toward the bb gun.

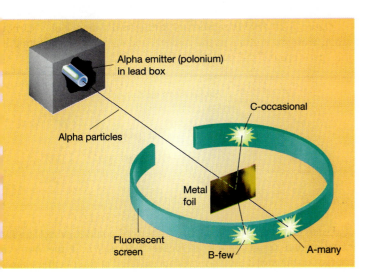

Alpha emitter (polonium) in lead box

Alpha particles

C-occasional

Metal foil

Fluorescent screen

B-few

A-many

Figure 8-8 *Rutherford bombarded metal foils with alpha particles emitted by radioactive polonium. Most particles were not deflected (point A); a few were deflected by small angles (point B); occasionally large-angle deflections occurred that could not be explained by Thomson's atomic model (point C).*

Teaching Strategy

The Rutherford Atom

More than 99.9 percent of atoms is empty space. Use the following analogies to illustrate how they can appear to be solid.

■ A soccer goalie who remains motionless would be easy to score upon. A goalie who moves around presents an almost impenetrable, "solid" surface.

■ A 1-cm wide flat propeller 20 cm long is turning incredibly fast in a horizontal plane. The propeller occupies only about 6 percent of the space (20 cm^2/314 cm^2 = 0.064 = 6%). Yet, if marbles were dropped on it they would bounce up as if the space were occupied by a solid.

particles after they had hit the target. Like the electrons in cathode rays, alpha particles also produce a small flash of light when they strike a fluorescent screen.

Rutherford's expectations, based on Thomson's model of the atom, are illustrated in Figure 8-9. The positively charged alpha particles should have been uniformly repelled by the evenly distributed positive charges in the atoms. These results would mean that the alpha particles should pass through the metal foil with little or no deflection from their original path. Indeed, Rutherford observed that most of the alpha particles passed straight through the metal foil, hitting the fluorescent screen at point A. Some alpha particles were deflected at small angles, striking the screen slightly off-center at points such as point B. The surprising result was that a few alpha particles were deflected at very large angles, striking the screen at points like point C. Rutherford was amazed at this result. He described his surprise in a lecture given some years later. "It was about as believable as if you had fired a 15-inch shell at a piece of tissue paper, and it came back and hit you."

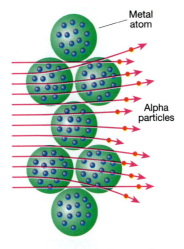

Metal atom

Alpha particles

Figure 8-9 *Using Thomson's atomic model as a guide, Rutherford expected the alpha particles to pass through the atoms of the metal foil almost undisturbed. (The blue spheres represent electrons distributed throughout each atom of metal.)*

8.7 The Rutherford Atom

Thomson's model of the atom failed to explain the deflection of alpha particles through large angles. Rutherford realized that the only reasonable explanation that could account for these large deflections was that an atom must contain a very small, dense center of positive charge. This center, called the **nucleus,** contains the atom's protons. Rutherford proposed that all of the positive charge of the atom and more than 99.9 percent of its mass are located in the nucleus. He further suggested that the electrons in an atom moved around the nucleus like bees around a hive.

Guided Practice

Review the Concept Check question on page 272 with students. Answers can be found in Appendix E on page 808.

Reteaching Idea

To crystallize your students' understanding of the Rutherford atom and to correct any misconceptions, divide your class into teams and challenge them to generate the longest possible lists of correct adjectives or phrases to describe the nucleus of an atom and the electrons of an atom. Have a member of each team put their lists on the chalkboard and have the class compare them, crossing out any entries that they decide are not correct. For the nucleus, expect descriptions such as tiny, dense, hard, positive, contains protons, takes up very little space in the atom; and for the electron, tiny, moving, negative, attracted to the nucleus.

≡CLOSE

Summing Up Main Ideas

Make a chart that summarizes the characteristics of alpha, beta, and gamma forms of radiation. Include the speed at which they travel, what they consist of, their ability to penetrate matter, and their charge. What characteristics made them ideal as tools to study the structure of the atom? How did knowledge of radioactive particles specifically contribute to Rutherford's atomic model?

Assign the Part Review questions.

Evaluating Skills

These skills are evaluated in the Part Review questions indicated. **Forming models: 6, 8; Determining main ideas: 8**

Figure 8-10 Right: *Rutherford proposed the dense center of an atom, called a nucleus. The electrons orbit in the space around the nucleus. (The size of the nucleus relative to the atom is greatly exaggerated in order to be visible.) Left: The occasional alpha particle that passes very close to a nucleus, or collides with a nucleus, is deflected by a large angle.*

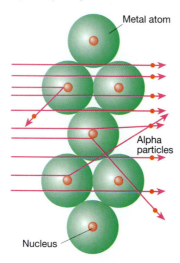

Metal atom

Alpha particles

Nucleus

PROBLEM·SOLVING
STRATEGY

*In the process of **verifying an answer** experimentally, Rutherford found results that could not be explained by Thomson's model, so this model had to be revised. (See Strategy, page 164.)*

Boxed numbers indicate questions that involve skills in interpretation, application, and analysis.

Figure 8-10 *(right)* represents Rutherford's model of a carbon atom, with six protons in the nucleus and six electrons orbiting in the space around the nucleus.

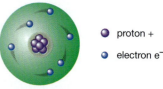

Rutherford's model

• proton +
• electron e⁻

1911

Using this model for an atom, Rutherford could now explain his experimental results. Look at Figure 8-10 *(left)*. If the positive charges of the target atoms were concentrated at their centers, most alpha particles would never come close enough to a nucleus to be deflected at all. Some alpha particles passing near a nucleus would be slightly deflected. Occasionally, however, an alpha particle would collide almost head-on with a nucleus. These alpha particles would deflect through very large angles.

By measuring the fraction of alpha particles deflected at each angle, Rutherford was able to calculate the size of the nucleus. The actual diameter of a nucleus is only 1/100 000 the diameter of an atom—about 10^{-15} meter. Consider this analogy—if the nucleus of a hydrogen atom were the size of a Ping-Pong ball, the diameter of the atom would be about 2 kilometers!

Rutherford assumed that the electrons moved at high speeds around the nucleus. However, according to the laws of physics known at the time, orbiting electrons should radiate light, causing them to lose energy and spiral into the nucleus. In Chapter 10, you will learn how further discoveries resolved Rutherford's dilemma, leading to new and unexpected laws of physics and yet another model of the atom. The revision of models when new data are obtained is one of the most fundamental processes of science.

PART 2 REVIEW

6. Make a drawing to illustrate the paths of alpha, beta, and gamma radiation as they pass between two oppositely charged plates. Be sure to label the positive and negative plates.

7. What unexpected result did Rutherford's gold foil experiment produce?

8. According to Rutherford's atomic model, why is most of an atom's mass located in its nucleus?

PART 2 REVIEW
ANSWERS
■ **Keyed to Objectives**

D 6.

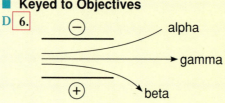

E 7. Some of the alpha particles bounced backwards.

E 8. A concentration of mass in a small region is required to make the alpha particles bounce backwards.

H I S T O R Y   O F   S C I E N C E

Atoms—From Philosophy to Science

It took 22 centuries to establish the concept of atoms and molecules. Scientific ideas often develop through discontinuous and indirect paths as ideas undergo rejection and revival over periods of time. The atomic theory is an example of this kind of development.

Around the year 400 B.C., the Greek philosopher Democritus theorized that all matter was composed of tiny, unseen particles, which he termed *atoms*, meaning "indivisible" in Greek. He proposed that atoms from different kinds of matter were different.

Twenty-one centuries later Robert Boyle proposed that gases were made up of tiny particles. But at the turn of the nineteenth century, it was John Dalton who revived Democritus' notions and promoted the concept that *all* matter consisted of these particles, or atoms. His idea differed from Democritus' in two significant ways. First, Democritus' approach would be described as philosophical, whereas Dalton's was empirical parallelism. Dalton explained the experimental results—those of Proust and Boyle—from the previous 150 years. Second, while Democritus had not attempted to describe the difference between different atoms, Dalton hypothesized the difference to be only one of mass.

Amadeo Avogadro, in 1811, introduced a new idea that further clarified the concept of atoms. Explaining the earlier works of Gay-Lussac and Ritter, Avogadro suggested that all gases having the same volume at the same temperature have the same number of particles. Avogadro is credited as the first chemist to make a distinction between atoms and molecules. Like Democritus' ideas, Avogadro's ideas suffered rejection by prominent chemists of his time—including Dalton—and he was ignored for almost half a century.

In the following years, chemists attempted to determine the composition of various substances. They tried to determine the relative proportions of the atoms that make up a substance, but they could not determine or agree upon precise chemical compositions. In 1860, the First International Chemical Congress convened to address this problem. At this meeting, the persuasive Italian chemist Stanislao Cannizzaro revived and championed Avogadro's ideas, observing that they could be used to determine the molecular masses and consequently the chemical formulas of various gases. Unfortunately Avogadro, who died in 1858, did not live to see his ideas accepted.

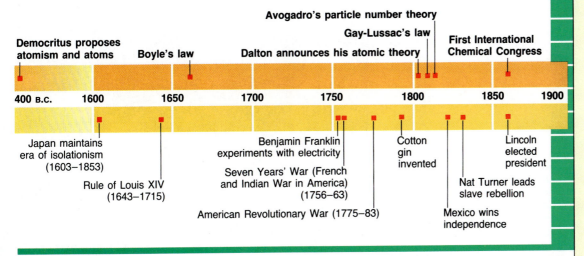

PART **3** **Atomic Number and Isotopes**

Developing Skills

Students may apply these skills in their study of Part 3.

Analyzing data: Have students use the data in Figure 8–14 to determine the number of protons and neutrons for all the isotopes of vanadium (V), strontium (Sr), and technetium (Tc).

Calculating: Have students use the data in Figure 8–14 to calculate the number of protons and neutrons and the mass number of the isotopes for zinc (Zn).

FOCUS

Activate Prior Knowledge

Part 3 of Chapter 8 discusses how neutrons were discovered by inference. Define the meaning of inference (the process of arriving at a conclusion by reasoning from evidence). Follow this by having students brainstorm a list of things they know exist, but cannot directly detect. Examples can be relatively concrete, such as knowing that an insect has eaten the edges of a chewed-up leaf, although no one actually saw this happen. Other examples may be abstract, such as students knowing they were once infants, although they have no conscious memory of that stage.

Objectives

Part 3

F. *Identify* the characteristics of subatomic particles.

G. *Distinguish* between atomic number and mass number.

H. *Determine* the number of protons, neutrons, and electrons in an isotope from its name or symbol.

Rutherford's atomic model suggested that atoms were made up of whole numbers of the subatomic particles—protons and electrons. However, some measurements of atomic masses could not be explained using this model. For example, a comparison of the charge and mass of different atoms indicated that the atomic masses of most atoms were approximately twice as large as expected, based on the mass of the protons thought to be present in them.

As early as 1920, Rutherford proposed that neutral particles with roughly the same mass as a proton existed in the nucleus of an atom. Indeed, the existence of such particles would account for the additional mass found in most atoms. However, detecting such neutral particles would be very difficult, since they would not be deflected by magnets or by charged plates, nor would they cause fluorescent screens to glow. In fact, the discovery of neutral particles in the atom is an example of discovery by inference.

8.8 The Neutron

In 1932, Irène and Frédéric Joliot-Curie performed experiments bombarding beryllium with alpha particles. They found that the beryllium emitted some kind of neutral radiation. If this radiation then struck a material containing hydrogen, such as paraffin wax, protons were emitted. The Joliot-Curies incorrectly assumed that the neutral radiation was gamma rays. By measuring the energy of the ejected protons, the Joliot-Curies calculated that the gamma rays must have a very high energy—about 50 MeV. (One MeV is equal to 1.6×10^{-13} J.)

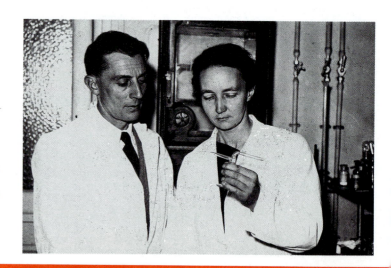

Figure 8-11 *Irène and Frédéric Joliot-Curie discovered in 1932 the particles that were predicted in 1923 by Rutherford to be neutrons. You will read more about Irène Joliot-Curie in Chapter 10.*

PART **3**

Section 8.8 *continued*

≡ T E A C H

Teaching Strategy

The Neutron

Have students draw models of a proton, neutron, and electron. Note the great difference in mass of an electron versus a proton or neutron.

It was difficult to understand how such high energy gamma rays could be produced when the energy of the bombarding alpha particles was only about 5 MeV. To resolve this dilemma, the British scientist James Chadwick proposed that the neutral radiation was not gamma rays, but a new type of particle called a neutron. A **neutron** has approximately the same mass as a proton, but no electric charge. Like protons, neutrons are found in the nucleus of the atom. Chadwick calculated that neutrons would need energies of only about 5 MeV—roughly corresponding to the alpha particle energy—in order to account for the energy of the protons ejected from the paraffin wax. Chadwick is credited with discovering neutrons by inferring their existence from other experimental evidence.

After Chadwick's discovery, scientists understood that the additional mass found in most atoms comes from the neutrons present in the nucleus. If an atom has approximately equal numbers of neutrons and protons, then its mass will be about twice as large as an atom with only protons. Rutherford's model of the atom was revised to incorporate Chadwick's discovery of the neutron.

Sodium atom
Na

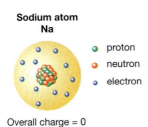

○ proton
○ neutron
○ electron

Overall charge = 0

Figure 8-12 *A sodium atom has 11 protons, 12 neutrons, and 11 electrons. Its net charge is zero.*

By 1932, the structure of the atom included protons and neutrons in the nucleus, with electrons occupying the space around the nucleus as shown in Figure 8-12. The number of protons equaled the number of electrons, so the atom as a whole had zero electric charge. Although physicists have discovered that protons and neutrons are actually composed of even smaller particles, for now it is sufficient to think of the atom in terms of three basic particles—protons, neutrons, and electrons. Table 8-1 compares the relative charges and masses of these three subatomic particles.

TABLE 8-1

Characteristics of Subatomic Particles			
	Electron	**Proton**	**Neutron**
Symbol	e	p	n
Relative charge	1−	1+	0
Relative mass (amu)	0.000549	1.007	1.009
Actual mass (g)	9.11×10^{-28}	1.673×10^{-24}	1.675×10^{-24}

The discovery of the structure of the atom was a progression of ideas and experiments carried out by many people. Figure 8-13 highlights some of the important events in this progression.

8.9 Atomic Number and Mass Number

In order to understand the basic chemical and physical properties of the elements, chemists must know the number of protons, neutrons, and electrons in the atoms that they investigate. To keep track of the numbers of different subatomic particles in each atom, chemists specify two quantities—atomic number and mass number.

Atomic number From his experiments with cathode-ray tubes, J. J. Thomson determined that the hydrogen nucleus has the smallest positive charge, corresponding to one proton. The nuclei of other elements have larger positive charges corresponding to a larger number of protons. For example, a calcium nucleus has 20 protons and carries a 20+ charge. The **atomic number** of an element is defined as the number of protons in the nucleus of one of its atoms. (The atomic number also equals the number of electrons in a neutral atom.) The atomic number of hydrogen is 1; the atomic number of helium is 2; for lithium it is 3; and so on. Elements are ordered in the periodic table according to their increasing atomic numbers.

A careful look at the periodic table shows that no two elements have the same atomic number. In fact, the atomic number defines an element. For example, silver's atomic number is 47. All atoms of silver have 47 protons in their nuclei. An additional proton

Figure 8-13 *The development of early models of the atom depended on the work of many people.*

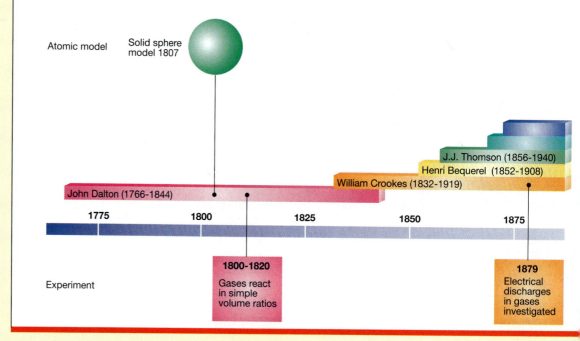

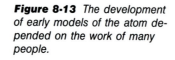

changes the element from silver to cadmium. Remember that for an atom to be neutral, the number of electrons must equal the number of protons. Thus a silver atom has 47 protons and 47 electrons.

Mass number Look again at the periodic table. Notice that from one element to the next, the atomic numbers increase by one. (This corresponds to one additional proton in the atoms of the element.) However, the atomic masses of elements increase by amounts greater than one. This is largely due to the neutrons in the nucleus. As you learned in Section 8.8, all atoms can contain neutrons in their nuclei. Neutrons add mass to a nucleus but do not change its charge. The total number of protons and neutrons in an atom's nucleus is called its **mass number.** (Generally, the actual atomic mass of an isotope, as expressed in atomic mass units, is not equal to its mass number.)

The mass number and the atomic number can be included in the symbol of an element. By convention, the atomic number is written as a subscript at the lower left of the symbol. The mass number is written as a superscript at the upper left of the symbol.

CONNECTING CONCEPTS

Models The nature of models in science varies. While the ideal gas law is mathematical, the early atomic models are visual. Yet each serves as a tool for understanding experimental observations.

Concept ✔ Check

If an atom of palladium could be changed to an atom of silver, which subatomic particles must be changed?

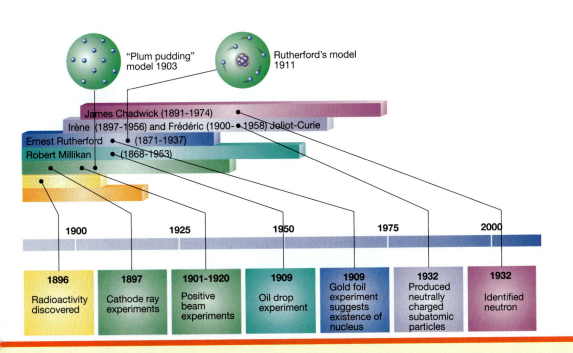

"Plum pudding" model 1903

Rutherford's model 1911

James Chadwick (1891-1974)

Irène (1897-1956) and Frédéric (1900-1958) Joliot-Curie

Ernest Rutherford (1871-1937)

Robert Millikan (1868-1953)

| 1900 | 1925 | 1950 | 1975 | 2000 |

1896	**1897**	**1901-1920**	**1909**	**1909**	**1932**	**1932**
Radioactivity discovered	Cathode ray experiments	Positive beam experiments	Oil drop experiment	Gold foil experiment suggests existence of nucleus	Produced neutrally charged subatomic particles	Identified neutron

Teaching Strategy

Isotopes

Have students use the data in Table 8–2 to write the symbols for the isotopes of all the diatomic elements.

PROBLEM-SOLVING STRATEGY

*By **using what you know** about atomic numbers and mass numbers, you should be able to derive this equation when you need it without memorizing it. (See Strategy, page 58.)*

CONNECTING CONCEPTS

Structure and Properties of Matter Most discoveries in science are interrelated. For example, the discovery of radioactivity provided the tools necessary to probe the structure of the nucleus.

For example, consider a potassium atom, which contains 19 protons, 19 electrons, and 20 neutrons. The chemical symbol for potassium is K. Its atomic number is 19, and its mass number is 19 plus 20, or 39. Thus the symbol for a potassium atom may be written as

atomic number

$$^{39}_{19}\text{K}$$

mass number

If the mass number and the atomic number of an atom are known, the number of neutrons present can be calculated easily using this formula.

mass number − atomic number = number of neutrons

The mass number of an atom of cobalt is 60. The atomic number of cobalt listed on the periodic table is 27. Thus the number of neutrons present in this atom of cobalt is 60 − 27, or 33.

8.10 Isotopes

Dalton had assumed that all atoms of the same element had identical masses. However, his assumption was incorrect, since atoms of the same element may contain different numbers of neutrons and therefore have different masses. (Remember that it is only the number of protons that determines an atom's identity.) For example, all atoms of lithium contain three protons; but some atoms of lithium contain three neutrons, while others contain four neutrons. These two forms of lithium are called isotopes. **Isotopes** are atoms of the same element that contain different numbers of neutrons and consequently have different atomic masses. Many elements occur in nature in several different isotopic forms. Hydrogen has two naturally occurring isotopes. Tin has ten naturally occurring isotopes—more than any other element.

Since the atomic number is always the same for any given element, it may be omitted when writing the symbol for an isotope. However, the mass numbers of different isotopes are not the same and must be retained. For example, there are two isotopes of lithium with 3 and 4 neutrons, respectively. These isotopes may be symbolized as $^{6}_{3}\text{Li}$ and $^{7}_{3}\text{Li}$, or they may be written as lithium-6 and lithium-7.

Table 8-2 is a partial list of elements and their naturally occurring isotopes. Different isotopes of each element are found in varying amounts as indicated by their percent of abundance in nature. The atomic mass of an element listed on the periodic table is an average based on the percent abundances of all the isotopes of that element. For example, the atomic mass of carbon is listed as 12.0111 amu. Because the average sample of carbon contains 1.11 percent carbon-13, the average atomic mass is slightly larger than 12.0000 amu, the mass of carbon-12.

Myths and Misconceptions

Students often mistakenly think that:
■ only certain elements have isotopes;
■ since they differ in atomic mass, isotopes should exhibit different chemical properties, and
■ isotopes are not considered atoms of the same element.
Stress that all elements have isotopes, but not all isotopes occur naturally. For 21 elements, the isotopes must be created artificially. Also,

although these atoms differ in the number of neutrons, they behave the same chemically because they have the same number of electrons. Since they have the same electron number, they are considered atoms of the same element. Ask students if they think isotopes of the same element have different physical properties?

TABLE 8-2

Components of Some Common Stable Isotopes

Isotope	Atomic number	Number of neutrons	Mass number	Mass of atom (in amu)	Nuclear charge	Number of electrons in neutral atom	Abundance in nature (%)
Hydrogen-1	1	0	1	1.0078	1+	1	99.985
Hydrogen-2	1	1	2	2.0140	1+	1	0.015
Helium-3	2	1	3	3.0160	2+	2	1.3×10^{-4}
Helium-4	2	2	4	4.0026	2+	2	~100
Lithium-6	3	3	6	6.0151	3+	3	7.5
Lithium-7	3	4	7	7.0160	3+	3	92.5
Beryllium-9	4	5	9	9.0122	4+	4	100
Boron-10	5	5	10	10.0129	5+	5	19.6
Boron-11	5	6	11	11.0093	5+	5	80.4
Carbon-12	6	6	12	12.0000*	6+	6	98.89
Carbon-13	6	7	13	13.0034	6+	6	1.11
Nitrogen-14	7	7	14	14.0031	7+	7	99.64
Nitrogen-15	7	8	15	15.0001	7+	7	0.36
Oxygen-16	8	8	16	15.9949	8+	8	99.76
Oxygen-17	8	9	17	16.9991	8+	8	0.04
Oxygen-18	8	10	18	17.9992	8+	8	0.20
Chlorine-35	17	18	35	34.9689	17+	17	75.77
Chlorine-37	17	20	37	36.9659	17+	17	24.23

* By definition, the mass of carbon-12 is exactly 12.0000—the standard for atomic masses.

Concept ✓ Check

Explain why the mass number varies for isotopes while the atomic number stays the same.

Of approximately 1500 known isotopes, only 264 are stable, meaning that they do not emit radiation spontaneously. The stability of an isotope depends partly on the number of neutrons in the nucleus relative to the number of protons present. Figure 8-14 is a graph comparing the number of neutrons (the y-axis) to the number of protons (the x-axis) present in the nuclei of different isotopes. The black dots indicate nuclei that are nonradioactive, or stable. Some isotopes are unstable, or radioactive. In order to become

PART 3

Section 8.10 continued

Guided Practice

Review the Concept Check questions on pages 279 and 280 with students. Answers can be found in Appendix E on page 808.

Reteaching Idea

If your students need to deal with the symbols for isotopes in a more concrete way, have them draw diagrams of B-10 and B-11. Have them use both sides of a full sheet of paper. On one side, have them represent the boron atom by a circle with a diameter equal to the full width of the paper (8.5 in.). Refer them to Table 8–2 and ask them to represent the nucleus of B-10 by drawing 5 neutrons (open circles) and 5 protons (shaded circles). The cluster of neutrons and protons should have a diameter no greater than 1/4 in. Have them add the electrons and then represent what they have drawn by the symbol for the B-10 isomer. On the reverse side of the paper, repeat the process for B-11. Ask students if they think the scale of their diagrams is proportional to an actual atom; then give them the approximate diameters for an atom (10^{-10} m) and nucleus (10^{-14} m). They can calculate that the actual diameter of an atom is 10 000 times greater than the diameter of a nucleus, whereas in their diagrams, the diameter of the atom is only 34 times greater than that of the nucleus. Ask how wide a sheet of paper would have to be to accommodate a scale diagram with a 1/4 inch nucleus (approximately 208 feet!).

⊟ CLOSE

Summing Up Main Ideas

Make a chart describing the characteristics of the three main subatomic particles. Include the particle's relationship to an element's atomic number, mass number, or atomic mass.

PART 3 REVIEW

Assign the Part Review questions.

Evaluating Skills

These skills are evaluated in the Part Review questions indicated.
Comparing/Contrasting: 9, 12;
Determining main ideas: 10, 13;
Calculating: 11, 14, 15

stable, radioactive isotopes decay by emitting radiation. Some radioactive nuclei contain too many neutrons relative to the number of protons (indicated by red dots), and others contain too few neutrons relative to the number of protons (indicated by blue dots). Some have both too many neutrons and too many protons (indicated by green dots). Unstable isotopes and radioactivity will be discussed in detail in Chapter 9.

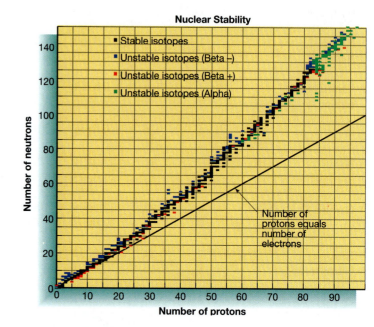

Figure 8-14 *This graph indicates the ratio of neutrons to protons in different atoms. In stable atoms with low atomic numbers, the number of protons is approximately equal to the number of neutrons. However, as the number of protons increases, the number of neutrons needed to maintain stability increases.*

PART 3 REVIEW

9. List two ways that a proton differs from an electron.

10. Which subatomic particle determines a specific element?

11. What is the mass number of an element that contains 20 protons and 22 neutrons?

12. How do the isotopes of oxygen listed in Table 8-2 differ from one another?

13. Write the symbol for calcium-41, including its mass number and atomic number.

14. An atom of zinc has an atomic number of 30 and a mass number of 65. How many protons, electrons, and neutrons are present in this zinc atom?

15. How many neutrons are in the following atoms?
   a. $^{108}_{47}Ag$ c. $^{94}_{40}Zr$
   b. $^{53}_{24}Cr$ d. $^{92}_{40}Zr$

Boxed numbers indicate questions that involve skills in interpretation, application, and analysis.

PART 3 REVIEW

ANSWERS

■ **Keyed to Objectives**

F **9.** Protons are positive in charge, while electrons are negative.
Protons have nearly 2000 times more mass.

H **10.** the proton

H **11.** 42

G **12.** They have different numbers of neutrons and different atomic masses.

G **13.** $^{41}_{20}Ca$

H **14.** 30 protons, 30 electrons (if atom is neutral), 35 neutrons

H **15. a.** 61
   b. 29
   c. 54
   d. 52

R E S E A R C H & T E C H N O L O G Y

Mass Spectrometer

J. J. Thomson's work with cathode-ray tubes laid the foundation for the development of an instrument, called a mass spectrometer, that can measure the masses of different isotopes of an element with great precision. A mass spectrometer works according to principles that are already familiar to you from your study of cathode-ray tubes.

There are two distinct regions in a mass spectrometer. In region A, a pair of charged plates produces an electric field, while magnets simultaneously produce a magnetic field perpendicular to the electric field. When a beam of ions passes through region A, the electric and magnetic fields bend the paths of ions with different velocities and by different amounts. Only ions with the same velocity will pass through the small hole at point P into region B. Region A is known as a velocity selector because it selects from the original ion beam only those ions having identical velocities.

In region B, there is only a magnetic field, which bends the ions into a circular path. Since all of the ions in the beam entering region B have the same velocities and charges, the radius of the curved path of any given ion depends only upon its mass. Thus, when an element is analyzed in a mass spectrometer, its different isotopes are separated because of their different masses.

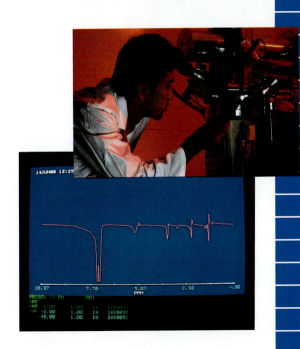

In older mass spectrometers, the radii of the curved paths were measured by locating the points at which the different isotopes struck a photographic plate. The intensity of the different lines on the photograph indicated the abundance of each isotope.

In modern mass spectrometers, the points of impact are recorded electronically. Information about the isotopes' masses and their abundances are directly displayed on a computer screen. Besides making precise measurements of isotope masses, mass spectrometers are used to separate isotopes and to analyze the chemical composition of unknown materials by determining which isotopes they contain. Applications of the mass spectrometer range from analyzing the components of air pollution to searching the Martian soil for traces of life. Archaeologists can use mass spectrometers to date archaeological objects, since the relative abundances of isotopes has varied slightly through the centuries.

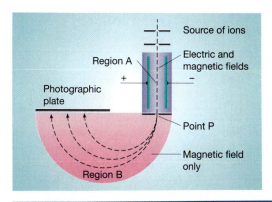

Source of ions

Region A

Electric and magnetic fields

+   −

Photographic plate

Point P

Magnetic field only

Region B

Decay: A Game for Radioactive Species

Estimated Time: (45 minutes)

Process Skills

Describing
Comparing/Contrasting
Determining cause and effect

Preparation

■ Materials

(for a class of 24, working in groups of 4)
6-sided dice (6); markers (one per person); Decay Cards, best placed on card stock and laminated (6); Tables of Radioactive Particles or Rays, or use the one in the book on page 285 (24)

Guiding the Investigation

■ Procedural Hints

For best results, try to seat the students in groups of four at a table. The Decay Cards should be lined up and properly put together. You may want to laminate the cards for future use. This will preserve them and also prevent students from writing on them.

Explain that the reason for moving the markers is more important than the movement of the marker. Beans, corn kernels, and small buttons all make excellent markers. All will allow four to fit in the space on the Decay Card at the beginning of the game.

To be sure that students know A and Z numbers before starting the game, encourage student dialogue.

L a b o r a t o r y

Investigation

Decay: A Game for Radioactive Species

Many elements disintegrate through radioactive decay. By emitting either an *alpha particle* or a *beta particle,* a *parent nuclide* will fall apart to form a new element or isotope, known as a *daughter nuclide.* If the daughter nuclide is stable, the radioactive chain will end. If not, the daughter will disintegrate further, forming a second new element or isotope. The sequence continues until a *stable* species is produced.

O b j e c t i v e s

Investigate a fundamental radioactive decay series that starts with an unstable nucleus and ends with a stable nucleus.

Determine what happens to the atomic number (Z) and the mass number (A) when an alpha particle is emitted.

Determine what happens to the atomic number (Z) and the mass number (A) when a beta particle is emitted.

■ Materials

☐ 1 6-sided die per team
☐ 1 marker for each player
☐ 1 Decay Card per team
☐ 1 Table of Radioactive Particles or Rays per person

1. Divide into groups of three or four. Each group should have a 6-sided die and a Decay Card. Each player should have a marker.

2. Place half of your Decay Card so that it lines up with the other half. When properly lined up, the 92 for atomic number (A) is in the upper right-hand corner, and the 206 for mass number (Z) is in the lower left-hand corner.

3. All player markers should be placed on the 92-Z and 238-A box at the beginning of the game. This appears in the upper right-hand corner of the Decay Card.

4. Each player rolls the die for a high roll. The person with the highest roll begins the game, after which rotation of turns is *counterclockwise* from the starter.

5. The starter begins play and follows these rules.

Roll	Play
1, 2	No radioactive decay; turn is over.
3, 4, 5	Beta decay occurs.
6	Alpha decay occurs.

6. For the die rolls that could result in decay, the player may move his or her marker only if the nucleus on which it resides undergoes that type of decay. A player's turn continues as long as radioactive decay continues to occur.

7. All members of the team consult the Radioactive Particles or Rays table on this page to see why movement is down or across or whatever. Alpha and Beta decay are highlighted on the table with heavier lines.

8. The radioactive decay winner is the first person on the team to arrive at the lower left-hand corner of the Decay Card at a spot with a stable nucleus.

9. Return all materials to the designated spot at the end of this investigation.

■ Conclusions

1. What does it mean for a nucleus to be radioactive?

2. Why does an alpha particle emission decrease the atomic number by two and decrease the mass by four?

3. Why does a beta particle emission raise the atomic number by one and leave the mass number the same?

Table of Radioactive Particles or Rays					
Symbol of Species	Name of Particle or Ray	Consequences of Addition		Consequences of Removal	
		Atomic Number (Z)	Mass Number (A)	Atomic Number (Z)	Mass Number (A)
$^{1}_{0}n$	neutron	no change	raise by 1	no change	lower by 1
$^{1}_{1}H$	proton	raise by 1	raise by 1	lower by 1	lower by 1
$^{0}_{-1}e\ \beta-$	beta particle	lower by 1	no change	raise by 1	no change
$^{0}_{+1}e\ \beta+$	positron	raise by 1	no change	lower by 1	no change
$^{4}_{2}He\ \alpha$	alpha particle	raise by 2	raise by 4	lower by 2	lower by 4
γ	gamma ray	no change/ creates instability	no change/ creates instability	no change/ creates stability	no change/ creates stability

Data Analysis
The Table of Radioactive Particles or Rays should be used to explain the general nature of radioactive decay. You may want to follow this laboratory investigation with a short discussion of some of the other natural decay schemes.

Conclusions

1. The word *radioactive* indicates an unstable nucleus, which reaches stability by emitting the appropriate particles or rays. See the Table of Radioactive Particles or Rays for particulars.

2. An alpha particle is a helium nucleus. When it is emitted from a nucleus, the mass number (A) is reduced by four units and the atomic number (Z) is reduced by two.

3. When a neutron changes into a proton, it emits a beta particle. This causes the transmutation of one element into another element with the same mass number (A) and a new atomic number (Z). Such a pair are called isobars. 24 Na and 24 Mg are isobars. Isobars are two different elements with the same mass number (A).

Chapter 8
Review
ANSWERS
begin on page
T291a.

Summary

The Discovery of Subatomic Particles

■ John Dalton proposed the first model of the atom. In his atomic model, an atom was an indivisible sphere with a uniform density throughout. He suggested that all atoms of the same element have the same mass and the same chemical behavior. Dalton also hypothesized that atoms of different elements always combine in fixed number ratios to produce specific compounds.

■ While studying electrical discharge in tubes containing gases at low pressure, Sir William Crookes found that beams composed of charged particles were produced. By measuring the deflection of these beams by magnetic and electric fields, J. J. Thomson was able to show that the particles were negatively charged, and he determined the ratio of their charge and mass. These negative particles are electrons.

■ Further study by Thomson showed that beams of positive particles were also formed in these tubes. The smallest positive particle was the hydrogen ion, later shown to be a proton. Thomson proposed a new atomic model, the plum-pudding model, in which electrons are evenly distributed throughout a sphere of positive charge in such a way that the atom is electrically neutral.

■ An ion is a particle that has either lost some of its electrons or gained additional electrons. As a result, an ion is an electrically charged atom or group of atoms.

■ Robert Millikan measured the size of the electric charge of an electron. The charge of the proton is equal to, but opposite that of an electron's. Millikan combined his results with J. J. Thomson's to calculate the masses of the electron and proton. He found that a proton's mass is 1836 times larger than an electron's mass.

Rutherford's Model of the Atom

■ While working with uranium in 1896, Henri Becquerel accidentally discovered that it emitted some kind of radiation. Radioactivity is the spontaneous emission of radiation from the nucleus of an atom.

■ By 1900, researchers had identified three types of radiation—alpha, beta, and gamma. Alpha radiation consists of positively charged, fast-moving helium atoms that have no electrons. Beta radiation consists of fast-moving electrons. Gamma radiation is a very energetic form of electromagnetic radiation with no electric charge and no mass.

■ Ernest Rutherford found that when alpha particles bombarded a target made of metal foil, some of the alpha particles were scattered through very large angles. To explain these results, Rutherford suggested that an atom has a densely packed center that contains all the positive charge and nearly all the mass of an atom. Rutherford called this center the nucleus.

Atomic Number and Isotopes

■ In 1932, James Chadwick proposed the existence of a third subatomic particle, the neutron, in order to explain the results of experiments that bombarded beryllium with alpha particles. Neutrons are found in the nuclei of most atoms; they have about the same mass as a proton, but no electric charge.

■ The atomic number of an element is the number of protons in the nucleus of one of its atoms. The mass number of an atom is the sum of the number of protons and the number of neutrons in the nucleus.

■ Atoms of the same element that have different numbers of neutrons, and therefore different atomic masses, are called isotopes. Many isotopes are radioactive and emit alpha or beta radiation in order to become more stable.

PROBLEM-SOLVING
▶ **S T R A T E G I E S**

Students apply these strategies in the following questions.

■ Factor-label method: 52, 53
■ Using what you know: 29, 34, 38, 51
■ Using similar problems: 52
■ Using patterns: 32, 33, 36, 37, 41, 42, 43, 44, 45, 46, 47, 48, 49, 50, 54
■ Using calculators: 52, 53
■ Verifying your answer: 52, 53

Chemically Speaking

alpha radiation 8.5
anion 8.3
anode 8.2
atomic number 8.9
beta radiation 8.5
cathode 8.2
cathode-ray tube 8.2
cation 8.3
electrode 8.2
electron 8.2

fluorescent 8.2
gamma radiation 8.5
isotopes 8.10
mass number 8.9
neutron 8.8
nucleus 8.7
proton 8.3
radiation 8.5
radioactivity 8.5

Concept Mapping

Using the method of concept mapping described at the front of the book, draw a concept map for the composition of the atom. Use the following concepts: *protons, neutrons, electrons, nucleus, atom, isotopes, ions, radioactivity, alpha radiation, beta radiation,* and *gamma radiation.*

Questions and Problems

THE DISCOVERY OF SUBATOMIC PARTICLES

A. Objective: Evaluate *the factors that influence the deflection of a charged particle.*

1. Imagine that a beam of calcium-40 ions and a beam of calcium-42 ions both pass through a magnetic field. Assume that the ions in each beam have the same velocities and charges. Which beam would be deflected more? Explain your reasoning.

2. Suppose that a beam passing between a pair of charged plates had some sulfur-32 ions with one extra electron and some sulfur-32 ions with two extra electrons. If all the ions had the same velocity, which particles would be deflected more? Explain your reasoning.

3. Which would be bent more by a magnet — a beam of sodium ions or a beam of potassium ions? Assume that all the ions have identical velocities and charges. Explain your reasoning.

4. Which would be bent more by a magnet — gamma rays or a beam of neutrons? Explain your reasoning.

5. Two beams of ions—germanium-74 and selenium-74—pass between a pair of charged plates. The ions have the same charge, but the velocity of the germanium ions is twice as large as the velocity of the selenium ions. Identify which beam will be deflected more and explain your reasoning.

6. Two beams of ions, one containing calcium-40 ions with a 1+ charge and the other containing argon-40 ions with a 1− charge, both travel at the same velocity. Explain how these two beams would be deflected if they passed through an electric field.

7. Make a drawing showing the deflection of these beams when passed between a pair of charged plates. Assume that all velocities are equal.
   a. sulfur-34 ions with a 2− charge and oxygen-16 ions with a 2−charge
   b. chromium-52 ions with a 2+ charge and chromium-52 ions with a 5+ charge
   c. chlorine-37 ions with a 1− charge and potassium-37 ions with a 1+ charge

B. Objective: Compare and contrast *the atomic models of Dalton and Thomson.*

8. List the experimental facts known to Thomson, but not known to Dalton, that led to the modification of Dalton's model of an atom.

9. Use Dalton's model of the atom to explain why sodium chloride is always 39.3 percent sodium and 60.7 percent chlorine by mass.

10. Use Dalton's model of the atom to explain why calcium chloride is always 36.1 percent calcium and 63.9 percent chlorine by mass.

Boxed numbers indicate questions that involve skills in interpretation, application, and analysis.

■ Breaking problems into manageable parts: 52

■ Making diagrams: 7, 12, 16, 22, 23, 28, 54

11. Which aspects of Dalton's model of the atom became outdated after Thomson's cathode-ray experiments?

12. Draw diagrams of the Thomson models of a boron atom and a fluorine atom.

C. Objective: **Differentiate** *between atoms and ions.*

13. How can a neutral atom become an ion with a charge of $2-$?

14. What subatomic change occurs when a neutral calcium atom becomes a calcium $2+$ ion?

15. Compare the composition of a neutral sodium atom with that of a sodium ion, Na^+.

16. Compare and contrast the subatomic particles contained in the following atoms or ions.
    a. a barium-137 atom and a barium-137 ion with a $2+$ charge
    b. a molybdenum-96 atom and a molybdenum-96 ion with a $6+$ charge
    c. a phosphorus-31 atom and a phosphorus-31 ion with a $3-$ charge

17. Identify the following ions as either cations or anions. Also indicate the number of electrons lost or gained from the neutral atoms.
    a. Cl^- b. Mg^{2+} c. S^{2-} d. Al^{3+}

RUTHERFORD'S MODEL OF THE ATOM

D. Objective: **Identify** *the characteristics of alpha, beta, and gamma radiation.*

18. List which of the three types of radiation—alpha, beta, or gamma—each of the following describes.
    a. is not deflected by a magnet
    b. has a negative charge
    c. moves with the greatest speed
    d. consists of ions
    e. is similar to light rays
    f. consists of the same particles as cathode rays

19. Compare and contrast the masses and charges of alpha, beta, and gamma radiation.

20. List the three types of radiation in order of decreasing penetrating ability.

E. Objective: **Analyze** *how Rutherford's atomic model explains the results of his gold foil experiment.*

21. List the two changes that Rutherford made in Thomson's model of the atom in order to explain why some alpha particles were deflected through very large angles.

22. Make a drawing of the Rutherford model of an atom of beryllium. Discuss the limitations of the drawing.

23. Make drawings of the Rutherford models of a fluorine-19 atom and a sodium-23 ion with a $1+$ charge.

24. Compare the number of fundamental particles in Dalton's atomic theory to the number of fundamental particles in Rutherford's model.

25. Describe the problem with Rutherford's model of the atom.

ATOMIC NUMBER AND ISOTOPES

F. Objective: **Identify** *the characteristics of subatomic particles.*

26. What observations led scientists to suspect that there must be neutral particles with about the same mass as protons in the nucleus of atoms?

27. Explain why most of an atom is empty space.

28. A proton beam, an electron beam, and a neutron beam pass between two charged plates. Assuming the velocities to be the same, draw a diagram showing the paths of each type of subatomic particle.

29. In less massive atoms, the ratio of neutrons to protons is about 1 to 1; while in more massive atoms, the ratio increases to 1.5 to 1. Considering the electric charges of these two subatomic particles, propose an explanation to account for this change in the ratio.

G. Objective: **Distinguish** *between atomic number and mass number.*

30. Calcium has five stable isotopes. How do these isotopes differ from one another? How are they similar?

31. Hydrogen-1 is the only isotope whose atomic number equals its mass number. What does that indicate about its composition?

32. An atom has 15 protons and 16 neutrons. What is the atomic number, the mass number, and the symbol of this element?

33. Write the symbol, including atomic number and mass number, for the following isotopes.
    a. helium-3
    b. helium-4
    c. nitrogen-13
    d. molybdenum-95
    e. uranium-238

34. How are chlorine-37 and calcium-40 similar?

35. Iodine-131 is a radioactive isotope often used in the treatment of thyroid disorders. Write the symbol for this element, including the atomic and mass numbers.

36. Copy and complete the table by filling in the symbol (including the atomic and mass numbers) for each isotope.

Isotope	Atomic number	Mass number	Symbol
magnesium	12	26	
iron	26	57	
antimony	51	123	

37. Copy and complete the table for the following isotopes.

Isotope	Atomic number	Mass number	Symbol
molybdenum		92	
	43	96	
			$^{55}_{25}Mn$

38. The following elements have only two naturally occurring isotopes. Use the average atomic mass listed on the periodic table to determine which isotope is more abundant. (Hint: The mass of an isotope is not the same as its mass number, but it is approximately equal to it.)
    a. iridium-191 and iridium-193
    b. vanadium-50 and vanadium-51
    c. antimony-121 and antimony-123
    d. thallium-203 and thallium-205
    e. silver-107 and silver-109

H. Objective: **Determine** *the number of protons, neutrons, and electrons in an isotope from its name or symbol.*

39. Cobalt-60 is used in radiation therapy to treat cancer. How many neutrons does each cobalt-60 atom contain?

40. Name three ways that isotopes differ from one another.

41. Neon in nature is 90.5 percent neon-20, 0.3 percent neon-21, and 9.2 percent neon-22. For each isotope, indicate the following.
    a. atomic number
    b. number of protons
    c. number of neutrons
    d. mass number
    e. nuclear charge

42. Copy and complete the table, assuming that each atom is neutral.

Symbol				P
Atomic number	36			
Mass number			235	32
Number of protons		25		
Number of neutrons	48	55		
Number of electrons			92	

43. Determine the number of protons, neutrons, and electrons in an ion of iodine-131 that has a charge of 1+.

COMPOSITION OF THE ATOM **289**

44. List the number of protons, neutrons, and electrons in a neutral atom of the following isotopes.
    a. boron-10
    b. boron-11
    c. chlorine-35
    d. chlorine-37

45. List the number of protons, neutrons, and electrons in a neutral atom of the following isotopes.
    a. $^{79}_{34}Se$
    b. $^{40}_{18}Ar$
    c. $^{133}_{55}Cs$
    d. $^{183}_{74}W$

46. List the number of protons, neutrons, and electrons in each of the following ions.
    a. $^{7}_{3}Li^{+}$
    b. $^{24}_{12}Mg^{2+}$
    c. $^{27}_{13}Al^{3+}$
    d. $^{31}_{15}P^{3-}$
    e. $^{127}_{53}I^{-}$

47. Suppose the discovery of a new element with two isotopes is announced. A research paper is published listing the isotopes as $^{265}_{106}X$ and $^{263}_{105}X$. What mistake has been made?

48. Copy the table below and fill in the missing information. Include the charge in the *Symbol* column.

Critical Thinking

SYNTHESIS WITHIN THE CHAPTER

49. Copy and complete the table for the composition of the following ions.

Symbol	Na		As	
Ion charge	1+		3−	
Number of protons		4		
Number of neutrons	12		42	10
Number of electrons		2		10
Atomic number				9
Mass number		9		

50. Elements in the periodic table are ordered according to increasing atomic number rather than increasing atomic mass. There are several places where the atomic number increases but the atomic mass decreases. Identify two of these places. Based on your understanding of atomic number, mass number, and isotopes, explain why these exceptions occur.

51. How many times more massive than an electron is an alpha particle? How many times more massive than a proton is an alpha particle?

Symbol	Number of protons	Number of neutrons	Number of electrons	Atomic number	Mass number
$^{34}_{16}S^{0}$		18	16		34
$_{31}Ga-$		40	31		
$^{107}_{-}Ag-$			47		
$^{182}_{-}$ _ −			74	74	
$^{56}_{-}$ _ −			23	26	
$_{8}$ _ −			10		16

SYNTHESIS ACROSS CHAPTERS

52. When the pressure of a gas in a cathode-ray tube is decreased to about 1×10^{-6} atm, cathode rays are no longer formed. At this point, how many molecules would there be in 1 liter of the gas, at 273 K?

53. Assume that the nucleus of a fluorine atom is a sphere with a radius of 5×10^{-13} cm. Calculate the density of a fluorine nucleus. Compare this density with the atomic density of iridium—the element whose density, 22.6 g/cm^3, is highest.

54. The table at the top of this page lists stable isotopes and the number of protons and neutrons in each isotope.

Element	Protons	Neutrons
Li	3	4
F	9	10
Ca	20	23
Se	34	43
Ba	56	79
Er	68	94
Re	75	110
Pb	82	126

a. Make a graph of the data by plotting the number of protons in each stable isotope along the x-axis and number of neutrons along the y-axis.

b. Make a best-fit straight line for the x-y coordinates to represent the data.

c. Determine the slope (to one place after the decimal) of the best-fit line (slope is $\triangle y / \triangle x$).

d. Describe the slope in words, using the value of the slope and the words *stable isotope, neutrons,* and *protons.*

e. What statement can you make about the relationship of numbers of protons to numbers of neutrons in stable isotopes?

Projects

55. Find a discarded television set (one that still produces a picture on the screen) and deflect the electron beam by placing a magnet near the screen. Run a plastic comb through your hair to see if the electron beam is also deflected by static electricity.

56. If an instrument that measures radiation is available, check the radiation levels of the following.
  a. a watch that glows in the dark
  b. a smoke detector
  c. a bunch of bananas

Research and Writing

57. Prepare a biographical report of one of the scientists mentioned in this chapter. Include background information not covered in the text about the scientist's experiments.

58. Find out how a television picture tube focuses and directs the beam of electrons in order to form the image that you see on the screen.

59. Winners of the Nobel Prize represent a very small portion of the scientific community. Scientists can work in many places, such as a water-treatment plant, an agricultural extension station, a university, a county health department, or local industries. Interview a scientist in your area and write a report about the person and his or her work.

60. Many different instruments are used to detect radiation. These include Geiger counters, cloud chambers, and scintillation detectors. Find out how these detectors work, which types of radiation they are sensitive to, and what discoveries they have made possible.

☐ Boxed numbers indicate questions that involve skills in interpretation, application, and analysis.

1. Calcium-40 would be deflected more because it has the smaller mass and all other factors are equal.

2. S^{2-} ions would be deflected more because they have a larger charge and all other factors are equal.

3. The beam of sodium ions would be bent more because sodium ions have less mass.

4. Neither are bent by a magnet because neither are charged particles.

5. The selenium ions are deflected more because they have a smaller velocity and therefore have less momentum.

6. Both beams would be bent by equal amounts but in opposite directions because they have equal masses, velocities and charges, but the charges are opposite in sign.

7. a.

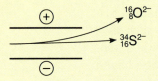

b.

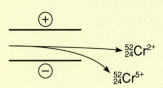

c.

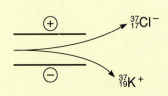

8. Atoms are not indivisible; they contain charged particles.

9. One atom of sodium with a mass of 22.99 combines with one atom of chlorine with a mass of 35.45, giving a total mass of 58.44. The percent composition of sodium is $22.99/58.44 \times 100 = 39.3\%$ and for chlorine $35.45/58.44 \times 100 = 60.7\%$.

10. One atom of calcium with a mass of 40.08 combines with two atoms of chlorine with a mass of 70.90 to give a total mass of 110.98. The percent composition of calcium is $40.08/110.98 \times 100 = 36.1\%$ and for chlorine $70.90/110.98 \times 100 = 63.9\%$.

11. Atoms were no longer considered indivisible, and the smallest particle was now an electron.

12.

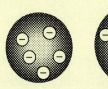

boron   fluorine

13. By gaining two electrons

14. Two electrons are lost.

15. Na^+ has ten electrons while a neutral sodium atom has eleven electrons.

16.

	Protons	Neutrons	Electrons
barium-137 atom	56	81	56
barium-137 ion	56	81	54
molybdenum-96 atom	42	54	42
molybdenum-96 ion	42	54	36
phosphorus-31 atom	15	16	15
phosphorus-31 ion	15	16	18

17. a. anion   1 electron gained
b. cation   2 electrons lost
c. anion   2 electrons gained
d. cation   3 electrons lost

18. a. gamma
b. beta
c. gamma
d. alpha
e. gamma
f. beta

19.

Radiation	Mass	Charge
alpha	4	2+
beta	1/1836	1−
gamma	0	0

20. gamma, beta, alpha

21. All of the positive charge and more than 99.9% of the mass of an atom is concentrated in a very small nucleus with a radius about 1/100 000 of the radius of the atom.

22.

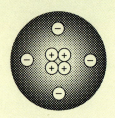

The nucleus is too large. If it were shown in the correct proportion, it would be too small to be seen.

23.

fluorine–19   sodium–23

24. Dalton proposed one fundamental particle for each element and Rutherford proposed two that are common to all elements.

25. The electron must be moving around the nucleus. However, a charge moving in a circle radiates energy. If that is true of the electron, it would lose energy and spiral into the nucleus, and the atom would collapse.

26. The masses of most atoms were twice as large as the mass of the number of protons they were thought to contain.

27. Electrons are extremely small but effectively occupy the space around the nucleus by appearing to be everywhere at once. Where the electron is not is empty space.

28.

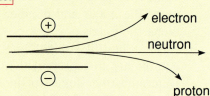

29. Neutrons are required to keep the like-charge protons from flying apart due to repulsive forces. As the number of protons increases, more neutrons are required.

30. All the isotopes of calcium have 20 protons in the nucleus and, if neutral, 20 electrons; but each nuclide has a different number of neutrons.

31. This isotope of hydrogen contains zero neutrons.

32. 15, 31, $^{31}_{15}P$

33. a. $^3_2$He

b. $^4_3$He

c. $^{13}_7$N

d. $^{95}_{42}$Mo

e. $^{238}_{92}$U

34. Both contain 20 neutrons in the nucleus.

35. $^{131}_{53}$I

36.

Isotope	Atomic number	Mass number	Symbol
magnesium	12	26	$^{26}_{12}$Mg
iron	26	57	$^{57}_{26}$Fe
antimony	51	123	$^{123}_{51}$Sb

37.

Isotope	Atomic number	Mass number	Symbol
molybdenum-92	42	92	$^{92}_{42}$Mo
technetium-96	43	96	$^{96}_{43}$Tc
manganese-55	25	55	$^{55}_{25}$Mn

38. a. iridium-193

b. vanadium-51

c. antimony-121

d. thallium-205

e. silver-107

39. 33

40. the number of neutrons, mass of atom, stability

41.

	Atomic number	Number of protons	Number of neutrons	Mass number	Nuclear charge
neon-20	10	10	10	20	10
neon-21	10	10	11	21	10
neon-22	10	10	12	22	10

42.

Symbol	Kr	Mn	U	P
Atomic number	36	25	92	15
Mass number	84	55	235	31
Number of protons	36	25	92	15
Number of neutrons	48	30	143	16
Number of electrons	36	25	92	15

43. 53 protons

78 neutrons

52 electrons

44.

	Protons	Neutrons	Electrons
a. boron-10	5	5	5
b. boron-11	5	6	5
c. chlorine-35	17	18	17
d. chlorine-37	17	20	17

45.

	Protons	Neutrons	Electrons
a.	34	45	34
b.	18	22	18
c.	55	78	55
d.	74	109	74

46.

Ion	Number of protons	Number of neutrons	Number of electrons
$^7_3$Li$^+$	3	4	2
$^{24}_{12}$Mg^{2+}	12	12	10
$^{27}_{13}$Al^{3+}	13	14	10
$^{31}_{15}$P^{3-}	15	16	18
$^{127}_{53}$I$^-$	53	74	54

47. Both elements should have the same atomic number—either 106 or 105.

48.

Symbol	Number of protons	Number of neutrons
$^{34}_{16}$S^0	16	18
$^{21}_{31}$GA^0	31	40
$^{107}_{47}$Ag^0	47	60
$^{182}_{74}$W^0	74	108
$^{56}_{26}$Fe^{3+}	26	30
$^{16}_8$O^{2-}	8	8

Number of electrons	Atomic number	Mass number
16	16	34
31	31	71
47	47	107
74	74	182
23	26	56
10	8	16

49.

Symbol	Na	Be	As	F
Ion charge	1+	2+	3-	1-
Number of protons	11	4	33	9
Number of neutrons	12	5	42	10
Number of electrons	10	2	36	10
Atomic number	11	4	33	9
Mass number	23	9	75	19

50. Cobalt is 58.93 and nickel is 58.69. Argon is 39.95 and potassium is 39.10. The stable isotopes of the first element have a greater average mass than those of the second.

51. 7290; 3.97

52. $PV = nRT$

$$n = \frac{PV}{RT} = \frac{(10^{-6}\ \text{atm})(1\ \text{L})}{(0.082\ \text{L·atm/mol·K})(273\ \text{K})}$$

$$n = 4.5 \times 10^{-8}\ \text{mol} \times 6.02 \times 10^{23}$$

molecules/mol = 2.7×10^{16} molecules

53. $V = \frac{4}{3}\pi r^3$

$= \frac{4}{3}\pi(5 \times 10^{-13}\ \text{cm})^3$

$= 5.2 \times 10^{-37}\ \text{cm}^3$

$m = 19\ \text{amu} \times 1.67 \times 10^{-24}\ \text{g/amu}$

$= 3.2 \times 10^{-23}\ \text{g}$

$D = \frac{3.2 \times 10^{-23}\ \text{g}}{5.2 \times 10^{-37}\ \text{cm}^3}$

$= 6 \times 10^{13}\ \text{g/cm}^3$

This density is 3×10^{12} times greater.

54.

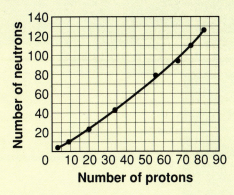

a. See graph.

b. See graph.

c. $m = 1.5$

d. The slope is the ratio of neutrons to protons for stable isotopes. There are 1.5 times as many neutrons as protons in stable isotopes.

e. Because the graph is a curve, there are more neutrons per proton as the number of protons increases.

CHAPTER 9
Planning Chart

Nuclear Chemistry

Investigations	Demonstrations	Texas Essential Elements★
Laboratory Manual 9–2 S In-text Investigation, page T318		**Content:** 13.1, 13.2, 13.4 **Process:** 10.2, 10.3, 10.4
Laboratory Manual 9–3 I		**Content:** 13.3, 13.4 **Process:** 10.1, 10.2, 10.4
Laboratory Manual 9–1 M		**Content:** 13.3 **Process:** 8.1, 10.1, 10.3, 10.4
		Content: 13.1 **Process:** 1.1, 1.2, 1.3, 4.3, 5.1, 5.2, 7.3, 8.2
		Process: 4.2, 4.3, 7.1, 10.1, 10.2, 10.3, 10.4
		Content: 13.3, 13.4 **Process:** 1.1, 5.1, 10.1, 10.2, 10.3, 10.4
KEY: **M**–*Microscale* **S**–*Structured* **I**–*Inquiry* **IM**–*Inquiry Microscale*		★*See pages T8–T11 for complete listing of Texas Essential Elements.*

9 Nuclear Chemistry

Chapter Rationale

Radioactivity is generally not well understood by people. Many think of radioactivity as a silent, deadly killer and have little knowledge of its uses and benefits. Chapter 9 provides a clear understanding of the causes, sources, and effects of radiation, both natural and artificial. Uses of radiation in understanding chemical processes and in the diagnosis and treatment of illness are described. Radioactive dating is explained, as well as its uses and limitations. Our technology and civilization depend on affordable sources of energy. We will need additional sources of energy as we exhaust easily obtainable fossil fuels. The pros and cons of nuclear power are presented to give students the background needed to participate in decision making.

About the Photograph

The Djenne/Mopti people of the twelfth century lived along the Niger River in present-day Mali. This sculpture is exhibited at the Detroit Institute of Arts in Detroit, Michigan. The thermoluminescence dating technique used to determine the artifact's age measures light emission as a sample of the artifact is heated from 350°C to 450°C on an electric heating plate. The amount of emitted radiation is a function of the age of the artifact. The theory behind thermoluminescence suggests that the number of electrons trapped in the structure of a material such as pottery, bone, or teeth increases with time. Heating excites the trapped electrons causing emission of radiation.

Chapter Planning Hints

Plan to complete the chapter, Lab Investigation, and Chapter Review in four to seven class sessions.

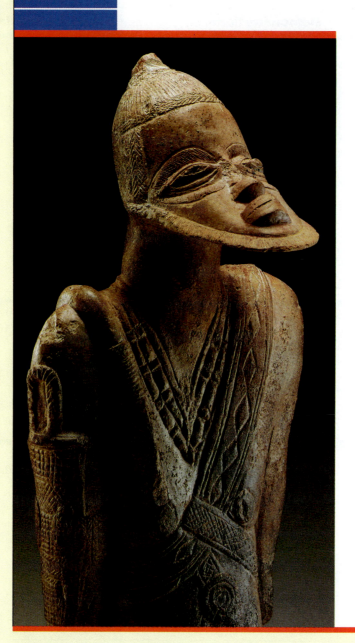

There are a variety of methods available for determining the age and composition of an artifact. This twelfth-century African sculpture from the Djenne/Mopti people was dated using a technique called thermoluminescence. In this chapter you will learn how objects are dated using radioactivity.

Myths and Misconceptions

Students may believe that a radioactive substance and radiation are the same thing. For example, they may think that irradiated food is radioactive, or that a person becomes radioactive by exposure to large doses of X rays. This misconception may be the result of inaccurate media reports about radioactivity. An accurate knowledge of nuclear chemistry is important in understanding radioactivity. Start a discussion of radioactivity by asking students for their ideas about how radiation affects them. Emphasize that radiation may cause damage to biological systems, but those systems do not become radioactive unless they are contaminated with radioactive elements. For example, food might *(continued on page T293)*

PART **1** Exploring Radioactivity

The atomic blasts that brought an end to World War II also brought with them the hope for cheap, clean energy for peaceful uses. The energy stored in the nucleus of an atom was immediately apparent; however, many of the long-term dangers were not. Today the use of nuclear reactions has tremendous impact on your life. At some power plants, nuclear reactions are used in fission reactors that produce electricity. Hospitals and research laboratories routinely use radioactive materials to diagnose diseases, treat some forms of cancer, and investigate scientific problems. How does radiation exposure to these sources compare with exposure to other sources that occur naturally? Some of these procedures generate hazardous radioactive waste. How can this hazardous material be stored safely? How can you assess the risks of using nuclear reactions and weigh these risks against potential benefits?

Issues regarding nuclear energy and radioactive waste can be found on ballots throughout the country. As other energy sources become scarce and more expensive, action on these issues will become necessary. On a larger scale, nuclear weapons are a reality that the world must struggle to deal with wisely. In a democracy, your ability to make intelligent decisions on these and related questions will depend to a large extent on how well you understand nuclear chemistry. To do so, you must take a closer look at the tiny nucleus you learned about in Chapter 8.

9.1 The Nucleus and Radiation

You have already learned that chemical changes can be explained by the behavior of atoms. Chemical changes involve the breaking of bonds between different atoms in the reactant molecules and the formation of new bonds in the product molecules. In a nuclear reaction, the situation is different. Changes occur involving the protons and the neutrons within the nucleus of a single atom.

In Chapter 8, you studied the composition of the nucleus. You learned that elements exist in different isotopic forms with different numbers of neutrons. For example, there are three naturally occurring isotopes of neon—neon-20, neon-21, and neon-22. You learned in Section 8.9 that the symbols for these isotopes are written as follows: $^{20}_{10}Ne$, $^{21}_{10}Ne$, and $^{22}_{10}Ne$. Remember that the superscripts *20, 21,* and *22* represent the mass numbers (that is, the total number of protons and neutrons) of the isotopes. The subscript *10* represents the atomic number (that is, the number of protons).

Objectives

Part 1

A. **Differentiate** between ionizing and nonionizing radiation.

B. **Identify** the different types of radioactive decay and **use equations** to represent the changes that occur.

C. **Determine** the mass loss in a given nuclear decay and using Einstein's equation, **calculate** the energy released.

D. **Predict** the fraction of radioactive nuclei that remain after a certain amount of time, given the half-life.

E. **List** some of the effects of ionizing radiation on life forms and the environment.

Developing Skills

Students may apply these skills in their study of Part 1.

Predicting: Have students predict the type of emission given off when phosphorus-30 decays to form silicon-30. Also, have them predict whether the nuclides formed by radioactive decay are stable when silicon-27 emits beta +, neon-24 emits beta −, and neon-23 emits beta −.

Calculating: Have students calculate the fraction of the fluorine-21 described in Example 9–3 after 2 minutes, 10 minutes, and 1 hour.

Comparing/Contrasting: Using the information given in Example 9–3, have students compare the fraction of phosphorus-30 with a half-life of 2.5 minutes to the fraction of fluorine-21 remaining after 1 hour.

☰ FOCUS

Activate Prior Knowledge

Students were introduced to isotopes in Chapter 8. Ask students to determine how many protons and neutrons are in carbon-14 and how carbon-14 differs from carbon-12. Then ask students how these isotopes of carbon compare chemically. (They are chemically the same.)

☰ TEACH

Teaching Strategy

The Nucleus and Radiation

The effects of small amounts of radiation on living systems are difficult to assess. Natural cellular processes include many changes, and among them are repair and replacement of molecules changed by radiation and other agents.

(continued on page T294)

Myths and Misconceptions

(continued from page T292)
be irradiated as a preservation technique, but the food would not become radioactive. Refer students to the **Science Technology & Society** feature at the end of this chapter, in which food irradiation is discussed.

(continued from page T293)

Knowledge of the characteristics of radiation is a first step in understanding its effects. The source of radiation determines its energy, penetrating ability, intensity, and persistence. Background radiation is unavoidable. Plants and animals must be able to repair the damage or use alternative processes to function successfully, or they will not survive. Generate a discussion about sources of radiation for inhabitants of Earth. Include information from pages 294 and 295 in the discussion. Get students to think of ways to (a) decrease sources of radiation, (b) make the population more aware of the sources, and (c) adequately protect members of the population from radiation.

Videodisc Connections

37247 to 38383, side 1
Alpha, beta, and gamma rays
(movie)

Do You Know?

A household smoke detector contains ionizing-type radioactive americium. If held 20 cm from your body for 1 year, you would receive 2 millirems of radiation.

Nuclide is a general name given to the nucleus of an atom. Since the nuclides of any one element differ only in their number of neutrons, a nuclide is identified by the mass number of its isotope. Remember that some isotopes are radioactive. Differences in the number of neutrons influence the kinds of nuclear reactions that each nuclide can undergo. (You will learn in Chapter 11 that all nuclides of any one element have a similar chemical nature.)

Types of radiation You learned in Chapter 8 that, by 1900, scientists had identified three types of radiation, or energy, given off by atoms—alpha, beta, and gamma radiation. Light, heat, microwaves, and radar are also forms of radiation.

Alpha radiation consists of rapidly moving helium nuclei. A helium nucleus has two protons and two neutrons. Alpha particles can be symbolized as either $_2^4\text{He}$ or α. The beta radiation identified by Rutherford consists of electrons, usually moving at tremendous speeds. These particles are symbolized as $_{-1}^0\text{e}$ or β^-. Since beta-minus particles are simply electrons, they have very little mass compared to a proton. Their charge is equal in magnitude, but opposite in sign, to that of a proton.

About 25 years after Rutherford's discoveries, a second type of beta radiation was found that consisted of positrons. A **positron** is a particle with the same mass as an electron but with a positive charge. A positron, often called a beta-plus particle, is symbolized as $_{+1}^0\text{e}$ or β^+. Gamma radiation is electromagnetic radiation similar to, but more energetic than X rays, radar waves, light, and microwaves. Gamma radiation is symbolized as γ. Electromagnetic radiation, including gamma radiation, travels through empty space at the speed of light, has no mass, and has no electric charge.

Radiation is classified as either ionizing or nonionizing. **Ionizing radiation** has sufficient energy to change atoms and molecules into ions. Remember that an ion is an atom that has either lost or gained electrons. Types of ionizing radiation include alpha, beta, X rays, and gamma rays. In contrast, radio waves and visible light are forms of **nonionizing radiation** because they do not have enough energy to ionize matter.

Concept ✔ Check

Explain the difference between alpha, beta, and gamma radiation.

Sources of radiation As you read this chapter, you are being bombarded with ionizing radiation. Some radiation comes from outer space and is called cosmic radiation. Other sources of ionizing radiation are emitted from Earth itself, the food you eat, and common building materials. For example, the building shown in Figure 9-1 is a source of radiation. Many common foods contain small amounts of radioactive elements. About half of the normal

Myths and Misconceptions

Some students may believe that food cooked in a microwave oven has been subjected to radioactivity. In fact, microwaves are a low-energy form of electromagnetic radiation. Microwaves are slightly higher in energy than radio waves, but lower in energy than infrared radiation. They penetrate only 2.5–3.5 cm into foods. Microwaves cook foods by exciting the molecules in the outer few centimeters, causing them to move faster. Heat is transferred to the inner part of the food by conduction from one molecule to another.

radioactivity in the body comes from potassium-40, and the rest is due to carbon-14 and hydrogen-3. All of these sources of natural radiation taken together constitute **background radiation.** One unit used to measure the amount of radiation is the **rem.** On average, you are exposed to 100 millirems of radiation per year from background sources.

In addition to background radiation, individuals are exposed to varying amounts of radiation, depending on their life-style and environment. A person who smokes two packs of cigarettes a day can be exposed to about 10 000 millirems per year. You can also increase your exposure to radiation through medical treatment, flying in airplanes, or living at high altitudes. Even though modern X-ray machines are designed to provide the maximum information with the minimum exposure to radiation, a chest X ray still exposes you to 50 millirems of ionizing radiation; a dental X ray exposes you to 20 millirems. When you fly in an airplane or live in a high-altitude city, you increase your exposure to cosmic radiation because there is less atmosphere to absorb it. The United States government recommends that exposure to radiation from sources other than background should be less than 500 millirems per year.

CONNECTING CONCEPTS

Processes of Science Measurement is an important part of every aspect of chemistry. It is vital to have a reliable, accurate method of measuring radiation.

Science Background

Effects of Radiation

The effects of a single dose of radiation over the whole body in a short time (a few minutes) are:
0–25 rem: no detectable effect
25–50 rem: the white blood cell count drops slightly
100–300 rem: nausea, fatigue, vomiting, and loss of hair
300–500 rem: the white blood cell count drops to near zero, and bleeding and sores develop
Greater than 500 rem: fatal to 50% of the population

Figure 9-1 Left: *Buildings made of granite, clay, and some kinds of brick emit more radiation than those made of wood.* Right: *If you lived in New York City's Grand Central Station, you would receive 570 millirems of additional radiation per year. Building materials do not emit enough radiation to pose a threat to life.*

Effects of radiation Ionizing radiation can cause changes in living cells. The effects of radiation exposure depend on the type and amount of radiation received. Massive doses of radiation result in harmful changes. DNA molecules are especially sensitive to ionizing radiation. The DNA molecule contains the information necessary for all cell functions. Changes in DNA can upset cell chemistry and result in either cell death or uncontrolled growth (cancer). Immature cells and cells that are undergoing rapid division—as in

Cooperative Learning

Types of Nuclear Decay

Teams of 3; **Time:** 20 minutes
Objective: Students will learn to write nuclear equations from information given in a handbook.
Task: One student is given a page from a handbook and chooses an unstable nuclide. The other two students write nuclear equations, given the type of radiation emitted.
Team responsibility: After each student has chosen nuclides, team members look for patterns in the type of radiation and note the tacit knowledge required to write the nuclear equations.
Evaluation: Have students share patterns they noticed. For example: (1) alpha emission does not occur in elements with atomic numbers less than 60, (2) nuclides with masses smaller than that of the most stable nuclide decay by beta + emission, (3) nuclides with masses larger than that of the most stable nuclide decay by beta − emission.

Give a quiz with 10 radioactive nuclides. For the last two, do not give the type of radiation emitted.

Figure 9-2 *The benefits of using ionizing x-radiation to discover tooth decay outweigh the possible negative effects. However, all uses of radiation should be carefully monitored.*

bone marrow, the reproductive organs, and the intestinal lining—are the most sensitive to radiation damage. If radiation causes changes in the chromosomal DNA of a sperm cell or an ovum, these changes are transmitted to the offspring.

What are the possible ill effects from long-term exposure to background and low-level radiation? There are two models of radiation damage. The threshold model assumes that receiving doses of radiation below a threshold level is not harmful. The linear model suggests that damage is proportional to the dose of radiation received and that even near-zero amounts of radiation do some harm. At present, there is not enough evidence to evaluate which model is correct. One problem in evaluating the effects of radiation is this: Since background radiation is unavoidable, you cannot have a control group of people who are exposed to zero radiation.

Most scientists think that the safest strategy is to minimize radiation exposure. However, the benefits of diagnosing bone damage, tooth decay, and other illnesses are considered to be much greater than the risks due to radiation exposure during these procedures. Controversy over the long-term effects of low-level radiation still exists, and scientists continue to investigate the issue.

9.2 Types of Nuclear Decay

Nuclear change, or decay, is an exothermic process. That is, every decay results in a nucleus that contains less energy. The emission of different types of radiation is one way that a nucleus can become less energetic, since the radiation carries away excess energy.

The stability of a nuclide partly depends on the relative number of neutrons and protons it contains. In some cases, having too few neutrons makes a nucleus unstable, and in other cases, having too many neutrons is the cause of instability. Nuclear physicists investigate why one nuclide, like neon-20, is stable and another nuclide, like neon-19, undergoes nuclear decay. Stable nuclides are recognized experimentally because they do not change. Unstable nuclides decay in order to form more stable nuclides. Changing to a stable nuclide may involve one or more decays.

In nuclear decay, the initial nucleus is called the **parent nuclide,** and the new nucleus that results is called the **daughter nuclide.** It is useful to write an equation to represent what occurs during a nuclear reaction. In Chapter 3, you balanced equations for chemical reactions by making sure that the numbers of each type of atom were conserved. An equation representing a nuclear reaction is balanced when the sum of the atomic numbers on the right is equal to the sum of the atomic numbers on the left. Also, the sum of the mass numbers on the right and left must be equal.

Alpha emission One type of nuclear reaction is decay by α (alpha) emission. In **alpha emission,** the parent nuclide decays into a daughter nuclide by emitting an α (alpha) particle.

EXAMPLE 9-1

Write an equation to represent the decay of thorium-230 by α (alpha) emission.

■ *Analyze the Problem* Begin by writing the symbol for thorium-230. The symbol should include the mass number as a superscript and the atomic number as a subscript. You can find the atomic number of thorium on the periodic table and write the symbol $^{230}_{90}\text{Th}$. Decay by α (alpha) emission means that an α (alpha) particle is given off by thorium-230. An alpha particle was described in Section 9.1 as a helium-4 nucleus, $^{4}_{2}\text{He}$. You can begin to write the equation as follows.

$$^{230}_{90}\text{Th} \rightarrow {}^{4}_{2}\text{He} + ?$$

■ *Apply a Strategy* Balancing an equation representing a nuclear reaction is very similar to balancing a chemical equation. However, rather than balancing the numbers of each type of atom, you must balance the sum of the atomic numbers of the nuclides and the sum of their mass numbers on each side of the equation.

■ *Work a Solution* Finding the identity of the daughter nuclide produced requires some simple math. Since the sum of the atomic numbers must be equal, the daughter nuclide in this case must have an atomic number of 88. Look at the periodic table. The element with this atomic number is radium, symbolized by Ra. Similarly, a mass number of 226 is required to make the sum of the mass numbers equal. Now you can complete the equation.

$$^{230}_{90}\text{Th} \rightarrow {}^{4}_{2}\text{He} + {}^{226}_{88}\text{Ra}$$

■ *Verify Your Answer* The sum of the mass numbers on the right side of the equation is 230, which equals the mass number on the left. The sum of the atomic numbers on the right is 90, which equals the atomic number on the left. Thus the equation is written correctly.

Practice Problems

1. Write an equation to represent the decay of radium-226 by α emission.

2. Write an equation to represent the decay of plutonium-240 by α emission.

3. The decay products from a nuclear reaction are an α particle and polonium-218. What is the parent nuclide in this reaction?

PROBLEM·SOLVING
S T R A T E G Y

*Balancing a chemical equation is a **similar problem** to balancing a nuclear equation. In a chemical equation, you must balance the number of atoms on both sides of the equation; in a nuclear equation, you must balance the atomic numbers and mass numbers. (See Strategy, page 65.)*

Practice Problems

Assign the Practice Problems.

PART 1

Section 9.2 continued

Teaching Strategy

Beta Emission

Although beta emission involves electrons, those electrons come from the nucleus. Within the nucleus, a neutron decays into a proton and an electron. The electron is emitted, leaving behind a proton to replace the neutron, thus transforming the element. (A neutrino is also produced and emitted in the process.)

CONNECTING CONCEPTS

Models Since nuclear reactions cannot be observed directly, equations are used to represent the changes that occur.

Beta emission Another type of nuclear reaction is decay by **beta emission,** in which either an electron or a positron is emitted by the parent nuclide. Consider the radioactive decay of the unstable nuclide neon-23 by β^- (electron) emission. The equation for this reaction is as follows.

$$^{23}_{10}\text{Ne} \rightarrow {}^{0}_{-1}\text{e} + {}^{23}_{11}\text{Na}$$

The subscript *10* in the symbol for neon-23 is the atomic number taken from the periodic table. The β^- particle, or electron, is symbolized by ${}^{0}_{-1}\text{e}$. Since the sum of the atomic numbers of the reactants and products must be equal, the atomic number of the daughter nuclide must be 11, the atomic number of sodium. Similarly, sodium's mass number must be 23. Notice that decay by β^- (electron) emission results in the conversion of a neutron to a proton. Neon has 10 protons and 13 neutrons, whereas sodium has 11 protons and 12 neutrons. Nuclides that decay by β^- (electron) emission have too many neutrons in the nucleus for the number of protons present.

In other cases, an unstable nuclide may emit a positron, or a β^+ particle. Remember that a β^+ (positron) particle has the same mass as an electron but has a positive charge. The result of β^+ (positron) emission is the conversion of a proton into a neutron. Nuclides that decay by β^+ (positron) emission have too few neutrons in the nucleus for the number of protons present.

TABLE 9-1

Examples of Nuclear Decay Processes		
α emission	β^- emission	β^+ emission
$^{238}_{92}\text{U} \rightarrow {}^{4}_{2}\text{He} + {}^{234}_{90}\text{Th}$	$^{27}_{12}\text{Mg} \rightarrow {}^{0}_{-1}\text{e} + {}^{27}_{13}\text{Al}$	$^{14}_{8}\text{O} \rightarrow {}^{0}_{+1}\text{e} + {}^{14}_{7}\text{N}$
$^{230}_{90}\text{Th} \rightarrow {}^{4}_{2}\text{He} + {}^{226}_{88}\text{Ra}$	$^{35}_{16}\text{S} \rightarrow {}^{0}_{-1}\text{e} + {}^{35}_{17}\text{Cl}$	$^{24}_{13}\text{Al} \rightarrow {}^{0}_{+1}\text{e} + {}^{24}_{12}\text{Mg}$
$^{226}_{88}\text{Ra} \rightarrow {}^{4}_{2}\text{He} + {}^{222}_{86}\text{Rn}$	$^{40}_{19}\text{K} \rightarrow {}^{0}_{-1}\text{e} + {}^{40}_{20}\text{Ca}$	$^{32}_{17}\text{Cl} \rightarrow {}^{0}_{+1}\text{e} + {}^{32}_{16}\text{S}$

Concept ✔ Check

The emission of gamma radiation often accompanies alpha and beta emission. Since gamma rays have no mass or charge, would gamma radiation change the mass number or atomic number of a nuclide?

Radioactive decay results in a daughter nuclide that is less energetic than the parent nuclide. The energy released when a decay process occurs is transformed either into kinetic energy of the α particles, β^- particles, and β^+ particles, or into a combination of rays and kinetic energy of particles. There are other kinds of nuclear reactions that an unstable nucleus can undergo. Some of these reactions involve subatomic particles that are not mentioned here.

9.3 Energy and Mass in Nuclear Reactions

You learned in Chapter 2 that matter is conserved in a chemical reaction. However, in a nuclear reaction, when the total mass of the reactants is compared to that of the products, a small portion of the mass seems to disappear. How is it that some matter disappears in a nuclear reaction? What happens to the missing matter?

Albert Einstein described a relationship between matter and energy, proposing that they can be interchanged. When a nuclear reaction takes place, the loss of mass is proportional to the energy released in the reaction. Einstein's theory can be expressed in this famous mathematical equation.

$$E = mc^2$$

Einstein's equation implies that matter can be converted into energy and that energy can be changed into matter. E is the energy released in the reaction (in joules), m is the mass (in kilograms), and c is the velocity of light (3.00×10^8 meters per second). Einstein's equation can be applied to calculate the amount of energy released when a sample of radioactive material undergoes a nuclear change.

EXAMPLE 9-2

How much energy is released when 1 mole of radium-226 decays by α emission to produce radon-222? Express your answer in kilojoules.

■ **Analyze the Problem** First write down the equation for the reaction.

$$^{226}_{88}\text{Ra} \rightarrow {}^{222}_{86}\text{Rn} + {}^4_2\text{He}$$

To calculate the energy released when a nuclear change takes place, you need to know how much mass was lost.

■ **Apply a Strategy** The mass of 1 mole of each of the nuclides involved is: radium-226 = 226.0254 g, radon-222 = 222.0175 g, and helium-4 = 4.0026 g. (The unusually high precision of these masses is necessary in the calculation because the change in mass is very small.)

The mass loss is found by subtracting the sum of the masses of the products from the mass of the reactant.

$$\text{mass } ^{226}_{88}\text{Ra} - (\text{mass } ^{222}_{86}\text{Rn} + \text{mass } ^4_2\text{He}) = \text{mass loss}$$
$$226.0254 \text{ g} - (222.0175 \text{ g} + 4.0026 \text{ g}) = 0.0053 \text{ g}$$

The combined mass of the products is 0.0053 g less than the mass of the reactant.

DO YOU KNOW?

Albert Einstein (1879–1955) developed his famous theory of relativity by the time he was 26 years old. Many brilliant people work in science, but Einstein is considered unique. His ideas greatly advanced knowledge in nuclear chemistry, physics, and astronomy. In 1905, Einstein published three papers, and each might have been worthy of a Nobel Prize!

Teaching Strategy

Energy and Mass in Nuclear Reactions

To understand the energy involved in nuclear processes, students need to work through some calculations.

Science Background

Energy and Mass in Nuclear Reactions

All radioactive processes release energy and result in the formation of more stable nuclides. Example 9–2 shows how the small mass deficit that occurs in nuclear reactions is converted by means of Einstein's equation to its energy equivalent. This energy, a product of the nuclear reaction, is evident in the kinetic energy of the emitted particles and often as gamma radiation. The release of gamma radiation alone does not change the identity of a nuclide, but results in lower energy and greater stability.

Practice Problems

Assign the Practice Problems.

PROBLEM-SOLVING

S T R A T E G Y

If you need to review the use of scientific notation, refer to Appendix B.

PROBLEM-SOLVING

S T R A T E G Y

Use what you know about symbols. An α particle is a helium-4 nucleus; a β^- particle is an electron, a β^+ particle is a positron.

■ **Work a Solution** Nuclear reactions involve the conversion of mass into energy, so now you can use Einstein's equation. To use this equation, mass must first be expressed in kilograms.

$$0.0053 \text{ g} \times \frac{1 \text{ kg}}{1000 \text{ g}} = 5.3 \times 10^{-6} \text{ kg}$$

Therefore,

$$E = mc^2$$
$$E = (5.3 \times 10^{-6} \text{ kg})(3.00 \times 10^8 \text{ m/s})^2$$
$$E = 4.8 \times 10^{11} \text{ kg m}^2/\text{s}^2$$

One joule is the equivalent of 1 kg m^2/s^2, so

$$4.8 \times 10^{11} \text{ kg m}^2/\text{s}^2 = 4.8 \times 10^{11} \text{ J or } 4.8 \times 10^8 \text{ kJ}$$

■ **Verify Your Answer** Just how much energy is 4.8×10^8 kJ? Compare this value to the energy produced during the combustion of octane, a chemical reaction you studied in Chapter 3. The complete combustion of 1 mole of octane produces 5.4×10^3 kJ of energy. This nuclear reaction produces 100 000 times more energy!

Practice Problems

4. When 1 mole of radon-222 decays by α emission, 5.4×10^8 kJ of energy are released. How much mass was converted into energy in this reaction?   **Ans.** 0.0060 g

5. How much energy in kilojoules is released when 1 mole of oxygen-14 decays by β^+ emission to form nitrogen-14? The molar masses are: oxygen-14 = 14.0086 g, β^+ = 0.0005 g, and nitrogen-14 = 14.0031 g.   **Ans.** 4.5×10^8 kJ

9.4 Half-Life

In a sample of radioactive nuclides, the decay of an individual nuclide is a random event. It is impossible to predict which nucleus will be the next one to undergo a nuclear change. How, then, do you make sense out of things that cannot be predicted on an individual basis? One approach is to predict change for a given amount of a very large number of nuclei—for example, one half. Scientists commonly discuss radioactive decay in terms of half-life. The time it takes for one half of the parent nuclides in a radioactive sample to decay is known as its **half-life**, or $t_{1/2}$.

The half-life of fluorine-21 is approximately five seconds. If a sample of fluorine-21 contains one million atoms, then 500 000 of the nuclei will decay within five seconds. Within another five seconds, 250 000 additional nuclei (one half of those remaining) will decay, and so on. Many radioactive nuclei have much longer half-lives. A sample of one million nuclei of strontium-90 will decay

DO YOU KNOW?

Chemical reactions also involve the loss of mass. However, this loss of mass is so small it cannot be detected on the most sensitive balance.

much more slowly because the half-life of strontium-90 is about 29 years. Half-lives may be used to calculate the fraction of parent nuclides that remain after a certain amount of time.

EXAMPLE 9-3

Fluorine-21 has a half-life of approximately 5 seconds. What fraction of the original nuclei would remain after 1 minute? If you began with 21 grams of fluorine, how many grams of fluorine would remain?

■ *Analyze the Problem* A half-life of 5 s means that 1/2 of the nuclei will remain after 5 s. At the end of 10 s, 1/2 of 1/2, or 1/4, will remain. You can express this mathematically as $1/2 \times 1/2 = 1/4$ or $(1/2)^2 = 1/4$. At the end of 15 s, or 3 half-lives, $1/2 \times 1/2 \times 1/2$, or 1/8, of the parent nuclides will remain. Express this as $(1/2)^3 = 1/8$.

■ *Apply a Strategy* Notice that a pattern can be found in the analysis you have done. Generally the fraction of nuclei that remain after a certain amount of time can be written as $(1/2)^n$, *n* being the number of half-lives in the given period of time. Now to determine the fraction of remaining nuclei, you just need to figure out how many half-lives are equal to 1 min.

■ *Work a Solution* One minute is equal to 60 s. The total time divided by the length of 1 half-life equals the number of half-lives. In this example, 60 s /5 s = 12, so $n = 12$. The fraction of parent nuclei remaining after 1 minute is calculated as $(1/2)^{12} = 1/4096$. Expressed as a decimal, this is 0.000 24, or 0.024 percent, which means that 99.976 percent of the original atoms have decayed. The mass of fluorine-21 that remains will be

$$21 \text{ g} \times \frac{1}{4\ 096} = 0.0051 \text{ g}$$

■ *Verify Your Answer* After many half-lives, the amount of fluorine-21 that remains should be very small.

Practice Problems

6. Iodine-131 has a half-life of 8 days. What fraction of the original sample would remain at the end of 32 days?

   Ans. 1/16

7. The half-life of chromium-51 is 28 days. If a sample contained 510 grams, how much chromium would remain after 56 days? How much would remain after 1 year?

   Ans. 130 g; 0.062 g

PROBLEM-SOLVING

S T R A T E G Y

Use what you know about half-lives to start working this problem. (See Strategy, page 58.)

PROBLEM-SOLVING

S T R A T E G Y

You can look for a pattern by working simple cases first (1 half-life, 2 half-lives, etc.). Then extend what you have learned to more complex cases (such as 12 half-lives). (See Strategy, page 100.)

PROBLEM-SOLVING

S T R A T E G Y

You can make a qualitative estimate of your answer to verify that it is reasonable. (See Strategy, page 125.)

Practice Problems

Assign the Practice Problems.

PART **1**
Section 9.5

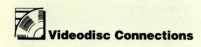

Videodisc Connections

43402 to 47551, side 1
Radon (movie)

Naturally occurring radioactive nuclides either have long half-lives compared to the age of Earth or they are daughter nuclides resulting from the decay of other radioactive isotopes. Many radioactive nuclides are human-made and cannot be found in nature. For example, technetium-97 has been produced as a daughter nuclide in a nuclear reactor. The half-life of technetium-97 is 2.6 million years. This may seem long, but it is short compared to the age of Earth—4.5 billion years! Any large amounts of technetium-97 that might have been present when Earth was formed would have decayed already. Therefore, no measurable amount can be found outside that produced in nuclear reactors today.

9.5 Nuclear Decay and the Environment

A nuclide like fluorine-21 has such a short half-life that in a few hours the radioactive atoms essentially disappear. The daughter nuclide, neon-21, is stable, so there is no more radiation emitted. Knowledge of both the half-life and the daughter products of a nuclide is needed in order to make decisions about how a particular radioactive substance can be used or stored.

The nuclides mentioned so far exhibit **spontaneous decay**, meaning their alpha and beta emissions occur naturally. Some nuclides undergo a series of spontaneous radioactive decays before a stable nuclide forms. In a **decay series**, a radioactive daughter nuclide from one decay becomes the parent nuclide of the next decay. The radioactive decay series of uranium-238 to lead-206 is depicted in Figure 9-3. This decay series produces fifteen radioactive daughter nuclides. Other decay series are the decay of uranium-235 into lead-207 and the decay of thorium-232 into lead-208.

Concept ✔ Check

Explain how a decay series operates.

Naturally occurring radon Identifying the daughter nuclides in a decay series of natural and human-made radioactive elements is important, since some of these nuclides are harmful. You can see in Figure 9-3 that radon-222 is one of the daughter products of the decay of uranium-238. Uranium-238 is present in small amounts in soil and rock, particularly in shale and granite. Radon-222 is different from the other daughter products in the uranium-238 series because it is a gas. Radon gradually escapes from porous rocks into the air. Radon can seep into a building through walls, water pipes, or cracks in the foundation.

Measures taken to conserve energy often make a home or building more airtight. Higher concentrations of radon result and pose

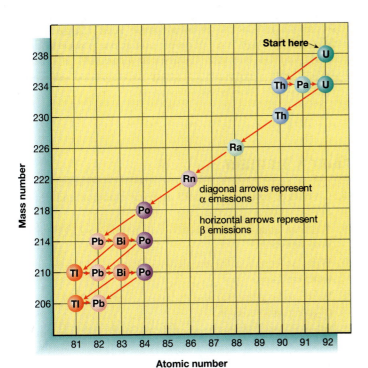

Figure 9-3 *The radioactive decay series of uranium-238 to lead-206 involves several steps. Alpha emissions result in the loss of two protons and thus a decrease in atomic number. Beta emissions involve the gain of a proton and an increase in atomic number.*

a potential health hazard. Radon can enter the body through the lungs. The thin walls of the lungs are particularly susceptible to radiation damage caused by the alpha particles that are emitted by radon-222. The daughter nuclide of radon decay is polonium-218 — a radioactive solid that can become lodged in the lungs and continue to emit radiation. The radiation from both radon-222 and polonium-218 can cause cancer.

The risk of cancer due to radon is much lower than the risk due to smoking. Still, in 1988, the Environmental Protection Agency considered it high enough to recommend that all homes be tested for radon. Instruments are now available that enable you to evaluate the amount of radon present in your home.

Nuclear-weapons testing Nuclear-weapons testing in the atmosphere has released significant amounts of radioactive material into the environment. The release of strontium-90 is particularly dangerous. Because it is chemically similar to calcium, strontium-90 is easily incorporated into the food chain and tends to accumulate in bones. Even very small amounts of strontium-90 may be harmful, since the radiation it emits can affect the red blood cell production in the bone marrow and can cause a form of cancer called leukemia. Atmospheric testing of nuclear weapons was banned in 1963. However, about half of the radioactive strontium-90 nuclides present in 1963 still remain in the environment.

PART 1

Section 9.5 *continued*

Guided Practice

Review the Concept Check questions on pages 294, 298, and 302. Answers can be found in Appendix E on page 808.

Reteaching Idea

If your students are having difficulty processing all the concepts in this part, have them work in small groups or pairs to develop a concept map starting with the phrase *nuclear reactions*. You could list on the chalkboard some of the words you think should be included.

Connected concepts might be *α emission* releases *helium nucleus* having symbol ^4_2He and also releases *daughter nuclide* having atomic charge $2-$, and produces *energy* in the form of *ionizing radiation*, specifically *alpha radiation* measured in *rems*. Similar connected concepts for $β^+$ *emission* and $β^-$ *emission* can be developed. Common to the three kinds of nuclear reactions is *energy* and the production of daughter nuclides.

≡CLOSE

Summing Up Main Ideas

Bismuth-210 decays via beta decay into polonium-210 with a half-life of 5 days. Have students write the nuclear equation and determine how many grams of a 500-g sample of bismuth-210 will remain after 20 days.

$$\left(^{210}_{83}\text{Bi} \rightarrow \, ^{0}_{-1}\text{e} + \, ^{210}_{84}\text{Po}\right.$$

$$\frac{1}{2} \times \frac{1}{2} \times \frac{1}{2} \times \frac{1}{2} = \frac{1}{16}$$
$$5 \quad 10 \quad 15 \quad 20$$

$$\left. \frac{1}{16} \times 500 \text{ g} = 31.3 \text{ g}\right)$$

PART 1 REVIEW

Assign the Part Review questions.

Evaluating Skills

These skills are evaluated in the Part Review questions indicated. **Classifying:** 8; **Analyzing data:** 9, 10, 11, 13, 14, 15, 16, 19; **Applying a strategy:** 9, 10, 11, 13, 14, 15, 16, 19; **Calculating:** 9, 10, 11, 13, 14, 15, 16, 19; **Verifying results:** 9, 10, 11, 13, 14, 15, 16, 19; **Determining main ideas:** 12, 17, 18; **Predicting:** 15

Boxed numbers indicate questions that involve skills in interpretation, application, and analysis.

PROBLEM·SOLVING

STRATEGY

*This problem will be easier to solve if you **break it into parts**. You might want to start with the nuclear equation for the decay process. (See Strategy, page 166.)*

Additional radioactive materials have been released into the environment through the operation of nuclear power plants and accidents like the one that occurred in Chernobyl in the Soviet Union in 1986. Environmental concerns associated with nuclear power plants will be discussed in Part 3.

PART 1 REVIEW

8. Give three examples of both ionizing radiation and nonionizing radiation.

9. Write an equation for the decay of polonium-218 by α (alpha) emission.

10. Write an equation for the decay of carbon-14 by β^- (electron) emission.

11. Write an equation for the decay of chlorine-32 by β^+ (positron) emission.

12. What happens to the matter that seems to disappear during a nuclear reaction?

13. The decay of 1 mole of cobalt-60 by β^- emission is represented by the equation $^{60}_{27}\text{Co} \rightarrow \, ^{0}_{-1}\text{e} + \, ^{60}_{28}\text{Ni}$. How much energy in kilojoules is released in this reaction if the products have 0.0032 g less mass than the reactant?
   Ans. 2.9×10^8 kJ

14. The half-life of phosphorus-30 is 2.5 min. What fraction of phosphorus-30 nuclides would remain after 10 min?
   Ans. 1/16

15. If 20.0 g of a radioactive isotope are present at 1:00 P.M. and 5.0 g remain at 2:00 P.M., what is the half-life of the isotope? Use the half-life to predict how much of the isotope would remain at 2:30 P.M. **Ans.** 30 min; 2.5 g

16. What fraction of radioactive strontium-90 nuclides, formed in the last atmospheric nuclear-bomb test in 1963, will be present in the environment in the year 2050? The half-life of strontium-90 is 29 years. **Ans.** 1/8

17. What two things must you know about a radioactive nuclide in order to evaluate its potential danger?

18. Name two health hazards associated with radon.

19. When the nuclei in 1 mole of polonium-211 decay by α emission to produce lead-207, how many kilojoules of energy are released? The mass in grams of 1 mole of each of the nuclei involved is: polonium-211 = 210.9866 g, lead-207 = 206.9750 g, and helium-4 = 4.0026 g.
   Ans. 8.1×10^8 kJ

PART 1 REVIEW

ANSWERS

■ Keyed to Objectives

A 8. ionizing radiation—alpha, beta, gamma, X rays; non-ionizing radiation—microwaves, infrared, radar

B 9. $^{218}_{84}\text{Po} \rightarrow \, ^{4}_{2}\text{He} + \, ^{214}_{82}\text{Pb}$

B 10. $^{14}_{6}\text{C} \rightarrow \, ^{0}_{-1}\text{e} + \, ^{14}_{7}\text{N}$

B 11. $^{32}_{17}\text{Cl} \rightarrow \, ^{0}_{1}\text{e} + \, ^{32}_{16}\text{S}$

C 12. The mass is converted into energy.

C 13.
$$0.0032 \text{ g} \times \frac{1 \text{ kg}}{1000 \text{ g}} = 3.2 \times 10^{-6} \text{ kg};$$
$$E = mc^2 = 3.2 \times 10^{-6} \text{ kg}$$
$$\times \left(3.00 \times 10^8 \text{ m/s}\right)^2$$
$$= 2.9 \times 10^{11} \text{ J};$$
$$2.9 \times 10^{11} \text{ J} \times \frac{1 \text{ kJ}}{1000 \text{ J}}$$
$$= 2.9 \times 10^8 \text{ kJ}$$

D 14. $\frac{10 \text{ min}}{2.5 \text{ min}} = 4$ half-lives
$$\left(\frac{1}{2}\right)^4 = \frac{1}{16}$$

D 15. $\frac{5.0 \text{ g}}{20.0 \text{ g}} = \frac{1}{4}$;

this is 2 half-lives = 1 hour. The half-life is 0.5 hour or 30 min. At 2:30, half of 5.0 (or 2.5) g will remain.

D 16. 2050 − 1963 = 87 years;

PART 2 Using Nuclear Reactions for Research

As soon as researchers began to unravel some of the mysteries of the nucleus, they looked for applications of the new science. Some applications were stumbled upon accidentally, like the production of new isotopes. From this step, nuclear scientists quickly moved to synthesize entirely new elements. New and better instruments were developed to accelerate subatomic particles and nuclei to greater speeds. Studying the rates of decay of different radioactive isotopes has enabled scientists to use these materials in research related to geology, biology, medicine, and genetics. Radioactive substances are used to determine the age of rocks from the moon and how chemical reactions work. Sometimes, the malfunctioning of certain body organs is diagnosed using radioactive isotopes.

Objectives

Part 2

F. *Explain* what is meant by transmutation.

G. *Determine* the age of a fossil using information about its rate of radioactive decay.

H. *Evaluate* the benefits and risks of radioisotopes used in medicine and research.

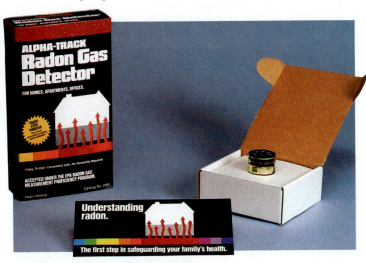

Figure 9-4 *A radon test kit is used to determine the concentration of radon gas in a home. These cans are untaped and exposed for one week.*

9.6 Synthetic Elements

Why are the reactions described in this chapter different from ordinary chemical reactions? Alpha and beta emissions produce elements that are different from the ones that began each reaction. The transformation of one element into another is known as **transmutation.** The idea of transmutation has fascinated people since ancient times. Alchemists, like the one shown in Figure 9-5, frequently tried to convert lead into gold. The work of alchemists provided knowledge that led to the science of chemistry. After many years of experimenting, chemists concluded that one element never changes into another element during chemical change. Only in a nuclear reaction, involving a change in atomic number, can transmutation occur. With this knowledge, it is now possible to use

Figure 9-5 *Alchemists, who flourished until the early 1700's, practiced a mixture of science, magic, and religion. Among other things, they attempted to change less costly metals into gold. They could not have known that only a nuclear process can change one element into another.*

PART **2**
Using Nuclear Reactions for Research
Section 9.6

Developing Skills

Students may apply these skills in their study of Part 2.

Determining sources of error: Have students suggest two possible sources of error in the dating of the plant fossil in Part Review question 23.

Predicting: Have students predict which of the radioisotopes listed in Table 9–2 will remain in the largest amounts at the end of one year if all begin with one-milligram amounts.

≡ FOCUS

Activate Prior Knowledge

The smoke detector is an application of nuclear chemistry with which students are familiar. Ask students to look at the smoke detectors they may have at home, or bring a smoke detector into the classroom. Ask students if they know how smoke detectors utilize a radioactive isotope such as americium-241. As Am-241 decays, it ionizes the air molecules in the chamber. A battery provides an electrical potential which causes the ions to flow across the chamber. This produces an electric current. Smoke impedes this current, causing the alarm to sound. Open the detector and show students what it looks like.

$\dfrac{87 \text{ years}}{29 \text{ years}} = 3$ half-lives;

$\left(\dfrac{1}{2}\right)^3 = \dfrac{1}{8}$

E 17. the half-life and the type of radiation emitted

E 18. lung cancer and genetic defects

C 19. $^{211}_{84}\text{Po} \rightarrow {}^{4}_{2}\text{He} + {}^{207}_{82}\text{Pb}$
mass change = 210.9866
− (206.9750 + 4.0026) = 0.0090 g

$9.0 \times 10^{-3} \text{ g} \times \dfrac{1 \text{ kg}}{1000 \text{ g}}$

$= 9.0 \times 10^{-6} \text{ kg}$

$E = mc^2 = \left(9.0 \times 10^{-6} \text{ kg}\right)$

$\times \left(3.00 \times 10^8 \text{ m/s}\right)^2$

$= 8.1 \times 10^{11} \text{ J}$

$8.1 \times 10^{11} \text{ J} \times \dfrac{1 \text{ kJ}}{1000 \text{ J}}$

$= 8.1 \times 10^8 \text{ kJ}$

PART 2
Section 9.6 *continued*

≡ TEACH

Teaching Strategy

Transuranium Elements

Have students use the periodic table to locate and identify the transuranium elements. Ask students if they can explain how synthetic elements such as the transuranium elements are made. Have students discuss how each of the transuranium elements received its name.

DO YOU KNOW?

The first synthetic element was actually produced in Italy in 1937. Technetium, atomic number 43, has no stable isotopes and does not exist in nature on Earth. The isotope that has the longest half-life has a mass number of 98, as given in parentheses on the periodic chart.

nuclear reactions to change lead into gold! Unfortunately, to produce one ounce of gold by transmutation costs more than one million dollars—much more than the value of the gold obtained. Still, transmutation reactions provide useful information about nuclear structure and produce special nuclides that are used in medical treatment and research.

Synthetic, or human-made, elements are produced by bombarding nuclei with different particles. Very often these particles have a positive charge. The target nuclei also have a positive charge that exerts a repulsive force. To overcome this force, the bombarding particles must be accelerated to very high speeds. This process requires large amounts of energy and special equipment, making such transmutations expensive.

Transuranium elements Since 1939, scientists have successfully synthesized elements with atomic numbers larger than that of naturally occurring uranium. Such an element, which does not exist in nature, is shown in Figure 9-6. It is known as a **transuranium element.** One example of a nuclear reaction that produces a transuranium element is

$$^{238}_{92}U + {}^{4}_{2}He \rightarrow {}^{242}_{94}Pu$$

In this reaction, uranium-238 is changed into the transuranium element—plutonium-242. As new elements are created, they may be used as the target nuclei for new transmutations unless these new elements are also radioactive and decay too rapidly.

Figure 9-6 *Left: A tiny sample of curium is less than 0.4 mm in diameter. Right: A material that contains plutonium.*

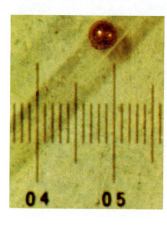

All of the transuranium elements that have been synthesized so far are radioactive and have short half-lives. Mendelevium-258 and fermium-257, with half-lives of 55 and 100 days respectively, are the only nuclides with 100 or more protons that have a half-life longer than a few days.

Plutonium-239 is a transuranium element that has been produced in large amounts through transmutation in reactors known as breeder reactors. The reactions that take place to make plutonium are the following

$$^{238}_{92}U + ^{1}_{0}n \rightarrow ^{239}_{92}U$$

$$^{239}_{92}U \rightarrow ^{239}_{93}Np + ^{0}_{-1}e$$

$$^{239}_{93}Np \rightarrow ^{239}_{94}Pu + ^{0}_{-1}e$$

Plutonium-239 is used as a fuel in nuclear power plants and can be used to make nuclear bombs. Plutonium-239, with a half-life of 24 000 years, is one of the most toxic substances known. Through production and processing, some plutonium-239 invariably leaks into the environment. As a citizen, you will have to help decide how much plutonium-239 should be allowed into the environment. The question is not simple because plutonium-239 may be needed as a fuel to produce electric energy as supplies of oil and coal become scarce and expensive.

Attempts to synthesize elements with more and more protons continue. Scientists in both the United States and the Soviet Union* claim priority in the synthesis of an element with atomic number 106. The synthesis of elements 107, 108, and 109 has been announced in Germany. Synthesis of element 107 has been reported also in the Soviet Union, but there is no independent verification yet of these discoveries. Independent verification is required before the element is given a name.

Concept Check

Explain and give an example of a transuranium element.

9.7 Radioactive Dating

Half-life measurements of radioactive elements in rocks and fossils can be used to determine their ages. For example, carbon-14 is a radioactive nuclide constantly produced in the atmosphere through collisions of nitrogen-14 nuclei with high-energy neutrons in cosmic radiation. Carbon-14 undergoes β^- emission, decaying back to nitrogen-14. The half-life of this decay is 5730 years. During photosynthesis, green plants absorb carbon dioxide, a percentage of which contains carbon-14. When the plant dies, photosynthesis stops and no more radioactive carbon dioxide is absorbed. However, decay of the carbon-14 already in the plant continues. The approximate time in history when a once-living plant died can be determined by measuring the radioactivity that is due to the remaining carbon-14.

The radioactivity of a substance can be measured by counting the number of decays that occur every minute in one gram of the substance. This rate decreases over time as the amount of radioactive material decreases. In a living organism, the radioactivity due to carbon-14 decay is 15.3 decays per minute per gram of carbon.

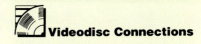

Videodisc Connections

38384 to 39484, side 1
Various commercial applications (movie)

DO YOU KNOW?

The ionizing radiation of radioactive polonium is used to eliminate the static electricity that results when plastic two-liter bottles are blown-dry after cleaning.

* Refers to the Soviet Union as it existed as of January 1, 1991.

PROBLEM-SOLVING
S T R A T E G Y

Finding the disintegration rate after **n** *half-lives is a* **similar problem** *to Example 9-3. To find the number of particles remaining after* **n** *half-lives, you multiply the original number by* $(1/2)^n$; *to find the disintegration rate, you multiply the original rate by the same fraction—*$(1/2)^n$. *(See Strategy, page 65.)*

Figure 9-7 *Radioactive carbon is formed when neutrons from space collide with nitrogen-14 in the atmosphere. Plants absorb carbon-14 in the form of* CO_2 *and convert it to other carbon compounds during photosynthesis. When a plant dies, radioactivity from carbon-14 decreases because no more of the isotope is being absorbed. The rate of radioactivity is used to find the age of the fossil plant.*

An organism that died 5730 years ago (the half-life of carbon-14) will have a decay rate one half as large, or 7.65 decays/min/g. One that died 2×5730 years ago (two carbon-14 half-lives) will have a decay rate $(1/2) \times (1/2)$, or one fourth, as large. That is, the fossil will undergo 3.83 decays/min/g. Generally the disintegration rate will equal $15.3 \times (1/2)^n$ decays/min/g, n being the number of half-lives that have passed since the organism died. Researchers can determine the age of a previously living substance by measuring its decay rate.

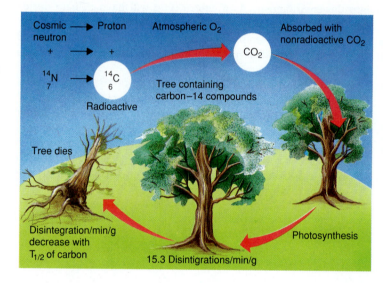

The half-life of carbon-14 is short compared to the age of most fossils. Radiocarbon dating is not useful for fossils older than 60 000 years. To determine the ages of older fossils, rocks, and minerals, researchers use other radioactive nuclides with longer half-lives, such as uranium-238 and potassium-40.

9.8 Radioactive Isotopes as Tracers

Isotopes of a given element behave the same way in a chemical reaction. Those isotopes that are radioactive can be detected by instruments sensitive to radiation. Suppose that a radioactive isotope of an element is substituted for a nonradioactive isotope in a chemical reaction. Instruments can be used to trace the steps of the chemical reaction, since all compounds containing the radioisotope (a shortened name for radioactive isotope) will be radioactive. A radioisotope used for tracking purposes is called a **tracer.**

When you studied biology, you probably studied such topics as photosynthesis, the importance of enzymes for speeding up chemical reactions in living cells, and the use of vitamins and minerals in cell functions. How was this information obtained? Researchers de-

Myths and Misconceptions

Students may think that all isotopes need to be radioactive to act as tracers. Explain that some nonradioactive, stable isotopes are used as tracers. For example, oxygen-18 is a stable isotope used to study photosynthesis. A mass spectrometer can detect the different mass numbers of these isotopes.

termined some of the reaction pathways by tracking molecules or nutrients through metabolic processes using tracers.

Radioactive tracers also are used in industry and environmental studies. Tracers can help detect the movement of groundwater through soil, the paths of certain industrial pollutants in the air and water, and the shifting of sand along coastlines. In industry, tracers help manufacturers test the durability of mechanical components and identify structural weaknesses in equipment.

Medical use of tracers In medicine, tracers are used to diagnose and treat diseases. A radioactive tracer is substituted for the nonradioactive form of a chemical that is normally used by a specific organ. Doctors then follow the tracer by detecting its radiation in order to help diagnose a possible malfunction. The radioisotope chosen for a procedure depends on the dosage, half-life, and chemical activity that are most suitable. As the organ absorbs the radioisotope, a scanner produces an image of the organ on a monitor. Areas of extremely high or low radioactivity signal the existence of cells that may be malfunctioning.

One isotope commonly used for medical diagnosis is iodine-131. Iodine is essential for the thyroid gland to function properly. Iodine-131 accumulates in the gland just like nonradioactive iodine and is detected easily. Table 9-2 lists some common radioisotopes used as tracers in medicine.

TABLE 9-2

Common Radioisotopes Used in Medicine		
Radioisotope	**Half-life**	**Target Organ**
chromium-51	27.7 days	spleen
iodine-131	8.1 days	thyroid gland, lungs, kidneys
gallium-67	3.2 days	lymph glands
phosphorus-32	14.3 days	liver
strontium-87m*	2.8 hours	bones
technetium-99m*	6.0 hours	brain, lungs, liver, spleen

* The *m* indicates an unstable form of a stable isotope. Sr-87 and Tc-99 are stable. Sr-87m and Tc-99m are unstable and decay by γ emission.

Radioisotopes for medical treatment Radioisotopes also are used in the treatment of cancerous tumors. In the case of thyroid cancer, iodine-131 is taken for a prescribed length of time in amounts larger than those used for diagnosis. The radioisotope accumulates in the gland and the radiation emitted destroys a higher proportion of cancer cells than healthy tissue. In other situations,

Figure 9-8 *Food can be preserved for special purposes by radiation. Irradiated foods have been developed for use in the military and the space program.*

Guided Practice

Review the Concept Check question on page 307 with students. Answers can be found in Appendix E on page 808.

Reteaching Idea

If your students need more help in sorting out the ways in which nuclear reactions are used in research and in everyday life, have a brainstorming session. Let them appoint one or two peers to take on chalkboard duty. Have students call out practical uses for nuclear reactions while the recorders put them on the board. All ideas should be recorded, but when the list is complete, have the class examine each use and decide whether it is correct or valid. Use the list as a means of reviewing the benefits and dangers of each application.

**Videodisc Connections**

39485 to 40208, side 1
Mammography (movie)

40209 to 43401, side 1
More medical applications (movie)

PART **2**
Section 9.8 continued

☰ CLOSE

Summing Up Main Ideas

Ask students to define transmutation and to write nuclear equations for the transmutation of plutonium-239 into curium-242 and a neutron. (Transmutation is the transformation of one element into another element.)

$$^{239}_{94}Pu + ^{4}_{2}He \rightarrow ^{242}_{96}Cu + ^{1}_{0}n$$

PART 2 REVIEW

Assign the Part Review questions.

Evaluating Skills

These skills are evaluated in the Part Review questions indicated.
Determining main ideas: 20, 25;
Describing: 21; **Analyzing data:** 22, 23, 24; **Applying a strategy:** 22, 23; **Calculating:** 22, 23; **Verifying results:** 22, 23; **Determining cause and effect:** 26, 27

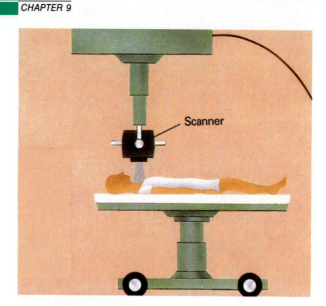

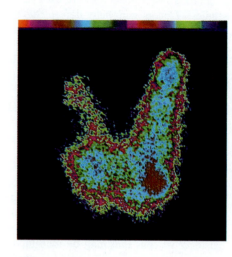

Figure 9-9 *A nuclear scan shows where radioactive iodine has been absorbed in a thyroid gland. Doctors use radioactive iodine-131 to identify areas of dysfunction and to treat tumors.*

a cancerous tumor is treated with radiation from an external source (such as cobalt-60). By changing the angle of bombardment, healthy cells are subjected to minimal amounts of radiation while tumor cells receive a concentrated dose. Radiation disrupts the fragile bonds of DNA molecules, and although healthy tissue is affected, the rapidly growing cancer cells are destroyed in greater numbers.

PART 2 REVIEW

20. What is transmutation?

21. Describe how scientists are able to synthesize elements with atomic numbers larger than that of uranium. Why is this process often expensive?

22. Write an equation for the production of the transuranium element obtained by bombarding americium-243 with high-speed nitrogen-14 nuclei.

23. What is the age of a plant fossil that emits 7.65 β^- particles/min/g from the radioactive decay of carbon-14?

Ans. 5730 y

24. Explain why radioactive dating using carbon-14 is not suitable for determining the ages of rocks.

25. List three ways that radioisotopes are used in research.

26. Why is iodine-131 useful in the treatment of thyroid disease?

27. What are some of the risks involved in using a radioactive tracer?

PROBLEM-SOLVING STRATEGY

To solve this problem, you will have to **use what you know** about the carbon-14 decay rate of living organisms (15.3 decays per minute per gram of carbon). (See Strategy, page 58.)

Boxed numbers indicate questions that involve skills in interpretation, application, and analysis.

PART 2 REVIEW

ANSWERS

■ Keyed to Objectives

F 20. The change of one element to another by a nuclear reaction

F 21. Large nuclei are bombarded with smaller nuclei such as hydrogen, helium, boron, carbon, nitrogen, and oxygen. Large amounts of energy are needed to overcome the repulsion of the target nucleus to the bombarding nucleus.

F 22. $^{14}_{7}N + ^{243}_{95}Am \rightarrow ^{257}_{102}No$

G 23. 7.65 disintegrations per minute per gram equals 5730 years.

G 24. Carbon-14 dating relies on the incorporation of carbon-14 into the object being dated. Carbon-14 is more likely to be incorporated into plants than rocks. Finally, rocks are much older than 50 000 years—the limit for carbon-14 dating.

H 25. Diagnosis of cell functions, tracking of materials, and identification of pathways in reactions

H 26. Iodine-131 accumulates in the thyroid gland and reduces the overgrowth that results in a goiter.

H 27. Harmful effects of radiation include damage to the chemical processes in cells or mutations or developmental defects in living organisms.

RESEARCH & TECHNOLOGY

Particle Accelerators

Imagine studying biology without a microscope or astronomy without a telescope! For a nuclear chemist, a particle accelerator is the tool needed to study the structure of a nucleus and synthesize new elements. Accelerator design is based on the principle that charged particles are accelerated when placed in an electric field.

In a Van de Graaf accelerator, a generator produces a large voltage on a metallic sphere at one end of an evacuated tube. The repulsive field of the sphere accelerates positive particles—such as protons, alpha particles, or positive ions—through the tube and toward a target. A Tandem Van de Graaf accelerator (with two generators) can accelerate protons to kinetic energies of 40 MeV and heavy ions to energies 10 times greater. (One MeV equals 1.6×10^{-13} J.)

A cyclotron consists of two semicircular, hollow conductors called dees. A voltage on the dees creates an electric field in the gap between them. Positive particles placed at the center of the cyclotron accelerate toward the negative dee. Inside the dee, a magnetic field forces the particles to move in a circular path. When the particles enter the gap again, the voltage is switched and they accelerate towards the second dee. As this process repeats itself, the particles gain speed, moving in larger circles until they are deflected out of the cyclotron to strike a target. Larger cyclotrons can accelerate protons, for example, to 60 MeV. Some large hospitals use cyclotrons to produce short-lived radioisotopes for research and diagnostic purposes.

In a linear accelerator (or linac), many conducting tubes are mounted in a straight line. A voltage on each tube produces an accelerating electric field in the gap between them. This voltage is alternated so that as a charged particle moves from one tube to the next, it gains additional energy. Some linacs have hundreds of tubes—the 50 000-MeV electron accelerator

Particle accelerators have advanced nuclear research, created the field of particle physics, and benefited medicine in the areas of research, diagnostic procedures, and radiation therapy.

at Stanford University is 2 miles long! Smaller, 10-MeV electron linacs are used in hospitals to produce gamma radiation to irradiate tumors.

The particle energies produced by these accelerators are sufficient to study nuclear reactions. Other accelerators, such as a synchrotron, can produce much higher energies—the synchrotron at Fermi National Accelerator Lab accelerates protons to 1 million MeV. A new synchrotron to be built in Texas called the superconducting supercollider (SSC) should accelerate protons to 20 million MeV! High-energy accelerators have opened up an entire new branch of physics—particle physics.

PART 3
Nuclear Reactions for
Energy
Section 9.9

Developing Skills

Students may apply this skill in their study of Part 3.

Comparing/Contrasting: Have students compare the estimated number of deaths per year due to the Chernobyl explosion to the current number of deaths from cancer. List and compare the risks from using nuclear fission for energy to the risks from using coal.

Compare the risks from nuclear waste to the risks from automobile emissions such as carbon monoxide and nitrogen oxides.

FOCUS

Activate Prior Knowledge

In Part 2 of Chapter 9, students studied common radioactive isotopes used in medicine. Ask students to study Table 9–2 and explain why they would or would not have reason for concern if hospitals were permitted to discard these radioactive isotopes into a landfill. (Possible reasons for concern include the known health problems, such as cancer and genetic defects, associated with exposure to radioactivity. Since all the radioisotopes in Table 9–2 have half-lives of less than 30 days, the radioactivity from waste in a landfill would soon disappear.

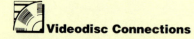

Videodisc Connections

33402 to 35349, side 1
Hiroshima bombing (movie)

PART 3 Nuclear Reactions for Energy

Objectives

Part 3

I. **Compare and contrast** nuclear fission and nuclear fusion.

J. **Analyze** the risks associated with nuclear waste and **evaluate** alternative disposal methods.

When you look at the stars, you see the results of some of the most energetic reactions in the universe. From Chapter 3, you know that chemical reactions absorb or release energy. Nuclear reactions give off about one million times more energy per gram of reactant than chemical reactions. The light and heat that reach Earth are the results of nuclear reactions within the sun.

9.9 Splitting Nuclei—Nuclear Fission

Fission is a nuclear reaction in which a nucleus is broken into two or more smaller nuclei, often by bombardment with neutrons of relatively low energy. Scientists first became aware of fission during their efforts to manufacture transuranium elements in the 1930's. They discovered that the uranium-235 nucleus breaks apart after absorbing a neutron.

The addition of a neutron makes the uranium nucleus unstable. As illustrated in Figure 9-10, the nucleus splits apart, forming two nuclei—usually with different atomic numbers—and emitting neutrons. Because the mass of the products is less than the mass of the reactants, energy is released. The neutrons emitted may be absorbed by other uranium-235 nuclei and cause them to undergo fission, which in turn releases more neutrons and more energy. This self-

Figure 9-10 In a fission chain reaction, a uranium-235 nucleus absorbs a neutron, becomes unstable, and breaks into two smaller nuclei. The neutrons produced are absorbed by other uranium nuclei and the process continues.

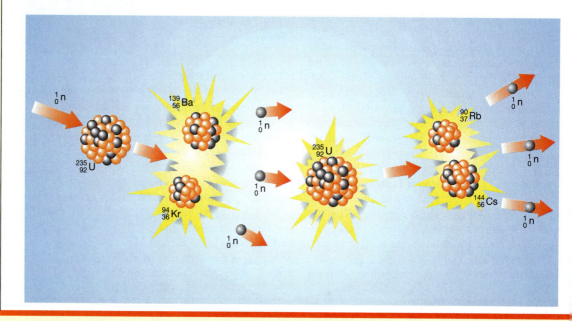

propagating reaction is called a **chain reaction.** If the amount of uranium-235 is small, many of the neutrons produced by the fission reaction pass through the material without being absorbed. As the amount of uranium-235 is increased, the chance of a neutron's striking a nucleus and being absorbed is also increased, thereby prolonging the reaction. The minimum amount of material needed to sustain the chain reaction is called the **critical mass.** The critical mass depends on the number of neutrons produced by each fission and on the concentration and shape of the uranium material.

How much energy is released during the fission of uranium-235? If 1 mole of uranium-235 completely fissioned, the mass loss would be approximately 0.22 gram. (Compare this to the 0.0053-gram mass loss calculated in Section 9-3 for the α decay of radium-226.) According to Einstein's equation, this fission reaction would produce 2.0×10^{10} kilojoules of energy—about forty times more energy than the α-decay reaction.

Concept ✔ Check

Explain how the energy produced by a chain reaction is so tremendous.

9.10 Nuclear Power Plants

Nuclear power plants use controlled fission reactions to produce energy to generate electricity. Uranium-235 is commonly used as fuel in nuclear reactors. Naturally occurring uranium ore contains only 0.7 percent uranium-235—a concentration too low to sustain a chain reaction. Therefore, the uranium ore must be enriched to a concentration of about 3 percent uranium-235 to enable a chain reaction to occur.

Structure of nuclear reactors Figure 9-11 shows the core of a fission reactor. Fuel rods containing the enriched uranium are inserted into the reaction chamber within the core. The reaction chamber of a pressurized nuclear reactor is illustrated in Figure 9-12. As the fission reaction proceeds, neutrons collide with other uranium atoms, continuing the chain reaction. If the neutrons are moving too fast, they cannot be readily absorbed by the uranium-235 nuclei. Therefore, in reactors using uranium-235 as a fuel, the neutrons are slowed down by collisions with **moderators.** The most effective moderators are water, beryllium, or graphite.

The rate of reaction is regulated by **control rods,** usually made of cadmium, that absorb some of the neutrons. Lowering the control rods into the fuel-rod assembly slows the rate of reaction. If control rods were not present inside the reactor, the heat of the reaction could raise the temperature high enough to cause a meltdown of the reactor core. Water acts as a coolant and transfers heat between

CONNECTING CONCEPTS

Change and Interaction The idea of a chain reaction is not limited to nuclear reactions. Sometimes chemical reactions proceed because the products continue to react with the initial substances.

Figure 9-11 *The water-covered core of a nuclear reactor contains the fuel rods and the mechanisms for controlling the reaction.*

PART **3**
Section 9.10

≣ TEACH

Science Background

Splitting Nuclei—Nuclear Fission

Nuclear fission of uranium-235 and plutonium-239 is a complicated process, and hundreds of daughter products are possible. The two daughter nuclei can range in atomic number from 30 to 65. Examples of possible equations include the following:

$$^{235}_{92}U + ^{1}_{0}n \rightarrow ^{141}_{56}Ba + ^{92}_{36}Kr + 3^{1}_{0}n$$
$$\rightarrow ^{101}_{40}Zr + ^{132}_{52}Te + 3^{1}_{0}n$$
$$\rightarrow ^{100}_{40}Zr + ^{134}_{52}Te + 2^{1}_{0}n$$
$$\rightarrow ^{99}_{39}Y + ^{135}_{53}I + 2^{1}_{0}n$$

The September 1991 issue of *The Journal of Chemical Education* lists the elements essential to all living species. The list includes hydrogen, carbon, oxygen, nitrogen, magnesium, phosphorus, sulfur, sodium, potassium, chlorine, calcium, iron, manganese, copper, zinc, lithium, iodine, boron, fluorine, silicon, vanadium, chromium, cobalt, nickel, molybdenum, selenium, and arsenic. The elements are also listed approximately in descending order of importance as judged by their amount, uniqueness, and the number of species that require them. If intensely radioactive, nuclides of these elements would pose a great threat to the environment. In addition, radioactive nuclides of elements that are chemically similar to the essential elements also pose a threat. Strontium is chemically similar to calcium. In the food chain, strontium can replace calcium and become a part of bone structure. Strontium-90 emits beta radiation and has a half-life of 29 years. Strontium-90 gives off substantial amounts of damaging radiation for about the average life span of a person.

PART **3**
Section 9.11

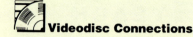

Videodisc Connections

47552 to 49616, side 1
Nuclear power plant (movie)

31520-31521, side 1
Three Mile Island power plant
(2-frame seq.)

Figure 9-12 *A typical commercial reactor contains thousands of fuel rods, each 4 meters long. The control rods are moved in or out to control the rate of reaction. Pressurized water is pumped through the reaction chamber to absorb heat energy. At the heat exchanger, this water heats a separate water system that makes steam to run a turbogenerator to make electricity.*

DO YOU KNOW?

A breeder reactor is a fission reactor that produces more fissionable material as it operates. These reactors use plutonium-239 fissions to produce both heat and more plutonium-239. Some nations discourage the construction of breeder reactors because plutonium-239 is used in building nuclear weapons.

the reactor and the steam turbines that produce electricity. Shielding, made of steel and high-density concrete, protects personnel by absorbing radiation.

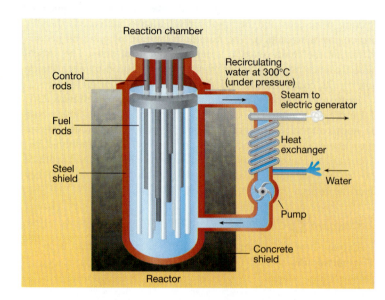

Reactor safety Despite strict safety guidelines, accidents can occur at nuclear power plants. In 1986, at the Chernobyl power plant in the Soviet Union, a runaway fission reaction caused a violent explosion. Radioactive material, including iodine-131, spewed into the atmosphere, affecting much of Scandinavia and eastern Europe. Thirty-one people were killed in this accident, and in the next 50 years there may be as many as 15 000 additional cancer deaths due to the radioactive fallout. The design of the nuclear reactors used in the United States is significantly different from that of the Chernobyl reactor, and it is unlikely that a similar accident could occur here. Still an explosion of radioactive steam might occur in the event of a meltdown. In 1979, there was a partial meltdown at the Three Mile Island plant in the United States. Although the possibility of a catastrophic accident is quite small, unanswered questions about nuclear-power safety remain. Of particular concern is the disposal of the radioactive waste generated. This issue will be examined more closely in Section 9.12.

9.11 Building Nuclei—Nuclear Fusion

In the nuclear reactions that occur within stars, energy is released when small nuclei join to form larger nuclei in a process called **fusion**. Fusion occurs for the same reason that fission does—the process leads to a more stable nucleus. In most stars, including the sun, hydrogen is converted into helium. The following equation,

Videodisc Connections

35351 to 37211, side 1
Fusion (movie)

illustrated in Figure 9-13, represents one hydrogen-to-helium fusion reaction produced in laboratory fusion experiments.

$$^3_1H + {}^2_1H \rightarrow {}^4_2He + {}^1_0n$$

The symbols ^2_1H and ^3_1H represent two isotopes of hydrogen—deuterium and tritium. In the production of 1 mole of helium-4, 1.7×10^9 kilojoules of energy are released. Helium can also be formed by combining two deuterium nuclides, but this reaction is more difficult to achieve in the laboratory. Generally nuclei with mass numbers less than 56 gain stability when they are fused into a larger nucleus.

Fusion reactions within the sun provide the solar energy necessary to sustain life on Earth. In one day, the energy reaching Earth from the sun equals all the energy ever used by humans on this planet! How does the amount of energy released when a kilogram of uranium fissions compare to that released when the same amount of hydrogen fuses? Although a single uranium fission event releases more energy than a single fusion event, one kilogram of hydrogen contains many more nuclei than one kilogram of uranium. The fission of one kilogram of uranium-235 produces energy equal to that obtained from the combustion of two million kilograms of coal, but the fusion of one kilogram of hydrogen into helium produces 20 times more energy than that!

Fusion reactors Fusion may be the power source capable of supplying the world's future energy needs. Scientists in the United States, the Soviet Union, and other countries are trying to achieve technically and economically feasible fusion reactions, but several problems remain. First, a huge input of energy is required to initiate the fusion process. Furthermore, in order to sustain the reaction, a temperature of 200-million kelvin is needed. No conventional fuel container can sustain the high temperatures required.

The Tokamak reactor, first developed in the Soviet Union, uses

Figure 9-13 Left: *The combination of deuterium and tritium to produce helium is one example of fusion. Nuclei of other elements of low atomic mass also can undergo fusion reactions to produce heavier, more stable nuclei and release energy.*
Right: *The Tokamak Fusion Test Reactor at Princeton University is one of the sites for fusion research in the United States. The reactor requires an electrical power supply equal to that of a city with a population of one half million.*

DO YOU KNOW?

The sun converts four million tons of hydrogen into helium every second. In addition to helium, fusion reactions in stars also produce elements such as carbon, nitrogen, silicon, and oxygen. The heavier elements (above iron in the periodic table) form during explosions of supernovas.

PART **3**
Section 9.12 ·

Teaching Strategy

Risk from Radioactive Waste

Energy is essential to support the world's current population and to maintain our standard of living. All energy consumption includes some risks. As oil and natural gas become scarce and more expensive, we may need to accept additional risks. Meanwhile, until a technological breakthrough makes unlimited safe energy available, everyone should conserve energy.

Guided Practice

Review the Concept Check question on page 313 with students. Answers can be found in Appendix E on page 808.

Reteaching Idea

If your students are unsure about issues surrounding the use of nuclear energy, have them stage a town meeting in which plans for construction of a nuclear power plant within their town boundaries are presented to the townspeople. The power plant is to use water from a local lake for cooling, and nuclear wastes are to be stored temporarily at the site until a permanent method of disposal can be found.
(continued on page T317)

Do You Know?

Only 10^{-13} percent of the deuterium available in sea water would be sufficient to meet the world's total energy needs for one year.

Figure 9-14 *Life on Earth would be impossible without the energy supplied by fusion reactions within the sun.*

a doughnut-shaped magnetic field to contain the nuclear fuel. In 1983, scientists using a Tokamak reactor at the Massachusetts Institute of Technology produced a fusion reaction at the break-even point. At the break-even point, there is the potential to obtain as much energy from the reaction as was used to initiate it.

There are several reasons why fusion reactions, especially those involving only deuterium, could be an important energy source. First, deuterium fuel is more readily available than uranium. In fact, deuterium can be extracted from ordinary sea water. Second, unlike the products of fission reactions, the helium produced in fusion is nonradioactive and does not pose a problem for waste disposal. Third, the reaction can be stopped at any time, eliminating the possibility of a nuclear meltdown. Fourth, the reaction would be a source of virtually inexhaustible energy and could eliminate most of the world's dependence on other fuels. Although scientists disagree about if and when economically feasible fusion will be achieved, research continues.

9.12 Nuclear Waste

The energy from fission has been harnessed in electric power plants to produce energy for consumption in many parts of the world. Unfortunately the waste materials from present nuclear-fission power plants pose a problem that is not easily solved. Disposal of radioactive waste is a very controversial issue. People are uncomfortable with the fact that radiation exposure has increased over the past 100 years. This increase has affected the way that people view the use of nuclear energy and the treatment of nuclear waste.

Risk from radioactive waste Several factors must be considered in order to calculate the risk from radioactive waste. *What is the half-life of the nuclide?* Nuclides that decay quickly may essentially disappear in a few days or weeks. *What are the daughter products of the decay?* A daughter product that is stable causes no further radiation problems. A daughter product that is radioactive will emit additional radiation. *What type of radiation is emitted?* Since alpha, beta, and gamma radiation have different energies and penetrating abilities, the risk of biological damage depends on the type of radiation emitted by a nuclide. *Can the radioactive waste be shielded effectively?* Gamma radiation is quite penetrating. Several centimeters of lead, or an even greater thickness of concrete, is required to shield against most gamma rays. β^- and β^+ particles are less penetrating; a few millimeters of aluminum is enough to stop them. α particles can be stopped by a single sheet of paper. *Are the radioactive nuclides easily incorporated into the food chain?* Nuclides that decay slowly and are essential elements for growth are more likely to enter the food chain.

PART 3 REVIEW

ANSWERS

■ Keyed to Objectives

I **28.** In fission, large nuclei are split; in fusion, small nuclei are fused together.

I **29.** Nuclear fission is started by the absorption of a neutron, which results in the splitting of the nucleus and the production of more neutrons. These can be absorbed, causing more nuclei to split, and so on.

I **30.** Control rods that absorb neutrons can be inserted into the nuclear pile to slow or stop the reaction.

I **31.** Water is a moderator that slows the speed of the neutrons. Slow neutrons are absorbed more readily by the nuclei of fissionable material. Water is also used to transfer heat and to produce steam for the turbine.

Possible waste-disposal solutions The problem of disposing of radioactive waste needs a reliable solution. A few nuclear waste products have half-lives of thousands of years and must be placed where they will not contaminate the environment. What is the cost of this storage? Is adequate security of the stored material possible? Consider some suggestions for waste disposal that have been rejected. Ocean dumping is not a viable solution because the canisters might corrode and release their contents. Incineration of nuclear waste produces gaseous radioactive products that would be released into the air. Sending waste into outer space to burn up near the sun is possible but expensive, and nobody can guarantee that the vehicle carrying the waste will successfully clear Earth's gravitational field without a mishap.

One current solution to the growing nuclear waste disposal problem is to bury the material in canisters deep underground in beds of salt. However, several questions remain unanswered about this disposal method. Will the canisters stay sealed over many hundreds or thousands of years? Is the site for storage geologically stable? Can the risk of accident in transporting dangerous materials to the storage sites be minimized?

Spent nuclear fuel rods can be reprocessed. The used rods are chemically dissolved and the uranium or plutonium is extracted and made into new fuel rods. The remaining radioactive waste is then converted into a solid—usually glass—by a process known as vitrification. This glass is stored underground. Currently the rate of waste production exceeds the rate at which the fuel rods are being reprocessed.

The potential for use of nuclear materials is enormous. Yet developing the technology needed to dispose of the waste products safely and economically will affect the growth of nuclear industries and the expansion of nuclear research in the future. People will have to make responsible decisions about how nuclear materials should be used. Understanding the issues is the first step in making those decisions.

Figure 9-15 *Radioactive wastes are mixed into molten glass that is then poured into graphite molds to harden. The wastes become trapped in the solid glass cylinders that result. The cylinders are placed in containers and can be stored underground.*

(continued from page T316)
Have students represent various interest groups, as well as ordinary citizens. One student should play the role of the chief executive officer of your local power company who presents the plan. After presentations by the interest groups, citizens should voice their concerns. Students should be able to back up their contributions to the debate with facts. Encourage students to prepare for their roles by finding other sources of information. For example, the long-running problems of getting the Seabrook Nuclear Power Plant in Seabrook, New Hampshire, built and licensed are instructive.

≡CLOSE

Summing Up Main Ideas

Have students compare the nuclear reaction that occurs in a nuclear power plant to the nuclear reaction that occurs in the sun. Also ask students to describe the fuel and waste products in both of these reactions. (A nuclear power plant uses fission, whereas fusion occurs in the sun. Fuels in a nuclear power plant are uranium-235 and plutonium-239. Fuels used by the sun include hydrogen, deuterium, and tritium. Fission produces a variety of radioactive nuclides. Fusion produces nonradiactive helium.)

PART 3 REVIEW

Assign the Part Review questions.

PART 3 REVIEW

28. Compare and contrast the processes of nuclear fission and nuclear fusion.

29. Describe the concept of a chain reaction.

30. How is a chain reaction controlled in a nuclear power plant?

31. What is the role of water in a nuclear power plant?

32. What is the greatest difficulty in producing energy from nuclear fusion?

33. Why is the disposal of nuclear wastes such an important problem?

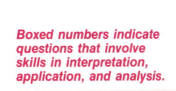
Boxed numbers indicate questions that involve skills in interpretation, application, and analysis.

Evaluating Skills

These skills are evaluated in the Part Review questions indicated. **Comparing/Contrasting:** 28; **Summarizing:** 29, 30, 33; **Stating a conclusion:** 32, 33

I 32. Sustaining a sufficiently high temperature in a confined space and then utilizing the energy produced

J 33. Radioactive waste materials frequently have long half-lives, and thus remain radioactive for a long time. If radioactive elements get into the food chain they can also get inside human bodies, where the elements are most harmful. (As the food chain proceeds, each higher level of consumers accumulates larger quantities of toxic substances. By this process of biological magnification, animals at the end of the food chain, where concentrations are highest, are most harmed.)

Determining the Half-Life of Barium-137m
Estimated Time: (40–50 minutes)

Process Skills

Measuring
Constructing tables and graphs
Predicting
Analyzing data

Preparation

■ Materials

(for demonstration or one lab group)

Apparatus

radiation detector (a nuclear scaler/timer is preferable, but a Geiger counter can be used); radioisotope generator—one of these types: (1) Isogenerator, from Oxford Tennelec/Nucleus Co., 601 Oak Ridge Turnpike, Oak Ridge, TN, 37830, or (2) Minigenerator, originally made by Union Carbide; no longer sold but still useful if it is available at your school; rubber gloves; beaker for the eluted Ba-137m; clock or stopwatch; graph paper

Reagents

■ For the Isogenerator, use the 0.1M EDTA solution as described in the kit.

■ For the Minigenerator, use 0.04M HCl as directed in the kit.

■ Safety

⚠ Wear rubber gloves. Keep the radioactive solution away from clothes, eyes, mouth, and skin. Wash off promptly if spills occur. After about 20 minutes, the radioactivity will have decreased so much that only background radiation can be detected, and at that point the solution can be flushed down the drain.

Laboratory

Investigation

Determining the Half-Life of Barium-137m

The term *half-life* refers to the average time required for one half of the nuclei in a sample of radioactive parent nuclides to emit radiation and become daughter nuclides. Each type of radionuclide has its own constant and characteristic half-life, varying from millions of years to mere seconds. With Ba-137m, you can determine the half-life of a radionuclide in one laboratory period.

In this experiment, you will pass a solution called an *eluent* through a cartridge of Cs-137. This unstable isomer is formed by the emission of a beta particle from the nucleus of cesium-137. Barium-137m remains unstable until the nucleus emits a gamma ray and becomes a stable nucleus, barium-137. Barium-137m is a natural by-product in the cartridge of cesium-137; it will be washed out of the cartridge along with the eluent solution. You will count samples of the eluent solution and record the counts for about 20 minutes, using a radioactivity detector.

O b j e c t i v e s

Explain how Ba-137m is obtained in the laboratory and *write the equation* for its formation.

Measure the rate of decay of Ba-137m using a radioactivity detector.

Construct and *interpret* a graph representing the decay of Ba-137m.

Determine the half-life of Ba-137m.

■ Materials

Apparatus	Reagents
□ radioactivity detector	□ Cs-137 cartridge
	□ eluent solution
□ beaker for eluted BA-137m	
□ rubber gloves	
□ clock or stopwatch	
□ graph paper	

  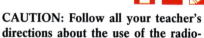

☢ **CAUTION: Follow all your teacher's directions about the use of the radioactivity detector and the radioactive sample.**

1. Turn on the radioactivity detector.

2. Put on your lab apron, safety goggles, and rubber gloves.

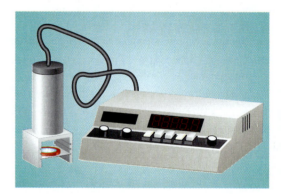

Data Table

Time (min)	Activity (cpm)	Corrected Activity (cpm)	Time (min)	Activity (cpm)	Corrected Activity (cpm)
0	11 905	11 855	12	489	439
2	6863	6813	14	342	292
4	4040	3990	16	199	144
6	2366	2316	18	103	53
8	1441	1391	20	91	41
10	828	778	Background radioactivity: 50 cpm		

3. Record the background radioactivity. Count the background for 1 minute. Average the values obtained by all of the teams. Record the average value at the bottom of your data table. This value must be subtracted from all readings of the radioactive sample to obtain the corrected counts per minute.

4. Your teacher will demonstrate the elution of the ion exchange column to obtain samples of Ba-137m and will distribute one of the samples to each team.

5. Using a radioactivity detector, count your sample for 1 minute and record the activity in counts per minute (cpm) in your data table. Wait 1 minute and then count for another minute. While waiting, you may start to calculate and record the corrected activity by subtracting the background count from each reading. Continue this procedure until the activity in cpm equals the background count. This will require about 18–20 minutes or about 11 readings.

6. Dispose of the sample as your teacher directs. Wash your hands thoroughly.

Data Analysis

Data Table

Time (min)	Activity (cpm)	Corrected Activity (cpm)
0		
2		
4		
6		
8		
10		
12		
14		
16		
18		
20		

Background radioactivity: _____ cpm

1. Finish subtracting the background count from each reading. Enter these values in the *Corrected activity (cpm)* column.

2. Draw a graph of your data by plotting corrected cpm on the vertical (*y*) axis and time in minutes on the horizontal (*x*) axis.

3. Draw a *smooth* curve connecting or coming as close as possible to the points on the line. Do *not* draw dot-to-dot lines.

4. To determine the half-life of Ba-137m, find the point on the *y*-axis where the activity is exactly one-half of the activity at time = zero. Draw a line parallel to the *x*-axis from that point to the curve. Then draw a vertical line down from the curve to the *x*-axis. The point at which the vertical line intersects the *x*-axis is the time required for half of the nuclei of the Ba-137m sample to decay. This is the half-life of Ba-137m.

5. To confirm your value, select any other convenient point in the middle range of the curve and determine the time for the activity to drop to half of this amount. Pool your information with that of other class members and obtain a class average for the half-life of Ba-137m. Compare this to the accepted value given to you by your teacher.

Conclusions

1. Write the nuclear reaction in which Cs-137 decays into Ba-137m.

2. Write the nuclear reaction in which Ba-137m decays into Ba-137.

3. Explain in your own words what is meant by a metastable barium-137m nucleus.

4. If a sample of Ba-137m gave an original corrected count of 12 000 cpm, what would its activity be 624 seconds later?

■ Procedural Hints

Be sure to measure the background radiation before eluting the sample. As soon as the sample is eluted, start counting. Follow the procedure of "count one minute; skip the next minute." Repeat until the corrected cpm equals the background cpm. This takes about 20 minutes. The one minute in between counting gives time to put the data on the blackboard or overhead projector and subtract the background. Assign one student to be timekeeper.

Make sure that students have graph paper to use for the plot. Using the chalkboard or overhead, show the class how to arrange the axes on the graph: "Time in minutes" on the *x*-axis and "Corrected cpm" on the *y*-axis. The half-life can be conveniently found from the graph without laborious calculations. The class average will usually be close to the accepted value of 2.6 minutes. (If students prepare their graph paper the day before, they can plot the curve as the data is being collected, and this speeds up the whole process.) In determining the half-life from the graph, students will get better results if they use values from the middle of the curve, rather than from the ends.

Data Analysis

■ Sample Data

(See table and data graphed below.)

Conclusions

1. Cs-137 → Ba-137m + e⁻ (beta particle)

2. Ba-137m → Ba-137 + (gamma ray)

3. "Metastable" means unstable or transient; thus the Ba-137m is stable for a short time and then decays.

4. The half-life of Ba-137m is 2.6 minutes or 156 seconds. Thus, 624 seconds/156 seconds per half-life = 4 half-lives. Therefore, the cpm would be 1/16 of the original cpm, or 750 cpm.

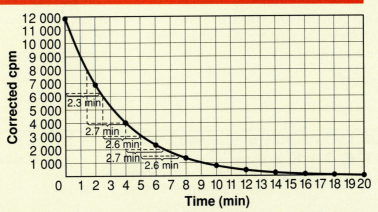

T319

Chapter 9
Review
ANSWERS
begin on page
T325a.

Summary

Exploring Radioactivity

- A nuclear change differs from a chemical change because nuclear reactions involve protons and neutrons, while chemical reactions involve electrons.

- Ionizing radiation has enough energy to change atoms and molecules into ions. Ionizing radiation can cause changes in the chemistry of cells and cell functions.

- Nuclear decay by the emission of different types of radiation results in a nucleus that contains less energy. In α emission, a helium-4 particle is emitted. In β^- emission, an electron is emitted and in β^+ emission a positron is emitted. The emission of gamma rays often accompanies alpha and beta emission.

- In nuclear decay, the initial nucleus is called the parent nuclide and the new nucleus that results is called the daughter nuclide. A nuclear reaction can be represented by an equation. The sum of the mass numbers and the sum of the atomic numbers on each side of the equation must be equal.

- Much larger amounts of energy are released in nuclear reactions than in chemical reactions. A detectable amount of mass is converted into energy, according to the equation $E = mc^2$.

- Since the decay of an individual nuclide is a random event, change is predicted for a given amount of a very large number of nuclei. The half-life of a radioactive nuclide is the time it takes for half of the nuclei in a given sample to decay.

- Radon-222 is a radioactive daughter nuclide produced in the decay series of uranium-238. Because it is a gas, radon can seep into buildings and enter the body through the lungs. High concentrations of radon pose a health hazard, since the radiation from both radon-222 and its daughter nuclide, polonium-218, can cause cancer.

Using Nuclear Reactions for Research

- The transformation of one element into another is known as transmutation. Transuranium elements and other radioactive nuclides that do not exist in nature can be synthesized in nuclear reactions produced by bombarding target nuclei with different particles.

- Radioactive dating, based on a knowledge of the half-lives and decay rates of radioactive nuclides, allows researchers to determine the age of certain objects.

- A tracer is a radioisotope used for tracking purposes in research in biology, chemistry, medicine, and physics.

Nuclear Reactions for Energy

- Fission is a nuclear reaction in which a nucleus is broken into two or more smaller nuclei, often by bombardment with neutrons of relatively low energy. The products of a fission reaction are energy, the smaller daughter nuclei, and additional neutrons. These additional neutrons can split other parent nuclei, initiating a chain reaction. The minimum amount of material needed to sustain the chain reaction is called the critical mass.

- The fission of uranium-235 is harnessed in modern nuclear reactors. Fission occurs in fuel rods containing enriched uranium. The neutrons emitted are slowed down by collisions with moderators, such as water or graphite. The rate of reaction is regulated by control rods, usually made of cadmium, that absorb some of the neutrons.

- Energy is released when nuclei with mass numbers less than 56 join together to form larger nuclei in a process called fusion. If the technology could be developed to economically produce fusion in reactors, hydrogen-to-helium

PROBLEM-SOLVING
▶ S T R A T E G I E S

Students apply these strategies in the following questions.

- **Factor-label method:** 8, 9, 10, 11, 12, 27, 57
- **Using similar problems:** 17
- **Using patterns:** 15, 16, 17, 18, 19, 20, 21, 39, 55
- **Using calculators:** 8, 9, 10, 11, 12, 15, 16, 17, 18, 19, 20, 21, 27, 35, 36, 37, 39, 55, 57, 59

T320

fusion could provide virtually limitless amounts of energy.

■ The amount of nuclear waste from power plants and industrial, medical, military, and research purposes continues to increase. Some nuclear waste products have half-lives of thousands of years and must be placed where they will not contaminate the environment. Scientists continue to search for reliable ways to dispose of this waste.

Chemically Speaking

alpha emission *9.2*
background radiation *9.1*
beta emission *9.2*
chain reaction *9.9*
control rods *9.10*
critical mass *9.9*
daughter nuclide *9.2*
decay series *9.5*
fission *9.9*
fusion *9.11*
half-life *9.4*

ionizing radiation *9.1*
moderators *9.10*
nonionizing radiation *9.1*
nuclide *9.1*
parent nuclide *9.2*
positron *9.1*
rem *9.1*
spontaneous decay *9.5*
tracer *9.8*
transmutation *9.6*
transuranium element *9.6*

Concept Mapping

Using the concept mapping method described at the front of this book, draw a concept map for nuclear chemistry, using the following concepts: *alpha emission, background radiation, beta emission, daughter nuclide, electron, parent nuclide, positron, radiation,* and *transmutation.*

Questions and Problems

EXPLORING RADIOACTIVITY

A. Objective: **Differentiate** *between ionizing and nonionizing radiation.*

1. Classify each of the following types of radiation as ionizing (I) or nonionizing (N):
   a. infrared   e. X rays
   b. gamma   f. radio waves
   c. microwaves   g. alpha radiation
   d. ultraviolet   h. beta radiation
2. Contrast ionizing and nonionizing radiation.
3. Which types of radiation listed in question 1 originate in the nucleus of atoms?

B. Objective: **Identify** *the different types of radioactive decay and* **use equations** *to represent the changes that occur.*

4. Write equations for the decay of bismuth-209 and radium-224 by α emission.
5. Write equations for the decay of cobalt-60 and calcium-39 by β^- emission.
6. Write an equation for the decay of copper-64 and nitrogen-12 by β^+ emission.
7. Fill in the correct symbol to complete each equation.

   a. $^{238}_{92}U \rightarrow$? $+ \, ^4_2He$

   b. $^{231}_{90}Th \rightarrow$? $+ \, ^0_{-1}e$

   c. ? $\rightarrow \, ^{20}_{10}Ne + \, ^0_{+1}e$

   d. $^{226}_{88}Ra \rightarrow \, ^{222}_{86}Rn +$?

   e. $^{40}_{19}K \rightarrow \, ^{40}_{20}Ca +$?

C. Objective: **Determine** *the mass loss in a given nuclear decay and using Einstein's equation,* **calculate** *the energy released.*

8. How much energy is released in a nuclear reaction if the mass loss is 1.68×10^{-4} g? Express your answer in kilojoules.
9. Bismuth-210 decays into polonium-210 by emitting a β^- particle. If 1 mole of bismuth decays, the mass loss is 7.0×10^{-4} g. How many kilojoules of energy are released in this reaction?
10. One mole of radium-226 decays by α emission to yield 4.8×10^8 kJ of energy. How

■ **Verifying your answer:** 8, 9, 10, 11, 12, 17, 18, 19, 20, 21, 27, 35, 36, 37, 55, 57, 59

■ **Breaking problems into manage-**

able parts: 11, 12, 57
■ **Writing chemical equations:** 4, 5, 6, 7, 32, 33, 44, 56

much energy is released when 1 g of radium-226 decays? (The nuclear mass of radium-226 is 225.9771 g/mol).

11. Calculate the energy given off in the following reaction.

$$^{222}_{86}Rn \rightarrow \, ^{218}_{84}Po + \, ^{4}_{2}He$$

The molar masses are radon-222 = 221.9703 g, polonium-218 = 217.9628 g, and helium-4 = 4.0026 g.

12. When the nuclei of 1 mole of polonium-210 decay by α emission to produce lead-206, how many kilojoules of energy are released? The molar masses are: polonium-210 = 209.9829 g, lead-206 = 205.9784 g, and helium-4 = 4.0026 g.

D. Objective: **Predict** *the fraction of radioactive nuclei that remain after a certain amount of time, given the half-life.*

13. Which will decay faster—carbon-14 or beryllium-10, which has a half-life of 1 600 000 years?

14. The half-life of uranium-238 is 4.5 billion years and the age of Earth is 4.5×10^9 years. What fraction of the uranium-238 that was present when Earth was formed still remains?

15. Chromium-48 decays by β^+ emission. After 6 half-lives, what fraction of the original nuclei would remain?

16. How many half-lives will pass before the fraction of remaining radioactive nuclides is less than 1/1 000 000?

17. The half-life of iodine-125 is 60 days. What fraction of iodine-125 nuclides would be left after 360 days?

18. Titanium-51 decays by β^- emission with a half-life of 6 min. What fraction of titanium would remain after 1 h?

19. A medical institution requests 1 g of bismuth-214, which has a half-life of 20 min. How many grams of bismuth-214 must be prepared if the shipping time is 2 h?

20. The half-life of radium-226 is 1602 years. What fraction of a sample of radium-226 would remain after 9612 years?

21. Show mathematically why the radioactivity in a sample is considered to be negligible after 10 half-lives.

E. Objective: **List** *some of the effects of ionizing radiation on life forms and the environment.*

22. List three harmful effects of ionizing radiation on living cells.

23. Describe three ways that ionizing radiation is useful.

24. Why is the maximum recommended level of radiation exposure lower for women of childbearing age than for older women?

25. Explain why the radiation from strontium-90 that has been incorporated into the bones is especially harmful.

26. Radioactive krypton-85 is a chemically inert gas that is released into the atmosphere during the reprocessing of nuclear fuel rods. Explain why inhaling krypton-85 is less harmful than ingesting strontium-90.

27. Astronauts in a spacecraft above the atmosphere receive about 100 millirems of radiation per day from cosmic sources. How long could they remain in space before they receive a dose of 5 rems—the maximum occupational dose allowed by the United States government?

28. Evaluate each of the following to determine which may result from exposure to radiation.
   a. genetic damage
   b. cancer
   c. skull shape
   d. hyperactivity
   e. drought
   f. leukemia
   g. birth defects
   h. food poisoning
   i. tooth decay
   j. nausea

29. Why is it difficult to study the effect of low doses of radiation on humans over a long period of time?

30. Look at the graph comparing two models of radiation damage. List which model(s) predict(s) risk for the following exposures.
    a. smoking two packs of cigarettes per day
    b. average background radiation
    c. two chest X rays
    d. six dental X rays
    e. weekly cross-country trip by airplane
    f. living in a home exposed to radon

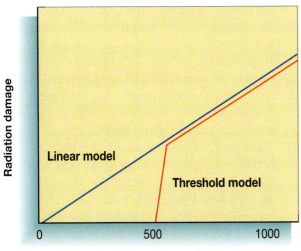

USING NUCLEAR REACTIONS FOR RESEARCH

F. Objective: **Explain** *what is meant by transmutation.*

31. Most transuranium isotopes have half-lives of less than 1 day. Why might these isotopes be so unstable?

32. Write an equation representing the synthesis of cobalt-60 from cobalt-59.

33. Describe a method of transmuting cobalt-59 to copper-63.

34. Why do neutrons require little energy in order to bombard target nuclei during the synthesis of nuclides?

G. Objective: **Determine** *the age of a fossil using information about its rate of radioactive decay.*

35. What is the age of a bone that emits β^- radiation from carbon-14 at the rate of 0.96 decays/min/g?

36. A sample of charcoal with a mass of 50.0 g was found in an ancient ruin. If the sample emits 382 β^- particles every minute from the decay of carbon-14, what is the approximate age of the ruin?

37. An organism died about 17 190 years ago. What would be the carbon-14 decay rate of a fossil formed from this organism?

38. Suppose that the production of carbon-14 decreased sharply for a 10 000-year period starting 40 000 years ago. If you determined a fossil's age by radioactive dating without knowing about this decrease, would you underestimate or overestimate the age of a fossil from this period? Explain your reasoning.

39. How many half-lives of carbon-14 and of uranium-238 have passed since Earth was formed about 4.5 billion years ago? (The half-life of carbon-14 is 5730 y and the half-life of uranium-238 is 4.5×10^9 y.) Use this information to explain why uranium-238 dating rather than carbon-14 dating is used for very old fossils.

H. Objective: **Evaluate** *the benefits and risks of radioisotopes used in medicine and research.*

40. Discuss how a radioactive tracer might be used to find a leak in a water pipe.

41. Sulfur will be used as a tracer to determine the method of nutrient transfer in a bean plant. Which of the two radioactive isotopes available would you choose—sulfur-35, with a half-life of 87 days, or sulfur-37, with a half-life of 5 minutes? Explain the reasons for your choice.

NUCLEAR CHEMISTRY **323**

42. Calcium phosphate is a major component of bones. Evaluate the benefits and risks of using calcium-47 to detect bone lesions.

43. The radioisotopes listed in Table 9-2 have relatively short half-lives. Why might a tracer with a short half-life be preferable to one with a long half-life?

NUCLEAR REACTIONS FOR ENERGY

I. Objective: Compare and contrast *nuclear fission and nuclear fusion.*

44. A typical fission reaction is represented as follows.

$$^1_0n + ^{235}_{92}U \rightarrow ^{141}_{56}Ba + ^{92}_{36}Kr + ?$$

How many neutrons must be released in this fission reaction?

45. What is the source of the energy released during nuclear fission?

46. Explain why a chain reaction keeps going.

47. List two advantages and two disadvantages of nuclear fusion as compared to nuclear fission.

J. Objective: Analyze *the risks associated with nuclear waste and* evaluate *alternative disposal methods.*

48. The water that circulates through the core of a fission reactor is used to heat a secondary water source that then runs the steam turbines (see Figure 9-10). Why is the water from the core not directly used to run the steam turbines instead?

49. Describe and compare two methods being proposed for the disposal of nuclear waste.

50. Consider the following radioactive decays.

$$^{31}_{14}Si \rightarrow ^0_{-1}e + ^{31}_{15}P \text{ and } ^{32}_{14}Si \rightarrow ^0_{-1}e + ^{32}_{15}P$$

The half-life of the first reaction is 2.62 h, while the half-life of the second reaction is 105 y. Although the first daughter product—phosphorus-31—is stable, phosphorus-32 is radioactive and further decays according to the equation

$$^{32}_{15}P \rightarrow ^0_{-1}e + ^{32}_{16}S$$

List two reasons why the release of silicon-31 should pose less threat to the environment than the release of silicon-32.

51. Polonium-210 is a radioactive nuclide that decays by α emission to the stable nuclide—lead-206. Hafnium-182 is a radioactive nuclide that decays by β^- emission to another radioactive nuclide—tantalum-182. Tantalum-182 further decays by emitting β^- particles, forming the stable nuclide—tungsten-182. The half-lives of these three reactions are 138 d, 9×10^6 y, and 115 d, respectively. Which of these radioactive nuclides—polonium-210 or hafnium-182—would pose more danger if accidentally released into the environment? List three reasons that support your answer.

52. Gallium-72 and xenon-133 are both radioactive nuclides that decay by β^- emission to stable nuclides. The half-life of xenon-133 is about 9 times longer than the half-life of gallium-72. Despite its longer half-life, why would xenon-133 be less dangerous than gallium-72 if both were released into the environment? (Hint: Think about the chemical activity of these isotopes.)

Critical Thinking

SYNTHESIS WITHIN THE CHAPTER

53. Explain why the decay of carbon-11 into boron-10 and a proton appears to be a valid nuclear reaction.

$$^{11}_6C \rightarrow ^{10}_5B + ^1_1H$$

Show that this reaction actually violates Einstein's equation. The molar masses of the nuclides are carbon-11 = 11.0114 g, boron-10 = 10.0129 g, and proton (^1_1H) = 1.007 g.

54. Does $E = mc^2$ apply to both fission reactions and fusion reactions?

55. After the 1986 Chernobyl reactor accident, several nations reported levels of iodine-131 contamination in milk. The reported decay rates per liter of milk are listed in the table, along with the safety limits set by each government.

Decay Rate of Iodine-131

| Nation | Decays/s/L | |
	Reported	Allowed
Poland	2000	1000
Sweden	2900	2000
Austria	1500	370
West Germany	1184	500

The half-life of iodine-131 is 8.1 days. Based on this information, list the order in which these countries resumed their consumption of milk.

56. A typical fission process occurs after a uranium-235 nuclide absorbs a neutron and becomes the unstable uranium-236 nuclide. Uranium-236 splits to produce tellurium-137, zirconium-97, and two neutrons. Write the two equations that represent the nuclear reactions.

SYNTHESIS ACROSS CHAPTERS

57. One fusion reaction studied in the laboratory is

$$^2_1H + {}^2_1H \rightarrow {}^3_2He + {}^1_0n$$

This reaction will release 1.6×10^8 kJ of energy for every mole of deuterium. The chemical burning of 1 mole of hydrogen releases 241.8 kJ of energy. How much hydrogen, in grams, would have to be burned in order to produce the same amount of energy as the fusion of 1 g of deuterium?

58. During World War II, the first practical method for separating the uranium-235 nuclide from the uranium-238 nuclide was to form uranium hexafluoride gas. The molecules of one of the nuclides diffuse faster than the molecules of the other. Which molecules diffuse faster?

59. Calculate the ratio of the rates of diffusion of the two isotopic forms of uranium hexafluoride.

60. Arrange the ionizing radiation in question 1 in order of increasing penetrating power.

Research and Writing

61. Read about and report on the events that took place at the Three Mile Island nuclear power plant in March 1979.

62. Read about and report on the events that took place at the Chernobyl nuclear power plant in 1986.

63. Read about the use of radioisotopes in cancer therapy. Find out details—not covered in the chapter—about how and when radioisotopes are used and how great is their effectiveness.

64. Read about the scientific contributions of the Curie family—Marie, Pierre, their daughter Irene, and her husband Frederic Joliot. Describe the history of their work and the roles they played in the development of nuclear science.

65. Investigate the irradiation of food. Find out what foods are good candidates for irradiation, how the process works, and why it is beneficial. Describe the controversies concerning the use of irradiation to treat food.

☐ Boxed numbers indicate questions that involve skills in interpretation, application, and analysis.

1. a. N
   b. I
   c. N
   d. N
   e. I
   f. N
   g. I
   h. I

2. Ionizing radiation has sufficient energy to produce ions in matter; nonionizing radiation does not.

3. b, g, h

4. $^{209}_{83}Bi \rightarrow ^4_2He + ^{205}_{81}Tl$
   $^{224}_{88}Ra \rightarrow ^4_2He + ^{220}_{86}Rn$

5. $^{60}_{27}Co \rightarrow ^0_{-1}e + ^{60}_{28}Ni$
   $^{39}_{20}Ca \rightarrow ^0_{-1}e + ^{39}_{21}Sc$

6. $^{64}_{29}Cu \rightarrow ^0_1e + ^{64}_{28}Ni$
   $^{12}_7N \rightarrow ^0_1e + ^{12}_6C$

7. a. $^{234}_{90}Th$ d. ^4_2He
   b. $^{231}_{91}Pa$ e. $^0_{-1}e$
   c. $^{20}_{11}Na$

8. $1.68 \times 10^{-4} g \times \frac{1\ kg}{1000\ g}$

   $= 1.68\ 10^{-7}\ kg$

   $E = mc^2 = 1.68 \times 10^{-7}\ kg$

   $\left(3.00 \times 10^8\ m/s\right)^2 = 1.51 \times 10^{10}\ J$

   $1.51 \times 10^{10}\ J \times \frac{1\ kJ}{1000\ J}$

   $= 1.51 \times 10^7\ kJ$

9. $7.0 \times 10^{-4} g \times \frac{1\ kg}{1000\ g}$

   $= 7.0\ 10^{-7}\ kg$

   $E = mc^2 = 7.0 \times 10^{-7}\ kg$

   $\left(3.00 \times 10^8\ m/s\right)^2 = 6.3 \times 10^{10}\ J$

   $6.3 \times 10^{10}\ J \times \frac{1\ kJ}{1000\ J}$

   $= 6.3 \times 10^7\ kJ$

10. $1\ g\ Ra \times \frac{4.8 \times 10^8\ kJ}{225.9771\ g\ Ra} = 2 \times 10^6\ kJ$

11. Change in mass = 221.9703 g
    $- (217.9628 + 4.0026)$

    $= 4.9 \times 10^{-3}\ g$

    $4.9 \times 10^{-3}\ g \times \frac{1\ kg}{1000\ g}$

    $= 4.9\ 10^{-6}\ kg$

    $E = mc^2 = 4.9 \times 10^{-6}\ kg$

    $\left(3.00 \times 10^8\ m/s\right)^2 = 4.4 \times 10^{11}\ J$

    $4.4 \times 10^{11}\ J \times \frac{1\ kJ}{1000\ J}$

    $= 4.4 \times 10^8\ kJ$

12. $^{210}_{84}Po \rightarrow ^4_2He + ^{206}_{82}Pb$
    Mass change = 209.9829 g
    $- (205.9784\ g + 4.0026\ g)$

    $= 1.9 \times 10^{-3}\ g$

    $1.9 \times 10^{-3}\ g \times \frac{1\ kg}{1000\ g}$

    $= 1.9\ 10^{-6}\ kg$

    $E = mc^2 = \left(1.9 \times 10^{-6}\ kg\right)$

    $\left(3.00 \times 10^8\ m/s\right)^2 = 1.7 \times 10^{11}\ J$

    $1.7 \times 10^{11}\ J \times \frac{1\ kJ}{1000\ J}$

    $= 1.7 \times 10^8\ kJ$

13. carbon-14

14. $\frac{1}{2}$

15. $\left(\frac{1}{2}\right)^6 = \frac{1}{64}$

16. $\left(\frac{1}{2}\right)^{20} = \frac{1}{1\ 048\ 576}$; therefore, 20 half-lives

17. $\frac{360\ days}{60\ days} = 6$ half-lives;

    $\left(\frac{1}{2}\right)^6 = \frac{1}{64}$

18. 1 hour = 60 min; $\frac{60\ min}{6\ min}$

    = 10 half-lives; $\left(\frac{1}{2}\right)^{10} = \frac{1}{1024}$

19. 2 hours = 120 min; $\frac{120\ min}{20\ min}$

    = 6 half-lives; $\left(\frac{1}{2}\right)^6 = \frac{1}{64}$

    At least 64 grams must be prepared.

20. $\frac{9612\ years}{1602\ years} = 6$ half-lives; $\left(\frac{1}{2}\right)^6 = \frac{1}{64}$

21. $\left(\frac{1}{2}\right)^{10} = \frac{1}{1024}$;

    if one gram were present at the start, less than one thousandth of a gram would remain and the radioactivity would be one thousand times smaller.

22. Damage to molecules in the cell and to the cell wall, changes in the chemical reactions resulting in disruption of cell functions, and genetic damage

due to changes in the chromosomal DNA of reproductive cells

23. Killing of harmful bacteria, diagnosis and treatment of disease, and beneficial mutations in the genetic structure of a cell

24. Radiation can cause genetic changes that result in birth defects.

25. Blood cells vital to body functions are produced inside the bones and are easily damaged by radiation. Strontium-90 can also cause leukemia.

26. Krypton-85 may be inhaled but it will most likely be exhaled before decaying; ingested strontium-90 will be incorporated into bones because it is chemically similar to calcium. There, it will emit radiation for a long time, damaging the blood cells produced.

27. $5\ rem \times \frac{1000\ millirem}{1\ rem} \times \frac{1\ day}{100\ millirem}$
    = 50 days

28. a, b, f, g, j

29. A noticeable effect may be due to some other causes or combination of causes. Also, everyone is exposed to background radiation, so it is impossible to design a control group.

30. Threshold Model: a, f
    Linear Model: b, c, d, e

31. The number of protons packed into the nuclei is too large.

32. $^{59}_{27}Co + ^1_0n \rightarrow ^{60}_{27}Co$

33. $^{59}_{27}Co + ^4_2He \rightarrow ^{63}_{29}Cu$

34. Because they are neutral, neutrons are not repelled by the positively charged nuclei.

35. The ratio of radioactive decay is $\frac{15.3}{0.96}$
    = 15.9. The radioactivity has decreased by a factor of 15.9, or approximately 16.

    $16^{\frac{1}{2}} = 4$ half-lives
    The half-life of carbon-14 is 5730

    years. $\frac{5730\ years}{half\text{-}life} \times 4\ half\text{-}lives$
    = 23 000 years

36. $\frac{382\ decays}{50.0\ g/min} = \frac{7.64\ decays}{g/min}$

    $\frac{15.3\ decays/g/min}{7.64\ decays/g/min} = 2.00$ half-lives

    $2.00\ half\text{-}lives \times \frac{5730\ years}{half\text{-}life}$
    = 11 500 years

37. $\frac{17\ 190\ years}{5730\ years} = 3$ half-lives

    $\left(\frac{1}{2}\right)^3 = \frac{1}{8}$

    $\frac{15.3\ decays}{g/min} \times \frac{1}{8} = \frac{1.91\ decays}{g/min}$

38. There would be less carbon-14 present initially, leading to a lower radioactive decay rate at the time of dating. The object would appear to be older than its correct age.

39. $4.5 \times \frac{10^9 \text{ y}}{4.5} \times 10^9 \text{ y} = 1$ half-life

    for uranium-238

    $4.5 \times \frac{10^9 \text{ y}}{5.73} \times 10^3 \text{ y} = 7.9 \times 10^5$

    half-lives for carbon-14

    The decay rate for carbon-14 after so many half-lives would be undetectably low, but it would still be fairly high for uranium-238.

40. A radioactive substance is mixed with the water, sent through the pipe, then removed. A radiation detector outside the pipe would reveal any leaks in the pipe.

41. Sulfur-35; the other isotope has such a short half-life, the radioisotope would be undetectable before the process could be traced.

42. Calcium-47 has a relatively short half-life, so the radiation level would be quite low in a few weeks. The damage done by the scanning process is small enough so that one should accept risk of using it to detect a life-threatening injury. On the other hand, calcium phosphate stays in the bones and is not eliminated from the body, so there is some risk to surrounding tissues while the radiation level is high.

43. The radioactivity given off by the tracer decreases rapidly when the half-life is short. This reduces radiation harm and environmental damage if the substance escapes.

44. $(235 + 1) - (141 + 92) = 3$

45. Matter is converted into energy.

46. Each time a neutron is absorbed, at least one new neutron (and usually three new neutrons) are produced to continue the reaction.

47. Advantages: less radioactive waste, 20 times as much energy produced per gram of matter; disadvantages: huge amounts of energy are needed to start the reaction, and the reaction is difficult to contain and sustain.

48. That water is likely to be radioactive

49. Burial in deep rock formations in glassed materials is safest if there are no geological upheavals, eruptions, or earthquakes that expose the material. Underground storage in canisters in salt beds requires geological stability and assumes the canisters will not leak. Corrosion of the canisters seems likely and makes this method appear risky.

50. Silicon is not likely to become a part of the food chain. Silicon-31 is a small hazard because it has a short half-life and loses radioactivity rapidly, becoming beneficial phosphorus-31. Silicon-32 decays more slowly and the daughter product, phosphorus-32, is radioactive and easily absorbed into the food chain. Thus, both silicon-32 and phosphorus-32 pose a long-term threat over hundreds of years.

51. Hafnium-182 is more dangerous because it produces radioactivity longer, has more radioactive daughters that may become part of the food chain, and the beta radiation produced is more penetrating.

52. Gallium is chemically similar to aluminum and is more likely to be found in the food chain. Xenon is chemically inert.

53. The nuclear reaction is apparently valid because the number of protons and neutrons are conserved. However, there is an increase in mass, since 10.0129 g + 1.007 g = 11.0179 g, which is greater than the mass of carbon-11. Spontaneous nuclear reactions are always exothermic, which means some matter is converted into energy and the mass decreases.

54. Yes

55. Sweden, Poland, West Germany, Austria

56. $^1_0\text{n} + ^{235}_{92}\text{U} \rightarrow ^{236}_{92}\text{U}$
    $^{236}_{92}\text{U} \rightarrow ^{137}_{52}\text{Te} + ^{97}_{40}\text{Zr} + 2^1_0\text{n}$

57. $1\ \text{g}\ ^2\text{H}_2 \times \frac{1.6 \times 10^8\ \text{kJ}}{4\ \text{g}\ ^2\text{H}_2} \times \frac{2\ \text{g}\ ^1\text{H}_2}{241.8\ \text{kJ}}$

    $= 3.3 \times 10^5\ \text{g}\ ^1\text{H}_2$

    Note: 1 mole of deuterium (D_2) has a mass of 4 g; 1 mole of hydrogen (H_2) has a mass of 2 g. $D_2 = {}^2H_2$; $H_2 = {}^1H_2$

58. Uranium-235 hexafluoride molecules diffuse faster.

59. $\text{rate} = \sqrt{\frac{352.0}{349.0}} = 1.0043$

60. gamma (greatest penetrating power), X ray, beta, alpha

C HEMICAL PERSPECTIVE

Critical Thinking Skills

These skills are applied in the feature.

- Identifying illogical thinking
- Making an informed decision
- Evaluating the relevance of information
- Evaluating an opinion or point of view
- Using resources

Focus

Activate Prior Knowledge

Ask students what feelings come to mind when they hear the word *radioactivity*. Do your students understand the relationship between radiation and radioactivity? Review the difference between ionizing and non-ionizing radiation.

Teach

Science Background

The incident at Chernobyl, coupled with other nuclear accidents and information released in a congressional report that some Americans were used as "nuclear guinea pigs," has bred misunderstanding and mistrust of the whole nuclear industry.

Teaching Strategy

Review the difference between alpha, beta, and gamma radiation. Discuss how skin can block alpha particles, but not beta particles and gamma radiation. Review that a gene mutation may be caused by the chemical rearrangement of DNA in a cell by radiation. Have students identify natural sources of radiation (the sun).

Look Ahead

Nucleic acids will be discussed in Chapter 23.

Radioactivity—Harmful or Helpful?

A scientific phenomenon discovered almost 100 years ago has the potential to destroy life on this planet or improve it greatly, depending on how it is used. This phenomenon is known as radioactivity. An educated public must decide if the benefits of using radioactive substances outweigh the risks. To arrive at an informed decision, you must evaluate the many beneficial uses as well as the inherent hazards of radiation.

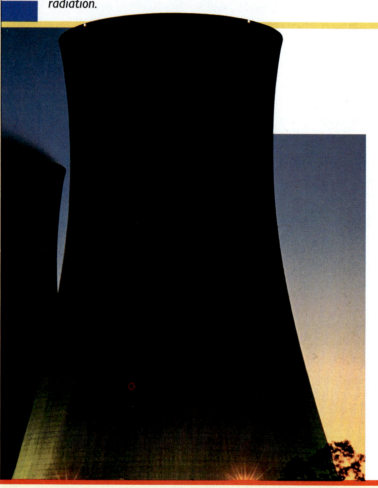

What comes to min when you hear th word *radioactivity* To some, it is the explosion the Chernobyl nuclear power plant, the grim aftermath of the bombing of Hiroshima, o the threat of a nuclear holocaust. To others, it is the fac that radioactivity can help dia nose diseases, rid the body o cancer, and save lives.

Radioactivity can be fright ening, since it easily penetrat living cells, damaging them to different degrees. The amour of damage depends upon the type of cell, the type of radia tion, and the dosage. If the dosage is high, it kills cells im mediately. But even slight ex posure may cause cells to reproduce abnormally. This, in turn, may cause cells to form cancerous tumor.

One of the most common uses of radioactivity is to fuel nuclear power plants. Some view nuclear power as the grand solution to the world's energy problems, since nuclear reactors do not contribute to the greenhouse effect, air pol lution, or acid rain as do foss fuels. Others view nuclear power as dangerous. The safety problems associated wi reactor operation and mainte

Some view nuclear power as the solution to energy problems, but others view it as dangerous.

...ance, the radioactive waste that is generated, and the risk of nuclear disaster concern many people. They point to Three Mile Island in 1979, when 1000 people were evacuated, and to Chernobyl in 1986, when a radioactive cloud killed 23 people, 40,000 people were evacuated, and parts of Western Europe and Scandinavia showed evidence of radiation.

Radioactive materials are used beneficially in medicine. Radioactivity, in the form of radiation therapy, can fight cancer. Radiation therapy involves administering a radioisotope that accumulates in the cancerous organ. Since rapidly dividing cancer cells are more sensitive to radiation than normal cells, more cancer cells are killed than normal ones. A series of such treatments can eliminate many types of cancer. Plutonium-238 is a radioactive material that powers cardiac pacemakers. A pacemaker that regulates the heartbeat of cardiac patients also exposes the wearer to radiation. This risk, however, offsets the risks associated with repeated surgical implantations of battery-powered pacemakers every two or three years.

Medical imaging is a new technique used in medical diag-

Radioactivity benefits several areas of medicine, including medical diagnosis.

...nosis. Imaging uses radioactive materials to enable doctors to look at organs inside the human body without surgery.

Doctors can also monitor processes inside the human body by injecting radioactive tracers.

Still another use of radioactivity is the irradiation of food. Food irradiation effectively sterilizes foods by killing bacteria that cause food to spoil. The Food and Drug Administration (FDA) found food irradiation so safe that it approved the irradiation of many foods—including fruits, vegetables, wheat, pork, and poultry. Critics of food irradiation say that not enough is known about the products formed when food is irradiated.

As with so many technical problems society faces today, decisions must be made by an informed public based on what it knows *now*. Is radiation more helpful than harmful? Evaluating the risks as well as the benefits will help you answer this question.

Discussing the Issues

1. Do you think the benefits of radioactivity outweigh the risks? Support your position.
2. Battery-operated smoke detectors contain americium-241, a radioactive isotope. Discuss the risks and benefits of using these devices in your home.

Take Action

1. Contact a radiology laboratory near your school to obtain permission to visit the facility. Observe those safeguards and precautions that workers practice in their jobs. Report your findings to the class.
2. Using a Geiger counter, compare various sites in your community. You may want to include your chemistry lab, homeroom, a playing field, a wooded area, an industrial parking lot, a residential driveway, and a local landfill.

327

Chemical Update
The idea of irradiating food with ionizing radiation has been around since the early 1960s. Gamma rays from cobalt-60 or cesium-137 kill microorganisms and prolong the shelf life of certain foods. Irradiation does not make food radioactive, but researchers are concerned that toxic by-products may be produced. The FDA has recently expanded its list of foods that can undergo irradiation.

*C*lose

Discussing the Issues
1. Answers will vary. This question provides an excellent opportunity for debates in cooperative learning groups. Encourage students to obtain additional information to support their position. Make sure students cite factual information to support their positions.
2. Answers will vary. Students may say that smoke detectors have saved many lives because they enable people to escape safely. Initially, radium-226 was used in smoke detectors. Once americium-241 was used, hazards of using a smoke detector became practically nonexistent because Am-241 does not release harmful gamma radiation.

Take Action
1. Students should contact hospitals and research facilities. Students will discover that workers use lead shielding, either in an apron or in walls, to protect themselves from radiation. Radiation-sensitive badges are used to monitor the amount of a worker's exposure.
2. Students will find that most locations will yield only background counts of radiation levels. They may find that some types of granite building materials give slightly elevated counts from background levels. Some students' families may have checked for radon gas in their basements; discuss their results.

T327

Electrons in Atoms

Investigations	Demonstrations	Texas Essential Elements★
	Creating a Spectrum, page T332	**Content:** 3.3 **Process:** 4.3
Laboratory Manual 10–1 M	The Puzzle of the Bright-Line Spectrum, page T338 Viewing Energy Levels As a Staircase, page T339 Electron Position in Atoms, page T343	**Content:** 2.6, 3.3, 3.4, 13.1 **Process:** 10.1, 10.4
Laboratory Manual 10–2 I In-text Investigation, page T354		**Content:** 3.7, 3.8
		Content: 3.7 **Process:** 1.2, 3.2, 4.3
		Process: 3.2, 4.2, 4.3, 7.1, 10.2, 10.4

KEY:
M–*Microscale* **S**–*Structured*
I–*Inquiry* **IM**–*Inquiry Microscale*

★*See pages T8–T11 for complete listing of Texas Essential Elements.*

10

Electrons in Atoms

Chapter Rationale

The quantum model of the atom is one of the greatest scientific achievements of this century. Because complete understanding of quantum mechanics requires extensive use of complex mathematical equations, the quantum mechanics dealt with in Chapter 10 will be very basic.

Several questions arise about quantum mechanics that are unanswerable. Is light a wave or particle? Sometimes light acts as a wave, other times as a particle. What is the path of an electron? In Niels Bohr's model of the atom, electrons circle the nucleus as planets circle a sun. However, the Heisenberg uncertainty principle shows that the path of an electron cannot be accurately determined.

Because electrons absorb and emit energy in the form of electromagnetic radiation, the study of waves, light, and the spectra of atoms is important for an understanding of the atom.

About the Photograph

The first fireworks were made in China by filling a bamboo tube with a mixture of potassium nitrate, sulfur, and charcoal. Metal filings, powdered magnesium, and aluminum were later added to produce brilliant sparkling effects. The combustion reaction excites the metals' electrons to enter higher energy levels. Color is emitted when these electrons return to their original energy state.

Chapter Planning Hints

Plan to complete the chapter, Laboratory Investigation, and Chapter Review in four to six sessions. You may wish to obtain The World of Chemistry videotape *Molecular Fingerprints.* There are four optional demonstrations for this chapter. They appear on pages T332, T338, T339, and T343.

Overview

Fireworks have their origin in black powder developed in China before A.D. 1000. During the nineteenth century, colors became part of fireworks when compounds were added whose atoms emitted light as a result of electrons absorbing and releasing energy.

PART

1 Waves and Energy

The modern picture of the atom is a radical departure from previous models. It is based on a mathematical description of the energy of an electron within an atom. The model does not tell where electrons are located within the atom. And, although the energies of the electrons are referred to as energy levels, these levels do not correspond to the location of electrons in the atom as the level of water corresponds to its height above a given reference point.

The modern view of the atom can be understood more fully with a knowledge of waves. You are familiar with some kinds of waves—water waves that you can see and sound waves that you cannot. There are other wave phenomena, important to the model of the atom, which you will learn about in this chapter.

The atomic model used today views electrons as having only certain amounts of energy, and not others. The energy of an electron changes by certain fixed values, so it is said to be *quantized*. What kind of model is consistent with this view of the atom? What conclusions can be drawn about the reactivity of atoms when the energy of electrons is described in this manner? These issues will be addressed after you have had an introduction to waves.

10.1 The Atomic Model Changes

In Chapter 8, you studied models of the atom proposed by John Dalton, J. J. Thomson, and Ernest Rutherford. Each of these scientists contributed to the understanding of atomic structure. John Dalton viewed the atom as a solid sphere. His model of the atom was based on evidence discovered from the combining ratios of elements and compounds in chemical reactions. Almost one hundred years later, J. J. Thomson proposed a new model that incorporated evidence of a new particle of the atom—the electron. Further experimental evidence suggested to Ernest Rutherford that the atom contained a nucleus of positive particles and electrons traveling about the nucleus. The model of the atom was later refined to include neutrons in the nucleus.

Why was it that Rutherford's model had to be changed? The nuclear atom he proposed had provided an explanation for the experiments on the scattering of alpha particles. However, it also set up a contradiction of facts. Rutherford suggested that the atom had negative charges surrounding a very small positive nucleus. Many experiments had shown that objects with unlike electric charges attract each other. If there is no force holding them back,

O b j e c t i v e s

Part 1

A. *Describe* properties of water waves and light waves.
B. *Explain* the relationship between energy and the frequency of light.
C. *Compare and contrast* different regions of the electromagnetic spectrum.

Developing Skills

Students may apply these skills in their study of Part 1.

Forming a hypothesis: Have students make waves in a bowl using their fingertip. Estimate the wavelength and predict how it will change as the waves are made faster.

Comparing/Contrasting: Have students compare the wavelength of the waves that could be made in a bowl of water to the amplitude of these waves.

Classifying: Have students make a list and classify the waves they find in their homes into the categories "electromagnetic" and "other."

Analyzing data: Have students use Table 10–1 to determine the color of light with a wavelength of 5.0×10^{-7} m.

≡ **FOCUS**

Activate Prior Knowledge

This activity will show students the relationship between frequency and wavelength. Set up a standing wave by shaking one end of a cord or Slinky coil that has been anchored. Point out that the frequency increases as the wavelength decreases.

≡ **TEACH**

Teaching Strategy

The Atomic Model Changes

Although Rutherford's model of the atom introduced the nucleus, it did not explain why atoms do not collapse. According to the laws of classical physics, coulombic forces should cause the negative electrons to lose energy as they spiral toward the positive nucleus. No such energy change was ever observed in the atom.

(continued on page T330)

(continued from page T329)

Later, Niels Bohr assumed that electrons can exist only in certain energy states, or levels. He also assumed a ground state, below which electrons cannot go. An electron may exist only in discrete energy levels, never between energy levels. This model of the atom successfully explained the bright-line spectrum emitted by glowing hydrogen gas.

Teaching Strategy

Waves

Emphasize that an understanding of waves is essential in understanding the modern model of the atom. Ask students to perform the "kitchen sink" experiment and report their findings the next day. Emphasize that although the waves transmit energy to the cork, the cork is not carried by the waves. Use the analogy of "The Wave" at a ball game. Energy is transported around the stadium by people standing up and sitting down. The people stay in the same place, while the wave moves.

the objects move toward each other. According to all experiments dealing with electric charge, the electrons should be pulled into the nucleus. Rutherford's model for the atom suggested an unstable structure, yet atoms are stable. They do not collapse. Evidently something was missing from the model.

10.2 Waves

You can study wave motion by trying this simple experiment. Fill your kitchen sink halfway with water. Float a cork or similar object in the center of the sink. Then generate some waves by dipping the back of a teaspoon into the water with a regular motion and observe what happens. You should notice that the waves spread out from the spoon rather quickly in all directions on the surface of the water. Does the cork bounce up and down with the rhythm of the passing waves? Does the cork move along the surface of the water with the waves?

Properties of waves Scientists have formalized some ideas to describe waves that include those you can observe in the sink experiment. The **frequency** of a wave is the number of waves that pass a point per unit of time. In the experiment, the cork bobs up and down every time a wave passes. This motion can be used to measure the frequency of the waves in the sink.

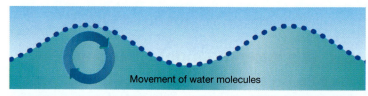
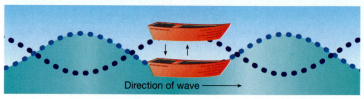

Figure 10-1 *The wave moves past the boat but does not carry the boat forward. The number of times the boat bobs up and down per unit of time is a measure of the frequency of the water waves.*

Figure 10-1 illustrates the effect of waves on a boat in water. As waves pass, the boat moves up and down. If the boat rises 10 times in one minute, the frequency is 10 cycles per minute. Frequency is usually symbolized by the Greek letter *nu*, ν, so for the boat $\nu = 10$ cycles per minute.

Another property of waves is **wavelength,** which is the distance between similar points in a set of waves, such as from crest to crest or trough to trough. The Greek letter *lambda*, λ, is often used to symbolize wavelength. Waves of differing wavelengths are illustrated in Figure 10-2.

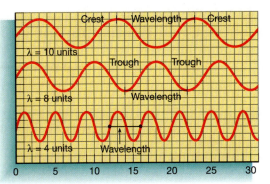
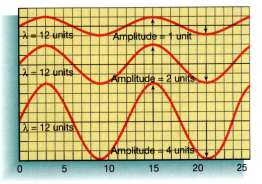

Figure 10-2 *Waves of different wavelengths but with the same amplitude are shown on the left. On the right, the waves shown have the same wavelengths but varying amplitudes. Notice that the wavelength is measured from crest to crest or trough to trough.*

A third measurable property of a wave is amplitude. Imagine a line, stretching in the direction of the wave, that is midway between the troughs and the crests. The **amplitude** of the wave is the distance from the crest (or the trough) to the imaginary line. The waves illustrated on the right in Figure 10-2 all have the same wavelengths but have different amplitudes.

Waves transmit energy If you did the floating cork experiment or watched a boat bobbing, you might have noticed that the cork did not move along the surface with the wave. Instead, it only bobbed up and down as the wave passed. The wave does not *carry* the water; it transmits energy *through* the water. The energy you used to move the spoon up and down at the surface of the water was transmitted by the wave. The amount of energy you used determines how far the cork moves up and down (amplitude), and how often a crest reaches the cork (frequency). It is the energy of waves that provides evidence for the current theory describing electrons in atoms.

10.3 Light

You are familiar with waves that you can see—for example, water waves. What about waves you cannot see? Sound waves travel through the air, creating a ripple effect analogous to that created by your spoon dipping in the water. You hear the sound if your ear is able to detect the wave. Light is made of waves you ordinarily do not notice, but these waves can be detected and measured under certain circumstances.

Characteristics of light waves Like water waves, light waves can be characterized by wavelength and frequency. For water

PART 1

Section 10.3

Teaching Strategy

Light

Although students have been exposed to the colors of the rainbow many times, Chapter 10 relates the colors to specific frequencies of light (see Table 10–1). Demonstrate the refraction of white light into colors with a prism.

waves on an ocean, the wavelength may be 12 meters and the frequency may be one wave every 20 seconds. For light, wavelengths are much shorter and frequencies are much greater. See Table 10-1 for some examples of wave measurements for comparison.

TABLE 10-1

Frequency and Wavelength of Different Kinds of Waves		
Wave	Frequency ν (number per second or hertz*)	Wavelength λ (meters)
Water	5.0×10^{-2}	1.2×10^{1}
Red light	4.3×10^{14}	7.0×10^{-7}
Yellow light	5.2×10^{14}	5.8×10^{-7}
Blue light	6.4×10^{14}	4.7×10^{-7}
Violet light	7.5×10^{14}	4.0×10^{-7}

* **Hertz** is a measure of frequency. One hertz (Hz) is one cycle per second.

The nature of light can be examined more closely using a filmstrip projector. If the white light coming from the projector passes through a narrow slit and prism, a rainbow of colors, or a **continuous spectrum,** is produced, such as the one in Figure 10-3. The light beam passing through the prism is bent, or refracted. The different frequencies that compose white light are bent to different angles, causing the light to separate into its component colors. Each color corresponds to waves of light within a particular range of frequency and wavelength.

Concept ✔ Check

Using Table 10-1, give two ways that you can describe blue light other than by color.

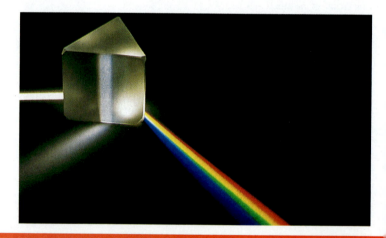

Figure 10-3 *A beam of white light is refracted by a prism and separated into a rainbow of colors. One mnemonic device to remember the sequence of colors from longest to shortest wavelength is ROY G BIV: red, orange, yellow, green, blue, indigo, violet.*

DEMONSTRATION

Creating a Spectrum

A large spectrum (24 cm) can be projected onto a screen by a slide projector and a prism. Carefully open a 2 × 2-inch slide. Place two pieces of exposed film, separated by about 2 mm, in the opened slide as illustrated. Carefully glue the slide back together.

(continued on page T333)

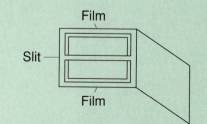

In Section 10-2, you learned that a water wave transmits energy. Light waves also transmit energy. This energy depends on several factors, including the length of time of exposure and the area over which the light is spread. A sunburn is the result of skin damage due to the energy from light. The amount of energy transmitted by the light also depends on the frequency of the light wave. Knowledge about the relationship between energy and frequency was advanced by the work of Max Planck and Albert Einstein.

Light as packets of energy In 1900, a German scientist named Max Planck analyzed data from the emissions of light from hot, glowing solids. An observation had been made that the color of the solids varied in a definite way with temperature. Planck suggested a relationship between the energy of atoms in the solid and the wavelength of light being emitted. According to Planck, the energy values of the atoms varied by small whole numbers. Soon after, Albert Einstein expanded on Planck's work by dealing specifically with light energy. He suggested that light was emitted in *packets* of energy and that the energy of each packet was proportional to the frequency of the light wave.

The idea that light energy comes in discrete packets may seem strange. You are more familiar with the concept that matter comes in packets called atoms; or that charge comes in packets, like the charge on an electron. The packets of light suggested by Einstein eventually became known as **photons.** The energy of a photon is described by an equation based on the work of Planck and Einstein.

$$E = h\nu$$

Energy, E, is measured in joules and is directly proportional to frequency, ν. The quantity h is known as Planck's constant and has a value of 6.6262×10^{-34} joule-second. In the visible light spectrum, the frequency of light increases from red to violet. As the frequency increases, so does the energy per photon, from red to violet. Each frequency of light has its own specific energy per photon *and no other.* Light is said to be quantized.

Einstein's suggestion—that light energy could be thought of as both particles and waves—was a tremendous leap in thinking for the time. This idea and the concept of specific amounts, or quantization, of energy are the basis for a theory that revolutionized atomic physics.

A closer look at quantization The concept of quantization is important for understanding the current model of the atom. The following experiment may help explain the idea more fully.

In some circumstances, you can make a wave appear to *stand still.* A rope about the length of a jump rope, a rubber hose, or a Slinky spring can be used for this experiment. Secure the rope or spring at one end. Move the other end side to side with one hand in rhythm until you notice that the crest of the wave produced does

Teaching Strategy

Light as Packets of Energy
The discussion of Planck's work and photons may confuse students. Although the text deliberately avoids a complex explanation of Albert Einstein's experiment on the photoelectric effect, you may want to clarify that the light energy absorbed by an electron depends only on the frequency of the light (electromagnetic radiation) and not on the intensity or length of exposure. Chemical proof of this is the reaction of hydrogen gas and chlorine gas to produce HCl. This requires light at or above a minimum frequency. Very intense light of a lower frequency will not initiate the reaction. Albert Einstein received the Nobel Prize for interpreting this fact to mean that energy is in "packets" or photons. The energy carried by each photon is directly proportional to the frequency.

DEMONSTRATION

(continued from page T332)
Place the slide in the projector with the slit vertical. Position a glass prism in the beam of light in front of the projector.

Project the spectrum through different colored plastic filters, which transmit only a limited number of wavelengths.

not seem to move along the rope, as shown in Figure 10-4. You have produced a *standing wave*. If you produced a wave that looks like Figure 10-4, the wave has three nodes—one in the middle and one at either end. A **node** is the location on the wave that has an amplitude of zero. As Figure 10-4 illustrates, a standing wave with three nodes has a distance across the spring of 1 wavelength. Now gradually increase the speed of your hand. For a short time the wave is out of sync and no standing wave is present. However, at just the right speed of your hand, a standing wave with four nodes can be produced (Figure 10-4). The length of the spring now is $1\frac{1}{2}$ wavelengths. By further increasing the speed of your hand, it may be possible to generate a standing wave with five nodes or even more.

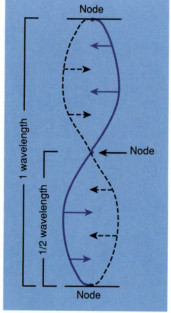
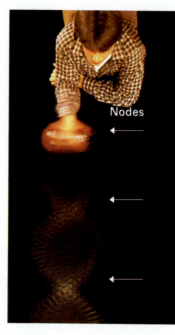

Figure 10-4 Left: *A Slinky anchored at one end will produce a standing wave only when the oscillation (side-to-side hand motion) at the other end is constant and at a particular rate. The standing wave pictured here has three nodes as shown in the diagram. Right: A faster oscillation will produce a standing wave with a shorter wavelength, the standing wave pictured here contains four nodes.*

Several relationships are important here. First, only a standing wave of $\frac{1}{2}$ wavelength, 1 wavelength, $1\frac{1}{2}$ wavelengths, 2 wavelengths, and so on, can be produced. It is impossible to produce a standing wave, given the conditions of the experiment, with $1\frac{2}{3}$ or $1\frac{3}{4}$ wavelengths. Wavelengths will change only by factors of one half—nothing less and nothing more. The wavelength of the stand-

CHEMICAL UPDATE

Supercomputers are used to process the vast amounts of information gathered in the study of the quantum model of the atom.

Now predictions can be made and molecules with a desired set of properties can be designed.

ing wave is said to be quantized. It will be helpful to keep the standing wave in mind for the discussion of the modern view of the atom.

Another relationship involves the frequency and the wavelength of the wave. All other things being equal, when you increase the side-to-side motion of your hand to produce three to four nodes, the frequency of the wave increases. At the same time, the wavelength decreases. Compare the wavelengths of the waves in Figure 10-4. The relationship between frequency and wavelength will be described in more detail in the next section.

10.4 The Electromagnetic Spectrum

When you walk outside on a sunny day, your face feels the warmth of the sun. The sun radiates energy that reaches Earth in the form of waves. The energy you feel as warmth and the light energy you see are part of a wide variety of energies that are categorized as electromagnetic radiation. **Electromagnetic waves** are produced by a combination of electrical and magnetic fields. You already have heard of many kinds of these waves. They include radio waves, microwaves, infrared radiation, ultraviolet radiation, X rays, gamma rays, and visible light. All electromagnetic waves travel at the speed of light, 3.00×10^8 m/s in a vacuum. (The speed of light in air is only slightly slower.)

Classifying electromagnetic waves Electromagnetic waves differ from each other by wavelength and frequency. The waves can be ordered by increasing frequency on a continuum, or spectrum, like the one pictured in Figure 10-5. Radio waves have the smallest frequency on the continuum, and gamma rays have the largest. Visible light is only a small part of the spectrum, with frequencies of about 10^{14} cycles per second.

DO YOU KNOW?

In January 1986, Voyager 2 detected a magnetic field around the planet Uranus. Characteristic radiowaves emitted by electrons that were escaping the planet through its magnetic field provided evidence for the field's presence.

Guided Practice

Review the Concept Check question on page 332 with students. Answers can be found in Appendix E on page 808.

Reteaching Idea

Before going on, you may want to give your students some extra help in understanding the terms introduced in this part. Have small groups work on concept maps beginning with the word *waves.* Have them include the terms *electromagnetic, frequency, wavelength, amplitude, node, standing, hertz, bright-line spectrum,* and *continuous spectrum.* When the maps have been completed and reviewed, ask for definitions, preferably oral, of each term.

Figure 10-5 *The named sections of the electromagnetic spectrum have no precise boundaries. They serve as a convenient way to classify radiation according to source.*

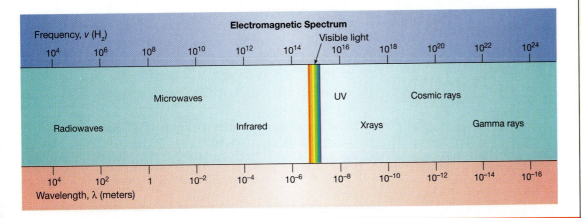

Electromagnetic Spectrum

Frequency, v (H$_z$)

10^4 10^6 10^8 10^{10} 10^{12} 10^{14} Visible light 10^{16} 10^{18} 10^{20} 10^{22} 10^{24}

Radiowaves   Microwaves   Infrared   UV   Xrays   Cosmic rays   Gamma rays

10^4 10^2 1 10^{-2} 10^{-4} 10^{-6} 10^{-8} 10^{-10} 10^{-12} 10^{-14} 10^{-16}

Wavelength, λ (meters)

PART 1

Section 10.4 *continued*

☰ CLOSE

Summing Up Main Ideas

Compare and contrast water waves, light waves, X rays, sound waves, and radio waves. Specify which kinds of waves

a. are part of the electromagnetic spectrum
b. transmit motion
c. transmit energy
d. have frequency
e. have wavelength
f. have amplitude
g. are emitted in packets of energy called photons.

PART 1 REVIEW

Assign the Part Review questions.

Evaluating Skills

These skills are evaluated in the Part Review questions indicated. **Describing:** 1, 3, 4, 5; **Classifying:** 2, 6; **Comparing/Contrasting:** 5, 7; **Determining main ideas:** 8, 9

DO YOU KNOW?

In about one second, a beam of light (if it were to curve) could travel around Earth's equator seven and a half times.

When you studied Table 10-1 earlier, did you see a regularity in the data? Look at the table again. Frequency increases as wavelength decreases. Each electromagnetic wave has its own wavelength and frequency. A mathematical relationship exists between the wavelength and frequency for any electromagnetic wave.

$$c = \lambda \times \nu \quad \text{or} \quad \nu = c\left(\frac{1}{\lambda}\right)$$

The quantity c is the velocity of light and is a proportionality constant that relates wavelength to frequency. Look at the electromagnetic spectrum in Figure 10-5. Note the same trend in the figure as in Table 10-1. For any electromagnetic wave, the product of wavelength and frequency must be equal to the velocity of light. Thus wavelength and frequency are inversely proportional. If you know the wavelength of the wave, you can calculate the frequency, and vice versa.

X rays In the previous section, you read that the greater the frequency of a wave, the greater its energy. Electromagnetic waves with very large frequencies, and therefore large amounts of energy, are X rays. They are produced by the bombardment of an anode (a positive electrode—for example, tungsten) by high-energy electrons. X rays are important in a variety of fields in science. You are familiar with dental and chest X rays. X rays also are used to investigate the structure of matter, and they are used in analytical chemistry to determine the composition of substances. X rays are even used to find metal fatigue in aircraft and machinery.

PART 1 REVIEW

1. Describe a significant weakness in Rutherford's model of the atom.
2. List five examples of waves.
3. Describe the difference between the frequency, wavelength, and amplitude of a wave.
4. Describe evidence from the kitchen sink experiment to support the statement *Water waves transmit energy, not matter.*
5. What is a photon? What is the difference between a photon of yellow light and a photon of violet light?
6. List seven colors of the visible light spectrum in *increasing* energy per photon.
7. How are frequency and wavelength of an electromagnetic wave related?
8. What does it mean to describe something as being quantized?
9. What wave characteristic determines the energy of a light wave?

Boxed numbers indicate questions that involve skills in interpretation, application, and analysis.

PART 1 REVIEW

ANSWERS

■ Keyed to Objectives

A 1. Rutherford's model suggested an unstable situation in which electrons would be pulled into the nucleus and the atom would collapse.

A 2. Answers may vary. Answers may include ocean or water waves, sound waves, light waves, radio waves, microwaves, infrared waves, or ultraviolet waves.

A 3. The frequency is the number of waves passing a point per unit of time. Wavelength and amplitude are not measured over time. Wavelength is the distance between corresponding points of a wave, and amplitude is the distance the wave deviates from an imaginary midline running in the direction of wave propagation. Wavelength and frequency are dependent upon each other, while amplitude is independent of both frequency and wavelength.

A 4. The cork moves up and down in the same location but does not move in the direction of the wave.

B,C 5. A photon is a packet of electromagnetic energy. A photon of violet

PART

2 The Hydrogen Atom

In Figure 10-6, the pattern you see was produced by a beam of electrons as they passed through a thin piece of metal foil. The diffraction (scattering) pattern produced by the electrons is similar to the pattern produced by X rays diffracted through a crystal. In 1927, when this phenomenon was first discovered, the idea that the behavior of particles could be described by the mathematics of wave motion seemed strange. However, it is a powerful idea that leads to a clearer understanding of the behavior of matter in general, and of electrons in atoms in particular.

The relationship between waves and atoms can be demonstrated in a rather striking, yet simple, experiment. The atom itself can be made to give off waves of definite frequencies, which serve as clues to the behavior of electrons in the atom. Hydrogen, the simplest of all atoms, contains only one electron, and will be described first.

10.5 The Puzzle of the Bright-Line Spectrum

If you were to view the brilliant red of neon advertising signs through a prism, you would see something unusual. Rather than a continuous spectrum, the light from the sign would be separated, or refracted, into several individual colors. This can be reproduced in the laboratory. Figure 10-7 on the next page shows several gases, each in a different tube connected to a source of electricity. When viewed through a prism, each gas is seen to have its own spectrum of bright lines. The **bright-line spectrum** of an element consists of several distinct (separate) lines of color, each with its own frequency. Compare the bright-line spectra in Figure 10-7 and you will notice that the spectrum for each element is unique.

Hydrogen spectrum Consider the bright-line spectrum of hydrogen gas. Table 10-2 lists the wavelengths and frequencies of visible light emitted by glowing hydrogen under low pressure.

TABLE 10-2

The Bright-Line Spectrum of Hydrogen		
Color	Frequency, ν (hertz)	Wavelength, (meters)
Red	4.57×10^{14}	6.56×10^{-7}
Blue-green	6.17×10^{14}	4.86×10^{-7}
Blue	6.91×10^{14}	4.34×10^{-7}
Violet	7.31×10^{14}	4.10×10^{-7}

Objectives

Part 2

D. Explain how the bright-line spectrum of hydrogen demonstrates the quantized nature of energy.

E. Predict the position(s) of electrons in an atom, using the concepts of quantum numbers and orbitals.

Figure 10-6 *The discovery that diffraction patterns like this are produced when electrons are passed through thin metal foil led to the idea that electrons could be described as if they were waves.*

Developing Skills

Students may apply these skills in their study of Part 2.
Predicting: Have students predict the order of filling seats at a sold-out concert. No seats are reserved.
Analyzing data: Have students use Table 10–2 to determine the color of light with a frequency of 7.3×10^{14} hertz.

FOCUS

Activate Prior Knowledge

In fluorescence, a substance absorbs energy and immediately re–emits that energy in the form of light. The light is a result of the excited electrons returning to their normal energy state. Television screens, fluorescent lamps, fluorescent paints and even brightening agents in laundry soaps designed to hide the natural yellowing of fabrics are all examples of the use of fluorescence in daily life.

Have students bring examples of fluorescent materials from home. Hold them under a light source. Turn off the classroom lights and observe.

TEACH

Teaching Strategy

The Puzzle of the Bright–Line Spectrum

Help students appreciate the relationship between hydrogen's bright-line spectrum and the energy levels for the electron in the atom. Make sure students do not rely on Bohr's planetary model of the atom.

(continued on page T338)

light carries more energy.

A **6.** red, orange, yellow, green, blue, indigo, violet

B **7.** Frequency times wavelength is equal to a constant, *c* (the speed of light). They are inversely proportional to each other. As frequency increases, wavelength decreases proportionally.

B,C **8.** That something exists only with or at specific energies

B,C **9.** Energy is dependent on (proportional to) frequency.

PART 2
Section 10.6

(continued from page T337)

Bohr developed a simple mathematical expression to calculate the potential energy for the electron in the hydrogen atom: $E = -k/n^2$ where $k = 1312$ kJ/mol and n is an energy level with an integer value of 1, 2, 3, 4. With this equation he was able to explain the bright-line spectrum of hydrogen in the visible, ultraviolet, and infrared regions. The equation is only valid for hydrogen or for any atom with only one electron. Bohr's calculations were based on his planetary model but confirmed by experiment.

Videodisc Connections

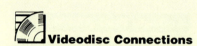

20002 to 27513, side 1
Emission spectra (movie)

8710, side 1
Atomic spectra; Lyman, Balmer series (1 frame)

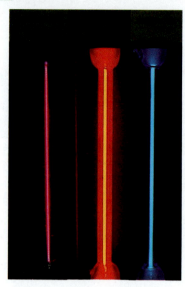

Figure 10-7 *The unrefracted lights from glowing gases (left) produce different bright-line spectra for each element (right). A continuous spectrum is provided for comparison.*

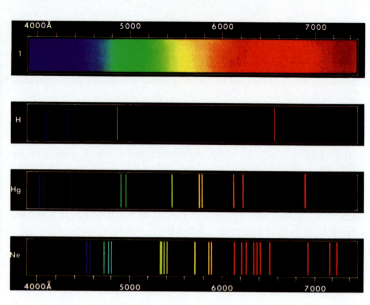

From the table, you can see that each bright line in the spectrum of hydrogen has a specific wavelength and frequency. Scientists were not able to explain why hydrogen or any other glowing gas did not form a continuous spectrum. They reasoned that since there were billions of atoms in the tube, there should be billions of different frequencies visible. Moreover, scientists wondered why each element exhibited a unique bright-line spectrum.

In 1885, a Swiss schoolteacher named Johann Balmer studied the bright-line spectrum of hydrogen. He discovered a mathematical progression in the sequence of lines. The progression can be expressed in the form of an equation:

$$E = \text{constant}\left(\frac{1}{2^2} - \frac{1}{n^2}\right) \qquad n = 3, 4, 5, \ldots$$

E is the energy of a spectral line, and n is an integer with a value greater than 2. The constant need not be specified here. The significance of Balmer's work was to become apparent as another scientist tackled the puzzle of the hydrogen atom.

10.6 Energy Levels and the Hydrogen Atom

In 1913, a Danish scientist, Niels Bohr, explained the bright-line spectrum of hydrogen. His reasoning went like this. Energy is being added to the hydrogen gas in the tube in the form of electricity. Energy is leaving the tube in the form of light. The energy of the light leaving the tube is quantized—that is, only certain frequencies of light are observed. (The frequencies for hydrogen are listed in Table 10-2). Bohr reasoned that the atoms of hydrogen in the tube

DEMONSTRATION

The Puzzle of the Bright-Line Spectrum

Students can view the spectrum of individual elements with a 2 × 2-inch diffraction grating replica, available from most scientific supply houses. The spectrum of various elements, such as H_2, He, Ar, and Hg can be produced from a spectrum power source and spectrum tubes. (Ask a physics teacher for these items.)

⚠️ **CAUTION: The spectrum power source is a high-voltage devise. Avoid touching exposed wires. Hg produces ultraviolet light; warn students not to look directly at a lighted spectrum tube. The spectrum tubes are fragile; handle with care.** Students can view the spectrum of the individual elements if they hold the diffraction grating about 2 cm from their eyes.

must be absorbing energy, then releasing it in the form of specific frequencies of light. He suggested that the hydrogen atoms themselves are quantized, that they exist only in certain, definite energy states, now called **energy levels.** The atoms absorb specific amounts of energy and then exist for a short time in higher energy levels. Such atoms are described as *excited*. Excited hydrogen atoms will emit energy as they return to lower energy levels.

Viewing energy levels as a staircase A helpful analogy to Bohr's idea of energy levels in the hydrogen atom is a staircase. Consider a house cat sitting on the second step of a staircase, as pictured in Figure 10-8 (left). The cat's potential energy is considered to be small because it is close to the ground. (In this case, potential energy is due to the gravitational attraction between the cat and Earth.) If the cat climbs to a higher step, as shown in Figure 10-8 (right), its potential energy increases. The energy change can be measured in specific values that correspond to the heights of the steps. If the cat moves from one step to a lower step, its energy decreases by a fixed amount.

Figure 10-8 *The cat may move either up or down on the staircase but must do so by whole numbers of steps. Since the cat's potential energy corresponds to the height at which it sits, only certain energy values are possible. Thus the cat's potential energy may be said to be quantized.*

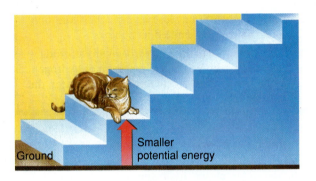

There are two points to be emphasized in this analogy. First, the cat must always change positions by an integral number of levels. It can move one, two, three, or more steps, but there is no way for it to move up or down by a half or a third of a step. Second, a change between two specific steps—for example, the second and the fourth—always involves the same change in energy. These ideas can be applied to the hydrogen atom with a few modifications.

A hydrogen atom is made up of a single electron-proton system. The negatively charged electron is attracted to the positively charged proton. This attraction gives the electron-proton system potential energy. Bohr concluded that the greater the electron-proton distance, the greater the potential energy in the system, and the higher the energy level. (He wrongly concluded that the electron in a given energy state keeps the same distance from the proton while moving around it in a circular path.) He surmised that since excited hydrogen atoms emit light energy of only specific frequencies, hydrogen atoms have specific energy levels and no others.

DO YOU KNOW?

A red sweater appears red because the molecules of the dye in the sweater are absorbing energy in the blue-green region of the visible spectrum. You see the wavelength of light not absorbed, red.

DEMONSTRATION

Viewing Energy Levels As a Staircase

Use a step stool to illustrate emission of energy from electron shells. Step down from the first step to the ground, and throw out a red ball (photon). Step down from the second step to the ground, and throw out a green ball. Step down from the third step to the ground, and throw out a blue ball.

Have students observe and analyze the process. The color of the ball corresponds to a given energy transmission. As the energy transition increases, the frequency increases from red to green to blue. What color is given off in going from step 3 to step 2? What color comes after violet?

The development of Bohr's theory There are some particularly significant facts about Bohr's theory. First, he used Einstein's idea of photons of energy to explain the specific amounts of energy observed in hydrogen's bright-line spectrum. Second, when Bohr did his calculations to find the energy levels of hydrogen, his values for the spectral lines matched the mathematical relationship found by Johann Balmer. Furthermore, Bohr predicted the existence of other spectral lines for hydrogen in the infrared and ultraviolet regions of the electromagnetic spectrum. The subsequent discovery of these spectral lines was a triumph for his theory.

Table 10-3 summarizes how Bohr's conclusions are applied to the bright-line spectrum of hydrogen:

TABLE 10-3

Bohr Model of the Hydrogen Atom
1. Hydrogen atoms exist in only specified energy states.
2. Hydrogen atoms can absorb only certain amounts of energy, and no others.
3. When excited hydrogen atoms lose energy, they lose only certain amounts of energy, emitted as photons.
4. The different photons given off by hydrogen atoms produce the color lines seen in the bright-line spectrum of hydrogen. The greater the energy lost by the atom, the greater the energy of the photon.

Energy levels of hydrogen Figure 10-9 is a diagram showing the energy levels of the hydrogen atom. Unlike the staircase in Figure 10-8, the *steps* of the hydrogen atom are not evenly spaced. (You will see later that the energy level *steps* are not actual distances between the electron and the nucleus of the atom.) Colored arrows indicate the amount of energy per photon that is given off when the atom changes from a higher level to level two. These energies correspond to the lines in the bright-line spectrum of hydrogen shown in Figure 10-7. The lines are known as the Balmer series. In a sense, analysis of the spectral lines of hydrogen provide a picture of the atom's "hidden staircase." Note in Figure 10-9 that the energies emitted per photon are much larger when an atom returns from a higher level to level one. These values are in the ultraviolet region and correspond to those predicted by Bohr. The difference in energy between level one and another level is considerably greater than between any other two levels.

Ionization energy An important value to note in the energy level diagram is 1312 kJ. If this amount of energy is absorbed by one mole of hydrogen atoms, all the electrons are removed, leaving

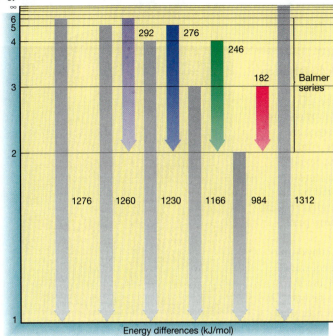

Figure 10-9 *Energy changes in the hydrogen atom between higher levels and level two are shown in the colors that correspond to its bright-line spectrum (the Balmer series). Energy lost in the transition from higher levels to level one yield photons with energy in the ultraviolet region (changes shaded in gray).*

one mole of hydrogen ions. The reaction can be expressed in an equation:

$$H(g) + 1312 \text{ kJ} \rightarrow H^+(g) + e^-$$

The value 1312 kJ is the ionization energy of hydrogen. **Ionization energy** for any element is the amount of energy needed to remove a mole of electrons from a mole of the gaseous atoms. Ionization energies are different for different elements.

Consider that if hydrogen ions and electrons recombine to form a mole of neutral hydrogen atoms, the energy emitted is 1312 kJ:

$$H^+(g) + e^- \rightarrow H(g) + 1312 \text{ kJ}$$

The fact that this energy is greater than any of the other energies listed in Figure 10-9 makes sense and lends support to the idea of energy levels in the hydrogen atom. The other energies in the diagram reflect instances when the electron moves from one energy level to another *without being removed* from the atom.

Concept ✔ Check

What is meant by ionization energy? Why is the ionization energy the largest amount of energy absorbed by the hydrogen atom?

C O N S U M E R   C H E M I S T R Y

Compact Disks

Over the past decade, a new technology for recording sound has been developed that offers improved sound clarity. The resulting recordings are known as compact disks, or CD's. They use an entirely new concept in recording information in a very small and rugged medium. CD's rely on a laser beam to stimulate a burst of excited atoms of a uniform level of energy. These uniform energy levels provide far greater fidelity than was achieved by previous recording methods—for example, records and magnetic tapes. These use analog principles to store sound waves.

CD's, on the other hand, store sound digitally, as a computer does. During recording, sounds are converted to a series of numbers, or digits. The digits are either zero or one. On the CD itself, a zero is recorded as a tiny pit in the surface of the CD. Ones are recorded as unpitted areas.

When a CD is played, a laser beam in the compact disk player aims a concentrated beam of light at the disk. The laser beam follows the concentric tracks of pitted and unpitted areas. The beam is reflected from the unpitted areas (ones) but passes through the pitted areas (zero). A light detector senses only the reflected signals. In this way, the original 16-bit code for a given voltage is reconstructed.

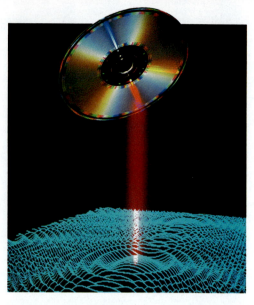

Combining the technology of computer storage and the laser beam, compact disc recordings have dramatically enhanced sound fidelity.

Your ear responds only to analog signals. The digital electric signal from the CD must be converted back to analog electronic signals. It is then amplified and sent to the speakers, which convert it to sound waves. The reconstructed sound waves are nearly identical to the original ones.

Applying the theory beyond hydrogen Niels Bohr viewed the hydrogen atom in some sense as a planetary system. According to Bohr, the circling electron remains at a particular distance from the nucleus until the atom absorbs enough energy to *boost* the electron to a higher energy level, or larger circular orbit. The Bohr theory was successful in predicting the frequencies of the bright-line spectrum of hydrogen. Yet, when his equations were applied to atoms with more than one electron, they failed to account for the bright-line spectra observed for these atoms. Bohr's theory was flawed because it could not be used to explain the experimental spectra of any element besides hydrogen. It was necessary to rethink the model of the atom once more.

10.7 The Modern Model of the Hydrogen Atom

A new model of the atom was needed that would account for the bright-line spectra of atoms with many electrons. The model also would have to be compatible with the periodic table. Elements are grouped together in the periodic table according to certain chemical and physical properties. Chemical properties of elements are directly related to the behavior of the electrons in atoms. The new theory would have to explain why groups of elements react similarly.

The new theory also needed to account for the energy of electrons in atoms described by Niels Bohr. Two new ideas in physics paved the way for the new model. In 1923, a French scientist named Louis de Broglie made a rather bold suggestion. Thinking about Einstein's theory that waves can have properties of particles (photons), de Broglie reasoned that perhaps particles could have properties of waves. If so, the behavior of electrons in atoms might better be understood using the mathematics of waves.

The energy of electrons described as waves Erwin Schrödinger, a German scientist, applied the idea of particle waves to electrons in atoms. He developed equations to describe the energy of electrons. Although the actual mathematics of Schrödinger's work is beyond the scope of this book, it is important to note that his conclusions provided further support to the concept that properties of waves can be used to describe electrons in atoms. (Schrödinger's equations also correctly described the behavior of waves in the electromagnetic spectrum.) The branch of physics that stems from the work of de Broglie and Schrödinger was first called wave mechanics. Since it describes the behavior of electrons in terms of quantized energy changes, it is more commonly called **quantum mechanics.**

Electron positions in atoms Quantum mechanics incorporates both particle-wave theory and probability into its description of the behavior of electrons in atoms. **Probability** is the likelihood of an occurrence. For example, the probability of finding a student in the hallway of your school during class time is small because the vast majority of students are in class at that time. However, the probability of finding a student in the hallway between class periods is much greater.

Since there is no experimental evidence that an electron has a definite *path* around the nucleus, as Bohr had thought, the notion of a path was discarded. How, then, can the position of an electron be described? Using the mathematics of quantum mechanics, you can predict the probability of finding an electron in a region of space around the nucleus. The region in space where there is a probability of finding an electron is called an **orbital.**

DO YOU KNOW?

In addition to Bohr, Schrodinger, and De Broglie, Werner Heisenberg contributed greatly to the model of the atom and quantum mechanics. While it was known that electrons move about the nucleus, according to Heisenberg their exact paths could not be determined. The Heisenberg uncertainty principle states that it is impossible to determine accurately the momentum and the position of a particle simultaneously.

Teaching Strategy

Electron Positions in Atoms

The mathematical equations that describe the energy of electrons are modifications of equations that describe waves.

The probability of finding an electron in an orbital can be explained using the analogy of a standing wave that appeared in Section 10.3. The amplitude of the standing wave is analogous to the wave function in Schroedinger's equation. The probability of finding an electron in a region of space around the nucleus is proportional to the square of the wave function. Since the amplitude at a node of a standing wave is zero, the probability of finding an electron at a node of an orbital (for example, 2*s* or 2*p*) is zero. The probability of finding an electron in a region of space gradually increases with the distance from the node, just as amplitude gradually increases with distance from a node. The amplitude, or probability of finding an electron, reaches a maximum and then it decreases to another node.

DEMONSTRATION

Electron Positions in Atoms

A rough approximation of the probability of finding an electron in an *s* orbital can be demonstrated by making a bull's-eye pattern on a piece of cardboard about 40 cm on a side, as illustrated below.

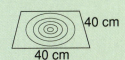

If dried beans, such as pinto or lentil, are dropped from about 10 cm directly above the center of the cardboard, the beans will distribute themselves around the cardboard so that the population distribution (beans per unit area) will gradually decrease with increasing distance from the center of the cardboard.

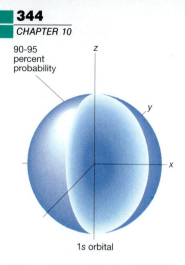

90-95 percent probability

1s orbital

Figure 10-10 *The 1s orbital of hydrogen is represented by a shaded sphere. Diagrams depicting orbitals normally enclose the region in which there is about a 95% probability of finding the electron. Areas of darker shading represent regions where the probability of finding the electron is greatest.*

The orbital description for an electron in an atom can be compared with the pattern of holes in a dart board. After it has been used for a long time, the dart board has many holes near the bull's-eye. The number of holes per unit area of the dart board decreases as you look farther from the center. The holes per unit area in the dart board is a measure of the probability that the next dart will land in the same region of the dart board. The holes in the dart board do not indicate anything about the order in which they were made or exactly where the next dart will land. The situation in the atom is similar. The orbital describes the probability that an electron will be found in a particular region about the nucleus, but it does not indicate the position or the path of the electron.

Orbitals and energy levels When a hydrogen atom is in its lowest energy state, often called the **ground state,** the energy of the electron is defined by an orbital shown in the model in Figure 10-10. Notice that the sphere does not have the same density of color throughout. You can think of the density of color as corresponding to the probability of finding the electron in that region of space. The relatively high density of the region close to the nucleus signifies that the electron is found closer to the nucleus more often than it is found farther away.

If the hydrogen electron absorbs energy, it can be found in a second, third, or even higher energy level. The energy levels of the electron of the hydrogen atom are each designated by a number, n. For the first energy level (the ground state), $n = 1$. For the second energy level, $n = 2$, and so on. The letter "n" is called the **principal quantum number.** Quantum numbers are used to describe an electron in an orbital. These labels serve much like an address that distinguishes one house from another.

In any one energy level, there is a specific number of orbitals possible. The value n^2 determines the number of possible orbitals

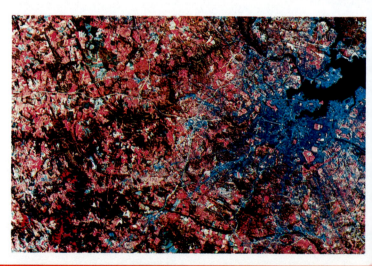

Figure 10-11 *This Landsat photo shows the distribution of populated areas around Baltimore, Maryland. The blue areas are those of greatest population density. Although the photo does not enable you to predict the location of any single person, it does show you those regions in which a person is most likely to be found.*

Myths and Misconceptions

Students often have the misconception that electrons orbit around the nucleus along regular pathways, or "shells." Although the electrons are in motion, their position and velocity cannot be determined simultaneously. Therefore, it is inaccurate to state that they orbit the nucleus in definite paths. As explained in this section, electrons have a higher probability of being found in regions called electron clouds, or orbitals.

for each energy level. Table 10-4 lists the total number of orbitals available for each of the first four energy levels of hydrogen.

TABLE 10-4

Orbitals of the Hydrogen Atom	
Energy Level	**Number of Orbitals**
(n)	(n^2)
1	1
2	4
3	9
4	16

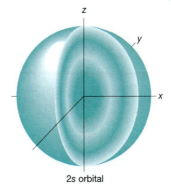

2s orbital

Figure 10-12 *The 2s orbital, like the 1s orbital, is spherically shaped. The 2s orbital for hydrogen has two regions where the probability of finding the electron is greatest.*

First energy level There is only one orbital for the first energy level. There are several orbitals that describe energy levels two, three, and four. The first orbital in an energy level is designated by the letter "*s*." For the first energy level ($n = 1$), the lone orbital is designated as the "1*s*" orbital. Figure 10-10, shown earlier, illustrates the 1*s* orbital of hydrogen.

Second energy level If the electron absorbs enough energy to be in level two, it may occupy any one of four orbitals. The 2*s* orbital (Figure 10-12) is shaped similarly to the 1*s* orbital but is larger. The larger size seems reasonable because the 2*s* orbital describes a higher energy state for the electron than does the 1*s* orbital. The probability of finding the electron in the 2*s* orbital is spread out over a larger region of space.

Three other orbitals exist in the second energy level. These three orbitals are not spherically shaped like the 1*s* and 2*s* orbital, but rather they are each double lobes, as represented by the structures in Figure 10-13. The double-lobe structure is signified by the letter *p*. Since the 2*p* orbitals are oriented around different axes in space, they are further differentiated by the labels $2p_x$, $2p_y$, and $2p_z$.

Figure 10-13 *The 2p orbitals of hydrogen are represented by three pairs of flattened lobes. Each 2p orbital has a region, known as the nodal plane, in which the probability of finding the electron is zero. When all three p orbitals are taken together, they describe a spherical shape.*

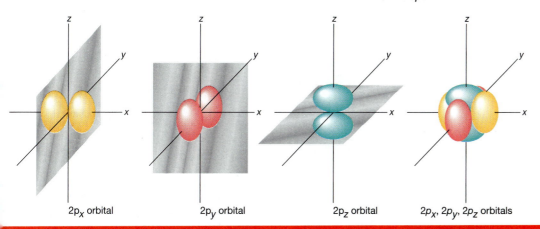

$2p_x$ orbital $\qquad$ $2p_y$ orbital $\qquad$ $2p_z$ orbital $\qquad$ $2p_x$, $2p_y$, $2p_z$ orbitals

PART **2**

Section 10.7 continued

Guided Practice

Review the Concept Check question on page 341 with students. Answers can be found in Appendix E on page 808.

Reteaching Idea

If your students need more help understanding the quantum mechanical model of hydrogen and how it relates to the bright-line spectrum, provide them with a sheet of paper on which horizontal lines representing energy levels are drawn, as in Figure 10–9. Have them label the lines n = 1, n = 2, and so on. Now have them draw electron orbitals on each level, as in Figure 10–14. Ask about the ground state, excited states, and how many orbitals are available to the hydrogen electron if its energy corresponds to quantum levels 2, 3, and 4. Have them place the electron at level 6 and draw an arrow to level 2. Do the same beginning at level 5, then 4, then 3. Relate these transitions to the Balmer series of bright lines. Ask what happens to the electron and to its energy. Ask if it is still in an excited state. Have students draw the transition from n = 2 to the ground state, then add transitions from other excited states to n = 1 (Lyman series). Have them compare the length of these arrows with those going to level 2. Ask whether more energy is involved and in what portion of the electromagnetic spectrum they could expect to find evidence of these transitions. If necessary, refer them to Figure 10–5. You can continue the exercise by looking at transitions from upper levels to n = 3 (Paschen series) found in the infrared.

PROBLEM-SOLVING

S T R A T E G Y

By **rereading information** you will be able to see relationships between concepts more easily. (See Strategy, page 201.)

Perhaps you are wondering how an electron can move from one lobe in a 2p orbital to another if the lobes are not touching. It is a good question. If you think of an orbital as describing the path of an electron, there is no answer to your question. Strictly speaking, an orbital does not describe a *house* in which an electron roams about. The orbital is a description of an electron wave. Recall from Section 10-3 that a standing wave has places, or nodes, where the amplitude is zero. In much the same fashion, some orbitals have places where the probability of finding an electron is zero. These places are also called nodes. Each 2p orbital has a node lying along the plane of the nucleus. The 2s orbital also has a node. Look carefully at Figure 10-12 and see if you can locate where the probability of finding the electron in the 2s orbital is zero.

Third energy level In level three, there are nine orbitals ($n^2 = 9$). One is the 3s orbital and three more are the 3p orbitals ($3p_x$, $3p_y$, and $3p_z$). Each of these has either a spherical or a double-lobed shape, but larger than their second energy level counterparts. Level three has five more orbitals, designated as 3d orbitals. They are differentiated in space on the x, y, and z axes as well. The shapes of the 3d orbitals are more complex than the s and p orbitals and are not shown.

Fourth energy level Figure 10-14 summarizes the energy levels of hydrogen and the orbitals present in each level. Notice that level four can have 16 orbitals ($n^2 = 16$). In energy level four, there is one 4s orbital, plus three 4p orbitals, five 4d orbitals, and seven additional orbitals, designated by the letter "*f*." The s, p, d, and f orbitals are often called *sublevels*.

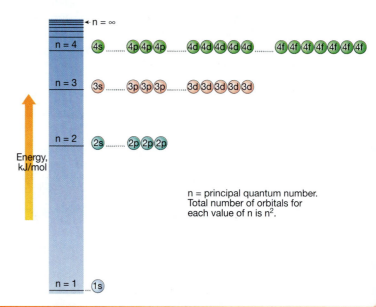

Figure 10-14 The energy levels of the hydrogen atom.

When the electron of the hydrogen atom absorbs enough energy to move to the fourth energy level, the electron can occupy any of the sixteen orbitals having exactly the same energy. If the electron loses energy and moves from the fourth to the second energy level, it can occupy any of the four orbitals for that level.

10.8 Quantum Numbers

You have been introduced to one of the four quantum numbers used to describe an electron in an orbital. These numbers specify the complete *address* for the electron in the atom. Orbitals are regions of space, oriented around the nucleus that can be designated uniquely by three quantum numbers. The principal quantum number, *n*, describes the *size* of the orbital. The value for *n* is an integer that ranges from 1, 2, 3, . . . to infinity.

The second quantum number, *l*, designates the *shape* of an orbital. The letters *s*, *p*, *d*, and *f* can be used to specify this second quantum number. An *s* orbital is spherical; a *p* orbital is composed of double lobes. The *d* and *f* orbitals also are composed of lobes, but are more complex.

The third quantum number, *m*, describes the orbital's *orientation* about the *x*, *y*, and *z* axes. For example, a $2p_x$ orbital is a double-lobed orbital of the second energy level, oriented around the *x*-axis. Three quantum numbers must be used to define a given orbital, and no two orbitals can have the same three quantum numbers.

A fourth quantum number designates the *spin* of the electron. Its meaning will be discussed in Section 10-9.

PART 2 REVIEW

10. What is a bright-line spectrum?

11 What is an energy level of an atom? Why are energy levels described as quantized?

12. Briefly explain why the bright-line spectrum of hydrogen is composed of discrete lines and is not a continuous spectrum.

13. What is an orbital?

14. Why is the ionization energy of hydrogen greater than the energy of any frequency in the bright-line spectrum for hydrogen?

15. How is a 3*s* orbital for the hydrogen atom different from a 2*s* orbital?

16. Explain what happens when the electron of a hydrogen atom changes from a 2*s* orbital to a 5*s* orbital.

17. Why is it not possible for two different orbitals to have the same first three quantum numbers?

Do You Know?

The letters s, p, d, *and* f *once stood for sharp, principal, diffuse, and fundamental, which were classifications of spectral lines in the emission spectra of elements.*

Boxed numbers indicate questions that involve skills in interpretation, application, and analysis.

≡CLOSE

Summing Up Main Ideas

Describe how the probability of finding an electron at a particular position can be predicted by specifying the size of the orbital, the shape of the orbital, and its orientation. Why can't an electron's exact position be described? How do the energy levels of an element correspond to its bright-line spectrum? How does ionization energy relate to an electron's position?

PART 2 REVIEW

Assign the Part Review questions.

Evaluating Skills

These skills are evaluated in the Part Review questions indicated. **Determining main ideas: 10, 11, 12, 15, 17; Comparing/Contrasting: 15, 16; Stating a conclusion: 17**

PART 2 REVIEW

ANSWERS

■ **Keyed to Objectives**

D **10.** A series of colored lines, each with its own specific frequency

D **11.** It is a way of describing the energy of an electron in reference to the nucleus of the atom. Electrons can be found only in certain specific energy levels.

D **12.** When the hydrogen electron drops from a higher energy level to a lower one, a discrete amount of energy is emitted.

E **13.** A region in space around the nucleus in which electrons are likely to be found

D **14.** Ionization energy is the energy needed to remove an electron from the influence of the nucleus. It is higher than the highest energy level available to the bound electron.

D **15.** The region of 0.99 probability of finding the electron in the 3*s* orbital is larger than that in the 2*s*.

D **16.** A specific quantum of energy is absorbed by the atom.

E **17.** Each orbital has its own unique set of three quantum numbers designating its size, shape, and orientation. They define an orbital and no two orbitals can have the same set.

HISTORY OF SCIENCE

Prized Women Scientists

Marie (Sklodowska) Curie is one of the most widely recognized female scientists. While her first interests focused on the magnetic properties of certain steels, investigations of radioactive substances ultimately captured her attention. Madame Curie studied the extremely radioactive mineral pitchblende. Since this ore seemed much more radioactive than pure uranium, she was convinced it contained an unknown element having a higher radioactivity than either thorium or uranium.

The discovery of polonium and radium In 1898, the Curies discovered a new element that was even more radioactive than uranium. Madame Curie named this element polonium in honor of her homeland, Poland. Although they discovered radium a few months later, it was not until 1910 that Madame Curie isolated pure radium metal. In 1903, the Curies shared the Nobel Prize in Physics with Henri Becquerel. After Pierre Curie was killed in an accident, Marie Curie continued their work alone. In 1911, she received the Nobel Prize in Chemistry for her isolation of radium and her studies of its properties.

A daughter takes up the work Irène Joliot-Curie, the elder daughter of Pierre and Marie Curie, worked as an assistant to her mother at the Radium Institute. After she met and married Frédéric Joliot in 1926, they worked together, continuing the work of Irène's parents. In 1934, they discovered the artificial production of radioactivity in nonradioactive substances, and for this discovery they shared the Nobel Prize in Physics.

Marie Goeppart-Mayer investigated the nucleus In 1930, Marie Goeppart, seven years younger than Irène Joliot-Curie, came from Germany to the United States, where she met and married another scientist named Joseph Mayer. Marie Goeppart-Mayer became primarily interested in nuclear physics. Her investigations corroborated earlier claims of closed shells in nuclei. She proposed that the movement of protons and neutrons in the nucleus was not only more independent than previously believed but that the direction of their spin was particularly important in determining the energy of nuclear orbits. In 1963 Dr. Goeppart-Mayer shared the Nobel Prize in physics with two other physicists.

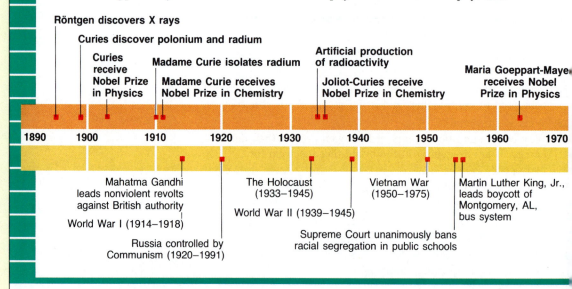

Röntgen discovers X rays

Curies discover polonium and radium

Curies receive Nobel Prize in Physics

Madame Curie isolates radium

Madame Curie receives Nobel Prize in Chemistry

Artificial production of radioactivity

Joliot-Curies receive Nobel Prize in Chemistry

Maria Goeppart-Mayer receives Nobel Prize in Physics

| 1890 | 1900 | 1910 | 1920 | 1930 | 1940 | 1950 | 1960 | 1970 |

Mahatma Gandhi leads nonviolent revolts against British authority

World War I (1914–1918)

Russia controlled by Communism (1920–1991)

The Holocaust (1933–1945)

World War II (1939–1945)

Supreme Court unanimously bans racial segregation in public schools

Vietnam War (1950–1975)

Martin Luther King, Jr., leads boycott of Montgomery, AL, bus system

PART

3 Electron Configurations

The hydrogen atom is the simplest of all atoms because it consists of only one electron and one proton. The electrons in more complex atoms (atoms with many electrons) can be understood in terms of the hydrogen atom if some modifications are made to the model. The material you study in this part provides the basis for what you will learn in the next two chapters. The modern theory of the atom successfully explains the relationships of elements in the periodic table. The theory also has been successful in explaining the behavior of atoms when they react with each other. Credibility in the model of the atom as described through quantum mechanics is strengthened because it is compatible with experimental data.

Objectives

Part 3

F. **Draw** and **write** electron configurations of neutral atoms and ions.

G. **Recognize** the filling order of electrons in many-electron atoms.

10.9 Orbital Sequencing in Many-Electron Atoms

Quantum mechanics can be applied to atoms that have more than one electron. Since most atoms have more than just a few electrons, many orbitals are occupied simultaneously by electrons in these atoms. This situation is different from that of hydrogen, in which the single electron can occupy only one orbital of the atom at a time depending on the energy of the electron.

Experimental data from the spectral analysis of elements also suggests that only two electrons can occupy the same orbital of a many-electron atom. Electrons behave as if they were spinning about their own axis. When two electrons occupy the same orbital, the electrons are said to spin in opposite directions. By convention, one electron is arbitrarily assigned a spin of $+\frac{1}{2}$, and the other electron is assigned a spin of $-\frac{1}{2}$. The spin characteristic of electrons is the fourth quantum number and is designated by the letter m_s. It is important to note here that if two electrons occupy the same orbital, they must have opposite spins. The energy of electrons is defined by their quantum numbers. No two electrons can have the same set of four identical quantum numbers. This concept is known as the **Pauli exclusion principle** (for Wolfgang Pauli, who devised it). Two electrons can have the same first three quantum numbers (when they are in the same orbital), but their spins must be opposite.

Concept ✓ Check

The fourth quantum number, m_s, designates the spin of the electron. What are the other three and what do they designate?

Developing Skills

Students may apply these skills in their study of Part 3.
Describing: Have students write the electron configurations for fluorine, chlorine, bromine, lithium, sodium, and potassium.
Comparing/Contrasting: Have students compare the electron configurations for lithium, sodium, and potassium to those for fluorine, chlorine, and bromine.

☰ FOCUS

Activate Prior Knowledge

This discussion will illustrate how chemical reactivity is related to electron configuration. Chlorine is a poisonous and reactive element. Argon is stable and does not react spontaneously with other elements. Chlorine's atomic number is just one more than that of argon. If two elements have almost the same number of protons and electrons, why are they so different? Also, why is the element fluorine, whose atomic number is almost half that of chlorine, so chemically similar to chlorine? Relate these questions to electron configurations and the periodic table.

☰ TEACH

Teaching Strategy

Orbital Sequencing in Many-Electron Atoms

The Pauli exclusion principle is an empirical statement based on the energy of electrons in orbitals and the periodic table. The fact that only two electrons may occupy an orbital is consistent with the arrangement of the elements in the periodic table in sets of two (two elements in the first period, eight in the next two

Videodisc Connections

18779 to 20001, side 1
Atomic theories (movie)

(continued on page T350)

(continued from page T349)
periods, and so on). Use the definition of the Pauli exclusion principle given in the text. However, if reference to quantum numbers is too confusing for students, another acceptable definition is: A maximum of two electrons may occupy any single orbital.

Teaching Strategy

Writing Electron Configurations

Remind students that there are differences between the orbitals for many-electron atoms and those of the hydrogen atom. Because of electron-electron repulsion in many-electron atoms all orbitals with the same principle quantum number (n) do not have the same energy as they do in the single-electron hydrogen atom. According to the Aufbau process, the $4s$ orbital is always filled before the $3d$ orbital is. Yet the $4s$ orbital is always above the $3d$ orbital. This will make more sense to students when they study the common ions of the transition elements. When a transition element loses electrons, it is the $4s$ electrons that are removed first. This anomaly also makes more sense when the promotion and hybridization of bonding electrons in a sp^3d or sp^3d^2 system (see the appendix) is studied.

A notable exception to the text's method of determining electron configurations of transition elements occurs when the Ti atom becomes Ti^{2+}. The electron configuration $1s^2\ 2s^2\ 2p^6\ 3s^2\ 3p^6\ 4s^2\ 3d^2$ becomes $1s^2\ 2s^2\ 2p^6\ 3s^2\ 3p^6\ 4s^2$ for the ion.

(continued on page T351)

DO YOU KNOW?

The process of adding electrons to the lowest available energy level is often referred to as the "aufbau" principle from the German word for "building up."

CONNECTING CONCEPTS

Structure and Properties of Matter Electric forces make atoms what they are. Electrons are attracted to the nucleus. Electrons also repel each other. They occupy specific orbitals in a many-electron atom in response to the forces of attraction and repulsion within the atom.

Writing electron configurations The procedure of organizing electrons in atoms from the orbital with the lowest energy to the orbital with the highest energy leads to the **electron configuration** of the atom. Organizing electrons in orbitals for the many-electron atoms is a relatively easy task which you will soon learn to do. The sequence of filling orbitals in many-electron atoms follows the scheme of the hydrogen atom to some extent. Table 10-5 shows the electron configurations of the first five elements in the periodic table, written in increasing order of atomic number. It is presumed that each atom is neutral in charge—that is, the number of protons in the nucleus and the number of electrons is equal. Do you see that the number of electrons placed in the orbitals of each element is the same as its atomic number?

TABLE 10-5

Electron Configurations for Elements 1 to 5				
Element	Symbol	$1s$	$2s$	$2p$
Hydrogen	$_1$H	↑	○	○ ○ ○
Helium	$_2$He	↑↓	○	○ ○ ○
Lithium	$_3$Li	↑↓	↑	○ ○ ○
Beryllium	$_4$Be	↑↓	↑↓	○ ○ ○
Boron	$_5$B	↑↓	↑↓	↑ ○ ○

All electron configurations given in Table 10-5 are listed in the atom's ground state—that is, in the lowest energy possible. The symbol ↑ represents one electron in an orbital. Two electrons in the same orbital are represented by the symbol ↑↓. The opposite directions of the arrows represent the opposite spins of the electrons. The order of *filling* up orbitals has a simple rule.

> Start with the $1s$ orbital. Then begin filling the next highest energy orbitals—for example, $2s$, $2p$—until all the electrons are accounted for.

The ground-state electron configurations for the next three elements after boron are given in Table 10-6.

TABLE 10-6

Electron Configurations for Elements 6 to 8				
Element	Symbol	$1s$	$2s$	$2p$
Carbon	$_6$C	↑↓	↑↓	↑ ↑ ○
Nitrogen	$_7$N	↑↓	↑↓	↑ ↑ ↑
Oxygen	$_8$O	↑↓	↑↓	↑↓ ↑ ↑

Notice that in carbon the 5th and 6th electrons are placed in separate $2p$ orbitals. If both electrons are placed in one $2p$ orbital, there

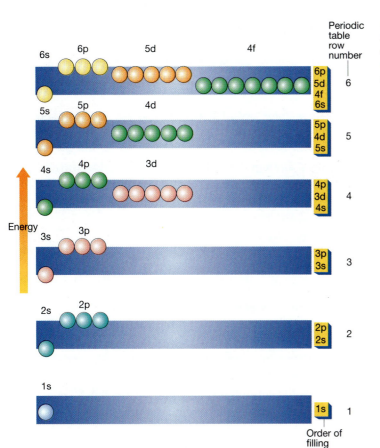

Figure 10-15 *The filling of orbitals in a many-electron atom occurs in the sequence that provides for the lowest potential energy of the system.*

PART **3**

Section 10.9 *continued*

(continued from page T350)

Several exceptions to the Aufbau process exist in the transition elements. Cr, Cu, Mo, Ag, and Au all contain either half-filled or completely filled *d* orbital systems. For example, the electron configuration of Cr is $1s^2\ 2s^2\ 2p^6\ 3s^2\ 3p^6\ 4s^1\ 3d^5$. The orbital system $4s^1\ 3d^5$ has lower energy than $4s^2\ 3d^4$.

Resources

The *World of Chemistry* videotape *Molecular Fingerprints* models the filling of orbitals with electrons.

would be a repulsion between them that would increase the energy of the system. The atom would then not be in the ground state. Remember that the ground state for an atom is the electron configuration with the lowest possible energy. By placing the electrons in different 2*p* orbitals, this repulsion is lessened. When adding electrons to a sublevel (such as the 2*p* sublevel system, or the 3*p* or 3*d*), the following rule is helpful to remember.

Put one electron in each orbital of the sublevel first; then go back and pair electrons in each orbital as necessary.

Figure 10-15 shows an energy level diagram for many-electron atoms. Study the chart carefully. The 1*s* orbital has the lowest energy and is filled first. While the 2*s* and 2*p* orbitals are filled next, they are shown in Figure 10-15 not to have the same energy. This becomes significant at the fourth energy level. The 4*s* orbital is at a lower energy level than the 3*d* orbital and is filled first. The filling sequence becomes 1s, 2s, 2p, 3s, 3p, 4s, 3d, 4p. Such differences in orbital sequencing has been confirmed by many types of experiments. The explanation for the order of the orbitals is complex and will not be discussed here.

PROBLEM-SOLVING STRATEGY

Look for patterns in the energy diagram to help you learn the filling order of electrons. (See Strategy, page 100.)

PART **3**
Section 10.9 *continued*

Practice Problems

Assign the Practice Problems.

Cooperative Learning

Teams of 4; **Time:** 30 minutes
Objective: Students will learn to write and interpret electron configurations.
Task: Write electron configurations for the first 56 elements. Classify the elements into groups with similar ending electron configurations.
Team responsibility: After doing 10 elements, stop and compare electron configurations. Detect and correct errors. Find group agreement on which elements have similar electron configurations.
Evaluation: Choose an element and ask students to name an element with a similar electron configuration.
Example: Calcium, $1s^2\ 2s^2\ 2p^6$ $3s^2\ 3p^6\ 4s^2$
Similar elements are magnesium, strontium, and barium. Note that all are in Group II of the periodic table.

Guided Practice

Review the Concept Check question on page 349 with students. Answers can be found in Appendix E on page 808.

Reteaching Idea

If your students need another way to connect electron configurations to energy levels, quantized energies, and bright-line spectra, this exercise may help. Take your class to the longest and broadest staircase available.

(continued on page T353)

PROBLEM·SOLVING
S T R A T E G Y

Use what you know.
The periodic table gives you the atomic number.

PROBLEM·SOLVING
S T R A T E G Y

Drawing diagrams helps you visualize the filling order of electrons. (See Strategy, page 216.)

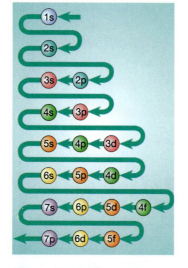

Figure 10-16 *When writing electron configurations, use this chart as an aid to remembering the sequence in which orbitals fill.*

EXAMPLE 10-1

Draw the electron configurations for atoms of neon, calcium, and manganese.

■ *Analyze the Problem* Recognize that you need to know the total number of electrons for each element. The total number of electrons is equal to the number of protons (atomic number).

■ *Apply a Strategy* Using Figure 10-16 as a guide, write out the order in which electrons fill orbitals. Then draw circles to represent the orbitals and use arrows to represent electrons.

■ *Work a Solution*

	1s	2s	2p	3s	3p	4s	3d
$_{10}$Ne	⬆⬇	⬆⬇	⬆⬇ ⬆⬇ ⬆⬇	◯	◯◯◯	◯	◯◯◯◯◯
$_{20}$Ca	⬆⬇	⬆⬇	⬆⬇ ⬆⬇ ⬆⬇	⬆⬇	⬆⬇ ⬆⬇ ⬆⬇	⬆⬇	◯◯◯◯◯
$_{25}$Mn	⬆⬇	⬆⬇	⬆⬇ ⬆⬇ ⬆⬇	⬆⬇	⬆⬇ ⬆⬇ ⬆⬇	⬆⬇	⬆ ⬆ ⬆ ⬆ ⬆

■ *Verify Your Answer* Count the total number of arrows to verify that you have represented the correct number of electrons equal to the atomic number.

Practice Problems

18. Draw the electron configurations for Na and Ar.
19. Draw the electron configurations for Sr and Kr.

The diagrams that you have drawn to represent the electron configurations in Example 10-1 are also known as **orbital diagrams**. As you probably have noticed, it is time-consuming to draw little arrows and circles. (Orbital diagrams will be useful when you study the periodic table and bonding in Chapters 11 and 13.) For now, it is simpler to use a shorthand method chemists have devised for writing electron configurations. The electron configuration for nitrogen can be written more succinctly as follows.

$$_7\text{N} \qquad 1s^2 2s^2 2p^3$$

The configuration is read "1s two, 2s two, 2p three" (not "1s squared", etc.). Notice that the sum of the superscripts is equal to the atomic number. Keep in mind the one drawback of the shorthand method: It does not tell you explicitly that the three electrons in the 2p sublevel are arranged with one electron each in the $2p_x$, $2p_y$, and $2p_z$ orbitals.

There is no real need to memorize the order of filling electrons for the many-electron atoms. However, Figure 10-16 is a mnemonic device that may help you work out electron configurations.

PART 3 REVIEW
A N S W E R S
■ **Keyed to Objectives**

F,G **18.** An electron configuration represents the ordered series of orbitals occupied by electrons in an atom.

10.10 Orbital Sequencing in Common Ions

Electron configurations can be written for simple ions. Chapter 11 will make clearer the relationship of electron configurations of ions and the periodic table. Here you need only understand that electron configurations of ions can be successfully predicted from what you already know. Some examples are given in Table 10-7.

TABLE 10-7

Electron Configurations of Atoms and Ions			
Element	Electron Configuration (Neutral Atom)	Ion	Electron Configuration (Ion)
$_{12}Mg$	$1s^2 2s^2 2p^6 3s^2$	Mg^{2+}	$1s^2 2s^2 2p^6$
$_{17}Cl$	$1s^2 2s^2 2p^6 3s^2 3p^5$	Cl^-	$1s^2 2s^2 2p^6 3s^2 3p^6$
$_{13}Al$	$1s^2 2s^2 2p^6 3s^2 3p^1$	Al^{3+}	$1s^2 2s^2 2p^6$

In the case of the magnesium ion, the symbol Mg^{2+} means that two electrons have been removed from the neutral atom. The two electrons that are removed are the ones with the highest energy—that is the $3s^2$. The magnesium ion, having lost two electrons, has ten remaining like the element neon. Therefore, Mg^{2+} has the same electron configuration as neutral neon. For Cl^-, one electron has been added to the neutral chlorine atom. It will occupy the lowest available energy orbital, a $3p$ orbital. The chloride ion, therefore, has 18 electrons like the element argon, and Cl^- has the same electron configuration as neutral argon.

In writing the electron configurations for simple positive ions, subtract the number of ionic charges (2 for magnesium) from the atomic number and proceed to fill the orbitals as if you were dealing with a neutral atom. For a negative ion, add the number of ionic charges (1 for chloride) to the atomic number and fill the orbitals as you would for a neutral atom.

PART 3 REVIEW

20. What is meant by the term *electron configuration*?

21. Draw an orbital diagram and write the electron configuration for atoms of each of the following elements:
Na, Cl, S, and Mg.

22. Write the electron configuration for each of the following ions:

$$Ca^{2+} \quad Al^{3+} \quad P^{3-} \quad F^-.$$

23. How do two electrons that occupy the same orbital differ?

CONNECTING CONCEPTS

Energy Electrons within atoms, atoms themselves and molecules exist only in certain energy states. This is the basis for the quantum theory.

(continued from page T352)
The steps will represent energy levels and the students will represent electrons in orbitals. Have students position themselves on the staircase in the orbital configuration of the element having an atomic number equal to the number of students. When the configuration is complete, throw a nerf ball to one of the "electrons" in the highest energy level. The ball will represent a photon of energy. The student who catches the ball should move up to a higher, unoccupied step and remain there until he/she throws the ball back to you. Other kinds of balls, for example a tennis ball or a soccer ball, can be used to represent photons with different energies. Inner electrons can also move to higher unoccupied energy levels. Relate the returning of the ball as the student returns to her/his original position to the bright-line spectrum.

☰ CLOSE

Summing Up Main Ideas

Discuss how the Pauli exclusion principle determines orbital sequencing. Include such factors as the spin, the number of electrons in an orbital, the four quantum numbers, and the order of filling up orbitals. Why is the $4s$ orbital filled before the $3d$ orbital?

PART 3 REVIEW

Assign the Part Review questions.

Evaluating Skills

These skills are evaluated in the Part Review questions indicated.
**Determining main ideas: 18;
Describing: 19, 20; Comparing/
Contrasting: 21**

F,G 19.

	1s	2s	2p	3s	3p
Na	⇅	⇅	⇅ ⇅ ⇅	↑	○ ○ ○
Cl	⇅	⇅	⇅ ⇅ ⇅	⇅	⇅ ⇅ ↑
S	⇅	⇅	⇅ ⇅ ⇅	⇅	⇅ ↑ ↑
Mg	⇅	⇅	⇅ ⇅ ⇅	⇅	○ ○ ○

Na	$1s^2$	$2s^2$	$2p^6$	$3s^1$	
Cl	$1s^2$	$2s^2$	$2p^6$	$3s^2$	$3p^5$
S	$1s^2$	$2s^2$	$2p^6$	$3s^2$	$3p^4$
Mg	$1s^2$	$2s^2$	$2p^6$	$3s^2$	

F,G 20.

	1s	2s	2p	3s	3p
Ca^{2+}	$1s^2$	$2s^2$	$2p^6$	$3s^2$	$3p^6$
Al^{3+}	$1s^2$	$2s^2$	$2p^6$		
P^{3-}	$1s^2$	$2s^2$	$2p^6$	$3s^2$	$3p^6$
F^-	$1s^2$	$2s^2$	$2p^6$		

F 21. They have opposite spins
$$(+\tfrac{1}{2} \text{ and } -\tfrac{1}{2})$$

The Electron Configuration Game

Estimated Time: (50 minutes; may require additional time as homework)

Process Skills

Forming models
Interpreting diagrams
Analyzing data

Preparation

■ Materials

(for a class of 24, working in teams of 4 and then individually) four-sided die, or regular six-sided die if four-sided are not available (6); pennies (6); quantum-atom energy distribution diagrams (7 per student, or 168); textbooks (24, or at least one per team); containers with all numbers from 1 to 30 on separate pieces of paper (6), rubber bands (if cards are used)

■ Preparation Hints

If possible, place the quantum-atom energy distribution diagrams on card stock. However, you may want to put them on paper and may even want to print more than one on a page to save paper and expense.

■ Safety

 Caution students not to shoot the rubber bands.

The Electron Configuration Game

The atoms of each element differ not only in the number of electrons they possess but also in the energies of their electrons. Electrons in atoms have discrete energies, depending upon their distance from the nucleus. The electrons are said to exist at discrete energy levels. These energy levels have electron orbitals associated with them. There are several types of orbitals, each having a different shape. Orbitals are arranged in order of increasing energy. In this investigation, you will first play a group game and then utilize what you have learned to determine the electron energy distribution for five elements.

Objectives

Compare the orbitals of the hydrogen atom to those of a many-electron atom (one having two or more electrons).

Determine the order in which electrons fill successive orbitals.

Apply the rules of electron ordering by completing *quantum-atom energy-distribution diagrams* for five elements.

■ Materials

☐ 4-sided die
☐ coin
☐ 8 quantum-atom energy-distribution diagrams
☐ container with all numbers from 1 to 30 on separate pieces of paper

■ Procedure

Part 1

1. Divide into groups of four players as directed by your teacher. Each group needs 1 four-sided die and 1 coin. Each player in the group needs 2 quantum-atom energy-distribution diagrams.

2. One member of the group randomly selects a number from the container. This is the atomic number of the first element to be considered by the group.

3. Each member of the group writes this number on the top of a quantum-atom energy-distribution diagram. Consult the periodic table to find the name of the element. In addition to the element's atomic number, write the symbol and electron configuration—for example, 11, Na, would be $1s^2\ 2s^2\ 2p^6\ 3s^1$.

4. The roll of the die determines n. If a four-sided die is used, the numbers $0, 1, 2,$ and 3 are painted on its sides. These faces represent the secondary quantum number l. Zero corresponds to s orbitals, 1 to p orbitals, 2 to d orbitals, and 3 to f orbitals.

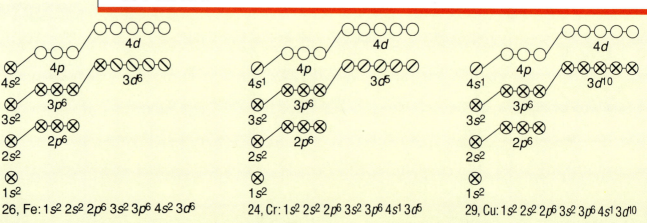

26, Fe: $1s^2\ 2s^2\ 2p^6\ 3s^2\ 3p^6\ 4s^2\ 3d^6$

24, Cr: $1s^2\ 2s^2\ 2p^6\ 3s^2\ 3p^6\ 4s^1\ 3d^5$

29, Cu: $1s^2\ 2s^2\ 2p^6\ 3s^2\ 3p^6\ 4s^1\ 3d^{10}$

If your group is using a six-sided die, 1 corresponds to s, 2 to p, 3 to d, and 4 to f. Five and 6 are ignored. When these numbers appear, the die is cast again.

5. The toss of a coin determines the spin value. A coin tossed heads represents a value of $+\frac{1}{2} m_s$; tails represents a value of $-\frac{1}{2} m_s$.

6. Play begins with the player who rolls and tosses the highest sum of $l + m_s$ value. Ties are broken by a reroll and retoss. Play proceeds clockwise around the group.

7. Play advances from one orbital to the next, as predicted by the level of n and the four rules printed on the quantum-atom energy-distribution diagram. If the roll of the die is successful, the spin is then determined by tossing the coin. Each player adds electrons to orbitals only if the roll of the die and the toss of the coin produce the correct l and m_s values. Each person rolls and tosses until a wrong value of l comes up.

8. The first person to place all electrons of the atom properly for both elements is the winner and is declared "Champion of the Atom."

Part 2

9. Compare your five quantum-atom energy-distribution diagrams to Figure 10-14 (the energy levels of the hydrogen atom) in your text. The degenerate nature of the hydrogen orbitals should be apparent.

10. Label your five diagrams as shown in the following example.

2, He: $1s^2$
12, Mg: $1s^2 \ 2s^2 \ 2p^6 \ 3s^2$
26, Fe: $1s^2 \ 2s^2 \ 2p^6 \ 3s^2 \ 3p^6 \ 4s^2 \ 3d^6$
24, Cr: $1s^2 \ 2s^2 \ 2p^6 \ 3s^2 \ 3p^6 \ 4s^1 \ 3d^5$
29, Cu: $1s^2 \ 2s^2 \ 2p^6 \ 3s^2 \ 3p^6 \ 4s^1 \ 3d^{10}$
Note that Fe, Cr, and Cu do not follow in numerical order. If you do not know why, check with your teacher.

Conclusions

1. In what ways has this investigation aided you in your understanding of electron configurations?

2. Create your own quantum-atom energy-distribution diagram for elements 19, 20, and 21 (potassium, calcium, and scandium).

Rules for Filling the Quantum-Atom Energy-Distribution Diagram

1. An orbital cannot hold more than two electrons.

2. Within any energy level, an incoming electron will occupy the orbitals that have the lowest energy.

3. When electrons enter a fixed energy level and subshell, available orbitals at that level are occupied singly before a second electron is put in an orbital.

4. Filled subshells are stable to loss of electrons.

Guiding the Investigation

■ Procedural Hints
In Part 2, you may want to substitute other elements in place of the five selected. Substitution will be important if you do not want to emphasize elements such as chromium and copper, which do not follow the n + 1 values exactly. You may want to eliminate the game and go directly to Part 2.

Data Analysis
Correct data quantum-atom energy-distribution diagrams are shown below. Students should be allowed free use of the textbook during Parts 1 and 2 of this laboratory investigation.

Conclusions
1. Students can learn the order of filling energy levels, and to fill all of one type of spin before filling the reverse spin electrons.

2. See diagrams below.

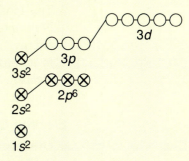

2, He: $1s^2$

12, Mg: $1s^2 \ 2s^2 \ 2p^6 \ 3s^2$

19, K: $1s^2 \ 2s^2 \ 2p^6 \ 3s^2 \ 3p^6 \ 4s^1$

21, Sc: $1s^2 \ 2s^2 \ 2p^6 \ 3s^2 \ 3p^6 \ 4s^2 \ 3d^1$

20, Ca: $1s^2 \ 2s^2 \ 2p^6 \ 3s^2 \ 3p^6 \ 4s^2$

Chapter 10
Review
ANSWERS
begin on page
T359a.

Summary

Waves and Energy

- The model of the atom used by scientists today is described by wave mechanics, or quantum mechanics.

- All waves have certain characteristics—such as frequency, wavelength, and amplitude. The wavelength of a standing wave is quantized.

- Visible light is electromagnetic waves. It occupies a small portion of the electromagnetic spectrum. White light contains all the colors of the rainbow. A prism refracts white light into its component colors, each having a wavelength and frequency different from the others.

The Hydrogen Atom

- The spectrum of hydrogen contains separate color lines. Each line is characterized by a wavelength and a frequency. These lines are explained by the concept of quantized energy levels in hydrogen atoms. An excited hydrogen atom can lose energy and "fall" to a lower energy level. In the process, an exact amount of energy in the form of a specific wavelength of light is emitted.

- The modern theory of the hydrogen atom is built upon wave mechanics and quantization of energy. The position and path of an electron in an atom cannot be determined. Instead, an electron is described in terms of an orbital volume.

Electron Configurations

- Orbitals are identified by symbols, such as 1s, 2s, 2p, etc., which describe the orbital's energy level, shape, and orientation in space.

- The arrangement of electrons around the nucleus of a many-electron atom is denoted in an electron configuration or drawn as an orbital diagram.

356 *CHAPTER 10*

Chemically Speaking

amplitude *10.2*
bright-line spectrum *10.5*
continuous spectrum *10.3*
electromagnetic waves *10.4*
electron configuration *10.9*
energy levels *10.6*
frequency *10.2*
ground state *10.7*
hertz *10.3*
ionization energy *10.6*
node *10.3*
orbital *10.7*

orbital diagrams
10.9
Pauli exclusion
principle *10.9*
photon *10.3*
principal quantum
number *10.7*
probability *10.7*
quantum
mechanics *10.7*
wavelength *10.2*

Concept Mapping

Using the method of concept mapping described at the front of this book, draw a concept map for the term *electron*.

Questions and Problems

WAVES AND ENERGY

A. Objective: **Describe** *properties of water waves and light waves.*

1. Give evidence that waves carry energy.
2. Describe a characteristic that is similar and a characteristic that is different between an ocean wave and a standing wave.
3. Describe the horizontal and vertical motion of a boat floating on ocean waves.
4. If you make a standing wave of wavelength 2.5 meters with a rope, what must be done to the rope in order to decrease the wavelength to 1.25 meters?
5. Briefly explain what a standing wave has in common with electrons in atoms.

PROBLEM-SOLVING
▶ S T R A T E G I E S

Students apply these strategies in the following questions.

- **Factor-label method:** 8, 9, 10, 11, 17, 18
- **Using what you know:** 8, 9, 10, 11
- **Using patterns:** 28, 29, 31, 32, 33, 34, 35, 36, 42, 43

- **Using calculators:** 8, 9, 10, 11, 17, 18
- **Verifying your answer:** 8, 9, 10, 11, 17, 18,
- **Making diagrams:** 28, 29

B. Objective: **Explain** *the relationship between energy and the frequency of light.*

6. Explain the statement: "The wavelength of a standing wave is quantized."

7. What is the significance of the equation $E = h\nu$? Explain in your own words how this equation is a mathematical statement of the quantization of energy.

8. A very bright line in the bright-line spectrum of sodium has a wavelength of 5.90×10^{-7} m. What is the frequency of this line?

9. Calculate the frequency of the electromagnetic waves produced when the electrons in a mole of hydrogen atoms change from the fifth to the second energy level. (Planck's constant has a value of 3.98×10^{-13} kJ·s/mol.)

10. What is the frequency of electromagnetic radiation emitted when the electrons of one mole of hydrogen atoms change from the 4s orbital to the 1s orbital? What is the wavelength of the radiation?

11. A radio station broadcasts at a frequency of 105.4 MHz. What is the wavelength of this electromagnetic wave? (MHz is the symbol for *megahertz*.)

C. Objective: **Compare and contrast** *different regions of the electromagnetic spectrum.*

12. List four regions of the electromagnetic spectrum.

13. Order the following regions of the electromagnetic spectrum according to energy per photon, from lowest energy to highest: X ray, infrared, ultraviolet, visible red, visible green, microwaves.

14. The electrons in hydrogen atoms will absorb energy that is equivalent to the energy in waves of the electromagnetic spectrum from the infrared to the ultraviolet. What are the magnitudes of nine frequencies and wavelengths of the electromagnetic waves involved?

Boxed numbers indicate questions that involve skills in interpretation, application, and analysis.

THE HYDROGEN ATOM

D. Objective: **Explain** *how the bright-line spectrum of hydrogen demonstrates the quantized nature of energy.*

15. Which colors appear in the bright-line spectrum of hydrogen?

16. Describe why hydrogen atoms in a spectrum tube emit energy in the blue region of the visible spectrum.

17. What is the energy given off by one hydrogen atom as it loses energy from level 3 to level 2 in joules per atom?

18. How much energy must a mole of hydrogen atoms absorb if the electrons are to be excited from the first level to the fifth level?

19. What must be done to a hydrogen atom to change its 2s electron to a 3s electron? What happens when a hydrogen atom with a 3s electron becomes a hydrogen atom with a 2s electron?

E. Objective: **Predict** *the position(s) of electrons in an atom, using the concepts of quantum numbers and orbitals.*

20. What is an orbital?

21. List all the orbitals available for the hydrogen atom when $n = 3$.

22. What orbital will the sixth electron of ground-state nitrogen occupy?

23. What are the three quantum numbers that describe an orbital?

24. Explain how the first three quantum numbers describe an orbital.

25. What is wrong with the following descriptions of an orbital?
    a. An orbital is a ball of uniform density.
    b. An orbital is a solar system, like a planet circling the sun at a fixed distance.
    c. An orbital tells you exactly where an electron can be found.
    d. An orbital can accommodate only one electron.

26. Which of the following statements about orbitals is false?
   a. Orbitals are distributed in space around the nucleus.
   b. Orbitals are regions of space in which electrons are likely to be found.
   c. Orbitals show the path of the electron.
   d. Orbitals are part of one model for atomic structure.

27. In what ways is the 4s orbital of a hydrogen atom different from a 1s orbital?

28. In which part of the electromagnetic spectrum would you observe the following energy changes for electrons of hydrogen atoms:

	Energy Level before the Change	Energy Level after the Change
1.	4s	2p
2.	5d	1s
3.	3p	2s

29. Order the changes in energy in problem 28 above according to the amount of energy given off, from the change with the least energy difference to the change with the greatest. Use only the principal energy level for this calculation.

ELECTRON CONFIGURATIONS

F. Objective: **Draw and write** *electron configurations of neutral atoms and ions.*

30. How are electron configurations for neutral atoms different from the electron configurations of the corresponding ions?

31. Write the electron configurations for elements 37, 38, and 39 (rubidium, strontium, and yttrium).

32. Write the electron configurations for the following elements: arsenic, krypton, bromine, and phosphorus.

33. Write the electron configurations for the following ions: K^+, O^{2-}, Br^-.

34. Draw the orbital diagrams and write the electron configurations for the following elements: potassium, silicon, fluorine, and argon.

35. Write the electron configurations for Be, Mg, Ca, and Sr. What is the similarity in the configurations of the outermost electrons of these elements?

36. Write the electron configurations for Sc, Ti, Ni, and Zn. Which set of orbitals is being filled last in these configurations?

G. Objective: **Recognize** *the filling order of electrons in many-electron atoms.*

37. Name the elements that correspond to each of the following electron configurations. (Assume all are neutral atoms in their ground states.)
   a. $1s^2 2s^2 2p^1$
   b. $1s^2 2s^2$
   c. $1s^2 2s^2 2p^6 3s^2 3p^2$

38. For each of the following electron configurations of neutral atoms, determine the name of the element listed and determine if the configuration as written is the ground state or an excited state.
   a. $1s^2 2s^2 2p^6$
   b. $1s^2 2s^2 2p^5 3s^2$
   c. $1s^2 2s^2 2p^6 3s^2 3p^6 4s^2 3d^3$
   d. $1s^2 2s^2 2p^6 3s^2 5s^1$

39. For each of the following electron configurations of neutral atoms, determine if the configuration as written is the ground state, an excited state, or if it is an impossible configuration:
   a. N $1s^2 2s^2 2p^3$
   b. Na $1s^2 2s^2 2p^6 4s^1$
   c. Ne $1s^2 2s^3 2p^5$
   d. V $1s^2 2s^2 2p^6 3s^2 3p^6 4s^2 3d^2 4p^1$

Critical Thinking

SYNTHESIS WITHIN THE CHAPTER

40. Imagine that you have a group of hydrogen atoms whose electrons are all occupying 2s orbitals. What could you do to the atoms so that the electrons will be occupying 4s orbitals?

41. Systems tend to exist in the lowest energy states possible. Cite evidence in this chapter to back up this statement.

SYNTHESIS ACROSS CHAPTERS

42. A lithium atom can combine with a chlorine atom in the reaction

$$Li(g) + Cl(g) \rightarrow LiCl(g)$$

a. Write electron configurations of the lithium atom, lithium ion, chlorine atom, and chloride ion.

b. Will the two ions attract? Why?

c. The electron configuration of which noble gases will each ion resemble?

d. Look up the ionization energy of lithium and compare it with the ionization energies of other elements. Do you think this reaction will take place readily? What other factor is important in making your decision?

43. Fill in the blanks for the table below:

Name of Particle	Number of Protons	Electron Configuration	Electric Charge on Particle
oxide ion	8		
	11	$1s^2 2s^2 2p^6$	
	18		0
phosphide ion			-3

Projects

44. While wearing safety goggles, use a sharp knife to carefully cut a large Styrofoam ball in half. Use a pen or wax pencil to draw circles on the flat surface to represent s-type orbitals and nodes.

45. Use Styrofoam eggs and lengths of wire cut from straightened coat hangers to make a model of p_x, p_y, and p_z orbitals. Caution: Wear safety goggles when cutting wire and inserting wire ends into the Styrofoam. The cut ends of the wires are sharp—use care when handling.

Research and Writing

46. One of the principles of the quantum theory is that molecules absorb only definite and distinct amounts of energy. The principle helps to explain how the greenhouse effect can take place in Earth's atmosphere. Research and report on the greenhouse effect and include the quantum theory in the report.

47. The year 1905 has been described as an important time for Albert Einstein. Investigate the work of Einstein, and report on why 1905 was such a significant year.

48. Atomic absorption spectroscopy is an important tool for the analytical chemist. Find out about this method of substance identification.

49. Chemiluminescence is used by the firefly to attract mates, and by children on Halloween night as "cold light lanterns." It can be used by the biochemist to identify trace amounts of certain molecules. Find out about the reactions that produce cold light. What is happening to the electrons in molecules when cold light is produced?

☐ Boxed numbers indicate questions that involve skills in interpretation, application, and analysis.

1. A cork bobs up and down on water, sunlight heats whatever it shines on, sound waves cause eardrums to vibrate, and so on.

2. Both kinds of waves have wavelengths. Standing waves have nodes whereas ocean waves do not.

3. The boat moves up and down vertically at the frequency of the passing waves. There is no horizontal motion of the boat due to the waves.

4. Increase the frequency of the shaking.

5. Both have restrictions in possible changes. A standing wave can have only specific wavelengths that are integral multiples of $\frac{1}{2}$. An electron in an atom can absorb energy only in amounts which are multiples of Planck's constant.

6. A standing wave only can have specific wavelengths that are integral multiples of $\frac{1}{2}$.

7. Answers will vary. E is energy, h is Planck's constant, v is frequency. Planck's constant is a proportionality constant that relates the energy in an electromagnetic wave to its frequency.

8. $c = \lambda \times v$

$v = \dfrac{3.00 \times 10^8 \text{ m/s}}{5.90 \times 10^{-7} \text{ m}}$

$= 5.08 \times 10^{14}$ hertz

9. $E = E_2 - E_5 = 275.52 \text{ kJ / mol}$

$E = h \times v$

$v = \dfrac{275.52 \text{ kJ/mol}}{(3.98 \times 10^{-13} \text{ kJ} \times \text{s/mol})}$

$= 6.92 \times 10^{14}$ hertz

10. $E_{photons} = E_1 - E_4 = 1230 \text{ kJ / mol}$

$= 1.23 \times 10^6$ J / mol $= 6.6262$

$\times 10^{-34}$ J·s / photon $\times 6.02$

$\times 10^{23}$ photons / mol $\times v$

$E = h v$

$v = \dfrac{1.23 \times 10^6 \text{ J/mol}}{\frac{(6.6262 \times 10^{-34} \text{ J} \cdot \text{s})}{\text{photon}} \times \frac{(6.02 \times 10^{23} \text{ photons})}{\text{mol}}}$

$= 3.08 \times 10^{15}$ hertz

11. $c = \lambda \times v$

105.4×10^6 hertz $=$ frequency of radio station

$\lambda = \dfrac{3.00 \times 10^8 \text{ m/s}}{105.4 \times 10^6 \text{ /s}} = 2.85$ m

12. Answers will vary. Some possible answers are radio waves, microwaves, infrared, visible light, ultraviolet, X rays, and gamma rays.

13. Microwaves, infrared, visible red, visible green, ultraviolet, X rays

14. See Table 10–2 and Figure 10–9. Given energy values for transitions from levels 2, 3, 4 and 5 to level 1, frequency and wavelength could be determined for each, using $E = hv$ and $c = \lambda v$

15. red, blue-green, blue, and violet

16. Excited atoms lose energy. If a change occurs from the fifth energy level to the second in hydrogen, energy is given off as blue light.

17. $E = E_3 - E_2 = \dfrac{182.8 \text{ kJ/mol} \times 1 \text{ mol}}{6.02 \times 10^{23} \text{ atoms}}$

$\times \dfrac{10^3 \text{ J}}{1 \text{ kJ}} = 3.04 \times 10^{-19}$ J / atom

18. $E_1 - E_5 = 1260$ kJ/mol absorbed

19. A specific amount of energy must be added to the atom. The same amount of energy is given off in the form of a photon.

20. a region in space around the nucleus of an atom in which an electron is likely to be found

21. $3s$, three $3p$ and five $3d$ orbitals

22. $2p$

23. n, l, and m

24. n describes the size of the orbital; l describes the shape, and m describes the orientation in space.

25. a. The orbital is not equally dense throughout. The probability of finding an electron varies within the orbital. Not all orbitals are ball-shaped.

 b. Orbitals do not describe the path of an electron around the nucleus. They describe a region in which electrons are likely to be found.

 c. An orbital describes a region where an electron can probably be found.

 d. An orbital can accommodate 2 electrons if their spins are opposite.

26. c.

27. The energy level is greater, so the energy of an electron in the orbital is greater, the probability distribution is farther from the nucleus, and a $4s$ orbital has nodes.

28. 1. blue-green
 2. ultraviolet
 3. red

29. 3 to 2, 4 to 2, 5 to 1

30. Depending on whether the ion is negative or positive, the total number of electrons represented would be more or less than the neutral atoms.

31. Rb $1s^2 2s^2 2p^6 3s^2 3p^6 4s^2 3d^{10} 4p^6$ $5s^1$
 Sr $1s^2 2s^2 2p^6 3s^2 3p^6 4s^2 3d^{10} 4p^6$ $5s^2$
 Y $1s^2 2s^2 2p^6 3s^2 3p^6 4s^2 3d^{10} 4p^6$ $5s^2 4d^1$

32. As $1s^2 2s^2 2p^6 3s^2 3p^6 4s^2 3d^{10} 4p^3$
 Kr $1s^2 2s^2 2p^6 3s^2 3p^6 4s^2 3d^{10} 4p^6$
 Br $1s^2 2s^2 2p^6 3s^2 3p^6 4s^2 3d^{10} 4p^5$
 P $1s^2 2s^2 2p^6 3s^2 3p^3$

33. K$^+$ $1s^2 2s^2 2p^6 3s^2 3p^6$
 O^{2-} $1s^2 2s^2 2p^6$
 Br$^-$ $1s^2 2s^2 2p^6 3s^2 3p^6 4s^2 3d^{10} 4p^6$

34.
 K $1s^2 2s^2 2p^6 3s^2 3p^6 4s^1$ ⇅ ⇅ ⇅⇅⇅ ⇅ ⇅⇅⇅ ↑

 Si $1s^2 2s^2 2p^6 3s^2 3p^2$ ⇅ ⇅ ⇅⇅⇅ ⇅ ↑↑○

 F $1s^2 2s^2 2p^5$ ⇅ ⇅ ⇅⇅↑

 Ar $1s^2 2s^2 2p^6 3s^2 3p^6$ ⇅ ⇅ ⇅⇅⇅ ⇅ ⇅⇅⇅

35. Be $1s^2 2s^2$
 Mg $1s^2 2s^2 2p^6 3s^2$
 Ca $1s^2 2s^2 2p^6 3s^2 3p^6 4s^2$
 Sr $1s^2 2s^2 2p^6 3s^2 3p^6 4s^2 3d^{10} 4p^6$ $5s^2$

 All the outermost s orbitals are occupied by two electrons.

36. Sc $1s^2 2s^2 2p^6 3s^2 3p^6 4s^2 3d^1$
 Ti $1s^2 2s^2 2p^6 3s^2 3p^6 4s^2 3d^2$
 Ni $1s^2 2s^2 2p^6 3s^2 3p^6 4s^2 3d^8$
 Zn $1s^2 2s^2 2p^6 3s^2 3p^6 4s^2 3d^{10}$
 The $3d$ orbitals are being filled.

37. a. boron
 b. beryllium
 c. silicon

38. Ne—ground; Na—excited; V—ground; Al—excited

39. N—ground; Na—excited; Ne—impossible; V—excited

40. Add energy with just the correct frequency, 6.17×10^{14} Hz.

41. Excited electrons emit energy until they reach the lowest possible energy state.

42. a. Li $1s^2 2s^1$
 Li$^+$ $1s^2$
 Cl $1s^2 2s^2 2p^6 3s^2 3p^5$
 Cl$^-$ $1s^2 2s^2 2p^6 3s^2 3p^6$

 b. Yes, because opposite charges attract.

c. Li$^+$ resembles He;
   Cl$^-$ resembles Ar.

d. The ionization energy for Li is 519 kJ/mol, which is low compared to other elements in Table 11–1. The reaction will take place readily.

43.

Name of Particle	Number of Protons	Electron Configuration	Electric Charge on Particle
oxide ion	8	$1s^2\,2s^2\,2p^6$	2^-
sodium ion	11	$1s^2\,2s^2\,2p^6$	1^+
argon atom	18	$1s^2\,2s^2\,2p^6\,3s^2\,3p^6$	0
phosphide ion	15	$1s^2\,2s^2\,2p^6\,3s^2\,3p^6$	3^-

The Periodic Table

Investigations	Demonstrations	Texas Essential Elements★
		Content: 4.1, 4.2, 11.2 **Process:** 4.2, 4.3, 7.3, 10.1
Laboratory Manual 11–1 S Laboratory Manual 11–2 M Laboratory Manual 11–3 IM		**Content:** 3.7, 3.10, 4.2, 4.4 **Process:** 4.3, 10.1, 10.3, 10.4
Laboratory Manual 11–4 IM In-text Investigation, page T386		**Content:** 4.3, 11.2 **Process:** 4.2, 4.3, 10.1, 10.2
		Content: 4.2, 4.3, 4.4 **Process:** 1.2, 3.2, 4.3, 6.1, 7.2
		Process: 4.2, 4.3, 7.1, 10.1, 10.2

KEY:
M–*Microscale* **S**–*Structured*
I–*Inquiry* **IM**–*Inquiry Microscale*

★*See pages T8–T11 for complete
listing of Texas Essential Elements.*

11

The Periodic Table

Chapter Rationale

Chapter 11 introduces the periodic table of the elements. The historical development, focusing on observation and classification, is presented. The utility of the periodic table as a predictor of chemical properties is emphasized. The discovery of the periodic nature of the elements leads to the discussion of the electron configurations of the elements, and the relationship between electron configuration and position in the periodic table. The periodic trends of the properties of the elements are emphasized.

About the Photograph

Most cultures organize their lives by charting periodic trends. The seasonal cycle, the lunar cycle, and the solar cycle are periodic events which calendars attempt to organize. Knowledge of these periodic trends allowed cultures such as the Mayans and Aztecs to know when to plant their crops and when to harvest. An early Roman calendar, borrowed from the Greeks, divided a 304-day year into 10 months and eventually made the calendar about three months ahead of the seasons. To correct the problem, Julius Caesar divided the year into 12 months, most with 30 or 31 days. The Julian calendar was widely used until the Gregorian calendar, used today, was developed in 1582 to make the solar and calendar years match more exactly.

Chapter Planning Hints

Plan to use four to seven class sessions to complete all three Parts, the Laboratory Investigation, and the Chapter Review. You may wish to obtain The World of Chemistry videotape The Periodic Table for use when introducing the periodic table. You may also wish to

(continued on page T361)

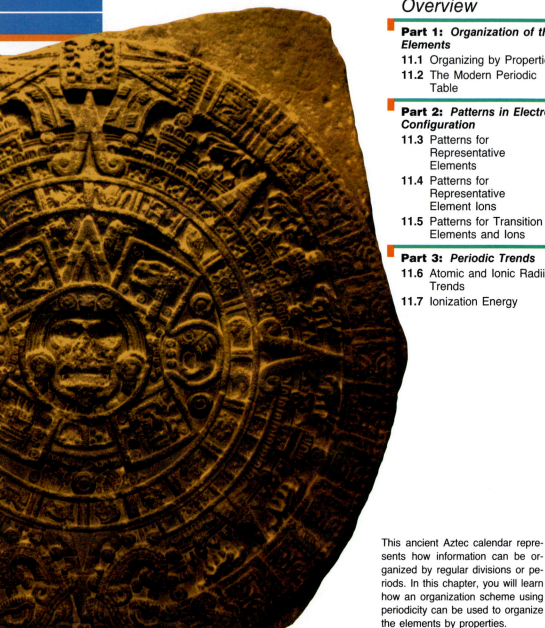

This ancient Aztec calendar represents how information can be organized by regular divisions or periods. In this chapter, you will learn how an organization scheme using periodicity can be used to organize the elements by properties.

PART 1 Organization of the Elements

Prior to the development of the modern atomic theory, chemists had made many macroscopic observations of elements and compounds. They became interested in organizing these observations for use in making predictions of the physical and chemical behavior of matter. However, deciding on a useful way to classify elements proved to be quite a challenge.

Elements could be grouped on the basis of physical or chemical characteristics. They could be organized into groups such as metals and nonmetals, or they could be ordered by increasing atomic mass. Elements could even be organized by how they react with other elements, such as oxygen or chlorine. However, developing an organizational scheme that would be useful for predicting both physical and chemical properties proved a more difficult task. An adequate model for prediction was not developed until the late 1860's. This model has become a tool still used by chemists today.

11.1 Organizing by Properties

In 1869, Dmitri Mendeleev (1834–1907), a Russian scientist, published an organizational scheme for the elements. His scheme, called a periodic table, arranged the elements in horizontal rows by increasing atomic mass, as shown in Figure 11-1 on the next page. Notice that not all rows contain the same number of elements. Mendeleev placed the elements in horizontal rows, so that elements with similar chemical reactivity were arranged in the same vertical column. For example, in Figure 11-1 all elements he tested in Gruppe I reacted with oxygen in a ratio of 2:1, such as Li_2O, while all elements in Gruppe II reacted with oxygen in a ratio of 1:1, such as MgO.

What Mendeleev did can be thought of as similar to putting together a large puzzle. However, in Mendeleev's puzzle, there seemed to be pieces missing, as indicated by dashes (—) in his version of the periodic table. Elements with the appropriate atomic mass and the necessary properties to fill those positions had yet to be discovered. Mendeleev not only predicted that the missing elements would be discovered, he also predicted the physical and chemical properties of some of those elements.

Arranging by atomic number Look at the atomic masses of the elements argon and potassium and the elements tellurium and iodine on the modern version of the periodic table, Table 11-3

Objectives

Part 1

A. **Describe** the classification schemes used to arrange elements in Mendeleev's periodic table and in the modern periodic table.

B. **Distinguish** between periods and groups on the periodic table.

DO YOU KNOW?

John Newlands applied his knowledge of music to his observations of the behavior of the elements. European music is based on a repeating scale of octaves. Every eighth note in the scale repeats: A, B, C, D, E, F, G, A, B, etc. Newlands observed a similar repetition in the properties of the known elements. He was able to organize the elements into a table that was seven elements wide. The eighth element in the table had properties similar to the first element.

(continued from page T360)

obtain the computer program, KC? Discoverer: *Exploring the Properties of the Chemical Elements,* for use when introducing periodic trends.

Developing Skills

Students may apply these skills in their study of Part 1.

Interpreting data: Have students compare the values of the first ionization energy of the elements in Period 2 and describe the pattern.

Comparing/Contrasting: Have students compare the classification scheme used to arrange the elements in Mendeleev's periodic table and that used in the modern periodic table.

Analyzing data and Forming a hypothesis: After examining Table 11–1 on page 363, have students form a hypothesis to explain why helium, neon, and argon are grouped together.

FOCUS

Activate Prior Knowledge

Try to get students to appreciate the insights of Mendeleev and others that led to the periodic table. Ask 6 to 10 students to come up to the front of the room and arrange themselves from shortest to tallest. Ask the rest of the students to see if there are any periodic patterns. Are there similarities between the students to the right or left of each student? For example, are all the students to the right of blondes wearing watches? Then focus on the first 20 elements arranged by increasing atomic number. The periodic table does show patterns; each element following a Group 8A element (noble gases) is a metal that reacts with water, and each element just preceding a Group 8A element is a nonmetal

(continued on page T362)

(continued from page T361)

that exists in nature as a diatomic molecule. (J. Finholt, *Journal of Chemical Education*, 61, 190, 1984.)

TEACH

Teaching Strategy

Organizing by Properties

Relate the story of Mendeleev's development of the periodic table and point out that good science often involves serendipity and the ability of a scientist to recognize it. You might simulate Mendeleev's task by challenging students to describe 10 missing pieces in a 50-piece puzzle.

Science Background

The Periodic Law

Mendeleev's periodic table was not the first effort that recognized a relationship between the atomic mass of an element and its properties. In 1829, Dobereiner noted that several triads (groups of three elements in which the atomic mass of the second element is approximately equal to the average of the atomic masses of the other two) had similar properties. In 1866, John Newlands noted that when elements are listed in order of increasing mass, the properties of the eighth element are similar to those of the first element. He compared his law of octaves to octaves on a musical scale. The periodic system of elements was developed independently and almost simultaneously by Lothar Meyer in Germany and by Mendeleev in Russia. The chief advantage of Mendeleev's table was that it was based on chemical properties and could be easily generalized and used. He grouped together the elements with similar properties and began to relate them to physical constants, especially atomic mass. One day in early 1869, he was arranging and rearranging

(continued on page T363)

TABELLE II

REIHEN	GRUPPE I. — R²O	GRUPPE II. — RO	GRUPPE III. — R²O³	GRUPPE IV. RH⁴ RO²	GRUPPE V. RH³ R²O⁵	GRUPPE VI. RH² RO³	GRUPPE VII. RH R²O⁷	GRUPPE VIII. — RO⁴
I	H=1							
2	Li=7	Be=9,4	B=11	C=12	N=14	O=16	F=19	
3	Na=23	Mg=24	Al=27,3	Si=28	P=31	S=32	Cl=35,5	
4	K=39	Ca=40	–=44	Ti=48	V=51	Cr=52	Mn=55	Fe=56, Co=59, Ni=59, Cu=63.
5	(Cu=63)	Zn=65	–=68	–=72	As=75	Se=78	Br=80	
6	Rb=85	Sr=87	?Yt=88	Zr=90	Nb=94	Mo=96	–=100	Ru=104, Rh=104, Pd=106, Ag=108.
7	(Ag=108)	Cd=112	In=113	Sn=118	Sb=122	Te=125	J=127	
8	Cs=133	Ba=137	?Di=138	?Ce=140	–	–	–	— — —
9	(–)	–	–	–	–	–	–	
10	–	–	?Er=178	?La=180	Ta=182	W=184	–	Os=195, Ir=197, Pt=198, Au=199.
11	(Au=199)	Hg=200	Tl=204	Pb=207	Bi=208	–	–	— — —
12	–			Th=231		U=240	–	— — —

Figure 11-1 *Mendeleev's periodic table, issued in 1872, had blank spaces left for elements that were not known at that time. Mendeleev predicted they would be discovered.*

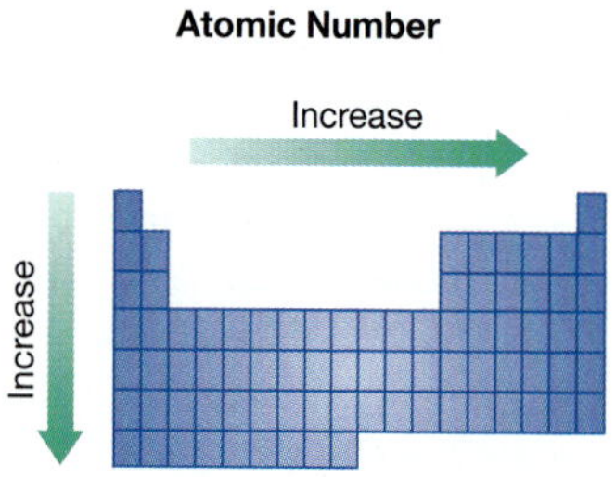

Atomic Number

Increase

Increase

on pages 366–367. You should find that these elements are not in order of increasing atomic mass. Because of their chemical properties, however, the elements' positions in the periodic table cannot be reversed. How can this discrepancy be resolved? In 1913, a British physicist, Henry Moseley, found that when the elements are arranged in order of increasing atomic number instead of atomic mass, these discrepancies disappear. The periodic table used today is arranged by increasing atomic number rather than by increasing atomic mass, as in Mendeleev's original periodic table.

The periodic law Mendeleev and others who developed schemes for the elements recognized that the repetition in properties of the elements was a fundamental pattern of nature. This fundamental pattern is known as the periodicity of the elements and is the basis of the **periodic law.** The modern periodic law states: *The properties of the elements repeat periodically when the elements are arranged in increasing order by their atomic numbers.*

The form of the periodic table has been modified since Mendeleev's time to reflect information learned about the structure of the atom and to accommodate newly discovered elements. However, the scheme of arranging the elements to provide regular repeating patterns of chemical and physical properties remains the same. As you will learn, these repeating patterns provide a strong basis from which to predict and explain the properties of elements.

Concept ✔ Check

How was Mendeleev able to predict the existence of undiscovered elements?

11.2 The Modern Periodic Table

Table 11-1 lists the first 20 elements and some of their physical and chemical properties. See if you can find some repeating properties among these elements for the purpose of classifying them as Mendeleev did.

TABLE 11-1

Symbol	Atomic Mass	Atomic Number	Physical State at 25°C 1 atm	Formula for Hydride	H to Element Ratio	Formula for Fluoride	F to Element Ratio	1st Ionization Energy (kJ/mol)
			Some Information About the First 20 Elements					
H	1.0	1	gas	H_2	1	HF	1	1312
He	4.0	2	gas	—		—		2372
Li	6.9	3	solid	LiH	1	LiF	1	519
Be	9.0	4	solid	BeH_2	2	BeF_2	2	900
B	10.8	5	solid	B_2H_6	3	BF_3	3	799
C	12.0	6	solid	CH_4	4	CF_4	4	1088
N	14.0	7	gas	NH_3	3	NF_3	3	1406
O	16.0	8	gas	H_2O	2	OF_2	2	1314
F	19.0	9	gas	HF	1	F_2	1	1682
Ne	20.2	10	gas	—		—		2080
Na	23.0	11	solid	NaH	1	NaF	1	498
Mg	24.3	12	solid	MgH_2	2	MgF_2	2	736
Al	27.0	13	solid	AlH_3	3	AlF_3	3	577
Si	28.1	14	solid	SiH_4	4	SiF_4	4	787
P	31.0	15	solid	PH_3	3	PF_3	3	1063
S	32.1	16	solid	H_2S	2	SF_2	2	1000
Cl	35.5	17	gas	HCl	1	ClF	1	1255
Ar	39.9	18	gas	—		—		1519
K	39.1	19	solid	KH	1	KF	1	418
Ca	40.1	20	solid	CaH_2	2	CaF_2	2	590

In looking at Table 11-1, did you notice that helium, neon, and argon are the only elements shown that do not form compounds with hydrogen and fluorine? Based on this observation, you could put these elements together in a group. These three elements do not react under usual conditions and had not been discovered when Mendeleev first proposed his periodic table. (In 1870, helium was discovered in the sun using spectroscopy.)

Chemical reactivity There seems to be a pattern to the ratios in which elements form compounds with hydrogen and fluorine (columns 6 and 8 in Table 11-1). The ratios for the elements lithium through fluorine are 1, 2, 3, 4, 3, 2, 1. This trend also exists for the elements sodium through chlorine.

PART **1**

Section 11.2

(continued from page T362) slips of paper on which he had written the name of each element and its atomic weight. He noted the relationship of atomic mass to the chemical properties of elements in the group when he arranged them like days on a calendar. Less than a month later, he announced his findings.

Look Back

You may wish to point out to your students how the Greek numbering system encountered in Section 2.9 of Chapter 2 is used to name elements and molecular compounds. For example, phosphorus pentachloride for PCl$_5$ and unnilpentium for element 105.

Science Background

Chemical Families

Hydrogen is in Group 1A but is not a metal like the other elements in the group. Hydrogen has other properties that also seem out of place for a Group 1A element. However, its electron configuration is consistent with the electron configurations of the other elements in 1A.

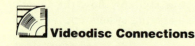

Videodisc Connections

903-908, side 6
Periodic Table: group identification (6-frame seq.)

9365 to 12353, side 6
Alkali metals (movie)

PART 1
Section 11.2 *continued*

First ionization energies Now compare the values for the first ionization energy, the energy required to remove one electron from an atom in the gaseous phase. The values, as shown in Table 11-2, generally increase from lithium to fluorine. You will learn more about ionization energy at the end of this chapter.

TABLE 11-2

Periodic Groups for the Elements Helium to Calcium First Ionization Energy							
							He 2 — 2372 kJ/mol
Li 3 LiF 519 kJ/mol	Be 4 BeF$_2$ 900 kJ/mol	B 5 BF$_3$ 799 kJ/mol	C 6 CF$_4$ 1088 kJ/mol	N 7 NF$_3$ 1406 kJ/mol	O 8 OF$_2$ 1314 kJ/mol	F 9 F$_2$ 1682 kJ/mol	Ne 10 — 2080 kJ/mol
Na 11 NaF 498 kJ/mol	Mg 12 MgF$_2$ 736 kJ/mol	Al 13 AlF$_3$ 577 kJ/mol	Si 14 SiF$_4$ 787 kJ/mol	P 15 PF$_3$ 1063 kJ/mol	S 16 SF$_2$ 1000 kJ/mol	Cl 17 ClF 1255 kJ/mol	Ar 18 — 1519 kJ/mol
K 19 KF 418 kJ/mol	Ca 20 CaF$_2$ 590 kJ/mol						

The periodic table today If you arranged elements 2 through 20 according to the trends in Table 11-1 that are observed for the formation of their fluorides and the systematic variation of their ionization energies, you would get a table similar to Table 11-2. Compare Table 11-2 with the complete modern version of the periodic table, shown in Table 11-3. You will find that elements in the same vertical columns have similar chemical properties.

In the modern periodic table, each vertical column identifies a **group** of elements, or a **chemical family.** The groups are identified by numbers across the top. The horizontal rows of elements are called **periods.** Table 11-4 on page 368 shows the elements with group numbers across the top and period numbers along the left-hand side.

CONNECTING CONCEPTS

Classifying Physical and chemical properties of the elements enable them to be classified into fundamental groups, such as metals and nonmetals.

Chemical families Some groups, or families, have special names. Group 1A is known as the **alkali metals** since these metals react with water to form an alkaline, or basic, solution. Sodium, for example, reacts with water very rapidly as seen in Figure 11-2. This reaction can be represented by the following equation.

$$2Na(s) + 2H_2O(l) \rightarrow 2NaOH(aq) + H_2(g) + \text{heat energy}$$

The sodium hydroxide, NaOH, produced contains the hydroxide ion, OH$^-$, and is classified as basic or alkaline. Each of the alkali metals undergoes a similar reaction. Although located in Group 1A, hydrogen is not considered an alkali metal because it is so different from the other members of Group 1A.

Group 2A is known as the **alkaline earth metals.** They also react with water to give basic solutions. Group 7A is called the **halogens,** meaning *"salt formers"*. You learned in Chapter 2 that elements in the last group of the periodic table, Group 8A, are called the noble gases because they are generally unreactive. Other groups on the periodic table are named by the first member of their family. Group 6A is known as the oxygen group, or oxygen family.

The elements in Groups 1A–8A, are known as the main group or **representative elements.** The B-group elements (between 2A and 3A) are called **transition metals.** Notice that in both Tables 11-3 and 11-4, there are two rows of elements removed from the main body of the periodic table. These elements are called the lanthanide and actinide elements, or—collectively—the **inner-transition metals.** The lanthanides are period 6 elements and follow the element 57, lanthanum; the actinides are in period 7 and follow element 89, actinium. They are separated from the main body of the periodic table only to make it easier to fit the table onto a single page.

Periods Periods have different numbers of elements. Period 1 has only two elements, H and He. Periods 2 and 3 have 8 elements each. Periods 4 and 5 have 18 elements each, including 10 transition elements. Period 6 has 32 elements including the lanthanides. These differences are easier to see using the long form of the periodic table (Table 11-3). The 7th row of the periodic table is not complete. Fewer than half of the elements in period 7 occur naturally on Earth. The rest have been synthesized by chemists or physicists, and all are radioactive.

Figure 11-2 *Sodium reacts with water to produce hydrogen gas, sodium ions, and hydroxide ions.* ⚠ CAUTION: *Three-tenths gram of sodium was placed in 200 mL of water for this picture. Using a larger amount of sodium would be dangerous. The transparent shield used to protect the photographer is not visible in the photo.*

Figure 11-3 *Sodium and calcium have properties that are characteristic of metals. Sulfur and bromine are both classified as nonmetals. As you can see the nonmetals look very different from the metals. To which group of the periodic table do each of these elements belong?*

Myths and Misconceptions

Students often regard the elements of the periodic table as abstract symbols, not as the concrete substances that they actually represent. Have students locate metals, nonmetals, and noble gases on the periodic table. Then show them actual samples or pictures of several metals (such as gold, silver, aluminum foil, iron nails, lead sinker, copper wire) and nonmetals (sulfur, charcoal). Ask students to describe some of the common properties of groups of elements on the periodic table. Students can also work together to develop a chart on which they identify the elements of an individual group, their sources, and uses.

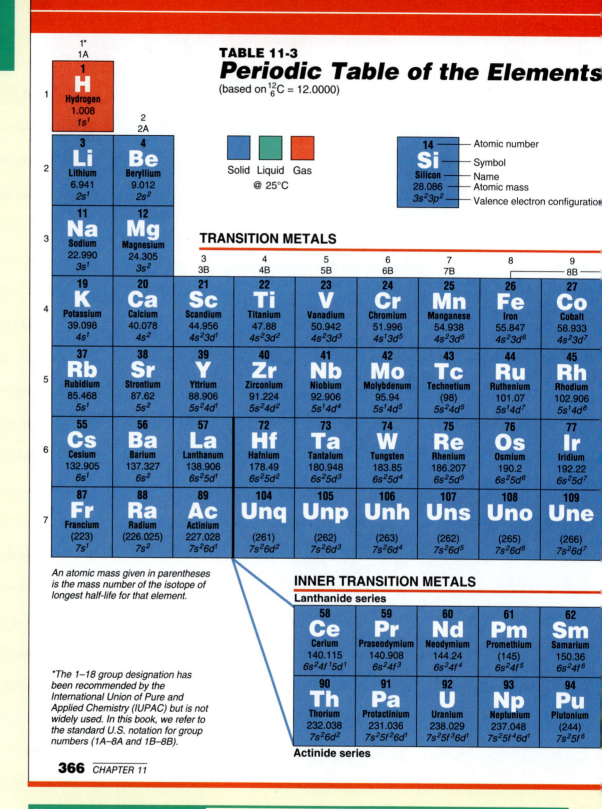

TABLE 11-3
Periodic Table of the Elements
(based on $^{12}_{6}C = 12.0000$)

Solid   Liquid   Gas
@ 25°C

14 — Atomic number		
Si — Symbol		
Silicon — Name		
28.086 — Atomic mass		
$3s^2 3p^2$ — Valence electron configuration		

1* 1A								
1 **H** Hydrogen 1.008 $1s^1$	2 2A							
3 **Li** Lithium 6.941 $2s^1$	**4** **Be** Beryllium 9.012 $2s^2$							
11 **Na** Sodium 22.990 $3s^1$	**12** **Mg** Magnesium 24.305 $3s^2$							

TRANSITION METALS

		3 3B	4 4B	5 5B	6 6B	7 7B	8	9 8B
19 **K** Potassium 39.098 $4s^1$	**20** **Ca** Calcium 40.078 $4s^2$	**21** **Sc** Scandium 44.956 $4s^2 3d^1$	**22** **Ti** Titanium 47.88 $4s^2 3d^2$	**23** **V** Vanadium 50.942 $4s^2 3d^3$	**24** **Cr** Chromium 51.996 $4s^1 3d^5$	**25** **Mn** Manganese 54.938 $4s^2 3d^5$	**26** **Fe** Iron 55.847 $4s^2 3d^6$	**27** **Co** Cobalt 58.933 $4s^2 3d^7$
37 **Rb** Rubidium 85.468 $5s^1$	**38** **Sr** Strontium 87.62 $5s^2$	**39** **Y** Yttrium 88.906 $5s^2 4d^1$	**40** **Zr** Zirconium 91.224 $5s^2 4d^2$	**41** **Nb** Niobium 92.906 $5s^1 4d^4$	**42** **Mo** Molybdenum 95.94 $5s^1 4d^5$	**43** **Tc** Technetium (98) $5s^2 4d^5$	**44** **Ru** Ruthenium 101.07 $5s^1 4d^7$	**45** **Rh** Rhodium 102.906 $5s^1 4d^8$
55 **Cs** Cesium 132.905 $6s^1$	**56** **Ba** Barium 137.327 $6s^2$	**57** **La** Lanthanum 138.906 $6s^2 5d^1$	**72** **Hf** Hafnium 178.49 $6s^2 5d^2$	**73** **Ta** Tantalum 180.948 $6s^2 5d^3$	**74** **W** Tungsten 183.85 $6s^2 5d^4$	**75** **Re** Rhenium 186.207 $6s^2 5d^5$	**76** **Os** Osmium 190.2 $6s^2 5d^6$	**77** **Ir** Iridium 192.22 $6s^2 5d^7$
87 **Fr** Francium (223) $7s^1$	**88** **Ra** Radium (226.025) $7s^2$	**89** **Ac** Actinium 227.028 $7s^2 6d^1$	**104** **Unq** (261) $7s^2 6d^2$	**105** **Unp** (262) $7s^2 6d^3$	**106** **Unh** (263) $7s^2 6d^4$	**107** **Uns** (262) $7s^2 6d^5$	**108** **Uno** (265) $7s^2 6d^6$	**109** **Une** (266) $7s^2 6d^6$

An atomic mass given in parentheses is the mass number of the isotope of longest half-life for that element.

*The 1–18 group designation has been recommended by the International Union of Pure and Applied Chemistry (IUPAC) but is not widely used. In this book, we refer to the standard U.S. notation for group numbers (1A–8A and 1B–8B).

INNER TRANSITION METALS

Lanthanide series

58 **Ce** Cerium 140.115 $6s^2 4f^1 5d^1$	59 **Pr** Praseodymium 140.908 $6s^2 4f^3$	60 **Nd** Neodymium 144.24 $6s^2 4f^4$	61 **Pm** Promethium (145) $6s^2 4f^5$	62 **Sm** Samarium 150.36 $6s^2 4f^6$
90 **Th** Thorium 232.038 $7s^2 6d^2$	91 **Pa** Protactinium 231.036 $7s^2 5f^2 6d^1$	92 **U** Uranium 238.029 $7s^2 5f^3 6d^1$	93 **Np** Neptunium 237.048 $7s^2 5f^4 6d^1$	94 **Pu** Plutonium (244) $7s^2 5f^6$

Actinide series

Myths and Misconceptions

Students often think that the inner transition metals are not part of the "true" periodic table, and they have difficulty recognizing how these elements are organized into the table. Stress that these elements are separated only for con-venience. To show how large the full periodic table would have to be to accommodate these elements, have students draw an outline of the table with all the elements, including the inner transition metals, in place.

13 3A	14 4A	15 5A	16 6A	17 7A	18 8A
					2 **He** Helium 4.003 $1s^2$
5 **B** Boron 10.811 $2s^22p^1$	6 **C** Carbon 12.011 $2s^22p^2$	7 **N** Nitrogen 14.007 $2s^22p^3$	8 **O** Oxygen 15.999 $2s^22p^4$	9 **F** Fluorine 18.998 $2s^22p^5$	10 **Ne** Neon 20.180 $2s^22p^6$
13 **Al** Aluminum 26.982 $3s^23p^1$	14 **Si** Silicon 28.086 $3s^23p^2$	15 **P** Phosphorus 30.974 $3s^23p^3$	16 **S** Sulfur 32.066 $3s^23p^4$	17 **Cl** Chlorine 35.453 $3s^23p^5$	18 **Ar** Argon 39.948 $3s^23p^6$

10	11 1B	12 2B						
28 **Ni** Nickel 58.693 $4s^23d^8$	29 **Cu** Copper 63.546 $4s^13d^{10}$	30 **Zn** Zinc 65.39 $4s^23d^{10}$	31 **Ga** Gallium 69.723 $4s^24p^1$	32 **Ge** Germanium 72.61 $4s^24p^2$	33 **As** Arsenic 74.922 $4s^24p^3$	34 **Se** Selenium 78.96 $4s^24p^4$	35 **Br** Bromine 79.904 $4s^24p^5$	36 **Kr** Krypton 83.80 $4s^24p^6$
46 **Pd** Palladium 106.42 $4d^{10}$	47 **Ag** Silver 107.868 $5s^14d^{10}$	48 **Cd** Cadmium 112.411 $5s^24d^{10}$	49 **In** Indium 114.82 $5s^25p^1$	50 **Sn** Tin 118.710 $5s^25p^2$	51 **Sb** Antimony 121.757 $5s^25p^3$	52 **Te** Tellurium 127.60 $5s^25p^4$	53 **I** Iodine 126.904 $5s^25p^5$	54 **Xe** Xenon 131.29 $5s^25p^6$
78 **Pt** Platinum 195.08 $6s^15d^9$	79 **Au** Gold 196.967 $6s^15d^{10}$	80 **Hg** Mercury 200.59 $6s^25d^{10}$	81 **Tl** Thallium 204.383 $6s^26p^1$	82 **Pb** Lead 207.2 $6s^26p^2$	83 **Bi** Bismuth 208.980 $6s^26p^3$	84 **Po** Polonium (209) $6s^26p^4$	85 **At** Astatine (210) $6s^26p^5$	86 **Rn** Radon (222) $6s^26p^6$

63 **Eu** Europium 151.965 $6s^24f^7$	64 **Gd** Gadolinium 157.25 $6s^24f^75d^1$	65 **Tb** Terbium 158.925 $6s^24f^9$	66 **Dy** Dysprosium 162.50 $6s^24f^{10}$	67 **Ho** Holmium 164.930 $6s^24f^{11}$	68 **Er** Erbium 167.26 $6s^24f^{12}$	69 **Tm** Thulium 168.934 $6s^24f^{13}$	70 **Yb** Ytterbium 173.04 $6s^24f^{14}$	71 **Lu** Lutetium 174.967 $6s^24f^{14}5d^1$
95 **Am** Americium (243) $7s^25f^7$	96 **Cm** Curium (247) $7s^26d^15f^7$	97 **Bk** Berkelium (247) $7s^25f^9$	98 **Cf** Californium (251) $7s^25f^{10}$	99 **Es** Einsteinium (252) $7s^25f^{11}$	100 **Fm** Fermium (257) $7s^25f^{12}$	101 **Md** Mendelevium (258) $7s^25f^{13}$	102 **No** Nobelium (259) $7s^25f^{14}$	103 **Lr** Lawrencium (260) $7s^25f^{14}6d^1$

Science Background

The Periodic Table Today

The names of elements 104 and beyond are symbolized by a 3-letter symbol representing systematic names that have been adopted by the International Union of Pure and Applied Chemistry (IUPAC). The names are as follows:

104, unnilquadium, Unq;
105, unnilpentium, Unp;
106, unnilhexium, Unh;
107, unnilseptium, Uns;
108, unniloctium, Uno;
109, unnilennium, Une.

Guided Practice

Review the Concept Check question on page 362 with students. Answers can be found in Appendix E on page 808.

PART **1**
Section 11.2 continued

Reteaching Idea

Students will be more successful in chemistry if they begin now to use the periodic table as a tool. You can provide them with more practice by reproducing tables such as the one shown. Ask students to locate and label the representative elements, the transition elements, the inner-transition elements, the oxygen family or group, the third period, the metals and nonmetals, the alkali metal family, the alkaline earth group, the halogens, the noble gases, and the oxygen, nitrogen, and carbon families.

Divide students into two teams. Develop a competition similar to a spelling bee, with questions on the positions of the first twenty elements in the table, the group number of each family, the period in which each element is found, and whether an element is a metal or nonmetal, gas or solid, atom or diatomic molecule.

≡ CLOSE

Summing Up Main Ideas

Have students explain the difference between the elements located in the second period and the second group in the periodic table. They should use concepts such as chemical activity and first ionization energies in their explanations.

PART 1 REVIEW

Assign the Part Review questions.

Evaluating Skills

These skills are evaluated in the Part Review questions indicated. **Determining main ideas:** 1; **Classifying:** 2, 4; **Analyzing data:** 5, 6

TABLE 11-4

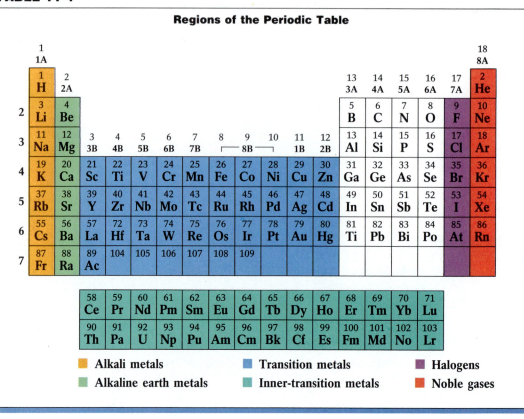

Regions of the Periodic Table

■ Alkali metals   ■ Transition metals   ■ Halogens
■ Alkaline earth metals   ■ Inner-transition metals   ■ Noble gases

PART 1 REVIEW

1. State the periodic law in your own words.

2. From the representative elements, name one group that contains only metallic elements and two groups that contain only nonmetallic elements.

3. What is the name and symbol for the element in each of the following positions on the periodic table?
   a. period 3, Group 7A   **b.** period 2, Group 6A

4. Which elements are inner-transition metals? Which are alkaline earth metals? K, Ca, Cl, U, La, Sr, Kr

5. Why did Mendeleev not place iodine in Group 6A and tellurium in Group 7A, as would be suggested by their atomic mass?

6. What general trend exists in the first ionization energy as you move from left to right on the periodic table?

Boxed numbers indicate questions that involve skills in interpretation, application, and analysis.

PART 1 REVIEW

ANSWERS

■ **Keyed to Objectives**

A **1.** Answers will vary. There should be mention of the cyclic nature of chemical and physical properties of the elements as a function of atomic number.

B **2.** Containing only metallic elements: Group 2A (some students may list

Group 1A since hydrogen is often considered separate from this group and Group 1A is called the alkali metal group); groups containing only nonmetallic elements: 7A and 8A.

B **3. a.** chlorine, Cl
   b. oxygen, O

A **4.** inner-transition metals: U; alkaline earth metals: Ca, Sr

B **5.** Mendeleev ordered the elements by

CAREERS IN CHEMISTRY

Science Director

Dr. Albert J. Snow is a Mohawk of the Iroquois Five Nations, born on the Kahnawake Reservation, which encompasses parts of Quebec, Ontario, and New York. For as long as he can remember, Albert has wanted to be a chemist.

Commitment to the science education process Currently Albert enjoys his new position as science director of the Discovery Museum in Bridgeport, Connecticut. One exciting part of Albert's job focuses on his coordinating the *Challenger* Learning Center, established by the families of the *Challenger* victims. He develops new exhibits and science programs, trains teachers and staff, and writes and implements grant proposals. Albert also works with school districts on curriculum development.

Albert J. Snow
Science Director

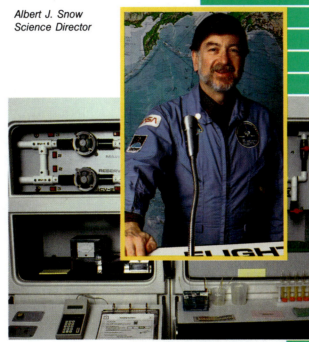

A multifaceted career Before Albert became science director, he taught high school chemistry for more than 25 years. He also served as science coordinator, science department chairman, and supervisor of instruction in science for grades K through 12. In addition, he has presented lectures, contributed to panels and committees, and written papers for publication.

A natural gravitation to science and education Albert received two master's degrees, one in chemistry and one in science education. He continued his studies and earned a doctorate in education, focusing on American Indian Ethno-Science. Studying science has helped him understand physical phenomena better and has increased his respect for nature and the environment, issues he believes are major concerns for the future. He also has realized that humankind must cooperate in order to survive. He hopes that today's students realize that future existence depends on individual contributions to society, and family.

Future existence depends on individual contributions to society and family.

A view of success Albert believes that success is attainable when commitment and dedication accompany your work. A concern for the science education process and a willingness to undertake difficult tasks also affect success. Albert feels rewarded in his work, gaining deep satisfaction from the importance of each completed mission.

---

increasing atomic mass, but the chemical and physical properties of iodine and tellurium indicate that they should be in Groups 7A and 6A, respectively.

A 6. The ionization energy generally increases going from left to right. (Observant students will notice the following anomalies: period 2, B and N; period 3, Al and P.)

CAREERS IN CHEMISTRY

Teaching Strategies

1. Individuals differ in their learning styles as evidenced by differences in the effectiveness of lectures, problem solving, hands-on experimentation, and cooperative learning. Have students consider how each of these different learning styles can be addressed in a science museum.

2. Have students investigate ethno-science and discuss the Native American philosophy of nature. They can then compare it to the Western view of the natural sciences.

3. Have students discuss the concept of science education as a process rather than a product.

Related Careers

Have students identify other careers in science that involve communication about science such as teaching, science illustration, and journalism. In addition, professions that involve science in the visual arts include science illustration, museum curatorship, art restoration, and taxidermy. For additional career information, contact the American Association of Museums, 1225 Eye St., NW, Suite 200, Washington, DC 20005; the Society of Illustrators, 128 E. 63rd St., New York, NY 10021; and the journalism department in your school or local college.

Resources

Contact your local museum of science or museum of natural history for additional information and materials.

PART **2**
Patterns in Electron
Configuration

Section 11.3

Developing Skills

Students may apply these skills in their study of Part 2.
Predicting: Have students predict the stable ion formed by a representative element using the periodic table.
Forming models: Have students draw electron configurations for period 4 transition elements and their ions.
Comparing/Contrasting: Have students compare the electron configuration for an element with its position on the periodic table.

≡ FOCUS

Activate Prior Knowledge

Ask students to write an electron configuration for sodium, potassium, fluorine, and chlorine. Follow the procedure found in Chapter 10, Part 3. Ask students to compare sodium with potassium and fluorine with chlorine and discuss observations.

Na $\quad 1s^2\ 2s^2\ 2p^6\ 3s^1$
K $\quad 1s^2\ 2s^2\ 2p^6\ 3s^2\ 3p^6\ 4s^1$
F $\quad 1s^2\ 2s^2\ 2p^5$
Cl $\quad 1s^2\ 2s^2\ 2p^6\ 3s^2\ 3p^5$

Sodium and potassium both have an s^1 electron in their valence level. They will have similar chemical properties. Fluorine and chlorine both have s^2p^5 valence electrons. They will have similar chemical properties.

≡ TEACH

Teaching Strategy

Patterns for Representative Elements

Students should begin to see the relationship between the valence electron configuration and chemical reactivity. For example, elements in Groups 1A–3A that
(continued on page T371)

PART **2** *Patterns in Electron Configuration*

Objectives

Part 2

C. *Relate* the electron configuration of an element to its position in the periodic table and to its chemical properties.
D. *Determine* the number of valence electrons for a representative element, using the periodic table.
E. *Predict* the stable ion formed by a representative element, using the periodic table.
F. *Draw* the electron configurations for period 4 transition elements or ions.

Mendeleev's organization of the elements was based on macroscopic chemical and physical properties. Once subatomic particles were discovered, scientists sought models of the atom that would relate the subatomic structure of the atom to its chemical properties. The wave mechanical model of the atom, which you learned about in Chapter 10, became popular because it provided a reasonable explanation for the periodic nature of the properties of the elements. As you will learn, the patterns in electron configurations and the arrangement of elements in the periodic table go hand in hand.

11.3 Patterns for Representative Elements

In Chapter 10, you studied the electron configurations of the elements. Electron configurations describe the arrangement of electrons in an atom and help to explain the similarities in the chemical properties of elements in the same group.

TABLE 11-5

Electron Configurations for Some Elements			
Alkali Metals	Alkaline Earths	Halogens	Noble Gases
Li	Be $1s^2 2s^2$	F	Ne
Na $1s^2 2s^2 2p^6 3s^1$	Mg	Cl	Ar
K	Ca	Br $1s^2 2s^2 2p^6 3s^2$ $3p^6 3d^{10} 4s^2 4p^5$	Kr

To practice writing electron configurations, copy Table 11-5 onto a sheet of paper. Refer to the periodic table to find the atomic number of each element. Remember that for a neutral atom, the number of electrons is equal to the atomic number. Also, give the ground state electron configuration—that is, the configuration showing the electrons occupying the lowest available energy levels. Some of the electron configurations are already given so you can be sure you are on the right track. You may refer to Figure 10-16, which gives the relative energies of orbitals in a many-electron atom.

Electron configurations of noble gases Are there similarities in the electron configurations of the elements in a given group? Look first at the noble gas elements listed in Table 11-5. Each has a total of 8 electrons in the outermost *s* and *p* orbitals.

The **outermost orbitals** are the orbitals with the highest principal quantum number that are occupied by electrons in the ground state electron configuration. Thus, for neon, the outermost orbitals are the $2s$ and $2p$ orbitals, and the electron configuration of the outermost electrons is $2s^2 2p^6$. Both argon and krypton also have 8 electrons in their outermost orbitals. The outermost orbital electron configurations are $3s^2 3p^6$ for argon and $4s^2 4p^6$ for krypton.

Electrons in the outermost orbitals are often the electrons involved in chemical bonding. For this reason, these electrons, which generally are in the outermost s and p orbitals, have a special significance and are referred to as **valence electrons.** The remaining electrons in an atom are referred to as **core electrons.** Remember that the maximum number of electrons in an orbital is 2 and that there are one s orbital and three p orbitals for a given principal quantum number. Therefore, the maximum number of valence electrons is 8. Each of the noble gases has its outermost s and p orbitals completely filled. Since the electron configuration of helium is $1s^2$, it has only 2 valence electrons; nevertheless, its valence orbital is filled just like the valence orbitals of the other noble gases.

Electron configuration of alkali metals

Each element in the alkali metal group has one valence electron in the outermost s orbital. Write the electron configuration for rubidium to see what orbital the electron with the highest energy occupies? You can get a clue from the fact that rubidium is in the 5th period. Lithium is in the 2nd period, and its valence electron is in a $2s$ orbital. As you can see, the principal quantum number describing the valence s electrons is the same as the period number.

Electron configurations of alkaline earth metals and halogens

For the alkaline earth metals, the two electrons with the highest energy fill the outermost s orbital. Write the electron configuration of strontium, Sr. What is the last orbital to be filled? It should also have the same number as the period number for strontium, which is 5.

The valence electrons of the halogens also show a pattern. Each atom has 7 valence electrons, 2 in the s orbitals and 5 in the p orbitals. Since chlorine is in period 3, the valence electron configuration of chlorine is $3s^2 3p^5$.

Determining the number of valence electrons

Figure 11-4 on the next page shows the relationship between the organization of the periodic table and the electron configurations of the elements. The orbital designations in Figure 11-4 indicate the filling order of orbitals and the valence electrons. Note the pattern that exists for each group of representative elements (Groups 1A–8A). In general, the number of valence electrons is equal to the group number. For example, aluminum has 3 valence electrons—its group number is 3A. As you will learn in the next section, similarities in

DO YOU KNOW?

Elements in you:
O, C, H, and N make up 96% of your body mass.
Ca and P make up 3%.
Na, K, S, Cl, and Mg make up 0.7%.
Fe, Co, Cu, Zn, I, Se, and F are trace elements.
Each of these elements is essential to life.

PROBLEM-SOLVING
STRATEGY

Looking for patterns in electron configurations and in placement of elements on the periodic table will lead to an understanding of many atomic properties. (See Strategy, page 100.)

Metallic Properties

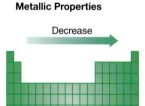

Decrease

Increase

PART 2
Section 11.3 *continued*

(continued from page T370)
form ions form positive ions by losing their valence electrons; elements in Groups 5A–7A that form negative ions do so by gaining electrons until they have the same electron configuration as the noble gas in the same period. Learning to equate the group number (of the representative or "A" group elements) with the number of valence electrons is an especially important concept.

Science Background

Electronic Theory

For years, the periodic table and periodic law were considered only empirical. Although they were useful tools, the underlying explanation of why they took the form they did was not understood. Today, we know the reason lies in the electronic theory. The properties of the elements repeat themselves as a periodic function of the arrangement of their electrons about the nucleus, the electron configuration.

Electron configurations can be written in two ways. The first lists the orbitals in the order they are filled according to the aufbau principle—for Br, $1s^2\ 2s^2\ 2p^6\ 3s^2\ 3p^6\ 4s^2\ 3d^{10}\ 4p^5$. The second is according to increasing principle quantum number—$1s^2\ 2s^2\ 2p^6\ 3s^2\ 3p^6\ 3d^{10}\ 4s^2\ 4p^5$. The latter makes it easier to see the valence electron configuration for those elements in Groups 3A through 8A in the fourth period and beyond.

Teaching Strategy

Patterns for Representative Element Ions

Again the emphasis should focus on the regularity of electron configurations of the valence electrons. The stability (unreactivity) of noble gases and the fact that the representative (A Group) elements form ions that are isoelectronic with the noble gases indicate that there is something unique about the electron configuration of noble gases.

Figure 11-4 *This diagram shows how the electron configurations of the elements are related to their positions on the periodic table. Prove to yourself that the group number of any element is the number of valence electrons it has.*

CONNECTING CONCEPTS

Classifying The physical and

chemical properties of the ele-

ments enabled Mendeleev to

classify them into families.

the valence electron configuration explain the experimental observation that elements in the same group have a tendency to react similarly.

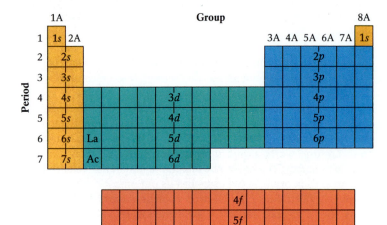

11.4 Patterns for Representative Element Ions

The most notable characteristic of the noble gas elements is that they are generally unreactive. None of the noble gases was known when Mendeleev proposed his periodic table. Noble gases were first called "inert gases" because the elements in this family were not observed to form compounds. In fact, it was not until 1962 that a xenon compound was prepared. The name "inert" is no longer applied to this group but the following generalization can be made: *When the valence orbitals of an atom are full, the atom tends to be unreactive.* All the noble gas atoms tend to be unreactive and have full valence orbitals. Helium has 2 electrons filling the $1s$ orbital, and the other noble gases have 8 electrons filling the valence s and p orbitals.

Alkali metals As you discovered in completing Table 11-5, alkali metals all contain one electron in the s valence orbital. The alkali metals are very reactive. In a typical reaction, an alkali metal loses one electron—the valence electron. When a neutral atom loses an electron, an ion is formed having a charge of $1+$. The neutral sodium atom has 11 protons and 11 electrons, and it has this electron configuration.

$$\text{Na} \quad 1s^2 2s^2 2p^6 3s^1$$

This electron configuration can be written in a shorthand notation.

$$[\text{Ne}]\, 3s^1$$

The symbol [Ne] represents the electron configuration of neon, $1s^2 2s^2 2p^6$. This is also the electron configuration of the core electrons

R E S E A R C H & T E C H N O L O G Y

Developing Products for the Future

About 13 000 years ago on the island of Japan, villagers discovered that if they heated their clay vessels in the fire, the vessels became harder and more durable. They found that the pottery's increased brittleness was a small price to pay for its greater usability.

These primitive people might be considered the world's first materials scientists—people who design new materials to meet specific needs. Modern-day materials scientists are also working with ceramic materials. They have developed ceramics that are far stronger, lighter, harder, and more durable than the most commonly used metals, including steel. Tests indicate that car engines built almost exclusively of ceramic parts run more efficiently than conventional metal engines and should last five times as long. Ironically, the problems that faced the ancient Japanese plague modern materials scientists—namely, that many of the modern ceramic materials are very brittle. Researchers are working to overcome this problem.

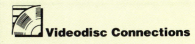

Videodisc Connections

632-636, side 6
Uses of ceramics (5-frame seq.)

23661 to 25170, side 6
Computer modeling (movie)

Many automotive components made from newly developed ceramics offer increased durability similar to that discovered by the Japanese 13 centuries ago.

for the sodium atom. The $3s$ valence electron is indicated in the usual way, $3s^1$.

If one electron is lost, a sodium ion forms that has 11 protons and 10 electrons, for a net charge of $1+$. The electron configuration of a sodium ion, Na^+, is

$$Na^+ \quad 1s^2 2s^2 2p^6$$

Look at the electron configuration you wrote for neon in Table 11-5. The neon atom has 10 electrons, and the electron configuration is the same as that of the sodium ion. The sodium ion, Na^+, and neon, Ne, are **isoelectronic** because they have the same electron configuration. Neon is unreactive because its valence orbitals are filled. A sodium atom can react to form a sodium ion, which has the same electron configuration as a neon atom.

DO YOU KNOW?

Cesium metal is found in some photocells, such as those controlling an automatic door, because of its low ionization energy. The energy in a beam of light shining on the cesium metal causes it to ionize. When the beam is interrupted, the ionization ceases, and this sends a signal for the door to open. This is an example of the photoelectric effect, for which Albert Einstein won his first Nobel Prize.

Figure 11-5 ⚠ CAUTION: *In this picture, sodium metal is reacting vigorously with chlorine. The flask is in a hood with the hood sash lowered because chlorine is a very poisonous gas. Only 0.1 g of sodium was used because the reaction is violent.*

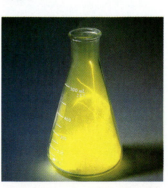

Concept ✔ Check

Write the electron configuration for another element in Group 1A, the potassium ion, K^+. Which noble gas is isoelectronic with the potassium ion?

Alkaline earth metals The alkaline earth elements (Group 2A elements) have two valence electrons. The alkaline earth metal, magnesium, has an atomic number of 12 and an electron configuration of

$$Mg \quad 1s^2 2s^2 2p^6 3s^2$$

or

$$[Ne]3s^2$$

Alkaline earth metals tend to form 2+ ions in chemical reactions. The electron configuration of the magnesium ion, Mg^{2+}, is

$$Mg^{2+} \quad 1s^2 2s^2 2p^6$$

Compare this configuration to the electron configuration for neon.

$$Ne \quad 1s^2 2s^2 2p^6$$

You find that the magnesium ion is isoelectronic with neon. When an atom of an alkaline earth element loses two electrons, it has an electron configuration like the noble gas in the preceding period of the periodic table.

Halogens The halogens in Group 7A contain seven valence electrons. The electron configuration of fluorine is

$$F \quad 1s^2 2s^2 2p^5$$

or

$$[He]2s^2 2p^5$$

If fluorine were to gain 1 electron, it would have 8 valence electrons and its outermost orbitals would be filled. When fluorine reacts to become an ion, it gains one electron. It becomes a fluoride ion with 10 electrons, and the electron configuration is

$$F^- \quad 1s^2 2s^2 2p^6$$

The fluoride ion has a 1– charge because it has one more electron than the neutral atom. Did you notice that the electron configuration is again the same as the configuration for neon? The fluoride ion and the neon atom are isoelectronic. In general, halogens form negative ions that have the same electron configurations as the noble gases immediately following them in the periodic table.

Forming ions When sodium reacts with chlorine as shown in Figure 11-5, the metallic element sodium forms positive ions by losing electrons. Chlorine, a halogen, forms negative ions by gaining an electron. In general, metals lose electrons and nonmetals gain electrons when they react together. You have just learned that the ions of representative elements formed from the loss and gain of electrons often have electron configurations that are identical to the electron configurations of the noble gases. A noble gas is unreactive because its valence orbitals are filled. In general, representative elements often react to form ions that have electron configurations identical to the unreactive noble gas electron configuration of eight valence electrons (or two valence electrons in the case of helium).

EXAMPLE 11-1

Predict the most likely charge on the ions formed from an atom of lithium, Li, and an atom of sulfur, S.

■ *Analyze the Problem* Work with the fact that an ion forms when an atom gains or loses electrons. These are ions of representative elements, and thus you would predict them to have electron configurations like the electron configurations of noble gases.

■ *Apply a Strategy* Compare the electron configuration of each element with the electron configuration of each noble gas to predict the charge that will occur on the ion. Identify whether or not electrons must be added or lost to obtain a noble gas configuration.

■ *Work a Solution*

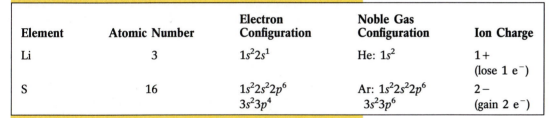

Element	Atomic Number	Electron Configuration	Noble Gas Configuration	Ion Charge
Li	3	$1s^2 2s^1$	He: $1s^2$	$1+$ (lose 1 e$^-$)
S	16	$1s^2 2s^2 2p^6$ $3s^2 3p^4$	Ar: $1s^2 2s^2 2p^6$ $3s^2 3p^6$	$2-$ (gain 2 e$^-$)

■ *Verify Your Answer* Look at the position of lithium and sulfur on the periodic table. Lithium is a metal, so it will tend to lose electrons. Since helium is the nearest noble gas, you reason that lithium would lose one electron to assume the helium electron configuration. Sulfur is a nonmetal, so it will tend to gain electrons. Sulfur is closest to argon on the periodic table, and it would most likely gain 2 electrons to assume that configuration.

Practice Problems

7. Predict the most likely charge on the ion formed by calcium.
8. Predict the most likely charge on the ion formed by chlorine.

PROBLEM·SOLVING

S T R A T E G Y

Look for patterns when writing electron configurations by organizing your data in a table. (See Strategy, page 100.)

Look for patterns when writing electron configurations by organizing your data in a table. (See Strategy, page 100.)

PART 2
Section 11.4 *continued*

Teaching Strategy

Patterns for Transition Elements and Ions

So far, we have looked at patterns for representative element ions. In the next section (11.5), students will see that the pattern for transition elements is not as simple as that for the representative elements. The reason is that electrons in both *s* and *d* orbitals can be involved in bonding. While representative elements tend to form only ions of a single charge, many transition elements form more than one ion. Predicting which elements form multiple ions or what the charge will be is not easy. However, given the ions that form, it is often easy to rationalize their formation. For example, many form 2+ ions that can correspond to a loss of the *s* electrons from the valence shell.

Practice Problems

Assign the Practice Problems.

11.5 Patterns for Transition Elements and Ions

Useful patterns that relate to electron configurations are also seen in the transition and inner transition metal regions of the periodic table. First count the number of transition elements in a given period. For example, in period 4, there are 10 elements from scandium to zinc. How many electrons can occupy d orbitals? A total of 10 electrons can occupy the five $3d$ orbitals that are being occupied as you progress from scandium to zinc. How many electrons can occupy the set of f orbitals? How many elements are classified as lanthanides? Again it is no coincidence that the answers to both of these latter two questions is 14.

Fourth period transition elements The electron configurations of transition elements are written in the same way as for the representative elements. However, the electron configuration is not always the same as would be predicted from the energy levels of the orbitals. The actual electron configuration can be determined only by experiment. However, the fourth period transition elements are, with two exceptions, what would be predicted. The electron configurations for the fourth period transition elements are shown in Table 11-6.

TABLE 11-6

Electron Configurations of the Fourth Period Transition Elements			
Element	Electron Configuration	Element	Electron Configuration
Sc	$[Ar]4s^23d^1$	Fe	$[Ar]4s^23d^6$
Ti	$[Ar]4s^23d^2$	Co	$[Ar]4s^23d^7$
V	$[Ar]4s^23d^3$	Ni	$[Ar]4s^23d^8$
Cr	$[Ar]4s^13d^5$	Cu	$[Ar]4s^13d^{10}$
Mn	$[Ar]4s^23d^5$	Zn	$[Ar]4s^23d^{10}$

Since the $3d$ orbital is the next higher energy orbital following the $4s$ orbital, once the $4s$ orbital is filled, you would expect the next electrons to occupy the five available $3d$ orbitals until a total of 10 electrons has been added. Generally this is what occurs. However, if you look at Table 11-6, you find two unexpected electron configurations. Chromium is $[Ar]4s^13d^5$ instead of the expected $[Ar]4s^23d^4$. Likewise, copper is $[Ar]4s^13d^{10}$ instead of $[Ar]4s^23d^9$. These unexpected configurations occur because a special stability occurs when sets of orbitals are exactly half filled or completely filled. For chromium, each of the $4s$ and $3d$ orbitals is half filled (has one electron). In the case of copper, the $3d$ orbital is completely filled, and the $4s$ orbital is half filled.

Science Background

Fourth Period Transition Elements

Actual electron configurations are determined by experiment. For many elements, a relatively simple pattern allows electron configurations to be predicted based upon the "aufbau" or building up principle. However, there are some cases that cannot be predicted. The first are those of Cr and Cu, fourth period transition elements. One can rationalize these anomalies, but it is important to remember that experiment is the only sure way to determine an electron configuration. In general, unexpected electron configurations are more likely to occur for the higher atomic number elements. This is in part because the differences in energy between orbitals become smaller as the principal quantum number of the orbitals increases.

Teaching Strategy

Fourth Period Transition Elements

Handle the Cr and Cu electron configurations as anomalies. Table 11–6 gives actual electron configurations. You may wish to have students try to find electron configurations in Table 11–6 that they would not expect.

Guided Practice

Review the Concept Check question on page 374 with students. Answers can be found in Appendix E on page 808.

CONNECTING CONCEPTS

Explaining Regularities Similar chemical and physical properties of elements are often due to similar outer electron configurations.

PART 2 REVIEW

ANSWERS

■ **Keyed to Objectives**

C 9. All noble gases have the maximum number of electrons possible in their outermost s and p orbitals; for He this is 2 in the $1s$ orbital, and for all others the number is 8 in the $s + p$ orbitals.

C 10. Isoelectronic means that both species have the same electron configuration.

E 11. O^{2-}: $1s^2 2s^2 2p^6$, 2− charge, isoelectronic with Ne

D 12. Rb, alkali metal, 1A, 1; Te, oxygen family, 6A, 6; Ca, alkaline earth metal, 2A, 2; Xe, noble gas, 8A, 8.

D 13. Be, 2; Ga, 3; As, 5; F, 7

Ion formation One of the characteristics of the transition metals that differentiates them from most representative elements is their tendency to form more than one ion. They do so because electrons can be lost from both the *s* and the *d* orbitals. For example, iron forms two ions, Fe^{2+} and Fe^{3+}. The electron configurations of the two ions also might surprise you. For Fe^{2+}, the configuration is $[Ar]3d^6$. The two electrons that are lost when the iron(II) ion forms are the $4s$ electrons. You might have expected that two $3d$ electrons would be lost, since the $3d$ orbitals are higher energy when the orbitals are being filled. However, the electrons lost come first from the orbital with the highest principal quantum number (the *n* quantum number), which is the $4s$ orbital rather than the $3d$ orbital. The electron configuration of the Fe^{3+} ion is $[Ar]3d^5$; the third electron lost comes from the $3d$ orbital.

What ion do you think scandium is likely to form? Table 11-6 shows that if scandium loses three electrons to form the ion Sc^{3+}, the electron configuration of the ion will be the same as that of argon. In fact scandium does form the ion Sc^{3+}. Titanium, however, forms three ions, Ti^{2+}, Ti^{3+}, and Ti^{4+}. The titanium ion, Ti^{4+}, is isoelectronic with argon but Ti^{2+} and Ti^{3+} are not. This is not unusual for transition metals. For example, the transition metal zinc forms the ion Zn^{2+} by losing two electrons. Its electron configuration is not isoelectronic with argon, but the ion has special stability due to the completely filled *d* orbitals.

PROBLEM·SOLVING STRATEGY

*You can **use what you know** to predict what ions are likely to form by becoming familiar with electron configuration trends on the periodic table. (See Strategy, page 58.)*

PART 2 REVIEW

9. How are the electron configurations of noble gases similar?

10. What does *isoelectronic* mean?

11. What is the electron configuration of the oxide ion? What is the charge on the oxide ion? With which noble gas is the oxide ion isoelectronic?

12. For each of the following elements, name the chemical group, or family. Then determine the number of valence electrons for each element: Rb, Te, Ca, and Xe.

13. Use the position in the periodic table to determine the number of valence electrons in the elements Be, Ga, As, F.

14. Use the position in the periodic table to determine how many electrons are in 3d orbitals for nickel.

15. Write the electron configurations (both the long form and the short-hand notation) for Ca, P, and B.

16. Write the electron configurations for the element copper and its 1+ and 2+ ions.

17. The electron configuration of silver is $[Kr]5s^14d^{10}$. What is the electron configuration of Ag^+?

CONNECTING CONCEPTS

Structure and Properties of Matter The chemical properties of elements depend on the number and arrangement of electrons in the atom.

Boxed numbers indicate questions that involve skills in interpretation, application, and analysis.

Reteaching Idea

If students have difficulty seeing how electron configurations are related to the periodic table, list electron configurations for a variety of elements on the chalkboard and refer students to Table 11–4. Ask them to locate each element by group number and period number. For representative elements ask students to explain why there is a relationship between group number and the number of valence electrons. Ask what the relationship is between the energy level of the valence electrons (principal quantum number) and the period number.

Write some noble gas configurations on the chalkboard. Focus on how elements lose or gain electrons to form ions with noble gas configurations. Have students write electron configurations for Cl^-, S^{2-}, K^+, and Ca^{2+}.

≡ CLOSE

Summing Up Main Ideas

Have students explain how the chemical properties of a particular element like sodium or chlorine can be related to the element's electron configuration. Have students determine the valence electrons of the element and the stable ion that it forms by using the periodic table.

PART 2 REVIEW

Assign the Part Review questions.

Evaluating Skills

These skills are evaluated in the Part Review questions indicated. **Determining main ideas:** 9; **Analyzing data:** 11, 12, 13, 14, 15, 16, 17; **Applying a strategy:** 11, 12, 13, 14, 15, 16, 17; **Verifying results:** 11, 12, 13, 14, 15, 16, 17; **Classifying:** 12

C 14. 8 electrons (nickel is the eighth element in the period 4 transition metals)

C 15. Ca: $1s^2 2s^2 2p^6 3s^2 3p^6 4s^2$ or $[Ar] 4s^2$; P: $1s^2 2s^2 2p^6 3s^2 3p^3$ or $[Ne] 3s^2 3p^3$; B: $1s^2 2s^2 2p^1$ or $[He] 2s^2 2p^1$

F 16. Cu: $[Ar] 4s^1 3d^{10}$ (note that the electron configuration is an exception to the building up principle), Cu^+: $[Ar] 3d^{10}$; Cu^{2+}: $[Ar] 3d^9$.

The first electron is lost from the $4s$ orbital, the second from the $3d$.

F 17. $[Kr] 5d^{10}$, the electron lost from the silver atom is the one with the highest principle quantum number, the $6s$ electron.

Developing Skills

Students may apply these skills in their study of Part 3.

Forming models: Have students use data collected on the atomic radius and ionization energy of atoms to formulate a model that relates any trends in these values to the positions of the elements on the periodic table.

Predicting: Have students predict the properties of an element using the periodic table.

Comparing/Contrasting: Have students compare the size of an atom to the size of its most stable ions. Note how the sizes of positive ions differ from negative ions.

≣FOCUS

Activate Prior Knowledge

Students learned how to draw electron configurations in Chapter 10. Have students draw the electron configurations for Li, Na, and K. Ask students to predict which of these three atoms would have a valence electron farthest away from the nucleus. Based on their predictions, ask students to explain why the sizes of atoms differ.

PART 3 Periodic Trends

Objectives

Part 3

G. *Describe* the periodic nature of atomic radius and ionization energy.

H. *Compare* the size of an atom to the size of its ion and give reasons for the difference.

I. *Predict* the properties of an element, using the periodic table.

So far you have seen that the periodic table was organized to illustrate the repetitive nature of the properties of the elements. Knowing the position of an element in the periodic table allows you to make predictions about its chemical behavior. You have also seen that the electron configuration of an element is related to its position in the periodic table and that the electron configuration of the valence electrons of the representative elements can be determined using the periodic table. The electron configuration and position in the table even enables you to predict the type of ion a representative element might form.

In this part of the chapter, you will study some additional properties of elements that can be related to the elements' positions in the periodic table. Such patterns are often referred to as **periodic trends.** An awareness of certain periodic trends is necessary for an understanding of chemical bonding, which you will learn about in Chapter 13.

11.6 Atomic and Ionic Radii Trends

How big is an atom? This simple question is, in fact, quite hard to answer. If someone were to ask you to measure the circumference of a volleyball, you might wrap a string around it, mark the point where the string overlaps, and then measure the distance from the end to the mark. If you were asked to measure the circumference of a football, you would have to ask for more information. Is it to be measured around the middle? Where is the middle? Do you want the circumference parallel or perpendicular to the longer axis?

One of the problems in determining the sizes of atoms is that atoms are incredibly small. Another is that in the case of atoms, size is hard to define. The size of an atom can have different meanings just as the circumference of a football can. Remember, the model you have learned for the atom describes electron configurations in terms of orbitals that have different energies. Just as an orbital does not have a definite size, the size of an atom cannot be precisely defined. Atoms cannot be accurately represented by a hard sphere model like a volleyball; such a representation for an atom is crude and imprecise.

In spite of the difficulty in measuring the size of an atom, size estimates are very useful and can be made in several ways. If you have a pure, crystalline sample of an element and can determine how the atoms are arranged, you can estimate the size of the atom. For example, a technique called X-ray diffraction can give an estimate of the distance between the nuclei of atoms in a solid crystal. Half of this distance is the **atomic radius.** For elements that exist as diatomic molecules, such as chlorine, Cl_2, measurements of the distance between nuclei of the atoms bonded in the molecule can also be estimated. The atomic radius is half of this distance.

Trends in atomic radii Table 11-7 lists the atomic radii of the representative elements. What trends do you observe in the representative elements? As you scan the table, the following should be apparent.

1. The atomic radius *decreases* as you go across a period from left (Group 1A) to right (Group 7A).

2. The atomic radius *increases* as you go down a group from the top to the bottom of the periodic table.

What explanation accounts for the first trend? You will recall that the higher the atomic number, the greater the number of protons in the nucleus. Thus the charge on the nucleus increases as the atomic number increases. The attractive force between the nucleus and any one electron depends on the charge of the nucleus. As the charge on the nucleus increases, the force of attraction on the elec-

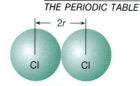

Figure 11-6 *The distance between two atoms in a diatomic molecule is two times the atomic radius.*

TABLE 11-7

Atomic Radii of Representative Elements (pm)						
Atomic radius decreases →						
1A	2A	3A	4A	5A	6A	7A
H 37						
Li 152	Be 111	B 88	C 77	N 70	O 66	F 64
Na 186	Mg 160	Al 143	Si 117	P 110	S 104	Cl 99
K 231	Ca 197	Ga 135	Ge 122	As 121	Se 117	Br 114
Rb 244	Sr 215	In 162	Sn 140	Sb 141	Te 137	I 133
Cs 262	Ba 217	Tl 171	Pb 175	Bi 146	Po 150	At 140

Atomic radius increases (↓ left side)

Atomic Radius

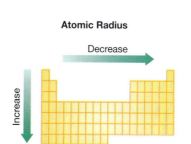

Decrease →

Increase ↓

PART 3
Section 11.6 *continued*

≡ TEACH

Science Background

Atomic and Ionic Radii Trends

Atomic size is a nebulous quantity but nevertheless it is very important. Students have a tendency to think of atoms as hard spheres, but of course they are not. Representing atoms on the printed page is problematic. Accurate models are given via mathematical representations, but such models are cumbersome. That is really the dilemma of all models; if they accurately represent nature, they may be too difficult to use. And if they are simple to use, they may not give accurate information in all applications. There are different ways to measure atomic sizes. Our atomic and ionic radii are based on solid-state crystals of the elements and ionic compounds. However, in covalent compounds, atomic sizes may be very different from these. A search of the literature will show that the way atomic or ionic size is determined is very carefully defined so that sizes based on different criteria will not be mistakenly compared.

Resources

Use the computer program KC? Discoverer: *Exploring the Properties of the Chemical Elements.* This program includes data for 45 properties of the elements. The elements meeting criteria specified can be selected. A set of data can be graphed versus any other set of data. The program can also be used to access the Periodic Table Videodisc which shows the elements and their reactions with air, water, acids, and bases. The program is an MS-DOS program. Both the program and the videodisc are available from JCE Software. (Address is listed in the front of the Teacher's Edition.)

Teaching Strategy

Trends in Atomic Radii

Shielding is a difficult concept for students. The main point is that the influence of the positively charged nucleus on valence electrons is decreased if there are core electrons. The concept of shielding is mentioned only in the most general way.

CONNECTING CONCEPTS

Making Predictions Knowing which group an element is in enables you to make many predictions about its physical properties, its chemical properties, and the compounds it will form.

trons increases. This causes the electrons to be drawn closer to the nucleus. Thus, in a period, as the atomic number (and therefore the nuclear charge) increases, the atomic radius decreases. Note in Table 11-7 that the radius of a boron atom is 88 pm; the radius of oxygen is 66 pm. The larger charge on the oxygen nucleus ($8+$ in oxygen compared to $5+$ in boron) causes the electrons in the oxygen atom to be drawn closer to its nucleus than the electrons in the boron atom are drawn to the boron nucleus.

To explain the second trend, recall that within a group, the valence electrons have the same configuration, but the outermost electrons are in higher energy orbitals (orbitals with higher principal quantum number) as the period number increases. As the number of electrons increases down a group, the valence orbitals have larger principal quantum numbers and a higher probability that the electrons will be found farther from the nucleus, resulting in a larger atomic radius.

A second factor affecting the size of the atom is called **shielding**. Core electrons will shield valence electrons from the full charge of the nucleus. This shielding effect lessens the force of attraction between the nucleus and the valence electrons. Compare the atomic radius of lithium to sodium—the atomic radius increases from 152 pm for lithium to 186 pm for sodium although the sodium nucleus has a charge of $11+$, compared to $3+$ for lithium.

Concept ✓ Check

In your own words, explain why atomic radius decreases as you go from left to right across a period of the periodic table. Explain why atomic radius increases as you go down a group.

Ion size versus atom size Like atomic radius, ionic radius can be determined by using X-ray diffraction methods on crystals of ionic solids. Look at the ionic radii of the representative elements in Table 11-8.

Compare the size of an ion to the size of the atom from which it is formed. For example, the atomic radius of the sodium atom is 186 pm, and the ionic radius of the sodium ion is 95 pm. That is quite a difference. Compare some other atomic and ionic radii for elements and their ions, using Table 11-7 and 11-8. As you can see, the general trend is for a positive ion to be smaller than the atom from which it is formed and a negative ion to be larger. What is the explanation for this size difference?

Size of positive ions The valence electron of the sodium atom is a $3s$ electron. To form an ion, the sodium atom loses this valence electron. The outermost electron configuration of the sodium ion is $2s^2 2p^6$. These electrons have a higher probability of being closer to the nucleus than the $3s$ electron present in the neutral atom. For this reason, the ion is smaller. As Figure 11-7 shows, the positive ion formed when an atom loses its valence electrons has

Positive Ion Radius

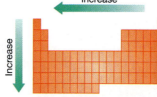

TABLE 11-8

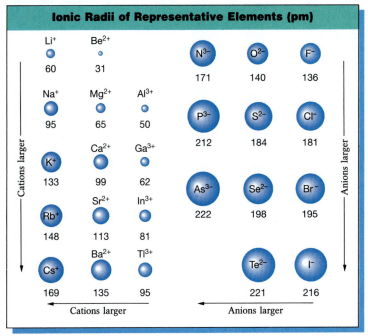

Ionic Radii of Representative Elements (pm)

a significantly smaller ionic radius than the atomic radius of the neutral atom.

Size of negative ions Why is the chloride ion larger than the chlorine atom? One additional electron is added to the seven valence electrons in a chlorine atom, while the positive charge in the nucleus stays the same. Recall that electrons have a natural tendency to repel one another. As a result, adding one more electron to the valence shell of the atom to form the ion increases the repulsion forces among electrons. This causes the ionic radius of the ion to be larger than the atomic radius of the element. Figure 11-7 shows size comparisons for some atoms and their ions.

11.7 Ionization Energy

Another important property that shows periodic trends is ionization energy. Recall that ionization energy is the energy needed to remove a mole of electrons from a mole of neutral gaseous atoms. This process can be represented as

$$\text{Element(g) + ionization energy} \rightarrow \text{Ion}^+(g) + e^-$$

Ionization energies of many elements were determined in the 1920's by bombarding gaseous samples of elements with electrons of precisely determined energy. When the bombarding electrons have enough kinetic energy, their collisions with atoms cause the atoms

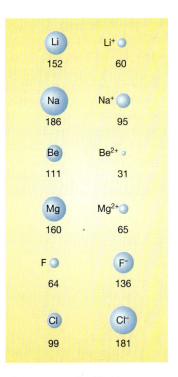

Figure 11-7 *Positive ions are smaller than the neutral atoms from which they are formed. Negative ions are larger than their neutral atoms. Can you account for this on the basis of electron configuration and nuclear charge?*

C O N S U M E R   C H E M I S T R Y

Essential Elements—The Chemistry of Life

In order to grow, to function, and to repair itself, your body needs a variety of chemical elements. These elements, which the body cannot synthesize, must be provided by the foods you eat, and are called essential elements. Some are needed in large quantities, and some are needed in minute amounts. All are important—you could not survive without them.

Iron and calcium are examples of essential minerals you must ingest in relatively large quantities. Much of the iron in your body is bound up in hemoglobin molecules, found in red blood cells, which transport oxygen throughout the body. Calcium plays an important role in building strong bones, regulating muscle contraction, and clotting blood. If dietary calcium is inadequate, the body will draw on reserves of calcium in the bones.

Many other minerals—including iodine, chromium and manganese—are needed in very small amounts. These trace elements are no less essential than the elements needed in larger amounts. Iodine, as the iodide ion, plays a part in regulating metabolism. Your diet

Essential elements can be found in a balanced diet.

should include only about 150 micrograms of iodine per day.

Eating a balanced diet generally provides you with the minerals you need. However, many people take mineral supplements to add to the levels of nutrients found in their diets. Although low-potency supplements can be beneficial in helping to ensure that you ingest adequate amounts of minerals, high-potency supplements can introduce harmful levels of minerals into your body. You can ask your physician if you have any questions about adding supplements to your diet.

to ionize. The first ionization energy is the energy required to eject the most weakly held electron from the atom. The result is a 1+ ion of the atom.

Ionization energies are important for predicting which elements will have a tendency to form positive ions. An element with low ionization energy can form a positive ion more easily than an element with a higher ionization energy. Elements with very high ionization energies do not usually form positive ions. However, they may form negative ions or nonionic compounds.

Ionization energy changes across a period

Ionization energies vary among the elements in a periodic pattern. The first ionization energy (abbreviated 1st IE) is the energy required to remove one of the valence electrons from the gaseous atom. Look back to Tables 11-1 and 11-2 at the 1st ionization energies of elements 1–20. Is there a periodic pattern? The regular pattern becomes evident when the values of first ionization energies from Tables 11-1 and 11-2 are graphed, as shown in Figure 11-8.

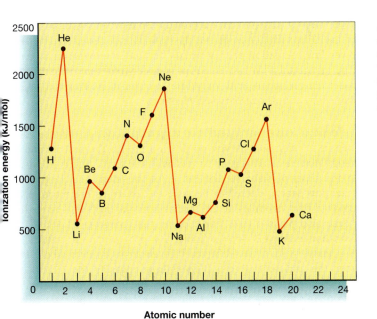

Figure 11-8 *The ionization energies of the first 20 elements are graphed. Study the graph with the periodic table for reference. How are ionization energies related to the periodic table and electron configurations?*

Science Background

Deviations in the Trend

Figure 11–8 shows the first ionization energy (IE) versus atomic number. Exceptions to the generally increasing IE within a period (for example, B and O in period 2) exist. These exceptions to the general trend can be rationalized by the type of orbital that the removed electron occupies and whether there is one or two electrons in the orbital. The lower first IE of boron is rationalized on the basis that it is easier to remove an electron from a $2p$ than from a $2s$ orbital. Removing the electron from the s orbital is more difficult because its electron density is closer to the nucleus than the $2p$ orbital. The lower value for oxygen is due to the electron's removal from a filled p orbital (two electrons) instead of a p orbital with only one electron, as is the case with nitrogen. Since electrons repel each other, the removal of one electron from a filled orbital requires less energy.

Notice that within a period, the first ionization energies of the alkali metals are the lowest and the noble gases are the highest. Low ionization energies mean that the electron removed is not held very tightly by the nucleus. Can the gradual increase in ionization energy as you cross a period from left to right be explained? Refer back to Table 11-7, which shows the atomic radii of the elements. As a period is crossed from left to right, the atomic radius decreases. The larger the size of the atom, the smaller the first ionization energy. Also, the amount of positive charge on the nucleus increases across a period. These two factors are related, and both are consistent with the oberved trend of ionization energy. The atomic radius for sodium is 186 pm, and the charge on its nucleus is 11 +. For argon, the atomic radius is 70 pm and the charge on its nucleus is 18 +. These values are consistent with the ionization energies of 498 kJ/mole for sodium and 1519 kJ/mole for argon.

Deviations in the trend If you closely examine Figure 11-8, you will find two decreases in the generally increasing ionization energies going across a period. In period 3, the first ionization energy of both aluminum and sulfur is lower than would be predicted by the preceding argument. These deviations depend on the type of orbital the electron is being removed from and the relative energies of various electron configurations.

The electron configuration of magnesium is $[Ne]3s^2$, and that of aluminum is $[Ne]3s^23p^1$. It is easier to remove an electron from a $3p$ orbital than from a $3s$ orbital because there is a higher probability that the $3p$ electron is farther from the nucleus. The electron configurations of phosphorus and sulfur are $[Ne]3s^23p^3$ and $[Ne]3s^23p^4$.

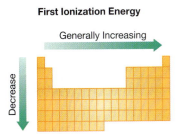

First Ionization Energy

Generally Increasing

Decrease

Teaching Strategy

Successive Ionization Energies

Point out the general relationship between size and IE; the larger the size, the lower the IE. Emphasize the general trend (increasing from left to right across a period). Do not be too concerned about the exceptions. Table 11–9 of successive ionization energies illustrates the difference in behavior of valence electrons and core electrons. Understanding this concept will enable students to see the reason that ionic compounds of the main group elements form with a specific charge for each ion. Emphasize that it is not the *difference* between successive ionization energies but the factor (*multiplier*) that is the key. For example, for sodium, the difference between IE_4 and IE_5 is about 5000 kJ, which to students often seems pretty big. But the multiplier is about 1.4 (13 400/9540). On the other hand, the difference between IE_1 and IE_2 is about 4000 kJ but the multiplier is more than 9 (4560/495). The fact that one multiplier is 9 and the other is only 1.4 indicates that there is a special significance to removing the second electron from sodium—i.e., that the second electron is not a valence electron.

Guided Practice

Review the Concept Check question on page 380 with students. Answers can be found in Appendix E on page 808.

Reteaching Idea

After showing students the equations for the first and second ionization of any element,

$$X(g) + IE_1 \rightarrow X^+(g) + e^-$$
$$X^+(g) + IE_2 \rightarrow X^{2+}(g) + e^-$$

point out that the equations state in symbols the definition of ionization energy. Have students write the equation for the third ionization energy.

(continued on page T385)

CONNECTING CONCEPTS

Models The periodic table is a model that accounts for past observations and accurately predicts future ones.

In the case of phosphorus, each of the 3*p* electrons is in an orbital by itself. In sulfur, one of the 3*p* orbitals has two electrons. The lower first ionization energy occurs because removing an electron from an orbital with two electrons is easier than removing an electron from an orbital with only one electron in it. This can be explained by repulsions between electrons.

Ionization energy within a group Look at the ionization energies of elements as you go down a group; the first ionization energy decreases. This is consistent with the trend that is predicted on the basis of size: As the radius of the atom gets larger, the ionization energy decreases because the electrons are more easily removed from orbitals that are farther from the nucleus. The nuclear charge also plays a role. For sodium, the charge is 11+ and the ionization energy is 489 kJ/mole; for potassium, the values are 19+ and 418 kJ/mole. How can it be easier to remove an electron when the nuclear charge is higher? In addition to the larger size, remember that the valence electron is shielded from the full influence of the nucleus charge by the core electrons. There is greater shielding in the potassium atom which has 8 more core electrons than the sodium atom. The observed ionization energies are the result of the combined effect of size and shielded nuclear charge.

Successive ionization energies More than one electron can be removed from an atom. The 2nd ionization energy is the energy required to remove a second electron. As you might expect, the ionization energy for each successive ionization becomes larger. For all elements, the second ionization energy will be larger than the first, since an electron is being removed from a 1+ ion instead of from a neutral atom. The ionization energies for the third, fourth, and subsequent electrons increase as well. Successive ionization energies for the period 3 elements are shown in Table 11-9.

TABLE 11-9 ■ Shaded area on table denotes core electrons.

General increase →

General decrease ↓

Element	IE_1	IE_2	IE_3	IE_4	IE_5	IE_6	IE_7
Na	498	4560	6910	9540	13 400	16 600	20 100
Mg	736	1445	7730	10 600	13 600	18 000	21 700
Al	577	1815	2740	11 600	15 000	18 310	23 290
Si	787	1575	3220	4350	16 100	19 800	23 800
P	1063	1890	2905	4950	6270	21 200	25 400
S	1000	2260	3375	4565	6950	8490	27 000
Cl	1255	2295	3850	5160	6560	9360	11 000
Ar	1519	2665	3945	5770	7230	8780	12 000

Successive Ionization Energies for Period 3 Elements

Videodisc Connections

909, side 6
Periodic Table: ionization energies (1 frame)

Look at the first through the seventh ionization energies of sodium. While each is larger than the previous ionization, there is a huge jump between the first and second; it takes about nine times as much energy to remove the second electron than to remove the first. But remember that the first electron removed from sodium is from a 3*s* orbital and the second electron comes from a 2*p* orbital. For the Group 2A element magnesium, the largest increase is between the 2nd and 3rd ionization energies. The biggest jump for aluminum occurs between the 3rd and 4th ionization energy. Does the same trend hold for the elements in other groups that are listed in Table 11-9? In general, once the valence electrons have been removed, there is a large increase in the amount of energy required to remove any of the core electrons.

Figure 11-9 *Some periodic trends are summarized here.*

Summary of Trends in the Periodic Table

Atomic number increase →
Atomic radii decrease →
Ionization energies increase →
Metallic properties decrease →

Atomic number increase ↓
Atomic radii increase ↓
Ionization energies decrease ↓
Metallic properties increase ↓

3 Li	4 Be											5 B	6 C	7 N	8 O	9 F	10 Ne
11 Na	12 Mg											13 Al	14 Si	15 P	16 S	17 Cl	18 Ar
19 K	20 Ca	21 Sc	22 Ti	23 V	24 Cr	25 Mn	26 Fe	27 Co	28 Ni	29 Cu	30 Zn	31 Ga	32 Ge	33 As	34 Se	35 Br	36 Kr
37 Rb	38 Sr	39 Y	40 Zr	41 Nb	42 Mo	43 Tc	44 Ru	45 Rh	46 Pd	47 Ag	48 Cd	49 In	50 Sn	51 Sb	52 Te	53 I	54 Xe
55 Cs	56 Ba	57 La	72 Hf	73 Ta	74 W	75 Re	76 Os	77 Ir	78 Pt	79 Au	80 Hg	81 Tl	82 Pb	83 Bi	84 Po	85 At	86 Rn
87 Fr	88 Ra	89 Ac	104	105	106	107	108	109									

PART 3 REVIEW

18. Explain why the size of atoms increases as you move down a group in the periodic table and decreases as you move across a period.
19. Why is a negatively charged ion larger than its corresponding neutral atom?
20. Predict the charge on the most common ion for each of the following elements: Mg, Cl, Al, S, Cs, I, O. Predict whether each ion would be smaller or larger than its neutral atom.
21. What is ionization energy?
22. Explain why the second ionization energy of barium is relatively small and the third ionization energy is very large.

Boxed numbers indicate questions that involve skills in interpretation, application, and analysis.

PART 3 REVIEW

ANSWERS

Keyed to Objectives

G 18. The size increases because the outermost electrons are in orbitals with a higher principal quantum number and a higher probability of being farther from the nucleus.

H 19. One or more electrons have been added to valence electrons present in the neutral atom, so increased repulsion between electrons increases the size.

I 20. Mg^{2+}, smaller; Cl^-, larger; Al^{3+}, smaller; S^{2-}, larger; Cs^+, smaller; I^-, larger; O^{2-}, larger

G 21. The energy needed to remove an electron from a neutral, gaseous atom

I 22. The 2nd electron is removed from a 6*s* orbital; the 3rd electron from a 5*p* orbital.

PART 3
Section 11.7 *continued*

(continued from page T384)

Ask students to write electronic configurations for Na, Mg, and Al. Then have them write equations for the ionization of the first electron, including in their equations the energies in kJ taken from Table 11–9. After each equation have them write the electron configuration for the ion formed. Repeat this procedure for the second ionization. Develop discussion concerning which electron is being removed and from what orbital. Have students compare the size of IE_1 and IE_2 for sodium (about 10X larger). Ask why IE_2 for sodium is so large. Have students predict how many times larger IE_3 for Mg will be than IE_2 for Mg. Then have them predict the size of IE_3 for Al.

CLOSE

Summing Up Main Ideas

Have students explain the reasons that the atomic radius and IE of elements are periodic properties. Have students cite reasons that the radius of an element is different from the radius of its ion. Have students predict the size of an ion as compared to the element it came from. Have students predict the first and successive ionization energies of elements using the periodic table as a reference. Refer students to Figure 11–9 and ask them to write a reason for each trend. For example, atomic number increases because the nuclei have increasing numbers of protons.

PART 3 REVIEW

Assign the Part Review questions.

Evaluating Skills

These skills are evaluated in the Part Review questions indicated. **Determining cause and effect:** 18, 19, 22; **Predicting:** 20; **Determining main ideas:** 21

Periodic Table of the Elements

Estimated Time: (30 minutes; may require additional time as homework)

Process Skills

Summarizing
Comparing/Contrasting
Constructing tables and graphs

Preparation

■ Materials

(for a class of 24, working individually or in groups of 4) textbooks (at least 1 per group of 4), blank periodic tables (24), CRC handbooks or other reference materials (at least 1 per group of 4)

■ Preparation Hints

Provide blank periodic tables of the elements printed on card stock, if possible.

Laboratory
Investigation

Periodic Table of the Elements

The handiest way to organize anything is the one that conveys the most information at a glance. Some information, or data, is best handled in tabular form, while other information is most conveniently illustrated graphically. The 109 known elements are arranged in the periodic table according to the *periodic law,* which states: *The chemical and physical properties of elements are a periodic function of their atomic numbers.*

Objectives

Classify 18 of the 109 elements by their physical and chemical properties.

Develop trends by placing elements into a "skeletal" periodic table of the elements.

■ Materials

☐ CRC Handbook of Chemistry and Physics
☐ blank periodic table
☐ textbook and other reference books

■ Procedure

In this exercise, you will be given some physical and chemical properties of various elements. You will identify each element and place it in its proper position on the periodic chart of the elements. A fictitious capital letter is assigned to all of the elements in one group. For example, an element, Af, with clues that tell you it is identical to sulfur, should be placed in group VIA, period 3. All elements in this group will then have symbols beginning with A. The second letter (*f* in this example) will not necessarily be in alphabetical order from the top of the group to the bottom of the group.

1. Group C

The Cc cation can be detected by its yellow flame in the flame test. Its compounds are used extensively in the manufacture of glass. It is easy to remove the one $3s$ electron from its outermost orbital, thus making a $+1$ ion.

Element Cb has a lower ionization energy than Cc. Green plants must have compounds containing ions of this element, which are added to the soil in fertilizer. A nitrate of Cb is used in making black gun powder and fireworks.

Cg has the lowest density and the smallest ionic radius of the group. Vaporized atoms of Cg give a crimson color to a flame.

2. Group A

Ad begins to melt at about 115°C. Near its boiling point, the nonmetal becomes more fluid. This yellow element exists in several allotropic (different atomic, or molecular, arrangements) forms. Its outermost orbital is $3s^2 3p^4$.

Ab is one of the most abundant elements in Earth's crust. Ab as a gas is somewhat denser than air. It will combine chemically with all elements except the noble gases.

3. Group B

Bd is obtained from the electrolytic reduction of its bauxite ore, $Bd_2O_3 \cdot 2H_2O$. Its ion has a charge of +3. This most abundant metal in the earth's crust is a self-protecting metal. On reacting with oxygen in the air, it forms Ba_2O_3.

Bb occurs in nature as $Na_2BbO_7 \cdot 10H_2O$. Bb_2O_3 dissolves to form a weak acid, H_3BbO_3, which can often be used as an eyewash. BbN is as hard as diamond.

4. Group D

Da's most abundant compound is the carbonate $DaCO_3$, or limestone. $Da(HCO_3)_2$ is often responsible for the temporary hardness of water. Human bone and tooth structure contain large percentages of $Da_3(PO_4)_2$. Vaporized Da atoms impart a red color to a flame.

Flame spectra of Db are green, and those of Df, red. Db is more dense than Df. Df is used to impart a crimson color to fireworks. $DbSO_4$ is often taken internally by patients who undergo X-ray examination of the gastrointestinal tract.

5. Group F

Elements of group F have four valence electrons. Fa and Fc have the greatest density of elements in the group and tend to form several ionic compounds. Fa is used to coat the steel that is used in food containers. An Fa fluoride is used in toothpaste to help prevent dental cavities.

Fc is the most metallic of the F group. Its compounds are poisonous and were once used in paint pigments. It is used extensively in the wet-cell type of car battery. Its great density makes it a suitable shield for nuclear reactors.

By weight, Fb is the second most abundant element in Earth's crust (25.7%). The compound FbO_2 is used in mortar, glass, and abrasives. It is a basic component of transistors, solar cells, rectifiers, and other solid-state devices.

6. Group G

Group G is an example of transition from nonmetallic to metallic properties down the group. Gc shows the highest ionization energy. Gc occurs in plant and animal protein and as the diatomic molecule, Gc_2, in the atmosphere. Compounds of Gc are used in fertilizers, foods, poisons, and explosives. It has 5 valence electrons.

Gb can exist in several allotropic forms. Its last electrons go into the third principle energy level. Compounds containing Gb are found in matches, protein, bone, and tooth structure. Gb was first prepared from and discovered in urine.

7. Group H

Ha has the highest ionization energy of any element in the group. Its attraction for hydrogen is so great that it will react explosively with most hydrides! Its hydro-acid is used to etch glass.

Hc is a gas, while Hb is a liquid at room temperature. Both are diatomic. Hc has a higher ionization energy than Hb. Hb is extracted from seaweed and used in photographic materials and sedatives.

Data Analysis

1. Read through the description of each element carefully. Consult the CRC handbook, the text, and other reference books to determine the correct element.

2. Place the letters for the coded element in its correct place in the blank periodic table. There are no duplicates, so if one of your elements seems to fall into a space already taken, you have made an error—go back and check your references again.

Conclusions

1. How was the periodic table useful in predicting the existence of elements before they were discovered?

2. Could you predict that other elements belong in group B besides Bd and Bb? What properties could you predict for them?

3. Three more elements—Cx, Cy, and Cz—make up the C group. Using the information you have about the first three members of the group, predict trends in density, ionic radius, and reactivity with water as you go down this group.

■ Procedural Hints

This investigation lends itself to a cooperative learning activity. Much can be learned when groups of four conscientiously work toward a common end. Provide only a limited number of CRC handbooks. Make it very clear to all students that all symbols are fictitious ones and that they are not necessarily in alphabetical order from top to bottom. You may use the entire exercise as a take-home one if you need to, but you will lose the cooperative learning aspect.

Data Analysis
(See periodic table below.)

Conclusions

1. By placing elements in the periodic table as they were discovered, researchers then knew what else to look for—certain elements with certain properties were needed to fill in certain places.

2. Yes; They would have atomic numbers of 31, 49, and 81. They would form ions with a 3+ charge.

3. These elements are alkali metals. As you go down this group, density and ionic radii increase; reactivity with water decreases.

Cg												Bb		Gc	Ab	Ha	
Cc												Bd	Fb	Gb	Ad	Hc	
Cb	Da															Hb	
	Df												Fa				
	Db												Fc				

Chapter 11
Review
ANSWERS
begin on page
T391a.

Summary

Organization of the Elements

- Elements were grouped by Dmitri Mendeleev into chemical families according to physical and chemical properties.

- The modern periodic table consists of elements listed according to increasing atomic number. Periods are listed horizontally in the periodic table, and chemical families (groups) are listed vertically.

Patterns in Electron Configurations

- Electron configurations can explain the chemical and physical properties of the elements.

- When atoms of the elements in Groups 1A–7A form ions, the ions also tend to have eight electrons in their outermost s and p orbitals. The positive ions tend to be isoelectronic with the noble gas in the preceding period, and the negative ions tend to be isoelectronic with the noble gas in the same period.

Periodic Trends

- Atomic radius and ionization energy trends generally follow predictable patterns, based on the position of an element in the periodic table.

Chemically Speaking

alkali metals *11.2*	isoelectronic *11.4*
alkaline earth metals *11.2*	outermost orbitals *11.3*
atomic radius *11.6*	periodic law *11.1*
chemical family *11.2*	periodic trends *11.6*
core electrons *11.3*	periods *11.2*
group *11.2*	representative elements *11.2*
halogens *11.2*	shielding *11.6*
inner-transition metals *11.2*	transition metals *11.2*
	valence electrons *11.3*

Concept Mapping

Using the method of concept mapping described at the front of this book, construct a concept map for the term *periodic table* using the concepts *elements, periods, groups, atomic number, noble gases,* and *halogens.* Use additional concepts from this chapter or previous chapters as necessary to expand your map.

Questions and Problems

ORGANIZATION OF THE ELEMENTS

A. Objective: Describe *the classification schemes used to arrange elements in Mendeleev's periodic table and in the modern periodic table.*

1. How did Mendeleev arrange the elements in his periodic table?
2. Give two examples of periodic relationships in everyday life (besides the periodic table).
3. What is periodic about the periodic table?
4. Why were none of the noble gases included in Mendeleev's periodic table?
5. In general, the atomic mass of elements increases as the atomic number increases. Find pairs of elements in the periodic table that are exceptions to this generalization.
6. Here is a list of chemicals: NaF, NaOH, H_2Se, CS_2, $AlCl_3$, Na_3PO_4. Use them and the periodic table to suggest the values of x and y in the following formulas:
   a. $Al_x(OH)_y$ c. Si_xCl_y
   b. $Tl_x(PO_4)_y$ d. $Ba_x(PO_4)_y$

B. Objective: Distinguish *between periods and groups on the periodic table.*

7. Name the elements in the halogen family.

PROBLEM-SOLVING
▶ **S T R A T E G I E S**
Students apply these strategies in the following questions.

- Factor-label method: 53
- Using what you know: 6, 12, 14, 15, 17, 18, 19, 20, 21, 22, 23, 24, 25, 26, 27, 28, 29, 30, 36, 37, 41, 43, 44, 50, 51
- Using patterns: 6, 12, 14, 15, 18, 19, 20, 21, 23, 24, 25, 26, 29, 30, 37, 41, 43, 44, 46, 47, 48, 54
- Using calculators: 53

T388

8. Write the symbols and names for the elements in period 2.

9. What trend in the number of electrons is observed in moving across a period in the modern periodic table?

10. Write the symbol for the elements in the following locations.
   a. period 3, Group 3A
   b. period 1, Group 8A
   c. period 4, Group 2B
   d. period 6, Group 5A

11. How are the elements in Group 6A similar?

12. Name the group in the periodic table in which each of the following elements falls, and categorize each as a metal or nonmetal.
   Rb, As, Xe, Sr, Sn, Bi, Br

PATTERNS IN ELECTRON CONFIGURATION

C. Objective: **Relate** *the electron configuration of an element to its position in the periodic table and to its chemical properties.*

13. At room temperature, nitrogen is a nonmetallic gas, and bismuth is a solid metal. Why are they both in Group 5A?

14. Name an element that has a filled *s* orbital.

15. Name an element that has a partially filled *p* orbital.

16. Explain why noble gases are unreactive.

17. Name the group of elements in the periodic table that has the following outer electron configurations.
   a. s^2
   c. elements filling the *d* orbitals
   b. s^2p^5
   d. s^2p^6

18. Name the elements with the following electron configurations.
   a. $[Ne]3s^23p^3$
   d. $1s^22s^22p^63s^1$
   b. $[Kr]5s^2$
   e. $1s^22s^22p^63s^23p^5$
   c. $[Ar]4s^23d^{10}4p^2$

D. Objective: **Determine** *the number of valence electrons for a representative element, using the periodic table.*

Boxed numbers indicate questions that involve skills in interpretation, application, and analysis.

19. How many valence electrons are in the following?
   a. elements of the oxygen family
   b. Na atom
   c. the element in Group 3A, period 5
   d. the element with the electron configuration $1s^22s^22p^5$

20. Use the periodic table to determine the electron configuration of the valence electrons for the following representative elements. (The principal quantum number is the same as the period number, and the total number of *s* and *p* electrons is the same as the Group number.)
   a. Ca, period 4, Group 2A
   b. As, period 4, Group 5A
   c. Cs   d. Ne   e. Po

E. Objective: **Predict** *the stable ion formed by a representative element using the periodic table.*

21. Predict the number of protons and electrons in stable ions of radium and iodine.

22. Use the periodic table to suggest formulas for compounds of the following pairs of elements.
   a. strontium-sulfur   c. calcium-chlorine
   b. gallium-fluorine   d. lithium-bromine

23. The metals of Group 2A of the periodic table combine with the halogens to form ionic solids. Write a general equation to represent these reactions, using M for the Group 2A metal and X for the halogen.

24. Predict the common ions formed when atoms of the elements listed gain or lose electrons. Then name the noble gas with which the ion is isoelectronic.
   a. magnesium   e. sulfur
   b. chlorine   f. barium
   c. aluminum   g. phosphorus
   d. potassium

25. The first three ionization energies of an element, in kJ/mole are these.
   IE$_1$ 403   IE$_2$ 2632   IE$_3$ 3859

■ Breaking problems into manageable parts: 23
■ Writing chemical equations: 45, 53
■ Making diagrams: 42

What is the charge on the most common ion of this element? How many valence electrons does the element have? Identify the element from the list: Ga, Rb, Ba.

F. Objective: Draw *the electron configurations for period 4 transition elements or ions.*

26. Use the position on the periodic table to determine the number of d orbital electrons in Fe, Zn, and Cr.
27. What element has the electron configuration
    a. $[Ar]4s^2 3d^2$?
    b. $[Ar]4s^1 3d^5$?
28. What is the electron configuration of Cr^{3+} and Ni^{2+}?
29. Which transition metal ion, Sc^{3+} or Zn^{2+}, is isoelectronic with Ar?

PERIODIC TRENDS

G. Objective: Describe *the periodic nature of atomic radius and ionization energy.*

30. For which of the following elements do you expect there to be a very large increase, going from the 2nd to the 3rd ionization energy (IE): Na, Mg, Al?
31. What trend is observed for the atomic radius of atoms
    a. going down a group?
    b. going left to right across a period?
32. Explain the observations in the previous problem.
33. How can the atomic radius of an element be experimentally determined?
34. How does core electron shielding affect the attraction of the nucleus for the valence electrons?
35. What is ionization energy (IE), and how is it determined?
36. Why does Na have a higher 2nd IE than a 1st IE?

37. Would you predict the 2nd IE of Be to be greater or less than its 3rd IE? Explain your answer.

H. Objective: Compare *the size of an atom to the size of its ion and give reasons for the difference.*

38. Which has the larger radius, Na^+ or Ne? Explain your answer.
39. What trend in the ionic radius of an element would you predict
    a. as you move from left to right across a period?
    b. as you move down a family?
40. Explain the basis of your predictions in the preceding problem.
41. Which of the following would you predict to be larger?
    a. Na or Na^+
    b. F or F^-
    c. Fe, Fe^{2+}, or Fe^{3+}
    d. H, H^+, or H^-
42. Choose an appropriate scale and using the data given in Table 11-7, make drawings that represent the size of the atoms in Group 2A.

I. Objective: Predict *the properties of an element, using the periodic table.*

43. If Rb_2O, MgO, and Al_2O_3 are stable compounds, what would be the formulas for stable oxides of Sr, K, and Ga?
44. Identify the two elements, using the information listed below:
    Element X:
    reacts with sodium to form the compound Na_2X
    is in the second period
    Element Y:
    reacts with oxygen to form the compound Y_2O
    has the lowest ionization energy of a fourth-period element
45. Write the formula of the ionic compound expected from the reaction of X and Y in question 44.

46. Chlorine is commonly used to purify drinking water. When chlorine dissolves in water, it forms hypochlorous acid.

$$Cl_2(g) + H_2O(l) \rightarrow$$
$$HOCl(aq) + H^+(aq) + Cl^-(aq)$$

Predict what happens when iodine, I_2, dissolves in water. Write the chemical equation for this reaction.

47. Sodium reacts with water to form a basic solution, as the following equation shows.

$$2\ Na(s) + 2\ H_2O(l) \rightarrow$$
$$2\ NaOH(aq) + H_2(g)$$

Write the equation for the reaction of the following metals with water:
a. K **b.** Li **c.** Mg **d.** Ca

48. Aluminum reacts with iodine to form aluminum iodide.
a. Write the equation for the reaction.
b. Write the equation for the reaction of gallium with bromine.

Critical Thinking

SYNTHESIS WITHIN THE CHAPTER

49. Which of the following electron configurations would you expect to have the lowest second ionization energy? Give reasons for your choice.
a. $1s^2 2s^2 2p^6$
b. $1s^2 2s^2 2p^6 3s^1$
c. $1s^2 2s^2 2p^6 3s^2$

50. Which element—Na, Si, Cl, or Cs—has
a. the highest first ionization energy?
b. the smallest atomic radius?
c. the most metallic character?

51. Use the periodic table to predict which species of each of these pairs has the smaller radius.
a. K, Br **c.** K^+, Ga^{3+}
b. Ne, F^- **d.** S, Se

52. Discuss the similarities between a calendar and the periodic table.

SYNTHESIS ACROSS CHAPTERS

53. When 25.0 grams of sodium metal reacts with excess oxygen gas, how many grams of sodium oxide will be formed?

54. Use the electron configurations for the following neutral atoms to answer questions a–f:
A $1s^2 2s^2 2p^6 3s^2$ D $1s^2 2s^2 2p^5$
B $1s^2 2s^2 2p^6 3s^1$ E $1s^2 2s^2 2p^3$
C $1s^2 2s^2 2p^6$
a. Which of the electron configurations would have the lowest first ionization energy?
b. Which configuration is a noble gas?
c. List the five configurations in predicted order of increasing first ionization energy.
d. Predict the configuration that should have the highest second ionization energy (IE_2).
e. Predict the configuration that should have the lowest second ionization energy (IE_2).
f. Predict the electron configurations for a compound of the formula x_3y_2.

Projects

55. Choose a family on the periodic table and list each element's uses in the everyday world. Consult reference materials such as the Merck Index to complete your list.

56. Find and bring to class as many different designs for the periodic table as you can.

Research and Writing

57. Read the labels to determine the difference between ordinary table salt and "lite salt." Look at each under a microscope. Write a paper describing the differences. Develop an advertising campaign to market each.

58. Find out about the periodic table developed by Lothar Meyer and write a short paper on why Mendeleev is given more recognition for his achievement than Meyer is for his.

☐ Boxed numbers indicate questions that involve skills in interpretation, application, and analysis.

1. Mendeleev arranged the elements in order of increasing atomic weight so that elements with similar chemical properties lined up in columns.

2. There are many possible answers. Some examples are the seasons, newspapers, school vacations, days of the week, and class periods in school.

3. Chemical and physical properties of the elements are periodic. Some specific examples of periodic properties are electron configurations, ionization energy, electron affinity, atom and ion size, ion charge, and reactivity.

4. None of the noble gases had been discovered when Mendeleev proposed his periodic table.

5. Exceptions to the increasing atomic masses in the periodic table are Ar and K, Co and Ni, Te and I, Th and Pa.

6.
	x	y
a.	1	3
b.	1	1
c.	1	4
d.	3	2

7. fluorine, chlorine, bromine, iodine, and astatine

8. Li, lithium; Be, beryllium; B, boron; C, carbon; N, nitrogen; O, oxygen; F, fluorine; Ne, neon

9. Each atom of an element has one more electron than does an atom of the element preceding it.

10. a. Al
   b. He
   c. Zn
   d. Bi

11. Many answers possible—some examples include 6 electrons in outermost shell, form 2− ions, nonmetals (with exception of Po)

12. Rb: alkali metal (1A), metal
   As: nitrogen group (5A), nonmetal
   Xe: noble gas (8A), nonmetal
   Sr: alkaline earth metal (2A), metal
   Sn: carbon group (4A), metal
   Bi: nitrogen group (5A), metal
   Br: halogen (7A), nonmetal

13. They both have 5 electrons in their outermost s and p orbitals.

14. Many possible; all representative elements with the exception of Group 1A; many of the transition elements

15. Any element without an np^6 electron configuration. From representative elements, any except 1A, 2A, and 8A elements.

16. They have their outermost s and p orbitals filled with electrons (2 in the case of He and 8 in all the other noble gases).

17. a. Group 2A
   b. Group 7A
   c. Groups 1B–8B
   d. Group 8A

18. a. phosphorus
   b. strontium
   c. germanium
   d. sodium
   e. chlorine

19. a. 6
   b. 1
   c. 3
   d. 7

20. a. $4s^2$
   b. $4s^24p^3$
   c. $6s^1$
   d. $2s^22p^6$
   e. $6s^26p^4$

21. radium: 88 protons, 86 electrons; iodine: 53 protons, 54 electrons

22. a. SrS
   b. GaF_3
   c. $CaCl_2$
   e. LiBr

23. $M + X_2 \rightarrow MX_2$

24. a. Mg^{2+}, neon
   b. Cl^-, argon
   c. Al^{3+}, neon
   d. K^+, argon
   e. S^{2-}, argon
   f. Ba^{2+}, xenon
   g. P^{3-}, argon

25. 1+, 1 valence electron (the difference between 1st and 2nd IE is a factor of about 6.5; between 2nd and 3rd, a factor of about 1.5). This implies that there is one valence electron, so it is a Group 1A element. From list, only Rb is a Group 1A element.

26. Fe: 6 d electrons
   Zn: 10 d electrons
   Cr: 5 d electrons (This is one of the anomalous cases—$4s^13d^5$ is the actual configuration.)

27. a. Ti
   b. Cr

28. Cr^{3+}: [Ar] $3d^3$
   Ni^{2+}: [Ar] $3d^8$

29. Sc^{3+}

30. Mg

31. a. Atomic radius increases.
   b. Atomic radius decreases.

32. a. Going down a group, the valence electrons are occupying orbitals with higher principle quantum number and have a higher probability of being found farther from the nucleus.
   b. Going across a group, the nuclear charge increases so the valence electrons are pulled more closely to the nucleus.

33. One technique is the use of X-ray diffraction of solid crystals.

34. Electron shielding lowers the amount of nuclear charge felt by the outermost electrons.

35. Ionization energy is the amount of energy required to remove an electron from a neutral gaseous atom. It can be determined by bombarding gaseous elements with electrons of known energy.

36. The first electron removed is a 3s electron, which is easier to remove than the 2nd electron, which is a 2p electron. As the principle quantum number decreases, the electrons are harder to remove.

37. Less; The 2nd IE is for an electron from the 2s orbital but the electron that is being removed by the 3rd IE is in a 1s orbital.

38. Ne; It has only 10 protons in its nucleus compared to 11 protons in Na^+.

39. a. Cations get smaller; anions get smaller but the anions are larger than the cations of the same period.
   b. Both cations and anions increase in size.

40. a. Cations of the same period are isoelectronic, so the more protons in the nucleus, the smaller the size. Anions of the same period are also isoelectronic (but not with the cations), so also get smaller.
   b. Outermost electrons are farther from the nucleus going down a family.

41. a. Na
   b. F^-
   c. Fe
   d. H^-

42. The drawings should increase in size from Be to Ra.

43. SrO, K_2O, and Ga_2O_3

44. X is O; Y is K

45. K_2O

46. Because I_2 is in the same group, it would be expected to react in a way

similar to chlorine.

$$I_2(s) + H_2O(l) \rightarrow HOI(aq) + H^+(aq) + I^-(aq)$$

47. The reactions for K and Li are identical to that of Na; products are KOH and LiOH, respectively.

   c. $Mg(s) + 2H_2O(l) \rightarrow Mg(OH)_2(aq) + H_2(g)$

   d. $Ca(s) + 2H_2O(l) \rightarrow Ca(OH)_2(aq) + H_2(g)$

48. a. $2Al(s) + 3I_2(s) \rightarrow 2AlI_3(s)$
   b. $2Ga(s) + 3Br_2(l) \rightarrow 2GaBr_3(s)$

49. The electron configuration in "c," because the second electron is removed from the $3s$ orbital

50. a. Cl
   b. Cl
   c. Cs

51. a. Br
   b. Ne
   c. Ga^{3+}
   d. S

52. Both are periodic in nature. For example, in a calendar, the day cycle repeats after every 7 days; for the first 20 elements in the periodic table, the cycle is 8 elements.

53. None; Sodium forms sodium peroxide, Na_2O_2, not the oxide.

54. a. B
   b. C
   c. B, A, E, D, C
   d. B
   e. A
   f. A and E (A_3E_2)

55. Uses for elements in a family may be similar.

56. Periodic tables may differ in their placement of hydrogen, lanthanide series, actinide series, and names of elements 93 to 109.

57. "Lite salt" contains a mixture of potassium chloride and sodium chloride.

58. See Science Background on page T362.

Elements: A Closer Look

Investigations	Demonstrations	Texas Essential Elements★
Laboratory Manual 12–2 S	Alkali Metals, page T395 Sodium and Potassium in Living Organisms, page T396 Aluminum, page T399	**Content:** 4.4, 5.2 **Process:** 10.1, 10.2
	Properties of Alloys, page T404	**Content:** 4.4 **Process:** 10.1, 10.4
		Process: 10.1, 10.2, 10.4
Laboratory Manual 12–1 S In-text Investigation, page T422		**Content:** 4.4 **Process:** 10.1
		Content: 4.4 **Process:** 1.1, 1.2, 1.3, 2.1, 2.2, 4.3, 5.1, 6.1
		Process: 4.2, 4.3, 7.1, 10.1, 10.2
		Content: 4.4 **Process:** 10.1, 10.2, 10.3, 10.4

KEY:
M–*Microscale* **S**–*Structured*
I–*Inquiry* **IM**–*Inquiry Microscale*

★*See pages T8–T11 for complete listing of Texas Essential Elements.*

12

Elements: A Closer Look

Chapter Rationale

Chapter 12 surveys some of the properties of the elements. The properties of metals are related to the model for metallic bonding. Metals, nonmetals, and metalloids are compared and contrasted. Students will relate the properties to the position of the elements on the periodic table. As principles are discussed in subsequent chapters, review how they relate to the properties presented in this chapter.

About the Photograph

Metallurgy is the science of extracting metals from their ores and preparing them for use. The Egyptians were separating iron from ore more than 4000 years ago. The photograph shows a gold Egyptian Collar representing the Vulture Goddess, Nekbet, from the tomb of King Tutankhamun, who ruled about 1300 B.C. Other valuable metals such as gold, silver, and copper have been found in a pure form and were used by the ancient Egyptians, Chinese, and American Indians. The pure metal was simply melted and molded into weapons, tools, or jewelry.

Chapter Planning Hints

Plan to spend two to four class sessions to complete the chapter, including the Laboratory Investigation and Chapter Review. You may wish to obtain the program KC? Discoverer: *Exploring the Properties of the Chemical Elements* to use with the chapter, as well as The World of Chemistry videotapes *The Periodic Table*, *Chemistry of the Earth*, and *Metals*. Four optional demonstrations are suggested for this chapter. They can be found on pages T395, T396, T399, and T404. You may wish to preview them at this time.

Metals were used by the ancient Chinese and Egyptians for utensils and ornaments.

Myths and Misconceptions

Students may describe metals as "hard, strong, and resistant to change." Thus they may have difficulty understanding that many metals are chemically reactive, given appropriate forms that allow the reactants to come in contact. Ask students to think of everyday examples of reactions of metals, such as the tarnishing of silver or the rusting of a car. Note that alkali metals such as sodium are not found in elemental form because of their high reactivity.

PART

1 Representative Metals

You have learned that the periodic table is arranged to emphasize important similarities in the properties of elements. These properties determine how certain elements can be used. For example, metals can be formed into shapes or drawn into flexible sheets. Nonmetals such as oxygen, carbon, and phosphorus have different properties and uses than metals. They do not conduct electricity and cannot be formed into tools the way many metals can. However, nonmetals are major components of Earth and its atmosphere, and they are found in many compounds that are essential to life. Elements called metalloids have properties of both metals and nonmetals. The properties of silicon, a metalloid, make it useful in electronic circuitry, and electric-wire insulations. In this chapter, you will look more closely at some of the properties of metals, nonmetals, and metalloids.

12.1 Properties of Metals

About three fourths of the known elements are classified as metals. You learned in Chapter 2 that with the exception of mercury, all metals are solids at room temperature. In the solid state, metals are crystalline, which simply means that their atoms are arranged in regular patterns.

Many metals are fairly reactive, and are found in nature combined with oxygen, sulfur, or carbon. Metallic elements have low ionization energies compared to ionization energies of nonmetallic elements. As a result, metals tend to give up electrons when they form compounds with other elements.

Explaining metallic properties Most properties of metals result from **metallic bonding**. This bonding is caused in part by the relative ease with which the valence electrons in metal atoms are lost. The low ionization energies of metals explain this tendency. As a result, the valence electrons of pure metals are not associated with particular atoms but instead can move rather freely among atoms throughout the metal.

Because they are not confined to a specific region, these delocalized electrons are often referred to as a "sea" of electrons. The electrons in this sea flow among the positively charged cores of the metal atoms. A crystal of sodium metal can be regarded as an array of sodium ions (Na^+) surrounded by a sea of electrons

Objectives

Part 1

A. ***Use models*** to explain some properties of metals.
B. ***Summarize*** some of the properties and uses of representative metals.

Developing Skills

Students may apply these skills in their study of Part 1.
Comparing/Contrasting: Have students compare and contrast properties of representative metals.
Forming models: Have students form models to explain some properties of metals.
Comparing/Contrasting: Have students compare the uptake of sodium and potassium by plants and animals and account for the difference.

☰ FOCUS

Activate Prior Knowledge

In Chapter 11 students learned that alkali metals react with water to form an alkaline solution. Obtain a very small piece of lithium metal.

⚠ **CAUTION: Wear safety goggles, a lab apron, and gloves. Protect students with a shield.** Show that lithium metal is soft by cutting it with a dull knife. Then drop the piece of lithium metal into a large beaker that contains about 100 mL of water. Direct students to write what they observe during the chemical reaction. Add a few drops of phenolphthalein indicator to confirm the presence of a base. Discuss with students how to safely test for the H_2 gas. Students should write the balanced chemical equation.
($2Li + 2H_2O \rightarrow 2LiOH + H_2$)

☰ TEACH

Teaching Strategy

Properties of Metals

Begin by asking students to name characteristics of a metal, such as whether it is shiny, a good conductor, malleable, and

Videodisc Connections

614, side 6
Metallic bonding (1 frame)

(continued on page T394)

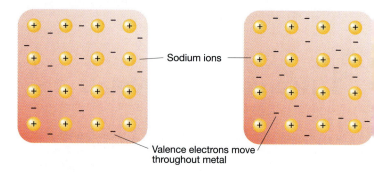

Sodium ions

Valence electrons move throughout metal

(continued from page T393)

so on. Students might also incorrectly suggest high density, high melting point, strength, and hardness. They will learn that these latter properties vary greatly among metals. For example, mercury is a liquid at room temperature and rubidium melts at less than 40°C; and some alkali metals are less dense than water and can be cut with a knife.

Figure 12-1 *A metal crystal is an array of positive ions in a "sea" of electrons.*

(e^-), as shown in Figure 12-1. Because a number of metal atoms share these highly mobile electrons, each metal atom is said to be bonded to the atoms that surround it. The greater the number of electrons per atom that participate in the metallic bonding, the stronger the bonds will be.

Malleability and ductility How does the electron-sea model explain the properties of metals? The ability to be hammered into shapes, *malleability*, and the ability to be stretched into wires, *ductility*, can be explained by the delocalized valence electrons of a metal being spread more or less uniformly throughout the crystal. When a piece of metal is hammered, as shown in Figure 12-2, the positive cores of the atoms slide past each other but are still held together by the delocalized sea of electrons. Crystals of other common materials, such as table salt, do not possess delocalized electrons. As a result, what happens when they are hit with a hammer?

Figure 12-2 *The atoms in a metal can slide past each other and still remain bonded in the "sea" of electrons.*

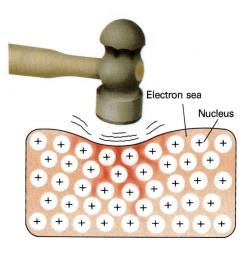

Electron sea

Nucleus

CONNECTING CONCEPTS

Models The electron-sea model of metallic bonding provides an explanation of thermal and electrical conductivity and malleability and ductility.

Electrical and thermal conductivity The electron-sea model also explains the high electrical and thermal conductivity of metals. Metals conduct electricity because the delocalized electrons can move rapidly through the metal. These mobile electrons also

Myths and Misconceptions

Students often have the misconception that all metals are solid, shiny, lustrous, strong, and hard. For example, they don't commonly think of potassium, sodium, or calcium as metals. This leads to difficulties in classifying the elements into the correct group of the periodic table. This misconception is especially true of the alkali metals and the alkaline earth metals. To help clarify this, have students compare the reactivity, density, hardness, and melting and boiling points of these metals to their electron configurations. They should conclude that these metals are more "metallic" than the transition metals or the noble metals with which they are most familiar.

carry some of the metal's thermal energy. When a part of the metal is heated, the kinetic energy of the delocalized electrons increases, causing the electrons to move more rapidly. Heat energy is moved throughout the crystal as these high-energy electrons collide and transfer some of their energy to the stationary metal ions. Heat is thus rapidly transmitted throughout the metal.

Would you expect there to be a connection between metals' ability to conduct electricity and their ability to conduct heat? If you have ever unplugged an electrical appliance and found the cord to be warm, you might suspect there is. Electrons moving through a metal bump into stationary metal ions, and transfer part of their energy to these stationary ions. This causes metals to heat up when current passes through them.

12.2 Alkali Metals

Recall from Chapter 11 that the elements within a group, or family of the periodic table have configurations of valence electrons that are similar. As a result, the elements in the same column show similar physical and chemical properties. It should not be surprising, therefore, that the metals in Group 1A are physically and chemically very much alike. These metals are called the **alkali metals.** They are lustrous, silvery solids that are soft enough to be cut with a knife.

Reactivity of alkali metals You learned in Chapter 11 that alkali metals get their name from the fact that they react with water to form basic, or alkaline, solutions. Alkali metals react not only with water but also with many other substances. Because of this high reactivity, they are not found in nature in the elemental state. Their reactivity also makes them difficult to purify, handle, and store. They must usually be stored in a nonreactive material such as kerosene or argon.

Alkali metals have a high reactivity because of their low ionization energies, which allow them to transfer their valence electrons to an atom of another element. This reactivity increases as you go down the group.

How would you predict potassium would react with water as compared to sodium? Figure 12-3 shows how vigorous the reaction is when a small piece of potassium is placed in water. It is much more violent and dangerous than the reaction of sodium with water. This reaction generates so much heat that the hydrogen produced by the reaction usually ignites. Rubidium and cesium react even more explosively with water.

Sodium and potassium Compared to the other alkali metals, sodium and potassium are relatively abundant in nature. Sodium is found most often in nature as sodium chloride. It can be mined as halite, or rock salt, $NaCl$, as well as crystallized from sea water. As you learned in Chapter 2, metallic sodium can be prepared by

CONNECTING CONCEPTS

Structure and Properties of Matter The reactivities of metals increase as you go down a group because the valence electrons are farther from the nucleus.

Figure 12-3 *The reaction of potassium with water is dangerous; it generates enough heat to ignite the hydrogen produced.*

PART **1**
Section 12.2

Science Background

Sodium and Potassium

Sodium is manufactured by the electrolysis of molten $NaCl$. Because pure sodium chloride melts at such a high temperature (801°C), it is usually mixed with $CaCl_2$ because the mixture has a melting point of about 580°C. An electric current is then run through this molten mixture to produce elemental sodium. Chlorine is a by-product of the process. One of the uses of sodium metal is in the manufacture of the dye indigo, which is used for "blue" jeans.

Videodisc Connections

9365 to 12353, side 6
Alkali metals (movie)

DEMONSTRATION

Alkali Metals

Have samples of sodium or potassium in glass jars for students to examine. The samples should be under an anhydrous liquid such as kerosene.

CAUTION: Jars are to remain sealed and should not be touched or moved.

running an electric current through molten sodium chloride in a process called electrolysis. Most sodium metal produced in the United States is used in sodium vapor lamps, as heat exchangers in nuclear reactors, and in the production of other metals, such as titanium and potassium.

Elemental potassium is most often produced by reacting molten potassium chloride, KCl, with sodium metal.

$$Na(l) + KCl(l) \rightarrow NaCl(l) + K(g)$$

The reaction is carried out at 870°C, which is above the boiling point of potassium but below the boiling point of sodium. At this temperature, potassium vaporizes and can be separated from the remaining liquid sodium chloride.

While potassium metal and sodium metal have similar properties, the increased reactivity, lower abundance, and higher cost of potassium limit its use in industrial processes.

Sodium and potassium in living organisms While potassium and sodium are essential elements for both plants and animals, most plants contain four to six times as much potassium as sodium. Animals get their potassium from plants, and plants get their potassium from the soil. To supplement the potassium naturally found in soil, many fertilizers contain potassium chloride, KCl.

Without an adequate intake of both potassium and sodium, your body would be unable to function. The transmission of nerve impulses relies on potassium and sodium, as illustrated in Figure 12-4. The membranes of nerve cells are able to maintain different concentrations of sodium and potassium ions inside and outside the cell. The transmission of a nerve impulse is accompanied by the

Figure 12-4 Nerve cells maintain different concentrations of ions on either side of the cell membrane. Top: *Stimulus of the nerve initiates an impulse.* Center: *The impulse moves as sodium ions flow into the cell and potassium ions flow out.* Bottom: *After the impulse has passed through, "pumps" in the membrane transport the ions back to their original positions.*

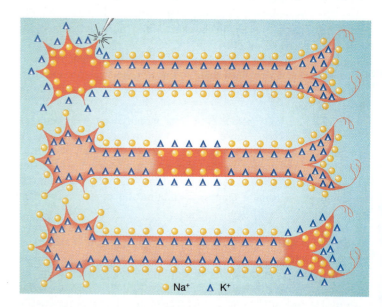

● Na⁺   ▲ K⁺

DEMONSTRATION

Sodium and Potassium in Living Organisms

Demonstrate the solubility of sodium and potassium salts in water and the ability of these aqueous solutions to conduct electricity. Dissolve about 6 g of NaCl and 7.5 g of KCl into 100 mL of cold water in separate 300-mL beakers.

Once the salts have completely dissolved, use a conductivity unit, powered by 1.5- or 9-volt batteries, to test how well each solution conducts electricity. For disposal, pour the liquids down the drain.

inward flow of sodium ions and the outward flow of potassium ions across the cell membrane. The original ion concentrations are then restored by "pumps" in the cell membrane. A second impulse can usually be transmitted after only a few thousandths of a second because that is the amount of time typically required to restore the initial ion concentrations.

Ion imbalance Periods of intense physical training can cause your body to lose both sodium and potassium. A deficiency of potassium can lead to muscle weakness and heart abnormalities. To avoid the effects of ion imbalance, athletes commonly consume foods high in potassium, such as bananas, which provide the necessary ions in a form that does not interfere with the natural checks and balances in the human body.

An excess of either sodium or potassium can be harmful to living organisms because it will upset the body's chemical balance and dehydrate the body. An excess of sodium can be partially responsible for high blood pressure. Your diet is more likely to provide you with too much sodium than too much potassium.

Concept ✔ **Check**

In your own words, relate the relatively low ionization energies of the alkali metals to the fact that they are not found in an uncombined state in nature.

12.3 Alkaline Earth Metals

The Group 2A elements are called **alkaline earth metals.** They are denser, harder, and have higher melting and boiling points than the corresponding alkali metals. This is primarily because each alkaline earth metal atom contributes 2, not 1, delocalized electrons to the electron sea and has a positive charge of $2+$, not $1+$, on the nucleus. As was the case with the alkali metals, the name of this group, alkaline earth metals, comes from the alkaline, or basic, solutions produced by reactions of the metals with water. The word *earth* is left over from alchemy days.

Reactivity of the alkaline earth metals Alkaline earth metals are less reactive than the alkali metals, but they are still too reactive to be found naturally as free metals. Their relatively low ionization energy accounts for their reactivity, which increases going down the alkaline earth family, just as it does for the alkali metals. For example, beryllium does not react with water; magnesium reacts very slowly with water and rapidly with steam. Calcium and the metals below it react readily with water, as shown in Figure 12-5 on the next page. The equation for the reaction of calcium with water is

$$Ca(s) + 2H_2O(l) \rightarrow Ca(OH)_2(aq) + H_2(g)$$

Teaching Strategy

Alkaline Earth Metals

Demonstrate the solubility of alkaline earth salts including magnesium carbonate and calcium sulfate. Try dissolving 1 g of each salt in 100 mL of water. Then filter the undissolved compound to illustrate how poorly each compound dissolves.

⚠ **CAUTION: Wear safety goggles and a lab apron.** For disposal, decant and pour the decantate down the drain. Wrap the solids in newspaper and put in the wastebasket.

PART 1

Section 12.3 continued

Resources

Use the program KC? Discoverer: *Exploring the Properties of the Chemical Elements*. The World of Chemistry videotapes *The Periodic Table, Chemistry of the Earth*, and *Metals* may be used throughout this chapter.

Figure 12-5 *Calcium reacts with water to produce bubbles of hydrogen, but there is no apparent reaction of magnesium with water.*

Magnesium and calcium are the most abundant of the alkaline earth metals. Both elements can be extracted through an electrolysis process from their chloride salts, $MgCl_2$ and $CaCl_2$, which are common in sea water.

Magnesium Commercially magnesium is the most important alkaline earth metal. It is a component of many useful alloys. An **alloy** is a mixture of two or more elements, at least one of which is a metal. Typically the components of an alloy are melted together and allowed to cool. The major commercial sources of magnesium are sea water, underground brines, and the minerals magnesite, $MgCO_3$, and dolomite, $CaCO_3 \cdot MgCO_3$.

Magnesium is used in large quantities to make aluminum alloys, which are harder and more corrosion-resistant than either metal alone. Because of their strength and low density, magnesium/aluminum alloys are used in aircraft and auto parts. You may even use sports equipment containing these alloys, such as bicycle frames, backpack frames, or tennis racquets.

When heated in air, magnesium burns to produce a mixture of magnesium oxide and magnesium nitride, releasing a great deal of energy. The brilliant white light you see given off by fireworks is produced by burning magnesium.

Magnesium oxide, MgO, which is also called magnesia, is produced when magnesium carbonate is heated.

$$MgCO_3(s) \xrightarrow{\text{heat}} MgO(s) + CO_2(g)$$

Magnesia reacts with water to form magnesium hydroxide, $Mg(OH)_2$, which is slightly soluble in water. A suspension of magnesium hydroxide in water is called *milk of magnesia* because of its milky white color. You may recognize this suspension as an antacid. Excess stomach acid, which can cause discomfort and lead to the formation of ulcers, can be neutralized by the magnesium hydroxide.

Calcium The most common naturally occurring compound of calcium is calcium carbonate, $CaCO_3$. This brittle white compound is commercially obtained from seashells and limestone.

PROBLEM-SOLVING

S T R A T E G Y

Writing chemical equations makes it easier to understand the reaction that is taking place. (See Strategy, page 244.)

Calcium carbonate is only slightly soluble in distilled water. However, if the water contains dissolved carbon dioxide, calcium carbonate will react to produce calcium hydrogen carbonate.

$$CaCO_3(s) + H_2O(l) + CO_2(g) \rightarrow Ca(HCO_3)_2(aq)$$

This reaction occurs in the formation of limestone caves. When rainwater containing dissolved carbon dioxide filters through limestone deposits, the rock is slowly dissolved and carried away. Any opening or crack in the rock formation will gradually enlarge. Many years of this process will result in a limestone cavern. As the water evaporates and carbon dioxide is released, solid calcium carbonate is deposited as stalactites and stalagmites, like those shown in Figure 12-6.

Figure 12-6 When underground water containing dissolved $Ca(HCO_3)_2$ emerges in a cavern, CO_2 and H_2O are released to the air, leaving $CaCO_3$ in the form of stalactites. Some water may drip off the stalactites to the floor, building up stalagmites by the same process.

Hard water Ground water in some areas contains dissolved calcium bicarbonate and magnesium bicarbonate, as well as other dissolved salts. Such water is called *hard water*. When this hard water evaporates or is heated, carbon dioxide is driven off and insoluble carbonate compounds form. These compounds are deposited in boilers and pipes used to heat and transport water as shown in Figure 12-7. You may also have noticed them coating or clogging teakettles, steam irons, coffeemakers, and other household objects.

12.4 Aluminum

Aluminum is the third most abundant element in Earth's crust after oxygen and silicon. It is usually found in aluminosilicate minerals (minerals containing aluminum, silicon, and oxygen). Weathering of these rocks forms the aluminum-containing clays that are a part of most soils.

Figure 12-7 Hard-water deposits can build up in pipes. Why is this buildup undesirable?

PART **1**

Section 12.4

Science Background

Properties of Aluminum

Precious stones such as diamonds, emeralds, rubies, and sapphires have known chemical compositions. Aluminum oxide is the basic mineral found in rubies and sapphires. Synthetic rubies and sapphires are made by melting aluminum oxide.

DEMONSTRATION

Aluminum

The reactivity of aluminum can be demonstrated by putting a small piece of aluminum foil (about 5 cm × 5 cm) into a container of 1 *M* NaOH and a separate small piece in a container of 1 *M* HCl under a hood. No reaction occurs with NaOH, but aluminum replaces hydrogen from HCl. Acidic corrosion of aluminum requires the presence of chloride ion. This can be

demonstrated by placing a small piece of aluminum foil into 1 *M* HNO₃. No reaction will occur until a few grams of solid sodium chloride are added to the nitric acid solution.

⚠️ **CAUTION: Wear safety goggles and a lab apron. Use a shield to protect yourself and students from spattering.** For disposal, neutralize the liquids and pour down the drain.

PART 1
Section 12.4 continued

Guided Practice

Review the Concept Check question on page 397 with students. Answers can be found in Appendix E on page 808.

Reteaching Idea

To reinforce the concept that elements with similar properties have similar electron structures, have students review the periodic table. Give students a blank periodic table. Have them identify the alkali metals, the alkaline earth metals and aluminum. They should color in each box, using a different color for each family. In addition, students can write the electron configuration for each element. Label each element and each group or family. Have students compare the chemical reactivities of Group 1 and Group 2 metals and explain how these differences are accounted for by the atomic sizes and nuclear charges of each.

≡ CLOSE

Summing Up Main Ideas

Show students several types of metals, such as magnesium, lead, tin, and aluminum. Have them describe the metallic properties of these elements. (Students are not to touch the lead sample.) Then ask students to list important uses for these metals.

PART 1 REVIEW

Assign the Part Review questions.

Evaluating Skills

These skills are evaluated in the Part Review questions indicated. **Determining main ideas:** 2, 4; **Predicting:** 2, 10; **Determining cause and effect:** 3, 5; **Summarizing:** 6, 8; **Analyzing data:** 7; **Applying a strategy:** 7; **Calculating:** 7; **Verifying results:** 7; **Comparing/Contrasting:** 9

DO YOU KNOW?

Only 5% of the energy used to extract aluminum from its ore is needed to recycle aluminum.

PROBLEM·SOLVING
STRATEGY

By looking for patterns among these substances, you can answer the question. (See Strategy, page 100.)

Boxed numbers indicate questions that involve skills in interpretation, application, and analysis.

Aluminum is the only Group 3A metal produced commercially in large quantities. It is in such wide use today that you might find it difficult to believe that aluminum was once considered a precious metal. Prior to 1886, the process used to produce aluminum metal from its compounds was so costly that it was more expensive than gold or silver.

Properties of aluminum Aluminum, a good electrical conductor, is a moderately soft, low-density solid with a moderate melting point of 660°C. Because of its high reactivity, aluminum metal quickly forms a thin, transparent, oxide coating, Al_2O_3, when exposed to air.

$$4Al(s) + 3O_2(g) \rightarrow 2Al_2O_3(s)$$

This aluminum oxide coating is very unreactive. If you scratch a piece of aluminum, it quickly forms a new layer of oxide on the damaged area. This oxide coating protects the rest of the metal from corrosion.

Small amounts of other elements—including copper, silicon, magnesium, and manganese—are often mixed with aluminum to form high-strength alloys. In this form, aluminum is used in auto parts, ladders, and airplanes. A typical large-passenger airplane contains more than 50 tons of aluminum alloy.

PART 1 REVIEW

1. Use the model of a sea of electrons to explain the property of malleability in metals.
2. What are the products of a reaction between an alkali metal and water?
3. Why don't alkali metals and alkaline earth metals occur as free elements in nature?
4. What is an alloy?
5. What is milk of magnesia? How is it produced from magnesium oxide?
6. Summarize the chemical events involved in the formation of limestone caves.
7. Write and balance the equation for the reaction of HCl with $CaCO_3$ to produce CO_2, H_2O, Ca^{2+}, and Cl^-.
8. How has humankind exploited the various properties of metals in present-day applications?
9. What do stalagmites and stalactites have in common?
10. If H_2 will react with sodium according to the equation

$$2Na(s) + H_2(g) \rightarrow 2NaH(s)$$

would you predict Cs to react with H_2? Write an equation for the reaction if it occurs.

PART 1 REVIEW
ANSWERS
■ **Keyed to Objectives**

A **1.** The mobile delocalized "sea of electrons" is able to maintain the metallic bonds as charged metal cores move as the wire is stretched.

B **2.** hydrogen gas and an aqueous solution of the metal hydroxide

B **3.** They react readily with both oxygen and water to form compounds.

B **4.** An alloy is a mixture of two elements, at least one of which is a metal.

B **5.** Milk of magnesia is a suspension of magnesium hydroxide in water. It is made by reacting MgO with H_2O to form $Mg(OH)_2$.

$$MgO + H_2O \rightarrow Mg(OH)_2$$

B **6.** When a limestone cave forms, water containing dissolved carbon

PART
2 Transition Metals

You have learned that the elements found in Groups 3B to 2B on the periodic table are called the **transition metals,** or d-block transition elements. Transition metals are used in many items you are familiar with—including tools, wire, jewelry, and coins. They also have important industrial applications as catalysts (chemicals that speed up the rate of chemical reactions), as well as important biological functions.

A special subset of the transition metals consists of the lanthanide and actinide series. These metals are called the **inner transition elements,** or f-block transition elements. Although some actinides are naturally occurring, most have been artificially produced since 1940. This section will highlight properties, reactions, and uses of some common transition metals.

12.5 Properties of Transition Elements

Iron and titanium are the most abundant of the transition elements. Iron is the fourth most abundant element in Earth's crust (after oxygen, silicon, and aluminum). Other transition elements, particularly some in period six, are very rare. Technetium (element 43) and promethium (element 61) are not found in nature. These are the only two elements of the first 83 that have no stable isotopes.

Reactivity Transition metals are typically less reactive than their counterparts in Groups 1A and 2A. In most cases, transition elements occur in nature as oxide or sulfide ores. However, a few transition metals—including gold, silver, and platinum are often found in the native or uncombined state in nature. The limited reactivity of these metals, called *noble metals,* contributes to their widespread use in coins, jewelry, and high-tech instrumentation.

Melting point, boiling point, and hardness All of the transition elements, except for those in Group 2B, are hard solids with relatively high melting points and high boiling points. Of the Period 4 transition metals, zinc melts and boils at the lowest temperatures, and mercury in Period 6 is a liquid with a melting point of $-39°C$. The elements in Groups 5B and 6B exhibit the highest melting points, boiling points, and hardnesses of the transition metals. In fact, tungsten in Group 6B has the highest melting point $(3410°C)$ of any metallic element.

Beyond Group 6B, the melting point, boiling point, and hardness of the metals decreases. This can be explained by the number of electrons that atoms contribute to the electron sea. The larger the

Objectives

Part 2

C. *Summarize* properties, uses, and abundances of some transition metals.

D. *Use models* to explain properties of transition metals and alloys.

CONNECTING CONCEPTS

Processes of Science—Classifying The inner transition elements are classified as a subdivision of the transition elements due to their filling of the *f*-block orbitals.

Developing Skills

Students may apply these skills in their study of Part 2.

Forming a hypothesis: Have students form a hypothesis to explain the properties of alloys.

Forming models: Have students form models to explain some of the properties of transition metals.

Comparing/Contrasting: Have students compare properties, uses, and abundance of transition metals.

☰ FOCUS

Activate Prior Knowledge

Students know some of the important functions of elements essential to life. Our bodies need to be constantly provided with certain elements to keep us healthy. Students are often surprised to learn that if they eat iron-fortified cereal they are likely consuming elemental iron. This activity provides evidence that food-grade iron filings are present in such cereals. Empty the contents of a package of dry, uncooked, iron-fortified hot wheat cereal into a bowl. (An individual-sized package works nicely because it can be opened in front of the students to show that you have not tampered with the contents.) Place a magnet in a small plastic bag. Stir the dry cereal mix with the magnet. Examine the iron filings attached to the bag.

(continue on page T402)

dioxide will react with calcium carbonate to produce calcium hydrogen carbonate. The limestone is slowly dissolved to produce cracks and eventually a cavern.

B **7.** $2HCl + CaCO_3 \rightarrow CO_2 + H_2O + Ca^{2+} + 2Cl^-$

B **8.** Metals have been used to make tools and strong structures because of the strength of some metallic bonds. The "sea of electrons" in

metals makes them useful for applications requiring ductility, malleability, or conductivity of heat and electricity.

B **9.** Stalagmites and stalactites contain compounds of alkaline earth elements.

A **10.** Cesium would react with hydrogen in a similar reaction.
$2Cs + H_2 \rightarrow 2CsH$

(continue from page T401)

You can further simulate what occurs to this elemental iron in the stomach by dissolving it in 0.1*M* HCl.

⚠️ **CAUTION: Wear safety goggles and a lab apron. Protect students with a shield.** This solution can then be tested with $K_4Fe(CN)_6$ (to get the deep blue precipitate of "Prussian" or "Turnbull's" blue, $Fe_4[Fe(CN)_6]_3$). This is a characteristic test for dissolved iron. Iron used by the body is in the 2+ oxidation state and is involved in the heme group of the protein hemoglobin in the oxygen transport system of the blood.

For disposal, neutralize with 0.1*M* or less concentrated base and pour down the drain.

☰ TEACH

Science Background

Color

Many of our beautiful dyes, pigments, and gemstones are due to the highly colored compounds of the transition metals, which usually result from the availability of unoccupied *d* orbitals. The color results from the absorption of light energy, which in turn causes the valence electrons to jump into higher energy *d* orbitals. Because light of a specific wavelength is absorbed from the white light of the room, the solutions appear colored. The particular wavelength that is absorbed depends not only on the transition metal cation, but also on the surrounding anion and solvent species.

Videodisc Connections

20277 to 22326, side 2
Superconductivity (movie)

Superconductors

Superconductivity is defined as a total absence of internal resistance to electric current. The phenomenon was discovered almost by accident in 1911 by Heike Kammerlingh Onnes, who had been studying the electrical conductivity of metals at very low temperatures. To his great surprise, he found that when mercury was cooled to near absolute zero (0 K or −273°C), an electric current induced in the material would continue to flow indefinitely.

Researchers discovered a total of 25 elements and a great number of alloys and compounds that possess this property. Unfortunately all the materials they studied at the time were found to completely lose their superconducting properties at temperatures above 23 K. To cool materials to these very low temperatures, liquid helium, with a boiling point of 4 K or −269°C, is used. However, the high cost of liquid helium makes it too expensive to use for practical applications.

In recent years, scientists have developed new classes of ceramic materials that superconduct above liquid nitrogen temperatures. (Liquid nitrogen has a boiling point of 77 K or −196°C and costs less per liter than milk.) These relatively high-temperature superconductors are complex compounds containing oxygen

as well as metals such as yttrium, barium, and copper.

The applications of high-temperature superconductors are exciting. Superconducting electromagnets, requiring much less electricity than ordinary electromagnets, are already in use. Trains that can travel at speeds up to 500 km/hr while levitating above superconducting tracks have been developed in Japan. Scientists are also working to develop superconducting wires, which could carry electricity over great distances with virtually no loss of energy.

DO YOU KNOW?

Many of the transition metals are very dense. The densest are iridium (Ir) at 22.61 g/cm^3 and osmium (Os) at 22.57 g/cm^3.

number of electrons, the stronger the metallic bond. If you look at the electron configuration for some of the transition elements, you find that scandium has one unpaired *d* electron to contribute, titanium has two, vanadium has three, and chromium has five unpaired *d* electrons and one unpaired *s* electron. Since the elements in Group 6B can have up to six unpaired electrons, they have the highest melting points, boiling points, and hardnesses. After this group, the electrons begin to pair up. Toward the end of the group, electrons are completely filling the 3*d* and 4*s* orbitals, and the melting points, boiling points, and hardness of the metals decrease.

Color Many compounds and solutions of transition metal ions are intensely colored. It is not uncommon for one transition metal to exhibit a variety of colors in different compounds or solutions. For example, an aqueous solution of Ni^{2+} is green, but if aqueous ammonia is added, the color of the solution changes to indigo, as shown in Figure 12-8. The color change is caused by electrons in the *d* orbitals of the nickel ions interacting differently with the electrons of the surrounding species.

Figure 12-8 *The Ni^{2+} ion is characteristically green in water (left) and blue in ammonia (right).* ⚠ CAUTION *Nickel ions and compounds are suspected carcinogens.*

Ferromagnetism Most transition metals are weakly attracted to magnets because of their unpaired electrons. However, with the exception of iron, cobalt, and nickel, transition metals do not remain magnetic when the magnet is removed. When a sample of Fe, Co, or Ni is brought into a magnetic field, the atoms of these metals line up and reinforce each other like a bunch of little magnets forming a large magnet. These metals remain magnetic even after the magnetic field is removed. This property is called **ferromagnetism**. Figure 12-9 illustrates this phenomenon at the atomic level.

12.6 Some Uses of the Transition Metals

The various properties of transition metals have led to many uses of these metals and of their alloys and compounds. In this section you will learn about some specific transition metals and how they are being used today.

Copper You probably are familiar with copper because of its widespread use. A copper-nickel alloy is used in the nickel, while the penny is made up of a very thin layer of copper covering a zinc core. The principal use of copper is as an electrical conductor—the *electrical conductivity* of copper is second only to silver, which is far less abundant. Copper is preferred to iron for applications involving the transport of water. This is because water pipes made of copper resist both corrosion and the formation of hard water deposits better than pipes made of iron or steel.

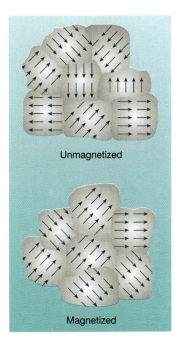

Unmagnetized

Magnetized

Figure 12-9 *When a ferromagnetic substance is magnetized, the magnetic moments of the atoms (represented by arrows) line up and reinforce each other.*

Science Background

Some Uses of the Transition Metals

Only seven metals were known to the ancients: gold, silver, mercury, copper, tin, iron, and lead. Some of these transition metals are found as native metals, while the others can be easily extracted from their ores using moderate heating.

Many different methods can be used to extract the transition metals from their ores, depending on the nature of the ore in which a particular metal is found. Transition metal ores typically fall into three categories:

- **Native (or Noble) metals**, such as gold and silver found in nature in elemental form, are often mixed with large amounts of rock and dirt.

- **oxides**, such as hematite, $Fe_2O_3 \cdot nH_2O$, which is the principal ore of iron

- **sulfides**, such as chalcocite, Cu_2S, and cinnabar, HgS—ores from which copper and mercury are extracted, respectively

It is important to note that many transition metals occur in more than one type of ore.

PART **2**
Section 12.6 continued

Science Background

Native Metals

Years ago, most gold was isolated by washing gold-bearing sand in skins or pans. When gold-bearing sand is swirled with water in a pan, the gold flakes or nuggets stay at the bottom because they are very dense (19.3 g/cm^3). The sand, which is less dense than gold, is swirled away with the wash water.

The gold content in most of the ores remaining today is too low for such mechanical separation to be profitable on a large scale. Instead, most gold is extracted through a cyanide treatment, which involves reacting the gold with sodium cyanide solution. The gold dissolves into the solution and the impurities, which do not react with the cyanide, remain behind. Elemental gold is obtained from the solution by a displacement reaction using zinc metal. Using this method, gold can be economically extracted from ore containing as little as 10 g of gold per ton of ore!

DO YOU KNOW?

The three metals in the copper subgroup (Cu, Ag, Au) have long been referred to as the coinage metals. In the United States this designation is a bit out of date, as our coins now contain primarily nickel, copper, and zinc.

CONNECTING CONCEPTS

Processes of Science—Predicting Alloys are predicted to be harder than pure metals because the atoms of the alloying metal fill unoccupied spaces in the crystalline structure.

Copper is relatively abundant in Earth's crust. It is often found in the elemental state in nature. Even when combined with another element, usually sulfur, it is easily separated through a process called roasting, which involves heating the ore in air.

Silver By far the greatest use of silver is in photographic film. Silver halides, the compounds formed when silver reacts with halogens such as bromine or chlorine, are sensitive to light. Photographic film has a thin coating of gelatin that contains microscopic crystals of a silver halide, such as silver bromide, $AgBr$. Color film contains color-producing dyes in addition to the silver compounds.

In the process of producing black-and-white images, silver ions, Ag^+, in the silver bromide crystals are changed to elemental silver, Ag, on exposure to light. The number of silver atoms formed depends on the amount of light that strikes a particular crystal. An invisible pattern, or latent image, of silver atoms is present in the exposed silver bromide crystals before developing. In the developing process, most of the silver compound in the exposed crystals is changed to silver metal creating a visible dark image where the film was exposed. To fix this image onto the film the unreacted silver bromide is removed by reacting it with an aqueous solution of sodium thiosulfate, commonly called "hypo." This process produces a negative, which is then washed, dried, and used to make a positive print.

Concept ✓ Check

What are some important modern uses of copper and silver?

Properties of alloys Many of the transition metals are used commercially in alloys. These alloys, including bronze, brass, and pewter, have been used for centuries. Alloys usually have different properties from those of the individual metals of which they are made. Their physical appearance may even be different, as when gold is alloyed with 10 percent or more palladium and looks almost silvery—thus accounting for its common name, white gold.

Alloys often exhibit increased strength and hardness. Stainless steel, for example, is iron alloyed with chromium and nickel. The strength of stainless steel makes it useful in tools. Iron hardened with manganese and small amounts of carbon forms spiegeleisen steel, which is so tough that it can be used in safes and armor plate. Gold used in jewelry is an alloy because pure gold is too soft. A 14-karat gold ring is 14/24 gold, with 10/24 being other elements.

Alloys usually have lower electrical and thermal conductivity than pure metals. This lower conductivity can be an advantage. For example, nichrome wire, made from an alloy of nickel, iron, and chromium, becomes red-hot when a current is passed through it and can be used as the heating element of hair dryers, toasters, and

DEMONSTRATION

Properties of Alloys

Use a low melting alloy (for example, Onion's fusible alloy, available from Flinn Scientific Company) to illustrate how an alloy can melt at a lower temperature than its constituent metals. Do this in a hood.

⚠ **CAUTION: Place a shield between the demonstration and students.**

Wear gloves, safety goggles, and a lab apron. Low melting alloys usually contain bismuth and/or antimony; the vapors of both are toxic. Do not allow a low melting alloy to touch your skin. Wash your hands after completing this demonstration.

space heaters. On the other hand, copper is valued for its high electrical conductivity. Copper used for electrical wiring must be extremely pure because even minute amounts of impurities can drastically lower its conductivity.

Alloys usually melt at a lower temperature than their constituent metals. A rather dramatic example is Wood's metal. This alloy is made of 50% Bi, 25% Pb, 13% Sn, and 12% Cd—each metal melting at temperatures above 200°C. Wood's metal has a melting point of only 70°C. Because of this low melting point, it is used in the fusible plugs that melt to set off automatic fire sprinkler systems.

Finally alloys may have chemical properties that are different from those of pure elements. For example, iron corrodes rapidly, but stainless steel resists corrosion. Pure silver tarnishes, but not when it is alloyed with gold.

Explaining properties of alloys Many properties of alloys can also be explained by considering the crystalline structures of metals. When a small amount of carbon is added to iron, the small carbon atoms occupy empty spaces among the iron atoms in the iron crystal, as shown in Figure 12-10. The carbon atoms make it more difficult for the iron atoms to slide past one another. Therefore, steel is harder than iron. Similarly, alloys have lower electrical and thermal conductivity because atoms of the impurity block the paths of electrons in the electron sea. Electrons are not able to move as freely through the metal crystal and cannot carry electrical or thermal energy as efficiently.

Alloys usually melt at a reduced temperature because they do not have perfect crystalline structure. Because the metal atoms are not in an orderly array, the metallic bonding is not as strong as it is in the pure metal. Therefore, less energy is needed to break down the crystal structure to melt the metal.

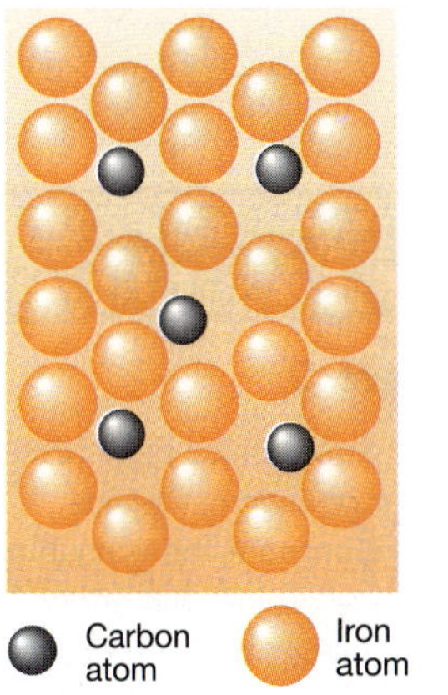

● Carbon atom   ● Iron atom

Figure 12-10 *Impurities, such as carbon, occupy the spaces between atoms, making an alloy stronger.*

PART 2 REVIEW

11. Explain why transition metals are harder and stronger than the alkali metals.

12. Describe the ways in which alloys differ from their component elements.

13. What qualities of copper make it important to electronics? To water transport?

14. Give at least two reasons why gold jewelry is not made of pure elemental gold.

15. Why would a small amount of arsenic impurity be a problem in copper that is to be used for electrical wiring?

16. What property of certain silver compounds makes them useful in photochromic lenses, which turn dark in the sun and become light again in the dark?

PART 2 REVIEW

ANSWERS

■ **Keyed to Objectives**

D 11. There are more electrons than in the alkali metal in the same period.

C 12. Appearance, hardness, strength, electrical and thermal conductivity, melting point, and chemical properties; in general, alloys can differ by both chemical and physical properties.

C 13. Cu has a high electrical conductivity and resists corrosion; it resists the formation of hard water deposits.

C 14. The cost; pure gold is too soft.

D 15. It lowers the conductivity of copper.

C 16. Light causes AgCl to change into Ag, which causes a darkening of the lens.

PART 2
Section 12.6 *continued*

Guided Practice

Review the Concept Check question on page 404 with students. Answers can be found in Appendix E on page 808.

Reteaching Idea

To help students distinguish between the different metals, their properties and uses, create a game "What Is It?" Divide students into teams. Each team will make up a number of questions based on the properties and uses of various elements. Another team will have to answer these questions. Devise a scoring system and award prizes to the winners. An example could be: "soft, silvery white, reacts violently with water, a deficiency of this necessary nutrient may lead to muscle weakness and heart abnormalities, commonly found in bananas." (potassium)

☰ CLOSE

Summing Up Main Ideas

Show students samples of the various transition metals, such as copper, silver, gold, zinc, and iron. Have students list the properties, uses, and relative abundance of these metals. Then ask students to make models that help explain different properties of these elements.

PART 2 REVIEW

Assign the Part Review questions.

Evaluating Skills

These skills are evaluated in the Part Review questions indicated. **Determining main ideas:** 11; **Describing:** 12, 13, 16; **Determining cause and effect:** 13, 14, 15, 16

PART **3**
Metalloids

Section 12.7

Developing Skills

Students may apply these skills in their study of Part 3.
Comparing/Contrasting: Have students compare and contrast the properties of metalloids and metals.
Forming models: Have students form models to explain the properties of metalloids.

≣ FOCUS

Activate Prior Knowledge

Some students may be familiar with microprocessor chips that are found in many pieces of electronic equipment. Display a microprocessor chip and discuss the reason that the chip is made from a metalloid such as silicon or gallium instead of a metal, such as copper, or a nonmetal, such as sulfur. Explain why the silicon used in this application initially must be very pure.

Objectives

Part 3

E. *Summarize* properties of common metalloids.

F. *Compare* the properties of metalloids with added impurities to the properties of metalloids without added impurities.

PART

3 Metalloids

In Chapter 11, you studied some of the general properties of metals and nonmetals. There are a few elements, however, that are difficult to classify as one or the other. These elements lie along the heavy zigzag line on the periodic table, which separates metals on the left from nonmetals on the right, as shown in Table 11-3 on pages 366–367. These elements are classified as metalloids or semimetals. Although aluminum falls along this line, it is usually considered a metal due to its metallic properties.

In this part of the chapter, you will look more closely at the properties and uses of three common metalloids: silicon, boron, and arsenic.

12.7 Properties and Uses of Metalloids

Metalloids exhibit properties of both metals and nonmetals. Although metalloids have nonmetallic crystalline structure and chemical behavior, they can exist in forms that have luster and conduct electricity—though not as well as metals. This latter property accounts for the term *semiconductors*.

Silicon The name silicon is derived from the Latin word for flint, a silicate mineral used by prehistoric people to make knives and other tools. Today you are surrounded by silicon-containing materials, including pottery, computer chips, and solar cells.

Pure silicon has some metallic properties, such as metallic luster, but it has a crystalline structure like that of diamond—a form of the nonmetal element carbon, shown in Figure 12-11. The electrons

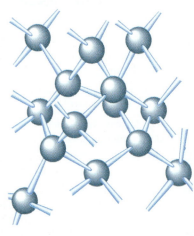

Figure 12-11 *Pure silicon crystals are composed of atoms of silicon covalently bonded to each other in a tetrahedral structure. Silicon crystals need to be grown with great care. They are very expensive to manufacture because of the purity required.*

in silicon are not free to move about in the crystal as they would be in true metals. As a result, a crystal of pure silicon is a poor conductor of electricity at low temperatures, although it can carry a moderate current at elevated temperatures.

The second most abundant element in Earth's crust, silicon is the most common metalloid. More than 90 percent of the rocks, minerals, and soils found in Earth's crust are composed chiefly of silicates. Figure 12-12 shows some silicate minerals, such as garnet, emerald, and asbestos, which are complex silicon-oxygen compounds.

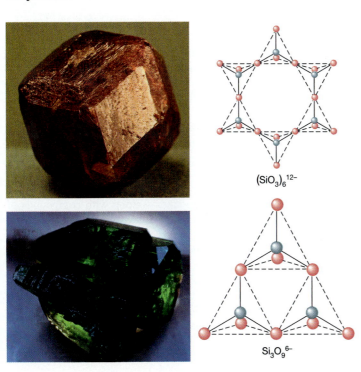

$(SiO_3)_6{}^{12-}$

$Si_3O_9{}^{6-}$

Figure 12-12 *Garnet and emerald are complex silicon-oxygen compounds.*

One common, simple silicon-containing compound is silicon dioxide, or silica, SiO_2. The mineral quartz is a pure crystalline form of silica. Both sand and sandstone are composed of small particles of quartz that form when larger quartz crystals are broken down due to weathering. When quartz melts at 1610°C, it gives a viscous liquid that cools to form silica glass. When silica is reacted with coke—a form of carbon—at 3000°C, elemental silicon—a gray, metallic-looking solid—is produced.

Boron Although boron is a nonconductor and resistant to heat, it has a characteristic metallic luster. Boron is very hard, partly because of the nonmetallic bonding that occurs among its atoms. Boron has been used to make filaments to reinforce plastic and metal parts. One of the compounds of boron, boron carbide, B_4C,

DO YOU KNOW?

Arsenic in the body tends to concentrate in the hair, which may show ten times as high an arsenic level as the body fluids. In modern forensic laboratories, analysis of hair samples can help to confirm or disprove arsenic poisoning. An analysis of a sample of Napoleon's hair suggests that he may have been a victim of arsenic poisoning. In 1991, the remains of President Zachary Taylor were exhumed and tested for arsenic. The results indicated he did not die of arsenic poisoning.

☰ **T E A C H**

Science Background

Silicon

Silicon and other metalloids have played a critical role in the development of computers and other aspects of the electronics industry. However, silicon glass and ceramic materials have also resulted in a materials revolution. A ceramic is composed of small plate-like crystals of aluminosilicate ion, which are cemented in silica glass, SiO_2. The Romans made a ceramic-glass combination called opal glass by adding antimony oxide to glass slurries. Today, LiO_2, Al_2O_3, TiO_2, and TiO are added to silica to form modern ceramic glass cookware. Ceramics are hard, porous, heat resistant, and generally unreactive. These characteristics make them useful in magnets, rocket nose cones, nuclear fuel rods, spark plugs, engine parts, windows in integrated circuits, and even human bone replacements.

Science Background

Metalloids as Semiconductors

To understand the conductivity differences in metal crystals (high conductivity), insulators (no conductivity), and semiconductors (some conductivity), the band theory is usually offered as an explanation. This theory is based on the molecular orbital theory. In a semiconductor, there are filled and empty molecular orbitals that have different energy levels. The empty orbitals form the conduction band and the filled orbitals form the valence band. The bands are separated by a moderately small energy gap, the forbidden zone. Some electrons in the valence band are able to cross the forbidden zone and enter the conduction band when the semiconductor material is heated. This is because the forbidden zone is sufficiently narrow to allow the electrons to be promoted. Semiconductors increase in conductivity when heated. The presence of impurities in the semiconductor materials allows electrons to cross the forbidden zone more easily.

(continued on page T409)

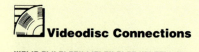

Videodisc Connections

41961 to 48498, side 4
Boron (movie)

36037 to 41960, side 4
Integrated circuits (movie)

Figure 12-13 *Boron and boron carbide form very hard crystals. Boron nitride can be treated with high pressure to form similar crystals.*

is extraordinarily hard and has a low density (2.5 g/cm^3), and a high melting point (2250°C). These properties make it an ideal material for use in bulletproof armor.

The mineral borax is a common source of boron. The chemical formula for borax is $Na_2B_4O_7 \cdot 1OH_2O$, and its systematic name is sodium tetraborate decahydrate. Borax is used in soaps and detergents. Large borax deposits are located in California and New Mexico. Much of the borax mined is converted into boric acid, H_3BO_3, which is used as a preservative for wood and leather, and in pottery enamels and glazes. Pure boric acid is a solid, making boric acid powder useful as roach poison.

Arsenic   Arsenic is obtained from various ores, such as the sulfides realgar, As_4S_4, and orpiment, As_2S_3. Elemental arsenic, which exists as As_4 molecules, is obtained by roasting orpiment in air and then reacting the oxide with coke (a form of elemental carbon).

Most elemental arsenic is used to create alloys with lead. Many years ago it was found that adding arsenic to lead used in lead shot would make the shot harder and more nearly spherical. Today an increasing amount of arsenic is used to make gallium arsenide semiconductors.

The toxicity of arsenic compounds—along with compounds of heavy metals, such as lead, mercury, and cadmium—results from their extraordinary affinity for sulfur. Sulfur is a part of nearly all enzymes, the essential catalysts for chemical reactions in cells. Arsenic and many heavy metals react with the sulfur in enzymes, dramatically hindering the functioning of the cells. As a result, cellular reactions can no longer take place normally, and the affected organism dies. Early weed killers and insecticides took advantage of the poisonous nature of arsenic compounds.

Concept ✔ Check

Explain why silicon, boron, and arsenic do not conduct electricity as well as true metals do.

12.8 Metalloids as Semiconductors

Computers have dramatically changed people's way of life. Uncountable bits of information are being processed and exchanged every day through this electronic medium. Silicon and other semiconducting elements have played a critical role in the development of the computer and are the basic elements of the electronics industry. At the heart of every computer are microchips, or integrated circuits, made mostly of silicon. Figure 12-14 shows how small a silicon chip is.

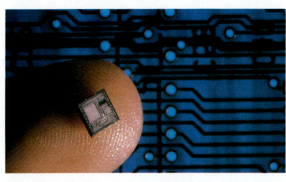

Figure 12-14 A single integrated circuit chip, smaller than a penny, is made mostly of silicon.

(continued from page T408)
There are several techniques used today to dope a semiconductor crystal. In a process called diffusion, the semiconductor base material is heated to a temperature below its melting point. In an atmosphere high in dopant concentration, the dopant diffuses into the semiconductor to a depth of only several micrometers. A second process, called ion implantation, involves the bombarding of the semiconductor material with a high-energy beam of dopant ions. The advantage of this technique is that the semiconductor material need not be heated to achieve the proper dopant concentration.

The process of making integrated circuits would make an excellent research project.

Doping metalloids Pure silicon is a poor conductor of electricity. However, when certain impurities such as arsenic, boron, or gallium are added, the conductivity increases dramatically. The semiconductor devices used in transistors and solar cells contain as few as 1 atom of impurity per 1,000,000 atoms of Si. Crystals of silicon containing added impurities are called **doped crystals.**

Impurities affect the conductivity of silicon in one of two ways. In the case of arsenic doping, the arsenic provides mobile electrons to the crystal. An arsenic atom, while approximately the same size as a silicon atom, has five valence electrons ($4s^2 4p^3$), whereas silicon has only four ($3s^2 3p^2$). When an arsenic atom replaces a silicon atom in the crystal, there is an extra electron, as shown in Figure 12-15. This extra electron is free to move through the crystal and will flow in the direction dictated by an electrical current. Semiconductors like this one, containing impurities that produce mobile electrons, are called **n-type semiconductors.**

Direction of electric field

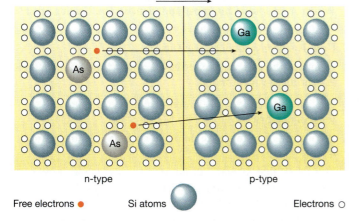

n-type   p-type

Free electrons ●   Si atoms 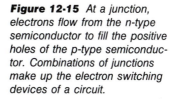   Electrons ○

Figure 12-15 At a junction, electrons flow from the n-type semiconductor to fill the positive holes of the p-type semiconductor. Combinations of junctions make up the electron switching devices of a circuit.

Concept ✔ Check

Explain what is meant by doping a silicon crystal with arsenic. How does doping affect the conductivity of silicon?

PART **3**
Section 12.8 continued

Guided Practice

Review the Concept Check questions on pages 408 and 409 with students. Answers can be found in Appendix E on page 808.

Reteaching Idea

To help students understand the differences in the conductivity of substances, have students review Figures 12–1, 12–2, (page 394), and 12–15, (page 409). They should compare the *n*-type semiconductor, which has an extra electron to move through the crystal, with the *p*-type semiconductors, which have a positive hole that can be filled by an electron, to the "sea of electrons," which is a description of the delocalized valence electrons that move freely among the positively charged cores of the metal atoms that characterizes metallic bonding.

≡CLOSE

Summing Up Main Ideas

Have students summarize the important properties of common metalloids and explain why pure metalloids sometimes have impurities added to them.

PART 3 REVIEW

Assign the Part Review questions.

Evaluating Skills

These skills are evaluated in the Part Review questions indicated. **Comparing/Contrasting:** 17, 20, 21, 23, 24; **Determining main ideas:** 18; **Determining cause and effect:** 19, 24; **Observing:** 22

DO YOU KNOW?

It is believed that the story of the Golden Fleece in Greek mythology was inspired by the ancient practice of washing gold-bearing sand over sheepskin. The gold would remain on the skins after the other impurities were washed out.

Boxed numbers indicate questions that involve skills in interpretation, application, and analysis.

Silicon can also be doped with impurities that result in a deficiency of electrons. Boron and gallium each have three valence electrons. Their outer electron configurations are $(3s^2 3p^1)$ and $(4s^2 4p^1)$, respectively. These three electrons can be shared with three neighboring silicon atoms, but there is no fourth valence electron to share with the fourth neighboring silicon atom.

The electron deficiency creates what is referred to as a *positive hole* in the crystal. When an electrical voltage is applied across the material, an electron will move from one atom to fill the hole on another atom. By doing so, it creates an electron deficiency around the atom it leaves. Another electron will leave its current position to move into that hole, and so on. Semiconductors of this type are called **p-type semiconductors.**

Placing a *p*-type semiconductor and an *n*-type semiconductor in contact will produce a **junction** through which current flows in only one direction. Because of the excess of electrons in the *n*-type semiconductor and the deficiency of electrons in the *p*-type semiconductor, current will tend to flow across the junction from the *n*-type to the *p*-type, but not the other way. Figure 12-15 illustrates the flow of electrons across such a junction.

Within the past few years, researchers have developed integrated circuits based on gallium arsenide, GaAs, and have achieved operating speeds five times faster than those of the fastest silicon chip. They also operate over a wider temperature range than that of silicon chips. However, the toxicity of gallium arsenide makes it difficult to work with.

PART 3 REVIEW

17. Which metalloid is the most abundant in the Earth's crust?

18. What is meant by doping?

19. How is silicon produced from its ore?

20. Compare the general properties of a metalloid with the general properties of a metal.

21. Explain the difference between *n*-type and *p*-type semiconductors.

22. Where can the metalloid elements be found on the periodic table?

23. You know that arsenic can be used to produce an *n*-type semiconductor. What other element could you use to produce an *n*-type semiconductor?

24. If you have a sample of ultrapure copper and a sample of ultrapure silicon and you dope each with a small amount of arsenic, how is the conductivity of each sample affected? Why are the two samples affected differently by the impurity?

PART 3 REVIEW

ANSWERS

■ **Keyed to Objectives**

E **17.** Si

F **18.** Doping is the addition of impurities to metalloids to increase conductivity.

E **19.** It is heated with coke to 3000°C.

E **20.** Metalloids have nonmetallic crystalline structure and chemical behavior; however, they can have luster and conduct electricity.

F **21.** An *n*-type semiconductor results when an element is replaced with an element having more valence electrons such as As in Si. A *p*-type semiconductor occurs when an element is replaced with an element having fewer valence electrons, such as B in Si.

PART 4 Nonmetals

Unlike the silvery-gray color that is typical of metals and metalloids, nonmetals have no one common color; in fact, they have vastly different colors. Similar variety is found in their physical states at normal conditions, their reactivity, their abundance, and their number of allotropic forms. While the number of nonmetals is small by comparison to the number of metals, the variety of nonmetals is great. Among the nonmetals are elements including H, C, N, P, O and S that play a vital role in maintaining life.

12.9 Carbon

Carbon is the only nonmetal in Group 4A. It is reasonably abundant on the planet Earth and is widely distributed. For example, large amounts of calcium carbonate, $CaCO_3$, are found in Earth's crust, and carbon-containing molecules are found in all plant and animal life. Carbon-containing materials, including diamonds, have even been discovered in meteorites.

Diamond Elemental carbon exists in two common yet different crystalline allotropes, diamond and graphite, which are shown in Figure 12-16. An **allotrope** is one of two or more forms of an element that exist in the same physical state but have different structures and properties. Both of these allotropes melt at around 3500°C. However, as you can see from Figure 12-16, the arrangement of carbon atoms within the crystals is quite different. The carbon atoms in diamond are arranged in a three-dimensional network, which accounts for its extraordinary hardness, relative in-

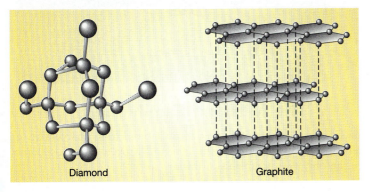

Diamond

Graphite

Figure 12-16 *The different submicroscopic structures of carbon in diamond and graphite account for the observable differences in the properties of the two allotropes.*

E **22.** Metalloids are found along the heavy zigzag line on the periodic table, which separates metals from nonmetals.

F **23.** P or Sb

F **24.** The conductivity of Cu is decreased and the conductivity of Si is increased. The conductivity of metals is decreased when impurities are added and the conductivity of Si is increased if As is added.

Objectives

Part 4

G. *Describe* properties and uses of some common nonmetals.

H. *Compare and contrast* the abundance and sources of some common nonmetals.

PROBLEM-SOLVING STRATEGY

By looking at diagrams, you can get a better understanding of the differences between allotropes of carbon at the submicroscopic level. (See Strategy, page 216.)

Videodisc Connections

35230 to 36036, side 4
Industrial diamonds (movie)

Developing Skills

Students may apply these skills in their study of Part 4.
Predicting: Have students predict the properties of nonmetals within a group or family.
Comparing/Contrasting: Have students examine the abundance and sources of some common nonmetals.
Forming models: Have students form models to explain the properties of nonmetals.

FOCUS

Activate Prior Knowledge

Students have previously been introduced to nitrogen fixation in their study of biology. Bring in a legume plant with its root nodules attached. Discuss the function of the nodule in the plant. (Bacteria in the nodules convert nitrogen in the air to usable nitrogen compounds.) Have students use their knowledge of synthesis reactions to write the equation for the commercial process of nitrogen fixation, which combines nitrogen gas and hydrogen gas under high pressure and temperature.
$[N_2(g) + 3H_2(g) \rightleftharpoons 2NH_3(g)]$

TEACH

Science Background

Carbon

Diamonds were first artificially made in 1954 by heating graphite to between 2000 and 2500°C at pressures ranging from 100 000 to 150 000 atmospheres. Under these conditions, the conversion takes only a few minutes. Once formed, the temperature and pressure are rapidly reduced, causing the carbon atoms to remain trapped in the diamond structure.

(continued on page T412)

PART **4**
Section 12.10

(continued from page T411)

There are three common non-crystalline forms of carbon. One is carbon black, which is commonly called soot. It is produced by the incomplete combustion of organic compounds. Charcoal is made by heating wood in the absence of air. Coke is an impure form of carbon made by heating coal in the absence of air. Enormous quantities of coke are consumed by the steel industry.

Teaching Strategy

Graphite

Tell students that diamond and graphite are both pure crystalline forms of carbon. Have students examine the lead of their pencils. It is made of graphite, with a clay binder to make it hard. Graphite itself is very soft. If pure graphite is available, show this to students.

The word *graphite* comes from the Greek word meaning "to write." If a diamond is available, show how it will scratch a piece of glass, whereas graphite will not. Explain to students that the bonding of the carbon atoms in the graphite and diamond account for these differences.

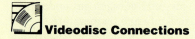

Videodisc Connections

21398-21400, side 4
Allotropes of carbon
(3-frame seq.)

DO YOU KNOW?

Molecules of crystalline carbon having the formulas C_{60} and C_{70} have recently been discovered. These molecules are called fullerenes because of their structural resemblance to geodesic domes designed by R. Buckminster Fuller. They are described in the Research and Technology feature on page 598.

Figure 12-17 *The space shuttle uses high-strength materials made of graphite and plastic in its payload baydoors.*

ertness, and extremely high thermal conductivity. In fact, diamond has the highest thermal conductivity of any known substance (about five times that of copper). For this reason, diamond-tipped tools do not overheat when used for drilling and cutting. Although the thermal conductivity is high, diamond is a very poor conductor of electricity. About 6 tons of diamonds are mined annually, most of which are used in industrial cutting and abrasion tools.

Graphite The graphite form of carbon is made up of weakly attracted sheets of carbon atoms that can easily slide past one another. This structure makes graphite soft, easily rubbed off, and useful as a lubricant. Graphite is contained in pencil lead. When you write, thin layers of graphite rub off onto the paper. Graphite is a good conductor of electricity and is commonly used as an electrode in chemical cells, including the common dry cell battery.

Because of its low cost and high melting point, graphite can be used as a liner for electric furnaces and containers that hold molten metals. At high pressures and temperatures (about 70 000 atm and 1800°C), diamonds can be synthesized from graphite for industrial use. Recently scientists have discovered that combining graphite with certain plastics creates special high-strength materials. These materials are currently used in the payload bay doors of the space shuttle and the cockpit of race cars. They are also used in tennis rackets and golf clubs.

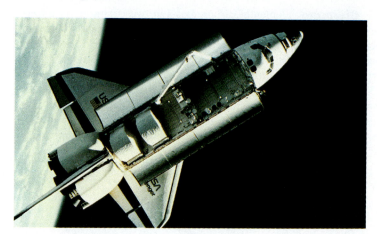

12.10 The Nitrogen Family

The Group 5A elements show a distinct trend from nonmetallic to metallic as you move down the family. Nitrogen and phosphorus are the only two nonmetals in this group.

Nitrogen Nitrogen exists in nature as a colorless, odorless gas consisting of N_2 molecules. Nitrogen gas accounts for 78.08 percent of Earth's atmosphere by volume.

Because nitrogen gas is relatively unreactive at normal temperatures, it can be used to protect certain reactive substances, just as kerosene is used to protect alkali metals. The electronics industry uses nitrogen as a protective atmosphere, or blanket, when making materials that would be adversely affected by the presence of oxygen or moisture. Certain foods are packaged in nitrogen, which excludes oxygen that might allow the food to spoil.

Nitrogen cycle Nitrogen compounds are important constituents of all living organisms. It has been known for more than a century that nitrogen is an essential component of all proteins, including enzymes. However, N_2 molecules in the air cannot be used directly by most organisms. Nitrogen-fixing bacteria are among the few organisms able to convert atmospheric nitrogen into nitrogen compounds. Many of these bacteria live in nodules on the roots of leguminous plants, such as peas, beans, and clover.

To complete the cycle, denitrifying bacteria convert nitrogen compounds into N_2 gas, a process that supplies energy to the bacteria. Figure 12-18 shows the steps in the nitrogen cycle, the circulation of nitrogen in the biosphere (the portion of Earth where life is found).

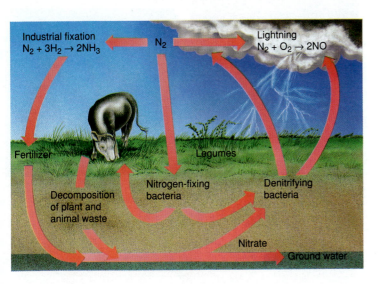

Commercial use of nitrogen Nitrogen and its compounds play a key role in the economy. Of the top 14 chemicals produced in the United States annually, five contain nitrogen. Today most nitrogen compounds are made from ammonia, which is synthesized by reacting nitrogen with hydrogen under special conditions in the presence of a catalyst. This important industrial process is called the Haber process.

$$N_2 + 3H_2 \rightarrow 2NH_3$$

DO YOU KNOW?

The largest diamond ever found weighed 3106 karats (0.61 kg). It was found in 1905 in the Premier Mine (now part of South Africa), and was cut into 9 large gems and 96 smaller gems.

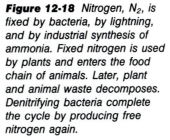

Figure 12-18 Nitrogen, N_2, is fixed by bacteria, by lightning, and by industrial synthesis of ammonia. Fixed nitrogen is used by plants and enters the food chain of animals. Later, plant and animal waste decomposes. Denitrifying bacteria complete the cycle by producing free nitrogen again.

Science Background

Nitrogen Cycle

Lightning causes nitrogen gas in the air to react with oxygen gas to form a variety of nitrogen oxides. These nitrogen oxides react further in the atmosphere to produce nitrates that dissolve in rain droplets and fall to the soil. Plants, and ultimately animals, rely on this fixed nitrogen to supply the nitrogen needed for protein production. Additional fixed nitrogen is added to the soil in the form of fertilizers, such as ammonium nitrate.

Science Background

Phosphorus

Black phosphorus is a third but much less common allotrope of phosphorus. It is obtained by heating white phosphorus under elevated pressure. Black phosphorus is stable in air at almost any temperature and has a texture and electrical conductivity similar to graphite.

Phosphorus The structures of the two most common allotropes of phosphorus are shown in Figure 12–19. White phosphorus, P_4, is the more reactive of the two forms. It is a soft, waxy substance with a low melting point (44°C) and boiling point (280°C). It is highly reactive and ignites in air at 30°C. Since it neither reacts with nor dissolves in water, it is usually stored underwater. White phosphorus is extremely toxic, and all contact with it should be avoided. As little as 0.01 g taken internally can be fatal, and contact with the skin produces painful burns.

Red phosphorus has a much higher melting point than white phosphorus. Its low volatility makes it less toxic than white phosphorus. Red phosphorus is insoluble in most common solvents and much less reactive than white phosphorus. In fact, it must be heated to 250°C before it will burn in air. These properties of the red allotrope result from its network structure, which is shown in Figure 12-19. Red phosphorus is made by heating white phosphorus to about 300°C in the absence of O_2 at atmospheric pressure. Red phosphorus is used in making matches—it is placed on the striking surface of the matchbox.

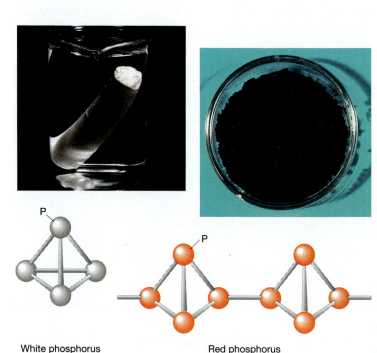

Figure 12-19 *The common allotropes of phosphorus are shown. White phosphorus has the formula P₄. Red phosphorus has a network structure, shown here in simplified form.*

White phosphorus　　　　Red phosphorus

Sources of phosphorus Over 200 different minerals are known to contain the phosphate ion, PO_4^{3-}, or its derivatives. These minerals are classified as orthophosphates. By far the largest commercial source of elemental phosphorus is the family of minerals called apatites, whose general formula is $3Ca_3(PO_4)_2 \cdot CaX_2$, in which X is commonly F^-, Cl^-, or OH^-. The impure form of apatite is called phosphate rock. Figure 12-20 shows many of the uses of phosphate-containing rock. Thousands of tons of elemental phosphorus, usually in the form of solid phosphorus, P_4, is produced each year by the reaction of apatite with coke. Eighty to ninety percent of this elemental phosphorus is used to make phosphoric acid. Of the remainder, much is converted to phosphorus sulfides. The heads of strike-anywhere matches contain the sulfide, P_4S_3.

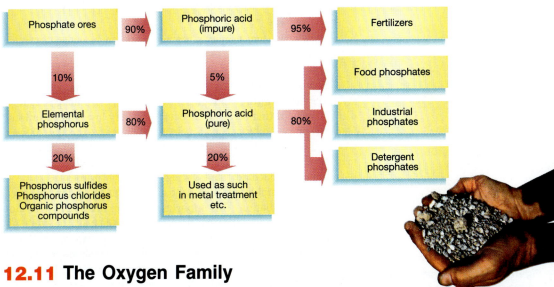

12.11 The Oxygen Family

The Group 6A elements show the same nonmetal-to-metal trend as Groups 4A and 5A. Oxygen and sulfur are nonmetals. Selenium and tellurium are predominantly nonmetallic, but they have semiconducting allotropes and are therefore classified as metalloids. Polonium is metallic.

Oxygen Oxygen is the most abundant element on Earth, making up 48 percent by mass of the crust, atmosphere, and surface water. However, many scientists think that elemental oxygen, O_2, did not appear in Earth's atmosphere until about two billion years ago, when the earliest green plants began to produce it via photosynthesis. The equation for the photosynthetic reaction is

$$CO_2(g) + H_2O(l) + \text{light energy} \rightarrow O_2(g) + \text{carbohydrates}$$

Oxygen gas, O_2, is a colorless, odorless gas at room temperature. Liquid and solid oxygen are pale blue. Oxygen forms compounds with almost every other element. This reactivity makes oxygen useful in a number of ways. Industrial applications of oxygen include the removal of impurities during the processing of iron and other metals. It is used medically in the treatment of patients who cannot get enough oxygen from breathing air normally. (Pure oxygen is obtained commercially by fractional distillation of liquid air).

Figure 12-20 *The table shows uses of phosphate-containing rock. Phosphate pebbles, shown in the hand, are used in the preparation of phosphoric acid.*

PART **4**

Section 12.11 continued

Science Background

Sulfur

Large deposits of the free element sulfur also occur in salt domes, which exist along the shore of the Gulf of Mexico. These deposits yield about 10 million tons of sulfur per year. Scientists think that the sulfur in these deposits was formed by anaerobic bacteria that fed on sedimentary sulfate deposits such as gypsum.

Oxygen is vital to life due to the roles it has in cellular functions, of which cellular respiration is the most important. During cellular respiration, cells release the energy stored in glucose molecules, $C_6H_{12}O_6$, by breaking the molecules down into water and carbon dioxide. This process is complex and involves many steps but can be summarized by this net equation.

$$C_6H_{12}O_6(s) + 6O_2(g) \rightarrow 6CO_2(g) + 6H_2O(l) + energy$$

Concept ✔ Check

How are the two previous reactions related to each other?

Ozone Ozone, O_3, is the less common allotrope of oxygen. At room temperature and pressure, ozone is a blue gas with a distinctive odor that makes it detectable at very low concentrations. Ozone is prepared by passing an electrical discharge through oxygen gas, O_2, or by irradiating oxygen gas with ultraviolet light. You may have noticed the odor of ozone near sparking electric motors, by photocopy machines, and during electrical storms.

Ozone is unstable and decomposes to form O_2 in the presence of ultraviolet radiation. This important reaction occurs in the stratosphere, where ozone absorbs, or filters out, much of the sun's ultraviolet radiation before this harmful radiation can reach Earth. Ozone is much more reactive than oxygen gas, which makes it more hazardous to handle. As a result, it is usually generated where it will be used. Its primary industrial application is in making oxygen-containing compounds.

Because of its ability to destroy bacteria, ozone can also be used to purify drinking water. However, ozone is more expensive than chlorine, and more difficult to handle. It also decomposes more rapidly and offers little or no protection against the bacteria that enter the water supply after treatment.

Oxygen molecule

Ozone molecule

Figure 12-21 *The structures of oxygen* (top) *and ozone* (bottom).

Sulfur Sulfur is about twice as abundant as carbon in the crust of Earth. In the solid state, sulfur can have more than 20 different allotropic forms due to the large number of ways sulfur atoms can form chains and rings. Sulfur compounds are present in coal, petroleum, and natural gas. Sulfur is also present in sulfur containing minerals, especially iron pyrites, FeS_2, commonly known as fool's gold, and gypsum, $CaSO_4 \cdot 2H_2O$, as seen in Figure 12-22. Free sulfur is found in some hot springs, geysers, and volcanic areas, including those in the western United States.

Two allotropes of sulfur At room temperature, the most stable allotrope of sulfur is the yellow, crystalline form called **rhombic** sulfur. Rhombic sulfur contains crown-shaped rings of eight sulfur atoms forming an S_8 molecule, as shown in Figure 12-23.

DO YOU KNOW?

Io, one of the moons of Jupiter, appears yellow because its surface is covered by deposits of sulfur from volcanic activity.

PART 4
Section 12.11 continued

Videodisc Connections

21373-21380, side 4
Processing sulfur (8-frame seq.)

When rhombic sulfur is heated above 96°C, it becomes opaque and the crystals expand into a second allotropic form called **monoclinic** sulfur. The molecular units of monoclinic sulfur are also crown-shaped S_8 rings, but these rings are packed together in a different way from those in the rhombic sulfur crystals. The monoclinic allotrope is stable from 96°C to the melting point, which occurs at 119°C. The S_8 ring structure is maintained in the thin yellow liquid that can exist from 119° to about 150°C. Above that temperature, the sulfur begins to thicken and turn reddish brown. By 200°C, the liquid is so thick that it will hardly pour.

The explanation for this behavior lies at the molecular level. Above 150°C, the S_8 rings break apart and form chains of sulfur atoms. These chains join together end to end to form longer chains, such as the one illustrated.

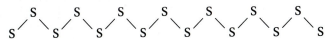

These chains range in length from eight to millions of atoms. They become entangled, causing the liquid to thicken. Above 250°C, the liquid sulfur begins to flow more easily because the thermal energy is enough to break the chains. At the boiling point, 445°C, liquid sulfur pours freely. The vapor that is formed contains a mixture of S_8, S_6, S_4, and S_2 molecules. Most allotropes of sulfur will slowly revert back to the stable rhombic form when kept at room temperature.

Sulfuric acid About 88 percent of the elemental sulfur produced is converted to sulfuric acid, the compound produced in greatest quantity by the chemical industry. Figure 12-24 on the next page shows many of the uses of sulfuric acid.

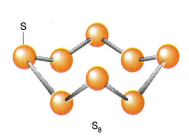

Figure 12-23 *The S_8 molecule of rhombic sulfur consists of a ring of eight atoms.*

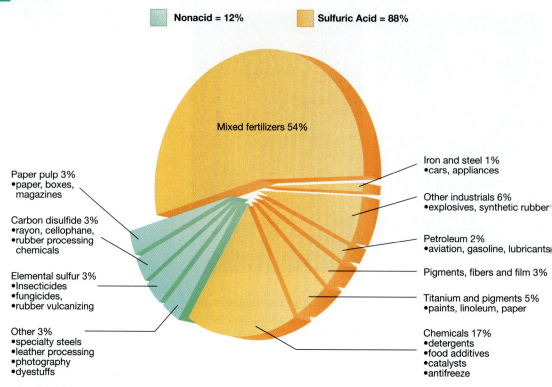

Nonacid = 12%   Sulfuric Acid = 88%

Mixed fertilizers 54%

Paper pulp 3%
•paper, boxes,
 magazines

Carbon disulfide 3%
•rayon, cellophane,
•rubber processing
 chemicals

Elemental sulfur 3%
•Insecticides
•fungicides,
•rubber vulcanizing

Other 3%
•specialty steels
•leather processing
•photography
•dyestuffs

Iron and steel 1%
•cars, appliances

Other industrials 6%
•explosives, synthetic rubber

Petroleum 2%
•aviation, gasoline, lubricants

Pigments, fibers and film 3%

Titanium and pigments 5%
•paints, linoleum, paper

Chemicals 17%
•detergents
•food additives
•catalysts
•antifreeze

Figure 12-24 *Modern life depends on sulfuric acid. About 88% of elemental sulfur produced each year is converted to sulfuric acid.*

Teaching Strategy

Halogen Reactivity

Point out to students the usefulness of the reactivity series of the halogens, which was studied in Chapter 3. This provides useful information about the chemistry of this family. The halogen at the top of the series can be used to replace a halogen below it in the series. Fluorine cannot be replaced because it is the most active member of the family. Fluorine reacts with most alloys. Fluorine will even react with xenon and krypton, which were once thought to be completely inert, to form compounds such as KrF_2, XeF_2, and XeF_4. Only He, Ne, and Ar are not known to react with fluorine. HF (hydrofluoric acid) is used to etch glass.

12.12 The Halogen Family

The members of the halogen family in Group 7A are reactive, nonmetallic elements that exist as diatomic molecules at normal conditions. Each has a distinctive color and odor and is poisonous. Under ordinary conditions, fluorine is a pale yellow gas and chlorine is a greenish-yellow gas. Bromine is a volatile, reddish-brown liquid with a reddish-brown vapor. Iodine is a shiny, black solid that sublimes readily to produce a violet vapor. Astatine is radioactive and has no stable isotopes.

Halogen reactivity   Because of their reactivity, the halogens are not found as free elements in nature. They occur primarily as halide salts—such as sodium chloride, NaCl, or cesium fluoride, CsF. The halogens react with almost all the other elements and with many compounds, including water. Fluorine reacts very vigorously with water. The reaction displaces the oxygen from the water molecule, as shown in the equation.

$$2F_2(g) + 2H_2O(l) \rightarrow 4HF(aq) + O_2(g)$$

Chlorine and bromine are far less reactive with water; they do not release oxygen but instead form other compounds. Iodine is the least reactive of the halogens and has no reaction with water.

Fluorine Because of its extreme reactivity, fluorine cannot be produced by reacting its minerals with other chemicals. The reason for this is that no other elements are reactive enough to displace fluorine from its compounds. Instead, fluorine is commercially prepared by running electricity through a mixture of potassium fluoride, KF, and hydrogen fluoride, HF. This process also produces hydrogen gas. The apparatus used to produce fluorine must be carefully set up to prevent contact between the fluorine and the hydrogen because the two react violently to produce hydrogen fluoride.

The principal commercial use of elemental fluorine is in the separation of uranium-235 from the more abundant isotope, uranium-238 in uranium ore. The separated uranium-235 is then made into uranium rods for nuclear fuel. In the separation process uranium hexafluoride, UF_6, containing both U-235 and U-238 is vaporized and passed through a series of porous barriers, as shown in Figure 12-25. Because uranium-235 is lighter than uranium-238, molecules of UF_6 containing U-235 pass through the barriers more rapidly and become concentrated.

Chlorine Chlorine is also prepared through an electrolysis process. Most chlorine is made by the electrolysis of aqueous solutions of sodium chloride. The equation for the reaction is

$$2NaCl(aq) + 2H_2O(l) \rightarrow Cl_2(g) + H_2(g) + 2NaOH(aq)$$

Chlorine is a major industrial chemical; about ten million tons of it is produced annually in the United States. Much of the chlorine is used to make chlorinated hydrocarbons (compounds containing chlorine, carbon, and hydrogen). These compounds are used as solvents, coolants, pesticides, and in compounds for many other applications. Additionally, large amounts of chlorine are used in water purification and as a bleach in the paper and textile industries.

Bromine and iodine Bromine and iodine are produced in much smaller quantities than chlorine. About 1000 metric tons of iodine and 2000 metric tons of bromine are produced annually in the United States from natural brines. The deep brine wells in Arkansas are the source of most bromide brines, and similar wells in Michigan are the source of iodide brines.

Halogens are used industrially, mainly as compounds, although chemists use elemental bromine and iodine for a variety of reactions. Examples of useful compounds include silver bromide and silver iodide (for photographic film), methyl bromide (a pesticide), and potassium iodide (a food additive).

Concept ✔ **Check**

Summarize the principal uses of fluorine, chlorine, bromine, and iodine.

CONNECTING CONCEPTS

Processes of Science—Classifying The similar properties of the elements in the Group 7A account for their inclusion in the halogen family.

Uranium-238   Uranium-235

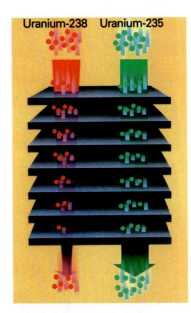

Figure 12-25 *Vaporized uranium hexafluoride is forced through porous barriers. Because molecules containing uranium-235 are lighter, they move through the barriers more easily and quickly than molecules containing uranium-238.*

Science Background

The Halogen Family

When discussing the chemistry of the halogen family, details of astatine chemistry are often omitted because very little is known about it. Astatine is thought to be the rarest of all of the naturally occurring elements, with perhaps only 25 mg of the element existing on the surface of Earth at any given time.

PART **4**
Section 12.13

Science Background

Uses of Noble Gases

In the United States, about 250 000 tons of argon are recovered annually by fractional distillation of liquid air. Small amounts of neon, krypton, and xenon are also recovered from air.

Guided Practice

Review the Concept Check questions on pages 416 and 419 with students. Answers can be found in Appendix E on page 808.

Reteaching Idea

If students have difficulty remembering all of the different nonmetals, their properties and uses, have them work in small groups to complete a chart of these elements that includes the group, forms normally found, uses, and any other special information. For example, iodine: Group 7, halogen, shiny black solid or a violet vapor, used in photography and as a food additive.

DO YOU KNOW?

Hospitals use a product called providone-iodine as a powerful antiseptic and disinfectant. It is diluted with water to the desired strength before use.

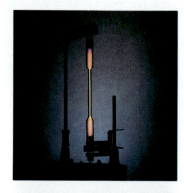

Figure 12-26 *Light of characteristic color is emitted when an electric charge is passed through tubes containing different gases. Shown here are helium (top), nitrogen (middle), and argon (bottom).*

12.13 The Noble Gases

On the far right side of the periodic table is a group of elements that exist as monatomic gases. Together they make up only about 1 percent of the atmosphere and are often called the "rare gases." Argon is the most abundant Group 8A element in Earth's atmosphere, making up about 1 percent of air. Helium is the lightest of the group, and the second most abundant element in the universe after hydrogen. However, the gravitational pull of Earth is not strong enough to retain large quantities of this low-density gas.

Uses of noble gases Noble gases are used to create an inert atmosphere for high-temperature metallurgical processes, including welding. Noble gases, particularly neon, are also used in gas discharge tubes. Figure 12-26 shows these gases glowing when excited by a high voltage. Helium gives a pink glow, neon a red-orange glow, and argon a purple glow.

Noble gases are used in lasers, such as the helium-neon laser, which emits red light at a wavelength of 632.8 nm. Xenon is readily soluble in blood and acts as an inhalation anesthetic in much the same way as dinitrogen oxide, N_2O,—more commonly referred to as laughing gas. Argon and krypton are also used in light bulbs to extend the lifetime of the filament. However, you may be most familiar with their use in neon signs.

Helium Most noble gases are obtained by distillation from liquid air. However, helium is obtained primarily from natural-gas wells in the western United States. The breathing gas used by deep-sea divers is helium mixed with oxygen. With a normal boiling point of only 4.1K ($-268.9°C$), liquid helium is the coldest liquid refrigerant available and it has very important applications in low-temperature research. For example, superconducting magnets, used in magnetic resonance imaging, are cooled by liquid helium.

Noble gas compounds In science, it is not uncommon for interesting discoveries to be the result of serendipity. The discovery of the first noble gas compounds illustrates the idea that "chance favors the prepared mind." While studying the chemistry of the extremely active compound, PtF_6, Neil Barlett quite accidentally noticed that exposing it to air led to the formation of O_2PtF_6, a complex compound that contains oxygen in the unusual form, O_2^+.

More importantly, Barlett recognized that the ionization energy of O_2 was comparable to that of Xe. He quickly proceeded to react PtF_6 with Xe to produce the first noble gas compound, $XePtF_6$. In 1962, Barlett's announcement of his synthesis of the orange-yellow compound was greeted with skepticism, since the scientific community had accepted the fact that noble gases were inert. Later the same year, however, chemists at the Argonne National Laboratory reported the reaction of xenon with fluorine at 400°C, to give XeF_4.

Among the best-known noble gas compounds is XeF_2. In view of the long-standing assumption that the noble gases were completely inert, it is ironic that this compound can be made by simply exposing a mixture of Xe and F_2 to ultraviolet light, which is present in sunlight.

PART 4 REVIEW

25. Use the structural difference between diamond and graphite to explain the difference in their hardness.

26. What is fixed nitrogen? Explain two ways it is produced.

27. What are the allotropic forms of oxygen? What is the major industrial use of each?

28. How do scientists believe the large deposits of elemental sulfur were formed?

29. What is the compound produced in greatest quantity by the chemical industry?

30. List two uses of noble gases.

31. Do allotropes of the noble gases exist? Why or why not?

32. What property of graphite makes it useful in pencils?

CONSUMER CHEMISTRY

Colored Gemstones

Of approximately 3 000 different minerals found on Earth, only about 100 are classified as gems. What gives gems their vast array of colors? In most cases, transition metal ions are responsible. Electrons in partially filled *d*-orbitals can sometimes absorb visible light. The wavelengths they absorb, and the resulting colors, depend upon the specific transition metal ion involved and the chemical environment surrounding the ion.

There are three types of colored gems, all of which depend upon transition metals for their color. In one type—which includes rubies, sapphires, emeralds, and amethysts—the color of the gem depends upon impurities in the crystal structure. In contrast, a second type of gemstone is inherently colored because of metals

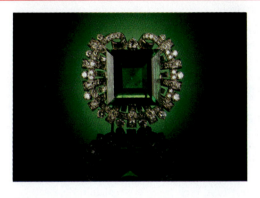

that are major components of the minerals themselves. For example, peridot is an iron-magnesium silicate.

The third type of gem contains transition metals both as major components and as impurities.

CLOSE

Summing Up Main Ideas

Have students list and compare the structure, properties, and uses for the common nonmetals that have different allotropes.

PART 4 REVIEW

Assign the Part Review questions.

Evaluating Skills

These skills are evaluated in the Part Review questions indicated. **Determining cause and effect:** 25, 28, 33; **Comparing/Contrasting:** 25, 30; **Applying a strategy:** 25; **Determining main ideas:** 26, 28, 29, 31; **Classifying:** 27; **Describing:** 30, 32

PART 4 REVIEW

ANSWERS
Keyed to Objectives

G 25. The carbon atoms in diamond are bonded together in a 3-dimensional network; in graphite, weak bonds exist between sheets of carbon atoms.

H 26. Nitrogen compounds formed from elemental nitrogen in the air.

Nitrogen-fixing bacteria and the Haber Process fix nitrogen.

G 27. O_2 (sometimes called dioxygen) and O_3, ozone; O_2 is used to remove impurities in the processing of iron and other metals. O_3 is used to manufacture oxygen-containing compounds.

H 28. By the action of anaerobic bacteria on sulfate mineral deposits such as gypsum

G 29. sulfuric acid, H_2SO_4

G 30. welding, gas discharge tubes ("neon" lights)

H 31. No, they are all monatomic gases.

G 32. It is soft, and layers easily rub off.

Discovering Trends in a Chemical Family
Estimated Time: (40–50 minutes)

Observing
Describing
Analyzing data
Predicting

Preparation

■ Materials

(for a class of 24, working in pairs)

Apparatus

(12 of each unless noted)
250-mL beakers (24), test tubes (24), pieces of fine sand paper, test-tube racks, 50-mL graduated cylinders, forceps

Reagents

■ 24 strips of magnesium (2–3 cm)

■ 24 small chunks of calcium

■ distilled water

■ 1 liter of 1.0M HCl

■ 12 100-mL dropper bottles of phenolphthalein (in a 50/50 mixture of water and alcohol)

■ Preparation Hints

Cut the magnesium strips ahead of time and ration the pieces. Keep the calcium turnings in a tightly capped bottle and dispense them with tongs, two to a pair, at the time of the lab.

■ Safety

⚠ Students must use forceps to handle the calcium. Be sure that students wear safety goggles and lab aprons. If you are making 1M HCl by diluting a more concentrated acid, use the fume hood and wear gloves, face shield, lab apron and safety goggles.

Guiding the Investigation

■ Procedural Hints

Allow the Mg+H$_2$O test tube to stand for 1 to 2 days to see evi-

---

Laboratory
Investigation

Discovering Trends in a Chemical Family

The periodic table gives clues to the properties of elements in each chemical family, or group (the vertical columns in the table). For example, for column 1, Li to Cs, you learned that the reactivity of these metallic elements with air and water increases with increasing atomic number (going down the table). By contrast, the nonmetallic elements in the next-to-last column, F to I, decrease in reactivity as the atomic number increases: F > Cl > Br > I. In this laboratory exercise, you will compare the reactivity of two metals in the alkaline earth family, magnesium and calcium, and from these data you will predict the activity trends in this group.

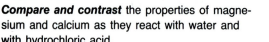

Objectives

Compare and contrast the properties of magnesium and calcium as they react with water and with hydrochloric acid.

Predict the reactivity trend for this chemical family.

Write and balance equations for each of the observed reactions.

1. Put on your lab apron and safety goggles.

2. Place 15 mL of distilled water in a test tube and 50 mL of water in a 250-mL beaker.

3. Put 1–2 drops of phenolphthalein indicator into both the test tube and the beaker. (Phenolphthalein turns pink in the presence of a base.)

Apparatus
□ 2 250-mL beakers
□ forceps
□ sandpaper
□ 2 test tubes
□ test-tube rack
□ 50-mL graduated cylinder

Reagents
□ 2 pieces of magnesium ribbon, 2–3 cm
□ 2 small chunks of calcium
□ phenolphthalein indicator
□ distilled or deionized water
□ 1.0M HCl

---

dence of a reaction. Add a drop of phenolphthalein, and the tube will eventually turn pink. If you do not wish to have students save their test tubes, save just one for demonstration later. You may have difficulty telling which metal reacts faster with 1.0M HCl, since the metal pieces are different masses and sizes.

Direct students to observe the reactions carefully.

Disposal

React the calcium completely with 1M HCl. Neutralize the acid and pour down the drain. Decant the acid from the magnesium. Wrap the magnesium in newspaper and put in the waste-

basket. Neutralize the decantate and pour down the drain.

CAUTION: Phenolphthalein solution is poisonous and flammable. Do not get it in your mouth; do not swallow any. Be sure there are no flames in the lab when you are using phenolphthalein.

4. Clean a small piece of magnesium ribbon with sandpaper to remove surface corrosion. Put the magnesium ribbon into the test tube.

5. Using the forceps, obtain a small chunk of calcium and put it into your beaker.

   CAUTION: Do not touch the calcium with your hands.

6. Observe the reaction for 5 minutes and record the observations in your data table. If you do not see anything happening in the test tube, set it aside until the next day and then observe it again.

7. Place 15 mL of 1.0M HCl in a test tube and 50 mL of 1.0M HCl in a 250-mL beaker.

8. Clean a piece of magnesium ribbon and obtain a small chunk of calcium, as described in steps 4 and 5. Place the magnesium in the test tube and the calcium chunk in the beaker. Observe and record your findings, including how fast the reaction occurred, in your data table.

Data Analysis

Data Table

Observations		
	Reaction with H$_2$O	**Reaction with HCl**
Mg		
Ca		

1. Which metal reacted faster with water?

2. Which metal reacted faster with acid?

3. Consult your text or other references and find out if beryllium reacts the same way as magnesium and calcium with water and acid.

4. Make a statement about the trends in reactivity as you move down the column of alkaline earth metals.

5. Predict the reactivity of strontium and barium, based on your activity in this lab.

6. Complete and balance these equations for the reactions that you observed.

$$Mg + H_2O \rightarrow$$
$$Ca + H_2O \rightarrow$$
$$Mg + HCl \rightarrow$$
$$Ca + HCl \rightarrow$$

Conclusions

1. How, do you think, are strontium and barium metals stored? Explain your answer.

2. If sufficient radium could be gathered for a test, predict its reactivity with water and hydrochloric acid.

3. Why would it be dangerous to handle even a small amount of radium?

Data Analysis

Sample Data
(See table below.)

Analysis

1. Calcium reacts with water faster than magnesium.

2. Calcium reacts with HCl faster than magnesium.

3. Beryllium is much less reactive than either magnesium or calcium.

4. Reactivity increases as one moves down the column of alkaline earth metals.
   Ba > Sr > Ca > Mg > Be

5. Strontium would be more reactive than Mg or Ca. Barium would react fastest of all.

6. $Mg(s) + 2H_2O(l) \rightarrow$
   $\qquad Mg(OH)_2(s) + H_2(g)$
   $Ca(s) + 2H_2O(l) \rightarrow$
   $\qquad Ca(OH)_2(s) + H_2(g)$
   $Mg(s) + 2HCl(l) \rightarrow$
   $\qquad MgCl_2(aq) + H_2(g)$
   $Ca(s) + 2HCl(l) \rightarrow$
   $\qquad CaCl_2(aq) + H_2(g)$

Conclusions

1. Strontium and barium have to be stored in inert gases to keep them from reacting with the oxygen and moisture in the air.

2. $Ra + 2HCl \rightarrow RaCl_2 + H_2(g)$,
   $Ra + 2H_2O \rightarrow Ra(OH)_2$
   $\qquad\qquad + H_2(g)$

3. Radium gives off ionizing radiation (gamma rays), which can burn the skin and cause cancer.

Data Table

	Observations	
	Reaction with H$_2$O	**Reaction with HCl**
Mg	Takes days to see phenolphthalein turn pink	Reacts in less than 1 minute
Ca	Reacts in less than 1 minute	Most reactive of all

Chapter 12
Review
ANSWERS
begin on page
T427a.

Summary

Representative Metals

- Most elements are metallic. In general, metallic elements exhibit the properties of malleability, ductility, thermal and electrical conductivity, and high melting temperatures. With the exception of mercury, metals are crystalline solids at room temperature. Most of the properties of metals are a result of the nature of the metallic bond.

- Alkali metals are the most reactive metals, and alkaline earth metals are slightly less reactive. Because of their reactivity, these metals are not found in the elemental state in nature.

- Alkali metals and alkaline earth metals both form basic solutions when they react with water.

Transition Metals

- A homogeneous mixture of a metal with one or more other elements is called an alloy. Alloys have useful properties that are often quite different from the properties of the pure elements.

- Many of the properties of transition metals result from their partially filled *d* orbitals. One property that distinguishes the transition metals from most other elements is the vast array of colors exhibited by their compounds and ores.

Metalloids

- Metalloids are elements that display properties of both metals and nonmetals.

- The microelectronics industry relies upon several metalloid elements, especially silicon. A crystal of silicon can be made to conduct electricity if it is doped with a minute amount of another element, such as gallium or arsenic.

- If distinct structural forms of an element exist in the same physical state (for example, solid or liquid), they are called allotropes. Allotropes often have strikingly different properties.

Nonmetals

- The properties of the nonmetals are quite varied. Some are found in their elemental form in nature, while others are not. At room temperature, some are solids, while others are gases; only one is a liquid. Several are highly colored. Some are relatively unreactive, while others are highly reactive.

- The elements of the halogen family are the most reactive of the nonmetals. The reactivity of the halogens decreases with increasing atomic mass.

- The elements of the noble gas family tend to be unreactive, although compounds of heavier noble gases have been prepared. The unreactive nature of noble gases makes them useful in a number of applications.

Chemically Speaking

alkali metals *12.2*
alkaline earth metals *12.3*
alloy *12.6*
doped crystal *12.8*
ferromagnetism *12.5*
inner transition elements *12.5*

junction *12.8*
metallic bonding *12.1*
n-type semiconductor *12.8*
paramagnetism *12.5*
p-type semiconductor *12.8*
transition metals *12.5*

Concept Mapping

Using the method of concept mapping described at the front of this book, construct a concept map for *transition elements*. Use additional concepts from this chapter or previous chapters as necessary to expand your map.

PROBLEM-SOLVING STRATEGIES

Students apply these strategies in the following questions.

- Factor-label method: 43, 44
- Using what you know: 5, 6, 18, 20, 21, 24, 34, 35, 39, 41, 42, 43, 44
- Using calculators: 43
- Breaking problems into manageable parts: 43
- Making diagrams: 3, 4

Questions and Problems

REPRESENTATIVE METALS

A. Objective: **Use models** *to explain some properties of metals.*

1. Describe the structure of metal crystals.
2. How does metallic bonding account for the malleability and ductility of metals?
3. Make a drawing of steel showing the carbon atoms as ● and the iron atoms as ○.
4. Use the electron-sea model to explain the high electrical conductivity of metals.

B. Objective: **Summarize** *some of the properties and uses of representative metals.*

5. Why are pure alkali metals stored in kerosene or an inert gas like argon?
6. Explain why a fire involving an alkali metal cannot be put out with water.
7. How did the alkali metals and the alkaline earth metals get their names?
8. List three properties of alkali metals.
9. What is the most common compound of calcium?
10. Explain what is meant by *hard water*. What is one method for softening hard water?
11. What type of compound forms on the surface of pure aluminum when it is exposed to air? What are the properties of this coating?

TRANSITION METALS

C. Objective: **Summarize** *properties, uses, and abundance of some transition metals.*

12. Which transition element has the highest melting point?
13. Which is the most abundant transition metal?
14. What three transition metals share the property of ferromagnetism?
15. Discuss the function of silver halides in black-and-white photography.

D. Objective: **Use models** *to explain properties of transition metals and alloys.*

16. How is stainless steel different from standard steel?
17. Why is steel harder than pure iron?
18. Why are manufacturers of copper for electrical wiring careful to remove even very small amounts of arsenic impurities?

METALLOIDS

E. Objective: **Summarize** *the properties of common metalloids.*

19. What common physical properties do most metalloids share?
20. Explain how the crystalline structure of silicon results in silicon being a poor conductor of heat.
21. Why is the term *semiconductor* used to describe metalloids?
22. What property of boron makes it useful for reinforcing plastics and metal parts? How can this property be explained?
23. What property of arsenic makes it poisonous?

F. Objective: **Compare** *properties of metalloids with added impurities to the properties of metalloids without added impurities.*

24. If pure silicon is a poor conductor of electricity, why has silicon played such a critical role in the development of semiconductor devices?
25. Account for the difference between arsenic-doped and boron-doped silicon semiconductors.
26. Why does a current flow in a specific direction across a junction?

NONMETALS

G. Objective: **Describe** *properties and uses of some common nonmetals.*

Boxed numbers indicate questions that involve skills in interpretation, application, and analysis.

■ Writing chemical equations: 6, 11, 15, 27, 31, 34, 41

27. Describe two ways that nitrogen gas can be converted into compound form, or fixed form.

28. Which family of elements is known as the salt formers?

29. What is the most reactive element?

30. What gases are commonly used to provide an inert atmosphere for welding?

31. Complete and balance the following equations. If no reaction occurs, write *NR*.
   a. $Cl_2(g) + I^-(aq) \rightarrow$
   b. $F_2(g) + Br^-(aq) \rightarrow$
   c. $I_2(s) + Br^-(aq) \rightarrow$
   d. $Br_2(l) + Cl^-(aq) \rightarrow$

32. White, black, and red phosphorus are all elemental forms of phosphorus, but the structure and properties of these substances are different. What are these different types of phosphorus called?

33. List the common allotropic forms of oxygen, carbon, phosphorus, and sulfur and give a description of each.

34. Name a nonmetal element that could be used in each instance to follow:
   a. a nonreactive liquid used to cool electrical wires to within a few kelvins of absolute zero
   b. a nonmetal used to disinfect water
   c. an element that reacts with hydrogen gas to produce a gas soluble in water forming an acid solution
   d. an element that combusts (combines with oxygen) to produce a nonmetal oxide

H. Objective: **Compare and contrast** *the abundance and sources of some common nonmetals.*

35. Why do scientists think that oxygen suddenly appeared in Earth's atmosphere approximately two billion years ago?

36. List three natural sources of sulfur or sulfur compounds.

37. What is the principal commercial use of oxygen?

38. What are some commercial uses of chlorine?

39. Nitrogen gas is commonly used as a protective blanket. What does this statement mean?

40. What important sulfur-containing chemical is produced commercially in the greatest quantity?

Critical Thinking

SYNTHESIS WITHIN THE CHAPTER

41. Identify each of the following substances from its description.
   a. a white, waxy solid, normally stored under water because it spontaneously bursts into flame at 30°C.
   b. an acid that etches glass
   c. a greenish-yellow gas that was used as a poisonous gas in World War I
   d. a yellow solid that burns in air to produce a choking odor

SYNTHESIS ACROSS CHAPTERS

42. The Hall-Heroult electrolysis process for extracting aluminum uses a mixture of alumina, Al_2O_3, and cryolite, Na_3AlF_6. This mixture melts at only 960°C, whereas pure alumina melts at temperatures above 2000°C. Cryolite is made by this reaction:

$$Al_2O_3(s) + HF(aq) + NaOH(aq) \rightarrow Na_3AlF_6(s) + H_2O(l)$$

   Balance the equation.

43. A teakettle contains 3.5 g of boiler scale, $CaCO_3$. What volume of vinegar, which is a 4.5% solution by mass of acetic acid, $HC_2H_3O_2$, will be required to react with the boiler scale to remove it if the reaction proceeds as follows?

$$CaCO_3(s) + 2HC_2H_3O_2(aq) \rightarrow Ca^{2+}(aq) + 2C_2H_3O_2^-(aq) + CO_2(g) + 2H_2O(l)$$

44. A copper ore is 6.0% copper(II) oxide. The copper(II) oxide is separated from the ore and

reacted with carbon (as coke). What mass of elemental copper can be obtained from 3500 kilograms of ore?

45. Both magnesium and calcium can be used to convert uranium(VI) fluoride to uranium metal. If both magnesium and calcium cost the same amount per kilogram, which could be used more economically to convert the fluoride to the metal?

46. Predict any other elements that could be used to produce uranium from uranium(VI) fluoride. Explain the basis for your prediction.

Projects

47. Contact a soil science specialist and learn what problems occur when water containing a high concentration of metallic salts, carbonates, and minerals is used to irrigate farmland. Find out how widespread these problems are. Develop a plan that could be implemented by a community to help overcome these problems.

48. Using old magazines and catalogs, collect pictures showing objects that use various elements. Construct a periodic table to hang on your classroom wall, using these pictures. If there are elements you cannot find pictures for, use reference books to find out the uses of those elements and draw pictures instead.

49. Using reference material, make a list of all the elements that are part of the composition of your body. Make a table that compares the relative amounts of these elements.

Research and Writing

50. Find out what kind of raw materials are used in the manufacture of computer chips. Write a paper on the sources of these materials. Include in your report how the cost of precious metals, such as gold, has been affected by their use in high-tech industries.

51. Different types of glass have different properties and applications. Find out how silica glass, soda glass, Pyrex, and other types of glass differ chemically. Include in a report how these types of glass are manufactured and how their uses vary.

52. Select an element that is of interest to you. Do a report on the history of the element. Include in your report who discovered the element, how it was discovered, and what its primary use is today.

☐ Boxed numbers indicate questions that involve skills in interpretation, application, and analysis.

1. An array of metal cations surrounded by a "sea" of electrons

2. The sea of electrons surrounding the metal cations allow for the atoms in a metal to slide past one another.

3.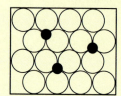

4. The electrons are mobile and can carry an electrical current.

5. They react with water and with oxygen in the air.

6. Alkali metals react with water to give hydrogen gas, which is a flammable gas and would itself catch fire.

7. They form alkaline (basic) solutions in water.

8. React vigorously with water, react with oxygen, soft, among others

9. calcium carbonate, $CaCO_3$

10. Hard water is water that contains dissolved $CaHCO_3$ or $MgHCO_3$. Hard water can be softened by removing the calcium and magnesium ions, using an ion exchange resin.

11. Al_2O_3; it bonds tightly to the surface of the metal protecting it from corrosion.

12. tungsten

13. iron

14. iron, cobalt, nickel

15. Upon exposure to light, they form elemental silver.

16. It has Cr and Ni added to produce an alloy that resists corrosion.

17. The atoms of the other elements fill empty space between iron atoms, which makes it harder for the iron atoms to slip past each other.

18. The impurity will lower the conductivity of copper.

19. They have luster and are poor conductors of electricity when pure.

20. The crystalline structure of silicon is a diamond-like network, so the electrons are not free to move, and heat cannot be easily conducted through the solid.

21. Metalloids are poor conductors at low temperatures, but they conduct moderately well at higher temperatures.

22. Boron is very hard due to the non-metallic bonding among the atoms.

23. It tends to combine with sulfur atoms in enzymes, which prevents the enzymes from their normal function. This in turn disrupts the normal biochemical reactions in cells.

24. It can be doped to create a better conductor.

25. As has one more valence electron than the Si atom and B has one less valence electron.

26. Current flows from the n-type (with excess electrons) to the p-type (with deficiency in electrons) semiconductor but will not flow in the opposite direction.

27. By lightning or by the action of nitrogen-fixing bacteria

28. halogens

29. fluorine

30. noble gases

31. a. $Cl_2(g) + 2I^-(aq) \rightarrow I_2(s) + 2Cl^-(aq)$
    b. $F_2(g) + 2Br^-(aq) \rightarrow Br_2(l) + 2F^-(aq)$
    c. NR
    d. NR

32. allotropes

33. Oxygen; O_2 (dioxygen) and O_3 (ozone); both gases
    Carbon: graphite (black, soft, conductor of electricity) and diamond (translucent, hard, nonconductor of electricity)
    Phosphorus: white and red. Both are solids. White is more toxic and consists of P_4 molecules. Red phosphorus is less reactive and exists as a network (Fig. 12–19). A third allotrope, black phosphorus, is less common.
    Sulfur: rhombic sulfur exists as S_8 molecules; it is yellow, and it is the stable form at room temperature; monoclinic is the stable form from 96 to 119°C and consists of S_8 molecules packed more closely than the rhombic form.

34. a. He
    b. Cl
    c. Cl
    d. C, N, P, S

35. The first green plants are believed to have evolved 2 billion years ago; oxygen is produced by photosynthesis that occurs in green plants.

36. Deposits of elemental sulfur, sulfur-containing minerals, coal, petroleum, and natural gas

37. Removal of impurities in the production of iron and other metals from their ores

38. The manufacture of chlorinated hydrocarbons used as solvents, pesticides, and so on; water treatment; bleach for paper and textile industry

39. It protects a substance from oxygen or moisture in the air.

40. sulfuric acid, H_2SO_4

41. a. phosphorus
    b. hydrofluoric acid
    c. chlorine
    d. sulfur

42. $Al_2O_3(s) + 12HF(aq) + 6NaOH(aq) \rightarrow 2Na_3AlF_6(s) + 9H_2O(l)$

43. $3.5 \text{ g } CaCO_3 \times \dfrac{1 \text{ mol } CaCO_3}{100.1 \text{ g } CaCO_3}$
    $\times \dfrac{2 \text{ mol } HC_2H_3O_2}{1 \text{ mol } CaCO_3} \times \dfrac{60 \text{ g } HC_2H_3O_2}{1 \text{ mol } HC_2H_3O_2}$
    $\times \dfrac{100 \text{ mL vinegar}}{4.5 \text{ g } HC_2H_3O_2} = 93 \text{ mL}$

44. $3500 \text{ kg ore} \times \dfrac{6.0 \text{ g } CuO}{100 \text{ g ore}}$
    $\times \dfrac{63.5 \text{ g } Cu}{79.5 \text{ g } CuO} = 1.7 \times 10^2 \text{ kg of Cu}$

45. Magnesium is more economical because it has a lower molar mass and would contain more moles per kilogram. The reactions are:
    $3Mg + UF_6 \rightarrow 3MgF_2 + U$
    $3Ca + UF_6 \rightarrow 3CaF_2 + U$

46. Other highly reactive metals such as Na or K

Science
Technology &
Society

Science
Technology &
Society

 CHEMICAL PERSPECTIVES

Critical Thinking Skills

The following skills are applied in the feature.
- Distinguishing between fact and opinion
- Evaluating an opinion or point of view
- Making an informed decision
- Using library resources

FOCUS

Activate Prior Knowledge

Refer to the information about metallurgical processes in Chapter 12. Discuss the importance of this technology to various industries. Metal alloys with greater strength, flexibility, heat resistance, and other qualities have advanced the automotive, construction, aircraft, and aerospace industries. Obtain NASA pictures that show 1960s spacecraft affected by reentry temperature and contemporary, heat-tolerant spacecraft. Or use pictures that contrast the damage caused by low-speed collisions to chrome automobile bumpers and modern metal/fiberglass bumpers.

Teach

Science Background

Platinum is used in catalytic converters to reduce the level of harmful gases in automobile exhaust. Manganese and its compounds are used in making paints and varnishes, disinfectants, deodorizers, and water purifiers. Point out that the U.S. deposits of low-grade strategic metals are not mined because it is more economical to buy them.

Look Ahead

Refer to the section on catalysts in Chapter 17 to discuss the use of platinum in catalytic converters.

Strategic Metals

The United States is blessed with a great variety of natural resources. Its coal, water, timber, and agricultural resources are the envy of many other countries. Nevertheless the United States must still import certain valuable resources that are important to its civilian economy and military power. Some of these materials, called strategic resources, are found in only a few locations around the globe. For example, deposits of many such strategic metals are found almost exclusively in the Soviet Union and South Africa. Historically United States relations with these countries have been somewhat unpredictable, and a war or an embargo could abruptly cut off the supply of strategic metals.

One strategic metal, platinum, is used in industry to catalyze many chemical reactions. All the platinum recovered from Earth in a year would fit inside an average-sized room; yet without this element the oil, chemical, and food industries of the western world would be devastated.

Chromium, another strategic metal, is an important component of many alloys. It is essential to the production of stainless steel, increasing the steel's strength, hardness, and durability. When chromium is added to other metals—such as nickel, aluminum, or cobalt—superalloys are formed that are exceptionally heat- and corrosion-resistant. Chromium is therefore vital to the aircraft and automotive industries. The United States imports more than 90 percent of the chromium it uses.

Manganese, a third strategic metal, is also used in the pro-

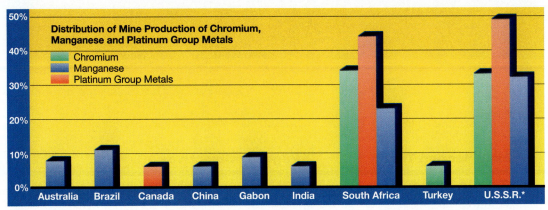

Distribution of Mine Production of Chromium, Manganese and Platinum Group Metals

- Chromium
- Manganese
- Platinum Group Metals

Australia | Brazil | Canada | China | Gabon | India | South Africa | Turkey | U.S.S.R.*

Most of the world's supply of platinum, chromium, and manganese is in South Africa and the U.S.S.R.*
*Refers to the USSR as it existed as of Jan. 1, 1991.

duction of steel. When manganese is added to raw steel, it reacts with naturally occurring impurities, making the steel much harder and more durable. Manganese steel, containing up to 14 percent manganese, is an important component of safes, electromagnets, and heavy machinery. The United States produces only 9 percent of the manganese it needs.

What can be done to reduce the nation's dependence on these imports? The United States maintains domestic stockpiles of some strategic metals to ensure a steady supply in case of some other emergency. They would not last very long, and more permanent solutions must be found.

In the future, new untapped sources of strategic metals may be discovered. Recently, scientists have found mountains submerged deep in the Pacific Ocean that are blanketed with ores including manganese. Sci-

The United States must still import certain valuable resources that are important to its civilian economy and military power.

entists have also found baseball-sized nodules on the ocean floor that contain manganese. Perhaps in the future, technological advances will recover strategic metals in a profitable and environmentally conscientious manner. Developing new materials to replace strategic metals and conserving and recycling the country's resources could also reduce its dependence upon foreign nations.

Discussing the Issues

1. Domestic sources of some strategic metals are found deep under environmentally protected lands. Can you think of any circumstances that would justify strip-mining these metals.
2. If the supply of platinum from South Africa was abruptly cut off, what should the United States government do? Why?

Take Action

1. Is there a recycling center in your community? What materials are recycled there? What steps could you take to encourage your community to set up such a facility?
2. Write to one of the large steel manufacturers. Find out if they use any recycled metals or if they are developing any substitutes for strategic metals. If they use recycled metals, ask them to suggest ways to recycle or conserve these metals.

429

Teaching Strategy

To connect the rarity, global locations, and technological importance of strategic metals to economic, political, and environmental issues, have small groups research such topics as:

- the impact of the political evolution from Rhodesia to Zimbabwe on the world chromium supply, 1966–71
- the impact of the 1978 takeover of Zaire's cobalt-producing Shaba province by guerillas
- the rationale for the U.S. government's refusal to impose economic sanctions on South Africa during the apartheid era
- the viability of deep-sea mineral mining
- the safety of mining in environmentally fragile areas

Close

Discussing the Issues

1. Answers will vary, but students should consider the effects of a scarcity of strategic metals on industries, national economy, or national security, and the availability of substitutes.
2. Answers will vary, but may include allowing price to rise so demand falls, rationing domestic stockpiles to U.S. industries, or opening new areas to mining, even in environmentally protected lands.

Take Action

1. Invite a representative of a local recycling center to speak about recycling techniques for metals or arrange a field trip. If there is no local recycling program, help students research information that could persuade local authorities or residents to start one.
2. Discuss responses from the steel companies. Ask students to assess if companies view recycling as an important economic benefit, as a corporate responsibility, or as a public relations consideration.

Chemical Bonding

Investigations	Demonstrations	Texas Essential Elements★
Laboratory Manual 13–1 S Laboratory Manual 13–2 IM	Ionic Bonds, page T432	**Content:** 3.9, 3.10, 5.1, 5.4, 5.5, 5.6 **Process:** 4.3, 10.1
		Content: 2.6, 3.9, 5.5, 5.7 **Process:** 4.3, 10.1
In-text Investigation, page T462	Molecular Shapes, page T453 Water Molecule and Polarity, page T459	**Content:** 3.9, 5.7 **Process:** 6.3, 8.2, 10.3, 10.4
		Content: 3.9, 5.7 **Process:** 1.2, 4.3, 6.3, 7.1, 8.2
		Process: 4.2, 4.3, 6.3, 7.1, 10.1

KEY:
M–Microscale   **S**–Structured
I–Inquiry   **IM**–Inquiry Microscale

★See pages T8–T11 for complete listing of Texas Essential Elements.

13

Chemical Bonding

Chapter Rationale

A study of molecular bonding and molecular geometry provides an exciting look into the nature of compounds. Additionally, it becomes a useful tool for understanding the subtleties of chemical reactions that provide researchers with valuable information for designing new pharmaceuticals, materials with special properties, and reaction catalysts.

About the Photograph

Water, the most abundant chemical compound on Earth, has unique properties based on its unusual structure and polarity. As water condenses and freezes in the upper atmosphere, the nature of its chemical bonds enables snowflakes to form in an infinite variety of hexagonal crystalline shapes as they fall.

Chapter Planning Hints

Plan to spend four to seven class sessions on the chapter, including the Laboratory Investigation and Chapter Review. You may wish to obtain The World of Chemistry videotape *Chemical Bonds* for use in introducing Part 1. Three optional demonstrations are suggested for this chapter. They are found on pages T432, T453, and T459. You may wish to preview them at this time.

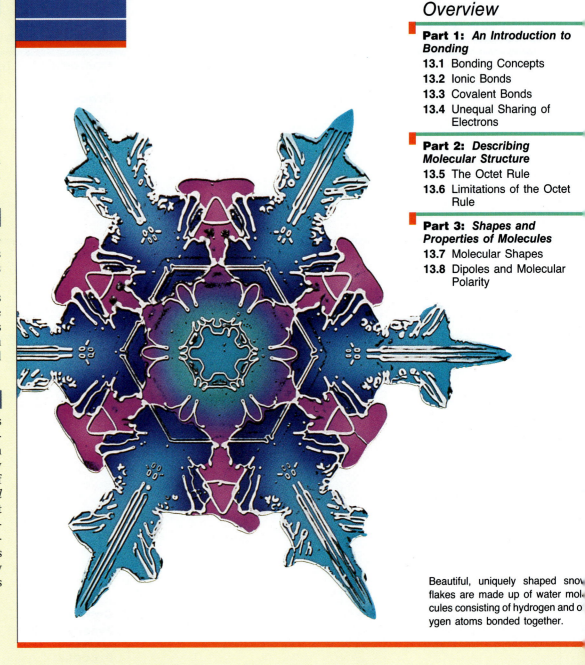

Beautiful, uniquely shaped snow flakes are made up of water molecules consisting of hydrogen and oxygen atoms bonded together.

PART 1 An Introduction to Bonding

Advances in chemical technology that directly affect your life are based on knowledge of submicroscopic particles and processes. Understanding how to combine molecules of hydrogen and nitrogen (from the air) to produce gaseous ammonia revolutionized the fertilizer industry and has helped farmers increase food supplies. Analyzing molecules that carry genetic codes helps in finding causes of diseases. An understanding of the chemistry of pollutants responsible for smog formation encourages the development of new technologies to protect the environment. This kind of understanding will not come unless differences and similarities of compounds are considered.

In this chapter, you begin looking at the differences between compounds by studying the concept of chemical bonds. You will look at simple models that can help explain properties of different types of compounds. How do elements come together, and why? What is the *glue* that holds the elements in compounds together?

O b j e c t i v e s

Part 1

A. *Describe* the nature of a chemical bond.
B. *Compare and contrast* ionic and covalent bonds.
C. *Predict* whether bonds are ionic, polar covalent, or nonpolar covalent using electronegativity values.
D. *Determine* the partial charge distribution of a polar covalent bond.

13.1 Bonding Concepts

A **chemical bond** is a strong attractive force between atoms or ions in a compound. In this chapter, you will study the electrical nature of chemical bonding. You will be introduced to theories that attempt to explain why certain atoms are strongly attracted to other atoms. As you consider the way in which atoms and ions combine, you need to focus on several key questions.

What do compounds have in common? There are millions of stable compounds formed from fewer than 100 naturally occurring elements. Despite the differences in properties of these elements, they do share one common characteristic. In almost all of the stable compounds of the representative elements, the atoms have acquired an electron configuration that is isoelectronic with that of a noble gas element. This observation serves as a basis for the explanation of how and why atoms bond to one another.

Why do only certain numbers of atoms combine to form a given compound? You will recall that the law of definite composition says that the proportion of elements in a given compound is fixed. The only way to know the formula of a compound is to determine experimentally the ratio of the elements in

Developing Skills

Students may apply these skills in their study of Part 1.
Comparing/Contrasting: Have students compare and contrast ionic and covalent bonds.
Predicting: Have students predict if bonds are ionic, polar covalent, or nonpolar.
Forming models: Have students draw diagrams of chemical bonding.
Interpreting data: Have students interpret data using differences in electronegativities to predict bond types.

☰ FOCUS

Activate Prior Knowledge

Covalent bonds form when a molecule achieves a state of the lowest potential energy. Students should have a concept of potential energy. Ask them to give examples of increasing and decreasing potential energy.

Demonstrate the concept of potential energy with two round foam rubber balls connected by a piece of elastic tied around each. Show that force can be applied either to pull the balls far apart or to squish them against each other. The potential energy is lowest when no one is pulling them apart or pushing them together. The potential energy is higher when either condition is taking place.

☰ TEACH

Teaching Strategy

Bonding Concepts

Bonding is the "glue" that holds atoms together in compounds. However, the glue isn't something that is easily understood. Try to get your students to think
(continued on page T432)

(continued from page T431)

in terms of balancing forces; if attractive forces are bigger than repulsive forces, a bond forms. If repulsive forces are larger than attractive forces, no bond forms.

Science Background

How Strong Is a Bond?

Both ionic and covalent bonds can be viewed in terms of changes in potential energy. Chemical bonds occur when the potential energy of the bonding atoms or ions is lower than that of the isolated atoms.

Consider the simultaneous attraction of the electrons to the two nuclei between which a bond might form. There are two sources of repelling forces, electron-electron repulsion and nucleus-nucleus repulsion. Work must be done to bring two electrons or two nuclei closer together, leading to an increase in potential energy. Likewise, there are attractive forces between the electrons and the nuclei. If the attractive forces are greater than both repelling forces, bonding occurs. As electrons approach nuclei, energy is released, and the potential energy of the system decreases.

Ionic bonding occurs when the attraction for an electron by one atom is so great that it can be thought of as being transferred from one atom to another. The atom that loses the electron is the cation and the atom gaining the electron is the anion. Since opposite charges attract, a bond results. The strength of an ionic bond depends on the size and charge of the ions.

the compound, as discussed in Chapter 4. However, predictions of the most likely formula of a compound can be made. Bonding theory will allow you to explain the fact that sodium and chlorine will react to form NaCl, but not Na_2Cl or $NaCl_2$.

How are atoms within a molecule arranged? The structure of a molecule shows the way in which the atoms are arranged. Information about this structure is important in predicting chemical properties. Conversely, information about chemical properties provides important clues about the structure of a molecule.

What is the shape of a molecule and why is it important? Shape is another aspect of the structure that influences chemical properties. If you have worked a jigsaw puzzle, you know that pieces of the wrong shape will not fit together. The same is true of molecules. Chemical reactions happen when atoms, molecules, or ions come in contact with one another. The shape of a molecule can be crucial in determining whether or not a reaction will occur. If the shape is not right, the species that need to be close to each other may not be able to come in contact. This requirement is especially important in the chemical reactions of living systems such as the action of the immune system, the effects of pharmaceuticals, the digestion of food, the production of food in plants, and the reproduction of cells in your body. In this chapter, you will study a model that provides a basis for predicting the shape of molecules.

How strong is a bond? The energy involved in the process of bond forming and bond breaking is known as **bond energy**. It is a measure of bond strength. Knowledge of bond energies will allow you to determine how much energy is obtained from digesting a gram of sugar or how much energy is stored when a tree produces cellulose. The strength of a bond indicates which bonds in a molecule come apart easily and which remain intact. The model that explains bonding will help you account for differences in bond energies.

As you can see, a good theory of bonding is necessary to understand many chemical facts. The simple theories that will be introduced in this chapter can provide you with some of this understanding. You may find it helpful to focus on these questions as you read the chapter.

13.2 Ionic Bonds

In Chapter 11, you learned that a cation is formed when an atom loses one or more electrons. The resulting ion has a positive charge equal to the number of electrons lost. Metals characteristically form cations. An anion is formed when an atom gains one or more electrons. The ion has a negative charge equal to the number of electrons gained. Nonmetals often gain electrons to form anions.

DEMONSTRATION

Ionic Bonds

⚠ **CAUTION: Protect your students with a shield and yourself with safety goggles and a lab apron.** Dissolve an ionic substance (i.e., a chloride of an alkali metal or alkaline earth metal) in water and check its conductivity or, alternatively, heat a low melting ionic substance—lithium chloride or sodium acetate—to show that these salts are made up of ions.

For disposal, pour aqueous solutions down the drain. Dissolve the lithium chloride or sodium acetate in water and pour down the drain.

It is a basic law of physics that particles of opposite charge attract one another; such an attraction is called an **electrostatic attraction.** An **ionic bond** is a chemical bond formed by the electrostatic attraction between a cation and an anion.

Properties of ionic compounds The compound sodium chloride contains sodium cations (Na^+) and chloride anions (Cl^-). Sodium chloride is classified as an ionic compound because of its physical and chemical properties. You learned in Chapter 2 that when solid sodium chloride melts into the liquid state, it conducts electricity. This indicates that sodium chloride must be composed of ions, because mobile charged particles are necessary in order for a substance to conduct an electrical current.

At room temperature, crystals of ionic compounds exist as regular, three-dimensional arrangements of cations and anions held together by electrostatic attractions. These arrangements are called **crystal lattices.** An entity consisting of one sodium ion and one chloride ion, therefore, does not exist. Sodium chloride is a collection of equal numbers of sodium and chloride ions arranged in a lattice, as shown in Figure 13-1.

Science Background

Properties of Ionic Compounds
The model for ionic bonds is simple; electrons are transferred between neutral atoms so two oppositely charged species attract one another. It is important to reemphasize here that ionic compounds are represented by empirical formulas. Using NaCl as an example, there is no entity consisting of one sodium ion and one chloride ion. There is in fact a network of equal numbers of sodium and chloride ions in a 1:1 ratio. Thus, reference to ionic species is by their empirical formulas.

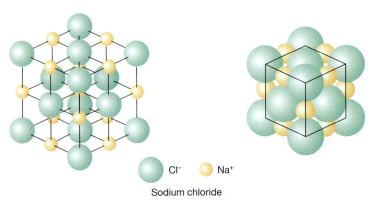

Cl⁻   Na⁺

Sodium chloride

Figure 13-1 *The arrangement of Na^+ and Cl^- ions in a crystal lattice leads to a cubic crystal on a macroscopic level. Note that the lines between ions are not bonds; they are reference lines showing the relative position of Na^+ and Cl^-.*

Forming ionic compounds One way to form an ionic compound is to react a metal with a nonmetal. For such a reaction to occur, the metal must transfer one or more electrons to the nonmetal. The formation of sodium chloride can be represented by using the electron configurations of sodium and chlorine as follows.

$$Na\ 1s^22s^22p^63s^1\ +\ Cl\ 1s^22s^22p^63s^23p^5\ \rightarrow$$

$$Na^+\ 1s^22s^22p^6\ +\ Cl^-\ 1s^22s^22p^63s^23p^6$$

Notice that the $3s$ valence electron in sodium is removed and added to a $3p$ valence orbital of chlorine. Both the sodium ion and the chloride ion have achieved stable noble gas configurations. The sodium ion is isoelectronic with neon. With which noble gas is the

PART 1
Section 13.2 *continued*

Teaching Strategy

Electron Dot Symbols

Students may think that electrons are different in different elements because elements have different symbols and different properties. Discuss with your students the fact that all electrons are the same; it is the number of electrons and their orbital position that result in diversity of elements and compounds. When introducing how to draw electron dot structures, be cautious when using dots, squares, or triangles to represent electrons. This can reinforce the misconception. It is important that students understand that different symbols are used only as a bookkeeping device and that there is absolutely no way of distinguishing one electron from another.

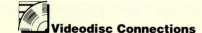

Videodisc Connections

5633-5636, side 3
Molecular graphics of NaCl
(4-frame seq.)

chloride ion isoelectronic? When the sodium ion achieves a noble gas configuration, it becomes positively charged. What charge does the chloride ion have? Because the sodium and chloride ions have opposite charges, an electrostatic attraction results which is responsible for the formation of an ionic bond.

Electron dot symbols In 1916, G. N. Lewis, an American chemist, developed a system of arranging dots—representing valence electrons—around the symbols of the elements, called **electron dot symbols** (also called Lewis electron dot symbols). In this representation, the element symbol denotes the *nucleus and the core electrons* of an atom, and the dots represent the *valence electrons*. The number of dots is equal to the number of valence electrons. The dots are placed, one at a time, along the sides of an imaginary square surrounding the element symbol. When there are more than four valence electrons, the dots are placed two to a side as necessary. Table 13-1 gives the electron configuration and the electron dot symbols for the second period elements. The exact placement of dots is arbitrary; the electron dot symbol for lithium can have the single dot on any of the four sides.

Electron dot symbols can also be used to represent ions. The formation of sodium chloride from atoms of sodium and chlorine represented earlier in the chapter by electron configurations can now be shown as

$$Na\cdot + \,:\!\ddot{C}l\!: \,\rightarrow Na^+ + [\,:\!\ddot{C}l\!:\,]^- \rightarrow Na^+ \,[\,:\!\ddot{C}l\!:\,]^-$$

TABLE 13-1

Element	Electron configuration	Orbital diagram			Electron dot symbol
		1s	**2s**	**2p**	
Li	$1s^2\,2s^1$	⇅	↑	○ ○ ○	Li·
Be	$1s^2\,2s^2$	⇅	⇅	○ ○ ○	Be·
B	$1s^2\,2s^2\,2p^1$	⇅	⇅	↑ ○ ○	·B·
C	$1s^2\,2s^2\,2p^2$	⇅	⇅	↑ ↑ ○	·Ċ·
N	$1s^2\,2s^2\,2p^3$	⇅	⇅	↑ ↑ ↑	·N:
O	$1s^2\,2s^2\,2p^4$	⇅	⇅	⇅ ↑ ↑	·Ö:
F	$1s^2\,2s^2\,2p^5$	⇅	⇅	⇅ ⇅ ↑	:F̈:
Ne	$1s^2\,2s^2\,2p^6$	⇅	⇅	⇅ ⇅ ⇅	:N̈e:

Table title: Electron Configurations, Orbital Diagrams, and Electron Dot Symbols of the Second Period Elements

EXAMPLE 13-1

Write the electron dot (Lewis) symbol for phosphorus.

■ *Apply a Strategy* Determine the number of valence electrons by referring to the periodic table. Then use dots to represent those electrons around the element symbol.

■ *Work a Solution* Since phosphorus is in Group 5A, it has 5 valence electrons. First, place one dot on each side of an imaginary box around the symbol, then pair up dots as needed, to attain the total number of valence electrons for the element.

$$\cdot \overset{\displaystyle \cdot}{\underset{\displaystyle \cdot}{P}} \colon$$

■ *Verify Your Answer* Compare the electron dot symbol of phosphorus with that of nitrogen in Table 13-1. Since both are Group 5A elements and have the same number of valence electrons, the electron dot symbol should be similar—and it is.

Practice Problems

Write the electron dot symbol for each of the following elements:

1. iodine   2. krypton   3. sulfur

> **PROBLEM·SOLVING**
> **S T R A T E G Y**
>
> *Use what you know* from Chapter 11 about groups of elements and their position on the periodic table to determine the number of valence electrons. (See Strategy, page 58.)

EXAMPLE 13-2

Use electron dot symbols to represent the formation of magnesium fluoride from atoms of magnesium and fluorine.

■ *Analyze the Problem* Recognize that to complete the problem, you must begin by determining the formula for magnesium fluoride.

■ *Apply a Strategy* Determine the number of valence electrons for magnesium and fluorine, using the periodic table.

■ *Work a Solution* Magnesium is from Group 2A and has 2 valence electrons, while fluorine is from Group 7A and has 7 valence electrons. The ions likely to form from these 2 elements are Mg^{2+} and F^-. In doing so, they both attain electron configurations that are isoelectronic with neon. As a result of the charges on the ions, you get a formula of MgF_2. The formation of magnesium fluoride can be written as

$$\colon\overset{\displaystyle \cdot}{\underset{\displaystyle \cdot}{F}}\cdot \ + \cdot Mg\cdot + \cdot\overset{\displaystyle \cdot}{\underset{\displaystyle \cdot}{F}}\colon \to [\colon\overset{\displaystyle \cdot\cdot}{\underset{\displaystyle \cdot\cdot}{F}}\colon]^- + [Mg]^{2+} + [\colon\overset{\displaystyle \cdot\cdot}{\underset{\displaystyle \cdot\cdot}{F}}\colon]^-$$

Balancing the charges, you get this formula.

$$MgF_2$$

> **PROBLEM·SOLVING**
> **S T R A T E G Y**
>
> *Break the problem into manageable parts.* Remember that the total charge for an ionic compound is zero. In all ionic compounds, the total positive charge must be equal to the total negative charge. (See Strategy, page 166.)

Practice Problems

Assign the Practice Problems.

PART **1**
Section 13.3

Practice Problems

Assign the Practice Problems.

Science Background

Covalent Bonds

Covalent bonding involves the overlap of unfilled orbitals as they approach each other. In a covalent bond, the shared pair of electrons will spend more time between the two nuclei. The mutual attraction of the two nuclei for the shared electrons is greater than the electron-electron or nucleus-nucleus repulsions.

Two helium atoms will not bond because both atoms have filled valence orbitals. As two helium atoms approach, the repulsive forces are greater than the attractive forces, so no bond forms.

Teaching Strategy

Covalent Bonds

Ask students to represent bonds by a mechanical analogy consisting of a hook and an eye (as in a door fastener). Challenge students to characterize some atoms as "hooks" and other atoms as "eyes." When a hook goes into an eye, a bond is formed. Ask which represents a metal and a nonmetal. [hooks—nonmetals; eyes—metals. Nonmetals can form compounds by either nonmetal-nonmetal bonds (hook-hook overlap), or nonmetal-metal bonds (hook-eye overlap), but metals form compounds only with nonmetals (hook-eye overlap). No "bond" is formed when two eyes overlap.]

■ **Verify Your Answer** Check that both the magnesium ion and the fluoride ion have an electron configuration isoelectronic with a noble gas element. Also check that the total positive charge is equal to the total negative charge.

Practice Problems

Use electron dot symbols to represent the formation of the following compounds from their elements.

4. strontium oxide

5. aluminum chloride

13.3 Covalent Bonds

Recall from Chapter 2 that hydrogen gas exists as a diatomic molecule, H_2. What is the force of attraction between two hydrogen atoms? In view of what you have just learned, you might think that an ionic bond is formed by one atom losing an electron and the other atom gaining it, but that is not the case. Experiments show that liquid hydrogen does not conduct electricity. Thus hydrogen cannot contain ions.

Even though a hydrogen molecule does not contain ions, each atom of hydrogen is still made up of charged particles—a proton with a positive charge and an electron with a negative charge. If two atoms of hydrogen are far apart, there is no significant force of attraction between the two atoms, and no bond exists. This is the case represented in Figure 13-2 *left*. For each atom, the plus sign represents the single proton in the nucleus, and the shaded area around the nucleus represents the electron in the 1*s* orbital. If the atoms are close enough to each other, an attraction between the electrons and protons develops. This force of attraction is a result of a pair of electrons being simultaneously attracted to both hydrogen nuclei. The pair of electrons is then shared between the two hydrogen atoms. This sharing of a pair of electrons between atoms is called a **covalent bond.** Figure 13-2 *right* is a representation of a hydrogen molecule.

Figure 13-2 *This figure illustrates two hydrogen atoms* (left) *before bonding and* (right) *after bonding.*

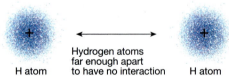

Hydrogen atoms
far enough apart
to have no interaction

H atom   H atom

H_2 molecule

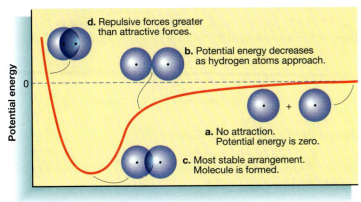

PART **1**

Section 13.3 *continued*

d. Repulsive forces greater than attractive forces.

b. Potential energy decreases as hydrogen atoms approach.

a. No attraction. Potential energy is zero.

c. Most stable arrangement. Molecule is formed.

Potential energy

0

Distance between nuclei

Figure 13-3 *The potential energy for two hydrogen atoms changes as they approach and form a covalent bond. The same principle can be applied to the formation of other covalent bonds.*

Potential energy changes and covalent bonds

Another way to look at the formation of a covalent bond is in terms of potential energy changes. Figure 13-3 shows the relative total potential energy of two hydrogen atoms.

The sequence *a* to *d* represents the nuclei of two hydrogen atoms, initially separated and then moving closer and closer together. If two hydrogen atoms are so far apart that they have no attraction for each other, as shown in *a*, the potential energy of the system is assigned a value of zero. As the atoms approach each other, however, forces between the atoms become important. There are repulsive forces between the electrons of the two atoms and between the protons of the two atoms. But there are also attractive forces between the proton of one atom and the electron of the other atom, and vice versa. If these attractive forces are larger than the repulsive forces, the potential energy will decrease. This change is shown in *b*. As the atoms get closer still, the energy drops more, as shown in *c*. Again the increase in attractive forces is larger than the increase in repulsive forces. However, as the two atoms get even closer together, repulsive forces increase more than the attractive forces. In *d*, the repulsive forces are larger than the attractive forces.

The most stable arrangement of the atoms is when the potential energy is lowest, as shown by *c*. The total potential energy of the molecule is less than the total potential energy of the individual atoms that form the molecule. Thus a molecule of hydrogen is more stable than two individual atoms of hydrogen.

Bond energy
When two atoms of hydrogen combine to form a molecule, energy is given off. It should seem reasonable, then, that energy is needed to break this covalent bond to form two separated hydrogen atoms. The energy needed to break a bond is the bond energy. The bond energy is the lowest potential energy shown in *c*. The distance between the two nuclei in *c* is referred to as the **bond length**.

CONNECTING CONCEPTS

Models Bonding models cannot be applied to every molecule. Models used in this chapter are chosen to help you achieve the goals of this course without being overly cumbersome. As you advance in your study of chemistry, you will be introduced to more sophisticated models that can be applied to a larger number of molecules.

Science Background

Potential Energy Changes and Covalent Bonds

Plots of potential energy as shown in Figure 13–3 indicate the bond energy, which is the magnitude of the minimum energy, and the bond length, which is the distance between the nuclei when the potential energy is at a minimum.

The text does not go into detailed models of covalent bonding. The valence bond approach treats covalent bond formation as an overlapping of atomic orbitals. Teachers may have used additional references in which the utility of this model has been expanded using wave equation treatments. However, this model does not adequately explain all covalent bonds. The molecular orbital theory is another approach to bonding. Both models have their advantages and disadvantages.

Videodisc Connections

385-389, side 3
Chemical bonds: forming bonds
(5-frame seq.)

Covalent bonds and electron dot symbols Electron dot symbols are also useful for representing covalent bonds. The formation of a molecule of hydrogen can be illustrated as

$$H\cdot \; + \; \cdot H \rightarrow \boxed{H : H}$$
2 electrons   2 electrons

The two circles emphasize that the two bonding electrons are associated with both hydrogen nuclei.

Can two chlorine atoms form a covalent bond? If you draw the electron dot symbol for a chlorine atom, you can see that there is one unpaired valence electron.

$$:\ddot{C}l\cdot$$

Just as in the case of hydrogen, when two chlorine atoms approach, the unpaired electrons are shared and a covalent bond is formed. The formation of molecular chlorine can be illustrated as

$$:\ddot{C}l\cdot \; + \; \cdot\ddot{C}l: \; \rightarrow \boxed{:\ddot{C}l \; \ddot{C}l:}$$
8 electrons   8 electrons

The shared pair of electrons in the equation represent the covalent bond.

Orbital diagrams and covalent bonds As two hydrogen atoms approach each other, the sharing of electrons in a covalent bond can be interpreted as the overlapping of orbitals. If you recall from Chapter 10 that any orbital can hold a maximum of two electrons, then a covalent bond may also be represented by drawing the orbital diagram for each atom and shading the orbitals that overlap.

	1s	2s	2p
F	⇅	⇅	⇅ ⇅ ↑
F	⇅	⇅	⇅ ⇅ ↑

Whether drawn using electron dots or orbital diagrams, a significant aspect of the representations is the fact that they show electrons being shared between atoms.

13.4 Unequal Sharing of Electrons

Could a covalent bond form between a hydrogen atom and a chlorine atom? If you draw the electron dot symbol for each atom, you will find that they both have an unpaired electron. If the unpaired electrons are shared by both the hydrogen and chlorine nucleus, a covalent bond is formed.

$$H\cdot \; + \; \cdot\ddot{C}l: \; \rightarrow \boxed{H : \ddot{C}l:}$$

Myths and Misconceptions

When learning about shared electrons, students may believe that electrons between atoms are always shared equally. It is true that electrons in a covalent bond between *identical* atoms are shared equally. However, in a covalent bond between *unlike* atoms, the electrons may spend more time in the vicinity of one atom than they do near the other atom. If students do not understand this phenomenon, they will have difficulty with electronegativity, polarity, and the identification of bond types.

Ask students to make drawings of the distribution of electrons in molecules such as HCl and H_2. Clarify electron sharing if students' drawings show an equal distribution of electrons forming the bond in the HCl molecule. Review the unequal sharing of electrons discussed in Section 13.4, emphasizing the model of HCl in Figure 13–4.

Could the electrons be unequally shared? Imagine a tug-of-war contest involving professional football defensive linemen and professional horse-racing jockeys. If two football players compete, they both pull on the rope, but the result is pretty much a standoff. Likewise a standoff occurs when two jockeys compete. However, if a lineman and a jockey compete against each other, the much stronger football player has the advantage and will be able to pull with a greater force. In a sense, the rope in a tug-of-war is analogous to the electron pair making up a bond. If both nuclei are identical, as in a hydrogen molecule or a chlorine molecule, the pair of electrons is shared equally. However, if one nucleus has a stronger attraction for electrons than the other nucleus, there is a high probability that the shared pair of electrons will be closer to that nucleus. Figure 13-4 shows a representation of the electron pair sharing in a molecule of HCl. Which nucleus has the stronger attraction for the electrons?

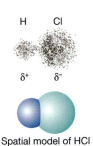

Spatial model of HCl

Figure 13-4 *There is an unequal distribution of the shared electrons in the bond between the hydrogen and the chlorine.*

Polar covalent bonds Even though electrons are shared, the fact that they are more strongly attracted to the chlorine atom results in a partial negative charge at the chlorine atom and a partial positive charge at the hydrogen atom. Such a bond is called a **dipole.** A dipole has two separated, equal but opposite charges. The lowercase Greek letter *delta*, δ, is used to indicate the partial charge at each end of the bond. A covalent bond that has a dipole is called a **polar covalent bond.** When two different elements form a covalent bond, the bond is usually a polar covalent bond, as in HCl. Covalent bonds in which electrons are equally shared by two nuclei, as in H_2 or Cl_2, are called **nonpolar covalent bonds.**

Electronegativity The measure of the attraction an atom has for a shared pair of electrons in a bond is called **electronegativity.** For example, in hydrogen chloride, chlorine has a greater attraction for the electron pair than hydrogen, so chlorine is said to be more electronegative than hydrogen. In general, bonding electrons will be more strongly attracted to the atom of higher electronegativity, and the partial negative charge, δ^-, will reside on that atom. Likewise the partial positive charge, δ^+, will reside on the atom of lower electronegativity value.

TABLE 13-2

Predicting Types of Bonds

Students often fail to see the continuum of bonding. Table 13–3 and Figure 13–5 illustrate that the different types of bonding are really just different degrees of the same phenomenon. Nonpolar covalent is equal sharing, polar covalent is unequal sharing, and ionic is unequal sharing to such an extent that the electron is considered to be transferred.

Electronegativities of the Elements																	
1A																	
2.1 **H**	**2A**												**3A**	**4A**	**5A**	**6A**	**7A**
1.0 **Li**	1.5 **Be**												2.0 **B**	2.5 **C**	3.0 **N**	3.5 **O**	4.0 **F**
0.9 **Na**	1.2 **Mg**												1.5 **Al**	1.8 **Si**	2.1 **P**	2.5 **S**	3.0 **Cl**
0.8 **K**	1.0 **Ca**	1.3 **Sc**	1.5 **Ti**	1.6 **V**	1.6 **Cr**	1.5 **Mn**	1.8 **Fe**	1.8 **Co**	1.8 **Ni**	1.9 **Cu**	1.6 **Zn**	1.6 **Ga**	1.8 **Ge**	2.0 **As**	2.4 **Se**	2.8 **Br**
0.8 **Rb**	1.0 **Sr**	1.2 **Y**	1.4 **Zr**	1.6 **Nb**	1.8 **Mo**	1.9 **Tc**	2.2 **Ru**	2.2 **Rh**	2.2 **Pd**	1.9 **Ag**	1.7 **Cd**	1.7 **In**	1.8 **Sn**	1.9 **Sb**	2.1 **Te**	2.5 **I**
0.7 **Cs**	0.9 **Ba**	1.1–1.2 **La–Lu**	1.3 **Hf**	1.5 **Ta**	1.7 **W**	1.9 **Re**	2.2 **Os**	2.2 **Ir**	2.2 **Pt**	2.4 **Au**	1.9 **Hg**	1.8 **Tl**	1.8 **Pb**	1.9 **Bi**	2.0 **Po**	2.2 **At**
0.7 **Fr**	0.9 **Ra**	1.1–1.7 **Ac–Lr**															

Decreasing electronegativity ↓

Increasing electronegativity →

Linus Pauling, an American scientist, devised a method of calculating the electronegativities of atoms in chemical bonds. In doing so, he assigned a value to each atom. Table 13-2 gives the electronegativity values for the elements. Notice that the values increase from left to right across the periodic table and decrease from top to bottom down a group. What is the least electronegative element on the table? Did you notice that metals tend to have lower values of electronegativity than nonmetals?

Concept **Check**

How can a bond between two atoms have a partial positive charge (δ^+) and a partial negative charge (δ^-).

Predicting types of bonds The difference between electronegativities of two atoms in a bond can be used as a guide to determine the degree of electron sharing in a bond. As the electronegativity difference between the atoms increases, the degree of sharing decreases. This difference in electronegativity can be used to predict the type of bonding. If the difference in electronegativities is 1.7 or more, the bond is generally considered more ionic than covalent. Sodium chloride has been given as an example of an ionic compound. What is the electronegativity difference between sodium and chlorine? If the electronegativity difference is between 0.1 and 1.7, the bond is a polar covalent bond that is more covalent than ionic. Does the electronegativity difference between hydrogen and

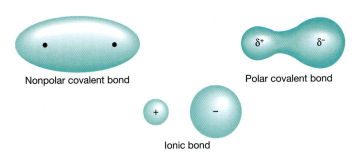

Nonpolar covalent bond

Polar covalent bond

Ionic bond

Figure 13-5 *These three types of bonds do not reflect different mechanisms for bonding; rather, a way to classify the degree of sharing electrons that occurs in any bond.*

chlorine in the HCl molecule confirm that it contains a polar covalent bond? Finally, if the difference is zero, the bond is considered nonpolar covalent, as in the case of a hydrogen or a chlorine molecule. Figure 13-5 shows a representation of the different types of bonds. Table 13-3 summarizes the relationship between bonding type and electronegativity differences.

TABLE 13-3

The Relationship between Electronegativity and Bond Type			
Electronegativity difference between the bonding atoms	Bond type	Covalent character	Ionic character
zero ↓ intermediate ↓ large	covalent ↓ polar covalent ↓ ionic	Increases	Increases

EXAMPLE 13-3

Classify the bond in each of the following as ionic, polar covalent, or nonpolar covalent: KF, O_2, ICl.

Show the partial charge for any polar covalent bonds.

■ **Analyze the Problem** Recall that the difference between electronegativities of two atoms is used to predict the type of bonding. You can reason that in a polar covalent bond, the negative end of the dipole will be the atom that attracts the electron pair more strongly, that is, the atom with the higher electronegativity.

■ **Apply a Strategy** Find the differences in electronegativity values for each pair of elements. Refer to Table 13-2 for the values you need. Make a table to organize the information as you obtain it.

PART 1

Section 13.4 *continued*

Guided Practice

Review the Concept Check question on page 440 with students. Answers can be found in Appendix E on page 808.

Reteaching Idea

If students are unsure about ionic, polar covalent, and nonpolar covalent bonds, revisit Tables 13–2 and 13–3. Focus on the arrows that indicate how ionic character increases as electronegativity increases. Ask students under what conditions a completely covalent bond forms. Have them draw a model of the chlorine molecule showing the bonding pair of electrons equidistant from each atom. Then have them use Table 13–2 to draw bonds between chlorine and each of the other elements in period three—sulfur, phosphorus, silicon, aluminum, magnesium, and sodium. The electron pair should be shown moving closer to chlorine as the electronegativity difference increases from right to left. Students should see that for NaCl, the sodium electron is virtually transferred to chlorine. Help students recognize that ionic bonds are the limiting case of polar covalent bonds—a complete removal of an electron resulting in a 1+ charge on the less electronegative atom.

PART 1

Section 13.4 continued

Practice Problems

Assign the Practice Problems.

☰ CLOSE

Summing Up Main Ideas

Have students use electron dot symbols to represent one element with an electronegativity of 1.5, one element with an electronegativity of 2.5, and one element with an electronegativity of 3.5. Students should use electron dot symbols to illustrate an ionic compound, a polar covalent compound, and a nonpolar covalent compound that could be formed using only the three elements they have selected. For example, Al (1.5), S (2.5), and O (3.5) could form Al_2O_3 (ionic), Al_2S_3 (polar covalent) and O_2 (nonpolar covalent).

PART 1 REVIEW

Assign the Part Review questions.

Evaluating Skills

These skills are evaluated in the Part Review questions indicated. **Determining main ideas:** 9, 10, 12; **Comparing/Contrasting:** 13, 15; **Classifying:** 14; **Predicting:** 17

■ **Work a Solution**

Compound	Elements	Electronegativity	Electronegativity difference	Bond type	Charge
KF	K	0.8			+
	F	4.0	3.2	ionic	−
O_2	O	3.5	0	nonpolar covalent	0
ICl	I	2.5		polar	$\delta+$
	Cl	3.0	0.5	covalent	$\delta-$

■ **Verify Your Answer** Check your math to be sure you have not made any errors. Also, if you know that the bond type of a particular compound—for example NaCl—is ionic, check to see if any of the compounds given in the problem have elements from the same families. In the case of KF, K and Na are in Group 1A, while F and Cl are in Group 7A. Elements in the same group have similar properties so if Na and Cl form an ionic bond, K and F will also. This agrees with the prediction in the problem.

Practice Problems

Identify the type of bond in the following substances.

6. HBr   7. NaF   8. N_2

PART 1 REVIEW

9. What is a chemical bond?

10. Explain how an ionic bond forms.

11. Use electron dot symbols to represent the formation of LiCl, K_2S, and $BaCl_2$.

12. Explain what is meant by electronegativity.

13. Distinguish between nonpolar covalent, polar covalent, and ionic bonds.

14. Classify the kind of bond contained in each of the following: HI, F_2, CsCl, MgO, Cl_2, NaBr, AsH_3, and PCl_3.

15. Choose the more polar covalent bond from the following pairs: H–Cl and H–I; C–H and C–O; S–Cl and P–S.

16. Indicate the partial-charge (δ) designation for the bonds in problem 15.

17. Using the three classifications of bonds discussed, predict the type that is most likely to be present in compounds made from elements of Groups 1A and 7A and Groups 6A and 7A.

Boxed numbers indicate questions that involve skills in interpretation, application, and analysis.

PART 1 REVIEW

ANSWERS

■ Keyed to Objectives

A 9. the strong attractive force between atoms or ions in a compound

A 10. An atom loses one or more electrons to form a cation and another atom gains one or more electrons to form an anion. The electrostatic attraction between the cation and the anion is the ionic bond.

A 11. $[Li]^+[:\ddot{C}l:]^-[K]^+[:\ddot{S}:]^{2-}[Ba]^{2+}[:\ddot{C}l:]^-$

C 12. the attraction that a bonded atom has for a pair of electrons

B 13. Nonpolar covalent—electron pair shared equally, both atoms have about the same EN; polar covalent—electron pair shared unequally, atoms have different EN; ionic—electrons transferred, atoms have very different EN.

C 14. HI—polar covalent; F_2—nonpolar covalent; CsCl—ionic; MgO—ionic; Cl_2—nonpolar covalent; NaBr—ionic; AsH_3—polar covalent; PCl_3—polar covalent.

D 15. H—Cl; C—O; S—Cl

D 16. $\overset{\delta^+}{H}—\overset{\delta^-}{Cl}$ $\overset{\delta^+}{H}—\overset{\delta^-}{I}$;
$\overset{\delta^-}{C}—\overset{\delta^+}{H}$ $\overset{\delta^+}{C}—\overset{\delta^-}{O}$;

PART 2 Describing Molecular Structure

One goal of this chapter is to increase your understanding of the way molecules behave. You have already been introduced to bonding models that tell you something about how atoms come together to form chemical bonds. The next step is to focus your attention on the resulting molecules. Being able to visualize molecules makes thinking about them easier.

While some simple molecules are relatively easy to visualize, there are also many subtleties to molecular structure. To make it easier not only to visualize molecules but to understand their chemical and physical properties, models have been devised for representing molecules. Because of the variety of molecules and because of the different models used to describe bonding, no single model for representing molecules is the best for all cases.

In this chapter, electron dot structures will be used to help you understand the properties of many different molecules. While this representation is not foolproof, it can serve as a guide. It provides a simple representation of many molecules, and predictions of properties based on this model can be verified by experimental evidence.

13.5 The Octet Rule

Predicting the bonding arrangements that occur between atoms in a molecule is based on two important observations. The first, which you have already learned, is that noble gases are unreactive and form very few compounds. The reason noble gases do not generally react is because the outermost *s* and *p* orbitals are filled, making them particularly stable. Helium has a filled valence orbital, with two electrons in the 1*s* orbital. All of the other noble gases have eight electrons in their valence orbitals corresponding to two electrons in the *s* orbital and six in the *p* orbitals. The second fact, related to what you learned in Section 13.2, is that ionic compounds of the representative elements are generally made up of anions and cations that have noble gas configurations.

From observations like these, chemists have formulated the **octet rule.** The octet rule is based on the assumption that atoms form bonds to achieve a noble gas electron configuration. Each atom would then have eight (an octet of) electrons in its valence orbitals. An important exception to this statement is hydrogen. Why is hydrogen an exception?

Electron dot structures of molecules You can use the octet rule to write electron dot structures (Lewis structures) for molecules. To do this, you need to know the following information.

O b j e c t i v e s

Part 2

E. *Apply* the octet rule to write electron dot structures of simple molecules and polyatomic ions.
F. *Identify* limitations to the octet rule.

Developing Skills

Students may apply these skills in their study of Part 2.
Forming models: Have students write electron dot and structural formulas of molecules.
Comparing/Contrasting: Have students compare the molecular structures of simple molecules.
Determining main ideas: Have students determine the limitations of the octet rule.

≡FOCUS

Activate Prior Knowledge

Discuss with students the concept that models are a way to visualize something that cannot be directly observed. Note that a given model may be adequate to explain certain properties of matter, but that different models may be required to more accurately reflect other properties. Ask students to draw or construct the different models that have been used to describe the atom, the nucleus of the atom, the electron configuration, and the ion. Remind students that throughout the book, several models are used to help visualize different aspects of chemical phenomena.

This will help students when they are learning to write Lewis dot structures. They will need to be aware that Lewis dot structures are useful but not universally applicable in representing molecular structures.

$$\overset{\delta^+ \; \delta^-}{\text{S—Cl}} \quad \overset{\delta^+ \; \delta^-}{\text{P—S}}$$

C 17. 1A and 7A—ionic; 6A and 7A— polar covalent

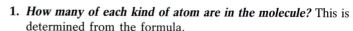

PART **2**
Section 13.5 *continued*

≡ TEACH

Teaching Strategy

The Octet Rule

Writing electron dot structures is a tool that will provide students with a basis for predicting the shape and polar characteristics of a molecule. It might appear that writing such structures is a trial-and-error process. However, a systematic approach can be used for virtually every case, including exceptions to the octet rule. Have students use the following strategy to write the electron dot structure for a molecule or an ion:

1. Determine the total number of valence electrons from all of the atoms. For a poly-atomic anion, *add* one electron for each unit of negative charge. For a cation, *subtract* one electron for each unit of positive charge.
2. Write the skeleton structure.
3. Place one pair of electrons between each set of bonded atoms.
4. Subtract the number of electrons used so far from the total available.
5. Complete the octets of the atoms attached to the central atom by adding pairs of electrons. (Hydrogen is an exception—it will have only two electrons.)
6. Count the electrons in the structure and subtract from the total to be used. Place the remaining electrons on the central atom in pairs.
7. If the central atom has an octet, the electron dot structure is complete. If the central atom does not have an octet of electrons, form double and triple bonds as necessary.

Electron dot structures are not difficult to construct, but it does take practice. Be sure to give students a number of examples by demonstrating several problems with different aspects.

1. *How many of each kind of atom are in the molecule?* This is determined from the formula.
2. *How many valence electrons are available?* Use the position of each atom in the periodic table to determine the number of valence electrons. This information will give the total number of electrons that will be used in the electron dot structure.
3. *What is the skeleton structure?* The skeleton structure shows which atoms are bonded to each other. The skeletal structure can be proven correct only by experimentation. However, for simple molecules, if there is a single atom of one element and several atoms of another element, the single atom is usually the central atom.
4. *Where do the dots go in the structure?* Place the dots around the atoms so that each atom has eight electrons—an octet structure. (Remember, hydrogen is an exception and will have only two dots.)

Electron dot structures of molecules are not difficult to construct, but it does take practice. The easiest way to learn is by doing several simple examples. You can then adapt the method to more complex molecules. The following examples will give you some practice.

EXAMPLE 13-4

Write electron dot structures for the following molecules: H_2O, and $CHCl_3$.

■ *Analyze the Problem* Recognize the fact that to write an electron dot structure, you must determine the number of valence electrons for the molecule and follow the octet rule.

■ *Apply a Strategy* Answer the four questions presented in this section. Organize your answer in a table format. Remember that in order to get the number of valence electrons for each kind of atom, you multiply the number of valence electrons per atom times the number of atoms in a molecule. Add up all of the electrons to get the total number of valence electrons in the molecule.

What is the skeleton structure? With H_2O, oxygen can form two bonds, whereas each hydrogen can form only one. Therefore, oxygen will be in the middle. In the case of $CHCl_3$, use the process of elimination to determine the central atom. It cannot be chlorine or hydrogen, because each of them forms only one bond. So the central atom must be carbon.

Where do the dots go in the structure? Place the dots so that each atom has eight electrons—except for hydrogen, which has two.

Videodisc Connections

387-389, side 3
Molecular structure: H_2O and NH_3 (3-frame seq.)

■ *Work a Solution*

Molecule	H$_2$O	CHCl$_3$
Number of each kind of atom in the molecule	O = 1 H = 2	C = 1 H = 1 Cl = 3
Valence electrons for each atom	O = 6 H = 1	C = 4 H = 1 Cl = 7
Total number of valence electrons	O = 1 × 6 = 6 H = 2 × 1 = 2 8	C = 1 × 4 = 4 H = 1 × 1 = 1 Cl = 3 × 7 = 21 26
Skeleton structure	H O H	H Cl C Cl Cl
Arrangement of dots	H $\ddot{\text{O}}$ H	H :Cl: C :Cl: :Cl:

■ *Verify Your Answer*

Make sure that the number of electron dots you drew in the last row equals the total number of dots you have written in your table.

Practice Problems

Write electron structures for the following molecules.

18. H$_2$S

19. SiF$_4$

Double and triple bonds Try to draw the electron dot structure for carbon dioxide, CO$_2$. When you use the method presented in the last example, you will encounter a problem. Carbon has four valence electrons, and the two oxygens together have 12, for a total of 16 valence electrons. Two possible structures that can be drawn for carbon dioxide include these.

$$:\ddot{\text{O}}:\text{C}:\ddot{\text{O}}: \quad \text{or} \quad :\ddot{\text{O}}:\ddot{\text{C}}:\ddot{\text{O}}:$$

In either case, carbon or oxygen will not have eight electrons represented. However, if each oxygen atom shares two pairs of electrons with the carbon atom, double bonds can be formed, and octets around both carbon and oxygen can be achieved.

$$:\ddot{\text{O}}::\text{C}::\ddot{\text{O}}:$$

Practice Problems

Assign the Practice Problems.

Science Background

The Octet Rule

The ultimate test of models is "does it fit the observed properties?" The utilization of Lewis structures and the octet rule is helpful in understanding bonding. As useful as it is, it does not take precedence over experimental observations. There are many molecules that do not fit the octet rule, some of which will be discussed in the next section.

A **double bond** is a covalent bond in which four electrons (two pairs) are shared by the bonding atoms. Double bonding is an arrangement that accounts for all electrons and satisfies the octet rule.

There is sound evidence for the existence of double bonds in molecules. Atoms believed to be bonded by double bonds are more difficult to break apart than similar atoms bonded by single bonds. Also, experimental measurements show that the bond distance of a double bond between two atoms is shorter than a corresponding single bond.

Evidence also has been found for the existence of triple bonds. A **triple bond** is a bond in which two atoms share three pairs of electrons. Nitrogen is an example of a molecule containing a triple bond. The electron dot structure for N_2 is

$$:N:::N:$$

EXAMPLE 13-5

Draw the electron dot structure for HCN.

■ **Apply a Strategy** Follow the strategy outlined in Example 13-4. Again use a table to organize your work. When drawing the structure, begin placing dots so each element is surrounded by its valence electrons. This makes it easier to visualize which electrons need to be moved if double or triple bonds are formed. To keep track of the dots, different symbols can be used for each element—for example, squares or triangles.

■ **Work a Solution**

Molecule	HCN
Number of valence electrons	H = 1 C = 4 N = 5
Total number of symbols	H = 1 (×1) = 1 C = 1 (×4) = 4 N = 1 (×5) = 5
Total number of valence e⁻	10
Skeleton structure	H C N
Arrangement of dots	H:C:::N:

■ **Verify Your Answer** Check that the total number of valence electrons is represented in your structures. With the exception of hydrogen, check that all elements have a total of eight dots (electrons), representing an octet structure.

Practice Problems
Draw the electron dot structure for

20. C_2H_4 **21.** CO

Structural formulas For convenience, bonding electron pairs are often represented as a line instead of a pair of dots. Nonbonding pairs of electrons, sometimes referred to as lone pairs, are still shown as dots. The resulting diagram is called a structural formula. Likewise, double and triple bonds are represented by two and three lines. The electron dot structures for molecules in Examples 13-5 and 13-6 are shown by using the line notation.

$$H-\overset{\cdot\cdot}{\underset{\cdot\cdot}{O}}-H \qquad :\overset{\cdot\cdot}{\underset{\cdot\cdot}{Cl}}-\overset{:\overset{\cdot\cdot}{Cl}:}{\underset{:\underset{\cdot\cdot}{Cl}:}{C}}-H \qquad H-C\equiv N:$$

Concept ✔ Check

Compare and contrast an electron dot structure with a structural formula.

Electron dot structure and polyatomic ions In Chapter 2, you learned about polyatomic ions. A polyatomic ion is a group of atoms with a charge. The individual atoms in a polyatomic ion are bonded to each other by covalent bonds.

You can write the electron dot structure for a polyatomic ion just as you wrote the electron dot structure for molecules. To do so, you need to recognize that the charge on the ion must be taken into account when determining the total number of valence electrons. For a polyatomic anion, you *add one electron* for each unit of negative charge; and for a cation, you *subtract one electron* for each unit of positive charge. Brackets are then placed around the structure and the charge indicated as shown in Example 13-6.

EXAMPLE 13-6

Write the electron dot structure for ClO_4^-.

■ ***Analyze the Problem*** Recognize that this is a polyatomic anion so you must account for the negative charge when writing

PART 2
Section 13.6

Practice Problems

Assign the Practice Problems.

PROBLEM-SOLVING
S T R A T E G Y

Review the list of common polyatomic ions given in Table 2-5.

PROBLEM-SOLVING
S T R A T E G Y

Use what you know from Examples 13-4 and 13-5 to write the structure of the ion. (See Strategy, page 58.)

---

the structure. There is one Cl and 4 oxygens, so Cl is most likely the central atom.

■ **Apply a Strategy** Determine the total number of valence electrons from all of the atoms. Then *add* one electron because the ion has a charge of -1.

■ **Work a Solution**

Ion	ClO_4^-
Number of valence electrons	Cl = 1 ($\times$7) = 7 O = 4 ($\times$6) = 24 Ion charge = 1
Total number of valence e^-	32
Skeleton structure	O O Cl O O
Arrangement of dots	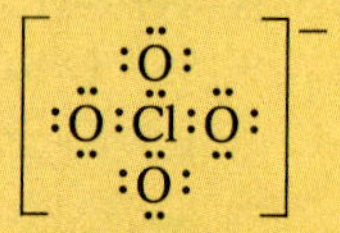 $\left[\begin{array}{c} :\ddot{O}: \\ :\ddot{O}:\ddot{C}l:\ddot{O}: \\ :\ddot{O}: \end{array}\right]^-$

■ **Verify Your Answer** Count to be sure that all 32 electrons are distributed and that each atom has an octet.

Practice Problems

Write the electron configuration for

22. NH_4^+

23. SO_4^{2-} (sulfur is the central atom)

13.6 Limitations of the Octet Rule

While the octet rule is a useful model that allows you to picture the structure of molecules, it is important to realize that molecules do not *obey* the octet rule or any other rule. The concept serves only as a scientific tool, or rule of thumb. Not surprisingly, molecules exist that cannot be explained using the octet rule. For example, nitric oxide, NO, one of the pollutants found in automobile exhaust, has an odd number of valence electrons (5 + 6 = 11). Since the octet rule requires that electrons be placed in pairs, NO cannot satisfy the octet rule.

Atoms without octets There are also some stable molecules that possess a central atom with fewer than eight electrons in the electron dot structure. Boron trifluoride is one example. The electron dot structure of BF_3 is written as follows.

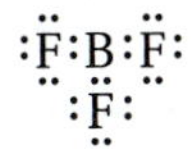

$$:\ddot{F}:B:\ddot{F}:$$
$$:\ddot{F}:$$

The boron atom has only six electrons around it. You could write an electron dot structure that would satisfy the octet rule.

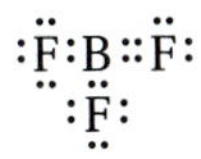

$$:\ddot{F}:B::\ddot{F}:$$
$$:\ddot{F}:$$

Such a structure, however, which shows one double bond and two single bonds, does not agree with experimental evidence indicating that each of the boron-fluorine bonds is close to a single bond. Remember, primary importance must be given to experimental results, and in this case it mandates that boron trifluoride be treated as an exception to the octet rule.

Atoms with more than an octet Compounds also exist in which the central atom has more than an octet of electrons. All of the compounds formed from the noble gas elements are examples. The existence of compounds of the noble gas elements was long thought to be an impossibility because the noble gas atoms already have complete octets. One of the first noble gas compounds to be synthesized was xenon tetrafluoride, XeF_4. The electron dot structure for XeF_4 has twelve electrons in the valence orbitals of xenon.

Phosphorus and sulfur also form stable molecules that have more than an octet of electrons. Phosphorus pentachloride shares 10 electrons in the valence shell, and sulfur hexafluoride shares 12 electrons in the valence shell. The electron dot structures for XeF_4, PCl_5, and SF_6 are shown below.

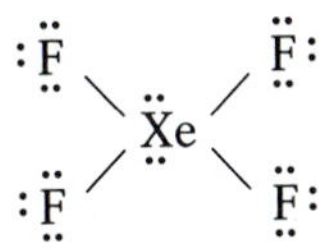

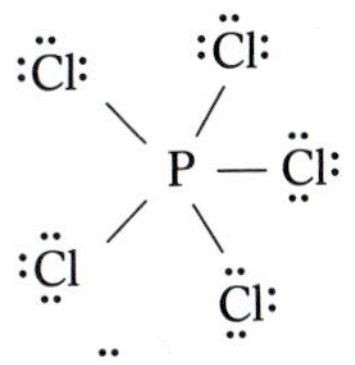

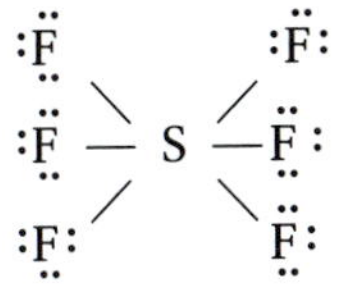

Molecules with more than an octet of electrons are possible because of the larger size of the central atom and because the central atom has bonding d orbitals in addition to the s and p orbitals.

Equivalent electron dot structures Some molecules and polyatomic ions have properties that cannot be adequately explained by a single electron dot structure. An example is the

Teaching Strategy

Equivalent Electron Dot Structures

While resonance structures seem artificial to students, these structures help to explain bond lengths and strengths in such molecules as O_3 and SO_2 and in ions such as CO_3^{2-} and NO_3^-.

Guided Practice

Review the Concept Check question on page 447 with students. Answers can be found in Appendix E on page 808.

PART 2

Section 13.6 continued

Reteaching Idea

Students may need more practice in writing electron dot structures and relating them to chemical bonds. Ask a student to draw the electron dot symbol for carbon on the chalkboard ($\cdot\dot{C}\cdot$). Ask another student to bond a hydrogen atom to the carbon by means of electron sharing. Ask two other students to add a chlorine and a fluorine atom. Challenge a fifth student to add a second fluorine atom. Point of emphasis: The structure with four bonds provides an octet of electrons around each atom (two around hydrogen). A fifth bond will not form.

≡ CLOSE

Summing Up Main Ideas

Have students list the four different kinds of bonding that electron dot structures are used to illustrate. (single, double, triple, and resonance) Also ask students to describe the experimental observations that are used to support the existence of different kinds of bonds. (Data on bond energies and bond distances support the existence of different types of bonds.)

PART 2 REVIEW

Assign the Part Review questions.

Evaluating Skills

These skills are evaluated in the Part Review questions indicated. **Determining main ideas:** 24, 25; **Summarizing:** 25; **Forming models:** 26, 27, 30, 31; **Analyzing data:** 26, 27, 30, 31; **Applying a strategy:** 26, 27, 30, 31; **Verifying results:** 26, 27, 30, 31

carbonate ion, $CO_3{}^{2-}$. One electron dot structure that fulfills the octet rule is

$$\left[:\ddot{O}:\ddot{O}::C::\ddot{O}: \right]^{2-}$$

However, two additional structures also fulfill the octet rule.

$$\left[:\ddot{O}::C:\ddot{O}: \right]^{2-} \quad \text{and} \quad \left[:\ddot{O}:C:\ddot{O}: \right]^{2-}$$

All three structures show the carbon atom as the central atom bonding to two oxygen atoms via a single bond and to the third oxygen atom by a double bond. The only difference is the position of the double bond. However, experimental studies of the carbonate ion indicate that all three of the carbon-oxygen bonds are identical; there is no evidence of both single and double bonds. In fact, the bonds are stronger than a carbon-oxygen single bond and weaker than a carbon-oxygen double bond. Once again the simple theory of bonding presented earlier cannot explain this phenomenon, which is called **resonance.** In cases where resonance occurs, more than one acceptable dot structure can be written without changing the arrangement of atoms. Resonance is often represented by writing each of the different electron dot structures and including double-headed arrows between the possible structures.

$$\left[:\ddot{O}:\ddot{O}:C::\ddot{O}: \right]^{2-} \longleftrightarrow \left[:\ddot{O}::C:\ddot{O}: \right]^{2-} \longleftrightarrow \left[:\ddot{O}:C:\ddot{O}: \right]^{2-}$$

While none of the three resonance structures shown for the carbonate ion actually exist, writing all three in this manner helps to emphasize the fact that the simple octet rule cannot correctly describe molecules that exhibit resonance. The resonance structures merely indicate that no single structure adequately represents the molecule.

PART 2 REVIEW

24. What is an electron dot (Lewis) structure?
25. Briefly describe how the electron dot structure of an atom is written.
26. Write the electron dot structure for an atom of each of the following elements: potassium, arsenic, bromine, silicon, tellurium, aluminum.
27. Draw the electron dot structure for each of the following molecules: Br_2, NH_3, $SiCl_4$, H_2S, C_3H_8.
28. What does a line represent in an electron dot formula?
29. What is a double bond? Give an example of a molecule containing a double bond.

Boxed numbers indicate questions that involve skills in interpretation, application, and analysis.

PART 2 REVIEW

ANSWERS

■ **Keyed to Objectives**

A 24. a symbolic representation of an atom and its valence electrons

E 25. The symbol of the element is surrounded by dots equal to the number of valence electrons.

E 26. $K\cdot$ $\cdot\ddot{A}s\cdot$ $\cdot\ddot{B}r:$

$\cdot\dot{S}i\cdot$ $\cdot\dot{T}e:$ $\dot{A}l\cdot$

E 27. $:\ddot{B}r:\ddot{B}r:$ $H:\ddot{N}:H$ with H below

$:\ddot{C}l:$
$:\ddot{C}l:\dot{S}i:\ddot{C}l:$ $H:\ddot{S}:H$
$:\ddot{C}l:$

$$\begin{array}{ccc} H & H & H \\ H:C:C:C:H \\ H & H & H \end{array}$$

30. Draw the electron dot structure for each of the following species:

$$C_2H_2, CO, NO^+, ClO_3^-.$$

31. Discuss how each of the following molecules is an exception to the octet rule: $BeCl_2$, NO_2, and SF_4.

32. Draw an electron dot structure of the nitrate ion, NO_3^-. Can this ion be represented by resonance structures? Explain your answer.

C O N S U M E R   C H E M I S T R Y

Practical Uses of Microwaves

What can be used to transport telephone conversations around the globe, cook food, and even explore molecular structure? You may be surprised to learn that microwaves are used for all of these applications.

Today systems of microwave satellites carry signals around the globe, thus improving long-distance transmission and greatly expanding in-

tercontinental communication. Additionally, microwaves can carry many more messages at the same time than wires. Microwaves are also used to transmit facsimile (FAX) messages, cellular telephone calls, and television signals.

What are microwaves? Microwaves are a relatively low-energy form of electromagnetic radiation, having wavelengths between 1 and 10 millimeters. Microwaves are higher in energy than FM radiowaves but lower in energy

than infrared radiation, the type of radiation given off by glowing charcoal briquettes.

Do you own a microwave oven or have you ever used a friend's? Microwaves are absorbed by polar molecules in food, primarily water. When water molecules absorb microwave radiation, they begin to move rapidly. They then transfer their heat energy to other

nearby molecules, and thus the food is warmed throughout.

Research uses Microwaves can also be used in microwave spectroscopy, a technique that helps chemists examine molecules at the submicroscopic level. By studying the way microwaves interact with the molecular bonds present, chemists can determine the molecule's size or shape or determine bond lengths or the magnitude of bond dipoles.

E **28.** a pair of electrons

E **29.** a bond formed by the sharing of two electron pairs; Many examples are possible.

E **30.**

F **31.** $BeCl_2$—Be has only two pairs of electrons; NO_2—has an odd number of electrons so all electrons cannot be paired and octets for each atom are not possible; SF_4—S has five pairs of electrons, four bonding pairs and one lone pair.

F **32.**

$$\left[:\ddot{O}:N:\ddot{O}: \atop :\ddot{O}: \right] \leftrightarrow \left[:\ddot{O}::N:\ddot{O}: \atop :\ddot{O}: \right] \leftrightarrow$$

$$\left[:\ddot{O}:N::\ddot{O}: \atop :\ddot{O}: \right]$$

PART **3**
Shapes and Properties
of Molecules

Section 13.7

Developing Skills

Students may apply these skills in their study of Part 3.
Predicting: Have students predict the shapes of molecules.
Forming models: Have students use the informaton in Table 13–4 to construct geometric shapes of some molecules.
Comparing/Contrasting: Have students compare the geometric shapes of the simple molecules.

≡FOCUS

Activate Prior Knowledge

Students may have had experience drawing and constructing geometric shapes in their study of geometry. Obtain sheets of acetate that are used to make overhead transparencies. Show students illustrations of the following geometric shapes: a regular tetrahedron, the sides of which are four equilateral triangles of the same size; a trigonal pyramid, which is a pyramid with a triangular base; a trigonal bipyramid, formed by putting the bases of two three-sided pyramids together; an octahedron, which can be constructed from two four-sided pyramids with their square bases together. Ask student volunteers to cut overhead transparencies and use transparent adhesive tape to assemble models of these geometric shapes. Pair students with partners who have had geometry. Use these structures as you study this part to show students where the central atom would be in a molecular structure with the same geometry.

PART **3** Shapes and Properties of Molecules

O b j e c t i v e s

Part 3

G. *Predict* the shapes of molecules.
H. *Determine* if a molecule is polar or nonpolar.

When engineers design a car, they must take into account how the shape of the car will affect the driver's performance and a passenger's comfort. That is why a model is built—to provide a three-dimensional view for analysis. The chemist, like the engineer, finds three-dimensional representations extremely important. For example, molecular biologists, scientists who analyze the structure of molecules in living systems, are concerned with large complex molecules called enzymes. Enzymes are responsible for facilitating many reactions in living systems and are composed of long chains of atoms that are twisted, bent, and turned into a maze of bonded atoms. However, each enzyme still has a definite, unique architecture that affects the nature of its properties and function.

When molecules are represented on a page in this book or when your teacher writes structures on the blackboard, you are restricted to two-dimensional representations. As a result, the electron dot structures you have studied may give the impression that molecules are two dimensional. Of course, for most molecules that is not true. In this section, photos and models will be used to help you visualize molecules as they exist in three dimensions.

13.7 Molecular Shapes

In this section, a simple model that will allow you to predict the shape, or geometry, of simple molecules will be introduced. This model, called the **valence shell electron pair repulsion (VSEPR) theory** has been tested and verified by the experimental determination of numerous molecular shapes. In most cases, the shape predicted by this model will be close to the actual shape of the molecule.

There are some basic principles that you will need to apply to the three-dimensional shape of molecules. You will recall that bonds between atoms are a result of the interaction of pairs of electrons. Electrons tend to repel other electrons because of their like charges. Thus it is reasonable to assume that the electron pairs around an atom will be spaced as far apart as possible. *The electron pairs orient themselves so that the repulsions between electron pairs are minimized.* This is the main idea behind the VSEPR theory.

Linear molecules Consider the compound beryllium chloride, $BeCl_2$. This compound, an exception to the octet rule, has an electron dot structure of

$$:\ddot{Cl}—Be—\ddot{Cl}:$$

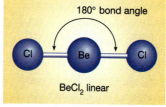

Figure 13-6 *A linear molecule, $BeCl_2$, is illustrated to show the placement of the electrons and the bond angle of 180°.*

You can see that there are two electron pairs on the central beryllium atom. How would you orient these two electron pairs so they would be as far apart as possible? If you place the pairs of electrons on opposite sides of the beryllium atom, repulsion is minimized. The result is an angle of 180° between the bonds. This angle is called the **bond angle** and represents the angle between the bonds connecting the atoms in the molecule. A model of the molecule is shown in Figure 13-6. Figure 13-7 shows how two balloons, representing electron pairs, naturally assume a linear spatial arrangement in the same way as the electron pairs in BeCl₂. The shape of the BeCl₂ molecule is described as *linear*.

Trigonal planar molecules Next look at the molecular shape of BF₃. The electron dot structure is

$$:\ddot{F}—B—\ddot{F}:$$
$$|$$
$$:\ddot{F}:$$

You will recall from Section 13-6 that this molecule also is an exception to the octet rule. To determine the actual arrangement of the fluorine atoms about the central boron atom, a balloon model is again useful. Figure 13-8 shows that three balloons spread out in space have the shape of a triangle.

If the balloons are thought to be analogous to the space occupied by the electron pairs associated with the boron atom, you would predict the electron pairs to be 120° apart from each other in order to minimize repulsion. This prediction has been verified by experiment. The ball-and-stick model of BF₃ in Figure 13-9 shows that all four atoms in the molecule lie in the same plane making the molecule *flat*. The F—B—F bond angle is 120° and because the central atom is joined to 3 identical atoms, all three bond angles are the same. This molecular shape is described as **trigonal planar** (a planar molecule with 3 atoms at the corners of a triangle and the central atom in the middle).

Tetrahedral molecules Methane, CH₄, has four covalent bonds. The electron dot structure of methane is

$$H$$
$$|$$
$$H—C—H$$
$$|$$
$$H$$

Consider two possibilities for the shape of the methane molecule and compare the H—C—H bond angles predicted for each shape with the experimentally measured bond angles. If the methane molecule were planar, each of the H—C—H bond angles would be 90°. Does a planar molecule allow the electron pairs on the carbon atom to be as far apart as possible? To give you a clue, look at four balloons tied together. The four balloons do not remain in a plane;

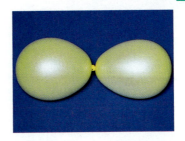
Figure 13-7 As illustrated by the balloon model, a linear arrangement of atoms for a molecule such as beryllium chloride allows for the greatest distance between the electron pairs.

Figure 13-8 Three balloons tied together are farthest apart when they are at angles of 120°. A molecule having this geometry, such as boron trifluoride, is called trigonal planar.

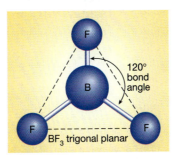
BF₃ trigonal planar
Figure 13-9 The BF₃ molecule is described as trigonal planar, with a bond angle of 120°. The dashed lines in the sketch give the outline of the trigonal (triangular) shape used to describe the molecule.

PART 3
Section 13.7 continued

≡ T E A C H

Teaching Strategy

Molecular Shapes

The geometry of many molecules can be determined from the number of bonded atoms and lone pairs of electrons surrounding the central atom. However, it often helps students to see the three-dimensional shapes of molecules to enhance thinking in three dimensions. Balloons provide a relatively simple alternative to commercial models. If you use the balloons in class, be sure that you emphasize that each balloon represents either a pair of bonded electrons or a lone pair of electrons and that the central atom is located at the position where the balloons are tied together. The central atom would take up a volume much larger than the tied neck of the balloons.

DEMONSTRATION
Molecular Shapes

Use balloons to demonstrate the natural repulsion of electrons. Inflate six balloons to equal size and tie them off. Take two balloons and tie the two ends together; do the same for the other two pairs of balloons. Then wrap one pair of balloons around the other a few times and do the same with the last pair. You will end up with all six balloons connected in the middle. Try to make the balloons flat. It is not a stable arrangement; they automatically assume the shape of an octahedron. Point out that this is the same behavior as electrons. Then pop one of the balloons with a pin. Now the five inflated balloons assume the shape of a trigonal bipyramid. Do the same for four, three, and two balloons.

Figure 13-10 *When four balloons are arranged so that they are as far apart as possible, a structure described as tetrahedral results. The angles between the balloons are all 109.5°.*

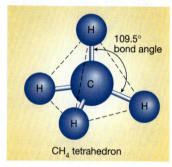

CH_4 tetrahedron

Figure 13-11 *The molecular structure of methane is called a tetrahedron, which means "four-sided."*

they assume the three-dimensional arrangement shown in Figure 13-10.

If the electrons in methane assume this arrangement, the angle between the H—C—H bonds is 109.5°, which is larger than the 90-degree angle that would exist if all the atoms were in one plane. The actual H—C—H bond angle measured experimentally is 109.5°. The geometric shape of the molecule can be shown by drawing lines between all the hydrogen atoms in the molecule. The shape outlined by the dashed lines in Figure 13-11 is called a tetrahedron, and the shape of the methane molecule is described as **tetrahedral.**

Trigonal pyramidal molecules In the structures described so far, all of the valence electrons of the central atom have been involved in bonding. How would you describe the shape of a molecule that has nonbonding (lone) electron pairs? To answer this, look at ammonia, NH_3.

$$H—\overset{\displaystyle\cdot\cdot}{N}—H$$
$$|$$
$$H$$

You can see from its electron dot structure that there are three pairs of bonding electrons and one lone pair of electrons. You will recall that the four balloons shown in Figure 13-10 provide a model to predict how four pairs of electrons will orient themselves to minimize repulsions. Any combination of bonding and nonbonding electron pairs giving a total of four electron pairs will assume the tetrahedral arrangement, as shown in Figure 13-12.

How would you describe the shape of the ammonia molecule? Look at the ball-and-stick model in Figure 13-12. When describing the shape of a molecule, it is important to focus only on the arrangement of the atoms in the molecule, as shown in Figure 13-12 *left*. In spite of the fact that you could not have determined the arrangement of the electron pairs without including nonbonding

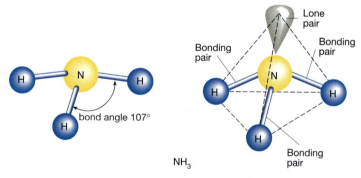

Figure 13-12 *In ammonia, three of the electron pairs on nitrogen form bonding pairs with hydrogen atoms. The fourth pair is a nonbonding polar pair at the fourth corner of the tetrahedron.*

pairs, the nonbonding electron pairs are *not* included in the description of molecular shape. Thus the shape of the ammonia molecule is described as **trigonal pyramidal,** a three-sided pyramid with triangular faces. If you summarize the information about the shape of an ammonia molecule, the arrangement of the electron pairs is tetrahedral, and the shape of the molecule is trigonal pyramidal.

What is the H—N—H bond angle in ammonia? Experimental measurements of the bond angle show that it is 107°, a little smaller than the tetrahedral angle of 109.5°. This means that the hydrogen atoms are a little closer together than you might predict. This difference can be explained by saying that a lone pair of electrons exerts larger repulsive force and thus occupies more space than a bonding pair of electrons. It is analogous to tying four balloons together when one balloon is a little larger than the others.

Concept ✔ Check

Do the lone pairs of electrons on the nitrogen in ammonia exert a larger repulsive force than the bonded pairs?

Bent structures You have previously written the electron dot structure of water as H:O:H. Does this structure give an accurate representation of the shape? Since there are four electron pairs around the central atom, what shape would you predict for the structure of water? You will recall that the arrangement of four electron pairs, both bonding and nonbonding, is tetrahedral. This is shown in Figure 13-13. The molecular shape for the water molecule is described as **bent.**

The H—O—H bond angle is 104.5°. As with ammonia, the fact that this bond angle is less than the tetrahedral bond angle is explained on the basis of the greater repulsion of the lone pairs compared to the bonding pairs.

Table 13-4 on page 457 summarizes the electron-pair arrangements and the molecular shapes for the molecules that you have been introduced to in this section.

EXAMPLE 13-7

Predict the shape of the following molecules.

H_2S, SiH_4, AsH_3, $InCl_3$ (an exception to the octet rule)

■ **Apply a Strategy** First draw the electron dot structure for each of the molecules. Once this is done, determine the arrangement of the electron pairs about the central atom. Then predict the molecular shape, based on the number of bonding and lone pairs of electrons on the central atom.

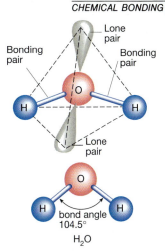

Figure 13-13 *The atoms in a water molecule lie in a plane and form an angle of 104.5°. The two lone pairs of electrons do not lie in that plane.*

PROBLEM·SOLVING STRATEGY

Use Table 13-4 for reference if you have difficulty.

Science Background

Bent Structures

The VSEPR theory (often pronounced "ves per") is an accurate predictor of geometric shape of molecules having a relatively small central atom. Molecules that have a large central atom from groups 5A or 6A and 4 units surrounding the central atom may not have tetrahedral structures. A possible explanation is that because the central atom is so large, there is less repulsion among the units of the central atom. VSEPR theory cannot be used to predict the shapes of molecules in which a transition metal is the central atom.

Practice Problems

Assign the Practice Problems.

■ **Work a Solution** The electron dot structure of H_2S is

$$H—\overset{\cdot\cdot}{\underset{\cdot\cdot}{S}}—H$$

The central sulfur atom has two bonding pairs and two lone pairs. The arrangement of electron pairs is tetrahedral. The molecular shape is bent.

The electron dot structure of SiH_4 is

$$\begin{array}{c} H \\ | \\ H—Si—H \\ | \\ H \end{array}$$

It has four bonding pairs. The arrangement of the electron pairs is tetrahedral. With all the electron pairs involved in bonding, the bond angle and the molecular shape are both tetrahedral.

The electron dot structure of AsH_3 is

$$\begin{array}{c} H—\overset{\cdot\cdot}{As}—H \\ | \\ H \end{array}$$

There are four pairs of electrons, in a tetrahedral arrangement, about the central arsenic atom. Since there are three bonding pairs and one lone pair, the molecular shape is trigonal pyramidal.

The electron dot structure of $InCl_3$ is

$$\begin{array}{c} :\overset{\cdot\cdot}{\underset{\cdot\cdot}{Cl}}—In—\overset{\cdot\cdot}{\underset{\cdot\cdot}{Cl}}: \\ | \\ :\overset{\cdot\cdot}{\underset{\cdot\cdot}{Cl}}: \end{array}$$

This is an exception to the octet rule, like BF_3 discussed earlier. There are only three pairs of electrons about the central indium atom and they are in a trigonal planar arrangement. Since all the pairs are also bonding pairs, the molecular shape is trigonal planar.

Notice that both $InCl_3$ and AsH_3 have similar molecular formulas but very different molecular shapes. The only way to predict the molecular shape is to write the electron dot structure first.

PROBLEM-SOLVING

S T R A T E G Y

*By **using patterns** of structures similar to those you have already seen, you can predict the shapes of unknown molecules. (See Strategy, page 100.)*

■ **Verify Your Answer** Compare your answers to molecules whose central atom is in the same family as the central atom of the unknown. In the case of H_2S, for example, sulfur and oxygen are in the same family and therefore have the same number of valence electrons. It is reasonable to assume that H_2S has a shape similar to that of H_2O which is bent.

Practice Problems

Predict the shape of the following molecules.

33. HOCl   **34.** CCl_4

TABLE 13-4

		Examples of Molecular Shapes				
Name	Structural Shape	Atoms Bonded to Central Atom	Lone Pairs of Electrons	Bond Angle	Sample Formula	Electron Dot Structure
Linear		2	0	180°	BeH_2	H:Be:H
Trigonal planar		3	0	120°	BF_3	
Tetrahedral		4	0	109.5°	CH_4	
Trigonal pyramidal		3	1	107°	NH_3	
Bent		2	2	104.5°	H_2O	
Trigonal bipyramidal		5	0		PCl_5	
Octahedral		6	0		SF_6	

VSEPR and double or triple bonds Can the VSEPR model be extended to molecules with double or triple bonds? The answer is yes. As far as molecular geometry is concerned, a multiple bond involving the central atom is treated just as if it were a single bonding pair. Here is how to reason why this is possible. The four electrons in a double bond or the six electrons in a triple bond must have a high probability of being in the region between the two nuclei of the bonded atoms. This is the same region that electrons in a single bond will occupy. Thus the fact that the central atom has multiple bonds has no effect upon the geometry predicted by the VSEPR theory.

Videodisc Connections

520-523, side 6
Buckyball images: fullerene
(4-frame seq.)

R E S E A R C H & T E C H N O L O G Y

Fullerenes

When predictions become reality, it is exciting, and this is no less true in chemistry. For years, two common forms of pure carbon were recognized: diamond and graphite. In May 1990, another new form of pure carbon was observed: a molecule with 60 carbon atoms that

observation they had made. In their new research, these predictions were realized, C_{60} was observed, and the pieces of this puzzle fell into place.

The excitement of fullerenes continues, since C_{60} has certain electronic properties that make it technologically promising. Already com-

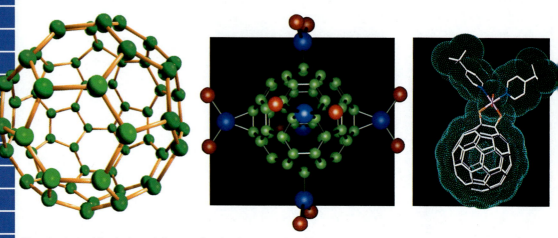

The structure of buckminsterfullerene, C_{60}, is shown on the left. A derivative containing six platinum atoms is shown in the middle, and another derivative, bunnyball, is on the right.

is shaped like a soccer ball. The structure of this molecule has a network of hexagonal and pentagonal connections made up of carbon atoms. Because of this structure, the molecule is extremely stable. This kind of symmetry and stability is expressed in the architectural principle of the geodesic dome, invented by American engineer and philosopher Buckminster Fuller. Although this molecule was not observed until 1990, the C_{60} molecule had been predicted five years earlier and had been named the buckminsterfullerene.

The C_{60} molecule has an interesting history. In 1985, a team of chemists found evidence of the existence of C_{60} but were not able to generate enough molecules to get definitive results. About five years later a group of American and German physicists thought that the C_{60} molecule might explain an earlier, unusual

pounds containing C_{60} have been found to act as conductors, insulators, and superconductors. For example, when potassium is added, a substance called a buckide salt, K_3C_{60}, forms and becomes a conductor. If too much potassium is added, the substance produced becomes an insulator. In addition, when K_3C_{60} is cooled to 18 kelvins, it becomes a superconductor. There are additional expectations that fullerene compounds will also serve as semiconductors. With the production of fully fluorinated bucky balls, called teflon balls, researchers boast the advent of an excellent, if not the best, lubricant.

Fullerenes have sparked a frenzy of research to exploit their properties. Some scientists caution that since fullerenes are costly to produce and possibly toxic, fullerenes, like CFC's, may not turn out to be the wonder chemicals first envisioned.

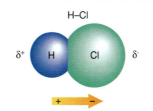

You have used the simple VSEPR model to predict the shapes of several molecules. This model is useful for predicting the shapes of a large number of molecules that have a main group element as the central atom. It is important to realize that this model addresses only the shapes of molecules. There are additional theories that explain other aspects of bonding that will not be discussed here.

13.8 Dipoles and Molecular Polarity

It is important to know about the shape of a molecule because the shape influences the properties of a molecule. Water is a molecule with polar covalent bonds. Water is also a polar molecule because of the bent shape of the water molecule. In Chapter 14, the unique properties of water will be related to the fact that it is a polar molecule. Proteins are large molecules that consist of many smaller molecules called amino acids, which are bonded together. A protein molecule, hemoglobin, is responsible for transporting oxygen in the blood. The basis of the disease sickle-cell anemia is a substitution of a nonpolar amino acid for a polar amino acid in the hemoglobin protein. Water and hemoglobin are but two examples of molecules whose properties are influenced by their shape and molecular polarity. In this section, you will focus on how the shape of a molecule is important in determining molecular polarity.

Polar bonds resulting in a polar molecule Recall the discussion of polar bonds in Section 13-4. In the HCl molecule, the more electronegative chlorine nucleus attracts the shared pair of electrons to a larger extent than the hydrogen nucleus. The result is a polar bond with separate centers of partial negative and positive charge. Figure 13-14 illustrates the dipolar nature of the HCl molecule. Since there is only one bond in HCl, the bond polarity dictates the polarity of the molecule. The fact that the bond in HCl is a polar bond causes HCl to be a polar molecule. The arrow beneath the molecule in Figure 13-15 indicates the direction the electrons are attracted toward. This arrow is used to indicate the direction of the *dipole moment,* which is the direction of the polar bond within a molecule.

Any diatomic (two-atom) molecule that has a polar bond will be a polar molecule, with its characteristic dipole moment. It can also be generalized that any molecule with only nonpolar bonds is a nonpolar molecule. The dipole moment of nonpolar molecules is zero and thus no arrow is used. For polyatomic molecules, the situation is not so simple—not all molecules with polar bonds are polar.

A nonpolar molecule with polar bonds Consider the molecule BeH_2. The two Be—H bonds are polar, since hydrogen has a higher electronegativity than beryllium. For each bond, the

Figure 13-14 *The arrow shown here is a common symbol for a dipole. By convention, the arrow points to the more electronegative end of the bond.*

CONNECTING CONCEPTS

Process of Science—Predicting Molecular polarity is an important property of molecules. To predict the polarity of a molecule, both the bond polarity and the molecular shape must be known.

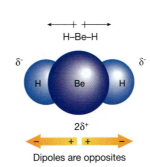

Figure 13-15 *BeH_2 has two polar bonds. However, the dipoles are oriented in opposite directions. The molecule is nonpolar overall.*

Teaching Strategy

Dipoles and Molecular Polarity

A principal objective of this section is the relationship between molecular geometry and molecular polarity. Uneven charge distribution in a molecule results in a molecular dipole moment. The dipole moment is determined by vector addition of the individual dipoles of the polar bonds in the molecule. The analogy of two tug-of-war teams pulling with equal force on a rope tied to a ring at an angle of 180° may help explain this concept. The ring will not move, because the forces cancel each other out. This situation is comparable to the two dipoles in a linear molecule such as CO_2. Even though both C=O bonds are polar towards the O, the molecule is nonpolar. Carbon monoxide on the other hand would be a polar molecule as there would be only one team pulling.

A similar analogy using bond angles of 120° can be used to explain BF_3. Extending the analogy to three dimensions and using a bond angle of 109.5°, the analogy provides an understanding of the polarity of tetrahedral molecules such as CH_4. The tug-of-war analogy quickly shows that bond polarities in the NH_3 molecule would not cancel themselves out and there would be a net dipole moment in that molecule.

Use some examples to tie aspects of this chapter together. For example ask about the polarity of CO_2 and SO_2. The similar formulas can be misleading. One must draw electron dot structures, determine the number of bonding and nonbonding pairs, and decide how to handle multiple bonds and molecules showing resonance in order to solve this problem. Finally, the importance of the shape of a molecule on the molecular polarity is illustrated.

DEMONSTRATION

Water Molecule and Polarity

Allow water to drain slowly from a buret. Bring a comb charged with static electricity in the vicinity of the water and the stream exiting the buret tip will be pulled toward the comb. Do the same thing with a non- polar liquid—use vegetable oil; the effect is not nearly so great. Students can try the former at home with a thin stream of water coming out of an ordinary faucet.

Guided Practice

Review the Concept Check question on page 455 with students. Answers can be found in Appendix E on page 808.

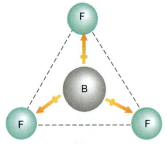

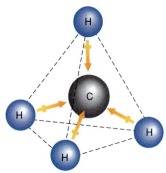

Figure 13-16 Top: *The three dipoles in BF₃ cancel, so the molecule is nonpolar. Bottom: In methane, CH₄, the four dipoles also cancel. Notice how in the B-F bond, the negative end of the dipole is directed away from the central atom, and in the C-H bond, it is directed toward the central carbon atom.*

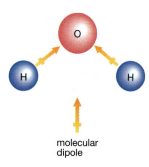

molecular dipole

Figure 13-17 *Water, like ammonia, is a polar molecule because the two dipoles do not cancel. The bonds do not orient in opposite directions, and the result is a net dipole.*

center of negative charge will be at the hydrogen atom and the center of positive charge at the beryllium atom. From the electron dot structure and the VSEPR theory, the shape of BeH₂ can be predicted to be linear. Thus the two dipoles in the molecule can be represented as shown in Figure 13-15.

As a result of the linear shape, the individual bond dipoles are directed exactly opposite each other, which causes them to cancel each other making the molecule nonpolar. An analogy to this is a tug-of-war between two evenly balanced teams. When the teams are pulling in opposite directions on the rope with equal force, the rope and the teams do not move.

Experimentally it has been shown that BeH₂ is a nonpolar molecule. Such confirmation strengthens the VSEPR model as an accurate means of predicting molecular shapes.

Other bonding situations involving identical polar bonds can also result in nonpolar molecules. Boron-fluorine bonds and carbon-hydrogen bonds are both polar bonds. But experimentation shows the dipole moment of both BF_3 and CH_4 to be zero. The shapes of the molecules are such that in both cases, the individual bond dipoles will cancel and the molecule will be nonpolar. Figure 13-16 illustrates the direction of the individual bond dipoles for BF_3 and CH_4.

Water molecule and polarity Water is a polar molecule. It behaves as if it has a positive end and a negative end. Look at Figure 13-17, which shows the bond dipoles in water.

From the geometric shape of the water molecule, can you predict whether it is polar or nonpolar? Molecules having bond dipoles that do not exactly cancel will be polar molecules. It is not an overstatement to say that life as we know it could not exist if water were a nonpolar molecule. The impact of the polar nature of water will be discussed in Chapter 14.

Predicting polarity In this chapter, you have learned concepts and skills that will allow you to predict whether or not a given molecule is polar or nonpolar. In order to predict the polarity of a molecule, you have to look beyond the simple molecular formulas. As Example 13-8 shows, you must apply what you have learned about writing electron dot structures, the VSEPR theory, and the electronegativity of elements.

EXAMPLE 13-8

Predict whether CO_2 is polar or nonpolar.

■ ***Analyze the Problem*** To determine molecular polarity, you need to know if the bonds are polar and what the shape of the molecule is.

PART 3 REVIEW

ANSWERS

■ **Keyed to Objectives**

G **38.** Pairs of electrons naturally repel each other so they spread themselves out in space as much as possible.

G **39.** They have like charges.

G **40.** No. They are two dimensional and molecules are often three dimen-

sional. Any three-dimensional molecule is an acceptable answer. Or a molecule such as water that is written as if it were linear when it is actually bent is also an acceptable answer.

G **41.** H₂O and CH₄: similar; both have four electron pairs arranged tetrahedrally about the central atom. NH₃ and BF₃: different; N has four pairs of electrons arranged tetrahe-

drally and B has three pairs arranged in a trigonal plane. BeH₂ and H₂S: different; Be has two pairs arranged linearly and S has four arranged tetrahedrally.

G **42.** GaH₃—trigonal planar, GeH₄—tetrahedral, PCl₃—trigonal pyramidal, and NH₄⁺—tetrahedral.

G **43.** Many are possible. Some likely choices are water, ammonia, carbon monoxide, and so on. The first

PART 3
Section 13.8 *continued*

■ *Apply a Strategy* Look up the electronegativities of C and O. Draw the electron dot structure for CO_2 and use the VSEPR theory to predict the shape.

■ *Work a Solution* The electron dot structure of CO_2 is

$$:\ddot{O}\!=\!C\!=\!\ddot{O}:$$

The electronegativity of C is 2.5 and of O is 3.5. Therefore, the C—O bond is polar. Because the molecule is linear, the bond dipoles cancel, and the molecule is nonpolar.

■ *Verify Your Answer* Check to make sure that each atom in the electron dot structure has an octet and that you have correctly recorded the electronegativity values.

Practice Problems

Predict whether the following molecules are polar or nonpolar.

35. H_2S
36. CCl_4
37. HF

PART 3 REVIEW

38. State the basis of the VSEPR theory for predicting molecular shape.

39. Why do pairs of electrons around a central atom repel each other?

40. Do electron dot structures accurately describe the shapes of molecules? Explain, using an example.

41. In which pairs of compounds do both molecules have similar bond angles? In which pairs are the bond angles very different? Explain your answers. H_2O and CH_4, NH_3 and BF_3, BeH_2 and H_2S.

42. Describe the shapes of the following species: GaH_3, GeH_4, PCl_3, and NH_4^+.

43. Give examples of two polar molecules. Sketch the bond dipoles and the molecular dipole.

44. Give examples of two nonpolar molecules containing polar bonds. Sketch the bond dipoles.

45. There are two resonance structures for SO_2. Draw the electron dot structures. Explain why, in spite of the fact that there are two structures, the molecular shape can be predicted.

> **PROBLEM·SOLVING**
> **STRATEGY**
>
> *Use what you know about VSEPR and double bonds. Double bonds are treated as if they were single bonds. (See Strategy, page 58.)*

> **PROBLEM·SOLVING**
> **STRATEGY**
>
> *By using similar problems, you can find that you already know many of the steps needed to solve this problem. (See Strategy, page 65.)*

Boxed numbers indicate questions that involve skills in interpretation, application, and analysis.

Practice Problems

Assign the Practice Problems.

Reteaching Idea

If students need more practice in determining the shapes of molecules, provide them with Styrofoam balls or balls of soft modeling clay and a bundle of toothpicks. With a bright-colored nontoxic magic marker, color the tips of some of the toothpicks. These can represent bonds to an atom. Toothpicks without colored tips can represent nonbonding electrons. Have students write the electron dot structures for $TeCl_2$, $SnCl_4$, PCl_3, and $GaCl_3$. (These have the same structures as the molecules in Example 13–7.) Have students arrange toothpicks on the Styrofoam balls to represent the bonding and nonbonding pairs on each central atom. Each pair should be as far from all the others as possible. When students remove the nonbonding toothpicks, they have a model for the molecular geometry.

☰CLOSE

Summing Up Main Ideas

Have students write the chemical formulas for molecules fitting the following descriptions: a nonpolar molecule of two atoms (O_2), a nonpolar molecule with four polar bonds (CCl_4), a polar molecule with ionic bonds (NaCl), and a nonpolar molecule with ionic bonds (BF_3).

PART 3 REVIEW

Assign the Part Review questions.

Evaluating Skills

These skills are evaluated in the Part Review questions indicated. **Determining main ideas:** 38; **Determining cause and effect:** 39; **Comparing/Contrasting:** 41; **Describing:** 42; **Forming models:** 43, 44, 45.

criterion is to have a polar bond—two atoms of differing EN. The second criterion is that the geometry is such that the bond dipoles do not cancel.

G 44. There are many examples. Carbon dioxide and boron trifluoride have polar bonds but the bond dipoles cancel and the molecules are nonpolar.

G 45.

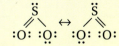

With both resonance structures, there are three groups of electrons to distribute themselves as far apart as possible from each other. In this case, the electron group distribution is trigonal planar. The geometry of the molecule is bent.

**Molecular Geometry and
beyond the Octet**
Estimated Time: (45 minutes)

Process Skills

Forming models
Measuring
Classifying

Preparation

■ Materials

(for a class of 24, working individually)

Apparatus

one box of toothpicks, 24 sheets of $8\frac{1}{2} \times 11$ white paper

Reagents

■ modeling clay, sufficient to make 1 large and 6 small balls per student

■ Preparation Hints

Although this lab can utilize elaborate model-building kits, it is suggested that the student can relate more easily to modeling clay than to balls and sockets.
Be prepared to name the geometric structures.

L a b o r a t o r y

Investigation

Molecular Geometry and beyond the Octet

Explaining the shapes of molecules is important in understanding how molecules react. The VSEPR (pronounced "Vesper") model is based on the premise that electron pairs around a central atom will position themselves to allow for maximum separation. Your task in this investigation is to construct a series of compounds using the VSEPR model and to use your model to determine the type of bonding and the geometry around each central atom.

Note: When you build your model, remember that lone-pair electrons cause more repulsion than electrons between atoms.

O b j e c t i v e s

Construct a series of compounds, using the VSEPR model.

Relate each constructed model to the electron-dot structure around the central atom.

Describe and name the molecular geometry of each model.

■ Materials

☐ 1 dozen toothpicks
☐ 24 modeling clay spheres (3-cm diameter)
☐ 24 modeling clay spheres (1-cm diameter)

■ Procedure

1. For each of the following molecules of ions, determine the number of lone pairs and bond pairs around the central atom.

   a. $HgCl_2$ e. PCl_5 i. SF_6
   b. CH_4 f. $TeCl_4$ j. BrF_5
   c. NH_3 g. ClF_3 k. XeF_4
   d. H_2O h. I^-_3 l. HCN

2. Build a model for each compound or ion, using a plain toothpick to represent the lone pairs and a toothpick and a small clay sphere to represent each pair bonded to an atom. Using the large clay sphere as the central atom, place the lone pairs (if any) first so they are as far apart as possible. Then add the bond pairs until all atoms are arranged at a maximum distance from each other. Fill in the first two columns of the data table.

3. Describe the structure you have created as linear, triangular planar, tetrahedral, trigonal bipyramidal, or octahedral. Record this information in the data table in the column headed Geometry with lone pairs.

4. Remove the lone-pair toothpicks from the structure and make any necessary minor alterations in the bond angles that are due to the lone pairs. Rename the shape you see. This name tells you the molecular geometry of the molecule. Record this in the last column.

5. Estimate and note the angle between the atoms attached to the central atom. Record this in the data table.

Data Table

Molecule or Ion	Number of Lone Pairs	Number of Bond Pairs	Geometry with Lone Pairs	Angle between Bonds in Central Atom	Geometry (shape) of Molecule
$HgCl_2$	0	1	linear	180	linear
CH_4	0	4	tetrahedral	109.5	tetrahedral
NH_3	1	3	tetrahedral	107	pyramid
H_2O	2	2	tetrahedral	104.5	bent
PCl_5	0	5	trigonal bipyramidal	90, 120	trigonal bipyramidal

Data Analysis

Molecule or Ion	Number of Lone Pairs	Number of Bond Pairs	Geometry with Lone Pairs	Angle between Bonds in Central Atom	Geometry (shape) of Molecule
$HgCl_2$					
CH_4					
NH_3					
H_2O					
PCl_5					
$TeCl_4$					
ClF_3					
I^-_3					
SF_6					
BrF_5					
XeF_4					
HCN					

Conclusions

1. What effect does the presence of lone-pair electrons have on the bond angles in a molecule?

2. What additional information does the VSEPR theory give you beyond electron-dot structures, in terms of molecular structure?

Guiding the Investigation

■ Procedural Hints

This lab can be one of the most enjoyable of the year. Hand out a sheet of white paper to put on each student's desk and then distribute six toothpicks, six small clay balls, and one large clay ball to each student or have them make the balls themselves.

To help students, have available a reference chart that relates the shape of the molecule (with lone pairs) with the geometry around the central atom. Also, briefly review the various molecular geometric shapes. If students have trouble estimating the angles between the atoms, have them use a protractor.

Data Analysis

■ Sample Data
(See table below.)

Conclusions

1. The lone pair of electrons takes slightly more space than electrons in a bond. Therefore, the bond angles are slightly reduced.

2. shape and number of lone pairs

Molecule or Ion	Number of Lone Pairs	Number of Bond Pairs	Geometry with Lone Pairs	Angle between Bonds in Central Atom	Geometry (shape) of Molecule
$TeCl_4$	1	4	trigonal bipyramidal	90, 120	trigonal bipyramidal
ClF_3	2	3	trigonal bipyramidal	120	triangle
I^-_3	3	2	trigonal bipyramidal	180	linear
SF_6	0	6	octahedral	90	octahedral
BrF_5	1	5	octahedral	90	square pyramidal
XeF_4	2	4	octahedral	90	square planar
HCN	0	4	linear	180	linear

Chapter 13
Review
ANSWERS
begin on page
T467a.

Summary

An Introduction to Bonding

■ It is convenient to classify chemical bonds as ionic or covalent. It is important to recognize that there is a continuum from ionic through polar covalent to nonpolar covalent bonding. Ionic bonding occurs when electrons are transferred from a metal to a nonmetal. Equal sharing of an electron pair by two identical atoms is a nonpolar covalent bond. Unequal sharing of electron pairs, as in a polar bond, is the middle ground between ionic and nonpolar covalent bonding.

Describing Molecular Structures

■ Electron dot diagrams are useful for assisting in the understanding of bonding. The valence electrons are represented as dots around the symbol of the element. In most cases, ionic and covalent bonds form so that each atom has an octet. One important exception is hydrogen, which has only two electron dots.

■ Some stable molecules do not fit the octet rule. Examples include NO, BeH_2, BF_3, PCl_5, SF_6. Because more than one acceptable electron dot structure can be drawn for some species— CO_3^{2-} and SO_2 for example—resonance structures are used.

Shapes and Properties of Molecules

■ The shape of a molecule depends on the number of bonded atoms and the number of unshared pairs of electrons surrounding the central atom. According to the valence shell electron pair repulsion theory, pairs of bonding electrons are oriented in space as far apart as possible. This theory can account for the shape of many molecules and explain why some molecules containing polar bonds are nonpolar, while others are polar.

Chemically Speaking

bond angle *13.7*
bond energy *13.1*
bond length *13.3*
chemical bond *13.1*
covalent bond *13.3*
crystal lattice *13.2*
dipole *13.4*
double bond *13.5*
electron dot symbol *13.2*
electronegativity *13.4*
electrostatic attraction *13.2*

ionic bond *13.2*
nonpolar covalent bond *13.4*
octet rule *13.5*
polar covalent bond *13.4*
resonance *13.6*
tetrahedral *13.7*
trigonal planar *13.7*
trigonal pyramidal *13.7*
triple bond *13.5*
VSEPR *13.7*

Concept Mapping

Using the method of concept mapping described at the front of this book, construct a concept map for the term *chemical bond* using concepts from this chapter or previous chapters as necessary.

Questions and Problems

AN INTRODUCTION TO BONDING

A. Objective: Describe *the nature of a chemical bond.*

1. What is a chemical bond?
2. Briefly explain how the potential energy changes as two hydrogen atoms approach each other.
3. Does the potential energy of a bonded system increase or decrease when a bond is broken? Explain your answer.
4. Which are more stable under ordinary conditions, hydrogen atoms or hydrogen molecules? Explain your answer.

▶ **PROBLEM-SOLVING STRATEGIES**

Students apply these strategies in the following questions.

■ **Using what you know:** 10, 11, 13, 17, 18, 22, 23, 24, 25, 26, 29, 31, 32, 33, 34, 38, 39, 40, 41, 43.

■ **Using patterns:** 10, 11, 13, 17, 22, 23, 24, 25, 26, 29, 31, 43.

■ **Verifying your answer:** 22, 23, 24, 25, 26.

■ **Breaking problems into manageable parts:** 22, 23, 24, 25, 26, 31, 32, 33

■ **Making diagrams:** 18, 27, 38, 39, 44

B. Objective: **Compare and contrast** *ionic and covalent bonds.*

5. How does an ionic bond form?
6. How does a covalent bond form?
7. What is a crystal lattice?
8. What types of elements usually form in an ionic bond?
9. What types of elements usually form in a covalent bond?
10. Write the symbol for the stable cation or anion that is likely to form from the following elements: ·
   a. Na
   b. S
   c. Ca
   d. N
   e. I
11. Using electron dot symbols, show the formation of an ionic bond between the following elements:
   a. K and Br
   b. Ca and S
   c. Sr and I
   d. Al and Cl
   e. Mg and N
12. What is similar about the electron configurations of ions of main group elements in an ionic bond?
13. Use electron dot structures to show the formation of covalent bonds between the following elements:
   a. H and Br
   b. two I atoms
   c. H and S
14. What type of electron dot structure does each main group atom in a compound usually exhibit?

C. Objective: **Predict** *whether bonds are ionic, polar covalent, or nonpolar covalent, using electronegativity values.*

15. What is electronegativity? How is it sometimes used to classify chemical bonds?

Boxed numbers indicate questions that involve skills in interpretation, application, and analysis.

16. Give one example of each of the following types of bonds.
   a. an ionic bond
   b. a nonpolar covalent bond
   c. a polar covalent bond
17. Classify bonds in each of the following substances as nonpolar covalent, polar covalent, or ionic.
   a. K_2O
   b. BeO
   c. NH_3
   d. KCl
   e. CBr_4
   f. N_2
   g. CS_2

D. Objective: **Determine** *the partial charge distribution of a polar covalent bond.*

18. Show the partial charge distribution in the following bonds:
   a. H–Br
   b. C–H
   c. C–Cl
   d. N–H
   e. N–O
   f. Be–H

DESCRIBING MOLECULAR STRUCTURES

E. Objective: **Apply** *the octet rule to write electron dot structures of simple molecules and polyatomic ions.*

19. State the octet rule.
20. What is a single bond? A double bond? A triple bond?
21. Relate the octet rule to the electron configuration of an element's valence electrons.
22. Draw the electron dot (Lewis) structures for:
   a. F_2
   b. HI
   c. NF_3

23. Draw the electron dot (Lewis) structures for the following molecules. In each case, the carbon atom is the central atom.
  a. CH_3Cl
  b. CH_2Cl_2
  c. $CHCl_3$

24. Draw the electron dot (Lewis) structures for the following polyatomic ions:
  a. IO_4^-
  b. IO_3^-
  c. IO_2^-
  d. IO^-
  e. SiO_4^{4-}
  f. PCl_4^+

25. What is the electron dot structure of the following isoelectronic species?
  a. N_2
  b. CN^-
  c. NO^+
  d. CO

26. Using the skeleton structures shown, draw the electron dot structures. Use lines to represent bonding pairs and dots to represent nonbonding pairs.
  a. F N N F
  b. Cl C C Cl
  c. H O O H
  d. H_3 C O H

F. Objective: *Identify limitations to the octet rule, including molecules that show resonance.*

27. Explain why each of following molecules is an exception to the octet rule.
  a. NO   **c.** XeF_2
  b. BeH_2 **d.** $TeCl_4$

28. What is resonance? Give an example of a molecule with resonance. Explain your choice.

29. Write the electron dot structures for each of the resonance forms for these species.
  a. SO_3
  b. NO_2^-
  c. O_3
  d. HCO_2^- (carbon is the central atom)

SHAPES AND PROPERTIES OF MOLECULES

G. Objective: **Predict** *shapes of molecules.*

30. Briefly explain how the valence shell electron pair repulsion theory (VSEPR) is used to predict the arrangement of the electron pairs about the central atom.

31. Describe the arrangement of the electron pairs for each of the following molecules.
  a. CCl_4
  b. SiH_4
  c. AsH_3
  d. H_2Se
  e. CS_2

32. Predict the shape of each of the molecules in the previous problem.

33. Predict the shapes of the following molecules. Each is an exception to the octet rule.
  a. BCl_3
  b. BeH_2

34. Look at Table 13-4. The bottom two molecules in the *Sample Formula* column are phosphorus pentachloride, PCl_5, and sulfur hexafluoride, SF_6. How are these molecules different from others you have studied in terms of their geometry and the bond angles of the atoms around the central atom?

H. Objective: **Determine** *whether a molecule is polar or nonpolar.*

35. What is the difference between a polar bond and a nonpolar bond?

36. Can a molecule with only nonpolar bonds be a polar molecule? Explain your answer.

37. Can a molecule with polar bonds be a nonpolar molecule? Explain your answer.

38. Show the bond dipoles and predict the molecular polarity of each of the molecules in question 31.

39. BF_3 is a flat, nonpolar molecule, and NF_3 a trigonal, pyramidal, polar molecule. Explain the reason that these two four-atom molecules have different properties.

Critical Thinking

SYNTHESIS WITHIN THE CHAPTER

40. What is the geometric structure of a water molecule? How many lone pairs and bonding pairs are associated with the oxygen atom? What is the approximate bond angle? What is the shape of the molecule? Is a water molecule polar or nonpolar?

41. Draw an electron dot structure for the oxygen molecule that fulfills the octet rule. Analyze this structure on the basis of experimental evidence which shows that oxygen molecules have unpaired electrons and that the distance between the two oxygen atoms is longer than the oxygen-oxygen double bond distance.

42. The two molecules named in question 34 violate the octet rule. What are the electron configurations for these molecules? How do these electron configurations provide some stability to the molecules?

SYNTHESIS ACROSS CHAPTERS

43. Write the formula for the compound or molecule, if any, that you would expect to form from the two elements listed. Identify each compound or molecule as ionic, polar covalent, or nonpolar covalent.

   a. F and Na   **d.** Ne and Ne
   b. C and F   **e.** As and Cl
   c. I and I

44. Why are the ammonium ion, NH_4^+, and the methane molecule, CH_4, said to be isoelectronic?

45. In some presentations of the periodic table, hydrogen is included in both Group 1A and Group 7A. Explain why this can be done.

Projects

46. Construct three-dimensional models of some of the molecules and ions studied in this chap-ter. Mount the models on poster board for display. You may even consider making a mobile for the classroom.

47. Use balloons to illustrate the arrangement of the valence electrons in cases where there are 2, 3, 4, 5, and 6 pairs of electrons around the central atom.

Research and Writing

48. Look up the values of the melting points and boiling points of some of the compounds discussed in this chapter. Write a paper discussing whether or not there is a relationship between these properties and the type of bonding.

49. Ask your teacher for some issues of *Journal of Chemical Education* or *Chem Matters*. Find some articles that relate to chemical bonding. Choose one and write a short report on how the information in the article relates to the VESPR model.

50. Do a report on phosphorus pentachloride, PCl_5, and sulfur hexafluoride, SF_6—the two molecules at the bottom of the *Sample Formula* column in Table 13-4. What are these chemicals, and what are they used for?

☐ Boxed numbers indicate questions that involve skills in interpretation, application, and analysis.

1. The force of attraction between two atoms in a molecular or an ionic compound.

2. As the hydrogen atoms get closer, the attractions get larger and the potential energy falls. At some point, the potential energy is at a minimum. When the atoms get closer still, the effect of repulsions causes the potential energy to rise.

3. The potential energy increases because energy is required to break a bond.

4. Hydrogen molecules; the potential energy of a molecule is less than for two separated atoms. Lower energy indicates more stability.

5. An electron (or electrons) is (are) transferred from a metal atom to a nonmetal atom and the resulting cation and anion are attracted by electrostatic forces.

6. An electron pair is shared by two atoms.

7. The structure representing the position that ions occupy in an ionic compound

8. metals and nonmetals

9. nonmetals with other nonmetals

10. a. Na^+
    b. S^{2-}
    c. Ca^{2+}
    d. N^{3-}
    e. I^-

11. a. $[K]^+ [:\ddot{Br}:]^-$
    b. $[Ca]^{2+} [:\ddot{S}:]^{2-}$
    c. $[:\ddot{I}:]^- [Sr]^{2+} [:\ddot{I}:]^-$
    d. $[:\ddot{Cl}:]^- [Al]^{3+} [:\ddot{Cl}:]^-$
       $[:\ddot{Cl}:]^-$
    e. $[Mg]^{2+}[:\ddot{N}:]^{3-}[Mg]^{2+}[:\ddot{N}:]^{3-}[Mg]^{2+}$

12. They are isoelectronic with that of a noble gas element.

13. a. $H:\ddot{Br}:$
    b. $:\ddot{I}:\ddot{I}:$
    c. $H:\ddot{S}:H$

14. Surrounded by an octet of electrons (except for hydrogen)

15. Electronegativity is a measure of the attraction of an atom for a bonded pair of electrons. Electronegativity differences indicate the type of bond: if they are very large, it is ionic, if zero, it is nonpolar covalent, and if intermediate, polar covalent.

16. a. NaCl
    b. Cl_2
    c. HCl

17. a. ionic
    b. ionic
    c. polar covalent
    d. ionic
    e. polar covalent
    f. nonpolar covalent
    g. nonpolar covalent

18. a. $\delta^+ \; \delta^-$
       H—Br
    b. $\delta^+ \; \delta^-$
       H—C
    c. $\delta^+ \; \delta^-$
       C—Cl
    d. $\delta^- \; \delta^+$
       N—H
    e. $\delta^+ \; \delta^-$
       N—O
    f. $\delta^- \; \delta^+$
       Be—H

19. Many atoms in compounds bond such that each atom has 8 electrons (an octet) in its valence shell.

20. A covalent bond formed by sharing one, two, and three pairs of electrons, respectively.

21. Each element generally shares or transfers electrons in such a way that it ends up with an octet of electrons in its outermost occupied orbitals.

22. a. $:\ddot{F}:\ddot{F}:$
    b. $H:\ddot{I}:$
    c. $:\ddot{F}:\ddot{N}:\ddot{F}:$
       $:\ddot{F}:$

23. a. $H:\ddot{C}:\ddot{Cl}:$ with H above and below
    b. $H:\ddot{C}:\ddot{Cl}:$ with H above and $:\ddot{Cl}:$ below
    c. $:\ddot{Cl}:\ddot{C}:\ddot{Cl}:$ with H above and $:\ddot{Cl}:$ below

24. a. $\left[\begin{array}{c} :\ddot{O}: \\ :\ddot{O}:I:\ddot{O}: \\ :\ddot{O}: \end{array} \right]^-$
    b. $\left[\begin{array}{c} :\ddot{O}: \\ :\ddot{O}:I:\ddot{O}: \end{array} \right]^-$

25. c. $\left[:\ddot{O}:I:\ddot{O}: \right]^-$
    d. $\left[:\ddot{O}:I: \right]^-$
    e. $\left[\begin{array}{c} :\ddot{O}: \\ :\ddot{O}:Si:\ddot{O}: \\ :\ddot{O}: \end{array} \right]^{4-}$
    f. $\left[\begin{array}{c} :\ddot{Cl}: \\ :\ddot{Cl}:P:\ddot{Cl}: \\ :\ddot{Cl}: \end{array} \right]^+$

25. a. $:N:::N:$
    b. $[:C:::N:]^-$
    c. $[:N:::O:]^+$
    d. $:C:::O:$

26. a. $:\ddot{F}:\ddot{N}=\ddot{N}:\ddot{F}:$
    b. $:\ddot{Cl}:C\equiv C:\ddot{Cl}:$
    c. $H—\ddot{O}—\ddot{O}—H$
    d.   H
           |
       $H—C—\ddot{O}—H$
           |
            H

27. a. odd number of electrons, not octet
    b. Be has only 2 pairs of electrons.
    c. Xe has 6 pairs of electrons around it.
    d. Te has 5 pairs of electrons around it.

28. Two equivalent electron dot structures that differ only in the position of multiple bonds. An example is
   $:\ddot{O}—S=\ddot{O}: \leftrightarrow :\ddot{O}=S—\ddot{O}:$

29. a. $:\ddot{O}=S—\ddot{O}: \leftrightarrow :\ddot{O}—S—\ddot{O}: \leftrightarrow :\ddot{O}—S=\ddot{O}:$
       $\quad\quad :\ddot{O}: \quad\quad\quad :O: \quad\quad\quad :\ddot{O}:$
    b. $[:\ddot{O}—N=\ddot{O}:]^- \leftrightarrow [:\ddot{O}=N—\ddot{O}:]^-$
    c. $:\ddot{O}—\ddot{O}=\ddot{O}: \leftrightarrow :\ddot{O}=\ddot{O}—\ddot{O}:$
    d. $\left[\begin{array}{c} H—C=\ddot{O}: \\ | \\ :\ddot{O}: \end{array} \right]^- \leftrightarrow \left[\begin{array}{c} H—C—\ddot{O}: \\ || \\ :O: \end{array} \right]^-$

30. Electron pairs assume the arrangement that maximizes the distance apart.

31. a. tetrahedral
    b. tetrahedral
    c. tetrahedral
    d. tetrahedral
    e. linear

32. a. tetrahedral
    b. tetrahedral
    c. trigonal pyramidal
    d. bent
    e. linear

33. a. trigonal planar
    b. linear

34. PCl_5 has a trigonal bipyramidal shape. Three Cl atoms form a triangle around the P, with Cl—P—Cl bond angles of 120°. One P—Cl bond is perpendicular to the plane above the plane and one P—Cl bond is perpendicular to the plane below the plane; thus these form Cl—P—Cl bond angles of 90° to the P—Cl bonds in the plane and an angle of 180° to each other.

SF_6 has an octahedral shape. Four F atoms form a square around the S, with F—S—F bond angles of 90°. Two more S—F bonds lie above and below the plane and perpendicular to it, forming more 90° F—S—F angles. The F—S—F angle from any F to the one opposite is 180°.

35. A polar bond has a partial positive charge on one atom and a partial negative charge on the other atom. No partial charges exist on the atoms in a nonpolar bond, because the electrons are shared equally.

36. No. To be a polar molecule, there must be polar bonds.

37. Yes. If the polar bonds are symmetrical so that the dipole of one bond cancels the dipole of the other bonds.

38. **a.** nonpolar   **d.** polar

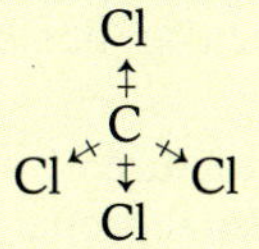

Cl
↕
C
Cl ⤪ ↕ ⤩ Cl
Cl

H ↔ Se
H

b. nonpolar   **e.** nonpolar bonds, nonpolar

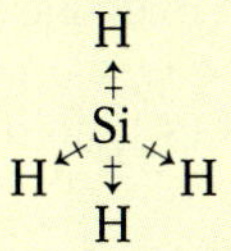

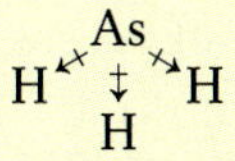

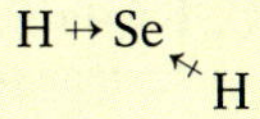

H
↕
Si
H ⤪ ↕ ⤩ H
H

S — C — S

c. polar

As
H ⤪ ↕ ⤩ H
H

39. BF_3 has 3 electron pairs surrounding the B atom and 3 symmetrical polar bonds so it is nonpolar. NF_3 has 4 electron pairs surrounding the N atom, 3 bonding and 1 nonbonding. The bonds are polar but not symmetrical so the molecule is polar.

40. Bent; 2 lone pairs, 2 bonding pairs; 105 degrees; bent; polar

41. The electron dot structure indicates that there should be a double bond and all electrons paired. Since this structure is not supported by the experimental evidence, the electron dot structure can not be correct.

42. In PCl_5, P is surrounded by 5 electron pairs, giving it a configuration of $3s^2\,3p^6\,3d^2$. In SF_6, S is surrounded by 6 electron pairs, giving it a configuration of $3s^2\,3p^6\,3d^4$. These configurations are similar to some transition metal ions and apparently provide stability to the molecules.

43. **a.** NaF, ionic
   b. CF_4, nonpolar covalent
   c. I_2, nonpolar covalent
   d. Ne, no compound expected
   e. $AsCl_3$, polar covalent

44. They both have the same number of electrons.

45. Hydrogen has one valence electron like the other group 1A elements. It also needs only one electron to have its valence shell filled like the other elements in group 7A.

Condensed States of Matter

Investigations	Demonstrations	Texas Essential Elements★
		Content: 2.2, 5.8, 8.1 **Process:** 4.3, 10.1
Laboratory Manual 14–3 IM In-text Investigation, page T492	Evaporation, page T477 Boiling Point, page T479 Heating Curves, page T481	**Content:** 2.3, 8.1 **Process:** 10.1, 10.4
Laboratory Manual 14–1 M	Surface Tension, page T485	**Content:** 8.1, 9.2 **Process:** 10.1, 10.4
Laboratory Manual 14–2 S		**Content:** 5.2, 8.1, 8.2 **Process:** 8.2, 10.4
		Content: 8.1 **Process:** 1.1, 1.2, 1.3, 2.1, 4.3, 5.1, 5.2, 6.2, 7.2
		Process: 4.2, 7.1, 7.2, 10.1, 10.2

KEY:
M–Microscale **S**–Structured
I–Inquiry **IM**–Inquiry Microscale

★See pages T8–T11 for complete
listing of Texas Essential Elements.

Chapter Rationale

The study of solids and liquids provides a contrast to gases, studied in Chapters 6 and 7. The kinetic molecular theory provides a model for gas behavior. Although kinetic molecular theory can be extended to solids and liquids, the model is not as simple. Chapter 14 covers intermolecular forces that are assumed to be negligible in the ideal gas model, but which are important in determining the state of matter in which a substance will exist at a given temperature.

About the Photograph

Steel can contain anywhere from 55 to 99.5 percent iron depending on the purpose of the steel. Other elements added to iron for making different types of steel include carbon, manganese, chromium, nickel, tungsten, molybdenum, and titanium. Heating iron ore to extremely high temperatures changes iron to a liquid that readily mixes with other elements. Heating also refines impurities from the iron ore. Molten iron mixed with other elements can be shaped into different forms using various hot-working methods such as forging, rolling, or extruding.

Chapter Planning Hints

Plan to complete the material in this chapter, including the Laboratory Investigation and the Chapter Review, in two to five class sessions. You may wish to obtain The World of Chemistry videotapes *States of Matter* for use when introducing intermolecular forces in solids and liquids, and *Water* for use when studying water. There are four optional demonstrations in this chapter. They appear on pages T477, T479, T481, and T485. You may wish to preview them at this time.

14

Condensed States of Matter

Overview

Generally when we encounter metals such as steel, it is a solid. However, at extremely high temperatures, steel becomes a liquid.

PART **1** *States of Matter*

Matter can exist in three commonly found states—gas, liquid, and solid. A liquid will change state to become a solid if its temperature is lowered below its freezing point. A liquid changes to a gaseous state if its temperature is raised above its boiling point. Such changes in state are called **phase changes.** You probably use phase changes every day without thinking about it. For example, you change water into a solid state when you put it in a freezer to make ice cubes. When you boil water to steam vegetables, you are taking advantage of water in the gaseous state.

It is important to realize that the particles that make up a substance do not change chemically during a phase change. The particles that make up water, steam, and ice are the same—molecules of H_2O. In other words, a phase change is a physical change, not a chemical change.

In this chapter, you will explore the arrangement of particles that make up a substance and the forces of attraction between the particles. By understanding the submicroscopic structure, you can better understand the macroscopic properties of substances in different states of matter.

14.1 Kinetic Molecular Theory: Liquids and Solids

You learned in Chapter 7 how to use the kinetic molecular theory to predict the behavior and properties of gases by examining the behavior of the particles that make up an ideal gas. You can now explain the properties of liquids and solids by adding to what you already know about gases.

Intermolecular forces in liquids and solids Recall that the kinetic molecular theory allows you to predict the properties of gases based on several simplifying assumptions: The particles of a gas are dimensionless points. The particles of an ideal gas are in constant, random, straight-line motion; collisions between gas particles are perfectly elastic; the average kinetic energy of gas particles depends upon the temperature; and gas particles exert no attractive or repulsive forces on one another. One of the reasons these assumptions work is that the particles that make up a gas are relatively far apart, compared to the particles in solids and liquids. Because gas particles are so far apart, the forces of attraction between them are very weak. For all practical purposes, the attraction

Objectives

Part 1

A. *Explain* how the three types of intermolecular forces arise.

B. *Compare and contrast* the physical properties of gases, liquids, and solids by comparing the strength of their intermolecular forces.

C. *Predict* which intermolecular forces will occur in a substance given its structure and composition.

PROBLEM-SOLVING STRATEGY

Use what you know about the kinetic molecular theory from Chapter 7 to help you understand intermolecular forces. (See Strategy, page 58.)

Developing Skills

Students may apply these skills in their study of Part 1.
Comparing/Contrasting: Have students compare and contrast the physical properties of gases, liquids, and solids.
Forming models: Have students form models for intermolecular forces.
Predicting: Have students predict the intermolecular forces that occur within a substance.

≡ FOCUS

Activate Prior Knowledge

In this activity, students may have previous knowledge of Brownian motion that they can use to explain their observations of particles in liquids and solids. They can also refer to Chapter 2, page 40.

Set up a high-power microscope. Sprinkle a small amount of talcum powder into a beaker of water. Place a drop of this mixture on a slide, cover with a cover slip, and observe under high power. Have students place a small amount of powder on a dry slide and observe that also. Is Brownian motion observed in a solid?

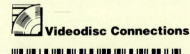
Videodisc Connections

22328 to 23515, side 2
States of matter (movie)

≡ T E A C H

Teaching Strategy

Intermolecular Forces in Liquids and Solids

Have students look up the densities of several common gases, liquids, and solids. Challenge them to determine the relationship between the density of these substances and the state of matter. A few possible examples are listed below. The data provided is for 25°C at 1 atm.

Substance	Density (g/mL)
hydrogen (g)	8.99×10^{-5}
fluorine (g)	1.55×10^{-3}
carbon dioxide (g)	1.98×10^{-3}
water (l)	1.00
ethyl alcohol (l)	0.79
mercury (l)	13.55
aluminum (s)	2.70
iron (s)	7.87
copper (s)	8.92
lead (s)	11.34
gold (s)	19.30

Resources

Use the videotape *States of Matter* from The World of Chemistry series.

Science Background

Effect of Pressure

Solids and liquids are typically over 1000 times more dense than gases. You can infer from this that in the gas phase, the particles making up a substance are the greatest distance apart.

DO YOU KNOW?

There is a fourth state of matter, called plasma, which consists of a mixture of atomic nuclei that have ionized completely and the electrons lost by these nuclei. A plasma is neutral because it contains an equal number of plus and minus charges from the protons and electrons. You learned about plasma while studying fusion in Chapter 9, Nuclear Chemistry. Plasma exists only at extremely high temperatures, such as those found in the sun, inside an atomic bomb, or in fusion experiments.

between gas particles at moderate temperatures and pressures is so small that it can be ignored.

In order to apply the kinetic molecular theory successfully to liquids and solids, attractive forces between particles must be considered because the particles are closer together. You know that covalent bonds are the forces that hold the atoms together within a molecule. But what holds one molecule close to another in a liquid or solid? The forces of attraction *between* two or more molecules are called **intermolecular forces.** In which state of matter would you expect there to be the weakest intermolecular forces? Because the particles are farthest apart in gases, you should expect the intermolecular forces to be weakest in the gaseous phase.

In liquids, the intermolecular forces are strong enough to hold the particles together, so liquids do not expand to fill their containers as gases do. But the intermolecular forces in liquids are weak enough to allow particles to move, or flow, past one another. Therefore, liquids, like gases, flow and assume the shape of their containers. Some liquids, like water, flow quickly; others, like oil, flow more slowly. The rate at which a liquid flows depends on the shape of the molecules, the temperature and pressure, and the strength of the intermolecular forces. In general, the stronger the intermolecular forces between particles of similar size and shape, the slower the liquid will flow.

In solids, the intermolecular forces are stronger than in liquids, and the molecules stay in a given position. Although a solid's particles vibrate, they do not move relative to one another. Therefore, solids have a definite shape and do not flow like gases and liquids.

Effect of temperature Why does a substance exist as a gas, a liquid, or a solid at a given temperature? You can answer this by examining how temperature affects the particles that make up a substance. The average kinetic energy of a gas increases with temperature. At a high temperature, if two gas particles get close enough to be momentarily attracted, they have enough kinetic energy to overcome this attraction. At lower temperatures, the average kinetic energy is lower. If the temperature is lowered sufficiently, particles that attract one another do not have enough kinetic energy to break away from each other, so they group together to form a liquid. This process is called **condensation.**

The temperature at which condensation occurs depends upon the strength of the intermolecular forces. If the intermolecular forces are large, condensation will occur at a higher temperature. If they are small, condensation will occur at a lower temperature.

Effect of pressure Increased pressure also can cause a gas to condense. Increasing the pressure forces gas particles closer together. The closer the particles, the stronger the intermolecular forces. If the pressure is increased sufficiently, the particles are forced close enough for the intermolecular forces to hold them together in the liquid state.

Science Background

Dispersion Forces

Dispersion forces are also called London forces. *Van der Waals forces* is a general term that includes dispersion forces, dipole-dipole forces, and hydrogen bonding.

Figure 14-1 *Fog occurs when water vapor condenses in pockets of cool air. What does this tell you about condensation?*

You may have seen butane stoves that are used for camping, like the one shown in Figure 14-2. Inside the fuel cartridge, the butane is a liquid at room temperature; if you shake the fuel cartridge, you can hear the butane slosh around. It would not make sense to transport butane as a gas because a gas occupies more volume than an equal mass of liquid. Instead, pressure is used to condense the butane so that it can be transported efficiently as a liquid. When you release the pressure by turning the valve, the butane liquid exits as a gas, which can then be ignited.

Do You Know?

Cake mixes give different directions for high altitudes because of the reduced air pressure.

14.2 Types of Intermolecular Forces

Because molecules are electrically neutral, you might think that there can be no forces of attraction between them. How do intermolecular forces arise? In this section, you will learn how three different kinds of intermolecular forces hold groups of molecules together: dispersion forces, dipole-dipole forces, and hydrogen bonding. Collectively, these intermolecular forces are called **van der Waals forces.**

Dispersion forces Momentary dipoles may form even in nonpolar molecules because the distribution of electrons in atoms is constantly changing. Thus, at a given moment, the distribution can be unsymmetrical. Figure 14-3 on the next page shows the momentary dipoles for two nonpolar hydrogen molecules. This results in a positive charge at one end of each molecule and a negative charge at the other end. **Dispersion forces** arise when the positive end of one momentary dipole is attracted to the negative end of another momentary dipole. Dispersion forces are the only intermolecular forces acting between nonpolar molecules.

You can get an idea of the strength of dispersion forces by investigating the boiling points of nonpolar liquids. For such liquids to boil, enough energy must be added to overcome the dispersion

Figure 14-2 *Butane, the fuel used in many camping stoves, is stored as a liquid. The butane remains a liquid in the canister because it is kept under high pressure.*

PART **1**

Section 14.2 *continued*

Videodisc Connections

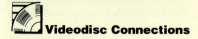

665-666, side 6
Van der Waals: toggle back and
forth (2-frame seq.)

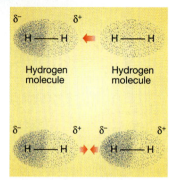

Figure 14-3 Top: *The hydrogen molecule on the left has a
momentary dipole. The electrons
in the nonpolar hydrogen molecule on the right are attracted
toward the positive end of the
momentary dipole.* Bottom: *Both
molecules have momentary dipoles, which are attracted toward each other.*

forces holding the particles together. Table 14-1 lists boiling points
for the halogens. Notice that the boiling points increase as molecular
mass increases from fluorine to iodine. The same trend is seen for
the boiling points of the carbon-hydrogen compounds shown in
Table 14-2. In general, as molecular mass increases, the dispersion
forces increase, because there are more electrons that can form
momentary dipoles. The larger the molecular mass of a nonpolar
compound, the greater the dispersion forces and the greater the
boiling point of the liquid.

TABLE 14-1

Boiling Points of Halogens			
Name	Formula	Molar Mass (g/mol)	Boiling Point (K, at 1 atm)
fluorine	F_2	38.0	85.0
chlorine	Cl_2	70.9	239.1
bromine	Br_2	159.8	331.9
iodine	I_2	253.8	457.4

TABLE 14-2

Boiling Points of Nonpolar Carbon-Hydrogen Compounds			
Name	Formula	Molar Mass (g/mol)	Boiling Point (K, at 1 atm)
methane	CH_4	16.0	111.7
propane	C_3H_8	44.1	231.1
hexane	C_6H_{14}	86.2	341.9
decane	$C_{10}H_{22}$	142.3	447.3
eicosane	$C_{20}H_{42}$	282.5	617.0

In small nonpolar molecules, such as fluorine, dispersion forces
are very weak compared to the kinetic energy of the molecules.
Only at very low temperatures is the average kinetic energy sufficiently low to allow dispersion forces to condense the gas into a
liquid. This explains why fluorine condenses at the frigid temperature of 85K ($-188°C$). But dispersion forces are not always weak.
You can infer from the high boiling points of eicosane and iodine
that large nonpolar molecules have very large dispersion forces.

Dispersion forces can arise even in atoms because electron dis-
tributions are constantly changing in atoms. Recall from Chapter
11 that the noble gases are monoatomic molecules because the
atoms are very stable. In noble gases, dispersion forces are the only
forces of attraction acting between the atoms. Because dispersion
forces are extremely weak in the noble gases, they condense at

very low temperatures. Helium, for example, condenses to the liquid phase at $-269°C$, only $4°C$ above absolute zero!

Concept ✔ Check

Why is measuring the boiling point of a substance a good method of determining the strength of the dispersion forces between molecules?

Dipole-dipole forces Like dispersion forces, **dipole-dipole forces** arise from the electrostatic attraction between the positive end of one dipole and the negative end of an adjacent dipole. However, unlike dispersion forces, which occur between nonpolar molecules, dipole-dipole forces exist only between polar molecules.

Substances with dipole-dipole forces tend to have greater intermolecular forces than substances with only dispersion forces, if their molecular masses are about the same. Consider, for example, carbon monoxide, CO, and nitrogen, N_2. These molecules have the same molecular mass and isoelectronic electron configurations, so you would expect them to have about equal dispersion forces. However, carbon monoxide is polar and therefore has dipole-dipole forces present. Nitrogen, however, is nonpolar and lacks dipole-dipole forces. Therefore, the fact that the boiling point of carbon monoxide (81K or $-192°C$) is 4 degrees higher than the boiling point of nitrogen (77K, $-196°C$) can be attributed to the added dipole-dipole force present in carbon monoxide.

Dipole-dipole interactions are only about one hundredth as strong as ionic or covalent bonds. Like dispersion forces, dipole-dipole forces are stronger when molecules are closer together, so these forces are relatively unimportant for molecules in the gas phase.

Hydrogen bonding Some polar molecules have much larger intermolecular forces than expected. Look at the graphs in Figure 14-4 on the next page. These graphs plot boiling point versus molecular mass for the hydrides of elements in Groups 4A, 5A, 6A, and 7A. What trend do you notice? The trend in Group 4A is what you would expect for nonpolar compounds. As the molecular mass of these compounds increases, the dispersion forces and the boiling points increase.

Does this pattern hold for the other three graphs? Notice that the boiling point of ammonia, NH_3, is much higher than you would expect based on the trend of boiling points for the other Group 5A hydrides. Notice also how the boiling points of water, H_2O, and hydrogen fluoride, HF, compare with boiling points of the other Group 6A and Group 7A hydrides. All three of these polar compounds have much higher boiling points than you would expect. If you apply the reasoning developed thus far in this chapter, you would predict that the dramatic increases in the boiling points of

CONNECTING CONCEPTS

Change and Interaction Interactions of electrical forces are fundamental to chemistry: Ions form salts; atoms bond together to form molecules; and molecules are attracted to other molecules. Each phenomenon is the result of forces that are electrical in nature.

Teaching Strategy

Hydrogen Bonding

Knowing when hydrogen bonding can occur is difficult for students. Show them some examples of molecules that do exhibit hydrogen bonding and some that do not hydrogen bond. Be sure to draw the structures using dotted lines to represent the hydrogen bonds between adjacent molecules.

 Videodisc Connections

652-653, side 6
Water molecules combining
(2-frame seq.)

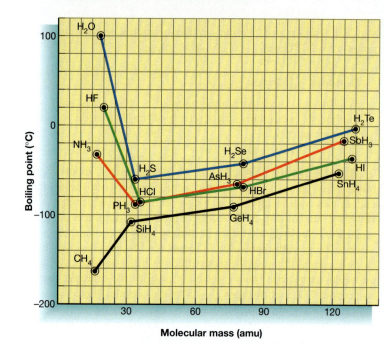

Figure 14-4 The boiling points of the covalent hydrides of elements in Groups 4A, 5A, 6A, and 7A. How are the patterns you see related to the strengths of intermolecular bonds?

these polar compounds must be the result of a relatively strong intermolecular force. This especially strong dipole-dipole force is called **hydrogen bonding.**

It is important to remember that hydrogen bonding is not the same as covalent bonding within a molecule. Hydrogen bonding occurs *between* molecules that have N—H, O—H, or F—H bonds. The electronegativity values of fluorine, oxygen, and nitrogen are 4.0, 3.5, and 3.0, respectively. Hydrogen's electronegativity is 2.1. Therefore, the covalent bonds between hydrogen and these elements are very polar, resulting in strong dipole-dipole interactions between molecules.

Another factor that explains the strength of hydrogen bonding is the small size of the atoms involved. The hydrogen atom in one molecule can get very close to the nitrogen, oxygen, or fluorine atom in an adjacent molecule because these atoms are relatively small. The closer two molecules can get, the stronger the intermolecular force that arises between them. Hydrogen bonding is about ten times stronger than ordinary dipole-dipole forces. Figure 14-5 shows how hydrogen bonding occurs between pairs of water, ammonia, and hydrogen fluoride molecules and in mixtures of two of these compounds. Hydrogen bonding can exist in other sub-

Concept ✔ Check

Why do polar molecules generally have higher boiling points than nonpolar molecules of similar mass?

PART 1 REVIEW

ANSWERS

■ Keyed to Objectives

A 1. They attract one another due to dispersion forces that arise due to an unsymmetrical electron distribution.

A 2. Dipole-dipole forces are the attractive forces between polar molecules. They arise from the attraction of the positive end of one polar molecule to the negative end of an adjacent polar molecule.

C 3. Hydrogen bonding is an especially strong dipole-dipole force exhibited between polar hydride molecules. Hydrogen bonding occurs between molecules that have N—H, O—H, and F—H bonds.

C 4. Because Ne is a monatomic molecule and I_2, CO_2, and CH_4 are nonpolar molecules, only dispersion

Hydrogen bonding in pure substances

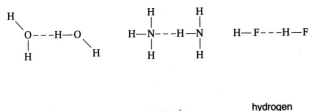

water   ammonia   hydrogen
fluoride

Hydrogen bonding in mixtures

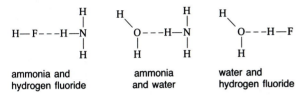

ammonia and   ammonia   water and
hydrogen fluoride   and water   hydrogen fluoride

Figure 14-5 *Hydrogen bonding occurs in molecules with N—H, O—H, and H—F bonds. Dashed lines represent hydrogen bonding between molecules. Solid lines represent covalent bonds within molecules.*

stances, but N—H, O—H, or F—H bonds must be present in the molecules.

Hydrogen bonding between molecules is weaker than covalent bonding within molecules. Figure 14-6 shows how hydrogen bonding occurs in a group of water molecules. Each water molecule can form hydrogen bonds with two other water molecules because of the two nonbonding electron pairs on each oxygen atom.

PART 1 REVIEW

1. Describe how two nonpolar molecules can attract one another.

2. What are dipole-dipole forces? Explain how these forces arise between molecules.

3. Explain what hydrogen bonding is. Under what conditions does hydrogen bonding occur?

4. In pure samples of each of the following, indicate the kinds of intermolecular forces that can occur: Ne, I_2, NH_3, CO_2, CH_4, and CH_3OH.

5. Which molecule would you expect to have a higher boiling point, GeH_4 or AsH_3? Explain your answer.

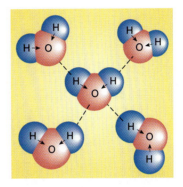

Figure 14-6 *Each water molecule is attracted to four other water molecules by hydrogen bonding.*

Boxed numbers indicate questions that involve skills in interpretation, application, and analysis.

forces occur. Both NH_3 and CH_3OH are polar (with a N—H and an O—H bond, respectively) and will exhibit both dispersion and dipole-dipole forces.

B 5. AsH_3 has the higher boiling point. Both compounds have about the same molar mass. However, AsH_3 is polar and GeH_4 is nonpolar. Thus, AsH_3 will have dipole-dipole forces and GeH_4 will not; the over-

all intermolecular forces will be higher for AsH_3.

PART **1**

Section 14.2 *continued*

Guided Practice

Review the Concept Check questions on pages 473 and 474 with students. Answers can be found in Appendix E on page 808.

Reteaching Idea

To assist students in distinguishing between the types of intermolecular forces, have them create a chart in which they compare and contrast dispersion forces, dipole-dipole forces, and hydrogen bonding. The chart should also include a description, with examples, of how these forces affect the physical properties of various substances.

≡CLOSE

Summing Up Main Ideas

Draw an arrow up the middle of a piece of paper. This represents increasing intermolecular forces. On the left side of the arrow, indicate how the strength of intermolecular forces changes as a substance changes phase from a gas to a liquid to a solid.

Place the different forces (dispersion, dipole-dipole, and hydrogen bonding) along the arrow according to their relative strength.

PART 1 REVIEW

Assign the Part Review questions.

Evaluating Skills

These skills are evaluated in the Part Review questions indicated. **Determining main ideas: 1, 2, 3, 4; Determining cause and effect: 2, 3; Comparing/Contrasting: 3, 4, 5**

PART **2**
Change of State
Section 14.3

Developing Skills

Students may apply these skills in their study of Part 2.

Comparing/Contrasting: Have students compare vapor pressure of different molecular substances to their intermolecular forces.

Forming models: Have students form models of phase changes at a molecular level.

Interpreting diagrams and Analyzing data: Have students interpret data using heating curves.

≣ FOCUS

Activate Prior Knowledge

This activity will reinforce students' awareness of the cooling effects of evaporation. Wrap the bulb of a thermometer with gauze; secure the gauze with a rubber band. Place the thermometer in a beaker and record the temperature. Wet the gauze with ten drops of alcohol and record the temperature every minute for five minutes. Remove the thermometer from the beaker and dispose of the gauze. Repeat the procedure using water as the liquid. Ask students which substance evaporates faster, and which caused the greatest temperature change. Which liquid is likely to have the lower boiling point?

⚠ **CAUTION: Remove all flames or sources of ignition. Wear a lab apron and goggles. Use a small capped bottle for the alcohol (containing no greater than 100 mL).**

PART
2 Change of State

Objectives

Part 2

D. *Explain* phase changes at the molecular level.

E. *Describe* the process of evaporation and *compare* vapor pressures of different substances by referring to intermolecular forces.

F. *Interpret* the features of heating curves.

PROBLEM-SOLVING
S T R A T E G Y ▶

Use what you know about real-world behavior of liquids and the kinetic molecular theory to understand phase changes. (See Strategy, page 58.)

Imagine that you are five billion times smaller than you really are, standing at the bottom of a large closed box filled with steam at 110°C. Most of the box is empty space, and you can see molecules of H_2O moving in all directions at a variety of speeds. Although there are plenty of collisions taking place, each molecule usually moves quite a long distance before it collides with another molecule.

What happens if the temperature goes down? Some molecules will move just as fast as before, but more of them will be moving more slowly. The average kinetic energy, and therefore the average speed of the molecules, decreases as the temperature goes down.

When the temperature drops to 100°C, something new and startling happens. Clusters of molecules are falling to the bottom of the box, crowding in close to you. As you struggle to swim up, you can see that these molecules have little space between them. Although they touch each other, you can easily push them past one another. When at last you swim high enough, you find yourself floating at the top of this churning crowd of molecules. Most of the box above you is empty, and only an occasional gaseous H_2O molecule can be seen darting by.

As the temperature drops below 100°C, the molecular motion slows down even more. Every once in a while you can observe a molecule plunging from above and mixing with the crowded scene around you. Just as often, one leaves the sea of molecules to escape upward into the space above.

14.3 Phase Changes

Water is undergoing phase changes. Did you notice that after most of the particles have condensed into the liquid phase, some particles escape to the gas phase even though the liquid is not boiling? How can this change of state occur?

Evaporation You may have noticed how quickly a puddle of water can disappear after a thunderstorm on a hot day. The liquid water changes into the gas phase, called water vapor. **Vapor** is the gaseous form of a substance that exists as a liquid or a solid under normal conditions of temperature and pressure. This change from liquid to vapor is called vaporization, or **evaporation.**

For a liquid to evaporate, the particles must have enough energy to overcome the intermolecular forces that hold them together in the liquid phase. According to the kinetic molecular theory, the particles of a liquid have a distribution of different energies, as shown in the graph in Figure 14-7. The graph shows that there is a minimum energy, E_{min}, required for particles to escape from the

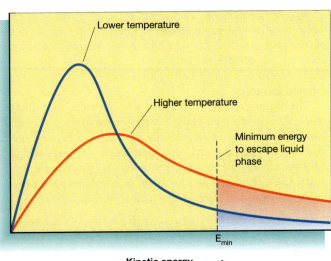

Figure 14-7 *Particles with kinetic energy greater than E_{min} can evaporate. More particles can evaporate at higher temperatures (red and blue areas) than at a lower temperature (blue area).*

liquid. As the temperature of the liquid increases, more particles have sufficient energy to escape from the liquid. For this reason, the rate of evaporation is higher at higher temperatures.

The rate of evaporation depends on temperature. At any given temperature, the rate of evaporation is constant, as shown by the red curve in Figure 14-8. As evaporation occurs, the number of vapor particles steadily increases. As more and more particles go into the vapor phase in a closed system, the numbers of gas particles hitting the surface of the liquid increases. Gas particles striking the liquid surface can become attracted to the liquid particles and condense back into the liquid phase. Therefore, as the number of particles in the gas phase increases, the rate of condensation increases, as shown by the blue curve in Figure 14-8. At some point in time, the rates of evaporation and condensation become equal.

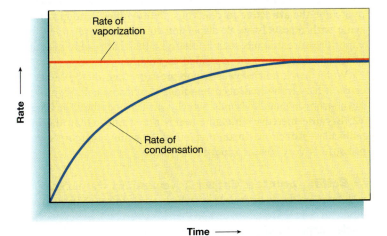

Figure 14-8 *The rates of condensation and vaporization of a liquid. In a closed system after a period of time, the two rates become equal.*

TEACH

Teaching Strategy

Evaporation

You can use the boiling process to emphasize the difference in densities of gases and liquids. The bubbles of vapor rise because they are many times less dense than the liquid.

⚠ **CAUTION: Wear safety goggles and a lab apron. Use a shield to protect students.**

DEMONSTRATION

Evaporation

Use cotton swabs to place different liquids on the chalkboard. Use only water, rubbing alcohol, and nail polish remover.

⚠ **CAUTION: Rubbing alcohol and nail polish remover vapors are flammable, can explode, and are harmful** if inhaled. Be sure there are no flames. **Wear safety goggles and a lab apron.** Rate the differences in the rate of evaporation to the relative strength of intermolecular forces.

Teaching Strategy

Vapor Pressure

Students may be concerned about the danger of breathing mercury vapors if liquid mercury is used in the laboratory. Refer to Figure 14–9 to compare the volatility of mercury and ether. Emphasize the fact that even though liquid mercury has a comparatively low volatility, its high toxicity necessitates avoiding contact with it.

Vapor pressure The partial pressure of the vapor above a liquid is called the **vapor pressure.** Recall from Chapter 6 that the partial pressure of a gas depends on the number of gas particles present. The greater the number of gas particles, the greater the vapor pressure. Thus as evaporation occurs, vapor pressure above a liquid increases.

The vapor pressure of a liquid also depends upon the temperature. At a given temperature, vapor pressure is constant. As the temperature increases, vapor pressure increases because the rate of evaporation is greater and vapor particles have more energy. Figure 14-9 shows plots of vapor pressure versus temperature for diethyl ether, $C_4H_{10}O$, water, and mercury. In each case, you can see that vapor pressure increases as the temperature increases.

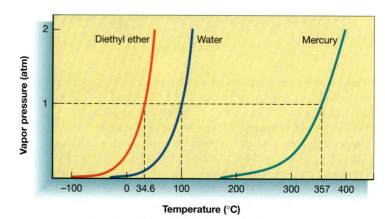

Figure 14-9 *Vapor pressure of diethyl ether, water, and mercury as temperature increases. The normal boiling point is the temperature at which the vapor pressure is equal to 1 atm.*

Why do these three liquids have such different vapor pressures at a given temperature? Vapor pressure depends on the strength of the intermolecular forces between the particles of the liquid. The stronger the intermolecular forces, the lower the vapor pressure will be, because fewer particles will have enough kinetic energy to overcome the attractive forces. Thus diethyl ether, a nonpolar molecule with relatively weak dispersion forces, has a relatively high vapor pressure. Liquids such as diethyl ether that readily evaporate at room temperature are classified as **volatile.**

Water has a much lower vapor pressure than diethyl ether because it has strong hydrogen bonding. Mercury is held together by even stronger metallic bonds, which you learned about in Chapter 12. Because mercury's metallic bonds are stronger than the intermolecular attractions in diethyl ether or water, mercury's vapor pressure is very low at room temperature.

Boiling point In Chapter 2, you learned that boiling point is defined as the temperature at which a substance changes from a liquid to a gas. Does this mean that boiling point is defined by a single temperature?

You may already know that water's boiling point is affected by altitude above sea level. At sea level, where the air pressure is about 1 atm, the boiling point of water is 100°C. In Denver, at an altitude of about 1600 m, or 1 mi., air pressure is only 0.83 atm, and water boils at about 95°C. Because boiling water is "colder" in Denver, foods take longer to cook there than at sea level.

If you think about what you have learned in this chapter, you will realize that boiling point must depend on the external pressure acting on a fluid. As external pressure increases, particles in a liquid are compressed slightly closer together, which increases the intermolecular forces holding the particles together. Boiling point therefore increases slightly at higher pressures because particles need more kinetic energy to overcome the intermolecular forces and escape to the gas phase.

A more sophisticated definition of boiling point can now be given in terms of vapor pressure. Boiling point is the temperature at which the vapor pressure equals the external pressure acting on a liquid. For example, at a pressure of 1 atm, water boils when it is heated to 100°C. At this temperature, the vapor pressure of water equals 1 atm. Because the vapor pressure equals the external pressure, vaporization can occur within the liquid, not just at its surface. Bubbles of vapor form in the liquid, rise to the surface, and escape, as shown in Figure 14-10.

The boiling point of any substance at 1 atm of pressure is called the normal boiling point. Thus the normal boiling point of water is 100°C. Look again at Figure 14-9. What are the normal boiling points of diethyl ether and mercury?

Pressure cookers speed up cooking by increasing the pressure to more than 1 atm. The increase in pressure causes water to boil at a higher than normal temperature and thus shortens the time needed to cook food.

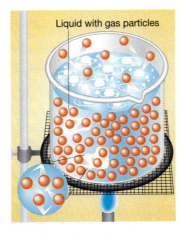

Liquid with gas particles

Figure 14-10 *During boiling, the particles of a liquid gain enough kinetic energy to escape as a gas.*

Concept ✔ **Check**

Explain why increasing the atmospheric pressure will increase the boiling point of a liquid.

Freezing point Freezing is the phase change at constant temperature and pressure from liquid to solid. The reverse process is called melting or *fusion*. For a substance at a given pressure, the melting point and freezing point are the same temperature. At this temperature, both the solid and liquid can exist simultaneously.

As you might expect, normal freezing point is defined as the freezing point at a pressure of 1 atm. Freezing point changes only slightly with small changes in external pressure because liquids are nearly incompressible. In other words, increasing the pressure on a liquid pushes the particles only slightly closer together, so it takes a large change in pressure to significantly change the freezing point.

D E M O N S T R A T I O N

Boiling Point

Use a vacuum pump to reduce the pressure above water in a vacuum flask. Put a thermometer in the water so students can see that the temperature does not increase even though the water is boiling as a result of the reduced pressure.

🔺 **CAUTION: The flask should be wrapped with cloth-backed adhe-** sive tape to confine any flying glass in case the flask implodes. Also use a shield, safety goggles, and a lab apron.

Alternatively, place 5 to 10 mL of water in a 50-mL plastic syringe. Expel any air, and seal with a syringe cap. Then pull on the plunger. Bubbles of water vapor will form as the pressure inside is lowered.

PART **2**

Section 14.3 *continued*

Videodisc Connections

383, side 2
States of matter: NaCl crystals
(1 frame)

41334 to 44458, side 2
Freeze drying (movie)

Solids have a wide range of melting points that depend upon the strength of their intermolecular forces. The stronger the intermolecular forces, the higher the melting point because molecules need more kinetic energy to break free from the structure of the solid. Which would you expect to have a higher melting point, a polar or a nonpolar substance, if their molecular masses are about equal? Because polar substances have dipole-dipole forces, they generally have higher melting points than nonpolar substances of the same molecular mass.

You can apply this reasoning to ionic solids, which consist of ions held together by ionic bonds. You learned in Chapter 13 that ionic bonds are quite strong; therefore ionic solids are characterized by high melting points. Similarly, metallic solids generally have high melting points because metallic bonds are also strong. Mercury is a familiar exception—it is the only metal that is liquid at normal temperature and pressure.

Sublimation How can a solid change phase directly to a gas? The answer must be that even solids have a vapor pressure. You probably have seen evidence of this. Wet clothes will freeze on a clothesline in winter, but after a period of time the clothes will be dry. You may have thought it mysterious that ice cubes in your freezer seem to get smaller if they are left there for a long time. In both cases, ice has changed directly into water vapor. The process by which a solid changes directly into a gas is called **sublimation**. The reverse process, a gas changing directly into a solid, is called condensation or deposition.

There are many practical applications of sublimation. Solid carbon dioxide, known as dry ice, is used to keep materials frozen while shipping. Instead of melting to form a liquid as water ice does, dry ice sublimes at normal pressure, and so remains dry. Naphthalene and paradichlorobenzene are commonly used to make mothballs. These substances are both solids that sublime at room temperature. The vapors produced by these solids have a distinctive odor that repels moths. Solid household air fresheners also work by sublimation. The solid sublimes to release a fresh smelling vapor into the air.

Figure 14-11 *A puddle forms around water ice because water changes from a solid to a liquid. No puddle forms around dry ice because it sublimes directly to the gas phase.*

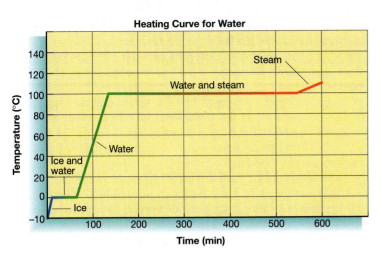

Heating Curve for Water

Figure 14-12 *The heating curve for 1 mole of water. Heat is added at the rate of 100 J per minute.*

Teaching Strategy

Heating Curves

Help your students understand the heating/cooling curves shown in this section. The horizontal axis is proportional to the amount of heat absorbed that causes a temperature or state change. Students may be surprised that the amount of energy required to change state is so much greater than to change temperature when no change of

Look Ahead

A quantitative treatment of the energy changes occurring during a change of state is covered in Section 16.3.

14.4 Heating Curves

A heating curve is a temperature-versus-time graph that is useful for illustrating the energy changes that take place as a substance is heated. Figure 14-12 shows a heating curve for water at 1 atm of pressure as the temperature changes from $-10°C$ to $110°C$. The curve shows what happens to 1 mole (18.0 g) of water when it is heated at a constant rate of 100 J per minute, starting with ice at $-10°C$ and ending with steam at $110°C$.

Heat of fusion As heat is added to the $-10°C$ ice, the temperature begins to rise. The water molecules in the ice increase their average kinetic energy but remain fixed in the solid state. After heating for just under 4 minutes, the ice reaches its melting point of $0°C$ and begins to melt. Once the ice begins to melt, the temperature stays constant until all of the ice has melted. During melting, all of the heat being added is used to overcome hydrogen bonds that hold water molecules in a fixed position in the solid phase.

The energy required to change 1 mole of ice into 1 mole of water at $0°C$ is called the **molar heat of fusion.** The intermolecular forces in the solid are so strong that it takes 60 minutes for the ice to melt. After the ice has completely melted, about 15 percent of the hydrogen bonding has been disrupted. As soon as the last bit of ice melts, the temperature again begins to rise and for the next 75 minutes more hydrogen bonding is disrupted as the molecules become more agitated.

Concept ✔ Check

Explain why the temperature of ice remains constant while ice is melting when heat is being added.

D E M O N S T R A T I O N

Heating Curves

Produce a portion of a heating curve by measuring the temperature of water (collected as snow or crushed ice) that has been cooled below 0°C and warmed to about 40°C.

CAUTION: Wear safety goggles and a lab apron.

PART 2

Section 14.4 continued

Guided Practice

Review the Concept Check questions on pages 479 and 481 with students. Answers can be found in Appendix E on page 808.

Reteaching Idea

To reinforce the concepts of boiling and change of state, set up an experiment with students where they heat water. **CAUTION: Have students wear safety goggles and lab aprons.** Have each pair of students fill a 250-mL beaker about half full with tap water. Measure the temperature of the water and place the beaker over a heat source. Students should heat the water to the boiling point, keeping track of the elapsed time, and they should write down any other observations. Once the boiling point is reached, they should continue to heat the water for an additional 5 minutes, taking temperature readings every 30 seconds. Assign them to make a data table and then graph their data. They should write a short conclusion explaining the phenomenon they observed.

Summing Up Main Ideas

Have students describe the processes that contribute to an atmospheric humidity level. They should answer such questions as: Why does the humidity level drop as the temperature decreases? How can there be water vaporized in the air when the temperature is below freezing? How can snow disappear when the temperature never exceeds 0°C?

PART 2 REVIEW

Assign the Part Review questions.

Boxed numbers indicate questions that involve skills in interpretation, application, and analysis.

Heat of vaporization At the end of this 75-minute period, the water has reached its boiling point. Once the liquid water reaches 100°C, it begins to boil, as molecules of water form gaseous steam. Once again, while the water is boiling, the temperature stays constant as long as both the liquid and gas are present. The amount of energy required to change 1 mole of water from the liquid state to the gaseous state is the **molar heat of vaporization.** This step takes 407 minutes! The heat of vaporization is very large because all of the hydrogen bonding must be disrupted before the liquid can completely vaporize.

Once all of the liquid is converted to steam at 100°C, it takes less than 4 minutes to heat the steam up to 110°C. The changes that occur in this entire process are all physical changes; no chemical reaction has occurred, and no covalent bonds have been broken.

A cooling curve is the reverse process of the one just described. If 1 mole of steam at 110°C was cooled to ice at −10°C, at a cooling rate of 100 J per minute, the cooling would take exactly the same time. The condensation of steam and the freezing of liquid water are the reverse of vaporization and melting, respectively.

Your body utilizes the high heat of vaporization of water as a cooling mechanism. As you sweat, water vaporizes. Because a large amount of heat is required to vaporize water, your skin cools as this heat is removed.

You can use the heating curve for water to explain why a steam burn is much more serious than a burn from boiling liquid water. A steam burn releases the heat of vaporization as the steam condenses on your skin. The damage is much greater than that caused by a burn from liquid water because the heat of vaporization is so great.

PART 2 REVIEW

6. Acetone has a greater vapor pressure than ethyl alcohol at 25°C. Predict which substance has larger intermolecular forces. Explain your answer.

7. The boiling point of ethyl alcohol is 78.5°C. Will the boiling point of acetone be lower or higher? Explain your answer.

8. What happens to the temperature of ice at −10°C when it is heated?

9. What happens at the submicroscopic level in terms of heat energy and intermolecular forces when ice at −10°C is heated until it becomes liquid water at +5°C?

10. What happens to the temperature when liquid water at 100°C and 1 atm is heated?

11. What happens at the molecular level when liquid water at 100°C and 1 atm is heated?

12. Compare the boiling point of water at 1 atm to the boiling point of water at 2 atm.

PART 2 REVIEW

ANSWERS

■ Keyed to Objectives

E **6.** Ethyl alcohol has larger intermolecular forces than acetone. As a result of the weaker attractive forces between molecules, acetone molecules can escape from the bulk liquid into the vapor phase, resulting in a higher vapor pressure at a given temperature.

E **7.** The boiling point of acetone will be lower (56.5°C). Less energy is required to overcome the weaker intermolecular forces in acetone, so the boiling point is lower.

D **8.** The temperature will rise. If enough heat is added to increase the temperature to 0°C, additional heat will cause the ice to begin melting.

D **9.** As the ice is heated, energy is trans-

HISTORY OF SCIENCE

The Continuing Process

The history of science reflects a continuing process of development. When you look at the periodic table, you view it as a finished product. However, about 50 of the elements listed there were discovered in the 1800's, about 30 more in the 1900's, and some as recently as the 1980's. These discoveries and many others like them contribute to the body of knowledge called science.

Notable inventions and inventors When scientific knowledge is applied to solve practical problems, inventions or technological developments occur. You are familiar with many inventions and inventors. For example, in 1876, when Alexander Graham Bell patented the telephone, the field of communications was advanced. In 1879, the flexibility and productivity of society were enhanced in the workplace and at home with the advent of the incandescent light bulb. It was invented and patented by Thomas Alva Edison. But did you know that a vacuum pan invented by Norbert Rillieux in 1846 changed the process of refining sugar, giving birth to granulated sugar? This revolutionized the worldwide production of sugar. Did you know that the lubricating cup invented by Elijah McCoy also had a dramatic impact on industry, saving valuable time? This device could lubricate machine parts automatically, so factory workers would not need to stop heavy machinery and lubricate parts by hand. Did you know that in 1884, Granville T. Woods invented a telephone transmitter that enabled moving trains to communicate with stations, greatly improving transportation safety?

Generations of contributions Unlike the names Bell and Edison, the names Rillieux, McCoy, and Woods are probably unfamiliar to you, even though these inventors made significant contributions to society. Many people take their contributions for granted and do not recognize these famous African Americans. Current scientific discoveries will undoubtedly lead to the unexpected ideas and inventions of the future, and it is important to understand that science and technology can grow only through the contributions of many people. One of the most urgent questions today is, Who will be doing science and technology tomorrow? The science of today will become the technology of tomorrow and part of the history of science.

Evaluating Skills

These skills are evaluated in the Part Review questions indicated. **Predicting:** 1, 7; **Comparing/ Contrasting:** 6, 7; **Determining cause and effect:** 8, 9, 10, 11; **Determining main ideas:** 10, 11

Resources

A new video entitled "Tracing the Path—African American Contributions to Chemistry in the Life Sciences" is available from the American Chemical Society. This 18-minute video traces scientific contributions by pre-colonial Africans in Africa, by African Americans in the late 1800s and early to mid-1900s in the United States, and by modern African Americans to the field of chemistry as it relates to the life sciences. The video comes with an extensive teacher's guide featuring hands-on activities, suggested discussion questions, and demonstrations. For more information write to A.C.S., P.O. Box 57136, Washington, DC 20037.

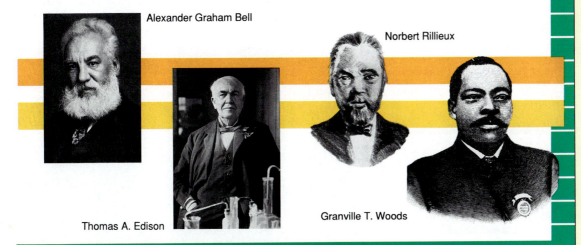

Alexander Graham Bell

Norbert Rillieux

Thomas A. Edison

Granville T. Woods

ferred to the ice. At 0°C, the energy of the water molecules is large enough to partly overcome the intermolecular forces (including some of the hydrogen bonding) that causes water to be solid below 0°C. Once melting begins, the temperature remains constant until all the ice is melted. Then the temperature begins to rise once again as more heat is added.

D 10. As heat is added, some of the water will vaporize, forming steam. The temperature will remain constant until all of the liquid is changed to the gas phase.

D 11. In the liquid below 100°C, the water molecules are in motion but attracted to adjacent molecules. At 100°C, the molecules have enough energy to overcome the attractive

forces, and the molecules go into the vapor phase.

E 12. The boiling point of water at 2 atm will be higher than 100°C, which is the boiling point at 1 atm. Particles need more energy to overcome the intermolecular forces when there is an increase in pressure.

PART **3**

Structure and Properties of Liquids

Developing Skills

Students may apply these skills in their study of Part 3.

Forming models: Have students form models that provide a molecular basis for surface tension.

Comparing/Contrasting: Have students compare the unusual properties of water to its structure and intermolecular forces.

≡ FOCUS

Activate Prior Knowledge

Discuss with students their previous observations of a sealed glass bottle containing a liquid such as milk or soda pop when the contents freeze. Demonstrate this phenomenon: Pour 25 mL of water into each of two plastic 50-mL graduated cylinders. Cover both with plastic wrap. Place one in a freezer and the other in a dark cupboard overnight. (Do not use a freezer that is used for storing food.) The next day, compare the water level in each.

≡ TEACH

Science Background

Surface Tension

The demonstration on page T485 shows the effect of soaps and detergents on the surface tension of water. Soaps are metallic salts of a carboxylic acid. They contain 12 to 18 carbon atoms in the

(continued on page T485)

Objectives

Part 3

G. *Explain* the molecular basis for surface tension.

H. *Explain* how the structure of water accounts for its unusual properties.

DO YOU KNOW?

It has been generally accepted that due to the pull of gravity, glass flows downward extremely slowly at room temperature. Indeed if you look at windows in very old houses, you can see the distortion as you look through the glass—it is thicker toward the bottom. However a recent report states that hand-made glass was thicker at one end than the other. It was customary to hang the thicker end down.

Figure 14-13 *Surface tension allows a water strider to walk on water.*

Liquids are the intermediate state of matter between gases and solids. Like solids, liquids are composed of particles in contact with one another, but like gases, liquids are fluid because the particles are not rigidly held in place. The properties of liquids are largely determined by the nature of the intermolecular forces between the particles that make up the liquid. In Part 3, you will see how intermolecular forces produce surface tension. You will also investigate some of the remarkable properties of water. Although water often is taken for granted, its unusual properties help make it essential to life as you know it.

14.5 Surface Tension

Have you ever seen bugs walking on water and wondered what holds them up? Water striders have specialized legs and feet that enable them to stay on the surface of the water, as shown in Figure 14-13. But the water also has a property that helps bugs to stay afloat—surface tension. **Surface tension** causes the surface of a liquid to act like a weak, elastic skin.

You can see in Figure 14-14 that surface tension allows a needle to float on water. Try this yourself. Carefully wipe any dirt or grease from a steel needle and cut a small square of tissue paper. Place the needle on the tissue paper and carefully lower both onto the surface of the water. Then use a pencil to gently push the tissue under the water. The tissue will sink, but the needle will remain on the surface, even though the density of steel is about eight times the density of water. If you observe the floating needle carefully, you can see that its weight stretches and deforms the water's surface.

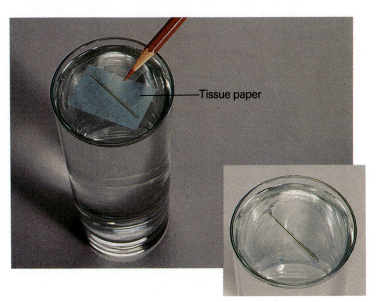

Tissue paper

(continued from page T484)

carbon chain forming the anion of the salt. The most common soap is sodium stearate, the sodium salt of stearic acid: $CH_3(CH_2)_{16}COONa$. Soaps commonly used as cleansing agents are the stearates and palmitates of sodium and potassium. Potassium soaps lather more readily than sodium soaps and are used in creams, cosmetics, and liquid soaps.

Soaps provide a cleansing action by lowering the surface tension of water and making it a better wetting agent. This occurs because the charged end of the soap is attracted to the polar water molecule, and the hydrocarbon end is attracted to nonpolar molecules of grease, oil, or dirt. The resulting mixture of soap, water, and greasy dirt can then be washed away.

Detergents are synthetic preparations that are not soaps but that act like them in their cleansing ability. Like soaps, they have polar and nonpolar ends. However, unlike soaps, they lather equally well in hard and soft water.

What causes surface tension? Figure 14-15 shows the intermolecular forces that act on the molecules within a liquid. The sum of these attractive forces between molecules of a single substance is called cohesion. In the interior of a liquid, cohesion pulls equally in every direction, and there is no net force exerted on each individual particle. In contrast, a particle on the surface is attracted by particles in the interior, and so experiences a net inward pull. As you can see in Figure 14-15, cohesion will pull a small amount of liquid into a sphere shape. It is cohesion that causes raindrops to be round.

What does the inward pull of cohesion do to the surface of a larger quantity of liquid? As you can see in Figure 14-15, the surface will be nearly flat, and the net inward pull will be downward. When you float a needle on water, the needle actually rests on the skinlike surface.

The strength of surface tension is related to intermolecular forces. The stronger the intermolecular forces in a liquid, the greater the cohesion and therefore the surface tension. Water has a large surface tension compared to most liquids because of hydrogen bonding. Try floating a needle on vegetable oil. The needle will sink because oil does not have a high surface tension.

Surface tension prevents water from being a good wetting agent. Have you ever noticed how water tends to bead up on the surface of a freshly waxed car but adheres to the surface of a dirty car? The force of attraction between two different substances is called adhesion. Whether a liquid will wet a solid depends upon the relative strength of cohesion and adhesion. Because water has a strong cohesion, it does not effectively wet many solids. This is why water is said to be a poor wetting agent.

DO YOU KNOW?

Mercury has a surface tension that is six times greater than the surface tension of water.

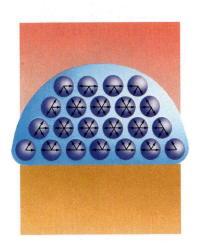

Figure 14-15 The arrows show how water molecules are attracted to each other in a drop.

DEMONSTRATION

Surface Tension

Demonstrate that a needle can be supported on water. When the needle is supported, add soap (for example, liquid dishwashing detergent) to the dish of water and watch the needle; as the soap disperses, the surface tension decreases and the needle will sink.

One of the functions of a soap is to make water a better wetting agent. If you add a few drops of soap to the water on which you are floating a needle, the needle will sink. The reason for this is that soap reduces the surface tension of water.

Teaching Strategy

Water: A Unique Liquid

Spend time discussing the truly unique properties of water. Have your students speculate how life on Earth would be different if water did not have its unique properties.

Resources

Use the videotape *Water* from The World of Chemistry series.

Guided Practice

Design experiments to predict the relative strength of intermolecular forces. What qualities or measurements would you observe experimentally? Help students brainstorm experimental designs that may include observing surface tension by seeing what will float on the surface of a liquid, observing the shape of a meniscus, freezing a liquid in a clear container, and determining how long to heat a liquid on a hot plate to raise the temperature 10°C. (Note: Experiments should not be carried out.)

Reteaching Idea

To enable students to further visualize and experience intermolecular forces, have them do the following experiment: Each student needs a large plastic drinking glass (6–8 ounces with no lip) and 50 to 60 pennies. Have students fill glasses carefully to the very top, but not overflowing. Holding a penny just above the surface of the water, they should *carefully* drop it, edge down, into the center of the water. Students continue this procedure until the glass overflows, counting the number of pennies used (50–60 or more). Have students record all observations and draw conclusions. If time permits, have them repeat the procedure using a soap or detergent solution or vegetable oil. Discard the drinking glasses in the wastebasket.

DO YOU KNOW?

If water is frozen very rapidly, it does not have time to form orderly crystals. If vegetables are flash-frozen (frozen rapidly at extremely low temperatures), the water in the individual cells does not crystallize and therefore does not rupture the cell wall. Flash-frozen foods taste fresher because little damage is done to the cell walls.

14.6 Water: A Unique Liquid

Water is one of the few liquid substances to be found in significant quantities on Earth. In fact, 70 percent of Earth's surface is covered with water. Water is essential to life as we know it. Historically people have settled where they have had access to adequate supplies of water. Because water is so common a substance, it is easy to overlook the fact that it has some truly remarkable properties.

The densities of water and ice Hydrogen bonding occurs in water molecules in the solid state as well as in the liquid state. When water freezes under normal conditions, hydrogen bonding holds molecules rigidly in a three-dimensional crystal, as shown in Figure 14-16. Notice that there are holes, empty spaces, within the ice crystal. As water freezes to form ice, it must expand to form this open crystal. As a result, the density of ice is less than the density of liquid water, which explains why ice floats. This is a very unusual phenomenon; most substances are more dense in the solid state than in the liquid state because their particles are closer together in the solid state. When ice melts, the hydrogen bonding partially breaks down, and the crystal collapses, bringing the molecules closer together.

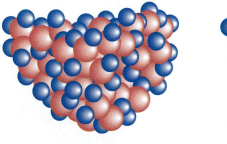
Liquid water

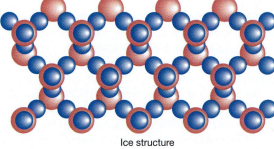
Ice structure

Figure 14-16 *Ice is less dense than water. The structure of ice keeps molecules further apart than they are in liquid water.*

Have you ever wondered why potholes form in roads during a freeze-thaw cycle? When water freezes, it increases in volume by about 9 percent. Repeated freezing and thawing can exert tremendous forces as water expands and contracts in a pothole, enlarging it rapidly. Rapid expansion of water during freezing can also burst water pipes in winter. One can prevent this by insulating pipes or

Myths and Misconceptions

Students often refer to density in terms of mass or volume alone. For example, a student may think that a larger chair has a greater density than a smaller chair, even if they are composed of materials with identical densities. A clear understanding of density is essential for comparing properties of solids, liquids, and gases. Initiate a discussion of density by referring to objects in the classroom. For example, using different sized pieces of chalk, demonstrate that the density of chalk in all the pieces is the same. Show students objects of similar size, but composed of substances with different densities, such as a steel marble and a marshmallow, or a Styrofoam ball and a lead sinker. Emphasize that density is not a measurement of mass or volume alone, but a ratio of mass divided by volume. Point out the unique density of water in the liquid and solid states.

by burying them underground. In barns or other unheated structures, people sometimes let water run at a trickle to prevent pipes from freezing. The water does not spend enough time cooling in the pipe to freeze solid.

There are some beneficial aspects to water's expansion during freezing. When a lake freezes, ice floats on the surface of the lake because it is less dense than liquid water. If the lake were to freeze solid, what problems would this cause for plant and animal life in the lake? Fortunately, the layer of ice on top of a lake insulates the warmer, denser water underneath. You can see in Figure 14-17 that the densest water, at 4°C, sinks to the bottom.

Water's heat capacity Another unusual property of water is that it absorbs much more energy than most liquids for a given change in temperature. You can compare this property in different substances by comparing their heat capacities. **Heat capacity** is the thermal energy required to raise the temperature of one kilogram of a substance by one kelvin. Water has a much higher heat capacity than most liquids because of water's strong hydrogen bonding. Although hydrogen bonding occurs in some other liquids, it is unique in water. As you saw in Figure 14-6, hydrogen bonding in water is three-dimensional because each oxygen atom has two non-bonding pairs of electrons. Water requires more energy to achieve a given temperature change because so much energy is used to overcome the hydrogen bonding.

Have you ever gone to the beach to cool off on a hot summer day? Why is it cooler near the shore than inland? Large bodies of water store large amounts of heat and this has a moderating effect on air temperature near the water. As the sun's rays heat the air, ocean water absorbs large amounts of heat, resulting in a more moderate air temperature. At night, as the air temperature drops, heat is transferred from the ocean to the air, creating warm breezes that once again moderate the air temperature. It might surprise you that palm trees grow on the southern coast of England. The warm climate needed for these trees is supplied by the ocean currents that carry warm water from the tropics to this region.

PART 3 REVIEW

13. Explain the surface tension of water on a molecular level.

14. Why would it not be a good idea to leave a bottle of carbonated soda in the freezer overnight?

15. Sketch the covalent bonds and hydrogen bonding occurring in several molecules of liquid water.

16. Why is the heat capacity of water so large? Explain your answer.

17. Use ice's structure to explain how the freeze-thaw cycle causes potholes.

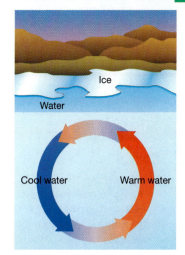

Figure 14-17 *In a lake, cool water sinks. Warmer water rises to the top.*

PROBLEM-SOLVING
S T R A T E G Y

Drawing a diagram will help you understand bonding at the submicroscopic level. (See Strategy, page 216.)

Boxed numbers indicate questions that involve skills in interpretation, application, and analysis.

PART 3
Section 14.6 *continued*

CLOSE

Summing Up Main Ideas

Ask students to imagine replacing water with methanol. Have them compare what would happen in the following examples in the presence of water and if the water were replaced with methanol. Pointing out the unique properties of water, discuss the implications on both a macroscopic and a molecular level.

■ a water strider walking on the surface of a stream
■ ice skaters waiting for a pond to freeze in winter
■ a small pothole in pavement
■ the air temperature on a summer day on a beach as compared to the surrounding countryside

PART 3 REVIEW

Assign the Part Review questions.

Evaluating Skills

These skills are evaluated in the Part Review questions indicated. **Summarizing:** 13; **Determining cause and effect:** 14, 17; **Forming models:** 15; **Determining main ideas:** 16

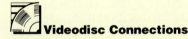

419 to 2336, side 2
Ice bomb (movie)

2337 to 4111, side 2
Superheated steam (movie)

PART 3 REVIEW

ANSWERS

■ **Keyed to Objectives**

G 13. The intermolecular forces between interior water molecules are the same in each direction. The forces on a molecule on the surface are not the same. The difference in the intermolecular forces for surface molecules and interior molecules creates surface tension.

H 14. Water expands when it freezes; the bottle is likely to break.

H 15. See Figure 14–5; make sure H—O—H bond angle is 105°.

H 16. The intermolecular forces in water are especially large because water molecules are polar and form hydrogen bonds.

(answers are continued on page T841)

PART 4 Structure and Properties of Solids
Section 14.7

Developing Skills

Students may apply these skills in their study of Part 4.
Forming models: Have students form models of crystalline solids.
Classifying: Have students classify crystalline solids based on the type of particles in the crystal lattice and the forces holding the particles in place.

≡ FOCUS

Activate Prior Knowledge

Observing snowflakes enables students to see crystal patterns on a macroscopic level. Students should also perceive how conditions at the molecular level influence properties of a solid.

Have students check library resources for illustrations of snowflakes. Then ask them to describe any crystal patterns they observe.

≡ TEACH

Teaching Strategy

Metallic and Covalent Solids

If possible, obtain and display several crystal shapes. Have students grow crystals of compounds as a project or construct models of crystals using Styrofoam balls, toothpicks, and glue.

⚠ **CAUTION: Observe the precautions on the labels and in the MSDSs for the compounds selected. Follow the disposal instructions in the MSDSs.**

**Videodisc Connections**

376, side 4
Metallic bonding (1 frame)

Objectives

Part 4

I. *Classify* crystalline solids based on the type of particles in the crystal lattice and the forces holding the particles in place.

J. *Explain* the properties of metallic solids, covalent network solids, molecular solids, and ionic solids by referring to their submicroscopic structure.

Figure 14-18 *The four solids in this photograph have very different properties.*

Figure 14-18 shows four familiar solids—an aluminum pan that contains a block of wax and a glass dish that contains a block of salt. Consider the behavior of these solids under some different conditions. If all four were put in an oven at 200°C, only the wax would change form; it would melt. If water was added to the pans, only the salt would be affected; it would dissolve. If struck by a hammer, the glass, wax, and salt would break, but the aluminum pan would just change shape.

Solids are classified as crystalline or amorphous according to their structure. A crystalline solid is composed of particles that are arranged in a regular pattern. Aluminum and salt are crystalline solids. In contrast, glass and wax are amorphous solids (amorphous means "without shape"). The particles in amorphous solids are not arranged in a regular pattern.

14.7 Metallic and Covalent Solids

How can you tell whether a solid is crystalline, and what type of solid it is? Sometimes the macroscopic properties of a solid reveal its crystalline structure. The crystals shown in Figure 14-19 have observable symmetry that must be the result of regular patterns at the submicroscopic level. Such crystals are all around you—from sand to snowflakes, and diamonds to salt. But crystal patterns are not always observable at the macroscopic level.

Metallic solids Although many metallic solids do not appear crystalline at the macroscopic level, special diffraction X-ray images reveal their regular structure at the submicroscopic level. Figure 14-20 shows a **unit cell,** which is the smallest blocklike unit from which the larger crystal can be built. Stacking unit cells in all directions will give the larger crystal. There are only seven different types of unit cells found in crystalline solids; four of these occur in metallic solids. Three are cube-shaped; the other is hexagonal.

As you learned in Chapter 13, metallic solids are good electrical conductors because of the sea of electrons that are free to move through the crystal lattice. You can use this property to distinguish metallic solids from most other crystalline solids. In addition, metallic solids are malleable because metallic bonds holding the atoms in place are nondirectional. When you hammer a metallic solid, the bonds are easily reoriented, which gives the solid a new shape.

Covalent network solids In contrast to metallic solids, which are held together by nondirectional metallic bonds, atoms in

covalent network solids are held together by an extensive network of directional covalent bonds. The entire network can be considered to be one giant molecule. In Chapter 12, you examined the structure of diamond, a covalent network solid, in Figure 12-19. Diamond and certain allotropes of silicon and germanium are arranged in a three-dimensional network. Each atom in these materials is covalently bonded to four other atoms arranged tetrahedrally about the center atom.

Covalent network solids can be two-dimensional and one-dimensional as well. Asbestos is based on a network of chains of silicon-oxygen covalent bonds. Graphite, the other allotropic form of carbon, consists of two-dimensional sheets of carbon atoms. You learned in Chapter 12 that graphite makes a good lubricant because the layers can slide. This is because the attractive forces between layers are relatively weak intermolecular attractions.

The amount of energy required to break the covalent bonds in a covalent network solid is large, and many bonds must be broken before the solid will melt. As a result, covalent network solids typically have extremely high melting points.

Figure 14-19 *Amethyst* (left) *and pyrite* (right) *are two examples of crystals that have obvious macroscopic regularities.*

14.8 Molecular and Ionic Solids

Molecular solids In contrast to metallic and covalent network solids, in which atoms are held together by bonds, the molecules in molecular solids are held in place only by relatively weak intermolecular forces. Common examples of molecular solids are ice, dry ice, sulfur, and iodine. In contrast to ionic solids and covalent network solids, no covalent or ionic bonds need to be broken to melt a molecular solid. Therefore, many molecular solids have relatively low melting points. Compare, for example, the melting point of ice, a molecular solid (0°C), with the melting point of graphite, a covalent network solid (3500°C).

The forces that exist among the molecules in a molecular crystal depend on the nature of the molecules. Many molecules such as CO_2, I_2, P_4, and S_8, are nonpolar and therefore are held together only by dispersion forces. Because these forces are weak, you might

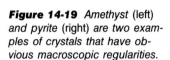
Unit cell

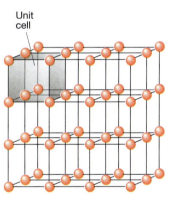
Crystal lattice

Figure 14-20 *One unit cell is the building block of the crystal structure.*

Science Background

Covalent Network Solids

Glass is a type of amorphous solid. When heated, glass shows no distinct melting point. Rather it becomes increasingly soft, melting gradually over a wide temperature range. As melted glass cools, it does not solidify at a particular temperature. Instead, it becomes more viscous. Glass is sometimes referred to as a supercooled liquid because it retains its ability to flow even when its temperature is below its typical freezing range.

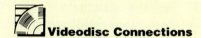**Videodisc Connections**

21398-21400, side 4
Nonmetals: allotropes of carbon
(3-frame seq.)

Guided Practice

Discuss the following questions with students.

1. Metallic bonds are nondirectional. How do these bonds differ from the bonding in amorphous solids? (While metallic bonds are nondirectional, they are arranged in a regular structure at the submicroscopic level. The particles in amorphous solids are not arranged in a regular pattern.)

2. Which class of solids would be useful as abrasives or to make cutting tools? Why? (Covalent network solids; they are very hard because the entire mass can be considered a single giant molecule. Their chemical bonds are very strong because the substance holds its electrons very tightly.)

Reteaching Idea

To review the difference between crystalline and amorphous structures of solids, arrange with a home economics teacher to bring a class to the home economics department or school kitchen to make candy. Have students prepare fudge and lollipops. In both cases, they will start with table sugar (sucrose in crystalline form). Once completed, the products should be carefully examined to observe the crystals. In fudge, if correctly prepared, the crystals will not be visible, nor detectable on the tongue, but they can be seen under a microscope. In lollipops, there are no crystals. Students should write a report using chemical terminology to explain how these products were formed. As an alternative activity, have students make labeled drawings of the particle structure of the different types of solids: amorphous, metallic, covalent network, molecular, and ionic. Have them summarize how the structure affects the physical properties of each type.

expect these substances to have very low melting and boiling points. Indeed, carbon dioxide is a gas at room temperature. However, the size and molecular mass of molecules also influence melting and boiling points. The larger the molecular mass, the greater the dispersion forces and the greater the energy needed to give molecules enough energy to become liquid or gaseous. Therefore, larger nonpolar molecules such as iodine, I_2, phosphorus, P_4, and sulfur, S_8, are solids at room temperature.

Other molecular solids contain molecules that are polar or exhibit hydrogen bonding. Ice and sugar are common examples of such molecular crystals that involve dipole-dipole interactions and hydrogen bonding as well as dispersion forces in their crystals.

Ionic solids Ionic solids are three-dimensional crystalline arrangements of positive and negative ions. The oppositely charged ions are held together by electrostatic attractions (ionic bonds). Because these bonds are relatively strong, ionic solids have high melting points. In a perfect ionic crystal, the array of ions could continue indefinitely in any direction.

The arrangement of cations and anions in an ionic solid depends partly upon the sizes of the ions. Figure 14-21 shows the unit cells for both sodium chloride and cesium chloride. Notice the difference in size between the sodium ion and the cesium ion. As a result of this size difference, these two ionic crystals have different packing arrangements.

A second factor that determines how the ions in a crystalline solid are arranged is the ratio of cations to anions. Aluminum oxide, Al_2O_3, contains two Al^{3+} ions and three O^{2-} ions. Therefore, the crystal structure of aluminum oxide is quite different from that of either sodium chloride, NaCl, or cesium chloride, CsCl.

Each ion in an ionic crystal is surrounded by ions of opposite charge. The charge and size of the ions affects the melting point of the solid. Sodium chloride, NaCl, melts at 801°C, whereas magnesium oxide, MgO, melts at 2800°C. This difference can be ex-

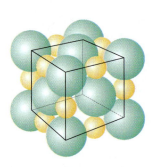
NaCl

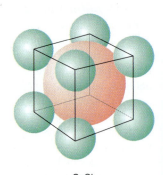
CsCl

Figure 14-21 *The structures of cesium chloride and sodium chloride differ because cesium ions are larger than sodium ions.*

Videodisc Connections

410, side 2
Salt crystal: model (1 frame)

25788 to 27044, side 2
Crystal growth under a microscope (movie)

plained in part by the charges on the ions in the crystal. The ions of magnesium and oxygen, with charges of 2 + and 2 − respectively, have a much stronger attraction for one another than the ions of sodium and chlorine, which have charges of 1 + and 1 − .

PART 4 REVIEW

18. What type of crystals do each of the following form?
    a. ice **b.** iron **c.** sodium chloride

19. Which type of intermolecular forces are involved in the crystalline structure of each crystal in problem 18?

20. Explain why carbon dioxide is a gas at room temperature, whereas iodine is a solid.

21. Why are three-dimensional network solids particularly hard substances?

Boxed numbers indicate questions that involve skills in interpretation, application, and analysis.

R E S E A R C H   &   T E C H N O L O G Y

Investigating Structure in Glass

Glassmaking was invented about 1500 B.C. in both Mesopotamia and Egypt. Although glass has been used in many applications for thousands of years, exciting new technologies have been developed in just the past decade. Fiber optics are now widely used for telephone communications and surgical procedures. Photosensitive glass that darkens when exposed to light is used in sunglasses and miniature computer switches. Soon, new discoveries may develop from research on the submicroscopic structure of glass.

Glass has traditionally been viewed as lacking the organized structure found in crystalline solids. The structure of glass was first investigated using X-ray diffraction. In this technique, X rays are scattered as they pass through a sample of glass. The scattered X rays are recorded on photographic film, and the resulting image can be used to infer the arrangement of particles in the glass. Glass was thought to be amorphous because X-ray crystallography images of glass have no organized pattern.

New evidence suggests, however, that glass can have an organized structure at the molecular level. Recently, the structure of glass has

been studied using neutron analysis, which reveals patterns on a much smaller scale than X-ray crystallography. The researchers beamed neutrons at silicate $[SiO_4]$ units. The scattering patterns of the neutrons indicated that units are evenly spaced within small regions of the crystal. Between these regions of order are disordered networks of silicate units.

With more research, engineers hope to control the structure of glass precisely. Some applications you may see in your lifetime include improved optical equipment, glass that conducts electricity, and glass containers that could safely store nuclear waste indefinitely.

≡CLOSE

Summing Up Main Ideas

Make a table comparing the physical properties of the five kinds of solids: amorphous, metallic, covalent network, molecular, and ionic. Include the following properties: particles arranged in a regular pattern, electrical conductivity, malleability, high or low melting point. In the table, place the following substances in the proper category: quartz (silicon dioxide), brass, carbon dioxide, rubber, limestone (calcium carbonate).

PART 4 REVIEW

Assign the Part Review questions.

Evaluating Skills

These skills are evaluated in the Part Review questions indicated. **Classifying:** 18; **Determining main ideas:** 19; **Comparing/Contrasting:** 20; **Understanding cause and effect:** 20, 21

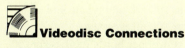Videodisc Connections

25149 to 30995, side 4
Specialty glass (movie)

30996 to 31796, side 4
Commercial glass applications (movie)

31797 to 35229, side 4
Fiberglass (movie)

PART 4 REVIEW

ANSWERS

■ Keyed to Objectives

I **18. a.** ice—molecular
   b. iron—metallic
   c. sodium chloride—ionic

I **19.** ice: dispersion, dipole-dipole, and hydrogen bonding; iron: metallic bonds; sodium chloride: ionic bonds

I **20.** Both are nonpolar, so only dispersion forces exist. Since iodine has a much larger molecular mass, its dispersion forces will be stronger than those in carbon dioxide.

I **21.** Each atom is covalently bonded to several adjacent atoms.

Laboratory

Investigation

Process Skills

Constructing tables and graphs
Describing
Measuring
Identifying and controlling
    variables

Preparation

■ Materials

(for a class of 24, working in groups of 4)
This lab suggests the use of Florence flasks; however, Erlenmeyer flasks may be used.

Apparatus
250-mL Florence flasks (24), ring stands with clamp (6), metersticks (6), 80-cm long glass tubing (6), 20 feet of vinyl tubing cut into 6 pieces, one-hole stoppers to fit Florence flasks (6), 10-cm long glass tubing (6)

Reagents

■ 100 mL ethyl alcohol
■ 100 mL methyl alcohol
■ 100 mL acetone
■ dropper bottle of glycerine
■ distilled or deionized water

■ Safety

All the solvents used are flammable and, when mixed with air, the vapors are explosive. Make certain that there are no flames, hot plates, or other sources of ignition in the laboratory. Ensure that at all times there is no more than 300 mL total of all flammable liquids in the room.

Vapor Pressure

A substance that is a liquid or a solid at room temperature is referred to as a vapor when it is converted to the gaseous state. Therefore, the vapor pressure of a substance is the pressure produced when an equilibrium exists between its gas and liquid phase. In this laboratory investigation, you will determine if different liquids have different vapor pressures and if the vapor pressure of a liquid can be changed by heating or cooling the liquid. You will also determine if there is a cumulative effect of mixing two liquids together.

Objectives

Compare the vapor pressures of different liquids.

Observe the effect of temperature on vapor pressure.

Observe the effect on vapor pressure when liquids are mixed.

■ Materials

Apparatus
☐ meterstick
☐ 80 cm of glass tubing
☐ clear vinyl tubing
☐ 4 250-mL Florence flasks
☐ one-hole rubber stopper
☐ 10-cm glass tubing
☐ ring stand and clamp

Reagents
☐ distilled or deionized water
☐ ethyl alcohol
☐ methyl alcohol
☐ glycerine
☐ acetone
☐ mixed solvent solution

■ Procedure

 CAUTION: Ethanol, methanol, and acetone are flammable. Make sure there are no flames anywhere in the laboratory. Methanol is poisonous. Do not get it in your mouth; do not swallow any.

1. Put on your safety goggles and lab apron.

2. Using a drop of glycerine on the end of the 10-cm glass tubing, insert the tubing into the one-hole stopper.

CAUTION: Wear gloves or use a cloth when you insert the tubing into the stopper.

Data Table

Solvent	Difference in Water Levels at Room Temperature (mm H_2O)	Difference in Water Levels after Warming with Hands (mm H_2O)
Acetone C_3H_6O	600	700
Methyl alcohol CH_3OH	450	500
Ethyl alcohol CH_3CH_2OH	300	350
Acetone and ethyl alcohol	400	450

3. Assemble the apparatus as shown. Fill the vinyl tubing completely with water before you attach the ends to the glass tubing.

4. Add 2 mL of acetone to a dry 250-mL Florence flask and reattach it to the apparatus. Observe and record the difference between the water levels in millimeters.

5. Gently cup the bottom of the Florence flask with both hands. Observe the effect this gentle warming has on the vapor pressure by measuring and recording the difference in the water levels.

6. To another dry flask, add 2 mL of methyl alcohol. Connect it to the apparatus and measure the difference between the water levels. Warm the flask with your hands and record your observations.

7. To a third dry flask, add 2 mL of ethyl alcohol. Connect it to the apparatus and measure the difference between the water levels. Warm the flask with your hands and record your observations.

8. Add 1 mL of acetone and 1 mL of ethyl alcohol to a dry flask and measure the difference between the water levels. Warm the flask and record your data.

Guiding the Investigation

■ Procedural Hints

If your class periods are short, you might set up the apparatus before class begins; however, the students do learn valuable skills in setting up the apparatus themselves.

Data Analysis

■ Sample Data

(See table and graph below.) Student graphs and data will depend on the atmospheric pressure at the time of the experiment. The more volatile substance has the higher vapor pressure.

Conclusions

1. Ketones exert more pressure than alcohols. Between the two alcohols, the one with the lower molecular mass exerts more pressure.

2. Warming the solvent increases vapor pressure.

3. Vapor pressure increases to the sum of the two individual liquids.

■ Data Analysis

Data Table

Solvent	Difference in Water Levels at Room Temperature (mm H_2O)	Difference in Water Levels after Warming with Hands (mm H_2O)
Acetone		
Methyl alcohol		
Ethyl alcohol		
Acetone and ethyl alcohol		

1. Prepare a bar graph of each liquid tested, showing the difference in heights of water in millimeters of mercury.

NOTE: The difference in water levels divided by 13.5 (the density of mercury) will convert mm of water to mm Hg.

■ Conclusions

1. Basing your answer on your observations, what correlations can you make between vapor pressure and the nature of the solution?

2. How did warming the solvent affect the vapor pressure?

3. What happened to the vapor pressure of individual liquids when they were part of a mixture of liquids?

Chapter 14
Review
ANSWERS
begin on page
T497a.

Summary

States of Matter

- The kinetic molecular theory can be used to predict the behavior of liquids and solids.

- The magnitude of intermolecular forces between particles determines whether a substance exists as a gas, a liquid, or a solid at a particular temperature.

- When particles in a liquid have enough energy to overcome attractive forces, they can escape from the liquid to become vapor particles. The boiling point of a liquid depends upon the magnitude of the intermolecular forces and the external pressure.

- The nature of intermolecular forces depends upon the molecular substance. Three intermolecular forces are dispersion forces, dipole-dipole forces, and hydrogen bonding.

Change of State

- Changing the temperature of a substance can cause it to change from one state of matter to another.

- Solids have a vapor pressure. The change of a solid directly into a gas is called sublimation.

- A heating curve enables you to see the effect of heat on the temperature of a substance. The temperature remains constant during melting and boiling.

Structure and Properties of Liquids

- Surface tension is a property of liquids. The properties of liquids depend upon the nature and magnitude of the intermolecular forces.

- Water has unusual properties compared to other liquids. It is more dense in the liquid than in the solid phase, has a high surface tension, and has a high heat capacity. Hydrogen bonding in water is responsible for these unusual properties.

Structure and Properties of Solids

- Solids with particles arranged in a regular pattern are classified as crystalline solids. Solids without a regular arrangement of particles are called amorphous solids.

- Atoms, molecules, or ions may be packed in several different ways in crystalline structures. Unit cells are the smallest unit from which a crystal can be constructed.

- Solids can be classified as metallic solids, covalent network solids, molecular solids, and ionic solids. Each type of solid has its own characteristic properties, such as melting point, hardness, and brittleness.

Chemically Speaking

condensation *14.1*	molar heat of vaporization *14.4*
dipole-dipole forces *14.2*	phase change *14.1*
dispersion forces *14.2*	sublimation *14.3*
evaporation *14.3*	surface tension *14.5*
heat capacity *14.6*	unit cell *14.8*
hydrogen bonding *14.2*	van der Waals forces *14.2*
intermolecular forces *14.1*	vapor *14.3*
molar heat of fusion *14.4*	vapor pressure *14.3*
	volatile *14.3*

Concept Mapping

Using the method of concept mapping described at the front of this book, draw a concept map for the term *solids*. Include the following terms: *ionic solids, amorphous solids, molecular solids, metallic solids,* and *covalent network solids.*

PROBLEM-SOLVING STRATEGIES

Students apply these strategies in the following questions.

- Factor-label method: 44
- Using what you know: 5, 6, 9, 10, 11, 12, 13, 19, 20, 21, 22, 23, 26, 27, 28, 30, 32, 33, 36, 38, 41, 43, 45
- Using patterns: 10, 11, 13, 23, 26, 41, 43
- Using calculators: 44, 46

Questions and Problems

STATES OF MATTER

A. Objective: **Explain** *how the three types of intermolecular forces arise.*

1. On a molecular level, describe dipole-dipole intermolecular forces.
2. Explain the origin of the dispersion forces between two molecules of nitrogen, N_2.
3. Describe the relationship between the polarity of individual molecules and the nature and strength of intermolecular forces.
4. Describe the relationship between molecular size and the strength of dispersion forces.

B. Objective: **Compare and contrast** *the physical properties of gases, liquids, and solids by comparing the strength of their intermolecular forces.*

5. The molar masses of two carbon compounds are listed below along with their boiling points. Explain the large difference in these boiling points.

Name	Formula	Molar Mass (g/mol)	Boiling Point (K, at 10/kpa or 1 atm)
ethane	C_2H_6	30	184
methanol	CH_3OH	32	338

6. When a piece of solid lead is dropped into a pool of liquid molten lead, will the solid lead sink or float? Explain your answer.
7. Which states of matter are fluid? Explain your answer at the submicroscopic level.
8. What effect do intermolecular forces have on the boiling point of a liquid?
9. Suggest an explanation for the fact that, at room temperature, carbon dioxide is a gas while silicon dioxide is a solid.

Boxed numbers indicate questions that involve skills in interpretation, application, and analysis.

C. Objective: **Predict** *which intermolecular forces will occur in a substance, given its structure and composition.*

10. What intermolecular forces are present between the molecules or atoms of the following substances?
    a. Ne   **b.** Br_2 **c.** HI   **d.** O_2 **e.** P_4
11. For each of the following liquids, list the types of intermolecular forces that you would expect to find.
    a. water, H_2O
    b. bromine, Br_2
    c. carbon tetrachloride, CCl_4
12. For each of the substances in problem 11, which would you expect to be stronger, the intermolecular forces or the covalent bonds?
13. Explain the reasons for the difference in boiling points between
    a. HF (20°C) and HCl (-85°C)
    b. HCl (-85°C) and LiCl (1360°C)
    c. CH_3OCH_3 (-24°C) and CH_3CH_2OH (79°C)

PHASE CHANGES

D. Objective: **Explain** *phase changes at the molecular level.*

14. What is a phase?
15. How does evaporation differ from boiling?
16. How can you increase the vapor pressure of a liquid? A solid?
17. What is the relationship between boiling point, external pressure, and vapor pressure?
18. Why does it take longer to boil an egg in water at high altitude?
19. What is the relationship between kinetic energy and temperature?
20. For a particular substance, why is the molar heat of fusion less than the molar heat of vaporization?
21. Describe how you could purify iodine by sublimation.
22. Explain why liquids cool as evaporation takes place.

■ Breaking problems into manageable parts: 13, 38, 45
■ Rereading the problem: 38
■ Making diagrams: 36

23. Four closed containers—A, B, C, and D— contain water at 100°C, 25°C, 0°C, and −10°C respectively, at 1 atm of pressure.
    a. Which sample has molecules with the greatest average kinetic energy?
    b. Which sample(s) have water vapor inside the container?

E. Objective: **Describe** *the process of evaporation and compare vapor pressures of different substances by referring to intermolecular forces.*

24. Describe vapor pressure on the molecular level.
25. Why does increasing the temperature increase the vapor pressure of a liquid?
26. Predict which substance in each of the following pairs would have a greater vapor pressure at 30°C.
    a. motor oil or gasoline
    b. water or rubbing alcohol
    c. perfume or vegetable oil
27. Both carbon tetrachloride, CCl_4, and mercury, Hg, are liquids whose vapors are harmful to humans. If carbon tetrachloride is spilled in a room, the danger can be removed by ventilating the room overnight. If mercury is spilled, someone must pick up the liquid droplets with a special chemical vacuum cleaner or a chemical reagent. Explain why the spills for mercury and carbon tetrachloride are handled differently.
28. Imagine traveling across the Sonoran Desert in Arizona when the temperature is 49°C (120°F). Your car's air conditioner is broken, but you have lots of water aboard. Suggest a way to keep cool as you travel.

F. Objective: **Interpret** *the features of heating curves.*

29. Why is the temperature of a substance constant during melting?

30. Explain why 12 g of steam at 100°C can melt more ice than 12 g of liquid water at 100°C.
31. In order to kill bacterial spores, the water in an autoclave must reach a temperature of 121°C. How is it possible to heat water to this temperature when water boils at 100°C?
32. How can water be made to boil at room temperature?
33. Which would cause a more severe burn, 1 mole of H_2O (g) at 100°C or 1 mole of H_2O (l) at 100°C? Why?

STRUCTURE AND PROPERTIES OF LIQUIDS

G. Objective: **Explain** *the molecular basis for surface tension.*

34. Explain surface tension in terms of cohesion. Why does water seem to have a skin?
35. Why are good wetting agents valued by manufacturers of soaps and detergents?

H. Objective: **Explain** *how the structure of water accounts for its unusual properties.*

36. Explain, on a submicroscopic level, why ice floats in water.
37. At what temperature does water have its highest density (at 1 atm of pressure)?
38. What would happen if you submerged a bottle of hot, colored water in a container of liquid water at 4°C and carefully removed the lid? What would happen if you submerged a bottle of colored water at 4°C in a container of hot water?

STRUCTURE AND PROPERTIES OF SOLIDS

I. Objective: **Classify** *crystalline solids based on the type of particles in the crystal lattice and the forces holding the particles in place.*

39. What distinguishes an amorphous solid from a crystalline solid?

40. What are two factors that determine the arrangement of ions in an ionic crystal?

41. Decide which type of solid each of the following elements would form—metallic, covalent network, molecular, or ionic.
    a. lithium   b. sulfur   c. nitrogen

J. Objective: **Explain** *the properties of metallic solids, covalent network solids, molecular solids, and ionic solids by referring to their submicroscopic structure.*

42. Why do molecular crystals have relatively low melting points?

43. Match each of the solids in the first column with two properties in the second column. Try to use each property at least once.
    a. metallic solid   I. low-melting
    b. covalent network   point
       solid   II. high-melting
    c. ionic solid   point
    d. molecular solid   III. conducts electricity when melted
                          IV. brittle
                           V. hard
                          VI. malleable

Critical Thinking

SYNTHESIS WITHIN THE CHAPTER

44. If a crystal of NaCl with a mass of 0.0585 gram is formed in three days, how many Na^+ and Cl^- ions are deposited on the crystal each second?

45. A teacher takes an empty soda can, adds a small amount of water to it, then heats the can over a bunsen burner. (The teacher is wearing safety goggles and a lab apron and is using tongs to hold the can.) After the water boils for a few minutes and the can fills with water vapor, the teacher quickly inverts the can and places it in a pan of cold water with the can's opening submerged. Explain why the can collapses when it hits the water.

SYNTHESIS ACROSS CHAPTERS

46. Using the graph below, calculate the total pressure of a mixture of acetone and ethanol at 30°C. Assume that one mole of each substance is present in the solution.

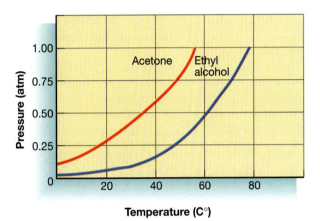

Projects

47. Look at "lite" salt and regular salt under a microscope and draw what you see. Read the labels on the salt containers and hypothesize why the two salts look so different.

Research and Writing

48. Most modern refrigerators use Freon as the coolant in the freezer compartment. Write a paper in which you discuss how Freon is used to cool the refrigerator and what environmental problems result from the involuntary release of Freon into the atmosphere.

49. Read about how X-ray diffraction patterns are made and what information they provide. Use this information to explain, in terms of the interference of waves, how an X-ray diffraction pattern is produced by a crystal.

CONDENSED STATES OF MATTER **497**

☐ Boxed numbers indicate questions that involve skills in interpretation, application, and analysis.

1. The oppositely charged regions of adjacent polar molecules are attracted to one another.

2. At a given instant, the distribution of electrons is unsymmetrical. This causes instantaneous dipoles that are the source of dispersion forces.

3. For polar molecules of similar molar mass, the stronger the molecular polarity, the stronger the dipole-dipole intermolecular force.

4. The higher the molar mass, the stronger the dispersion forces.

5. Ethane is nonpolar; methanol is polar and can form hydrogen bonds. The only intermolecular forces in ethane are dispersion forces. It has the lowest boiling point because it takes the least amount of energy to overcome the intermolecular attractive forces in ethane. For molecules of similar molecular mass, as the intermolecular forces increase, the boiling point of the substance increases.

6. Most solids are more dense than the corresponding liquid, so the solid lead will probably sink.

7. Gases and liquids. The magnitude of intermolecular forces are not so large as to prevent molecules from moving relative to adjacent molecules.

8. As the magnitude of intermolecular forces increases, the boiling point of a liquid increases.

9. Silicon dioxide exists as a covalent network solid held together by very strong bonds. Carbon dioxide exists as individual nonpolar molecules.

10. a. Ne: dispersion
    b. Br_2: dispersion
    c. HI: dispersion, dipole-dipole
    d. O_2: dispersion
    e. P_4: dispersion

11. a. water: dispersion, dipole-dipole, hydrogen bonding
    b. bromine: dispersion
    c. carbon tetrachloride: dispersion

12. Covalent bonds are always stronger than intermolecular forces.

13. a. Hydrogen bonding occurs between HF molecules.
    b. LiCl is ionic and ionic bonds are much stronger than intermolecular forces in HCl.
    c. CH_3OCH_3 is nonpolar and has only dispersion forces; CH_3CH_2OH is polar, forming dipole-dipole forces, and forms hydrogen bonds in addition to dispersion forces.

14. Phase is a name for a state of matter, for example, solid, liquid or gas.

15. Evaporation occurs at a temperature below the boiling point.

16. Increase the temperature of the liquid or solid.

17. At the boiling point of a liquid, the vapor pressure is equal to the external pressure.

18. Water boils at a lower temperature since the external pressure is lower at higher altitudes. Since the temperature is lower, it takes longer for foods to cook.

19. The average kinetic energy is proportional to the absolute temperature.

20. To exist in the gas phase, all of the attractive intermolecular forces must be overcome, so the heat required is very much greater.

21. Heat solid iodine and allow the vapor to cool on a cold, clean surface. Solid iodine crystals will deposit.

22. Evaporation occurs because the high energy molecules are escaping from the bulk liquid. As a result, the average kinetic energy of the molecules remaining is less, so the temperature is lower.

23. a. A
    b. all four

24. For any substance, some higher energy molecules will escape from the surface into the vapor phase. The pressure of the gas phase is the vapor pressure. In a closed system of liquid and vapor, some liquid molecules are escaping to the gas phase and some gas molecules are condensing to a liquid. At equilibrium, both processes still occur, but at the same rate. Thus it is a dynamic process.

25. At a higher temperature, a larger fraction of the liquid molecules have sufficient energy to overcome the intermolecular attractive forces and escape to the vapor phase.

26. a. gasoline
    b. isopropyl alcohol (the alcohol component in rubbing alcohol)
    c. perfume

27. The vapor pressure of carbon tetrachloride, a nonpolar liquid at room temperature, is much higher than that of metallic mercury. Thus the rate of evaporation of mercury is very slow. If the spill is not cleaned up, it will release mercury vapor into the room continuously for a long period of time.

28. Splash water on your face and clothes. As the water evaporates, you will be cooled.

29. All the energy is absorbed by the molecules undergoing the phase change.

30. Steam at 100°C has more energy (by the amount of the heat of vaporization) than water at 100°C.

31. At pressures above 1 atmosphere, water's boiling point increases.

32. Lower the pressure to less than the vapor pressure of water at room temperature.

33. 1 mole of $H_2O(g)$, because it would transfer the energy of the heat of vaporization to your skin as it condensed.

34. The unbalanced intermolecular force on the surface molecules of a liquid gives rise to surface tension; cohesion pulls surface molecules inward.

35. They lower the surface tension of water to make water a more effective wetting agent, so the soaps and detergents can clean better.

36. The three-dimensional structure of ice is less dense than that of liquid water. As water freezes, the hydrogen bonds in the solid hold molecules rigidly in a three-dimensional crystal. This results in empty spaces forming in ice as it expands to form this open crystal. Thus, the density is less.

37. 4°C

38. The less dense hot colored water will rise out of the bottle and mix quite rapidly. The more dense colored water would stay in the jar.

39. The particles in an amorphous solid are not arranged in a regular pattern; those in a crystalline solid are.

40. The sizes and the charges of the ions

41. a. metallic
    b. molecular
    c. molecular

42. The intermolecular forces are relatively weak compared to ionic, covalent, and metallic bonds present in other crystals.

43. a. II, III, VI
    b. II, V
    c. II, III, IV, V
    d. I

44. (0.0585 g NaCl/3 days) × (1 mol NaCl/58.5 g NaCl) × (2 × 6.02 × 10²³ ions/1 mol NaCl) × (1 day/24 hr) × (1 hr/60 min) × (1 min/60 s) = 4.64×10^{15} ions/s

45. The can is filled with steam. When it is placed upside down in the cold water, the steam condenses. When the steam condenses to liquid water, hardly any gas is left in the can. The pressure inside the can is significantly less than the atmospheric pressure outside the can. As a result, the atmospheric pressure squashes the can.

46. $P_{total} = P_1 + P_2$

From graph:

P_1 = acetone's partial pressure at 30°C

P_2 = ethyl alcohol's partial pressure at 30°C

$P_{total} = 0.4 \text{ atm} + 0.1 \text{ atm}$

$P_{total} = 0.5 \text{ atm}$

Solutions

Investigations	**Demonstrations**	**Texas Essential Elements★**
Laboratory Manual 15–1 M Laboratory Manual 15–2 S Laboratory Manual 15–3 I	Temperature, page T506	**Content:** 9.1, 9.2, 9.3, 9.4, 9.5, 9.6 **Process:** 4.3, 8.2, 10.1, 10.2, 10.4
In-text Investigation, page T524	Forming a Precipitate, page T510	**Content:** 11.2 **Process:** 4.1, 4.3, 10.2
		Content: 9.7, 9.8 **Process:** 4.3, 9.1, 9.2, 10.1
		Content: 9.1, 11.2 **Process:** 1.1, 1.2, 1.3, 2.1, 4.1, 6.1, 8.1, 8.2
		Process: 4.1, 4.2, 4.3, 5.2, 7.1, 10.1, 10.2, 10.4
		Content: 9.1, 9.2 **Process:** 10.1, 10.2, 10.3, 10.4
KEY: M–*Microscale* S–*Structured* I–*Inquiry* IM–*Inquiry Microscale*		★*See pages T8–T11 for complete listing of Texas Essential Elements.*

15 Solutions

Chapter Rationale

A basic understanding of solutions is very important not only in chemistry, but also in everyday living. Much of the matter we encounter is in solution form. Concepts learned in this chapter form the basis for concepts in upcoming chapters.

About the Photograph

The thiosulfate ion is a common ligand. In a water solution thiosulfate ions cluster around a central positive ion forming a complex ion. By forming complex ions, thiosulfate ions can initiate crystallization.

Chapter Planning Hints

Plan to complete the chapter, including the Laboratory Investigation and Chapter Review, within five to seven class sessions. You may wish to obtain the video *Solutions* to use when you introduce Part 1. Two optional demonstrations are suggested for this chapter on pages T506 and T510. You may wish to preview them at this time.

Look Ahead

You may want to consider incorporating Chapter 21 into Part 2 of this chapter if you have not already done so. Precipitation reactions in aqueous solutions and Chapter 21, Chemical Analysis, provide an excellent opportunity to introduce a number of laboratory experiences that enhance critical thinking.

Overview

A seed crystal of sodium thiosulfate can provide a pattern for crystal growth in a precipitation reaction of a solid from a solution. The reaction releases heat and is used in some heat packs that are applied to sports injuries or used as hand warmers.

PART 1 The Nature of Solutions

Solutions are very much a part of your life. The water you drink, the air you breathe, and the blood coursing through your veins are all solutions. What these and other solutions have in common are ions or molecules of one substance evenly dispersed throughout another substance.

For centuries, people have investigated the properties of solutions. They have used their findings in a wide range of technological advances that have included the creation of metal alloys, the refining of petroleum, the desalination of sea water, and survival in environments that lack sufficient oxygen for life—such as in the oceans and in space.

You also have investigated the properties of solutions at home though you may not be aware of it. Have you ever wondered why when you made an oil and vinegar salad dressing, the ingredients never remain mixed? No matter how much you shake the dressing, these liquid components will never form an actual solution. As soon as the dressing is allowed to stand, the oil and vinegar separate, forming two distinct layers.

Have you ever tried to clean paintbrushes with water? Some paints, such as water colors and certain latex paints, rinse from the brush. Oil-based paints, however, require a special solvent for cleansing.

These common encounters illustrate the importance of understanding the solution process. Within this part of the chapter, you will see how submicroscopic models are used to explain your macroscopic observations of the behavior of solutions.

15.1 What Is a Solution?

The word *solution* usually conjures up thoughts of sugar water, salt water, or some of the colorful solutions you use in the chemistry laboratory. However, you may be surprised to learn that air, brass, and window glass also are solutions. A few examples of solutions are shown in Figure 15-1 on the next page. Any substance—solid, liquid, or gas—that is evenly dispersed or distributed throughout another substance—solid, liquid, or gas—is a **solution**. Solutions are often called **homogeneous mixtures** because they are not pure substances, yet the substances that comprise them are evenly dispersed throughout the mixture. A solution has the appearance of a pure substance, even though it is a mixture. The brass faucet in Figure 15-1 is a solid solution made of copper and zinc atoms that are dissolved in various proportions.

Objectives

Part 1

A. **Distinguish** solutions from other mixtures.
B. **Describe** the dissolving process.
C. **Analyze** the factors that affect solubility.

Developing Skills

Students may apply these skills in their study of Part 1.
Classifying: Challenge students to think of several solutions that are nonaqueous.
Forming models: Have students form models of particles in solution.
Analyzing data: Have students interpret data about solubility.
Applying a strategy: Have students apply their knowledge of molecular polarity to predict solubility.

FOCUS

Activate Prior Knowledge

Have students, wearing safety goggles and lab aprons, describe what happens when a few small crystals of sodium chloride are added to 1 mL of water in one test tube; a few small crystals of sodium chloride are added to 1 mL of ethanol in another.

⚠ **CAUTION: Ethanol is flammable; be sure there are no flames or other sources of ignition in the room.** 1 mL of water is mixed with 1 mL of ethanol in the third test tube; and 1 g of ammonium chloride is added to 2 mL of water in the fourth. Students should watch for evidence of dissolving and change in temperature. Does stirring help the substance dissolve?

To dispose of liquids, combine them and dilute with ten volumes of water and pour down the drain.

PART **1**
Section 15.2

TEACH

Teaching Strategy

What Is a Solution?

Many of the concepts in this chapter are extensions of ideas presented in earlier chapters. You may want to take the opportunity here to increase in-class group learning and outside-class reading.

Teaching Strategy

What Is a Solution?

Stress the diversity of the various types of solutions. Have students examine various types of solutions such as brass, steel, carbonated beverages, vinegar, sea water, and ethylene glycol (antifreeze) solution.

Science Background

Types of Solutions

In Table 15-1, the example given for a gas dissolved in a solid, that is, carbon dioxide in ice, is significant in environmental science. Ice cores taken from deep within the Antarctic ice fields are being studied for the concentration of carbon dioxide in the ice. The ice contains bubbles of air trapped hundreds of years ago when the water froze. The air bubbles are analyzed for carbon dioxide content to compare the concentrations of this greenhouse gas then and now.

Figure 15-1 *You could add many household liquids to those shown in this photo of everyday solutions.*

Within a solution, the substance that is the dissolving medium is known as the **solvent.** The **solute** is the substance dissolved in the solvent. Some liquids are so soluble in each other, like alcohol and water, that as you add more and more water to alcohol, the concentration of the water exceeds the concentration of the alcohol. The water is then said to be the solvent, and the alcohol becomes the solute. Because the same substance can be referred to as a solute in one instance and a solvent in another, the terms *solute* and *solvent* should not be thought of as absolutes. Table 15-1 describes some examples of solutions and lists each solvent and solute. What do you notice about the states of the solutions as compared to their respective solvents and solutes?

Not all mixtures are homogeneous. If you were to stand on the shore and scoop up a handful of sea water, sand would quickly separate from the water. The sea water-sand mixture cannot be called a solution, because the sand is not evenly distributed throughout the sea water. Mixtures characterized by observable segregation of component substances are called **heterogeneous mixtures.** Indeed, the sand itself is a heterogeneous mixture made of small crystals of silicon dioxide and various kinds of rock. A sample of sand on one end of a beach may be made up of components quite different from sand on the other end.

TABLE 15-1

Types of Solutions			
Solution	State of Solution	State of the Solvent	State of the Solute(s)
Earth's atmosphere	gas	gas—N_2	gas—O_2, Ar, CO_2
ocean water	liquid	liquid—H_2O	solid—salts—NaCl gas—O_2, CO_2
gold jewelry	solid	solid—Au	solid—Ag, Cu
aquarium water	liquid	liquid—H_2O	gas—O_2, CO_2
carbon dioxide in ice	solid	solid—ice	gas—CO_2

15.2 The Process of Solvation

Have you ever looked closely at table salt as it dissolves in a glass of water? The crystals of sodium chloride become smaller and eventually disappear. Many other ionic substances dissolve similarly in water. Figure 15-2 shows crystals of potassium permanganate, $KMnO_4$, dissolving in water. As the crystals dissolve, the solution takes on the characteristic color of $KMnO_4$. As you learned in Chapter 13, ionic bonds are relatively strong. How can water molecules break the bonds and dissolve these solids?

Cooperative Learning

Teams of 5; **Time:** 30 min.
Objective: Students will identify five household solutions.
Task: Household solutions may be liquid solvent solutions, but you may want to challenge students by asking them to name two or three solutions that are not aqueous. The groups should also identify the solvent and solute in each solution.
Team responsibility: If possible, have each member of a group bring in an example of a solution to class the next day. If students bring any household solutions to school, require the solutions to be in their original manufacturer's containers.
Evaluation: Have students quickly identify solute and solvent in their sample solutions to the group and then to the whole class.

Resources

Show the video *Solutions* from Coronet Films, Inc.

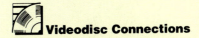 **Videodisc Connections**

23516 to 23915, side 2
Sodium chloride dissolving in water (movie)

Figure 15-2 *The discussion of dissociation that follows will help you relate the macroscopic events shown in the photo to what is happening on the submicroscopic level. The purple substance is potassium permanganate.*

Dissociation To answer the question, think about what you already know about water. Recall from Chapter 13 that water is a polar molecule, as illustrated in Figure 15-3. The oxygen end is somewhat negatively charged, and the hydrogen end is somewhat positively charged. You also know that opposite charges attract. It is reasonable to expect the negative ends of water molecules to be attracted to the positive sodium ions on the surface of the NaCl crystal. The positive ends of other water molecules are similarly attracted to negative chloride ions. Figure 15-4 on the next page illustrates this process. At the surface of the crystal the water molecules become associated with the ions in the crystal. A group of these water molecules will isolate an ion from its neighbors, surrounding it and shielding it from the attractive force of oppositely charged ions. When the charged ions are surrounded by water molecules, they are said to be **hydrated.** It is the interaction of attractive forces between the water molecules and the ions in the crystal of sodium chloride that are responsible for the dissolving process. The process of dissolving a solute in a solvent is called **solvation.**

Eventually the distances between ions increase, allowing the hydrated ions from the solute surface to disperse throughout the solvent. The hydrated ion cannot easily rejoin the crystal, because it is surrounded by a layer of water molecules. The process of decomposition of a crystal into hydrated ions is called **dissociation.** The dissociation of NaCl can be expressed by the following equation. The symbol, (aq), following each ion tells you that water molecules, usually more than one, are associated with each ion in solution.

$$NaCl(s) \rightarrow Na^+(aq) + Cl^-(aq)$$

Many of the compounds you work with in the laboratory contain ionic bonds and dissolve in water as a result of dissociation.

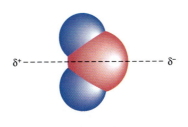

δ^+ -------------------- δ^-

H_2O

Figure 15-3 *Because the water molecule is polar, as this diagram suggests, the water is an excellent solvent for other polar substances.*

PART **1**

Section 15.2 continued

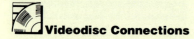

Videodisc Connections

7838 to 12104, side 2
Polystyrene in acetone (movie)

12105-12114, side 2
Polystyrene in acetone: molecular graphics (10-frame seq.)

12414-12419, side 6
Isotactic polystyrene
(6-frame seq.)

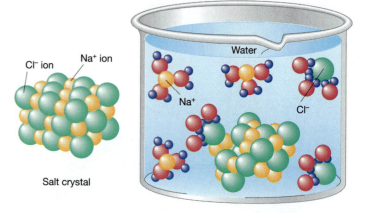

Figure 15-4 Water molecules surround and separate positive and negative ions in a dissolving ionic solid. The polarity of the water molecule is the important factor in this process.

Molecular solvation Many molecular substances will also dissolve in water. For example, ethanol, C_2H_5OH, is a polar molecule, as illustrated in Figure 15-5. When water and ethanol are mixed, a solution forms. Solvation occurs because of the attraction between polar solute molecules and polar solvent molecules. The polar ends of the solute molecules are attracted to the oppositely charged polar regions of the solvent molecules and vice versa. In this fashion, the solute molecules disperse throughout the solution. Many sugars, including table sugar, dissolve in water in a similar manner because like ethanol, they also are polar molecules.

Attractions between polar molecules may draw the solution components into a smaller volume. Figure 15-6 illustrates what happens when 50 mL of ethanol is added to 50 mL of water. Notice that the resultant volume is less than the sum of the two component volumes. What could account for the decrease in volume? Look again at the structure of ethanol, shown in Figure 15-5. The molecule contains oxygen and hydrogen atoms, as does water. Recall from Chapter 14 that hydrogen bonding takes place between liquid water molecules. The same is true for ethanol. In this case, additional

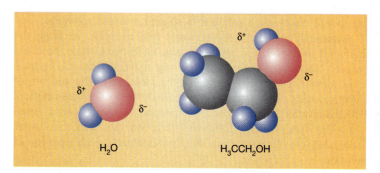

Figure 15-5 Compare the separation of charge indicated here for the ethanol molecule with that of water. Can you see why ethanol and water form solutions in all proportions?

Myths and Misconceptions

Students often mistakenly believe that ionic compounds and molecules are the same and that they behave the same in solutions. Stress that ionic compounds dissolve in water by the process of dissociation, in which ions are separated from each other. Relate this to the polarity of the water molecule. In contrast, when some molecules such as covalent molecules that are nonelectrolytes dissolve in water, they remain intact. Students should understand the distinction between dissociation and molecular solvation before proceeding to study the ionic reactions described in Part 2.

hydrogen bonding takes place between water and ethanol molecules when the two liquids are mixed. The ability of water and alcohol molecules to form hydrogen bonds with each other causes the volume to decrease. This is because in a liquid the distance between molecules held together by a hydrogen bond is less than the average distance between separated molecules.

Concept ✓ Check

How is the polarity of water a factor in the dissolving of an ionic solid?

Videodisc Connections

32209 to 33841, side 2
Making mayonnaise (movie)

28741 to 30417, side 2
Soap (movie)

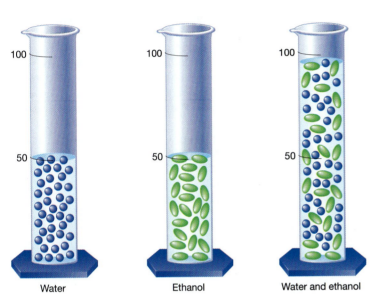

Water   Ethanol   Water and ethanol

Figure 15-6 When equal volumes of water and ethanol are mixed the resulting volume is less than the sum of the individual volumes since water molecules take positions between ethanol molecules.

Miscibility Water and ethanol will mix in any desired proportion, always resulting in a solution. Components of gaseous solutions demonstrate a similar tendency. When there is no apparent limit to the solubility of one substance in another, the components are said to be **miscible.** Not all molecular substances dissolve easily in water, however. If you have ever tried to use water to clean a paint brush coated with oil-based paint, you know the awful mess that is created. Oil-based paints are composed of nonpolar molecules. When polar and nonpolar substances are mixed, they show very little attraction for each other. The particles remain separated and solvation does not occur. An oil and vinegar salad dressing is another example. When agitated, the components mix, but when left to stand, the vinegar (which is itself a solution of two polar substances, acetic acid and water) separates from the nonpolar oil, making a liquid with two distinct layers, as seen in Figure 15-7 on the next page. The attractive forces among the molecules in the vinegar solution are stronger than the attractive forces between the

PART **1**

Section 15.3

Science Background

Like Dissolves Like

The rule of thumb *like dissolves like* should not be thought of as a hard and fast rule. Solubility involves more than the polar and nonpolar molecules. Benzene and carbon tetrachloride are soluble in ethanol, and methanol is soluble in benzene. Make sure students realize that *like dissolves like* is merely a handy rule and not a law of nature.

Videodisc Connections

44459 to 49526, side 2
Microcellular foam (movie)

28016 to 28740, side 2
Oil spill (movie)

Do you know?

If water gets into an automobile engine's fuel lines, it may interfere with the combustion process. To prevent this undesired effect, a solution known as dry gas is added to the fuel. Dry gas consists of a methanol solution that will solvate water found within the fuel system. Since the methanol solution is flammable, it combusts within the engine. The water contaminant exits the engine along with other combustion products.

Figure 15-7 *Oil and water are immiscible, which means they do not mix.*

vinegar solution molecules and the nonpolar oil molecules. Two liquids, such as oil and vinegar, that do not mix are said to be **immiscible.**

Like dissolves like Solvation is determined by the compatibility of the solute and the solvent. You have seen that two polar molecules, like water and ethanol, are soluble in each other. However, nonpolar molecules, like oil, will not dissolve in water, which is composed of polar molecules. Many nonpolar molecules, like iodine, will dissolve in nonpolar solvents, such as mineral oil. In summary, solvation compatibility may be simply stated as *like dissolves like.* If both solution components are nonpolar or if both are significantly polar, solvation may occur.

You should remember that there are many exceptions to this rule. For example, sugar, composed of polar molecules, is not very soluble in ethanol, also composed of polar molecules. It is also good to remember that small amounts of unlike molecules will dissolve in each other. For example, trace amounts of the banned pesticide, DDT, can be found in water. DDT is nonpolar, and its solubility in water is very low (about 1 part per billion, 1 gram of DDT per 1 billion grams of water), but its presence even in this small amount is troublesome. Because DDT is concentrated in the fatty tissues of animals, its accumulation in the food chain has caused damage to fish, birds, and other organisms. DDT's limited solubility has not prevented it from persisting in the environment.

Concept ✔ Check

Explain what is meant by *like dissolves like.* How does this expression relate to polar and nonpolar molecules?

15.3 Solubility

When 39.0 g of cobalt(II) chloride is dissolved in 50 mL of distilled water at 25°C and left undisturbed in an open container, crystals will begin to grow as the water evaporates. Solid cobalt(II) chloride and its solution are shown in Figure 15-8. The maximum mass of cobalt(II) chloride that will dissolve in 50 mL of water at 25°C is 39.0 g. No more cobalt(II) chloride can be dissolved in the solution at that temperature. Any additional compound added would simply settle to the bottom of the container. A solution that cannot dissolve any more solute at a given temperature is said to be **saturated.** A solution that is able to dissolve more solute is called **unsaturated.**

Measuring solubility **Solubility** is the amount of substance needed to make a saturated solution at a specified temperature. The solubility of cobalt(II) chloride at 25°C is 78 g per 100 mL of water.

The solubility of a solid in different liquids varies widely. For example, 35.7 g of sodium chloride dissolves in 100 g of water at

Figure 15-8 *When more CoCl₂ is added to a saturated solution of CoCl₂ at a given temperature, the additional solid will not dissolve.*

0°C. Yet very little sodium chloride dissolves in ethanol. Tincture of iodine is a solution of elemental iodine, I_2, in ethanol and water. Ethanol is a necessary ingredient because iodine is not very soluble in water. Because ethanol is soluble in water, it is often used to help dissolve materials that would not be soluble in water alone.

In the same liquid, solubilities of different solids vary considerably. Silver nitrate, for example, has a solubility in water exceeding 250 g per 100 g of water. On the other hand, silver chloride has a solubility of 0.000 193 g per 100 g of water. These differences in solubilities can be used to identify products in chemical reactions, as you will see later in this chapter. Table 15-2 lists the solubilities of some ionic substances.

Under these circumstances, which substance in Table 15-2 is the most soluble? Which is the least soluble?

Because of this range of solubilities, the word *soluble* does not have a precise meaning. There is an upper limit to the solubility of the most soluble solid. On the other hand, even the least soluble solid furnishes a few dissolved particles per liter of solution. Glass containers are used for much of the work done in the lab because glass has such low solubility in water. In this book, the word *soluble* will be used to mean that more than 0.1 mole of solute dissolves per liter of solution.

15.4 Factors Affecting Solubility

You may have noticed that you can get your hands cleaner and wash them more quickly if you use warm water rather than cold water. The same can be said of many laundry detergents. The hotter the water, the better they clean.

TABLE 15-2

Solubilities of Various Compounds	
Substance	**g/100 g H₂O at 0°C**
NH_4Cl	29.4
NH_4I	155.0
$Ca(C_2H_3O_2)_2$	37.4
$CuSO_4 \cdot 5H_2O$	23.1
$FeCl_3$	74.4
PbI_2	0.044
$MgSO_4$	22.0
KI	128.0
$NaCl$	35.7
$NaOH$	42.0

CONNECTING CONCEPTS

Models The concept of equilibrium is a model used to explain why the pressure in a closed system remains constant. Dynamic equilibrium exists whenever two opposing reactions are occurring at the same rate. Equilibrium models are also helpful in explaining reaction rates and solubility in saturated solutions.

Figure 15-9 *Many substances dissolve more readily at higher temperatures as this graph shows. The solubility of which substance is affected least by changes in temperature?*

Temperature One of the reasons why most soaps and detergents work better in hot water is that they are able to remove more dirt and grease and hold these unwanted substances in solution when the water is hot. For many substances, *solubility increases with an increase in the temperature of the solution.* Figure 15-9 shows how the solubility of several ionic compounds increases with an increase in temperature. The solubility of silver nitrate, $AgNO_3$, increases substantially with an increase in temperature. The solubility of sodium chloride, on the other hand, remains almost constant from 0°C to 100°C.

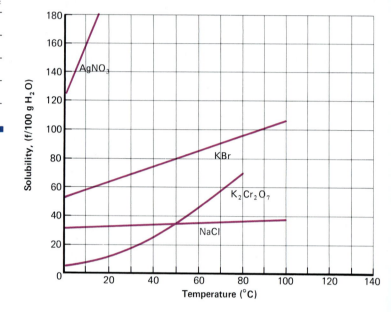

A method of crystal growing takes advantage of decreasing solubility with decreasing temperature. When, for example, a heated saturated sugar solution is allowed to cool, crystals begin to grow inside the solution, as shown in Figure 15-10. The crystals continue to grow as long as the solution is left uncovered so that water can evaporate.

Sometimes, if left undisturbed, a solution that has been heated to dissolve added solute can cool without crystals forming. The cooled solution contains more solute than it usually would hold at that temperature. Under these circumstances a solution is said to be **supersaturated.** If a seed crystal is dropped into a flask containing a supersaturated solution, crystals will often begin to precipitate out in a wonderfully cascading display.

The solubility of a dissolved gas decreases as the temperature of the solution increases. Have you ever noticed that if a bottle of carbonated beverage is left uncovered at room temperature, it goes flat? The carbon dioxide in the beverage comes out of solution,

PART 1
Section 15.4 *continued*

Teaching Strategy

Connecting Concepts

Equilibrium is an important concept that is covered in Chapter 18. Since this is the first time students will encounter equilibrium, they should understand what equilibrium means. In an equilibrium system, the rate of the forward reaction is equal to the rate of the reverse reaction. The reactants and products need not be present in equal amounts.

DEMONSTRATION

Temperature

The principle of supersaturation can be demonstrated in the following way. Place a ratio of 10 g of sodium acetate hydrate to 1 mL of distilled water into a small flask. Slowly heat to dissolve the crystals. No crystals of solute should remain on the neck of the flask. Allow the solution to come to room temperature undisturbed. Place a few crystals of sodium acetate in a beaker on a table. From a buret, slowly drip the solution over the crystals. Crystallization forms a tall column of sodium acetate.

⚠️ **CAUTION: Wear safety goggles and a lab apron. Protect your students with a shield.** For disposal of sodium acetate, save and reuse, or dissolve in water and pour down the drain.

Figure 15-10 A sugar-water solution becomes supersaturated by dissolving as much sugar as possible at a high temperature. As the solution cools and some solvent evaporates beautiful crystals come out of solution.

forms bubbles on the side of the bottle and eventually escapes. A cold carbonated beverage can dissolve more carbon dioxide than a warm beverage. Now can you explain why you feel the fizz on your tongue when you drink a carbonated beverage?

The change in solubility of a gas with a change in temperature has more significance than its effect on carbonated drinks. Fish use the oxygen dissolved in water for respiration. Many game fish, like trout, need a higher concentration of dissolved oxygen than do many scavenger fish or bottom-dwellers. A small change in the temperature of a body of water could have a great effect on the kinds of fish populations that a river or lake could support. A factory that uses river water for cooling may change the population of fish living in a river by returning water to the river at a higher temperature. This sort of pollution is called thermal pollution. Such contamination of a body of water must be taken into consideration when permits are given for industrial usage of water.

Pressure   When a bottle containing a carbonated beverage is opened, bubbles rise to the liquid's surface. This sometimes violent release of carbon dioxide gas can be stopped if the bottle's cap is retightened. If the beverage is at room temperature, an even more energetic evolution of gas occurs, as shown in Figure 15-11. How might these observations be explained on the submicroscopic level?

The solubility of a gas depends on the pressure acting upon the system. If the pressure of the system is reduced, the dissolved gas rapidly leaves the solution phase as small bubbles. As these bubbles rise within the solvent, they increase in size because they are encountering pressure. On reaching the liquid's surface, the bubbles burst.

When the container is closed, there is an equilibrium between the gas above the liquid and the gas dissolved in the solvent. If the container is opened, the pressurized gas escapes. The reduced pressure on the liquid's surface allows additional gas molecules to leave the solution. Beverages are packaged in sealed bottles and cans to prevent the escape of carbon dioxide. The beverages can be kept indefinitely without losing their carbonation until they are opened by the consumer.

DO YOU KNOW?

The gas bubbles appearing on the inside edge of a pot of water before it boils are bubbles of air that become undissolved as the water is heated. The bubbles that are constantly produced as water boils contain water vapor.

Figure 15-11 The solubility of CO_2 in a carbonated beverage decreases with increases in temperature. Opening a bottle of warm soda shows how quickly the gas comes out of solution once the pressure on the solution is reduced.

Guided Practice

Review the Concept Check questions on pages 503 and 504 with students. Answers can be found in Appendix E on page 808.

Reteaching Idea

If students are unclear about the definition of solubility and how solubility is affected by temperature, refer them to Figure 15–9 and ask questions using the terms introduced in this part (solvent, solute, solvation, dissociation, hydration, miscible, saturated, unsaturated, supersaturated). Some questions might be these:

- What is the solvent used?
- Are $AgNO_3$, NaCl, $K_2Cr_2O_7$, and KBr miscible with water at temperatures from 0°C to 100°C?
- What is the solubility of $AgNO_3$ at 0°C?
- What is the solubility of $AgNO_3$ at 10°C?
- If a solution contains 80 grams of KBr at 50°C, is the solution saturated, unsaturated, or supersaturated?
- What would you see happening if a solution of 80 grams of KBr at 50°C cooled to 30°C? How many grams of KBr would precipitate as the temperature decreased from 50°C to 30°C?
- Would the KBr solution at 30°C be saturated, unsaturated, or supersaturated?
- Which substance, $K_2Cr_2O_7$ or NaCl, has the greater solubility at 40°C? Which has the greater solubility at 70°C?
- What two processes take place when each of the four substances dissolves? (hydration, dissociation)

 Videodisc Connections

4112 to 7837, side 2
Standard ammonia fountain
(movie)

10584 to 12844, side 1
Chemiluminescent NH_3 fountain
(movie)

PART 1

Section 15.4 *continued*

≡ CLOSE

Summing Up Main Ideas

Have students identify the solvent in ocean water as well as two solid solutes and two gas solutes in ocean water. Then ask students to describe how an increase in water temperature from 15°C to 25°C would affect the solubility of each solute. Students can use Table 15–1 to find water is the solvent, salts are solid solutes, and CO_2 and O_2 are gas solutes. Salts other than NaCl will be more soluble in water at 25°C. The solubility of NaCl will remain constant. The solubilities of CO_2 and O_2 will be less at 25°C.

PART 1 REVIEW

Assign the Part Review questions.

Evaluating Skills

These skills are evaluated in the Part Review questions indicated. **Classifying:** 1; **Stating a conclusion:** 2, 3; **Analyzing data:** 4; **Predicting:** 5, 6, 7

Boxed numbers indicate questions that involve skills in interpretation, application, and analysis.

PART 1 REVIEW

1. Of the following, which are homogeneous mixtures and which are heterogeneous mixtures: black coffee, household bleach, tea, maple syrup, cream of mushroom soup?

2. On the basis of the principle like dissolves like, determine which is more soluble in water, ammonia or carbon dioxide? Explain your choice. Use a reference book to evaluate your choice. The Merck Index is useful.

3. Why is using water to clean a paintbrush covered with oil-based enamel not an effective cleanup method?

4. Using Figure 15-9, derive a rule of thumb about the relationship between the solubility and the temperature of a solution. List any exceptions.

5. Predict what will happen when solute is added to a saturated solution at a constant temperature?

6. Write the dissociation reaction for each of the following ionic substances in water.
   a. NaI(s)   c. $FeCl_3$(s)
   b. MgS(s)   d. $(NH_4)_2CO_3$(s)

7. How can a supersaturated solution be prepared?

C O N S U M E R   C H E M I S T R Y

Paints

Paleolithic hunters of 15 000 years ago drew and painted scenes on the walls of their caves. Studies of Egyptian tombs of 2000 B.C. not only provide evidence of social life but also indicate how similar ancient paint was to paint made today.

Paint has four ingredients: pigment, a binder, a solvent, and additives. Pigment gives paint its color and its covering power, or opacity. Pigment also contributes to a paint's durability and adhesive qualities. Prehistoric paint included natural pigment from vegetables or the earth mixed with water or oil.

A binder carries pigment and binds it to a surface. Binders contain one or more resins, sticky substances made from plants or manufactured. Drying oils can also be used as binders. The binder affects the adhesive quality, drying time, and hardness of paint. In Egypt,

paint was made from ground pigment, resins, and drying oils.

The solvent keeps paint a liquid. Solvents are also called thinners. Turpentine is a familiar one and was used in ancient Egypt. The type of solvent needed is determined by the composition of the binder used. Recently petroleum solvents have replaced turpentine. Such solvents are necessary for oil-based paint. However, water has become the preferred solvent with the advent of latex paints, since they contain resins that are water soluble.

PART 1 REVIEW

ANSWERS

■ **Keyed to Objectives**

A **1.** Homogeneous mixtures: black coffee, household bleach, tea, maple syrup. Heterogeneous mixtures: cream of mushroom soup

C **2.** Ammonia is more soluble in water because both ammonia and water are polar molecules. The solubility

of ammonia is 47 percent by mass at 0°C and the solubility of carbon dioxide is 0.14 percent at 0°C.

C **3.** Water, which is composed of polar molecules, is not a good solvent for oil-based paint, which is nonpolar. The oil-based paint will bead in the water and cause a mess.

C **4.** For many substances, solubility increases with an increase in temperature. Exceptions include sodium chloride and gases.

C **5.** No more solute will dissolve. The added solute will settle to the bottom of the container. The added solute and the solution will come to equilibrium.

B **6. a.** NaI(s) → Na^+(aq) + I^- (aq)
   b. MgS(s) → Mg^{2+}(aq) + S^{2-} (aq)
   c. $FeCl_3$(s) → Fe^{3+}(aq) + 3Cl^-(aq)
   d. $(NH_4)_2CO_3$(s) →
      2NH_4^+(aq) + CO_3^{2-}(aq)

PART 2 Ionic Equations and Precipitation Reactions

In Part 1 of this chapter, you learned that ionic substances have different solubilities. You can use these solubilities to produce desirable reactions in solution. For example, your chemistry teacher has accumulated solutions made up of ionic substances that may be harmful to the environment if poured down the drain. For example solutions containing lead, mercury, barium ions and other heavy metal ions should not be disposed of casually. If a solution containing an anion that will react with the heavy metal ions is added to a waste container, a precipitate containing the heavy metal ions will settle to the bottom of the container. The remaining solution is then relatively free of these ions and can be safely poured down the drain. The precipitated compounds can then be disposed of in an environmentally responsible manner.

In this part of the chapter, you will investigate one kind of reaction that takes place in aqueous solutions. You will investigate the nature of the reactants and products of this type of reaction. You will also use this knowledge to write equations for the reactions.

15.5 Reactions in Solution

You are familiar with reactions that take place in aqueous solution. Many of the substances you have used in the laboratory are ionic compounds that dissociate in water and react to form new substances.

Silver nitrate, $AgNO_3$, and potassium chloride, KCl, are ionic solids that are soluble in water. If a solution of $AgNO_3$ and a solution of KCl are combined, milky-white crystals form within the mixture, as shown in Figure 15-12, and eventually collect on the bottom of the reaction flask as a **precipitate**. You first read about precipitation reactions in Chapter 3, where they were also described as double displacement reactions. How can this reaction be explained in terms of solubility?

The equation for the reaction shown in Figure 15-12 is

$$AgNO_3(aq) + KCl(aq) \rightarrow AgCl(s) + KNO_3(aq)$$

The equation lists the formulas of the ionic substances dissolved in water and also the formula of the precipitate, silver chloride, $AgCl$. Notice the state symbols indicating that all the substances except $AgCl$ are dissolved in water. The products, $AgCl$ and KNO_3, have different solubilities. A chemistry handbook would show you that $AgNO_3$, KCl, and KNO_3 are very soluble in water, while $AgCl$ is not soluble. Using this information, you can see how the state symbols in the equation were determined. Potassium nitrate does not form a precipitate, because it is soluble. Silver chloride forms

Figure 15-12 *The formation of a precipitate when two solutions of ionic compounds are mixed tells you that a new insoluble compound has formed from the ions in solution.*

O b j e c t i v e s

Part 2

D. *Identify* ionic substances that precipitate from aqueous solutions.

E. *Write* ionic equations and net ionic equations for precipitation reactions in aqueous solutions.

Developing Skills

Students may apply these skills in their study of Part 2.
Classifying: Have students classify reactions as precipitation or other.
Predicting: Have students predict precipitation reactions.
Analyzing data: Have students interpret a solubility table.
Analyzing data: Have students use data to determine the products of precipitation reactions.
Verifying results: Have students verify results by comparing predicted products with data obtained from experiments.
Designing experiments: Have students design experiments for precipitation reactions. (Note: Experiments should not be carried out.)

≡ FOCUS

Activate Prior Knowledge

Students are already familiar with balancing chemical equations and predicting double displacement reactions (Chapter 3). Mix together a $0.2M$ solution of strontium chloride and a $0.2M$ solution of sodium carbonate. Have students make observations and write the balanced chemical equation for the reaction.
$$[SrCl_2(aq) + Na_2CO_3(aq) \rightarrow$$
$$SrCO_3(s) + 2NaCl(aq)]$$
⚠ **CAUTION: Wear safety goggles, lab apron, gloves, and a face shield. Dispose of $SrCO_3$ by wrapping precipitate in newspaper and placing in wastebasket. Pour the decantate down the drain.**

C **7.** A saturated solution is gently heated as more solute is dissolved. Then the solution is allowed to cool back to room temperature.

☰ T E A C H

Teaching Strategy

Reactions in Solution

You may want to teach this section in Chapters 8 and 9. Students would have the background to perform precipitation reactions and qualitative analysis in the lab. See also Chapter 21 for more chemical analysis. With this sequence of topics, students can continue with lab work while they investigate atomic structure. Students will derive important skills from labs in ionic reactions in aqueous solutions.

Teaching Strategy

Writing Ionic Equations

Some students have a difficult time understanding the symbolism of ionic particles. Review with them the meaning of the example below.

$$SO_4^{2-}$$

The *4* means four oxygen atoms attached to one sulfur atom. The *2* means that the unit composed of five atoms has a net negative charge of two, that is, the unit has two more electrons than protons.

a precipitate because it is insoluble. To be able to predict the products of a reaction and write equations accurately, you need to have information about the solubilities of substances. Some regularities in the solubility of various ionic compounds are given in the solubility table in Appendix D. This information is based on experimental results.

15.6 Writing Ionic Equations

In aqueous solutions, soluble ionic substances dissociate into component ions. The dissociation of the two reactants discussed in the previous section are represented as follows.

$$AgNO_3(s) \rightarrow Ag^+(aq) + NO_3^-(aq)$$
$$KCl(s) \rightarrow K^+(aq) + Cl^-(aq)$$

Using ions instead of formulas, you can represent the reaction another way. The equation for the formation of AgCl can be rewritten as follows:

$$Ag^+(aq) + NO_3^-(aq) + K^+(aq) + Cl^-(aq) \rightarrow$$
$$AgCl(s) + K^+(aq) + NO_3^-(aq)$$

Known as an **ionic equation,** this representation lists reactants and products as hydrated ions rather than in formula form. Ionic equations produce a more accurate picture of what is occurring between the components of the reaction than formula equations.

Figure 15-13 illustrates the two component solutions being mixed. Notice that the potassium ions and nitrate ions stay in solution, while silver chloride precipitates out. Because the K^+ and NO_3^- ions do not participate in the reaction, they are called **spectator ions.** The ionic equation is simplified by dropping the spectator ions from the equation. The resulting **net ionic equation** for the reaction may be written as follows.

$$Ag^+(aq) + Cl^-(aq) \rightarrow AgCl(s)$$

Figure 15-13 *When soluble silver nitrate and potassium chloride are mixed, the positive and negative ions "change partners" resulting in the formation of a precipitation of silver chloride.*

☐ D E M O N S T R A T I O N

Forming a Precipitate

Add 1 g of lead(II) nitrate crystals to a large test tube containing 10 mL of deionized water. Add 3 g of potassium iodide crystals to another large test tube containing 10 mL of deionized water. Dissolve by swirling the test tubes. Quickly pour the contents of one tube into the other. Immediately, a bright yellow precipitate forms. Have students discuss speed of

reaction and the nature of the precipitate.

⚠ **CAUTION: Do not allow students to handle the test tube. Use a shield to protect students. Wear safety goggles, lab apron, and gloves.** For disposal, decant the supernate down the drain. Save the lead iodide in a sealed, labeled container for a disposal contractor. Wash hands thoroughly.

EXAMPLE 15-1

Using the solubility table in Appendix D, write an ionic equation for the reaction that occurs when equal volumes of $0.2M$ solutions of barium chloride and sodium carbonate are mixed. Then write the net ionic equation for the reaction.

■ **Analyze the Problem** To write the ionic equation, you must determine what ions you have in solution and what products are possible. You are told that barium chloride and sodium carbonate are both in solution. Therefore, you know that each substance has dissociated into its component ions as follows.

$$BaCl_2(s) \rightarrow Ba^{2+}(aq) + 2Cl^-(aq)$$
$$Na_2CO_3(s) \rightarrow 2Na^+(aq) + CO_3{}^{2-}(aq)$$

■ **Apply a Strategy** When you mix the two solutions, you now know that you have four types of ions in the mixture: Ba^{2+}, Cl^-, Na^+, and $CO_3{}^{2-}$. Write the left-hand side of the ionic equation.

$$Ba^{2+}(aq) + 2Cl^-(aq) + 2Na^+(aq) + CO_3{}^{2-}(aq) \rightarrow$$

You know that positive ions combine with negative ions, so the two possible products are $BaCO_3$ and $NaCl$.

Before writing the rest of the equation, refer to the solubility table to determine if either product forms an insoluble precipitate. Is either barium carbonate or sodium chloride insoluble?

■ **Work a Solution** The solubility table tells you that NaCl is soluble, and that $BaCO_3$ is not soluble. Therefore, $BaCO_3$ must be a precipitate. The ionic equation for this reaction must be

$$Ba^{2+}(aq) + 2Cl^-(aq) + 2Na^+(aq) + CO_3{}^{2-}(aq) \rightarrow$$
$$BaCO_3(s) + 2Na^+(aq) + 2Cl^-(aq)$$

The sodium ions and chloride ions remain in solution and do not participate in the reaction. By removing these spectator ions, you end up with the net ionic equation

$$Ba^{2+}(aq) + CO_3{}^{2-}(aq) \rightarrow BaCO_3(s)$$

■ **Verify Your Answer** From past experience with one of the products, you may deduce a reasonable answer. If you recognize sodium chloride as a soluble salt, you should be able to predict that $BaCO_3$ would be the precipitate.

Practice Problems

8. Write an ionic equation for the reaction that occurs when equal volumes of $0.3M$ solutions of lead nitrate and ammonium sulfate are mixed. Identify the spectator ions.

9. Write an ionic equation for the reaction that occurs when equal volumes of $0.2M$ solutions of barium sulfide and iron(II) sulfate are mixed.

PROBLEM-SOLVING
STRATEGY

Use information that you know or that you can look up. (See Strategy, page 58.)

PROBLEM-SOLVING
STRATEGY

To solve this problem, you are breaking it into manageable parts—identifying ions, writing and balancing equations, and identifying spectator ions. (See Strategy, page 166.)

Practice Problems

Assign the Practice Problems.

Cooperative Learning

Teams of 4; **Time:** 20 minutes
Objective: Students will identify ionic substances that precipitate from solutions. They will also identify the precipitate.
Task: Assign each member of a group one of the rows of ions in Table 3–4 (page 108) that form precipitates. Each member of the group should present a problem, i.e., a combination of cations and anions that produces a precipitate. Specifically, a problem should consist of two solutions that when mixed will produce a precipitate containing an ion in a student's assigned row of ions. For example, student A is assigned precipitates with sulfate. Student A's problem for his or her group members might be "find the precipitate formed when solutions of sodium sulfate and barium chloride are mixed."
Team responsibility: Each student is responsible for making sure that all group members understand their problems.
Evaluation: Randomly ask individuals to present their problems to the class. Ask volunteers to provide answers to make sure the teams carried out their responsibilities.

PART **2**

Section 15.6 *continued*

Guided Practice

Write an ionic equation for the reaction that occurs when equal volumes of $0.4M$ solutions of barium chloride and potassium sulfate are mixed.

$Ba^{2+}(aq) + 2Cl^-(aq) + 2K^+(aq)$
$\quad + SO_4{}^{2-}(aq) \rightarrow BaSO_4(s)$
$\quad + 2K^+(aq) + 2Cl^-(aq)$

Reteaching Idea

Students sometimes have difficulty predicting whether a precipitate will form when ionic solutions are mixed because they are not comfortable using Table 3–4 or Appendix D. Provide them with extra practice by listing the names of some ionic substances. Ask students to show what would happen to each substance if it were placed in water by writing its formula either as a solid—if it does not dissolve—or as aqueous ions if it does [e.g., $AgCl(s)$ or $Na^+(aq) + Cl^-(aq)$]. Include substances not specifically mentioned in the table (e.g., iron(II) sulfide, gallium nitrate, nickel hydroxide, cobalt sulfate, magnesium acetate, ammonium chromate).

For more practice in predicting precipitate formation, make lists of cations and anions and challenge students to find all possible combinations of these ions that would form precipitates. Compare class results.

Cations: $NH_4{}^+$, Co^{2+}, Fe^{3+}, Ba^{2+}, Sr^{2+}, Pb^{2+}, Na^+, $Hg_2{}^{2+}$
Anions: $CO_3{}^{2-}$, $PO_4{}^{3-}$, Br^-, S^{2-}, $SO_4{}^{2-}$, Cl^-, $NO_3{}^-$, OH^-

---

Other reactions of solutions Precipitates do not always form when reagents react in solution. When, for example, aqueous solutions of sodium hydroxide and hydrogen chloride (hydrochloric acid) are mixed, the following reaction occurs.

$$Na^+(aq) + OH^-(aq) + H^+(aq) + Cl^-(aq) \rightarrow$$
$$Na^+(aq) + Cl^-(aq) + H_2O(l)$$

The net ionic equation for this reaction is

$$OH^-(aq) + H^+(aq) \rightarrow H_2O(l)$$

This reaction between solutions containing hydrogen ions and hydroxide ions to form water is a common reaction in chemistry. It will be discussed at length in Chapter 19.

Some metals react with hydrogen ions in solution to form metallic ions and hydrogen gas. Consider the example of zinc and hydrochloric acid:

$$Zn(s) + 2HCl(aq) \rightarrow H_2(g) + ZnCl_2(s)$$

When written as a net ionic equation, the reaction is represented as

$$Zn(s) + 2H^+(aq) \rightarrow H_2(g) + Zn^{2+}(aq)$$

Still another ionic reaction is illustrated by mixing baking soda and nitric acid, $NaHCO_3$ and HNO_3. The ionic equation is written as follows.

$$Na^+(aq) + HCO_3{}^-(aq) + H^+(aq) + NO_3{}^-(aq) \rightarrow$$
$$Na^+(aq) + NO_3{}^-(aq) + H_2CO_3(aq)$$

The products appear to remain in solution. However, one product, carbonic acid, H_2CO_3, decomposes readily to form carbon dioxide and water.

$$H_2CO_3(aq) \rightarrow CO_2(g) + H_2O(l)$$

The overall reaction can be described by the following net ionic equation.

$$HCO_3{}^-(aq) + H^+(aq) \rightarrow CO_2(g) + H_2O(l)$$

These are but a few reactions that occur when ionic solutions are mixed. As you continue your study of chemistry, you will find out about other reactions of solutions.

PART 2 REVIEW

10. Predict the identity of the precipitate formed during the reaction between lead(II) nitrate and potassium iodide, and write a balanced ionic equation.

11. Write a balanced ionic equation for the reaction between solutions of silver nitrate and sodium chloride.

12. Make a submicroscopic drawing which shows separate solutions of silver nitrate and sodium chloride each containing

---

PART 2 REVIEW

ANSWERS

■ **Keyed to Objectives**

D **10.** Lead(II) iodide, PbI_2, is formed.
$Pb^{2+}(aq) + 2NO_3{}^-(aq) + 2K^+(aq)$
$\quad + 2I^-(aq) \rightarrow PbI_2(s) + 2K^+(aq)$
$\quad + 2NO_3{}^-(aq)$

E **11.** $Ag^+(aq) + NO_3{}^-(aq) + Na^+(aq)$
$\quad + Cl^-(aq) \rightarrow AgCl(s) + NO_3{}^-(aq)$
$\quad + Na^+(aq)$

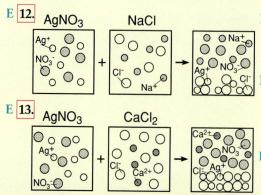

E **12.**   AgNO₃   NaCl

E **13.**   AgNO₃   CaCl₂

E **14.** **a.** $Ag^+(aq) + Cl^-(aq) \rightarrow AgCl(s)$
b. $Pb^{2+}(aq) + 2Br^-(aq) \rightarrow PbBr_2(s)$
c. $SO_4{}^{2-}(aq) + Ba^{2+}(aq) \rightarrow$
$\quad\quad\quad\quad\quad\quad\quad BaSO_4(s)$

D **15.** **a.** soluble   **d.** soluble
b. soluble   **e.** soluble
c. insoluble   **f.** soluble
Soluble means that more than 0.1 mole of solute dissolves per liter of solution.

E **16.** Spectator ions are ions that are not involved in a reaction. They must ten dissolved $AgNO_3$ and ten dissolved NaCl particles. Make a drawing after the solutions have been mixed.

13. Make a submicroscopic drawing which shows separate solutions of silver nitrate and calcium chloride each containing twelve dissolved particles. Make a drawing after the solutions have been mixed.

14. Write the net ionic equation for the reactions between each of these pairs of ionic compounds.
  a. silver nitrate and sodium chloride
  b. lead(II) nitrate and potassium bromide
  c. sodium sulfate and barium chloride

15. Interpret the data in the solubility table in Appendix D to determine which of the following compounds are insoluble in water. What is the definition of soluble in terms of mol/L?
  a. sodium hydroxide
  b. ammonium acetate
  c. calcium sulfate
  d. lead(II) chloride
  e. potassium chloride
  f. calcium bromide

16. Explain why spectator ions are not included in net ionic equations.

17. Predict the products and write net ionic equations for the following reactions. Use the solubility table in Appendix D to help you in determining solubilities. If no reaction occurs, write N.R.
  a. $NaOH(aq) + HCl(aq) \rightarrow$
  b. $Bi(NO_3)_3(aq) + NaOH(aq) \rightarrow$
  c. $Pb(C_2H_3O_2)_2(aq) + K_2SO_4(aq) \rightarrow$
  d. $CuSO_4(aq) + FeCl_3(aq) \rightarrow$
  e. $FeSO_4(aq) + (NH_4)_2S(aq) \rightarrow$
  f. $K_2CO_3(aq) + Sr(NO_3)_2(aq) \rightarrow$
  g. $NaCl(aq) + KOH(aq) \rightarrow$
  h. $NaI(aq) + AgNO_3(aq) \rightarrow$
  i. $Al_2(SO_4)_3(aq) + CaCl_2(aq) \rightarrow$
  j. $Na_2SO_4(aq) + CaCl_2(aq) \rightarrow$
  k. $K_2SO_4(aq) + Ba(C_2H_3O_2)_2(aq) \rightarrow$
  l. $MgSO_4(aq) + CaBr_2(aq) \rightarrow$

18. Write an equation for the reaction of solutions of barium hydroxide and nitric acid, HNO_3.

19. Write the net ionic equation for the reaction of magnesium with sulfuric acid, H_2SO_4, and explain in your own words what happens in the reaction.

Boxed numbers indicate questions that involve skills in interpretation, application, and analysis.

PART **2**
Section 15.6 *continued*

☰ CLOSE

Summing Up Main Ideas

Have students indicate compounds that will form a precipitate when mixed with calcium chloride in aqueous solutions. Also ask them to write ionic equations to describe at least two precipitate-forming reactions involving calcium chloride. Refer students to Table 3–4 to determine positive ions that form precipitates with Cl^- and negative ions that form precipitates with Ca^{2+} in water.

PART 2 REVIEW

Assign the Part Review questions.

Evaluating Skills

These skills are evaluated in the Part Review questions indicated.
Predicting: 10, 17, **Applying a strategy:** 11, 14, 18, 19; **Verifying results:** 11, 14, 18, 19; **Analyzing data:** 11, 14, 15, 18, 19; **Forming models:** 12, 13; **Stating a conclusion:** 16, 19

---

be present, however, to maintain a balanced charge.

E **17. a.** $H^+(aq) + OH^-(aq) \rightarrow H_2O(l)$
  b. $Bi^{3+}(aq) + 3OH^-(aq) \rightarrow$
          $Bi(OH)_3(s)$
  c. $Pb^{2+}(aq) + SO_4^{2-}(aq) \rightarrow$
          $PbSO_4(s)$
  d. no reaction
  e. $Fe^{2+}(aq) + S^{2-}(aq) \rightarrow FeS(s)$
  f. $Sr^{2+}(aq) + CO_3^{2-}(aq) \rightarrow$
          $SrCO_3(s)$

  g. no reaction
  h. $Ag^+(aq) + I^-(aq) \rightarrow AgI(s)$
  i. $Ca^{2+}(aq) + SO_4^{2-}(aq) \rightarrow$
          $CaSO_4(s)$
  j. $Ca^{2+}(aq) + SO_4^{2-}(aq) \rightarrow$
          $CaSO_4(s)$
  k. $Ba^{2+}(aq) + SO_4^{2-}(aq) \rightarrow$
          $BaSO_4(s)$
  l. $Ca^{2+}(aq) + SO_4^{2-}(aq) \rightarrow$
          $CaSO_4(s)$

E **18.** $Ba^{2+}(aq) + 2OH^-(aq) + 2H^+(aq)$
          $+ 2NO_3^-(aq) \rightarrow 2H_2O(l)$
          $+ Ba^{2+}(aq) + 2NO_3^-(aq)$
E **19.** $Mg(s) + 2H^+(aq) + SO_4^{2-}(aq) \rightarrow$
          $H_2(g) + Mg^{2+}(aq) + SO_4^{2-}(aq)$
Magnesium replaces hydrogen ion from the solution, liberating hydrogen gas.

PART **3**
Colligative Properties of Solutions

Section 15.7

Developing Skills

Students may apply these skills in their study of Part 3.
Analyzing data: Have students interpret data for colligative properties.
Comparing/Contrasting: Have students compare colligative properties for molecular and ionic solutions.
Analyzing data: Have students organize data from a table of boiling and melting points.
Calculating: Have students calculate the molar mass of a molecule.

≡FOCUS

Activate Prior Knowledge

Students should be familiar with molarity (Chapter 4) and density (Chapter 1). Have students calculate how much NaCl must be added to water to get a 0.5M and a 1.0M solution of salt water (2.93 g NaCl in 100 mL of water for 0.5M, and 5.85 g NaCl in 100 mL of water for 1.0M). Have students make the solutions and try to layer one of the solutions on top of the other in a test tube.

⚠ **CAUTION: Students should wear safety goggles and lab aprons.** The solutions will layer if the more concentrated, or denser, of the two solutions is on the bottom. They will mix if the more concentrated solution is on the top. To dispose of solutions, pour down the drain.

Objectives

Part 3

F. *Relate changes* in boiling and freezing temperature to the concentration of solute in a solution.

G. *Calculate changes* in boiling and freezing temperatures of solutions.

If you live in one of the northern states, you are familiar with the scene featured in Figure 15-14. Salt, either sodium chloride or calcium chloride, is spread on snowy and icy roads. Salt lowers the temperature at which a saltwater solution freezes. The surface of the treated road will not freeze, unless the air temperature gets down below −20°C (−4°F). These salts are used because they are inexpensive and effective. Unfortunately they also are corrosive to vehicle exteriors.

Have you ever made your own ice cream? The directions ask you to place ice and salt in the exterior chamber to freeze the cream mixture. Rock salt lowers the temperature at which ice melts to below 0°C. A salt/ice/water mixture can maintain a temperature of about −18°C or 0°F. The ice-cream-making process takes advantage of the fact that solutions have properties different from those of pure solvents. In the remainder of this chapter, you will read about how these differences are put to use in everyday life.

Figure 15-14 *If you live in the north this scene is common-place in winter. Salting roads helps clear them of ice. How?*

15.7 Boiling Point Elevation and Freezing Point Depression

If you added table sugar to water to make a solution and brought the solution to a boil, you would find that boiling would begin at a temperature greater than 100.0°C, the boiling point of pure water. If you froze the same sugar-water solution, freezing would begin at a temperature below 0.0°C, the freezing point of pure water.

When other solutions are tested, the results are similar to the sugar-water solution. Table 15-3 lists the temperatures at which each solution is expected to begin boiling or freezing.

TABLE 15-3

Boiling and Freezing Point Data for Some Aqueous Solutions				
Solution	Temperature at which boiling begins (°C)		Temperature at which freezing begins (°C)	
	Concentration A	Concentration B	Concentration A	Concentration B
sucrose	100.10	100.73	−0.35	−2.68
glycerol	100.10	100.77	−0.35	−2.68
sodium chloride	100.20	101.46	−0.70	−5.36
calcium chloride	100.30	102.19	−1.05	−8.04

Look at Table 15-3. Notice that in all cases, the boiling point of the pure solvent, water, is increased when a solute is added.

Boiling point elevation is the property of solutions that describes the temperature difference between the boiling point of a pure solvent and the temperature at which a solution begins to boil. On the other hand, the freezing point of water is lowered when a solute is added to the water. **Freezing point depression** is the property of solutions that describes the temperature difference between the freezing point of a pure solvent and the temperature at which a solution begins to freeze.

Examine Table 15-3 more closely. Assume that Concentration B is greater than Concentration A. What do you notice when you compare the initial boiling temperatures for the two concentrations? What about the two groups of freezing temperatures? You should see that the boiling temperatures are greater in the Concentration B column than in the Concentration A column for each substance. The freezing temperatures are lower in the Concentration B column than in the Concentration A column. The data seem to follow the pattern that the higher the concentration of the solute, the greater the solution deviates from the boiling temperature and freezing temperature of the pure solvent.

What do you notice about the boiling temperatures or freezing temperatures of the four solutes in any one column? Does sodium chloride seem to deviate more from the boiling temperature and freezing temperature of pure water than the sucrose and glycerol solutions? Why should this be?

When sodium chloride, NaCl, dissociates in water, it produces two ions, sodium, Na^+, and chloride, Cl^-, in the following dissociation reaction.

$$NaCl(s) \rightarrow Na^+(aq) + Cl^-(aq)$$

DO YOU KNOW?

Coffee contains more than 100 oils and various chemicals, which are responsible for its flavor. Freshly brewed coffee has the most attractive flavor because many of these chemicals are thermally sensitive and degrade to less palatable substances. Freeze-dried instant coffee is prepared by brewing coffee, quick-freezing it with liquid nitrogen before the thermal breakdown occurs, and evaporating the solid water under a high vacuum.

PART 3
Section 15.7 *continued*

≡ TEACH

Teaching Strategy

Boiling Point Elevation

Although many students drive to school, most do not understand the cooling system of an internal combustion engine. Hand out a diagram illustrating a cross section of such an engine. Identify the water jackets and explain the function of the water pump, radiator, and thermostat.

Teaching Strategy

Freezing Point Depression

At home, have students try to freeze tap water, a saturated table salt solution, and a saturated sugar solution in the freezer. They should use small plastic containers (not glass) for this experiment. The center of a freezer compartment should be about 0°F or −18°C. Have students report their data to the class.

**Videodisc Connections**

39695 to 40631, side 2
Antifreeze (movie)

Science Background

Boiling Point Elevation and Freezing Point Depression

Boiling point elevation and freezing point depression can be explained in terms of equilibrium. At the normal boiling point of a pure liquid, the rate of vaporization equals the rate of condensation, and boiling occurs. However, when a non-volatile solute is dissolved in the liquid, the solute molecules reduce the access of solvent molecules to the surface of the liquid, where those with sufficient kinetic energy can escape to the vapor phase. This lowers the rate of vaporization, while the rate of condensation remains equal to that of the pure solvent. For the solution to begin boiling, the temperature must be increased to raise the average kinetic energy of the solvent and thereby increase the rate of vaporization. When the rate of vaporization equals the rate of condensation, the solution begins to boil. Similar considerations hold for the lowering of the freezing point of a solution. At the normal freezing point of the pure solvent, the rate of melting is unaffected by the presence of dissolved solute in the liquid phase, but the rate at which solvent molecules solidify is lower because not every molecule in the solution can take a place in the crystal lattice. The kinetic energy of the molecules must be reduced by lowering the temperature until the rate of melting becomes equal to the rate of fusion.

DO YOU KNOW?

Some insects can make their own antifreeze. They may accumulate glycerol in their bodies during the fall. Then, during the winter months their cells are not destroyed by freezing temperatures. A particular moth's eggs can be cooled to −45°C before its cells freeze.

One formula unit of NaCl produces two particles—that is, two ions. When one formula unit of sucrose dissolves in water, it can produce only one particle, a hydrated sucrose molecule. Therefore, theoretically, sodium chloride is twice as effective as sucrose in raising the boiling temperature and reducing the freezing temperature. Sodium chloride is sometimes called an **electrolyte** because when dissolved in water, it can carry an electric current. The hydrated sodium and chloride ions are mobile enough to carry the current.

Further inspection of Table 15-3 reveals that calcium chloride, $CaCl_2$, another electrolyte, has the greatest effect on changing the freezing or boiling points of solutions. Calcium chloride produces three ions when it dissociates in water.

$$CaCl_2(s) \rightarrow Ca^{2+}(aq) + 2Cl^-(aq)$$

You would expect it to be three times as effective as sucrose in changing boiling and freezing temperatures. And it is—theoretically. Actually, in solution some units do not dissociate into ions. This means that the change in freezing temperatures for dilute solutions of electrolytic solutes are somewhat less than if they were completely dissociated. You need not be concerned with the mechanics or the mathematics of this effect here. Yet it is generally true that electrolytes are more effective than molecular solutes in changing the boiling and freezing temperatures of solutions.

The discussion so far seems to be pointing to the general principle that: ***the number of solute particles, not their size or whether they are molecules or ions, determines to a large extent how the solute will affect the boiling and freezing points of water.***

Boiling point elevation and freezing point depression are two characteristics of solutions called **colligative properties** because they do not depend on the size or type of particles present as a solute, but only upon the concentration of the particles.

Concept ✓ Check

Spreading salt on icy roads is a practical application of freezing point depression. Would $CaCl_2$ be more effective than NaCl? Why?

15.8 Molality

You have learned that colligative properties are directly dependent on the concentration of the solute in a solution. Throughout this course, you have been using molarity—that is, moles of solute per liter of solution, as the means of measuring concentration. However, for predicting temperature changes in the initial boiling points and freezing points of solutions, another method of measuring concentration is used. **Molality** is the number of moles of solute per kilogram of solvent. Molality should be used in calculating boiling and freezing point changes. The following example gives you an illustration of molality, abbreviated by the lowercase letter, *m*.

EXAMPLE 15-2

How would you prepare a 0.50m solution of sucrose, $C_{12}H_{22}O_{11}$, using 500.0 grams of water?

■ **Analyze the Problem** In this problem you are asked for a procedure. You are given the mass of water to use and need to know how much sucrose to measure out.

■ **Apply a Strategy** Find the number of grams of sucrose to measure by first finding the number of moles of sucrose needed to make a 0.50m solution.

■ **Work a Solution** By definition, 0.50m can be expressed as follows.

$$\frac{0.50 \text{ moles sucrose}}{1 \text{ kg water}}$$

Change 500.0 g of water to kg.

$$500.0 \text{ g} \times \frac{1 \text{ kg}}{1000 \text{ g}} = 0.5000 \text{ kg}$$

When 0.500 kg is multiplied by the molality, the number of moles of sucrose is the result.

$$0.5000 \text{ kg} \times \frac{0.50 \text{ moles sucrose}}{1 \text{ kg water}} = 0.25 \text{ mol sucrose}$$

Converting moles to grams using the molar mass of sucrose gives this.

$$0.25 \text{ mol sucrose} \times \frac{342.3 \text{ g sucrose}}{\text{mol sucrose}} = 86 \text{ g sucrose}$$

The solution is prepared by mixing 86 g of sucrose with 500.0 g of water.

■ **Verifying Your Answer** It should make sense to you that if you are preparing a solution with the same concentration but using half the amount of solvent (500.0 g vs. 1 kg), you should need less than 1 mole of solute.

Practice Problems

20. How many grams of glucose, $C_6H_{12}O_6$, are there in a 0.77m glucose solution made with 450. g of water?   **Ans.** 62.5 g

21. How many grams of NaCl would you need to prepare a 0.0050m saline solution (NaCl) using 2.0 kg of water?
    Ans. 0.58 g

22. How many grams of BaCl$_2$ would you need to prepare a 0.40m BaCl$_2$ solution using 100.0 g of water?
    Ans. add 8.3 g

PROBLEM·SOLVING STRATEGY

It may help to think of **similar problems** to solve new ones. The molarity problems of Chapter 4 are very similar to these problems. (See Strategy, page 65.)

PROBLEM·SOLVING STRATEGY

You can **simplify** the problem by **using what you know** about the definition of molality to think about the problem as a simple ratio. 0.50m means 1/2 mole of solute in 1 kg of water. (See Strategy, page 58.)

PROBLEM·SOLVING STRATEGY

Use the **factor-label method** to help you set up the ratios necessary to solve this problem. (See Strategy, page 12.)

PART **3**
Section 15.8 continued

Practice Problems

Assign the Practice Problems.

Science Background

Calculations Involving Colligative Properties

The boiling point elevation and freezing point depression of NaCl is not necessarily two times greater than that expected for a molecular solute. Sodium chloride and other ionic substances behave as if they do not completely dissociate into ions in solution. For instance, you may find three species of solute particles in a sodium chloride aqueous solution: Na^+, Cl^-, and NaCl. The ions may be present to only 90 percent. In other words, sodium chloride in this instance is only 90 percent dissociated. The van't Hoff factor (i) may be incorporated into the formula for the freezing point of an electrolyte as follows:

$$\Delta T_f = k_f \times m \times i$$

where i is a number less than 2 but greater than 1 for sodium chloride. The greater the concentration of the electrolytic solution, the smaller the value of i.

DO YOU KNOW?

Over 97 percent of the Earth's water is sea water. About 2 percent is fresh water in the polar ice caps. That leaves only 1 percent that is usable for drinking water—in groundwater, rivers, lakes, glaciers, and in the atmosphere.

15.9 Calculations Involving Colligative Properties

Now you can apply your knowledge of molality to solve problems that ask you to find the boiling point elevation or freezing point depression of a solution.

As you read in Section 15-7, the change in boiling or freezing temperature is related to the concentration of solute. The equation that relates these concepts to the difference in boiling temperatures between a solution and the pure solvent is

$$\Delta T_b = k_b \times m$$

In the equation ΔT_b is the *change* (increase) in the boiling point of the pure solvent and the temperature at which the solution begins to boil; k_b is the constant that relates ΔT to the molality of the solute, m. Most of the solutions you work with are water solutions. The value of k_b for water is

$$k_b = 0.51 \frac{°C \times kg\ H_2O}{mol_{solute}}$$

The equation that relates the difference in the freezing point of a pure solvent and the initial freezing point of the solvent in a solution is much like the previous equation.

$$\Delta T_f = k_f \times m$$

Here ΔT_f represents the difference between the freezing point of the pure solvent and the temperature at which the solution begins to freeze; k_f is the constant that relates ΔT to the molality of the solute, m. The value of k_f for water is

$$k_f = 1.86 \frac{°C \times kg\ H_2O}{mol_{solute}}$$

Example 15-3 shows you how these equations can be applied to a typical problem that you might encounter in chemistry.

EXAMPLE 15-3

At what temperature will a solution that is composed of 0.73 moles of glucose in 650. mL of water begin to boil?

■ **Analyze the Problem** This problem first asks you to find ΔT_b, the difference between the boiling point of pure water, 100°C, and the temperature at which the solution begins to boil.

■ **Apply a Strategy** Write the equation for calculating the change in boiling temperature.

$$\Delta T_b = k_b \times m$$

You have been given the value of k_b in this section of the chapter. Calculate the molality, m, from the information given in the problem. Recognize that before you can find the molality of the solution, you must convert 650 mL of water to kg of water. If you remember that the density of water is 1.00 g/mL, then the number of kg of water can be calculated.

■ **Work a Solution** Calculate the mass of the water.

$$? \text{ kg} = 650.0 \text{ mL} \times \frac{1.00 \text{ g}}{1.00 \text{ mL}} \times \frac{1.00 \text{ kg}}{1000 \text{ g}} = 0.650 \text{ kg H}_2\text{O}$$

Find the value of m.

$$\text{molality} = \frac{\text{mol}_{\text{solute}}}{\text{kg}_{\text{solvent}}} = \frac{0.73 \text{ mol glucose}}{0.650 \text{ kg H}_2\text{O}} = 1.1m$$

Now you can substitute the known values in the equation to find ΔT_b.

$$\Delta T_b = 0.51 \frac{°C \times \text{kg H}_2\text{O}}{\text{mol glucose}} \times \frac{1.1 \text{ mol glucose}}{\text{kg H}_2\text{O}} = 0.57°C$$

Since the increase in boiling temperature is 0.57°C and the boiling point of pure water is 100.00°C, the temperature at which the solution will begin to boil is 100.57°C. According to the rules governing significant digits, the result is 100.6°C.

■ **Verifying Your Answer** Solutes cause an elevation in boiling temperature, so you would expect the answer to be above 100°C. Check your calculations to be sure you have not introduced any errors.

◀ **PROBLEM-SOLVING STRATEGY**

Recall information that you know. The relationship between milliliters of water and grams of water is 1 to 1. (See Strategy, page 58.)

Practice Problems
Assign the Practice Problems.

Practice Problems

23. At what temperature will a sucrose solution boil if it contains 1.55 moles of sucrose in 600.0 mL of water?

Ans. 101.3°C.

24. At what temperature will a solution of ethylene glycol (the major ingredient in automotive antifreeze) freeze if it contains 120 g of ethylene glycol in 500.0 mL of water? (The molar mass of ethylene glycol is 62.1 g/mol.)

Ans. −7.1°C

You may be asked to solve problems involving solutes that are ionic substances. The procedure for these problems is similar to those in Examples 15-2 and 15-3. However, you must remember that an ionic substance that is dissociated lowers the freezing point or elevates the boiling point of water more than a molecular substance of the same concentration. Because ionic compounds dissociate into ions, it is the total concentration of these ions that must be taken into account, rather than the original concentration of the undissociated ionic compounds.

Practice Problems

Assign the Practice Problems.

EXAMPLE 15-4

What is the lowest freezing temperature for a saltwater solution? The solubility of sodium chloride is 280 g per 1000 g of water at 0°C.

■ *Analyze the Problem* The problem is asking for a temperature change from the freezing point of pure water to the temperature at which a saltwater solution freezes. The more salt that is added to the solution, the lower the freezing temperature of the solution. The maximum amount of salt that could be added to 1000 g of water at 0°C is 280 g.

■ *Apply a Strategy* You can calculate the molality of the solution from the solubility data given in the problem. *The effective molality will be two times the calculated molality because NaCl produces two ions, Na^+ and Cl^-.* Then you can use the equation given in the previous section to solve the problem.

■ *Work a Solution* The calculated molality is

$$280 \text{ g NaCl} \times \frac{1 \text{ mol NaCl}}{58.5 \text{ g NaCl}} \times \frac{1}{1 \text{ kg water}} = 4.8 \text{ } m$$

The effective molality is twice the calculated molality:

$$4.8m \times 2 = 9.6m$$

The ion concentration is $9.6m$.
The equation for finding freezing temperatures of solutions is

$$\Delta T_f = k_f \times m$$

Substituting the values for this problem, you get the following.

$$\Delta T_f = 1.86 \frac{°C \times kg_{solvent}}{mol_{solute}} \times 9.6 \text{ } m = 18°C$$

The temperature is depressed 18° below the freezing point of water, which is 0°C. Therefore, the freezing temperature is −18°C.

■ *Verify Your Answer* Since 280 g is about 4.5 moles of salt, and salt has twice the effect on the freezing temperature, then 9 moles of ions times the constant, 1.86, yields about an 18 degree difference in temperature. An estimate such as this is a good check on the reasonableness of your answer.

Practice Problems

25. At what temperature will a sodium chloride solution boil if 120 g of salt is dissolved in 1000 g of water?   ***Ans.*** 102.1°C

26. At what temperature will a solution begin to freeze if 200.0 g of calcium chloride, $CaCl_2$, is dissolved in 850.0 mL of water?   ***Ans.*** −11.8°C

PROBLEM-SOLVING

S T R A T E G Y

Break the problem into manageable parts. *By sorting out the problem into the several concepts it contains, you can identify the steps needed to solve the problem. (See Strategy, page 166.)*

Constants for solvents other than water Chemists use a wide variety of solute/solvent combinations, depending on the specific application. For example, the molar mass of some organic substances can be found by using camphor as a solvent. The boiling and freezing constants for many solvents have been determined experimentally. Table 15-4 lists the boiling point and freezing point constants as well as the boiling and freezing points of some important solvents. Chemists are particularly interested in solvents that have large values for K_b and K_f, since these produce larger changes in boiling and freezing temperature and improve the accuracy of measurement.

TABLE 15-4

Properties of Some Solvents				
Substance	Boiling Point °C	k_b $\dfrac{°C \times kg_{solvent}}{mol_{solute}}$	Freezing Point °C	k_f $\dfrac{°C \times kg_{solvent}}{mol_{solute}}$
benzene C_6H_6	80.1	2.53	5.50	5.12
camphor $C_{10}H_{16}O$	208.0	5.95	179.8	40.0
carbon disulfide CS_2	46.2	2.34	−111.5	3.83
acetic acid	80.1	3.07	16.6	3.9
ethyl ether	34.5	2.02	−116.2	1.79
ethanol	78.5	1.22	−114.1	
acetone	56.5	1.71	−94.0	

The data in this table will be helpful in solving some of the problems at the end of Part 3 and in the Chapter Review.

15.10 Calculating Molar Mass

One of the practical applications of colligative properties is that the molar mass of the solute can be calculated from freezing point determinations. The molar masses of vitamin C and nicotine, for example, can be determined from the temperatures at which water solutions of these substances begin to freeze. This technique is especially helpful when identifying an unknown compound or determining the formula of a newly isolated compound. The molar masses of many organic substances that are not soluble in water, like fat-soluble vitamins and other natural products, can be found by dissolving known amounts in a nonpolar solvent, such as camphor. The temperature at which the solution begins to freeze is noted. Then the molar mass of the solute is determined from the rearrangement of the freezing point equation that you studied earlier in this section.

DO YOU KNOW?

Condensed milk cannot be made simply by heating milk to evaporate some of the water. Milk scorches at high temperatures. Instead, the water is evaporated by reducing the pressure over the milk. This technique saves energy and avoids the breakdown of the complex chemicals in milk.

Guided Practice

Review the Concept Check question on page 516 with students. Answers can be found in Appendix E on page 808.

Reteaching Idea

To help students perform problems dealing with colligative properties, provide time for extra practice using whatever format works best—discussion at the chalkboard, working in pairs or small groups, or individual work. The following problems are variations of Examples 15–3, 15–4, and 15–5.

At what temperature will a solution begin to boil if it is composed of 3.00 g of carbon tetrachloride, CCl_4, in 130 g of benzene? (80.5°C)

What is the temperature at which a solution containing 1.50 g of potassium nitrate, KNO_3, in 35.0 mL of water begins to freeze? (−0.4°C)

A solution consisting of 6.25 g of an unknown hydrocarbon dissolved in 100 g of benzene was found to begin freezing at 3.42°C. What is the molar mass of the hydrocarbon? (154 g/mol)

> **PROBLEM-SOLVING**
> **STRATEGY**
>
> *Break this problem into* **manageable parts** *to help you find the answer. (See Strategy, page 166.)*

> **PROBLEM-SOLVING**
> **STRATEGY**
>
> *Use the* **factor label** *method to help you solve this part of the problem. (See Strategy, page 12.)*

EXAMPLE 15-5

When 36.0 g of a nonvolatile, molecular substance is dissolved in 100. g of water, the solution begins to freeze at −3.72°C. What is the molar mass of solute?

■ *Analyze the Problem* The molar mass of a substance is usually expressed as grams per mole. Mass is given in the problem. The moles of solute need to be determined from other data in the problem.

■ *Apply a Strategy* From previous problems in this chapter, you know that molality is expressed as moles of solute per kilogram of solvent. You also know that the relationship between freezing point depression and molality is

$$\Delta T_f = k_f m$$

You can then take the problem step-by-step to solve for moles of solute.

■ *Work a Solution* Solve the formula that determines freezing point depression for molality.

$$m = \frac{\Delta T_f}{k_f}$$

Substitute for the values of ΔT_f and k_f.

$$m = \frac{3.72°C}{1.86°C \times kg/mol}$$

$$m = \frac{2.00 \text{ mol solute}}{kg \text{ solvent}}$$

Determine the moles of solute used in this problem.

$$\text{mol solute} = \frac{2.00 \text{ mol solute}}{kg \text{ water}} \times \frac{0.100 \text{ kg water}}{1}$$

mol solute = 0.200 mol solute

Since the molar mass of a substance is grams per mole, the molar mass of the unknown solute can be found by dividing the mass of the solute by the moles of solute.

$$\text{molar mass} = \frac{36.0 \text{ g}}{0.200 \text{ mol}}$$

molar mass = 180. g/mol

■ *Verifying Your Answer* The problem involves many steps. Therefore, you may not be able to estimate the answer easily. Check each step to make sure that your answer is reasonable. You may want to check your answer to see if the molar mass is greater than one. No molar mass can be less than one, since the lightest element, hydrogen, has a molar mass of one.

PART 3 REVIEW

ANSWERS

■ **Keyed to Objectives**

F 29. The colligative properties of solutions are boiling point elevation and freezing point depression. (Osmotic pressure and vapor pressure lowering are also colligative properties.)

F 30. The freezing point depression of the $MgCl_2$ solution will be greater than the freezing point depression of the KCl solution. There are more particles in a solution containing $MgCl_2$ than KCl, mole per mole.

F 31. A concentrated solution of ethylene glycol will significantly increase the boiling temperature and decrease the freezing temperature of the engine's coolant.

G 32. a. $\dfrac{\dfrac{0.60\,g}{153.8\,g/mol}}{\dfrac{420.0\,g}{1000\,g}} = 0.0093 m$

b. $\dfrac{\dfrac{0.45\,g}{63\,g/mol}}{\dfrac{905\,g}{1000\,g}} = 0.0079 m$

Practice Problems

27. When 27.3 g of a nonvolatile molecular substance is dissolved in 300. g of water, the solution begins to freeze at −0.49°C. What is the molar mass of solute?

Ans. 350 g/mol

28. In an experiment to determine the molar mass of an unknown substance that is not soluble in water, 10.0 g of the unknown were dissolved in 100. g of liquid carbon disulfide. The solution was placed in a fume hood and heated until boiling first occurred at 47.8°C. What is the molar mass of the unknown? *Ans.* 150 g/mol

The determination of the molar mass of a substance is only one of the valuable uses of colligative properties of substances. Compare the uses of sodium chloride or calcium chloride as solutes on icy roads and ethylene glycol, the solute and major ingredient in automobile antifreeze. Sodium or calcium chloride are more effective than ethylene glycol in reducing the freezing temperatures of ice. They are less expensive and actually aid tire friction, whereas ethylene glycol is slippery. On the other hand, even though a solution of sodium chloride would be more effective in expanding the liquid temperature range of water in the cooling system of an engine, it is corrosive and not a good lubricant.

PART 3 REVIEW

29. Identify the colligative properties of solutions.

30. Compare/contrast the effect of 1 mole of $MgCl_2$ with 1 mole of KCl on the freezing point of a water solution.

31. Explain the purpose of adding ethylene glycol to the cooling system of automobile engines.

32. Calculate the molality of the following solution components.
    a. 0.60 g of CCl_4 in 420.0 g of benzene   *Ans.* 0.0093 m
    b. 0.45 g of HNO_3 in 905 g of water   *Ans.* 0.0079 m
    c. 7.8 g of $MgCl_2$ in 5.24 kg of water   *Ans.* 0.016 m
    d. 52 g of C_2H_5OH in 160.0 g of water   *Ans.* 7.1 m

33. When 5.0 g of $CaCl_2$ is dissolved in 50. g of water, at what temperature will the solution begin to boil?

Ans. 101.5°C.

34. What is the temperature at which a solution composed of 15 g of paradichlorobenzene, $C_6H_4Cl_2$, dissolved in 100. g of camphor begins to freeze? Use Table 15-5 as a reference.

Ans. 139.0°C

35. Devise an experiment that would determine the molar mass of vitamin C from the freezing temperature of an aqueous solution of this substance.

PROBLEM-SOLVING
STRATEGY
Use what you know about converting units to help you solve this problem. (See Strategy, page 58.)

Boxed numbers indicate questions that involve skills in interpretation, application, and analysis.

Practice Problems

Assign the Practice Problems.

≡ CLOSE

Summing Up Main Ideas

Have students determine how much 100 g of NaCl will lower the freezing point of 1 kg of water. Then have them make the same determination for 100 g of sucrose ($C_{12}H_{22}O_{11}$). After students have completed these calculations, ask them to give two reasons for the difference between the two freezing points. 100 g of NaCl will lower the freezing point of 1 kg of water to −6.4°C. 100 g of sucrose will lower the freezing point to -0.54°C Two reasons for the difference between the two freezing points are the dissociation of NaCl and the higher molecular weight of $C_{12}H_{22}O_{11}$.

PART 3 REVIEW

Assign the Part Review questions.

Evaluating Skills

These skills are evaluated in the Part Review questions indicated. **Summarizing:** 29; **Comparing/Contrasting:** 30; **Determining cause and effect:** 31; **Calculating:** 32, 33, 34; **Analyzing data:** 32, 33, 34; **Applying a strategy:** 32, 33, 34; **Verifying results:** 32, 33, 34; **Designing and performing experiments:** 35

c. $\dfrac{\dfrac{7.8\ \cancel{g}}{95.2\ \cancel{g}/\text{mol}}}{\dfrac{5.24\ \text{kg}}{1\ \text{kg}}} = 0.016m$

d. $\dfrac{\dfrac{52\ \cancel{g}}{46\ \cancel{g}/\text{mol}}}{\dfrac{160.0\ \cancel{g}}{1000\ \cancel{g}}} = 7.1m$

G **33.** $\Delta T_b = k_b \times m \times 3$
$= (0.51 \times 0.9m) \times 3$
$= 1.5°C$
The boiling temperature is 101.5°C.

G **34.** $\Delta T_f = k_f \times m$
$= 40.0 \times 1.02m$
$= 40.8°C$
Since the freezing point of camphor is 179.8°C, the freezing temperature of the solution is 139.0°C.

F **35.** You would need to know the freezing point of pure water, the mass of vitamin C used, the mass of the water in which the solute was dissolved, and the freezing point constant for water. For the experiment you would need an environment that was below 0°C.

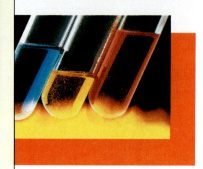

Process Skills

Observing
Forming Models
Analyzing data
Applying a strategy

Preparation

■ Materials

(for a class of 24, working in pairs)
Apparatus
petri dishes with covers (12), Scoopulas (24), disposable plastic gloves (24 pairs)
Reagents
■ 200 mL distilled or deionized water
■ 5 g copper(I) chloride
■ 5 g potassium iodide
■ 5 g magnesium hydroxide
■ 5 g sodium sulfate
■ 5 g calcium chloride

■ Preparation Hints

Crystals of the reagents will be used directly from the bottle. This experiment can be demonstrated on an overhead projector.

Laboratory
Investigation

Ionization—Observing an Ionic Reaction

A teaspoon of salt is added to a glass of water, and the crystals disappear. You hear about a factory river's mercury salts contaminating an entire fishing industry. Ironically, even though these are very common events, the actual process of how a solid dissolves remains one of the least understood processes in science. However, it is known that many dissolving crystals form ions that migrate and diffuse in a suitable liquid medium. These released ions can then recombine by attracting other oppositely charged ions to them. If the solubility of this newly formed compound is very low, the result is that a precipitate forms. It can be said that an ionic reaction has taken place.

In this investigation, you will observe reactions very closely and will be able to watch actual precipitates form.

Objectives

Observe the mechanics of a typical ionic reaction.

Determine what ions are formed and what new substances might be created.

Interpret an ionic reaction by drawing a series of pictures.

■ Materials

Apparatus	Reagents
□ petri dish with cover	□ copper(I) chloride crystals
□ 2 Scoopulas	□ potassium iodide crystals
□ distilled or deionized water	□ calcium chloride crystals
□ disposable plastic gloves	□ sodium sulfate crystals
	□ magnesium hydroxide

■ Procedure

1. Put on your safety goggles, laboratory apron, and gloves.

2. Open a petri dish and fill it with distilled water. Place it on a lab bench and allow the water to settle for a minute or two.

3. One lab partner should have a scoopula with one or two crystals of potassium iodide, and the other partner should have a scoopula with one or two crystals of copper(I) chloride. Carefully add the crystals to the water on opposite sides of the petri dish.

4. Make as many observations as possible for the next five minutes. In Box A, draw submicroscopic pictures of what you think happened. Using colors for the different ions present might be helpful.

5. Add distilled water to the second petri dish and allow it to stand for one or two min-utes. Now add one or two small calcium chloride crystals to the top of the dish (twelve o'clock position). As soon as possible, add crystals of magnesium hydroxide and sodium sulfate to the dish, equidistant from the calcium chloride (that is, at the four o'clock and eight o'clock positions). Observe and record observations for the next five minutes.

6. In Box B, draw what you think happened at the submicroscopic level.

7. Before you leave the laboratory, wash your hands thoroughly with soap and water.

SOLUTIONS **525**

Data Analysis

Potassium iodide and copper(I) chloride

Calcium chloride, magnesium hydroxide, and sodium sulfate

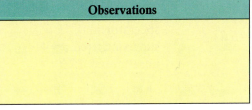

Box A

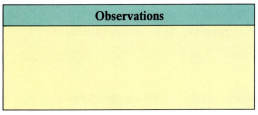

Box B

1. Write the chemical equation for the reaction of potassium iodide and copper(I) chloride.

2. Basing your findings on your observations and the drawing in Box B, write the equations for any one ionic chemical reaction that you observed.

Conclusions

1. Which possible chemical reactions did not happen? Why?

2. Define *ionization* and explain its role in the chemical reactions you observed.

Guiding the Investigation

■ Procedural Hints

The use of petri dishes is an excellent way to allow students to visualize the solid dissolving and the ions migrating to the interface where the reaction takes place.

Disposal

Save unused reagents for future use or wrap the solids separately in newspaper and put in the waste basket. Combine liquid and precipitated waste products and pour down the drain.

Data Analysis

■ Sample Data

(See Boxes A and B below.)

■ Analysis

1. $KI(s) + CuCl(s) \rightarrow CuI(s) + K^+(aq) + Cl^-(aq)$
2. $CaCl_2(s) + Mg(OH)_2(s) \rightarrow Ca(OH)_2(s) + Mg^{2+}(aq) + 2Cl^-(aq)$

Conclusions

1. $Mg(OH)_2$ and Na_2SO_4 do not react because they do not form precipitates.

2. Ionization is the formation of an ion from an ionic solid. When ionic compounds dissolve, the ions are free to migrate and to react with other ions they come in contact with.

Observations

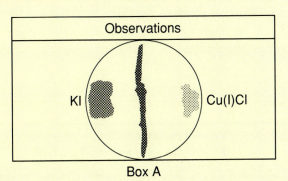

Box A

Observations

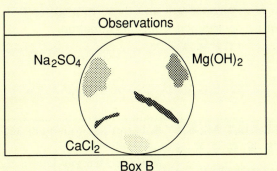

Box B

Chapter 15
Review
ANSWERS
begin on page
T529a.

Summary

The Nature of Solutions

- Solutions are homogeneous mixtures that contain a solute dissolved in a solvent. Solutions can be made up of one, two, or even three phases of matter, such as solids dissolved in liquids, liquids dissolved in liquids, and so forth. The concentrations of solutes may be measured as molarity or molality.

- Many ionic and molecular substances are soluble in water. Solubility depends on many factors, including the polar or nonpolar nature of the solutes and solvents, the temperature, bonding characteristics, and the pressure (for gases).

Ionic Equations and Precipitation Reactions

- Insoluble ionic products of a chemical reaction precipitate out of solution. An ionic equation can be written to describe this type of double displacement reaction. Spectator ions are not involved in the reaction, and are omitted from net ionic equations that contain only the ions that react.

Colligative Properties of Solutions

- Two properties of solutions that are called colligative properties are boiling point elevation and freezing point depression. The concentration of the solute and whether the particles are molecules or ions determine the extent to which the colligative properties of a solution will deviate from the properties of the pure solvent. Molality is the unit for determining the concentration of solute per kilogram of solvent when colligative properties are measured. The difference between the boiling or freezing temperatures of a pure solvent and those of a solution can be determined from this equation.

$$\Delta T = k \times m.$$

Chemically Speaking

boiling point elevation 15.7
colligative properties 15.7
dissociation 15.2
electrolyte 15.7
freezing point depression 15.7
heterogeneous mixtures 15.1
homogeneous mixtures 15.1
hydrated 15.2
immiscible 15.2

ionic equation 15.6
miscible 15.2
molality 15.8
net ionic equation 15.6
precipitate 15.5
saturated 15.3
solubility 15.3
solute 15.1
solution 15.1
solvation 15.2
solvent 15.1
spectator ions 15.6
supersaturated 15.4
unsaturated 15.3

Concept Mapping

Using the concept mapping method described at the front of this book, complete a concept map for the term *solution* using words from this chapter and previous chapters as necessary.

Questions and Problems

THE NATURE OF SOLUTIONS

A. Objective: Distinguish *solutions from mixtures.*

1. How do heterogeneous mixtures differ from homogeneous mixtures?
2. Give an example of how water may be either a solvent or a solute.
3. Give an example of each of the following types of solution.

PROBLEM-SOLVING
► **S T R A T E G I E S**
Students apply these strategies in the following questions.

- **Factor-label method:** 36, 37, 38, 39, 40, 41
- **Using what you know:** 32, 33, 36, 37, 38, 39, 40, 41
- **Using patterns:** 9, 21, 22
- **Verifying your answer:** 36, 37, 38, 39, 40, 41

T526

a. a gaseous solute in a liquid solvent
b. a solid solute in a solid solvent
c. a liquid solute in a liquid solvent

4. Make a submicroscopic drawing for each of the following mixtures that were stirred vigorously and then allowed to stand for an hour:
   a. fifteen molecules of oil and fifteen molecules of water
   b. fifteen molecules of methyl alcohol and fifteen molecules of water.

B. Objective: **Describe** *the process of dissolving.*

5. Describe the process by which sodium chloride dissociates within an aqueous solution.

6. What particles are present when 5 g of each of the following substances is placed in 200 mL of water and then stirred?
   a. NaCl(s)
   b. ethanol, C_2H_5OH(l)
   c. a diamond(s)

7. Explain the statement that "Substances whose molecules can form hydrogen bonds are likely to be soluble in water."

8. If like dissolves like, why would it be incorrect to say that there are no nonpolar molecules in the water you drink?

9. Predict which of the following pairs of substances will form solutions when mixed:
   a. water and methanol
   b. methanol and carbon tetrachloride
   c. carbon tetrachloride and benzene
   d. ethanol and methanol
   e. ammonia and carbon tetrachloride

10. Will carbon tetrachloride solvate an ionic solid? Explain your answer.

11. How many layers would you encounter in a mixture containing oil, water, alcohol, and carbon tetrachloride? Explain your answer.

12. How are saturated solutions and unsaturated solutions alike? How do they differ?

13. What factors are equal when a saturated solution is in equilibrium?

14. Explain how a solution may be both dilute and saturated.

15. In what units may solubility be measured?

16. Growing pure crystals is an important industrial process. Describe two methods of growing crystals from aqueous solutions.

C. Objective: **Analyze** *the factors that affect solubility.*

17. How does temperature affect solubility?

18. How could you determine experimentally that a solution of LiBr is saturated?

19. NaCl is quite soluble in water but MgO is not. Explain the difference in solubility of these two compounds, based on the chemical properties of the compounds.

20. How will an increase in temperature affect the solubility of a gas dissolved in a liquid?

IONIC EQUATIONS AND PRECIPITATION REACTIONS

D. Objective: **Identify** *ionic substances that precipitate from aqueous solutions.*

21. Which of the following ionic compounds are soluble in water?
    a. cesium chloride
    b. lithium sulfate
    c. strontium carbonate
    d. potassium phosphate
    e. magnesium sulfide
    f. silver iodide

22. Some of the solutions listed below cannot be made because the solute is not very soluble. Use the solubility table in Appendix D to identify which solutions cannot be made.
    a. 0.1 *M* silver acetate
    b. 0.1 *M* nickel acetate
    c. 0.1 *M* nickel hydroxide
    d. 0.1 *M* nickel sulfide

23. Assume that each of the following compounds dissolves in water to form separate,

Boxed numbers indicate questions that involve skills in interpretation, application, and analysis.

- Breaking problems into manageable parts: 28, 29, 37, 38, 39, 40
- Making diagrams: 44
- Writing chemical equations: 24

mobile ions in solution. Write the formulas and names of the ions that can be expected.

a. HI
b. Na_2CO_3
c. $Ba(OH)_2$
d. KNO_3
e. NH_4Cl
f. $Ca(C_2H_3O_2)_2$
g. $(NH_4)_3PO_4$
h. $(NH_4)_2SO_4$

24. A 1.0*M* solution of each of the following ionic compounds is prepared. Write the dissociation equation for each compound. What is the concentration of each kind of ion present in solution?

a. potassium fluoride
b. sodium carbonate
c. lead nitrate
d. iron(III) chloride
e. aluminum sulfate

E. Objective: **Write** *ionic equations and net ionic equations for precipitation reactions in aqueous solutions.*

25. What is a spectator ion?
26. What are the disadvantages of using net ionic equations?
27. What is the advantage of representing a reaction by a net ionic equation?
28. Write net ionic equations for the following reactions. Use the solubility table in Appendix D to help determine solubilities:

a. $AgNO_3(aq) + KBr(aq) \rightarrow$
b. $FeCl_3(aq) + NaOH(aq) \rightarrow$
c. $K_2SO_4(aq) + BaCl_2(aq) \rightarrow$
d. $Mg(NO_3)_2(aq) + KOH(aq) \rightarrow$
e. $CaCl_2(aq) + K_2CO_3(aq) \rightarrow$

29. Write an ionic equation and a net ionic equation for the reaction produced when 0.2*M* solutions of each pair of ionic substances are mixed.

a. silver nitrate and lithium bromide
b. iron(III) chloride and sodium carbonate
c. ammonium sulfate and magnesium iodide
d. zinc acetate and potassium hydroxide
e. sodium sulfide and chromium(III) nitrate
f. aluminum sulfate and strontium sulfide

COLLIGATIVE PROPERTIES OF SOLUTIONS

F. Objective: **Relate** *changes in boiling and freezing temperature to the concentration of solute in a solution.*

30. What effects will the addition of a solute have on the boiling and freezing points of a solution?
31. Would ocean water in which ice has been formed and then removed be a better source of salt than untreated ocean water? Explain.
32. At the onset of arctic winter, large regions of the sea's surface freeze. Explain what happens to the freezing point of the ocean water found beneath the ice masses as winter progresses.
33. The temperature at which a pure liquid boils remains constant until all the liquid has changed to a gas. If a solution is heated to boiling, however, the temperature required to maintain the boiling state steadily increases. Explain why this is so.
34. Would spreading crystals of barium chloride on a layer of snow affect the melting process? Explain your answer.
35. In the process of fermentation, yeast can produce a solution that is about 15% alcohol (30 proof). At higher concentrations of alcohol, the yeast cannot survive. How, then, are the more concentrated alcoholic beverages obtained? Explain your answer.

G. Objective: **Calculate** *changes in boiling and freezing temperatures of solutions.*

36. Calculate the molality of the following solutions.

a. 0.050 g CO_2 in 652 g of water (H_2O)
b. 56 g NH_3 in 200 g of water (H_2O)
c. 3.21 g C_6H_{12} in 231 g of benzene (C_6H_6)
d. 320. g CCl_4 in 3.5 kg of benzene (C_6H_6)
e. 157 g H_2O in 1.25 kg of ethanol (C_2H_5OH)
f. 50.5 g C_7H_{18} in 742 g of hexane (C_6H_{14})

37. What mass of solute is needed to dissolve in the given amount of solvent to obtain the indicated solution molality?
    a. $FeCl_3$ to 1000. g H_2O for a 0.238m solution
    b. Br_2 to 500. g CCl_4 for a 0.356m solution
    c. C_6H_6 to 100. g C_7H_{18} for a 0.550m solution
    d. CCl_4 to 30.0 g C_6H_6 for a 2.25m solution
    e. C_2H_5OH to 750. g H_2O for a 1.50m solution

38. Determine the freezing point depression of the following aqueous solutions. Each solute is dissolved in 200. g of water.
    a. 50. g sucrose, $C_{12}H_{22}O_{11}$
    b. 100. g glycerol, $C_3H_8O_3$
    c. 24 g urea, CH_4N_2O
    d. 35 g sodium chloride, NaCl
    e. 18 g ammonium phosphate, $(NH_4)_3PO_4$

39. At what temperature will a solution composed of 6.0 g of naphthalene, $C_{10}H_8$, in 35 g of benzene begin to boil?

40. When 2.55 g of a substance is dissolved in 150. g of water, the solution freezes at $-0.42°C$. What is the molar mass of the substance?

41. Find the molar mass of an unknown nonvolatile molecular solute if the solution begins to freeze at $-0.186°C$. The solution was prepared by dissolving 1.80 g of the unknown in 1000. g of water.

Critical Thinking

SYNTHESIS WITHIN THE CHAPTER

42. Why is it necessary to have a concentration standard other than molarity?

SYNTHESIS ACROSS CHAPTERS

43. How might a compound's molecular geometry relate to its solubility in water?

44. Antifreeze/antiboil automotive products prevent the engine coolant from boiling by raising the temperature at which the solution will boil. The following table is taken from the instructions on the back of an antifreeze container.

Percent Concentration	Boiling Temperature
40%	125.5°C
50%	128.3°C
55%	130.0°C

Graph the data. Can the temperature versus percent concentration be made into a direct proportion? Explain your answer.

45. From your knowledge of the size of ions and their charges, determine for each of the following pairs which ionic compound is more soluble in water:
    a. KCl or PbO
    b. NaCl or KCl
    c. LiBr or LiF

Projects

46. Design an experiment to separate the components of a glucose-water solution.

47. Grow some crystals. Try growing crystals of sugar, copper(II) sulfate, and potassium alum $[KAl(SO_4)_2 \cdot 12H_2O]$ in different containers.

Research and Writing

48. Find out how soaps and detergents clean. In an essay, summarize the information you learn.

49. Prepare a report on the different methods of desalinating sea water.

50. Prepare a report on the chemistry behind the cooling system of an automobile engine.

☐ Boxed numbers indicate questions that involve skills in interpretation, application, and analysis.

1. Heterogeneous materials are characterized by an observable segregation of component substances. Homogeneous materials remain uniformly mixed.

2. In a 5% alcohol solution, water is the solvent. In a 70% alcohol solution, water is the solute.

3. **a.** soda pop
   b. brass
   c. vinegar; acetic acid in water

4. **a.**

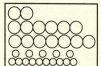

oil

water

   b.

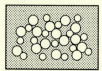

○ methyl alcohol
○ water

5. The positive and negative ions attract the oppositely charged ends of the water molecules. As the ions become isolated, the reduced effects of the interionic forces allow them to diffuse into the solvent.

6. **a.** Na^+, Cl^- and H_2O
   b. CH_3CH_2OH and H_2O
   c. the diamond and H_2O

7. Since water is capable of hydrogen bonding, other molecules that also are capable of hydrogen bonding will be soluble in water.

8. Water is the "universal solvent." Trace amounts of molecules that are considered not soluble in water are found in drinking water.

9. **a.** miscible
   b. immiscible
   c. miscible
   d. miscible
   e. immiscible

10. No; The nonpolar carbon tetrachloride does not demonstrate a significant attraction for ionic solids to cause solvation.

11. Two layers—water/alcohol layer; oil/carbon tetrachloride layer

12. Both saturated and unsaturated solutions are solutions containing solute particles in a solvent. An unsaturated solution, however, can support additional solute. A saturated solution contains the maximum amount of solute at a given temperature.

13. In a saturated solution when undissolved solute is present, the rate the solute particles are becoming solvated is equal to the rate the solute particles are returning to the solid solute.

14. Saturation means that the solution contains the maximum amount of solute it can hold at a given temperature. If that maximum amount is relatively small, the solution is dilute.

15. In parts per million or billion; in grams per 100 grams of water; in molarity; in molality

16. Heat a solution and let it cool so that it becomes supersaturated. Crystals will fall out of solution when a seed crystal is added. Another method is to let a solution evaporate with a seed crystal suspended inside the solution.

17. In general, the amount and rate of dissolving will go up as the temperature increases. However, the solubility of gases decreases as temperature increases.

18. If you added more LiBr, stirred the solution for a long time and some LiBr fell to the bottom of the container, then the solution is saturated.

19. Since magnesium and oxide ions are relatively small ions and have a multiple charge (2+ and 2− respectively) you can assume that they are bonded rather strongly in a solid lattice structure. It would take much energy to separate the ionic bonds. On the other hand, sodium and chloride are both singly charged ions and water can easily hydrate these ions.

20. As the temperature rises, the solubility of gas decreases.

21. **a.** soluble
    b. soluble
    c. insoluble
    d. soluble
    e. insoluble
    f. insoluble

22. Only "b" is soluble.

23. **a.** H^+—hydrogen ion; I^-—iodide ion
    b. Na^+—sodium ion; CO_3^{2-}—carbonate ion
    c. Ba^{2+}—barium ion; OH^-—hydroxide ion

   d. K^+—potassium ion; NO_3^-—nitrate ion
   e. NH_4^+—ammonium ion; Cl^-—chloride ion
   f. Ca^{2+}—calcium ion; $C_2H_3O_2^-$—acetate ion
   g. NH_4^+—ammonium ion; PO_4^{3-}—phosphate ion
   h. NH_4^+—ammonium ion; SO_4^{2-}—sulfate ion

24. **a.** $KF(s) \rightarrow K^+(aq) + F^-(aq)$
    $1M$—each ion.
    b. $Na_2CO_3(s) \rightarrow$
    $2Na^+(aq) + CO_3^{2-}(aq)$
    $2M$ sodium ions and $1M$ carbonate ions
    c. $Pb(NO_3)_2(s) \rightarrow$
    $Pb^{2+}(aq) + 2NO_3^-(aq)$
    $1M$ lead ions and $2M$ nitrate ions
    d. $FeCl_3(s) \rightarrow Fe^{3+}(aq) + 3Cl^-(aq)$
    $1M$ iron(III) ions and $3M$ chloride ions
    e. $Al_2(SO_4)_3(s) \rightarrow$
    $2Al^{3+}(aq) + 3SO_4^{2-}(aq)$
    $2M$ aluminum ions and $3M$ sulfate ions

25. A spectator ion is an ion that remains unchanged during a reaction.

26. Additional information about the reaction may be needed. Additional reactions not indicated by the net ionic equation may occur.

27. A net ionic equation is a quick and easy way to represent the ions involved in a precipitation reaction.

28. **a.** $Ag^+(aq) + Br^-(aq) \rightarrow AgBr(s)$
    b. $Fe^{3+}(aq) + 3OH^-(aq) \rightarrow$
    $Fe(OH)_3(s)$
    c. $SO_4^{2-}(aq) + Ba^{2+}(aq) \rightarrow BaSO_4(s)$
    d. $Mg^{2+}(aq) + 2OH^-(aq) \rightarrow$
    $Mg(OH)_2(s)$
    e. $Ca^{2+}(aq) + CO_3^{2-}(aq) \rightarrow$
    $CaCO_3(s)$

29. **a.** $Ag^+(aq) + NO_3^-(aq) \rightarrow$
    $Li^+(aq) + Br^-(aq) \rightarrow$
    $AgBr(s) + NO_3^-(aq) + Li^+(aq)$
    $Ag^+(aq) + Br^-(aq) \rightarrow AgBr(s)$
    b. $2Fe^{3+}(aq) + 6Cl^-(aq) + 6Na^+(aq)$
    $+ 3CO_3^{2-}(aq) \rightarrow Fe_2(CO_3)_3(s)$
    $+ 6Cl^-(aq) + 6Na^+(aq)$
    $2Fe^{3+}(aq) + 3CO_3^{2-}(aq) \rightarrow$
    $Fe_2(CO_3)_3(s)$
    c. NR
    d. $Zn^{2+}(aq) + 2CH_3COO^-(aq)$
    $+ 2K^+(aq) + 2OH^-(aq) \rightarrow$
    $Zn(OH)_2(s) + 2CH_3COO^-(aq)$
    $+ 2K^+(aq)$
    $Zn^{2+}(aq) + 2OH^-(aq) \rightarrow$
    $Zn(OH)_2(s)$
    e. $6Na^+(aq) + 3S^{2-}(aq) + 2Cr^{3+}(aq)$
    $+ 6NO_3^-(aq) \rightarrow Cr_2S_3(s)$
    $+ 6Na^+(aq) + 6NO_3^-(aq)$
    $2Cr^{3+}(aq) + 3S^{2-}(aq) \rightarrow Cr_2S_3(s)$

f. NR; SrS is insoluble.

30. A solute will elevate the boiling point and depress the freezing point of the solution.

31. Yes; Since salt would be restricted from sea ice, the solution left behind after the ice was removed would have a higher concentration of salt than untreated ocean water.

32. Since the ice that forms is almost pure water, the ocean water under the ice is more concentrated in salt than it was before. The freezing temperature of the water under the ice is therefore lower than it would be without the ice.

33. The boiling temperature of a solution constantly increases as the pure solvent boils away. The solute becomes more concentrated, thus increasing the boiling temperature of the remaining solution.

34. Yes. The barium chloride would melt the snow because the solution of barium chloride would have a lower freezing temperature than the ice. Of course, if the air temperature drops below the freezing temperature of the solution, the solution/ice mixture will freeze.

35. Distillation units (stills) can be used to obtain a more concentrated alcohol distillate.

36. a. $\dfrac{0.050\,g}{44\,g/mol} = 0.0011$ mol;

$\dfrac{0.0011\ mol}{0.652\ kg} = 0.0017 m$

b. $\dfrac{56\,g}{17\,g/mol} = 3.3$ mol;

$\dfrac{3.3\ mol}{0.200\ kg} = 16.5 m$

c. $\dfrac{3.21\,g}{84.2\,g/mol} = 0.0381$ mol;

$\dfrac{0.0381\ mol}{0.231\ kg} = 0.165 m$

d. $\dfrac{320\,g}{154\,g/mol} = 2.1$ mol;

$\dfrac{2.1\ mol}{3.5\ kg} = 0.60 m$

e. $\dfrac{157\,g}{18.0\,g/mol} = 8.72$ mol;

$\dfrac{8.72\ mol}{1.25\ kg} = 6.98 m$

f. $\dfrac{50.5\,g}{102\,g/mol} = 0.495$ mol;

$\dfrac{0.495\ mol}{0.742\ kg} = 0.667 m$

37. a. $1.000\ \text{kg H}_2\text{O} \times \dfrac{0.238\ \text{mol FeBr}_3}{1\ \text{kg H}_2\text{O}}$

$\times \dfrac{162\ \text{g FeBr}_3}{1\ \text{mol FeBr}_3} = 38.6\ \text{g FeBr}_3$

b. $0.500\ \text{kg CCl}_4 \times \dfrac{0.356\ \text{mol Br}_2}{1\ \text{kg CCl}_4}$

$\times \dfrac{160\ \text{g Br}_2}{1\ \text{mol Br}_2} = 28.5\ \text{g Br}_2$

c. $0.100\ \text{kg C}_7\text{H}_{18} \times \dfrac{0.550\ \text{mol C}_6\text{H}_6}{1\ \text{kg C}_7\text{H}_{18}}$

$\times \dfrac{78.1\ \text{g C}_6\text{H}_6}{1\ \text{mol C}_6\text{H}_6} = 4.30\ \text{g C}_6\text{H}_6$

d. $0.0300\ \text{kg C}_6\text{H}_6 \times \dfrac{2.25\ \text{mol CCl}_4}{1\ \text{kg C}_6\text{H}_6}$

$\times \dfrac{154\ \text{g CCl}_4}{1\ \text{mol CCl}_4} = 10.4\ \text{g CCl}_4$

e. $0.750\ \text{kg H}_2\text{O} \times \dfrac{1.50\ \text{mol C}_2\text{H}_5\text{OH}}{1\ \text{kg H}_2\text{O}}$

$\times \dfrac{46.1\ \text{g C}_2\text{H}_5\text{OH}}{1\ \text{mol C}_2\text{H}_5\text{OH}} = 51.9\ \text{g C}_2\text{H}_5\text{OH}$

38. $\Delta T_f = k_f \times m$

a. moles $= \dfrac{50\,g}{342\,g} = 0.15$ mol

$= \dfrac{1.86°C}{1\,m} \times \dfrac{0.15\ mol}{0.200\ kg} = 1.4°C$

b. moles $= \dfrac{100\,g}{92.1\,g} = 1.09$ mol

$= \dfrac{1.86°C}{1\,m} \times \dfrac{1.09\ mol}{0.200\ kg} = 10.1°C$

c. moles $= \dfrac{24\,g}{60\,g} = 0.40$ mol

$= \dfrac{1.86°C}{1\,m} \times \dfrac{0.40\ mol}{0.200\ kg} = 3.7°C$

d. moles $= \dfrac{35\,g}{58.5\,g} = 0.60$ mol

$= \dfrac{1.86°C}{1\,m} \times \dfrac{0.60\ mol}{0.200\ kg} \times 2 = 11.2°C$

e. moles $= \dfrac{18\,g}{149\,g} = 0.12$ mol

$= \dfrac{1.86°C}{1\,m} \times \dfrac{0.12\ mol}{0.200\ kg} \times 4 = 4.5°C$

39. moles $= \dfrac{6.0\,g}{128\,g} = 0.047$ mol

$\Delta T_b = k_b \times m$

$= \dfrac{2.53°C}{1\,m} \times \dfrac{0.047\ mol}{0.035\ kg} = 3.4°C$

Since the boiling point of pure benzene is 80.1°C, the solution will boil at 83.5°C.

40. Since ΔT is 0.42°C,

$m = \dfrac{0.42°C}{1.86°C/m} = 0.22 m$

$\text{mol} = \dfrac{0.22\ mol}{1\ kg} \times \dfrac{0.150\ kg}{1}$

$= 0.033$ mol

molar mass $= \dfrac{2.55\ g}{0.033\ mol} = 77\ g/mol$

41. Since ΔT is 0.186°C,

$m = \dfrac{0.186°C}{1.86°C/m} = 0.10 m$

$\text{mol} = \dfrac{0.10\ mol}{1\ kg} \times \dfrac{1.00\ kg}{1}$

$= 0.10$ mol

molar mass $= \dfrac{1.80\ g}{0.10\ mol} = 18\ g/mol$

42. Concentrations can be measured more conveniently or more accurately using other standards. Calculations with freezing point depressions and boiling point elevations work more accurately when molality is used instead of molarity.

43. Molecular geometry will determine the polarity of a particle. For example, although the C—Cl bond is polar, the CCl_4 molecule is nonpolar. A molecule's polarity or lack of it will determine solubility.

44.

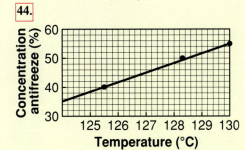

Although the boiling temperature does increase with concentration, it is not a direct proportion because the ratio of concentration/temperature is not a constant.

45. a. KCl
b. KCl
c. LiBr

CHEMICAL PERSPECTIVES

Critical Thinking Skills

These skills are applied in the feature.

■ Using library resources
■ Devising multiple solutions
■ Evaluating an opinion or point of view

*F*ocus

Activate Prior Knowledge

Have students bring the list of contents from boxes of laundry detergent. Draw attention to lists that include phosphates. Ask students if they know how phosphates contribute to water pollution. (Excess phosphates in water can cause algae to grow in large numbers. As the algae die, the decomposers that break them down use up most of the dissolved oxygen in the water. This can cause fish and other organisms to die, leading to more pollution.) Laundry detergent manufacturers are required to limit the phosphates in their products.

*T*each

Science Background

Pollutants can be divided into eight types: sewage, disease-causing agents (bacteria and parasites), inorganic chemicals and minerals, organic chemicals, plant nutrients, sediments, radioactive substances, and heat. Some of the inorganic chemicals are acids, salts, lead, mercury, cadmium, and chromium. The organic chemicals include oil, pesticides, herbicides, and industrial solvents and chemicals.

Teaching Strategy

Ask students to generate a definition of water pollution. (Water pollution is the addition of any harmful material that degrades *(continued on page T531)*

Polluted Waters

"From the contaminated sediment of New Bedford Harbor to the closed beaches of Long Island, from the declining shellfish harvests of Chesapeake Bay to the rapidly disappearing wetlands of Louisiana, from the heavily polluted waters of San Francisco Bay to the Superfund sites in Puget Sound, the signs of damage and loss are pervasive." So says a Congressional subcommittee report of 1991.

Water pollution is a serious environmental problem. Water covers approximately 75 percent of Earth's surface. You may not realize that only 3 percent of water is fresh and less than 1 percent of water suitable for drinking! Frequently referred to as the universal solvent, water dissolves many compounds. While water can carry essential salts, minerals, and oxygen, it can also carry undesirable toxic substances over large distances. When scientists studied the poisoning of marine life in the Great Lakes, they found traces of about 400 chemicals, some originating from as far away as Latin America.

Chemicals resulting from industrial waste are one source of water pollution. Many factories on rivers and lakes have

 **Videodisc Connections**

830, side 6
Australia and surrounding seas:
IR imaging (1 frame)

Only 3 percent of water is fresh and less than 1 percent of water suitable for drinking!

been disposing of chemicals in nearby waters. Even after the water passes through a water treatment plant, some of the chemicals stay behind in the drinking water. In one city, for example, between 1951 and 1969, the death rate due to cancer was 32 percent higher than the national rate. The water supply was found to contain almost 200 different industrial chemicals.

Sewage is another contributor to water pollution. Disposing of untreated, or raw, sewage in nearby waterways can drastically affect the aquatic environment and the spread of disease. About 80 percent of the disease in the world today is caused by water polluted with human waste and sewage. Also 30 million people in the United States use drinking water that is contaminated with this kind of pollution.

Coastal areas all over the world have been polluted by oil spills. The less dense oil stays on top of the water, spreading thinly out over areas that can stretch for miles. This thin layer of oil deprives fish of their oxygen supply, contains oil-soluble contaminants that are toxic to plant and animal life, and coats the feathers of birds and the gills of fish. Massive cleanup efforts are required to remove oil from

Lake scenes like this one may be jeopardized. In order to have bodies of water as inviting as this one, pollutants must be reduced and efforts to clean-up polluted waterways must be endorsed.

beaches and water.

During the 1970's, the United States Congress passed several laws for the control of water pollution. The Safe Drinking Water Act was adopted in 1974. Despite this legislation, many Americans are still worried about their drinking water: More and more of it is not fit to drink. What is it going to take and how long will it be before water is clean and safe?

Discussing the Issues

1. What is the source of drinking water in your community? How is it treated? Who decides if the water is fit to drink? Discuss the lead content of your school's drinking water.
2. What are some alternatives to the federal regulation of water pollution? Do you think these measures would be more or less successful than federal regulation? Explain your answer.

Take Action

1. If there is a particular industry, or utility company, that discharges pollutants into your water supply, find out what regulations it must comply with.
2. Find out if your community has a toxic-waste collection day. If it does, volunteer to help with the next one. If it does not, discuss with community groups the possibility of starting one.

531

(continued from page T530)
the quality of a body of water so that it doesn't meet specified standards.)

Chemical Update
New EPA standards are expected to help reduce contamination by hazardous chemicals in the water supply of 3 million people and to prevent an estimated 75 cases of cancer per year. Newer standards may increase the water and sewage bills of municipal customers by 50 to 70 percent over a five-year period.

Close

Discussing the Issues
1. Answers will vary. Possible answers include lakes, rivers, streams, reservoirs, wells, springs, or aquifers. If students point out that their water comes from municipal water treatment facilities, ask them where the water comes from that feeds into it. For information on control of water standards and lead content, students could visit the library or the local water treatment plant.
2. One alternative to federal regulation of industries is self regulation. However, since pollution control measures are costly, industries may not be willing to make major changes in their waste disposal practices. As people become more knowledgeable about industrial pollution, they may be able to pressure industries to be more responsible for their actions.

Take Action
1. Ask students to gather information about water quality from their state's natural resources department, the local office of the Geological Survey, or the local EPA office.
2. Have students contact a local automotive service to find out how motor oil is discarded. Students could make educational posters or circulars concerning the proper way to discard motor oil.

Thermodynamics

Investigations	Demonstrations	Texas Essential Elements★
Laboratory Manual 16–1 S Laboratory Manual 16–2 IM	Energy, Heat, and Temperature, page T534 Storing Energy, page T536 Constant Temperature During a Change of State, page T539	**Content:** 2.3, 2.6 **Process:** 4.1, 4.3, 10.1
Laboratory Manual 16–3 I In-text Investigation, page T560	Exothermic and Endothermic, page T546	**Content:** 2.7, 10.3 **Process:** 4.3, 8.2, 10.1
		Content: 2.7, 10.3, 10.4
		Content: 2.7 **Process:** 1.1, 1.2, 1.3, 4.3, 5.1, 6.1, 6.2, 8.1
		Process: 4.2, 4.3, 7.1, 8.2, 10.1, 10.2

KEY:
M–*Microscale*   **S**–*Structured*
I–*Inquiry*   **IM**–*Inquiry Microscale*

★*See pages T8–T11 for complete listing of Texas Essential Elements.*

16 Thermodynamics

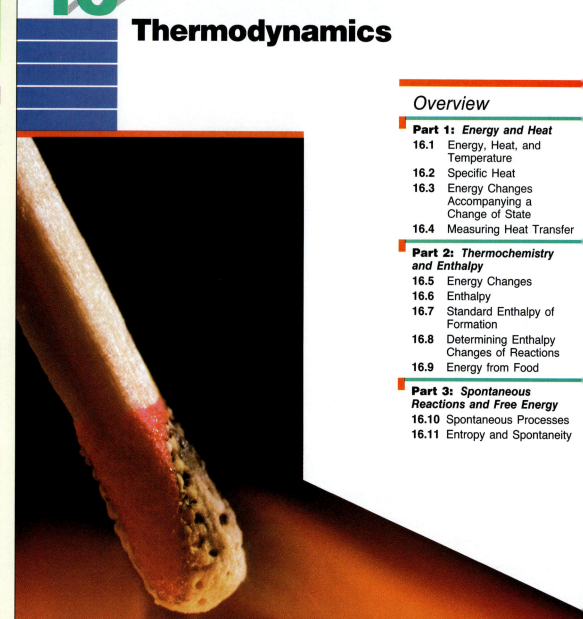

This exothermic reaction was initiated by heat generated by friction. Energy is released in the form of heat and light.

Chapter Rationale

Thermodynamics is a very precise area of chemistry with its own language and rigor. Chapter 16 aims to provide insights into thermodynamics without overwhelming students.

Parts 1 and 2 emphasize thermochemistry, focusing on heat changes as a result of chemical reactions and physical changes of state. Part 3 is a nonquantitative description of entropy and free energy, discussing factors involved in a reaction's spontaneity.

About the Photograph

Potential energy contained in the chemicals of the match tip and the match itself is transformed by a chemical reaction to heat and light.

Chapter Planning Hints

Plan to complete the chapter, including the Laboratory Investigation and Chapter Review, in four to eight class sessions. You may wish to contact the Environmental Protection Agency, Occupational Safety and Health Administration, and the Nuclear Regulatory Commission for materials to use when introducing Careers in Chemistry at the end of Part 1 of this chapter. You will find four optional demonstrations suggested for this chapter on pages T534, T536, T539, and T546. You may wish to preview them at this time.

Myths and Misconceptions

One of the most common misconceptions is the confusion between the terms *heat* and *temperature*, which students tend to use interchangeably. *Temperature* refers to the measure of the average kinetic energy of the particles in matter. The temperature of a substance is measured in degrees. *Hotness* and *coldness* are relative terms comparing the temperature of one object with another. *Heat* is the quantity of thermal energy transferred from one substance to another, as a result of differences in temperature. The energy transfer, or heat flow, describes what happens to all of the particles in a substance. If heat is gained by a system, the particles speed up, which increases the internal kinetic energy and therefore the temperature.

(continued on page T533)

PART
1 Energy and Heat

The term *energy* is used in many contexts. Did you ever tell your parents, "I just don't have the energy to clean my room"? What is the meaning of *energy* in chemistry?

In Chapter 3, you learned that energy can cause a change in matter. Another way to define *energy* is "the capacity to do work or to produce heat." If you wind the spring of a grandfather clock, you do work on the spring. In this way, the spring acquires energy, which in turn can do work by moving the hands of the clock. In this chapter, you will learn about the concepts of heat and energy and how they are related.

The total energy in a system is the sum of potential and kinetic energy. Consider again the example of a clock. A wound-up clock spring has potential energy. This potential energy is converted into kinetic energy as the hands of the clock move. The food you eat has chemical energy that is released when the food is digested. This energy can be converted into kinetic energy as you walk or run, into electric energy responsible for nerve impulses, and into thermal energy that warms your body.

Chemists are interested primarily in the energy change that accompanies a chemical reaction or a change of state. Understanding energy changes will help you determine which fuel to use for heating your home, economical ways to produce electricity, and the significance of a balanced diet.

16.1 Energy, Heat, and Temperature

Heat is energy that is transferred from one object to another because of a difference in their temperatures. Heat always flows from the warmer object to the colder object. The transfer of energy can be detected by measuring the resulting temperature change. Qualitatively, you may sense temperature as the hotness or coldness of an object. If you touch a hot pan, heat flows from the pan to your hand, and you perceive that the pan is at a higher temperature than your hand. Your hand gets hotter and the pan gets colder as a result of the energy transfer. A more precise definition of temperature is based on the kinetic molecular theory that you studied in Chapter 7. The **temperature** of an object is proportional to the average kinetic energy of its atoms or molecules. A model of the relationship between temperature and kinetic energy is shown in Figure 16-2 on the next page.

O b j e c t i v e s

Part 1

A. *Distinguish* between energy, heat, and temperature.

B. *Calculate* the quantity of heat absorbed or released when a substance changes temperature.

C. *Calculate* the quantity of heat absorbed or released during a phase change.

D. *Measure* the specific heat of a substance, using a calorimeter.

Developing Skills

Students may apply these skills in their study of Part 1.
Comparing/Contrasting: Have students compare and contrast energy, heat, and temperature.
Measuring: Have students describe how to use a calorimeter to measure the specific heat of a substance.
Calculating: From data that you supply, have students calculate the heat absorbed or released as a result of a physical change.

≡ **FOCUS**

Activate Prior Knowledge

Students may already understand that more energy is required to heat a substance as its mass increases.

 CAUTION: Wear safety goggles and lab aprons.

Set up two hot plates and place a 500-mL beaker on each one. Pour 50 mL of water into one and 250 mL into the other. Heat both beakers at the same setting on the hot plates. Compare the lengths of time necessary to bring the beakers of water to a boil.

≡ **TEACH**

Teaching Strategy

Energy, Heat, and Temperature

The SI unit of energy is the joule. The metric unit of the calorie, originally defined as the amount of energy needed to raise 1 g of water from 14.5°C to 15.5°C, is now defined as 1 cal = 4.184 J. This is an exact definition, just as 100 cm = 1 m and 1 foot = 12 inches are exact definitions.

Myths and Misconceptions

(continued from page T532)
The amount of heat in a system depends not only on the average kinetic energy of the particles in a substance, but also on the number of particles. To help students distinguish between these terms, have them compare the temperature and the amount of heat of: an ice cube and an iceberg, a drop of boiling water and a cup of boiling water, a match that has been lit and a log that is burning, a huge mass of molten lava erupting from a volcano and a tiny stream of lava a distance away. For example, a drop of boiling water and a cup of boiling water have the same temperature, but the amount of heat transferred from the cup is much greater than the amount transferred from the drop of water.

Figure 16-1 *Explain how the transfer of energy allows the measurement of body temperature.*

Heat and temperature As the temperature of a substance increases, the average velocity of its atoms or molecules increases. Thus the total heat energy of the substance must increase also. However, the total energy also depends on the number of atoms or molecules present. Recall from Chapter 1 that properties that depend on the amount of matter in an object are called extensive properties, while those that are independent of the amount of matter are called intensive properties. For example, mass is an extensive property, but density is an intensive property. Similarly, heat is an extensive property, while temperature is an intensive property. The total sum of the energies of all the atoms or molecules will be larger if more molecules are added to a sample. However, as long as the additional molecules have the same average kinetic energy as the other molecules, the temperature of the sample remains the same.

Consider the following example, shown in Figure 16-3. The water in both the teacup and the pail has the same temperature. Therefore, the average kinetic energy of the water molecules in both containers is the same. However, the energy of the water in the pail is greater. There are many more water molecules in the pail, so the sum of all their kinetic energies is greater. Thus, because the water in the pail has more mass, it has more energy, even though both containers of water have the same temperature.

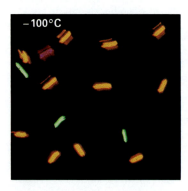

−100°C

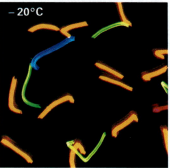

−20°C

30°C

Figure 16-2 *These lights are a model of the movement of atoms or molecules at different temperatures. The higher the temperature, the faster the particles move.*

Measuring energy The SI unit of energy is called the joule [jewl]. One joule is a very small amount of energy—a heartbeat produces about 1 joule of energy. Chemists typically express energies in kilojoules—1 kJ = 1000 J.

Chemists have often used a non-SI energy unit—the calorie. The **calorie** is defined as 1 cal = 4.184 J. The former metric system definition of the calorie is the amount of energy needed to increase the temperature of one gram of water one degree Celsius. You are familiar with the nutritional energy unit called the Calorie (with a capital *C*). This unit of energy is actually one kilocalorie. Did you realize that your diet of 3000 Calories per day is actually providing you with 3,000,000 calories?

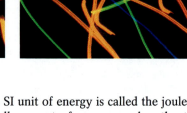

DEMONSTRATION

Energy, Heat, and Temperature

Pour equal volumes of 1*M* HCl and 1*M* NaOH into separate beakers.

⚠️ **CAUTION: Wear safety goggles and a lab apron. Use a shield to protect students.**

Measure the temperature of each solution and record it. Pour the solutions together and measure the final temperature. Ask

students why the temperature increased, and where the heat came from. Now repeat the experiment with double the volume of acid and base. Before pouring the two solutions together, ask students to predict the final temperature. Most will predict that the temperature increase will double. Mix the
(continued on page T535)

16.2 Specific Heat

Look again at Figure 16-3. Imagine that you add the same quantity of heat to both containers. Can you predict which sample of water will warm up more? The energy that is transferred to the cup of water will be distributed among fewer molecules. Therefore, the average kinetic energy of those molecules will increase more than the average kinetic energy of the molecules in the pail. In other words, the resulting water temperature in the cup will be greater than the temperature in the pail.

Factors determining heat transfer The amount of heat transferred depends on three factors: the capacity of a substance to absorb heat, its mass, and its change in temperature. In fact, the amount of heat transferred is directly proportional to each of these factors—as any one of them increases, so does the amount of heat transferred. Often chemists are interested in comparing the capacity of different substances to absorb heat. In order to make this comparison, equal masses and temperature changes are necessary. The **specific heat** is a measure of this property and is defined as the quantity of heat needed to raise one gram of a substance one degree Celsius. The SI units of specific heat are J/g°C.

Table 16-1 on the next page lists the specific heats of some common substances. If you had 1 gram of each substance listed, you could use the specific heat to determine the quantity of heat needed to raise its temperature 1°C—for example, from 19.5°C to 20.5°C. You would need 0.803 J of energy to raise the temperature of 1 g of granite by 1°C. Lead has the lowest specific heat of the substances listed—only 0.128 J of energy is needed to raise the temperature of 1 g of lead 1°C. Which substance listed requires the greatest quantity of heat per gram to raise its temperature 1°C?

To evaluate the heat transferred to or from a substance, you must know its specific heat, its mass, and the temperature change, ΔT. (The symbol Δ—the greek letter *delta*—means "change in.")

Figure 16-3 *The pail and the cup contain water at the same temperature. The pail has more heat energy because it has more mass.*

Teaching Strategy

Factors Determining Heat Transfer

The symbol for changes in heat, ΔH, will not be introduced until Part 2. In Part 1, all heat transfers are treated as positive values. Heat energy gained (absorbed) or lost (released) is described as a "gain" or "loss" of a positive value. For a specific system, if heat is gained, temperature rises. If heat is lost, the temperature decreases.

EXAMPLE 16-1

Calculate the quantity of heat, in kilojoules, needed to warm water from 25.0°C to 95.0°C to prepare a cup of coffee. The cup holds 250.0 mL of water.

■ *Analyze the Problem* In order to find the quantity of heat needed, you must know the specific heat of water, the mass of water, and the temperature change it will undergo. The specific heat of water at 20°C, listed in Table 16-1, is 4.18 J/g°C.

Figure 16-4 *Photos like this reveal relative heat losses from various parts of homes. Energy is always transferred if there is a difference in temperature.*

DEMONSTRATION

(continued from page T534)
solutions, measure the temperature, and record it. (The temperature rise should be the same as in the first experiment.) Ask students to explain the result. Discuss with students why the temperature did not dou-

ble, even though the amount of heat produced in the second experiment did double. For disposal, neutralize the acid and base to about pH 7 and pour down the drain.

TABLE 16-1

Specific Heat of Common Substances at 20°C	
Substance	Specific Heat (J/g°C)*
air	1.00
aluminum	0.895
carbon (diamond)	0.502
carbon (graphite)	0.711
carbon dioxide	0.832
copper	0.387
ethyl alcohol, C_2H_6O	2.45
gold	0.129
granite	0.803
iron	0.448
lead	0.128
paraffin	2.9
silver	0.233
stainless steel	0.51
water	4.18

* SI units for specific heat is J/kgK since 1°C = 1 K then J/kg°C = J/kgK.

Practice Problems

Assign the Practice Problems.

■ **Apply a Strategy** You can break this problem down into three parts. First, if you know the volume of water in the cup, you can calculate the mass, using the value of the density of water. The density of water is listed in Table 1-5 as 1.00 g/cm³. Next, the temperature change can be found by subtracting the initial temperature from the final temperature. Finally, using these values of mass, ΔT, and the specific heat of water, you can calculate the quantity of heat needed to make a cup of coffee.

■ **Work a Solution** First determine the mass of the water. Recall that 1 mL = 1 cm³, so 250.0 mL = 250.0 cm³. Using the factor-label method, determine the mass from the volume and density.

$$250.0 \, \cancel{cm^3} \times 1.00\frac{g}{1 \, \cancel{cm^3}} = 250.0 \, g$$

You can also use the equation mass = density × volume to determine the mass of water.

The change of temperature, ΔT = 95.0°C − 25.0°C = 70.0°C. Finally, using the value for the specific heat of water found in Table 16-1, you can find the quantity of heat needed as follows.

$$\text{heat transferred} = \left(4.18\frac{J}{g°C}\right)(250.0 \, g)(70.0°C)$$

$$\underset{\substack{\text{specific} \\ \text{heat}}}{} \quad \underset{\text{mass}}{} \quad \underset{\substack{\text{change in} \\ \text{temperature}}}{}$$

heat transferred = 73150 J

heat transferred = 73.2 kJ

■ **Verify Your Answer** Checking units is a good way to make sure that you have solved a problem correctly. You know that *quantity of heat* refers to the amount of energy transferred in order to increase the temperature of the water. Therefore, your answer should be expressed in units of energy. The kilojoule is a unit of energy.

The relationship between heat transferred, specific heat, mass, and change in temperature is given by this mathematical expression.

$$q = s \times m \times \Delta T$$

The symbol *q* represents the heat transferred, *s* is the specific heat, *m* is the mass and ΔT is the change in temperature. The following practice problems can be solved using this equation.

Practice Problems

1. How much energy is required to heat a #10 iron nail with a mass of 7.0 g from 25°C until it becomes red hot at 750°C?

   Ans. 2.3 kJ

DEMONSTRATION

Storing Energy

Use two or three large plastic foam cups stacked together as a calorimeter. Prepare one calorimeter for each solid to be checked. Add 100 mL of water at room temperature to each of the calorimeters and place a thermometer and stirring rod in each. Place pieces of assorted metals or other solids in a beaker of water and heat to boiling.

⚠ **CAUTION: Wear safety goggles and a lab apron. Use a shield to protect students.**

The demonstration is more effective and easier for students to interpret if the solid samples have the same mass. Samples with a mass of 10–25 g should give suit-

(continued on page T537)

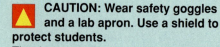

2. If 5750 J of energy are added to a 455-g piece of granite at 24.0°C, what is the final temperature of the granite?

Ans. 39.7°C

3. A 30.0-g sample of an unknown metal is heated from 22.0°C to 59.2°C. During the process, 1.00 kJ of energy is absorbed by the metal. What is the specific heat of the metal? Using Table 16-1, identify the metal.

Ans. 0.896 J/g°C

DO YOU KNOW?

Another energy unit is the Btu, which stands for British thermal unit. One Btu is the amount of energy needed to raise 1 pound of water 1°F, from 63°F to 64°F. You will usually find the energy ratings of air conditioners, gas grills, and home heating systems listed in Btus rather than joules (1 Btu = 1055 J).

Storing energy Can you store energy? Yes, a substance with a large value of specific heat has the capacity to store a large amount of energy. Compare the specific heats of water and granite with the values for other substances listed in Table 16-1. Both water and granite have relatively large values of specific heat and are used in solar heated homes to store energy from the sun. During the day, the granite or water is heated by the sun's energy. During the night, the energy stored in the water or granite is transferred to the air, warming the inside of the home.

Figure 16-5 *Many solar homes gather energy from the sun by circulating water in pipes in rooftop installations.*

16.3 Energy Changes Accompanying a Change of State

The specific heat of a substance indicates the amount of energy that must be added to or removed from one gram of a substance to change the substance's temperature by one degree Celsius. You will recall that changing the temperature of a substance can also cause it to change from one state to another. For example, a gas can be cooled until it condenses to a liquid. Further cooling can cause the liquid to freeze. These are changes of state that were discussed in Section 14.3.

DEMONSTRATION

(continued from page T536)
able results. Allow the water containing the solid samples to boil for several minutes to allow them to come to thermal equilibrium. Remove the samples and place one in each calorimeter. Stir and take temperature readings until the temperature no longer rises. Compare the temperature rise in each calorimeter and relate it to the specific heat of each solid. (If you do not use solids of equal mass, it will be necessary to do calculations before comparisons can be made.) Save the various solids for reuse.

Science Background

Energy Changes Accompanying a Change of State

Because the concept of a system and its surroundings is not introduced until Section 16.5, Section 16.3 does not assign a positive or negative value to heat transfer. Normally the quantity of heat transferred is negative if the system is losing heat energy (an exothermic reaction or change of state), and is positive if the system is gaining heat energy (an endothermic reaction or change of state).

During a change of state, a phase change, the energy of a substance changes. The change from the liquid phase to the gas phase is called vaporization. The quantity of heat that must be absorbed to vaporize one gram of a liquid is called the **heat of vaporization.** Likewise, the quantity of heat needed to cause one gram of a solid to melt into its liquid phase is called the **heat of fusion.** Heats of vaporization and fusion are measured in joules per gram, J/g. Table 16-2 lists the heats of fusion and vaporization for some common substances.

TABLE 16-2

Heats of Fusion and Vaporization for Some Common Substances		
Substance	Heat of Fusion (J/g)	Heat of Vaporization (J/g)
copper	205	4726
ethyl alcohol	109	879
gold	64.5	1578
lead	24.7	858
silver	88	2300
water	334	2260

The quantity of heat transferred as a result of a phase change is the product of the mass of the substance and the heat of the phase change.

$$\text{heat transferred} = \text{mass} \times \text{heat of the phase change}$$

EXAMPLE 16-2

Calculate the heat required to change a 250.0-g sample of liquid water at 100°C into steam, also at 100°C.

■ *Analyze the Problem* The change in the water is from a liquid to a gas. Therefore, the heat of vaporization and the mass are required.

■ *Apply a Strategy* To determine the energy transferred, you need the mass of the water, which is given, and its heat of vaporization, which is found in Table 16-2.

■ *Work a Solution*

$$\text{energy transferred} = \text{mass} \times \text{heat of vaporization}$$

$$= 250.0\,\cancel{g} \times 2260\frac{J}{\cancel{g}} = 565\,000\ J$$

$$= 565\ kJ$$

Thus 565 kJ of energy is required to vaporize 250.0 g of water at 100°C into steam at 100°C.

■ **Verify Your Answer** Check your units; the product of J/g × g gives J, an energy unit. The energy transferred is large, but the numbers multiplied are also large, so you expect a large answer.

Practice Problems

4. Calculate the heat required to melt a 15-g ice cube at 0°C to give water, also at 0°C.   **Ans.** 5.0 kJ

5. How much heat is released when 15 g of steam at 100°C condenses to give 15 g of water at 100°C?   **Ans.** 34 kJ

Constant temperature during a change of state Figure 16-6 is the temperature-versus-time heating curve for water that you saw in Chapter 14. The two horizontal portions of the heating curve correspond to melting and vaporization. Notice that no temperature change occurs during these changes of state. However, the energy of the water must increase because heat is being absorbed. Heat is absorbed when a liquid vaporizes. When

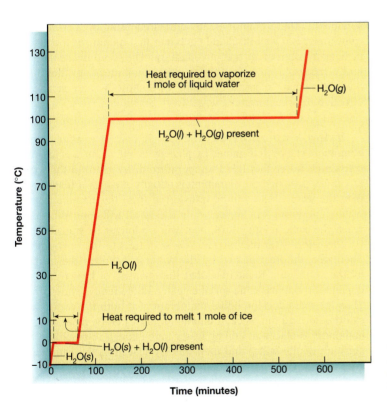

Figure 16-6 The heating curve for 1 mole of water starting with ice at −10°C and continuing until the water is steam at 110°C. The energy is added as heat at the rate of 100 J per minute.

PART 1

Section 16.3 *continued*

Practice Problems

Assign the Practice Problems.

Teaching Strategy

Constant Temperature During a Change of State

Emphasize that temperature is constant during a change of state. Help your students with the interpretation of heating/cooling curves.

DEMONSTRATION

Constant Temperature During a Change of State

Use a supersaturated solution, such as sodium acetate, to show that energy is released as heat during crystallization. A convenient supersaturated solution is the commercial product Heat Solution. Sodium acetate is packaged inside a plastic bag and a metal disk initiates crystallization. By heating in hot water, the Heat Solution can be reused. Point out the reversibility of thermodynamics; heat is given off during crystallization and heat is stored by heating the bag.

⚠ **CAUTION: If you prepare your own solution, wear safety goggles and a lab apron. Use a shield to protect students. Follow the manufacturer's precautions if you use a manufactured pack.**

PART **1**
Section 16.4

Teaching Strategy

Measuring Heat Transfer

At this point in Chapter 16, temperature differences are described with the terms "heat gained" when heat is absorbed and "heat lost" when heat is released. Example 16–3 illustrates this strategy. The more sophisticated method to determine ΔT is by the equation: $\Delta T = T_f - T_i$. When heat is lost by the system, ΔT is negative. When heat is gained, ΔT is positive. If Example 16–3 were approached in this way, the setup would be: $(4.18 \text{ J/g}°C)(100.00 \text{ g})(32.9°C - 22.4°C) = -(S_{aluminum}) \times (75.25 \text{ g})(32.9°C - 99.3°C)$ Since the water is gaining heat, it has a positive value of q. In contrast, since aluminum is losing heat, its q has a negative value.

Science Background

Using a Calorimeter

Calorimeters are not perfectly insulated. The heat capacity of the calorimeter (sometimes referred to as the calorimeter constant) is determined experimentally using a reaction of known ΔH. Careful calorimetry measurements, such as combustion reactions, are carried out in special calorimeters called bomb calorimeters. The principles are the same as for the styrofoam cup calorimeter seen in Figure 16–8, but experimental measurements are more precise and accurate when using a bomb calorimeter.

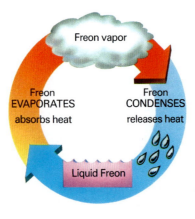

Figure 16-7 *Freon absorbs heat from inside a refrigerator and is vaporized. Outside the refrigerator, the Freon condenses, releasing heat into the air.*

Freon vapor

Freon
EVAPORATES
absorbs heat

Freon
CONDENSES
releases heat

Liquid Freon

Figure 16-8 *A simple calorimeter can be made from two Styrofoam cups and a Styrofoam lid. The thermometer measures the temperature change of the reacting mixture as the mixture is gently stirred.*

a gas condenses, heat is released. Since 2260 J of energy must be absorbed to change 1 g of water at 100°C into steam at 100°C, then 2260 J of energy are released when 1 g of steam at 100°C condenses into water at 100°C. A steam burn is very serious because such a large amount of energy is released when steam condenses on the skin.

Similarly, heat is absorbed when a solid melts and released when a liquid freezes. Since 334 J of energy are absorbed to melt 1 g of ice at 0°C, 334 J of energy are released when 1 g of water at 0°C freezes. Farmers often protect their crops from frost damage by spraying water into the air. When the water freezes, heat is released, raising the temperature of the surrounding air.

Concept ✓ Check

Explain in your own words what is happening to the water being heated in Figure 16-6 when the curve slants upward and when it is horizontal.

16.4 Measuring Heat Transfer

The values of specific heat, heat of vaporization, and heat of fusion listed in Tables 16-1 and 16-2 are based on experimental measurements. These quantities are measured using a calorimeter. A **calorimeter** is a well-insulated container that minimizes the amount of heat transferred to the surroundings. The word *calorimeter* literally means "heat measurer"—from *calor* meaning "heat" and *meter* meaning "measure". Figure 16-8 shows a very simple but effective calorimeter constructed from Styrofoam cups.

Using a calorimeter The specific heat of a metal, such as aluminum, can be determined by placing the metal into a calorimeter containing water that has a temperature different from that of the metal. Suppose that the aluminum is initially at a higher temperature than the water. Heat will be transferred from the aluminum to the water. The water will warm, while the metal will cool. When both reach the same temperature, heat will no longer be transferred.

The calorimeter minimizes any loss of heat to the surroundings. Therefore, the heat gained by the water is equal to the heat lost by the aluminum. Remember that the quantity of heat transferred depends on the mass, the specific heat, and the temperature change. Thus the mass and the initial temperature of both the water in the calorimeter and the piece of aluminum must first be measured. The aluminum is placed in boiling water long enough to reach the temperature of the water and then quickly placed in the calorimeter. After the water and aluminum reach the same temperature, the final temperature of both substances is measured. Since the specific heat of water is 4.18 J/g°C, the specific heat of the aluminum can be calculated from the data. Example 16-3 shows you how.

EXAMPLE 16-3

Suppose that 100.00 g of water at 22.4°C is placed in a calorimeter. A 75.25-g sample of aluminum is removed from boiling water at a temperature of 99.3°C and quickly placed in the calorimeter. The substances reach a final temperature of 32.9°C. Determine the specific heat of aluminum.

■ *Analyze the Problem* The initial temperature of the aluminum sample is the same as that of the boiling water—99.3°C. Assuming that the calorimeter is perfectly insulated, all of the heat lost by the metal is gained by the water. The specific heat of water is 4.18 J/g°C. Recall from Example 16-2 that heat transferred can be calculated using this relationship.

$$\text{heat transferred} = s \times m \times \Delta T$$

■ *Apply a Strategy* Organizing your data into a table will help you sort out what you have been given to allow you to calculate the specific heat of aluminum.

Specific Heat of Aluminum		
	Aluminum Sample	Water in Calorimeter
Mass (g)	75.25	100.00
Specific heat (J/g°C)	?	4.18
Initial temperature (°C)	99.3*	22.4
Final temperature (°C)	32.9	32.9

* Temperature of boiling-water bath initially containing aluminum sample.

First, you can use the data for the water to calculate the quantity of heat gained by the water. Since this value must be the same as the quantity of heat lost by the aluminum, you can then find the specific heat of aluminum.

■ *Work a Solution* First, calculate the heat gained by the water.

$$\text{heat gained by water} = s_{(water)} \times m_{(water)} \times \Delta T_{(water)}$$

$$\text{heat gained by water} = \left(4.18\frac{J}{g°C}\right)(100.00\ g)(32.9°C - 22.4°C)$$

$$\text{heat gained by water} = 4390\ J$$

If you assume that the system is perfectly insulated, the heat lost by the aluminum must be 4390 J. You can write an equation for the heat lost by the aluminum that is similar to the previous equation for water. Substitute the value for the heat lost—4390 J—and solve for specific heat.

PROBLEM-SOLVING STRATEGY

Use what you know. The boiling point of a substance depends on the pressure. In this case, the pressure must be less than 1 atm since the boiling point of water is less than 100°C. (See Strategy, page 58.)

PART 1
Section 16.4 *continued*

Guided Practice

Review the Concept Check question on page 540 with students. Answers can be found in Appendix E on page 808.

Reteaching Idea

If your students are unclear about heat-absorbing and heat-releasing processes covered in this part, have an individual or competitive activity designed to put the material into perspective. However you decide to frame the activity, be sure that a chart of the results is put on the chalkboard so that you can discuss any misconceptions.

Give students a list of energy events and ask them to decide, (1) whether each event is energy-absorbing or -releasing, (2) what kind of energy is involved (heat of vaporization, heat of fusion, specific heat), (3) the units of the energy specified (J/g or J/g°C), and (4) what additional information they would need in order to calculate the energy. Examples of events:

■ Ice on a pond melts in spring.
■ Water droplets form on a cold window.
■ Perspiration evaporates and cools the runner.
■ Molten lava solidifies.
■ An iron heating coil becomes red-hot.
■ A puddle of ethyl alcohol disappears after an hour.
■ Granite paving blocks are hot to bare feet on a sunny day.
■ Liquid solder seals a joint.
■ Water pipes on a roof installation provide heat at night.
■ A microwave prepares a cup of tea.

When students have answered (4), ask them to make up some data for selected events and, using Tables 16–1 and 16–2, solve for the kJ involved.

PART 1
Section 16.4 continued

Practice Problems

Assign the Practice Problems.

CLOSE

Summing Up Main Ideas

Consider two teaspoons, each having a mass of 10 g. One is made of silver and the other of stainless steel. They are immersed in boiling water for two minutes.

1. Which spoon would have a higher temperature? (neither)

2. Which spoon would have a greater amount of stored heat? (steel)

3. Which spoon's molecules would have the greater kinetic energy? (neither)

4. Calculate how much heat would be released if the spoons were cooled to room temperature (25°C).

   ($q = s \times m \times \Delta T$
   Silver: $q = (0.233 \text{ J/g°C})$
   $\times 10 \text{ g} \times 75°C = 175 \text{ J}$.
   Steel: $q = (0.51 \text{ J/g°C}) \times 10 \text{ g}$
   $\times 75°C = 382 \text{ J}$)

PART 1 REVIEW

Assign the Part Review questions.

Evaluating Skills

These skills are evaluated in the Part Review questions indicated.
Comparing/Contrasting: 7, 8, 9;
Determining cause and effect: 8, 9; **Analyzing data:** 9, 10, 11;
Applying a strategy: 9, 10, 11;
Calculating: 9, 10, 11; **Verifying results:** 9, 10, 11

DO YOU KNOW?

Some appliances use phase changes to transfer energy. The cooling system of a refrigerator is filled with liquid Freon. The Freon absorbs heat from inside the refrigerator and vaporizes. The vapor is circulated to the refrigerator's exterior, where it is condensed. You can feel this heat being released behind or underneath your refrigerator when the compressor is running.

PROBLEM-SOLVING
STRATEGY

*You will need to **use what you know** from Table 16-1 to compare your calculated value with the accepted value. (See Strategy, page 58.)*

Boxed numbers indicate questions that involve skills in interpretation, application, and analysis.

heat lost by aluminum = $s_{(aluminum)} \times m_{(aluminum)} \times \Delta T_{(aluminum)}$

$4390 \text{ J} = s_{(aluminum)}(75.25 \text{ g})(99.3°C - 32.9°C)$

$$s_{(aluminum)} = \frac{(4390 \text{ J})}{(75.25 \text{ g})(99.3°C - 32.9°C)}$$

$s_{(aluminum)} = 0.879 \text{ J/g°C}$

■ **Verify Your Answer** The value for the specific heat of aluminum listed in Table 16-1 is 0.895 J/g°C. This is very close to the calculated value of 0.879 J/g°C. The values recorded in Table 16-1 were determined using calorimeters that make more precise measurements than are possible with a simple calorimeter.

Practice Problem

6. A 25-g sample of a metal at 75.0°C is placed in a calorimeter containing 25 g of water at 20.0°C. The temperature stopped changing at 29.4°C. What is the specific heat of the metal.
   Ans. 0.89 J/g°C

PART 1 REVIEW

7. Compare and contrast energy and heat. How can you measure the transfer of energy?

8. The same quantity of heat is added to an iron nail (3.5 g) and to a metric ton (1000 kg) of iron. Which would reach the higher temperature? Explain your reasoning.

9. Solar homes often use granite or water to absorb heat from the sun by day. This heat is released into the house at night. If the temperature of 1000 kg of granite was raised 10°C in one house and the temperature of 1000 kg of water was raised 10°C in another house, which house absorbed more heat? Explain your answer.

10. How much heat is transferred when 25.0 g of ethyl alcohol vapor at its boiling point condenses to form a liquid at the same temperature? Is energy absorbed or released?
    Ans. 22.0 kJ

11. A 30.00-g sample of an unknown metal was removed from boiling water and placed in a coffee-cup calorimeter containing 100.00 g of water. The water in the calorimeter was initially 20.0°C, while the boiling water was 99.0°C. When the temperature of the water in the calorimeter became constant, the final temperature of water and metal was 22.4°C. Identify the unknown metal by calculating its specific heat and comparing the calculated value with the accepted values of the substances, listed in Table 16-1.
    Ans. 0.44 J/g°C

PART 1 REVIEW
ANSWERS
■ Keyed to Objectives

A **7.** Energy is the capacity to do work or produce heat. Heat is a quantitative measure of energy transferred. Energy can take forms other than heat, such as light, sound, and so on.

B **8.** The nail will reach a higher temperature because it has less mass.

B **9.** Because the specific heat of water is greater than that of granite, the house using water would absorb more heat.

C **10.** (25.0 g)(879 J/g) = 21 975 J
= 22.0 kJ
Heat is released.

CAREERS IN CHEMISTRY

Environmental Health and Safety Technologist

People, increasingly concerned with the quality of the air they breathe and the water they drink are looking for stricter environmental regulations to protect their health. David Goodwin, an Environmental Health and Safety Technologist is already doing this.

Job description David is currently working for Genetics Institute, a biotechnology company. He is responsible for helping the company comply with local, state, and federal regulations regarding health and safety. David develops and implements training programs for the employees. In addition, he conducts hazardous chemical tests for people involved in the laboratory and pharmaceutical manufacturing facility.

Educational background David always knew he wanted to work in science but was unsure of the particular area. As a freshman in college, he took a career alternatives class, where he discovered the field of environmental health. In this class, he learned that there would be a number of jobs in the environmental and health fields in the future. David went on to earn his B.S. in Environmental Health.

Personal rewards For David, a major reward of his job is the opportunity to work with experts in the biotechnology field. He is impressed with how these scientists devote their lives to discovery research in an effort to improve the quality of life. His study of environmental health has helped to show David the seriousness of major illness, such as cancer. He strongly believes that any contribution in his field enhances not only the life of others but his life as well.

Part of David's key to success is keeping a positive attitude and welcoming new ideas and knowledge. David recalls an old African proverb that says, "Not to know is bad, but not to wish to know is worse." He urges students to follow the wisdom of this proverb by identifying personal goals and then learning as much as possible to achieve these goals.

Looking to the future David urges students to take environmental courses to become more aware of environmental issues. David expects they will take a positive stand for both people and the environment.

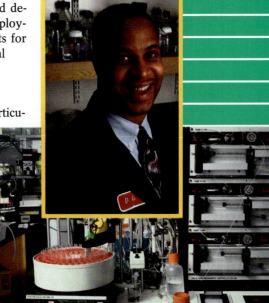

David Goodwin
Environmental Health
and Safety Technologist

"Not to know is bad, but not to wish to know is worse."

(Old African proverb)

CAREERS IN CHEMISTRY

Teaching Strategies

1. Have students identify various types and sources of pollution, including sound, air, and water.

2. Have students identify various sources of indoor pollution, such as chemicals used in the manufacture of laminated woods, paints, carpets, and furniture. Tie in this topic with the **Science Technology & Society** feature on household chemicals, pages 78–79.

Look Ahead

Discuss these topics in connection with outdoor air pollution and the **Science Technology & Society** feature on acid rain, pages 676–677.

Related Careers

Some related professions that students can discuss are environmental law, public health medicine, and epidemiology. For more information on related careers, contact the Environmental Protection Agency, 401 M St., SW, Washington, DC 20460; the U.S. Centers for Disease Control, 1600 Clifton Rd., NE, Atlanta, GA 30333; and the U.S. Department of Health and Human Services, 200 Independence Ave., SW, Washington, DC 20201.

Resources

Contact the Environmental Protection Agency, the Occupational Safety and Health Administration, and the Nuclear Regulatory Commission for additional information.

D **11.** $\left(4.18\ \frac{J}{g\,^\circ C}\right)(100.0\ g)(22.4\,^\circ C - 20.0\,^\circ C)$

$= (s)(30.0\ g)(99.0\,^\circ C - 22.4\,^\circ C)$

$s = \frac{0.44\ J}{g\,^\circ C}$; the metal is iron.

PART **2**
Thermochemistry and Enthalpy

Section 16.5

Developing Skills

Students may apply these skills in their study of Part 2.

Comparing/Contrasting: Have students compare and contrast the energy changes that occur during endothermic and exothermic reactions.

Calculating: Have students apply Hess's Law to calculate the enthalpy change for a reaction.

Forming models: Have students draw models representing the formation of a mole of a compound from the elements.

≡ FOCUS

Activate Prior Knowledge

In Chapter 3 students were introduced to exothermic and endothermic reactions. This activity demonstrates that some reactions generate heat, whereas others absorb heat.

Set up two stirring hot plates, each with a 250-mL beaker and a magnetic stirring bar. Pour 150 mL water into each and turn the stirring plates on low.

Slowly pour 5 g ammonium chloride into one beaker and 5 g sodium hydroxide into the other. Have students carefully feel the outside of each beaker and note the temperature of each.

⚠ **CAUTION: Wear safety goggles and gloves.**

≡ TEACH

Teaching Strategy

Energy Changes

This section introduces the fundamentals of the precise language of thermodynamics. The text strives to present the flavor of thermodynamics without intimidating students with unnecessary jargon.

Objectives

Part 2

E. **Describe** the energy changes that occur in the system and surroundings for an exothermic and an endothermic reaction.

F. **Apply** Hess's Law to **calculate** the enthalpy change for a reaction using the enthalpy changes for other reactions.

G. **Identify** the equation that corresponds to the standard enthalpy of formation of a compound.

H. Given ΔH_f° for each reactant and product, **calculate** ΔH° for a reaction.

Figure 16-9 *This familiar exothermic reaction releases 393.5 kJ/mole of energy to the surroundings.*

PART
2 Thermochemistry and Enthalpy

In Part 1, you learned about the transfer of heat that results when a hot object comes in contact with a cooler object. You also learned that a substance absorbs or releases heat when it changes from one physical state to another.

Many chemical reactions release energy in the form of heat along with the chemical products. For example, in a Bunsen burner, methane—or natural gas—combines with oxygen in the air to produce carbon dioxide and water. In this reaction, heat is also produced. The heat from burning methane can be used to cook food on a gas stove or to heat a building using a gas furnace. In Part 2, you will learn about **thermochemistry**—the study of heat transfers that accompany chemical reactions.

16.5 Energy Changes

You saw in Chapter 13 that energy is always involved in the making and breaking of chemical bonds. Bond making is an exothermic process—energy is always released. Bond breaking is an endothermic reaction—energy is always absorbed.

It is not easy to evaluate the energy change resulting from the breaking and forming of individual chemical bonds, but fortunately chemists gain much valuable information by studying the overall energy change that occurs in a chemical reaction. For example, if you are wondering how much natural gas must be burned in your Bunsen burner to carry out some reaction, you want information about the heat released as a result of the reaction rather than details about the energies of the individual bonds in the reactant and product molecules.

System and surroundings It might not be readily apparent how a chemical process can be exothermic or endothermic and also be consistent with the law of conservation of energy. To understand how energy is conserved, you must divide the universe into two parts, the **system** and the **surroundings.** When you study a chemical reaction, you are interested in the system, a specific part of the universe. Everything outside the system is referred to as the surroundings. For example, if a reaction is carried out in a test tube, the system is the reactants and products. The test tube itself, the air in contact with the reagents, and the rest of the universe are considered the surroundings. Figure 16-10 shows a representation of these terms.

The law of conservation of energy refers to the universe. When natural gas burns in a furnace, the methane, oxygen, carbon dioxide,

Myths and Misconceptions

Students have difficulty understanding that energy is not created or destroyed in a chemical reaction. This misconception is perpetuated by the use of phrases such as, "heat is lost in this reaction," implying that it is gone. Check for this misconception by probing students with questions such as "What happens to the energy that is released in the chemical reaction?" Be careful with the terminology you use in class, and emphasize the distinction between "system" and "surroundings."

16.6 Enthalpy

Enthalpy (en-thal'-pē), symbolized by the letter *H*, is a measure of the energy content of a system. Often chemical and physical changes occur under constant pressure. For example, a reaction in an open flask or test tube occurs under the constant pressure of the atmosphere. When a process occurs at constant pressure, the **enthalpy change,** ΔH (called delta H), is a measure of the heat change accompanying the process. All energy changes discussed in this text will be at constant pressure and thus will be enthalpy changes.

The enthalpy change for any chemical reaction depends only on the values of the initial enthalpy—the energy content of the reactants, and the final enthalpy—the energy content of the products. It does not depend upon the way in which the chemical change is accomplished. For example, consider two different processes for the burning of carbon. In the first, carbon is converted directly to CO_2 when unlimited oxygen is available to react.

$$C(s) + O_2(g) \rightarrow CO_2(g) \qquad \text{Energy released} = 393.5 \text{ kJ}$$

In the second, a limited amount of oxygen results in the formation of carbon monoxide, CO.

$$C(s) + \frac{1}{2}O_2(g) \rightarrow CO(g) \qquad \text{Energy released} = 110.5 \text{ kJ}$$

If the carbon monoxide formed then reacts with more oxygen, CO_2 is formed.

$$CO(g) + \frac{1}{2}O_2(g) \rightarrow CO_2(g) \qquad \text{Energy released} = 283.5 \text{ kJ}$$

Combine the equations for the two steps just as you would algebraic equations and add the energies released. The result is this.

$$C(s) \quad + \frac{1}{2}O_2(g) \rightarrow CO(g) \qquad \text{Energy released} = 110.5 \text{ kJ}$$

$$CO(g) + \frac{1}{2}O_2(g) \rightarrow CO_2(g) \qquad \text{Energy released} = 283.0 \text{ kJ}$$

$$C(s) \quad + CO(g) + O_2(g) \rightarrow CO(g) + CO_2(g)$$
$$\text{Energy released} = 393.5 \text{ kJ}$$

Since CO(g) appears on both sides of the equation in equal amounts, it can be eliminated to give the same overall equation as the one-step process. Notice that the total energy released is also the same as the one-step reaction.

$$C(g) + O_2(g) \rightarrow CO_2(g) \qquad \text{Energy released} = 393.5 \text{ kJ}$$

Figure 16-10 *A yellow precipitate, cadmium sulfide, is formed when aqueous solutions of sodium sulfide and cadmium nitrate are mixed. The materials—$Na_2S(aq)$, $Cd(NO_3)_2(aq)$, and $CdS(s)$—make up the system. The surroundings are the test tube, the tongs, and the air.*

◄ **PROBLEM-SOLVING**
S T R A T E G Y

Usually fractional coefficients are not used in chemical equations. However, it is often convenient to use them in thermochemistry, as has been done here.

Science Background

System and Surroundings

Give students several examples of systems and surroundings. The reacting species and the products are included in the system. Everything else, including the container in which a reaction occurs, comprise the surroundings.

Teaching Strategy

Enthalpy

Refer Students to Figure 16–9 and Table 16–3. To many, it seems counterintuitive to have a negative ΔH for an exothermic reaction because a positive amount of heat is given off. However, it does make sense in the context of the system losing heat.

Fractional coefficients are often used in writing equations in thermochemistry. This is, however, not the case with most stoichiometry applications. Help students get used to this convention. Help students understand that calculations deal with moles rather than with molecules or atoms. It is logical to consider the reaction of half a mole of O_2, but it is not logical to consider the reaction of half of a molecule of O_2.

Two or more equations can be added together. Adding the corresponding enthalpy changes will give the overall enthalpy change. Treat chemical species the same as algebraic quantities. If the same species occurs on both sides of an equation, the smaller amount can be subtracted from each side to give the net equation.

Science Background

Enthalpy

$C_6H_{12}O_6(s) + 6O_2(g) \rightarrow 6CO_2(g) + 6H_2O(l)$ $\Delta H°_r = -2808$ kJ is a thermochemical equation. A thermochemical equation tells us the enthalpy change for the reaction, in addition to the reactants and products with their physical state. If a thermochemical equation is reversed, the sign of ΔH is reversed.

(continued on page T546)

(continued from page T545)

Enthalpy is the energy measured for processes occurring at constant pressure. Most reactions that students will encounter occur in open containers at the pressure of the atmosphere. These are constant pressure processes. Energy changes under constant volume conditions (as in a bomb calorimeter, for example) are not the same as enthalpy changes, but can be corrected to give enthalpy changes.

Videodisc Connections

3264 to 5632, side 3
Sodium chloride (movie)

5637 to 6477, side 3
Zinc and sulfur (movie)

12554 to 17619, side 3
The chef (movie)

11593 to 12553, side 3
Ethanol explosion (movie)

Figure 16-11 Top: *When barium hydroxide and ammonium thiocyanate are mixed, an endothermic reaction takes place.* Middle: *If placed on a board with a puddle of water, the flask will freeze to the board.* Bottom: *Because the difference in enthalpy is +130 kJ/mole, heat is transferred from the surroundings to the system—the reacting materials.*

Chemists have been able to show repeatedly that in all chemical reactions, the path from reactants to products does not affect the overall enthalpy change. The energy released or absorbed depends only on the initial enthalpy and the final enthalpy.

$$\Delta H = H_{final} - H_{initial}$$

Another way to express the relationship is this.

$$\Delta H = H_{products} - H_{reactants}$$

Exothermic reactions You have seen that the burning of carbon results in a release of energy. This means that the enthalpy of the products is lower than the enthalpy of the reactants. The equation for ΔH shows that this results in a negative value for ΔH. When ΔH is negative, energy is removed from the system and released to the surroundings. Thus when one mole of carbon is burned at constant pressure to form one mole of carbon dioxide, 393.5 kJ of energy is released. Therefore, $\Delta H = -393.5$ kJ.

Endothermic reactions Consider a different example. When solid barium hydroxide octahydrate, $Ba(OH)_2 \cdot 8H_2O$, and ammonium thiocyanate, NH_4SCN, react, the reaction container cools. In fact, the flask gets cold enough to freeze water, as shown in Figure 16-11. The equation for the reaction is this.

$$Ba(OH)_2 \cdot 8H_2O(s) + 2NH_4SCN(s) \rightarrow$$
$$Ba(SCN)_2(aq) + 2NH_3(aq) + 10H_2O(l)$$

As illustrated in Figure 16-11, the reactants must gain 130 kJ of energy from the surroundings in order for this reaction to occur. This means that the enthalpy of the products is greater than the enthalpy of the reactants, or $\Delta H = +130$ kJ. ΔH is positive for an endothermic reaction because energy must be added to the system by transferring heat from the surroundings. Because heat is transferred from the surroundings, the surroundings (flask, board, puddle of water) become cooler.

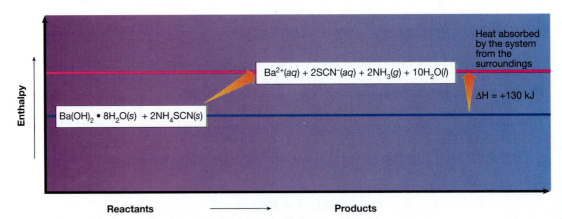

Enthalpy

Ba²⁺(aq) + 2SCN⁻(aq) + 2NH₃(g) + 10H₂O(l)

Ba(OH)₂ • 8H₂O(s) + 2NH₄SCN(s)

Heat absorbed by the system from the surroundings

ΔH = +130 kJ

Reactants   Products

DEMONSTRATION
Exothermic and Endothermic

Use commercial hot and cold packs to demonstrate the terms endothermic and exothermic. Your athletic department may be a source of hot and cold packs.

CAUTION: Follow the manufacturer's precautions on the packs.

The enthalpy changes for exothermic and endothermic reactions are summarized in Table 16-3.

TABLE 16-3

Enthalpy Changes for Exothermic and Endothermic Reactions			
Type of Reaction	Experimental Observation	Enthalpy Change for the System	Sign of ΔH
Exothermic	Reaction container warms. (Heat is released to the surroundings.)	Energy is removed from the system.	−
Endothermic	Reaction container cools. (Heat is absorbed from the surroundings.)	Energy is added to the system.	+

Concept ✔ Check

What change occurs in the temperature of the *system* when an exothermic reaction occurs? What change occurs in the temperature of the *surroundings* when an endothermic reaction occurs?

16.7 Standard Enthalpy of Formation

It is impossible to measure the energy content or absolute enthalpy of a substance. But chemists have been able to set up an arbitrary system based on an agreed-upon reference point. Through experiments and calculation, the enthalpies of many substances have been placed on a scale above and below the reference point. The situation is similar to that of measuring temperature. For example, to create the Celsius temperature scale, a particular temperature was arbitrarily assigned a value of zero. The zero point is the temperature at which water freezes or melts. A positive temperature on the scale simply indicates that the average kinetic energy of molecules is greater than the average kinetic energy of water molecules at 0°C. A negative temperature indicates that the average kinetic energy of the molecules is less than the average kinetic energy of water molecules at 0°C.

A similar tactic is used to describe enthalpy changes. Scientists have agreed to assign a zero value to the energy of all elements in their standard state. The precise meaning of *standard state* is subtle, and you need not worry about it in this course. You may think of the standard state of an element as the form in which the pure element exists at 1 atmosphere pressure. For example, oxygen ordinarily exists as a diatomic gas at a pressure of one atmosphere

Teaching Strategy

Standard Enthalpy of Formation
Write several thermochemical equations that represent standard heat of formation reactions. In each case, 1 mole of a compound will be the product and its elements will be the reactants. If reactants exist as molecules (e.g., H_2, Cl_2), they must be written that way. Likewise, their normal state, usually at 25°C and 1 atm pressure, is indicated [e.g., Hg(l), Fe(s)].

Videodisc Connections

23547 to 25287, side 3
Thermite reaction (movie)

36811 to 38406, side 3
Goose egg explosion (movie)

27026 to 30819, side 3
Ammonium dichromate (movie)

PART **2**

Section 16.7 continued

Science Background

Compounds on an Enthalpy Scale

There is no way to measure values of enthalpy, H. However, changes of enthalpy, ΔH, are comparisons and can be measured. The standard enthalpy of formation, ΔH_f°, is assigned an arbitrary value of 0 for elements in their standard state.

Videodisc Connections

36811 to 38406, side 3
Goose egg explosion (movie)

DO YOU KNOW?

Thermodynamics predicts which processes are possible, but not how fast they will occur. The reaction of methane and oxygen spontaneously yields carbon dioxide and water. However, at room temperature, the rate is so slow that nothing appears to happen. Once the reaction is started with a match, though, it proceeds on its own. In Chapter 17, you will study kinetics—the branch of chemistry that deals with the rate at which reactions occur.

and a temperature of 25°C. This is its standard state at 25°C. Aluminum ordinarily exists as a cystalline solid, and that is its standard state. It is important to keep in mind that enthalpy changes are involved in any temperature change or pressure change, so the standard state of an element always applies to a particular temperature and pressure as well as to a particular physical state (solid, liquid, or gas).

Compounds on an enthalpy scale Once a reference point is established for the enthalpy of elements in their standard state, you might ask if enthalpies of compounds such as water can be determined. The answer is yes. This can be done by measuring how much energy is involved in the formation of one mole of water from the elements hydrogen and oxygen when they are in their standard states. The energy change for this reaction is called the **standard enthalpy of formation** of water and is given the symbol ΔH_f°. The superscript *o* indicates that the value of ΔH is measured when all substances are in their standard states. The subscript *f* indicates that the energy is associated with the formation of *one mole* of a compound from its elements in their standard states. For this discussion you can assume a temperature of 25°C.

To determine ΔH_f° for water, hydrogen and oxygen are burned in a calorimeter. The equation for the reaction is one that you are familiar with, but now it can be identified as a standard enthalpy of formation equation.

$$H_2(g) + \frac{1}{2}O_2(g) \rightarrow H_2O(l)$$

In a standard enthalpy of formation equation, the reactants are elements in their standard states. In this equation, the coefficient $\frac{1}{2}$ is used for oxygen because only $\frac{1}{2}$ mole of oxygen is required to form one mole of water. Standard enthalpy of formation equations always represent the formation of one mole of the product.

The energy released in this experiment is 285.8 kJ. Recall that ΔH for any reaction is the difference between the enthalpy of the reactants and products.

$$\Delta H = \Delta H_f^\circ \text{ product} - \Delta H_f^\circ \text{ reactants} = -285.8 \text{ kJ}$$

Since the reactants are elements in their standard states, their enthalpies of formation are zero. The value of ΔH for the reaction is therefore the enthalpy of formation of one mole of liquid water.

$$\Delta H = \Delta H_f^\circ \text{ product} - 0$$
$$\Delta H = \Delta H_f^\circ \text{ liquid H}_2\text{O} = -285.8 \text{ kJ}$$

Experiments similar to this in which other compounds are formed from their elements have allowed chemists to tabulate enthalpy of formation data for hundreds of compounds. Some of them are listed in Table 16-4. The availability of standard enthalpy of formation data for compounds will allow you to calculate the enthalpy change for many reactions, as shown in Example 16-4 on page 550.

TABLE 16-4

Standard Enthalpies of Formation, ΔH_f°, at 25°C		
Substance	Formula	ΔH_f° (kJ/mole)
water	$H_2O(l)$	− 285.8
water	$H_2O(g)$	− 241.8
hydrogen peroxide	$H_2O_2(l)$	− 187.6
hydrogen sulfide	$H_2S(g)$	− 20.1
carbon monoxide	$CO(g)$	− 110.5
carbon dioxide	$CO_2(g)$	− 393.5
glucose	$C_6H_{12}O_6(s)$	−1268
sucrose	$C_{12}H_{22}O_{11}(s)$	−2222
methane	$CH_4(g)$	− 74.8
acetylene	$C_2H_2(g)$	+ 227
ethylene	$C_2H_4(g)$	+ 52.30
ethane	$C_2H_6(g)$	− 84.7
carbon	$C(s, diamond)$	+ 1.90
calcium oxide	$CaO(s)$	− 653.6
calcium carbonate	$CaCO_3(s)$	−1206.9
ammonia	$NH_3(g)$	− 46.3
nitric oxide	$NO(g)$	+ 90.4
nitrogen dioxide	$NO_2(g)$	+ 33.9
sulfur dioxide	$SO_2(g)$	− 296.1
sulfur trioxide	$SO_3(g)$	− 395.2

Science Background

Determining Enthalpy Changes of Reactions

Hess's Law provides a convenient way to evaluate enthalpy changes for a large number of reactions using a limited amount of data. Tables of data such as Table 16–4 are available to allow computation of reaction enthalpy changes.

16.8 Determining Enthalpy Changes of Reactions

In Section 16.6 you learned that equations for reactions can be combined in the same way as algebraic equations. The enthalpy of the resulting reaction is the sum of the enthalpies of the combined reactions. The Swiss chemist Germaine Henri Hess first stated the principle underlying this observation. He proposed that when reactants are converted to products, the enthalpy change is the same, regardless of whether the conversion occurs in one step or in a sequence of several steps. This is called **Hess's Law.**

To apply Hess's Law you will need to write equations that correspond to the standard enthalpy of formation of compounds. These equations describe the formation of one mole of a compound in its standard state from the elements in their standard states. For example, the equation for the formation of calcium carbonate is this.

$$Ca(s) + C(s) + \frac{3}{2}O_2(g) \rightarrow CaCO_3(s)$$

Notice that the reactants are elements and the product is a compound. All are in their standard states as shown in Table 16-4. To balance the equation for *one mole* of $CaCO_3$, it is necessary to use a fractional coefficient for oxygen. Example 16-4 will show you how enthalpies of formation are used in applying Hess's Law.

EXAMPLE 16-4

Calculate the enthalpy change that occurs during the combustion of methane, when the water is formed as a liquid.

■ **Analyze the Problem** Write and balance the equation for the combustion of methane. Remember that the water is formed as a liquid.

$$CH_4(g) + 2O_2(g) \rightarrow CO_2(g) + 2H_2O(l)$$

In order to determine ΔH°, you must know ΔH_f° for each reactant and product. These values can be found in Table 16-4. You must also be able to write the enthalpy of formation equations for each compound in the combustion equation.

■ **Apply a Strategy** Organizing your data into a table will help you to solve this problem. The enthalpy of formation equations and their ΔH_f° can be combined according to Hess's Law to form the equation for the combustion of methane.

	Substance	Number of Moles, n	ΔH_f° (kJ/mole)
Reactants	$CH_4(g)$	1	−74.8
	$O_2(g)$	2	0
Products	$CO_2(g)$	1	−393.5
	$H_2O(g)$	2	−285.8

■ **Work a Solution** Write the enthalpy of formation equation and the enthalpy of formation, ΔH_f°, for each of these compounds: $CH_4(g)$, $CO_2(g)$, and $H_2O(l)$.

$$C(s) + 2H_2(g) \rightarrow CH_4(g) \qquad \Delta H_f^\circ = -74.8 \text{ kJ}$$
$$C(s) + O_2(g) \rightarrow CO_2(g) \qquad \Delta H_f^\circ = -393.5 \text{ kJ}$$
$$H_2(g) + \frac{1}{2}O_2(g) \rightarrow H_2O(l) \qquad \Delta H_f^\circ = -285.8 \text{ kJ}$$

These equations must be manipulated so that they add up to the equation for the combustion of methane, CH_4. Since methane is a reactant, the equation for the formation of methane must be reversed. When an equation is reversed the sign of the energy change is changed. This means that the sign of the enthalpy change becomes positive. Since two moles of water are formed in the combustion of methane, the equation for the formation of water must be rewritten to show the formation of two moles of water. As a result, the enthalpy change for that reaction is doubled.

$$CH_4(g) \rightarrow C(s) + 2H_2(g) \qquad\qquad \Delta H° = +74.8 \text{ kJ}$$
$$C(s) + O_2(g) \rightarrow CO_2(g) \qquad\qquad \Delta H° = -393.5 \text{ kJ}$$
$$2H_2(g) + O_2(g) \rightarrow 2H_2O(l) \qquad\qquad \Delta H° = 2(-285.8)$$

Add the equations according to Hess's law.

$$CH_4(g) + C(s) + 2H_2(g) + 2O_2(g) \rightarrow$$
$$C(s) + 2H_2(g) + CO_2(g) + 2H_2O(l)$$

Eliminate terms that appear on both sides of the equation in equal numbers.

$$CH_4(g) + 2O_2(g) \rightarrow CO_2(g) + 2H_2O(l)$$

Add the enthalpies of the three equations to find the $\Delta H°$ for the combustion of methane.

$$+74.8 + (-393.5) + 2(-285.8) = -890.3 \text{ kJ} = \Delta H°$$

Note that the change in enthalpy is a negative number. The reaction is exothermic—heat is released to the surroundings.

■ *Verify Your Answer* For each equation changed, check to make sure that the value of ΔH was also changed correctly. If an equation was reversed, the sign of ΔH must change. If coefficients were changed by multiplication, then ΔH must also be multiplied by the same factor. Figure 16-12 is a diagram of this reaction.

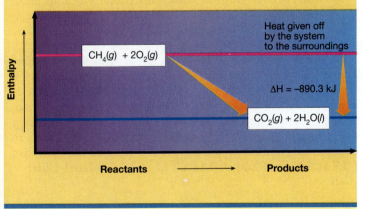

Figure 16-12 *The combustion of methane is an exothermic reaction. The enthalpy of the reactants is greater than the enthalpy of the products. The difference in enthalpy is −890.3 kJ. Therefore, 890.3 kJ is transferred from the system to the surroundings.*

Practice Problems

12. Calculate the enthalpy change for each of the following reactions, using the values of $\Delta H_f°$ listed in Table 16-4.

   a. $2H_2O_2(l) \rightarrow O_2(g) + 2H_2O(l)$ *Ans.* −196.4 kJ

   b. $2CO(g) + O_2(g) \rightarrow 2CO_2(g)$ *Ans.* −566.0 kJ

PART **2**

Section 16.9

Science Background

Energy from Food

The energy our bodies require varies depending on factors such as age, size, and activity level. A typical 15- to 18-year-old female requires about 2300 kcal/day, and a typical 15- to 18-year-old male requires about 3000 kcal/day. If the total mass of carbohydrate, fat, and protein contained in foods is known, students can determine the energy content using the values given in this section.

Guided Practice

Review the Concept Check question on page 547 with students. Answers can be found in Appendix E on page 808.

Reteaching Idea

Your students may not fully appreciate the relative basis for standard heats of formation. Ask them to draw a vertical scale of kJ extending from +300 to −300 and having divisions of 100 kJ. To the right of zero, have students locate $N_2(g)$, $H_2(g)$, $O_2(g)$, and any other elements, in their standard states, that you or they choose. Then have them locate $H_2O(l)$ at −285.8 kJ, $NO_2(g)$ at +33.9 kJ, $NH_3(g)$ at −46.3 kJ. Add any other compounds you wish using data from Table 16–4.

(continued on page T553)

Figure 16-13 *Strenuous activity like this requires high-energy foods.*

Having worked Example 16-4 and the practice problems, you may have noticed a regularity that provides a shortcut in calculations. Did you see that when you added up the standard enthalpies of formation, the resulting $\Delta H°$ was the difference between the sum of $\Delta H_f°$ for all the products and the sum of $\Delta H_f°$ for all the reactants?

$$\Delta H = (\text{sum of } n\Delta H_f° \text{ of products}) - (\text{sum of } n\Delta H_f° \text{ of reactants})$$

In this expression, n is the number of moles of each reactant and product in the balanced equation. Check the calculations you did for the practice problems and verify this conclusion for yourself.

16.9 Energy from Food

Most of the food that you eat is converted into energy that is used to sustain life. Energy from food keeps your heart and lungs functioning, provides heat to maintain your body temperature, and provides electrical energy for nerve impulses. Whenever you use a muscle to walk, to run, or even to turn the pages of a chemistry textbook, you use energy. The chemical reactions that take place when food is digested and metabolized are multistep processes, but as long as you know the enthalpy change for both the reactants and the products, you can determine the overall enthalpy change. Information about the reactions of carbohydrates, fats, and proteins can be used to estimate the energy obtained from these nutrients. In Chapter 23, you will learn about the actual structure of these classes of compounds.

Carbohydrates in your diet Most people's diets are about 60 percent carbohydrates. Sugars, starch, and cellulose are all carbohydrates. Starch and more complicated sugars break down to yield glucose—a simple sugar with the formula $C_6H_{12}O_6$.

The combustion of glucose results in the formation of carbon dioxide and water. Therefore, the combustion of a carbohydrate in a calorimeter will give the same value of ΔH as the total value of ΔH for the series of metabolic reactions that convert the carbohydrate to carbon dioxide and water. In a calorimeter the energy released by the combustion of glucose is 2808 kJ/mole. This is an enthalpy change of 15.6 kJ per g of glucose digested, the equivalent of 3.7 kcal (since 1 kcal = 4.18 kJ) or to 3.7 Cal (since 1 kcal = 1 Cal).

Fats and proteins Fats also make up a significant portion of your diet. In the United States, most people's diets are 30 to 40 percent fat. A typical fat molecule is tristearin, $C_{57}H_{110}O_6$. Fats are used by animals to store energy. The average enthalpy change that occurs during the digestion of fat is 38 kJ/g, or 9 kcal/g. This is more than double the caloric content for a gram of carbohydrate.

PART 2 REVIEW

ANSWERS

■ **Keyed to Objectives**

E **13.** exothermic; Drano and water is the system; the pipe and the rest of the universe comprise the surroundings. Heat flows from the system to the surroundings.

F **14.** $\Delta H° = (-325 \text{ kJ}) + (-186 \text{ kJ})$
$= -511 \text{ kJ}$

G **15.** $K(s) + \frac{1}{2}Cl_2(g) + \frac{3}{2}O_2(g) \rightarrow$
$KClO_3(s)$

G **16.** a; one mole of $CO_2(g)$ is formed from its elements in their standard state, $C(s)$ and $O_2(g)$.

H **17.** $[2(-393.5) + 1(-285.8)] - [1(+227) + \frac{5}{2}(0)] = -1299.8 \text{ kJ}$, which rounds to -1300.00 kJ when recording the proper number of significant digits.

About 10 percent of your diet is protein. Proteins are very large molecules, with molar masses of up to 100 000 g/mole. They are made from simpler compounds called amino acids and contain primarily the elements carbon, hydrogen, oxygen, and nitrogen. The proteins you eat are used to synthesize other biological molecules. Protein is not used for energy unless there is a shortage of fats and carbohydrates in the body. The average enthalpy change when protein is metabolized is 17 kJ/g, or 4 kcal/g, about the same as for a carbohydrate.

PART 2 REVIEW

13. When Drāno is poured into a pipe containing water, the temperature of the water increases. Classify the reaction as endothermic or exothermic. Identify the system and the surroundings and indicate the direction of heat flow.

14. Given the following equations,

$$Sn(s) + Cl_2(g) \rightarrow SnCl_2(s) \quad \Delta H^\circ = -325 \text{ kJ}$$
$$SnCl_2(s) + Cl_2(g) \rightarrow SnCl_4(l) \quad \Delta H^\circ = -186 \text{ kJ}$$

calculate ΔH° for this reaction.

$$Sn(s) + 2Cl_2(g) \rightarrow SnCl_4(l) \qquad \textbf{Ans. } -511 \text{ kJ}$$

15. Write the equation that represents the standard enthalpy of formation for potassium chlorate, $KClO_3$.

16. Which of these equations represents the standard enthalpy of formation for carbon dioxide? Explain your reasoning.
    a. $C(s) + O_2(g) \rightarrow CO_2(g)$
    b. $CO(g) + \frac{1}{2}O_2(g) \rightarrow CO_2(g)$
    c. $2C(s) + 2O_2(g) \rightarrow 2CO_2(g)$
    d. $CaCO_3(s) \rightarrow CaO(s) + CO_2(g)$

17. Calculate ΔH° for the combustion of 1 mole of acetylene, C_2H_2, when water is formed in the liquid state. Use values of ΔH_f° listed in Table 16-4. $\qquad$ **Ans.** -1300 kJ

18. Calculate the energy (in kcal) that is released when a "quarter-pound" hamburger is digested. The mass of the hamburger is 114 g. It is 41 percent water, 16 percent protein, 14 percent fat, and 29 percent carbohydrate.
    $\qquad$ **Ans.** 349 kcal

19. Compare the energy available in an 8-oz. (240 g) glass of milk to that available in a 12-oz. (360 g) can of a cola soft drink. Assume that milk is 87.6 percent water, 3.3 percent protein, 2.8 percent fat, and 4.7 percent carbohydrate. Assume that the soft drink is 89.0 percent water and 11.0 percent sugar (a carbohydrate).
    $\qquad$ **Ans.** milk, 140 kcal; soda, 160 kcal

Boxed numbers indicate questions that involve skills in interpretation, application, and analysis.

H **18.** 114 g × 0.16 × 4 kcal/g = $\quad$ 73
$\qquad$ 114 g × 0.14 × 9 kcal/g = 144
$\qquad$ 114 g × 0.29 × 4 kcal/g = $\underline{132}$
$\qquad\qquad\qquad\qquad\qquad$ 349

H **19.** milk:
$\qquad$ 240 g × 0.033 × 4 kcal/g = $\quad$ 32
$\qquad$ 240 g × 0.028 × 9 kcal/g = $\quad$ 60
$\qquad$ 240 g × 0.047 × 4 kcal/g = $\underline{\quad 45}$
$\qquad\qquad\qquad\qquad\qquad$ 137
$\qquad$ (rounded to 140)

soda:
360 g × 0.11 × 4 kcal/g = $\quad$ 158
$\qquad\qquad$ (rounded to 160)

Note: Although only one significant digit is justified, two have been kept to allow comparison.

PART 2

Section 16.9 *continued*

(continued from page T552)
Ask students to write the equations for the formation of $NO_2(g)$, $NH_3(g)$, and $H_2O(l)$ and the value of ΔH_f° for each reaction. Focus on the change in energy on the scale as the compounds are formed from the elements. Emphasize that the change in energy is the energy of the products minus the energy of the reactants. Then have students calculate ΔH° for this reaction.

$$4NH_3(g) + 7O_2(g) \rightarrow 4NO_2(g) + 6H_2O(g)$$

Students can either add heat of formation equations and their energy changes, or use the relationship

$\Delta H^\circ = $ (sum of $n\Delta H_{f\ products}^\circ$) − (sum of $n\Delta H_{f\ reactants}^\circ$).
($\Delta H = -1130$ kJ)

≡ CLOSE

Summing Up Main Ideas

Have students prepare a three-column table with the following heads: *Changes, Exothermic,* and *Endothermic.* Under the head labeled *Changes,* include *energy change* (released or absorbed), *sign of change* (+ or −), *change for system* (higher or lower E), and *change for surroundings* (higher or lower E). In the other two columns students should briefly describe each of the four changes for an exothermic reaction and an endothermic reaction.

PART 2 REVIEW

Assign the Part Review questions.

Evaluating Skills

These skills are evaluated in the Part Review questions indicated. **Classifying:** 13, 16; **Analyzing data:** 14, 15, 17, 18, 19; **Calculating:** 14, 17, 18; **Applying a strategy:** 14, 15, 17, 18, 19; **Verifying results:** 14, 15, 17, 18, 19; **Comparing/Contrasting:** 19

PART 3
Spontaneous Reactions
and Free Energy
Section 16.10

Developing Skills

Students may apply these skills in their study of Part 3.
Comparing/Contrasting: Have students compare and contrast spontaneous and nonspontaneous processes.
Forming models: Have students form models for the relationship between entropy and enthalpy.
Calculating: Have students calculate the free energy of a system.

≡ FOCUS

Activate Prior Knowledge

Students already are familiar with the difference between order and disorder.

Set up a game of tiddlywinks between two students in the front of the classroom. Begin by handing the students the playing pieces in stacked columns. As they play, point out the increase in disorder as the tiddlywinks become more and more dispersed. As the students gather up the playing pieces after the game is over, instruct them to stack the tiddlywinks carefully according to color. Is this an increase or decrease in disorder? What would seem to be the more natural state: tiddlywinks stacked in columns or randomly spread over the bottom of their container?

≡ TEACH

Teaching Strategy

Spontaneous Processes

Give students examples of spontaneous processes and explain that spontaneous processes tend to occur in nature. A nonspontaneous process occurring spontaneously appears odd. When a

(continued on page T555)

PART 3 Spontaneous Reactions and Free Energy

Objectives

Part 3

I. *Describe* the changes in enthalpy and entropy that indicate a tendency for a reaction to be spontaneous.

J. Using the Gibbs free energy equation, ***explain*** the conditions required for a spontaneous reaction.

Figure 16-14 *As soon as the diver's feet leave the diving board, a spontaneous process begins.*

The study of energy changes as they relate to macroscopic quantities such as pressure, volume, temperature, and enthalpy is known as **thermodynamics.** Thermodynamics is important because it tells you which reactions can occur for a given set of conditions. In Part 1, you learned how to calculate the quantity of heat absorbed or released because of temperature changes or changes of state. In Part 2, you learned that a change in enthalpy, ΔH, measures the amount of heat absorbed or released during a chemical reaction or a physical change at constant pressure. In Part 3, you will study two additional functions—entropy and Gibb's free energy—that will enable you to predict whether or not a chemical reaction or change of state will occur.

16.10 Spontaneous Processes

- A brick held above the floor falls when released.
- Wet clothes dry when hung outside.
- A hot cup of coffee cools when left on the table.
- Ice melts at room temperature.
- A drop of food coloring added to a glass of water spreads throughout the water.
- An Alka-Seltzer tablet dissolves and produces bubbles of carbon dioxide when added to water.

You will not be surprised to find that these are examples of spontaneous physical and chemical processes. **Spontaneous** reactions are those that can occur, under specific conditions, without any assistance. Most familiar reactions occur spontaneously. Under the right conditions they proceed on their own. For example, once the gas in your Bunsen burner starts to burn, it burns spontaneously. The combustion of natural gas is a spontaneous reaction. It is also an exothermic reaction. You might conclude that all exothermic reactions are spontaneous because the reactants have more energy than the products, like the raised brick that falls to the floor. However, energy is not the only factor that determines whether a process is spontaneous or not. Consider the diagram in Figure 16-15. Two flasks are connected by a closed stopcock. Initially a gas is contained in one flask; the other flask is a vacuum. When the stopcock is opened, the gas expands to fill both flasks. The temperature of the gas remains constant, so there is no change in energy. Yet the process occurs spontaneously. Similarly the drop of food color spreads slowly throughout the glass of water, even without stirring, until the water is uniform in color.

Spontaneous endothermic reactions Can endothermic processes happen spontaneously? Consider the example of clothes hung outside to dry. Water turns into vapor spontaneously. Yet the conversion of liquid water to water vapor requires energy and is an endothermic process. Likewise, you studied in Section 16-6 the reaction that occurs when ammonium thiocyanate, NH_4SCN, and barium hydroxide, $Ba(OH)_2 \cdot 8H_2O$, are mixed. This reaction, shown in Figure 16-11, occurs spontaneously, even though it is endothermic. Clearly, having a knowledge of the enthalpy change for a reaction does not provide enough information to predict whether or not the reaction will occur.

Exothermic processes do *tend* to be spontaneous. However, this is not always the case. In the next section, you will study another factor that affects whether or not a process is spontaneous.

16.11 Entropy and Spontaneity

Imagine that you open a new box of playing cards. The cards are arranged in numerical order by suit. In this condition, the cards are well ordered, as shown in Figure 16-16. After you shuffle the cards, the order is gone. The cards are placed randomly. This is a situation with a large amount of disorder. ***Entropy,*** symbolized by S, is a measure of disorder. The shuffled cards are a high-entropy situation. Moving from a condition of low entropy to one of high entropy— that is, from order to disorder—tends to be spontaneous. There is a natural tendency to move from order to disorder. Have you ever noticed this trend occurring in your room at home?

The expansion of gas into a vacuum, diagramed in Figure 16-15, occurs spontaneously because the entropy of the system increases. Initially the positions of the gas molecules can be specified within one flask. After the stopcock is opened, their positions become more disordered, since they can now be located anywhere within the two flasks. Thus, when the gas molecules are spread throughout both flasks, they are more disordered than when they are all in one flask. Again the spontaneous change is from a lower entropy condition to a higher entropy condition.

Figure 16-15 Top: *When the stopcock is closed, the gas molecules are confined to a smaller volume. This represents a lower-entropy condition. Bottom: When the stopcock is opened, the gas molecules expand to fill a volume twice as large. This represents a higher-entropy condition.*

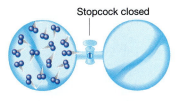

Stopcock closed

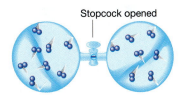

Stopcock opened

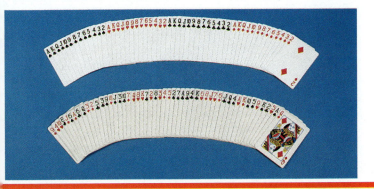

Figure 16-16 Top: *A newly opened deck of cards is very ordered and has a low entropy. Bottom: A shuffled deck is more disordered and has a higher entropy.*

(continued from page T554)
film is played backwards people laugh because they know nature does not behave that way. You may wish to run a film backwards and ask students to respond.

Science Background

Entropy and Spontaneity

Unlike enthalpy, absolute values of entropy can be determined. A perfectly ordered crystal at 0 K has an entropy of 0. Above 0 K entropy is a positive quantity. The quantitative aspects of entropy are not discussed in the text.

Teaching Strategy

Increasing Disorder

Focus on the qualitative aspects of entropy rather than the quantitative aspects. Reactions that increase entropy (ΔS is positive) tend to proceed spontaneously. Free energy change is the only predictor of reaction spontaneity. If ΔG is negative, the reaction is spontaneous. The value of ΔG depends upon the values of ΔH, ΔS, and the absolute temperature.

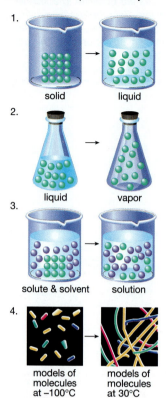

Figure 16-17 *These processes have positive values of ΔS and tend to occur spontaneously.*

1.

solid — liquid

2.

liquid — vapor

3.

solute & solvent — solution

4.

models of molecules at $-100°C$ — models of molecules at $30°C$

5.

$2H_2O_2$ — $2H_2O + O_2$

Increasing disorder Changes in entropy are measured using the same convention as is used for enthalpy.

$$\Delta S = S_{final} - S_{initial}$$

For chemical reactions, this can be rewritten as follows.

$$\Delta S = S_{products} - S_{reactants}$$

What is the algebraic sign of ΔS for a reaction that tends to be spontaneous? Since a spontaneous process tends to go from an initial condition of lower disorder, or lower entropy, to a final condition of greater disorder, or higher entropy, ΔS will be positive. Therefore, spontaneous processes *tend* to proceed with an increase in entropy for the system and ΔS tends to be positive.

Look at the processes illustrated in Figure 16-17. They have positive values of ΔS, and represent increases in disorder.

1. *A solid changing to a liquid.* The structure of a liquid has more disorder than a solid. Example: Ice changing to liquid water.

2. *A liquid changing to a gas.* The structure of a gas has more disorder than a liquid. Example: Liquid water changing to water vapor.

3. *A solute dissolving in a solvent.* The solute particles and the solvent particles mix, so the solution has more disorder than the pure solute or solvent. Example: Sugar dissolving in water.

4. *Heating a system.* Particles move faster and increase disorder.

5. *A reaction increasing the numbers of particles in the system.* Example: The decomposition of hydrogen peroxide forms 3 product molecules from 2 reactant molecules.

$$2H_2O_2 \rightarrow 2H_2O + O_2$$

Predicting spontaneous processes Table 16-5 summarizes the effects of enthalpy and entropy on the spontaneity of reactions.

TABLE 16-5

Factors That Determine Spontaneity		
Factor	**Sign**	**Reaction Tendency to Be Spontaneous**
ΔH	−	Exothermic reactions *tend* to be spontaneous.
ΔS	+	Reactions that increase disorder *tend* to be spontaneous.
ΔH	+	Endothermic reactions *tend* to be nonspontaneous.
ΔS	−	Reactions that increase order *tend* to be nonspontaneous.

DO YOU KNOW?

There are more than 8×10^{67} ways to order a deck of playing cards. Only one of these ways results in the cards' ending up in numerical order by suit. How likely is it that you would shuffle a deck of cards and end up with it in the same order as a new, unopened deck?

In order to make a prediction about spontaneity, you must consider both the enthalpy change and the entropy change. If ΔH is negative and ΔS is positive, then the reaction will always be spontaneous. For example, the decomposition of hydrogen peroxide, H_2O_2, is an exothermic reaction (ΔH negative) *and* it proceeds with an increase in entropy (ΔS positive). Therefore, this reaction is always spontaneous. Conversely, if ΔH is positive *and* ΔS is negative, the reaction will always be nonspontaneous.

Concept ✔ Check

If the conversion of oxygen to ozone, O_3, is always nonspontaneous, what are the signs of ΔH and ΔS for the reaction?

DO YOU KNOW?

Josiah Willard Gibbs was an American physicist and one of the founders of thermodynamics. His contributions to thermodynamics are honored by attaching his name to the free-energy function.

The effect of temperature What happens if a reaction is endothermic with a positive value of ΔS? In such a case, you must determine which factor, enthalpy or entropy, predominates. Consider the example of ice melting. Changing from the solid to the liquid state is endothermic and has a positive change in entropy. The enthalpy factor does not favor a spontaneous change, but the entropy factor does. Will the melting process occur spontaneously? As you think about this question, you may realize that the answer can be either yes or no, depending upon the temperature and pressure of the surroundings. At atmospheric pressure, if the temperature is above 0°C, ice melts spontaneously. But at the same pressure, if the temperature is below 0°C, ice does not melt spontaneously. At high temperatures, the entropy factor predominates; but at low temperatures, the enthalpy term predominates.

Temperature is also important in any process in which both ΔH and ΔS are negative. Such processes are spontaneous at low temperatures and nonspontaneous at high temperatures. The reason for this is that the enthalpy factor favoring spontaneity predominates at low temperatures and the entropy factor predominates at high temperatures. Can you explain the spontaneous condensation of steam to liquid water at temperatures below 100°C, based upon the enthalpy and entropy changes that occur?

Gibbs free energy predicts spontaneity Free energy, often called *Gibbs free energy* and symbolized as *G,* is a quantity defined to take into account the relative contributions of enthalpy and entropy in predicting whether or not a reaction will occur under a given set of conditions. As with changes of enthalpy and entropy, changes in free energy depend only on the initial and final conditions.

$$\Delta G = G_{final} - G_{initial}$$

For chemical reactions, this can be expressed as follows.

$$\Delta G = G_{products} - G_{reactants}$$

Guided Practice

Review the Concept Check question on page 557 with students. Answers can be found in Appendix E on page 808.

Reteaching Idea

Students are sometimes confused when asked to combine enthalpy and entropy changes in the Gibb's equation and decide whether a reaction is spontaneous. First help them to understand the equation as a tally of energy "types." Enthalpy (ΔH) is the total energy released or absorbed; $T\Delta S$ is that portion of the released energy that is unavailable for work. ΔG is what remains after the "useless" energy has been subtracted from the total energy. ΔG is the energy available to do work. A negative value for ΔG means that a reaction is spontaneous.

Table 16–6 graphically represents all combinations of signs for ΔH and ΔS at temperatures high and low. The magnitudes and directions (+ or −) are represented by arrows (vectors). Although your students may be unfamiliar with vectors, they can grasp the pictorial representation readily. Tell them that vectors can be subtracted by reversing the direction of the vector to be subtracted and placing its tail on the head of the first. In each block, $T\Delta S$ is subtracted from ΔH to give the resultant, ΔG. Go over each combination carefully. Ask students if they understand why the arrow for $T\Delta S$ is longer when the temperature is high.

Relating enthalpy, entropy, and free energy
Changes in free energy that occur at constant pressure and at constant temperature are a function of enthalpy, entropy, and temperature, as given by the following equation.

$$\Delta G = \Delta H - T\Delta S$$

T is the temperature on the Kelvin scale. For all spontaneous reactions, $G_{products}$ will be smaller than $G_{reactants}$. In other words, ΔG must be negative for a reaction to be spontaneous. Table 16-6 summarizes the characteristics of ΔG, based on the possible signs of ΔH and ΔS. The effect of temperature in determining whether a reaction will be spontaneous is also indicated.

The Gibbs free energy equation is valuable in providing a way to determine whether a reaction is spontaneous. If you know the enthalpy change, ΔH, and the entropy change, ΔS, at a particular temperature, you can solve the equation for ΔG. If ΔG is negative, the reaction is spontaneous. A positive value of ΔG indicates that the reaction is nonspontaneous. For example, the value of ΔG for the freezing of one mole of water at −10°C is −224J. The negative sign of ΔG for this reaction confirms what you already know from experience—that water freezes spontaneously at −10°C. At temperatures above the freezing point of water, $T\Delta S$ is larger than ΔH, and ΔG becomes positive. You know that water does not freeze spontaneously at temperatures above its freezing point.

The conversion of oxygen to ozone, $3O_2(g) \rightarrow 2O_3(g)$, is nonspontaneous at all temperatures because ΔH is positive and ΔS is negative. What about the reverse reaction, $2O_3(g) \rightarrow 3O_2(g)$? Recall that the algebraic sign of ΔH is changed for the reverse reaction. The same is true for ΔS and ΔG. Thus, for the reverse reaction, the conversion of ozone to oxygen, ΔH is negative and ΔS is positive. This means that ΔG will be negative and the reaction is spontaneous. In general, if a reaction is spontaneous, the reverse of that reaction will be nonspontaneous.

Energy to do work When gasoline is burned in an automobile engine, only a portion of the released energy is used to move the car forward. Some energy is lost as heat, since the engine and the exhaust gases become hot. This energy is not available to propel the car. A measure of the efficiency of an automobile engine is its *miles per gallon* rating.

Can an automobile engine be made more efficient? Consider the free energy change, ΔG, for the burning of gasoline. In a chemical reaction or a physical change, free energy is a measure of the energy available to do work. An exothermic reaction, such as the burning of gasoline, might be expected to produce considerable useful energy, but if the entropy term $T\Delta S$ is a large positive number, much of the energy released will be used to increase entropy and will be unavailable to do work. The free energy change tells you how much energy remains to do work after the energy used in increasing entropy has been subtracted from the enthalpy change.

PART 3 REVIEW

ANSWERS

■ **Keyed to Objectives**

I **20. a.** steam; gases have higher entropy (more disorder) than liquids.

b. iodine vapor; gases have higher entropy (more disorder) than solids.

c. 7 heads and 5 tails are less

The free energy change is a measure of the maximum energy available for useful purposes. The efficiency of an automobile engine can be measured by comparing the *theoretical* value of ΔG to the actual performance of the engine. Although one hundred percent efficiency can never be attained, knowing how much energy is theoretically available helps engineers attempting to maximize the performance of their design.

TABLE 16-6

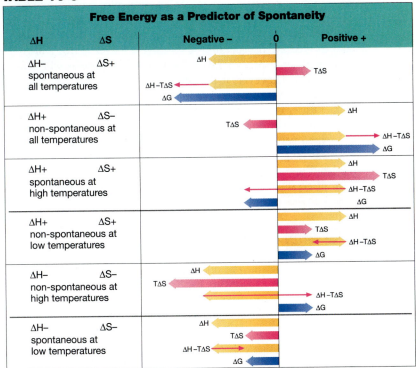

		Free Energy as a Predictor of Spontaneity		
ΔH	ΔS	Negative –	0	Positive +
$\Delta H-$ $\Delta S+$ spontaneous at all temperatures				
$\Delta H+$ $\Delta S-$ non-spontaneous at all temperatures				
$\Delta H+$ $\Delta S+$ spontaneous at high temperatures				
$\Delta H+$ $\Delta S+$ non-spontaneous at low temperatures				
$\Delta H-$ $\Delta S-$ non-spontaneous at high temperatures				
$\Delta H-$ $\Delta S-$ spontaneous at low temperatures				

PART 3 REVIEW

20. Which has more entropy? Explain your reasoning.
    a. 1 g of liquid water or 1 g of steam
    b. 1 g of iodine vapor or 1 g of solid iodine?

21. Predict the sign of ΔS for the following processes. Explain your reasoning.
    a. $I_2(s) \rightarrow I_2(g)$
    b. heating liquid water from 20°C to 50°C

22. Which of the following processes tend to be spontaneous changes? Explain your answer in terms of disorder.
    a. Sugar dissolves in water.
    b. A pile of bricks changes into a brick wall.

Boxed numbers indicate questions that involve skills in interpretation, application, and analysis.

CLOSE

Summing Up Main Ideas

Have students consider the decomposition of $KClO_3(s)$ to $KCl(s)$ and $O_2(g)$.

When this reaction takes place, heat is absorbed from the surroundings. What is the likelihood of this being a spontaneous reaction? Is entropy increasing or decreasing? Why?

This reaction takes place spontaneously at temperatures exceeding 370°C. What can be said about the ΔH and ΔS of this reaction? Is ΔG a positive or negative value above 370°C? Below 370°C?

What is the likelihood of the reverse reaction—$KCl(s)$ and $O_2(g)$ combining to form $KClO_3(s)$—taking place?

⚠ **CAUTION:** The thermal decomposition of a chlorate or a perchlorate to produce oxygen in the laboratory is extremely dangerous. Do not allow anyone to undertake this procedure.

Assign the Part Review questions.

Evaluating Skills

These skills are evaluated in the Part Review questions indicated.
Comparing/Contrasting: 20;
Determining main ideas: 20;
Determining cause and effect: 21, 22

ordered (higher entropy) than 12 heads

I **21. a.** ΔS is positive because S_{final} is larger than $S_{initial}$.
   b. ΔS is positive because S at 50° is greater than S at 20°.
   c. ΔS is positive. Ions in solution have less order (higher entropy) than ions in a solid crystal.

I **22. a.** spontaneous; sugar displays more disorder in solution than in the solid crystal.
   b. nonspontaneous; bricks display less disorder in a wall than in a pile.
   c. spontaneous; a liquid has more disorder than a solid.

Thermodynamics and the Rubber Band

Estimated Time: (35 minutes)

Process Skills

Observing
Describing
Forming hypotheses
Analyzing data
Predicting
Verifying results

Preparation

■ **Materials**

(for a class of 24, working in pairs)

Apparatus

(12 of each, unless noted)
Bunsen burners (can be shared); clean, wide rubber bands; ring stands with rings; test tubes; Scoopulas; 10-ounce steel nuts (or any available weights); thermometers; rulers; 1 roll each of fishing line (nylon), heavy-duty polyester thread, and heavy-duty silk thread

Reagents

■ 100 mL of distilled water
■ 200 g of sodium acetate

■ **Preparation Hints**

The best results are obtained with the type of rubber band used by the U.S. Postal Service. These can be purchased at an office supply store.

■ **Safety**

Students may attempt to misuse the rubber bands by shooting them across the room. Reinforce that this is neither appropriate nor safe.

Make sure students understand that they must apply the Bunsen burner to the stretched rubber band in ONE QUICK MOTION. Do not allow students to burn the rubber.

Laboratory

Investigation

Thermodynamics and the Rubber Band

Based on your everyday experiences, two rules seem to govern why processes occur the way they do. First, processes tend to be exothermic—that is, the enthalpy decreases. Second, processes tend to increase the amount of disorder—that is entropy increases. When a process favors both rules the process will definitely occur. However, if the process favors one rule but not the other, the deciding factor will be the temperature. The higher the temperature, the greater the molecular motion. When molecules move faster, the amount of randomness, or disorder, increases. In this experiment you will use a rubber band that in its relaxed state has long, randomly oriented polymers. When you stretch the band you organize the chains (decreasing the randomness). A form of crystallization actually occurs along parts of the polymer.

Objectives

Determine if the process of stretching a rubber band is exothermic or endothermic.

Determine if the process of crystallization from a supersaturated solution is exothermic or endothermic.

Interpret the data to make a hypothesis and predict what will happen if you heat a stretched rubber band.

Materials

Apparatus
☐ wide, clean rubber band
☐ ring stand
☐ test tube
☐ thermometer
☐ Bunsen burner
☐ ruler
☐ 250-g steel nut

☐ nylon fishing line
☐ polyester thread
☐ silk thread

Reagents
☐ sodium acetate
☐ deionized or distilled water

Procedure

1. Put on your lab apron and safety goggles.

2. Prepare a supersaturated solution of sodium acetate by adding 15 grams of sodium acetate to a clean test tube that contains 5 mL of water.

   ▲ **CAUTION: When heating material in a test tube, move the test tube continually back and forth through the flame. Stop the heating process temporarily any time you see bubbles start to form. Do not point the open end of a heated test tube directly at anyone.**
   Heat this material until all the solid has dissolved. Allow the solution to cool to room temperature. While you are waiting, do steps 3 and 4.

3. Using both hands, gently place the rubber band against your upper or lower lip and quickly stretch the rubber band. Record what you experience in your data table.

4. Hold the stretched rubber band on your lip for a few minutes and then slowly allow the rubber band to relax. Again record what you experience in your data table.

5. To the cooled solution, add a thermometer and a few crystals of sodium acetate. Hold or clamp the thermometer so it does not rest in the test tube. Note what happens to the temperature during the crystallization process. Record this in your data table.

6. Based on the data in the table, write a simple hypothesis that might account for what you experienced with the stretched and relaxed rubber band. Then make a prediction based on your hypothesis as to what will happen if a stretched rubber band is heated.

7. Set up the ring stand. Tie one end of the rubber band to a clamp on the ring stand and tie a 250-g steel nut to the other end of the rubber band. Measure the distance from the table top to the bottom of the nut. Now, while still holding the ruler, quickly pass a low flame over the stretched rubber band and observe how the length of the rubber band changes. Record your observations in the data table.

   ⚠ CAUTION: Do not burn the rubber.

8. Repeat step 7 with nylon fishing line, polyester thread, and silk thread. Make a prediction first whether you think each material will shrink or stretch when heated. Then tie one end of the material to the clamp on the ring stand and tie the weight to the other end. Heat the material very gently and observe how the length of each material changes.

Data Analysis

1. Was your prediction for the reaction of the rubber band to heating correct? If not, develop a new hypothesis that would account for your data.

Data Table

Rubber Band

Temperature change
1. Rubber band stretched ———
2. Rubber band relaxed ———
3. During crystallization process ———
Prediction:
Observation:
Explanation:

2. Were your predictions for the reactions of the nylon fishing line, polyester thread and silk thread to heating correct? If not, restate other hypotheses that would account for your data.

Conclusion

1. Was the process of stretching a rubber band an exothermic or endothermic process? Explain your answer.

2. Rewrite the equation below, placing the word *heat* on the appropriate side of the equation.
   Relaxed rubber band →

   　　　　　　　　Stretched rubber band

3. Was the process of crystallization of sodium acetate an exothermic or endothermic process? Explain your answer.

4. If you were given samples of threads of unknown composition, could you use the information you learned in the investigation to determine whether or not some samples had similar compositions? Explain your answer.

Guiding the Investigation

■ Procedural Hints

Students should see that the crystallization process will release heat. Therefore, have them prepare a supersaturated solution of sodium acetate and actually measure the increase in temperature when it crystallizes.

Data Analysis

■ Sample Data
(See data table below.)

■ Analysis

1. Answers will vary. In order to develop students' higher-level skills, allow sufficient time to formulate the hypotheses. A discussion on the previous day may be advisable.

2. Answers will vary. Students must be able to account for their new data. Small group discussions or a class discussion comparing results and hypotheses may be helpful.

Conclusions

1. The temperature increases, indicating an exothermic reaction.

2. Equation should read: Relaxed rubber band → stretched rubber band + heat

3. The temperature increases as crystals form, indicating an exothermic reaction.

4. Yes; If the thread had a similar reaction to heat, it *may* have a similar composition.

Data Table

Rubber Band

Temperature change
1. Rubber band stretched —feels warmer—increased temperature
2. Rubber band relaxed —feels cooler—decreased temperature
3. During crystallization process —feels warmer—increased temperature
Prediction: Rubber band would get longer (stretch).
Observation: Rubber band contracted when heated.
Explanation: Stretching rubber band is exothermic. When heat is added, the reaction reverses and shrinks the rubber band (Le Châtelier's Principle, presented in Chapter 18).

Chapter 16 Review ANSWERS begin on page T565a.

Summary

Energy and Heat

- Energy is the capacity to do work or produce heat.

- Heat is energy that is transferred from one object to another because of a difference in their temperatures. Heat always flows from the warmer object to the colder object. The transfer of energy can be detected by measuring the resulting temperature change.

- Specific heat is the quantity of heat needed to raise the temperature of one gram of the substance one degree Celsius. The quantity of heat transferred is expressed mathematically by the equation $q = s \times m \times \Delta T$, in which s is specific heat, q is quantity of heat, m is mass, and ΔT is temperature change. Every substance has its own characteristic value of specific heat.

- The quantity of heat that must be absorbed to vaporize one gram of a liquid is called the heat of vaporization. The quantity of heat needed to cause one gram of a solid to melt into its liquid phase is called the heat of fusion.

- Calorimeters are used to measure heat changes that accompany a change of state or a chemical reaction. The SI unit for energy is the joule. One calorie is defined as 4.18 joules.

Thermochemistry and Enthalpy

- Compounds have potential energy because of the bonds between atoms. Breaking bonds requires energy and is always endothermic; forming bonds releases energy and is always exothermic.

- The quantity of heat absorbed or released during a reaction that occurs at constant pressure is called the enthalpy change, ΔH. The standard enthalpy of formation, ΔH_f^o, is the amount of energy released or absorbed when one mole of a substance is formed from its elements in their standard state. Reactions of known enthalpy can be combined according to Hess's law to determine $\Delta H°$ for an unknown reaction.

Spontaneous Reactions and Free Energy

- Entropy, S, is a measure of disorder. The more disordered a system, the higher the entropy. ΔS is the entropy change that occurs during a given process.

- Exothermic reactions and reactions that increase the entropy of a system tend to be spontaneous. The change in free energy, ΔG, is a predictor of spontaneity. ΔG is expressed by the equation $\Delta G = \Delta H - T\Delta S$. If ΔG is negative, the reaction is spontaneous.

- The quantities enthalpy, entropy, and free energy depend only on the initial and final conditions—the reactants and products.

Chemically Speaking

calorie *16.1*	Hess's Law *16.9*
calorimeter *16.4*	specific heat *16.2*
enthalpy change, ΔH *16.7*	spontaneous *16.11*
entropy, S *16.12*	standard enthalpy of formation, ΔH_f^o *16.8*
free energy, G *16.14*	surroundings *16.6*
heat *16.1*	system *16.6*
heat of fusion *16.3*	temperature *16.1*
heat of vaporization *16.3*	thermochemistry *16.5*

Concept Mapping

Using the method of concept mapping described at the front of this book, draw a concept map for thermodynamics. Include the following terms in your map—*energy, heat, temperature, enthalpy change, entropy change, free energy change, system, surroundings,* and *spontaneous.*

Students apply these strategies in the following questions.

- **Factor-label method:** 3, 5, 6, 7, 29, 31
- **Using what you know:** 4, 8, 9, 10, 11, 15, 18, 24, 25, 26, 27, 28, 29, 30, 31, 32

- **Using similar problems:** 5, 6, 7, 20, 21, 22, 29, 30, 31, 32
- **Using calculators:** 3, 5, 6, 7, 16, 20, 21, 22, 29, 30, 31, 32
- **Verifying your answer:** 3, 5, 6, 7,

Questions and Problems

ENERGY AND HEAT

A. Objective: Distinguish *between energy, heat, and temperature.*

1. Define *energy, heat,* and *temperature.* What units are commonly used to measure each?
2. Compare and contrast the units of calories and Calories.
3. A 1-oz. bar of chocolate contains about 147 Calories. This is equivalent to what quantity of energy in kilojoules?
4. Explain why a cup of boiling water contains less energy than a large iceberg?

B. Objective: Calculate *the quantity of heat absorbed or released when a substance changes temperature.*

5. When a 50.0-g piece of nickel absorbs 350.0 J of heat, the temperature of the nickel changes from 20.0°C to 36.0°C. What is the specific heat of nickel?
6. A solar-heating specialist is considering paraffin as a possible solar-heat collector. How many kilograms of paraffin would be needed to collect as much energy as 4.78×10^3 kg of water? The specific heat of paraffin is listed in Table 16-1. (*Hint:* Assume same temperature change.)
7. Calculate the quantity of heat that must be removed from 200.0 g of ethyl alcohol to cool it from 25.0°C to 10.0°C.

C. Objective: Calculate *the quantity of heat absorbed or released during a phase change.*

8. One mole of steam at 100°C could accidentally burn your hand more severely than 1 mole of water at that same temperature. Use the concept of heat of vaporization to explain this statement. Justify your explanation with calculations.

Boxed numbers indicate questions that involve skills in interpretation, application, and analysis.

9. Many solar homes store heat by letting the sun melt a solid material like sodium sulfate decahydrate, $Na_2SO_4 \cdot 10H_2O$, which has a melting point near normal room temperature. Even small amounts of this liquid can store large quantities of heat. Use the concept of heat of fusion to explain how this is possible.

D. Objective: Measure *the specific heat of a substance, using a calorimeter.*

10. Describe what happens when a hot piece of metal is placed in cool water inside a calorimeter. Be sure to include a statement about the final temperature in your description.
11. If a cold piece of metal is placed in an equal mass of warm water, will the final temperature be closer to the original temperature of the metal or the water?

THERMOCHEMISTRY AND ENTHALPY

E. Objective: Describe *the energy changes that occur in the system and surroundings for an exothermic and an endothermic reaction.*

12. The following reaction is exothermic.

$$2Na(s) + Cl_2(g) \rightarrow 2NaCl(s)$$

   a. What is the sign of ΔH for this reaction?
   b. Is the enthalpy of the product greater or less than that of the reactants? Explain.
   c. What is the sign of ΔH for the reverse reaction?

13. Since energy must be conserved in an exothermic reaction, where does the energy come from and where does it go?

14. Consider the following reaction.

$$S(s) + O_2(g) \rightarrow SO_2(g) \qquad \Delta H = -297 \text{ kJ}$$

   a. Is this reaction exothermic or endothermic?
   b. How does the enthalpy of the product compare to that of the reactants?
   c. What is the value of ΔH for the reverse reaction?

16, 20, 21, 22, 29, 30, 31, 32
- Breaking problems into manageable parts: 16, 20, 21, 22, 26, 28, 29, 30, 31, 32
- Making diagrams: 10, 11, 29

- Writing chemical equations: 17, 19, 21, 22, 30

F. Objective: **Apply** *Hess's Law to calculate the enthalpy change for a reaction using the enthalpy changes for other reactions.*

15. The heat of sublimation for water is the enthalpy change for this reaction.

$$H_2O(s) \rightarrow H_2O(g)$$

Relate heat of sublimation to heat of fusion and heat of vaporization.

16. The standard enthalpies of reaction for the following reactions can be measured directly.

$$\frac{1}{2}N_2(g) + \frac{1}{2}O_2(g) \rightarrow NO(g) \quad \Delta H^o = +90.4 \text{ kJ}$$

$$\frac{1}{2}N_2(g) + O_2(g) \rightarrow NO_2(g) \quad \Delta H^o = +33.8 \text{ kJ}$$

   a. Find the standard enthalpy of reaction for the combustion of nitric oxide, NO.

$$NO(g) + \frac{1}{2}O_2(g) \rightarrow NO_2(g)$$

   b. Is the reaction exothermic or endothermic? Explain your answer.

G. Objective: **Identify** *the equation that corresponds to the standard enthalpy of formation of a compound.*

17. Write the equation that corresponds to the standard enthalpy of formation of $H_2S(g)$.

18. Why would the heat produced by the reaction described below not be the standard enthalpy of formation, ΔH_f^o, for water?

$$H_2(l) + \frac{1}{2}O_2(l) \rightarrow H_2O(l)$$

19. Translate the following statements into equations that include enthalpy changes.

   a. The standard enthalpy of formation for magnesium oxide, MgO(s), is -607.1 kJ/mole.

   b. The standard enthalpy of formation for ammonia, $NH_3(g)$, is -46.3 kJ/mole.

   c. The quantity of heat released during the combustion of octane, C_8H_{18}, is -5470.6 kJ/mole of octane.

H. Objective: **Given** ΔH_f^o *for each reactant and product,* **calculate** ΔH^o *for a reaction.*

20. What is the value of the enthalpy change for this reaction? Use the standard enthalpies of formation listed in Table 16-5.

$$SO_2(g) + \frac{1}{2}O_2(g) \rightarrow SO_3(g)$$

Is this reaction endothermic or exothermic?

21. Write an equation for the combustion of 1 mole of ethylene, $C_2H_4(g)$. Use the standard enthalpies of formation listed in Table 16-5 to calculate the amount of heat absorbed or released by this reaction.

22. Calculate the ΔH^o for the combustion of sucrose, $C_{12}H_{22}O_{11}(s)$—table sugar. Use Table 16-3 for the values of ΔH_f^o that you may need.

SPONTANEOUS REACTIONS AND FREE ENERGY

I. Objective: **Describe** *the changes in enthalpy and entropy that indicate a tendency for a reaction to be spontaneous.*

23. What is a spontaneous process? Give three examples of spontaneous processes. Give three examples of nonspontaneous processes.

24. The ΔS value for a certain reaction has a negative value. What does that tell you about the reaction?

25. Predict the sign of ΔS for the following reactions.

   a. $CaO(s) + CO_2(g) \rightarrow CaCO_3(s)$

   b. $2HgO(s) \rightarrow 2Hg(l) + O_2(g)$

   c. $C_6H_{12}O_6(s) \rightarrow 2C_2H_5OH(l) + 2CO_2(g)$
       (glucose)   (ethanol)

J. Objective: **Using** *the Gibbs free energy equation,* **explain** *the conditions required for a spontaneous reaction.*

26. The following reaction is spontaneous.

$$CaO(s) + SO_3(g) \rightarrow CaSO_4(s)$$

Which sign would you expect for the values of the following and why?

a. ΔG   **b.** ΔS   **c.** ΔH

27. The following reactions are spontaneous. What is the sign of ΔS?

a. $NaCl(s) \rightarrow NaCl(aq)$ $ΔH = +3.9 \text{ kJ}$

b. $H_2O(s) \rightarrow H_2O(l)$ $ΔH = +6.0 \text{ kJ}$

28. Consider the following change of state.

$$H_2O(l) \rightarrow H_2O(s)$$

a. Is this reaction spontaneous at 298K?

b. What is the sign of ΔH for this reaction?

Critical Thinking

SYNTHESIS WITHIN THE CHAPTER

29. A 25-g piece of gold and a 25-g piece of aluminum, both heated to 100.0°C, are put in identical calorimeters. Each calorimeter contains 100.0 g of water at 20.0°C.

a. Which sample will heat the water to the higher temperature and why?

b. What is the final temperature in the calorimeter containing the gold? In the calorimeter containing the aluminum?

c. Which piece of metal undergoes the greater change in energy and why?

30. A simple fat molecule has the formula $C_3H_5(OH)_2OCO(CH_2)_2CH_3$. The standard enthalpy of reaction when it undergoes combustion to form carbon dioxide and water is −6405 kJ/mole or −1531 kcal/mole of fat. Calculate the amount of energy released per gram of fat. Compare it to the amount of energy released when a carbohydrate is burned (4 kcal/g). Which provides more energy per gram?

SYNTHESIS BETWEEN CHAPTERS

31. The amount of solar radiation received in Arizona annually is about $8.4 \times 10^6 \text{ kJ/m}^2$. The area of Arizona is $3.0 \times 10^{11} \text{ m}^2$. How much coke (C) must be combusted to produce the same amount of energy? The equation for the reaction is this.

$$C(s) + O_2(g) \rightarrow CO_2(g)$$

32. The standard enthalpy of formation for sodium chloride, NaCl, is −411 kJ/mole. Calculate the enthalpy change when 1.37 moles of sodium chloride are formed.

Projects

33. Biologists and biochemists frequently talk about energy being stored in chemical bonds. They may even say that energy is released when high energy bonds are broken. However, in this text, you have learned that energy is required to break bonds. Find a reference to high energy bonds in a biology or biochemistry book. What is really meant by *high energy bonds*?

Research and Writing

34. You are the consulting chemical engineer on a fuel-efficiency project and have been asked to prepare a report on the best applications for three readily available fuels: hydrogen, methane (natural gas), and octane (a major component of gasoline).

a. Look up the enthalpy change for the combustion of these three fuels. Calculate which has the greatest enthalpy change per gram.

b. Look up the density of these materials at standard conditions and use this data to determine the enthalpy change per liter.

c. Use the information you have gathered to prepare a justification for using octane in automobile engines, hydrogen in rockets, and methane for home heating.

☐ Boxed numbers indicate questions that involve skills in interpretation, application, and analysis.

1. Energy is the ability to do work or to produce heat. Heat is energy that is transferred from one object to another. Temperature is proportional to the kinetic energy. Energy and heat are measured in joules; temperature is measured in °C or K.

2. 1000 calories = 1 Calorie or 1 kcal

3. $147 \text{ Cal} \times \frac{1000 \text{ cal}}{1 \text{ Cal}} \times \frac{4.184 \text{ J}}{1 \text{ cal}}$
   $\times \frac{\text{kJ}}{1000 \text{ J}} = 615 \text{ kJ}$

4. Assume both are being cooled to a temperature lower than either. Although ΔT is larger for boiling water, the mass of an iceberg is so large compared to the mass of a cup of water, the total energy transferred is more from the iceberg.

5. $350 \text{ J} \left(\frac{1}{50.0 \text{ g}}\right) \times \left(\frac{1}{36.0°C - 20.2°C}\right)$
   $= 0.438 \text{ J/g°C}$

6. For convenience, assume a 1°C temperature change:
   $\left(4.18 \frac{\text{J}}{\text{g°C}}\right)\left(4.78 \times 10^3 \text{ kg}\right)\left(\frac{1000 \text{ g}}{1 \text{ kg}}\right)$
   $\times \left(1°C\right) = \left(2.00 \times 10^7\right) \text{J for the water}$
   $\left(2.00 \times 10^7\right)\left(\frac{1}{1°C}\right)\left(\frac{1 \text{ g°C}}{2.9 \text{ J}}\right)\left(\frac{1 \text{ kg}}{1000 \text{ g}}\right)$
   $= 6.9 \times 10^3 \text{ kg paraffin}$

7. $\left(200.0 \text{ g}\right)\left(2.45 \frac{\text{J}}{\text{g°C}}\right)\left(25.0°C - 10.0°C\right)$
   $= 7350 \text{ J} = 7.35 \text{ kJ}$

8. When steam condenses, heat equal to the heat of vaporization (the heat of condensation) is transferred from the steam to your hand in addition to the heat transferred as the 100°C water cools in contact with your hand. For 1 mole of steam at 100°C, the extra heat transferred would be:
   $1 \text{ mol} \times \frac{18 \text{ g}}{1 \text{ mol}} \times \frac{2260 \text{ J}}{\text{g}} \times \frac{1 \text{ kJ}}{1000 \text{ J}}$
   $= 41 \text{ kJ}$

9. When melted $Na_2SO_4 \cdot 10H_2O$ solidifies, it will give off heat equal in magnitude to the heat of fusion.

10. Heat is transferred from the hotter metal to the cooler water. Heat transfer will continue until the water and the metal are at the same temperature. The final temperature will be between the original temperatures of the water and the metal.

11. The final temperature will be closer to the temperature of the water since all metals have a specific heat less than that of water. Thus, the metal will undergo a larger temperature change.

12. a. negative
    b. The enthalpy of NaCl is less than that of reactants. The excess energy is released.
    c. positive

13. The larger amount of energy stored in the reactants relative to the energy of the products is transferred to the surroundings. Heat is transferred from the system to the surroundings.

14. a. exothermic
    b. ΔH_f of product lower than ΔH_f of reactants
    c. +297 kJ

15. The heat of sublimation is the sum of heat of fusion and heat of vaporization if the phase changes occur at the same temperature. If they are at different temperatures, the relationship is only approximate.

16. a. $NO(g) \rightarrow \frac{1}{2}N_2(g) + \frac{1}{2}O_2(g)$
    $\Delta H = -90.4 \text{ kJ}$
    $\frac{1}{2}N_2(g) + O_2(g) \rightarrow NO_2(g)$
    $\Delta H = +33.8 \text{ kJ}$
    $NO(g) + \frac{1}{2}O_2(g) \rightarrow NO_2(g)$
    $\Delta H = -56.6 \text{ kJ}$
    b. exothermic, because ΔH is negative

17. $H_2(g) + S_8(s) \rightarrow H_2S(g)$
    Some may show S as S_8 molecules; this is more correct since S exists primarily as molecules.
    $H_2(g) + \frac{1}{8}S_8(s) \rightarrow H_2S(g)$

18. The standard state of hydrogen and oxygen is not liquid.

19. a. $Mg(s) + \frac{1}{2}O_2(g) \rightarrow MgO(s)$
    $+ 607.1 \text{ kJ}$
    b. $\frac{1}{2}N_2(g) + \frac{3}{2}H_2(g) \rightarrow NH_3(g)$
    $+ 46.3 \text{ kJ}$
    c. $C_8H_{18}(l) + \frac{25}{2}O_2(g) \rightarrow 8CO_2(g)$
    $+ 9H_2O(l) + 5470.6 \text{ kJ}$

20. $[(1)(-395.2)] - [(1)(-296.1)$
    $+ (1/2)(0)]$
    $= -99.1 \text{ kJ, exothermic}$

21. $C_2H_4(g) + 3O_2(g) \rightarrow 2CO_2(g)$
    $+ 2H_2O(l)$
    $[(2)(-393.5) + (2)(-285.8)]$
    $- [(1)(+52.30) + (3)(0)] = -1410.9 \text{ kJ}$

22. $C_{12}H_{22}O_{11}(s) + 12O_2(g) \rightarrow 12CO_2(g)$
    $+ 11H_2O(l)$
    $[(12)(-393.5) + (11)(-285.8)]$
    $- [(1)(-2222) + (12)(0)] = -5644 \text{ kJ}$

23. A spontaneous process is a reaction that occurs by itself once it begins. Spontaneous processes include combustion of fuel, rusting of iron, or fermentation. Nonspontaneous processes include photosynthesis, the decomposition of water, or the separation of metals from their ores.

24. The entropy of the reactants is larger than the entropy of the products. The products are more ordered than the reactants.

25. a. negative
    b. positive
    c. positive

26. a. ΔG is negative since the reaction is spontaneous.
    b. ΔS is negative since a solid is formed from a gas and a solid.
    c. ΔH must be negative in order for ΔG to be negative even though ΔS is negative.

27. a. positive
    b. positive

28. a. no
    b. negative

29. a. aluminum; It has a higher specific heat.
    b. gold:
    $\left(0.129 \frac{\text{J}}{\text{g°C}}\right)(25 \text{ g})(100°C - T_f)$
    $= \left(4.18 \frac{\text{J}}{\text{g°C}}\right)(25 \text{ g})(T_f - 20.0°C)$
    $T_f = 21°C$
    aluminum:
    $\left(0.895 \frac{\text{J}}{\text{g°C}}\right)(25 \text{ g})(100°C - T_f)$
    $= \left(4.18 \frac{\text{J}}{\text{g°C}}\right)(25 \text{ g})(T_f - 20.0°C)$
    $T_f = 24°C$
    c. aluminum; It has a higher specific heat.

30. $\left(\frac{1531 \text{ kcal}}{1 \text{ mol}}\right)\left(\frac{1 \text{ mol}}{162.2 \text{ g}}\right) = 9.439 \text{ kcal/g}$
    The fat provides more energy per gram.

31. $\left(3.0 \times 10^{11} \text{ m}^2\right)\left(\frac{8.4 \times 10^6 \text{ kJ}}{1 \text{ m}^2}\right)$
    $\times \left(\frac{1 \text{ mol}}{393.5 \text{ kJ}}\right)\left(\frac{12.01 \text{ g}}{1 \text{ mol}}\right) = 7.7 \times 10^{16} \text{ g}$

32. $1.37 \text{ mol} \left(\frac{-411 \text{ kJ}}{1 \text{ mol}}\right) = -563 \text{ kJ}$

T565b

Reaction Rates

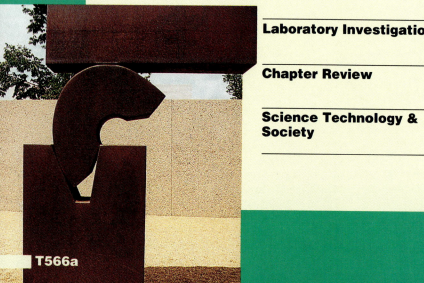

Investigations	Demonstrations	Texas Essential Elements★
		Content: 10.1 **Process:** 2.2, 4.3, 7.1
Laboratory Manual 17–1 M Laboratory Manual 17–2 IM Laboratory Manual 17–3 IM In-text Investigation, page T588	Collision Theory and Concentration, page T577 Nature of Reactants, page T578 Effect of Temperature, page T579	**Content:** 10.1, 10.2 **Process:** 2.2, 7.3, 10.1, 10.4
		Content: 10.2
		Content: 9.7, 10.2 **Process:** 1.1, 1.2, 1.3, 2.2, 4.3, 5.1, 5.2, 6.1, 6.2, 8.1
		Process: 4.2, 4.3, 5.2, 7.1, 8.1, 9.1, 9.2, 10.1
		Content: 10.1 **Process:** 10.1, 10.2, 10.3, 10.4
KEY: **M**–Microscale **S**–Structured **I**–Inquiry **IM**–Inquiry Microscale		★*See pages T8–T11 for complete listing of Texas Essential Elements.*

17

Reaction Rates

Chapter Rationale

This chapter introduces students to various aspects of reaction kinetics. The chapter begins with a discussion of reaction rates: what a rate means qualitatively, and how it can be quantitatively determined. Most students will have little difficulty understanding visual evidence for a faster reaction or a slower reaction. However, many students do not fully understand distance-rate-time problems. Take time to carefully develop the quantitative relationships your students will need to determine and to compare reaction rates. In particular, notice how students will be asked to use a graph in (for them) an unusual way. They will be interested in not only the points on a curve, but also the slopes of tangent lines to the curves.

After students have explored the meaning of the word *rate*, they will study the factors affecting reaction rates. The chapter ends with a discussion of the relationship between rates and reaction mechanisms.

About the Photograph

Steel sculptures eventually corrode due to the oxidation of iron to iron(III) oxide. For a steel sculpture to endure for decades, it can be coated with paint or a metal that oxidizes in air less readily than iron does. Metal sculptures that have endured for centuries are usually made from bronze. Bronze is an alloy of copper and tin.

Chapter Planning Hints

Plan to complete this chapter, including the Laboratory Investigation and the Chapter Review, in three to five class sessions. There are three optional demonstrations in this chapter. They appear on pages T577, T578, and T579.

One often thinks of chemical reactions as occuring quickly. However, many chemical reactions, such as the rusting of metal that has occurred on this sculpture, happen extremely slowly.

Myths and Misconceptions

Many students have a misconception that unless you see obvious signs of a reaction immediately, there is no reaction occurring. They are taught that evidence of a reaction includes color change, formation of a precipitate, gas release, and heat production. In slow reactions such as rusting, it takes a long time for the evidence of the reaction to be seen. Discuss with your students the fact that the central concept of this chapter is reaction rate, or how long it takes for a reaction to occur.

PART **1** Determining Rates of Reactions

At this point in your study of chemistry, you are familiar with a wide variety of chemical and physical changes. You recognize evidence of a chemical change when you drop an Alka-Seltzer tablet into water, strike a match across the front of its matchbook, or watch bubbling occur as a commercial preparation for unclogging a stopped-up sink begins to mix with water.

Besides the fact that all three of these occurrences are chemical reactions, do you see anything else that they have in common? One response you might make is that they all take place quickly. Within a short period of time, you can observe the formation of products from each reaction.

Do all reactions take place so quickly? With a little thought, you will realize that some reactions are not very fast. For example, although it may take several years to be noticed, a brand-new automobile may rust if it is exposed to saltwater spray from the ocean or if it is driven on roads treated with salt in winter. A nail may also rust, but not so fast that you can observe it within a matter of minutes. These are examples of the reaction of iron with oxygen to form iron oxide. Under certain conditions, however, this slow reaction can occur rapidly. When finely divided iron is heated in pure oxygen, the reaction occurs almost instantaneously.

Chemists are interested in the factors that make some reactions go faster than others. In order to study these factors, a chemist must have some way to measure how fast a reaction is taking place. What data should be collected to measure rates? In this section, you will take a closer look at the meaning of a reaction rate.

Objectives

Part 1

A. Explain what is meant by a rate and **identify** the data necessary to **determine** a rate.

B. Determine whether the rate of a reaction is increasing, decreasing, or remaining constant and **calculate** the rate of a reaction.

C. Identify an appropriate reactant or product for determining the reaction rate and **describe** how to measure the rate experimentally.

17.1 What Is a Rate?

Before answering the question—What is a rate?—you might find it helpful to think about how people use the word *rate*. When factory managers talk about the rate of production, they are referring to the number of products finished per unit of time. The interest rate that bankers apply to your savings account tells you how much money is earned by your savings per unit of time. When you use the word *rate* in ordinary conversation, you are referring to how fast something takes place. This is similar to the way chemists talk about the rates of reactions.

Rates and speeds You can begin to understand reaction rates by comparing a chemical reaction with a trip in an automobile.

Developing Skills

Students may apply these skills in their study of Part 1.
Interpreting diagrams and Analyzing data: Ask students how they can distinguish between a constant rate and a changing rate in Figure 17–2.
Forming hypotheses: Using Figure 17–4, ask students why they think the reaction would slow down at the end.

≡ FOCUS

Activate Prior Knowledge

Give students some small pieces of magnesium, zinc, and tin metals, along with a 0.1*M* HCl solution and test tubes.

⚠ **CAUTION: Be sure students are wearing safety goggles and lab aprons.** Direct students to mix the metals with no more than 5 mL of acid. Ask students which reaction was the fastest, and how they were able to determine this. During the subsequent class discussion, you should point out the similarity of the three reactions they were studying:
$$Mg + 2HCl \rightarrow MgCl_2 + H_2$$
(fastest)
$$Zn + 2HCl \rightarrow ZnCl_2 + H_2$$
$$Sn + 2HCl \rightarrow SnCl_2 + H_2$$
For disposal, combine all spent acid solutions, neutralize with 0.1*M* or less concentrated base, and pour down the drain. Wrap solids in newspaper and put in the wastebasket.

PART **1**
Section **17.1** continued

≡ TEACH

Cooperative Learning

Teams of 3; **Time:** 20 minutes
Objective: Students will learn about rates by studying the flow of water from a buret.
Task: Wearing safety goggles, students will fill a 25-mL or 50-mL buret with water. One student will watch a clock and call time every 15 seconds once the stopcock is opened. Another student will read the level of the water inside the buret. The third student will record the readings.
Team responsibility: Determine how the rate of water flow varied over time (if at all). Students should be challenged to find some way to organize their data so that it is usable (for example, make a chart).
Evaluation: Hold a class discussion to compare team responses.

The speed at which a car travels can be calculated using

$$\text{speed} = \frac{\text{distance}}{\text{time}}$$

Suppose a car traveling at a constant speed goes a distance of 50 kilometers in a half-hour time period. Its speed would then be 100 kilometers per hour, about the maximum speed allowed on most superhighways.

When you state an average speed for an automobile, you know that the vehicle will not be traveling at that speed during an entire journey. Suppose you are traveling by car from Chicago to Milwaukee to visit a friend. Your journey will be about 90 miles long and take about 2 hours. By using the equation given earlier, you can calculate that the average speed during the trip would be 45 miles per hour. Does this mean that your car's speedometer will register 45 miles per hour during the entire journey? Of course not. You will travel slower as you go along the city streets at both ends of the journey. You will travel faster than the average speed when you are on the interstate highway between the two metropolitan areas. You may even stop to buy gas.

An overall, or average, speed, then, does not necessarily tell you how fast a car is going at a particular point in its journey. Sometimes an overall speed is what you need to know—for example, to estimate your time of arrival. For other purposes, you need to be aware of how fast you are traveling during a certain portion of the trip—for instance, when you pass a highway patroller using a radar gun.

Figure 17-1 Top: *A time-lapse illustration of a car traveling at a constant speed over a distance of 150 meters. Bottom: A graph of time versus distance traveled by the car. Because the car is traveling at a constant velocity, the line on the graph is straight with a positive slope.*

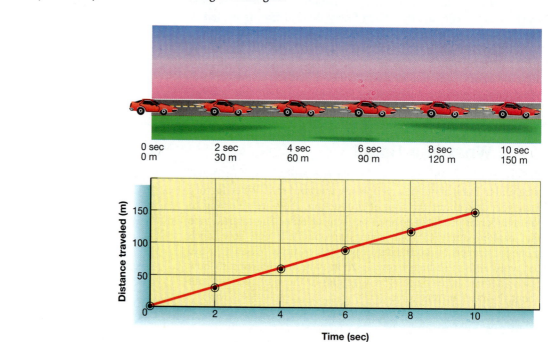

Using graphs to determine rates A graph can be used to visualize both overall speed and speeds over shorter distances. Figure 17-1 shows you how to construct a distance-time graph for an automobile. In the illustration, you see an automobile traveling at a constant speed. Its position after every 2.0 seconds is indicated. Just beneath the illustration is a graph of these distances and times. The graph is a straight line that has a positive slope—that is, the line is moving upward rather than downward. This straight line is an indication that the automobile is moving at a constant speed. Since it goes 150 meters in 10.0 seconds, its speed is 15.0 meters per second.

Figure 17-2 Top: *A time-lapse illustration of a car accelerating over a distance of 150 meters.* Bottom: *A graph of time versus distance traveled by the car. Because the car is accelerating, the line on the graph is a curve moving upward.*

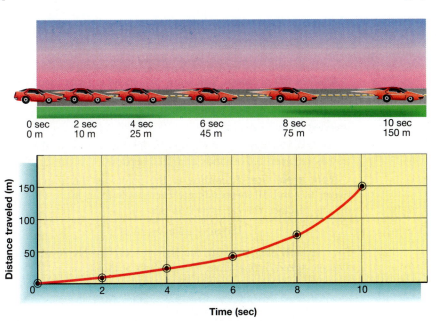

In Figure 17-2, you see an automobile whose speed is not constant. You can conclude from the photograph that the car must be accelerating—that is, traveling at a faster and faster speed. Notice that the car travels a longer distance over the last two seconds in the illustration than it does during the first two seconds. The graph for this car is shown directly below its illustration. The curve shown here is continually going upward, like the line in the previous figure. This indicates that the car is continually moving forward over the ten-second time interval. However, unlike Figure 17-1, the graph is a curve, not a straight line. The curve indicates that the speed of the automobile is *not* constant; it is changing during the time interval. In fact, since the curve goes upward more sharply at the end of the graph, the car must be speeding up. This, of course, is exactly the conclusion that you had already drawn from the picture. The graph verifies what you already learned from the picture: the car is accelerating.

Science Background

Using Graphs to Determine Rates

By using a graph, it is possible to determine the rate of a reaction. The average rate of a reaction is the slope of the line connecting the initial and final points. The instantaneous rate at a given point is the slope of the line tangent to the curve at that point. This concept, of course, is covered in a calculus class. Another way of expressing the instantaneous rate is to say that it is the first derivative of the curve at that point. Using the notation of calculus, it may be said that the rate of this reaction:

$$aA + bB \rightarrow cC + dD$$

is given by any one of these four derivatives:

$$\text{rate} = \frac{(-d[A]/dt)}{a}$$
$$= \frac{(-d[B]/dt)}{b}$$
$$= \frac{(+d[C]/dt)}{c}$$
$$= \frac{(+d[D]/dt)}{d}$$

If any of your students are taking calculus, you might want to show how what they already know is related to the rates of chemical reactions.

Practice Problems

Assign the Practice Problems.

It is not difficult to determine the speed of the car from the first graph, because it is the same at every point. Can you determine the speed from the second graph? You cannot determine the speed at any point in time without using more complicated mathematics, but you can determine the *average* speed of the car over any particular *interval* of time. In the following Example, you will see how to use the graph to determine average speed.

EXAMPLE 17.1

What is the average speed shown by the graph between 6.0 and 10.0 seconds?

- ■ *Analyze the problem* You know that speed is a rate involving distance and time. You have been given a four-second time interval and a graph from which you can obtain data about distance traveled in that interval.

- ■ *Apply a strategy* Use the graph to determine how far the car travels between 6.0 seconds and 10.0 seconds.

- ■ *Work a solution* According to the points on the graph, between 6.0 and 10.0 seconds the car travels from 80 m to 150 m. The distance the car travels is this.

$$150 \text{ m} - 80 \text{ m} = 70 \text{ m}$$

Four seconds elapse during the time the car travels 70 m. The average speed during these four seconds is this.

$$\frac{70 \text{ m}}{4.0 \text{ s}} = 17.5 \text{ m/s} = 18 \text{ m/s}$$

- ■ *Verify your answer* Since you are working a problem involving an automobile, your answer should represent a realistic speed for the vehicle. You may be able to judge whether or not your answer is reasonable by changing it into more familiar units.

$$18 \frac{\text{m}}{\text{s}} \times \frac{1 \text{ km}}{1000 \text{ m}} \times \frac{60 \text{ s}}{\text{min}} \times \frac{60 \text{ min}}{\text{hr}} = 65 \frac{\text{km}}{\text{hr}}$$

This speed is a bit faster than 35 miles per hour.

PROBLEM-SOLVING
S T R A T E G Y

*Use the **factor-label method** to help you convert m/s to km/hr. (See Strategy, page 12.)*

Practice Problems

1. Using the data from the graph shown in Figure 17-2, calculate the average speed of a car during the first 4.0 seconds of travel.   ***Ans.*** 6.3 m/s

2. Use the data from the same graph to calculate the average speed of a car over the entire 10.0 seconds shown by the graph.   ***Ans.*** 15.0 m/s

How would the graph of a car that was slowing down appear? You can see such a graph in Figure 17-3. Notice how the curve rises upward sharply at the beginning but soon levels out. This first portion of the graph corresponds to a car that is gradually slowing down.

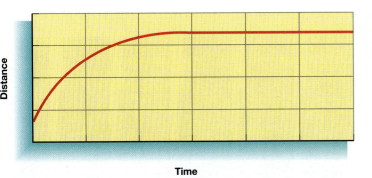

Figure 17-3 *A time-versus-distance graph of a car slowing down. When the slope of the line becomes zero, the car has stopped moving.*

What about the straight-line portion on the right of this graph? If you said that this indicates a constant speed, then you're doing a good job of interpreting graphs! However, you can be even a little more specific about this constant speed. Contrast this straight-line portion with the straight line of Figure 17-1. In the previous figure, the line slopes upward, while in Figure 17-3 the line is parallel with the x-axis. This means that the distance traveled is not changing. The right-hand portion of this graph corresponds to a car whose speed is constant because the car has stopped.

17.2 Reaction Rates

After reading the last section, you may have concluded that watching the speedometer is a much easier way to determine the speed of a car! Unfortunately there is no speedometer that you can use to follow the speed of a chemical reaction, but you can use the method just described. Just as the speed of a car can be determined by measuring its distance over an interval of time, the rate of a chemical reaction can be found by measuring the change in amount of reactant or product over a time interval.

The rate of a chemical reaction   What happens to the rate of a reaction as it proceeds? A fairly simple reaction to follow is the reaction of magnesium with hydrochloric acid. Magnesium displaces hydrogen gas from the hydrochloric acid, as shown by this chemical equation.

$$Mg(s) + 2HCl(aq) \rightarrow H_2(g) + MgCl_2(aq)$$

One way to determine the rate of this reaction is to measure the volume of hydrogen gas that forms. A method for collecting

PART 1
Section 17.2 continued

Teaching Strategy

Graphing Reaction Rates

After students have completed the cooperative learning activity and after they have completed Section 17.2, ask them to graph their water flow data and determine the rate in mL/sec at various points on their graphs.

and measuring the gas can be seen in Figure 17-4. A strip of magnesium is placed into a gas-collecting tube full of 0.2*M* HCl. As the reaction proceeds, the tube fills with hydrogen gas, displacing some of the hydrochloric acid that flows out past the loosely fitting cork. The gas-collecting tube has milliliters marked on the side, making it possible to read the volume of gas that has formed at any given time.

Figure 17-4 Top: *A time-lapse photograph of Mg reacting with 0.2M HCl. The reaction rate can be determined by the volume of hydrogen gas generated over 3-minute intervals. Bottom: A graph of the reaction rate. At what point on the graph does the reaction rate begin to slow down?*

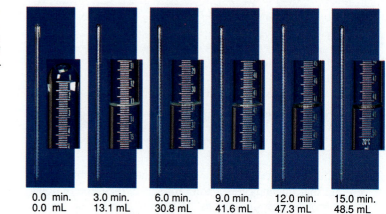

| 0.0 min. | 3.0 min. | 6.0 min. | 9.0 min. | 12.0 min. | 15.0 min. |
| 0.0 mL | 13.1 mL | 30.8 mL | 41.6 mL | 47.3 mL | 48.5 mL |

Rate of Production of Hydrogen Gas

PROBLEM·SOLVING
STRATEGY

Use what you know about everyday objects, such as automobiles, to help solve problems involving the rates of chemical reactions.
(See Strategy, page 58.)

Graphing reaction rates The amount of hydrogen gas collected over time can be plotted on a graph, as seen in Figure 17-4. Notice that time is plotted on the *x*-axis of this graph, just as it was on the graphs showing the speed of an automobile. The *y*-axis shows the volume of hydrogen gas produced. This variable (volume of hydrogen) changes with time, as "distance" changes on the speed graphs.

When you understand the relationship between the speed of an automobile and the rate of a chemical reaction, you can use this relationship to help you solve rate problems. The average speed of a car is calculated from this equation.

$$\text{speed} = \frac{\text{distance}}{\text{time}}$$

Similarly, the average rate of any chemical reaction may be determined from this equation.

$$\text{reaction rate} = \frac{\text{amount of product formed}}{\text{time interval}}$$

What can you learn about the reaction of magnesium and hydrochloric acid by studying the graph? First, notice that for most of the time period covered by this graph, the plot of volume versus time is very nearly a straight line. Just as a straight line for the automobile speeds meant that the speed of the car was constant, so the straight-line portion of this graph indicates that the rate of this reaction remains nearly constant for most of the time.

Second, you see that the reaction did not proceed at a constant rate throughout the experiment. In fact, a changing rate is characteristic of most chemical reactions. Notice that at the beginning of the graph, the slope of the curve is not as steep as it becomes later. This indicates that early in the reaction, the production of gas does not take place quickly. Did you also notice that the graph flattens slightly at the end? This corresponds to a gradual decrease in the amount of hydrogen produced and a slower rate of reaction after most of the hydrochloric acid has reacted.

Concept ✓ Check

What does the slope of the line on a reaction rate graph indicate about the rate of the reaction?

17.3 Reaction Rates from Experiments

The rate of a reaction is expressed either in terms of the amount of product formed in a period of time or as the amount of reactant consumed in a period of time. Therefore, changes in either the amount of a reactant or a product can be studied. You have already seen that by measuring the amount of hydrogen produced when magnesium and hydrochloric acid react, you can learn about the rate at which that reaction proceeds. It turns out that the rate at which the mass of the magnesium disappears is the same as the rate of appearance of the hydrogen gas (in mol/L). In other reactions, you can measure any change that is related to the amount of any substance present in the reaction mixture.

Reactions involving gases The data for the reaction of magnesium and hydrochloric acid, shown in Figure 17-4, was obtained by measuring the hydrogen gas at constant pressure. It would also be possible to measure changes in the amount of gas produced at constant volume. If the reaction takes place in a rigid container, the volume remains constant. As you learned in Chapter 6, the pressure of a gas will increase as more and more gas accumulates,

CONNECTING CONCEPTS

Change and Interaction How fast does a reaction take place? This is yet another way to characterize chemical reactions. If you understand the factors that control the rate of a reaction, then you can manipulate these factors to speed up or slow down reactions.

Myths and Misconceptions

When students make predictions about reaction rates, they sometimes are confused in stating whether altering a factor such as concentration will increase or decrease the reaction rate. When they study graphs of reaction rates and the various factors affecting them, they have difficulty stating a conclusion regarding the reaction rate. Emphasize that reaction rate means how fast something happens, and that if the *rate* is increased, the *time* is decreased (and vice versa).

PART 1

Section 17.3 *continued*

Guided Practice

Review the Concept Check questions on pages 573 and 574 with students. Answers can be found in Appendix E on page 808.

Reteaching Idea

To help students organize the information in Part 1 on determining the rate of a chemical reaction, have them make a concept map for the term *reaction rate.* They should incorporate terms such as *amount of product formed, amount of reactant consumed, volume of gas formed, graphing, pressure of gas, changes in concentration, color of solution, change in mass.*

provided that its volume and temperature remain constant. You could follow the pressure changes by connecting the reaction flask to a manometer, a pressure-measuring device.

Reactions involving colors Another way to measure the change in the reactants or products of a reaction is to measure changes in their concentration. This can be especially convenient when one substance in the reaction is colored. An example is provided by this reaction.

$$Zn(s) + Cu(NO_3)_2(aq) \rightarrow Zn(NO_3)_2(aq) + Cu(s)$$

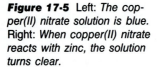

Since copper(II) nitrate has a blue color and a zinc nitrate solution is colorless, you expect to see the blue color fade, as this reaction takes place. (Color is directly related to concentration.) By using an instrument called a spectrophotometer, which measures how intensely colored the solution is, you can determine how the concentration of the solution changes as the reaction proceeds. Figure 17-5 gives you visual evidence.

Figure 17-5 Left: *The copper(II) nitrate solution is blue.* Right: *When copper(II) nitrate reacts with zinc, the solution turns clear.*

Three observable properties for studying reaction rates experimentally include the volume of a gas, the pressure of a gas, or the color of a solution. For other reactions, it may be desirable to follow the changes in mass of one of the reactants or products.

Concept ✔ Check

What other observable properties could you use to measure rates?

PART 1 REVIEW

3. Relative to automobile travel, which of these three variables does a reaction rate most closely resemble: the speed of the automobile, the distance it travels, or the time of travel?

4. A friend tells you that you can recognize a fast reaction because it produces more product than a slow reaction. What other factors must be included to make this a correct statement?

5. Suppose substances A and B react to form C, as shown below.

$$A + B \rightarrow C$$

The rate of this reaction can be followed by measuring the mass of substance C, which forms over time. The two graphs below show two of the many possible results that may be found for this reaction. Determine whether the reaction rate is increasing, decreasing, or remaining constant over time for graph I and for graph II.

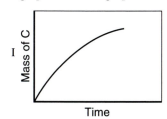
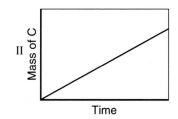

6. Explain how you can tell from a plot of product concentration versus time—without actually calculating reaction rates—whether the reaction rate is increasing, decreasing, or remaining constant.

7. Using the graph shown in Figure 17-4, calculate the average rate of the formation of hydrogen gas between the fifth and tenth minutes. **Ans.** 3.8 mL/s

8. Look at the graph in Figure 17-4 over the last minute. Without doing another computation, determine how the rate of the reaction at this point compares with the rate you calculated in the last question.

9. What reactant or product would you choose to measure in order to determine the rate of this reaction? Explain how you would measure the substance you chose.

$$Zn(s) + 2HCl(aq) \rightarrow H_2(g) + ZnCl_2(aq)$$

10. What reactant or product would you choose to measure in order to determine the rate of this reaction? Explain how you would measure the substance you chose.

$$Cu(s) + 2AgNO_3(aq) \rightarrow 2Ag(s) + Cu(NO_3)_2(aq)$$

Boxed numbers indicate questions that involve skills in interpretation, application, and analysis.

☰CLOSE

Summing Up Main Ideas

Give two examples of chemical reactions, one with a slow and one with a fast reaction rate. For each reaction, ask students to specify which reactant or product would be used to determine the reaction rate. Students should also describe how the formation of the product and the depletion of the reactant would be measured. Ask students to tell how graphs illustrating the rates of each reaction would be alike and different. (Both graphs would have increasing slopes. Slopes would also be different. One may be more linear than the other.)

PART 1 REVIEW

Assign the Part Review questions.

Evaluating Skills

These skills are evaluated in the Part Review questions indicated. **Identifying and controlling variables: 3, 4; Determining main ideas: 4, 9, 10; Interpreting diagrams: 5, 6, 7, 8; Analyzing data: 5, 6, 7, 8; Applying a strategy: 5, 7, 8; Calculating: 7; Verifying results: 7; Designing and performing experiments: 9, 10**

PART 1 REVIEW

ANSWERS

■ **Keyed to Objectives**

A **3.** the speed of an automobile

A **4.** A fast reaction produces more product per unit time than a slow reaction.

B **5.** The rate is decreasing in Graph I, because the curve becomes less steep. Graph II has a line of constant slope, so its reaction rate is constant.

B **6.** The rate increases if a curve slopes upward, decreases if a curve flattens, and remains constant if the curve is a line.

B **7.** Draw a line between these two points. The slope of this line is 3.8 mL/s.

B **8.** Because the curve becomes less steeply sloped at the end, the rate decreases.

C **9.** You could measure the volume of H_2 gas produced at constant pressure.

C **10.** You could measure the intensity of the blue color that appears as $Cu(NO_3)_2$ forms.

PART **2**
Factors Affecting
Reaction Rates
Section 17.4

Developing Skills

Students may apply these skills in their study of Part 2.
Analyzing data and Interpreting diagrams: Ask students how the kinetic-molecular theory they learned earlier in the course is related to the graph shown in Figure 17–12.

≡ FOCUS

Activate Prior Knowledge

Students have observed temperature and surface area affecting a reaction rate if they have made a gelatin dessert. Study how changing temperature or surface area affects the gelling process by dividing the class into three groups.

⚠ **CAUTION: Safety goggles and lab aprons must be worn. Remind students that nothing is eaten in the chemistry lab or classroom.** The first group will dissolve gelatin dessert mix in boiling water while stirring the solution. The second group will add boiling water to gelatin, but will not stir the mixture. The third group will add cold water to gelatin while stirring the solution. Three minutes after adding water to the gelatin, stop students and have them observe and compare the results.

For disposal, combine, add double the volume of water, heat until dissolved, and let cool. If still liquid, pour down the drain. If gelled, add more water and repeat.

Objectives

Part 2

D. *Identify* factors that can affect the rate of a reaction and *recognize* how a change in each factor can affect the rate.

E. *Explain,* using collision theory, why reaction rates change when reaction conditions change.

F. *Compare* the rate of a reaction with and without a catalyst.

Figure 17-6 *Particles must have a specific orientation when they collide in order for the collision to be successful and a new product to form.*

PART 2 Factors Affecting Reaction Rates

In a combustion reaction, a substance reacts with oxygen, and energy is released. The substance can be a burning candle or the food that you have eaten. Your body obtains energy through the combustion of food as this equation for the reaction of glucose with oxygen shows.

$$C_6H_{12}O_6(s) + 6O_2(g) \rightarrow 6CO_2(g) + 6H_2O(l) + energy$$

There are certainly some important differences between the combustion of a candle and the combustion of glucose in your body. For example, part of the energy of the candle's wax is released in the form of light, while the energy released when your body burns glucose is converted into chemical energy. In addition, you don't tend to think that combustion is possible when something is dissolved in water or when the temperature is as low as your body's temperature (about 37°C). How is the glucose dissolved in your body's fluids able to undergo combustion at such a low temperature? You know that sugar will not burn in a sugar bowl at room temperature.

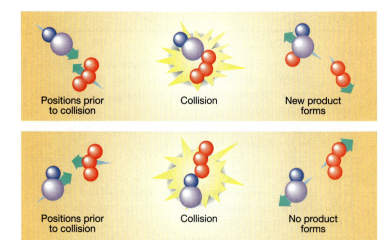

Positions prior to collision — Collision — New product forms

Positions prior to collision — Collision — No product forms

This question can be answered in part by studying the factors that affect the rates of reactions. Explaining why these factors cause rates to vary will involve a submicroscopic model called **collision theory.** According to this theory, the rates of chemical reactions depend upon the collisions between reacting particles. Any kind of change that affects the collisions will also affect the rate of reaction. As you read the next section, notice how this model provides an explanation for the observations that are made.

17.4 Effect of Surface Area

Both physical and chemical changes can be affected by the amount of surface area of a solid in a reaction. For example, if you put a sugar cube into one glass of water and an equal amount of granulated sugar into another glass and stir the contents of both glasses equally, the granulated form dissolves before the cube does.

Similarly, in a chemical reaction such as that between hydrochloric acid and zinc metal, the reaction rate is slower when large chunks of zinc are used rather than an equal mass of smaller pieces. Figure 17-7 shows the bubbles of hydrogen forming on the surface of the zinc.

$$Zn(s) + 2HCl(aq) \rightarrow ZnCl_2(aq) + H_2(g)$$

Using collision theory, it is not difficult to explain why smaller pieces of a solid react faster than larger pieces. The atoms of zinc in the interior of the pieces cannot react until they come in contact with the acid. As Figure 17-8 shows, if a piece is cut in half, additional zinc atoms will be on the surface and can react. Cutting the pieces into smaller pieces will further increase the surface area and therefore the rate of reaction. You can predict that increasing the surface area increases the number of collisions between reacting molecules and that the reaction will take place faster.

17.5 Collision Theory and Concentration

You now know how a change in the surface area of the solid reactant affects the rate of the reaction between zinc and hydrochloric acid. Can the reaction rate be changed by changing the hydrochloric acid in some way? Yes, you can change the concentration of the acid that is used.

What would happen to the reaction rate if the concentration of hydrochloric acid is increased? Figure 17-9 shows that zinc reacts more rapidly with concentrated hydrochloric acid than with dilute hydrochloric acid.

Figure 17-7 *Hydrogen gas is produced on the surface of zinc metal when zinc reacts with hydrochloric acid.*

Figure 17-8 *The cube has a surface area of 96 cm². When the cube is cut into eight pieces, the total surface area is 192 cm². More surface area is exposed to other reactants.*

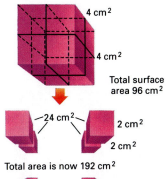

4 cm²

4 cm²

Total surface area 96 cm²

24 cm²   2 cm²

2 cm²

Total area is now 192 cm²

24 cm²

Figure 17-9 *The rate of the reaction between zinc and hydrochloric acid increases when the concentration of hydrochloric acid is increased from 0.5M (left) to 6M (right).*

PART 2
Section 17.5

≡TEACH

Teaching Strategy

Effect of Surface Area

Bring in several wooden building blocks or sugar cubes to help illustrate the point made about surface area. Stack several blocks together, and show students how the overall surface area increases as you pull the blocks apart. Ask them how the collision theory explains the faster reaction rate with greater surface area.

⚠ **CAUTION: Remind students that nothing is eaten in the chemistry lab or classroom.**

Videodisc Connections

25288 to 27025, side 3
Micro grain elevator (movie)

31626 to 36210, side 5
KMnO₄ in glycerine (movie)

DEMONSTRATION

Collision Theory and Concentration

Fill a 15 × 150 mm test tube with 1.0*M* HCl. Insert a 0.50 cm strip of magnesium and measure the length of time it takes the magnesium to react. Repeat with 0.50*M* and 0.10*M* solutions of HCl.

⚠ **CAUTION: Wear safety goggles and a lab apron. Use a shield to protect students.** For disposal, combine liquids and neutralize with 0.1*M* or less concentrated base and pour down the drain.

Does collision theory explain this result? In the more concentrated solution, there are more reactant particles for every milliliter of solution. The more reactant particles there are, the more collisions you can expect to take place. This leads to an increase in the rate.

17.6 Nature of Reactants

Lithium metal reacts with water at 25°C to produce the results seen in Figure 17-10. The bubbles in the picture on the left show that one of the products of this reaction is gaseous. The glowing light bulb on the right shows that there must be a product that consists of ions. Measurement of the temperature of the solution just after the reaction shows that heat has been released. This equation is consistent with these observations.

$$2Li(s) + 2H_2O(l) \rightarrow 2Li^+(aq) + 2OH^-(aq) + H_2(g) + energy$$

The gas produced is elemental hydrogen, and the electrical conductivity is caused by lithium and hydroxide ions in solution.

Other Group 1 metals, such as potassium, react in a similar manner. When metallic potassium is placed in water, this reaction takes place.

$$2K(s) + 2H_2O(l) \rightarrow 2K^+(aq) + 2OH^-(aq) + H_2(g) + energy$$

Figure 17-10 Left: *The photograph shows the reaction of lithium with water.* Right: *The presence of lithium ions in solution is shown by the lit bulb of the conductivity apparatus.*

Figure 17-11 *The reaction of potassium with water is shown. Compare the reaction with that of lithium above. In which reaction is energy released more rapidly?*

Although the equation looks similar to that of lithium and water, the observations that you can make during the reaction are different. Hydrogen gas evolves much more rapidly when the potassium reacts with water. Energy is also produced more rapidly as shown in Figure 17-11. By comparing the evolution of hydrogen and of energy from both reactions, you can tell that potassium reacts more rapidly with water than does lithium. The difference in the rates is because of differences in the reactants involved.

DEMONSTRATION

Nature of Reactants

To demonstrate rate of reaction varying with nature of reactants: Add 1 g of $Fe(NO_3)_2$ to a large test tube half-filled with distilled water. Add 10 drops of $1 M H_2SO_4$. Add 1 g of $Na_2C_2O_4$ to a large test tube half-filled with distilled water. Add 10 drops of $1 M H_2SO_4$. Add a very dilute solution of $KMnO_4$ a drop at a time to each test tube.

The reaction rate is very fast in the Fe^{2+} solution but very slow in the $C_2O_4{}^{2-}$ solution (about 1 hour).

⚠️ **CAUTION: Use a shield to protect students. Wear safety goggles and a lab apron.** For disposal, neutralize the solutions and pour down the drain.

17.7 Effect of Temperature

Earlier in this course, you learned how temperature affects molecular motion. From your study of the kinetic molecular theory, you know that raising the temperature increases the average velocity and kinetic energy of gas molecules. It is not surprising, then, to learn that temperature also affects the rate of a reaction, since a reaction is due to collisions between reactant molecules.

When the concentration of a reactant increases, more collisions take place, and the reaction rate goes up. Is this what happens when the temperature increases? For many reactions near room temperature, an increase in the temperature by ten degrees (from about 293 K to 303 K, if you assume that room temperature is around 20°C) will *double* the rate of a reaction. This is a large increase in rate for such a small increase in temperature! Although the number of collisions increases, this factor alone does not explain the increase in the reaction rate.

High-energy collisions You can begin to understand what is happening if you keep in mind that collisions by themselves are not sufficient to cause a reaction to take place. The colliding particles must have sufficient energy to react. To understand this principle, consider the following analogy. If a stalled car is being pushed by another car, there are gentle bumps from the car behind, but no damage is done to either car. The situation changes when two cars collide head-on on an interstate highway. Such high-energy collisions cause extensive car damage. Similarly, high-energy molecular collisions cause molecular damage. The result of this damage is that bonds may be broken and new bonds may take their place. That is, a chemical reaction occurs and new chemical compounds form.

When you read about the kinetic molecular theory in Chapter 7, you learned that molecules move faster as their temperature increases. However, this does not mean that all molecules travel with the same speed at the same temperature. In fact, gas molecules at a particular temperature show a wide range of molecular energies. A few molecules travel at very high speeds and have high kinetic energy. If one of these molecules collides with another molecule, you would expect molecular damage to take place. Most molecules have much lower speed and energy and do not react.

Concept ✓ Check

What is the relationship between the temperature of a molecule and its kinetic energy? Do all molecules at a particular temperature have the same kinetic energy?

The energy sufficient for reaction A chemical reaction takes place only if the two colliding molecules bring enough energy to the collision that a rearrangement of atoms occurs to form new

CONNECTING CONCEPTS

Structure and Properties of

Matter It is important to remember that the submicroscopic model of matter uses particles that are in motion; even in solids, atoms and molecules have motion due to vibration. This is the basic idea behind collision theory. It is this motion that helps explain variations in reaction rate.

Science Background

Effect of Temperature

A chemical rule of thumb is that as the temperature increases by 10°C, the rate of a reaction doubles. This rule of doubling the reaction rate for an increase in temperature of 10°C only applies to certain reactions over a moderate temperature range. However, the rule is useful in predicting the effect of temperature on reaction rates.

DEMONSTRATION

Effect of Temperature

Make up two large test tubes of $Na_2C_2O_4$ as in the demonstration on page T578.

⚠️ **CAUTION: Wear safety goggles and a lab apron. Use a shield to protect students.** Warm one tube to about 40°C before adding the MnO_4^-.

Compare the rates of the reaction between room temperature and at 40°C. For disposal, neutralize the solutions with 0.1 *M* or less concentrated base and pour down the drain.

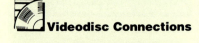

Videodisc Connections

20505 to 23658, side 6
Elephant toothpaste (movie)

molecules. The two curves in Figure 17-12 show the distribution of energies of colliding molecules at two different temperatures, T_1 and T_2. The minimum amount of energy required for a reaction to occur is called the threshold energy, or **activation energy,** and is shown by a vertical line in the figure. The shaded area to the right of this line represents the fraction of collisions that will occur with energy greater than the minimum amount required.

Figure 17-12 *The graph shows the distribution of energy levels for molecules at two different temperatures, T_1 and T_2. Note that at the higher temperature, T_2, there are more molecules that have kinetic energies equal to or greater than the activation energy than at the lower temperature level, T_1.*

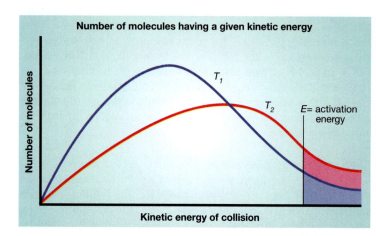

Number of molecules having a given kinetic energy

T_1

T_2

$E =$ activation energy

Number of molecules

Kinetic energy of collision

At a lower temperature, T_1 (shown by the gray line), not as many molecules have energies high enough to react. Few of the collisions lead to a chemical reaction. What happens when the temperature is increased to T_2 (shown by the violet line)? The distribution curve flattens and spreads out. The average speed of the molecules is greater, so more of the collisions involve energy greater than the activation energy that is needed for reaction. Because there are more effective collisions at higher temperatures, the reaction rate is greater. The degree to which the rate changes varies from one reaction to another reaction.

17.8 Catalysts

Factors that affect reaction rates include the surface area of a solid reactant, the concentration of reactants, the nature of the reactants themselves, and the temperature at which a reaction takes place. One additional factor that can make a reaction go faster is the presence of a catalyst. A **catalyst** is a substance that can increase the rate of a reaction without being consumed during the reaction. The decomposition of hydrogen peroxide, H_2O_2, will help you understand what a catalyst is and how it works. Hydrogen peroxide decomposes according to this equation.

$$2H_2O_2(aq) \rightarrow 2H_2O(l) + O_2(g)$$

You might buy a bottle of hydrogen peroxide to use as a disinfectant.

DO YOU KNOW?

Hydrogen peroxide decomposes very slowly because an inhibitor has been added. An inhibitor slows the rate of a reaction by blocking low energy pathways and raising the activation energy.

Myths and Misconceptions

Students initially have a misconception about catalysts. They find it difficult to recognize that the catalyst itself does not participate in the reaction, but its presence enables the reaction to occur or to occur more rapidly. A useful analogy to explain this phenomenon is that a catalyst acts like a person who introduces two strangers to one another. If they had not been introduced by their mutual acquaintance, they might never have spoken to one another. Once they are introduced to each other, the person (catalyst) who made the introduction may not take part in the conversation that follows.

You would not want this reaction to have taken place because then your bottle might contain only water. Fortunately the rate of this reaction is quite slow. In fact, in a properly stored bottle—at 25°C—this reaction takes place so slowly that it would be months before you noticed the disappearance of the peroxide.

Why do some reactions take place so slowly? You know that in order for the reaction to occur, the colliding molecules must have relatively high energy. If the activation energy is high, then only a few molecules will collide with enough energy to react, and the rate of the reaction will be slow. For this reason, you would store a bottle of hydrogen peroxide in a relatively cool place.

Increasing reaction rates with catalysts The rate of decomposition of hydrogen peroxide can be changed by adding manganese dioxide. In Figure 17-13, you see a solution of hydrogen peroxide that has had a small amount of manganese dioxide, MnO_2, added to it. The decomposition reaction now proceeds briskly, even at room temperature. The evidence for this increase in rate is provided by the fact that a glowing splint, placed above the reacting mixture, bursts into flames as it reacts with the oxygen gas escaping from the decomposing peroxide.

Figure 17-13 Left: *The decomposition of hydrogen peroxide takes place very slowly. There is not enough oxygen produced to ignite the splint.* Right: *The catalyzed decomposition of hydrogen peroxide proceeds quickly. The presence of O_2 product ignites the glowing splint.*

There are two things to note about the role of manganese dioxide in this process. First, the MnO_2 speeds up the reaction. Second, when the reaction is complete, the manganese dioxide can be recovered unchanged. Just as much manganese dioxide is present at the end of the reaction as there was at the beginning. The overall equation for the reaction is the same. The manganese dioxide increased the rate of the reaction without being consumed and therefore is a catalyst.

Guided Practice

Review the Concept Check question on page 579. Answers can be found in Appendix E on

Reteaching Idea

To help students identify and compare the factors affecting the rate of a reaction, have them complete a summary table.

Factors Affecting Reaction Rate	Mechanism Involved	Effect on Reaction Rate
Surface area		
Concentration		
Nature of reactants		
Temperature		
Catalysts		

Once students have made the table, have them explain it in their own words.

PART **2**
Section **17.8** continued

☰ CLOSE

Summing Up Main Ideas

Have students list five factors that affect the rate of a chemical reaction. Also ask students to specify how the reaction rate is affected by a change in each factor and describe how the collision theory may explain the factor's effect on the reaction rate. (Increasing surface area and concentration increases the reaction rate because the number of collisions between reacting molecules increases. Increasing temperature also increases reaction rate by increasing the number of collisions and the energy of the colliding particles. The nature of the reactants can increase or decrease the reaction rate. Catalysts increase reaction rates by causing more reactant molecules to collide with sufficient energy for a reaction.)

PART 2 REVIEW

Assign the Part Review questions.

Evaluating Skills

These skills are evaluated in the Part Review questions indicated. **Determining cause and effect: 11, 15, 16; Comparing/Contrasting: 12, 13, 14, 16; Predicting: 12; Determining main ideas: 17**

DO YOU KNOW?

Catalysts used for automobile emission control use platinum or palladium that is attached to a honeycomb ceramic. The metals do not always adhere well to the ceramic. Tin(IV) oxide adheres well to both metals and to the ceramic surface and has made the catalytic converter ten times more effective.

Boxed numbers indicate questions that involve skills in interpretation, application, and analysis.

Enzymes: biological catalysts Certain proteins called **enzymes** serve as catalysts that help reactions in your body take place at 37°C. For example, you have a series of enzymes that catalyze the burning of glucose.

$$C_6H_{12}O_6(aq) + 6O_2(g) \rightarrow 6CO_2(g) + 6H_2O(l)$$

This equation summarizes reactions which take place in a series of three steps. The six-carbon glucose molecule is broken down into successively smaller molecules. As these processes occur energy is released, and some of it is stored as chemical energy in the bonds of specific molecules.

This complex sequence of reactions is unlikely to take place in solution at body temperature without enzymes. Enzymes are biological catalysts that increase the rate of each reaction in the process. They are large, complex molecules designed to work with only one specific molecule or with a limited class of molecules. Therefore, your body contains a wide array of enzymes, each one carrying out a limited but necessary role. Their role in biological systems is to act as catalysts in the same way that manganese dioxide does in the decomposition of hydrogen peroxide. After the reaction has taken place, enzymes are left intact so that they can continue to catalyze more reactions. In many respects your body runs a large chemical factory, but the reactions occurring in living systems are far more complex and efficient than any chemical process yet devised.

Other catalysts The chemical industry produces a variety of catalysts that have useful applications. A mixture of catalysts, for example, has been designed for use in the catalytic converter in your automobile. These catalysts, which include a variety of transition metals such as rhodium, convert possible pollutants into less harmful chemicals. Carbon monoxide is converted into carbon dioxide, and unburned gasoline is changed into carbon dioxide and water. At the same time catalytic converters were developed, it was important that unleaded gasoline was available to the market. The reason for this is that lead in gasoline poisons (inactivates) the catalysts in the converter, making it impossible to catalyze the reactions just described.

PART 2 REVIEW

11. How does increasing the concentration of a reactant affect the rate of a reaction?

12. One piece of zinc reacts with 6.00*M* hydrochloric acid at 25°C. Another piece of zinc of equal size and shape reacts with 1.00*M* hydrochloric acid at 25°C. Predict which reaction occurs at a faster rate.

13. A chunk of zinc reacts with 1.00*M* hydrochloric acid at 25°C. An equal mass of powdered zinc reacts with 1.00*M*

PART 2 REVIEW

ANSWERS

■ **Keyed to Objectives**

D 11. Increasing the concentration increases the reaction rate.

D 12. Since 6.00*M* HCl is more concentrated than 1.00*M* HCl, the zinc reacts faster with the 6.00*M* solution.

E 13. Due to its greater surface area, the powdered zinc reacts faster. More exposed surfaces allow for more collisions leading to a reaction to occur.

E 14. Potassium reacts faster, illustrating the effect of the changing nature of reactants.

E 15. Increasing the temperature increases the average kinetic energy of colliding molecules.

F 16. The decomposition is faster in the presence of the catalyst manganese dioxide.

F 17. Manganese dioxide increases the rate of decomposition without being consumed during the reaction.

hydrochloric acid at 25°C. Compare the reaction rates. Use collision theory to explain your answer.

14. Which reacts faster with water, lithium or potassium? Explain your answer.

15. How does temperature affect the average kinetic energy of colliding reactant particles?

16. Does the decomposition of hydrogen peroxide take place faster when manganese dioxide is present or when manganese dioxide is absent?

17. Why is manganese dioxide referred to as a catalyst for the decomposition of hydrogen peroxide?

R E S E A R C H & T E C H N O L O G Y

The Driving Force behind Explosives

Few materials are more destructive than the explosives that can level a building in seconds or propel a bullet. Yet similar explosives can be used to create beautiful displays of fireworks.

Explosions proceed by a self-contained decomposition reaction: Atoms present in the explosive material recombine to form more stable molecules but not with oxygen in the air. This contrasts with ordinary combustion reactions that consume oxygen.

Most commercially available explosives, including nitroglycerin, trinitrotoluene (TNT), and dynamite, are based on organic compounds containing nitrogen. When these compounds decompose, the relatively weak bonds between the elements present (usually hydrogen, oxygen, nitrogen, and carbon) are broken. Among the gaseous products formed are nitrogen, carbon monoxide, carbon dioxide, and water, all of which contain much stronger bonds. When these strong bonds form, an enormous amount of energy is released.

In a powerful explosion, the decomposition reaction can occur in less than a millionth of a second. The gaseous products may quickly ex-

pand to more than 10 000 times the volume of the original explosive. The pressure created by the rapidly expanding gases provides the tremendous force that is used for many important applications in industry today.

For example, certain explosives are used to mold large pieces of metal. Nose cones for rockets are cast underwater, using explosives that force the metal into a mold. Also, in cases where conventional welding is difficult or impossible, explosives can be used to force dissimilar metals to join. High-pressure vessels used in the chemical industry and joints used in ships are made in this way. This process of shaping or changing metals using explosions is known as explosive forming.

PART **3**
Reaction Pathways
Section 17.9

Developing Skills

Students may apply these skills in their study of Part 3.

Analyzing data and Interpreting diagrams: Ask students to use the graphs in Figure 17–17 to explain why a catalyzed reaction takes place faster.

Forming models: Ask students to form their own analogies for the rate-determining step of a reaction. (See the dishwashing analogy in Section 17.10.)

FOCUS

Activate Prior Knowledge

Students were introduced to the catalytic role of enzymes in Part 2. This activity demonstrates the action of a biological enzyme, protease, found in common household products.

Have students stain swatches of fabric with a protein substance, such as egg albumen. Allow the swatch to set overnight. The following day cut the swatches in half. Wearing rubber gloves, hand-scrub one piece with a paste of water and soap flakes. Scrub the other swatch with a paste made of a detergent that contains protease or protein-digesting enzyme (as labeled on the container). Rinse and dry the fabric overnight. Compare the results of the two treatments.

⚠️ **CAUTION: Safety goggles must be worn. Also be aware that some individuals are allergic to these enzymes.**

Objectives

Part 3

G. **Demonstrate** how the potential energy of the substances involved in a chemical reaction changes as the reaction progresses, using a graph.

H. **Define** a reaction mechanism and **explain** how the rate-determining step of the mechanism affects the overall rate of the reaction.

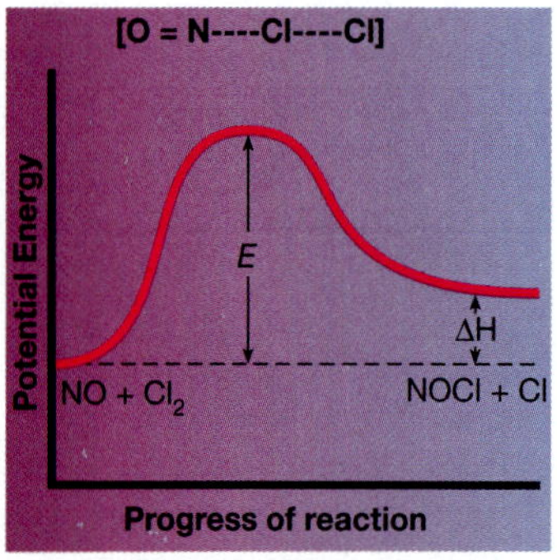

Figure 17-14 *The graph shows that a high amount of kinetic energy is needed to form an activated complex [O = N—Cl—Cl] from the reactants, NO + Cl$_2$. Once the activation complex is formed, the kinetic energy is transformed into a high potential energy.*

PART
3 Reaction Pathways

As you have seen, a variety of factors can be changed to make reactions go faster or slower. In order to understand reaction rates more fully, you need to look at the pathways that reacting molecules take and how the reaction pathway affects the reaction rate.

17.9 Activation Energy and Catalysts

The concept of activation energy is worth looking at from another point of view. Imagine a bowler trying to roll a ball up a steep hill. On most attempts, the ball slows down and stops before it reaches the top of the hill, rolling back down toward the bowler. Occasionally the bowler rolls the ball with enough energy that it is able to reach the top of the hill and roll down the opposite side. On each trip up, the ball slows down (loses kinetic energy) and gains potential energy because of its position above its starting point. It has its maximum potential energy at the top of the hill.

Collisions of molecules Imagine a similar situation for molecules in a chemical reaction. When molecules collide with each other, their kinetic energy is converted to potential energy. A collision results in a high-energy arrangement of reactant molecules, called an **activated complex.** An activated complex has high potential energy just like the ball at the top of the hill as illustrated in Figure 17-14. It also has a very short lifetime. While it exists, old bonds are partially breaking, and new bonds are beginning to form. The activated complex for the reaction which occurs between NO and Cl$_2$ is shown in Figure 17-15.

The products will form if the Cl----Cl bond breaks; but reactants will remain if the N----Cl bond breaks. Like the bowling ball at the top of the hill, the reaction can go in either direction. If the new N----Cl bond becomes strong, the old Cl----Cl bond will break and products will form. In effect the product molecules will "roll down the other side of the hill." However, the activated complex could simply break apart into reactant molecules once again.

Like the bowling ball that must be given sufficient kinetic energy to carry it over the hill, reactant molecules must collide with sufficient energy—the activation energy—to allow them to get over a potential energy barrier that separates reactants and products.

In Figure 17-16, you can see the relationship between the distribution curve for molecular kinetic energies and the potential energy "hill" for a chemical reaction. To react, molecules must collide with enough energy to assume the high-energy configuration of atoms (the activated complex) represented by the top of the

Myths and Misconceptions

Students may have misconceptions about chemical bonds that can lead to difficulties in understanding chemical reactions. We often refer to the "energy necessary to break bonds between atoms." As a result, students often think that bonds between atoms are actual physical entities, similar to sticks that are snapped apart. This misconception can be reinforced when you have students construct "ball-and-stick" models of molecules. Review the concept of bonding, reminding students that bonds result from the sharing or transferring of electrons between atoms and that a chemical reaction is the breaking and making of chemical bonds.

barrier. With less energetic collisions, the molecules do not react, even though the products are at a lower energy level than the reactants. Several values are marked on the energy distribution curve with circles. When molecular collisions having those energies occur, the system reaches the corresponding circles on the potential-energy diagram. Obviously these collisions are not successful.

Lowering the activation energy The action of the catalyst manganese dioxide in the decomposition of hydrogen peroxide can be explained in terms of the activation energy for the reaction. As you know, a catalyst makes a reaction go faster, which means that more molecules must be exceeding the activation energy. Yet this cannot be due to an increase in the kinetic energy of the molecules. You learned earlier that the average kinetic energy of the molecules changes proportionally with the temperature, yet nothing has taken place to affect the temperature. The explanation must involve something other than a change in the distribution of molecular energies.

$$O = N + Cl - Cl$$
$$\downarrow$$
$$[O = N\text{---}Cl\text{---}Cl]$$
Activated complex

$$[O = N\text{---}Cl\text{---}Cl]$$
$$\downarrow$$
$$O = N - Cl + Cl$$
Products

$$[O = N\text{---}Cl\text{---}Cl]$$
$$\downarrow$$
$$O = N + Cl - Cl$$
Reactants

Figure 17-15 *An activated complex either can go on to form the products of the reaction or can revert back to the reactants.*

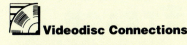
Videodisc Connections

12845 to 14468, side 1
Cl_2 and H_2 gases (movie)

5252 to 9358, side 6
Magnesium and dry ice (movie)

911 to 5251, side 6
Magnesium and sand (movie)

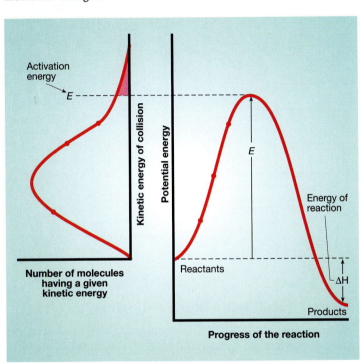

Activation energy

E

Kinetic energy of collision

Potential energy

E

Energy of reaction

Reactants

ΔH

Number of molecules having a given kinetic energy

Products

Progress of the reaction

Figure 17-16 *These graphs show a comparison between the kinetic energy distribution curve and the activation energy diagram. The graph on the left is turned on its side to relate the activation energy value, E, on both curves. Note that only a small number of collisions have sufficient kinetic energy to reach the top of the potential energy hill.*

If the molecules are not moving faster, then why does the reaction rate increase? Think again about the bowling ball analogy. How could the bowler be successful more often even if he doesn't increase the average energy he gives to each throw? Suppose that the top of the hill was lowered, so that the ball did not have such

PART **3**

Section 17.10

≡ T E A C H

Teaching Strategy

Reaction Mechanisms

Give students this analogy for the rate-determining step. Tell them that they are shopping for a gift for a friend in a crowded store on December 23. What part of this shopping expedition might take longest? How could it be speeded up? Make a relationship between their responses and the mechanisms of chemical reactions.

Guided Practice

The reaction mechanism for the formation of iron(III) hydroxide includes these two steps.
1. $4Fe(s) + 3O_2(g) \rightarrow$
$$2Fe_2O_3(s) \text{ (slow)}$$
2. $2Fe_2O_3(s) + 6H_2O(l) \rightarrow$
$$4Fe(OH)_3(s) \text{ (fast)}$$
Have students write an equation for the net reaction and identify the rate-determining step.
[$4Fe(s) + 3O_2(g) + 6H_2O \rightarrow$
$$4Fe(OH)_3(s)$$
Step 1 is the rate-determining step.]

DO YOU KNOW?

Preservatives in food delay spoiling by slowing chemical reactions.

Figure 17-17 *These graphs show another comparison of the relationships for a catalyzed versus an uncatalyzed reaction. There are more collisions with sufficient kinetic energy to produce products for the catalyzed reaction. Note that the energy of the reaction does not change.*

a high peak to climb. Then the bowler, with the same effort, could more often roll the ball over the hill.

A catalyst has a similar effect on a chemical reaction. It speeds a reaction along by providing a lower-energy pathway from reactants to products. The catalyzed reaction takes place in a different way from the uncatalyzed reaction. The catalyzed path has a lower activation energy because it involves a different reaction mechanism and the formation of a different activated complex. Many catalysts cause a more favorable orientation of the colliding particles, so the collisions are more effective. In Figure 17-17, you can see the effect that a catalyst has on the energy pathway of a reaction.

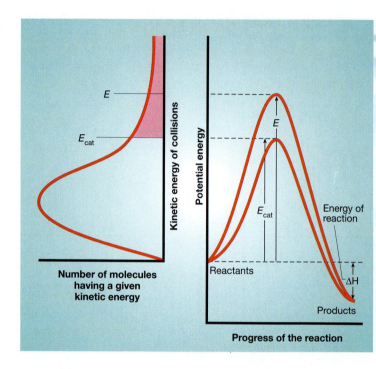

17.10 Reaction Mechanisms

When hydrogen bromide and oxygen react, water and elemental bromine are formed, as represented by this chemical equation.

$$4HBr(g) + O_2(g) \rightarrow 2H_2O(g) + 2Br_2(g)$$

Four molecules of hydrogen bromide react with one molecule of oxygen. Does this mean that four molecules of hydrogen bromide must *simultaneously* collide with one molecule of oxygen? The probability that five gaseous molecules will collide simultaneously is very small. Instead, experiments show that this reaction takes place in a series of steps.

HBr(g) + O₂(g) → HOOBr(g)	slow

$$HBr(g) + O_2(g) \rightarrow HOOBr(g) \quad \text{slow}$$
$$HOOBr(g) + HBr(g) \rightarrow 2HOBr(g) \quad \text{fast}$$
$$2HOBr(g) + 2HBr(g) \rightarrow 2H_2O(g) + 2Br_2(g) \quad \text{fast}$$

The first reaction takes place slowly, while the second and third reactions are fast. This sequence of reactions that produce bromine and water is called the **reaction mechanism** for the overall reaction. Notice that when you add the three reaction steps and cancel terms, the result is the overall equation.

Because the first reaction is the slowest reaction in the mechanism, it determines the overall rate. The second and third reactions cannot occur until HOOBr is formed. The slowest reaction in a reaction mechanism is called the **rate-determining step.** An analogy might help you understand the rate-determining step better. Imagine five people working together to wash dishes. The first two clear the table and hand the dishes to a third person, who washes them. The last two people dry and stack them. Since only one person is washing the dishes, this step is likely to be the bottleneck that determines how fast all five people can finish the job.

If reactions take place by two or more steps, you can control the speed of the overall reaction by controlling the slowest step. You have learned in this chapter, for example, that increasing the concentration of a substance can increase the rate of the reaction. In the reaction of hydrogen bromide and oxygen, you can see that both reactants are involved in the rate-determining (slow) step. Therefore, you can change the concentration of *either* reactant (HBr or O_2) to increase the rate of the overall reaction. For some reactions, one or more of the reactants does *not* appear in the rate-determining step. For these reactions, changing the concentrations of reactants that are *not* in the rate-determining step would not affect the overall reaction rate.

PROBLEM-SOLVING STRATEGY

Use what you know to add these three equations to get the overall equation. Remember that if a species appears on both sides of a chemical equation, it can be canceled out just as in a mathematic equation. (See Strategy, page 58.)

PART 3 REVIEW

18. How does a catalyst affect the activation energy of a reaction?

19. Does manganese dioxide *increase* or *decrease* the activation energy for the decomposition of hydrogen peroxide? Explain.

20. What is a reaction mechanism?

21. Suppose a reaction takes place according to this reaction mechanism.

$$A + B \rightarrow C \quad \text{fast} \quad A + C \rightarrow D \quad \text{slow}$$

Which step in the mechanism is the rate-determining step?

22. If you want to increase the overall rate of the reaction, would you increase the concentration of A or of B? Explain.

Boxed numbers indicate questions that involve skills in interpretation, application, and analysis.

Reteaching Idea

Some students may need practice in the use of graphs to show potential energy changes of substances involved in chemical reactions. Have students draw potential-energy curves showing the pathways of exothermic, endothermic, catalyzed, and uncatalyzed reactions. On the curves they should indicate energy of reactants and products, the activated complex, activation energy, and change in enthalpy (ΔH). Students should explain the curves in their own words. Once they have done so, show students several other comparison graphs and ask them to interpret the graphs in terms of potential energy changes and activation energy and to predict which reactions will proceed faster.

☰CLOSE

Summing Up Main Ideas

Consider the following theoretical reaction mechanism:
Step 1: $2C_6H_{12}O_6 + 2H^+ \rightarrow 2(C_6H_{13}O_6^+)$ (slow)
Step 2: $2(C_6H_{13}O_6^+) \rightarrow C_{12}H_{24}O_{11}^{2+} + H_2O$ (fast)
Step 3: $C_{12}H_{24}O_{11}^{2+} \rightarrow C_{12}H_{22}O_{11} + 2H^+$ (fast)
Have students write the net reaction, identify the rate-determining step and any catalysts for the reaction.
$[2C_6H_{12}O_6(s) + 2H^+ \rightarrow C_{12}H_{22}O_{11}(s) + H_2O(l) + 2H^+$
Step 1 is the rate-determining step and H^+ is the catalyst.]

PART 3 REVIEW

Assign the Part Review questions.

Evaluating Skills

These skills are evaluated in the Part Review questions indicated. **Determining cause and effect:** 18, 19, 21, 22; **Determining main ideas:** 20

PART 3 REVIEW
ANSWERS
■ Keyed to Objectives

G **18.** A catalyst lowers the activation energy of a reaction.

G **19.** Since manganese dioxide is a catalyst, it decreases the activation energy for the decomposition.

H **20.** A reaction mechanism is the series of individual steps that occur during an overall chemical reaction.

H **21.** The slow step is the rate-determining one.

H **22.** Increase the concentration of A. A appears in the slow (rate-determining) step, but B does not.

The Sulfur Clock

Estimated Time: (45-minute lab, 15-minute postlab; may require some homework time)

Process Skills

Measuring
Constructing tables and graphs
Interpreting data
Analyzing data
Stating a conclusion

Preparation

■ Materials

(for a class of 24, working in pairs)

Apparatus

(12 of each unless specified) graph paper (1 piece per student), 125-mL flasks (48 optimum; may use other size flasks), 50-mL graduated cylinders, 10-mL graduated cylinders, 5-mL graduated cylinders (if available), marking pencils, timing devices (can be student watches with second hand or wall clock with second hand)

Reagents

■ 2 liters of 0.161M $Na_2S_2O_3 \cdot 5H_2O$ (40.0 g of the salt per liter of solution)

■ 500 mL of 1.0M HCl(aq) solution (84 mL 12M hydrochloric acid per liter)

■ 1 liter of distilled water (avoid deionized water if possible)

■ Safety

If you dilute 12M hydrochloric acid to make the 1.0M or 2M acid, use the hood and wear safety goggles, a lab apron, face shield, and gloves. Use the same equipment if you use 2M acid in a demonstration. Use a shield to protect students. All students present at a demonstration using acid or base greater than 1M concentration should wear safety goggles.

Laboratory

Investigation

The Sulfur Clock

It is known that the thiosulfate ion, $S_2O_3^{2-}$(aq), decomposes in the presence of the hydrogen ion, H^+(aq), in the following manner.

$$S_2O_3^{2-}(aq) + 2H^+(aq) \rightarrow S(s) + H_2SO_3(aq)$$

When sulfur is produced, it makes the solution opaque. When the solution becomes opaque, it is no longer possible to see through it. You will use this fact to determine reaction time, which is defined in this experiment to be the time when you no longer see a mark on a piece of paper under the flask. If you start timing the reaction as soon as the hydrogen ion is added, very good *rate* data can be obtained.

Objectives

Compare the time that it takes for opaqueness to occur when thiosulfate ion at different concentrations are added to a constant concentration of hydrogen ion.

Measure the time in seconds for opaqueness to occur and **plot** it against the concentration of thiosulfate ion.

Determine what relationship, if any, exists between the rate and the concentration of the thiosulfate ion.

■ Materials

Apparatus
☐ graph paper
☐ 4 125-mL flasks
☐ 50-mL graduated cylinder
☐ 10-mL graduated cylinder
☐ 5-mL graduated cylinder or pipet
☐ marking pencil

Reagents
☐ 150 mL of 0.161M $Na_2S_2O_3 \cdot 5 H_2O$ (called hypo) solution
☐ 50 mL of 1.00M HCl(aq) solution
☐ distilled or deionized water

Procedure

1. Put on your laboratory apron and safety goggles.

   CAUTION: 1M hydrochloric acid is corrosive to skin and eyes. Wash off spills or splashes with plenty of water. Use

the eyewash fountain if 1*M* HCl gets in your eyes. Call your teacher.

2. Label your four flasks A, B, C, and D with a marking pencil.

3. Take a piece of white paper and place on it whatever mark you wish to utilize during the experimental procedure. It is very important that you use the same mark for all four runs.

4. Into flask A, put 10 mL of the thiosulfate solution and 30 mL of distilled water. Set flask A aside for now.

5. Into flask B, put 20 mL of the thiosulfate solution and 20 mL of distilled water. Set flask B aside for now.

6. Into flask C, put 30 mL of the thiosulfate solution and 10 mL of distilled water. Set flask C aside for now.

7. Into flask D, put 40 mL of the thiosulfate solution and *no* distilled water. Place flask D aside for now.

8. Return to flask A and swirl the contents to make certain the contents are thoroughly mixed to a uniform concentration. Place the flask over the mark. Measure, very carefully, 10.0 mL of 1.0*M* HCl(aq). Get ready to start timing. When ready, quickly pour the acid into flask A. Start timing. Swirl the flask and peer through the solution until the mark is no longer visible. Stop the timing. Record this time in seconds in your data table.

9. Swirl flask B and give the contents a chance to be thoroughly mixed. Place the flask over the same mark. Once again, measure carefully 5.0 mL of 1.0*M* HCl(aq). Get ready to start your timer. Pour the 5.0 mL of acid into the flask and start timing immediately. Record in your data table the time at which you can no longer see the mark.

10. Continue with the same process you used for flasks A and B, using the remaining solutions in flasks C and D. Record these times in your data table.

11. The products of these reactions can be rinsed down the drain and the flasks cleaned with detergent. Make certain that you clean up your laboratory station. Put your laboratory equipment away before you do the calculations or analysis of data.

■ Data Analysis

Data Table

Time in Seconds	
Flask A	_____
Flask B	_____
Flask C	_____
Flask D	_____

1. Obtain a piece of graph paper from your instructor. Label the *x*-axis (abscissa) *time in seconds.* Be certain to use the whole *x*-axis and use all of the spaces available to you. Do not clutter your labels; that is, label only every fifth unit or so. Label the *y*-axis (ordinate) *volume of thiosulfate* in mL. Expand your graph to utilize the entire page of graph paper.

■ Conclusions

1. What kind of graph results when you plot mL of thiosulfate against time in seconds?

2. What does this tell you about the rate of the reaction?

3. What do you think would have happened to the reaction time if you had reduced the hydrochloric acid by half? Why?

Guiding the Investigation

■ Procedural Hints

The same person should swirl all four flasks. If you decide to have different people do parts of the set, establish a uniform swirl technique.

A uniform mark generated by the computer and taped on the underside of a glass plate makes the data gathered from different individuals relatively consistent. This will be less important if one person has the time to do all four runs.

This lab can be done in less time as a demonstration on an overhead projector using 2.0*M* HCl solution (166 mL 12*M* HCl per liter).

Data Analysis

■ Sample Data
(See sample data table and graph below.)

Conclusions

1. The curve obtained is a hyperbola. See sample graph for an example. This type of curve indicates a nonlinear relationship between concentration and time. The *rate of reaction* is decreasing as the concentration of sodium thiosulfate decreases.

2. The less concentrated the hydrochloric acid, the slower the rate.

Data Table

	Time in Seconds
Flask A	162.0
Flask B	63.0
Flask C	38.5
Flask D	28.7

Note that the data for flask A have not been plotted, but the graph would flatten out at that point.

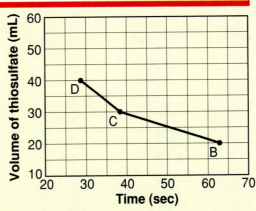

Summary

Determining Rates of Reactions

- The rate of a chemical reaction is a measure of how fast a reaction is taking place. The average rate of a reaction can be calculated if you have information about how the amounts of either a reactant or a product change over time.

- Changes in a reaction rate can be shown on a graph. The rate of a reaction is constant wherever there is a straight-line portion to the graph.

Factors Affecting Reaction Rates

- Many factors change the rate of a reaction. These include the surface area of a solid reactant, the concentration of a substance, the nature of the reactants themselves, the temperature at which a reaction takes place, and the presence or absence of a catalyst.

- Collision theory provides an explanation for why reaction rates vary when conditions are changed. The rate of a reaction depends on the number of collisions between reacting particles and the fraction of the particles that collide with sufficient energy to cause a reaction.

Reaction Pathways

- Only collisions with enough energy to form an activated complex can result in the formation of products. The amount of energy required to form an activated complex is called the activation energy. Reactions with relatively low activation energies take place quickly; reactions with high activation energies take place slowly.

- Catalysts increase reaction rates by providing an alternate reaction pathway having a lower activation energy. Enzymes are biological catalysts that make it possible for otherwise unlikely reactions to take place at our body's temperature.

- Many reactions occur in a series of steps, called the reaction mechanism. For these reactions, the overall rate of the reaction is dependent on the speed of the slowest step, which is the rate-determining step.

Chemically Speaking

activated complex 17.9

activation energy 17.7

catalyst 17.8

collision theory 17.4

enzyme 17.8

rate-determining step 17.10

reaction mechanism 17.10

Concept Mapping

Using the method of concept mapping described at the front of this book, make a concept map for the term *rate of reaction*.

Questions and Problems

DETERMINING RATES OF REACTION

A. Objective: **Explain** *what is meant by a rate and* **identify** *the data necessary to* **determine** *a rate.*

1. What metric units would you use to discuss the rate of each of these?
   a. gasoline consumption in a car
   b. coal production in a mine
   c. formation of hydrogen gas when zinc reacts with hydrochloric acid

2. Suppose you are trying to explain reaction rates to a friend by drawing an analogy with the speed of an automobile on a highway. What feature about the reaction would be analogous to each of these?
   a. the distance traveled by the automobile
   b. the amount of time the automobile travels
   c. the speed at which the automobile travels

- Factor-label method: 6, 7, 8, 9, 10, 11, 43, 46, 47
- Using what you know: 3, 4, 5, 6, 12, 13, 14, 15, 16, 17, 18, 19, 20, 21, 22, 24, 25, 26, 27, 39, 41, 42, 44, 45
- Using similar problems: 6, 8, 9, 10, 11, 16, 23, 36, 38, 45, 46, 47
- Using patterns: 16, 44

3. Plotting distance on the y-axis and time on the x-axis, draw curves that show an automobile in each of these situations.
   a. traveling at a constant speed
   b. continually speeding up as it travels
   c. gradually slowing down as it travels

4. Zinc reacts with hydrochloric acid according to the following equation.

   $$Zn(s) + 2HCl(aq) \rightarrow ZnCl_2(aq) + H_2(g)$$

   You can carry out the reaction in the same way that magnesium was reacted with hydrochloric acid in Section 17.2.
   a. Suppose you plotted the concentration of HCl along the y-axis and time along the x-axis. Why would this plot be unlikely to resemble any of the three graphs from question 3?
   b. Suppose you plotted the concentration of $ZnCl_2$ along the y-axis. Would this plot resemble any of the graphs in question 3?

5. Describe two ways that you could follow the rate of this reaction in the laboratory.

   $$Co(s) + 2HCl(aq) \rightarrow H_2(g) + CoCl_2(aq)$$

B. Objective: **Determine** *whether the rate of a reaction is increasing, decreasing, or remaining constant and* **calculate** *the rate of a reaction.*

6. At 20°C, a small strip of magnesium reacts with $3.0M$ hydrochloric acid to produce 0.00050 mole of H_2 gas in 20 seconds.
   a. What is the rate of this reaction in mol/minute?
   b. Suppose $6.0M$ hydrochloric acid is substituted for the $3.0M$ acid. Predict whether the new rate of reaction will be faster or slower than before.

7. Refer to the data in question 6 to answer these questions.
   a. How much magnesium reacts to form 0.00050 mole of hydrogen gas?
   b. How many moles of hydrochloric acid (HCl) react to form 0.00050 mole of hydrogen gas?

c. What would be the rate of disappearance of the magnesium metal? Of the hydrochloric acid in mol/s?

8. Iodine-137 is a radioactive substance that has been used medically to detect whether the thyroid is functioning normally. Over a four-day period, a 100-mg sample of this isotope decays at an average rate of 7.3 mg/day. What mass of I-137 has decayed after four days?

9. Carbon dioxide reacts with water in animal cells according to the following reaction.

   $$CO_2(g) + H_2O(l) \rightarrow H^+(aq) + HCO_3^-(aq)$$

   Without a catalyst, two molecules of CO_2 react with two molecules of H_2O per minute when the temperature is 37°C. How many molecules of carbon dioxide will react in one day? A single molecule of the enzyme carbonic anhydrase can catalyze 3.6×10^7 molecules of carbon dioxide in one minute. How many molecules of carbon dioxide will react in one day, using one molecule of the enzyme?

10. At 20°C, a 3-percent solution of hydrogen peroxide produces 15 mL of oxygen gas in 120 seconds. What is the rate of this reaction?

11. In 60 seconds, 90 percent of 50 mL of a 3-percent solution of hydrogen peroxide decomposes at 20°C in the presence of a catalyst. If the rate of this reaction doubles for each 10-degree increase in temperature, how long might it take for the same amount of this solution to decompose at 40°C?

C. Objective: **Identify** *an appropriate reactant or product for determining the reaction rate and* **describe** *how to measure the rate experimentally.*

12. Write the equation for the reaction that takes place when you mix magnesium metal with nitric acid, HNO_3. What product of this reaction could you use to follow the rate of this reaction?

REACTION RATES **591**

■ Using calculators: 6, 7, 8, 9, 10, 11, 43, 46, 47

■ Verifying your answer: 6, 7, 8, 9, 10, 11, 43, 46, 47

■ Breaking problems into manageable parts: 23, 43, 46, 47

■ Making diagrams: 3, 23, 32, 33, 34

■ Writing chemical equations: 12, 13, 15, 16, 41, 42, 46, 47

13. Describe an experiment you could carry out to compare the reaction rate of magnesium metal and 1*M* HBr with the reaction rate of magnesium metal and 0.25*M* HBr.

14. A solution of copper(II) sulfate is blue. When you put zinc into this solution, the following reaction takes place.

$$CuSO_4(aq) + Zn(s) \rightarrow ZnSO_4(aq) + Cu(s)$$

What property of this reaction mixture could you follow if you were interested in comparing the rates of its reaction under different conditions?

FACTORS AFFECTING REACTION RATES

D. Objective: **Identify** *factors that can affect the rate of a reaction and* **recognize** *how a change in each factor can affect the rate.*

15. **a.** Write the equation for the reaction you expect to take place if a sample of sodium is placed inside a bottle of chlorine gas.
   b. Write the equation for the same reaction involving lithium rather than sodium.
   c. If the metal samples of sodium and lithium are of equal size, shape, temperature, and purity and the temperature of the chlorine gas is 25°C in both bottles, would you expect the two reactions to take place at the same rate? Explain.

16. When calcium is placed in water, it reacts as shown by this equation.

$$Ca(s) + 2H_2O(l) \rightarrow$$
$$Ca^{2+}(aq) + H_2(g) + 2OH^-(aq)$$

Write the equation for the reaction of magnesium with water. Will these reactions take place at the same rate?

17. Hydrogen and iodine react at 400°C, according to the equation.
$$H_2(g) + I_2(g) \rightarrow 2HI(g)$$
How would the rate of reaction be affected by the following?
   a. increasing the temperature

   b. increasing the concentration of hydrogen
   c. increasing the concentration of both the hydrogen and the iodine
   d. adding a catalyst

18. Which will react faster, zinc and 3*M* hydrochloric acid or zinc and 1*M* hydrochloric acid?

19. Use collision theory to explain why increasing the concentration of hydrochloric acid would cause an increase in the rate of its reaction with zinc.

20. Which will burn faster, a solid log, a split log, or wood shavings?

21. When you pour a solution of lead nitrate, $Pb(NO_3)_2$ into a solution of potassium iodide, KI, you notice the formation of a yellow solid as soon as the solutions meet. Would you expect this reaction to take place at the same rate if you mixed solid lead nitrate with solid potassium iodide? Explain.

22. Why is 6*M* hydrochloric acid more hazardous to skin and eyes than 0.2*M* hydrochloric acid?

E. Objective: **Explain,** *using collision theory, why reaction rates change when reaction conditions change.*

23. You have a cube of zinc measuring 1000 cm on each edge.
   a. Calculate the surface area of the cube.
   b. If the cube is cut into smaller cubes that are 10 cm on each edge, find the surface area of each cube, the total number of cubes, and the total surface area of all the cubes.
   c. The cubes are then cut into cubes that are 1 cm on each edge. Find the surface area of one of these cubes, the number of these cubes, and the total surface area of all the 1-cm cubes.
   d. In which of the three forms described will the zinc react fastest with 1*M* HCl? Explain, using collision theory.

24. Using collision theory described in this chapter, explain the following.

a. Sugar dissolves faster in a cup of hot coffee than in cold lemonade.

b. A sugar cube dissolves more slowly than granulated sugar.

c. Stirring a teaspoon of sugar helps it dissolve faster than not stirring it.

25. You hang your clothes outside to dry on two consecutive days. Both days have similar conditions of temperature and humidity. However, on the first day, the wind blows fiercely, while on the second day the air is completely calm. Will the clothes dry faster on the first day or the second? Why?

26. White phosphorus reacts rapidly with oxygen when exposed to air. What can you say about the magnitude of the activation energy for this reaction?

27. The metallic luster of fine copper wool doesn't readily change unless it is put into a crucible and heated at a high temperature. This causes the copper to darken as it reacts with oxygen. How, do you think, does the activation energy of this reaction compare with that of the phosphorus reaction described in question 26?

F. Objective: Compare *the rate of a reaction with and without a catalyst.*

28. Describe the effect that manganese dioxide has on the rate of the decomposition reaction of hydrogen peroxide.

29. If you add 1.0 g of manganese dioxide to 1.0 liter of 3-percent hydrogen peroxide, the solution will fizz. When the fizzing stops, how much manganese dioxide would you expect to recover? Explain your answer.

30. The reaction represented by this equation takes place very slowly (if at all) at room temperature.

$$CH_3CH_2OH(l) \rightarrow CH_2CH_2(g) + H_2O(aq)$$

However, in the presence of an acid (H^+), the reaction takes place much faster. It is believed to follow this mechanism.

$$CH_3CH_2OH + H^+ \rightarrow CH_3CH_2OH_2^+$$
$$CH_3CH_2OH_2^+ \rightarrow CH_3CH_2^+ + H_2O$$
$$CH_3CH_2^+ \rightarrow CH_2CH_2 + H^+$$

Give two reasons why the acid can be considered a catalyst for the reaction.

31. Sugar does not burn upon exposure to the air at room temperature. What enables your body to carry out this reaction at just a slightly higher temperature?

REACTION PATHWAYS

G. Objective: Demonstrate *how the potential energy of the substances involved in a chemical reaction changes as the reaction progresses, using a graph.*

32. Sketch a potential-energy curve for an endothermic reaction. Label the parts representing the activated complex, activation energy, and change in enthalpy.

33. Repeat the last question for an exothermic reaction.

34. How does a catalyst affect the activation energy for a reaction? Sketch two potential-energy curves for a reaction, one showing the uncatalyzed reaction and the other showing the catalyzed reaction. Label each curve.

H. Objective: Define *a reaction mechanism* and **explain** *how the rate-determining step of the mechanism affects the overall rate of the reaction.*

35. For the dishwashing analogy at the end of Section 17.10, explain why the person washing the dishes can be considered as the rate-determining step.

36. For the same analogy referred to in the last question, describe the effects on the reaction rate if a sixth person is added to do the following.

a. clear the tables

b. wash dishes

c. dry dishes

37. Along some toll roads, you pay the toll at plazas set up at regular intervals along the road. Quite often the road widens considerably when you come to these plazas. Explain why there are usually more toll booths than there are lanes of traffic on the highway between the toll booths. Compare this example to a chemical reaction.

38. A group of students is assembling a 10-page document for mailing. There are 50 copies of each typed page in separate stacks. The pages must be
(1) assembled in order,
(2) straightened,
(3) stapled, and
(4) inserted into envelopes for mailing.
   a. If 4 students work together, each performing a different operation, which of the 4 steps might be the rate-determining step?
   b. What would be the effect on the overall rate if 5 more people assembled the pages (step 1)?
   c. What would be the effect on the rate if the 5 helpers worked on the second step? The third step? The fourth step?
   d. What would be the effect if the envelopes had to be addressed, stamped, and mailed in the fourth step?

39. The equation for the formation of ammonia is this.

$$N_2(g) + 3H_2(g) \rightarrow 2NH_3(g)$$

Explain why this equation is not likely to represent the reaction mechanism.

40. You want to contact Indiana Jones to give a short motivational speech to your graduating class. Your sources indicate that his agent in New York has pinpointed his current location in the rain forests of South America. You telephone the agent in New York, who sends a telegram via satellite to South America. The telegram is given to a messenger who must travel a few hundred kilometers by boat and several hundred meters on foot before hand-

ing the message to Indiana Jones. The messenger returns to the telegraph office with the reply, and the process is reversed. Which is the rate-determining step in this process?

41. In this question, you will work with this hypothetical overall reaction.

$$2AB \rightarrow A_2 + B_2 + energy$$

Suppose this reaction has been found to take place in these two steps.

$$2AB \rightarrow A_2 + 2B + energy \qquad slow$$
$$2B \rightarrow B_2 \qquad fast$$

   a. Show that by adding these two reactions you obtain the overall reaction.
   b. Which of the two steps in this reaction mechanism is likely to have the higher activation energy? Why?

42. Hydrogen peroxide reacts with hydrogen ions and iodide ions according to the following equation.

   a. $H^+ + I^- + H_2O_2 \rightarrow H_2O + HOI$

A possible mechanism for this reaction is this.

   b. $H^+ + H_2O_2 \rightarrow H_3O_2^+ \qquad fast$
   c. $H_3O_2^+ + I^- \rightarrow H_2O + HOI \qquad slow$

   a. Show that adding equations b and c gives equation a.
   b. How would you expect the rate to be affected if the concentration of I^- is doubled?

43. In an important industrial process for producing ammonia, the overall reaction is as follows.

$$N_2(g) + 3H_2(g) \rightarrow 2NH_3(g) + 100.3 \text{ kJ}$$

A yield of about 98 percent can be obtained at 200°C and 1000 atm. The process makes use of a catalyst of finely divided iron oxides containing small amounts of potassium oxide and aluminum oxide.
   a. Is the above reaction endothermic or exothermic?
   b. How many grams of hydrogen must react to form 25 grams of ammonia?

c. Is it likely that the equation for the overall reaction represents the reaction mechanism?

Critical Thinking

SYNTHESIS WITHIN THE CHAPTER

44. Explain why a catalytic converter is honeycombed in shape and operates at a high temperature.

SYNTHESIS ACROSS CHAPTERS

45. Explain why it takes longer to hard-boil an egg in a pan of boiling water on Pikes Peak than in Boston.
46. The catalyzed decomposition of 55 mL of 3.0-percent hydrogen peroxide, H_2O_2, is 90-percent complete in 60 seconds at 20°C. What is the volume of oxygen gas produced at 95.5 kPa in 60 seconds?
47. A strip of magnesium with a mass of 0.22 grams reacts with 65 mL of 3.0M HCl at a temperature of 30°C and a pressure of 92 kPa in 25 seconds. Calculate the rate at which hydrogen gas is produced in milliliters per second.

Projects

48. Design an experiment to measure the rate of production of carbon dioxide gas when calcium carbonate is dropped into a solution of hydrochloric acid. After obtaining your teacher's approval, conduct the experiment and write a lab report explaining your results.

Research and Writing

49. Considering that very little energy (about 1.9 kJ/mol) is required to convert graphite to diamond, find out why this process is so difficult.
50. To spice up a gelatin dessert, a cook often adds fruit before it sets completely. Many boxes of gelatin contain a warning similar to this: Do not add fresh or frozen pineapple, but canned pineapple may be used. Find out why fresh pineapple cannot be used (perhaps by doing a kitchen experiment). Then use a reference source to learn what happens when the pineapple is added. Why is it all right to add canned pineapple? Do you think that the fruit could be added to the dessert if it's cooked first?

☐ Boxed numbers indicate questions that involve skills in interpretation, application, and analysis.

1. a. liters per kilometer
   b. metric tons per day
   c. mL (or L) per minute

2. a. the amount of product produced
   b. the time required to produce the product
   c. the reaction rate

3. a.

b.

c.

4. a. The concentration of HCl decreases as the reaction goes on.
   b. It would probably have components of all three graphs, but mostly resemble the graph in 3c. The concentration of $ZnCl_2$ would increase rapidly at first, level off at a steady rate, and finally slow down near the end.

5. Measure the rate at which Co disappears, measure the decreasing concentration of HCl, measure the volume of H_2 produced (the easiest method), or measure the changing color of the solution as the pink product, $CoCl_2$, is produced.

6. a. $(0.00050 \text{ mol}/20 \text{ s}) = (0.000025 \text{ mol}/1 \text{ s}) \times (60 \text{ s}/1 \text{ min})$
   $= 0.0015 \text{ mol/min}$
   b. The rate will be faster.

7. $Mg + 2HCl \rightarrow H_2 + MgCl_2$
   a. $0.00050 \text{ mol } H_2 \times \dfrac{1 \text{ mol Mg}}{1 \text{ mol } H_2}$
   $= 0.00050 \text{ mol Mg}$
   b. $0.00050 \text{ mol } H_2 \times \dfrac{2 \text{ mol HCl}}{1 \text{ mol } H_2}$
   $= 0.0010 \text{ mol HCl}$
   c. $0.000050 \text{ mol Mg}/20 \text{ s}$
   $= 0.000025 \text{ mol Mg}/s,$
   $0.0010 \text{ mol HCl}/20 \text{ s}$
   $= 0.000050 \text{ mol HCl}/s$

8. $4 \text{ days} \times 7.3 \text{ mg/day} = 29.2 \text{ mg}$

9. $2 \text{ molecules/min} \times 60 \text{ min/hr} \times 24 \text{ hr/day} = 2880 \text{ molecules/day}$
   $3.6 \times 10^7 \text{ molecules/min} \times 60 \text{ min/hr} \times 24 \text{ hr/day}$
   $= 5.2 \times 10^{10} \text{ molecules/day}$

10. $15 \text{ mL}/120 \text{ s} \times 60 \text{ s/min} = 7.5 \text{ mL/min}$

11. At 30°C, the reaction is twice as fast. At 40°C, the reaction is four times as fast. Therefore, it should take only 1/4 as long for decomposition to occur:
   $1/4 (60 \text{ seconds}) = 15 \text{ seconds}$

12. $Mg(s) + 2HNO_3(aq) \rightarrow Mg(NO_3)_2(aq) + H_2(g)$
   Measure the volume of H_2 gas.

13. Follow the relative rates of production of hydrogen gas by measuring its volume as the two reactions proceed.

14. Measure the rate of disappearance of $CuSO_4$ by using a spectrophotometer to measure the decreasing intensity of its blue color in solution.

15. a. $2Na(s) + Cl_2(g) \rightarrow 2NaCl(s)$
   b. $2Li(s) + Cl_2(g) \rightarrow 2LiCl(s)$
   c. No, because changing the nature of the reactants changes the reaction rate.

16. $Mg(s) + 2H_2O(l) \rightarrow Mg^{2+}(aq) + H_2(g) + 2OH^-(aq)$
   No, because the reactants are different.

17. a. Reaction rate increases.
   b. Reaction rate increases.
   c. Reaction rate increases.
   d. Reaction rate increases.

18. $3M$ HCl reacts faster.

19. Because there are more HCl molecules per liter in concentrated HCl, there will be more molecular collisions between HCl and Zn, leading to a faster reaction rate.

20. wood shavings

21. No; The ions in two solids are not as free to move and come in contact with each other as the ions dissolved in solution.

22. Any deleterious reactions involving HCl take place faster with the more concentrated solution.

23. a. Surface area $= (1000 \text{ cm})^2$ per face $\times 6$ faces $= 6 \times 10^6 \text{ cm}^2$
   b. Surface area of one 10-cm cube $= 6 \times 10^2 \text{ cm}^2$
   As the 1000-cm cube is cut into 10-cm cubes, there will be 1000/10 = 100 small cubes on each edge of the large cube. So there are $(100)^3$ cubes or 10^6 cubes. The total surface area is $10^6 \times 6 \times 10^2 \text{ cm}^2 = 6 \times 10^8 \text{ cm}^2$
   c. Surface area of each cube is $6 \times (1 \text{ cm})^2 = 6 \text{ cm}^2$. Each 10-cm cube produces $10^3 = 1000$ 1-cm cubes, so 10^6 10-cm cubes will produce $10^6 \times 1000$ cubes or 10^9 cubes; the total area is $10^9 \times 6 \text{ cm}^2$ or $6 \times 10^9 \text{ cm}^2$.
   d. The smallest cubes will react fastest, because the greatest amount of surface area is exposed for possible collisions.

24. a. Effective collisions take place more often when the temperature is higher.
   b. Granulated sugar exposes more surface area for collisions with water.
   c. Sugar is exposed to more water faster when it is stirred, so more collisions occur.

25. Clothes dry faster on the windy day, because the water molecules are exposed to more air per unit time.

26. Fast reactions have a relatively small activation energy.

27. The reaction between copper and oxygen has a higher activation energy, because its reaction proceeds more slowly at room temperature.

28. Manganese dioxide increases the rate of the decomposition of hydrogen peroxide by catalyzing the reaction.

29. All of it, because a catalyst is not consumed during a reaction.

30. The acid makes the reaction take place faster, but it is not used up during the reaction. Note that for every one mole of H^+ consumed in the first step of the mechanism, one mole is produced in the last step.

31. Your body contains enzymes that catalyze this reaction so it can occur at body temperature.

32.

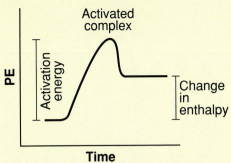

33.

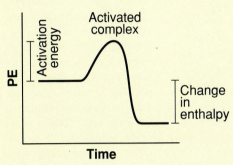

34. A catalyst lowers the activation energy for a reaction.

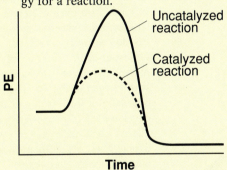

35. The step of "washing the dishes" is the slowest step, especially with only one person doing it.

36. a. no change

b. overall rate increases

c. no change

37. Paying your toll is the slow step in traveling down a toll superhighway; providing more lanes increases the rate of this step. This is similar to a chemical reaction in that by increasing the rate of the slowest step you can increase the rate of the overall reaction.

38. a. Assembly is probably the rate-determining step.

b. The rate would increase. (Inserting the document into envelopes may be the new rate-determining step.)

c. Second step no change; third step no change; fourth step no change unless more people were added to the first step.

d. Step 4 would then be the rate-determining step.

39. It is unlikely that 4 molecules (one N_2, three H_2) will collide together at the same time to react.

40. The messenger who goes by boat and on foot

41. a. $2AB \rightarrow A_2 + 2\cancel{B}$

$$\frac{2\cancel{B} \rightarrow B_2}{2AB \rightarrow A_2 + B_2}$$

b. The first step (the slower step) has the higher activation energy.

42. a. $H^+ + H_2O_2 \rightarrow \cancel{H_3O_2^+}$

$$\frac{\cancel{H_3O_2^+} + I^- \rightarrow + H_2O + HOI}{H^+ + I^- + H_2O_2 \rightarrow H_2O + HOI}$$

b. The reaction will go faster, because I^- is a reactant in the slow step.

43. a. exothermic

b. $25 \, \cancel{g \, NH_3} \times \frac{1 \, \cancel{mol \, NH_3}}{17 \, \cancel{g \, NH_3}} \times \frac{3 \, \cancel{mol \, H_2}}{2 \, \cancel{mol \, NH_3}}$

$\times \frac{2.0 \, g \, H_2}{1 \, \cancel{mol \, H_2}} = 4.4 \, g \, H_2$

but since the yield is only 98%,

$4.4 \, g / 0.98 = 4.5 \, g \, H_2$ must react

c. No; the overall equation implies that three molecules of H_2 must simultaneously collide with one molecule of N_2.

44. Increased surface area and increased temperature favor increased reaction rates.

45. Water boils at a lower temperature on Pikes Peak, causing reaction rates to be slower.

46. $2H_2O_2(aq) \rightarrow 2H_2O(l) + O_2(g)$

The reaction is 90% complete in 60 seconds, so only 0.90×55 mL of the solution reacts.

$0.90 \times 55 \, \cancel{mL \, H_2O_2} \times \frac{3.0 \, \cancel{g \, H_2O_2}}{100 \, \cancel{mL \, H_2O_2}}$

$\times \frac{1 \, \cancel{mol \, H_2O_2}}{34 \, \cancel{g \, H_2O_2}} \times \frac{1 \, mol \, O_2}{2 \, \cancel{mol \, H_2O_2}}$

$= 0.022 \, mol \, O_2$

$PV = nRT$

$V = \frac{nRT}{P}$

$= \frac{0.022 \, \cancel{mol} \times 8.31 \, L \cdot \cancel{kPa} / \cancel{mol} \cdot \cancel{K} \times 293 \, \cancel{K}}{95.5 \, \cancel{kPa}}$

$= 0.56 \, L$

47. $Mg + 2HCl \rightarrow MgCl_2 + H_2$

$0.22 \, \cancel{g \, Mg} \times \frac{1 \, \cancel{mol \, Mg}}{24.3 \, \cancel{g \, Mg}} \times \frac{1 \, mol \, H_2}{1 \, \cancel{mol \, Mg}}$

$= 0.0091 \, mol \, H_2$

$V = \frac{nRT}{P}$

$= \frac{0.0091 \, \cancel{mol} \times 8.31 \, L \cdot \cancel{kPa} / \cancel{mol} \cdot \cancel{K} \times 303 \, \cancel{K}}{92 \, \cancel{kPa}}$

$= 0.25 \, L$

rate per second $= \frac{0.25 \, \cancel{L}}{25 \, s} \times \frac{1000 \, mL}{1 \, \cancel{L}}$

$= 10 \, mL/s$

**Science
Technology &
Society**

CHEMICAL PERSPECTIVES

Food Additives—Food for Thought

If you walked down the food aisles in any supermarket today, you would find many people examining cans and boxes closely. Some would simply be comparison-shopping. But many more would be reading the content labels, trying to find what type of additives may have been put into the food they are about to purchase. The presence of many of these food additives is offensive to some people. They regard food additives as unnecessary and, in some cases, even harmful. Other people consider additives essential for an abundant, safe, nutritious, and available food supply.

Food additives are any ingredients intentionally added to food products by the food manufacturers. As people become more aware of the harmful nature of some chemicals, they increasingly question the need for putting them into food. Over 2,800 additives are used. Some additives increase the nutritional value of foods. Others improve color, texture, or flavor. Still others are food preservatives.

Food preservation is a broad term for any process that slows the normal spoilage rate of food. Two main causes of spoilage are oxidation and decay due to microorganisms. Oxidation is the reaction of natural components in food with oxygen in the air. The browning of fresh fruit and the development of rancid fats and oils are some examples of oxidation. Microorganisms such as bacteria, molds, and yeast cause another type of food spoilage that alters the color, odor, and appearance of food.

Antioxidants and antimicrobials are two general types of additives used for food preservation. Antioxidants prevent or slow down the oxidation of foods. Antimicrobials prevent spoilage by inhibiting the

ients: Salt, Monosodium
ate, Modified Cornstarch,
, Chicken Fat, Dehydrated
and Parsley, Oleoresins of
and Paprika, BHA and BHT
ect color and Sodium Silico

Critical Thinking Skills

These skills are applied in the feature.

- Devising multiple solutions
- Evaluating the relevance of information
- Making an informed decision
- Using library resources

FOCUS

Activate Prior Knowledge

In Chapter 3, decomposition reactions were introduced. Demonstrate the enzymatic decomposition of hydrogen peroxide. Wearing safety goggles and a lab apron, chop a piece of fresh liver into fine pieces and put it into a large test tube. Add about 10 mL of 3 percent hydrogen peroxide. Place a glowing splint into the test tube to test for oxygen. Have students record their observations. An enzyme in the liver will catalyze the decomposition of hydrogen peroxide into water and oxygen.

$$2H_2O_2 \rightarrow 2H_2O + O_2$$

This reaction goes very quickly due to the catalysis of the enzyme from the liver. Many preservatives slow down the decomposition of molecules in food by removing the conditions that catalyze decomposition.

Teach

Science Background

There are many different classes of food additives, such as preservatives and antioxidants, emulsifiers, stabilizers, thickeners, nutritive additives, flavor and color enhancers, sequestrants, clarifying agents, curing agents, foaming and nonfoaming agents, and leavening agents. The additives of interest in this chapter are those used to preserve food—preservatives, antioxidants, and sequestrants.

To prevent fruit from oxidizing to a brown color, dip it in orange juice, which contains the antioxidants citric acid and ascorbic acid.

growth and action of bacteria, mold, and yeasts.

Proponents of food additives argue that additives are essential. The incidence of food poisoning has dropped dramatically over the past 30 years due largely to food additives. To help foods survive long-distance shipments and storage, as well as to meet the demands for ease in preparation, the use of food additives is supported by many people.

On the other hand, opponents of food additives argue that additives are unnecessary and dangerous. Some foods contain nitrates, which the body may convert to a carcinogen, a potential cancer-causing compound. Moreover, some chemicals used as additives are suspected of being harmful. Similarly, the long-term deleterious effects of others may not be known at this time. Furthermore, some food additives can cause allergic reactions in certain people. Still other foods contain so

Some foods contain so many chemicals that you may wonder if they are foods at all!

many chemicals that you may wonder if they are foods at all!

Clearly the issue of food additives is controversial. Both the risks and the benefits must be weighed before you can decide to support or reject their general use. On another level, you may want to make a personal decision about particular additives—whether you feel safe ingesting them.

Discussing the Issues

1. Make a list of the food additives that are in the prepared foods that you eat in any given day. Use reference books to identify the purpose of each of these additives.
2. What changes would you have to make if you chose not to eat any food containing food additives?

Take Action

1. Write a letter of inquiry to the Food and Drug Administration to find out what procedures are required before a suspicious product can be removed from the marketplace.
2. Write to a company that produces a food additive that interests you to determine what kinds of tests that product underwent and the time involved before it became marketable.

597

Teaching Strategy

Read the ingredients on the label of your students' favorite snack foods. Write the ingredients on the board. Cross off those ingredients that students can identify. Ask them if they know what the remaining ingredients are. Most likely you will have a list of some common food additives. Have students research and report on food additives of note, such as Alar.

Close

Discussing the Issues

1. Answers will vary depending on students' diets. The references should give information on each class of food additives. Food additives that help preserve food enable it to be shipped farther and stored longer. Additives ensure that food supplies are nutritious and safe. In certain regions of the world, essential vitamins and minerals are supplied. Other classes of food additives generally make food more desirable.

2. Answers will vary. Students may point out that they will have to spend more time preparing foods. They may also mention having a less varied diet since they will only be able to eat those items that are in season and grown locally. They may plan to eat more frozen foods or foods preserved by methods other than food additives. They could also plan to eat fewer prepared snacks.

Take Action

1. In their letters of inquiry to the FDA, students could mention specific food items. For example, they could inquire about the procedure used for removing cyclamate (a sweetener) from the market.

2. Students may want to ask the food additive company (Dow, DuPont) what the purposes of food additives are, such as preservation, flavor enhancement, or to make the color or appearance more pleasing.

T597

Reaction Equilibrium

Investigations	Demonstrations	Texas Essential Elements★
	What Is Equilibrium?, page T600 Equilibrium Involving Solutions of Solids, page T605	**Content:** 2.4, 9.1, 10.5 **Process:** 10.1
Laboratory Manual 18–2 IM Laboratory Manual 18–3 IM		**Content:** 10.5, 10.6, 10.8 **Process:** 4.3, 10.1
Laboratory Manual 18–1 M In-text Investigation, page T626	Changes in Concentration, page T620	**Content:** 9.7, 10.5, 10.7 **Process:** 10.1
		Content: 10.7 **Process:** 1.1, 1.2, 1.3, 4.3, 5.1, 6.1, 6.2, 8.1, 8.2, 9.1, 9.2
		Process: 4.1, 4.2, 4.3, 7.1, 8.2
		Content: 8.9, 10.2, 10.7 **Process:** 10.2, 10.3, 10.4

KEY:
M–Microscale **S**–Structured
I–Inquiry   **IM**–Inquiry Microscale

★*See pages T8–T11 for complete listing of Texas Essential Elements.*

18

Reaction Equilibrium

Chapter Rationale

This chapter helps tie together previous work on stoichiometry and reaction rates with the treatment of acids and bases to follow. The concept of equilibrium is introduced by looking at reactions that come to equilibrium in light of assumptions previously made about stoichiometry problems. One of these assumptions is that all reactions go to completion. Students are now introduced to reactions that obviously do not go to completion, but seem to stop with leftover reactants present. Equilibrium is defined on both a macroscopic and submicroscopic level. Submicroscopic equilibrium is defined in terms of equal rates of the forward reaction and reverse reaction. Understanding submicroscopic equilibrium is an important foundation for understanding strong and weak acids discussed in the next chapter. This chapter also provides another opportunity to have students form a model of the submicroscopic world and use that model to explain events at the macroscopic level.

The equilibrium constant expression and LeChâtelier's principle are introduced to give students an appreciation of the power of these regularities and how they can be manipulated to change or control reactivity.

About the Photograph

Use the photograph as an analogy for equilibrium. Bees moving in and out of the hive are analogous to the rates of the forward and reverse reactions at equilibrium. Just as the number of bees in the hive remains constant, the observable properties of a physical or chemical system remain constant at equilibrium.

Overview

An example of equilibrium is the number of bees in a hive population that remains constant as individual bees move in and out.

PART **1** *Reactions That Appear to Stop*

A football stadium is an exciting place. Two opposing teams on the field provide a lot of action to watch: long runs, touchdown passes, field goals, quarterback sacks, interceptions, and other plays. On the sidelines, you can see the cheerleaders supporting the team and hear the band playing the school song. Even in the stands, there is hustle and bustle among the fans.

Chemical reactions can also be exciting. In many reactions, the formation of new substances from other substances proceeds in a spectacular way. For instance, think about the big bang when a spark is brought to a mixture of hydrogen and oxygen gases. At the submicroscopic level, you can imagine a busy rearrangement of atoms into new molecules when this chemical reaction takes place.

What connection could there be between the action at a football stadium and the action of a chemical reaction in progress? The similarity may be greater than you think.

18.1 What Is Equilibrium?

Not every chemical reaction proceeds vigorously to convert all the reactants to products. Many reactions seem to stop completely, even with leftover amounts of all the reactants present. It seems as if such reactions should continue to form more products, but they do not. Reactions of this type are said to reach **equilibrium.**

How can you recognize a reaction that does not go to completion but instead reaches equilibrium? You can begin to find out by considering how two familiar acids react with water. The acids are hydrochloric acid, HCl, and acetic acid, CH_3COOH, the acid that accounts for the sour taste of vinegar. One reacts completely with water, the other only partially. Observing their behaviors at the macroscopic level can lead to an understanding of the submicroscopic phenomenon of equilibrium. The equations for the two reactions are these.

$$HCl(aq) + H_2O(l) \rightarrow Cl^-(aq) + H_3O^+(aq)$$
$$CH_3COOH(aq) + H_2O(l) \rightarrow CH_3COO^-(aq) + H_3O^+(aq)$$

Since all the reactants and products in these reactions are clear and colorless solutions, you need a way to identify the products. One way to make the products "visible" is to test the solutions for conductivity. The equations indicate that ions are present. These ions are free to move in solution and therefore can complete an

Objectives

Part 1

A. *Explain* and *apply* the macroscopic and submicroscopic definitions of *equilibrium.*

B. *Identify* chemical reactions that come to equilibrium and *describe* the process of reaching equilibrium.

Chapter Planning Hints

Plan to complete this chapter in three to six class sessions. You may wish to obtain the article, "The 'Bean' Lab," Dickenson and Erhardt, *Journal of Chemical Education*, November 1991, Volume 11, pp. 930–931 to introduce Section 18.2. You will find three optional demonstrations suggested for this chapter. They appear on pages T600, T605, and T620. You may wish to preview them at this time.

Developing Skills

Students may apply these skills in their study of Part 1.

Predicting: When lead chloride, a relatively insoluble solid, is placed into water, it establishes this equilibrium: $PbCl_2 \rightleftharpoons Pb^{2+} + 2Cl^-$. Ask students about the rates of the forward and reverse reactions: (a) when lead chloride is first placed into water; (b) at some intermediate point before equilibrium has been reached; and (c) when equilibrium is established between the reactants and the products.

Comparing/Contrasting: Ask students to provide their own analogies about the difference between a steady-state situation and equilibrium.

Constructing tables and graphs: Ask students to construct a graph showing the nitrogen dioxide/dinitrogen tetroxide reaction coming to equilibrium if the reaction starts with dinitrogen tetroxide only. Compare with the graph in Section 18.2 on page 604.

Determining main ideas: Have students use the definition of submicroscopic equilibrium to explain why the macroscopic properties of a system must remain constant for equilibrium to be reached.

☰ FOCUS

Activate Prior Knowledge

This activity will help students visualize a chemical reaction that has both a forward and reverse direction. Obtain a set of objects that can be easily put together and taken apart. Plastic eggs that come in two halves would be acceptable. Put about fifty of these objects into a large box. Start with all of the objects put together.

Assign one student the task of taking the objects apart and assign another the task of putting them together. Have the two students take the objects apart and put them back together, stopping at one-minute intervals to count the number of complete objects versus incomplete objects. Record on the chalkboard how the number of incomplete and whole objects changes from one one-minute interval to another. After several minutes a condition in which the number of objects in each category remains relatively constant will be reached.

Discuss why some "reactants" and some "products" were left at the end of each time period. Did this "reaction" ever go to completion? What was true about the rates at which the students worked at the beginning? What was true about their rates of working near the end of the activity? Develop the idea that some chemical reactions work in the same way.

Keep the data from this demonstration for later use (Section 18.2).

electrical circuit. If you test the conductivity of these solutions with the apparatus shown in Figure 18-1, you will see that the reactions have produced ions.

When a $1M$ solution of HCl is used, a light bulb glows brightly. With a $1M$ solution of CH_3COOH, the light bulb also glows, but much less brightly. What conclusion can you draw from these observations? There are more ions present in the $1M$ HCl reaction with water than in the $1M$ CH_3COOH reaction with water. Since the ions are products of these reactions, you can conclude that the acetic acid reaction did not produce as much product as the hydrochloric acid reaction did.

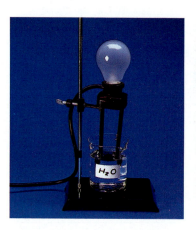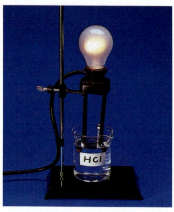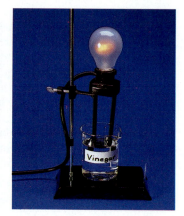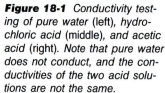

Figure 18-1 Conductivity testing of pure water (left), hydrochloric acid (middle), and acetic acid (right). Note that pure water does not conduct, and the conductivities of the two acid solutions are not the same.

Careful analysis shows that the hydrochloric acid reacts almost completely with water to form ions. Such a reaction is said to *go to completion*. But when you put acetic acid into water, only a small portion of it reacts to form ions. Only some of the original reactant (CH_3COOH) is used up. Not as many CH_3COO^- and H_3O^+ ions are produced by this reaction as Cl^- and H_3O^+ ions are produced by the reaction of hydrochloric acid and water. The reaction of acetic acid with water is said to reach equilibrium.

Macroscopic equilibrium Why do some reactions produce less product than others? To understand what is taking place, you can consider a simple analogy involving a football game. Spectators fill the seats in the stadium that surrounds the field. There is a concession area just behind the seats. The entire complex is surrounded by a fence. Well into the first quarter of the game, all of the spectators have arrived. No more spectators will be admitted after this point.

During the second quarter, the announcer says that 20 000 people are present at the stadium. Are all of these people sitting in their seats? No! Some are leaving their seats in the stands to go to the concession area. Others are returning to their seats. However,

DEMONSTRATION

What is Equilibrium?

⚠ **CAUTION: Wear safety goggles and a lab apron.** For disposal, neutralize with $0.1M$, or less concentrated, acid and pour down the drain. Test $0.1M$ solutions of sodium hydroxide and ammonia with a conductivity apparatus powered by 1.5- or 9-volt batteries. Point out to students the reasons for the differences in

conductivity. Even though the solutions have the same concentration, the sodium hydroxide solution yields more ions than the ammonia solution. Show that the sodium hydroxide dissolves completely in water, while the ammonia reacts only partially with water and then comes to equilibrium.

(continued on page T601)

at any given moment during the second quarter, you will find that there are 500 people outside the main arena and 19 500 in the stands. But not the same people are sitting in the stands at all times. Thus the count of the people in both areas remains constant while individuals move back and forth during the entire second quarter.

A shorthand notation shows the movements of individuals during the game. The process of moving from the stands to the concession area can be represented this way.

$$\text{spectator} \rightarrow \text{buyer}$$

The process of returning to the stands can be shown this way.

$$\text{buyer} \rightarrow \text{spectator}$$

What must be true about these two processes during the second quarter? If the net number of people in the stands is not changing, then these processes must be occurring at the same rate. You can combine the two equations into a single expression.

$$\text{spectator} \rightleftharpoons \text{buyer}$$

The double arrow symbol $\rightleftharpoons$ shows two opposing processes that take place at the same rate.

Submicroscopic equilibrium If you could actually observe the molecules participating in the reaction of acetic acid with water, you would see the same kind of movement just described at the football stadium. There is a forward reaction, as shown by this equation.

$$CH_3COOH(aq) + H_2O(l) \rightarrow CH_3COO^-(aq) + H_3O^+(aq)$$

The opposite reaction is also taking place.

$$CH_3COO^-(aq) + H_3O^+(aq) \rightarrow CH_3COOH(aq) + H_2O(l)$$

These equations show that both acetic acid molecules, CH_3COOH, and acetate ions, CH_3COO^-, are continually reacting in solution. In order for the amounts of the four substances present to remain constant, these two opposing reactions must be taking place at the same rate. The system is at equilibrium and can be represented by the following equation using a double arrow.

$$CH_3COOH(aq) + H_2O(l) \rightleftharpoons CH_3COO^-(aq) + H_3O^+(aq)$$

On the other hand, the reaction between hydrochloric acid and water is nearly 100 percent complete. Reactions that go to completion may be shown with the single arrow you are accustomed to using.

$$HCl(aq) + H_2O(l) \rightarrow H_3O^+(aq) + Cl^-(aq)$$

Defining equilibrium—macroscopic Now that you have learned some of the characteristics of a reaction that reaches equilibrium, you are ready to define *equilibrium*. You will be introduced to two definitions, one emphasizing what you can see at

PROBLEM-SOLVING

S T R A T E G Y

*When **writing a chemical equation**, use a double arrow to indicate a system at equilibrium. (See Strategy, page 244.)*

TEACH

Teaching Strategy

A closed system is an important condition of equilibrium. Evaluate several experiments that students have done or that you have demonstrated to provide examples of closed systems.

DEMONSTRATION

(continued from page T600)
$$NaOH \rightarrow Na^+ + OH^-$$
$$NH_3 + H_2O \rightleftharpoons NH_4^+ + OH^-$$

Discuss the rates of the forward and reverse reactions for the ammonia reaction when equilibrium is attained.

PART **1**

Section 18.1 continued

Teaching Strategy

Defining Equilibrium—
Macroscopic

Try to get students to devise a closed system using a plastic foam cup with a small hole in the bottom and a small battery operated water pump. The water leaving the cup enters the pump and is pumped back into the cup.

Videodisc Connections

823-829, side 6
Chemical cycles (7-frame seq.)

Figure 18-2 Top: *A sealed terrarium must have a delicate balance of air, water, nutrients, and plant and animal life. Bottom: The biosphere, which began a two-year experiment in 1991, is a larger scale version of an Earth microcosm.*

PROBLEM·SOLVING

S T R A T E G Y

*To make sure you understand the definition of equilibrium, **reread** this paragraph.*

the macroscopic level, the other emphasizing the invisible submicroscopic level. Here is the macroscopic definition.

A reaction taking place in a closed system has reached equilibrium when all reactants and products are present and their observable properties are not changing.

This definition states some factors that you have already learned about equilibrium. First, all reactants and products must be present. This eliminates reactions that go to completion, such as the reaction of magnesium and oxygen to form magnesium oxide. Second, the observable properties of the system do not change. One important observable property is the concentration of reactants and products, as indicated by the constant glow of the light bulb illustrated in Figure 18-1.

The definition specifies a closed system. A reaction that reaches equilibrium must somehow be set apart from the rest of its environment. In the football stadium analogy, the fence around the stadium separates the people under consideration (those people who shuffle between their seats and the concession area during the game) from those who decided not to attend the game. The acetic acid-water reaction is a closed system if you consider a bottle of vinegar with its cap on. No more water or acetic acid is being added, and no reactant or product can escape.

Is it possible to design a system that is not closed but has constant observable properties? Consider a plastic foam cup with a hole in the bottom. The cup is held underneath a faucet. The faucet is adjusted so that water flows into the cup just as fast as it drains out of the hole in the bottom. Although the level of the water remains constant under these conditions, this is not an example of equilibrium. Water is both entering and leaving the cup. One condition for equilibrium is for nothing to enter or leave the system.

Since processes that reach equilibrium are taking place in a closed environment, there are several observable properties other than the mass or concentration of reactants and products that you can also monitor. These properties also must remain constant. They include the temperature, the volume of the reaction system, the color of the system that is related to concentration, and the pressures of any gases involved. For reactions that take place in solution, one of the most important properties is the concentrations of the dissolved substances.

Note that this definition of equilibrium says that the observable properties of a system are constant, including the concentrations of dissolved substances. It does *not* say that these concentrations are equal. When acetic acid comes to equilibrium in water, there is a larger amount of the reactant CH_3COOH present than there is product, CH_3COO^-. What is equal at equilibrium? Read on.

Defining equilibrium—submicroscopic The submicroscopic definition of *equilibrium* brings to your attention the underlying processes that are taking place. It can be stated this way.

When a reaction has come to equilibrium, the reactants are forming products at the same rate as the products are forming reactants.

This definition helps you understand why the observable properties must remain constant. If product and reactant molecules are being produced at the same rate, then their amounts do not change.

Even though a system at equilibrium does not visibly change, there is a flurry of submicroscopic activity taking place. Together both the macroscopic and the submicroscopic definitions provide a foundation for understanding that equilibrium is not a static state but an active, dynamic process.

Concept ✔ Check

What is equal when a reaction is at equilibrium?

18.2 When Reactions Come to Equilibrium

Exactly what is going on at the submicroscopic level as a process reaches equilibrium? The chemical reaction represented by this equation will help you discover the answer.

$$2NO_2(g) \rightleftharpoons N_2O_4(g)$$

To carry out this reaction, 0.0500 mole of nitrogen dioxide, NO_2, is placed into a flask that has a fixed volume of 1 liter, as shown in Figure 18-3. Initially there is no dinitrogen tetraoxide, N_2O_4, in the flask. However, this substance forms as the nitrogen dioxide gradually reacts. Table 18-1 shows how the amounts of both reactant and product change as the reaction proceeds.

TABLE 18-1

Amounts of NO_2 and N_2O_4 as Reaction Proceeds to Equilibrium	
Amount of NO_2	**Amount of N_2O_4**
0.0500 mol	0.0000 mol
0.0428 mol	0.0036 mol
0.0320 mol	0.0090 mol
0.0220 mol	0.0140 mol
0.0154 mol	0.0173 mol
0.0120 mol	0.0190 mol
0.0106 mol	0.0197 mol
0.0102 mol	0.0199 mol
0.0100 mol	0.0200 mol
0.0100 mol	0.0200 mol
0.0100 mol	0.0200 mol

CONNECTING CONCEPTS

Models Chemical equilibrium is a model. Like other chemistry models, it proposes a submicroscopic explanation for macroscopic observations. All models are subject to change to accommodate new observations.

Figure 18-3 Nitrogen dioxide, NO_2, and dinitrogen tetroxide, N_2O_4, are both present here.

PART **1**
Section 18.2

Resources

When Reactions Come to Equilibrium

Try a simple activity involving different types of beans as a simulation for reaching equilibrium. This activity is set up for small groups of students to do, and is described in an article called "The 'Bean' Lab," Dickenson and Erhardt, *Journal of Chemical Education*, November 1991, Volume 11, pp. 930–931.

CONNECTING CONCEPTS

Change and Interaction Reaction equilibrium exists whenever two opposing reactions are occurring at the same rate. Some examples of equilibrium include vapor–liquid systems, saturated solutions, and the reactions of weak acids and weak bases with water.

You can learn more about this reaction if these numbers are presented in a different format. In Figure 18-4, you see this reaction in pictorial form and as a graph of the data in Table 18-1. The pictures are actually a submicroscopic representation of the changing amounts of NO_2 and N_2O_4 as the mixture approaches equilibrium. Notice that the concentration of NO_2 decreases at first and finally comes to a plateau at $0.0100M$, where it no longer changes. The initial concentration of the product is zero; the concentration of N_2O_4 gradually increases until it reaches a final plateau of $0.0200M$.

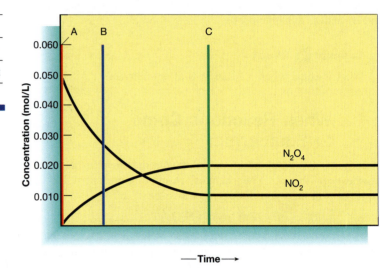

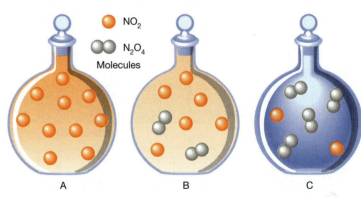

Figure 18-4 *You can follow the changing concentrations of both NO_2 and N_2O_4 as equilibrium is approached.*

The graph shows a region where there is no equilibrium and a region where equilibrium exists. The region of equilibrium is where both curves flatten out; at this point, the observable properties of the system (for example, the concentration of both species) are no longer changing. The portion of the curve before the plateau does not represent equilibrium. Rather, this is an area where the concentrations of reactants and products are changing as the reaction approaches equilibrium.

Myths and Misconceptions

Students may have difficulty interpreting the double arrow ($\rightleftharpoons$) as an indication of a reversible reaction. Emphasize that the double arrow indicates two reactions (forward and reverse) occurring at equal rates, but in opposition, so that the reactions approach a state of equilibrium. Sometimes students think that the double arrow means "equal." Stress that this is not the case, and the reactants do not equal the products (either in mass or in concentration).

Students also tend to overlook the significance of arrow length, as in $\rightleftharpoons$. Clarify that for some reactions at equilibrium, a K_{eq} that is greater than one indicates that the products are favored (and K_{eq} values less than one indicate the reverse). Students also may not realize that $\rightarrow$ can indicate the equilibrium lies so far to the right that no arrow to the left is used, as in shifting equilibrium (Section 18.8).

How could you follow the changes in concentrations of these gases? Nitrogen dioxide is a brown gas, while dinitrogen tetraoxide is colorless. Compare the pictures accompanying the graph. At the start, all of the gas was brown NO_2. But since the total amount of NO_2 gradually decreases from *A* to *B* to *C*, the intensity of the color also decreases. When equilibrium is reached, the color no longer changes. Color is an observable property of this reaction, which must be constant when equilibrium is attained. The properties you observed (colors, concentrations) are those that can be measured in the macroscopic world. But the models represent the submicroscopic world. How does the second definition of equilibrium apply?

Moving toward equilibrium In the three cases—*A*, *B*, and *C*—visualize the molecules in constant motion. In Figure 18-4, the reactant molecules are bouncing into each other. Some of the collisions result in the formation of the product N_2O_4. Is it possible for the reverse reaction ($N_2O_4 \rightarrow 2NO_2$) to take place in *A*? Of course not! Since there are no product molecules at the beginning of the reaction, there cannot be any reaction taking place in the reverse direction.

As the reaction progresses, there is a gradual buildup of N_2O_4 and a gradual decrease of NO_2, as represented by the configuration shown in *B*. Now that some product molecules are present, they can interact to reform reactant molecules. At the same time, several reactant molecules are left. They can continue to form product molecules through the forward reaction.

How does the rate of the forward reaction in *B* compare with its rate at the beginning of the reaction in A? You can apply concepts from Chapter 17 to answer this question. When the concentrations of the reactants decrease, the rate of the reaction decreases. In *B*, the forward reaction is proceeding more slowly than it was in *A*.

How do the rates of the forward and reverse reactions compare in *B*? You can answer this question by looking at the accompanying graph. The amount of N_2O_4 continues to increase before and after the picture shown by *B*. N_2O_4 must be produced faster than it is being used. For this to occur, the forward reaction must be proceeding at a faster rate than the reverse reaction. These relative rates also explain what is happening to the concentration of the reactant. The amount of nitrogen dioxide decreases because the forward reaction is taking place at a faster rate. This description of the relative rate applies anywhere between *A* and *C*, even when the amount of N_2O_4 is greater than the amount of NO_2. As long as N_2O_4 is increasing, the forward reaction is faster than the reverse reaction.

What is going on at *C* and beyond? The amounts of both substances no longer change. Equilibrium has been established. The forward reaction has slowed down, and the reverse reaction has speeded up—until the rates of the two reactions are equal. Both reactions will continue at this rate.

PROBLEM·SOLVING STRATEGY

*By **breaking down the process** of equilibrium **into steps**, it becomes easier to understand how a reaction reaches equilibrium. (See Strategy, page 166.)*

Teaching Strategy

If you have done the **Activate Prior Knowledge** activity (page T600), have students plot the data on a graph similar to the one shown in Figure 18–4. Because students physically performed the "reaction" and collected the data themselves, they will have a more concrete understanding of the submicroscopic concepts discussed in Section 18.2. After students make the graph, ask them to interpret it. In which region are the rates of assembly/disassembly increasing? decreasing? Can they identify a region where equilibrium is attained?

DEMONSTRATION

Equilibrium Involving Solutions of Solids

Show students that solubility equilibrium has been established when a saturated solution is prepared. Add a small amount of baking soda, sugar, or table salt to water and allow it to dissolve completely. Ask students if a solubility equilibrium (involving the solid and its aqueous solute) has been

established. Solubility equilibrium is not reached for an unsaturated solution. Add more solid until students declare that equilibrium is reached.

⚠ **CAUTION: Wear safety goggles and a lab apron.** For disposal, pour down the drain.

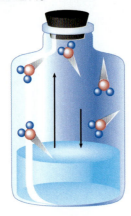

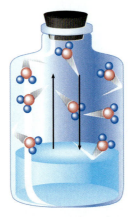

Figure 18-5 Top: *After water is placed in a stoppered bottle, molecules escape into the vapor phase at a steady rate, but the return of water molecules to liquid is slow.* Bottom: *When sufficient gas molecules have accumulated, the rates of evaporation and condensation become equal.*

18.3 Processes That Reach Equilibrium

The principles of equilibrium apply to a wide variety of reactions. Some reactions are familiar to you, while others will be discussed in later chapters. Both physical and chemical changes provide examples of equilibrium. An example of physical change that reaches equilibrium is the vaporization of a liquid.

Vapor-liquid equilibrium As you already know, liquids can change into their gaseous form without boiling. For example, if you leave an open pan of water at room temperature for a period of several days, you will notice that the water level gradually decreases before disappearing entirely. This is not an example of equilibrium, because the amount of water (an observable, macroscopic property) is continually changing because you have an open system. However, if you put some water into a bottle and cap it, only a small portion of the water evaporates. Very quickly **vapor-liquid equilibrium** will be established between these two opposing reactions as shown in Figure 18-5.

$$H_2O(l) \rightleftharpoons H_2O(g)$$

This equation shows that liquid water is evaporating at the same rate as gaseous water vapor is condensing. Equilibrium involving a substance changing from one physical state to another is called phase equilibrium.

Equilibrium involving solutions of solids Equilibrium can be established by dissolving a solute (solid, liquid, or gas) in a solvent. For example, when water is exposed to air, a certain amount of oxygen gas becomes dissolved in the water. This is an equilibrium that is very important to the survival of fish.

$$O_2(g) \rightleftharpoons O_2(aq)$$

Solids dissolved in water are another example. In the case of solids, you need to be careful about identifying when equilibrium has been reached. Suppose you are dissolving blue solid copper sulfate in water. If you take 1.0 g of the salt and put it in 100 mL of water, it dissolves completely. There is no solid left over for the reverse reaction to take place. In other words, this is a reaction that goes to completion.

$$CuSO_4(s) \rightarrow CuSO_4(aq)$$

Typically, chemists refer to solubility equilibrium when they talk about relatively insoluble substances, such as lead iodide, PbI_2, barium sulfate, $BaSO_4$, or cadmium sulfide, CdS. Since very little of these solids dissolves in water, equilibrium is quickly established between the solid and the dissolved solute, as shown by this equation.

$$PbI_2(s) \rightleftharpoons Pb^{2+}(aq) + 2I^-(aq)$$

PART 1
Section 18.3

Teaching Strategy

Equilibrium Involving Solutions of Solids

If you have previously covered the solubility of ionic solids, you may wish to review the table of solubility data in Appendix D at this time. Ask students to identify three substances on the table that can reach solubility equilibrium by dissolving only a small portion of solid. Then have them identify three other substances in which a much larger amount of solute must be dissolved.

Guided Practice

Review the Concept Check question on page 603 with students. Answers can be found in Appendix E on page 808.

Reteaching Idea

Before going on to the quantitative aspects of equilibrium, make sure your students understand the terms and concepts presented in Part 1. Have them draw concept maps, or help you do so, starting with the word *equilibrium*. They should include the terms *reversible reactions, closed system, constant observable properties, equal rates, all reactants and products present*. Also include the four types of equilibrium introduced in Part 1: *vapor-liquid, solutions of solids, gas-phase,* and *acid-base*. Have students define each term and/or give examples.

PART 1 REVIEW

ANSWERS

■ Keyed to Objectives

A 1. The Alka-Seltzer tablet is *not* at equilibrium with the products because the system is open. The fizzing indicates that one of the products of this reaction is escaping.

A 2. The double arrow shows that the forward and reverse reactions are taking place at the same rate.

B 3. At the beginning, only the forward reaction takes place, because there are no products. As time passes, the rate of the forward reaction (producing NH_3) decreases as reactants disappear, and the rate of the reverse reaction (producing N_2 and H_2) increases as more product appears. Finally, equilibrium is established when the rates of both reactions are the same.

Gas-phase equilibrium When a chemical reaction involving only gases takes place in a closed system, the reaction may proceed to equilibrium, as you saw in the reaction of NO_2 and N_2O_4. Another example of a reaction between gases that reaches **gas-phase equilibrium** is the production of ammonia from its elements, as shown by this equation.

$$N_2(g) + 3H_2(g) \rightleftharpoons 2NH_3(g)$$

Equilibria involving acids and bases Both acetic acid and ammonia, a base, react with water when they dissolve, but they react in different ways, as these equations show.

$$CH_3COOH(aq) + H_2O(l) \rightleftharpoons CH_3COO^-(aq) + H_3O^+(aq)$$
$$NH_3(aq) + H_2O(l) \rightleftharpoons NH_4^+(aq) + OH^-(aq)$$

The first equation is typical of an **acid-base equilibrium** involving a water solution of an acid, while the second equation is typical of an equilibrium involving a water solution of a base. Notice the difference in the two reactions. Ammonia, NH_3, receives a hydrogen ion, H^+, from the water when it reacts, while the acetic acid molecule loses a hydrogen ion to the water. The properties and reactions of chemicals classified as acids and bases are so important that an entire chapter will be devoted to them.

PART 1 REVIEW

1. You put an Alka-Seltzer tablet into water. You see it fizz and dissolve. As it fizzes, is the solid tablet (a reactant) in equilibrium with the products of this reaction? Explain your answer.

2. What does the double arrow indicate in the following chemical equation?

$$Mg^{2+}(aq) + 2OH^-(aq) \rightleftharpoons Mg(OH)_2(s)$$

3. According to the text, the following gas-phase reaction reaches equilibrium.

$$N_2(g) + 3H_2(g) \rightleftharpoons 2NH_3(g)$$

Suppose you start with a mixture of nitrogen and hydrogen gases. Briefly describe how the rates of the forward and reverse reactions change as the system comes to equilibrium.

4. Equations involving substances containing zinc are shown. Briefly describe what you might see as these reactions take place.
   a. When the solid zinc nitrate is put into water, it readily dissolves. The equation for this change is this.

$$Zn(NO_3)_2(s) \rightarrow Zn^{2+}(aq) + 2NO_3^-(aq)$$

   b. When you add some sodium hydroxide to this solution, the following equilibrium is set up.

$$Zn^{2+}(aq) + 2OH^-(aq) \rightleftharpoons Zn(OH)_2(s)$$

◄ **PROBLEM-SOLVING STRATEGY**

Draw a diagram to help you describe the rates of the forward and reverse reactions. (See Strategy, page 216.)

Boxed numbers indicate questions that involve skills in interpretation, application, and analysis.

PART 1
Section 18.3 *continued*

≡CLOSE

Summing Up Main Ideas

Describe both the macroscopic and submicroscopic equilibrium in an unopened bottle of soda pop. (CO_2 in the solution is in equilibrium with the CO_2 present in the air space at the top of the bottle. The amount of H_2O vapor at the top is also in equilibrium with the H_2O in the soda pop. For every molecule of CO_2 or H_2O that enters the air space, another molecule enters the solution.) How does this compare to what was happening inside the bottle when it was first sealed? (Before the system reached equilibrium, CO_2 and H_2O were vaporizing and entering the air space at the top of the bottle faster than these molecules were redissolving in the soft drink.) If the bottle is opened, why is it no longer considered to be in equilibrium? (The system is no longer closed.)

PART 1 REVIEW

Assign the Part Review questions.

Evaluating Skills

These skills are evaluated in the Part Review questions indicated. **Determining main ideas:** 1, 2; **Describing:** 3, 4

Videodisc Connections

376 to 3534, side 5
Multicolor ammonia fountain (movie)

B **4.** **a.** The solid dissolves totally in the water, if only a small amount is used, since zinc nitrate is quite soluble. Under these circumstances, this is *not* an example of equilibrium (as the single arrow suggests in the equation) because no reactant is leftover.

b. Upon the addition of the hydroxide ion, some white solid will appear in the solution. Since equilibrium is established quickly, the amount of the white solid present will remain constant provided that no more hydroxide is added.

CAREERS IN CHEMISTRY

CAREERS IN CHEMISTRY

Teaching Strategies

1. Discuss with students the patent process and the role of patents in the development of technology. Have them identify other intellectual property rights such as trade secrets, trademarks, and copyrights and how they differ. Also have them consider the drawbacks of patents and why they have a finite duration.

2. Have students identify growth areas for patents such as computer software, biotechnology, pharmaceuticals, and biomedical devices.

3. Have students discuss the experiences of relatives and friends who have careers that may be different from the ones they expected to pursue.

Related Careers

Discuss with students other legal specialties and other professions where an understanding of math and science is a valuable complement to other components of the field, for example, environmental law, medical malpractice, architecture, journalism, management, and teaching. For additional career information, contact the American Bar Association, 750 N. Lake Shore Dr., Chicago, IL 60611; the Environmental Protection Agency, 401 M Street, SW, Washington, DC 20460; and the architecture department of a nearby university.

Resources

Contact the Bar Association in your state to identify a local patent attorney or other lawyer with a scientific background and invite him or her to your class to discuss the role of science in the profession.

Patent Attorney

The number of different career opportunities has increased over the last few years. New careers are emerging that either blend or apply seemingly unrelated disciplines.

Ellen Joy Kapinos
Patent Attorney

■ *Changes in the direction of your career serve only to strengthen the fund of knowledge and expertise you have to offer.*

A mixture of science and law Ellen Joy Kapinos was working toward her master's degree in biological sciences when she decided to combine her interest and training in science with a degree in law. After completing her master's degree, she went to law school. It was there she decided to become a patent attorney. Now, as Senior Patent Attorney for a biotechnology company, Ellen deals with legal issues surrounding the awarding of patents for inventions made through her company's scientific research.

Patents for front-runners in technology A patent grants to an inventor the exclusive right to make, use, or sell an invention for a specific period of time. Ellen's major tasks include preparing applications for U.S. and foreign patents, following the legal process through to the securing of patents for her company, and providing the legal expertise in support of her company's patent positions. Ellen finds the combination of scientific and legal issues to be stimulating and rewarding, especially since patent law always involves the latest in technology.

Patent law opportunities Ellen believes that opportunities in her field will increase and that law schools will make patent law a more important part of their curricula. To become a patent attorney, you must demonstrate special knowledge by passing a patent bar exam in addition to the state bar exam. A patent agent differs from a patent attorney in that a degree in law is not required. However, a patent agent must have a science background and must have successfully completed the patent bar examination. As a patent agent, you are able to present cases before the Patent and Trademark Office, but not before the courts.

Indirect career paths can be right Ellen stresses that the study of science provides the underpinnings for a wide range of career choices. Your first choice of career may not prove to be right, but changes in the direction of your career serve only to strengthen the fund of knowledge and expertise you have to offer.

PART
2 Quantitative Aspects of Equilibrium

At the beginning of this chapter, you contrasted reactions that go to completion with reactions that reach equilibrium. You have already learned how to do calculations involving reactions that go to completion. But what about reactions that come to equilibrium? Can you determine the amount of reactants and products present at equilibrium? The answer to this question is yes. In this section, you will learn a relationship that will let you make quantitative predictions about these reactions too.

18.4 The Equilibrium Constant Expression

Consider this reaction involving phosphorus trichloride, PCl_3, Chlorine, Cl_2, and phosphorus pentachloride, PCl_5, which has come to equilibrium.

$$PCl_3(g) + Cl_2(g) \rightleftharpoons PCl_5(g)$$

By determining the concentrations of the reactants and product, you can study this equilibrium. If you start with 1.00 mole of PCl_3 and 1.00 mole of Cl_2 inside a rigid 1.00-L reaction vessel, the initial concentration of each of the reactant gases is 1.00 mol/L. A shorthand way of writing the *concentration of* a reactant or product is to place its formula inside brackets. For instance, the symbol $[PCl_3]$ stands for the *concentration of phosphorus trichloride,* measured in units of moles per liter. Therefore, $[PCl_3] = [Cl_2] = 1.00$ mol/L. If this reaction goes to completion, you can calculate the final concentration of PCl_5 to be 1.00 mol/L. Instead, the concentrations of all three gases become constant when $[PCl_5] = 0.26$ mol/L. This is called the **equilibrium concentration** of PCl_5. What is the equilibrium concentration of PCl_3 and Cl_2? Before going on, calculate what it would be.

An equilibrium concentration of PCl_5 of 0.26 mol/L corresponds to only 26 percent of the product you would expect if the reaction had gone to completion. As a first guess, you might assume that whenever this reaction takes place, you will obtain 26 percent of the predicted possible product.

Finding an equilibrium regularity You can try out this guess by looking at more equilibrium concentrations. Table 18-2 on the next page shows the results of four experiments involving this reaction. These experiments were carried out by mixing different initial concentrations of PCl_3 and Cl_2 and measuring the concentrations of all three gases when equilibrium was established.

O b j e c t i v e s

Part 2

C. *Write* the equilibrium constant expression for any reaction at equilibrium.

D. *Calculate* the equilibrium constant for any reaction at equilibrium.

E. *Determine* equilibrium concentrations, using the equilibrium constant expression.

F. *Apply* the solubility product constant to saturated solutions of ionic solids.

Developing Skills

Students may apply these skills in their study of Part 2.

Forming a hypothesis: Have students use Section 18.4 and the equilibrium concentrations in Table 18–2 to look for a constant relationship involving the numbers in the table.

Calculating: Have students determine the values of equilibrium constants and the equilibrium concentrations of reactants and products. (See Practice Problems 5, 6, and 7.)

Determining main ideas: Ask students why the answer to Practice Problem 5 should be the same as that of Example 18–1.

☰ FOCUS

Activate Prior Knowledge

This activity will use students' knowledge of solubility to demonstrate equilibrium.

⚠ **CAUTION: Have students wear safety goggles and lab aprons.** Have students add 25 grams of NaCl to 50 mL of water in a 100-mL beaker. Stir for two minutes. Let the solution settle for five minutes. Then, carefully pour off as much liquid as possible and discard. Allow the remaining salt in the beaker to dry. After it is dry and cool, measure the mass of the salt.

Have several groups of students perform this activity and compare the results to show that the equilibrium between salt entering and leaving the solution is constant.

TABLE 18-2

	Initial Concentrations		Equilibrium Concentrations			Predicted Concentration if 100% Complete	Percent of Predicted Product
Experimental Data for the Reaction of PCl_3 and Cl_2							
Exp.	$[PCl_3]$	$[Cl_2]$	$[PCl_3]$	$[Cl_2]$	$[PCl_5]$	$[PCl_5]$	$[PCl_5]$
1	$0.1000\,M$	$0.1000\,M$	$0.0956\,M$	$0.0956\,M$	$0.0044\,M$	$0.1000\,M$	4.4%
2	$0.500\,M$	$0.500\,M$	$0.417\,M$	$0.417\,M$	$0.083\,M$	$0.500\,M$	17%
3	$1.00\,M$	$1.00\,M$	$0.74\,M$	$0.74\,M$	$0.26\,M$	$1.00\,M$	26%
4	$5.00\,M$	$5.00\,M$	$2.35\,M$	$2.35\,M$	$2.65\,M$	$5.00\,M$	53%

PART **2**

Section 18.4 continued

TEACH

Teaching Strategy

The Equilibrium Constant Expression

Many students become confused with rules for writing equilibrium expressions. To combat this, start by having students write equilibrium constants for reactions in which each reactant and product has a coefficient of one. When you proceed to reactions that contain coefficients greater than one, such as $2H_2$ or $3N_2$, have students write out these terms as $H_2 + H_2$ or $N_2 + N_2 + N_2$ respectively. Have students note that the coefficients in the chemical equation become exponents in the equilibrium constant expression. You can use the **Cooperative Learning** activity which follows to reinforce this concept.

Cooperative Learning

Teams of 2; **Time:** 20 minutes
Objective: Students will write equilibrium constant expressions.
Task: Direct students to use the eleven equations in Table 18–4. (Or you can make up your own list of equations, if you prefer.) Only one student per team should have the list. The student with the list will give the other student the equation for an equilibrium reaction. This student will write the equilibrium constant expression for the reaction. If the expression is written incorrectly, the student with the book should alert the partner of this; however, the student with the book should not tell the other student the correct expression. After six equations are done, partners should switch roles.

(continued on page T611)

Notice that the actual concentration of PCl_5 is not a regular percentage of the amount predicted by stoichiometry calculations. However, don't discard the idea that there might be an equilibrium regularity. Although the first hypothesis was wrong, there may be some other way you can manipulate the concentrations to uncover a regularity. Good problem solvers keep looking for a pattern when they suspect there might be one.

There are many ways that you could try combining $[PCl_3]$, $[Cl_2]$, and $[PCl_5]$ into a relationship. You might want to guess some possibilities and try them out yourself before you read any further. One possibility is this ratio.

$$\frac{[PCl_5]}{[PCl_3][Cl_2]}$$

What happens when you substitute the equilibrium concentrations from the four experiments into this expression?

1. $$\frac{[PCl_5]}{[PCl_3][Cl_2]} = \frac{(0.0044)}{(0.0956)(0.0956)} = 0.48$$

2. $$\frac{[PCl_5]}{[PCl_3][Cl_2]} = \frac{(0.083)}{(0.417)(0.417)} = 0.48$$

3. $$\frac{[PCl_5]}{[PCl_3][Cl_2]} = \frac{(0.26)}{(0.74)(0.74)} = 0.47$$

4. $$\frac{[PCl_5]}{[PCl_3][Cl_2]} = \frac{(2.65)}{(2.35)(2.35)} = 0.48$$

This expression gives a constant result. Now you have a relationship that describes the equilibrium of this reaction.

$$\frac{[PCl_5]}{[PCl_3][Cl_2]} = 0.48$$

This relationship wouldn't be very important if it worked only for this reaction. Fortunately experiments with other equilibrium reactions show that a simple relationship involving the equilibrium concentrations also gives a constant value. Look at the expressions that give rise to a constant for the reactions in Table 18-3. See if you can find a pattern based on these expressions.

TABLE 18-3

Some Equilibria and Equilibrium Constant Expressions	
Reaction	**Equilibrium Constant Expression**
$COCl_2(g) \rightleftharpoons CO(g) + Cl_2(g)$	$K_{eq} = \dfrac{[CO][Cl_2]}{[COCl_2]}$
$H_2(g) + Cl_2(g) \rightleftharpoons HCl(g) + HCl(g)$	$K_{eq} = \dfrac{[HCl][HCl]}{[H_2][Cl_2]} = \dfrac{[HCl]^2}{[H_2][Cl_2]}$
$Fe^{3+}(aq) + SCN^-(aq) \rightleftharpoons FeSCN^{2+}(aq)$	$K_{eq} = \dfrac{[FeSCN^{2+}]}{[Fe^{3+}][SCN^-]}$

The symbol K_{eq} stands for the **equilibrium constant**,—that is, the (constant) number you calculate when you substitute the equilibrium concentrations of the reactants and products of a given reaction into the equilibrium expressions shown. Notice that in each case, the expression has the form of a quotient (fraction). The numerator (top half) of the quotient has product concentrations multiplied together; the denominator (bottom half) has the reactant concentrations multiplied together. You can express this pattern in the form of a rule: The **equilibrium constant expression** for a reaction that comes to equilibrium is written by dividing the product of the equilibrium concentrations of the products by the product of the equilibrium concentrations of the reactants.

If you know the equilibrium concentrations of all of the reactants and products in the reaction, you can use the equation for the reaction to write the equilibrium constant expression and calculate the value of the equilibrium constant. Example 18-1 shows you how this is done.

Figure 18-6 *Forces are balanced in the human pyramid just as they are in chemical reactions at equilibrium.*

EXAMPLE 18-1

This reaction involving hydrogen iodide, hydrogen, and iodine reaches equilibrium at 425°C.

$$2HI(g) \rightleftharpoons H_2(g) + I_2(g)$$

The equilibrium concentrations of the three gases are these: $[HI] = 0.0175M$; $[H_2] = 0.0045M$; $[I_2] = 0.00125M$. What is the value of the equilibrium constant for this reaction?

■ **Analyze the Problem** This problem involves a reaction that comes to equilibrium. Equilibrium concentrations are given. You

PART **2**

Section 18.4 *continued*

(continued from page T610)
Team responsibility: For those cases where a partner could not write the correct expression, the partners should work together to come up with the correct answer. Do this after each partner has had the chance to try five or six expressions.
Evaluation: Ask students if they noticed a relationship between the coefficients in the chemical equation and the exponents in the equilibrium constant expressions.

PART **2**

Section 18.4 *continued*

Practice Problems

Assign the Practice Problems.

PROBLEM-SOLVING

S T R A T E G Y

Break this problem into **manageable** *steps in order to solve for* K_{eq}. *(See Strategy, page 166.)*

will need to know the equilibrium constant expression to solve the problem.

■ **Apply a Strategy** First you need the equilibrium constant expression for the reaction. The chemical equation has a coefficient of 2 in front of HI. How can you handle this coefficient? Try rewriting the chemical equation without using any coefficients.

$$HI(g) + HI(g) \rightleftharpoons H_2(g) + I_2(g)$$

Now you can write the equilibrium constant expression.

$$K_{eq} = \frac{[H_2][I_2]}{[HI][HI]} = \frac{[H_2][I_2]}{[HI]^2}$$

To determine the value of K_{eq}, you will need to substitute the equilibrium concentrations into this expression.

■ **Work a Solution** Substitute the given equilibrium concentrations in the equilibrium constant expression.

$$K_{eq} = \frac{[H_2][I_2]}{[HI]^2} = \frac{(0.0045)(0.00125)}{(0.0175)^2} = 0.018$$

■ **Verify Your Answer** Check your work to make certain that you have written the equilibrium constant expression correctly and that you have not made any mathematical errors.

Practice Problems

5. Another mixture of hydrogen, iodine, and hydrogen iodide gases reaches these equilibrium concentrations at 425°C: $[H_2] = 0.0091M$, $[I_2] = 0.00059M$, $[HI] = 0.0173M$. What is the value of the equilibrium constant for this mixture? (Hint: What *should* the value of the constant be?)

6. At a different temperature, the same mixture of these three gases reaches equilibrium at these concentrations: $[H_2] = [I_2] = 0.00078M$, and $[HI] = 0.0035M$. What is the value of the equilibrium constant now? **Ans.** 0.050

Example 18-1 showed you one way to handle a reaction in which a reactant or product had a coefficient other than one. When you read 2HI, you wrote [HI] two times in the equilibrium constant expression. If some other equation says $3NH_3$, you could write $[NH_3]$ three times in the equilibrium constant expression.

Is there another simpler way to handle such equations? Take another look at these two equations and equilibrium expressions.

$$2HI(g) \rightleftharpoons H_2(g) + I_2(g) \qquad K_{eq} = \frac{[H_2][I_2]}{[HI]^2}$$

$$H_2(g) + Cl_2(g) \rightleftharpoons 2HCl(g) \qquad K_{eq} = \frac{[HCl]^2}{[H_2][Cl_2]}$$

Do you see how the number 2 shows up both as a *coefficient* in the chemical equation and as an *exponent* in the equilibrium expression? This coefficient-exponent relationship is true for all equilibrium reactions. You may restate the rule for the equilibrium constant expression this way.

The following reaction is at equilibrium.

$$aA + bB \rightleftharpoons cC + dD$$

The equilibrium constant expression is this.

$$K_{eq} = \frac{[C]^c[D]^d}{[A]^a[B]^b}$$

TABLE 18-4

Some Equilibrium Systems and Constants		
Reaction	**Equilibrium Constant Expression**	K_{eq}*
$2NO_2(g) \rightleftharpoons N_2O_4(g)$	$K_{eq} = \dfrac{[N_2O_4]}{[NO_2]^2}$	1.20 at 55°C
$N_2(g) + 3H_2(g) \rightleftharpoons 2NH_3(g)$	$K_{eq} = \dfrac{[NH_3]^2}{[N_2][H_2]^3}$	626 at 200°C
$2HI(g) \rightleftharpoons H_2(g) + I_2(g)$	$K_{eq} = \dfrac{[H_2][I_2]}{[HI]^2}$	1.85×10^{-2} at 425°C 85 at 25°C
$2SO_2(g) + O_2(g) \rightleftharpoons 2SO_3(g)$	$K_{eq} = \dfrac{[SO_3]^2}{[SO_2]^2[O_2]}$	261 at 727°C
$PCl_5(g) \rightleftharpoons PCl_3(g) + Cl_2(g)$	$K_{eq} = \dfrac{[PCl_3][Cl_2]}{[PCl_5]}$	2.24 at 227°C 33.3 at 487°C
$COCl_2(g) \rightleftharpoons CO(g) + Cl_2(g)$	$K_{eq} = \dfrac{[CO][Cl_2]}{[COCl_2]}$	8.2×10^{-2} at 627°C
$2NO(g) + O_2(g) \rightleftharpoons 2NO_2(g)$	$K_{eq} = \dfrac{[NO_2]^2}{[NO]^2[O_2]}$	6.45×10^5 at 227°C
$C(s) + 2H_2(g) \rightleftharpoons CH_4(g)$	$K_{eq} = \dfrac{[CH_4]}{[H_2]^2}$	8.1×10^8 at 25°C
$CO(g) + H_2O(g) \rightleftharpoons CO_2(g) + H_2(g)$	$K_{eq} = \dfrac{[CO_2][H_2]}{[CO][H_2O]}$	1.02×10^5 at 25°C 10.0 at 690°C 3.59 at 800°C
$H_2(g) + Cl_2(g) \rightleftharpoons 2HCl(g)$	$K_{eq} = \dfrac{[HCl]^2}{[H_2][Cl_2]}$	1.8×10^{33} at 25°C
$C(s) + H_2O(g) \rightleftharpoons CO(g) + H_2(g)$	$K_{eq} = \dfrac{[CO][H_2]}{[H_2O]}$	1.96 at 1000°C

* Equilibrium reactions are affected by temperature; therefore values of K_{eq} are for a specific temperature.

Myths and Misconceptions

In calculating the value of the equilibrium constant expression, students are often confused when changing the coefficients of the formulas in the balanced equation to exponents in the equilibrium expression. In addition, students may have difficulty in deciding which substances to use in the calculations and which substances are not factors in the equilibrium. Use a number of examples to demonstrate this concept to students and to provide them with practice in writing equilibrium constant expressions.

18.5 Equilibrium Involving Liquids and Solids

All of the reactions in the last section involved either gases or solutes dissolved in water. But solids and liquids are also involved in many equilibrium reactions. One example is the chemical reaction you studied at the beginning of this chapter.

$$CH_3COOH(aq) + H_2O(l) \rightleftharpoons CH_3COO^-(aq) + H_3O^+(aq)$$

Another example is this reaction involving solid barium sulfate and its ions dissolved in water.

$$BaSO_4(s) \rightleftharpoons Ba^{2+}(aq) + SO_4^{2-}(aq)$$

Based on what you have just learned, it seems reasonable to write these equilibrium constant expressions this way.

$$K = \frac{[CH_3COO^-][H_3O^+]}{[CH_3COOH][H_2O]} \quad \text{and} \quad K = \frac{[Ba^{2+}][SO_4^{2-}]}{[BaSO_4]}$$

However, chemists typically do *not* write these expressions this way. They omit the terms $[H_2O]$ and $[BaSO_4]$. Why?

Solid and liquid concentrations are constant

Equilibrium constant expressions show the relationship between variables, such as dissolved solutes like CH_3COOH and $BaSO_4$. Can you expect changing concentrations for a solid such as $BaSO_4$ or a liquid such as H_2O? The answer is no. The density of pure solids and liquids—that is, the number of grams per unit of volume—doesn't depend on the amount of solid or liquid that is present. No matter how large or small the sample, the density of liquids and solids is the same. Similarly, the number of moles of a solid or liquid per unit volume (their concentration) also does not change.

Since their concentrations are constant, there is no need to include terms for solids and liquids in equilibrium constant expressions. However, when you write the expression, you automatically incorporate the values of solid and liquid concentrations into the value of the equilibrium constant, as shown here.

$$[BaSO_4]K = [Ba^{2+}][SO_4^{2-}]$$
2 constants

$$K_{eq} = [Ba^{2+}][SO_4^{2-}]$$
1 new constant

The accepted equilibrium constant, therefore, is the product of $[BaSO_4]$ and K, but you do need to know either of those values.

Concept Check

Write the equilibrium constant expression for this reaction.

$$CaCO_3(s) \rightarrow CaO(s) + CO_2(g)$$

18.6 Using the Equilibrium Constant Expression

Writing equilibrium expressions enables you to calculate the concentrations of reactants and products when reactions reach equilibrium. In this section, you will deal with a solution of Ca^{2+} in water. When ions such as Ca^{2+} and Mg^{2+} are dissolved in water, to the concentration of $0.01M$ or more, that water is often called *hard* water. You may be familiar with some of the adverse effects of hard water, such as depositions of calcium-containing solids in water pipes or the formation of scummy residues with soaps. One way to remove the calcium ions from the water is to precipitate them in a solid such as calcium carbonate, $CaCO_3$. Example 18-2 presents a problem based on this precipitation.

DO YOU KNOW?

Another agent for softening water goes by the name ethylenediaminetetraacetic acid. Instead of saying this mouthful, chemists usually abbreviate the name to EDTA. EDTA works by forming complex ions with the calcium or magnesium ions in hard water. Hence it is called a complexing agent. The next time you buy a bottle of shampoo, see if EDTA or tetrasodium EDTA is listed among the ingredients. Shampoos work better with soft water.

EXAMPLE 18-2

When Ca^{2+} ions are mixed with CO_3^{2-} ions, they form a precipitate of calcium carbonate, $CaCO_3$. The equation for the equilibrium between the precipitate and the dissolved ions is this.

$$CaCO_3(s) \rightleftharpoons Ca^{2+}(aq) + CO_3^{2-}(aq)$$

Suppose you add enough sodium carbonate to a sample of hard water (containing Ca^{2+} ions) that the equilibrium concentration of the carbonate ion is $0.010M$. What is the resulting concentration of the calcium ion in solution? The value of the equilibrium constant for this reaction is 3.9×10^{-9}.

■ **Analyze the Problem** Since this problem describes an equilibrium, you will need to apply an equilibrium constant expression to solve it.

■ **Apply a Strategy** Begin by compiling what you already know about this reaction.

$$K_{eq} = 3.9 \times 10^{-9}$$
$$[CO_3^{2-}]_{eq} = 0.010M$$
$$[Ca^{2+}]_{eq} = ?$$

The variables listed are related by the equilibrium constant expression. Use it to obtain the unknown concentration.

■ **Work a Solution** Write the equilibrium constant expression.

$$K_{eq} = [Ca^{2+}][CO_3^{2-}]$$

Note that $[CaCO_3]$ is not included. Why not? Now substitute what you know, rearrange, and solve for $[Ca^{2+}]$.

PART 2
Section 18.7

Practice Problem

Assign the Practice Problem.

Teaching Strategy

To give students some basic practice with solubility product constants, the illustrations in this section and the problems assigned to students involve only salts that break up into a one-to-one cation to anion ratio. This eliminates difficult expressions such as $(2x)^2$ from the problem solutions. If you wish to extend what is done in this section, you might want to have students work a few problems involving other insoluble salts, such as lead chloride, $PbCl_2$, or calcium hydroxide, $Ca(OH)_2$.

PROBLEM·SOLVING
STRATEGY

*You can **use what you know** to evaluate if your answer is correct. (See Strategy, page 58.)*

$$3.9 \times 10^{-9} = [Ca^{2+}](0.010)$$

$$[Ca^{2+}] = \frac{3.9 \times 10^{-9}}{0.010} = 3.9 \times 10^{-7}M$$

■ **Verify Your Answer** Note that the final answer is a small number. This is just what you would expect from the fact that the carbonate ion is used as a water softener to reduce the high level of calcium ions in hard water.

Practice Problem

7. Suppose you add carbonate ions to a solution containing Ca^{2+} ions so that a precipitate forms. The concentration of the carbonate ion is $0.50M$. What is the concentration of the calcium ion? (Hint: The product of $[Ca^{2+}]$ and $[CO_3^{2-}]$ cannot exceed the K_{eq}. Precipitation begins if $[Ca^{2+}][CO_3^{2-}] > K_{eq}$, and continues until $[Ca^{2+}][CO_3^{2-}] = K_{eq}$.)

Ans. 7.8×10^{-9} mol/L

Figure 18-7 *The formation of stalactites and stalagmites is an example of equilibrium in natural processes.*

18.7 Solubility Equilibrium

The reaction in Example 18-2 is representative of a type of equilibrium called **solubility equilibrium**. This is an equilibrium that exists between an ionic solid and its ions in solution. There can be equilibrium in such a system only if the solution is saturated. Solid reactant must be present if the forward reaction (dissolving) and the reverse reaction (precipitating) are occurring at the same rate. Some reactions and their equilibrium constant expression are shown below.

$$AgCl(s) \rightleftharpoons Ag^+(aq) + Cl^-(aq) \qquad K = [Ag^+][Cl^-]$$
$$PbCl_2(s) \rightleftharpoons Pb^{2+}(aq) + 2Cl^-(aq) \qquad K = [Pb^{2+}][Cl^-]^2$$
$$CaSO_4(s) \rightleftharpoons Ca^{2+}(aq) + SO_4^{2+}(aq) \qquad K = [Ca^{2+}][SO_4^{2-}]$$

The solubility product constant As you might guess from these examples, whenever you write a chemical equation for the dissolving of an ionic substance, you always obtain an equilibrium expression in which there is no denominator. The reason is simple: The solid (the only reactant) is omitted from the expression. Thus the expression is always the product of the anions and cations raised to powers equal to their coefficients. Since these reactions involve solubilities, the equilibrium constant for these reactions is called a **solubility product constant.** You may show that you are working with a solubility process by writing K_{sp} for the equilibrium constant rather than K. However, there is no difference between a K_{sp} and any other equilibrium constant. Some K_{sp} values are shown in Table 18-5. Practice writing the equations for these K_{sp} values. The next example illustrates how K_{sp}'s can be calculated and used.

Concept ✔ Check

Write the equation for the dissolving of AgBr(s) in water and the equilibrium constant expression for the reaction.

Equilibrium constant expressions are really mathematical equations with unknowns (the concentrations of the products and reactants) and a constant (K_{eq}). You can use these equations to solve problems—for example, if you know that the concentration of a saturated solution of silver bromide is $7.1 \times 10^{-7}M$, you can calculate the value of K_{sp}. To do so you must recognize that the equilibrium equation and expression are these.

$$AgBr(s) \rightleftharpoons Ag^+(aq) + Br^-(aq)$$
$$K_{sp} = [Ag^+][Br^-]$$

Since there is one bromide ion for each silver ion, the concentration of both ions is 7.1×10^{-7} mol/L. When this value is substituted into the K_{sp} expression for each of the unknowns, you find that K_{sp} is 5.0×10^{-13}. Example 18-3 shows you how to do another problem using the solubility product expression.

EXAMPLE 18-3

Determine the equilibrium concentration of Ca^{2+} formed by dissolving calcium carbonate, $CaCO_3$, in water. The value of K_{sp} for calcium carbonate is 3.9×10^{-9}.

■ **Analyze the Problem** This problem involves a dissolution reaction, so you need to use the solubility product constant and the equation for dissolving calcium carbonate.

■ **Apply a Strategy** The equation for the reaction and the K_{sp} expression are the following.

$$CaCO_3(s) \rightleftharpoons Ca^{2+}(aq) + CO_3{}^{2-}(aq)$$
$$K_{sp} = [Ca^{2+}][CO_3{}^{2-}]$$

The problem states the value of K_{sp}. There are still two unknowns in the last expression. How can you proceed? You learned that the relationship between the two ions can be found from the balanced chemical equation. In this problem, the one-to-one mole ratio tells you that at equilibrium $[Ca^{2+}] = [CO_3{}^{2-}]$. This relationship tells you that there is only one unknown and makes it possible to solve the problem with the information given.

■ **Work a Solution** Since you do not know the concentration of either Ca^{2+} or $CO_3{}^{2-}$, use the letter x to represent their equilibrium concentrations.

$$x = [Ca^{2+}] = [CO_3{}^{2+}]$$

TABLE 18-5

Some Solubility Product Constants at 25°C	
Compound	K_{sp}
AgCl	1.7×10^{-10}
AgBr	5.0×10^{-13}
AgI	8.5×10^{-17}
BaCO₃	5.1×10^{-9}
CaCO₃	3.9×10^{-9}
MgCO₃	3.5×10^{-8}
SrCrO₄	3.6×10^{-5}
BaCrO₄	8.5×10^{-11}
PbCrO₄	2.8×10^{-13}
CaSO₄	2.4×10^{-5}
SrSO₄	7.6×10^{-7}
PbSO₄	1.3×10^{-8}
BaSO₄	1.6×10^{-9}

◀ **PROBLEM-SOLVING STRATEGY**

Use what you know about the coefficients in a balanced equation to determine equilibrium concentrations. (See Strategy, page 58.)

PART 2

Section 18.7 *continued*

Guided Practice

Have students answer the Concept Check questions on pages 614 and 617. Answers can be found in Appendix E on page 808.

Reteaching Idea

If your students need practice writing equilibrium constant expressions and using them to solve problems, have them work in pairs writing expressions for each of the following equations. Have a member of each pair put one expression on the chalkboard so that the class can decide whether each one is correct.

1. $Cu(s) + 2Ag^+(aq) \rightleftharpoons Cu^{2+}(aq) + 2Ag(s)$
2. $PbI_2(s) \rightleftharpoons Pb^{2+}(aq) + 2I^-(aq)$
3. $4Fe(s) + 3O_2(g) \rightleftharpoons 2Fe_2O_3(s)$
4. $CN^-(aq) + H_2O(l) \rightleftharpoons HCN(aq) + OH^-(aq)$
5. $CoS(s) \rightleftharpoons Co^{2+}(aq) + S^{2-}(aq)$
6. $2CO(g) + O_2(g) \rightleftharpoons 2CO_2(g)$
7. $2HI(g) \rightleftharpoons H_2(g) + I_2(g)$
8. $H_2O(l) \rightleftharpoons H_2O(g)$
9. $Ag^+(aq) + 2NH_3(aq) \rightleftharpoons Ag(NH_3)_2{}^+(aq)$
10. $4HCl(g) + O_2(g) \rightleftharpoons 2H_2O(g) + 2Cl_2(g)$

The equilibrium constant for equation 1 is 2×10^{15} at 25°C and the equilibrium constant for equation 5 is 3.0×10^{-26} at 25°C. Ask students which reaction will have more product when equilibrium is established. (Reaction 1)

Ask students to determine the solubility of CoS at 25°C. (1.7×10^{-13} mol/L).

If the reaction described by equation 5 is at equilibrium and H_2S gas is bubbled through the solution until the concentration of S^{2-} is 0.0010 mol/L, what will be the concentration of Co^{2+}? (3.0×10^{-23} mol/L)

PART 2
Section 18.7 continued

Practice Problems

Assign the Practice Problems.

≡CLOSE

Summing Up Main Ideas

For the theoretical reaction
$$A_2 + B_2 \rightleftharpoons 2AB,$$
write the equilibrium constant expression.

$$K = \frac{[AB]^2}{[A_2][B_2]}$$

Calculate K at 25°C if A_2 and B_2, initially present in concentrations of 3.00 mol/L each, yield 4.64 mol/L of AB.

$$[A_2] = [B_2] = 3 - \left(\frac{1}{2}\right)(4.64)$$
$$= 0.68 \text{ mol/L}$$

$$K = \frac{[AB]^2}{[A_2][B_2]} = 46.6$$

PART 2 REVIEW

Assign the Part Review questions.

Evaluating Skills

These skills are evaluated in the Part Review questions indicated. **Determining main ideas: 10; Analyzing data: 11; Applying a strategy: 12; Calculating: 12; Verifying results: 12**

Boxed numbers indicate questions that involve skills in interpretation, application, and analysis.

Replace the ion concentrations with x in the K_{sp} expression.

$$K_{sp} = [Ca^{2+}][CO_3{}^{2-}]$$
$$3.9 \times 10^{-9} = (x)(x) = x^2$$

Solve for x.

$$x = \sqrt{3.9 \times 10^{-9}} = 6.2 \times 10^{-5}M$$
$$x = [Ca^{2+}] = 6.2 \times 10^{-5}M$$

Since the calcium ion comes from calcium carbonate, this answer also represents the amount of $CaCO_3$ that dissolves in water. You have determined that the solubility of $CaCO_3$ is $6.2 \times 10^{-5}M$.

■ **Verify Your Answer** Qualitatively, the solubility of $CaCO_3$ has been shown to be a small number, which you would expect for an insoluble compound. Quantitatively, you may verify your answer by substituting it into the K_{sp} expression to see if you obtain the original value.

$$[Ca^{2+}][CO_3{}^{2-}] = (6.2 \times 10^{-5})(6.2 \times 10^{-5}) = 3.8 \times 10^{-9}$$

Practice Problems

8. Calculate the solubility of AgBr in water.
   Ans. 7.1×10^{-7} mol/L

9. Determine how many moles of $PbSO_4$ dissolve in 1 liter of water.
   Ans. 1.1×10^{-4}

PART 2 REVIEW

10. At 25°C, the concentration of 0.500 L of pure water is 55.4 mol/L. Without doing any calculations, give the concentration of 1.75 L of pure water at 25°C. Explain why no calculation is necessary.

11. Write the equilibrium constant expression for these equations.
   a. $2NO_2(g) \rightleftharpoons N_2O_4(g)$
   b. $Sn^{2+}(aq) + Pb(s) \rightleftharpoons Sn(s) + Pb^{2+}(aq)$
   c. $2CO(g) + O_2(g) \rightleftharpoons 2CO_2(g)$
   d. $2Fe_2O_3(s) + 3C(s) \rightleftharpoons 3CO_2(g) + 4Fe(s)$

12. Magnesium carbonate can be precipitated from a solution containing the magnesium ion by adding a solution of sodium carbonate.

$$Mg^{2+}(aq) + CO_3{}^{2-}(aq) \rightleftharpoons MgCO_3(s)$$

What is the equilibrium concentration of Mg^{2+} if enough carbonate is added to 0.20M Mg^{2+} solution so that the equilibrium concentration of $CO_3{}^{2-}$ is 0.175M? K_{sp} is 3.5×10^{-8}.

PART 2 REVIEW

ANSWERS

■ **Keyed to Objectives**

E **10.** The concentration is 55.4 mol/L because the concentration of a pure liquid does not depend on its sample size. The concentration remains the same as long as the temperature does not change.

C **11. a.** $K = \dfrac{[N_2O_4]}{[NO_2]^2}$

   b. $K = \dfrac{[Pb^{2+}]}{[Sn^{2+}]}$

   c. $K = \dfrac{[CO_2]^2}{[CO]^2[O_2]}$

   d. $K = [CO_2]^3$

E **12.** K_{sp} always refers to the dissolution of a solid, not its formation, so the chemical equation must be rewritten this way:
$$MgCO_3 \rightleftharpoons Mg^{2+} + CO_3{}^{2-}$$
$$K = [Mg^{2+}][CO_3{}^{2-}]$$

PART 3 Predicting Changes in Equilibrium

So far you have seen that equilibrium is a dynamic situation in which the rate of the forward reaction is equal to the rate of the reverse reaction. You learned how to combine the concentrations of reactants and products to get a constant value, the equilibrium constant. Now you will examine how an equilibrium can be shifted when changes are made that disturb it in some way.

18.8 Changes in Concentration

To study the effects of a change in concentration on equilibrium, the easiest kind of reaction to use is one that takes place in solution. The reaction you will use is the equilibrium that is established between two simple ions, Fe^{3+} and SCN^- (the thiocyanate ion), and the complex ion $FeSCN^{2+}$.

$$Fe^{3+}(aq) + SCN^-(aq) \rightleftharpoons FeSCN^{2+}(aq)$$

The photograph in Figure 18-8 illustrates this reaction. The test tube on the left, *A*, contains a solution of the Fe^{3+} ion. Test tube *B* contains the thiocyanate ion. When the contents of these two test tubes are mixed, the resulting solution is shown in test tube *C*. The color you see in test tube *C* can be explained by the fact that $FeSCN^{2+}$ is dark red in color. The new red color in the third tube provides visual evidence for the formation of the product. If you add water to test tube *C*, you obtain the solution shown in test tube *D*. The additional water reduces the intensity of the color, making it easier to note color changes. This solution, which is at equilibrium, will be used to see what happens when the concentrations of the individual ions are changed.

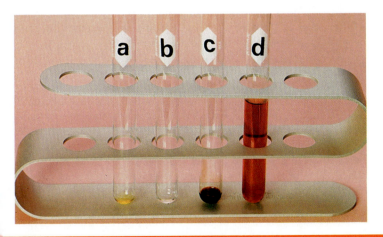

Objectives

Part 3

G. *Explain* Le Châtelier's principle.

H. *Predict* changes in equilibrium, using Le Châtelier's principle.

Figure 18-8 *Test tube A contains 0.20 M Fe(NO₃)₃, and test tube B contains 0.20 M KSCN. When the contents of A and B are mixed, the solution in test tube C results. Dilution of C produces the solution in D.*

When sodium carbonate is added to a solution containing magnesium ion, magnesium will precipitate until its equilibrium concentration is reached.

$$[Mg^{2+}] = \frac{K_{sp}}{[CO_3^{2-}]}$$

$$= \frac{3.5 \times 10^{-8}}{0.175} = 2.0 \times 10^{-7}\ M$$

Developing Skills

Students may apply this skill in their study of Part 3.
Analyzing data: Ask students to interpret their observations from Figures 18–9 and 18–10 using LeChâtelier's principle.

FOCUS

Activate Prior Knowledge

This activity will use students' knowledge of solutions to demonstrate how equilibrium can shift. Wearing safety goggles and a lab apron, set up three 100-mL beakers. To each add 25 grams of KCl. Add 50 ml of ice-cold water to the first, 50 ml of 40°C water to the second, and 50 ml of a room temperature solution of 2M NaCl to the third.

Stir each solution for two minutes with a stirring rod. Let stand for 5 minutes to allow undissolved KCl to settle; keep the ice-cold solution on ice. Carefully remove as much liquid as possible. Dry and weigh the remaining salt. Compare the results. For disposal, pour the liquid down the drain. Wrap the solid in newspaper and put in the wastebasket.

TEACH

Teaching Strategy

Changes in Concentration

Illustrate the reactions described in Section 18.8 for students as you talk about the effect of changing concentrations. Wearing safety goggles and a lab apron prepare solutions of iron(III) nitrate and potassium thiocyanate. Dilute the mixture as suggested in the text if the color is too intense. Add solid potassium thiocyanate to the mixture to shift the equilibrium in favor of the
(continued on page T620)

PART 3

Section 18.8 *continued*

(continued from page T619)

complex ion, and add silver nitrate to shift the equilibrium in favor of the simple ions, Fe^{3+} and SCN^-. For disposal, evaporate to dryness. Put the residue in a labeled, sealed container for an EPA-approved waste disposal contractor.

Figure 18-9 *The test tube on the left shows the original solution from test tube D in Figure 18-8. The test tube on the right shows the darker color of the solution when solid KSCN is added.*

DO YOU KNOW?

Physicians determine the effects of some drugs by monitoring the concentrations of various chemicals in the blood. These concentrations depend on equilibrium reactions that shift with varying conditions. For instance, in the treatment of sickle-cell anemia, physicians observe the effects of drugs on the concentration of bound oxygen in the blood.

Shifting equilibrium What happens if you add some solid potassium thiocyanate (KSCN) to a sample of the solution from test tube *D*? The KSCN provides more of the reactant ion SCN^-. You can see the result in Figure 18-9. The solution becomes even darker. More of the product, the complex ion $FeSCN^{2+}$, must have formed. This conclusion seems reasonable, since you expect to see more product as more reactant is added.

Concept ✓ Check

Describe in your own words how the concentrations of Fe^{3+}, SCN^- and $FeSCN^{2+}$ change if a crystal of KSCN is added to the test tube on the left in Figure 18-9. What stays constant?

This increase in the concentration of the complex ion is also consistent with the equilibrium constant expression for the reaction.

$$K_{eq} = \frac{[FeSCN^{2+}]}{[Fe^{3+}][SCN^-]}$$

When SCN^- is added to the solution, the concentration of this ion increases. However, at equilibrium, the ratio of products to reactants in the equilibrium constant expression always has the same value at a given temperature. The larger value of $[SCN^-]$ must be counterbalanced by a *decrease* in the value of $[Fe^{3+}]$ and an *increase* in the value of $[FeSCN^{2+}]$. These changes in concentration must occur because the following reaction takes place.

$$Fe^{3+}(aq) + SCN^-(aq) \rightarrow FeSCN^{2+}(aq)$$

Notice that the process that restores equilibrium is represented by the equation in which the arrow points to the right. This is referred to as a shift to the right. After this takes place, the concentration of Fe^{3+} is decreased, and the concentration of $FeSCN^{2+}$ is increased. The shift uses up some of the added SCN^-, but not all. The new concentration of SCN^- is greater than before the solid KSCN was added. Equilibrium is reestablished, with new equilibrium concentrations of all reactants and products.

Now try another change that shifts the equilibrium in test tube *D*. By adding some drops of silver nitrate, $AgNO_3$, a precipitate of

---

DEMONSTRATION

Changes in Concentration

A simple way to illustrate the effects of changing concentration is to add a few drops of concentrated hydrochloric acid to a saturated solution of sodium chloride. This equilibrium is shifted to the left:
$NaCl(s) \leftarrow Na^+(aq) + Cl^-(aq)$
Students will notice the formation of more white solid.

CAUTION: Wear safety goggles, face shield, lab apron, and rubber gloves. Do the addition behind a shield to protect students. For disposal, neutralize the solutions and pour down the drain.

silver thiocyanate, AgSCN, immediately forms. To produce this precipitate, some SCN^- is removed from the system at equilibrium. In Figure 18-10, you can see that the color of the solution lightens when the silver thiocyanate precipitate forms. You may interpret this as evidence for a decrease in the concentration of the $FeSCN^{2+}$ ion. This decrease takes place because the equilibrium shifts to the left.

$$Fe^{3+}(aq) + SCN^-(aq) \leftarrow FeSCN^{2+}(aq)$$

After this shift has occurred and equilibrium has been restored, the concentration of Fe^{3+} is found to have increased and the concentration of $FeSCN^{2+}$ to have decreased. The shift has added to the concentration of SCN^-, but has not brought it back to the concentration it had before SCN^- was precipitated as AgSCN(s). The shift to the left resulted in new equilibrium concentrations, but they combine to give the same equilibrium constant.

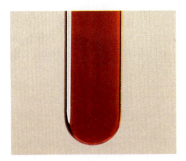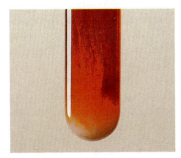

Figure 18-10 *The test tube on the left shows the solution from test tube D of Figure 18-8. The test tube on the right shows that when a solution of silver nitrate is added, a solid forms and the solution becomes lighter in color.*

18.9 Le Châtelier's Principle

Toward the end of the nineteenth century, Henri Louis Le Châtelier stated this principle regarding changes in equilibrium.

> *If you do something to disturb a system at equilibrium, the system responds in a way that undoes partially what you have just done.*

What can you do to a system to disturb its equilibrium? You have already studied changes in concentration. There are also changes in temperature, changes in system volume, and changes in pressure. When changes in any of these factors occur, the equilibrium can be disturbed. The system partially counteracts the disturbance by reacting in one of two ways. The equilibrium may shift to the right, favoring the formation of more products at the expense of some reactants, or the equilibrium may shift to the left, favoring the formation of more reactants at the expense of the products.

Changes in temperature Consider this equation for a gas equilibrium as you study the effect of increasing or decreasing the temperature of a reaction at equilibrium.

$$2NO_2(g) \rightleftharpoons N_2O_4(g) + 57.2 \text{ kJ}$$

brown   colorless

This is the reaction you studied earlier in this chapter. Remember that NO_2 is a brown gas, while N_2O_4 is a colorless gas. This color difference makes it possible to observe a shifting equilibrium. Notice that the equation for this reaction is written to show that this is an exothermic reaction. Heat is given off when the reaction proceeds to the right. What happens if you change the temperature? If you submerge the flask in boiling water, the temperature increases. Heat energy is added to the system. How can the system react to undo this change? If the reaction moves to the left, some of the added energy will be consumed. Notice that the reverse reaction is endothermic. More NO_2 will form, and less N_2O_4 will be left. When equilibrium is established again, you can expect to see a darker color in the flask, as shown in Figures 18-11 and 18-12.

If an increase in temperature favors the formation of more NO_2, what would happen if the temperature went down from room temperature? If you said that you expected to see less NO_2 and more N_2O_4, then you are starting to understand Le Châtelier's principle. Lowering the temperature removes energy from the system, so you expect a response that will partially restore some of that energy. The system must shift to the right, the direction in which energy is released. The light color of the flask in the middle photograph clearly shows a new position of equilibrium in which less nitrogen dioxide is present.

Figure 18-11 *The same sample of nitrogen dioxide gas is shown at three different temperatures—0°C, 25°C, and 100°C. What accounts for the color differences?*

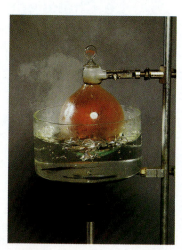

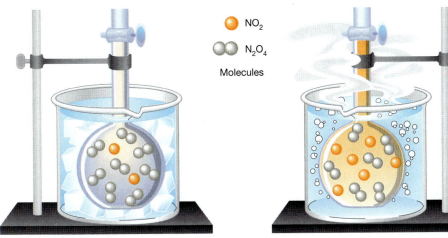

Flask A at 0°C

Flask B at 100°C

PART **3**
Section 18.9 *continued*

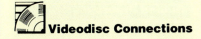

Videodisc Connections

35230 to 36036, side 4
Industrial diamonds (movie)

Changes in pressure and volume You learned in Chapter 6 how gases are affected by changes in pressure and volume. Can you predict that equilibria involving gases will also be affected? The equilibrium between NO_2 and N_2O_4 is useful again in studying how a system will respond to changes in volume and pressure.

$$2NO_2(g) \rightleftharpoons N_2O_4(g)$$

Suppose you increase the overall pressure on this system. According to Le Châtelier's principle, the system will shift in a direction that tends to *reduce* the pressure. How can the system do this? Notice that the chemical equation shows two gas molecules on the left and only one on the right. The pressure of the system decreases when it moves in the direction of *fewer* gas molecules. This system responds to the increased pressure by moving to the right, forming more N_2O_4. Figure 18-13 on the next page provides a model to help you visualize the change.

How does a change in volume affect the equilibrium of a system? Think about what happens to the pressure when changes in volume occur. For instance, in the last example, you could have asked what happens to the equilibrium when you decrease the volume. Decreasing the volume increases the overall pressure. The system adjusts to this change by moving to the right, as described before.

Predicting the results of pressure and volume changes What would happen if the pressure on the following reactions was reduced by increasing their overall volume?

$$NH_3(g) + HCl(g) \rightleftharpoons NH_4Cl(s)$$
$$H_2(g) + I_2(g) \rightleftharpoons 2HI(g)$$

For the first reaction, the system can partially undo the pressure change by producing more gas molecules. On the reactant side, there are two molecules in the gas phase. On the product side, there

Figure 18-12 Left: *When NO_2 gas is cooled, the molecules react to form molecules of the colorless gas, N_2O_4. Right: Heating the gas results in decomposition of N_2O_4 to produce more molecules of the brown gas, NO_2.*

DO YOU KNOW?

In 1955, the process to convert graphite to industrial diamonds was developed. High pressure favors the formation of diamond, since its density is greater than that of graphite.

C(graphite) + 18 kJ $\rightleftharpoons$

                C(diamond)

The conversion is carried out at temperatures near 2000°C and pressures between 50 000 and 100 000 atmospheres. Catalysts are used to obtain a suitable rate of reaction.

Guided Practice

Review the Concept Check question on page 620 with students. Answers can be found in Appendix E on page 808.

Reteaching Idea

If your students need more practice in applying Le Châtelier's principle, divide them into an even number of teams of three or four. Challenge pairs of teams to find ways to apply stresses to a reaction at equilibrium. One team in each pair should be the supporter of the reactants and find ways to apply stresses that will increase the amount of reactants present at equilibrium. The other team should support the products and find ways to increase the amount of products at equilibrium. You might have them work with this reaction.

$$4HCl(g) + O_2(g) \rightleftharpoons 2H_2O(g) + 2Cl_2(g) + 113 \text{ kJ}$$

Some stresses might be: increasing or decreasing the temperature, removing or adding moles of any of the reactants or products, increasing or decreasing the partial pressure of any reactant or product, increasing or decreasing the total pressure on the system, increasing or decreasing the volume of the system.

When the teams have exhausted the possibilities, review their responses so that there are no misconceptions. Ask what they think would happen if the temperature of the reaction were lowered to the point where the gaseous water froze to ice. (The reaction would continue in the forward direction until almost all reactants were used up.)

Figure 18-13 *The pressure is increased on the gas inside the sealed syringe by depressing the plunger. Note how the system responds to this change. On the right, there are more molecules of N_2O_4 but fewer gas molecules in all.*

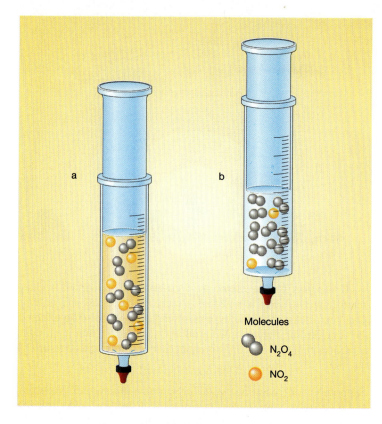

Molecules

N_2O_4

NO_2

are no molecules in the gas phase. Since NH_4Cl is a solid, not a gas, you ignore it when you predict a response to a pressure change. This is because the volume of a solid does not change significantly as pressure changes. The system can increase its pressure by shifting to the left, producing more NH_3 and HCl. For the second reaction, there are two molecules of gas on each side of the equation. There is no direction for a shift to counteract a change in the overall pressure. As a result, the equilibrium amounts of H_2, I_2, and HI do not change when the volume of the system is increased.

Another way to change the pressure of a system is to introduce more gas—either a reactant or product. For example, suppose you add more $I_2(g)$ to the reaction involving H_2, I_2, and HI, which has already come to equilibrium. This increases the partial pressure of I_2 in the system. The partial pressure of a gas in a mixture can be taken as a measure of its concentration. Therefore, with an increase in the concentration of I_2, the system shifts to the right, reducing the partial pressure of the added I_2 as it reacts with H_2 to form more HI. When equilibrium is established again, the partial pressure of HI has increased. The partial pressure of H_2 has decreased. By shifting to the right, some of the added I_2 has been used up, but the new partial pressure of I_2 is greater than it was before the addition was made.

PART 3 REVIEW

ANSWERS

■ Keyed to Objectives

H **13.** Iron(III) ions and nitrate ions are introduced. Since nitrate does not appear in the equilibrium reaction, only iron ions affect the equilibrium. The position of equilibrium is shifted to the right, in order to reduce the effect of the additional iron(III) ions. Since this produces more $FeSCN^{2+}$ ion, the color of the final solution becomes darker.

H **14.** Since an exothermic reaction results in energy being given off, the word "energy" should be written on the right side of this equation. If you raise the temperature, this system will respond by moving in the endothermic direction; that is, the system will shift to the left.

PART 3 REVIEW

13. You have a test tube in which the following equilibrium is established.

$$Fe^{3+}(aq) + SCN^-(aq) \rightleftharpoons FeSCN^{2+}(aq)$$

What two ions would you introduce to this test tube if you put in some solid iron(III) nitrate, $Fe(NO_3)_3$? Which ion affects this reaction? What happens to the position of equilibrium when this ion is added? What would you see happening in the test tube as you added the $Fe(NO_3)_3$?

14. The reaction between molecular hydrogen and molecular iodine to form hydrogen iodide is an exothermic reaction that comes to equilibrium.

$$H_2(g) + I_2(g) \rightleftharpoons 2HI(g)$$

If you include the word *energy* in this equation, should it be on the left side or the right side? Why? If you add energy to this system by raising its temperature, would there be more HI, less HI, or the same amount of HI when the new equilibrium is attained? Why?

15. The following equation represents a chemical reaction that is allowed to come to equilibrium.

$$4NH_3(g) + 5O_2(g) \rightleftharpoons 4NO(g) + 6H_2O(g)$$

How will this system respond if the overall pressure is increased by reducing the volume of the reacting system? How will the system respond if the partial pressure of NH_3 is increased by adding more ammonia? How will the system respond if the partial pressure of H_2O is increased by adding more water vapor?

16. The following reaction is at equilibrium.

$$Ba(ClO_3)_2(s) \rightleftharpoons Ba^{2+}(aq) + 2ClO_3^-(aq)$$

$$\Delta H = +28.0 \text{ kJ}$$

Use Le Châtelier's principle to determine whether the following changes shift the equilibrium to the left or the right.
  a. The temperature is increased.
  b. Barium nitrate is added.
  c. More $Ba(ClO_3)_2(s)$ is added.

PROBLEM-SOLVING

S T R A T E G Y

Look for regularities in chemical reactions to help you answer this question. (See Strategy, page 100.)

Boxed numbers indicate questions that involve skills in interpretation, application, and analysis.

≡CLOSE

Summing Up Main Ideas

Going in the forward direction, the reaction
$$2CO(g) + O_2(g) \rightleftharpoons 2CO_2(g)$$
is exothermic.
Describe the effect that the following changes will have on the equilibrium state, and why.
  a. an increase in temperature (The reaction will shift to the left. By increasing the rate of the endothermic reaction, the extra heat will be partially absorbed.)
  b. an increase in pressure (Shifts the reaction to the right. The increase in pressure favors the reaction where 3 moles of gas molecules are converted to 2 moles.)
  c. removal of CO_2 from the reaction vessel (The equilibrium will shift to the right in order to partially replace the CO_2 that has been removed.)

PART 3 REVIEW

Assign the Part Review questions.

Evaluating Skills

These skills are evaluated in the Part Review questions indicated.
Predicting: 13, 14, 15, 16;
Determining cause and effect: 13, 14, 15, 16; **Analyzing data:** 13, 14, 15, 16

When the new position of equilibrium is attained, there will be less HI than before.

H 15. There are 9 moles of gas on the left side but only 10 moles on the right side. When the overall pressure is increased by reducing the volume, the system will respond by shifting to the left (the side with fewer moles of gas). If more ammonia is added, the system responds by shift-

ing to the right. If more water vapor is added, the system responds by shifting to the left.

H 16. a. The equilibrium shifts to the right, the direction in which energy is absorbed.

  b. The equilibrium shifts to the left to partially relieve the "stress" of additional barium ion.

  c. The equilibrium does not shift, because the concentration of barium chlorate does not change.

Qualitative Observations of an Equilibrium System

Estimated Time: (45 minutes)

Measuring
Predicting
Verifying results
Interpreting data
Analyzing data
Forming hypotheses
Stating a conclusion

Preparation

■ **Materials**

(for a class of 24, working in pairs)

Apparatus
(12 of each unless noted)
13 × 100-mm test tubes (60), 150-or 250-mL beakers (24), heat sources (12 unless shared), Beral pipettes (36), well plates, graduated cylinders (10-mL preferred), balances (12 unless shared), test-tube racks, test-tube holders, marking pencils, ice

Reagents

■ 100 mL of 1.5M CuCl$_2$ (aq) solution (25.6 g CuCl$_2$·2H$_2$O per 100 mL)

■ 50 mL of 0.050M AgNO$_3$(aq) solution (0.425 g AgNO$_3$ per 50 mL)

■ 60 mL of 4M NaCl solution (14 g NaCl per 60 mL solution)

■ distilled water

Safety

⚠ See student text for safety precautions for skin contact with silver nitrate. Gloves should be used. Wash hands after the experiment is concluded; students should wash their hands before leaving the lab.

L a b o r a t o r y
Investigation

Qualitative Observations of an Equilibrium System

Le Châtelier's Principle states that when a system equilibrium is disturbed by a change in an external factor, the net reaction occurs in such a way as to offset the changes, and a new equilibrium is reached. Examples of external changes include changes in temperature, pressure, or concentration. The equilibrium system that you will be using in this investigation is the following:

$$CuCl_4^{2-}(aq) \leftrightharpoons Cu^{2+}(aq) + 4\ Cl^-(aq) + heat$$

The net reaction shift to the left or right can be monitored by observing a color change. The tetrachlorocuprate(II) ion, $CuCl_4^{2-}$(aq), is green; the copper(II) ion, Cu^{2+}(aq), is blue; and the chloride ion, Cl^-, is colorless. Therefore, the production of a *green* color is *net reaction to the left,* and the formation of a *blue* color is *net reaction to the right.*

O b j e c t i v e s

Predict and subsequently **confirm** the effect that a change in temperature would have on an equilibrium system.

Predict and then **confirm** the effect that a change in concentration would have on a system at equilibrium.

Determine what effect a temperature and a concentration change would have on this system.

■ Materials

Apparatus
□ 6 13 × 100 mm test tubes
□ test tube rack
□ hot-water bath
□ 3 Beral pipettes

□ well plates
□ 10-mL graduated cylinder
□ ice-water bath
□ balance
□ test tube holder
□ marking pencil

Reagents
□ 6.0 mL of 1.5M CuCl$_2$(aq) solution
□ 3.0 mL of 0.050M AgNO$_3$(aq) solution

□ distilled water
□ 4M NaCl

■ Procedure

Part 1

1. Put on a lab apron and safety goggles.

2. Prepare a boiling-water bath on a hot plate. Also prepare an ice-water bath.

3. Label two 13 × 100 mm test tubes A-1 and A-2. Into each tube, place 3.0 mL of 1.5M copper(II) chloride, CuCl$_2$(aq), solution. The tube labeled A-1 will be used as a reference for equilibrium comparisons.

4. Place the tube labeled A-2 in a boiling water bath. In the space provided on the

data table predict one of the following: a. Net shift left, b. Net shift right, c. No net change.

5. After several minutes, remove test tube A-2 from the boiling water. Record your results in the data table. Compare the results to your predictions.

6. Predict what will happen when you cool the solution and enter your prediction on the data table. Put the test tube labeled A-2 into an ice-water bath. After one minute, examine the color. Record your results.

Part 2

7. Place 3.0 mL of 0.05M silver nitrate solution, $AgNO_3$(aq), into a clean test tube labeled B-1.

   ☠ ✋ 🧤 **CAUTION: Silver nitrate is poisonous and corrosive to skin and eyes. Wear gloves. Wash off spills and splashes. If any gets in your eyes, use the eyewash fountain immediately. Do not get it in your mouth; do not swallow any.**

8. Obtain a well plate. Into each of two wells, place 3.0 drops of copper(II) chloride, $CuCl_2$(aq), solution. Label one well B-2 and the other well B-3. The well labeled B-3 will be used as a reference.

9. Predict what will happen if you increase the chloride concentration in solution. Write your predictions on the table.

10 Add two drops of the 4.0M sodium chloride, NaCl(aq), solution to well B-3. This will increase the concentration of the chloride ions in the solution. Observe the color of the solution in well B-3 and compare it to the color of well B-2. Compare the result to your prediction.

11. Predict what will happen if you decrease the chloride concentration in your solution. Record your prediction.

12. Add 1 drop of silver nitrate, $AgNO_3$(aq), solution to well B-3. This decreases the concentration of chloride ions, Cl^-(aq), be-cause it produces the white solid silver chloride, AgCl(s). Compare the color of the solution in B-3 to the color in B-2. Compare your results to your prediction.

Part 3

13. Label two test tubes C-1 and C-2. In each, put 1.0 mL of 1.5M $CuCl_2$(aq) solution.

14. Design your own experiment in which you alter C-2 with respect to temperature and concentration. Get your teacher's permission before conducting your experiment. Make your prediction on the data table.

15. Perform your experiment and enter your results on the data table. Compare your results to your predictions.

■ **Data Analysis**   **Data Table**

Treatment	Prediction	Result
Part 1 Heat Solution Cool Solution		
Part 2 Increase Cl^- concentration Decrease Cl^- concentration		
Part 3		

■ **Conclusions**

1. Based on the color change, how does a decrease in temperature affect the concentrations of $CuCl_4^{2-}$(aq) and Cu^{2+}(aq)?

2. Based on the color change, how does an increase in temperature affect the concentrations of $CuCl_4^{2-}$(aq) and Cu^{2+}(aq)?

3. What effect does adding NaCl(aq) have on the color of the solution? Why?

Guiding the Investigation

■ **Procedural Hints**
Make all solutions ahead of time.
Disposal
Save for future use or pour the copper and sodium chloride solutions down the drain. Combine and reserve the silver-containing solutions in a labeled, sealed container for disposal by an EPA-approved waste disposal contractor.

Data Analysis

■ **Sample Data**
(See table below.)

Conclusions
1. decreases concentration of $[CuCl_4^{2-}]$ and increases both $[Cu^{2+}]$ and $[Cl^-]$
2. increases concentration of $[CuCl_4^{2-}]$ and decreases both $[Cu^{2+}]$ and $[Cl^-]$
3. Color becomes green. More complex formed, which is green in color.

Data Table

Treatment	Prediction	Result
Part 1		
Heat solution	green	green
Cool solution	blue	blue
Part 2		
Increase Cl^- concentration	green	green
Decrease Cl^- concentration	blue	blue
Part 3	varies with experiment	varies with experiment

Chapter 18
Review
ANSWERS
begin on page
T631a.

Summary

Reactions That Appear to Stop

- A reaction is said to reach equilibrium if it takes place in a closed system, if all reactant and product species are present, and if the observable properties of the system are not changing. Reactions that reach equilibrium take place in both the forward and backward directions.

- When equilibrium is reached, the forward and reverse reactions take place at equal rates.

- Examples of reactions that reach equilibrium are found in physical changes (e.g. vaporization) and chemical changes (e.g. gas-phase reactions and the reactions of acids and bases).

Quantitative Aspects of Equilibrium

- An equilibrium constant expression is the product of the equilibrium concentrations of the products divided by the product of the equilibrium concentrations of the reactants all raised to a power equal to their coefficients in the balanced chemical equation.

- The concentrations of pure solids and liquids remain constant and are omitted from the equilibrium constant expression.

- If an ionic solid XY does not completely dissolve when it is mixed with water, the equilibrium constant, called a solubility product constant (K_{sp}), can be written.

$$K_{sp} = [X^+][Y^-]$$

Predicting Changes in Equilibrium

- When a system at equilibrium undergoes a change, processes occur that tend to counteract the change and establish a new equilibrium. Le Châtelier's principle can be applied to predict how changes in the temperature, pressure, volume, or concentration of reactants and products affect a system at equilibrium.

Chemically Speaking

acid-base equilibrium
18.3
equilibrium 18.1
equilibrium
concentration 18.4
equilibrium constant
18.4
equilibrium constant
expression 18.4
gas-phase equilibrium
18.3

Le Châtelier's
principle 18.9
solubility equilibrium
18.7
solubility product
constant 18.7
vapor-liquid
equilibrium 18.3

Concept Mapping

Using the method of concept mapping described at the front of this book, make a concept map for the term *reaction equilibrium*.

Questions and Problems

REACTIONS THAT APPEAR TO STOP

A. Objective: **Explain** *and* **apply** *the macroscopic and submicroscopic definitions of equilibrium.*

1. Assume that this reaction takes place in an open container. The reaction will not reach equilibrium. Why not?

$$MgCO_3(s) + 2HCl(aq) \rightarrow$$
$$MgCl_2(aq) + H_2O(l) + CO_2(g)$$

2. State the macroscopic conditions necessary for equilibrium to be attained.

3. State the submicroscopic conditions necessary for equilibrium to be attained.

4. Using your answers to questions 2 and 3, explain why students may focus on the static aspect of equilibrium, forgetting the dynamic aspect.

PROBLEM-SOLVING
► **S T R A T E G I E S**
Students apply these strategies in the following questions.

- Factor-label method: 36, 37
- Using what you know: 31, 32, 33, 34
- Using similar problems: 17, 18,

19, 24, 25, 26, 27,
- Using patterns: 12, 13, 14, 15, 17, 18, 19, 22, 23, 24, 25, 26, 27
- Making an estimate: 16

T628

B. Objective: **Identify** *chemical reactions that come to equilibrium and* **describe** *the process of reaching equilibrium.*

5. Describe the submicroscopic events taking place at equilibrium for this reaction.

$$NH_3(aq) + H_2O(aq) \rightleftharpoons$$
$$NH_4^+(aq) + OH^-(aq)$$

6. Give an example of each equilibrium type.
   a. vapor-liquid equilibrium,
   b. solubility equilibrium,
   c. gas-phase equilibrium,
   d. acid-base equilibrium.
7. Suppose this reaction reaches equilibrium by adding solid lead chloride to water.

$$PbCl_2(s) \rightleftharpoons Pb^{2+}(aq) + 2Cl^-(aq)$$

Briefly describe how the lead ion concentration changes as equilibrium is reached.
8. When hydrochloric acid is poured into a solution of lead nitrate, a precipitate of lead chloride is formed, and this equilibrium is established.

$$Pb^{2+}(aq) + 2Cl^-(aq) \rightleftharpoons PbCl_2(s)$$

Briefly describe how the lead ion concentration changes as equilibrium is reached.

QUANTITATIVE ASPECTS OF EQUILIBRIUM

C. Objective: **Write** *the equilibrium constant expression for any reaction at equilibrium.*

9. What is an equilibrium constant expression? How is it related to the equation for the reaction that comes to equilibrium?
10. What is meant by the symbol $[CH_3COOH]$?
11. Why are the concentrations of solids and liquids omitted from the equilibrium constant expression?
12. Write the equilibrium constant expression for the following reactions.
    a. $A + B \rightleftharpoons C + D$
    b. $H_2(g) + Cl_2(g) \rightleftharpoons 2HCl(g)$
    c. $COCl_2(g) \rightleftharpoons CO(g) + Cl_2(g)$

Boxed numbers indicate questions that involve skills in interpretation, application, and analysis.

13. Write the equilibrium constant expression for each of these reactions:
    a. $CaCO_3(s) \rightleftharpoons CaO(s) + CO_2(g)$
    b. $AgCl(s) \rightleftharpoons Ag^+(aq) + Cl^-(aq)$
    c. $NH_3(aq) + H_2O(l) \rightleftharpoons$
       $NH_4^+(aq) + OH^-(aq)$

D. Objective: **Calculate** *the equilibrium constant for any reaction at equilibrium.*

14. In the following reaction at 448°C, the equilibrium concentrations are $[HI] = 0.0040M$, $[H_2] = 0.0075M$, and $[I_2] = 0.00043M$.

$$2HI(g) = H_2(g) + I_2(g)$$

Calculate the equilibrium constant at this temperature.
15. When acetic acid reacts with water, these equilibrium concentrations are found.

$$[CH_3COOH] = 0.20M, [CH_3COO^-] =$$
$$0.0019M, [H_3O^+] = 0.0019M.$$

The equation for the reaction is this.

$$CH_3COOH(aq) + H_2O(l) \rightleftharpoons$$
$$CH_3COO^-(aq) + H_3O^+(aq)$$

What is the equilibrium constant expression for this reaction, and what is the value of the equilibrium constant?

E. Objective: **Determine** *equilibrium concentrations, using the equilibrium constant expression.*

16. At room temperature, the value of the equilibrium constant for the following reaction is 2×10^{33}.

$$H_2(g) + Cl_2(g) \rightleftharpoons 2HCl(g)$$

When this reaction reaches equilibrium, do you expect more products or more reactants to be present? Explain.
17. Consider this equation for a reaction at equilibrium.

$$H_2(g) + Br_2(g) \rightleftharpoons 2HBr(g)$$

REACTION EQUILIBRIUM **629**

■ Using calculators: 14, 15, 17, 18, 19, 24, 25, 26, 27, 36, 37
■ Verifying your answer: 14, 15, 17, 18, 19, 24, 25, 26, 27, 36, 37
■ Making diagrams: 8, 35
■ Writing chemical equations: 21, 23, 24, 25, 26, 27, 35

The value of K at 25°C is 1.02. At equilibrium, the concentration of HBr is found to be 0.050M. Assuming that H_2 and Br_2 are present in equal amounts, calculate the concentration of H_2 at equilibrium.

18. When ammonia dissolves in water, it reaches the equilibrium described by this equation.

$$NH_3(aq) + H_2O(l) \rightleftharpoons$$
$$NH_4^+(aq) + OH^-(aq)$$

The value of the equilibrium constant is 1.8×10^{-5}. If $[NH_3] = 0.25M$ and $[NH_4^+] = 0.075M$, what is the equilibrium concentration of $[OH^-]$?

19. Water reacts with itself to set up the equilibrium represented by this equation.

$$2H_2O(l) \rightleftharpoons H_3O^+(aq) + OH^-(aq)$$

a. What is the equilibrium constant expression for the reaction $K_{eq} = 1.00 \times 10^{-14}$?
b. Using the value for $[OH^-]$ that you calculated in question 18, what is the equilibrium concentration of H_3O^+ in the solution described in that question?

F. Objective: **Apply** *the solubility product constant to saturated solutions of ionic solids.*

20. What is meant by the symbol K_{sp}?
21. Write a balanced chemical equation for the solubility equilibrium set up when these insoluble ionic solids are mixed with water.
   a. $CaCO_3(s)$ b. $AgBr(s)$ c. $PbSO_4(s)$
22. Write the solubility product constant (K_{sp}) expression for each of the solids listed in question 21.
23. Write the solubility product constant (K_{sp}) expression for each of the following solids as they mixed with water.
   a. $PbCl_2(s)$ b. $Mg(OH)_2(s)$ c. $Fe(OH)_3(s)$
24. When you prepare a saturated solution of calcium sulfate, $CaSO_4$, you find that the concentration of both the Ca^{2+} ions and SO_4^{2-} ions is 0.0049M. What is the value of K_{sp} for calcium sulfate?

25. Sea water is saturated with AgCl. The chloride ion concentration in sea water is 0.53M, and the solubility product constant for AgCl is 1.7×10^{-10}. Calculate the concentration of silver ion in sea water.
26. Using data found in Table 18-5 for silver iodide, calculate the solubility of AgI in water at 25°C. Report your answer in units of grams of silver iodide per liter of solution.
27. The solubility product constant for lead chloride is 1.7×10^{-5}. How many moles of lead nitrate can dissolve in 1.00 liter of a 0.1M solution of sodium chloride? (Hint: One of the ions found in $PbCl_2$, the chloride ion, is already present in the solution. That can be taken to be its equilibrium concentration.)

PREDICTING CHANGES IN EQUILIBRIUM

G. Objective: **Explain** *what is meant by Le Châtelier's principle.*

28. State Le Châtelier's principle.
29. When an equilibrium is shifted to the right, do the concentrations of the reactants increase or decrease? What happens to the concentrations of the products?
30. Suppose a change causes the following reaction to shift to the right. What will happen to the color?

$$Fe^{3+}(aq) + SCN^-(aq) \rightleftharpoons FeSCN^{2+}(aq)$$

H. Objective: **Predict** *changes in equilibrium, using Le Châtelier's principle.*

31. Use Le Châtelier's principle and the following chemical equation to answer the questions.

$$energy + 2HI(g) \rightleftharpoons H_2(g) + I_2(g)$$

What is the effect on the equilibrium concentration of hydrogen iodide if the following changes are made?
   a. hydrogen gas is added

b. the pressure of the system is increased by decreasing the volume

c. the temperature of the system is increased

d. the volume of the system is increased

32. Predict how the equilibrium shifts if the following changes take place in this reaction.

$$H_2(g) + Cl_2(g) \rightleftharpoons 2HCl(g) + energy$$

a. The pressure is increased by decreasing the overall volume.

b. The temperature is increased.

c. Hydrogen chloride is removed.

33. How will this equilibrium be affected by the changes listed below?

$$N_2O_4(g) + energy \rightleftharpoons 2NO_2(g)$$

a. The pressure is increased by decreasing the volume.

b. The pressure is increased by adding NO_2.

c. The pressure is increased by adding N_2O_4.

34. If you want to obtain a greater yield of products from the following gas-phase equilibria, would you want to increase or decrease the overall pressure by changing the volume? Do any of these equilibrium mixtures remain unaffected by such a change in pressure?

a. $N_2(g) + 3H_2(g) \rightleftharpoons 2NH_3(g)$

b. $H_2(g) + Br_2(g) \rightleftharpoons 2HBr(g)$

c. $2SO_2(g) + O_2(g) \rightleftharpoons 2SO_3(g)$

Critical Thinking

SYNTHESIS WITHIN THE CHAPTER

35. The box on the left shows an equilibrium mixture of the gases AB and A_2B_2.

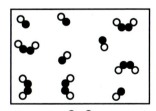 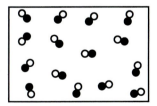

$\infty\bullet$ = AB, $\overset{\bullet}{\infty}\bullet$ = A_2B_2

a. What is the balanced chemical equation for the equilibrium reaction that takes place between AB (the reactant) and A_2B_2 (the product)?

b. Suppose you start with the amount of gas AB represented by the box on the right. Draw a picture, different from the one on the left, showing what the contents of this box might look like when equilibrium is attained.

c. Suppose you added enough AB to double the amount of AB in the equilibrium mixture on the left. How would the system respond? Explain.

SYNTHESIS ACROSS CHAPTERS

36. Using the value of 1.00 g/cm^3 for the density of water, calculate the concentration of pure water in mol/L.

37. Aluminum metal has a density of 2.7 g/cm^3. What is the concentration in mol/L of a cube of aluminum measuring 3.0 cm on each side? What is the concentration in mol/L of 25 g of aluminum?

RESEARCH AND WRITING

38. The name of Fritz Haber is often associated with the industrial production of ammonia. Using appropriate reference materials, try to find the details of Haber's process. What role does Le Châtelier's principle play in finding appropriate conditions for this reaction? Are the temperature and pressure conditions used in the Haber process chosen to maximize the amount of ammonia in the equilibrium process?

☐ Boxed numbers indicate questions that involve skills in interpretation, application, and analysis.

1. This is not a closed system, and carbon dioxide will escape.

2. The observable properties of a system remain constant, all reactants and products are present, and the system is closed.

3. The rates of the forward and reverse reactions are equal.

4. The static aspects are at the macroscopic level, while the dynamic aspect cannot be observed directly at the submicroscopic level.

5. The rate at which ammonia and water react to form ammonium ion and hydroxide ion is equal to the rate at which ammonium ion and hydroxide ion react to form ammonia and water.

6. a. $H_2O(l) \rightleftharpoons H_2O(g)$
   b. $CaCO_3(s) \rightleftharpoons Ca^{2+}(aq) + CO_3^{2-}(aq)$
   c. $2NO_2(g) \rightleftharpoons N_2O_4(g)$
   d. $NH_3(aq) + H_2O(l) \rightleftharpoons NH_4^+(aq) + OH^-(aq)$

7. Lead ion concentration increases rapidly at first; gradually the formation of lead ions slows down and finally reaches an equilibrium concentration, which does not change.

8. Lead ion concentration decreases rapidly at first, then decreases more slowly until it reaches a lower unchanging equilibrium value.

9. This expression shows how the equilibrium concentrations are related to each other. It is a ratio of the product of the concentrations of the products in a reaction to the product of the concentrations of the reactants. It has a constant value at a given temperature.

10. [CH_3COOH] stands for the concentration of the CH_3COOH in units of moles per liter.

11. Concentrations of liquids and solids remain constant and are incorporated into the equilibrium constant.

12. a. $K = \dfrac{[C][D]}{[A][B]}$
   b. $K = \dfrac{[HCl]^2}{[H_2][Cl_2]}$
   c. $K = \dfrac{[CO][Cl_2]}{[COCl_2]}$

13. a. $K = [CO_2]$
   b. $K = [Ag^+][Cl^-]$
   c. $K = \dfrac{[NH_4^+][OH^-]}{[NH_3]}$

14. $K = \dfrac{[H_2][I_2]}{[HI]^2} = \dfrac{(0.0075)(0.000\ 43)}{(0.0040)^2}$
    $= 0.20$

15. $K = \dfrac{[CH_3COO^-][H_3O^+]}{[CH_3COOH]}$
    $= \dfrac{(0.0019)(0.0019)}{0.20} = 1.8 \times 10^{-5}$

16. More products, because products are in the numerator of the expression. A large equilibrium constant indicates that the equilibrium favors the products.

17. $K = \dfrac{[HBr]^2}{[H_2][Br_2]} = 1.02$
    $\dfrac{(0.050)^2}{x^2} = 1.02$
    $x = \sqrt{\dfrac{(0.050)^2}{1.02}} = 0.050M$
    $[H_2] = 0.050M$

18. $K = \dfrac{[NH_4^+][OH^-]}{[NH_3]}$ $[OH^-] = \dfrac{K[NH_3]}{[NH_4^+]}$
    $= \dfrac{(1.8 \times 10^5)(0.25)}{(0.075)} = 6.0 \times 10^{-5}\ M$

19. a. $K = [H_3O^+][OH^-]$
    $= 1.00 \times 10^{-14}$
   b. $[H_3O^+] = \dfrac{K}{[OH^-]}$
    $= \dfrac{1.00 \times 10^{-14}}{6.0 \times 10^{-5}} = 1.7 \times 10^{-10}\ M$

20. K_{sp} is the solubility product constant, the equilibrium constant for a reaction involving the dissolution of an insoluble ionic solid.

21. a. $CaCO_3(s) \rightleftharpoons Ca^{2+}(aq) + CO_3^{2-}(aq)$
    b. $AgBr(s) \rightleftharpoons Ag^+(aq) + Br^-(aq)$
    c. $PbSO_4(s) \rightleftharpoons Pb^{2+}(aq) + SO_4^{2-}(aq)$

22. a. $K_{sp} = [Ca^{2+}][CO_3^{2-}]$
    b. $K_{sp} = [Ag^+][Br^-]$
    c. $K_{sp} = [Pb^{2+}][SO_4^{2-}]$

23. a. $K_{sp} = [Pb^{2+}][Cl^-]^2$
    b. $K_{sp} = [Mg^{2+}][OH^-]^2$
    c. $K_{sp} = [Fe^{3+}][OH^-]^3$

24. $CaSO_4(s) \rightleftharpoons Ca^{2+}(aq) + SO_4^{2-}(aq)$
    $K_{sp} = [Ca^{2+}][SO_4^{2-}]$
    $= (0.0049)(0.0049) = 2.4 \times 10^{-5}M$

25. $AgCl(s) \rightleftharpoons Ag^+(aq) + Cl^-(aq)$
    $K_{sp} = [Ag^+][Cl^-]$
    $[Ag^+] = \dfrac{K_{sp}}{[Cl^-]} = \dfrac{1.7 \times 10^{-10}}{0.53}$
    $= 3.2 \times 10^{-10}\ M$

26. $AgI(s) \rightleftharpoons Ag^+(aq) + I^-(aq)$
    $K_{sp} = [Ag^+][I^-]$
    $8.5 \times 10^{-17} = x^2$
    $x = \sqrt{8.5 \times 10^{-17}}$
    $= 9.2 \times 10^{-9}$ mol/L
    $\times\ 234.8$ g / mol
    $= 2.2 \times 10^{-6}$ g/L

27. $K_{sp} = [Pb^{2+}][Cl^-]^2$
    $[Pb^{2+}] = \dfrac{K_{sp}}{[Cl^-]^2} = \dfrac{1.7 \times 10^{-5}}{(0.1)^2}$
    $= 1.7 \times 10^{-3}\ M$
    0.0017 moles of $Pb(NO_3)_2$ can dissolve in this solution.

28. If something is done to disturb a system at equilibrium, then the system responds by partially undoing this change.

29. The concentrations of reactants decrease and the concentrations of products increase.

30. The intensity of the color increases, as more of the colored ion $FeSCN^{2+}$ forms.

31. a. [HI] increases
    b. No change
    c. [HI] decreases
    d. No change

32. a. No change
    b. The equilibrium shifts to the left.
    c. The equilibrium shifts to the right.

33. a. The equilibrium shifts to the left.
    b. The equilibrium shifts to the left.
    c. The equilibrium shifts to the right.

34. a. Decrease the volume to increase the overall pressure.
    b. Volume changes will not affect this reaction.
    c. Decrease the volume to increase the overall pressure.

35. a. $2AB \rightleftharpoons A_2B_2$

   b. Notice that the contents of this box can react to produce the mixture shown in the box on the left, so this will be the equilibrium mixture.

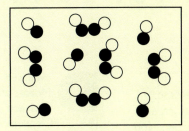

   c. The equilibrium will shift to produce more A_2B_2 and decrease the concentration of AB so that the equilibrium constant is maintained.

36. $\dfrac{1.00 \text{ g } H_2O}{cm^3} \times \dfrac{1 \text{ mol } H_2O}{18.02 \text{ g } H_2O} \times \dfrac{1000 \text{ cm}^3}{L}$

   $= 55.5 \text{ mol } H_2O / L$

37. For both samples, the concentration is: $\dfrac{2.7 \text{ g Al}}{cm^3} \times \dfrac{1 \text{ mol}}{26.98 \text{ g Al}} \times \dfrac{1000 \text{ cm}^3}{L}$

   $= 100 \text{ mol } / L$

CHEMICAL PERSPECTIVES

Chlorofluorocarbons— Wonder Chemicals?

Sunbathing is still an enjoyable summertime activity for many people. When a dark tan is the desired outcome, people pass up the bottle of suntan lotion with sunscreen. The next time you are in the market for suntan lotion, you may want to think again about passing up the sunscreen. Nature's own sunscreen, the ozone layer, is being destroyed by a group of chemicals known as CFC's, or chlorofluorocarbons. If something is not done soon to stop this dangerous trend, sunbathing may become a dangerous activity. In fact, bottles of suntan lotion may someday carry this warning: Sunbathing may be hazardous to your health.

Developed by General Motors and Du Pont between 1928 and 1930, CFC's were often called wonder chemicals. CFC's were tested and found to be non-toxic, stable, noncorrosive, and nonflammable. To add to their overall appeal, CFC's were in-expensive to produce. As a result of these desirable qualities, CFC's were integral parts of many industries. Until recently, they were used as propellants in aerosol cans. They are still used in refrigeration and air-conditioning. Not until the early 1970's did CFC's begin to lose some of their appeal. Ironically the same qualities that made them industrial wonder chemicals also made them dangerous to the atmosphere.

CFC's are considered the primary suspects in the deple-tion of the ozone layer. The ozone layer, extending from 18 to 30 miles above Earth, protects the planet from the sun's dangerous ultraviolet rays, acting as nature's own sunscreen. In 1974, scientists reported that chlorine released into the atmosphere could de-stroy ozone for decades. A single chlorine atom destroys thousands of ozone molecules.

Critical Thinking Skills

These skills are applied in the feature.

- Evaluating an opinion or point of view
- Using library resources
- Making an informed decision
- Identifying valid/invalid inter-pretations
- Devising multiple solutions/interpretations

Focus

Activate Prior Knowledge

Suggest to students that they may have experienced or know someone who has experienced a severe sunburn. Elicit student knowledge of cell damage from mild or severe sunburn; for example, pain and peeling indi-cate cell damage.

Teach

Science Background

In the upper layers of Earth's atmosphere a layer of ozone normally filters out most of the high-frequency UV light from the sun. Ultraviolet light is a form of high-energy radiation that can harm living cells by damaging genetic material. In humans, this damage can lead to skin cancers, cataracts, and sup-pression of the immune system. UV light can also damage farm crops and ocean ecosystems. NASA satellite data have con-firmed a British report of 1985, which described an area of greatly reduced ozone concen-tration over Antarctica. This area appears to be growing.

Teaching Strategy

Have students find out how existing CFCs are being disposed of in their area. As a start, they can contact air conditioner sales

and service shops and junk yards that dispose of refrigerators.

Compare current CFCs and their uses with possible replace-ment chemicals/processes by making a chart with chemicals, uses, and the added environmen-tal and financial cost of using replacement chemicals. Obtain the American Cancer Society poster, "Fry Now—Pay Later"

and connect to earlier discussion of sunburns and cell damage. Contact eye and skin specialists to find out their recommenda-tions regarding sun exposure and protective measures.

1. $Cl + O_3 \rightarrow$
$$ClO + O_2$$
2. $ClO + O \rightarrow$
$$Cl + O_2$$

Later that year it was reported that CFC's migrate to the upper atmosphere, above the ozone layer, where they react with ultraviolet radiation.

3. $CF_2Cl_2 + UV\ light \rightarrow$
$$CF_2Cl + Cl$$

The chlorine atoms produced then react with ozone, according to reactions 1 and 2. In this reaction sequence, the chlorine atoms act as catalysts, set free to attack other ozone molecules. As the concentration of CFC's is increased, the equilibrium of reaction 3 is shifted to the right, according to Le Châtelier's principle. As a result, increasing numbers of chlorine atoms are available to catalyze the destruction of thousands more ozone molecules.

In September 1987, a treaty was signed that has become known as the most significant international environmental agreement in the history of the world. The Montreal Protocol on substances that deplete the ozone layer mandated significant reductions in the use and production of CFC's. Over 46 countries—including the United States, the Soviet Union, and members of the European Economic Community—signed this agreement. It had profound social, political, and economic effects. In the

Chlorine atoms are rapidly destroying thousands of ozone molecules, thus depleting the ozone layer and reducing nature's own sunscreen.

United States alone, CFC production is a $750 million industry. The value of products and services directly dependent upon CFC's is about $27 billion. In addition, the industrial growth may need to be sacrificed in many developing nations, where the cost of using CFC substitutes would require financial assistance from other nations. However, the Montreal Protocol remains an international commitment to protect the ozone layer, despite the many obstacles to overcome.

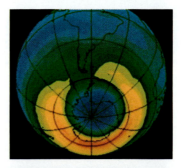
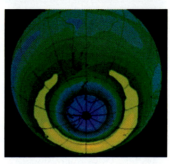

Ozone levels range from high, indicated by yellow areas, to very low, indicated by purple areas. The top image is from 1980 and the lower one from 1990. What trend do you see?

Discussing the Issues

1. In January 1989, industries voluntarily began developing CFC recycling programs. Do you think this is a good substitute for eliminating CFC's altogether? Explain.
2. Why do any uncertainties about the role of CFC's in the ozone depletion not prevent significant action from being taken, even though this action will be costly in both dollars and jobs?

Take Action

1. Automobile air conditioners are the single biggest source of CFC's in the upper atmosphere. What can you do to reduce this form of CFC pollution?
2. Find out what major companies are doing to find alternatives to CFC's and to develop new products that do not depend upon CFC's.

633

Look Back
Connect the ozone layer with another atmospheric problem by referring back to the **Science Technology & Society** feature, "Global Warming," in Chapter 5.

Chemical Update
In the U.S. Federal Clean Air Act amendments of 1990, Congress banned production of most CFCs by January 1, 2000. Worldwide measures such as this may be too late; severe damage may have already been done. Researchers in Antarctica have found up to a 12 percent decline in the growth of phytoplankton, the tiny photosynthetic algae that form the base of the marine food chain.

Close

Discussing the Issues
These questions provide opportunities for students to use their research skills. Students could write to a senator or representative to discover measures Congress supports to control the damaging effects of CFCs.

1. Answers will vary. Student responses should indicate understanding that this is an interim measure. Some students may guess that there are public relations benefits or financial advantages to getting a head start on the obligatory phase-out in January, 2000.
2. Answers will vary. Some students may realize that preventive measures are taken based on worst-case scenarios. An effect has been observed and the possible long-term damage could be much more expensive than short-term problems. No one is certain that damage will occur or be prevented by banning CFCs. However, the probability of both damage from CFCs and some alleviation of the problem from CFC banning is high.

Take Action
1. Answers will vary. The most obvious answers are replacing CFCs with other coolants or reducing coolant exhaust to the environment.
2. General Motors, DuPont, Ford, General Electric, Procter and Gamble, Dow Chemical, and Hyundai are among the companies that may be researching possible substitutes for CFCs. Have students select one or more of these companies and write a letter of inquiry concerning the progress of the research.

Acids and Bases

Investigations	Demonstrations	Texas Essential Elements★
	Indicators, page T637 Acid and Base Strength, page T642	**Content:** 8.1, 9.2, 11.1, 11.4 **Process:** 4.3, 7.2, 8.1, 8.2, 10.1
Laboratory Manual 19–1 S Laboratory Manual 19–4 I	Cabbage Juice Indicator and Neutralization, page T647	**Content:** 11.7 **Process:** 2.1, 3.2, 7.1, 8.1, 9.1
Laboratory Manual 19–2 M Laboratory Manual 19–3 S Laboratory Manual 19–5 IM In-text Investigation, page T668	pH Scale, page T654 pH and Ion Concentration, page T655 Buffers, page T664	**Content:** 11.3, 11.5, 11.6 **Process:** 4.3, 8.2, 10.1, 10.4
		Content: 11.5 **Process:** 1.1, 1.2, 1.3, 2.1, 3.1, 4.3, 7.2
		Process: 4.2, 7.1, 7.2, 8.2, 9.1, 9.2, 10.1
		Content: 8.9, 11.5 **Process:** 10.1, 10.2, 10.4
KEY: **M**–*Microscale* **S**–*Structured* **I**–*Inquiry* **IM**–*Inquiry Microscale*		★*See pages T8–T11 for complete listing of Texas Essential Elements.*

19

Acids and Bases

Chapter Rationale

Chapter 19 provides an introduction to acids and bases. Following an exposition of the observable properties of acids and bases, students are taught to apply the Brønsted definition, which is reinforced throughout the chapter.

Most teachers will want to cover at least part of this chapter, as the concepts of acid and base are fundamental to future studies in both biology and chemistry. These concepts are also important to understanding terminology students may encounter in everyday life, such as the pH of a swimming pool, acid rain, and so on. In Part 1, students have the opportunity to practice their skills in writing chemical equations; in Part 2, students can review stoichiometry and solution concentration as they solve titration problems.

About the Photograph

The photograph provides you with an opportunity to remind students that all acids are not equally dangerous—some, in fact, are important for normal body functioning. For example, ascorbic acid, or vitamin C, is an important vitamin obtained from citrus fruits. After you finish Part 1, you may wish to ask students to identify other everyday substances that are acids or bases, such as vinegar (acid) and ammonia (base).

Chapter Planning Hints

Plan to complete the chapter, Laboratory Investigation, and Chapter Review in five to seven class sessions. You may wish to obtain The World of Chemistry videotape *Acids and Bases* for use in this chapter. There are six optional demonstrations that are found on pages T637, T642, T647, T654, T655, and T664.

Do you realize that acids are a part of the food you eat? These fruits are high in vitamin C, which is also known as ascorbic acid.

PART **1** Introduction to Acids and Bases

Acids and bases are familiar substances. Not only are they common chemicals found in a laboratory, but many kinds of acids and bases can be found right in your own home. Citrus fruit contains ascorbic acid, better known as vitamin C, while the vinegar used on a salad contains acetic acid. Some automobile batteries contain sulfuric acid, the same substance you have used in the laboratory. Ammonia is a common base found in many household cleaners. Many recipes call for the base sodium hydrogen carbonate. You know it better as baking soda.

Not only are acids and bases familiar substances, but they also undergo important chemical reactions. For example, sulfuric acid is the top chemical produced in the United States, with an annual production of about 40 billion kilograms. It is used in the production of a wide variety of materials—including fertilizers, detergents, plastics, and drugs—as well as being a component in the processing of metals and petroleum. In this chapter, you will begin your study of acids and bases by learning the macroscopic characteristics used to describe these important compounds. You will then take a closer look at the kinds of reactions that make acids and bases an important part of chemistry and the world around you.

19.1 Properties of Acids and Bases

Acids and bases comprise two groups of substances that can be categorized by their physical and chemical properties. Let's consider those properties that differentiate acids and bases from other substances and from each other.

1. *Taste* Perhaps there is no simpler distinguishing characteristic than this one. From your own experience of tasting acidic foods such as lemons, oranges, cherries, or even yogurt, you know that acids taste sour. If you have ever accidentally tasted soap, then you would recognize a bitter taste as one way to identify a base. (⚠ *Caution: Never use taste to identify a lab chemical or unknown substance.*)

2. *Feel* Your sense of touch provides another way to distinguish between acids and bases. A soap-and-water mixture feels slippery. Solutions of ammonia, another base, also feel slippery. Slipperiness is a characteristic property of bases. In fact, when you work with bases in the lab (such as sodium hydroxide), this slipperiness may alert you to the fact that your skin has

Objectives

Part 1

A. *Distinguish* between an acid and a base, using observable properties.

B. *Define* acids and bases by *applying* the Brønsted definition of acids and bases.

C. *Identify* conjugate acid-base pairs in a reaction.

Developing Skills

Students may apply this skill in their study of Part 1.
Comparing/Contrasting: The process of formulating an operational definition is discussed on page 638. Ask students how this type of definition compares and contrasts with a dictionary definition. Why might operational definitions be especially useful in science?

☰FOCUS

Activate Prior Knowledge

Set out some familiar substances containing acids and bases—vinegar (acetic acid, CH_3COOH), an ammonia-based cleaner, baking soda ($NaHCO_3$, sodium bicarbonate), powdered chalk (calcium carbonate, $CaCO_3$), orange juice (citric acid). You may also wish to set out some bottles containing $0.1M$ or less concentrated "laboratory" acids and bases—hydrochloric acid, sulfuric acid, sodium hydroxide. Identify these substances with labels containing their names, formulas, and precautionary information, along with the designator *acid* or *base*. Also set out some litmus paper.

⚠ **CAUTION: Everyone must wear safety goggles and lab aprons.**

Ask students these two questions:

1. Do you notice any similarities in the formulas of acids? of bases?

2. How does litmus paper react with these substances?

(continued on page T636)

PART 1

Section 19.1 continued

(continued from page T635)
Students may respond that acids all contain "H," but may see nothing in common for bases. Explain that when they begin the chapter, they will learn how hydrogen transfers between acids and bases. They should be able to provide the proper changes for litmus paper: acids make blue litmus paper turn red, and bases make red litmus paper turn blue.

Videodisc Connections

366, side 5
Common household acids and bases (1 frame)

367-372, side 5
Acid and base indicators (6-frame seq.)

7104 to 14185, side 5
Shakhashire: Red cabbage indicator (movie)

DO YOU KNOW?

The English word *acid* comes from the Latin word *acidus*, referring to a sour substance.

accidentally come in contact with a base and needs to be washed immediately with water. (▲ *Caution: Never touch any lab chemicals or unknown substances with bare skin.*)

Dilute acids, on the other hand, do not feel much different from water. However, if you have ever had a cut on your hand or a canker sore in your mouth, you know the sharp feeling that fruit juice or some other acid can produce.

3. ***Reaction with metals*** Figure 19-1 shows what happens when magnesium ribbon and mossy zinc are placed separately into hydrochloric acid and acetic acid. In both cases, a vigorous reaction takes place and bubbles form rapidly. By collecting the gas that is given off and testing it with a burning splint, you could verify (from the popping noise) that the gas is hydrogen. It is a characteristic of acids to react with active metals and produce hydrogen gas. The equation for the reaction of zinc with hydrochloric acid is

$$Zn(s) + 2HCl(aq) \rightarrow H_2(g) + ZnCl_2(aq)$$

Do all metals react with acids to form hydrogen gas? Look back at the activity series described in Chapter 3. Hydrogen may be replaced only by metals that are listed higher in the series. Metals such as copper, silver, platinum, and gold do not replace hydrogen from an acid. While active metals react with acids, they generally do not react with bases.

Figure 19-1 One macroscopic property of acids is the release of hydrogen gas when acids react with certain metals. Why is copper an exception?

4. ***Electrical conductivity*** Figure 19-2 shows water and two solutions being tested with a conductivity apparatus: 1M hydrochloric acid and 1M sodium hydroxide. Both solutions conduct an electric current quite well. What you see is representative of what happens when acids or bases dissolve in water. While this characteristic does not help differentiate between an acid or a base, it does help distinguish whether a substance might be an acid or a base in the first place. It also tells you something about the chemical behavior of acids and bases in water solutions. You have learned in earlier chapters that a solution

Figure 19-2 *Conductivity testing of pure water, hydrochloric acid, and sodium hydroxide is shown. Note that pure water does not conduct and the conductivity of the other two solutions is similar.*

will conduct electricity if it contains ions. Since a solution containing an acid or a base conducts electricity, you can conclude that acids and bases produce ions when they dissolve in water, forming electrolytic solutions.

5. *Indicators* An **indicator** is a substance that is one color in an acid solution and another color in a basic solution. One of the most common indicators used in the laboratory is litmus. Litmus comes from a rare form of lichen that grows in the Netherlands. In Figure 19-3 *(left)*, you can see that blue litmus paper turns red when dipped in an acid and red litmus paper turns blue when dipped in a base. Phenolphthalein is another indicator of acids and bases. Note in Figure 19-3 *(right)* that phenolphthalein is colorless in an acid but has a distinct pink color in a base.

Figure 19-3 Left: *Litmus is an indicator. Blue litmus paper turns red in the presence of an acid. Red litmus turns blue in the presence of a base.* Right: *The indicator phenolphthalein is colorless in an acidic solution and pink in a basic solution.*

⚠️CAUTION: *A solution of phenolphthalein and alcohol is poisonous and flammable. Take care when using it in the lab.*

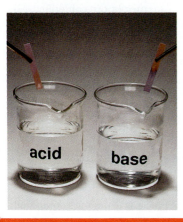

DEMONSTRATION

Indicators

Add 10 drops of 1 *M* HCl solution to 50 mL of distilled water in a 600-mL beaker. Place on an overhead projector. Add 20 mL of universal indicator. Drop in one Phillips antacid tablet. Stir slowly for 2 minutes as the pH increases and the color of the indicator changes from orange to blue.

⚠️ **CAUTION: Wear safety goggles and a lab apron. Use a shield to protect students.**
For disposal, pour down the drain.

≡ T E A C H

Teaching Strategy

Defining Acids and Bases

Three definitions of acids and bases are commonly used: the Arrhenius definition (an acid produces H_3O^+ in water, whereas a base produces OH^-); the Brønsted definition (an acid is a proton donor, whereas a base is a proton recipient); and the Lewis definition (an acid is an electron acceptor, whereas a base is an electron donor). This chapter covers only the first two definitions, but emphasizes the Brønsted viewpoint. Because several definitions for a new concept may interfere with students' learning, you may also wish to emphasize only the Brønsted definition as you cover the chapter.

Science Background

Arrhenius Definition

The hydrogen ion, H^+, does not exist independently in aqueous solution. H^+ is always hydrated with one or more water molecules. With one water molecule, $H+$ becomes H_3O^+; with two, it becomes $H_5O_2^+$; with three, $H_7O_3^+$; and so on. We typically represent all of these forms of the hydrated species by simply writing the hydronium ion, H_3O^+.

DO YOU KNOW?

An easy way to remember how litmus reacts with an acid or base is this. RE**D** **B**LUE ACI**D** **B**ASE

PROBLEM·SOLVING
S T R A T E G Y

*Use what you know about atomic structure to understand the terms used here. When the hydrogen atom loses its one electron, all that remains is the proton, which is the H^+ ion. The words **proton** and **hydrogen ion** can be used interchangeably, since both refer to the same particle. (See Strategy, page 58.)*

Summarizing the properties At this point, you have read about five properties that you can use to characterize acids and bases. The information is summarized for you in Table 19-1.

TABLE 19-1

Characteristic Properties of Acids and Bases	
Acids Dissolve in Water to Form Solutions That	**Bases Dissolve in Water to Form Solutions That**
Taste sour	Taste bitter and feels slippery
Release hydrogen gas when they react with active metals	Generally do not react with active metals
Conduct an electric current	Conduct an electric current
Turn blue litmus red	Turn red litmus blue
Turn phenolphthalein colorless	Turn phenolphthalein pink

19.2 Defining Acids and Bases

Now that you can distinguish between an acid and a base macroscopically, you can formulate your own definitions of these substances. For example, you might say that "an acid is a substance that reacts with most metals releasing hydrogen and turns litmus red, while a base is a substance that does not react with most metals and turns litmus blue." This kind of definition is an operational definition, which means you can apply the definition by carrying out the operations that are asked for. For example, you could test a solution with litmus paper.

An operational definition such as this one for acids and bases relates to observable, macroscopic properties of the compounds. In order to explain the behavior of acids and bases, macroscopic properties need to be explained on the submicroscopic level.

Arrhenius definition To distinguish between acids and bases on the submicroscopic level, consider what happens when hydrogen chloride gas dissolves in water. The result of this process is a solution of hydrochloric acid. Because this solution is a good conductor of electricity, you have evidence that there are ions in the solution. This equation describes the ionization reaction that takes place.

$$HCl(g) + H_2O(l) \rightarrow H_3O^+(aq) + Cl^-(aq) + energy$$

Note that one of the products of this reaction is the hydronium ion,

H_3O^+. The **hydronium ion** is the result of a hydrogen ion, H^+, donated by the acid combining with water. A model for the formation of the hydronium ion is shown in Figure 19-4.

As you have just learned, bases also form aqueous solutions that conduct electricity. These equations show the ions that form when sodium hydroxide and ammonia dissolve in water.

$$NaOH(s) \rightarrow Na^+(aq) + OH^-(aq)$$

$$NH_3(g) + H_2O(l) \rightarrow NH_4^+(aq) + OH^-(aq)$$

Svante Arrhenius, a Swedish chemist, proposed the following distinction between acids and bases: Acids form hydronium ions in aqueous (water) solution, while bases form hydroxide ions.

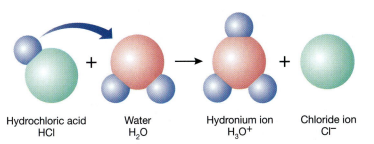

| Hydrochloric acid | Water | Hydronium ion | Chloride ion |
| HCl | H_2O | H_3O^+ | Cl^- |

Figure 19-4 *The formation of the hydronium ion involves a proton transfer from the acid to the water molecule. This reaction is a Brønsted acid-base reaction.*

Brønsted definition Water is not the only solvent in which acids and bases can dissolve. However, you must have an aqueous solution in order to apply the Arrhenius definition. A broader viewpoint was proposed independently by Danish chemist Johannes Brønsted and English chemist Thomas Lowry.

Arrhenius defined acids and bases by looking at what ions they produced in aqueous solution. In essence, he focused on the products of the reaction. Brønsted's definition is based on what happens *during* an acid-base reaction.

Let's take a look at three reactions involving acids, whose equations are given below.

$$CH_3COOH + H_2O \rightarrow H_3O^+ + CH_3COO^-$$

$$HCl + NH_3 \rightarrow NH_4^+ + Cl^-$$

$$HSO_4^- + OH^- \rightarrow H_2O + SO_4^{2-}$$

DO YOU KNOW?

Some drain cleaners work because of the reaction between aluminum and the base sodium hydroxide. When added to water, these chemicals in the cleaner react, producing hydrogen bubbles that loosen the materials clogging the drain.

PROBLEM-SOLVING STRATEGY

Finding patterns and regularities in these equations will help you understand the definition of an acid. (See Strategy, page 100.)

CHEMICAL UPDATE

Brønsted Definition

Working independently, both Johannes Brønsted and Thomas Lowry proposed a proton-transfer theory of acids and bases. For this reason, the theory has often been referred to as the Brønsted-Lowry theory.

However, because Brønsted described a more fully developed theory than Lowry, there has recently been a trend to shorten this name to the Brønsted theory, a convention this text follows.

Teaching Strategy

Brønsted Definition

Students often master the movement of the hydrogen when they write acid-base equations, but they have more difficulty with the changing charges in these reactions. In fact, they often see so many examples involving neutral acids, such as HCl + H$_2$O → Cl$^-$ + H$_3$O$^+$, that they incorrectly "learn" that the conjugate base of an acid always has a 1− charge. Use a variety of examples, such as

$$H_2PO_4^- + H_2O \rightarrow HPO_4^{2-} + H_3O^+$$
$$NH_4^+ + H_2O \rightarrow NH_3 + H_3O^+$$

to show that the charge is reduced by one when an acid loses its proton (and increases by one when a base gains a proton).

PROBLEM-SOLVING
S T R A T E G Y

Use what you know to recognize that the H$^+$ is actually transferred to a water molecule. You will find that H$^+$(aq) and H$_3$O$^+$(aq) are used interchangeably when studying acids and bases. (See Strategy, page 58.)

The first reactant in each of these reactions is an acid. In the first reaction, an H$^+$ ion is donated by acetic acid, CH$_3$COOH, to water. After the acetic acid has lost an H$^+$ ion, it becomes the acetate ion, CH$_3$COO$^-$. Similarly, HCl donates an H$^+$ ion to ammonia as it becomes the chloride ion, Cl$^-$, and HSO$_4^-$ donates an H$^+$ ion to OH$^-$ and becomes the sulfate ion, SO$_4^{2-}$.

Bases too can be defined on the basis of the movement of H$^+$ ions. Examine these equations, in which a base is listed first.

$$SO_3^{2-} + H_2O \rightarrow HSO_3^- + OH^-$$

$$NH_3 + HNO_3 \rightarrow NH_4^+ + NO_3^-$$

Notice that both SO$_3^{2-}$ and NH$_3$ accept an H$^+$ ion to become HSO$_3^-$ and NH$_4^+$, respectively.

These examples illustrate Brønsted's definition of **acids** and **bases.** The definition is summarized in Table 19-2.

TABLE 19-2

Brønsted Definitions	
Brønsted acid	**Brønsted base**
A substance that donates an H$^+$ ion (proton) to another substance	A substance that accepts an H$^+$ ion (proton) from another substance

Water as an acid and a base Look at the reactions of HCl and NH$_3$ with water.

$$HCl + H_2O \rightarrow H_3O^+ + Cl^-$$

$$NH_3 + H_2O \rightarrow NH_4^+ + OH^-$$

Did you notice that when HCl acts as a proton donor, H$_2$O acts as a proton acceptor? In that reaction, H$_2$O can be identified as a Brønsted base. What happens in the reaction of NH$_3$ and water? There NH$_3$ molecules act as proton acceptors, with water a proton donor. This process makes water a Brønsted acid.

It may seem contradictory to say that water is both an acid and a base. However, under differing circumstances, water is able either to give up a proton or accept a proton. A particular water molecule can undergo only one of these reactions at a time. Substances such as water, which have the ability to act both as an acid and as a base, are said to be **amphiprotic**.

Concept ✔ Check

How is the Brønsted definition of an acid and base different from the Arrhenius definition?

H I S T O R Y   O F   S C I E N C E

Development of Acid-Base Definitions

Several chemists influenced the current definitions of acids and bases. In 1884, Svante August Arrhenius presented a theory of ionic dissociation as part of his Ph.D. thesis. After observing that some substances when dissolved in water conduct electricity, he explained that molecules dissociate into positively and negatively charged atoms. Arrhenius's idea was revolutionary, but earned him only the lowest passing mark on his thesis. In 1903, he won the Nobel Prize in Chemistry for work based on his thesis.

One of the remarkable coincidences in the history of science is the occurrence of simultaneous and independent discoveries. In 1923, the concept of acids and bases was revisited by 3 scientists in 3 different publications. Johannes Nicolaus Brønsted published a paper that extended the concept of acids and bases. The definition of an acid as a proton donor remained similar to Arrhenius's, but the definition of a base as a proton acceptor was broader.

Thomas Martin Lowry, another chemist, is also credited with this acid-base theory. Currently the Brønsted-Lowry theory of acids and bases is called the Brønsted theory.

Gilbert Newton Lewis was the third chemist who furthered the concept of acids and bases. His definitions were even more general than Brønsted's and Lowry's: An acid can accept an electron pair, while a base is a substance that can donate an electron pair.

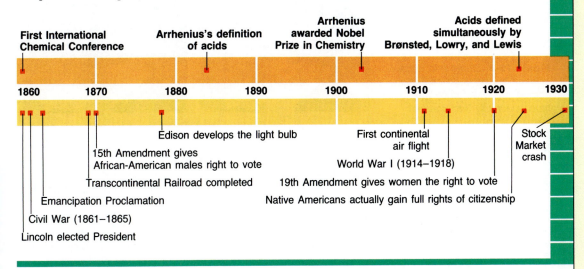

PART *1*
Section 19.3

Teaching Strategy

Acid and Base Strength

Students easily confuse "strength" with "concentration." You may want to give them some pairs such as the following, and ask which acid is stronger and which acid is more concentrated.

- 0.1*M* HCl vs. 0.1*M* HF (HCl is stronger; they have equal concentrations.)
- 0.1*M* HCl vs. 0.01*M* HF (HCl is stronger and more concentrated.)
- 0.01*M* HCl vs. 0.1*M* HF (HCl is stronger, whereas HF is more concentrated.)
- 0.1*M* HCl vs. 0.01*M* HCl (The strengths are equal, whereas the first sample is more concentrated.)

Point out to students that any acid that ionizes (nearly) 100 percent is a strong acid, regardless of its concentration.

19.3 Acid and Base Strength

You may have heard the terms *strong* and *weak* used in describing an acid or base. In everyday speech, *strong* and *weak* generally refer to concentration. However, chemists do *not* use the words *strong* and *weak* to refer to the concentration of an acid or base. They simply describe the solution as either concentrated or dilute. In chemistry, the words *strong* and *weak* refer to something different from its concentration.

Strong and weak acids Figure 19-5 shows the use of a conductivity apparatus to test the conducting properties of two acid solutions—acetic acid and hydrochloric acid. Although the molar concentration of each acid solution is the same, the light intensities differ. The dimmer bulb indicates there is less electricity conducted by the acetic acid solution. How can this difference be explained?

Strong acid You have learned that acids form ions when they donate H^+ ions to water to produce the hydronium ion, H_3O^+. The strength of an acid depends on the number of hydronium ions produced per mole of acid. Acids of similar concentration can differ in the amount of hydronium ion produced. This is what has happened in the solutions of hydrochloric acid and acetic acid.

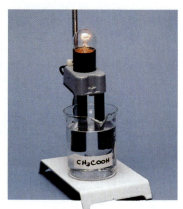

Figure 19-5 *Strong and weak acids of the same concentration can be differentiated by how much electricity they conduct.*

When HCl ionizes in water, the conductivity experiment indicates that a larger number of the HCl molecules react to form hydronium ions. In fact, almost all the HCl molecules react with water, making HCl a **strong acid.**

$$HCl(aq) + H_2O(l) \longrightarrow H_3O^+(aq) + Cl^-(aq)$$

Essentially all of the HCl molecules ionize, so a single arrow is used; it is said that the HCl is 100 percent ionized.

DEMONSTRATION

Acid and Base Strength

Use a conductivity apparatus to compare the conductivity of these substances:
- pure (distilled or deionized) water
- 0.1*M* HCl (strong acid)
- 0.1*M* CH₃COOH (weak acid)
- 0.1*M* NaOH (strong base)
- 0.1*M* NH₃

⚠ **CAUTION: Use only conductivity apparatus with 1.5- or 9-volt bat-** teries as the power source. Wear safety goggles and a lab apron. Use a shield to protect students. Use the relative conductivities to initiate a discussion of the relative number of ions in solution for each of the last four substances. Explain how equilibrium is involved for the weak substances, CH₃COOH and NH₃. For disposal, neutralize and pour down the drain.

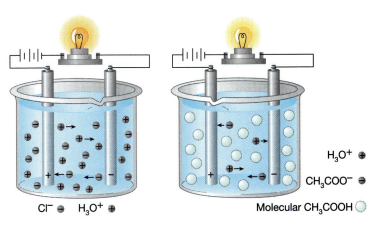

Figure 19-6 *These diagrams present submicroscopic models to explain the conductivity differences shown for HCl and CH₃COOH. Note that the presence of fewer ions for CH₃COOH affects the conductivity.*

H_3O^+

CH_3COO^-

Molecular CH_3COOH

Cl^- H_3O^+

Weak acids When acetic acid ionizes in water, at equilibrium a considerable amount of CH_3COOH molecules remain.

$$CH_3COOH(aq) + H_2O(l) \rightleftharpoons H_3O^+(aq) + CH_3COO^-(aq)$$

Only a small proportion of hydronium ions and acetate ions are present, so the solution is a weak conductor of electricity, as shown in Figure 19-6. In this reaction, are the reactants or products favored at equilibrium? Acids such as acetic acid that do not ionize completely in an aqueous solution are called **weak acids.**

Since the reactions of HCl and CH_3COOH with water have been described as two-way equilibriums, you may also consider the reverse of these equations, as shown here.

$$\underset{\text{base}}{Cl^-} + H_3O^+ \longleftarrow \underset{\text{acid}}{HCl} + H_2O$$

$$\underset{\text{base}}{CH_3COO^-} + H_3O^+ \rightleftharpoons \underset{\text{acid}}{CH_3COOH} + H_2O$$

Notice how both the chloride ion, Cl^-, and acetate ion, CH_3COO^-, function as proton acceptors in these equations. According to the Brønsted definition, they may be identified as bases.

Concept ✔ Check

Could an acid be both a concentrated acid and weak acid? Explain why or why not.

Myths and Misconceptions

When referring to acids and bases, students frequently confuse the terms *weak* (or *strong*) and *dilute* (or *concentrated*). Clarify that *weak* or *strong* refers to the degree of ionization, whereas *dilute* or *concentrated* refers to the concentration of the acid or base.

(continued on page T645)

PART 1
Section 19.3 continued

Science Background

Conjugate Acid-Base Pairs

Make sure that students understand the distinction between the terms *ionization* and *dissociation*. The proper term to use for a reaction like this

$$HCl + H_2O \rightarrow Cl^- + H_3O^+$$

is *ionization*, because ions are formed only when the HCl reacts with H_2O; the HCl itself is not an ionic substance.

This process may be contrasted with the dissolution of ionic substances in water:

$$NaCl(s) \rightarrow Na^+(aq) + Cl^-(aq)$$

This time the proper term is *dissociation*, because the ions already existed in the solid. Ions are not forming when the solid dissolves; they are merely being separated from each other in solution.

Guided Practice

Review the Concept Check questions on pages 641, 643, and 644 with students. Answers can be found in Appendix E on page 808.

Reteaching Idea

To reinforce the concept that the strength of acids and bases depends on the degree of ionization, have students write chemical equations for the reaction of several strong and weak acids and bases with water. For example, $HCl(aq) + H_2O(l) \rightleftharpoons H_3O^+(aq) + Cl^-(aq)$.

Conjugate acid-base pairs The equations also illustrate a relationship often referred to as conjugate acid-base pairs. *Conjugate* means "paired together." Two substances such as HCl and Cl^- that are related to each other by the donating and accepting of a single proton are sometimes referred to as a **conjugate acid-base pair.** Similarly, the conjugate base of the Brønsted acid CH_3COOH is CH_3COO^-. Conjugate acid-base pairs are very important in the human body. You will learn about that importance in Section 19.8 on buffers.

The strength of HCl as compared to CH_3COOH can be better understood by considering the relationship between the acid and its conjugate base. In the case of HCl, water has a stronger attraction for the proton than the Cl^- ion, making Cl^- a relatively weak conjugate base. A strong acid such as HCl therefore has a weak conjugate base.

$$\underset{\substack{\text{strong} \\ \text{acid}}}{HCl(aq)} + H_2O(l) \rightleftharpoons H_3O^+(aq) + \underset{\substack{\text{weak} \\ \text{conjugate} \\ \text{base}}}{Cl^-(aq)}$$

By comparison, a weak acid has a strong conjugate base. In the reaction of acetic acid and water, the water molecule is not a strong enough base to remove the H^+ ion from all the acetic acid molecules. This means that the acetate ion is a stronger base than water since it has a greater attraction for the H^+ ion.

Concept ✓ Check

In your own words, describe what is meant by a conjugate acid-base pair.

Comparing acid and base strength Just as weak acids react only partially with water, there are also weak bases that react the same way. Ammonia is a typical example of a weak base. Dissolved in water, far more NH_3 is found in solution than NH_4^+ as this reaction occurs.

$$NH_3(aq) + H_2O(l) \rightleftharpoons NH_4^+(aq) + OH^-(aq)$$

There are far more weak acids and weak bases than strong acids and bases. Some of the most common strong acids include HCl, HBr, HI, HNO_3, and H_2SO_4. Among the strong bases are all the hydroxides of Group 1A metals (such as NaOH) and of Group 2A metals (except for Be). In this course, you may assume that any other acid or base you encounter is weak, unless you are told otherwise.

PART 1 REVIEW

ANSWERS

■ **Keyed to Objectives**

A **1.** Acids react with magnesium and with zinc to form hydrogen gas, acids have a sour taste, phenolphthalein remains colorless in the presence of acids, and acids make blue litmus turn red.

A **2.** They both conduct electricity in aqueous solution.

A **3.** Spoiled milk is acidic, as evidenced by its characteristic sour taste.

A **4.** Use an indicator, such as litmus. It is easy to test, and you can obtain the result without harming yourself. (Don't even think about tasting an unknown substance!)

B **5.** **a.** $Zn + 2HCl \rightarrow ZnCl_2 + H_2$
b. $Mg + H_2SO_4 \rightarrow MgSO_4 + H_2$

B **6.** **a.** $HI + H_2O \rightarrow I^- + H_3O^+$
b. $NH_4^+ + H_2O \rightarrow NH_3 + H_3O^+$
c. $H_2CO_3 + H_2O \rightarrow HCO_3^- + H_3O^+$
d. $HNO_3 + H_2O \rightarrow NO_3^- + H_3O^+$

C **7.** The conjugate base is the species formed when these substances lose a proton (H^+). These bases are also shown as the first product in the equations written in the last question:
a. I^- **b.** NH_3

PART 1 REVIEW

1. Name two properties of acids that are not shared by bases.

2. Name one property that acids and bases have in common.

3. On the basis of information you have read so far in this chapter, name one substance you are familiar with that is probably an acid but has not been mentioned in this chapter. Explain how you know that it is an acid.

4. Review the list of observable properties of an acid given in Table 19-1. If you had to use only one of these properties to identify an unknown substance as an acid or a base, which one would you use? Why?

5. Write a chemical equation for the following reactions of metals and acids. If no reaction takes place, then simply write N.R. ("no reaction") instead of products.
   a. the reaction of zinc with hydrochloric acid
   b. the reaction of magnesium with sulfuric acid

6. The following substances act as Brønsted acids in water. Write a chemical equation for each that illustrates its reaction with water.
   a. hydroiodic acid, HI
   b. ammonium ion, NH_4^+
   c. H_2CO_3
   d. HNO_3

7. Give the conjugate base of the following.
   a. HI   c. H_2CO_3
   b. NH_4^+ d. HNO_3

8. The following substances act as Brønsted bases in water. Write a chemical equation for each that illustrates its reaction with water.
   a. cyanide ion, CN^-
   b. oxide ion, O^{2-}
   c. CH_3COO^-
   d. NH_3

9. Give the conjugate acid of the following.
   a. CN^- c. CH_3COO^-
   b. O^{2-} d. NH_3

10. Identify each reactant and each product in these equations as either a Brønsted acid or a Brønsted base.

    a. $HNO_3(aq) + H_2O(l) \rightleftharpoons NO_3^-(aq) + H_3O^+(aq)$

    b. $H_2S(aq) + H_2O(l) \rightleftharpoons HS^-(aq) + H_3O^+(aq)$

11. Which of these bases is stronger, NO_3^- or HS^-? Explain your answer.

12. What does an indicator "indicate"?

◀ **PROBLEM-SOLVING STRATEGY**

Writing a chemical equation, as you did in the previous problem, may help you to identify conjugate acids and bases. (See Strategy, page 244.)

Boxed numbers indicate questions that involve interpretation, application, and analysis.

PART 1
Section 19.3 *continued*

(continued from page T644)

In each reaction, ask students to identify the conjugate acid or base. For each equation, indicate the position of equilibrium, then have students classify the acids and bases as strong or weak. Ask students to compare the conducting properties of each acid or base solution. Students can make a table to summarize their conclusions, using these terms as headings: acid (or base), equilibrium reaction, strength, conducting property, conjugate base (or acid), strength of conjugate base (or acid).

☰ CLOSE

Summing Up Main Ideas

Have students explain how the Arrhenius and Brønsted theories can be used to explain the difference between a strong acid and a weak acid. (Arrhenius: a strong acid produces more hydronium ions in water solutions than a weak acid does. Brønsted: a strong acid donates more hydrogen ions to other substances than a weak acid does.)

PART 1 REVIEW

Assign the Part Review questions.

Evaluating Skills

These skills are evaluated in the Part Review questions indicated.
Comparing/Contrasting: 1, 2, 11; **Observing:** 3; **Describing:** 3; **Determining main ideas:** 3, 4, 12; **Applying a strategy:** 5, 6, 7, 8, 9; **Classifying:** 10

---

    c. HCO_3^- d. NO_3^-

B 8. a. $CN^- + H_2O \rightarrow HCN + OH^-$
   b. $O^{2-} + H_2O \rightarrow OH^- + OH^-$
   c. $CH_3COO^- + H_2O \rightarrow CH_3COOH + OH^-$
   d. $NH_3 + H_2O \rightarrow NH_4^+ + OH^-$

C 9. The conjugate acid is the species formed when these substances gain a proton. These acids are also shown as the first product in the equations written in the last question:

    a. HCN   c. CH_3COOH
    b. OH^- d. NH_4^+

B 10. a. HNO_3 is the proton donor, so it is the acid; H_2O receives the proton, so it is the base.
    NO_3^- = base, H_3O^+ = acid
   b. H_2S is the proton donor (acid); H_2O receives the proton (base).
    HS^- = base, H_3O^+ = acid

B 11. From the position of equilibrium indicated by question 10, HNO_3 is a stronger acid than H_2S. Since stronger acids have weaker conjugate bases, NO_3^- is the weaker base, and HS^- is the stronger base.

A 12. An indicator helps differentiate between an acid and a base by taking on one color in an acid and a different color in a base. Instead of having a color, some indicators may be colorless in one of these two forms.

Developing Skills

Students may apply this skill in their study of Part 2.

Determining main ideas: Have students formulate an operational definition for the neutralization of a sodium hydroxide solution by hydrochloric acid, using litmus as an indicator.

≡ FOCUS

Activate Prior Knowledge

Students may recognize acid-base neutralization reactions as double displacement reactions they learned about in Chapter 3. Have students predict the products of the double displacement reaction between HBr and $Mg(OH)_2$ and write the balanced equation.

$$2HBr + Mg(OH)_2 \rightarrow$$
$$MgBr_2 + 2H_2O$$

≡ TEACH

Science Background

Neutralization

It is easy to confuse the terms "neutralization" and "neutral solution." An acid is neutralized when it is mixed with a stoichiometrically equivalent amount of a base. A neutral solution has a pH of 7. Neutralizations do not necessarily result in neutral solutions. For example, when acetic acid is neutralized with sodium hydroxide, the resulting solution of sodium acetate is basic, because the acetate ion is a weak base.

PART 2 Acid-Base Reactions

Objectives

Part 2

D. **Distinguish** between the nature of the reactants and the nature of the products when a strong acid neutralizes a strong base.

E. **Describe** titration and **calculate** the concentration of an acid or base, using the results of a titration.

What you have learned about acids and bases so far has provided you with the essential tools to begin investigating how acids and bases react with each other. You have learned that the Brønsted definition describes an acid as a substance that donates a proton, and a base as a substance that accepts a proton. This definition also describes the chemical reaction between the two.

Exactly what happens when an acid and a base are mixed together? How could you tell that a chemical reaction has taken place? To answer these questions, let's begin by considering a representative reaction between two common substances found in the laboratory, hydrochloric acid and sodium hydroxide.

19.4 Neutralization

When HCl is mixed with NaOH, an acid-base reaction takes place, forming NaCl and H_2O.

$$HCl(aq) + NaOH(aq) \rightarrow NaCl(aq) + H_2O(l)$$

The mixture resulting from the reaction of HCl with NaOH is shown in Figure 19-7. Does there seem to be any physical evidence of a reaction? The products form a clear, colorless solution that looks the same as the reactants. When you think about it, this observation should not seem surprising. Look again at the products, salt and water. Table salt dissolves readily in water, and since they are the only two products, the result shown in Figure 19-7 is exactly what you would expect. But how can you tell that you now have a solution of sodium chloride rather than a mixture of hydrochloric acid and sodium hydroxide?

Figure 19-7 *When HCl is mixed with NaOH, is there any macroscopic evidence of a reaction?*

Evidence of exothermic reaction In this case, one indication of a reaction can be found by feeling the flasks before and after the reaction. The solution is distinctly warmer after mixing. You could use a thermometer to verify that an exothermic reaction has occurred. However, this observation does not prove that the process was a chemical reaction. Changes in temperature can also accompany physical changes, such as when a solution forms or when a supersaturated solution crystallizes.

Analysis of products What other indication is there that a chemical change has occurred? If you look at the product side of the equation, you should see a clue. Salt dissolved in water is a mixture. If you evaporate the water from a mixture, you can recover the solid and test its properties to see if it is sodium chloride.

There is another, easier way to demonstrate that a chemical reaction has taken place. You can show that the product is neither an acid nor a base. When the resulting solution is tested, red litmus remains red and blue litmus remains blue. If there had been no chemical reaction, the litmus papers would have changed color.

As you might guess, some other properties of the mixture shown in Figure 19-7 have also changed. Magnesium metal does not vigorously react with this mixture. If you were to taste the mixture, you would find it tastes salty rather than sour or bitter. If you were to touch the solution, it would not feel slippery, as bases do. (⚠ *Caution: You should never test an acid-base mixture made in the lab by taste or touch. Some acids and bases and the products of their reactions are toxic or skin irritants or both.*)

Defining neutralization Acids and bases can be considered opposites because their behaviors can be described as either proton donors or proton acceptors. Chemists say that an acid neutralizes a base when the two react completely, leaving no excess acid or base. If you read espionage novels, you may have seen this word before. Spies are sometimes said to be *neutralized* if they are made ineffective. Similarly, when sodium hydroxide neutralizes hydrochloric acid, the resulting solution has neither acidic nor basic properties. Reactions between an acid and a base may be classified as a **neutralization.**

Neutralization may occur between acids and bases other than HCl and NaOH. Some examples are listed in Table 19-3.

TABLE 19-3

Neutralization Reactions
$HCl(aq) + KOH(aq) \rightarrow KCl(aq) + H_2O(l)$
$H_2SO_4(aq) + Mg(OH)_2(s) \rightarrow MgSO_4(aq) + 2H_2O(l)$
$H_2SO_3(aq) + NaOH(aq) \rightarrow NaHSO_3(aq) + H_2O(l)$
$H_2SO_3(aq) + 2NaOH(aq) \rightarrow Na_2SO_3(aq) + 2H_2O(l)$

PROBLEM-SOLVING STRATEGY

Use information you know about the properties of mixtures and compounds to identify the products of the reaction. (See Strategy, page 58.)

PROBLEM-SOLVING STRATEGY

Look for a pattern in this series of chemical equations to see what you can learn about neutralization reactions. (See Strategy, page 100.)

DEMONSTRATION

Cabbage Juice Indicator and Neutralization

Put enough red cabbage into a beaker to fill it. Add distilled water. Bring it to a boil for about five minutes. Decant and save the remaining liquid. Allow it to cool for five minutes. The liquid can be used as an indicator.

Put 40 mL of the juice into a beaker on an overhead projector. Add 10 drops of 1.0*M* HCl, one drop at a time, swirling as acid is added. Then add 20 drops of 1.0*M* NaOH, one drop at a time.

⚠ **CAUTION: Wear safety goggles and a lab apron. Use a shield to protect students.**

Notes: Neutral juice is blue. Decreasing the pH turns it purple, then red. Increasing the pH above 7 will yield a blue-green, then finally a green color. For disposal, neutralize and pour down the drain.

PART **2**
Section 19.5

Resources

You may wish to show The World of Chemistry videotape *Acids and Bases* at this point. The videotape covers the properties of acids and bases, definition of pH, neutralization (including the neutralizing action of antacid tablets), and acid rain.

CONNECTING CONCEPTS

Processes of Science One question commonly asked in chemistry is this: "How much do I have?" Titration is one analytical technique that can be used to answer that question.

DO YOU KNOW?

The concentration of acids and bases can be expressed not only in terms of molarity but also in terms of normality. Normality takes into account the moles of hydrogen ions that can be supplied by an acid and the moles of hydroxide ions that can be supplied by a base.

Do you notice any similarity in the products of these reactions? In each case, two products have formed: One is an ionic compound and the other is water. The ionic products in these reactions are called **salts.**

Complete neutralization   Notice in the last two equations in Table 19-3 that sulfurous acid, H_2SO_3, reacts in different proportions with NaOH to form two different salts. Sodium hydrogen sulfite, $NaHSO_3$, is formed in the first reaction; sodium sulfite, Na_2SO_3, is formed in the second. The salt produced depends on whether the acid reacts with the base in a one-to-one ratio or a one-to-two ratio. Acids that can donate more than one proton are called **polyprotic** acids. In this reaction, sulfurous acid can donate two protons to a base. A reaction in which all of the acidic protons leave the acid, the term *complete neutralization* is used.

19.5 Titrations

You have learned that one question chemists routinely ask about a substance is: How much of it do I have? To answer this question, you can again apply what you already know to answer the question of how much acid or base you have. From previous work in this course and in the laboratory, you know that molarity (moles per liter) is a common way of expressing the concentration of a solution. In addition, if you know both the molarity and the volume of a sample of an acid or base, you can calculate the number of moles.

What if you do not know the concentration? You could find it experimentally by using what you know about acid-base reactions and by applying the principles of stoichiometry that you have practiced several times in this course.

Determining concentration experimentally   Suppose you have a sample of hydrochloric acid of unknown concentration. If you react the acid with a known concentration and volume of sodium hydroxide, this neutralization reaction happens.

$$HCl(aq) + NaOH(aq) \rightarrow NaCl(aq) + H_2O(l)$$

According to this balanced equation, there is a 1-to-1 mole relationship between hydrochloric acid and sodium hydroxide as they react. For every *one* mole of hydrochloric acid that reacts, *one* mole of sodium hydroxide reacts. *Five* moles of hydrochloric acid reacts with *five* moles of sodium hydroxide, *ten* moles of hydrochloric acid reacts with *ten* moles of sodium hydroxide, and so forth. When you have added just enough sodium hydroxide (and no more) to react completely with a sample of the acid, then you have reached the **equivalence point.** If you know the number of moles of base used to reach the equivalence point, you can calculate the number of moles of acid you began with.

Using a buret In the laboratory, you carry out this reaction with a buret, as shown in Figure 19-8. The buret is helpful in two ways. First, it lets you conveniently measure the volume of the base that you use. Second, the flow of base into the sample of acid can be precisely controlled. At the bottom of the buret is a stopcock, which can be opened fully to let the base flow quickly into the acid, opened partially to let the base flow slowly, and closed completely to stop the flow of the base, as shown in Figure 19-9.

Figure 19-9 *Note the position of the stopcock. Horizontal is "closed," while "vertical" is open.*

Figure 19-8 *Most simple titrations involve the use of burets.*

How do you know when you have reached the equivalence point? That is, how do you know that you have added just enough base to react with all of the acid? Indicators are useful in answering these questions. Phenolphthalein, as you have already seen, is colorless in an acid and pink in a base. One or two drops of this indicator can be put into the sample of HCl before you add the base. Before you reach the equivalence point, not all of the acid has reacted. The solution remains colorless. When you reach the equivalence point, all of the acid is gone and no excess base is present. As soon as you have surpassed the equivalence point by the smallest amount (by one drop or less), excess (unreacted) sodium hydroxide begins to accumulate. The solution turns pink. When you obtain a pink color that will not disappear as you swirl the solution, you stop adding NaOH and read the buret to determine the volume of base you used.

Calculating the answer This process of gradually adding one reactant from a buret to another reactant until a color change signals that equivalent amounts of reactants have been reacted is called **titration.** You can combine information about the volume of NaOH used in the titration and its concentration (which is known) to calculate the number of moles of NaOH needed to reach the equivalence point. The balanced equation helps you determine how many moles of the acid must have originally been present. The following Example illustrates how you can use the results of a titration to determine the concentration of an acid.

EXAMPLE 19-1

When 42.5 mL of 1.03 *M* NaOH is added to 50.0 mL of vinegar (a solution of acetic acid, CH_3COOH), the phenolphthalein in the solution just turns pink. What is the concentration of the acetic acid in vinegar?

■ ***Analyze the Problem*** You know that when the first pink color of phenolphthalein appears, you have reached the point of the titration at which the number of moles of acid is stoichiometrically equivalent to the number of moles of added base. Therefore, you can reason that if you find the number of moles of NaOH used to neutralize the moles of acetic acid in 50.0 mL of vinegar, you can calculate the concentration of the acetic acid.

■ ***Apply a Strategy*** Diagram a road map and look for relationships that can be used to calculate what you want to find. The road map will also help you organize your work.

42.5 mL of 1.03 *M* NaOH   *M* of CH_3COOH

$$\frac{1 \text{ L NaOH}}{1000 \text{ mL NaOH}}$$

liters of NaOH

$$\frac{1.03 \text{ moles NaOH}}{1 \text{ L NaOH}}$$ $$\frac{\text{moles } CH_3COOH}{\text{liter of soln}}$$

moles of NaOH $$\frac{1 \text{ mole } CH_3COOH}{1 \text{ mole NaOH}}$$ moles of CH_3COOH

■ ***Work a Solution*** Do the calculations indicated on the road map in steps. Begin by calculating the number of moles of NaOH involved in the reaction. Since molarity is defined as moles per liter, convert 42.5 mL to liters.

$$42.5 \text{ mL NaOH} \times \frac{1 \text{ L}}{1000 \text{ mL NaOH}} = 0.0425 \text{ L NaOH}$$

PROBLEM·SOLVING

S T R A T E G Y

Break the problem down into manageable steps by using a road map to understand it better. (See Strategy, page 166.)

PROBLEM·SOLVING

S T R A T E G Y

Use the factor-label method to help you set up your mathematical statements. Make sure units cancel to give you the units you need in your answer. (See Strategy, page 2.)

Next use the definition of molarity (moles/liter) to determine the number of moles of NaOH in 0.0425 L of a 1.03M solution.

$$0.0425 \, \cancel{L} \times \frac{1.03 \text{ mol}}{1 \, \cancel{L}} = 0.0438 \text{ mol NaOH}$$

To determine the ratio in which the acid and base react, write the balanced equation.

$$\text{NaOH} + \text{CH}_3\text{COOH} \rightarrow \text{H}_2\text{O} + \text{CH}_3\text{COONa}$$

Since the ratio of sodium hydroxide to acetic acid is one to one, there must also have been 0.0438 mol of acetic acid in the vinegar.

$$0.0438 \, \cancel{\text{mol NaOH}} \times \frac{1 \text{ mol CH}_3\text{COOH}}{1 \, \cancel{\text{mol NaOH}}} = 0.0438 \text{ mol CH}_3\text{COOH}$$

Now you can calculate the molarity of the vinegar. Since you have data in mL, convert that to L and divide the number of moles by the volume.

$$50.0 \, \cancel{\text{mL}} \times \frac{1 \text{ L}}{1000 \, \cancel{\text{mL}}} = 0.0500 \text{ L}$$

$$\frac{0.0438 \text{ mol CH}_3\text{COOH}}{0.0500 \text{ L}} = 0.876 \, M$$

■ **Verify Your Answer** First estimate to see if your answer is reasonable. Notice that the volume of vinegar is slightly *greater* than that of the sodium hydroxide solution. You would expect it to be slightly *less concentrated* than the NaOH, and your answer is consistent with this estimate. Now work the problem in reverse by calculating the concentration of NaOH in a 42.5-mL solution if 50.0 mL of 0.876M vinegar must be added to just turn the solution pink. If the answer just calculated is correct, you should get an answer of 1.03M for sodium hydroxide, which is the molarity given in the original problem.

Practice Problems

13. In a titration of another sample of vinegar, you find that it requires 11.10 mL of 0.748M NaOH to neutralize a 10.0-mL sample of vinegar. What is the concentration of acetic acid in this sample of vinegar? **Ans.** 0.830M

14. What is the concentration of acid in rainwater when 100.0 mL is titrated with 25.12 mL of 0.00105M NaOH? Since acid rain contains several acids, use the symbol HA to represent the acids that are present.

PROBLEM-SOLVING
S T R A T E G Y

Use what you know about neutralization reactions to write this equation. Remember that a neutralization reaction produces a salt and water. (See Strategy, page 58.)

PART **2**
Section 19.5 *continued*

Practice Problems

Assign the Practice Problems.

Guided Practice

Have students replace the 10.0-mL vinegar sample with a 10.0-mL sample of sulfuric acid in Practice Problem 13 on page 651. (Answer: 0.415)

Reteaching Idea

Titration problems provide an opportunity to review stoichiometry problems. To help students solve these problems, advise them to draw a solution road map before they calculate an answer. Have students draw road maps for Practice Problems 13 and 14 (page 651). Ask them to share their road maps with each other.

PART **2**
Section 19.5 *continued*

☰ CLOSE

Summing Up Main Ideas

Have students write a balanced equation for the reaction between stomach acid (HCl) and milk of magnesia [Mg(OH)$_2$]. Also, ask students to determine the volume of 0.11M HCl that is neutralized by 10.0 mL of 0.25M Mg(OH)$_2$.

[2HCl + Mg(OH)$_2$ → MgCl$_2$ + 2HOH]

0.0100$\cancel{L}$ × 0.25 mol /$\cancel{L}$

= 2.5 × 10^{-3} mol of Mg(OH)$_2$

2.5 × 10^{-3} $\cancel{\text{mol Mg(OH)}_2}$

× $\dfrac{2 \text{ mol HCL}}{1 \text{ mol Mg(OH)}_2}$

= 5.0 × 10^{-3} mol of HCL

$\dfrac{5 \times 10^{-3} \cancel{\text{mol}}}{0.11 \cancel{\text{mol}}/L}$ = 0.045 L = 45 mL

PART 2 REVIEW

Assign the Part Review questions.

Evaluating Skills

These skills are evaluated in the Part Review questions indicated. **Classifying:** 15, 17; **Analyzing data:** 16, 18; **Determining main ideas:** 19; **Calculating:** 20, 23, 24; **Applying a strategy:** 21, 23, 24; **Determining sources of error:** 22; **Verifying results:** 23, 24

PART 2 REVIEW

15. The following unbalanced equation represents the complete neutralization of phosphoric acid, H$_3$PO$_4$, with magnesium hydroxide, Mg(OH)$_2$.

    $\underline{?}$ H$_3$PO$_4$(aq) + $\underline{?}$ Mg(OH)$_2$(aq) →

    $\underline{?}$ Mg$_3$(PO$_4$)$_2$$^+$(s) + $\underline{?}$ H$_2$O(l)

    a. Complete this equation by balancing it.
    b. Identify the salt in this equation.

> **PROBLEM·SOLVING STRATEGY**
>
> *Use what you know* about neutralization reactions to answer this question. (See Strategy, page 58.)

16. Write the balanced equation for the neutralization of the following acids with potassium hydroxide, KOH.
    a. HCl
    b. CH$_3$COOH

17. Identify the salts in the equations you wrote in the last question. Can either of these salts also act as a base? If so, which one(s)?

18. Suppose you wanted to make potassium bromide by using an acid-base reaction. Which acid and which base would you use? Write the equation for the reaction.

19. What is meant by the term *equivalence point*?

> **PROBLEM·SOLVING STRATEGY**
>
> This problem is easier to solve if you **break it into parts** as stated by the question. (See Strategy, page 166.)

20. Write the equation representing the complete neutralization of sulfuric acid with potassium hydroxide. If you have a sample containing 2.5 moles of sulfuric acid, then how many moles of potassium hydroxide must be added to reach the equivalence point? ***Ans.*** 5.0 moles KOH

21. One brand of antacid tablets contains calcium carbonate as its active ingredient. You could use the process of titration to determine the mass of calcium carbonate in each tablet. Which of these two substances would you use to titrate calcium carbonate: hydrochloric acid or sodium hydroxide? Explain your answer.

22. You and a friend are both carrying out a titration to determine the concentration of acetic acid in the same bottle of vinegar. Your friend claims that you must both use the same size sample of vinegar if you are to both come up with the same concentration when you finish. Do you agree with this claim? Explain your answer.

23. What is the concentration of 50.0 mL of a sodium hydroxide solution that is neutralized by 30.0 mL of 0.500M HCl? ***Ans.*** 0.300M

24. What is the concentration of NH$_3$ in household ammonia if 48.25 mL of 0.5248M HCl is needed to neutralize 22.00 mL of the ammonia? ***Ans.*** 1.151M

Boxed numbers indicate questions that involve interpretation, application, and analysis.

PART 2 REVIEW

ANSWERS

■ **Keyed to Objectives**

D 15. a. 2H$_3$PO$_4$ + 3Mg(OH)$_2$ →

Mg$_3$(PO$_4$)$_2$ + 6H$_2$O

b. magnesium phosphate, Mg$_3$(PO$_4$)$_2$

D 16. a. HCl + KOH → KCl + H$_2$O

b. HC$_2$H$_3$O$_2$ + KOH → KC$_2$H$_3$O$_2$ + H$_2$O

D 17. The salts are potassium chloride, KCl, and potassium acetate, KC$_2$H$_3$O$_2$. Since the acetate ion is the conjugate base of a weak acid, the salt potassium acetate is also a base. Potassium chloride, however, is not a base, since the chloride ion is the conjugate base of a strong acid.

E 18. You may obtain the potassium ion from the base potassium hydroxide, KOH, and you may obtain the bromide ion from hydrobromic acid, HBr. The equation for this reaction is

HBr + KOH → KBr + H$_2$O

D 19. The term *equivalence point* refers to the point during a neutralization reaction at which just enough base (but no more) has been added to react completely with all the acid originally present.

PART **3** pH and Acid-Base Equilibrium

You have just learned some of the reactions that acids and bases undergo. But acids and bases are also important because they can influence other reactions. The chemical reactions occurring in the cells in your body depend greatly on the hydrogen ion concentration. This dependence is why the acid-base balance of the body must be regulated precisely. The normal $[H_3O^+]$ is $4 \times 10^{-8}M$. Even in times of illness, the $[H_3O^+]$ almost never becomes greater than $10 \times 10^{-8}M$ or less than $1.6 \times 10^{-8}M$.

Chemists have found that $[H_3O^+]$ concentrations have a wide range and, as in the case of cells, can be extremely small. To get some idea of the range of $[H_3O^+]$ concentrations, try to imagine spreading out 100 million sheets of typing paper. They would cover 6 km^2; or said another way, they would cover a square measuring about 2.46 km on each side. Now compare the size of one tenth of the period at the end of this sentence with that huge square of typing paper. The difference in size is comparable to the difference in hydrogen ion concentrations that can occur in water solutions. In this part of the chapter, you will see how such a wide range of concentrations can be represented and how reaction equilibrium concepts can be used to understand that representation.

19.6 pH Scale and Indicators

To illustrate difficulties in trying to represent something that varies over a wide range of values, let's look at some data representing the $[H_3O^+]$ during the neutralization of a $1M$ solution of NaOH with a $1M$ solution of HCl. You start with 100 mL of the $1M$ NaOH solution. The $1M$ HCl is added a little at a time until all of the NaOH has reacted and there is an excess of HCl. Each time some of the acid is added, the $[H_3O^+]$ of the solution is measured with a pH meter like that shown in Figure 19-10. Figure 19-11 is an

Figure 19-10 A pH meter measures changes in $[H_3O^+]$ in the lab, but it is also used in environmental studies to monitor the acidity of water.

Objectives
Part 3

F. Apply the concept of pH to the description of acid and base solutions.

G. Interpret the pH scale using the ion-product constant of water, K_w.

H. Compare the strengths of acids using the acid dissociation constant, K_a.

I. Explain how a buffer works to prevent changes in pH.

Developing Skills

Students may apply this skill in their study of Part 3.

Interpreting diagrams: Ask students to compare the graphs in Figures 19–11, 19–12, and 19–13. What are the advantages and disadvantages of using a logarithmic scale?

≣ FOCUS

Activate Prior Knowledge

Students are familiar with neutralization and titration from Part 2 of this chapter. Prepare $1M$ solutions of HCl and NaOH.

⚠ **CAUTION: Everyone must wear safety goggles and lab aprons.**
Have students add 10 ml of $1M$ HCl to an evaporating dish. Add two drops of bromthymol blue to the acid and observe the color (yellow). Add the NaOH dropwise to the HCl until the solution turns green. Have students record the volume of NaOH added. Ask students how the volume of $1M$ NaOH added to make the solution green compares with the initial volume of $1M$ HCl.

D **20.** $H_2SO_4 + 2KOH \rightarrow$
$$2H_2O + K_2SO_4$$
$$2.5 \text{ mol } H_2SO_4 \times \frac{2 \text{ mol KOH}}{\text{mol } H_2SO_4}$$
$$= 5.0 \text{ mol KOH}$$

D **21.** If you are planning on doing this titration by adding a substance that reacts directly with the calcium carbonate, then you should choose an acid (such as HCl), because calcium carbonate is a base.

E **22.** This claim is not true. The concentration of the vinegar is the same no matter what size sample you choose. If your sample is larger than your friend's then you will use more base to titrate your vinegar.

D **23.** $HCl + NaOH \rightarrow NaCl + H_2O$
$$30 \text{ mL HCl} \times \frac{1 \text{ L}}{1000 \text{ mL}}$$
$$\times \frac{0.500 \text{ mol HCl}}{1 \text{ L HCl}} \times \frac{1 \text{ mol NaOH}}{1 \text{ mol HCl}}$$
$$= 0.0150 \text{ mol NaOH}$$

$$\frac{0.0150 \text{ mol NaOH}}{0.0500 \text{ L NaOH}} = 0.300M$$

D **24.** $HCl + NH_3 \rightarrow NH_4^+ + Cl^-$
$$48.25 \text{ mL HCl} \times \frac{1 \text{ L}}{1000 \text{ mL}}$$
$$\times \frac{0.5248 \text{ mol HCl}}{1 \text{ L HCl}} \times \frac{1 \text{ mol } NH_3}{1 \text{ mol HCl}}$$
$$= 0.02532 \text{ mol } NH_3$$
$$\frac{0.02532 \text{ mol } NH_3}{0.02200 \text{ L } NH_3} = 1.151M$$

≡ TEACH

Teaching Strategy

pH and Acid-Base Equilibrium

Understanding the vast range of concentrations of the hydronium ion is critical for understanding the need for a pH scale. Ask your students to develop other analogies similar to that in the introduction in Part 3.

Figure 19-11 *The data from Table 19-4 are graphed to show the change in hydronium ion concentration as 1M HCl is added to 1M NaOH. On this scale it appears that there is no change in [H₃O⁺] until 100 mL of the acid have been added.*

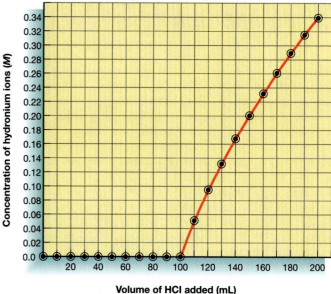

Graph of H₃O⁺ conc. vs. vol of HCl

attempt to plot a graph of these data. The $[H_3O^+]$ is shown along the y-axis, and the volume of HCl added is shown along the x-axis.

The problem in analyzing these data is selecting a scale for the $[H_3O^+]$ that will allow you to place all of the data on a single graph and still give an accurate picture of what is taking place. Figure 19-11 shows a graph that includes all of the data points, but the scale is so large that there appears to be no change in the $[H_3O^+]$ until

TABLE 19-4

[H₃O⁺] as 1M HCl Is Added to 100 mL of 1M NaOH			
Volume of HCl added (mL)	[H₃O⁺]	Volume of HCl added (mL)	[H₃O⁺]
0	1.0×10^{-14}	99.99	2.0×10^{-10}
10	1.2×10^{-14}	100	1.0×10^{-7}
20	1.4×10^{-14}	100.01	5.0×10^{-5}
30	1.8×10^{-14}	100.1	5.0×10^{-4}
40	2.3×10^{-14}	101	5.0×10^{-3}
50	3.0×10^{-14}	105	2.4×10^{-2}
60	4.0×10^{-14}	110	4.8×10^{-2}
70	5.6×10^{-14}	120	9.1×10^{-2}
80	9.1×10^{-14}	130	1.3×10^{-1}
90	2.0×10^{-13}	140	1.7×10^{-1}
95	3.8×10^{-13}	150	2.0×10^{-1}
99	2.0×10^{-12}	200	3.3×10^{-1}
99.9	2.0×10^{-11}		

 DEMONSTRATION

pH Scale

Using a pH meter, show students how the pH changes from the beginning to the equivalence point and beyond as an acid is titrated with a base. To provide some variety from the text, you may wish to use fruit juice (undiluted) or nitric acid with ammonia. Acids and bases should be 0.1M or less.

CAUTION: Wear safety goggles and a lab apron. Use a shield to protect students. As you carry out the titration, have students write data on the board and ask them to prepare a graph showing the results. At various points on their graph, ask them to calculate what the hydronium ion concentration is from the pH you measured.

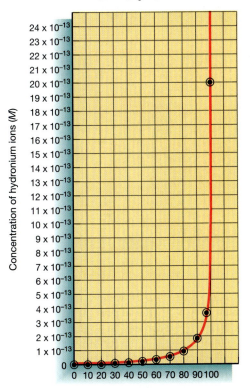

Graph of [H₃O⁺] vs. vol of HCl

Concentration of hydronium ions (M)

Volume of HCl added (mL)

Figure 19-12 *A portion of the graph in Figure 19-11 is plotted using a different scale for the hydronium ion concentration. Note that the hydronium ion concentration changes rapidly when 90–100 mL of acid are added. Using this scale makes it difficult to get all the data from Table 19-4 on a conveniently sized graph.*

Teaching Strategy

Using a Logarithmic Scale

To give students a better idea of the use of log scales (similar to pH scales), point out other log scales in common use, such as decibels for measuring sound intensity (a 10-unit increase in the decibel level corresponds to a tenfold increase in intensity) or the Richter scale for reporting the intensity of an earthquake (in which a one-unit increase in the Richter value corresponds to a tenfold increase in intensity).

100 mL of HCl has been added. Looking at Table 19-4, you know that this is not the case. The $[H_3O^+]$ had doubled by the time 30 mL of acid had been added, and it had increased tenfold by the time 90 mL of acid had been added. This change does not show on the graph in Figure 19-11. The only way to make it show is to use a different scale.

Figure 19-12 shows the data from Table 19-4 plotted with a new scale. Now the change in $[H_3O^+]$ that occurs during the addition of the first 99 mL of acid can be seen. The problem is that the rest of the data cannot be shown. Is it possible to select a scale that shows the changes taking place and gets all the data on the graph?

Using a logarithmic scale One solution to this problem is to transform the wide range of values to a logarithmic scale. The **logarithm** of a number is the power to which 10 must be raised to equal that number. An increase of 1 in the logarithm of a number represents a tenfold increase in the number.

The $[H_3O^+]$ after 90 mL of acid was added is shown as $2.0 \times 10^{-13} M$, and the logarithm of that number is -12.7. When 99 mL of acid had been added, the $[H_3O^+]$ had increased 10 times

PROBLEM-SOLVING

S T R A T E G Y

Use what you know *from algebra to interpret logarithms.*
$\log 2 \times 10^{-13}$ *is*
$\log 2 + \log 10^{-13} =$
$.3 - 13 = -12.7$ *(See Strategy, page 58.)*

DEMONSTRATION

pH and Ion Concentration

Students have a difficult time understanding pH and ion concentration. Use a pulley and string to represent the idea of (pH + pOH) = 14. Then the idea of H_3O^+ increasing as OH^- decreases can be understood.

One drawback of this visual system is that it indicates the relationship is linear rather than logarithmic.

The demonstration can be used throughout acid-base concepts.
$$pH + pOH = 14$$
$$K_w = 1.00 \times 10^{-14} \text{ at } 25°C$$
At a pH of 7 $[H_3O^+] = [OH^-]$
$$= 1.0 \times 10^{-7} \text{ mol/L}$$
$$pH = -\log[H_3O^+]$$

Figure 19-13 *In this graph, the hydronium ion concentrations now appear as logarithms. All the data from Table 19-4 now fit on a conveniently sized graph. Note that the logarithms are all negative giving a graph that does not have its origin in the lower left corner.*

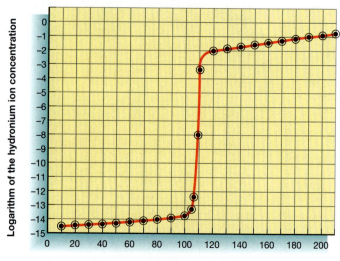

Graph of log H_3O^+ vs. vol of HCl

to a value of $2.0 \times 10^{-12}M$. However, the logarithm increased only 1 to a value of -11.7 (the log of 2.0×10^{-12}).

When the $[H_3O^+]$ recorded in Table 19-3 varies from 0.000 000 000 000 01 to 0.33 (a factor of over 10 million million), the log $[H_3O^+]$ changes only from -14 to nearly 0. Although the $[H_3O^+]$ cannot be represented conveniently on a graph, the log $[H_3O^+]$ can be. The data are plotted again in Figure 19-13. Note that the changes in $[H_3O^+]$ during the early stages of the addition of acid are shown and that all of the data are plotted.

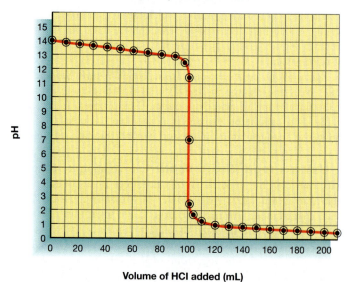

Graph of pH vs. vol of HCl

Figure 19-14 *Using the pH scale the data from Table 19-4 can be plotted showing a graph with its origin in the lower left corner.*

Dealing with negative logs Can you identify one thing that is inconvenient about the graph shown in Figure 19-13? All of the values for the log $[H_3O^+]$ are negative. You are probably more accustomed to working with positive numbers.

Any time the log of the hydronium ion concentration is represented, you are likely to get a negative number. In most analytical experiments involving acids, the hydronium ion concentration is seldom greater than $1M$, so the log $[H_3O^+]$ is usually negative. (The logarithm of any number between 1 and 0 is negative.) Not willing to bother with negative numbers all the time, chemists defined a term to describe the log of the hydronium ion concentration. The term is **pH**.

$$pH = -\log [H_3O^+]$$

Since the logarithm of the hydronium ion concentration is almost always negative, minus the logarithm of the hydronium ion concentration is almost always positive. The log $[H_3O^+]$ and pH are the same numeral but with opposite signs. As a result, as $[H_3O^+]$ increases, the pH value decreases (-5 is larger than -6, but $+5$ is less than $+6$). With pH, you can use positive numbers and plot graphs in the upper right quadrant, where you are more accustomed to seeing them.

Figure 19-14 shows the data from Table 19-4 expressed as pH. It is just like Figure 19-13 but rotated 180° on the x-axis. (It is what you would see in a mirror placed along the x-axis of Figure 19-13.)

The midpoint of the pH scale is labeled as 7. Acid solutions have a pH less than 7 while basic solutions have a pH greater than 7. Table 19-5 lists pH values for some common substances. In the next section of the chapter, you will learn how the value of 7 was determined to represent neutrality.

Concept ✓ Check

In your own words, explain why a logarithmic scale is used to change $[H_3O^+]$ values into pH values.

DO YOU KNOW?

Flowers are sensitive to the pH of the soil in different ways. Hydrangeas, for example, produce blue flowers when grown in an acid soil and pink blossoms when grown in an alkaline soil.

TABLE 19-5

pH Values for Some Common Substances*			
pH	**Substance**	**pH**	**Substance**
1	gastric (stomach) juice	7	pure water
2	lemon juice	7.4	human blood
3	grapefruit, soft drinks	8	seawater
4	tomato juice	10	soap and detergent
6	cow's milk		solutions

* Note that the values listed represent an average point in a pH range for each material. For example, tomato juice has a pH that ranges from 4 to 4.5. Detergent solutions can vary from 9.5 to 10.5.

Myths and Misconceptions

Students often confuse *pH* and *acidity*. This can lead to further difficulty in interpreting the pH scale. For example, students may think that a "low pH" must mean a weak acid and vice versa. Stress that pH means percent $[H_3O^+]$. Clarify its numerical value as $-\log [H_3O^+]$. Make sure that students understand that a log is an exponent, as well as the difference between *log* and *antilog*.

PART **3**
Section 19.6 continued

Practice Problems
Assign the Practice Problems.

EXAMPLE 19-2

What is the pH of a 0.01M nitric acid solution, HNO_3? Nitric acid is a strong acid.

■ **Analyze the Problem** Recognize that since nitric acid is a strong acid, it ionizes nearly 100% in solution. The equation for the ionization is

$$HNO_3 + H_2O \rightarrow H_3O^+(aq) + NO_3^-(aq)$$

One mole of HNO_3 produces one mole of H_3O^+ ions. Therefore, $0.01M$ HNO_3 produces a solution that is $0.01M$ in $H_3O^+(aq)$.

■ **Apply a Strategy** In this case, the strategy is to use the definition of pH to solve the problem.

■ **Work a Solution** Write the $[H_3O^+]$ in scientific notation.

$$[H_3O^+] = 0.01M = 1 \times 10^{-2}M$$

By definition,

$$
\begin{aligned}
pH &= -\log [H_3O^+] \\
&= -\log (1 \times 10^{-2}) \\
&= -(\log 1 + \log 10^{-2}) \\
&= -(0 + -2.0) \\
pH &= -(-2.0) = 2.0
\end{aligned}
$$

■ **Verify Your Answer** Since you know from the problem statement that the solution is acidic, you could have estimated that the pH was less than 7. Your answer is consistent with that prediction.

> **PROBLEM-SOLVING**
> **STRATEGY**
>
> *You can **use a calculator** to obtain this answer. With most calculators, you will enter 1×10^{-2}, press the log key, change the sign, and the display should read 2. (See Strategy, page 134.)*

> **PROBLEM-SOLVING**
> **STRATEGY**
>
> ***Making an estimate** can be helpful in judging the correctness of your answer, especially when you are working with new and unfamiliar concepts. (See Strategy, page 125.)*

Practice Problems

25. What is the pH of a $0.05M$ solution of hydrochloric acid, HCl? Hydrochloric acid is a strong acid.　　**Ans.** 1.3

26. Find the pH of a solution whose H_3O^+ concentration is
    a. $0.1M$;
    b. $1.0 \times 10^{-7}M$;
    c. $2.55 \times 10^{-3}M$.　　**Ans. a.** 1.0　**b.** 7.00　**c.** 2.593

Hydronium ion concentration from pH You have just learned how to find the pH of any solution by calculating the negative log of the hydronium ion concentration. It is also useful to be able to go in the opposite direction—calculate the hydronium ion concentration in a solution from its pH. The $[H_3O^+]$ is the antilog of $-pH$, or the number whose logarithm is $-pH$. Example 19-3 provides you with an illustration.

EXAMPLE 19-3

What is the H_3O^+ concentration of a solution that has a pH of 3?

- **Analyze the Problem** Recognize that this problem is the reverse of Example 19-2. You need to determine how to convert from pH to concentration.

- **Apply a Strategy** Use the concept of antilogs to solve this problem. The antilog of a number is the number equal to 10 raised to the power of a given number.

$$\text{antilog } x = 10^x$$

- **Work a Solution**

$$\text{pH} = -\log[H_3O^+] = 3$$
$$= \log[H_3O^+] = -3$$
$$[H_3O^+] = \text{antilog of } -3$$
$$[H_3O^+] = 10^{-3}M = 1 \times 10^{-3}M$$

- **Verify Your Answer** Start with a concentration of $1 \times 10^{-3}M$ and find the pH. Your answer should be a pH of 3.

Practice Problems

27. Find the value of $[H_3O^+]$ in a solution that has a pH of 2.
    Ans. $1 \times 10^{-2}M$

28. Find the value of $[H_3O^+]$ in a solution that has a pH of 13.
    Ans. $1 \times 10^{-13}M$

PROBLEM-SOLVING STRATEGY

You can **use a calculator** if it has log and antilog functions to solve this problem. Enter -3, press the INV and log keys, and the display will read 0.001. (See Strategy, page 134.)

Indicators You have learned that indicators can be used to identify an acid from a base by a color change. The color change is due to the changing proportion of the indicator molecules in the acid or base form. This changing of proportions occurs over various pH values as shown in Figure 19-15.

Look at methyl orange in Figure 19-15. You find that when the pH is 3 or less, the color is red. This is because virtually all of the methyl orange molecules have hydrogen ions attached and are in the acid form which is red. Also notice that when the pH is 5 or greater, the color is yellow. This is because almost all of the methyl orange molecules have donated a proton to another more basic substance. Having donated a proton, the methyl orange molecules are in their base form which is yellow. At a pH of about 4, there are almost equal numbers of molecules in the acid form (red) and the base form (yellow) and the color is orange, the color obtained when red and yellow are mixed. The pH range over which the color changes is the transition range of the indicator. More precise pH

PART 3
Section 19.6 continued

Practice Problems

Assign the Practice Problems.

DO YOU KNOW?

The pOH can be calculated just like the pH, with the relationship $pOH = -\log[OH^-]$. If you know the pH, you can also find the pOH, using the relationship that $pH + pOH = 14$.

PART **3**

Section 19.6 continued

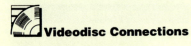

Videodisc Connections

3535 to 3539, side 5
Ammonia fountain: molecular
graphics (5-frame seq.)

376 to 3534, side 5
Multicolor ammonia fountain
(movie)

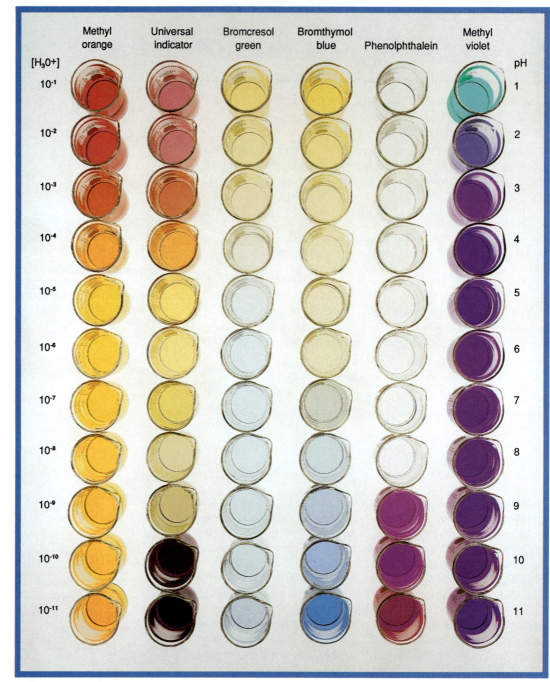

Figure 19-15 Acid-base indicators show a wide range of colors in solutions with different $[H_3O^+]$ concentrations.

measurements show that the transition range for methyl orange is between pH 3.2 and 4.4.

Figure 19-16 shows the transition range for six indicators. Notice that all six of the indicators change color between the point where 99.90 mL of HCl has been added to the 100.00 mL of NaOH and the point where 100.10 mL have been added. The difference between 99.90 mL and 100.10 mL is about 4 drops of acid added. Therefore, any of the indicators can be used to determine the equivalence point for the HCl titration of NaOH.

Concept ✔ Check

In one or two sentences, explain how an indicator works.

DO YOU KNOW?

Some everyday substances are also indicators. If you boil a red cabbage in water, you extract a dye that turns different colors in acids and bases. Some colored sheets of paper (or even colored clothing!) also change color if an acid or a base is applied.

Look Back

Acid-Base Equilibrium: K_w and K_a
This chapter does not describe how to use K_a values or how to compute K_a values from equilibrium concentrations. The background for doing equilibrium calculations such as these has already been covered in Chapter 18. If you would like your students to do such calculations, you may wish to assign them question 84 at the end of this chapter. In addition, you may wish to assign some problems similar to these:
1. What is the hydronium ion concentration of a 0.010M acetic acid solution?
($4.2 \times 10^{-4}M$)
2. What is the pH of a 0.10M HCN solution? (5.10)

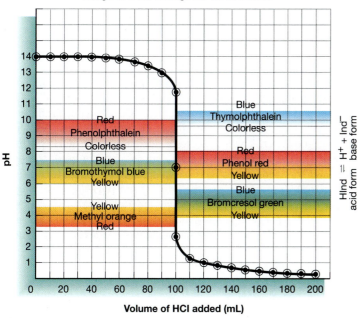

Range of Color Change for Six Indicators

Figure 19-16 *The pH range over which six indicators change color. Note that all of these indicators change color in the region of rapid change in pH.*

19.7 Acid-Base Equilibrium: K_w and K_a

If you tested pure water with a pH meter, you would find it has a pH of 7.00, or a value of $1.00 \times 10^{-7}M$ for its $[H_3O^+]$. This may seem surprising. How can $[H_3O^+]$ form if no acid has been added to water? Water undergoes a self-ionization reaction, where it acts simultaneously as the acid and the base.

$$H_2O(l) + H_2O(l) \rightleftharpoons H_3O^+(aq) + OH^-(aq)$$

This equation represents an equilibrium in which there are far more reactants than products. You have already learned to write

CONNECTING CONCEPTS

Models The concept of equilibrium as applied to acid-base reactions is a model used to explain macroscopic observations and to make predictions for other acid-base reactions.

an equilibrium constant expression for such reactions. Do not forget that the concentrations of liquids such as H_2O are typically omitted from these expressions, as shown here.

$$K_w = [H_3O^+][OH^-]$$

The value for K_w at 25°C is 1.00×10^{-14}. Thus,

$$[H_3O^+][OH^-] = 1.00 \times 10^{-14}$$

K_w is the usual way K_{eq} for the ionization of water is expressed. Notice how small the value for K_w is. This information is consistent with what you have just learned about this reaction: Its position of equilibrium lies far to the left. When water ionizes, it forms as many hydronium ions as hydroxide ions. Looking back at the chemical equation, you will see that H_3O^+ and OH^- are in a 1-to-1 mole ratio. Since $[H_3O^+] = [OH^-]$ in pure water, you may substitute in the equation to obtain

$$[H_3O^+][H_3O^+] = 1.00 \times 10^{-14}$$

Taking the square root of each side you find

$$[H_3O^+] = 1.00 \times 10^{-7}M$$

PROBLEM·SOLVING STRATEGY

Use what you know about inverse proportions to recognize that as $[H_3O^+]$ increases then $[OH^-]$ must decrease and vice versa.

Changes in $[H_3O^+]$ and $[OH^-]$ In pure water, the concentrations of H_3O^+ and OH^- are equal. But what happens if NaOH or gaseous HCl is added to the water? HCl acts as a strong acid when it dissolves in water, forming H_3O^+ and Cl^- ions. All acids increase the $[H_3O^+]$, which causes a decrease in the $[OH^-]$ of the system. On the other hand, NaOH acts as a strong base, forming OH^- and Na^+ ions. Bases increase the $[OH^-]$ and cause a decrease of the $[H_3O^+]$. In both cases, the $[H_3O^+]$ and $[OH^-]$ are no longer equal. Although their *concentrations* are not equal, experiments show that for every aqueous solution, the product of $[H_3O^+]$ and $[OH^-]$ remains the same. This means that K_w is a constant. When

Figure 19-17 *From the number line for pH note that as pH increases $[H_3O^+]$ decreases. What is the relationship between pH and $[OH^-]$? What value does pH + pOH always equal for a given $[H_3O^+]$?*

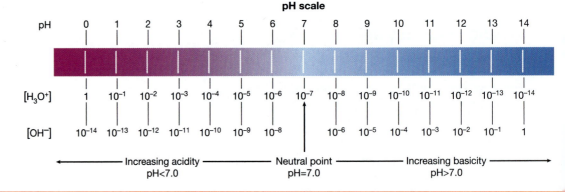

the temperature is 25.0°C, the product has this value.

$$K_w = [H_3O^+][OH^-] = 1.00 \times 10^{-14}$$

The relationship among $[H_3O^+]$, $[OH^-]$, and pH is shown in Figure 19-17.

Concept ✔ Check

Using Figure 19-17 as a guide, write a mathematical relationship between pH and pOH.

Acid dissociation constant Hydrofluoric acid, HF, is a weak acid whose hydronium ion concentration is unknown. The equation for the ionization of HF is

$$HF(aq) + H_2O(l) \rightleftharpoons H_3O^+(aq) + F^-(aq)$$

You can write the equilibrium constant expression just as you did for water by dividing the product concentrations by the reactant concentrations. Remember to leave out the liquid, $H_2O(l)$, from this expression.

$$K_a = \frac{[H_3O^+][F^-]}{[HF]}$$

Acid dissociation constants for various acids are listed in Table 19-6. K_a is the usual way to express K_{eq} for the ionization of a weak acid just as K_w is the way K_{eq} is expressed for water. The numerical value of K_a indicates the ability of an acid to donate a proton. The larger the value, the greater that ability.

Table 19-6 does not show K_a values for strong acids, because their ionization reaction with water is very nearly complete. You may consider any strong acid as if it has totally formed H_3O^+ ions and its conjugate base.

PROBLEM·SOLVING STRATEGY

Use what you already know about equilibrium to find a useful expression for the equilibrium of a weak acid and its conjugate base.

TABLE 19-6

Dissociation Constants for Some Weak Acids		
Acid	**Reaction**	**K_a (at 25°C)**
hydrofluoric	$HF + H_2O \rightleftharpoons H_3O^+ + F^-$	6.6×10^{-4}
formic	$HCOOH + H_2O \rightleftharpoons H_3O^+ + HCOO^-$	1.8×10^{-4}
acetic	$CH_3COOH + H_2O \rightleftharpoons H_3O^+ + CH_3COO^-$	1.8×10^{-5}
carbonic	$H_2CO_3 + H_2O \rightleftharpoons H_3O^+ + HCO_3^-$	4.4×10^{-7}
hydrogen sulfite ion	$HSO_3^- + H_2O \rightleftharpoons H_3O^+ + SO_3^{2-}$	6.2×10^{-8}
hypochlorous	$HClO + H_2O \rightleftharpoons H_3O^+ + ClO^-$	2.9×10^{-8}
hydrocyanic	$HCN + H_2O \rightleftharpoons H_3O^+ + CN^-$	6.2×10^{-10}
hydrogen carbonate ion	$HCO_3^- + H_2O \rightleftharpoons H_3O^+ + CO_3^{2-}$	4.7×10^{-11}

C O N S U M E R   C H E M I S T R Y

Lost Memories—Deteriorating Paper Treasures

Do you have a collection of old letters, comic books, baseball cards, or newspaper clippings stashed away in your room or attic? When was the last time you took a look at these treasures? You may not realize it, but these paper treasures will not last forever.

The cause of this deterioration is the acid that forms in the paper made from wood pulp.

Paper made from wood pulp can deteriorate due to the formation of acid in the paper.

Before wood pulp, paper was made from cotton fibers that required very little chemical treatment. Paper made from cotton pulp has lasted for hundreds of years without decaying. But since the nineteenth century, as a result of the great demand for paper, papermakers have used pulp derived from wood as a less expensive alternative to cotton rag.

Paper made from wood must be treated with a chemical sizing agent to prevent the ink from blurring. Rosins are added to the paper as the sizing agent, while alum and potassium aluminum sulfate is added to bind the rosin to the paper. When exposed to warm temperatures and humidity, the alum reacts with the moisture in the air to form an acidic solution. The cellulose fibers of the paper are broken down by this solution. The result is a weaker paper that crumbles much like a dead, dried leaf.

Paper manufacturers are now making wood-fiber paper that is basic rather than acidic. This paper is both more durable and stronger than acid paper. They are using new sizing agents that do not contain alum rosin. In addition, during the manufacturing process, they are dipping the paper in calcium carbonate, which neutralizes acids that may be present or form with age.

19.8 Buffers

You have learned that the addition of small amounts of acid or base to water can shift the $[H_3O^+]$–$[OH^-]$ equilibrium. In Figure 19-18, you can see what happens as increasing amounts of the strong acid HCl or the strong base NaOH are added to pure water. Notice how the indicators in these test tubes change color. Pure water is not very resistant to changes in pH; in fact, its pH changes quite dramatically as even small amounts of an acid or base are added.

In certain situations, however, it is crucial to have a solution that can withstand the addition of an acid or base without substantially changing the pH. For example, in human blood, the pH must remain very close to 7.35 for the body to function normally. Blood has the characteristic of maintaining a nearly constant pH when small amounts of acid or base are added. A solution that

D E M O N S T R A T I O N

Buffers

⚠ **CAUTION: HCl and NaOH are corrosive. Wash any spills or splashes immediately with plenty of water. A face shield and gloves should be used.** To 100 mL of 2*M* acetic acid solution (115 mL acid/L), add 2.0 g of sodium acetate. Test for pH with the pH meter. To 25 mL of this buffer, slowly add some distilled water while the pH electrode is immersed in the beaker. To 25 mL of this buffer, slowly add 1*M* HCl (85.5 mL acid/L) one drop at a time and note the pH reading. To 25 mL of this buffer, slowly add 1*M* NaOH (40 g/L) one drop at a time and note the pH reading. Note: Dilution will not change the pH. The addition of a strong acid or a strong base (in limited quantities) will not change the pH.

resists changes in pH even when acids or bases are added is called a **buffer.** The pH of blood is maintained by several different buffering systems.

How buffering works Why is a buffer able to prevent large changes in pH while an ordinary solution cannot? The resistance of a buffer to added acid or base is due to the presence of a conjugate acid-base pair in the solution. For example, carbonic acid, H_2CO_3, is a weak acid, and its conjugate base is the hydrogen carbonate ion, HCO_3^-. In the blood, this conjugate acid-base pair undergoes reactions to help control the pH. When excess hydronium ions enter the blood, the hydrogen carbonate ion undergoes the following reaction to reduce the $[H_3O^+]$ concentration.

$$HCO_3^-(aq) + H_3O^+(aq) \rightleftharpoons H_2CO_3(aq) + H_2O(aq)$$

In this way, excess H_3O^+ cannot build up and drastically affect the pH.

Whenever excess hydroxide ions form in the blood they have a strong affinity for H^+. Carbonic acid provides a source of protons for the OH^-, and the following reaction occurs.

$$H_2CO_3 + OH^- \rightleftharpoons HCO_3^- + H_2O$$

Just as your body uses a weak acid and conjugate base pair for buffering, chemists use this same concept to make buffers in the lab. For example, a buffer can be made in the laboratory by using the weak acid, acetic acid and its conjugate base, sodium acetate.

Figure 19-18 *The pH of pure water changes rapidly as small amounts of acid or base are added. Left: 1M HCl added to water containing methyl orange. Right: 1M NaOH added to water containing phenolphthalein.*

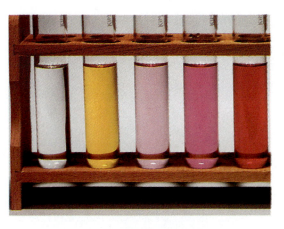

Applying Le Chatelier's principle The two carbonic acid reactions occurring in the blood can be written as a single chemical equation.

$$H_2CO_3 + H_2O \rightleftharpoons H_3O^+ + HCO_3^-$$

According to Le Chatelier's principle, which you learned in Chapter 17, when excess H_3O^+ enters the blood, the equilibrium will shift

Science Background

How Buffering Works

Le Châtelier's principle and the following equation

$$CH_3COOH(aq) \rightarrow H^+(aq) \\ + CH_3COO^-(aq)$$

explain how an acetic acid-sodium acetate buffer maintains a constant pH.

Dilution with distilled water does not change the pH because both CH_3COOH and CH_3COO^- are equally diluted.

The addition of strong acid does not change the pH dramatically because the equation shifts to the left as new H+ from the strong acid reacts with CH_3COO^- to form CH_3COOH.

The addition of a strong base does not change the pH because the equation shifts to the right. As OH^- is added from the strong base, H^+ from dissociating CH_3COOH neutralizes additional OH^-.

Guided Practice

Review the Concept Check questions on pages 657, 661, and 663 with students. Answers can be found in Appendix E on page 808.

Reteaching Idea

Students may be intimidated at first by the use of logarithms. Explain that a logarithm is simply an exponent. Therefore, the logarithm (log) of 10^{-2} is −2, and the log of 10^{-12} is −12. Since pH = −log $[H_3O^+]$, a solution that has $[H_3O^+] = 10^{-4}$ has a pH of 4. Without referring to Figure 19–17, have students complete their own table of pH values (from 0–14) indicating the strength of the acid or base ($[H_3O^+]$ or $[OH^-]$ in moles/liter). In the table, have students indicate strong, moderate, and weak acids; neutrality; weak, moderate, and strong bases. Ask them to state the relationship between pH value and strength. They should also explain why a difference of 1 in pH value represents a tenfold difference in strength. Thus, even small changes in pH indicate definite changes in acid or base strength. Relate this to the human body, where the pH of the blood must be maintained within the narrow range of 7.35–7.45. Finally, have students indicate in the table where the pH of common substances (such as those in Table 19–5) would fall.

to the left, keeping the H_3O^+ concentration relatively constant in the solution. When a base containing OH^- is added, the equilibrium will shift to the right because the added OH^- reacts with H_3O^+ to produce water. This shift temporarily lowers the H_3O^+ concentration. A shift in the equilibrium to the right will replenish the H_3O^+ to near its original concentration.

Preparing a buffer You can prepare a buffer by mixing a weak acid and its conjugate base in the same solution. For example, one of your blood buffers is the H_2CO_3/HCO_3^- combination already described. Another blood buffer is a mixture of the weak acid $H_2PO_4^-$ and its conjugate base, HPO_4^{2-}.

Mixtures of weak acids and their salts can form buffer solutions. Mixtures of strong acids and their salts cannot. In a buffer, you need an acid that can donate protons to added base and a conjugate base that can accept protons from added acid. Strong acids and their conjugate bases are unable to do this. For example, consider the strong acid HCl. Its conjugate base, the chloride ion, is so weak that it is unable to accept protons from any added acid. However, the conjugate base of a weak acid, such as H_2CO_3 or CH_3COOH, can serve as a proton acceptor.

Take note of everyday products that claim to be buffered, such as aspirin as shown in Figure 19-19. By reading their ingredient labels, you may be able to identify the weak acids and their conjugate bases that are being used to provide the buffers.

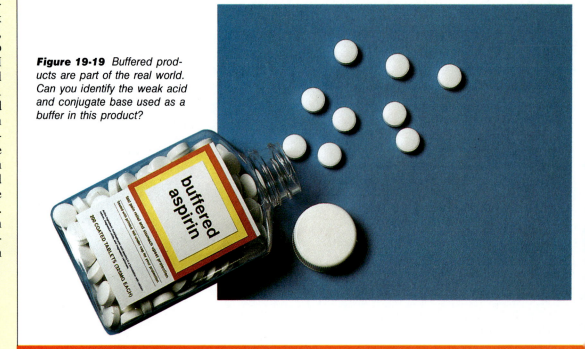

Figure 19-19 *Buffered products are part of the real world. Can you identify the weak acid and conjugate base used as a buffer in this product?*

PART 3 REVIEW

ANSWERS

■ **Keyed to Objectives**

F **29.** pH = −log$[H_3O^+]$

F **30.** pH = −log(0.010) = 2.00

F **31.** $[H_3O^+]$ = antilog(−9) = $10^{-9}M$
Since the pH is greater than 7, this solution is a base.

F **32.** The smaller the pH value of a solu-

tion, the more hydronium ion and the less hydroxide ion that solution contains. Therefore, Solution A has more hydronium ion, whereas Solution B has more hydroxide ion. Since both solutions have pH values less than 7, they are both acids.

F **33.** Bromphenol blue is yellow if the pH is less than 3.0, whereas phenolphthalein is colorless if the pH is less than 8.2. The solution must have a pH of less than 3.0.

F **34.** In pure water, the OH^- concentration is already $1.00 \times 10^{-7}M$. By adding OH^- ion to water (in the form of KOH), you would expect this concentration to increase. Therefore, in a solution of KOH, $[OH^-] > 1.00 \times 10^{-7}$.

G **35.** This is the relationship sometimes referred to as the K_w expression (or the ionization of water relationship): $[H_3O^+][OH^-] = 1.00 \times 10^{14}$

PART 3 REVIEW

29. What is the mathematical relationship between the hydronium ion concentration and the pH?

30. A 0.010M solution of hydrochloric acid has a hydronium ion concentration of 0.010M. What is the pH of this solution?

31. A solution containing sodium acetate is found to have a pH of 9. What is the hydronium ion concentration of this solution? Is the solution acidic or basic?   ***Ans.*** $1 \times 10^{-9}M$

32. Solution A has a pH of 3.0, while Solution B has a pH of 6.0. Which solution has the greater hydronium ion concentration? Which solution has the greater hydroxide ion concentration? Identify each solution as acidic or basic.

33. When you test a solution with bromphenol blue and with phenolphthalein, you find that the first indicator turns yellow and the second indicator is colorless. What can you say about the pH of the solution?

34. If you dissolved some solid potassium hydroxide in water, would you expect the OH$^-$ concentration to be *greater* than $1.00 \times 10^{-7}M$, *less* than $1.00 \times 10^{-7}M$, or *equal* to $1.00 \times 10^{-7}M$? Explain your answer.

35. What is the mathematical relationship between [H$_3$O$^+$] and [OH$^-$] in any aqueous solution?

36. A solution containing ammonia, NH$_3$, has a hydronium ion concentration of $1.0 \times 10^{-12}M$. What is the hydroxide ion concentration of this solution? Would you classify this solution as acidic or basic?   ***Ans.*** 1.0×10^{-2}

37. Find the pH of the following solutions.
    a. 0.0010M HCl   ***Ans.*** pH = 3.00
    b. $4.5 \times 10^{-3}M$ HNO$_3$ ***Ans.*** pH = 2.35
    c. $9.1 \times 10^{-5}M$ HCl   ***Ans.*** pH = 4.04
    d. $3.7 \times 10^{-4}M$ HI   ***Ans.*** pH = 3.43

38. What is the [H$_3$O$^+$] for each solution listed below?
    a. pH = 5.08   ***Ans.*** $8.3 \times 10^{-6}M$
    b. pH = 11.50   ***Ans.*** $3.16 \times 10^{-12}M$
    c. pH = 7.00   ***Ans.*** $1.0 \times 10^{-7}M$

39. Which acid is stronger, HF or H$_2$CO$_3$? How do you know?

40. What is the equilibrium constant expression for the ionization of HClO? What is the value of K_a for this acid?

41. What substance might you mix with CH$_3$COOH to produce a buffered solution? Explain how the buffer would work.

42. Using appropriate chemical equations, show how a mixture of H$_2$PO$_4^-$ and HPO$_4^{2-}$, acting as conjugate acid and base respectively, can respond to the addition of the following.
    a. HCl   **b.** NaOH

◀ **PROBLEM·SOLVING**
STRATEGY

If you **use what you know** *about pH, you can answer this question without doing any calculations. (See Strategy, page 58.)*

◀ **PROBLEM·SOLVING**
STRATEGY

Be sure to use your calculator as you work problems 37 and 38. (See Strategy, page 134.)

Boxed numbers indicate questions that involve skills in interpretation, application, and analysis.

≡CLOSE

Summing Up Main Ideas

Ask students to write a definition for pH and to describe how pH is related to K_w and K_a. (pH is the negative logarithm of the hydronium ion concentration. The pH of a solution is never more than 14 because the ionization constant for water [K_w] is 1.0×10^{-14}. The acid dissociation constant [K_a] indicates the strength of an acid, and the K_a is used to predict how much a specific acid will change the pH of a solution.)

PART 3 REVIEW

Assign the Part Review questions.

Evaluating Skills

These skills are evaluated in the Part Review questions indicated.
Determining main ideas: 29, 35, 40; **Calculating:** 30, 31, 36, 37, 38; **Applying a strategy:** 30, 31, 36, 37, 38; **Verifying results:** 30, 31, 36, 37, 38; **Classifying:** 31, 32, 36; **Analyzing data:** 39; **Forming a hypothesis:** 41

G 36. Using the relationship stated in the last question:

$$[OH^-] = \frac{1.00 \times 10^{-14}}{[H_3O^+]}$$

$$= \frac{1.00 \times 10^{-14}}{1.00 \times 10^{-12}} = 0.0100M$$

$$= 1 \times 10^{-2}\ M$$

The solution is a base.

F 37. **a.** pH = $-\log(0.0010) = 3.00$
     b. pH = $-\log(4.5 \times 10^{-3}) = 2.35$
     c. pH = $-\log(9.1 \times 10^{-5}) = 4.04$
     d. pH = $-\log(3.7 \times 10^{-4}) = 3.43$

F 38. **a.** [H$_3$O$^+$] = antilog(-5.08)
         = $8.3 \times 10^{-6}M$

     b. [H$_3$O$^+$] = antilog(-11.50)
         = $3.16 \times 10^{-12}M$

     c. [H$_3$O$^+$] = antilog(-7.00)
         = $1.0 \times 10^{-7}M$

H 39. HF is stronger because K_a is larger.

H 40. HClO(aq) + H$_2$O(l) →
         H$_3$O$^+$(aq) + OCl$^-$(aq)

$$K_a = \frac{[OCl^-][H_3O^+]}{[HClO]} = 2.9 \times 10^{-8}$$

I 41. Since a buffer solution may be prepared by mixing a weak acid with its conjugate base, you could add some sodium acetate to the acetic acid already present. Acetate ion is the conjugate base of acetic acid.

(answers are continued on page T841)

Indicators

Estimated time: (50–60 minutes; could be extended to 2 periods if additional indicators are used in Part 1)

Process Skills

Calculating
Determining sources of errors
Comparing/Contrasting
Determining cause and effect

Preparation

■ Materials

(for a class of 24, working in pairs)
Apparatus
24-well spot plates (12), toothpicks, wax marking pencils (12), 10-mL graduated cylinder
Reagents (in Beral pipettes or dropper bottles)

■ pH solutions: vinegar
seltzer water
neutral solution (pH 7)
0.1M NaHCO$_3$
household ammonia
unknown pH solution

■ Indicators: bromthymol blue
phenolphthalein
Universal Indicator

■ Titration solutions:
0.10M HCl
0.20M NaOH

■ Buffer capsules

■ Preparation Hints

Part 1: Vinegar, seltzer water, and household ammonia are used "as is." 0.1M NaHCO$_3$: Dissolve 8.4 g NaHCO$_3$ in 1 liter of distilled water.
pH 7 solution:
(1) Use prepared buffer capsules.
(2) Make a solution of Epsom salts, MgSO$_4$·10H$_2$O (1 tablespoon to a pint of distilled water), and adjust the pH to 7 with HCl or NaOH (should be green when bromthymol blue is added).

Laboratory

Investigation

Indicators

You learned that acid-base indicators are molecules that can be found in a weak-acid form or a weak-base form. Each of these forms usually has a different color. For example, the acidic form of bromthymol blue is yellow, while the basic form is blue. Because of these colors, indicators can be used to identify the pH of a solution and determine the point at which a neutralization reaction has occurred.

In this activity, you will investigate the colors of three indicators: bromthymol blue, phenolphthalein, and Universal Indicator (a mixture of several indicators). Then you will use that information to determine the pH of an unknown solution.

Objectives

Compare the colors of bromthymol blue, phenolphthalein, and Universal Indicator in a series of different pH solutions.

Estimate the pH of an unknown solution.

Materials

Apparatus
□ 10-mL graduated cylinder
□ 24-well plate
□ 24 toothpicks
□ wax marking pencil

Reagents
□ dropper bottles containing:
□ vinegar
□ seltzer water
□ household ammonia
□ 0.1M NaHCO$_3$
□ pH 7 solution
□ solution of unknown pH
□ Indicators:
Universal Indicator
bromthymol blue
phenolphthalein

Procedure

1. Put on your lab apron and safety goggles.
2. Obtain a well plate and one bottle of each solution listed under reagents.
3. Using a wax pencil, label your well plate to match the data table for Part 1. Notice that each box on the data table corresponds to a well on the plate. The solutions with various pH values and unknown pH value are listed across the top, and the indicators are listed along the side.

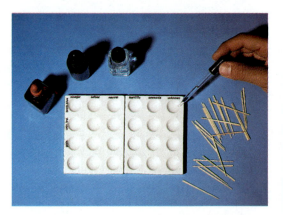

Unknown pH solution suggestions: Any dilute acid (less than 1.0M of HCl, HNO$_3$, H$_2$SO$_4$) or base (less than 1.0M of NaOH, KOH, NH$_4$OH)
Part 2: 0.10M HCl: Use 10 mL of 1M HCl and 90 mL of water.

Unknown M NaOH: To make a 0.20M solution, dissolve 8.00 g NaOH in 1 L distilled water; for a 0.15M solution, use 6.00 g, and for a 0.25M solution, use 10.00 g NaOH.

4. Put 20 drops of each solution in the proper well. Then add 1 drop of bromthymol blue to each well in the first row and 1 drop of Universal Indicator to each well in the second row.

☠ 🔥 **CAUTION: Phenolphthalein solution is poisonous and flammable. Do not get it in your mouth. Be sure there are no flames in the lab.**

Add 1 drop of phenolphthalein to each well in the third row. Stir the wells to mix the solutions completely, using 1 toothpick in each well. Record the resulting colors in the data table. Estimate the pH of the unknown solution.

5. Before leaving the laboratory, clean up all materials and wash your hands thoroughly.

Data Analysis

Data Table

Indicators	pH Solutions					
	Vinegar pH = 3	Seltzer water pH = 5	Neutral pH = 7	0.1M NaHCO₃ pH = 10	Household ammonia pH = 12	Unknown pH solution
Bromthymol blue						
Universal indicator						
Phenolphthalein						

1. At what pH does bromthymol blue, phenolphthalein, and Universal Indicator change color?

2. Which indicator gives no information in the acid-to-neutral pH range?

Conclusions

1. When bromthymol blue is green, what is the relationship between the amounts of OH^- and hydronium ions, H_3O^+, in the solution? (>, <, or equal) Explain your answer.

2. What is the approximate pH of your un-

known solution? Explain your reasoning.

3. Is your unknown an acidic, a basic, or a neutral solution? How do you know?

4. Which indicator would be most useful in testing a wide variety of solutions? Explain your answer.

Data Table

Indicators	pH Solutions					
	Vinegar pH=3	Seltzer water pH=5	Neutral pH=7	0.1M NaHCO₃ pH=10	Household ammonia pH=12	Unknown pH solution
Bromthymol blue	yellow	yellow	green	blue	blue	
Universal Indicator	red	pink/orange	green	blue/green	purple	
Phenolphthalein	clear	clear	clear	light pink	pink	

■ **Safety**
Ammonia should be used under the hood.

Guiding the Investigation

■ **Procedural Hints**
Part 1: In the interest of lab efficiency, provide one set of reagents for each pair of students. If the experiment is done with Beral pipets, a minimum of reagents will be used.

Part 2: Be sure to make the NaOH solution a *different* concentration from the 0.10M HCl, so that students do not get the mistaken impression that titration involves using the same volumes of solutions. The concentration must not exceed 0.3M.

The green color of bromthymol blue in neutral solutions is quite stable once it is reached. Thus, students must be reminded to agitate the spot plate (or stir with toothpicks) to mix the solutions well. Stress to the students that at pH 7,

$[H^+]$	=	$[OH^-]$
(yellow)		(blue)

Equal amounts of the yellow and blue colors will give green color (neutral). The titration will go so quickly that students should have time to repeat it 2 or 3 times and average their results.

Disposal
Combine all liquids and neutralize with 0.1M or less concentrated acid or base, as necessary, and pour down the drain.

Data Analysis

■ **Sample Data**
(See table below.)

■ **Analysis**
1. Bromthymol blue at pH 7, phenolphthalein at about pH 9, and Universal Indicator all along.

2. phenolphthalein

Conclusions
1. $H_3O^+ = OH^-$ because the solution is neutral (pH = 7).

2. Answers may vary.

3. Answers may vary.

4. Universal Indicator, because it has a wide variety of colors and covers the range from pH 2 to pH 12.

Chapter 19
Review
ANSWERS
begin on page
T675a.

Summary

Introduction to Acids and Bases

■ Acids and bases are classes of compounds that may be identified by observable properties.

■ The Brønsted definition provides a sub-microscopic-level explanation for acids and bases. According to Brønsted, an acid is any compound that can donate a hydrogen ion to another substance, while a base is any compound that can accept a hydrogen ion.

■ After an acid loses its proton, the remaining species is its conjugate base. Similarly, when a base accepts a proton, the new species is its conjugate acid.

■ Litmus and phenolphthalein are examples of indicators, substances that can change color when exposed to acids or bases.

Acid-Base Reactions

■ A neutralization reaction is one in which an acid reacts with a base. If the base is a hydroxide, the products of this reaction are a salt and water.

■ A titration is a laboratory technique in which the volume of a solution having a known concentration is carefully measured to determine how much of the solution is needed to completely react with a solid or a solution with an unknown concentration.

pH and Acid-Base Equilibrium

■ The pH scale gives a convenient method for reporting the $[H_3O^+]$ of a solution. Mathematically the relationship between $[H_3O^+]$ and pH may be expressed this way.

$$pH = -\log[H_3O^+]$$

■ Water undergoes self-ionization.
$$H_2O(l) + H_2O(l) \rightleftharpoons H_3O^+(aq) + OH^-(aq)$$

The equilibrium expression for this reaction is
$$K_w = [H_3O^+][OH^-] = 1.00 \times 10^{-14}$$

■ Because the reaction of a weak acid with water is an example of equilibrium, the principles of equilibrium may be applied to such reactions.

■ The value of the equilibrium constant may be used to compare strengths of weak acids. The larger the K_a, the stronger the acid.

■ A buffer is a solution that is able to resist changes in pH as acid or base is added.

Chemically Speaking

acid 19.2
acid-dissociation
  constant, K_a 19.9
amphiprotic 19.2
base 19.2
buffer 19.8
conjugate acid-base
  pair 19.3
equilibrium constant
  for water, K_w 19.8
equivalence point 19.5

hydronium ion 19.2
indicator 19.1
logarithm 19.6
neutralization 19.4
pH 19.6
polyprotic 19.4
salt 19.4
strong acid 19.3
titration 19.5
weak acid 19.3

Concept Mapping

Using the method of concept mapping described at the front of this book, draw a concept map for *acids* and *bases*, using terms from this chapter and previous chapters as necessary.

Questions and Problems

INTRODUCTION TO ACIDS AND BASES

A. Objective: **Distinguish** between an acid and a base, using observable properties.

1. You are told that an unknown substance is either an acid or a base. Explain whether or

PROBLEM-SOLVING
▶ **S T R A T E G I E S**
Students apply these strategies in the following questions.

■ **Using what you know:** 1, 2, 4, 8, 11, 12, 20, 21, 22, 29, 36, 39, 43, 44, 53, 58, 67, 73
■ **Using similar problems:** 5, 25, 26,

31, 32, 33, 34, 35, 37, 38
■ **Using patterns:** 3, 8, 16, 17, 18, 19, 45, 46, 69, 70
■ **Making an estimate:** 36, 45, 46, 72

T670

not each of the following properties could be used to determine the kind of substance you have.

a. color of solution
b. electrical conductivity
c. reaction with litmus paper

2. What property of a lemon-lime soda helps you identify it as an acid?

3. When you test a sample of baking soda dissolved in water with a strip of litmus paper, you find that red litmus turns blue. What color do you expect to see when you add a drop of phenolphthalein to this sample? Explain your answer.

4. What gas is given off when magnesium is placed in hydrochloric acid?

5. When small pieces of cobalt metal are placed in acetic acid, you observe that bubbles are emitted as the solution takes on a slightly pink color. Write a chemical equation for the reaction between cobalt and the following substances.

a. hydrochloric acid
b. sulfuric acid

B. Objective: **Define** *acids and bases by* **applying** *the Brønsted definition of acids and bases.*

6. State the Brønsted definition of an acid and provide an example of a Brønsted acid.

7. State the Brønsted definition of a base and provide an example of a Brønsted base.

8. Identify each of the following reactants as either a Brønsted acid or a Brønsted base.

a. $HF + H_2O \rightarrow F^- + H_3O^+$
b. $NH_3 + HCl \rightarrow NH_4^+ + Cl^-$
c. $H_2O + H_2O \rightarrow H_3O^+ + OH^-$
d. $PO_4^{3-} + 3HNO_3 \rightarrow H_3PO_4 + 3NO_3^-$
e. $HClO_4 + OH^- \rightarrow ClO_4^- + H_2O$
f. $CO_3^{2-} + 2CH_3COOH \rightarrow CO_2 + H_2O + 2CH_3COO^-$

9. Write a chemical equation representing the reaction of the following substances with the Brønsted acid H_3O^+.

a. NH_2^-
b. NH_3
c. CN^-
d. OH^-

10. Write a chemical equation representing the reaction of the following substances with the Brønsted base OH^-.

a. H_2SO_3
b. $HOCN$
c. HCl
d. NH_4^+

11. Explain why the ion F^- cannot possibly be a Brønsted acid.

12. Suppose you had an aqueous solution that has a $0.1M$ concentration of hydronium ions. Was a Brønsted acid or a Brønsted base added to the water? Did the water itself act like a Brønsted acid or a Brønsted base? Explain your answer.

13. Why is water considered to be amphiprotic?

14. The anion $H_2PO_4^-$ is amphiprotic. Write chemical equations that illustrate why this anion is amphiprotic.

C. Objective: **Identify** *conjugate acid-base pairs in a reaction.*

15. What is meant by the term *conjugate base?*

16. Identify the conjugate base of the first reactant in each of these chemical equations.

a. $H_2S + H_2O \rightarrow HS^- + H_3O^+$
b. $HClO_4 + H_2O \rightarrow ClO_4^- + H_3O^+$
c. $H_2O + NH_3 \rightarrow NH_4^+ + OH^-$

17. Identify the conjugate acid of the first reactant in each of these chemical equations.

a. $CO_3^{2-} + H_2O \rightarrow HCO_3^- + OH^-$
b. $CH_3COO^- + HCl \rightarrow CH_3COOH + Cl^-$
c. $H_2O + HNO_3 \rightarrow NO_3^- + H_3O^+$

18. What is the conjugate base of these Brønsted acids?

a. H_2SO_4
b. HBr
c. NH_4^+
d. H_2O
e. HPO_4^{2-}

19. What is the conjugate acid of each of these Brønsted bases?

a. OH^-
b. CN^-
c. SO_3^{2-}
d. H_2O
e. HPO_4^{2-}

Boxed numbers indicate questions that involve skills in interpretation, application, and analysis.

ACIDS AND BASES **671**

■ **Using calculators:** 31, 32, 33, 34, 35, 37, 38, 48, 50, 52, 54, 65, 66
■ **Verifying your answer:** 31, 32, 33, 34, 35, 37, 38, 54, 65, 66
■ **Breaking problems into manageable parts:** 31, 32, 34, 35, 37, 38, 54, 65, 66
■ **Making diagrams:** 57
■ **Writing chemical equations:** 5, 9, 10, 12, 14, 18, 19, 22, 23, 24, 25, 26, 28, 31, 32, 33, 34, 35, 59, 76, 77, 78

T671

ACID-BASE REACTIONS

D. Objective: *Distinguish between the nature of the reactants and the nature of the products when a strong acid neutralizes a strong base.*

20. Explain why this reaction may be classified as a neutralization reaction.

$$HCl + LiOH \rightarrow LiCl + H_2O$$

21. What is the name of the class of substances that can be used to neutralize a solution of $1.0M$ HNO_3?

22. Name a specific substance that you can use to neutralize phosphoric acid to produce sodium phosphate, Na_3PO_4.

23. Write equations for the reactions that take place when aqueous solutions of the following substances are mixed. If no reaction occurs, then write *NR*.
    a. CH_3COOH and $NaOH$
    b. HF and NH_3
    c. HCl and HCN
    d. HNO_3 and $NaOCl$

24. Write an equation for the neutralization reaction that takes place when you mix the following.
    a. 1 mole of H_3PO_4 and 1 mole of $NaOH$
    b. 1 mole of H_3PO_4 and 3 moles of $NaOH$

25. What acid and what base could you mix together to form these salts?
    a. sodium chloride
    b. potassium fluoride
    c. magnesium sulfate

26. Write chemical equations for two different reactions that you could use to produce the salt zinc chloride.

27. Lead(II) chloride and lead(II) hydroxide are both white, insoluble, ionic solids. Explain why lead chloride may be called a salt, but lead hydroxide is not.

28. Write a chemical equation that shows why the problem of excess stomach acid, HCl, can be partially relieved by milk of magnesia, which contains $Mg(OH)_2$.

E. Objective: *Describe titration and calculate the concentration of an acid or base, using the results of a titration.*

29. If you want to find out the concentration of a sample of an acid, one of the things you might want to find out about that sample is how many moles of acid it contains. What else would you need to know to determine its concentration?

30. Why is a buret used for many titrations?

31. The concentration of a solution of potassium hydroxide is determined by titration with nitric acid. A 30.0-mL sample of KOH is neutralized by 42.7 mL of $0.498M$ HNO_3. What is the concentration of the potassium hydroxide solution?

32. What volume of $0.28M$ NaOH is required to neutralize 28.73 mL of $0.15M$ HCl?

33. How many grams of lithium bromide would be present after evaporation when 500.0 mL of $1.00M$ HBr and 500.0 mL of $1.00M$ LiOH are mixed together?

34. Oxalic acid, $H_2C_2O_4$, is a solid diprotic acid that is only slightly soluble in water. However, as it reacts with KOH or any other strong base, it continues to dissolve. When 6.25 g of oxalic acid is placed in water containing phenol red, the suspension is yellow. A solution of KOH is added until the color changes to red. This color change is obtained at the equivalence point of this titration. What is the molarity of KOH if 32.2 mL is required to reach the equivalence point?

35. A 1.2-g tablet of $Mg(OH)_2$ neutralizes 450.0 mL of stomach acid. What is the molarity of the HCl in the solution?

36. Suppose you are given a solution of an acid whose concentration is known to be between $0.10M$ and $0.25M$. You use the process of titration to determine more precisely what the concentration is. You have a choice of two sodium hydroxide solutions to use: one that is $0.1150M$ and one which is $0.01500M$. Which of these two solutions would be the

better choice to use? Explain your answer.

37. You carry out a titration based on the following reaction:

$$H_2SO_4 + 2NH_3 \rightarrow SO_4^{2-} + 2NH_4^+$$

How many moles of sulfuric acid must be added to 6.35 moles of ammonia to reach the equivalence point?

38. Suppose you react solid sodium carbonate with a solution of hydrochloric acid, as shown by the following equation.

$$Na_2CO_3(s) + 2HCl(aq) \rightarrow$$
$$2NaCl(aq) + CO_2(g) + H_2O(l)$$

If 10.0 g of sodium carbonate reacts, then how many moles of hydrochloric acid have you added?

39. If you titrate nitric acid with sodium hydroxide, you will probably add a drop or two of phenolphthalein to the sample of acid before you begin adding the sodium hydroxide. Why is the indicator added?

40. You are carrying out the titration described in the last question, but realize that you have forgotten to add the indicator after you have started. You decide to add two drops of phenolphthalein even though some of the base has already been used. Would you prefer to see the solution remain colorless at this point or would you prefer to see it turn pink? Explain your answer.

41. There are two common ways that students miss the equivalence point of a titration. They either forget to put in the indicator at the beginning of the titration, or they add the base too quickly to the acid, so that they cannot read the volume of the base in the buret at the instant where the indicator changes color. Besides starting completely over, what could you do to finish a titration if you have missed the equivalence point?

42. Look back at your work on the quantitative problems you have solved in this section, as well as any other problems in this chapter involving a titration. Make a list of as many ways as possible for you to verify that your solutions to these problems are correct.

pH AND ACID-BASE EQUILIBRIUM

F. Objective: *Apply the concept of pH to the description of acid and base solutions.*

43. Which solution has the lower pH value: $0.1M$ HNO_3 or $0.001M$ HNO_3?

44. Which solution has the higher pH value: $0.1M$ HCl or $0.1M$ NaOH?

45. Solution A has a pH of 5.0. Solution B has a hydronium ion concentration that is 1000 times greater than that of solution A. What is the pH of solution B?

46. If the pH of a solution changes from 10 to 8, by what factor does the hydroxide ion concentration change?

47. Determine the pH of
   a. $0.10M$ HCl;
   b. $0.010M$ HCl;
   c. $0.00010M$ HCl.

48. Determine the pH of
   a. $0.50M$ HCl;
   b. $0.025M$ HCl;
   c. $0.00158M$ HCl.

49. Determine the pH of
   a. $1.0M$ NaOH;   **b.** $0.0010M$ NaOH.

50. Determine the pH of
   a. $0.075M$ NaOH;   **b.** $0.00839M$ NaOH.

51. Give the hydronium ion concentration, $[H_3O^+]$, of a solution whose pH is
   a. 3.00   **b.** 8.00

52. Give the hydronium ion concentration, $[H_3O^+]$, of a solution whose pH is
   a. 2.26   **b.** 7.69

53. Given the following pH values, state whether each solution is acidic or basic.
   a. pH = 1.0   **c.** pH = 6.50
   b. pH = 5.0   **d.** pH = 7.2

54. A basic solution is prepared by dissolving 1.25 g of sodium hydroxide pellets in enough water to make 250.0 mL of solution. What is the pH of the prepared solution?

55. You test a solution with the indicator bromphenol blue. The solution turns green. What conclusion can you draw about the pH of this solution?

G. Objective: *Interpret* the pH scale using the ion-product constant of water, K_w.

56. The self-ionization of water can be represented by this equation:

$$H_2O + H_2O \rightleftharpoons H_3O^+ + OH^-$$

Can this reaction also be classified as a Brønsted acid-base reaction? Explain your answer.

57. Does the relationship between the hydronium ion concentration and the hydroxide ion concentration in an aqueous solution more closely resemble the relationship between the volume and pressure of a gas or the relationship between the volume and absolute temperature of a gas? Explain your answer.

58. Is $[H_3O^+]$ greater than, less than, or equal to $[OH^-]$ in an acidic solution?

59. In a sample of household cleaner containing ammonia, which concentration is greater, the hydroxide ion concentration or the hydronium ion concentration?

60. A friend claims that a $1.0M$ HCl solution contains no hydroxide ions. Do you agree? Explain your answer.

61. Calculate the $[H_3O^+]$ of a $0.0010M$ KOH solution.

62. Determine the $[H_3O^+]$ of $0.025M$ NaOH.

63. If some HCl is added to the solution described in the last question, will the $[H_3O^+]$ increase or decrease? Will the $[OH^-]$ increase or decrease? Explain your answers.

64. Determine the $[OH^-]$ of $0.10M$ HCl.

65. Calculate $[H_3O^+]$ and $[OH^-]$ in a solution made by mixing 50.0 mL of $0.200M$ HCl and 25.0 mL of $0.200M$ NaOH.

66. Calculate $[H_3O^+]$ and $[OH^-]$ in a solution made by mixing 50.0 mL of $0.200M$ HCl and 40.0 mL of $0.200M$ NaOH.

67. What volume of $0.200M$ NaOH must be added to 50.0 mL of $0.200M$ HCl to produce a solution in which $[H_3O^+] = 1 \times 10^{-7}M$?

H. Objective: *Compare* the strengths of acids using the acid dissociation constant, K_a.

68. Why are K_a values not listed in Table 19-6 for strong acid?

69. List the following acids in order of decreasing ability to donate a proton: carbonic, hydrofluoric, hypochlorous, and acetic.

70. The equation for the ionization of the weak acid HCN in water is

$$HCN(aq) + H_2O(l) \rightleftharpoons$$
$$CN^-(aq) + H_3O^+(aq)$$

Write the equilibrium expression for this reaction.

71. When the reaction described in the previous question comes to equilibrium, which is present in the greater concentration: reactants or products? Explain your answer.

72. Without performing any calculations, determine whether a $0.1M$ solution of hydrofluoric acid or a $0.1M$ solution of hypochlorous acid has the greater H_3O^+ concentration. Explain your answer.

73. Which solution described in the last question has the higher pH? Explain your answer.

I. Objective: *Explain* how a buffer works to prevent changes in pH.

74. What is a buffer?

75. Name one of the weak acid–weak base pairs that your blood uses to guard against large swings in pH.

76. What salt might you add to a solution of HCN to create a buffered solution?

77. Could you create a buffer by mixing HI(aq) and NaI(aq)? Explain your answer.

78. Using appropriate chemical equations, show how a buffer composed of sodium acetate, CH_3COONa, and acetic acid, CH_3COOH, is able to guard against pH changes when
   a. HCl is added.
   b. NaOH is added.

Critical Thinking

SYNTHESIS WITHIN THE CHAPTER

79. Because many household items are caustic in nature, poison prevention is an important issue in storing them. For example, if liquid Drano is accidentally swallowed, the base causes severe damage to the esophagus. However, the base usually does not harm the stomach. Explain why. Directions on the Drano container advise you *not* to induce vomiting in case of ingestion. Explain.

80. Use the four graphs to answer **a–c**.

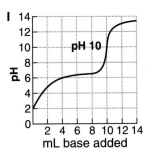

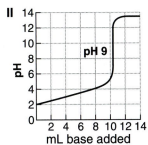

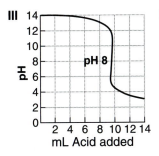

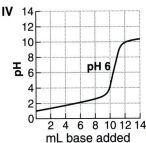

a. Which graph represents the titration of a strong acid with a strong base?

b. Which graph represents the titration of a weak acid with a strong base?

c. Which graph represents the titration of a strong acid with a weak base?

SYNTHESIS ACROSS CHAPTERS

81. Explain why ammonia may act as both a Brønsted acid and Brønsted base, but an ammonium ion may act as a Brønsted acid only.

82. You are given a solid monoprotic acid, and you are asked to determine its molecular mass. You weigh out a 0.115-g sample of this acid. You find out that 5.58 mL of 0.101M sodium hydroxide is required to titrate the acid to its equivalence point. What is its molecular mass?

83. Describe how you could use the process of titration to determine the molar mass of a solid monoprotic acid.

84. A 0.25M solution of benzoic acid is found to have a $[H_3O^+]$ equal to $4 \times 10^{-3}M$. Calculate the value of K_a for benzoic acid.

Projects

85. Find out what chemicals are used in swimming pool maintenance. How is the concentration of these chemicals controlled? What role does pH play in the analysis of the water? What happens if the pH is not correct?

86. Devise an experiment to find out how tea responds to changes in pH. After obtaining your teacher's permission, conduct the experiment. Write a report indicating what conclusions you made.

Research and Writing

87. Whenever *Chemical and Engineering News* publishes its list of the top fifty chemicals produced in the United States, sulfuric acid consistently appears in the top position. Find out what you can about this important chemical. How is it produced from sulfur? What industries make use of sulfuric acid?

88. G. N. Lewis, an American chemist who was born in 1875, proposed a definition of acids and bases that differs from those stated by Arrhenius and by Brønsted. What definition did he propose and how does it compare with the two definitions you met in this chapter?

ACIDS AND BASES **675**

Review ANSWERS

☐ Boxed numbers indicate questions that involve skills in interpretation, application, and analysis.

1. **a.** No
   b. No
   c. Yes. Red litmus indicates an acid; blue litmus indicates a base.

2. Its sour taste

3. Since the litmus test shows that baking soda is a base, a drop of phenolphthalein should give the solution a pink color.

4. hydrogen

5. **a.** $Co + 2HCl \rightarrow CoCl_2 + H_2$
   b. $Co + H_2SO_4 \rightarrow CoSO_4 + H_2$

6. A Brønsted acid donates a proton to a base. Example: HCl donates a proton to H_2O.

7. A Brønsted base accepts a proton from an acid. Example: NH_3 accepts a proton from H_2O.

8. **a.** HF = acid, H_2O = base
   b. NH_3 = base, HCl = acid
   c. H_2O = acid, H_2O = base
   d. PO_4^{3-} = base, HNO_3 = acid
   e. $HClO_4$ = acid, OH^- = base
   f. CO_3^{2-} = base, CH_3COOH = acid

9. **a.** $NH_2^- + H_3O^+ \rightarrow NH_3 + H_2O$
   b. $NH_3 + H_3O^+ \rightarrow NH_4^+ + H_2O$
   c. $CN^- + H_3O^+ \rightarrow HCN + H_2O$
   d. $OH^- + H_3O^+ \rightarrow H_2O + H_2O$

10. **a.** $H_2SO_3 + OH^- \rightarrow HSO_3^- + H_2O$
    b. $HOCN + OH^- \rightarrow OCN^- + H_2O$
    c. $HCl + OH^- \rightarrow Cl^- + H_2O$
    d. $NH_4^+ + OH^- \rightarrow NH_3 + H_2O$

11. F^- does not have a proton to donate.

12. $[H_3O^+] = 0.1M$; pH = 1.0
    $[H_3O^+] > 1.0 \times 10^{-7}M$ when a Brønsted acid is added to water. Since the water is a proton acceptor in this case, it acted like a Brønsted base.

13. Water can both accept protons from Brønsted acids (such as HCl) and donate protons to Brønsted bases (such as NH_3).

14. $H_2PO_4^- + OH^- \rightarrow HPO_4^{2-} + H_2O$
    acid　　　base
    $H_2PO_4^- + HCl \rightarrow H_3PO_4 + Cl^-$
    base　　　acid

15. The conjugate base is the chemical species that is formed after a Brønsted acid has donated its proton.

16. **a.** HS^-
    b. ClO_4^-
    c. OH^-

17. **a.** HCO_3^-
    b. CH_3COOH
    c. H_3O^+

18. **a.** HSO_4^-
    b. Br^-
    c. NH_3
    d. OH^-
    e. PO_4^{3-}

19. **a.** H_2O
    b. HCN
    c. HSO_3^-
    d. H_3O^+
    e. $H_2PO_4^-$

20. Because it represents the reaction of an acid (HCl) with a base (LiOH), forming a salt (LiCl) and water.

21. bases

22. NaOH
    ($H_3PO_4 + 3NaOH \rightarrow$
    　　　　　$Na_3PO_4 + 3H_2O$)

23. **a.** $CH_3COOH + NaOH \rightarrow$
    　　　　　$CH_3COONa + H_2O$
    b. $HF + NH_3 \rightarrow F^- + NH_4^+$
    c. $HCl + HCN \rightarrow NR$
    d. $HNO_3 + NaOCl \rightarrow HOCl + NaNO_3$

24. **a.** $H_3PO_4 + NaOH \rightarrow$
    　　　　　$NaH_2PO_4 + H_2O$
    b. $H_3PO_4 + 3NaOH \rightarrow$
    　　　　　$Na_3PO_4 + 3H_2O$

25. **a.** HCl and NaOH
    b. HF and KOH
    c. H_2SO_4 and $Mg(OH)_2$

26. $2HCl + Zn(OH)_2 \rightarrow ZnCl_2 + 2H_2O$
    $Zn + 2HCl \rightarrow ZnCl_2 + H_2$

27. Lead(II) chloride may be produced by the reaction of an acid and a base (see equation below), but lead(II) hydroxide cannot. Because lead(II) hydroxide contains the OH^- ion, it is a base.
    $Pb(OH)_2 + 2HCl \rightarrow PbCl_2 + 2H_2O$

28. $Mg(OH)_2 + 2HCl \rightarrow MgCl_2 + 2H_2O$

29. Its volume

30. Because a buret is a convenient instrument for delivery and measuring volumes of acids and bases.

31. $HNO_3 + KOH \rightarrow KNO_3 + H_2O$

$$\frac{0.0427 \text{ L HNO}_3 \times \frac{0.498 \text{ mol HNO}_3}{\text{L HNO}_3} \times \frac{1 \text{ mol KOH}}{1 \text{ mol HNO}_3}}{0.0300 \text{ L KOH}}$$
$$= 0.709 M$$

32. $HCl + NaOH \rightarrow NaCl + H_2O$
    $0.02873 \text{ L HCl} \times \frac{0.15 \text{ mol HCl}}{1 \text{ L HCl}}$
    $\times \frac{1 \text{ mol NaOH}}{1 \text{ mol HCl}} \times \frac{1 \text{ L NaOH}}{0.28 \text{ mol NaOH}}$
    $= 0.015 \text{ L NaOH} = 15 \text{ mL NaOH}$

33. $HBr + LiOH \rightarrow LiBr + H_2O$
    Note that stoichiometrically equiva-

lent amounts of reactants have been mixed.
$0.5000 \text{ L HBr} \times \frac{1.00 \text{ mol HBr}}{1 \text{ L HBr}}$
$\times \frac{1 \text{ mol LiBr}}{1 \text{ mol HBr}} \times \frac{86.8 \text{ g LiBr}}{1 \text{ mol LiBr}}$
$= 43.4 \text{ g LiBr}$

34. $H_2C_2O_4 + 2KOH \rightarrow K_2C_2O_4 + 2H_2O$
$$\frac{6.25 \text{ g H}_2\text{C}_2\text{O}_4 \times \frac{1 \text{ mol H}_2\text{C}_2\text{O}_4}{90.03 \text{ g H}_2\text{C}_2\text{O}_4} \times \frac{2 \text{ mol KOH}}{1 \text{ mol H}_2\text{C}_2\text{O}_4}}{0.0322 \text{ L KOH}}$$
$$= 4.31 M$$

35. $Mg(OH)2 + 2HCl \rightarrow MgCl2 + 2H2O$
$$\frac{1.2 \text{ g Mg(OH)}_2 \times \frac{1 \text{ mol Mg(OH)}_2}{58.3 \text{ g Mg(OH)}_2} \times \frac{2 \text{ mol HCl}}{1 \text{ mol Mg(OH)}_2}}{0.4500 \text{ L HCl}}$$
$$= 0.091 M$$

36. Use the 0.1150M NaOH solution, since you will use approximately equal volumes of acid and base to reach the equivalent point. Otherwise, you will use almost 10 times as much base as acid.

37. $6.35 \text{ mol NH}_3 \times \frac{1 \text{ mol H}_2\text{SO}_4}{2 \text{ mol NH}_3}$
    $= 3.18 \text{ mol H}_2\text{SO}_4$

38. $10.0 \text{ g Na}_2\text{CO}_3 \times \frac{1 \text{ mol Na}_2\text{CO}_3}{105.99 \text{ g Na}_2\text{CO}_3}$
    $\times \frac{2 \text{ mol HCl}}{1 \text{ mol Na}_2\text{CO}_3} = 0.189 \text{ mol HCl}$

39. So that you know when equivalent amounts of nitric acid and sodium hydroxide have been mixed together

40. You would prefer to see it remain colorless. This shows that there is still some excess acid and you may continue adding base until you see a color change.

41. Add a measured amount of acid to the mixture, and continue titration with the base. In your calculations, do not forget to use the entire volume of acid (that is, what you put in at the beginning plus the excess acid added later).

42. Answers will vary. Students should be encouraged to share their lists.

43. 0.1M HNO_3

44. 0.1M NaOH

45. In A, $[H^+] = 10^{-5}M$. In B, $[H^+] = 1000 \times (10^{-5}) = 10^{-2}M$, so pH of solution B = 2.

46. pH = 10 $\Rightarrow$ pOH = 4 $\Rightarrow$ $[OH^-] = 10^{-4}M$
    pH = 8 $\Rightarrow$ pOH = 6 $\Rightarrow$ $[OH^-] = 10^{-6}M$
    $\frac{10^{-4}}{10^{-6}} = 100$, so $[OH^-]$ changes by a factor of 100.

47. **a.** pH = 1.0
    b. pH = 2.0
    c. pH = 4.0

48. **a.** pH = $-\log(0.50) = 0.30$
    b. pH = $-\log(0.025) = 1.60$

c. pH $= -\log(0.001\ 58) = 2.801$

49. a. $[H_3O^+] = \dfrac{10^{-14}}{1.0} = 10^{-14}$

pH $= 14.0$

b. $[H_3O^+] = \dfrac{10^{-14}}{0.0010} = 10^{-11}$

pH $= 11.0$

50. a. pH $= -\log\left(\dfrac{10^{-14}}{0.075}\right) = 12.88$

b. pH $= -\log\left(\dfrac{10^{-14}}{0.00839}\right) = 11.924$

51. a. $1.00 \times 10^{-3} M$
b. $1.00 \times 10^{-8} M$

52. a. $[H_3O^+] = 10^{-2.26} = 5.50 \times 10^{-3} M$
b. $[H_3O^+] = 10^{-7.69} = 2.04 \times 10^{-8} M$

53. a. acidic
b. acidic
c. acidic
d. basic

54. $[OH^-] = \dfrac{1.25\ g \times \frac{1\ mol}{40.00\ g}}{0.2500\ L} = 0.125 M$

$[H_3O^+] = \dfrac{10^{-14}}{0.125} = 8.0 \times 10^{-14}\ M$

pH $= -\log(8.0 \times 10^{-14}) = 13.10$

55. The pH must be in the range of 3.0 to 4.6, because bromphenol blue is yellow below 3.0 and blue above 4.6.

56. Yes, because water acts as both a proton donor (acid) and a proton acceptor (base)

57. Volume and pressure, because both relationships are inverse proportionalities.

58. $[H_3O^+]$ is greater than $[OH^-]$ in an acidic solution.

59. Because ammonia is a base, the hydroxide ion concentration is greater.

60. No, because all aqueous solutions contain *both* hydronium ions and hydroxide ions.

61. $[H_3O^+] = \dfrac{1 \times 10^{-14}}{0.0010}$

$= 1.0 \times 10^{-11}\ M$

62. $[H_3O^+] = \dfrac{1 \times 10^{-14}}{0.025}$

$= 4.0 \times 10^{-13}\ M$

63. Because HCl is an acid, adding it to a solution will increase $[H_3O^+]$ and decrease $[OH^-]$.

64. $[OH^-] = \dfrac{1 \times 10^{-14}}{0.10}$

$= 1.0 \times 10^{-13}\ M$

65. 25.0 mL of the acid will react with 25.0 mL of the base, leaving 25.0 mL of unreacted acid in 75.0 mL of solution.

$[H_3O^+] = \dfrac{0.0250\ L \times 0.200\ \frac{mol}{L}}{0.0750\ L}$

$= 0.0667 M$

66. 40.0 mL of the acid reacts with 40.0 mL of the base, leaving 10.0 mL of unreacted acid in 90.0 mL of solution.

$[H_3O^+] = \dfrac{0.0100\ L \times 0.200\ \frac{mol}{L}}{0.0900\ L}$

$= 0.0222 M$

$[OH^-] = \dfrac{1 \times 10^{-14}}{0.0222}$

$= 4.50 \times 10^{-13}\ M$

67. Stoichiometrically equal amounts must be used, so 50.0 mL of NaOH will neutralize the acid.

68. Since strong acids dissociate (nearly) completely, there is no need to report a value which, in essence, gives the degree of dissociation.

69. Hydrofluoric > acetic > carbonic > hypochlorous

70. $K_a = \dfrac{[CN^-][H_3O^+]}{[HCN]}$

71. Reactants, because weak acids undergo very little dissociation.

72. Hydrofluoric acid. Because it has the larger K_a, it is the stronger acid.

73. The weaker acid, hypochlorous acid, has a lower $[H_3O^+]$, so it has a higher pH.

74. A solution whose pH does not easily change as acid or base is added is a buffer.

75. The carbonic acid/ hydrogen carbonate buffers

76. NaCN (or any salt containing CN^-)

77. No, because I^- is unable to compete for protons in an aqueous solution. (HI is a strong acid.)

78. a. $CH_3COO^- + H_3O^+ \rightarrow CH_3COOH + H_2O$

b. $CH_3COOH + OH^- \rightarrow CH_3COO^- + H_2O$

79. Your stomach contains hydrochloric acid, which neutralizes the base. If you induce vomiting, any unneutralized base can damage the esophagus once again.

80. a. Graph II
b. Graph I
c. Graph IV

81. Ammonia is able to both donate and accept a proton, but the ammonium ion is unable to accept a proton, because it has no electron pairs left to share with H^+:

82. $0.005\ 58\ L \times \dfrac{0.101\ mol\ OH^-}{1\ L}$

$\times \dfrac{1\ mol\ acid}{1\ mol\ OH^-} = 0.000\ 563\ 6\ mol$

$\dfrac{0.115\ g}{0.000\ 563\ 6\ mol} = 204\ g/mol$

83. Wearing safety goggles and a lab apron, weigh out a sample of the acid, keeping track of its mass. Dissolve the acid in water and titrate it with a base (such as NaOH) of known concentration. Use the titration results to determine the number of moles of acid, and divide its mass by the moles to obtain the molar mass.

84. $HA + H_2O \rightleftharpoons H_3O^+ + A^-$

$[HA] = (0.25M - 4 \times 10^{-3})$

$[H_3O^+] = [A^-] = 4 \times 10^{-3}\ M$

$K_a = \dfrac{[H_3O^+][A^-]}{[HA]}$

$= \dfrac{(4 \times 10^{-3})(4 \times 10^{-3})}{(0.25 - 4 \times 10^{-3})}$

$= 6.5 \times 10^{-5}$

CHEMICAL PERSPECTIVES

Critical Thinking Skills

The following skills are applied in the feature.
- Identifying valid/invalid interpretations
- Making an informed decision
- Devising multiple solutions/interpretations

*F*ocus

Activate Prior Knowledge

Show a picture of city traffic or the skyline in Athens, Mexico City, or Los Angeles—all cities that have been forced to enact laws to reduce traffic in order to relieve air pollution. Ask students to predict the effects of pollution on historic buildings and statues in these cities, based on their study of acids and the concept of pH in Chapter 19.

*T*each

Science Background

Catalytic converters on automobile exhaust systems use a mixture of platinum-palladium pellets as a catalyst. As carbon monoxide passes over the catalyst, it is converted to carbon dioxide. The catalytic converter also catalyzes the conversion of nitrogen oxides to nitrogen and oxygen. The platinum-palladium pellets merely serve as catalysts and are not consumed in the chemical reactions. Largely because of the catalytic converter, carbon monoxide emissions from automobile exhausts have been reduced by 96% and nitrogen oxides by 76% since 1970.

Teaching Strategy

Have student groups call or write authorities for information on air pollution or acid rain in your state or region, and for the respondent's position on reduc-

Air Pollution and Acid Rain

Over the past two decades, scientists have collected a great deal of evidence that air pollutants from the combustion of fossil fuels and the smelting of metallic ores are causing acid rain. In addition, it is becoming more and more clear that acid rain is emerging as a growing environmental problem that is threatening forests, animal life, and even your health.

The effects of acid rain are evident on this sculpture.

Acid rain is any form of precipitation that has a pH of less than 5.6. Why a pH of 5.6 and not 7, which is neutral? Normal rainfall itself is slightly acidic. When water mixes with carbon dioxide in the air, carbonic acid is formed. A pH of 5.6 results.

Although acid rain was recognized over a century ago, it has become a widespread environmental problem only in the last three decades. During this time, the pH of precipitation in industrialized areas worldwide has decreased from 10 to 30 percent.

What is causing this increase in the acidity of precipitation? Air pollution from the combustion of fossil fuels, both coal and oil, is the primary cause. Coal and oil contain sulfur and nitrogen, which are released into the atmosphere as gaseous oxides when the fuel is burned. When sulfur oxides and nitrogen oxides react with water in the atmosphere, sulfurous, sulfuric, nitric, and nitrous acids are formed.

Seventy-nine percent of sulfur oxide emissions, about 20 million tons per year, come from coal-burning electric-power plants. Most of the remaining sulfur oxide emissions

ing it. Sources might include the state or federal EPA, the local electric utility, the organizations named in **Take Action** section below, local chapters of environmental and health organizations, your state senator and representative, your members of Congress, and ecology specialists from a local university. When responses arrive, have the groups make a chart showing the

nature of pollutants in your area and their health and environmental consequences.

Look Back

Review relevant concepts from Chapters 3, "Chemical Equations and Reactions"; 15, "Solutions"; and 19, "Acids and Bases" to introduce the discussion.

This forest illustrates the effects of acid rain on plant life.

come from smelting of ores and automobiles. These same sources produce over 60 percent of the nitric oxide emissions.

Acid rain has had a wide range of damaging effects on the environment. The pH of some lakes is now so low that fish can no longer reproduce successfully. Acid rain is also responsible for the presence of toxic metals in lakes, rivers, streams, and drinking water. Aluminum, cadmium, and lead salts are leached out of surrounding rocks and collect in bodies of water, where they poison plant and animal life.

Environmental scientists have warned that forests will become wastelands if something is not done to curb acid rain. Trees weakened by the stress of acid rain are more susceptible to damage as a result of natural events such as drought, insect attacks, and frosts. Breathing gaseous air

Although acid rain was recognized over a century ago, it has become a widespread environmental problem only in the last three decades.

pollutants that are associated with acid rain can cause respiratory diseases such as bronchitis, asthma, and emphysema.

Something must be done to curb acid rain. If additional steps are not taken to reduce the emissions of sulfur and nitrogen oxides into the atmosphere, today's threat will be tomorrow's catastrophe.

Discussing the Issues

1. What steps can be taken to curb sulfur oxide and nitrogen oxide emissions?
2. The controversy over acid rain is no longer about its cause and effects, but rather about who should pay for its control. Explain why this is such a controversial issue.

Take Action

1. Prepare and take a survey of people in your community to find out how aware they are of the causes and effects of acid rain.
2. Contact the Acid Rain Foundation, 1630 Blackhawk Hills, St. Paul, MN 55122, or the Acid Rain Information Clearinghouse, 33 S. Washington St., Rochester, NY 14608, to find out how you can support their efforts to curb acid rain.

677

Videodisc Connections

24679 to 26455, side 5
Acid rain (movie)

*C*lose

Discussing the Issues
Use the students' chart to focus the discussion on changes that could be made by individuals, industries, communities, and governments at each level to solve problems.

1. Answers will vary. Students may suggest conserving heat, driving less, recycling, requiring factories and power plants to install pollution-control devices or convert to nuclear power, developing electric cars, using alternative energy sources, devising city policies on mass transit/traffic, forming a national energy policy, and encouraging international cooperation on reducing pollution.
2. Answers will vary, but students should know that some people believe dangers are exaggerated and no new measures are necessary or that we cannot afford to make changes until our economy is stronger. There is disagreement about how much responsibility individual polluters, states, and the federal government should take. States that produce high-sulfur coal or that have large industries using it fear the loss of jobs and damage to their economy if they cannot use their traditional fuel. These states say they cannot afford to pay for expensive programs to benefit other areas. Other disagreements include the relative costs of health and environmental harm versus the costs to prevent the damage.

Take Action
1. Advise interested students on writing survey questions, targeting a survey population, and organizing the data.
2. Advise interested students about disseminating the information they received from environmental groups or forming a club to work on local issues.

Electrochemistry

Investigations	Demonstrations	Texas Essential Elements★
Laboratory Manual 20–1 M		**Content:** 2.6, 12.1, 12.2 **Process:** 2.1, 10.4
Laboratory Manual 20–2 S	Reactions That Drive Voltaic Cells, page T688 Anodes and Cathodes, page T689 Comparing Voltaic Cells, page T690	**Content:** 12.4 **Process:** 4.1, 4.2, 8.1, 10.1
Laboratory Manual 20–3 I In-text Investigation, page T704		**Content:** 12.3, 12.5, 12.6 **Process:** 10.1, 10.2
		Content: 12.4 **Process:** 1.1, 1.2, 1.3, 2.1, 4.1, 4.3, 5.1, 6.1, 7.1, 8.1
		Process: 3.2, 4.1, 4.2, 4.3, 7.1, 10.1

KEY:
M–*Microscale* **S**–*Structured*
I–*Inquiry* **IM**–*Inquiry Microscale*

★*See pages T8–T11 for complete listing of Texas Essential Elements.*

Chapter Rationale

If you are running out of time but you feel that your students need to have an understanding of the essentials of electrochemistry, your minimum goals should be that students be able to (1) recognize a redox reaction, (2) balance simple redox reactions, and (3) have a working knowledge of some applications of redox chemistry, such as dry cells.

About the Photograph

Nearly any object can be electroplated if its surface can be made to conduct electricity. Positive metal ions in the electroplating bath are attracted to a negatively charged surface. Once in contact with the negatively charged surface, metal ions such as copper, gold, or silver gain electrons and plate on the object.

Chapter Planning Hints

Plan to complete the chapter, including the Laboratory Investigation and the Chapter Review, within eight to ten class sessions. You will find four optional demonstrations suggested for this chapter. They appear on pages T681, T688, T689, and T690. You may wish to preview them at this time. Before beginning Part 3 you may wish to obtain a battery guide from a battery manufacturer.

20
Electrochemistry

Overview

The plating of metal is one example of a class of reactions that you will learn about in this chapter.

PART

1 Oxidation and Reduction

Many familiar chemical processes belong to a class of reactions called oxidation-reduction, or redox, reactions. Every minute, redox reactions are taking place inside your body and all around you. Reactions in batteries, burning of wood in a campfire, corrosion of metals, ripening of fruit, and combustion of gasoline are just a few examples of the wide range of redox reactions.

You already have seen some examples of oxidation and reduction reactions, when you classified reactions in Chapter 3. Recall that in a combustion reaction, such as the combustion of methane or the rusting of iron, oxygen is a reactant.

$$CH_4(g) + 2O_2(g) \rightarrow CO_2(g) + 2H_2O(g)$$
$$4Fe(s) + 3O_2(g) \rightarrow 2Fe_2O_3(s)$$

You learned that these reactions can be classified as synthesis or combustion. The term *oxidation* also seems reasonable for describing these reactions because, in both cases, a reactant combines with oxygen. The term *reduction* is used to describe the reverse process. You may recall one example of reduction from Chapter 3—the decomposition of water.

$$2H_2O(l) \rightarrow 2H_2(g) + O_2(g)$$

However, not all oxidation or reduction reactions involve oxygen. There are many similar reactions between metals and nonmetals that are classified as oxidation or reduction reactions. In this chapter, you will learn how to identify oxidation and reduction reactions and discover how these reactions work in the world around you.

20.1 Redox Reactions

A simple reaction will serve to demonstrate oxidation and reduction. When a piece of solid copper is immersed in a colorless silver nitrate solution, you can tell that a chemical reaction occurs because the solution turns blue over a period of time. You also notice a silvery coating that forms on the piece of copper, as shown in Figure 20-1 on the next page. What is the nature of this chemical change? You know that copper(II) ions in solution are blue, so copper(II) ions must be forming. The silver nitrate solution contains silver ions; these ions must be coming out of solution to form the solid silver-colored material. The unbalanced equation for the reaction between solid copper and silver ions is this.

$$Cu(s) + Ag^+(aq) \rightarrow Cu^{2+}(aq) + Ag(s)$$

Objectives

Part 1

A. *Differentiate* between *reduction, oxidation, reducing agent,* and *oxidizing agent.*

B. *Calculate* the oxidation numbers of atoms and ions.

C. *Apply* conservation laws to balance oxidation-reduction equations.

Developing Skills

Students may apply these skills in their study of Part 1.

Classifying: Have students classify reactions as oxidation or reduction.

Forming models: Have students draw diagrams of electron transfer in atoms and ions.

Predicting: Have students infer electron gain or loss in atoms or ions.

≡ FOCUS

Activate Prior Knowledge

In Chapter 2, students used ion charge to predict the formula of a compound. In Chapter 10, students determined possible ions that atoms will form based on the electron configurations of the atoms. Have students write the electron configurations for iron and oxygen. Then ask them to write the formulas for two different compounds formed from ions of iron and oxygen. (FeO, Fe_2O_3)

≡ TEACH

Teaching Strategy

Oxidation and Reduction

The definition for oxidation originally referred to an element combining with oxygen. In many combustion reactions, an element is oxidized and oxygen is reduced. The definition for oxidation was later expanded to refer to an atom losing electrons. This expanded definition can be used with reactions that do not involve oxygen. Section 20.1 offers students a definition of

(continued on page T680)

PART 1
Section 20.1 *continued*

(continued from page T679)
oxidation and reduction that does not include the concept of loss or gain of electrons. The definitions presented here are more intuitive than the LEO GER definitions of oxidation and reduction.

Cooperative Learning

Half-reactions

Teams of 3; **Time:** 20 minutes
Objective: Students will create models of electron transfer in atoms and ions.
Task: Student groups will design illustrations of electron transfer in atoms and ions. They may want to draw an atom of iron with an electron charge cloud and a nucleus. Then, they can draw the iron(III) ion. Have students practice with several different ions, both metals and nonmetals.
Team responsibility: Make sure that all team members participate in drawing the illustration and check each others' work.
Evaluation: Ask students at random to share one of their team's illustrations and explain it to the class.

Figure 20-1 Left: *A clean strip of copper metal has just been placed in a solution of silver nitrate.* Right: *After a period of time has passed, what observations tell you that a chemical reaction has taken place?*

The equation tells you that solid copper atoms are changing to copper ions at the same time that silver ions are changing to solid silver atoms.

Half-reactions Consider what is happening to the two reactants independently. Each copper atom loses two electrons to form a copper(II) ion, as described by the following equation.

$$Cu(s) \rightarrow Cu^{2+}(aq) + 2e^-$$

Each neutral copper atom acquired a 2+ charge by losing two electrons. Whenever an atom or ion becomes more positively charged (positive charge increases) in a chemical reaction, the process is called **oxidation.**

You know that electrons do not exist alone. In this reaction, electrons are transferred to the silver ions in solution, as described by the following equation:

$$Ag^+(aq) + e^- \rightarrow Ag(s)$$

When a silver ion acquires one electron, it loses its 1+ charge and becomes a neutral atom. Whenever an atom or ion becomes less positively charged (positive charge *reduces*) in a chemical reaction, the process is called **reduction.**

Figure 20-2 *Oxidation and reduction always occur together.*

Each of these equations describes only half of what takes place when solid copper reacts with silver ions. Reactions that show just half of a process are, logically enough, called **half-reactions.** You always need two half-reactions—one for oxidation and one for reduction—to describe any **redox reaction.** The reason for this is that it is impossible for oxidation to occur by itself. The electrons given up by oxidation cannot exist alone; they must be used by a reduction reaction. Thus, there will always be an oxidation half-reaction whenever there is a reduction half-reaction, and *vice versa.*

To find the net equation for a redox reaction, you might simply add the equations for the half-reactions. But doing this may not give you a balanced equation. You learned in Chapter 3 that a balanced equation must show the same number of atoms or ions on each side in order to satisfy the law of conservation of mass. Because redox reactions involve the transfer of electrons, balancing the net equation for a redox reaction also requires consideration of the number of electrons in each of the half-reaction equations. If electrons appear in the net equation for the redox reaction, you know you have made a mistake, because electrons cannot exist by themselves.

As you can see in Figure 20-3, each copper atom gives up two electrons, but each silver ion accepts only one electron. The overall equation is balanced only when the number of electrons lost in one half-reaction equals the electrons gained in the other half-reaction. The following example shows you how to balance the overall equation for the reaction between solid copper and silver ions.

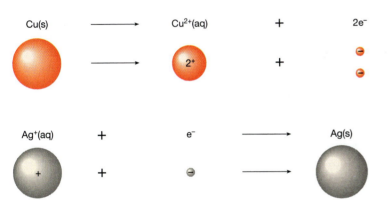

Figure 20-3 *Each copper atom loses two electrons, but each silver ion gains only one electron.*

EXAMPLE 20-1

Balance the following redox equation.

$$Cu(s) + Ag^+(aq) \rightarrow Cu^{2+}(aq) + Ag(s)$$

Analyze the Problem You are given the reactants, products, and the charges on the ions. To balance the equation, you must make sure that atoms and ions are balanced in the net equation and that electrons are balanced in the equations for the half-reactions.

D E M O N S T R A T I O N

Half-reactions

Add about 7 grams of copper(II) chloride to 50 mL of deionized water. Dissolve the crystals. Add a 10-cm square of aluminum foil to the solution. In a few seconds the aluminum will begin to disintegrate. Use this demonstration to introduce the concepts of oxidation and reduction; the aluminum is oxidized and the copper(II) ions are reduced. Hydrogen gas is also produced.

CAUTION: Wear safety goggles and a lab apron. Use a shield to protect students. For disposal, wrap the solids in newspaper and put in the wastebasket. Let the decantate evaporate; put the residue in a sealed, labeled container for an EPA-approved waste disposal contractor.

PART 1
Section 20.1 continued

PROBLEM SOLVING

▶ As an exercise in problem solving, ask students to devise a way to balance the equation without writing half-reactions (balance charges). The two solutions should be compared to show that the results are the same.

Encourage students to write out half-reactions neatly and accurately. They should also arrange the half-reactions so that the arrows line up one below the other. This is especially important for more complex redox equation balancing.

Some students will have difficulty understanding ionic charges. You may want to review with them the fundamentals of atomic structures (protons and electrons) and particle charge.

Students saw pre-algebra equation writing in Chapter 2, when they were writing formulas of ionic substances. Refer them to Chapter 2, Example 2–6, where they had to determine the charge on ions given the formula of the ionic compound.

Practice Problems

Assign the Practice Problems.

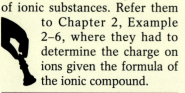

Videodisc Connections

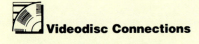

26478 to 31625, side 5
Red hots get oxidized (movie)

31626 to 36210, side 5
KMnO$_4$ and glycerine (movie)

36211 to 43242, side 5
Shakhashire: copper and hydrogen (movie)

PROBLEM-SOLVING STRATEGY

When you **write chemical equations** for the half-reactions, writing one equation above the other, with the arrows lined up, will make the addition easier.

PROBLEM-SOLVING STRATEGY

Use what you know about electrons to **verify** that the net equation makes sense. The balanced net equation does not have electrons because free electrons do not exist in solution.

■ **Apply a Strategy** Start by writing equations for the half-reactions. First balance the number of electrons in the two half-reactions, and then add the equations to give the balanced equation for the overall reaction.

■ **Work a Solution** The equations for the half-reactions can be written like this.

$$Cu(s) \rightarrow Cu^{2+}(aq) + 2e^-$$
$$Ag^+(aq) + e^- \rightarrow Ag(s)$$

Balance the number of electrons in the two half-reactions by multiplying the second equation by two.

$$Cu(s) \rightarrow Cu^{2+}(aq) + 2e^-$$
$$2Ag^+(aq) + 2e^- \rightarrow 2Ag(s)$$

The number of electrons in both equations is now equal. Add the equations for the two half-reactions to give the balanced redox equation:

$$Cu(s) \rightarrow Cu^{2+}(aq) + 2\cancel{e^-}$$
$$\underline{2Ag^+(aq) + 2\cancel{e^-} \rightarrow 2Ag(s)}$$
$$2Ag^+(aq) + Cu(s) \rightarrow Cu^{2+}(aq) + 2Ag(s)$$

■ **Verify Your Answer** Check to make sure the atoms or ions on both sides of the equation are equal. Looking at the balanced equation, you can see that there are 2 silver particles and 1 copper particle on each side.

Another way to check the answer is to determine whether the net charge is equal on both sides of the overall equation. To do this, look at the left side of the net equation. You can see that 2 silver ions, each with a 1+ charge, have a total charge of 2+. On the right side of the equation, the copper(II) ion has a charge of 2+. The total charge is therefore the same on both sides of the net equation.

Practice Problems

1. Balance the following equation for a redox reaction.

$$Cr^{3+}(aq) + Zn(s) \rightarrow Cr(s) + Zn^{2+}(aq)$$

2. Write a balanced equation for the reduction of iron(III) ions to iron(II) ions by the oxidation of nickel atoms to nickel(II) ions in aqueous solution.

Oxidation and reduction occur together. The solid copper is called the **reducing agent,** because it brings about the reduction of silver ions. If the silver ions were not present, the copper would not oxidize. The silver ion is the **oxidizing agent,** because it causes the oxidation of copper atoms. Notice that the substance that is reduced is the oxidizing agent and the substance that is oxidized is the reducing agent.

Concept ✓ Check

In the reaction $Fe^{2+}(aq) + Mg(s) \rightleftharpoons Fe(s) + Mg^{2+}(aq)$

Which reactant is the oxidizing agent? The reducing agent?

20.2 Oxidation Numbers

To keep track of electron transfers in redox reactions more easily, oxidation numbers have been assigned to all atoms and ions. An **oxidation number** is the real or apparent charge an atom or ion has when all bonds are assumed to be ionic. The oxidation number of an atom is determined by pretending that electrons are not shared in chemical bonds, but instead belong to the atom having the higher electronegativity. For example, in the water molecule, the oxygen atom is more electronegative than hydrogen—that is, oxygen has the greater tendency to gain electrons. Oxygen is assigned the two electrons contributed by the two hydrogen atoms. These extra electrons give oxygen a charge of -2 just as if it were an ion. But you know this is not actually true. The chemical bonds in the water molecule are covalent. In a sense, assigning oxidation numbers is arbitrary, but it is useful because it allows you to follow the exchange of electrons that occurs in oxidation and reduction reactions.

Rules for assigning oxidation numbers You are already familiar with the oxidation numbers shown in Table 20-1. Here are some easy-to-follow rules for assigning others.

Rule 1: The oxidation number for any atom in its elementary state is zero.

Rule 2: The oxidation number for any simple ion is the charge on the ion.
    a. The oxidation number of alkali metals in compounds is $+1$—for example, Li^+, Na^+, and K^+.
    b. The oxidation number of alkaline earth metals in compounds is $+2$—for example, Mg^{2+}, Ca^{2+}, and Ba^{2+}.

Rule 3: The oxidation number for oxygen usually is -2. In peroxides, it is -1.

Rule 4: The oxidation number for hydrogen is $+1$ in all its compounds except metal hydrides like NaH and BaH_2, in which it is -1.

Rule 5: All other oxidation numbers are assigned so that the sum of oxidation numbers equals the net charge on the molecule or polyatomic ion.

These rules will allow you to determine the oxidation number of the atoms in most compounds or polyatomic ions. If no rule applies to the compound or ion with which you are working, draw the electron dot structure to predict their oxidation numbers.

TABLE 20-1

Oxidation Numbers of Simple Ions	
Ion	**Oxidation Number**
Mg^{2+}	$+2$
Al^{3+}	$+3$
Cl^-	-1
S^{2-}	-2

DO YOU KNOW?

Only one element, fluorine, is more electronegative than oxygen. When oxygen bonds to fluorine, oxygen assumes an oxidation number of $+1$ or $+2$. Such compounds are rare.

Teaching Strategy

Oxidation Numbers

Usually with the introduction of oxidation numbers, students ask, "Why do we have to know this anyway?" Oxidation numbers are handy tools for determining whether or not a reaction is redox. If it is redox, oxidation numbers tell which species is oxidized and which is reduced. Discuss with students the fact that oxidation numbers are arbitrary numbers used to define a system.

PART 1

Section 20.2 continued

Practice Problems

Assign the Practice Problems.

PROBLEM-SOLVING

S T R A T E G Y

Recognize the pattern that the rules are general guidelines. You must decide which rules are appropriate for assigning oxidation numbers in a particular problem.

PROBLEM-SOLVING

S T R A T E G Y

*It may help to **think of similar problems** that you have solved involving charges of ions—for example, predicting formulas, which you did in Section 2.11.*

EXAMPLE 20-2

What is the oxidation number of each atom in the sulfite ion, $SO_3{}^{2-}$?

■ *Analyze the Problem* There are two different elements, oxygen and sulfur, in this ion. The problem is asking you to find the oxidation number of each element.

■ *Apply a Strategy* Check to see which rules for assigning oxidation numbers might apply. Then draw a table to organize your data.

■ *Work a Solution* The sulfite ion is polyatomic, so the sum of the oxidation numbers must equal the charge of the ion (Rule 5). Since the net charge on the sulfite ion is $2-$, the sum of the oxidation numbers of sulfur and the three oxygen atoms must be equal to -2. According to Rule 3, each oxygen atom has an oxidation number of -2. The following table will help to determine the oxidation number of sulfur.

Atoms	Total oxidation number
S	$1(?)\ = ?$
$3O$	$3(-2) = -6$
SO_3	$= -2$

You are looking for the oxidation number of sulfur. Rephrasing the problem in terms of algebra may be helpful. What is the result when you subtract -6 from -2? The answer is $+4$. Therefore, the oxidation number of each sulfur atom is $+4$. The oxidation number of each atom of oxygen is -2. Another approach to the problem is to set up your table as a subtraction. Place SO_3 at the top and subtract the contribution of oxygen.

■ *Verify Your Answer* Try checking your answer by working backward. You know that the sum of oxidation numbers for all atoms in a polyatomic ion should equal the total charge of the ion. The oxidation number of sulfur is $+4$, and the total of the oxidation numbers for three oxygen atoms is $3(-2) = -6$. The sum of $+4$ and -6 is -2, which is the same as the charge of $SO_3{}^{2-}$. This confirms that you have not made an error in addition.

Practice Problems

3. What is the oxidation number of each atom in the nitrate polyatomic ion, $NO_3{}^-$?   ***Ans.*** $N = +5; O = -2$

4. What is the oxidation number of each hydrogen atom in a hydrogen gas molecule, H_2?   ***Ans.*** $H = 0$

5. What is the oxidation number of each element in $MgBr_2$?   ***Ans.*** $Mg = +2; Br = -1$

20.3 Balancing Complicated Redox Reactions

Most chemical reactions are complex, and unless the reaction has been studied very carefully, exactly what happens during the reaction is not known. Nevertheless, you can begin to write the balanced equation by starting with what you know. For example, in the reaction between zinc metal and the vanadate ion, VO_3^-, the two reactants can be written down on the left side of an arrow and the products on the right.

$$Zn(s) + VO_3^-(aq) \rightarrow Zn^{2+}(aq) + VO^{2+}(aq)$$

Notice that the number of oxygen atoms on both sides of the equation are not equal and the equation is not balanced with respect to charge. Moreover, not all the reacting species are represented. Because this reaction takes place in acid solution, hydrogen ions, H^+, must be involved. You can balance an equation for this reaction by writing equations for the half-reactions, balancing the increase and decrease in oxidation numbers and then summing up the equations to get an overall equation. Zinc reacts to give zinc ions. Its half-reaction is this.

$$Zn(s) \rightarrow Zn^{2+}(aq) + 2e^-$$

The oxidation number of vanadium decreases from $+5$ to $+4$ when the vanadate ion, VO_3^-, changes to the vanadyl ion, VO^{2+}.

Atoms	Total oxidation number
V	$1(?) = +5$
3 O	$1(-2) = -6$
VO_3^-	$= -1$

Atoms	Total oxidation number
V	$1(?) = +4$
O	$1(-2) = -2$
VO^{2+}	$= +2$

The unbalanced equation for the reduction half-reaction is this.

$$VO_3^- \rightarrow VO^{2+}$$

First balance the oxygen atoms. There are three oxygen atoms on the left and only one on the right. Since the reaction is taking place in acid solution, there will be many hydrogen ions in the solution. Experiments show that hydrogen ions react with the excess oxygen to form water, though almost certainly through a complicated series of steps. Thus it is common practice to balance redox equations in acid solutions by assuming that hydrogen ions combine with excess oxygen to form water.

$$VO_3^-(aq) + 4H^+(aq) \rightarrow VO^{2+}(aq) + 2H_2O(l)$$

PROBLEM-SOLVING STRATEGY

Use what you know about acid solutions to determine that H^+ ions are present.

PART 1
Section 20.3

Teaching Strategy

Balancing Complicated Redox Reactions

The section on balancing redox reactions is not meant to be comprehensive. Only one method of balancing is presented here, that is, the half-reaction method. This method is more universal than the oxidation number method and can be applied more habitually to a wide range of redox reactions. Also, balancing redox equations for reactions in basic conditions is more complex, and need not be introduced in a beginning chemistry course.

PROBLEM SOLVING

▶ To strengthen problem-solving skills, encourage students to think of other strategies that might be used to balance such equations. Compare results from several procedures. Comparable results should strengthen faith that the answer derived is the correct one.

Guided Practice

Review the Concept Check question on page 683 with students. Answers can be found in Appendix E on page 808.

PART 1

Section 20.3 *continued*

Reteaching Idea

If students have difficulty with oxidation numbers and the definitions of oxidation and reduction, provide them with more practice by having them determine the oxidation numbers of each sulfur (i.e., apparent charge per sulfur atom) in the following molecules and ions.
SO_2, SO_4^{2-}, S_8, S_2O_3, H_2S, $S_2O_3^{2-}$ (4+, 6+, 0, 3+, 2−, 2+)
Have them arrange the molecules and ions in order of the most highly reduced sulfur to the most highly oxidized sulfur. Reinforce the historic definition of oxidation as the combining of an atom with oxygen, but more importantly, stress the more inclusive definition of oxidation as an increase in positive oxidation number.

☰ CLOSE

Summing Up Main Ideas

Have students write two balanced equations for redox reactions involving oxygen as the oxidized element and as the reduced element.
$$2H_2O(l) \rightarrow 2H_2(g) + O_2(g)$$
$$4Fe(s) + 3O_2(g) \rightarrow 2Fe_2O_3(s)$$
Ask students to explain why a definition of oxidation and reduction that describes reactions in terms of gaining or losing positive charge is better than defining oxidation and reduction in terms of oxygen.

PART 1 REVIEW

Assign the Part Review questions.

Evaluating Skills

These skills are evaluated in the Part Review questions indicated. **Determining main ideas:** 6, 8, 9, 11; **Classifying:** 7; **Analyzing data:** 10; **Applying a strategy:** 10; **Calculating:** 10; **Verifying results:** 10

Two water molecules were added to the right side in order to have a total of three oxygen atoms on each side of the equation. You then add four hydrogen ions to the left side in order to balance hydrogen on both sides of the equation.

Now that the atoms are balanced on each side of the equation, you can balance the charge. The net charge on the left is $3+$, and the net charge on the right is $2+$. In order to balance the charge, you can add one electron on the left. (Remember, electrons are produced from the reaction of zinc.)

$$VO_3^-(aq) + 4H^+(aq) + e^- \rightarrow VO^{2+}(aq) + 2H_2O(l)$$

Since there were two electrons produced by the reaction of each zinc atom, two must be consumed by the reaction of the vanadate ion. This can be shown by multiplying the entire equation by two.

$$2VO_3^-(aq) + 8H^+(aq) + 2e^- \rightarrow 2VO^{2+}(aq) + 4H_2O(l)$$

Then add the two half-reactions.

PROBLEM-SOLVING STRATEGY

*You **solved a similar problem** in Section 15.6 when you balanced net ionic equations.*

$$Zn(s) \rightarrow Zn^{2+}(aq) + 2e^-$$
$$2VO_3^- + 8H^+ + 2e^- \rightarrow 2VO^{2+} + 4H_2O$$
$$\overline{2VO_3^-(aq) + Zn(s) + 8H^+(aq) \rightarrow 2VO^{2+}(aq) + Zn^{2+}(aq) + 4H_2O(l)}$$

Notice that the equation only tells you what happens in the reaction between vanadate ions and zinc. You were told that the reaction takes place in acid solution. If the solution is acidified by sulfuric acid, there will be sulfate ions present; if the solution is acidified by nitric acid, there will be nitrate ions present. It is impossible to obtain vanadate ions by themselves; they are always produced together with a positive ion. However, these spectator ions do not take part in the reaction and often are omitted from the balanced equation.

PART 1 REVIEW

6. Define *oxidation* and *reduction*.

7. Determine which of the following processes are oxidations and which are reductions.
   a. Co^{2+} becomes Co c. Fe^{3+} becomes Fe^{2+}
   b. $2I^-$ becomes I_2 d. Sn^{2+} becomes Sn^{4+}

8. What is an oxidizing agent?

9. How do you know when a redox equation is balanced?

10. Balance the following redox equations. Identify what has been reduced and what is the reducing agent.
    a. $Na(s) + Cl_2(g) \rightarrow NaCl(s)$
    b. $Cu^{2+}(aq) + Mg(s) \rightarrow Cu(s) + Mg^{2+}(aq)$
    c. $Fe^{3+}(aq) + Al(s) \rightarrow Fe^{2+}(aq) + Al^{3+}(aq)$
    d. $Au^{3+}(aq) + Cd(s) \rightarrow Au(s) + Cd^{2+}(aq)$

11. Define *oxidation number*.

Boxed numbers indicate questions that involve skills in interpretation, application, and analysis.

PART 1 REVIEW

ANSWERS

■ **Keyed to Objectives**

A **6.** Oxidation is the process in which an atom or ion gains positive charge. Reduction is the process in which an atom or ion loses positive charge.

A **7. a.** reduction
   b. oxidation
   c. reduction
   d. oxidation

A **8.** An oxidizing agent is the reagent that is reduced in a redox reaction.

C **9.** A redox equation is balanced when both the number of each kind of atom or ion on both sides of the equation is equal, and when the total electric charge on the reactant side equals the total charge on the product side.

R E S E A R C H & T E C H N O L O G Y

Solar Cells

The sun has been shedding its light on Earth for billions of years. Only recently, however, has it been possible to make use of sunlight for something other than heat. In 1839, the French scientist Edmund Becquerel observed that a weak electric current could be produced when sunlight fell on certain materials. Exploitation of this property later gave birth to the solar cell. Solar cells can change light energy from the sun directly into electrical energy.

Solar cells were first developed as power sources for satellites. Banks or arrays of solar cells unfold once the satellite is in orbit. The solar cells produce electricity to power the equipment in the satellite and to recharge batteries that are used when the satellite is in Earth's shadow. The amazing thing about them is that these miniature electric power plants don't have any movable parts.

Solar cells are made of layers of a semiconducting crystal such as silicon. Silicon semiconductors can be made more efficient by a process called *doping*. Doping involves adding impurities to the crystal structure of the sili-con. If some arsenic atoms replace silicon atoms in the crystal lattice, an n-type semiconductor is produced. Because arsenic atoms have more valence electrons than silicon atoms, excess electrons are available in n-type semiconductors. Doping the crystal with boron produces a p-type semiconductor. Boron atoms have one less electron than is necessary to bond with the neighboring silicon atoms. Therefore, electron vacancies, or *holes,* are created in p-type semiconductors.

In an individual solar cell, an n-type and a p-type semiconductor are sandwiched in layers. When exposed to sunlight, the p-type semiconductor gives up its extra electrons. These electrons are then free to flow into the holes in the n-type semiconductor, producing an electric current.

By the end of this century, solar cell power plants may rival conventional fossil fuel power plants, according to the Electric Power Research Institute. Many people find this method of electricity production very desirable because solar cell power plants are nonpolluting and silent.

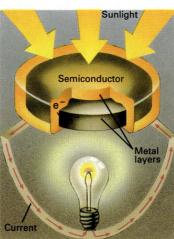

Arrays of photovoltaic cells collect energy from the sun for direct and efficient conversion to electricity.

C **10.** **a.** $2Na(s) + Cl_2(g) \rightarrow 2NaCl(s)$
$Cl_2(g)$ is reduced.
Na(s) is the reducing agent.
b. $Cu^{2+}(aq) + Mg(s) \rightarrow Cu(s) + Mg^{2+}(aq)$
Cu^{2+} is reduced. Mg is the reducing agent.
c. $3Fe^{3+}(aq) + Al(s) \rightarrow 3Fe^{2+}(aq) + Al^{3+}(aq)$
Fe^{3+} is reduced. Al is the reducing agent.

d. $2Au^{3+}(aq) + 3Cd(s) \rightarrow 2Au(s) + 3Cd^{2+}(aq)$
Au^{3+} is reduced. Cd is the reducing agent.

B **11.** Oxidation number is the real or apparent charge an atom or ion has when assigned a certain number of electrons.

PART **2**
Spontaneous Redox Reactions

Section 20.4

Developing Skills

Students may apply these skills in their study of Part 2.

Forming models: Have students form models of electrochemical cells.

Analyzing data: Have students interpret data from electrochemical cells.

Predicting: Have students use Table 20–2 to predict spontaneity in redox reactions.

Analyzing data: Have students relate half-cell potentials to electrochemical cells.

Determining cause and effect: Have students apply concepts in electrochemistry to industrial and household uses.

Analyzing data: Have students devise multiple solutions to voltage in electrochemical cells.

≡ FOCUS

Activate Prior Knowledge

Students have observed the movement of electrons in their experiences with electricity. Initiate a discussion about electricity by demonstrating static electricity. Have students name other common experiences in which they have observed electrons flowing. These can include seeing a spark when an appliance is turned on or when a car is jump-started and observing lightning discharge.

≡ TEACH

Teaching Strategy

Simple Voltaic Cells

Do not introduce the students to half-cell potentials yet. Let students deal with the qualitative aspects of electrochemistry first.

Objectives

Part 2

D. *Predict* whether or not a redox reaction will occur spontaneously.

E. *Calculate* the voltage of a voltaic cell, using a table of standard reduction potentials.

Figure 20-4 *Without batteries, many of the things we need or enjoy would "go dead."*

PART 2 Spontaneous Redox Reactions

Stop for a moment to think how strange and amazing it is that a chemical reaction can light a flashlight or power a portable radio. The reactions that cause battery-operated items to work are oxidation-reduction reactions. An **electrochemical cell** is a chemical system in which an oxidation-reduction reaction can occur. When electrons flow from the reducing agent to the oxidizing agent, an electric current is established in the cell. Electrochemical cells in which the redox reaction occurs spontaneously are called batteries, or **voltaic cells.** The current produced by batteries can do useful electrical work, such as running an electric motor, which converts electrical energy into mechanical energy.

Today's society depends on voltaic cells. An automobile uses one type of voltaic cell, a storage battery, to start its engine. A common battery, or dry cell, is another kind of voltaic cell. Flashlights, toys, games, watches, and portable computers all operate on power supplied by voltaic cells.

20.4 Simple Voltaic Cells

A voltaic cell can easily be constructed so that it can do useful work, as shown in Figure 20-5. The beakers contain $1M$ solutions of copper(II) sulfate, $CuSO_4$, and zinc sulfate, $ZnSO_4$. Both copper(II) sulfate and zinc sulfate are electrolytes, which, as you learned in Chapter 15, are substances whose water solutions conduct an electric current. A zinc strip is placed in the zinc sulfate solution, and a copper strip is placed in the copper(II) sulfate solution. These metal strips are *electrodes*, electrically conducting solids that are placed in contact with the electrolyte solutions. The **salt bridge** is composed of a concentrated solution of a strong electrolyte, such as potassium nitrate. The salt bridge can be a U-tube containing the solution or simply a ribbon of filter paper saturated with potassium nitrate solution. The purpose of the salt bridge will become apparent soon.

In order to complete the circuit, a wire is connected to each electrode, and those wires are attached to an LED (light emitting diode). As soon as the circuit is complete, the LED lights up. The voltaic cell is doing useful electrical work. However, in a matter of minutes, the glow in the LED begins to fade and will eventually go out.

Reactions that drive voltaic cells A very simple observation helps to explain how the zinc-copper voltaic cell works. When the mass of each electrode is measured before and after the

---

DEMONSTRATION

Reactions That Drive Voltaic Cells

Demonstrate a rather surprising reaction when a strip of Mg and a strip of Cu are placed in $1M\,Cu^{2+}$ solution. The Mg is the anode and the Cu acts as a cathode. No salt bridge is needed, but do not short out the cell by touching the two electrodes. See if you can play a small portable radio using this cell as the energy source.

⚠ **CAUTION: Wear safety goggles and a lab apron.** For disposal, wrap the solids in newspaper and put in the wastebasket. Let the decantate evaporate; put the residue in a sealed, labeled container for an EPA-approved disposal contractor.

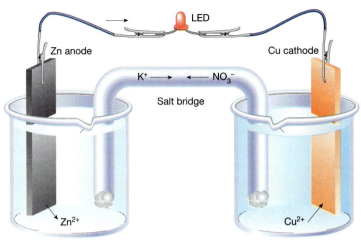

1M zinc sulfate 1M copper sulfate

Figure 20-5 *When connected by wires and a simple salt bridge, electric charge flows through the circuit and causes the LED to light up.*

reaction, it is found to be different. The copper electrode has a greater mass after the reaction, and the zinc electrode has less mass. The explanation for the change in mass is rather simple. As the cell works, the zinc electrode is oxidized, forming zinc ions that are released into solution.

$$Zn(s) \rightarrow Zn^{2+}(aq) + 2e^-$$

The copper ions from the copper(II) sulfate solution are reduced at the copper electrode.

$$Cu^{2+}(aq) + 2e^- \rightarrow Cu(s)$$

The zinc electrode loses electrons, while the copper electrode gains electrons. The electrons flow through the wire from the zinc electrode to the copper electrode, as shown in Figure 20-5. Sufficient current flows to cause the LED to light up.

What is the purpose of the salt bridge? If charges build up at either electrode, they will repel like charges, and current will stop flowing. The salt bridge is necessary to complete the circuit and prevent the buildup in each beaker of excess positive or negative charges. As positively charged zinc ions, Zn^{2+}, are formed in the left cell compartment, negatively charged nitrate ions, NO_3^-, are attracted from the salt bridge and enter the beaker. At the same time, positively charged copper(II) ions, Cu^{2+}, are removed from the solution in the right cell compartment and potassium ions, K^+, enter the beaker to take their place. The contents of both beakers remain electrically neutral, even as the concentrations of reactants and products change during the reaction. The current will continue to flow in the cell until the cell reaches equilibrium.

Anodes and cathodes Zinc metal is more easily oxidized than copper metal. Copper ions are more easily reduced than zinc

DO YOU KNOW?

Battery *actually means "a series of galvanic cells," such as in a 12-volt car battery. Flashlight batteries are more accurately called dry cells.*

DEMONSTRATION

Anodes and Cathodes

An electrochemical cell can be made from a lemon, a copper penny (cathode), and a strip of zinc (anode). Stick the Zn and penny into a lemon about 1 cm apart. Attach a voltmeter. It should register about 0.15 volt.

CAUTION: Wear safety goggles and a lab apron. For disposal, save the electrodes for future use or wrap in newspaper and put in the wastebasket.

TABLE 20-2

Oxidation Properties for Some Common Metals	
Easily Oxidized	**Strong Reducing Agents**
	Li
	K
	Cs
	Ca
	Na
	Mg
	Al
	Mn
	Zn
	Cr
	Fe
	Cd
	Co
	Cu
	Ag
	Au
Not Easily Oxidized	**Weak Reducing Agents**

ions. The spontaneous reaction in the voltaic cell is expressed as the sum of the equations for the two half-reactions.

$$Zn(s) \rightarrow Zn^{2+}(aq) + 2e^-$$
$$Cu^{2+}(aq) + 2e^- \rightarrow Cu(s)$$
$$\overline{Zn(s) + Cu^{2+}(aq) \rightarrow Zn^{2+}(aq) + Cu(s)}$$

In this example, the zinc electrode is called the anode, and the copper electrode is called the cathode. The **anode** is the site of oxidation, and the **cathode** is the site of reduction.

How can you tell which of two metals will be the cathode and which will be the anode? Table 20-2 lists some common metals according to their relative ease of oxidation. Given any two metals in the table, the one that is closer to the top will be the anode, because it is more easily oxidized.

Concept ✔ Check

Which is more easily oxidized, iron or cobalt? If paired in a voltaic cell, which would be the anode?

20.5 Comparing Voltaic Cells

There are so many different combinations of oxidation and reduction half-reactions that the number of possible electrochemical cells is enormous. How could you determine which cells would be the most effective in producing electricity?

Comparing electricity to flowing water Three concepts about the nature of electricity will be helpful in comparing electrochemical cells. Perhaps these concepts will be more meaningful if the flow of electric current through a wire is compared to the flow of water through a pipe. Suppose you were a fire fighter trying to put out a raging fire. You hook up your hose to a fire hydrant and hope that the water flows through the hose as usual. As a fire fighter, you would be interested in three things.

1. ***Is there enough water available*** to put out the fire?
2. ***How fast can water flow*** from the fire hydrant?
3. ***How high will you be able to reach*** with the water?

The amount of water, its flow rate, and its pressure are important in fighting a fire. The same kinds of things are important to consider when working with voltaic cells. Cells need enough electricity, moving at an adequate rate, with sufficiently high pressure to do the job at hand. Table 20-3 compares important quantities in water systems with those in voltaic cells.

The SI unit used to measure the amount of electricity flowing through a wire is the **coulomb.** One coulomb is the charge of 1.04×10^{-5} mol of electrons.

D E M O N S T R A T I O N

Comparing Voltaic Cells

You can make a "flash cube" go off by setting up a cell made from a strip of magnesium and copper and 3*M* sulfuric acid as the electrolyte.

⚠ **CAUTION: Sulfuric acid is corrosive. Wear safety goggles, face** shield, lab apron, and gloves. Conduct the reaction behind a shield.

For disposal, rinse the electrodes with water. Neutralize the acid by slowly adding 0.5*M* or less concentrated base until the pH is about 7; then pour down the drain.

TABLE 20-3

Comparing Flow of Water to Flow of Electricity		
Quantity Measured	Units Used with Water	Units Used with Electricity
amount of flow	gallons	coulombs
rate of flow	gallons/minute	coulombs/second (amperes)
tendency to flow (pressure)	pounds/inch^2	volts

The rate of flow is the amount transported divided by the time it takes to transport. Gallons per minute for water and coulombs per second for electricity are used to indicate the rate of flow. One coulomb per second is also called an **ampere,** one of the seven base SI units. A circuit through which one coulomb is passing per second is said to be carrying a current of one ampere.

Electrical pressure is expressed in volts. **Voltage** is a measure of the tendency of electrons to flow.

Cell voltages Voltaic cells can be tested for their ability to produce an electric current by comparing the tendency of the electrons to flow, or the voltage. A voltaic cell with a high voltage is one that can do a large amount of work in a given amount of time. Each half-reaction contributes to the total voltage of the cell.

A copper-hydrogen voltaic cell is set up as shown in Figure 20-6. In the beaker on the right, the copper is being reduced.

$$Cu^{2+}(aq) + 2e^- \rightarrow Cu(s)$$

In the beaker on the left, hydrogen gas is being oxidized.

$$H_2(g) \rightarrow 2H^+(aq) + 2e^-$$

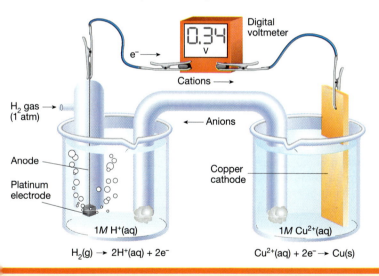

Figure 20-6 *The standard hydrogen half-cell on the left uses a platinum electrode because platinum does not react with hydrogen ion. Hydrogen is oxidized when the standard half-cell is connected to a Cu/Cu^{2+} half-cell.*

DO YOU KNOW?

Have you ever been shocked when you walked on a plush carpet and then touched a metal doorknob? The voltage in the shock is about 10 000 volts. However, the amperage is very low.

PART 2

Section 20.5 *continued*

Science Background

Cell Voltages

Table 20–3 suggests that volts are comparable to water pressure. This is a useful concept for students; however, pressure and voltage are expressed in fundamentally different units. The equation upon which the definition of electric potential is based states that the electric potential energy, U_e, due to two like charges, q_1 and q_2, separated by a distance r is:

$$U_e = k\frac{q_1q_2}{r}$$

where k is a constant. If q_2 is a *unit* charge, the electric potential energy due to its position at distance r from q_1 becomes $\frac{kq_1}{r}$.

This potential energy per unit charge is called the *electric potential* V at distance r, i.e.:

$$V = k\frac{q_1}{r}$$

The definition of voltage is developed from a consideration of the effect of moving a charge q between points A and B having electric potentials V_A and V_B. The resulting change in *potential energy*, ΔU, is given by the equation

$$\Delta U = q(V_B - V_A)$$

If ΔU is expressed in joules and q in coulombs, then the potential difference ($V_B - V_A$) is expressed in volts. Thus the volt is defined as one joule per coulomb. Emphasize that the volt is always a difference unit. At students' homes, electric outlets have a potential difference of 115 volts between the hot side and the ground side of the line, which provides the driving force for the electric current to light lamps and heat toasters.

The voltmeter, a device for measuring voltage, reads 0.34 volts as the electric current flows.

In Chapter 19, you learned that Brønsted acid-base systems can be thought of in terms of competition for protons. In much the same way, oxidation-reduction reactions can be thought of as a competition for electrons. In a copper-hydrogen cell, copper ions have a greater tendency to gain electrons than do hydrogen ions. The electrons flow away from hydrogen toward the copper ions, not the other way around. The spontaneous reaction between copper ions and hydrogen gas can be expressed like this.

$$Cu^{2+}(aq) + H_2(g) \rightarrow Cu(s) + 2H^+(aq)$$

Copper atoms do not give up electrons to hydrogen ions.

In Figure 20-7, a zinc-hydrogen cell is depicted. In this cell, the zinc is being oxidized and the hydrogen is being reduced. The cell voltage is 0.76 volts. The two half-reactions are these.

$$Zn(s) \rightarrow Zn^{2+}(aq) + 2e^-$$
$$2H^+(aq) + 2e^- \rightarrow H_2(g)$$

Figure 20-7 *Hydrogen is reduced when the standard hydrogen half-cell is connected to a Zn/Zn^{2+} half-cell.*

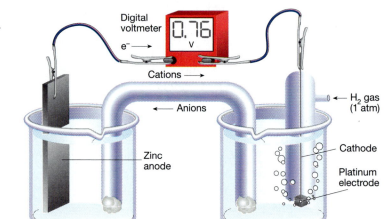

In the competition for electrons, the hydrogen ions win out over the zinc ions. Electrons flow from the zinc atoms to the hydrogen ions. The overall equation for the spontaneous reaction is this.

$$Zn(s) + 2H^+(aq) \rightarrow Zn^{2+}(aq) + H_2(g)$$

The copper-hydrogen and zinc-hydrogen cells provide information about the relative abilities of copper, zinc, and hydrogen ions to compete for electrons. Since both cells have a common reactant, hydrogen, the ability of the three ions to gain electrons can be compared. In the first cell, copper(II) ions are more easily reduced than hydrogen ions. In the second cell, hydrogen ions are more easily reduced than zinc ions. These ions, listed in order of decreasing tendency to be reduced, are Cu^{2+}, H^+, and Zn^{2+}.

Concept ✔ Check

What do you think happens to the zinc anode when it is paired with a hydrogen electrode? Does the same change occur with a copper electrode and hydrogen?

Half-cell potentials The tendency of an atom or ion to gain electrons can be determined by looking at the reactions in the electrochemical cell. The voltage of a particular electrochemical cell is a measure of the tendency of electrons to flow from the substance that is oxidized to the substance that is reduced. The voltage for a cell is determined by the contribution made by each half-reaction. The contribution to the cell voltage made by each half-reaction is called the **half-cell potential,** a term that emphasizes the relationship between voltage and potential energy. Half-cell potentials are symbolized by the letter E. The voltage of a cell depends on the concentration of the reactants and products present in the solution; therefore, a standard cell potential needs to be defined. The symbol $E°$ refers to the standard half-cell potential for $1M$ solutions, at 1 atm of pressure for gases, and 25°C.

The hydrogen half-cell is used as the standard to which all other half-cell potentials will be compared. Choosing a particular half-cell as the standard is something like designating the freezing point of water as zero on a Celsius thermometer. The standard hydrogen half-cell potential is assigned a value of $E° = 0.00$ volts.

Calculating cell voltages from half-cell potentials You can add or subtract voltages much as you would temperatures. (For example, it was four degrees Celsius colder today than yesterday.) The voltage of a cell equals the sum of the two half-cell potentials. You can use the hydrogen half-cell potential to calculate any other half-cell potential. For example, the voltage of the copper-hydrogen cell, which is 0.34 volts, equals the sum of the copper half-cell potential and the hydrogen half-cell potential. Thus, the copper half-cell potential is 0.34 volts, because the hydrogen half-cell potential is 0.00 volts.

$$Cu^{2+}(aq) + 2e^- \rightarrow Cu(s) \qquad E° = +0.34 \text{ volts}$$

In the zinc-hydrogen cell, the half-cell potential for the oxidation of zinc is 0.76 volts, since the zinc-hydrogen cell produces 0.76 volts.

$$Zn(s) \rightarrow Zn^{2+}(aq) + 2e^- \qquad E° = +0.76 \text{ volts}$$

However, this equation represents the oxidation of zinc. To make it easier to compare different substances, half-cell potentials usually are given as reduction potentials. Therefore, the equation for the zinc half-reaction is reversed and written as a reduction equation. The sign of the half-cell potential also is reversed.

$$Zn^{2+}(aq) + 2e^- \rightarrow Zn(s) \qquad E° = -0.76 \text{ volts}$$

CONNECTING CONCEPTS

Change and Interaction Acid-base reactions involve the exchange of protons, H^+. Redox reactions can be thought of as the exchange of electrons, e^-.

The negative sign indicates that zinc ions have less tendency to be reduced than do hydrogen ions. The three ions you have been studying and their half-cell potentials are listed in the following order.

$$Cu^{2+}(aq) + 2e^- \rightarrow Cu(s) \quad E° = +0.34 \text{ volts}$$
$$2H^+(aq) + 2e^- \rightarrow H_2(g) \quad E° = 0.00 \text{ volts}$$
$$Zn^{2+}(aq) + 2e^- \rightarrow Zn(s) \quad E° = -0.76 \text{ volts}$$

You can see that if the sign of a half-cell potential is positive, the atom or ion will more easily accept electrons than will hydrogen ions. If the sign of a half-cell potential is negative, the atom or ion will not accept electrons as easily as hydrogen ions. Table 20-4 lists some substances in order of their ability to gain electrons. Notice that hydrogen is set in the middle of the table as a reference point, with an $E°$ value of 0.00 volts.

When a voltaic cell is set up between zinc and a $1.0M$ solution of zinc sulfate and copper and a $1.0M$ solution of copper(II) sulfate, there is a potential difference between the two half-cells. Figure 20-8 illustrates such a cell. Notice that the voltmeter reads about 1.1 volts. This is reasonable, considering the standard conditions involved. The standard half-cell potential for the reduction of copper(II) ions is 0.34 volts, and the standard half-cell potential for the reduction of zinc ions is −0.76 volts. Yet in this electrochemical cell, zinc is being oxidized; therefore, the standard half-cell potential for zinc is +0.76 volts. This voltaic cell has a total voltage of 1.10 volts.

Figure 20-8 When a Zn/Zn^{2+} half-cell is actually connected to a Cu/Cu^{2+} half-cell, a potential of about 1.1 V is obtained. What reasons could you cite as to why the reading is not exactly 1.1 V?

20.6 Predicting Redox Reactions

Chemists use half-cell potentials to predict whether an oxidation-reduction reaction will occur spontaneously. If the cell voltage for an overall reaction is positive, the reaction will proceed as written. If, however, the cell voltage is negative, the reaction will not pro-

---

Myths and Misconceptions

There are several student misconceptions associated with redox reactions:

■ Students sometimes think that oxidation always involves the combination of a substance with oxygen. Stress that oxidation is a reaction involving a *loss* of electrons by an atom.

■ Students interpret reduction as "losing something." Although reduction reactions do result in a decrease in oxidation number, they involve an atom *gaining* an electron.

These misconceptions can contribute to difficulty when calculating cell voltages using half-cell potentials. When using a table of Standard Reduction Potentials for calculations comparing <u>oxidation</u> reactions, the sign for the half-cell potential must be reversed.

(continued on page T695)

TABLE 20-4

Standard Reduction Potentials	
Half-Reaction*	**$E°$ (volts)**

Easily reduced

Not easily oxidized

Half-Reaction	$E°$ (volts)
$F_2(g) + 2e^- \longrightarrow 2F^-$	$+2.87$
$H_2O_2 + 2H^+ + 2e^- \longrightarrow 2H_2O$	$+1.77$
$4H^+ + SO_4^{2-} + PbO_2 + 2e^- \longrightarrow PbSO_4 + 2H_2O$	$+1.68$
$MnO_4^- + 8H^+ + 5e^- \longrightarrow Mn^{2+} + 4H_2O$	$+1.52$
$Au^{3+} + 3e^- \longrightarrow Au$	$+1.50$
$Cl_2(g) + 2e^- \longrightarrow 2Cl^-$	$+1.36$
$Cr_2O_7^{2-} + 14H^+ + 6e^- \longrightarrow 2Cr^{3+} + 7H_2O$	$+1.33$
$MnO_2 + 4H^+ + 2e^- \longrightarrow Mn^{2+} + 2H_2O$	$+1.28$
$\frac{1}{2}O_2(g) + 2H^+ + 2e^- \longrightarrow H_2O$	$+1.23$
$Br_2(l) + 2e^- \longrightarrow 2Br^-$	$+1.06$
$NO_3^- + 4H^+ + 3e^- \longrightarrow NO(g) + 2H_2O$	$+0.96$
$Ag^+ + e^- \longrightarrow Ag$	$+0.80$
$Fe^{3+} + e^- \longrightarrow Fe^{2+}$	$+0.77$
$O_2(g) + 2H^+ + 2e^- \longrightarrow H_2O_2$	$+0.68$
$I_2 + 2e^- \longrightarrow 2I^-$	$+0.53$
$Cu^+ + e^- \longrightarrow Cu$	$+0.52$
$Cu^{2+} + 2e^- \longrightarrow Cu$	$+0.34$
$SO_4^{2-} + 4H^+ + 2e^- \longrightarrow SO_2(g) + 2H_2O$	$+0.17$
$Cu^{2+} + e^- \longrightarrow Cu^+$	$+0.15$
$Sn^{4+} + 2e^- \longrightarrow Sn^{2+}$	$+0.15$
$\frac{1}{8}S_8 + 2H^+ + 2e^- \longrightarrow H_2S(g)$	$+0.14$
$2H^+ + 2e^- \longrightarrow H_2(g)$	0.00
$Pb^{2+} + 2e^- \longrightarrow Pb$	-0.13
$Sn^{2+} + 2e^- \longrightarrow Sn$	-0.14
$Ni^{2+} + 2e^- \longrightarrow Ni$	-0.25
$Co^{2+} + 2e^- \longrightarrow Co$	-0.28
$PbSO_4 + 2e^- \longrightarrow Pb + SO_4^{2-}$	-0.36
$Cr^{3+} + e^- \longrightarrow Cr^{2+}$	-0.41
$Fe^{2+} + 2e^- \longrightarrow Fe$	-0.44
$Cr^{3+} + 3e^- \longrightarrow Cr$	-0.74
$Zn^{2+} + 2e^- \longrightarrow Zn$	-0.76
$2H_2O + 2e^- \longrightarrow H_2(g) + 2OH^-$	-0.83
$Mn^{2+} + 2e^- \longrightarrow Mn$	-1.18
$Al^{3+} + 3e^- \longrightarrow Al$	-1.66
$Mg^{2+} + 2e^- \longrightarrow Mg$	-2.37
$Na^+ + e^- \longrightarrow Na$	-2.71
$Ca^{2+} + 2e^- \longrightarrow Ca$	-2.87
$Sr^{2+} + 2e^- \longrightarrow Sr$	-2.89
$Ba^{2+} + 2e^- \longrightarrow Ba$	-2.90
$Cs^+ + e^- \longrightarrow Cs$	-2.92
$K^+ + e^- \longrightarrow K$	-2.92
$Li^+ + e^- \longrightarrow Li$	-3.00

Not easily reduced

Easily oxidized

* Ionic concentrations, 1M in water at 25°C.

Myths and Misconceptions

(continued from page T694)
Consider a role-playing experience with students. Have students represent atoms by wearing signs (+) or (−) as appropriate. When the atoms are oxidized or reduced, have students give away or accept the appropriate sign.

Guided Practice

Review the Concept Check questions on pages 690 and 693 with students. Answers can be found in Appendix E on page 808.

Reteaching Idea

If students are uncertain about how to use a table of standard reduction potentials to decide whether a redox reaction is spontaneous, you can provide some practice by challenging individuals or small groups of students to design electrochemical cells that will perform a particular function—for example, reduce cobalt ions. The reduction reaction can be combined with any half reaction below cobalt in Table 20–4. Have students combine the reduction and oxidation half-reactions, balance the overall equation and calculate the cell voltage. Focus on the fact that students' cells must have a positive voltage. Compare class results. On the basis of the magnitude of the cell voltages obtained for the various cells, ask students which might be most effective in providing useful current. If more practice is needed, ask students to design a cell to oxidize any element in Table 10–4.

DO YOU KNOW?

Biting into a piece of aluminum foil can demonstrate the current an electrochemical cell is capable of generating. Aluminum acts as the anode, silver fillings in your mouth act as the cathode, and saliva acts as the electrolyte. The nerve of the tooth detects the current.

PROBLEM-SOLVING STRATEGY

You have **solved similar problems** using half-reactions and can apply the same strategies here. Remember that when you reverse a reaction, you must reverse the sign of the voltage.

PROBLEM-SOLVING STRATEGY

Reread the problem to determine what the two oxidation half-reactions are that you are asked to compare.

ceed spontaneously in the forward direction. Some examples will demonstrate how potentials can be used to predict whether or not an oxidation-reduction reaction will occur spontaneously.

Silver tarnish is a film of silver sulfide, Ag_2S, formed when silver is oxidized by hydrogen sulfide, H_2S, in the air. One way to restore the luster to silverware is to immerse it in an electrolyte solution and bring the solution into contact with a metal that is more easily oxidized than silver. The silver sulfide forms silver and sulfide ions. The more active metal is oxidized and transfers electrons to the silver, causing silver atoms to plate out on the silverware. The silver ions are reduced.

EXAMPLE 20-3

Can aluminum foil immersed in an electrolyte solution be used to restore the luster to silverware? Justify your answer by using the cell potential for the overall reaction. (Assume $1M$ solutions and 25°C.)

■ **Analyze the Problem** You are asked to calculate the cell potential; if the cell potential is positive, then the reaction will proceed spontaneously.

■ **Apply a Strategy** Use Table 20-4 to compare the ease of oxidation of silver and aluminum. Then use the half-cell potentials to calculate the cell voltage.

■ **Work a Solution** Look up the silver ion and aluminum ion half-cell potentials in Table 20-4. Because it is lower in the table than silver, aluminum will be more easily oxidized than silver and can be used to reduce silver ions to silver atoms. The equation for the reduction half-cell is this.

$$Ag^+(aq) + e^- \rightarrow Ag(s) \quad E° = +0.80 \text{ volts}$$

Reverse the equation for the aluminum half-cell reaction to show that aluminum will be oxidized.

$$Al(s) \rightarrow Al^{3+}(aq) + 3e^- \quad E° = +1.66 \text{ volts}$$

The balanced equation of the reaction and the cell potential for the overall reaction are obtained by adding together the two half-cell equations and their voltages. To balance the electrons in the half-reactions, the silver half-reaction first is multiplied by three.

$3Ag^+(aq) + 3e^- \rightarrow 3Ag(s)$	$E° = +0.80$ volts
$Al(s) \rightarrow Al^{3+}(aq) + 3e^-$	$E° = +1.66$ volts
$3Ag^+(aq) + Al(s) \rightarrow 3Ag(s) + Al^{3+}(aq)$	$E° = +2.46$ volts

The cell potential for the overall reaction is positive, so the reaction occurs spontaneously, and the tarnish is removed.

Verify Your Answer Look at the problem a different way to confirm your result. Examination of Table 20-4 tells you that Ag^+ ions are more easily reduced because Ag^+ is higher on the table than Al^{3+}. Aluminum therefore is a good reducing agent for silver ions.

Practice Problems

12. Can a zinc strip immersed in an electrolyte solution be used to restore the luster to silverware? Show the balanced equation and the cell potential for the overall reaction. (Assume a $1M$ solution and 25°C.)

13. Will a reaction take place when a strip of zinc is placed in a $1.0M$ solution of nickel(II) sulfate solution? Write a balanced equation for the reaction, if one takes place.

Figure 20-9 *When a tarnished silver fork is placed in the electrolyte, nothing happens. What occurs when aluminum foil is added to the beaker?*

Notice that in the silver half-reaction, the moles of silver were multiplied by three so that the overall equation would be charge-balanced. But you do not multiply the half-cell potential listed in Table 20-4 by three. The presence of three times as many electrons does not mean that they will have three times the tendency to flow. The voltage remains unchanged, no matter how many atoms react. In a similar way, the pressure of water flowing from a larger reservoir would not necessarily be greater than the pressure of water flowing from a smaller reservoir.

As you learned in Example 20-3, a positive cell potential means that the reaction proceeds spontaneously and that the products of the reaction predominate. Figure 20-10 will help you remember the relationship of cell potential and the direction of the reaction.

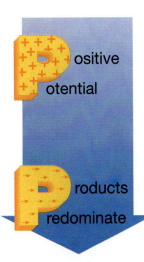

Figure 20-10 *When the cell potential is positive, the products predominate. The net redox reaction proceeds spontaneously in a forward direction, producing the products.*

PART 2

Section 20.6 *continued*

Practice Problems

Assign the Practice Problems.

CLOSE

Summing Up Main Ideas

The following terms are used to describe the action of voltaic cells: coulomb, ampere, voltage, half-cell potential. Have students make a table that lists the definition of each of these terms. In the same table ask students to describe the relationship between coulomb and ampere and between voltage and half-cell potential.

PART 2
Section 20.6 *continued*

PART 2 REVIEW

Assign the Part Review questions.

Evaluating Skills

These skills are evaluated in the Part Review questions indicated. **Describing:** 14, 16; **Predicting:** 16, 19, 21, 22, 23; **Comparing/Contrasting:** 15; 16; **Determining cause and effect:** 16; **Forming models:** 17; **Analyzing data:** 18, 24; **Applying a strategy:** 18, 20, 24; **Calculating:** 18, 20, 24; **Verifying results:** 18, 20, 24; **Constructing tables and graphs:** 20

CONNECTING CONCEPTS

Change and Interaction Qualitative electrochemical problems emphasize again the need for you to understand the mole concept.

Boxed numbers indicate questions that involve skills in interpretation, application, and analysis.

PART 2 REVIEW

14. What kind of chemical reaction occurs at a cathode? At an anode?

15. Explain the difference between the rate of electrical flow and voltage.

16. Is it likely that a reaction will take place when magnesium metal is placed in a $1M$ solution of hydrochloric acid? What is the equation for the reaction? Describe what you will see when the reaction is taking place. What are the products?

17. Make two submicroscopic drawings of the substances that are changing in question 16, one before the reaction starts, and then after the reaction is complete. Analyze the drawings to determine which substances are gaining electrons and which are losing electrons.

18. Calculate the cell potentials expected for the following redox reactions. Assume that all ion concentrations are $1M$, gas pressures are 1 atm, and the temperature is 25°C.
    a. $Co(s) + Fe^{3+}(aq) \rightarrow Co^{2+}(aq) + Fe^{2+}(aq)$
    b. $H_2(g) + Cl_2(g) \rightarrow 2H^+(aq) + 2Cl^-(aq)$
    c. $I^-(aq) + MnO_4^-(aq) \rightarrow I_2(aq) + Mn^{2+}(aq)$ (acid solution)

19. Will silver metal in a solution of chloride ions produce silver ions and chlorine gas?

20. An ampere is a measure of the rate of flow of electricity.
    a. Express an ampere as a labeled factor using SI base units.
    b. For a current of constant amperage, what is the relationship between the number of electrons passing through the wire and the amount of time the current flows?
    c. A certain flashlight draws a current of 0.40 amps. Construct a graph of coulombs on the y-axis and time in seconds on the x-axis for this current drain of the batteries.
    d. How many coulombs of electrical charge pass through the bulb operating the flashlight in ten seconds?
    e. How many electrons have passed through the bulb after ten seconds?
    f. Explain how you can use current and time in this situation to count electrons.

21. Predict what will happen if an aluminum spoon is used to stir a $1M$ solution of iron(II) nitrate, $Fe(NO_3)_2$ (at 25°C).

22. What will happen if an iron spoon is used to stir a $1M$ solution of aluminum chloride, $AlCl_3$ (at 25°C)?

23. Can a $1M$ solution of iron(III) sulfate, $Fe_2(SO_4)_3$, be stored in a container made of nickel metal? Explain your answer.

24. Most of the bromine produced in the United States is made by oxidizing bromide ions, Br^-, to bromine gas, Br_2, using chlorine gas, Cl_2. What is $E°$ for this reaction?

PART 2 REVIEW

ANSWERS

■ **Keyed to Objectives**

D 14. Reduction occurs at the cathode and oxidation occurs at the anode.

D 15. The rate of electrical flow is a measure of the electric charge (coulombs) flowing through a circuit per unit time (seconds). One coulomb per second is an ampere.

Voltage is a measure of electric pressure. Actually, voltage is the potential difference between the anode and cathode in an electrochemical cell.

D 16. The reaction will take place.
$$Mg(s) + 2HCl(aq) \rightarrow$$
$$Mg^{2+}(aq) + 2Cl^-(aq) + H_2(g)$$
The magnesium will corrode, resulting in bubbles of hydrogen gas.

D 17.

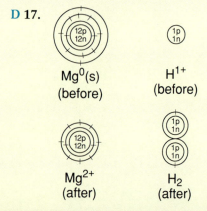

$Mg^0(s)$ (before)

H^{1+} (before)

Mg^{2+} (after)

H_2 (after)

PART 3 Putting Redox Reactions to Work

Both spontaneous and nonspontaneous redox reactions are useful in different ways. Spontaneous redox reactions can do useful work, such as powering batteries in toys, watches, and automobiles. Nonspontaneous redox reactions, on the other hand, need an external energy source to make them happen. Nonspontaneous redox reactions are simply the reverse of spontaneous reactions. The plating of metals, the reduction of metals from their ores, and the separation of valuable elements from compounds all depend on reversing spontaneous redox reactions.

Objectives

Part 3

F. *Describe* how commercial cells produce an electric current.

G. *Explain* the processes of electrolysis and corrosion.

20.7 Voltaic Cells and Storage Batteries

There are many kinds of voltaic or electrochemical cells on the market today. Some familiar examples are the cells used in flashlights, radios, and calculators and the lead storage batteries used for starting automobiles. Although batteries differ in size, chemical composition, and voltage, they all derive energy from the same source—from the making and breaking of chemical bonds.

Electrons flow out of and back into batteries as part of a redox reaction, but this happens only when the battery becomes part of a closed electrical circuit. Chemical potential electrical energy can be stored in a battery for a long time before it is released by completing the circuit. That is why batteries are so practical; they supply electrical energy when and where you want them to.

Dry cells Not all electrochemical cells contain water solutions of their electrolytes like those you have been studying. A common battery, or **dry cell,** is an electrochemical cell in which the electrolytes are present as solids or as a paste. For example, one common type of dry cell, the Leclanché cell, is filled with a paste of manganese dioxide, MnO_2, water, and ammonium chloride, NH_4Cl. A zinc strip can act as the anode, and the cathode is a graphite rod located in the center of the cell. Zinc is oxidized, and manganese dioxide is reduced to Mn_2O_3.

Another common dry cell is shown in Figure 20-11 on the next page. This is an alkaline manganese cell, commonly called an alkaline battery. This cell consists of a powdered zinc anode and a cathode made of manganese dioxide and carbon. The cell uses potassium hydroxide, KOH, an alkaline substance, as the electrolyte that maintains the charge balance in the cell. The chemistry of the alkaline battery is complicated, but the overall reaction can be summarized in the following redox equation.

DO YOU KNOW?

Modern maintenance-free car batteries can be sealed because they do not lose water. When an older battery is being charged, water is changed to hydrogen and oxygen gas by electrolysis. Newer batteries use an alloy of lead and calcium that prevents the decomposition of water.

Developing Skills

Students may apply these skills in their study of Part 3.

Observing and describing: Have students observe and describe the chemical reactions in electrochemical cells.

Classifying: Have students classify electrolysis.

Applying a strategy: Have students apply knowledge of electrochemistry to build a better battery.

Calculating: Have students calculate current in electrochemical cells.

≡ FOCUS

Activate Prior Knowledge

Students are familiar with a variety of cells and batteries. Begin a discussion by having students name cells and batteries with which they are familiar. Have them make a list of the various purposes for batteries. Then have them list characteristics that would be important for batteries used for these purposes. For example, batteries for toys would need to be safe and inexpensive. Batteries for a cardiac pacemaker would need to be reliable, long-lasting, and small.

≡ TEACH

Resources

Write to Duracell or Eveready for informative battery guides and applications of electrochemical cells.

Videodisc Connections

26472, side 5
Electrochemistry: lemon battery
(1 frame)

E **18.** **a.**
$$Co \rightarrow Co^{2+} + 2e^-$$
$$\underline{2Fe^{3+} + 2e^- \rightarrow 2Fe^{2+}}$$
$E°$ = +0.28 volts
$E°$ = +0.77 volts
$E°$ cell = +1.05 volts

b.
$$H_2 \rightarrow 2H^+ + 2e^-$$
$$\underline{Cl_2 + 2e^- \rightarrow 2Cl^-}$$
$E°$ = +0.00 volts
$E°$ = +1.36 volts
$E°$ cell = +1.36 volts

c.
$$10I \rightarrow 5I_2 + 10e-$$
$$\underline{2MnO_4^- + 16H^+ + 10e^- \rightarrow 2Mn^{2+} + 8H_2O}$$
$E°$ = −0.53 volts
$E°$ = +1.52 volts
$E°$ cell = +0.99 volts

D **19.** No; Both half-reactions are oxidations.

(answers are continued on page T841)

PART **3**
Section **20.7** continued

Science Background

Dry Cells

The role of carbon in the alkaline battery is to carry electrons and increase the conductivity of the cathode.

Teaching Strategy

Storage Batteries

Review the connection between density and concentration so students understand why measuring the density of sulfuric acid solution in a car battery can be useful.

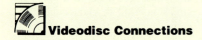
Videodisc Connections

46419 to 47488, side 5
Car batteries (movie)

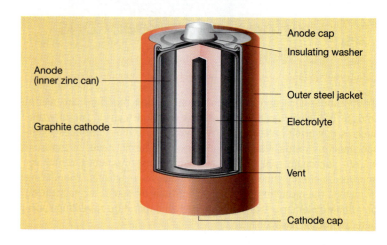

Figure 20-11 *The alkaline battery has a longer life than ordinary batteries and a more dependable current during continuous usage.*

$$Zn(s) + 2MnO_2(s) + H_2O(l) \rightarrow Zn(OH)_2(s) + Mn_2O_3(s)$$

Zinc is oxidized, and the manganese in manganese dioxide is reduced. The alkaline battery is more efficient than the Leclanché cell because the alkaline battery delivers five to ten times more electrical energy and is more reliable after long periods of storage.

Storage batteries The lead storage battery used in an automobile is not a dry cell. It contains several compartments, or cells, connected together. Lead is oxidized to form lead(II) sulfate, $PbSO_4$, at the anode; and lead(IV) oxide, PbO_2, is reduced to lead(II) sulfate at the cathode. Sulfuric acid, H_2SO_4, is the electrolyte used to maintain the charge balance of the cell. The reactions that occur during discharge (use) of this electrochemical cell are these.

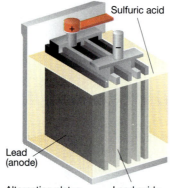

One of six cells in a lead storage battery

Sulfuric acid

Lead (anode)

Alternating plates of lead and lead oxide

Lead oxide (cathode)

Figure 20-12 *This cell produces about 2 volts. How many of these cells do you think a 12-volt car battery has?*

$Pb + SO_4^{2-} \rightarrow PbSO_4 + 2e^-$		$E° = +0.36$ volts
$PbO_2 + SO_4^{2-} + 4H^+ + 2e^- \rightarrow PbSO_4 + 2H_2O$		$E° = +1.68$ volts
$PbO_2 + Pb + 4H^+ + 2SO_4^{2-} \rightarrow 2PbSO_4 + 2H_2O$		$E° = +2.04$ volts

When the battery is being charged by the car's generator, the reverse reaction occurs. Because the reverse reaction is nonspontaneous, it requires an input of energy, in the form of electricity from the generator.

New batteries: smaller and stronger Both dry cells and alkaline cells use a zinc anode and a graphite cathode. Another popular battery is the "button" cell. The 1.3-volt mercury button cell uses powdered zinc as the anode and mercury(II) oxide as the cathode. A variation of this cell is the 1.6 volt silver oxide cell.

The lithium cell, actually lithium/manganese dioxide, yields about 3.3 volts and has many applications. The anode is lithium metal, which is oxidized as shown in the following equation.

$$Li(s) \rightarrow Li^+ + e^-$$

Myths and Misconceptions

Students and the public in general frequently have misconceptions regarding the terms *dry cell* and *battery*. An electrochemical cell is a system in which an oxidation-reduction reaction can occur spontaneously to produce power. A dry cell is an electrochemical cell that uses moist paste as the electrolyte. Most consumers use the term battery to describe the dry cell that is used to operate such devices as flashlights, radios, watches, and toys. A battery is a series of two or more electrochemical cells connected together. For example, an automobile battery typically consists of six electrochemical cells. The misnomer has been used so extensively that recent dictionaries now give an alternate definition of battery as a single cell to furnish electric current, as in a flashlight.

This half-cell reaction can yield a large potential difference in a cell. Table 20-4 tells you that under standard conditions, this half-cell potential is 3.00 volts. The cathode material is originally manganese dioxide, MnO_2. When the battery is being used, the electrons flow from the anode to the cathode through the external circuit. At the same time, the Li^+ ions migrate through an electrolyte to the cathode, where the manganese dioxide is reduced to manganese(III) oxide when it picks up an electron. The equation for the reduction reaction is this.

$$MnO_2 + Li^+ + e^- \rightarrow MnO_2(Li^+)$$

The lithium cell is typical of the kind of innovation that is taking place in the power-cell industry. Not only are the shapes and sizes varied, as seen in Figure 20-13, but there are many different reactions that run the cells. Table 20-5 lists some of the characteristics of various cells.

Figure 20-13 *Batteries come in a variety of sizes and shapes for a variety of purposes.*

Science Background

Electrolysis

One kilogram of good quality bituminous coal provides 3.3×10^4 kJ of energy, enough to produce about 55 g of aluminum from its ore, bauxite. The same amount of coal will provide the energy to recycle about 55 kg of aluminum.

TABLE 20-5

Some Common Electrochemical Cells		
Name	**Use**	**Description**
zinc-carbon	flashlights, radios, toys	1.5 volts; has a relatively short lifespan
mercury(II) oxide	hearing aids, digital watches, calculators	1.3 volts, high energy for its size
lithium-solid electrolyte	computer memories, sensor circuits	1.9 volts, very long life at low current drainage
lithium-SO_2	walkie-talkies, lanterns, sonar buoys	2.9 volts, long life but limited commercial life because sulfur dioxide is a toxic gas
zinc-air	electronic games, calculators, crib monitors	1.45 volts, inexpensive, must be sealed until used
nickel-cadmium	radios, flashlights, small power tools	rechargeable, expensive, does not stay charged long when not in use
fuel cell	space program, supplements municipal power supplies	uses hydrogen and oxygen gases to yield water and electricity; not very portable

20.8 Electrolysis

Each year millions of metric tons of aluminum and other valuable elements are reduced from ores to salts by a process called electrolysis. In **electrolysis,** an external source of electricity causes a

PART 3
Section 20.9

Guided Practice

Review the Concept Check question on page 702 with students. Answers can be found in Appendix E on page 808.

Reteaching Idea

Make sure that your students can verbalize the difference between electrochemical cells and electrolytic cells, and that they know the uses of each. They should know that voltaic and electrochemical are two adjectives that describe the same type of cell, and that batteries are voltaic cells. Ask your students if iron is galvanized in order to set up an electrochemical or electrolytic cell.

☰ CLOSE

Summing Up Main Ideas

Have students complete the following outline.

I. Electrochemical Cells and Storage Batteries
  A. Dry Cells
    1. Leclanché cell
      a. Zinc is oxidized.
      b. Mn is reduced.
    2. Alkaline manganese cell
      a. Zinc is oxidized.
      b. Mn is reduced.
  B. Storage Batteries
    1. Half-cell reactions on discharge
      a. $Pb(s) \rightarrow Pb^{2+}(aq)$ $+ 2e^-$
      b. $Pb^{4+}(aq) + 2e^- \rightarrow Pb^{2+}(aq)$
    2. Half-cell reactions when being charged
      a. $Pb^{2+}(aq) + 2e^- \rightarrow Pb(s)$
      b. $Pb^{2+}(aq) \rightarrow Pb^{4+}(aq) + 2e^-$

II. Electrolysis
  A. Definition: An external source of electricity causes a nonspontaneous redox reaction to occur.

(continued on page T703)

DO YOU KNOW?

Fossil fuels are the major energy source for transportation, heating, and electricity generation in the world. As the supply of these fuels diminishes, hydrogen gas may become the fuel of the future, and the electrolysis of water may become one of the most important sources of hydrogen gas.

DO YOU KNOW?

It takes about 100 years for a tin-coated steel can (a common tin can) to degrade completely, about 400 years for an aluminum can, and about 100 000 years for a glass bottle.

Videodisc Connections

18538 to 21367, side 4
Aluminum recycling (movie)

11360 to 18537, side 4
Steel (movie)

---

nonspontaneous redox reaction to occur. Electrolysis also is used to separate commercially important substances from aqueous solutions.

Aluminum metal is obtained from its ore by electrolysis. Most aluminum ore is composed of the mineral bauxite, $Al_2O_3 \cdot 2H_2O$, and impurities of iron and silicon oxides. The bauxite is first refined to aluminum oxide, which is then dissolved at high temperatures in the mineral cryolite. When enough electricity is applied to the molten solution, aluminum metal is produced at the cathode. Simplified versions of the half-reactions are these.

$$4Al^{3+} + 12e^- \rightarrow 4Al$$
$$6O^{2-} \rightarrow 3O_2 + 12e^-$$
$$\overline{4Al^{3+} + 6O^{2-} \rightarrow 4Al + 3O_2}$$

This process for manufacturing aluminum is effective, but it is expensive. The process uses about 60 kilojoules of electrical energy for each gram of aluminum produced.

Approximately ten million metric tons of aluminum is produced each year worldwide. The amount of energy needed to produce all this aluminum is enormous. As a step toward energy conservation, more and more communities are recycling aluminum. Only about 5 percent of the energy used to extract aluminum from its ore is needed to recycle aluminum.

20.9 Corrosion

When it comes to corrosion, iron is the champion. In the United States, the rusting (corrosion) of iron costs many billions of dollars per year. About one fifth of the iron produced each year is used to replace and repair items that are being destroyed by corrosion.

You probably know from your own experience that the steel in cars corrodes for the same reasons that an iron nail rusts or a ship's hull becomes so full of holes it has to be scrapped. In all these examples, the iron in steel is returning to its ore. When iron rusts, the iron is being oxidized.

Water and oxygen are necessary for rusting to occur, and the presence of hydrogen ions—from acid rain, for example—hasten the process. Corrosion occurs most rapidly at points where iron is strained by pressure or by bending or where iron comes in direct contact with other metals.

Iron corrodes in several steps. First the iron oxidizes while oxygen is reduced in the presence of water.

$$Fe(s) \rightarrow Fe^{2+}(aq) + 2e^-$$
$$H_2O(l) + \tfrac{1}{2}O_2(g) + 2e^- \rightarrow 2OH^-(aq)$$

The iron(II) and hydroxide ions then combine to form iron(II) hydroxide.

$$Fe^{2+}(aq) + 2\,OH^-(aq) \rightarrow Fe(OH)_2(s)$$

PART 3 REVIEW

ANSWERS

■ Keyed to Objectives

F **25.** An alkaline battery is an electrochemical "dry" cell. It generates electricity from a redox reaction within the can whenever a complete circuit is available. Zn is the anode and MnO_2 is the cathode. The electrolyte is a solution of KOH in a gelling agent.

Concept ✓ Check

What is the difference between electrolytic cells and those that are called electrochemical or voltaic?

This ionic substance is unstable in the presence of water and is quickly oxidized to iron(III) hydroxide.

$$2Fe(OH)_2(s) + H_2O(l) + \tfrac{1}{2}O_2(g) \rightarrow 2Fe(OH)_3(s)$$

Both iron(III) hydroxide and iron(III) oxide, Fe_2O_3, which is formed when iron(III) hydroxide is heated by the sun, are components of rust.

Corrosion can be prevented by using a metal that is less easily oxidized than iron. Look again at Table 20-4. Which metals are more easily oxidized than iron? Copper may be a good substitute for iron, but it is expensive. Gold and silver are, of course, prohibitively expensive. One solution is to coat iron with copper, but paint is much cheaper than copper. Much time and effort is spent each year painting iron and steel to prevent moisture and oxygen from corroding the metal, as seen in Figure 20-14. The iron can also be coated with tin (as in tin cans), plastic, or grease.

Another method that provides corrosion protection is the use of a metal that is more easily oxidized than iron. If iron is coated with zinc, the zinc oxidizes first but leaves behind a protective oxide that prevents moisture or oxygen from corroding the iron. Steel coated with a thin layer of zinc is said to be galvanized. Blocks of zinc or magnesium can also be bonded to the hulls of ships. Magnesium rods are placed inside home water heaters to prevent corrosion. These active metals corrode first and leave the hull or external steel components relatively free of corrosion.

Figure 20-14 *Painting is one of the cheapest ways to prevent corrosion.*

(continued from page T702)
   B. Half-cell reactions for electrolysis of aluminum
     1. $Al^{3+} + 3e^- \rightarrow Al(s)$
     2. $2O^{2-} \rightarrow O_2 + 4e^-$
III. Corrosion
   A. Reactions for the oxidation of iron
     1. $Fe(s) \rightarrow Fe^{2+} + 2e^-$
     2. $Fe^{2+} \rightarrow Fe^{3+} + 1e^-$
   B. Prevention of iron corrosion
     1. Using a metal that is less easily oxidized
     2. Using a metal that is more easily oxidized

PART 3 REVIEW

Assign the Part Review questions.

Evaluating Skills

These skills are evaluated in the Part Review questions indicated. **Describing:** 25; **Determining cause and effect:** 25, 26, 28, 29; **Analyzing data:** 27; **Applying a strategy:** 27; **Calculating:** 27; **Verifying results:** 27

Videodisc Connections

378 to 6974, side 4
Copper (movie)

43534 to 46418, side 5
Platinum in copper sulfate (movie)

6975 to 11359, side 4
Statue of Liberty (movie)

PART 3 REVIEW

25. Briefly describe how an alkaline battery generates an electric current.

26. Why is acid used in the lead storage battery in a car?

27. At the anode in the zinc-air electrochemical cell, zinc metal reacts with hydroxide ions to produce zinc hydroxide and electrons. At the cathode, oxygen from the air reacts with water and electrons to produce hydroxide ions. Write equations for the half-reactions at the anode and cathode and a balanced overall redox equation.

28. If you were designing a pacemaker, what characteristics of electrochemical cells would you be interested in? Which type of cell would you use?

29. Briefly explain how iron rusts.

Boxed numbers indicate questions that involve skills in interpretation, application, and analysis.

F 26. Sulfuric acid is the electrolyte in the lead storage battery. The acid solution also provides hydrogen ions for the reduction of lead(IV) oxide to lead(II) sulfate.

F 27. $O_2 + 2H_2O + 4e^- \rightarrow 4OH^-$
$2Zn + 4OH^- \rightarrow 2Zn(OH)_2 + 4e^-$
The overall reaction is:
$O_2 + 2Zn + 2H_2O \rightarrow 2Zn(OH)_2$

F 28. You may be looking for dependability, long life, and a source of constant voltage. A silver oxide battery may be a good choice.

G 29. Iron rusts as Fe is oxidized to Fe^{2+}. Oxygen gas is reduced in the presence of H_2O to form OH^-. The Fe^{2+} and OH^- produce unstable $Fe(OH)_2$. This substance reacts with water and oxygen to form $Fe(OH)_3$.

Electrochemical Cells

Estimated Time: (2 40-minute periods)

Process Skills

Observing
Measuring
Applying a strategy

Preparation

■ Materials

(for a class of 24, working in groups of 4)

Apparatus

(6 of each unless noted)
alligator clips with wire (12), voltmeters, 400-mL beakers, standard test tubes (18), 9-volt batteries, petri dishes, paper clips (12), small light bulbs (12), solid stoppers, test tubes, 100-mL graduated cylinders, 50-mL graduated cylinders, tongs, knives

Reagents

- 6 lemons or oranges
- 6 zinc metal strips (2–3 cm each)
- 6 copper metal strips (2–3 cm each)
- 6 lead metal strips (2–3 cm each)
- 2 liters of saturated sodium sulfate solution
- 200 mL 1M CuSO$_4$ solution
- 200 mL bromthymol blue
- 100 g mossy zinc
- distilled water

■ Preparation Hints

To make 1M CuSO$_4$: 50 g CuSO$_4$·5H$_2$O in 200 mL total volume

To make saturated sodium sulfate solution: 140 g of Na$_2$SO$_4$·10H$_2$O in 500 mL water
When you add the bromthymol blue solution, it should be a green color. If not, adjust with an acid or base that is 0.5M or less in concentration.

Laboratory
Investigation

Electrochemical Cells

Electrochemical, or voltaic, cells spontaneously convert chemical energy to electrical energy. This energy is the result of the transfer of electrons during an oxidation-reduction reaction. By separating the oxidation and reduction sites, you can get a usable electric current. Electrons flow from the oxidation site to the reduction site.

Electrolytic cells are different from electrochemical cells. Electrolytic cells use electrical energy to cause a reaction that would not normally occur.

In Part 1, you will work with an electrochemical cell and measure the flow of electrons created during an oxidation-reduction reaction. In Part 2, you will construct an electrolytic cell, which will convert water to hydrogen and oxygen gas.

Objectives

Construct a voltaic cell, using a lemon and various metal strips.

Determine the potential differences with various combinations of metal strips.

Observe and describe an electrolytic cell.

Identify and use a simple electrolytic cell to separate water into hydrogen and oxygen gas.

■ Materials

Apparatus
- petri dish
- 400-mL beaker
- 2 alligator clips with wire
- 2 paper clips
- small light bulb and socket
- 9-volt battery
- voltmeter

- 2 standard-sized test tubes
- 2 solid stoppers
- test tube
- 100-mL graduated cylinder
- 50-mL graduated cylinder
- tongs
- knife

Reagents
- bromthymol blue indicator
- lemon or orange
- lead strip
- copper strip
- zinc strip

- mossy zinc
- saturated sodium sulfate solution
- 1M copper(II) sulfate solution
- deionized or distilled water

■ Procedure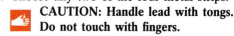

Part 1 Spontaneous oxidation-reduction

1. Put on your lab apron and goggles.

2. Add 10 mL of 1M CuSO$_4$ to your test tube and add a small piece of mossy zinc. Let the test tube stand and make several observations during your lab period.

3. Connect the two alligator clips to the voltmeter.

4. Choose any two of the four metal strips.
   CAUTION: Handle lead with tongs. Do not touch with fingers.
   Make two slits through the lemon skin with the knife. Insert the two strips into

■ Safety

Do not eat the fruit. Do not handle the lead with bare hands; use tongs. Wear safety goggles and a lab apron.

the slits. Do not allow the metals to touch each other. Connect the alligator clips to each metal and read the voltage. Record the readings in your data table.

5. Replace the strips with other combinations of two different strips. Record all voltages in your data table.

6. Attach a small light bulb socket to your circuit, using the two metal strips that give the highest voltmeter reading.

Part 2 Nonspontaneous oxidation-reduction

7. Connect the alligator clip wires to the 9-volt battery.

8. Pour about 25 mL of the saturated sodium sulfate solution in the petri dish and add a few drops of bromthymol blue indicator. Allow the liquid to settle and unbend the two paper clips. Allow them to lie in the liquid. Connect an alligator clip to each paper clip and observe.

9. Pour about 100 mL of water into the beaker and add about 200 mL of the saturated sodium sulfate solution. Fill two test tubes with water and carefully turn them upside down into the beaker. Make sure you have no air bubbles trapped in the test tube.

10. Place the 9-volt battery into the beaker and place the mouth of the test tubes over each electrode and collect the gas. Note the volumes of gas collected in each test tube and make a prediction as to the identity of each gas. If there is time, you should test the gas to confirm your predictions. Remove the battery from the solution as soon as possible.

11. Wash your hands with soap and water. Clean up and put equipment away.

■ **Data Analysis**

Data Table

Test Metals	Voltmeter Reading
Cu + Zn	
Cu + Pb	
Zn + Pb	

Part 1

1. Describe and draw a picture of what you think happened in the test tube with the mossy zinc and the $1.0M$ copper(II) sulfate solution.

2. Using your data on the lemon battery, make a list of voltages for each metal.

3. Compare your results with the standard reduction half-cell reactions found in your text.

4. How much voltage did you use to light the light bulb?

Part 2

5. Basing your answers on the colors of the indicator, tell which electrode produced an acidic product and which produced a basic product.

6. Note your prediction of the gases produced.

7. Write the oxidation and reduction reaction that would account for these gases.

■ **Conclusions**

1. Assuming that the H^+ ion is responsible for the acidic conditions and that the OH^- ion is responsible for the basic conditions, explain how these ions were formed at each electrode.

2. What would have happened if you had used a nonacidic fruit like an apple instead of a lemon in Part 1? Why?

Data Table

Test Metals	Voltmeter Reading
Cu + Zn	0.90
Cu + Pb	0.31
Zn + Pb	0.58

■ **Procedural Hints**

Lab time can be cut in half by doing only one type of cell. Make sure that the slits in the fruit are large enough to allow the lead strips to be pushed into the fruit without crumpling.

Disposal

Unused reagents: Put the fruit in the school's food garbage. Save the solutions and metals, or pour the liquids down the drain. Put the lead in a labeled, sealed container for an EPA-approved waste disposal contractor. Wrap the solids separately in newspaper and put in the wastebasket. Waste products: To dispose of the fruit, combine all the liquids and squeeze out the fruit juice into them. Squeeze the juice out through the slits in the skin. Discard the fruit (wrapped in paper) in the wastebasket. Make the liquid mixture slightly basic with $1M$ Na_2CO_3 solution. Add sodium polysulfide solution to precipitate lead and sulfides; pour the decantate down the drain. Reserve the precipitate in a labeled, sealed container for disposal by an EPA-approved waste disposal contractor.

Data Analysis

1. The blue solution became lighter and students should immediately have seen copper metal forming on the zinc. The zinc appeared to dissolve. This is a single displacement reaction.

2. See table below.

3. Standard potentials are:
   for the copper-zinc pair—1.10 volts
   for the copper-lead pair—0.47 volts
   for the zinc-lead pair—0.89 volts

4. 1.10 volts was used when the light bulb lit up for the copper-zinc pair.

5. Base (blue color) was produced at the cathode.

6. Hydrogen gas would be produced at the cathode. Oxygen gas would be produced at the anode.

7. $2H_2O(l) \rightarrow 2H_2(g) + O_2(g)$

Conclusions

1. At the cathode: $4H_2O + 4e^- \rightarrow 2H_2 + 4OH^-$
   At the anode: $2H_2O \rightarrow O_2 + 4H^+ + 4e^-$

2. With fewer H^+ ions available, the circuit would not be completed and there would be no reaction.

Chapter 20
Review
ANSWERS
begin on page
T709a.

Summary

Oxidation and Reduction

■ Oxidation is an increase in the oxidation number of an atom or ion. Reduction is a decrease in the oxidation number of an atom or ion.

■ Oxidation numbers help describe redox reactions more clearly. The ions and atoms in compounds are assigned oxidation numbers according to a set of rules.

■ An oxidizing agent is the substance in a reaction that is reduced, and the reducing agent is the substance that is oxidized. Oxidation and reduction half-reactions must occur together in a reaction.

■ A balanced redox equation must be mass- and charge-balanced and should not contain electrons in the net equation.

Spontaneous Redox Reactions

■ An electrochemical cell is a chemical system capable of producing an electric current.

■ Cell voltage is a measure of the tendency of electrons to flow. If two substances have a great difference in their tendency to lose electrons, the voltage of the cell will be high. Cell voltage can be used to predict whether a particular redox reaction will occur spontaneously.

Putting Redox Reactions to Work

■ Batteries are voltaic cells. They are examples of spontaneous redox reactions.

■ An electric current can be used to drive redox reactions that do not occur spontaneously. This process is called electrolysis.

■ Rust is a product of the corrosion of iron. When iron is oxidized, it forms iron(III) oxide and iron(III) hydroxide.

Chemically Speaking

ampere *20.5*
anode *20.4*
cathode *20.4*
coulomb *20.5*
dry cell *20.7*
electrochemical cell *20.4*
electrolysis *20.8*
half-cell potential *20.5*
half-reaction *20.1*

oxidation *20.1*
oxidation number *20.2*
oxidizing agent *20.1*
redox reaction *20.1*
reducing agent *20.1*
reduction *20.1*
salt bridge *20.4*
voltage *20.5*
voltaic cell *20.4*

Concept Mapping

Using the method of concept mapping described at the front of this book, draw a concept map for the term *electrochemical cell*. Include the following terms: *anode, cathode, electrode, oxidation, reduction, salt bridge,* and *voltage*.

Questions and Problems

OXIDATION AND REDUCTION

A. Objective: **Differentiate** *between reduction, oxidation, reducing agent, and oxidizing agent.*

1. If a neutral atom becomes an ion with a 1+ charge, has it been oxidized or reduced? Write a general equation using M to represent the neutral atom.

2. If an ion, X^-, acquires a 2− charge, has it been oxidized or reduced? Write a general equation.

3. Determine which of the following elements are in their common oxidized state and which are in their common reduced state. Use Table 20-4 as a reference if necessary.

PROBLEM-SOLVING STRATEGIES
Students apply these strategies in the following questions.

■ Factor-label method: 34, 35
■ Using what you know: 3, 5, 14, 15, 20, 23, 24, 25, 26, 33, 34, 35, 36, 37

■ Using similar problems: 14, 15, 35, 36, 37
■ Using patterns: 3, 5
■ Verifying your answer: 33, 34, 35,

a. Mg   **c.** O_2 **e.** Al^{3+} **g.** Cr^{3+}
b. I^- **d.** Na^+ **f.** S^{2-} **h.** Mn

4. Consider this equation.
   $$Mg(s) + Co^{2+}(aq) \rightarrow Co(s) + Mg^{2+}(aq)$$
   a. Which substance is oxidized?
   b. Which substance is reduced?
   c. Which substance acts as the reducing agent?
   d. Which substance acts as the oxidizing agent?

5. Which of these elements might be used as an oxidizing agent and which might be used as a reducing agent? Use Table 20-4 as a reference if necessary.
   a. Ca^{2+} **c.** Fe^{3+} **e.** F^-
   b. Au   **d.** Na   **f.** Mn

B. Objective: **Calculate** *the oxidation numbers of atoms and ions.*

6. What steps would you use to determine the oxidation number of each atom in nitrogen dioxide, NO_2?

7. Determine the oxidation number of each atom in the following substances.
   a. H_2SO_4 **c.** UO_3 **e.** VO_3^-
   b. P_4 **d.** U_2O_5 **f.** ClO_2^-

8. State whether the change represents an oxidation, a reduction, or neither.
   a. $MnO_2 \rightarrow Mn_2O_3$ **b.** $NH_3 \rightarrow NO_2$
   c. $O_2 \rightarrow O^{2-}$ **d.** $P_2O_5 \rightarrow P_4O_{10}$
   e. $HClO_4 \rightarrow HCl + H_2O$

9. One method of obtaining copper metal is to let a solution containing Cu^{2+} ions trickle over scrap iron. Write the equations for the two half-reactions. Assume that Fe^{2+} forms. Indicate in which half-reaction oxidation is taking place.

C. Objective: **Apply** *conservation laws to balance oxidation-reduction equations.*

10. What two quantities must be equal in a balanced redox equation?

11. Aluminum metal will react with the hydrogen ions in acidic solutions to liberate hydrogen gas. Write equations for the two half-reactions and the balanced redox reaction.

12. Make two submicroscopic drawings of the substances that are changing in question 11, one before the reaction starts, and one after the reaction is complete. Analyze the drawings to determine which substances are gaining electrons and which are losing electrons.

13. Write a balanced equation for the reaction between tin(II) ions, Sn^{2+}, and permanganate ions, MnO_4^-, in an acid solution to produce tin(IV) ions, Sn^{4+}, and manganese(II) ions, Mn^{2+}.

14. Write balanced equations for each of the following reactions.
    a. $H_2O_2 + I^- + H^+ \rightarrow H_2O + I_2$
    b. $In + BiO+ \rightarrow In^{3+} + Bi$
    c. $V^{2+} + H_2SO_3 \rightarrow V^{3+} + S_2O_3^{2-}$
    d. $Mn + IrCl_6^{3-} \rightarrow Mn^{2+} + Ir + Cl^-$

15. Write balanced equations for each of the following reactions. Identify what has been oxidized and what the oxidizing agent is.
    a. $HBr + H_2SO_4 \rightarrow SO_2 + Br_2 + H_2O$
    b. $NO_3^- + Cl^- + H^+ \rightarrow NO + Cl_2 + H_2O$
    c. $Zn + NO_3^- + H^+ \rightarrow Zn^{2+} + NH_4^+ + H_2O$
    d. $BrO^- \rightarrow Br^- + BrO_3^-$

SPONTANEOUS REDOX REACTIONS

D. Objective: **Predict** *whether or not a redox reaction will occur spontaneously.*

16. Draw a complete diagram representing a copper-silver electrochemical cell.
    a. Label all parts of the cell including the solutions.
    b. Show the half-reactions that are occurring.
    c. Give the cell voltage that would be generated for $1M$ solutions at standard temperature and pressure.
    d. Show the direction of electron flow

Boxed numbers indicate questions that involve skills in interpretation, application, and analysis.

36, 37   22, 24, 25, 26, 31, 32, 33
■ Breaking problems into manageable parts: 34
■ Writing chemical equations: 20,

through a voltmeter connected to the electrodes.

e. Show the direction of ion movements through the salt bridge.

17. What is the function of a salt bridge in an electrochemical cell?

E. Objective: **Calculate** *the voltage of a voltaic cell, using a table of standard reduction potentials.*

18. Briefly explain voltage. What other words come to mind when you think of voltage?
19. What is a half-cell potential?
20. If you wished to replate a silver spoon, would you make it the anode or the cathode in a cell? What would you use as the other electrode? Use half-reactions in your explanation.
21. Use the half-cell potentials in Table 20-4 to decide if the reaction in question 20 will occur spontaneously at standard conditions.
22. Steel screws and bolts can be plated with cadmium to minimize rusting. From this balanced redox equation, find the half-cell potential for the reduction of cadmium.

$$Cd^{2+} + Fe \rightarrow Cd + Fe^{2+}$$
$$E° = +0.15 \text{ volts}$$

23. Complete and balance each of the following equations. Using the half-cell potentials from Table 20-4, predict whether each reaction will proceed spontaneously under standard conditions.
    a. $Mg(s) + Sn^{2+}(aq) \rightarrow$ ____
    b. $Mn(s) + Cs^+(aq) \rightarrow Mn^{2+}(aq) +$ ____
    c. $Cu(s) + Cl_2(g) \rightarrow Cu^{2+}(aq) +$ ____
    d. $Fe(s) + Fe^{3+}(aq) \rightarrow Fe^{2+}(aq)$
24. What will happen if a piece of copper metal is dipped into a $1M$ solution of Cr^{3+} ions? Explain, using $E°$ values.
25. Which of the following reducing agents will spontaneously reduce $Cu^{2+}(aq)$ to $Cu(s)$ under standard conditions? (All ions are $1M$.)
    a. $Sn^{2+}(aq) \rightarrow Sn^{4+}(aq)$
    b. $Cl^-(aq) \rightarrow Cl_2(g)$

c. $Au(s) \rightarrow Au^{3+}(aq)$
d. $MnO_4^-(aq) \rightarrow Mn+(aq)$

26. Which of the following oxidizing agents will spontaneously oxidize $Fe^{2+}(aq)$ to $Fe^{3+}(aq)$?
    a. $Ag^+(aq) \rightarrow Ag(s)$
    b. $Pb^{2+}(aq) \rightarrow Pb(s)$
    c. $Al^{3+}(aq) \rightarrow Al(s)$
    d. $MnO_4^-(aq) \rightarrow Mn^{2+}(aq)$

PUTTING REDOX REACTIONS TO WORK

F. Objective: **Describe** *how commercial cells produce an electric current.*

27. Describe a chemical reaction that occurs in an alkaline manganese dry cell.
28. The mercury button cell is used in calculators, hearing aids, and watches. It is very reliable for its size. The cell produces a current by the redox reaction of zinc and mercury(II) oxide in a potassium hydroxide electrolyte. The two half reactions are these.

$$Zn + OH^- \rightarrow ZnO + H_2O + e^-$$
$$HgO + H_2O + e^- \rightarrow Hg + OH^-$$

   a. Balance the two half-reactions.
   b. Write the overall equation for the cell.
   c. What materials are found at the cathode? At the anode?
   d. Even though the zinc and hydroxide reaction produces water, there is no danger of water leaking from the cell. Why?
   e. Is there any evidence to suggest that zinc atoms have more affinity for ions of oxygen than for electrons, but that mercury(II) ions have more affinity for electrons than for ions of oxygen? Explain.
   f. As the redox reaction proceeds, what happens to the mass of the zinc present in the cell? To the mass of the mercury present in the cell? When the cell dies, what can you say about the masses of zinc and mercury in the cell?
29. In a nickel-cadmium rechargeable cell—when the cell is doing useful electrical work—the half reactions are these.

$$Cd + OH^- \rightarrow CdO + H_2O + e^-$$
$$NiO + H_2O + e^- \rightarrow Ni + OH^-$$

a. Balance the half-reactions.
b. Identify the cathode and anode.
c. An external source of electricity can be used to recharge the cell. Write half-reactions for this electrolysis.

G. Objective: Explain *the processes of electrolysis and corrosion.*

30. Explain how the process of electrolysis differs from what occurs in an electrochemical cell.
31. Describe the anode and cathode reactions in the corrosion of iron.
32. Would copper metal make a good cathodic protector to prevent iron from rusting? Explain your answer.

Critical Thinking

SYNTHESIS WITHIN THE CHAPTER

33. A half-cell consisting of a palladium electrode in a $1M$ palladium(II) nitrate solution, $Pd(NO_3)_2$, is connected with a standard hydrogen half-cell. The overall cell potential is 0.99 volts. The platinum electrode in the hydrogen half-cell is the anode. Determine the $E°$ value for the reaction.
$$Pd(s) \rightarrow Pd^{2+}(aq) + 2e^-$$
34. Concentrated nitric acid, HNO_3, is $15.9M$ and contains 68 percent nitric acid by weight in water. How many liters of concentrated acid are needed to react with 0.100 kg of copper metal in the following reaction?
$$Cu(s) + H^+(aq) + NO_3^-(aq) \rightarrow$$
$$Cu^{2+}(aq) + NO_2(g) + H_2O(l)$$

SYNTHESIS ACROSS CHAPTERS

35. Titanium metal will react with iron(II) oxide, FeO, to form titanium oxide, TiO_2, and iron metal.

a. Write a balanced equation for the reaction.
b. How many grams of iron will be produced from the reaction of 57.3 grams of titanium with excess iron(II) oxide?
36. Iodine is recovered from iodates in Chilean saltpeter by the reaction described in this unbalanced equation.
$$HSO_3^-(aq) + IO_3^-(aq) \rightarrow$$
$$I_2(g) + SO_4^{2-}(aq) + H^+(aq) + H_2O(l)$$
a. How many grams of sodium iodate, NaIO, will react with 1.00 mole of potassium bisulfite, $KHSO_3$?
b. How many grams of iodine are produced?
37. A 1.2-volt lead storage battery contains sulfuric acid, made from 700.0 grams of pure hydrogen sulfate, H_2SO_4, dissolved in water.
a. If this acid solution were spilled, how many grams of solid sodium carbonate, Na_2CO_3, would you need to neutralize it (producing carbon dioxide gas and water)?
b. How many liters of $2.0M$ sodium carbonate solution would be needed?
c. Suggest a reason why you do not need to know the volume of sulfuric acid solution.

Projects

38. Using a digital multimeter and $1M$ solutions of various metal ions, find the cell potentials of some electrochemical cells.

Research and Writing

39. Research the contribution Sir Humphry Davy made to the field of electrochemistry.
40. Research the chemical reactions that take place in several different kinds of batteries.

☐ Boxed numbers indicate questions that involve skills in interpretation, application, and analysis.

1. $M \rightarrow M^+ + e^-$
   The substance has become oxidized.
2. $X^- + e^- \rightarrow X^{2-}$
   The ion has been reduced.
3. **a.** Mg—reduced state
   b. I^-—reduced state
   c. O_2—oxidized state
   d. Na^+—oxidized state
   e. Al^{3+}—oxidized state
   f. S^{2-}—reduced state
   g. Cr^{3+}—oxidized state
   h. Mn—reduced state
4. **a.** Mg
   b. Co^{2+}
   c. Mg
   d. Co^{2+}
5. **a.** oxidizing agent
   b. reducing agent
   c. oxidizing agent
   d. reducing agent
   e. reducing agent
   f. reducing agent
6. **a.** Determine the charge on the molecule, NO_2, = 0
   b. Determine the oxidation number of each atom of oxygen, = 2−
   c. Determine the oxidation number of nitrogen. [?] + 4− = 0
   The oxidation number of N is 4+.
7. **a.** H = 1+; S = 6+; O = 2−
   b. P = 0
   c. U = 6+; O = 2−
   d. U = 5+; O = 2−
   e. V = 5+; O = 2−
   f. Cl = 3+; O = 2−
8. **a.** reduction
   b. oxidation
   c. reduction
   d. neither
   e. reduction
9. $Cu^{2+} + 2e^- \rightarrow Cu(s)$; reduction
   $Fe(s) \rightarrow Fe^{2+} + 2e^-$; oxidation
10. The charge and number of atoms of each element must be equal. Also, the number of electrons lost must equal the number of electrons gained.
11. $2Al \rightarrow 2Al^{3+} + 6e^-$
    $6H^+ + 6e^- \rightarrow 3H_2$
    The overall reaction is:
    $2Al + 6H^+ \rightarrow 2Al^{3+} + 3H_2$

12.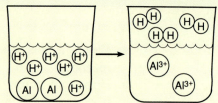

The H^+ ions gained electrons to form $H_2(g)$. The Al(s) lost electrons to form $Al^{3+}(aq)$.

13. $5Sn^{2+} \rightarrow 5Sn^{4+} + 10e^-$
    $10e^- + 16H^+ + 2MnO_4^- \rightarrow$
    $\qquad\qquad 2Mn^{2+} + 8H_2O$
    _____
    $5Sn^{2+} + 2MnO_4^- + 16H^+ \rightarrow$
    $\qquad 5Sn^{4+} + 2Mn^{2+} + 8H_2O$
14. **a.** $H_2O_2 + 2H^+ + 2e^- \rightarrow 2H_2O$
    $2I^- \rightarrow 2e^- + I_2$
    _____
    $2I^- + H_2O_2 + 2H^+ \rightarrow I_2 + 2H_2O$
    b. $In \rightarrow In^{3+} + 3e^-$
    $BiO^+ + 2H^+ + 3e^- \rightarrow Bi + H_2O$
    _____
    $In + BiO^+ + 2H^+ \rightarrow$
    $\qquad\qquad In^{3+} + Bi + H_2O$
    c. $4V^{2+} \rightarrow 4V^{3+} + 4e^-$
    $2H_2SO_3 + 2H^+ + 4e^- \rightarrow$
    $\qquad\qquad S_2O_3^{2-} + 3H_2O$
    _____
    $4V^{2+} + 2H_2SO_3 + 2H^+ \rightarrow$
    $\qquad 4V^{3+} + S_2O_3^{2-} + 3H_2O$
    d. $3Mn \rightarrow 3Mn^{2+} + 6e^-$
    $2IrCl_6^{3-} + 6e^- \rightarrow 2Ir + 12Cl^-$
    _____
    $3Mn + 2IrCl_6^{3-} \rightarrow$
    $\qquad 3Mn^{2+} + 2Ir + 12Cl^-$
15. **a.** $2HBr \rightarrow Br_2 + 2H^+ + 2e^-$
    $2H^+ + H_2SO_4 + 2e^- \rightarrow$
    $\qquad\qquad SO_2 + 2H_2O$
    _____
    $2HBr + H_2SO_4 \rightarrow$
    $\qquad Br_2 + SO_2 + 2H_2O$
    HBr is oxidized; H_2SO_4 is the oxidizing agent.
    b. $2NO_3^- + 8H^+ + 6e^- \rightarrow$
    $\qquad\qquad 2NO + 4H_2O$
    $6Cl^- \rightarrow 3Cl_2 + 6e^-$
    _____
    $2NO_3^- + 8H^+ + 6Cl^- \rightarrow$
    $\qquad 2NO + 3Cl_2 + 4H_2O$
    Cl^- is oxidized; NO_3^- is the oxidizing agent.
    c. $4Zn \rightarrow 4Zn^{2+} + 8e^-$
    $NO_3^- + 10H^+ + 8e^- \rightarrow$
    $\qquad\qquad NH_4^+ + 3H_2O$
    _____
    $4Zn + NO_3^- + 10H^+ \rightarrow$
    $\qquad 4Zn^{2+} + NH_4^+ + 3H_2O$
    Zn is oxidized; NO_3^- is the oxidizing agent.
    d. $2BrO^- + 4H^+ + 4e^- \rightarrow$
    $\qquad\qquad 2Br^- + 2H_2O$
    $BrO^- + 2H_2O \rightarrow$
    $\qquad\qquad BrO_3^- + 4H^+ + 4e^-$
    _____
    $3BrO^- \rightarrow 2Br^- + BrO_3^-$
    BrO^- is oxidized and is the oxidizing agent.

16.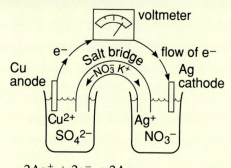

$2Ag^+ + 2e^- \rightarrow 2Ag$
$\qquad\qquad E° = +0.80$ volts
$Cu \rightarrow Cu^{2+} + 2e^-$
$\qquad\qquad E° = -0.34$ volts
_____
$2Ag^+ + Cu \rightarrow 2Ag + Cu^{2+}$
$\qquad\qquad E°_{cell} = +0.46$ volts
In the salt bridge, K^+ moves toward the Ag side; NO_3^- moves toward the Cu side.
17. The salt bridge maintains the electric neutrality in the solutions of an electrochemical cell.
18. In this context, voltage is the tendency of electrons to flow through an electrochemical cell. Other words for voltage are electric pressure or more properly, potential difference.
19. A half-cell potential (reduction potential) is the tendency of a half-cell reaction to gain electrons in comparison to the tendency of hydrogen ions to gain electrons. A positive $E°$ value means that the half-cell has a greater tendency to be reduced than hydrogen ions. A negative value means that the half-cell has less tendency to gain electrons than hydrogen ions. $E°$ is measured at a $1M$ effective concentration for solutions and 1 atm pressure for gases.
20. To plate out any metal, positive metallic ions must be changed to neutral atoms:
    $M^{n+} + ne^- \rightarrow M(s)$
    Such a reaction involves reduction. Since reduction takes place at the cathode, the spoon to be plated should be made the cathode. Pb may be a good choice for the other electrode.
    $2Ag^+ + 2e^- \rightarrow 2Ag$
    $Pb \rightarrow Pb^{2+} + 2e^-$
21. $2Ag^+ + 2e^- \rightarrow 2Ag \qquad E° = +0.80$ volts
    $Pb \rightarrow Pb^{2+} + 2e^- \quad E° = +0.13$ volts
    The overall reaction is:
    $2Ag^+ + Pb \rightarrow 2Ag + Pb^{2+}$
    $E° = +0.93$ volts (spontaneous)
22. $Cd^{2+} + 2e^- \rightarrow Cd \quad E° = ?$
    $Fe \rightarrow Fe^{2+} + 2e^-$
    $\qquad\qquad E° = +0.44$ volts
    _____
    $Cd^{2+} + Fe \rightarrow Cd + Fe^{2+}$

$$E°_{cell} = +0.15 \text{ volts}$$
$$E° \text{ for } Cd^{2+} = +0.15 - (+0.44)$$
$$= -0.29 \text{ volts}$$

23. a. $Mg \rightarrow Mg^{2+} + 2e^-$
$$E° = +2.37 \text{ volts}$$
$Sn^{2+} + 2e^- \rightarrow Sn$
$$E° = -0.14 \text{ volts}$$
$\overline{Mg + Sn^{2+} \rightarrow Mg^{2+} + Sn}$
$$E°_{cell} = +2.23 \text{ volts}$$
Spontaneous as written.

b. $Mn \rightarrow Mn^{2+} + 2e^-$
$$E° = +1.18 \text{ volts}$$
$2Cs^+ + 2e^- \rightarrow 2Cs$
$$E° = -2.92 \text{ volts}$$
$\overline{Mn + 2Cs^+ \rightarrow Mn^{2+} + 2Cs}$
$$E°_{cell} = -1.74 \text{ volts}$$
Nonspontaneous as written.

c. $Cu \rightarrow Cu^{2+} + 2e^-$
$$E° = -0.34 \text{ volts}$$
$Cl_2 + 2e^- \rightarrow 2Cl^-$
$$E° = +1.36 \text{ volts}$$
$\overline{Cu + Cl_2 \rightarrow Cu^{2+} + 2Cl^-}$
$$E°_{cell} = +1.02 \text{ volts}$$
Spontaneous as written.

d. $Fe \rightarrow Fe^{2+} + 2e^-$
$$E° = +0.44 \text{ volts}$$
$2Fe^{3+} + 2e^- \rightarrow 2Fe^{2+}$
$$E° = +0.77 \text{ volts}$$
$\overline{Fe + 2Fe^{3+} \rightarrow 3Fe^{2+}}$
$$E°_{cell} = +1.21 \text{ volts}$$
Spontaneous as written.

24. $3Cu \rightarrow 3Cu^{2+} + 6e^-$
$$E° = -0.34 \text{ volts}$$
$2Cr^{3+} + 6e^- \rightarrow 2Cr$
$$E° = -0.74 \text{ volts}$$
$\overline{3Cu + 2Cr^{3+} \rightarrow 3Cu^{2+} + 2Cr}$
$$E°_{cell} = -1.08 \text{ volts}$$
No visible spontaneous reaction occurs.

25. $Cu^{2+} + 2e^- \rightarrow Cu$ $E° = +0.34 \text{ volts}$
The other half-reaction must give up electrons and be positive or no more negative than -0.34 volt. Reaction (a) is the only one that satisfies the conditions.

26. $Fe^{2+} \rightarrow Fe^{3+} + e^-$ $E° = -0.77 \text{ volts}$
The other half-reaction must gain electrons and be more positive than $+0.77$ volts.
Reactions (a) and (d) will spontaneously oxidize Fe^{2+}.

27. A reaction that occurs in an alkaline cell is:
$Zn + 2MnO_2 + H_2O \rightarrow$
$$Zn(OH_2) + Mn_2O_3$$
Zn is the anode and MnO_2 is the cathode.

28. a. $Zn + 2OH^- \rightarrow ZnO + H_2O + 2e^-$
$HgO + H_2O + 2e^- \rightarrow Hg + 2OH^-$

b. $Zn + HgO \rightarrow ZnO + Hg$

c. At the cathode HgO is being reduced to Hg. At the anode Zn is being oxidized to ZnO.

d. Water is being used up by the reduction of HgO.

e. The overall reaction proceeds spontaneously. ZnO is favored over Zn in the oxidation half-reaction, and Hg is favored in the reduction half-reaction.

f. The mass of zinc and the mass of mercury do not change as the reaction proceeds, because no atoms are created or destroyed, even when Zn atoms become Zn^{2+} ions and Hg^{2+} ions become Hg atoms. When the cell dies, the mass of zinc and mercury in the cell is still the same, but the Zn has been oxidized and the Hg^{2+} reduced.

29. a. $Cd + 2OH^- \rightarrow CdO + H_2O + 2e^-$
$NiO + H_2O + 2e^- \rightarrow Ni + 2OH^-$

b. The site of the reduction of NiO is the cathode and the site of the oxidation of Cd is the anode.

c. $CdO + H_2O + 2e^- \rightarrow Cd + 2OH^-$
$Ni + 2OH^- \rightarrow NiO + H_2O + 2e^-$

30. In electrolysis an external source of electricity is needed to carry out a redox reaction. A spontaneous reaction occurs in an electrochemical cell.

31. At the anode the following reaction takes place:
$Fe \rightarrow Fe^{2+} + 2e^-$
At the cathode the reaction is
$H_2O + \frac{1}{2}O_2 + 2e^- \rightarrow 2OH^-$

32. No; Copper is less likely to be oxidized than iron.

33. $H_2 \rightarrow 2H^+ + 2e^-$ $E° = 0.00 \text{ volts}$
$Pd^{2+} + 2e^- \rightarrow Pd$ $E° = ?$
$\overline{Pd^{2+} + H_2 \rightarrow 2H^+ + Pd}$
$$E°_{cell} = +0.99 \text{ volts}$$
$Pd(s) \rightarrow Pd^{2+} + 2e^-$
$$E° = -0.99 \text{ volts}$$

34. The balanced reaction is
$Cu + 4H^+ + 2NO_3^- \rightarrow$
$$Cu^{2+} + 2NO_2 + 2H_2O$$
$0.100 \text{ kg Cu} \times \frac{1 \text{ mol Cu}}{0.0635 \text{ kg Cu}}$
$\times \frac{2 \text{ mol HNO}_3}{1 \text{ mol Cu}} \times \frac{1 \text{ L HNO}_3}{15.9 \text{ mol HNO}_3}$
$= 0.198 \text{ L HNO}_3$

35. The equation is
$Ti + 2FeO \rightarrow TiO_2 + 2Fe$
$57.3 \text{ g Ti} \times \frac{1 \text{ mol Ti}}{47.9 \text{ g Ti}} \times \frac{2 \text{ mol Fe}}{1 \text{ mol Ti}}$
$\times \frac{55.8 \text{ g Fe}}{1 \text{ mol Fe}} = 134 \text{ g Fe}$

36. The balanced equation is
$5HSO_3^- + 2IO_3^- \rightarrow$
$$I_2(g) + 5SO_4^{2-} + 3H^+ + H_2O$$
a. $1.00 \text{ mol KHSO}_3 \times \frac{2 \text{ mol NaIO}_3}{5 \text{ mol KHSO}_3}$
$\times \frac{198 \text{ g NaIO}_3}{1 \text{ mol NaIO}_3} = 79.2 \text{ g NaIO}_3$

b. $1.00 \text{ mol KHSO}_3 \times \frac{1 \text{ mol I}_2}{5 \text{ mol KHSO}_3}$
$\times \frac{254 \text{ g I}_2}{1 \text{ mol I}_2} = 50.8 \text{ g I}_2$

37. The reaction is
$H_2SO_4 + Na_2CO_3 \rightarrow$
$$CO_2 + H_2O + Na_2SO_4$$
a. $700.0 \text{ g H}_2SO_4 \times \frac{1 \text{ mol H}_2SO_4}{98.1 \text{ g H}_2SO_4}$
$\times \frac{1 \text{ mol Na}_2CO_3}{1 \text{ mol H}_2SO_4} \times \frac{106 \text{ g Na}_2CO_3}{1 \text{ mol Na}_2CO_3}$
$= 756 \text{ g Na}_2CO_3$

b. $756 \text{ g Na}_2CO_3 \times \frac{1 \text{ mol Na}_2CO_3}{106 \text{ g Na}_2CO_3}$
$= 7.14 \text{ mol}$
volume $Na_2CO_3 = 7.14 \text{ mol}$
$\times \frac{1 \text{ L}}{2.0 \text{ mol}} = 3.57 \text{ L}$

c. You only need to know the number of moles of H_2SO_4 spilled.

Chemical Analysis

Investigations	Demonstrations	Texas Essential Elements★
	Equations Describe Submicroscopic Events, page T712	**Content:** 6.4, 9.4 **Process:** 1.1, 1.2, 1.3, 2.1, 4.2, 4.3, 6.1, 9.1, 9.2, 10.1, 10.4
Laboratory Manual 21–1 S Laboratory Manual 21–2 IM Laboratory Manual 21–3 IM In-text Investigation, page T732		**Process:** 3.2, 4.2, 4.3, 7.1, 8.1, 8.2, 9.2, 10.1, 10.4
		Content: 12.2 **Process:** 1.1, 1.2, 1.3, 2.1, 3.1, 4.3, 5.1, 8.2, 10.1
		Process: 1.1, 1.2, 1.3, 3.2, 4.2, 4.3, 5.1, 6.1, 7.1, 8.1, 8.2, 9.1, 9.2, 10.1, 10.2

KEY:
M–Microscale **S**–Structured
I–Inquiry **IM**–Inquiry Microscale

★See pages T8–T11 for complete listing of Texas Essential Elements.

21

Chemical Analysis

Chapter Rationale

The material here is suitable as an extension of Chapter 15, Solutions. Part 1 of this chapter is a review of ionic and net ionic equations of Chapter 15, Part 2.

Qualitative labs can be used to maintain students' lab skills as they discover the atom in Chapters 8 through 10. This chapter could be assigned as background reading for those labs.

You also may want to present this chapter to your students as a reading assignment when they perform qualitative analysis experiments in the lab. A series of qualitative analysis experiments is a fine way to end the year in chemistry. Students will remember these investigations for years to come.

About the Photograph

Chemical analysis plays an important role in agriculture and horticulture. Many essential plant nutrients are water soluble cations or anions. Soil pH also has a large influence on plant growth. Analytical chemists test soil samples to determine the presence and concentration of individual ions as well as the pH of the soil. The results of chemical analysis help determine how soil should be prepared before planting.

Chapter Planning Hints

Plan to complete this chapter, including the Laboratory Investigation and the Chapter Review, in nine to ten class sessions. An optional demonstration appears on page 712. You may wish to preview it at this time.

Overview

Part 1: *The Tools of Analysis*
21.1 Analysis Using Equations
21.2 Analysis Using Solubility Tables
21.3 Going beyond Precipitates

Part 2: *Multiple-Ion Mixtures*
21.4 More Tools and Techniques
21.5 Analyzing Multiple-Ion Mixtures

Often gardeners want to find out the quality of their soil. This can be done using chemical analysis.

PART

1 The Tools of Analysis

One of the most interesting activities of chemistry is a kind of chemical sleuthing, in which you determine the identity of an unknown substance produced in a reaction. Much like a detective, you formulate a plan of action, you gather evidence (data), determine what is relevant to the case, and then draw conclusions based on the evidence. However, as a chemist you have an advantage over a detective. The detective must reconstruct the events of the case; you will be able to observe the events from the beginning. Whether a detective or a chemist, though, careful observation is important.

An unknown substance might be a safe substance, such as water, or it could be a dangerous substance, such as an acid. Never assume that a substance you are working on is safe. To be safe, you must follow all laboratory safety procedures if you work in the laboratory with unknowns. Most of the compounds and solutions discussed in this chapter are toxic. Some are very toxic, and some, such as the compounds and solutions of nickel or chromium, are suspected to cause cancer. Do not work in the laboratory with any of these compounds and solutions except under the supervision of your teacher. Wear safety goggles, a laboratory apron, and rubber gloves. Perform flame tests only under a hood. Wash your hands thoroughly and scrub under your nails with a fingernail brush before you leave the laboratory.

Once you have made observations in the laboratory, you will need to organize the data you obtained and apply strategies to analyze it. For example, in this chapter you will be investigating reactions that take place in aqueous solutions. Consider the reaction between two ionic salts, lead(II) nitrate, $Pb(NO_3)_2$, and potassium iodide, KI. Both ionic salts are soluble in water. If a solution of lead(II) nitrate and a solution of potassium iodide are combined, bright yellow crystals form within the mixture, as shown in Figure 21-1 on the next page. The colorful reaction product eventually collects on the bottom of the vessel. What is the yellow solid? Now the detective work begins!

21.1 Analysis Using Equations

Figure 21-1 provides macroscopic evidence for a reaction between lead(II) nitrate and potassium iodide. To analyze the reaction, you need to find out what is happening on the submicroscopic level. Writing an equation will help you do this.

Objectives

Part 1

A. *Use* ionic equations and solubility data to *identify* ionic products.

B. *Analyze* experimental data to determine the patterns of behavior of ions in solution.

C. *Predict* products of ionic reactions, using problem-solving skills and experimental data.

Developing Skills

Students may apply these skills in their study of Part 1.

Classifying: Have students classify combinations of ions into those that form precipitates and those that do not.

Predicting: Have students predict the products of reactions occurring in solution.

Constructing tables and graphs: Have students organize the data in tables.

Comparing/Contrasting: Have students compare the results of mixing solutions from one experiment to another.

Analyzing data: Have students devise multiple interpretations for possible precipitates.

≡ FOCUS

Activate Prior Knowledge

Students are familiar with several reactions from Chapter 15 in which two water soluble compounds combine to form a precipitate. Dissolve about 0.5 g of potassium iodide in 7 mL of distilled water in a test tube. Dissolve about 0.5 g of lead(II) nitrate in another test tube.

⚠ **CAUTION: Lead and its compounds are toxic. Do not allow students to handle the test tubes. Use a shield to protect students. Wear safety goggles, a lab apron, and gloves.**
While the students are paying close attention to you, pour the potassium iodide solution into the tube containing lead(II) nitrate solution. Discuss the results. For disposal, decant the supernatant down the drain and save the lead iodide in a sealed, labeled container for an EPA-approved waste disposal contractor. Wash your hands when finished.

Myths and Misconceptions

When students first learn to write and balance equations, they arrange and account for all the atoms in the reactants and in the products that are formed. Once they gain a knowledge of ionic equations and solubility tables, they can begin to predict more accurately the actual product(s) of a reaction. Stress with students that when two ionic solutions are combined and a precipitate is formed, the other ions in the solution are spectator ions. These ions do not react to form a product, and they can be eliminated to arrive at the net ionic equation for the reaction.

PART 1
Section 21.1 continued

☰ T E A C H

Teaching Strategy

Analysis Using Equations

Encourage students to use problem-solving skills that they learned throughout the course to identify precipitates. The table of solubilities, Appendix D, should be used only to verify results or as a last resort. Encourage students to THINK! They can use their own experience with chemicals at home. For example, they should know from everyday experience that sodium chloride is soluble. This kind of knowledge is important in solving precipitate problems.

One of the major goals of this chapter is to provide an environment in which students can think independently. Therefore, don't demand from them skills required to read solubility tables and to devise flow charts of more complex situations. Let them tinker with their own methods of predicting precipitates.

Cooperative Learning

Analysis Using Equations

Teams of 4; **Time:** 15 minutes
Objective: Students write and analyze dissociation equations.
Task: Give the students time to work in groups writing dissociation equations like this one:
$Na_2SO_4(s) \rightarrow 2Na^+(aq) + SO_4^{2-}(aq)$
Students need to practice these skills because they will use them throughout the chapter.
Team responsibility: Students quiz each other about the meaning of subscripts, superscripts, and coefficients in these equations.
Evaluation: Hold a brief discussion about subscripts, superscripts, and coefficients in dissociation equations.

Figure 21-1 *When lead(II) nitrate, Pb(NO₃)₂, and potassium iodide, KI, are mixed together, bright yellow crystals are formed. This observation can be used to determine what reactions are taking place.*

Equations describe submicroscopic events You learned in Chapter 3 that when an ionic salt dissolves in water, the salt undergoes dissociation. This means that it separates into positive and negative ions. Lead(II) nitrate and potassium iodide dissociate according to the following equations.

$$Pb(NO_3)_2(s) \rightarrow Pb^{2+}(aq) + 2NO_3^-(aq)$$
$$KI(s) \rightarrow K^+(aq) + I^-(aq)$$

Also recall that when two ionic solutions are mixed, a double replacement reaction may take place. The precipitate that forms can be an ionic compound or a mixture of two ionic compounds. In this case, the precipitate is a yellow solid that could be either potassium nitrate, KNO_3, or lead iodide, PbI_2, or a mixture of both. If you investigate the properties of potassium nitrate and lead iodide in the laboratory or look them up in a handbook, you will find that potassium nitrate is a white solid that is very soluble in water. Lead iodide is a yellow solid that is not very soluble in water. The yellow product must be lead iodide. You can now sum up the results by writing the equation that represents the submicroscopic events.

$$Pb^{2+}(aq) + 2NO_3^-(aq) + 2K^+(aq) + 2I^-(aq) \rightarrow$$
$$PbI_2(s) + 2K^+(aq) + 2NO_3^-(aq)$$

The equation shows that lead ions and iodide ions join together and precipitate as insoluble lead iodide. The other ions are spectator ions. They do not react and can be eliminated to give this concise net ionic equation.

$$Pb^{2+}(aq) + 2I^-(aq) \rightarrow PbI_2(s)$$

The case is closed! By using a knowledge of ionic equations and reference material on solubility, the unknown product of a reaction was identified. Now use Example 21-1 to develop your skill in applying these tools of analysis.

☰ D E M O N S T R A T I O N
Equations Describe Submicroscopic Events

⚠️ **CAUTION: Lead compounds are toxic. Wear gloves, an apron, and safety goggles. Use a shield to protect students. Do not allow students to handle the flask. Wash your hands when finished.**

To show a dramatic change in solubility with temperature, prepare the following supersaturated solution. Mix 75 mL of 0.01 M Pb(NO₃)₂ with 75 mL of 0.01 M NaI.

[Pb(NO₃)₂ : 3.3 g/L; NaI : 1.5 g/L]. Filter into a 250-mL flask and save some of the precipitate. Heat the solution almost to boiling. Add precipitate until it just disappears as the solution reaches about 90°C. Stopper the flask after it has cooled.

As the solution cools, beautiful golden crystals of PbI₂ precipitate are produced.

(continued on page T713)

EXAMPLE 21-1

What precipitate forms when 0.2M solutions of barium chloride and zinc sulfate are mixed at 20°C?

■ *Analyze the Problem* To solve the problem you need to know the ions that are present in each solution. Then you must determine whether any combination of these ions forms an insoluble ionic compound.

■ *Apply a Strategy* Write the formulas for all the positive and all the negative ions present in the two solutions. Generate the formulas of the new substances that could be formed by combining these ions. Check the solubilities of each of these possible products.

■ *Work a Solution* The chemical equations for the dissociations of barium chloride, $BaCl_2$, and zinc sulfate, $ZnSO_4$, are written below.

$$BaCl_2(s) \rightarrow Ba^{2+}(aq) + 2Cl^-(aq)$$
$$ZnSO_4(s) \rightarrow Zn^{2+}(aq) + SO_4^{2-}(aq)$$

The 2 ionic compounds yield 4 different ions. When the 2 solutions are mixed, the 4 ions can combine to form 2 new ionic compounds, barium sulfate and zinc chloride. The solubility table in Appendix D shows that barium sulfate is not soluble in water, but zinc chloride is. Therefore, barium sulfate is the precipitate formed by the reaction.

■ *Verify Your Answer* Recheck your work to make sure that you have correctly identified the two possible products of the reaction—barium sulfate and zinc chloride. With your teacher's permission, try doing a laboratory test to confirm that barium sulfate is the precipitate. Dissolve a sample of each of both solids in water. Do your observations confirm the conclusion? **CAUTION: These chemicals are toxic. Make sure to wear safety goggles, a lab apron, and rubber gloves. Wash your hands thoroughly before leaving the laboratory.**

Practice Problems

1. When 0.2M solutions of strontium chloride and lithium carbonate are mixed at 20°C, a precipitate forms. Use ionic equations and reference tables to determine the product. Write the net ionic equation.

2. No precipitate forms when a dilute solution of iron(III) nitrate is mixed with calcium chloride. What are the four ions mixed in the solution? What can you conclude about the solubility of all possible combinations of the four ions in this solution?

Practice Problems

Assign the Practice Problems.

PROBLEM-SOLVING

S T R A T E G Y

*In determining solubility, **use what you know** about molarity and solubility. In Chapter 15, you learned that a substance is considered soluble if the molarity is at least .1M at 20°C. (See Strategy, page 58.)*

DEMONSTRATION

(continued from page T712)
Swirling the flask produces a beautiful display of iridescent color.
For disposal, combine all liquids and solids. Decant and pour the decantate down the drain. Save the PbI_2 in a sealed, labeled container for disposal by an EPA-approved waste disposal contractor.

21.2 Analysis Using Solubility Tables

Suppose you are to conduct an experiment in which you mix pairs of ionic solutions and observe whether a precipitate forms. Figure 21-2 shows a set of 5 solutions, each with the name of the dissolved ionic substance. Notice that 3 of the solutions are colorless, 2 have a distinct color, and all 5 are clear. The solutions are mixed 2 at a time. Some mixings result in the formation of a precipitate, and others do not, as shown in Figure 21-3. For these solutions, you can assume that when there is no precipitate, no reaction occurs.

Teaching Strategy

Analysis Using Solubility Tables

Students should be asked to predict precipitates solely from the data in Table 21–1. Encourage them not to rely at this point on the Table of Solubilities, Appendix D. They should be able to determine the identity of precipitates from the data given in this section and from their everyday experiences with solutions.

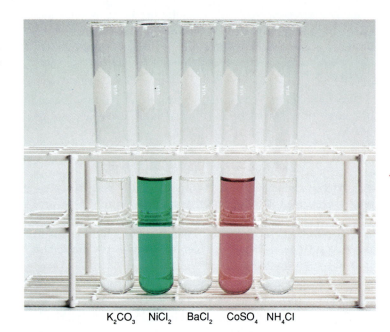

Figure 21-2 *These five test tubes contain different known ionic solutions. By mixing known solutions two at a time, it is possible to determine which ones react and the color of the precipitate formed.*

K_2CO_3 $NiCl_2$ $BaCl_2$ $CoSO_4$ NH_4Cl

TABLE 21-1

Ions Present	Reactions of Some Ionic Compounds in Solution				
	Ammonium Chloride	Nickel(II) Chloride	Barium Chloride	Cobalt(II) Sulfate	Potassium Carbonate
	$NH_4^+ + Cl^-$	$Ni^{2+} + Cl^-$	$Ba^{2+} + Cl^-$	$Co^{2+} + SO_4^{2-}$	$K^+ + CO_3^{2-}$
$K^+ + CO_3^{2-}$	N.R.	green ppt.	white ppt.	red ppt.	X
$Co^{2+} + SO_4^{2-}$	N.R.	N.R.	white ppt.	X	
$Ba^{2+} + Cl^-$	N.R.	N.R.	X		
$Ni^{2+} + Cl^-$	N.R.	X			
$NH_4^+ + Cl^-$	X				

All solutions are 0.2*M* at 25°C.

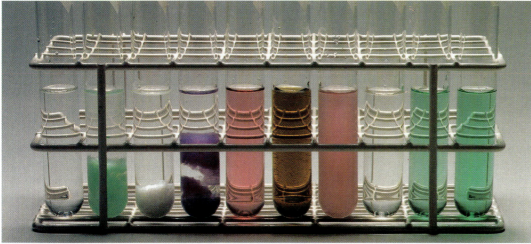

K₂CO₃ + NH₄Cl   K₂CO₃ + NiCl₂   K₂CO₃ + BaCl₂   K₂CO₃ + CoSO₄   CoSO₄ + NH₄Cl   CoSO₄ + NiCl₂   CoSO₄ + BaCl₂   BaCl₂ + NH₄Cl   BaCl₂ + NiCl₂   NiCl₂ + NH₄Cl

Figure 21-3 *Ionic solutions from Figure 21-2 are mixed two at a time. In which mixtures do reactions take place?*

Organizing data Table 21-1 shows you how the results of the mixing experiments can be arranged to allow patterns to emerge and comparisons to be made. For example, there are no reactions when ammonium chloride, NH_4Cl, in the first vertical column, is mixed with each of the other four solutions. From that information, you can conclude that no combination of the ions in the other four solutions will produce a precipitate with NH_4^+ or Cl^- ions. This is evidence that can be used to make deductions about the identity of a precipitate when a reaction does occur. Example 21-2 will help you learn how to do that.

EXAMPLE 21-2

Using the experimental data in Table 21-1, determine the identity of the precipitate that forms when nickel(II) chloride and potassium carbonate are mixed.

■ *Analyze the Problem* To solve the problem you need to realize that mixing the two ionic solutions could result in no reaction, the formation of one of two possible precipitates, or the formation of both precipitates.

■ *Apply a Strategy* Begin by writing the formulas for the two possible precipitates. You can do this by analyzing the formulas $NiCl_2$ and K_2CO_3 or by writing ionic equations. Examine the table of data for evidence that in other mixings, one of these two possible precipitates did not form when its ions were present in solution.

Teaching Strategy

Organizing Data

Since one of the major objectives of this chapter is to have students observe and find patterns in chemical reactions, it may not be a good idea to call attention to the rules of solubility they may have learned in Chapter 15. We are not trying to "streamline" students' learning. They need to develop the mental tools to analyze a range of data dealing with a set of chemicals.

Practice Problems

Assign the Practice Problems.

PROBLEM-SOLVING

S T R A T E G Y

Look for patterns and regularities in a reaction in Table 21-1. You need to find a reaction with products similar to those formed when nickel chloride, NiCl$_2$, reacts with potassium carbonate, K$_2$CO$_3$. (See Strategy, page 100.)

CONNECTING CONCEPTS

Structure and Properties of

Matter A substance is identified

by its characteristic properties.

Characteristic properties include

solubility, color, odor, and the

chemical reactions that take

place when it is mixed with dif-

ferent reagents.

■ ***Work a Solution*** In Table 21-1, potassium carbonate (K$^+$, CO$_3^{2-}$) is listed in the first horizontal row; nickel(II) chloride (Ni^{2+}, Cl$^-$) is in the second vertical column. When they are mixed, a green precipitate results. Because a double replacement reaction occurs when nickel chloride and potassium carbonate are mixed, the new combinations that could form are potassium chloride, KCl, and nickel carbonate, NiCO$_3$.

Now examine Table 21-1. Notice that when ammonium chloride (NH$_4^+$ + Cl$^-$) and potassium carbonate (2K$^+$ + CO$_3^{2-}$) are mixed, there is no reaction. Since one of the possible combinations of this mixing is potassium chloride, the absence of a precipitate means that potassium chloride is soluble. By the process of elimination, the green precipitate must be nickel carbonate.

■ ***Verify Your Answer*** You can use the tools of analysis that you learned earlier to verify your answer: Write the ionic equation and refer to a table of solubilities. The ionic equation is written below.

$$Ni^{2+}(aq) + 2Cl^-(aq) + 2K^+(aq) + CO_3^{2-}(aq) \rightarrow$$
$$NiCO_3(s) + 2K^+(aq) + 2Cl^-(aq)$$

Check the solubility table in Appendix D to be certain that NiCO$_3$ is insoluble and KCl is soluble in water.

Practice Problems

3. Using the experimental data given in Table 21-1, determine the identity of the precipitate that forms when barium chloride (Ba^{2+} + 2Cl$^-$) and cobalt(II) sulfate (Co^{2+} + SO$_4^{2-}$) are mixed.

4. Using only the data that is provided in Table 21-1, would you be able to determine the identity of the red precipitate that forms when potassium carbonate (2K$^+$ + CO$_3^{2-}$) and cobalt(II) sulfate (Co^{2+} + SO$_4^{2-}$) are mixed? Explain your answer.

21.3 Going beyond Precipitates

Your detective work so far has involved only evidence of reaction in the form of precipitates. Some combinations of ionic solutions provide other macroscopic evidence that a reaction has occurred. For example, when two ionic solutions are mixed, there might be a temperature change, the release of gas bubbles, the evolution of an odor, or a color change. As a chemical detective, you can use these results, just as you use the formation of a precipitate, to help you deduce the product of a reaction. To do so, you need to draw on your knowledge of different types of reactions and make deductions from experimental data.

TABLE 21-2

Ions Present	Lead Nitrate	Potassium Nitrate	Copper Sulfate	Hydro-chloric Acid	Sodium Hydroxide	Potassium Carbonate	Cobalt(II) Sulfate	Barium Chloride	Ammonium Iodide	Nickel(II) Chloride
	Pb^{2+}, NO_3^-	K^+, NO_3^-	Cu^{2+}, SO_4^{2-}	H^+, Cl^-	Na^+, OH^-	K^+, CO_3^{2-}	Co^{2+}, SO_4^{2-}	Ba^{2+}, Cl^-	NH_4^+, I^-	Ni^{2+}, Cl^-
Ni^{2+}, Cl^-	white ppt.	N.R.	N.R.	N.R.	green ppt.	green ppt.	N.R.	N.R.	N.R.	X
NH_4^+, I^-	yellow ppt.	N.R.	N.R.	N.R.	NH_3 odor	N.R.	N.R.	N.R.	X	
Ba^{2+}, Cl^-	white ppt.	N.R.	white ppt.	N.R.	white ppt.	white ppt.	white ppt.	X		
Co^{2+}, SO_4^{2-}	white ppt.	N.R.	N.R.	N.R.	red ppt.	red ppt.	X			
K^+, CO_3^{2-}	white ppt.	N.R.	blue ppt.	bubbles of gas	N.R.	X				
Na^+, OH^-	white ppt.	N.R.	blue ppt.	gets warm	X					
H^+, Cl^-	white ppt.	N.R.	N.R.	X						
Cu^{2+}, SO_4^{2-}	white ppt.	N.R.	X							
K^+, NO_3^-	N.R.	X								
Pb^{2+}, NO_3^-	X									

Note: All solutions are 0.2M at 25°C.

Reactions of Ten Compounds in Aqueous Solution (table title)

Expanding your data base Table 21-2 gives the results of the experimental mixing of ten different ionic compounds, including some of those you saw in Table 21-1. Some patterns are readily apparent. Potassium nitrate ($K^+ + NO_3^-$) gives no evidence of a reaction with any of the other nine solutions, but lead(II) nitrate ($Pb^{2+} + NO_3^-$) produces a precipitate with every other solution. From these two observations, can you determine which ion in lead nitrate is part of the precipitating product? If your answer is Pb^{2+}, you can confirm it by referring to the table in Appendix D, which shows that all combinations of positive ions with NO_3^- are soluble.

Heat and odor as evidence Heat is evolved in the mixing of hydrochloric acid and sodium hydroxide. As you learned in Chapter 19, this is the reaction of an acid and a base. The product, a salt dissolved in water, gives no visual evidence of its formation, but the heat released can be felt by the warming of the test tube if concentrations are 3M. At lower concentrations, any temperature

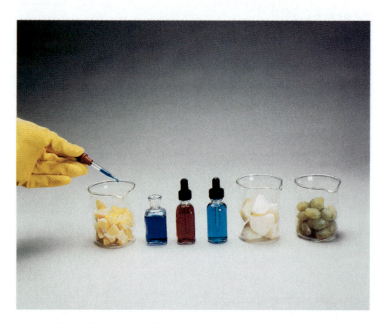

Figure 21-4 *Chemical analysis can be done on food to determine the presence of different nutrients. For example, indophenol can be used to test for vitamin C, iodine can be used to test for starch, and Benedict's solution can be used to test for simple sugars such as glucose and fructose.* ▲ **CAUTION: Some people can have an allergic reaction to indophenol. Do not get it on your skin.**

change can be measured with a thermometer. The reaction of ammonium iodide ($NH_4^+ + I^-$) with sodium hydroxide ($Na^+ + OH^-$) is also an acid-base reaction, but this time the most observable evidence of a reaction is the evolution of a faint odor of ammonia.

Concept ✓ Check

Why is the availability of a solubility table often essential for doing chemical analysis of ionic compounds?

Evidence from gaseous products The identity of the gas evolved when hydrochloric acid and potassium carbonate are mixed cannot be determined from the data given in the table. However, you could make a guess. Notice that the reacting ionic compounds contain the elements hydrogen, chlorine, carbon, and oxygen. Hydrogen gas, chlorine gas, oxygen gas, or carbon dioxide might be reasonable first guesses. However, your knowledge of acids and bases could lead you to carbon dioxide as the most likely. In acid solution, the hydrogen carbonate ion, HCO_3^-, forms and establishes this equilibrium.

$$HCO_3^- + H^+ \rightleftharpoons H_2O + CO_2$$

All compounds containing carbonate ion release carbon dioxide when treated with hydrochloric acid. This is a test used by geologists to determine if a rock contains carbonates. A drop of hydrochloric acid is placed on the rock. If bubbles of carbon dioxide are released, carbonates are assumed to be present.

Working with a large array of experimental data can be confusing, but Example 21-3 should help you hone your deductive skills as a chemical detective.

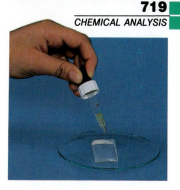

Figure 21-5 *Formation of gas is evidence that a reaction is occurring. Here, carbon dioxide bubbles form on the surface of calcite after hydrochloric acid is added with a dropper.*

EXAMPLE 21-3

You have been given four test tubes labeled *A, B, C,* and *D.* Each contains one of the solutions in Table 21-2. In tests using hydrochloric acid and sodium hydroxide, the following happened: Unknown *A* did not react with hydrochloric acid but formed a blue precipitate with sodium hydroxide; Unknown *B* formed white precipitates with both solutions; Unknown *C* did not react with hydrochloric acid, but formed a white precipitate with sodium hydroxide; Unknown *D* produced an odor when mixed with sodium hydroxide but did not react with hydrochloric acid. Deduce the identity of *A, B, C,* and *D.*

■ *Analyze the Problem* Identification depends on differences in the way the four unknown solutions react with sodium hydroxide and hydrochloric acid. You are told that the unknown solutions are in Table 21-2.

■ *Apply a Strategy* Make a table for recording the data given in the problem. Study your table and Table 21-2 and deduce the identity of *A, B, C,* and *D.*

■ *Work a Solution* A table helps you organize the given data.

Unknowns	Test Solution	
	NaOH	HCl
A	blue ppt.	N.R.
B	white ppt.	white ppt.
C	white ppt.	N.R.
D	odor	N.R.

Since *A, B, C,* and *D* are solutions on Table 21-2, take each of the ten solutions in turn and check its reactions with sodium hydroxide and hydrochloric acid. Starting from the left, lead nitrate forms white precipitates with both sodium hydroxide and hydrochloric acid; it could be Unknown *B.* Potassium nitrate forms no precipitates; therefore, it cannot be one of the un-

> **PROBLEM-SOLVING**
> **S T R A T E G Y**
>
> *Organize your data to make it easier to see relationships.*

> **PROBLEM-SOLVING**
> **S T R A T E G Y**
>
> **Look for patterns and regularities** *between your table and Table 21-2. (See Strategy, page 100.)*

PART 1
Section 21.3 continued

Practice Problems

Assign the Practice Problems.

Guided Practice

Review the Concept Check question on page 718 with students. Answers can be found in Appendix E on page 808.

Reteaching Idea

If your students have not mastered the thought processes needed to reason through an analysis, give them more practice with this problem, which can be solved either as a small group enterprise or a class exercise.

Solutions A, B, and C all reacted with $Pb(NO_3)_2$ to give white precipitates. A formed bubbles when HCl was added, but B and C did not react. When NaOH was added to the three unknowns, A did not react, B produced a blue precipitate, and C formed a green precipitate.

Have students arrange the data in a table and identify the unknown. They should be able to articulate their reasoning. (A is K_2CO_3, B is $CaSO_4$, and C is $NiCl_2$.)

PROBLEM·SOLVING
S T R A T E G Y

Summarize the data in the solubility table by **looking for patterns.** (See Strategy, page 100.)

knowns. Copper sulfate forms a blue precipitate with sodium hydroxide but does not react with hydrochloric acid. Unknown A could be copper sulfate.

Potassium carbonate releases bubbles of gas when treated with hydrochloric acid. Since no bubbles are noted, potassium carbonate cannot be one of the unknowns. Cobalt sulfate forms a red precipitate with sodium hydroxide; therefore, it is not one of the unknowns. Barium chloride forms a white precipitate with sodium hydroxide but does not react with hydrochloric acid. It could be Unknown C. Ammonium iodide produces an odor with sodium hydroxide and does not react with hydrochloric acid. Unknown D could be ammonium iodide.

At this point, all four solutions have been tentatively identified, but you have not looked at reactions of the tenth solution. Nickel chloride forms a green precipitate with sodium hydroxide. Since there is no evidence of a green precipitate, you can deduce that A is copper sulfate, B is lead nitrate, C is barium chloride, and D is ammonium iodide.

■ **Verify Your Answer** Check to see that there are no other possibilities. Write the equations for the reactions. If needed, check a solubility table to be sure that precipitates do form.

Practice Problems

5. Three test tubes designated *1*, *2*, and *3* contain clear solutions. They are to be identified using solutions of sodium hydroxide and ammonium iodide. When test tube 1 is mixed with sodium hydroxide, a green precipitate forms, but there is no reaction with ammonium iodide. Test tube 2 forms a white precipitate with sodium hydroxide but no precipitate with ammonium iodide. Test tube 3 forms a white precipitate with sodium hydroxide and a yellow precipitate with ammonium iodide. Use the data in Table 21-2 to determine the identity of the three solutions.

6. You are given an unknown solution containing one of the compounds in Table 21-2. Outline a procedure to determine the identity of the unknown. Include safety procedures.

7. The labels came off two bottles of solutions. One was known to be ammonium iodide and the other potassium carbonate. Describe two tests that could identify the solutions.

PART 1 REVIEW

8. Make a table to classify all the compounds used or produced in Table 21-1 as soluble or insoluble. Which substances cannot be classified, based on the information you have?

PART 1 REVIEW

ANSWERS

■ **Keyed to Objectives**

B **8.**

insoluble	soluble	?
$NiCO_3$	NH_4Cl	$CoCO_3$
$BaSO_4$	KCl	K_2SO_4
$BaCO_3$	$CoCl_2$	
	$NiCl_2$	
	$BaCl_2$	

soluble
$(NH_4)_2 CO_3$
$(NH_4)_2 SO_4$
$NiSO_4$
$CoSO_4$

B **9.** Chloride compounds are usually soluble. Carbonate compounds are often insoluble.

A **10.** $Pb^{2+}(aq) + 2NO_3^-(aq) + Ni^{2+}(aq) + 2Cl^-(aq) \rightarrow PbCl_2(s) + Ni^{2+}(aq) + 2NO_3^-(aq)$

$Pb^{2+}(aq) + 2NO_3^-(aq) + 2NH_4^+(aq)$

$+ 2I^-(aq) \rightarrow PbI_2(s) + 2NH_4^+(aq) + 2NO_3^-(aq)$

$Pb^{2+}(aq) + 2NO_3^-(aq) + Ba^{2+}(aq) + 2Cl^-(aq) \rightarrow PbCl_2(s) + Ba^{2+}(aq) + 2NO_3^-(aq)$

$Pb^{2+}(aq) + 2NO_3^-(aq) + Co^{2+}(aq) + SO_4^{2-}(aq) \rightarrow PbSO_4(s) + Co^{2+}(aq) + 2NO_3^-(aq)$

$Pb^{2+}(aq) + 2NO_3^-(aq) + 2K^+(aq) + CO_3^{2-}(aq) \rightarrow PbCO_3(s) + 2K^+(aq) + 2NO_3^-(aq)$

$Pb^{2+}(aq) + 2NO_3^-(aq) + 2Na^+(aq)$

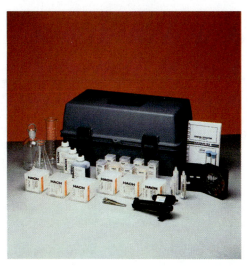

Figure 21-6 *Chemical analysis can be done on drinking water to test for the presence of compounds such as chlorine and ammonia.*

9. Make a list of any patterns you note from the solubility table you made in question 8—for example, *Chlorides usually are (or are not) soluble.*

10. Write ionic equations for all the reactions that yield precipitates in Table 21-2.

11. Write net ionic equations for all the reactions in question 10.

12. Do all of the white precipitates in the first column of Table 21-2 contain lead? Explain.

13. Expand the solubility table you made in answering question 8 to include the new substances in Table 21-2.

14. Expand the list of solubility patterns you made for question 9.

15. You are given an unknown solution containing one of the compounds in Table 21-2. Outline the procedure you would use to determine the identity of the unknown.

16. What gas is produced when HCl(aq) is mixed with K_2CO_3(aq)? Write the equations for the reactions that occur.

17. After an experiment involving the solutions listed in Table 21-2, three beakers lost their labels. Mixing the contents of each of the beakers produces the following results.

Unknowns	Beaker A	Beaker B
beaker *C*	white ppt.	gets warmer
beaker *B*	white ppt.	

What is the identity of solution *A*?

18. Can you determine the identities of solutions *B* and *C* without further tests? Explain.

Boxed numbers indicate questions that involve skills in interpretation, application, and analysis.

≡CLOSE

Summing Up Main Ideas

One of the compounds found in Table 21–2 on page 717 reacts with NaOH in aqueous solution, forming a blue precipitate. Have students identify the compound and write an ionic equation for its reaction with NaOH to form the blue precipitate. Have them verify the identity of the precipitate using Appendix D. (Using Table 21–2, the compound that forms a blue precipitate with NaOH is copper(II) sulfate. The ionic equation is:
Na^+(aq) + $2OH^-$(aq)
+ Cu^{2+} (aq) + SO_4^{-2}(aq) →
Na^+(aq) + SO_4^{-2}(aq) + $Cu(OH)_2$(s)
The blue precipitate is copper(II) hydroxide.)

PART 1 REVIEW

Assign the Part Review questions.

Evaluating Skills

These skills are evaluated in the Part Review questions indicated.
Comparing/Contrasting: 8;
Classifying: 8; **Constructing tables and graphs:** 8, 13, 14;
Analyzing data: 8, 9, 10, 11, 16, 17, 18; **Observing:** 9; **Applying a strategy:** 10, 11, 16; **Verifying results:** 10, 11, 16; **Determining main ideas:** 12; **Determining cause and effect:** 16

+ $2OH^-$(aq) → $Pb(OH)_2$(s)
        + $2Na^+$(aq) + $2NO_3^-$(aq)
Pb^{2+}(aq) + $2NO_3^-$(aq) + $2H^+$(aq)
+ $2Cl^-$(aq) → $PbCl_2$(s)
        + $2H^+$(aq) + $2NO_3^-$(aq)
Pb^{2+}(aq) + $2NO_3^-$(aq) + Cu^{2+}(aq)
+ SO_4^{2-}(aq) → $PbSO_4$(s)
        + Cu^{2+}(aq) + $2NO_3^-$(aq)
Ba^{2+}(aq) + $2Cl^-$(aq) + Cu^{2+}(aq)
        + SO_4^{2-}(aq) → $BaSO_4$(s)
        + Cu^{2+}(aq) + $2Cl^-$(aq)
$2K^+$(aq) + CO_3^{2-}(aq) + Cu^{2+}(aq)

+ SO_4^{2-}(aq) → $CuCO_3$(s)
        + $2K^+$(aq) + SO_4^{2-}(aq)
$2Na^+$(aq) + $2OH^-$(aq) + Cu^{2+}(aq)
+ SO_4^{2-}(aq) → $Cu(OH)_2$(s) +
        $2Na^+$(aq) + SO_4^{2-}(aq)
Ni^{2+}(aq) + $2Cl^-$(aq) + $2Na^+$(aq)
+ $2OH^-$(aq) → $Ni(OH)_2$(s)
        + $2Na^+$(aq) + $2Cl^-$(aq)
Ba^{2+}(aq) + $2Cl^-$(aq) + $2Na^+$(aq)
+ $2OH^-$(aq) → $Ba(OH)_2$(s) +
        $2Na^+$(aq) + $2Cl^-$(aq)
Co^{2+}(aq) + SO_4^{2-}(aq) + $2Na^+$(aq)

+ $2OH^-$(aq) → $Co(OH)_2$(s)
        + $2Na^+$(aq) + SO_4^{2-}(aq)
Ni^{2+}(aq) + $2Cl^-$(aq) + $2K^+$(aq)
+ CO_3^{2-}(aq) → $NiCO_3$(s) +
        $2K^+$(aq) + $2Cl^-$(aq)
$2K^+$(aq) + CO_3^{2-}(aq) + Ba^{2+}(aq)
+ $2Cl^-$(aq) → $BaCO_3$(s)
        + $2K^+$(aq) + $2Cl^-$(aq)

(answers are continued on page T841)

CAREERS IN CHEMISTRY

PART 1

Section 21.3 continued

CAREERS IN CHEMISTRY

Teaching Strategies

1. Have students identify the skills required of a research scientist, such as writing, financial management, teaching concepts, and laboratory techniques.

2. Discuss the rewards of a career in research, such as opportunities to make a fundamental contribution to understanding of a scientific field, variety in professional activities, and travel.

3. Highlight some of the rewards Prof. Phillips gains from teaching. You may want to share your feelings of reward in teaching chemistry.

Related Careers

Many research scientists work for companies or research foundations where there is little or no opportunity to engage in formal teaching. On the other hand, at some academic institutions teaching is primary, and significantly less emphasis is placed on independent research. Have students consider the differences in work environment and job requirements for these different settings.

Contact your local junior college to find out which career opportunities are available to people with two-year degrees. Also write to a nearby university for information on careers in teaching science in elementary and secondary schools.

Resources

Contact the American Chemical Society, the Association for Women in Science, or a local academic institution for additional information and to identify individuals who might speak to your class. Consider a panel of your fellow teachers to discuss their interests in science and teaching.

Professor of Chemistry

As a professor of chemistry, Dr. Philip Phillips finds his job both demanding and rewarding. He is teacher and researcher combined.

> Essential to success in research is a certain amount of healthy disregard for dogma, that is, what you have learned to be truth.

Inspiring understanding As a teacher, he hopes to provide his students with clear explanations of difficult concepts so that their knowledge of chemistry is based firmly on understanding. As a researcher, he finds great rewards in being able to choose the topics of his studies and in the anticipation that his research will change the way people think about science.

Education to gain and give

Philip's route to his academic job involved years of study and research. He earned his bachelor's degree in math and chemistry and followed it with a doctoral degree in physical chemistry. Then came two years of postdoctoral research. Finally it was his turn to give back to other students what he had learned under the guidance of his professors.

Each semester Philip teaches one class and directs the work of a research group made up of two postdoctoral fellows and a graduate student. They are currently working on electron transport in polymers and transport in biological systems. Besides guiding the study itself, Philip must secure grants to fund the work and write papers on the ongoing work.

Philip Phillips
Professor of Chemistry
at M.I.T.

Science is creative Philip says that to be successful in research you must have innovative ideas on key problems. Success in research may come only after many hours of hard work and of being lost. Also "Essential to success in research is a certain amount of healthy disregard for the accepted dogma, that is, what you have learned to be truth. If you find yourself constantly finding fault with accepted explanations, you probably have a promising career ahead of you in research. Students should be encouraged to be different."

PART 2 Multiple-Ion Mixtures

In this chapter, you have acquired some of the sleuthing skills needed by a chemical detective. You learned how to use ionic equations and solubility data to help you identify precipitates. You used experimental data from ionic reactions organized in a way that allowed patterns to emerge. Using that data, you developed deductive reasoning that led to the identification of unknown solutions. Now you are ready to tackle more complicated problems—problems in which more than one ion is present in a solution.

21.4 More Tools and Techniques

If a solution contains more than one unknown, precipitates may form that are mixtures of more than one solid, as shown in Figure 21-7. How do you tell that more than one precipitate is present? If both are white, it would be impossible to tell. If one is colored, you could not say for sure that the colored precipitate was not masking a white precipitate that was also present. A mixture of two colored precipitates could produce a combined color that was different from any reference data. Sometimes a colored solution will prevent your recognizing the true color of the precipitate. For example, a white precipitate of barium sulfate, $BaSO_4$, will appear pink if cobalt ions are present in the test tube, as in Figure 21-8. Techniques and procedures are needed to overcome these complications.

Objectives

Part 2

D. *Recognize* techniques useful for identifying ions in solution.
E. *Apply* skills of analysis to identify an unknown in a mixture containing more than one unknown.

Figure 21-7 *The precipitate in this test tube is actually a mixture of $NiCO_3(s)$ and $CoCO_3(s)$.*

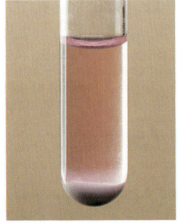

Figure 21-8 *A barium sulfate precipitate appears pink due to Co^{2+} ions in solution. After centrifuging and washing, the precipitate is distinctly white.*

Developing Skills

Students may apply these skills in their study of Part 2.
Analyzing data: Have students identify unknowns from flame tests and other data.
Interpreting diagrams: Have students organize data to form a flow chart.
Analyzing data: Have students analyze data to determine the identity of a mixed precipitate.

FOCUS

Activate Prior Knowledge

Have students use problem-solving skills emphasized in Part 1 to solve this problem. If $0.5M$ solutions of sodium hydroxide, potassium nitrate, and lead nitrate were placed in identical unlabeled bottles, which tests should be performed to determine which bottles contain sodium hydroxide, potassium nitrate, and lead nitrate? Have students work in teams or small groups to come up with lists of appropriate tests. (Note: Tests are not to be carried out.)

TEACH

Teaching Strategy

More Tools and Techniques

Descriptive analytical chemistry is most effectively learned in the laboratory. If the students share the data they obtain, they will be able to gather much information in a matter of minutes. If they are to gather the information on Table 21–2, it may take them two or three 45-minute periods. Each student will have an opportunity to observe some of the chemical reactions.

(continued on page T724)

PART **2**

Section 21.4 continued

(continued from page T723)
You may find that the reagents suggested in the Heath Chemistry Laboratory Manual are different. Substances that are especially toxic have not been included in the laboratory exercises.

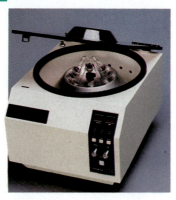

Figure 21-9 A centrifuge is used to separate precipitates from solutions. As the centrifuge turns, the force of gravity pulls the precipitate to the bottom of the test tube.

DO YOU KNOW?

It has been known for centuries that certain substances would color a flame when burned. The Chinese, when they invented fireworks, used this principle to add colors to the displays.

Figure 21-10 The flame color for lithium ions. ▲**CAUTION: This flame test produces toxic fumes; it should be conducted in a fume hood.**

Separations One of the most useful techniques of analysis is the physical separation of a liquid solution from a precipitate. In an unknown solution containing more than one type of positive ion, you might begin a separation by adding a solution that will precipitate only one of the ions. Think about the mixture of cobalt ion and barium ion just referred to. The addition of the sulfate ion results in the precipitation of barium sulfate. The cobalt ion remains in solution. The barium ion and the cobalt ion can be separated by pouring off the liquid containing the cobalt ion, Co^{2+}(aq), leaving barium in the form of $BaSO_4$(s) in the test tube. To separate the two more effectively, chemists use a **centrifuge.** This machine, shown in Figure 21-9, operates like the spin cycle of a washing machine, spinning the test tube at high speed. After centrifuging, the solid is packed into the bottom of the tube, which allows a more precise separation of solid and liquid.

Washing precipitates The $BaSO_4$(s) left in the test tube could still retain some pink color from the cobalt solution. To verify that the precipitate is actually white, water can be added and thoroughly mixed with the solid to remove any traces of cobalt. Then the mixture can be centrifuged and the water discarded. This is called washing a precipitate. It is done to purify the precipitate.

Flame tests Not every positive metal ion permits identification by precipitation. You know from the solubility table in Appendix D that all alkali metal ions—lithium, sodium, potassium, rubidium, and cesium—remain in solution no matter what negative ion is added. To identify these and some other metal ions, a technique called a **flame test** is used. The test identifies each ion by the characteristic color it produces when heated. Figure 21-10 shows a platinum wire that has been dipped in a solution of lithium chloride. The scarlet color of the flame is characteristic of lithium. The same result can be obtained if the wire is dipped into a solution of any other soluble lithium salt. Figure 21-11 shows the flame tests for potassium, sodium, calcium, strontium, barium, and copper. Notice that the flame test for strontium is very similar to the flame test for lithium, but with some experience you should be able to tell the crimson of strontium from the scarlet of lithium.

Special tests You already know about specific tests for the ions CO_3^{2-} and NH_4^+. Adding an acid to carbonate ion causes the release of bubbles of carbon dioxide gas. When hydroxide ion is added to ammonium ion, NH_4^+, the faint odor of ammonia is evidence that the ammonium ion has reacted to form ammonia.

$$OH^- + NH_4^+ \rightarrow NH_3 + H_2O$$

There are other tests for individual ions that you will learn about as you continue to study this chapter. Some are specific only when an ion has been separated from other ions in the unknown.

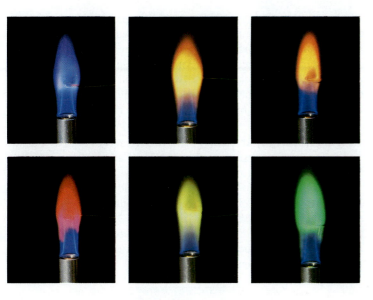

Figure 21-11 *Flame tests for various ions, from left to right on top—potassium, sodium, calcium; bottom—strontium, barium, copper.* ▲***CAUTION: These flame tests produce toxic fumes; they should be conducted in a fume hood.***

Reagents When chemists analyze ionic solutions, they use test solutions, called **reagents,** to find out what positive metal ions (cations) or what negative ions (anions) are present. This chapter will deal only with the identification of positive metal ions. In solution, positive ions are of course associated with negative ions, but reagents can be designed to cause a reaction only with positive ions. The solutes in these reagents will be negative ions combined with a hydrogen ion or an alkali metal ion. Remember that alkali metal ions and hydrogen ions do not form precipitates with any anions. Therefore, any precipitate that results when a reagent is added to an unknown solution must be caused by a reaction between cations in the unknown and anions in the reagent. When sulfuric acid, H_2SO_4, for example, is added to a solution that contains barium ion, a precipitate of barium sulfate forms. If you add sulfuric acid to an unknown solution, and no precipitate forms, could the unknown solution contain barium ion?

Flowcharts In carrying out an analysis, tests are done in a systematic way to allow the separation of each ion from any other ions that are present. The chemical detective must be familiar with the chemistry of every ion that could be present in the unknown solution and must devise a strategy for separating the ions. This strategy can be mapped out on a **flowchart,** a step-by-step diagram of separations and tests that lead to the identification of all the ions. For example, suppose that you have an unknown that could contain barium and cobalt ions. You know from Table 21-2 that barium precipitates when sulfate ions are added, but cobalt does not. Adding sulfuric acid could be the first step in separating the two ions. Barium is now in the form of $BaSO_4(s)$, and the cobalt is in the form of

CONNECTING CONCEPTS

Processes of Science—Interpreting Data Chemical analysis requires careful interpretation of data. The sequence of reagents used is as important as the observed reaction products in interpreting analytical data.

Teaching Strategy

Analyzing Multiple Ion Mixtures

Many of the substances mentioned in this section are toxic. Some ions, such as mercury and lead, may have been eliminated from use in your high school. The intent here is not to encourage their use, but to illustrate a method of analysis. Other substances, such as calcium, strontium, and magnesium can be used by the students in the laboratory. The same end will be achieved, that is, students will have the opportunity to separate and identify a mixture of cations in solution.

With the popularization of small-scale chemistry, qualitative analysis should become a substantial component of the lab program. A few grams of silver nitrate may last the whole year. Student exposure to caustic substances, such as sodium hydroxide and hydrochloric acid, is greatly reduced.

PROBLEM-SOLVING
S T R A T E G Y

Break the procedure into a series of steps and then make the flowchart based on these steps. (See Strategy, page 166.)

the aqueous ion, Co^{2+}(aq). The two can be separated by centrifuging and pouring off the solution containing the cobalt ion, leaving the solid barium sulfate behind. To prove that the cobalt ion is present in the clear solution, you could look for a negative ion that would cause cobalt to precipitate. Hydroxide ion will combine with cobalt to form a red precipitate. Adding a sodium hydroxide solution will confirm the presence of cobalt ions.

Diagraming a strategy A flowchart serves both as a guide and as a summary of steps in the analysis of an unknown solution. The separation of barium and cobalt is shown in the flowchart in Figure 21-12. When you add a reagent, it is shown along the vertical line under the test ions. A reagent may cause an ion or ions to precipitate while others remain in solution. If precipitation takes place, the formulas for the solid or solids are written to the left and the aqueous components to the right. Flowcharts will help you plan your strategies and verify your results.

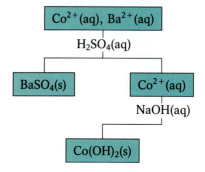

Figure 21-12 *A flowchart for the separation of barium and cobalt ions.*

Concept ✓ Check

Explain why it is so important to make a flowchart before beginning a chemical analysis.

21.5 Analyzing Multiple-Ion Mixtures

The power of the techniques and tools you have been learning can be appreciated by studying a small part of a well-known system for the analysis of positive ions. Imagine having 20 or more positive ions in one solution. How could you possibly separate each one from all the others and establish its identity? First you must know the chemistry of all the ions. Without that, even the most skilled detective could not break the case. However, in this section only three positive ions will be considered.

The three insoluble chlorides Of all the common cations, only silver, Ag^+, lead, Pb^{2+}, and mercury(I), Hg_2^{2+}, precipitate with the chloride ion. This behavior, which these three metal ions share, provides a means of separating them from all the other ions that could be present in a solution. Once they are separated from the larger group, they can be further separated from each other and finally identified. Table 21-3 on the next page gives experimental data obtained by testing the ions Ag^+, Pb^{2+}, and Hg_2^{2+} and the chlorides they form. These are the data a chemical detective needs in order to develop a logical scheme for separating the three ions. The reagents used in the tests are listed above the vertical columns. The substances tested are listed down the left-hand side of the table. Wherever an X appears, no test was done. The flowchart shown in Figure 21-13 was developed using the data in the table. Refer to the data table while following the steps in the flowchart.

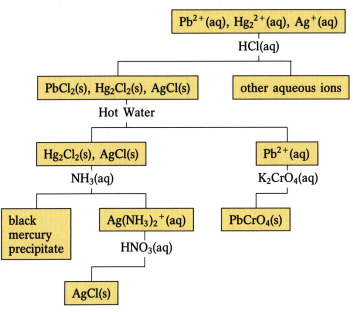

Figure 21-13 *A flowchart for the separation of lead, mercury, and silver ions.*

Mapping a strategy After adding hydrochloric acid, you are faced with the possibility of three white precipitates mixed together. How can they be separated? The data table shows that lead chloride is soluble in hot water. If the mixed precipitates are heated in water, lead chloride will dissolve and can be centrifuged and poured off, leaving behind silver chloride and mercury chloride. Now the lead ion, if present, is in solution as $Pb^{2+}(aq)$. If you wanted to identify the presence of lead in the unknown, you would need a confirmatory test. Table 21-3 shows that $Pb^{2+}(aq)$ forms a yellow precipitate with chromate ion, CrO_4^{2-}. If a yellow precipitate forms when potassium chromate is added to the solution that was poured off, then lead is present in the unknown. Why would it not be possible to test for lead in this way before precipitating the chlorides? Table 21-3 shows that precipitates of all three ions form when potassium chromate is added. Although their colors are different, a mixture of two or three precipitates could be confusing. Therefore, whenever you identify an ion by precipitating it with a reagent, you should be certain that interfering ions have been removed from the solution.

Separating silver chloride and mercury chloride In the other test tube, the precipitate containing the two solid chlorides of Ag^+ and Hg_2^{2+} are mixed together. Some method for separating them must be found. Fortunately both silver chloride and mercury chloride react in unique ways with ammonia, NH_3. Notice in the data table that silver chloride dissolves when mixed with ammonia. The complex ion formed, $Ag(NH_3)_2^+$, is soluble. Mercury(I) chloride, on the other hand, reacts with ammonia to form a solid black product. Here is a way you can separate the two metal ions and at the same time identify mercury(I). When ammonia is added, the formation of a black solid confirms the presence of Hg_2^{2+}.

Using the data table, can you devise a test that will confirm the presence of silver? If silver ion is present in the unknown, it will be in the form of $Ag(NH_3)_2^+(aq)$. First separate the solution from the black precipitate by centrifuging and pouring off the solution. Adding nitric acid, HNO_3, which neutralizes the ammonia and causes silver chloride to precipitate again, this time by itself. Because both Pb^{2+} and Hg_2^{2+} have been removed, a white precipitate is a specific test for the presence of silver.

There is excitement in identifying the contents of a colorless solution. In Example 21-4, you can learn more about how to develop a scheme of analysis.

TABLE 21-3

Reactions of Silver, Lead, and Mercury(I)					
Test Substance	**Reagent Added**				
	HCl	**Hot Water**	**K₂CrO₄**	**NH₃**	**HNO₃**
Ag^+	white ppt.	X	red ppt.	X	X
Pb^{2+}	white ppt.	X	yellow ppt.	X	X
Hg_2^{2+}	white ppt.	X	red ppt.	X	X
AgCl	X	N.R.	X	dissolved	N.R.
PbCl₂	X	dissolved	X	X	N.R.
Hg₂Cl₂	X	N.R.	X	black ppt.	turns grey
$Ag(NH_3)_2^+$	white ppt.	X	X	X	precipitates again

Note: *X* means no test was done.

EXAMPLE 21-4

An unknown solution may contain Pb^{2+}, Ba^{2+}, and Cu^{2+}. Draw a flow chart for the analysis, using the experimental data in the following data table.

Test Substance	Reagent Added		
	HCl	H_2SO_4	Na_2CO_3
Pb^{2+}	white ppt.	white ppt.	white ppt.
Ba^{2+}	N.R.	white ppt.	white ppt.
Cu^{2+}	N.R.	N.R.	blue ppt.

■ **Analyze the Problem** You have been given data that can be used to separate the three ions from one another. Draw a flow-chart that describes the separation and identification.

■ **Apply a Strategy** Look for a reagent that will precipitate only one of the ions. Look for one that will separate the other two. Look for a reagent that will form a precipitate with the third.

■ **Work a Solution** The reagent hydrochloric acid precipitates only one of the three ions, Pb^{2+}. Hydrochloric acid should be added to the solution, and if Pb^{2+} is present, it will precipitate as $PbCl_2(s)$. The ions $Ba^{2+}(aq)$ and $Cu^{2+}(aq)$ can be separated from the $PbCl_2$ by centrifuging and pouring off the solution in which they are dissolved.

Sulfuric acid, H_2SO_4, precipitates Ba^{2+}, but not Cu^{2+}. If a precipitate forms upon the addition of SO_4^{2-}, then Ba^{2+} is present. If Cu^{2+} is present in solution, it can be separated from $BaSO_4(s)$ by centrifuging and pouring it off. Since Cu^{2+} forms a blue precipitate with CO_3^{2-}, adding Na_2CO_3, sodium carbonate, will confirm its presence. Following the steps in the separation, a flowchart can be drawn.

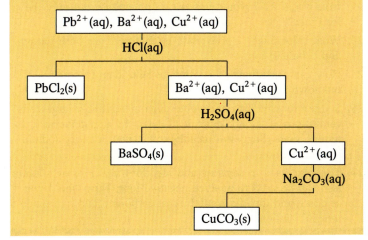

PART 2
Section 21.5 continued

Guided Practice

Review the Concept Check question on page 726 with students. Answers can be found in Appendix E on page 808.

Reteaching Idea

If your students need practice in drawing flow charts, have them practice with this problem. A solution contains the cations Ag^+, Cu^{2+}, and Ba^{2+}. The three ions can be separated and identified using the reagents HCl, H_2SO_4, and K_2CO_3. Have them make a table of the results of testing the three cations against the three reagents. After they have identified the unknowns, encourage them to translate their reasoning into a flow chart.

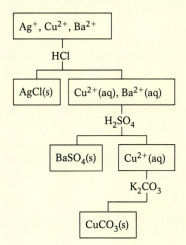

PART **2**
Section 21.5 *continued*

Practice Problems

Assign the Practice Problems.

≡CLOSE

Summing Up Main Ideas

An unknown solution yields a white precipitate when HCl is added to it. After adding hot water, the resulting solution is separated from the white precipitate. Treating the solution with potassium chromate yields a yellow precipitate. The white precipitate completely dissolves in ammonia. Have students identify which of the following ions were present in the unknown solution: lead, silver, and/or mercury, and give reasons for their answers. (Lead ion is present; lead chloride dissolves in hot water and then precipitates lead chromate. Silver ion is also present. Silver chloride dissolves in ammonia.)

PART 2 REVIEW

Assign the Part Review questions.

Evaluating Skills

These skills are evaluated in the Part Review questions indicated. **Classifying:** 21, 23; **Determining main ideas:** 21, 25; **Analyzing data:** 22, 23, 27; **Applying a strategy:** 22, 23, 27; **Verifying results:** 22, 23, 27; **Describing:** 24; **Predicting:** 24; **Determining cause and effect:** 26

Boxed numbers indicate questions that involve skills in interpretation, application, and analysis.

■ **Verify Your Answer** Check the solubility data in Appendix D and the data in Table 21-2 for further evidence that the deductions you made are correct.

Practice Problems

19. You are given a solution that contains barium nitrate and copper(II) nitrate. What procedure would you follow to separate the metal ions?
20. Design a flowchart for the separation of the metal ions Ba^{2+}, Ag^+, and Mg^{2+} in a solution containing a mixture of these ions. The products of the reaction of these ions with three different reagents are listed in the following data table.

Test Substance	Reagent Added		
	NaCl(aq)	Na₂SO₄(aq)	NaOH(aq)
Ba^{2+}	N.R.	white ppt.	white ppt.
Ag^+	white ppt.	white ppt.	brown ppt.
Mg^{2+}	N.R.	N.R.	white ppt.

PART 2 REVIEW

21. List two problems you might encounter when trying to identify a mixture of ionic substances rather than a single ionic substance.
22. What reagent from Table 21-2 would you add to a solution containing cobalt(II) and copper(II) ions to precipitate out both of these ions?
23. A solution contains lead and barium ions. Which reagent from Table 21-2 would you use to precipitate out only the lead ions?
24. What color might a precipitate be that contains both barium and cobalt(II) ions?
25. How can centrifuging a precipitate help identify an unknown?
26. Sodium ions tend to be soluble even at relatively large concentrations. They are difficult to detect by precipitation techniques alone. Suggest a technique that may identify sodium ions in solution.
27. The logic used to separate and identify metal ions in solution also can be used to analyze negative ions. How would you separate and identify a mixture of carbonate and hydroxide ions in solution?

PART 2 REVIEW

ANSWERS

■ **Keyed to Objectives**

D 21. A single reagent may precipitate more than one cation, and the color of the precipitate may be masked by the color of the solution.

D 22. Add sodium hydroxide. The hydroxide ion precipitates both cobalt and copper ions.

D 23. Add hydrochloric acid. The chloride ions precipitate out only the lead ions.

E 24. The precipitate may have a pink color.

D 25. The centrifuge packs the precipitate in the bottom of the test tube, allowing a soluble ion to be separated by pouring off the supernatant liquid.

R E S E A R C H   &   T E C H N O L O G Y

Chemistry of Crime

Forensic science is the branch of science dealing with solving crimes. Through careful investigation, observation, and interpretation, forensic scientists provide an objective analysis of physical evidence found at the scene of a crime.

One of the first steps in a criminal investigation involves the collection of evidence from the scene of a crime by police officers or technicians from a crime laboratory. Forensic scientists, or criminalists, then examine the evidence in a crime laboratory. Each laboratory has a chemical section, often subdivided into many specialized areas. These areas focus on analyzing bodily fluids, identifying physical markings on bullets and firearms, and examining handwriting and typewritten materials. Other areas deal exclusively with microchemistry or explosives and arson. In the case of fires, chemists may study the evidence to identify fire accelerants, such as gasoline, in order to determine the origin of a fire. Clearly, the chemist is an important member of the forensic science team. Since the crimes committed and the evidence collected are so varied, modern forensic chemists are crime detectives who use a wide variety of analytical instruments and techniques to help solve crimes.

Evidence often consists of specks of paint, glass, plastic, metal, or even tiny pieces of clothing. Using instruments such as chromatographs, spectrophotometers, X-ray instruments, and mass spectrometers, the forensic chemist can analyze even minute samples of evidence. For example, small pieces of clothing from the body of a hit-and-run victim can be matched with the paint of a suspect's automobile by using infrared spectroscopy.

Some elaborate techniques are used to identify drugs and poisons. Often a series of complex separation and purification procedures must be performed before a substance can be identified. Drugs and poisons may have to be

The physical evidence at the scene of a fire is carefully collected for analysis. It is later examined to determine if a crime may have been committed.

extracted from the vital organs, blood, and sometimes even the urine of victims. In addition, the source of the drug or poison must be determined so foods, drinks, and other objects found near the victim can be tested.

The results of a forensic chemist's work extend beyond the laboratory. While the analytical data collected may be used to find an individual guilty of a crime, it may be used just as well to clear an innocent person of suspicion.

D **26.** Sodium may be identified by a flame test. Sodium ions emit a bright yellow color when excited.

E **27.** Add hydrochloric acid solution to the mixture. The formation of bubbles confirms the presence of carbonate ions. If the solution becomes warm, hydroxide ions are present.

The Strength of Commercial Bleaches

Estimated Time: (40–50 minutes)

Calculating
Interpreting data
Comparing/Contrasting
Analyzing data
Verifying results
Stating a conclusion

Preparation

■ Materials

(for 24 students working in pairs)
Apparatus
Beral pipettes (48), 13 × 100
mm test tubes (48), marking
pencils (12); masking tape or colored tape

Reagents

- (30 mL each)
- diluted bleach samples
- starch solution
- $0.1M$ $Na_2S_2O_3 \cdot 5 H_2O$
- $0.5M$ KI
- $6M$ acetic acid

■ Preparation Hints

Use several samples of bleach including "name" brands, as well as generic brands. Have at least one sample from a container that was previously opened several months earlier. To make diluted bleach samples, dilute 5 mL of bleach to 100 mL with deionized or distilled water.
$0.1M$ $Na_2S_2O_3 \cdot 5 H_2O$ solution: Dissolve 2.48 g in 100 mL distilled water.
$0.5M$ KI solution: Dissolve 8.30 g in 100 mL distilled water.
$6M$ acetic acid: Dilute 50 mL glacial acetic with 50 mL distilled water. Wear safety goggles, lab apron, and gloves when preparing $6M$ acetic acid.
Starch solution: (1) Make a slurry of 1.0 g soluble starch (such as potato starch) in 10 mL cold distilled water. Add to 100 mL of boiling water; stir rapidly until clear; cool. Make it one day

Laboratory

Investigation

The Strength of Commercial Bleaches

Chlorine bleach is prepared commercially by bubbling chlorine gas through a concentrated solution of sodium hydroxide:

$$Cl_2(g) + 2NaOH(aq) \rightarrow NaOCl(aq) + NaCl(aq) + H_2O(l)$$

The OCl^- ion (hypochlorite) is the active ingredient in bleach; it can kill bacteria as well as oxidize stains and colors, and thus it is useful both as a disinfectant and as a laundry aid. In this lab activity, you will be able to determine the percent of OCl^- in a bleach sample, and you will also be able to compare the strength of several different brands of bleach.

The analysis of the amount of hypochlorite in bleach is accomplished in two steps and is known as the *indirect iodine titration* method. In the first step, the bleach is allowed to react with potassium iodide to produce iodine, $I_2(aq)$. In the second step, the iodine is titrated with a solution of sodium thiosulfate, $0.1M$ $Na_2S_2O_3$, until a visible end point appears.

O b j e c t i v e s

Balance oxidation-reduction equations.

Titrate and **calculate** the percent of hypochlorite in bleach samples.

Evaluate and compare results with other bleach samples.

Identify possible sources of error.

■ Materials

Apparatus
☐ 4 Beral pipets
☐ 4 13×100-mm test tubes
☐ marking pencil

Reagents
☐ diluted bleach samples
☐ starch solution
☐ $0.1M$ $Na_2S_2O_3$
☐ acetic acid ($3M$)
☐ $0.5M$ KI

■ Procedure

1. Put on your safety goggles and lab apron.

2. Obtain Beral pipets and approximately 2 mL each of the dilute bleach, the starch, and the thiosulfate in separate test tubes. Label them for easy identification.

3. Put 20 drops of the diluted bleach solution into a labeled test tube. Have your instructor add 20 drops of the ($3M$) acetic acid solution to this tube.

   CAUTION: Acetic acid is very corrosive to skin and eyes. Use it only in a fume hood. Wash off spills and splashes. If acetic acid gets in your eyes, use the eyewash fountain immediately.

4. Add 10 drops of the KI solution. Note the color change that occurs. Add 1 drop of the starch solution, which will act as the indica-

before or on day of lab; or (2) Spray aerosol-type starch into distilled water; test with an alcohol solution of iodine, which you make by adding 10 to 20 drops of tincture of iodine to 5 mL denatured alcohol. Add more starch if necessary to get a blue-black color.

Disposal

All liquids can be poured down the drain, except any that contain elemental iodine; these will be brown or dark blue in color. For these, convert the iodine to iodide by adding sodium thiosulfate solution, with stirring, until decolorized. Then pour down the drain.

tor for the titration. The titration end point is made obvious by this drop of starch solution. As long as free I_2 remains, a complex of starch-iodine gives the solution a dark blue color. As soon as all the I_2 has reacted with the thiosulfate ion ($S_2O_3^{2-}$), the solution becomes colorless. This sudden change from blue to colorless is the end point.

5. Titrate by adding drops of the $Na_2S_2O_3$ solution and counting the drops. After every 2 to 3 drops, agitate the test tube to mix the contents well.

6. Record in your data table the number of drops necessary to make the dark blue starch-iodine color disappear.

7. Repeat the analysis twice. Average the results and report your findings.

8. Allow a sample of bleach to be exposed to sunlight and air for several days. Repeat this analysis on this sample.

9. Repeat the experiment with a sample of bleach that has been in an opened bottle for several months. Perform this analysis on this sample.

Data Analysis

Data Table

Sample Tested	Drops of $Na_2S_2O_3$ Used			
	Trial 1	Trial 2	Trial 3	Average

1. The equation for the first step is as follows.
$NaOCl + I^- + H^+ \rightarrow I_2 + Cl^- + NaOH$
Balance this equation. Which element is oxidized? Which element is reduced? What is the molar ratio of $NaOCl/I_2$?

2. The equation for the second step is as follows.
$I_2 + S_2O_3^{2-} \rightarrow$
$I^- + S_4O_6^{2-}$ (tetrathionate ion)
Balance this equation. Which element is oxidized? Which element is reduced? What is the molar ratio of $I_2/S_2O_3^{2-}$?

3. Combine the molar ratios determined in the previous two questions to find the molar ratio of $NaOCl/S_2O_3^{2-}$.

4. The label on a bleach bottle usually says that it contains 5.25% active ingredient, or 5.25% NaOCl. Your teacher will tell you how many drops of the 0.1M $Na_2S_2O_3$ solution are required for a bleach sample having 5.25% NaOCl. Use this information to calculate the percent of NaOCl in your samples.

Conclusions

1. What causes the color changes in step 4?

2. How does your sample of bleach compare with the value on the label? Compare the class results for different brands of bleach.

3. Does a generic brand of bleach have the same percent of NaOCl as a name brand?

4. Find out the price of each bottle if you can. Which bleach was the best value for the money?

5. Does exposure to sunlight affect the percent of NaOCl in the sample? Why, do you suppose, does bleach come in opaque bottles?

Data Table

Sample Tested	Drops of $Na_2S_2O_3$ Used			
	Trial 1	Trial 2	Trial 3	Average
				15

Guiding the Investigation

■ Procedural Hints
Have students label the pipettes by using colored tape or masking tape. Test each sample of bleach ahead of time to find out approximately how many drops of 0.1M $Na_2S_2O_3$ solution are required for the titration of 5.25% bleach.

Data Analysis

■ Sample Data
(See table below.)

■ Analysis
1. $NaOCl + 2I^- + H^+ \rightarrow$
$I_2 + Cl^- + NaOH$
Oxidized: iodine (1− to 0)
Reduced: chlorine (1+ to 1−)
Molar ratio of $NaOCl/I_2$ is 1/1.

2. $I_2 + 2S_2O_3^{2-} \rightarrow 2I^- + S_4O_6^{2-}$
Oxidized: sulfur (2+ to 2.5+)
(Elements CAN have fractional oxidation numbers.)
Reduced: iodine (0 to 1−)
Molar ratio of $I_2/S_2O_3^{2-}$ is 1/2.

3. Molar ratio of $NaOCl/S_2O_3^{2-}$ is 1/2.

4. (# drops actual/# drops theoretical) × 5.25% = % NaOCl

Conclusions
1. The first color change in step 4 is caused by formation of elemental iodine, I_2, which is brown in a water solution containing KI. The second is caused by formation of a complex of starch and iodine. When this color disappears, the iodine has all been changed into colorless iodide ion.

2. Fresh samples may test higher than 5.25% NaOCl, since manufacturers sometimes produce a stronger concentration to ensure that the bleach will be at least 5.25% at the time of purchase.

3. Answers will vary.

4. Usually generic brands are the best value.

5. Yes. Sunlight can cause bleach to decompose.

T733

Chapter 21
Review
ANSWERS
begin on page
T737a.

Summary

The Tools of Analysis

■ The analysis of an unknown requires application of many previously developed problem-solving skills, such as writing ionic equations and determining solubilities.

■ The presence and color of a precipitate can be used to identify an unknown. Solubility tables are useful in identifying precipitates that form.

■ Several other observations—such as heat, bubbles, or an odor—are further evidence that can be used to identify an unknown.

Multiple-Ion Mixtures

■ Several techniques are useful in analyzing solutions. A flame test can be used to help identify an unknown. Separation can be done by precipitating, centrifuging, and washing.

■ To determine the presence of an unknown in a multiple-ion mixture, it is necessary to utilize the experimental data and then reason correctly from the data. A flow chart can help.

■ Some identification techniques are very specific, such as the acid test for carbonate compounds or the odor of ammonia when hydroxide ion is added to solutions containing ammonium ion.

■ Some ions are most easily identified after a series of tests. When a reagent is added to a mixture of ions, it is necessary to consider the possible effects of several ions. Some ions interfere with the tests of other ions, making it necessary to separate the ions first.

Chemically Speaking

centrifuge *21.4*   flow chart *21.4*
reagent *21.4*   flame test *21.4*

734 *CHAPTER 21*

Concept Mapping

Using the method of concept mapping described at the front of this book, draw a concept map for the term *reagent*. Include the following terms: *cation, anion, precipitate, color change, unknown, flame test,* and *flow chart.*

Questions and Problems

THE TOOLS OF ANALYSIS

A. Objective: **Use** *ionic equations and solubility data to* **identify** *ionic products.*

1. Write the equation for the solution process that occurs when each of these substances dissolves in water.
   a. sulfuric acid
   b. potassium hydroxide
   c. sodium carbonate
   d. strontium nitrate
   e. ammonium sulfate
   f. potassium sulfate
2. What are the cations in solutions *a, b,* and *c* of question 1?
3. What are the anions in solutions *d, e,* and *f* of question 1?
4. Name two ions that are yellow in solution.
5. List the different ions contained in a solution that is a mixture of potassium chloride and magnesium sulfate.
6. List the different ions contained in a solution that is a mixture of sodium carbonate and ammonium carbonate.
7. Write ionic equations for two reactions that may occur when solutions of sodium sulfate and barium chloride are mixed.
8. Write ionic equations for two reactions that may occur when solutions of lead(II) nitrate and potassium chloride are mixed.

PROBLEM-SOLVING

Students apply these strategies in the following questions.

■ **Using what you know:** 2, 3, 4, 11, 14, 15, 16, 17, 18, 19, 21, 22, 23, 24, 40, 41

■ **Using similar problems:** 42, 43, 44, 45, 46, 47, 48, 49

■ **Using patterns:** 10, 12, 20, 25, 26, 27, 28, 29, 30, 31, 32, 33, 35, 37, 38, 39

■ **Using calculators:** 42, 43, 44, 45, 46, 47, 48, 49

T734

B. Objective: **Analyze** *experimental data to determine the patterns of behavior of ions in solution.*

Questions 9 through 13 refer to the data table below, which shows the results when 0.2*M* solutions of each table entry are mixed. (Each reaction gives only one precipitate.)

9. Determine the ions present in each solution.

10. You can infer from evidence in the table that two of the ions do not form a precipitate with any of the other ions in the table. What are the two ions? Explain your reasoning.

11. Determine the formula of the precipitate formed when potassium hydroxide is mixed with cobalt(II) nitrate.

12. Potassium chloride and lithium chloride are soluble. Determine the formula of the precipitates formed when iron(III) chloride is mixed with potassium hydroxide and lithium hydroxide.

13. Write net ionic equations for the reactions in question 12.

C. Objective: **Predict** *products of ionic reactions, using problem-solving skills and experimental data.*

14. How would you test for the presence of hydroxide ions in a solution?

15. How would you test for the presence of silver ions in a solution?

16. How would you test for the presence of sulfite ions in a solution?

17. When sulfuric acid and sodium carbonate are mixed, bubbles can be seen rising in the solution. What is the name and formula of the gas produced?

18. When 1*M* nitric acid and 1*M* sodium hydroxide are mixed, what evidence is there that a reaction is taking place?

19. When a potassium hydroxide solution is poured over a solid, the smell of ammonia is detected. What positive ion is present in the solid?

20. An unknown solution is placed in two test tubes. Sodium hydroxide solution is added to

Data Table						
	Iron(III) Chloride	**Cobalt(II) Nitrate**	**Cobalt(II) Chloride**	**Lithium Hydroxide**	**Potassium Hydroxide**	**Potassium Nitrate**
Potassium nitrate	N.R.	N.R.	N.R.	N.R.	N.R.	X
Potassium hydroxide	reddish-brown ppt.	pale red ppt.	pale red ppt.	N.R.	X	
Lithium hydroxide	reddish-brown ppt.	pale red ppt.	pale red ppt.	X		
Cobalt(II) chloride	N.R.	N.R.	X			
Cobalt(II) nitrate	N.R.	X				
Iron(III) chloride	X					

Boxed numbers indicate questions that involve skills in interpretation, application, and analysis.

- Verifying your answer: 42, 43, 44, 45, 46, 47, 48, 49
- Breaking problems into manageable parts: 20, 33, 34, 42, 43, 44, 45, 46, 47, 48, 49
- Rereading the problem: 20, 33
- Making diagrams: 33, 34
- Writing chemical equations: 1, 7, 8, 11, 12, 13, 25, 26, 27, 28, 29, 30, 31, 32, 33, 34, 36, 42, 43, 44, 45, 48, 49

one of the tubes. The smell of ammonia is detected. Hydrochloric acid is added to the other test tube. Bubbles of a gas are seen rising in the solution. What is the formula of the unknown?

MULTIPLE-ION MIXTURES

D. Objective: **Recognize** *techniques useful for identifying ions in solution.*

21. Using the compounds in question 1, determine which ion would give a violet flame in a flame test.

22. Using the compounds in question 1, determine which ion would give a crimson flame in a flame test.

23. Lithium compounds are very soluble in water. They rarely form precipitates in concentrations normally dealt with in laboratory analysis. How would you test for the presence of lithium ions in solution?

24. Describe how two metal ions can be separated by the following.
    a. precipitating one ion and using a centrifuge
    b. precipitating one ion and filtering

E. Objective: **Apply** *skills of analysis to identify an unknown in a mixture containing more than one unknown.*

25. An unknown might contain barium nitrate, barium chloride, or sodium sulfide. When a silver nitrate reagent is added, no reaction occurs. Does the unknown contain more than one of the three compounds? Explain.

26. An unknown is a solution of barium nitrate, barium chloride, or sodium sulfide. Name a reagent that, when added to the unknown will identify it. Explain your answer.

27. An unknown is a solution of zinc sulfate, cobalt(II) nitrate, or lead(II) nitrate. When a solution of barium chloride is added, no reaction occurs. What is the identity of the unknown?

28. An unknown is a solution of zinc sulfate, cobalt(II) nitrate, or sulfuric acid. Name one reagent that, when added to the unknown will identify it. Explain your answer.

29. An unknown is a solution of sodium iodide, sodium hydroxide, or sodium carbonate. When a solution of lead(II) nitrate is added a yellow precipitate is formed. What is the identity of the unknown?

30. An unknown contains a solution of sodium iodide, sodium hydroxide, or sodium carbonate. Name a reagent that when added to the unknown, will identify it. Explain.

31. An unknown is a solution of barium chloride, sodium carbonate, lead(II) nitrate, or potassium hydroxide. When a solution of sodium iodide is added, a yellow precipitate forms. What is the identity of the unknown?

32. An unknown is a solution of barium chloride, sodium carbonate, lead(II) nitrate, or potassium hydroxide. Name a reagent that when added to the unknown, will identify it. Explain your answer.

33. Design a flowchart for the separation of the metal ions Hg_2^{2+}, Cu^{2+}, and Al^{3+} in a solution containing a mixture of these ions. The products of the reaction with three different reagents are as follows.

Data Table			
Test Substance	Reagent Added		
	HCl(aq)	H₂S(aq)	NH₃(aq) forming OH⁻ ions
Hg_2^{2+}	white ppt.	black ppt.	white ppt.
Cu^{2+}	N.R.	black ppt.	pale blue ppt.
Al^{3+}	N.R.	N.R.	white ppt.

34. Make a flowchart for the separation of a solution containing a mixture of the following anions: Cl^-, SO_4^{2-}, and OH^-.

Critical Thinking

SYNTHESIS WITHIN THE CHAPTER

35. A mixture contains silver and magnesium ions. Magnesium chloride is relatively soluble, but silver chloride is insoluble. Suggest a method of separating the silver and magnesium ions.

36. Write an ionic equation and net ionic equation for the reaction between sodium hydroxide and ammonium chloride.

37. Suggest a test to identify the presence of the carbonate ion in solution.

38. Suggest a test to identify the presence of the ammonium ion in solution.

39. A solution contains S^{2-} and SO_3^{2-}. How would you separate these ions?

SYNTHESIS ACROSS CHAPTERS

40. Iron(III) chloride is soluble in acid but not very soluble in base. Suggest a reason why.

41. Explain why a precipitate of lead chloride might not appear if you mixed $0.02M$ solutions of lead nitrate and potassium chloride.

42. The solubility of strontium sulfite, Sr_2SO_3, at 17°C is $0.00020M$. Will a precipitate form when 10.0 mL of a $0.030M$ solution of strontium chloride is mixed with 10.0 mL of a $0.0020M$ solution of potassium sulfite at 17°C? What is the formula of the precipitate?

43. The maximum concentration of cobalt(II) fluoride in water at 25°C is $0.16M$. Will a precipitate of cobalt(II) fluoride form when equal volumes of $0.25M$ cobalt(II) nitrate and $0.25M$ sodium fluoride solutions are mixed at 25°C?

44. When 40.0 mL of a $0.50M$ solution of sodium carbonate is reacted with an excess of hydrochloric acid, what volume of carbon dioxide gas will be formed at 25°C and a pressure of 95 kilopascals.

45. When 20.0 mL of $0.50M$ lead(II) nitrate reacts with 20.0 mL of $1.00M$ potassium io-dide, what mass of lead(II) iodide will be formed?

46. What is the molarity of a solution in which 10.8 g of sodium nitrate is added to enough water to make 175 mL of solution?

47. Describe how you would prepare 1.50 L of a $0.50M$ solution of magnesium sulfate heptahydrate.

48. How many milliliters of a $0.50M$ solution of sulfuric acid are required to react completely with 10.0 mL of a $0.50M$ solution of potassium hydroxide?

49. How many milliliters of a $0.25M$ solution of nitric acid are required to completely react with 20.0 mL of a $0.050M$ solution of barium hydroxide?

Projects

50. Using a reference source, find a specific test for phosphate in water. Analyze the water in a local stream or lake for phosphates.

51. Ask your teacher if the school has a spectrophotometer. Design an experiment (including safety procedures) to determine the concentration of a solution of cobalt(II) nitrate. Write a research proposal and submit it to your teacher. If the proposal is approved, carry out the experiment.

Research and Writing

52. Research the problem of ozone depletion. Find out what chemical reactions are involved. Report your findings.

53. Find out the relationship between the use of fertilizers and water pollution.

54. Find out the smallest concentration of lead ions in water that is measurable. What effects can lead ions in the water system have on human health? What are the risks? What are the solutions?

☐ Boxed numbers indicate questions that involve skills in interpretation, application, and analysis.

1. a. $H_2SO_4(l) \rightarrow H^+(aq) + HSO_4^-(aq)$
b. $KOH(s) \rightarrow K^+(aq) + OH^-(aq)$
c. $Na_2CO_3(s) \rightarrow 2Na^+(aq) + CO_3^{2-}(aq)$
d. $Sr(NO_3)_2(s) \rightarrow Sr^{2+}(aq) + 2NO_3^-(aq)$
e. $(NH_4)_2SO_4(s) \rightarrow 2NH_4^+(aq) + SO_4^{2-}(aq)$
f. $K_2SO_4(s) \rightarrow 2K^+(aq) + SO_4^{2-}(aq)$

2. Cations:
a. $H^+(aq)$
b. $K^+(aq)$
c. $Na^+(aq)$

3. Anions:
a. $NO_3^-(aq)$
b. $SO_4^{2-}(aq)$
c. $SO_4^{2-}(aq)$

4. Iron(III) and CrO_4^{2-} are both yellow in solution.

5. The ions present are K^+, Cl^-, Mg^{2+}, SO_4^{2-}.

6. The ions present are Na^+, CO_3^{2-}, NH_4^+.

7. $Ba^{2+}(aq) + 2Cl^-(aq) + 2Na^+(aq) + SO_4^{2-}(aq) \rightarrow BaSO_4(s) + 2Na^+(aq) + 2Cl^-(aq)$
or
$Ba^{2+}(aq) + 2Cl^-(aq) + 2Na^+(aq) + SO_4^{2-}(aq) \rightarrow 2NaCl(s) + Ba^{2+}(aq) + SO_4^{2-}(aq)$

8. $Pb^{2+}(aq) + 2NO_3^-(aq) + 2K^+(aq) + 2Cl^-(aq) \rightarrow PbCl_2(s) + 2K^+(aq) + 2NO_3^-(aq)$
or
$Pb^{2+}(aq) + 2NO_3^-(aq) + 2K^+(aq) + 2Cl^-(aq) \rightarrow 2KNO_3(s) + Pb^{2+}(aq) + 2Cl^-(aq)$

9. potassium nitrate = K^+, NO_3^-
potassium hydroxide = K^+, OH^-
lithium hydroxide = Li^+, OH^-
cobalt(II) chloride = Co^{2+}, Cl^-
cobalt(II) nitrate = Co^{2+}, NO_3^-
iron(III) chloride = Fe^{3+}, Cl^-

10. Potassium ions and nitrate ions do not form precipitates. There are no reactions with any combination of these ions with other ions in the table.

11. $Co(OH)_2$ is formed.

12. The precipitate formed in both reactions is $Fe(OH)_3$.

13. $Fe^{3+}(aq) + 3OH^-(aq) \rightarrow Fe(OH)_3(s)$

14. When hydrochloric acid is added to a solution containing hydroxide ions, the reaction vessel should feel warm. Also, iron(III), cobalt(II), copper(II), and nickel(II) ions will precipitate with hydroxide ions.

15. When hydrochloric acid is added to a solution containing silver ions, a precipitate of silver chloride forms. When ammonium hydroxide solution is added to the silver chloride, it dissolves. The solution is then treated with dilute nitric acid. If a precipitate reforms, silver ions are present.

16. Addition of a strong acid to a solution containing sulfite ions produces SO_2 gas, which has a choking odor.

17. Carbon dioxide, CO_2, is formed.

18. You should feel the test tube getting warmer.

19. Ammonium ions, NH_4^+, are present.

20. Using the limited information in the chapter, the unknown should be ammonium carbonate, $(NH_4)_2CO_3$.

21. The compounds containing potassium (b. and f.) will give a violet flame.

22. The compound containing strontium (d.) will give a crimson-colored flame.

23. If the solution is concentrated enough, a sample of the solution should give a scarlet-colored flame, revealing the presence of lithium ions.

24. a. After precipitation, the mixture is centrifuged and the liquid is poured off.
b. The precipitated ion will be in the solid on the filter paper; the other ion will be in the solution that passes through the paper.

25. The unknown might contain only barium nitrate. The other two anions would form a precipitate with silver ions.

26. Silver nitrate will identify it.
no reaction, x = $Ba(NO_3)_2$
white precipitate, x = $BaCl_2$
black precipitate, x = Na_2S

27. The unknown is cobalt(II) nitrate.

28. Sodium carbonate will identify the unknown.
A white precipitate will indicate the presence of $ZnSO_4$.
A red precipitate will indicate the presence of $Co(NO_3)_2$.
Bubbles of gas will indicate the presence of H_2SO_4.

29. The unknown is sodium iodide.

30. Hydrochloric acid will identify the unknown.
No reaction will result from NaI.
Heat will be produced from NaOH.
Odorless bubbles will evolve from Na_2CO_3.

31. The unknown is lead(II) nitrate.

32. Hydrochloric acid will identify the unknown.
No reaction will result from $BaCl_2$.
Odorless bubbles will evolve from Na_2CO_3.
A white precipitate will result from $Pb(NO_3)_2$.
Heat will be produced from KOH.

33.

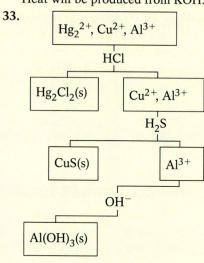

34.

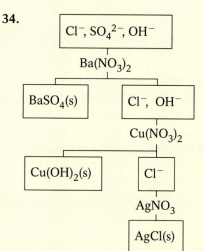

35. Add chloride ions to precipitate silver chloride. Centrifuge the mixture, then pour off the supernatant liquid containing the magnesium ions.

36. The ionic equation is
$Na^+(aq) + OH^-(aq) + NH_4^+(aq) + Cl^-(aq) \rightarrow H_2O(l) + NH_3(aq) + Na^+(aq) + Cl^-(aq)$
The net ionic equation is
$NH_4^+(aq) + OH^-(aq) \rightarrow H_2O(l) + NH_3(aq)$

37. Add hydrochloric acid to the solution. If the carbonate ion is present, an odorless gas, CO_2, should evolve.

38. Add sodium hydroxide solution. If the ammonium ion is present, the odor of ammonia will be present.

39. Add barium nitrate solution to these anions. A precipitate of barium sulfite will form and the sulfide ions will remain in solution.

40. Insoluble iron(III) hydroxide would be formed in the basic solution that contains a high concentration of hydroxide ions. An acid has a relatively low concentration of hydroxide ions.

41. The solubility table states that lead chloride is not soluble at a concentration of $0.1M$ or greater. The concentration of the ions may not be sufficient to cause a precipitate to form.

42. Since the solubility is $0.000\ 20M$, K_{sp}
$$= [Sr^{2+}][SO_3^{2-}]$$
$$= (2.0 \times 10^{-4})(2.0 \times 10^{-4})$$
$$= 4.0 \times 10^{-8}.$$
The number of moles of each ion present is

$0.010\ \cancel{L} \times \frac{0.030\ mol}{1\cancel{L}} = 0.0003$ mol

Sr^{2+} and

$0.010\ \cancel{L} \times \frac{0.0020\ mol}{1\cancel{L}} = 0.000\ 02$ mol

SO_3^{2-}

The concentration of each ion in the solution at the instant of mixing is:

$\frac{0.0003\ mol}{0.020\ L} = 0.015M$ in Sr^{2+}

and

$\frac{0.000\ 02\ mol}{0.020\ L} = 0.001M$ in SO_3^{2-}

If the ion product $[Sr^{2+}][SO_3^{2-}]$ exceeds the K_{sp} for $SrSO_3$, a precipitate forms.
$[0.015M][0.001M] = 1.5 \times 10^{-5}$
Since 1.5×10^{-5} is greater than 4.0×10^{-8}, a precipitate forms. The formula of the precipitate is $SrSO_3$.

43. Since the solubility of CoF_2 is $0.16M$,
$K_{sp} = [Co^{2+}][F^-]^2 = (0.16)(0.32)^2$
$= 1.6 \times 10^{-2}$
The concentration of each of the ions in the solution at the instant of mixing is $0.25M/2 = 0.12M$
The ion product in this solution is
$[0.12M][0.12]^2 = 1.7 \times 10^{-3}$
Since this value is less than K_{sp}, no precipitate forms.

44. $Na_2CO_3(aq) + 2HCl(aq) \rightarrow$
$\qquad 2NaCl(aq) + H_2O(l) + CO_2(g)$

$40.0\ \cancel{mL\ Na_2CO_3} \times \frac{0.50\ \cancel{mol\ Na_2CO_3}}{1000\ \cancel{mL\ Na_2CO_3}}$

$\times \frac{1\ mol\ CO_2}{1\ \cancel{mol\ Na_2CO_3}} = 0.020$ mol CO_2

$PV = nRT$

$V = nRT / P$

$\frac{0.020\ \cancel{mol} \times 8.31\ L \cdot \cancel{kPa/mol} \cdot \cancel{K} \times 298\ \cancel{K}}{95\ \cancel{kPa}}$

$= 0.52$ L

45. $Pb(NO_3)_2(aq) + 2KI(aq) \rightarrow$
$\qquad PbI(s) + 2KNO_3(aq)$

$20.0\ \cancel{mL\ Pb(NO_3)_2}$

$\times \frac{0.50\ mol\ Pb(NO_3)_2}{1000\ \cancel{mL\ Pb(NO_3)_2}}$

$= 0.010$ mol $Pb(NO_3)_2$

$20.0\ \cancel{mL\ KI} \times \frac{1.00\ mol\ KI}{1000\ \cancel{mL\ KI}}$

$= 0.020$ mol KI

The mole ratio is the correct stoichiometric ratio. Therefore, either reactant can be used to calculate the product.

$20.0\ \cancel{mL\ KI} \times \frac{1.00\ \cancel{mol\ KI}}{1000\ \cancel{mL\ KI}} \times \frac{1\ \cancel{mol\ PbI_2}}{2\ \cancel{mol\ KI}}$

$\times \frac{461\ g\ PbI_2}{1\ \cancel{mol\ PbI_2}} = 4.6$ g PbI_2

46. $\frac{10.8\ \cancel{g\ NaNO_3}}{175\ \cancel{mL}} \times \frac{1\ mol\ NaNO_3}{85.0\ \cancel{g\ NaNO_3}}$

$\times \frac{1000\ \cancel{mL}}{1\ L} = 0.726M$

47. $1.50\ \cancel{L\ MgSO_4 \cdot 7H_2O}$

$\times \frac{0.50\ \cancel{mol\ MgSO_4 \cdot 7H_2O}}{1\ \cancel{L\ MgSO_4 \cdot 7H_2O}}$

$\times \frac{246.4\ g\ MgSO_4 \cdot 7H_2O}{1\ \cancel{mol\ MgSO_4 \cdot 7H_2O}}$

$= 185$ g $MgSO_4 \cdot 7H_2O$

To 185 g $MgSO_4 \cdot 7H_2O$, add enough distilled water so that the final volume is 1.50 L when all solute is dissolved.

48. $H_2SO_4(aq) + 2KOH(aq) \rightarrow$
$\qquad K_2SO_4(aq) + 2H_2O(l)$

$10.0\ \cancel{mL\ KOH} \times \frac{0.50\ \cancel{mol\ KOH}}{1000\ \cancel{mL\ KOH}}$

$\times \frac{1\ \cancel{mol\ H_2SO_4}}{2\ \cancel{mol\ KOH}} \times \frac{1000\ mL\ H_2SO_4}{0.50\ \cancel{mol\ H_2SO_4}}$

$= 5.0$ mL H_2SO_4

49. $2HNO_3(aq) + Ba(OH)_2(aq) \rightarrow$
$\qquad Ba(NO_3)_2(aq) + 2H_2O$

$20.0\ \cancel{mL\ Ba(OH)_2} \times \frac{0.50\ \cancel{mol\ Ba(OH)_2}}{1000\ \cancel{mL\ Ba(OH)_2}}$

$\times \frac{2\ \cancel{mol\ HNO_3}}{1\ \cancel{mol\ Ba(OH)_2}} \times \frac{1000\ mL\ HNO_3}{0.25\ \cancel{mol\ HNO_3}}$

$= 8.0$ mL HNO_3

Organic Chemistry

Investigations	Demonstrations	Texas Essential Elements★
	Nylon, page T748	**Process:** 4.2, 4.3, 10.1, 10.4
Laboratory Manual 22–1 S Laboratory Manual 22–2 M Laboratory Manual 22–3 I In-text Investigation, page T764	Oxidation, page T760 Polymerization, page T761	**Content:** 12.1 **Process:** 3.1, 3.2, 4.2, 4.3, 10.1, 10.4
		Process: 1.2, 4.2, 7.1
		Process: 3.1, 4.2, 7.1, 8.2, 10.1, 10.2

KEY:
M–*Microscale* **S**–*Structured*
I–*Inquiry* **IM**–*Inquiry Microscale*

★*See pages T8–T11 for complete listing of Texas Essential Elements.*

22

Organic Chemistry

Chapter Rationale

The properties and reactions of some organic chemicals have been integrated into each chapter. Knowledge of formulas, the mole concept, atoms, molecules, bonding, and reactions is needed to understand organic chemistry. Organic compounds are considered separately because they make up more than 90 percent of the known compounds. To organize this information, a system of nomenclature, the use of diagrams to represent structures, the identification of common functional groups, and typical reactions are presented.

Equations for reactions that indicate stoichiometric proportions, such as those in Chapter 5, do not convey enough information. Structural representations show which bonds are broken and how the new compound is different. Conditions of the reaction such as the temperature, the reactants' state, and catalysts needed are more important in organic reactions.

About the Photograph

In the production of rayon, plant fibers are cleaned, dried, and converted into a colloidal suspension using several processes. One of these processes, the viscose process, makes a suspension of cellulose by treating wood fibers or cotton fibers with sodium hydroxide and carbon disulfide. The resulting rayon is often used as a replacement for silk.

Chapter Planning Hints

To complete this chapter, the Laboratory Investigation, and the Chapter Review will require five to eight classes. You may wish to obtain The World of Chemistry videotape *Organic Chemistry*. You will find three optional demonstrations in this chapter on pages T748, T760, and T761.

Overview

Research in organic chemistry has resulted in the development of real-world products, such as synthetic fibers.

PART 1 Introducing Carbon Compounds

It is obvious that carbon compounds contain carbon. However, unlike compounds formed from other elements, carbon compounds are far more numerous and varied. There are more than 6 million different carbon compounds known, and over 300,000 new ones are synthesized each year! Most of these compounds are combinations of carbon with a handful of other elements. The most common elements found with carbon are hydrogen, oxygen, nitrogen, sulfur, phosphorus, and the halogens.

Because there are so many carbon compounds, an entire branch of chemistry has developed around them. As a result of many experimental observations, some general chemical and physical properties of carbon compounds are known. For example, most carbon compounds are either nonelectrolytes or weak electrolytes, and as a group they tend to have low melting points. Carbon compounds made solely from carbon and hydrogen are generally nonpolar and insoluble in water, whereas other classes of carbon compounds include some substances that are quite soluble. In this chapter, you will take a closer look at the properties of a few groups of carbon compounds. You also will find out why they are significant in today's world.

Objectives

Part 1

A. **Recognize** the relationship of fossil fuels to organic chemistry.

B. **Define** a hydrocarbon and **identify** homologous series of alkanes, alkenes, and alkynes.

C. **Distinguish** isomers of hydrocarbons.

D. **Draw** structural formulas and **name** straight-chain and cyclic hydrocarbons, using the IUPAC system.

22.1 Where Do Carbon Compounds Come From?

Millions of years ago, climatic conditions on Earth resulted in the rapid growth of vegetation, as shown in Figure 22-1 on the next page. As plants and trees later died, they fell to the floors of forests, swamps, and marshes. The continuing cycle of growth and decay resulted in vast deposits of plant material. As the material accumulated, pressure and heat began altering the chemical structure of the buried compounds. In time, the layers were pressed into hard beds of **coal,** composed chiefly of carbon atoms with appreciable amounts of oxygen, hydrogen, nitrogen, and sulfur compounds incorporated into its structure.

Carbon compounds from coal Until the onset of the Industrial Revolution, the wealth of chemicals stored in coal deposits was seldom utilized. Through a process called **destructive distillation,** in which coal is heated in the absence of air, a wide array of carbon compounds was liberated. Coke, a residue of the process,

Developing Skills

Students may apply these skills in their study of Part 1.
Classifying: Have students classify the compounds on pages 741 and 742 as straight chain or branched.
Comparing/Contrasting and Interpreting diagrams: Have students compare the compounds in Figure 22–2 to those in Figure 22–3 and contrast their shapes.

☰ FOCUS

Activate Prior Knowledge

Show examples of organic compounds in sealed containers. Possible examples are phthalic acid, stearic acid, paraffin, cyclohexane, ethanol, salicylic acid, phenolphthalein, bromthymol blue, methylethyl ketone, methyl salicylate, oxalic acid, butane (in a lighter, taped to prevent use), pentane, and octane.

☰ TEACH

Teaching Strategy

Where Do Carbon Compounds Come From?

A note of conservation is appropriate here. Millions of years were required to produce the petroleum and natural gas we are pumping from Earth. We have been refining crude oil only about 150 years and already the supply is becoming scarce. The amount of oil on Earth is finite so we should try to take appropriate measures to conserve our resources and to support research for alternatives.

PART **1**
Section 22.1 *continued*

Videodisc Connections

12392-12399, side 6
Analysis of crude oil
(8-frame seq.)

Figure 22-1 *The coal deposits of North America formed from swampy forests that existed during the Carboniferous Period, which began about 345 million years ago.*

was substituted for charcoal in iron making. Subsequently people began to investigate how to use the by-products of distillation, such as coal gas and coal tar. Coal tar was separated into over 200 different carbon compounds. These substances could then either be used directly or treated in the laboratory to produce additional compounds.

The origin of petroleum and natural gas

At about the same time that Earth's prehistoric environment was dominated by land plants, its shallow seas supported heavy growth of algae, bacteria, and plankton. As these microscopic organisms died, their bodies settled into the ooze of the seafloor. Microbes, living within the ooze, began decomposing the accumulated matter, producing methane gas, CH_4. As the ooze grew deeper, high temperatures and pressures altered the molecular structures of the compounds that were present (sugars and other carbon-based substances). Huge deposits of crude oil and natural gas were produced during these reactions. Under tremendous pressure, these mixtures of compounds diffused into the porous space of nearby sandstone. There they remained, until an industrialized society recognized the value of petroleum and natural gas.

Living organisms synthesize carbon compounds

Plants and animals are highly efficient chemical factories. Living organisms must synthesize numerous carbon-based molecules. The synthesized compounds include proteins, sugars, cellulose, starches, vitamins, oils, waxes and fats. Useful products found in plants can include dyes, drugs and fibers, to name a few. Since all the sources of carbon compounds originally came solely from living organisms, the chemistry of carbon was called **organic chemistry.** This name comes from the belief—now discarded—that living materials, containing a special ingredient absent in nonliving matter, were organized in a unique way. Although organic chemicals are now routinely synthesized in laboratories, the name continues to be applied to the chemistry of carbon compounds.

DO YOU KNOW?

One of the largest organic molecules is found in the chromosome of the fruit fly Drosophila melanogaster. *The chromosome is about 2 cm long but only 0.000 002 cm in diameter. Its formula is approximately* $C_{614\,000\,000}H_{759\,000\,000}N_{217\,000\,000}P_{62\,000\,000}O_{496\,000\,000}$, *or a little over 2 billion atoms! Its molar mass is about 23 100 tons!*

22.2 Sorting Out Organic Compounds

Why are there so many different carbon compounds in comparison to compounds made from other elements? One reason is the bonding behavior of carbon. In Chapter 13, you learned that carbon atoms have four electrons available for bonding and that these electrons can be shared in four covalent bonds with other atoms. Figure 22-2 shows the tetrahedral arrangement of bonding electrons around the carbon atom. However, sometimes carbon may form double or triple bonds. Additionally, carbon atoms have an unusual ability to link together to form chains of varying length. This bonding behavior can produce carbon chains of astounding proportions.

Since the properties of any substance depend upon both the composition and the structure of the molecule, different arrangements of the same atoms result in different substances, each with a unique chemical and physical identity. For example, the 92 atoms of the molecule $C_{30}H_{62}$ may be arranged to form about four billion possible compounds! You will have an opportunity to look at some simpler molecules and the several structural arrangements the atoms of these molecules can have.

Hydrocarbons and derivatives Compounds containing only carbon and hydrogen atoms are called **hydrocarbons.** Organic compounds in which some or all of the hydrogen atoms have been replaced by other atoms are considered to be **derivatives** of hydrocarbons. Although simple in structure, hydrocarbons constitute the building blocks for more complex organic molecules. Coal, petroleum, natural gas, and certain species of trees are the most common natural sources of hydrocarbons.

The longest carbon chain in a hydrocarbon molecule is frequently referred to as the **carbon backbone.** When structural diagrams of hydrocarbons are made, often only the carbon backbone and associated bonds are drawn. It is assumed that the identity of the atoms not shown is hydrogen. For example, the structural formula for ethane, C_2H_6, can be drawn in either of these ways.

$$
\begin{array}{cc}
\text{H H} \\
| \quad | \\
\text{H}-\text{C}-\text{C}-\text{H} \qquad -\text{C}-\text{C}- \\
| \quad | \qquad\qquad | \quad | \\
\text{H H}
\end{array}
$$

In the second case, only the carbon backbone of two carbons and their bonds are represented. The simplest hydrocarbon molecules consist of a single linear chain of carbon atoms with hydrogens bonded as shown here.

$$C_3H_8 \qquad\qquad C_7H_{16}$$

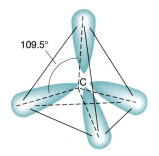

Figure 22-2 A carbon atom can form covalent bonds with up to four other atoms.

109.5°

C

CONNECTING CONCEPTS

Structure and Properties of Matter The structure and composition of organic compounds determines their properties and reactivities.

Teaching Strategy

Sorting Out Organic Compounds

To whet students' interest in organic chemistry and its importance to everyday life, assign a brief research project. Students may work individually or in small groups of two to four. Topics should be selected by the students and they should appeal to their particular interests. Have students share their reports with the class in a five to ten minute presentation that may include visuals, if applicable. Suggested topics could be health related (for example, drugs and their effect on the body) or environmentally related (for example, oil spills, hazardous waste, recycling issues, contaminated water supplies, or the effects of pesticides and herbicides).

CONNECTING CONCEPTS

Models Understanding the structure of organic compounds is easier if you use models such as space-filling, ball and stick, or accurate diagrams to represent them.

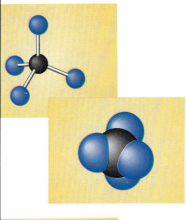

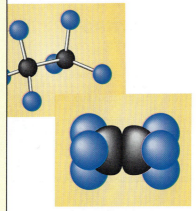

Figure 22-3 *The space-filling models in the foreground more accurately represent the structures of methane, top, and ethane, bottom, but the ball and stick models help you visualize the tetrahedral geometry around each carbon atom.*

These simple molecules are called **straight-chain** or **unbranched** hydrocarbons. More complex hydrocarbons may be composed of several carbon chains that cross, such as those below. These molecules are called **branched** hydrocarbons. The carbon backbone of each molecule is shown in blue.

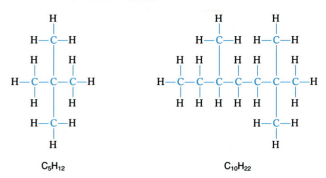

C_5H_{12} $C_{10}H_{22}$

Saturated and unsaturated hydrocarbons Hydrocarbons may contain all single bonds or combinations of single, double, and triple bonds. The reactivity of a hydrocarbon is dependent upon the number and type of bonds found within the molecule. Molecules made entirely of single carbon-carbon bonds are relatively stable. They cannot incorporate additional atoms into their structure, so they are said to be **saturated.** When double or triple bonds are found between carbon atoms, the possibility exists for opening some of the bonds and introducing additional atoms to the structure. Hydrocarbons containing at least one double or triple carbon-carbon bond are referred to as **unsaturated.**

saturated
ethane

unsaturated
ethene   ethyne

Carbon-carbon bonds themselves also may be described as saturated or unsaturated, depending on whether they are single bonds or double or triple bonds.

Representing structures The structural formulas of saturated hydrocarbons are shown above as flat molecules, but this way of representing molecules is only a convenience. The structures are, in fact, three-dimensional. Did you notice in Figure 22-2 that carbon's four bonding electrons are positioned at 109.5° angles around the nucleus? This means that when carbon forms four single bonds, the arrangement of the bonds in space will have the geometry of a tetrahedron. Figure 22.3 shows the simplest hydrocarbon methane, CH_4, and the two-carbon chain ethane, C_2H_6.

While the geometry around a saturated carbon atom (one forming four bonds) is three-dimensional, the atoms around a carbon forming a double bond lie in a plane. A structural model for ethene is shown in Figure 22.4.

What do you think is the geometry around a carbon atom which forms a triple bond? If you said that the atoms bonded to carbon should lie along a straight line, you are correct. The geometry is linear. The formula for ethyne, C_2H_2, correctly represents the geometry of the molecule when it is written this way: $H—C≡C—H$.

Condensed formulas As you begin to draw your own structural formulas for hydrocarbons, you will appreciate the convenience of condensed formulas. For example, ethane can be represented as $CH_3—CH_3$. The straight chain hydrocarbon, C_7H_{16}, can be represented in either of these ways.

$$CH_3—CH_2—CH_2—CH_2—CH_2—CH_2—CH_3 \quad or \quad CH_3—(CH_2)_5—CH_3$$

A branched hydrocarbon can be represented like this.

$$\begin{array}{c} CH_3 \\ | \\ CH_3—C—CH_3 \\ | \\ CH_3 \end{array}$$

Organizing hydrocarbons Hydrocarbons exist in such huge numbers that learning about them could be bewildering. To complicate matters, some hydrocarbons have the same chemical formula but differ in the way their atoms are arranged. As a result, organic compounds are studied by classifying them into logical groups.

Concept ✓ Check

Can saturated and unsaturated hydrocarbons also be straight-chain and branched hydrocarbons? Explain what is meant by each term.

22.3 Alkanes

Petroleum can be subjected to fractional distillation, in which volatile substances with different condensation temperatures (boiling points) separate as they are cooled. Some of the products that result from this process are a group of closely related hydrocarbons called alkanes. **Alkanes** are straight- or branched-chain saturated compounds containing only single bonds. The first four members of the alkane series are listed in Table 22-1 on page 745.

Boiling points and intermolecular attraction Notice the relatively low boiling points of the compounds listed in the table. This should not come as a surprise. Boiling points of liquids depend, in part, on the strength of intermolecular attractions. In Section 22.1, you read that hydrocarbons are generally nonpolar. As a result, the only intermolecular attractions are dispersion forces.

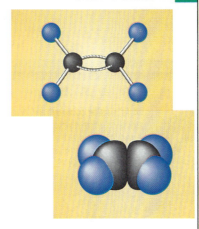

Figure 22-4 *All the atoms in ethene lie in one plane. Can you estimate the size of the H—C—H angle?*

CONNECTING CONCEPTS

Processes of Science—Classifying Organic compounds can be classified on the basis of their composition and structures.

PART **1**
Section 22.3

Cooperative Learning

Alkanes

Teams of 3; **Time:** 30 minutes
Objective: Students will learn to draw the structures and name the isomers of an organic compound.
Task: Students will draw and name the five isomers of hexane.
Team responsibility: Structures and their names will be compared and errors will be identified and corrected.
Evaluation: Have students draw and name the nine isomers of heptane. Give a bonus to every member of a team if the team succeeds in drawing and naming all nine isomers.

PROBLEM-SOLVING
S T R A T E G Y

*It is easier to **look for a pattern** in a homologous series if you start with the simpler compounds in the series. (See Strategy, page 100.)*

Figure 22-5 *Natural gas is a commonly used fuel. It consists mostly of methane with smaller amounts of other hydrocarbons.*

On the other hand, the boiling points of compounds listed in the table increase with increasing numbers of atoms. How can this observation be explained? Recall from Chapter 13 that even non-polar molecules are affected by dispersion forces. The more atoms there are in the molecule, the larger the overall strength of the intermolecular attractions. The greater the attractive forces between molecules, the higher the boiling point.

Methane begins a series The simplest alkane is methane gas, CH_4. It is produced during the anaerobic decomposition of organic substances (decomposition without oxygen) and is the major constituent of natural gas. The presence of methane in coal mines and swamps supports its association with decaying organic materials. Some biologists think methane was produced in Earth's primitive atmosphere from reactions with hydrogen and carbon gases. Further reactions involving methane, water, nitrogen, carbon dioxide, carbon monoxide, and hydrogen may have played a vital role in the evolution of life. Note methanes in Figure 22-5.

The next member of the alkane series is ethane, C_2H_6. The ethane molecule contains one carbon-carbon single bond and six carbon-hydrogen bonds. Along with methane, ethane is a constituent of natural gas.

Propane, C_3H_8, also is found in natural gas and often is used as a fuel in portable stoves, lanterns, and low-temperature torches. Propane's molecular structure differs from that of ethane by the presence of a unit made of one carbon atom and two hydrogen atoms, represented as $—CH_2—$. Notice in Table 22-1 that as alkane molecules increase in length, each successive compound has an additional $—CH_2—$ group in its structure. A series of compounds, whose members differ by the addition of the same structural unit, is called a **homologous series.** The alkanes are an example of one homologous series. Study the chemical formulas in the table. Do you see a pattern? The general formula for an alkane is C_nH_{2n+2}. The subscript n is the number of carbon atoms in the molecule. Can you predict the formulas for the nine-carbon and ten-carbon compounds in this series?

22.4 Naming Hydrocarbons

In the early history of organic chemistry, the number of compounds known was limited. Their names came from a variety of sources and have become well established. However, as the number of known compounds increased, there was a need for a more systematic method of naming new ones. The current procedure for naming organic compounds is based on a set of rules formulated by the International Union of Pure and Applied Chemistry (IUPAC).

Unbranched alkanes, like those in Table 22-1, are the simplest to name. Hydrocarbons above butane derive their names from the longest straight chain of carbon atoms found in the molecule. For

TABLE 22-1

Representative Alkanes				
Chemical Formula	**Structural Formula**	**Condensed Formula**	**Name**	**Boiling Point (°C)**
CH_4	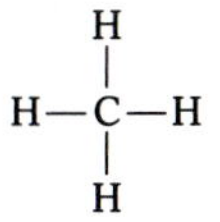 H | H—C—H | H		methane	−162
C_2H_6	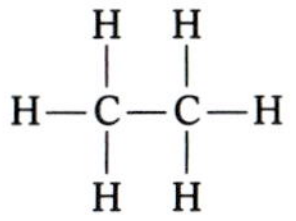 H H | | H—C—C—H | | H H	CH_3—CH_3	ethane	−89
C_3H_8	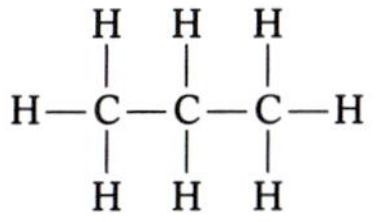 H H H | | | H—C—C—C—H | | | H H H	CH_3—CH_2—CH_3	propane	−42
C_4H_{10}	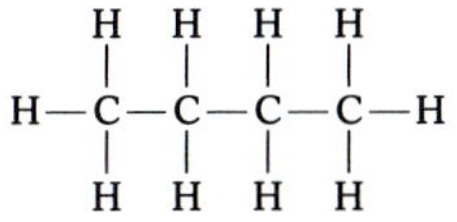 H H H H | | | | H—C—C—C—C—H | | | | H H H H	CH_3—$(CH_2)_2$—CH_3	butane	0

these compounds, the name is based on the Greek word for the number of carbons. The prefix *pent, hex, hept,* or *oct* is followed by the family ending *ane.* The names for the next two compounds in the alkane series are nonane (nine carbons) and decane (ten carbons).

Branched-chain saturated hydrocarbons There are many saturated hydrocarbon compounds that have branched chains—for instance, molecule A to the right. Clearly the black portion of this structure is almost the same as heptane, and the colored portion is very much like methane. You could call the molecule methane-heptane, but that is a bit awkward to say. More importantly, it does not distinguish the first molecule from the others in the figure, which also are forms of methane-heptane. According to the IUPAC rules, the name of the smaller portion, or branch, is modified so that *yl* replaces the *ane* ending. (The branch is known as an alkyl group.) The name for molecule A then becomes methylheptane. This name is less awkward to say, but there is still a small problem to solve: how to distinguish between molecules B and C, which are different from molecule A and from each other. In molecule A, the methyl group is on the third carbon atom of the long chain, so the name of the compound is 3-methylheptane. If you count from the other end of the molecule, the methyl group is on the fifth carbon. However, by convention, the lowest "address" is always used to locate a branch. Molecule B is 2-methylheptane, and molecule C is 4-methylheptane.

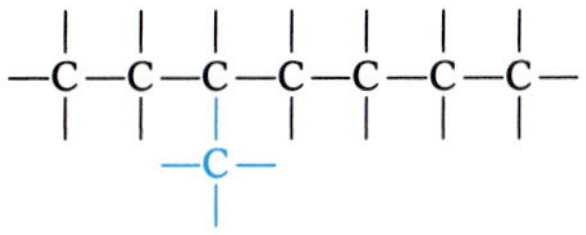

Molecule A

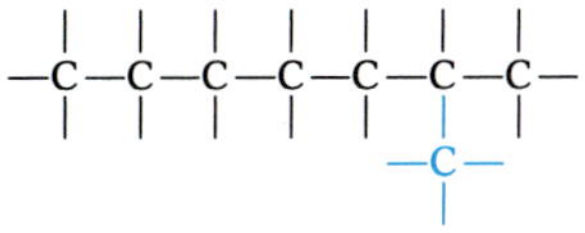

Molecule B

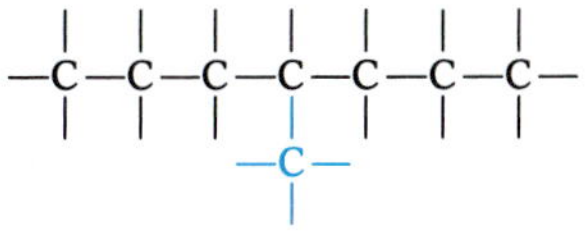

Molecule C

Myths and Misconceptions

When writing formulas and naming organic compounds, students often have the misconception that two different names for a structure represent two different isomers. In fact, the two names may refer to the same molecule. For example,

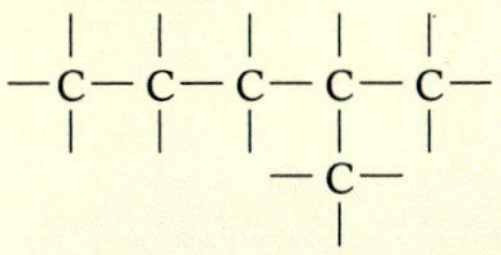

and

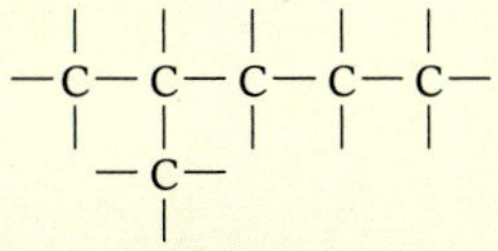

are the same molecule, not isomers. You can determine this by giving students several formulas and asking them to correctly name them. If students disagree about which answer is correct, have them build three-dimensional ball-and-stick models of the molecules.

PART **1**

Section 22.4 *continued*

Teaching Strategy

Naming Hydrocarbons

Contact a local industrial chemical plant, manufacturing plant, refinery, waste treatment facility, recycling plant, or lawn service to arrange for a guest speaker for the class. This could be a chemist, plant manager, chemical engineer, or environmental engineer or ecologist. The speaker could describe the chemicals used in that plant, the function of these chemicals and their effects on the environment, if any (for example, what emissions into the air or groundwater may be of concern and how wastes are handled). After the talk, students could use their knowledge to look up the background of these substances and predict their impact on living organisms. As students discuss individual substances, they should identify their structural formulas and physical and chemical properties. They can relate these properties to the chemical's use, such as industrial solvent, pesticide, and so on.

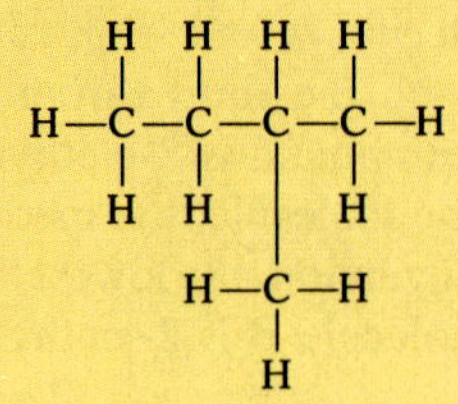

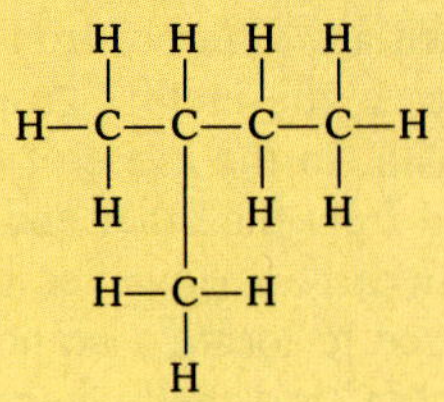

CONNECTING CONCEPTS

Processes of Science—

Communicating Dealing with the enormous number of organic compounds became easier when chemists agreed on a way to name them.

Isomers have different structures and properties The three molecules shown on the previous page are examples of **structural isomers**, compounds with the same chemical formula but different arrangements of atoms. In the case of the methylheptanes, all three molecules have the formula C_8H_{18}, but the atoms are arranged differently. Many organic compounds exist as structural isomers. Such isomers differ somewhat in physical properties—such as melting points, boiling points, and solubilities in different solvents. The numbering system described here is a way to distinguish between the compounds by name.

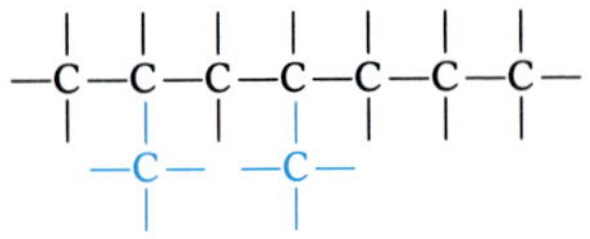

Using prefixes Now consider a slightly more complicated example in which two methyl groups are present. In the molecule shown to the left, there are seven carbon atoms in the longest unbranched chain, so heptane is used as the last part of the name. One methyl group is on the second carbon atom, and the other methyl group is on the fourth carbon atom. The name for the molecule could be 2-methyl-4-methyl-heptane. It is descriptive and accurate, but there is a shorter way of showing the presence of two methyl groups. The prefix *di*, meaning "two," is used. The name for the compound is then 2,4-dimethylheptane.

EXAMPLE 22-1

One compound with the chemical formula C_5H_{12} is pentane. Pentane has three structural isomers. For each isomer, draw the structural diagram and determine its IUPAC name.

■ ***Analyze the Problem*** You know that the structural formula for pentane is a straight-chain skeleton of five carbons. You should also realize that isomers will be branched chains of carbons, providing 12 sites for the hydrogens. When the structures are drawn, you must apply the IUPAC rules for naming them.

■ ***Apply a Strategy*** Begin with a 4-carbon chain. Place the fifth carbon on other carbons to form branched chains. Do the same for a 3-carbon chain. Add hydrogens so that each carbon has 4 bonds.

■ ***Work a Solution*** A chain of 4 carbons has 2 carbons that are not on the ends.

To name the isomers, you first need to name the longest chain. Chains of 4 carbons have the name butane. Next you need to number the butane chains in such a way as to give the methyl group the lowest address. That means the first isomer should be numbered starting from the right, giving the name 2-methylbutane. The second should be numbered from the left, giving the same name! You have just shown that the 2 structural formulas are not two isomers of each other but are the same molecule written in two different ways. A chain of 3 carbons can accommodate branches only at the single carbon in the center of the chain.

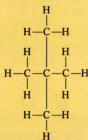

A 3-carbon chain is called propane. The location of its 2 branches is the second carbon, counted from either direction. Therefore, the name of this isomer is 2,2-dimethylpropane.

■ **Verify Your Answer** Check that each carbon is shown with 4 bonds and each hydrogen with 1. See what happens if you place the methyl groups in any other positions. Can you conclude that there are only 3 structural isomers of C_5H_{12}?

Practice Problems

1. There are two structural isomers of C_4H_{10}. Draw the structural formula and write the IUPAC name of each.

2. Draw the straight-chain structures for nonane and decane.

3. Match each name in a–d with the correct structure in e–h.
   a. 3-ethyl-2-methylhexane c. 2,2,4-trimethylhexane
   b. 3-ethyl-4-methylhexane d. 3-ethylhexane

PROBLEM-SOLVING STRATEGY

Break this task of naming isomers **into manageable steps.** *(See Strategy, page 166.)*

PART **1**

Section 22.4 *continued*

Practice Problems

Assign the Practice Problems.

PART **1**
Section 22.4 continued

Videodisc Connections

39878 to 41996, side 6
Nylon (movie)

37012 to 39877, side 6
Rayon (movie)

---

4. Write the IUPAC names of the following alkanes.

a.

b.

c.

5. How many hydrogen atoms are there in a molecule of an alkane containing 15 carbon atoms? 50 carbon atoms?

C O N S U M E R   C H E M I S T R Y

Nylon—Fabric from a Beaker

The discovery of nylon is an example of planned research coupled with unexpected observations. Researchers were seeking a synthetic fabric to replace silk, a widely used but very expensive fabric. Silk, a natural product made from the fiber of the silkworm cocoon, is soft, durable, versatile, and warm. However, production of silk required so much manual labor that the cost of silk fabric was beyond the reach of most people.

Silk is a protein. Most protein molecules are polymers made of hundreds or even thousands of amino acids. Silkworms combine these acids into long chains to form silk fibers. In 1927, the DuPont Company financed a research project to learn more about the characteristics of polymers and how to make them. If polymers could be produced on an industrial scale, the fibers would be less expensive and, therefore, available to more people.

A young American chemist, Wallace Carothers, was employed to organize the research program. Since other chemists previously had difficulty making molecules join each other in long chains, Carothers decided to use longer starting molecules. He chose diaminohexane and adipic acid, two molecules that did

combine into a polymer chain. He named this new compound nylon 6,6, since there were 6 carbon atoms in each of the original monomers.

Ironically the actual discovery of nylon was partially an accident. While studying reactions using different combinations of starting monomers, Carother's associate, Julian Hill, happened to pull a stirring rod out of the thick, syrupy mixture of one combination. Long threads appeared along the stirring rod.

The fibers, which did not break, solidified when cooled, and when pulled, stretched like rubber but did not snap back. The first synthetic fiber had been made.

D E M O N S T R A T I O N

Nylon

⚠ **CAUTION: This demonstration must be performed in a hood. Wear safety goggles, lab apron, and rubber gloves. Wash thoroughly afterwards. Do not allow students to handle any of the reagents or nylon polymer.** Place 150 mL of 1,1,1-trichloroethane and 3 mL of decanedioyl chloride into a 600-mL beaker. Into a separate 600-ml beaker,

place 150 mL of 0.4M NaOH (16 g/L) and 70 drops of hexamethylene diamine (premeasured). Add 4 drops of phenolphthalein to this beaker. Slowly pour the contents of the first beaker (containing trichloroethane solution) into the second beaker. Using tongs, lift up the skin that forms at the solution interface. You can wrap this fiber (continued on page T749)

22.5 Alkenes

When petroleum is heated to high temperatures in the presence of certain catalysts, the larger alkanes composing it may be broken into different alkanes and another type of hydrocarbon called alkenes. This process, known as **cracking**, is used to produce organic molecules containing double-bonded carbon atoms. Hydrocarbons containing at least one double carbon-carbon bond belong to the **alkene** series. Some examples of alkenes are listed in Table 22-2.

TABLE 22-2

Members of the Alkene Series of Hydrocarbons		
Chemical Formula	Structural Formula	Name
C_2H_4	$\begin{array}{c} H \quad\quad H \\ \diagdown\quad\diagup \\ C = C \\ \diagup\quad\diagdown \\ H \quad\quad H \end{array}$	ethene
C_3H_6	$\begin{array}{c} H \quad\quad H \\ \diagdown\quad\diagup \\ C = C \\ \diagup\quad\diagdown \\ H \quad\quad CH_3 \end{array}$	propene
C_4H_8	$\begin{array}{c} H \quad\quad H \\ \diagdown\quad\diagup \\ C = C \\ \diagup\quad\diagdown \\ H \quad\quad CH_2{-}CH_3 \end{array}$	1-butene
C_4H_8	$\begin{array}{c} H \quad\quad CH_3 \\ \diagdown\quad\diagup \\ C = C \\ \diagup\quad\diagdown \\ CH_3 \quad\quad H \end{array}$	2-butene

Study the chemical formulas of the four compounds listed in the table. There is a pattern similar to that of the alkanes. In this case, the general formula for an alkene is C_nH_{2n}. The name of each alkene is similar to the alkane having the same number of carbon atoms. However, the ending of the name is changed from *ane* to *ene*.

Naming alkene structural isomers The last two compounds in the table are isomers, differing only in the location of the double bond. Since the location of the double bond will influence the chemical behavior of the alkene, its position needs to be identified. The double bond is identified by the lowest number of the carbon atom involved in the bond. For example, the following molecule is called 2-pentene. Note that the double bond is between the second and third carbon atom.

Resources

The World of Chemistry video-tape *Organic Chemistry* shows fractional distillation, structural formulas, space filling models of molecules, and functional groups. Several demonstrations that are too difficult, too expensive, or too hazardous to do in the classroom are shown. Applications of organic chemistry to daily life as well as some industrial processes are also shown and described.

PART 1

Section 22.5

DEMONSTRATION

(continued from page T748)
around a pencil and continue collecting the nylon polymer. To dispose of liquids and solutions, save for reuse, or reserve in separate, clearly marked, sealed containers for disposal by an EPA-approved waste disposal contractor. To dispose of the nylon, wrap in newspaper and put in the wastebasket.

PART **1**

Section 22.6

Teaching Strategy

Aromatic Hydrocarbons

Contact a chemist at the local water treatment plant. The Environmental Protection Agency tests a sample of water each month for a variety of organic compounds such as trichloroethylene, benzene, toluene, chloroform, and xylene. Obtain a list of the organics currently being evaluated. Some are listed by common names such as chloroform (trichloromethane). Have students look up the IUPAC name and draw the structure.

If you have a large river or other body of water in your area, contact the agency responsible for water testing to find out what it entails. Perhaps students can participate in such a testing program.

DO YOU KNOW?

Ethene (ethylene) is a ripening agent for apples, bananas, and tomatoes.

In general, alkenes are more reactive than the corresponding alkanes. Recall from Chapter 13 that one bond of a carbon-carbon double bond is more easily broken than the other. As a result, the alkenes are more likely to react with chemical reagents than similar alkanes.

The simplest alkene is ethene, C_2H_4. This compound (commonly known as ethylene) is a gas with a slightly sweet odor. Certain plants naturally produce ethene. A small amount is chemically produced during the refining of hydrocarbons. Ethene is one of the most important organic compounds in the chemical industry. It is used in the production of such varied products as ethyl alcohol, solvents, plastics, gasoline additives, antifreeze, detergents, and synthetics. It is even used to hasten the ripening of fruit.

22.6 Alkynes

The third series of hydrocarbon compounds contains a triple carbon-carbon bond and is known as **alkynes.** All members of this unsaturated series are also reactive. (Recall from Chapter 13 that very little energy is needed to break one bond of a triple carbon-carbon bond.) Alkynes have the general formula C_nH_{2n-2}. They are named by replacing the *ane* ending of the parent alkane with the ending *yne*. Table 22-3 lists a few alkynes.

TABLE 22-3

Members of the Alkyne Series of Hydrocarbons		
Chemical Formula	**Structural Formula**	**Name**
C_2H_2	H—C≡C—H	ethyne
C_3H_4	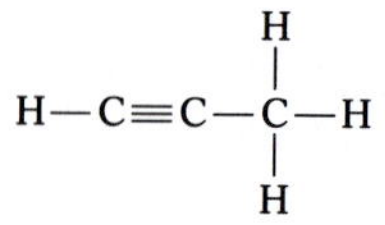 H—C≡C—C—H (with H above and below the third C)	propyne
C_4H_6	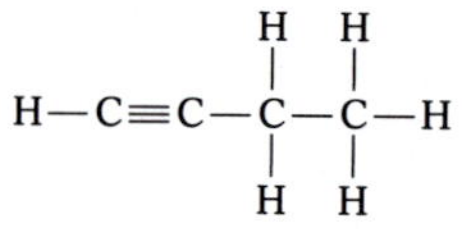 H—C≡C—C—C—H (with H's on the two end carbons)	1-butyne
C_4H_6	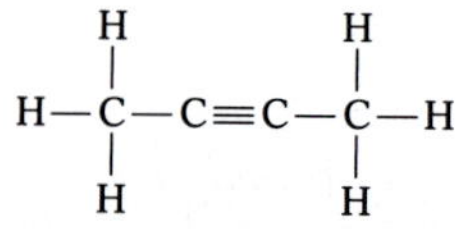 H—C—C≡C—C—H (with H's on end carbons)	2-butyne

As with the alkenes, the location of the triple bond affects the properties of the compound, so it is identified by assigning it the lowest number of the carbon involved in the bond. Procedures for naming the branches on alkyne molecules are the same as those for alkenes and alkanes. Note that the last two compounds in the table are structural isomers.

The simplest and most common alkyne is ethyne, C_2H_2. More commonly known as acetylene, this explosive gas is an important industrial hydrocarbon. Its use in oxyacetylene torches, as shown in Figure 22-6, produces temperatures sufficient to cut and weld steel.

Concept Check

Draw the structural formula for 1-butyne. Could you have a compound named 2-methyl-l-butyne? Would 3-methyl-l-butyne be possible? Does 3-methyl-l-butyne have an isomer?

22.7 Aromatic Hydrocarbons

Another important class of organic compounds is the aromatic hydrocarbons. The name *aromatic* was originally used to describe these compounds because most of them possess rather distinctive fragrances, or aromas. Aromatic hydrocarbons were previously obtained from the distillation of coal tar, which is a by-product of the preparation of coke from coal. Some aromatic compounds are still derived this way, but the most important one, benzene, is obtained chiefly from petroleum.

Benzene, C_6H_6, is the simplest of the aromatics. All of these compounds have a basic structure of one or more rings made of six carbon atoms. The structure of the six-carbon ring, called the benzene ring, is represented this way.

A carbon atom is at each corner of the hexagon. Each carbon is bonded by a single bond to a hydrogen atom. The circle within the hexagon is a way of representing the fact that the six bonds joining the carbon atoms in the ring are neither single bonds nor double bonds. The unique character of the benzene bonds accounts for the special reactivity of aromatic compounds.

Countless derivatives of benzene Benzene is the starting material for thousands of compounds. Combinations of other atoms besides carbon and hydrogen can be attached to the carbons of a benzene ring to create organic chemicals of incredibly varied characteristics. Benzene rings may even fuse together to form aromatic compounds of increasing complexity, which in turn are used for raw materials in other processes. Although benzene and some of its derivatives are carcinogens, you come in contact with the products of aromatic compounds every day. Benzene and its derivatives are used to produce plastics, synthetic fibers, dyes, medicines, anesthetics, synthetic rubber, food additives, paints, and ex-

Figure 22-6 *An oxyacetylene torch uses a mixture of oxygen and ethyne (acetylene).*

DO YOU KNOW?

Gasoline fuels, obtained by the simple distillation of petroleum, contain various volatile hydrocarbon compounds. Occasionally these fuels may explode prematurely, producing engine knock. To reduce this problem, branched-chain alkanes, alkenes, and aromatic hydrocarbons are added to the fuel.

PART 1
Section 22.7

Teaching Strategy

Countless Derivatives of Benzene
Use a Merck Index to look up the formula, structure, and properties of some household organic substances. Have students identify which of the substances are benzene derivatives. Examples: caffeine ($C_8H_{10}N_4O_2$),
oil of wintergreen or methyl salicylate ($C_8H_8O_3$),
pepperine (in pepper: $C_{17}H_{19}N_2O_4$),
aspirin (acetylated salicylic acid: $C_9H_8O_4$),
oxalic acid (in rhubarb: $H_2C_2O_4$),
naphthalene (moth balls: $C_{10}H_8$),
isopropyl alcohol (2-propanol: C_3H_7OH),
acetone [dimethyl ketone, fingernail polish remover: $(CH_3)_2CO$],
acetic acid (ethanoic acid, vinegar: CH_3COOH),
formaldehyde (methaldehyde: H_2CO)

Guided Practice

Review with students the Concept Check questions on pages 743 and 751. Answers can be found in Appendix E on page 808.

Reteaching Idea

To enable students to gain more experience naming and recognizing the structures of various hydrocarbons, play a game, "Name That Hydrocarbon!" Students can assist in the preparations and procedures for the game. The format and results can be patterned on popular TV game shows. Obtain oaktag or similar stock and markers. Make a list of all the compounds to be named, and have students create cards with the name of a hydrocarbon on one side and the structural formula on the other. Divide the class into teams and begin the game. Have a time limit for each team to name the compound correctly. Devise a scoring system and award prizes to the winning team.

☰ CLOSE

Summing Up Main Ideas

Have students write the IUPAC name and draw structural formulas for an alkane, an alkene, an alkyne, and an aromatic compound that has six carbon atoms. (Several structures are possible for each classification. Make sure students' structures each have only six carbon atoms, the appropriate bonding, and number of hydrogen atoms for each classification.)

PART 1 REVIEW

Assign the Part Review questions.

Evaluating Skills

These skills are evaluated in the Part Review questions indicated. **Recognizing main ideas: 6, 7, 8, 9, 12, 13; Determining cause and effect: 8, 9; Classifying: 10, 12, 13; Forming models: 11, 12, 13**

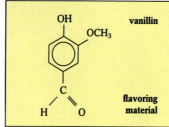
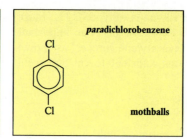
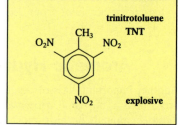
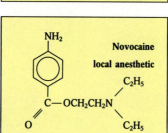
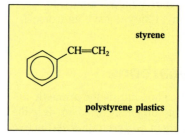
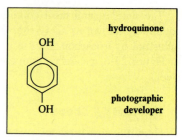

Figure 22-7 *Here are just a few examples of familiar substances that are benzene derivatives. Styrene is a monomer from which polystyrene is produced.*

plosives—to name just a few. You can see in Figure 22-7 how various groups, substituted on the benzene ring, create derivatives that have very different properties.

PART 1 REVIEW

6. What elements are most commonly found in organic compounds?

7. Name four gases that may have played a vital role in the evolution of life.

8. Describe two factors that account for the multitude of carbon compounds.

9. Why is it possible to use fractional distillation to separate hydrocarbons in petroleum?

10. Write the general formula for an alkene.

11. Draw the structural formulas for the following alkenes: 2-pentene, 3-hexene, 4-decene.

12. The formula C_6H_{12} can exist as several straight-chain and branched-chain structural isomers. Draw the structural formula for the straight-chain compound and one of the branched-chain isomers.

Boxed numbers indicate questions that involve skills in interpretation, application, and analysis.

13. Explain why it is necessary to give the positions of alkyl groups and double or triple bonds when naming hydrocarbons.

PART 1 REVIEW

ANSWERS

■ Keyed to Objectives

B **6.** carbon, hydrogen, nitrogen, sulfur

A **7.** water, methane, ammonia, carbon dioxide

B,C **8.** Carbon-carbon chains of varying length and the possibility of many different structures are two factors.

A **9.** Each hydrocarbon has a characteristic boiling point.

B **10.** C_nH_{2n}

D **11.**

C,D **12.**
straight–chain compound

one branched-chain isomer

C **13.** Giving the positions of alkyl groups and multiple bonds distinguishes one isomer from another.

HISTORY OF SCIENCE

A Dream Solution

"Let us learn to dream, gentlemen, and perhaps we shall learn the truth." This was written by the German chemist August Kekule in 1865 after having a dream that helped him solve a chemical mystery. Before exploring Kekule's dream, it is helpful to understand some of the ideas Kekule promoted.

Carbon connections In 1858, before chemical formulas had universal acceptance and agreement, Kekule believed that atoms of a substance had a fixed combination and a specific arrangement. Focusing on the valence of the carbon atom and the arrangement of carbon atoms in different substances, he theorized that the carbon atom could be connected to four other atoms, including other carbon atoms. Based on this notion, he further suggested that chains of carbon atoms could be formed.

A eureka experience Seven years later Kekule had a dream that influenced his making an important discovery. In his written account of the experience, he reported feeling unable to write his textbook because his mind was too preoccupied with other things. After turning away from his work and unexpectedly falling asleep, he recalled seeing dancing chains of molecules and then seeing the ends of one dancing, snakelike chain attach to form a circle. Next he remembered awakening quickly to work on the notion that benzene might have a ring structure, an idea implied by the circular, snakelike chain in his dream.

Theories in science result from a creative process of putting ideas together as well as from rigorous research based on verifiable experiments and data. Lest you believe that dreams alone produce great discoveries, it is important to recognize that Kekule had been involved with the same work in chemistry for many years and had been an architect before becoming a chemist. While Kekule writes of truths through dreams, his education was reflected in his dream, and he unconsciously combined his knowledge of architecture and chemistry to suggest the benzene structure.

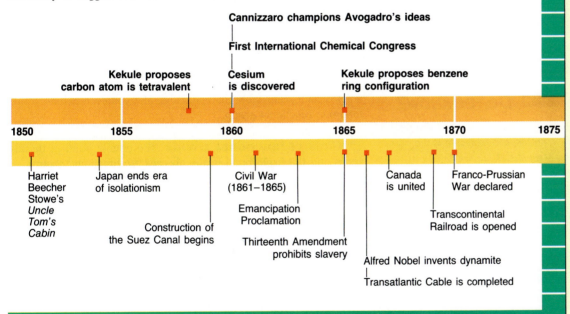

PART 2 Reactions of Organic Compounds

Developing Skills

Students may apply these skills in their study of Part 2.

Classifying: Have students classify the functional groups shown in the condensation polymerization reaction on page 762.

Forming models and Interpreting diagrams: Have students draw models that represent the structures of the compounds in Table 22–4 when a methyl group is substituted for each ethyl group.

≣ FOCUS

Activate Prior Knowledge

Students are familiar with the properties of acetic acid from Chapter 19. Using a sample of $6M$ acetic acid, find its pH and test its conductivity using a conductivity indicator.

⚠ **CAUTION: Wear safety goggles and a lab apron. Use a conductivity apparatus powered by 1.5- or 9-volt batteries.** Have students write the formula for acetic acid and draw a probable structure. Then ask students to study the structure and determine where the molecule is most likely to release a hydrogen ion.

For disposal, neutralize with $0.1M$ or less concentrated base and pour down the drain.

Objectives

Part 2

E. Identify functional groups and **describe** how they affect the properties of the compounds in which they occur.

F. Differentiate types of organic reactions.

DO YOU KNOW?

If your eyes tear when you peel onions, this molecule is the culprit.

It is water soluble, so cut and peel onions under water. No tears!

"Organic chemistry nowadays almost drives me mad. To me it appears like a primeval tropical forest full of the most remarkable things, a dreadful endless jungle into which one does not dare enter for there seems to be no way out."

—Friedrich Wöhler, 1835

When Wöhler made this statement, he had no notion of the vast number of carbon compounds yet to be synthesized. As chemists learned how to manipulate the reactions of compounds, the science of organic chemistry boomed. In addition to carbon and hydrogen, organic compounds can contain other elements whose atoms may be arranged in a variety of bonding combinations. Even the slightest difference in composition or structural arrangement may result in two compounds of very different chemical and physical properties. Through a process called polymerization, small molecules are linked together to form chains. The result is a class of giant molecules used to manufacture everything from videocassettes to parachutes to nonstick cookware. In this part of the chapter, you will have an opportunity to learn about several groups of organic compounds besides the hydrocarbons and to find out what kinds of reactions these compounds can undergo.

22.8 Functional Groups

The characteristics of organic molecules depend on their composition and their arrangement of atoms. Any atom, group of atoms, or organization of bonds that determines specific properties of a molecule is known as a **functional group**. The functional group generally is a reactive portion of a molecule, and its presence signifies certain predictable characteristics. Many molecules have more than one functional group.

Kinds of functional groups The double bond in the alkenes and the triple bond in the alkynes are functional groups. A functional group also may be an atom or group of atoms that is attached to a carbon atom in place of a hydrogen. The functional groups that are most commonly encountered contain oxygen, nitrogen, or both. A functional group can even be a single halogen atom. (Sulfur and phosphorus also are components of functional groups.) Table 22-4 lists examples of some of the functional groups found in organic comounds, and Figure 22.8 shows their geometry. In the structural formula, R— represents the rest of the molecule to which the structural group is attached. R— may be a methyl, ethyl or other alkyl group.

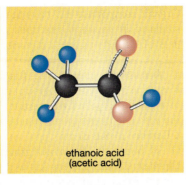

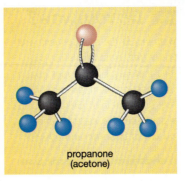

ethanol
(ethyl alcohol)

ethanoic acid
(acetic acid)

propanone
(acetone)

Figure 22-8 *Models reveal the geometry around functional groups.*

TABLE 22-4

Common Functional Groups Found in Organic Compounds			
General Structure	**Group Name**	**Structural Formula**	**Example**
R—O—H	alcohol	H—C—C—O—H	ethanol
R—O—R'*	ether	H—C—C—O—C—C—H	ethoxyethane
R—C(=O)H	aldehyde	H—C(=O)H	methanal
R—C(=O)—R'	ketone	H—C—C(=O)—C—H	propanone
R—C(=O)OH	acid	H—C—C(=O)OH	ethanoic acid
R—C(=O)—O—R'	ester	H—C—C(=O)—O—C—C—H	ethyl ethanoate
R—N(H)(H)	amine	H—C—N(H)(H)	methylamine

* R and R' symbolize the general alkyl hydrocarbon group of the molecule. They may be the same group or different groups.

PART 2

Section 22.8 *continued*

☰ TEACH

Teaching Strategy

Functional Groups

Help students use their problem-solving skills to develop a systematic way (such as index cards, tables, or charts) of recognizing and remembering functional groups and of naming the resulting compounds.

Science Background

Aldehydes and Ketones

The December, 1990, issue of the *Journal of Chemical Education* contains an article titled, "Sherlock Holmes and the Fraudulent Ketone." The story is written for students and teachers and presents a scientific problem in mystery format.

DO YOU KNOW?

Methanol is the main constituent of dry gas, an additive for gasolines that helps to prevent frozen fuel lines in automobiles during very cold weather. Gasohol, sold at some service stations, is a mixture of gasoline and ethanol.

Organic compounds that have the same functional group will behave similarly in chemical reactions. Some general characteristics and uses of the groups are summarized here.

Alcohols contain the functional group —OH. This group, known as the **hydroxyl group,** may be bonded to a carbon atom of a chain or cyclic hydrocarbon. Alcohols are named by replacing the *e* ending of the parent alkane with *ol.* Because of the significant difference in the electronegativities of oxygen and hydrogen in the O—H bond, the hydroxyl group is polar. From your studies in Chapters 13 and 15, you know that a polar structure such as —OH can be involved in hydrogen bonding. Predictably, alcohols of low molecular mass are more soluble in water than their corresponding alkane. However, as the molar mass of the molecule increases, the effect of the —OH group is counterbalanced by the increasing portion that is nonpolar. Alcohols of larger molecular mass do not dissolve well in water.

Methanol, CH_3OH, is the simplest alcohol. It is commonly known as methyl alcohol or wood alcohol and is used in the synthesis of plastics and fibers. Ethanol (known also as ethyl alcohol) has been produced by human societies since ancient times from the fermentation of fruits and grains. (Another name for ethanol is grain alcohol.) In addition to its presence in alcoholic beverages, ethanol is used in gasohol and in industrial processes as the starting material for other compounds and in the preparation of medicines.

Ethers have an oxygen atom bonded between two hydrocarbon portions of the molecule. There is much less opportunity for a significant amount of polarity in the molecule, and as a result, ethers demonstrate no hydrogen bonding and have relatively low boiling points. The substance commonly called ether is ethoxyethane (also known as diethyl ether). Its structure is shown in Table 22-4. Diethyl ether is a volatile, highly flammable liquid that was once used extensively as an anesthetic. Its present role as an anesthetic is limited, but it continues to be used as a solvent for oils and fats.

Aldehydes and ketones both contain the **carbonyl** functional group, which has this structure.

In aldehydes, the carbonyl group is attached to a carbon atom that has at least one hydrogen atom attached to it. The chemical formula for an aldehyde usually is written as RCHO. In ketones, the carbonyl group is attached to a carbon atom that is attached to two other carbon atoms. The chemical formula for a ketone is usually written as RCOR'.

Aldehydes are named by replacing the *e* ending of the parent alkane with *al.* The simplest aldehyde is methanal, HCHO, which

PART 2
Section 22.8 *continued*

is commonly known as formaldehyde. It has a sharp, penetrating odor and was once frequently used to preserve biological specimens. Its primary uses now are in the industrial preparation of plastics and resins. Aldehydes of considerably larger molar mass and aromatic aldehydes have more pleasant odors. Some common flavorings, such as vanillin, oil of cinnamon, and oil of almonds, fall into the latter category.

Ketones are named by replacing the *e* ending of the parent alkane with the ending *one*. The simplest ketone is propanone, CH_3COCH_3, known better by its common name, acetone. It is a volatile liquid, used extensively as a solvent for paints and lacquers but most popularly used to dissolve nail polish.

Organic acids (or carboxylic acids) contain the **carboxyl** functional group, —COOH, which makes the molecules polar. These compounds also are weak acids because of the dissociation of the hydrogen atom from the carboxyl group. Organic acids are named by replacing the *e* ending of the parent alkane with *oic* acid. Many organic acids have common names because they have been well-known since before the establishment of a naming system. You probably have come in contact with a variety of organic acids because some of them are components of common foods, like those shown in Figure 22-9. Ethanoic acid, usually called acetic acid, is particularly well known. In diluted form (five percent solution with water), it is called vinegar and is produced by oxidation of ethanol. Other organic acids are found in sour milk, yogurt, and a variety of fruits.

Videodisc Connections

14469 to 18777, side 1
Photochemical smog (movie)

Figure 22-9 Citric acid derives its name from citrus fruit in which it is found along with another organic acid, ascorbic.

PART 2

Section 22.8 *continued*

Teaching Strategy

Substitution and Addition

Obtain games for students to play based on how pesticides such as DDT (dichlorodiphenyl-trichloroethane) and herbicides have entered the food or water supply, or how they have affected the wildlife population. Examples: "Bald Eagle Game" from Massachusetts Audubon Society, South Great Road, Lincoln, MA 01773; "Deadly Links" from Western Regional Environmental Education Council.

Esters are produced from a reaction between organic acids and alcohols. The process, known as **esterification,** is a reversible dehydration reaction in which the alcohol loses a hydrogen atom and the acid loses the —O—H part of its carboxyl group. The reaction occurs only in the presence of an acid catalyst. Water is generated as a by-product.

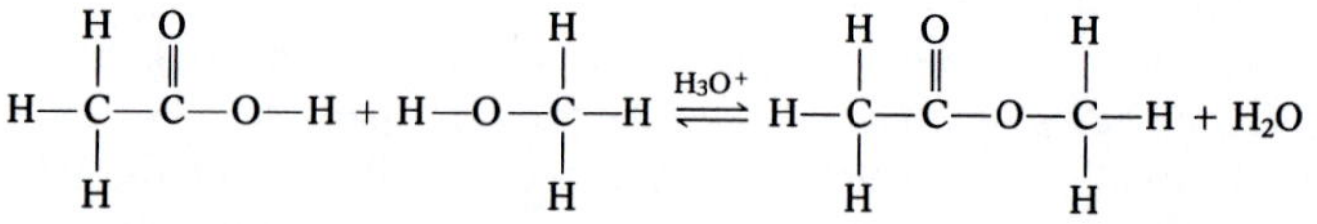

$$H-\underset{\underset{H}{|}}{\overset{\overset{H}{|}}{C}}-\overset{\overset{O}{\|}}{C}-O-H + H-O-\underset{\underset{H}{|}}{\overset{\overset{H}{|}}{C}}-H \underset{}{\overset{H_3O^+}{\rightleftharpoons}} H-\underset{\underset{H}{|}}{\overset{\overset{H}{|}}{C}}-\overset{\overset{O}{\|}}{C}-O-\underset{\underset{H}{|}}{\overset{\overset{H}{|}}{C}}-H + H_2O$$

Most esters possess distinctive aromas and flavors. Fragrant foods, such as fruits, are a natural source of these compounds. For example, the fragrance of pineapple is due to the ester ethyl buanoate. Synthetic esters of low molar mass are often used as perfume additives and in artificial flavorings.

Amines are organic compounds closely related to ammonia. It is possible for organic R— groups to replace one, two, or three hydrogens in the ammonia molecule to produce molecules like those illustrated here.

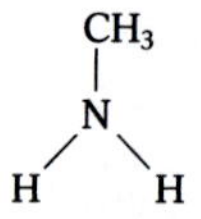

methylamine 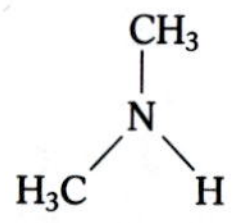   dimethylamine 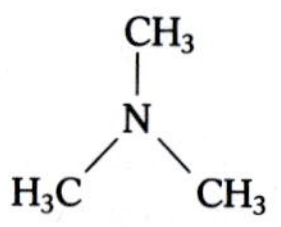   trimethylamine

If an amine or ammonia is heated with an organic acid, an important group of biological compounds called **amides** is produced. Amides contain a carbonyl group bonded to the nitrogen atom of an amine.

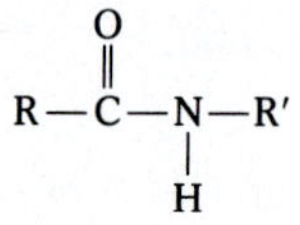

$$R-\overset{\overset{O}{\|}}{C}-\underset{\underset{H}{|}}{N}-R'$$

amide linkage

Perhaps the most important property of the amides is their ability to form unusually strong intermolecular bonds. These intermolecular bonds are responsible for the naturally occurring linkages between regions in protein molecules. (You will read more about these bonds later in this chapter.) Amides also are important because they provide links between other molecular units (besides amino acids) to form larger molecules. Nylon is a product of this kind of linkage.

Concept ✔ Check

Write formulas for the simplest alcohol, ether, aldehyde, ketone, organic acid, ester, and amine. Check your formulas by referring to Table 22-4. Are all the formulas in the table the simplest?

22.9 Substitution and Addition

Methane, the simplest hydrocarbon, can be treated with chlorine gas in the presence of heat or high-energy light waves. The reaction may be represented by either of these equations.

$$CH_4 + Cl_2 \longrightarrow CH_3Cl + HCl$$

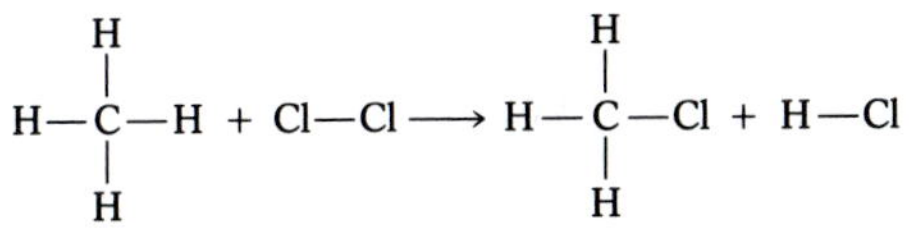

A chlorine atom has taken the place of one hydrogen atom in the methane molecule. The new compound that results is an alkyl halide called chloromethane. This reaction, in which a hydrogen atom is replaced by another atom or group of atoms, is called **substitution.** Substitution of chlorine for additional hydrogen atoms in the methane molecule can result in three other compounds.

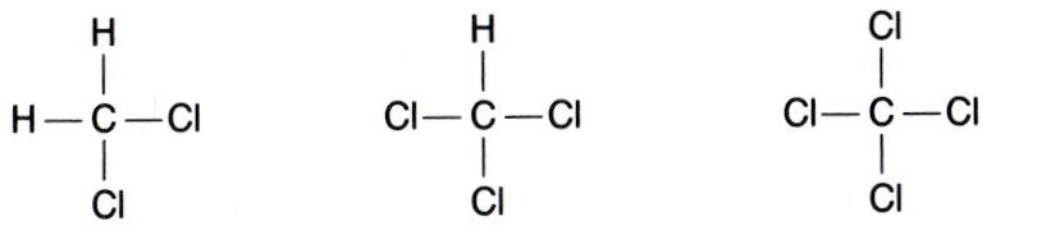

dichloromethane   trichloromethane   tetrachloromethane

Each compound has unique chemical and physical properties. Chloromethane, CH_3Cl, is used as a refrigerant. Dichloromethane, CH_2Cl_2, is used as a solvent, a spray-can propellant, and most recently in a controversial method (due to possible health hazards) for extracting caffeine from coffee. Trichloromethane, $CHCl_3$, is better known as chloroform. Although it is seldom used today as an anesthetic, it remains an important organic solvent. The last product of chlorine substitution, CCl_4, is a grease solvent more commonly known as carbon tetrachloride.

Addition reactions Another reaction of organic molecules is addition. In an **addition** reaction, a carbon compound containing one or more double (or triple) bonds is reacted with another substance in order to open the double bond and add new constituents to the carbon atoms involved. For example, the demand for ethanol is much greater than what could be supplied through natural fermentation. To meet the demand, ethanol is synthesized in an addition reaction between ethene and water.

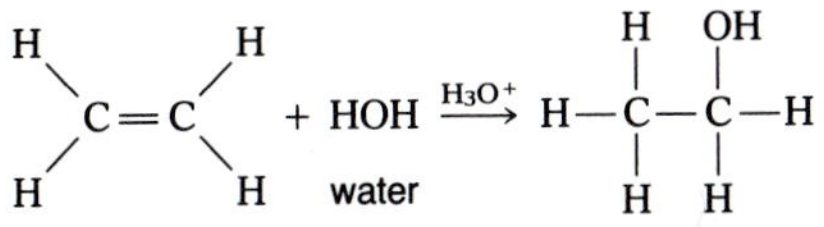

In the overall reaction (which is acid catalyzed), the hydrogen of water is added to one of the carbon atoms and the —OH portion is added to the other carbon. A single carbon-carbon bond remains.

Cooperative Learning

Modeling Reactions

Teams of 4; **Time:** 30 minutes
Objective: Students will model the molecules and changes in reactions.
Task: Have students use clay balls and toothpicks to make models of the molecules reacting in Sections 22.9 to 22.11.
Team responsibility: Have students construct the molecules and explore spatial relationships during the reactions.
Evaluation: Have a brief discussion in which students share ideas and insights gained from using the models.

Videodisc Connections

7838 to 12104, side 2
Polystyrene in acetone (movie)

12414-12419, side 6
Isotactic polystyrene graphics
(6-frame seq.)

44459 to 49526, side 2
Microcellular foam (movie)

14482 to 20504, side 6
Polyurethane foam (movie)

22.10 Oxidation and Reduction

Many organic compounds can be converted to other compounds through an oxidation reaction. The reaction you are probably most familiar with is the combustion of alkanes to produce carbon dioxide and water. (See Section 3.7.) For example, the combustion of methane, the main constituent of natural gas, may be represented by this equation.

$$CH_4 + 2O_2 \longrightarrow CO_2 + 2H_2O$$

Oxidation You learned in Chapter 20 that oxidation is defined as an increase in oxidation number. For example, an alcohol may be oxidized to an aldehyde.

The oxidizing agent, represented by [O] in the equation, may be a substance like copper oxide or potassium dichromate.

In the alcohol, the oxidation number of carbon is $2-$. In the aldehyde, carbon has an oxidation number of zero. (Recall the rules you learned in Chapter 20 for finding oxidation numbers. Oxygen in compounds is usually $2-$ and hydrogen is $1+$. (The total for the molecule is zero.) The oxidation number of carbon has increased, so carbon is said to be oxidized. Note that hydrogen has been removed. Methanal has only 2 hydrogen atoms while methanol has 4.

Depending on the location of the —OH group, a ketone may form instead of an aldehyde.

Aldehydes are readily oxidized to produce an organic acid. Notice that in the process oxygen is added.

Reduction The reverse of these processes, in which oxygen is removed from a molecule or hydrogen is added, is known as reduction. Again, the terminology is consistent with what you learned in Chapter 20. If an aldehyde is reduced to yield an alcohol, the oxidation number of carbon decreases from zero to $2-$. The oxidation number of carbon also decreases when an acid is reduced to an aldehyde.

 CAUTION: Wear safety goggles and a lab apron. Do this demonstration only in the hood and do not generate formaldehyde for longer than ten minutes. Do not inhale formaldehyde vapors. ⟶

 D E M O N S T R A T I O N

Oxidation

Demonstrate the oxidation of methanol to formaldehyde using a copper catalyst. Put 10 mL of methanol in a 100-mL beaker and cover with a watch glass. Wait five minutes to allow methanol vapor to accumulate inside the beaker. Place a shield in front of the beaker, and make sure that the stock container of methanol is removed from the hood. Then, heat one end of a coiled #16 copper wire until it glows, remove the watch glass and hold the glowing end of the copper wire just inside the beaker within the vapor but above the liquid methanol. The exothermic oxidation of methanol to formaldehyde will make the copper wire continue to glow.

Organic chemists make use of oxidation and reduction to change one functional group into another. These processes, in combination with substitution and addition reactions, serve as steps in the synthesis of a tremendous variety of desired end products.

Concept Check

Starting with ethanol, show by equations how an aldehyde can be formed by oxidation. Then show how the aldehyde can be converted to an acid.

22.11 Polymerization

As organic molecules of increasing complexity are formed, trends in the physical and chemical properties of the resulting compounds may be observed. For example, the boiling temperatures of the straight-chain alkanes tend to increase as the number of carbon atoms in the chain is increased. Ethane, C_2H_6, is a gas under standard conditions; octane, C_8H_{18}, is a liquid: octadecane, $C_{18}H_{38}$, is a solid.

Chemical reactivity may be similarly influenced by the presence of functional groups, which can be arranged in chains along the molecule. The key to this chemical treasure chest is the process of polymerization in which extended chain structures are formed from simple molecules called **monomers**. This chemical behavior pattern may produce molecular chains of astounding lengths which are made up of basic repeating units. Molecules composed of a regularly repeating structural sequence are known as **polymers.**

Addition polymerization Two types of polymers are addition and condensation polymers. An example of **addition polymerization** is polyethylene, the plastic used in milk cartons and wash bottles. The structure of polyethylene is shown to the right. The monomer is ethylene. In the structure, one of the ethylene repeating units is blue. A typical polyethylene molecule will be made up of several thousand ethylene units. The reaction for the formation of polyethylene can be represented by the equation

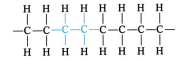

where n is equal to the number of monomer units that have reacted. The double bond in the ethylene monomer is the reactive part of the molecule. The reaction requires a suitable catalyst.

One or more of the hydrogen atoms in ethylene may be replaced by groups such as —F, —Cl, —CH$_3$, and —COOCH$_3$. Synthetic polymers—with trade names such as Teflon, Saran, and Plexiglas—result. By varying additional components of the molecule, it is possible to create compounds with customized properties.

Figure 22-10 *At one time, parachutes were made from silk. The less expensive, synthetic polymers nylon and Dacron are now the more frequently used materials.*

PART 2
Section 22.11

Teaching Strategy

Polymerization

Show students a selection of plastic items made from polymers commonly found in the home. Look for similarities and differences in strength, flexibility, density, transparency, and so on.

Teaching Strategy

Polymerization

Examine a collection of polymers for the recycling classification (a triangle with a number inside). Find out which types are being recycled in your area.

Videodisc Connections

41997 to 45984, side 6
Synthetic fibers (movie)

45985 to 48984, side 6
Manufactured fibers (movie)

25171 to 26147, side 6
Stereolithography (movie)

DEMONSTRATION

Polymerization

In this demonstration, two clear liquids turn into a semisolid, slime-like polymer when mixed. Prepare liquid A by slowly sprinkling 4 g of powdered polyvinyl alcohol into 100 mL of tap water at 70°C while stirring vigorously. For liquid B, add 1 g of sodium borate to 25 mL of water and stir until dissolved. Show that both solutions are liquid by stirring or pouring. To form the polymer, mix A with B while stirring. For disposal, wrap the solid in newspaper and put in the wastebasket.

CAUTION: Wear safety goggles, a lab apron, and plastic gloves. Do not inhale the dust generated when handling sodium borate; wear a dust respirator around your nose and mouth. Handle sodium borate only in the hood. Wash your hands thoroughly when finished. Students should not handle the polymer.

Guided Practice

Review the Concept Check questions on pages 758 and 761. Answers can be found in Appendix E on page 808.

Reteaching Idea

To further reinforce the importance of organic chemistry to everyday life, have students make a list of all the chemical substances in their clothing and in what they used, consumed, or otherwise encountered up to the time they arrived in class. Have them complete a table listing each substance, its chemical name (if it can be identified), whether it is an organic compound, and its structural formula. Students will need assistance with information about fuels, sources of electric power and heat, and with labels from foods, personal care products, and clothing.

≡CLOSE

Summing Up Main Ideas

Have students write balanced equations using structural formulas for each of the following reactions.
a. esterification reaction between propanoic acid and ethanol

$$CH_3CH_2C-OH + HO-CH_2CH_3 \rightarrow$$
$$CH_3CH_2\overset{O}{\overset{\|}{C}}-O-CH_2CH_3 + HOH$$

b. the addition reaction between 1–butene and chlorine gas

$$CH_3CH_2CH=CH_2 + Cl_2 \rightarrow$$

$$CH_3CH_2\underset{Cl}{\overset{H}{\underset{|}{C}}}-\underset{Cl}{\overset{H}{\underset{|}{C}}}-H$$

c. the oxidation of ethanol to acetic acid

$$CH_3CH_2-OH + [O] \rightarrow$$
$$CH_3\overset{O}{\overset{\|}{C}}-H + H_2O$$
$$CH_3\overset{O}{\overset{\|}{C}}-H + [O] \rightarrow CH_3\overset{O}{\overset{\|}{C}}-OH$$

Condensation polymerization When the formation of a polymer is accompanied by the elimination of atoms, the process is called **condensation polymerization.** For example, monomeric units known as amino acids may combine to form chains of polypeptides. If the chains are very long, they are called proteins. **Amino acids** contain both an amine and an organic acid group. The structure of the simplest amino acid, glycine, is shown to the left. When the amine end of the molecule is joined with the acid end of another molecule, a molecule of water is eliminated.

The result is a molecule made from the two amino acids linked by an amide bond. This particular kind of bond is called a **peptide bond.** You will read more about amino acids in Chapter 23.

PART 2 REVIEW

14. What is a functional group?

15. Write the name of the functional group contained in each of the following four molecules.

16. Why does a 4-carbon ether have a lower boiling point than a 4-carbon alcohol?

17. From the names of the compounds listed, identify the functional group each molecule contains.
    a. propanol   c. methoxymethane   e. butanone
    b. ethylamine   d. ethanal   f. methyl methanoate

18. Draw the structural formula for the ester made from ethanol and acetic (ethanoic) acid.

19. How do substitution and addition reactions differ?

20. Write the equation for the addition of water to ethene. What is the name of the product formed?

21. Identify the type of organic reaction represented by each of the following.

    a. $CH_3-CH_3 + Br_2 \xrightarrow{heat} CH_3-CH_2-Br + HBr$

    b. $CH_3-CH=CH_2 + H_2O \xrightarrow{H_3O^+} CH_3-CH_2-CH_2-OH$

PROBLEM-SOLVING STRATEGY

Look for regularities in the names to help determine functional groups. (See Strategy, page 65.)

PART 2 REVIEW

Assign the Part Review questions.

Evaluating Skills

These skills are evaluated in the Part Review questions indicated.
Classifying: 14, 17, 19, 21;
Determining main ideas: 14, 15, 16, 19, 21; **Forming models:** 18;
Comparing/Contrasting: 19

PART 2 REVIEW

ANSWERS

■ **Keyed to Objectives**

E **14.** atoms, groups of atoms, or organizations of bonds that determine a specific property

E **15.** aldehydes, carboxyl, carbonyl, ether

E **16.** Hydrogen bonding in the alcohol causes a higher boiling point.

CAREERS IN CHEMISTRY

On-Scene Emergency Response Coordinator

Oil spills alter the environment and pose health hazards. In addition to the efforts being made to minimize the occurrence of accidental spills, great efforts are also being made to remedy the effects of any previous spills. When an accidental spill of hazardous chemicals or oil occurs, Maureen O'Mara might be called to the site.

> ■ *Science gives us a greater appreciation of nature, which we must have if we are going to protect our environment from ourselves.*

To the rescue In her role as on-scene coordinator for the U.S. Environmental Protection Agency (EPA), she evaluates the emergency and decides what immediate action should be taken to protect people and the environment. Then Maureen organizes, supervises, and manages the cleanup. Managing the cleanup means overseeing the allocation of funds, supervising personnel, providing technical assistance, and communicating with the media and the local community. But not all Maureen's responsibilities involve cleaning up after a disaster has occurred. She is now engaged in preparedness planning for a potential earthquake on the New Madrid Fault in Missouri.

Maureen O'Mara   On-Scene Emergency Response Coordinator for the EPA

Changes along the way With a B.S. in chemistry, Maureen started out as an analytical chemist. Part of her job involved the disposal of hazardous chemicals. Soon the environmental aspects of the job became more interesting to her than her lab work, so she pursued other job options to gain more experience.

Personal rewards Maureen enjoys her involvement in all the complex technical, financial, and personnel-management issues. Each project is unique, with challenging problems requiring new solutions. She enjoys knowing that her efforts serve to protect people's lives and the environment.

For the future Many colleges provide a more direct approach to Maureen's field by offering both bachelor's and master's degree programs in environmental science. But Maureen thinks that the most important thing is to study science. "Studying science gives us a greater understanding of ourselves and our relationship to the earth. It also gives us a greater appreciation of nature, which we must have if we are going to protect our environment from ourselves."

CAREERS IN CHEMISTRY

Teaching Strategies

1. Recognition of the need to clean up spills is relatively recent. Have students discuss what would happen to oil and chemical spills if they were not cleaned up.

2. Discuss similarities and differences in cleaning up after the derailment of a train pulling tank cars of chemicals such as chlorine gas or weed killer versus a train of box cars containing nuclear waste from hospitals and biomedical research facilities.

3. Ms. O'Mara is involved in preparedness in the event of a disaster. Have students discuss other approaches to preparedness and prevention, such as the routing and transportation of hazardous substances.

4. Have students research and discuss different methods of clean-up including containment and biodegradation.

Related Careers

Have students identify related careers. Ecologists, marine biologists, and oceanographers must understand some of the same environmental and biological interactions as Ms. O'Mara. Forest management, meteorology, and agriculture require similar knowledge. For information on related careers, contact the Institute for Environmental Education, 32000 Chagrin Blvd., Cleveland, OH 44124; the Environmental Quality Division, National Wildlife Federation, 1400 16th St., NW, Washington, DC 20036; and the American Society of Agricultural Engineers, 2950 Niles Rd., St. Joseph, MI 49085.

Resources

Contact the DEP and the EPA for additional information.

E **17. a.** hydroxyl
   b. amine
   c. carbonyl
   d. oxygen
   e. carbonyl
   f. ester

E **18.**

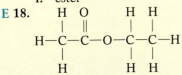

F **19.** In substitution, an atom or group of atoms is replaced by another group. In addition, new atoms are added across a double or triple bond.

F **20.** $H_2O + C_2H_4 \rightarrow CH_3CH_2OH$ (ethanol)

F **21. a.** substitution
        b. addition

The Molecular Structure of Organic Compounds

Estimated Time: (50–60 minutes; 2 days if demonstrations are done)

Process Skills

Forming models
Applying a strategy
Classifying
Interpreting diagrams
Comparing/Contrasting
Measuring
Stating a conclusion
Predicting

Preparation

■ Materials

(for a class of 24, working in groups of 4)
ball-and-stick molecular models (6), protractors (6)

Guiding the Investigation

■ Procedural Hints

Explain the difference between a 3-dimensional drawing of a molecule and the usual way that these compounds are shown.

Explain the shorthand in this notation of the same compound.

Models help us visualize the shape of molecules, but all models have limitations. The ball-and-stick models do not show molecular vibrations or bond bending and stretching, nor do they show the electrons. Make sure that students understand that each bond represents 2 shared electrons. Review the differences between structural, geometric, and functional isomers before the lab.

Laboratory Investigation

The Molecular Structure of Organic Compounds

Understanding the molecular geometry of organic molecules is essential in order to understand their properties and chemical reactions. In this lab activity, you will construct models of a number of organic compounds and study their structure.

Objectives

Explain the different types of carbon bonds.

Design representations of organic molecules, using chemical shorthand.

Construct models of organic compounds.

Diagram and construct several types of organic isomers.

Relate molecular structure to chemical properties.

Materials

□ set of ball-and-stick molecular models
□ protractor

Procedure

Part 1

For each of the following compounds, construct a model, draw a structural formula, and answer the questions.

CH_4, methane

1. Using a protractor, estimate the bond angle between any two bonds connecting C to H. Are all bond angles the same? Explain.

2. To which hydrocarbon family does methane belong?

C_2H_6, ethane

1. Estimate the bond angle between any carbon and two of its hydrogens.

2. To which hydrocarbon family does ethane belong? What portion of the name is the family name?

3. Which of the following belong to ethane's family: ethylene, butene, pentane, propane, octane?

C_3H_8, propane

1. Estimate the bond angle between any carbon and two of its hydrogens.

2. Describe the shape of the carbon backbone of propane.

3. Compare your structural-formula drawing with the model you made. List similarities and differences. Which do you think more accurately represents the actual molecule?

4. Why, do you think, do chemists use drawings such as this?

$$\begin{array}{c} -C- \\ -C-C-C-C-C- \\ -C- \qquad ? \end{array}$$

C_4H_{10}, butane

1. Find two different ways to make models of this compound.

2. Draw both structural formulas.

■ Answers to Questions in the Procedure

Part 1

Methane
1. about 110° (109.5°); Yes, because the bonds form a regular tetrahedral shape.
2. Methane belongs to the alkane family.

Ethane
1. about 110° (109.5°)
2. alkane family; the –ane portion
3. pentane, propane, and octane

Propane
1. about 110° (109.5°)
2. The shape is zig-zag.
3. Similarities: same number and arrangement of atoms;
   Differences: model is 3-dimensional, drawing is only 2-dimensional; Model can show C—C bond twisting.
4. for convenience in representing molecules; Hydrogen atoms are at each bond.

3. What is the term that is applied to compounds that have the same number of atoms but are arranged differently?

4. The C_4H_{10} molecule, with its carbon backbone in a continuous chain, is called butane. Use the IUPAC system of naming to write the correct name for the other model.

C_2H_4, ethene (ethylene)

1. Estimate the bond angle between one of the carbons and its two hydrogens.

2. To which hydrocarbon family does ethene belong?

3. Which term applies to ethene: *saturated* or *unsaturated*? What types of C-to-C bonds do all unsaturated compounds have?

C_2H_2, ethyne (acetylene)

1. To which hydrocarbon family does ethyne belong?

2. The C-to-C bond is a

_____ bond.
(single, double, triple)

3. Ethyne is a/an

_____ compound.
(saturated, unsaturated)

C_5H_{10}, pentene

1. To which hydrocarbon family does this molecule belong?

2. Is it saturated or unsaturated?

3. How many isomers of this molecule can you draw?

4. Construct two of these isomers.

$C_3H_6O_2$, ethyl methyl ether

1. To which hydrocarbon family does ethyl methyl ether belong?

2. What is the bond angle between the two carbons of the ethyl portion of the molecule?

3. What is the bond angle around the oxygen atom?

4. Build models and draw the possible isomers of this compound.

5. What are the correct names for these isomers?

C_3H_8, 3-propylamine

1. To what family does propylamine belong?

2. Describe the shape of the carbon backbone of propylamine. How does it compare with propane?

3. Draw and construct an isomer of propylamine. What is the full name of this compound?

Part 2 Geometric isomers (optional)

The carbon atoms in a double bond are not free to rotate, which results in the existence of geometric isomers. Consider the example of 2-butene. With *cis*-2-butene, both of the methyl groups attached to the double-bonded carbons are on the same side. In the case of *trans*-2-butene, the methyl groups are on opposite sides of the molecule.

1. Construct *cis*-2-butene and *trans*-2-butene.

2. Can *trans*-2-butene be twisted and turned into *cis*-2-butene? Explain your answer.

■ *Conclusions*

1. Describe the differences in bonds in ethane, ethene, and ethyne. Which of these compounds is saturated?

2. As the number of carbon atoms in the alkanes increases, what happens to the boiling point?

3. What do the changes in boiling points imply about the molecular attractions between molecules?

4. How many isomers of propanol can you draw? Name them.

5. Draw a structural formula for C_6H_{12}; determine whether or not it is saturated. To which hydrocarbon family does it belong?

4.

5. 1-propanol (n-propanol) or 2-propanol (isopropanol)

3–propylamine
1. the amine family

2. It is zig-zag, the same as propane.

3. Several are possible; 3-propylamine

Part 2
Geometric Isomers (optional)
1. *cis*-2-butene   *trans*-2-butene

2. No; because of the double bond.

Conclusions
1. Ethane has all single bonds; it is saturated. Ethene has a double bond; it is unsaturated. Ethyne has a triple bond; it is unsaturated.

2. The boiling point increases.

3. Increase in boiling point implies that attraction between molecules increases as size of molecules increases.

4. The isomers of propanol are:
1-propanol
(n-propanol)

2-propanol
(isopropanol)

5. Various structures are possible. It is not saturated. It belongs to the alkenes.

Butane

1.
n-butane

2-methylpropane
(isobutane)

2. See above.   **3.** isomers

4. 2-methyl propane (isobutane)

Ethene

1. 120°   **2.** alkene family

3. *unsaturated*; Saturated compounds have single C—C bonds.

Ethyne

1. Ethyne belongs to the alkyne family.

2. triple **3.** unsaturated

Pentene

1. alkene family

2. unsaturated

3. five isomers:
1-pentene   2-pentene

2-methyl-2-butene

2-methyl-1-butene

2-methyl-3-butene

4. See above.

Ethyl methyl ether

1. the ether family

2. about 110° (or 109.5°)

3. about 110° (or 109.5°)

Chapter 22
Review
ANSWERS
begin on page
T771a.

Summary

Introducing Carbon Compounds

■ Originally, the processing of fossil fuels provided a variety of useful compounds. Now far more are routinely synthesized in the laboratory, using the compounds of fossil fuels as starting materials. These compounds have played a major role in the evolution of industrialized society. Carbon compounds have had global applications because of their use as building materials, fabrics, dyes, explosives, drugs, flavorings, solvents, and fuels.

■ Hydrocarbons contain only two elements, carbon and hydrogen. Yet these simple molecules are the building blocks for many complex organic compounds. Hydrocarbons are classified according to structure and composition into alkanes, alkenes, alkynes, or aromatics. The first three groups are composed of simple carbon chains. The aromatics have different reactivity from either saturated or unsaturated compounds.

Reactions of Organic Compounds

■ Hydrocarbon molecules may incorporate atoms other than hydrogen and carbon into their structure. Known as functional groups, these components alter the chemical behavior of the resulting molecule. Many of the functional groups contain the element oxygen. Included in this category are such significant classes of compounds as alcohols, ethers, carboxylic acids, aldehydes, ketones, and esters. Amines and amides are compounds that contain the element nitrogen.

■ Organic compounds can undergo a variety of chemical reactions, which allows for the production of endless numbers of compounds. Depending on the functional group or groups in a molecule, compounds may react through substitution, addition, esterification, oxidation, polymerization, or combinations of these. One compound can be converted to another or used to synthesize something new.

■ Chemists can synthesize compounds with desired characteristics by controlling chain length and functional groups. Long molecules, composed of repeating molecular units, are produced by polymerization of simple molecules called monomers. The resulting polymers include familiar synthetic materials, such as polyethylene.

Chemically Speaking

addition *22.10*	destructive distillation *22.1*
addition polymerization *22.12*	ester *22.9*
alcohol *22.9*	esterification *22.9*
aldehyde *22.9*	ether *22.9*
alkane *22.3*	functional group *22.9*
alkene *22.5*	homologous series *22.3*
alkyne *22.6*	
amide *22.9*	hydrocarbons *22.2*
amine *22.9*	hydroxyl group *22.9*
amino acid *22.12*	ketone *22.9*
branched *22.2*	monomer *22.12*
carbon backbone *22.2*	organic acid *22.9*
carbonyl *22.9*	organic chemistry *22.1*
carboxyl *22.9*	peptide bond *22.12*
coal *22.1*	polymer *22.12*
condensation polymerization *22.12*	saturated *22.2*
	straight-chain *22.2*
cracking *22.5*	structural isomer *22.4*
cycloalkane *22.7*	substitution *22.10*
delocalized *22.8*	unbranched *22.2*
derivatives *22.2*	unsaturated *22.2*

Concept Mapping

Using the method of concept mapping described at the front of this book, make a concept map for the term *hydrocarbons*.

PROBLEM-SOLVING
► **S T R A T E G I E S**
Students apply these strategies in the following questions.

■ **Using what you know:** 9, 18, 19, 27, 28, 29, 30, 31, 47, 48, 49, 58, 61, 62

■ **Using patterns:** 9, 18, 22, 23, 24,

27, 31, 38, 39, 40, 41, 43, 47, 49, 54, 55, 59, 61, 62

■ **Making diagrams:** 12, 20, 21, 22, 23, 24, 26, 27, 31, 38, 39, 40, 41,

Questions and Problems

INTRODUCING CARBON COMPOUNDS

A. Objective: **Recognize** *the relationship of fossil fuels to organic chemistry.*

1. Why are coal, natural gas, and petroleum often called fossil fuels?
2. What role did bacteria play in creating fossil fuel deposits?
3. What physical conditions are thought to have transformed organic compounds from organisms into petroleum?
4. What is a hydrocarbon?
5. How is coal tar produced?
6. Why was the chemistry of carbon originally called organic chemistry?
7. What are the chief sources of organic compounds that are used in industry?
8. List two general characteristics associated with organic compounds.

B. Objective: **Define** *a hydrocarbon and* **identify** *homologous series of alkanes, alkenes, and alkynes.*

9. What is the general formula for members of the alkane series?
10. Why are methane, ethane, and propane considered members of a homologous series?
11. What is the difference between a saturated organic compound and an unsaturated compound?
12. Draw both the complete structural formula and the carbon backbone that represent the formula C_3H_8. Is this molecule straight-chained or branched?
13. Suggest a reason for the chemical stability of alkanes.
14. What is a saturated organic compound?
15. **a.** What is the simplest alkene? How is it used?
    b. Describe its geometry.

16. Compare the chemical reactivity of alkanes to alkenes.
17. **a.** What is the simplest alkyne? How is it used?
    b. Describe its geometry.
18. Explain why most hydrocarbons are insoluble in polar solvents.

C. Objective: **Distinguish** *among isomers of hydrocarbons.*

19. What is a structural isomer?
20. Draw an example of a branched, unsaturated hydrocarbon.
21. In naming propene, why is it unnecessary to identify the double bond location?
22. Draw three structural isomers of pentane.
23. Draw the four structural isomers of C_4H_9Cl.
24. Draw three structural isomers of pentene.

D. Objective: **Draw** *structural formulas and* **name** *straight-chain and cyclic hydrocarbons, using the IUPAC system.*

25. Describe how the location of a branch in an alkane molecule is identified.
26. How many carbons are in each branch of the molecule 2,2-diethyl-3-methyl-4-propyldecane?
27. Draw the structural formulas for the following compounds.
    a. 2-methylbutane
    b. 3,3-dichlorohexane
    c. 4-ethyl-3,3,4-trimethyldecane
    d. 5-methyl-4-ethyl-1-nonene
    e. 1,3-hexyne
28. Write the correct name for each of the following structures.

a.

43, 47, 54, 55
■ **Writing chemical equations:** 53, 60

b.
$$
\begin{array}{c}
\text{H} \quad \text{H} \qquad \text{H} \quad \text{H} \quad \text{H} \quad \text{H} \quad \text{H} \\
\text{H}-\text{C}-\text{C}-\!\!-\!\!-\text{C}-\text{C}-\text{C}-\text{C}-\text{C}-\text{H} \\
\text{H} \quad | \qquad \text{H} \quad | \quad \text{H} \quad \text{H} \quad \text{H} \\
\text{H}-\text{C}-\text{H} \quad \text{H}-\text{C}-\text{H} \\
\text{H} \qquad\qquad \text{H}-\text{C}-\text{H} \\
\qquad\qquad\qquad \text{H}
\end{array}
$$

c.
$$
\begin{array}{c}
\text{H} \quad \text{Cl} \quad \text{H} \quad \text{H} \quad \text{H} \\
\text{H}-\text{C}-\text{C}-\text{C}-\text{C}-\text{C}-\text{H} \\
\text{H} \quad \text{H} \quad \text{Cl} \quad \text{H} \quad \text{H}
\end{array}
$$

d.
$$
\begin{array}{c}
\qquad \text{H} \qquad\qquad \text{H} \\
\qquad \text{H}-\text{C}-\text{H} \quad \text{H}-\text{C}-\text{H} \\
\text{H} \quad \text{H} \quad | \quad \text{H} \qquad \text{H} \quad \text{H} \\
\text{H}-\text{C}-\text{C}-\text{C}-\text{C}-\!\!-\!\!-\text{C}-\text{C}-\text{H} \\
\text{H} \quad \text{H} \quad | \quad \text{H} \qquad \text{H} \quad \text{H} \quad \text{H} \\
\qquad\qquad \text{H}-\text{C}-\text{H} \\
\qquad\qquad\qquad \text{H}
\end{array}
$$

29. Write the correct name for each of the following structures.

a.
$$
\begin{array}{c}
\text{H} \qquad \text{H} \quad \text{H} \\
\text{H}-\text{C}-\text{C}=\text{C}-\text{C}-\text{H} \\
\text{H} \quad | \quad \text{H} \\
\text{H}-\text{C}-\text{H} \\
\text{H}
\end{array}
$$

b.
$$
\begin{array}{c}
\text{H} \quad \text{H} \qquad \text{H} \\
\text{H}-\text{C}-\text{C}=\text{C} \\
\text{H} \qquad\qquad \text{H}
\end{array}
$$

c.
$$
\begin{array}{c}
\text{H} \quad \text{H} \qquad\qquad \text{H} \\
\text{H}-\text{C}-\text{C}-\text{C}\equiv\text{C}-\text{C}-\text{H} \\
\text{H} \quad \text{H} \qquad\qquad \text{H}
\end{array}
$$

d. $\text{H}-\text{C}\equiv\text{C}-\text{H}$

30. Draw the structural formula for each of the following compounds.

a. 2-methyl-3-heptene
b. bromobenzene
c. 1-ethyl-2-methyl-3-propylbenzene
d. methylacetylene

31. What is the maximum number of triple bonds that can be present in a 3-carbon hydrocarbon? A 4-carbon hydrocarbon? A 5-carbon hydrocarbon? (Consider both straight-chain and cyclic forms.)

REACTIONS OF ORGANIC COMPOUNDS

E. Objective: **Identify** *functional groups and* **describe** *how they affect the properties of the compounds in which they occur.*

32. How does the presence of a hydroxyl group influence an alcohol's solubility in water?
33. What functional group is present in vinegar?
34. How do aldehyde and ketone structures differ?
35. What is a common source of esters?
36. Name two substances that contain amide bonds.
37. What two classes of organic compounds contain the carbonyl functional group?
38. Draw possible structures for compounds with the molecular formula C_2H_7N.
39. Draw the structural formula of each of the following as derived from a parent ethane molecule.
a. an alcohol
b. an aldehyde
c. a carboxylic acid
40. Draw the structural formula for each of the following.
a. methoxymethane
b. 1-pentanol
c. 2-aminobutane
d. propanal
Draw the structural formulas for the carboxylic acids containing 1, 2, and 3 carbon atoms.
41. Draw the structural formulas for the following compounds.
a. 2-propanol

b. 2-methyl-4-octanol
c. 2-methoxypropane
d. propyl acetate

42. Make drawings to show the simplest possible ketone.

43. Make a drawing showing the bonding and unpaired electrons in dimethyl ether.

44. What products would result from the hydrolysis of an ester?

45. Draw the structural formula for each of the following compounds.
   a. chloroethyne
   b. methyl propionate
   c. diethyl amine
   d. ethyl-methyl-propylamine
   e. 1,4-diaminobutane
   f. 1,2 dichloro-1,2-dibromoethene
   g. 1,3-dibromopropene

46. Write the correct name for each of the following structures.

a. 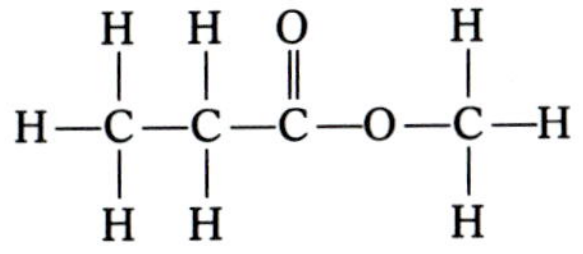 H—C—C—C—O—C—H (with H, H, O, H substituents)

b. 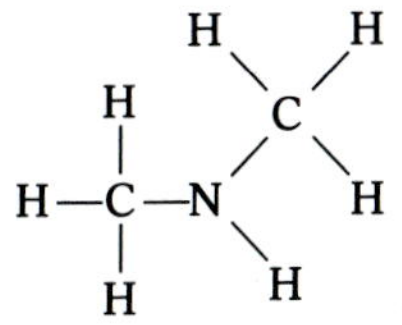 H—C—N (with C and H groups)

47. The chemical formula C_2H_6O exists as two structural isomers. Draw each isomer and identify the functional group in each case. Predict how the boiling points and solubilities in water of the two compounds differ. Explain the basis of your predictions.

48. Write the correct name for each of the following structures.

a. 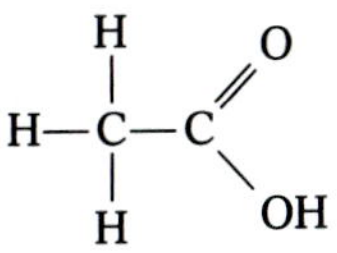 H—C—C (with H, O, OH)

b. H—C—C—C—C—H (with H, O, H, H)

c. H—C (with O and H)

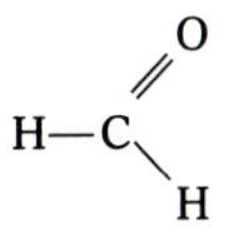

d. 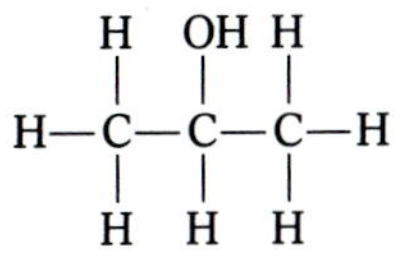 H—C—C—C—H (with H, OH, H)

e. 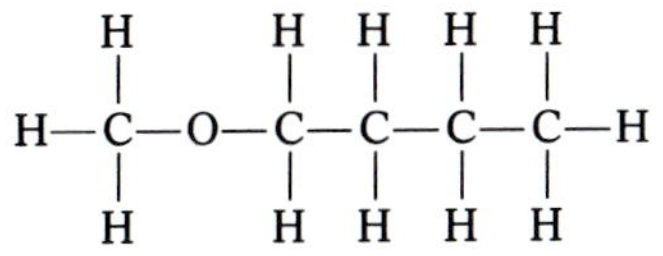 H—C—O—C—C—C—C—H (with H substituents)

f. 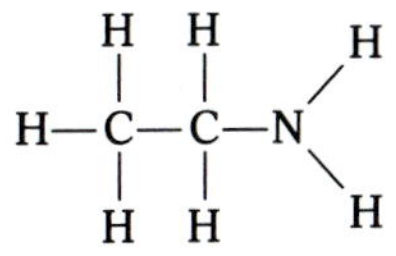 H—C—C—N (with H and H substituents)

g. H—C—C—C—C—C—H (with H, H, O, H, H)

h. H—C—C—C—C—OH (with H substituents)

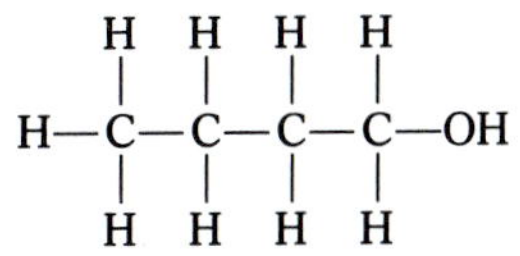

i. 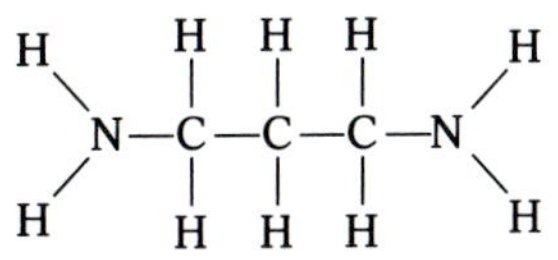 N—C—C—C—N (with H substituents)

j. 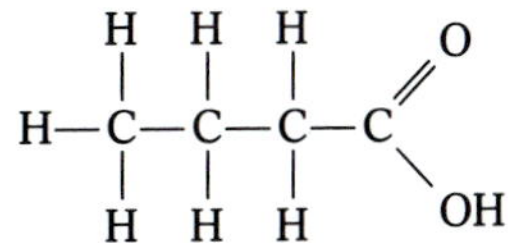 H—C—C—C—C (with H substituents and O, OH)

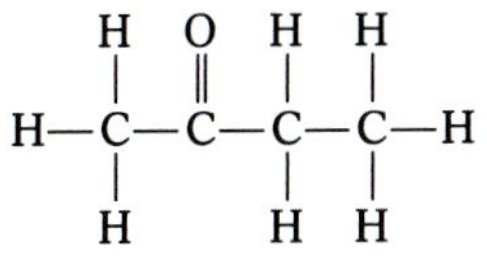

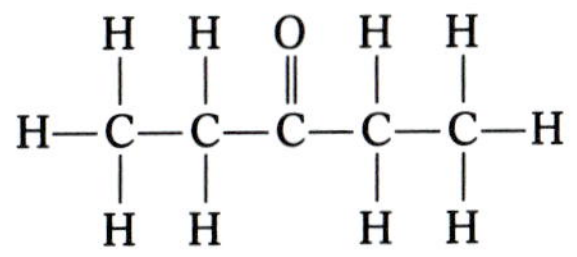

F. Objective: **Differentiate** *types of organic reactions.*

49. Identify the type of organic reaction represented by each of the following equations.

ORGANIC CHEMISTRY **769**

a. (structural formula reaction) ⟶ ... + $3H_2O$

b. (structural formula reaction) $\xrightarrow{H_3O^+}$ ...

c. (structural formula reaction) $\xrightarrow{heat}$ ... + $2HCl$

d. $R\!-\!\overset{\displaystyle O}{\overset{\|}{C}}\!-\!OH + HO\!-\!R' \rightleftharpoons R\!-\!\overset{\displaystyle O}{\overset{\|}{C}}\!-\!OR' + H_2O$

e. (structural formula) $\xrightarrow{K_2Cr_2O_7}$ (structural formula)

50. How may carbon tetrachloride be produced?

51. What are some characteristics of a carbon chain that may be altered to produce tailor-made compounds?

52. What is a polymer?

53. Using structural formulas, write the reaction of the esterification of propanoic acid and ethanol.

54. Ethane reacts with chlorine to substitute first one chlorine for hydrogen, then two, and so on until C_2Cl_6 is formed. Draw structural formulas for all the chlorinated derivatives of ethane from this series of reactions.

55. Lucite is an addition polymer of methyl-methacrylate. Draw a portion of the Lucite structure.

(structural formula of methylmethacrylate)

56. How do oxidation and reduction of organic compounds differ from each other?

57. How might the presence of air affect the process of destructive distillation?

Critical Thinking

SYNTHESIS WITHIN THE CHAPTER

58. When hydrocarbons are heated to high temperatures in the absence of air, they often decompose into related compounds of similar properties. Describe a method that might be used to separate these mixtures into pure substances.

59. Science-fiction writers sometimes describe alien worlds whose life forms are based upon the element silicon. What characteristics of the silicon atom might justify such a premise?

SYNTHESIS ACROSS CHAPTERS

60. When low-grade coal is burned, toxic sulfur dioxide gas is produced. In the atmosphere, this gas is oxidized to sulfur trioxide, which associates with water to form sulfuric acid.
   a. Write a set of three balanced equations showing the reactions responsible for the formation of this acid rain component.
   b. Describe how acidic precipitation may be reduced.

61. Use the kinetic molecular theory to explain why the boiling points of the alkanes in Table 22-1 increase with increasing molecular mass.

62. In the preparation of methyl acetate, the yield of the ester is rather low at equilibrium. Study the equation below, and apply Le Châtelier's principle to explain what can be done to increase the yield.

$$CH_3COOH + CH_3OH \xrightleftharpoons{H_3O^+} CH_3\overset{\overset{\displaystyle O}{\|}}{C}-O-CH_3 + H_2O$$

   acetic   methyl   methyl   water
   acid   alcohol   acetate

Projects

63. Using toothpicks to represent bonds and Styrofoam spheres to represent atomic nuclei, construct molecular models of the first five members of the alkane series.

64. Use toothpicks and marshmallows to construct molecular models of the first five members of the alkene family.

Research and Writing

65. Prepare a report on the techniques used by geologists to locate and extract petroleum.

66. Find out what type of fuel is burned at the nearest power plant. Investigate what problems may be associated with released air pollutants.

67. Investigate the difference between saturated and unsaturated fats in human diets. How is the body's use of these materials affected by the differences?

68. Investigate how the cracking process affects the efficiency of gasoline fuels.

☐ Boxed numbers indicate questions that involve skills in interpretation, application, and analysis.

1. They are derived from decayed matter of both plants and animals that lived millions of years ago.
2. Bacteria decomposed the accumulated matter into new organic compounds, including methane.
3. high temperatures and pressures
4. a carbon compound containing only carbon and hydrogen atoms
5. by the destructive distillation of coal
6. from the discarded belief that carbon compounds originally came solely from living organisms.
7. coal, petroleum, and natural gas
8. They tend to be either nonelectrolytes or weak electrolytes and to have low melting points.
9. C_nH_{2n+2}
10. They differ by the addition of the same structural unit, $—CH_2—$
11. Saturated compounds contain only single bonds between carbon atoms. Unsaturated compounds contain at least one double or triple carbon-carbon bond.
12.

    H H H   H H H
    | | | | | |
H — C — C — C — H   — C — C — C —
    | | | | | |
    H H H

    straight-chained

13. All of the carbon-carbon bonds are saturated.
14. a compound whose molecules contain only single carbon-carbon bonds
15. **a.** ethene; raw material for making polymers
    b. linear
16. Alkenes are more reactive.
17. **a.** ethyne; It is often used as a fuel in oxyacetylene torches.
    b. linear
18. Most hydrocarbon molecules are nonpolar. Polar solvents will not dissolve nonpolar compounds.
19. a compound with the same chemical formula as another compound but a different arrangement of atoms
20. Answers will vary considerably. Two possibilities include

21. There is only one possible site for the double bond in the molecule.
22.

23.

24.

25. by the number of the carbon atom to which the branch is attached
26. 2 carbons in each of the ethyl groups, 1 carbon in the methyl group, and 3 carbons in the propyl group
27. **a.**

b.

c.

d.

e.

28. **a.** 2,2,3-tribromo-3-methylhexane
    b. 4-ethyl-2-methylheptane
    c. 2,3-dichloropentane
    d. 3,3,5-trimethylheptane
29. **a.** 2-methyl-2-butene
    b. propene
    c. 2-pentyne
    d. ethyne or acetylene
30. **a.**

b.

c.

d.

propyne

31. 3 carbons: 1 triple bond
    4 carbons: 2 triple bonds
    5 carbons: 2 triple bonds
32. The polar nature of the hydroxyl group allows alcohols of low molecular masses to be soluble in water.
33. the carboxyl group, COOH
34. In aldehydes the carbonyl group is attached to a terminal carbon. In ketones the carbonyl group is attached to a carbon atom that is attached to two other carbon atoms.
35. fragrant foods such as fruit
36. protein molecules and nylon
37. aldehydes and ketones
38.

39. **a.**

b.

c.

40. **a.**

b. $-C-C-C-C-C-OH$

c. structure with NH_2: $-C-C-C-C-$

d. $-C-C-C\overset{O}{\underset{H}{\diagdown}}$ $\quad -C\overset{O}{\underset{OH}{\diagdown}}$

$-C-C\overset{O}{\underset{OH}{\diagdown}}$ $\quad -C-C-C\overset{O}{\underset{OH}{\diagdown}}$

41. a. structure with OH: $-C-C-C-$

b. branched structure with $-C-$ and OH: $-C-C-C-C-C-C-C-C-$

c. $-C-O-C-C-$ with $-C-$ branch

d. $-C-C-C-O-\overset{O}{\overset{\|}{C}}-C-$

42. $-C-\overset{O}{\overset{\|}{C}}-C-$

43. $-C-\overset{..}{\underset{..}{O}}-C-$

44. an acid and an alcohol

45. a. $H-C\equiv C-Cl$

b. $-\overset{|}{C}-O\diagup$ $\overset{O}{\underset{\diagdown O}{C}}-C-C-$ ... $C-C-C$

c. $C_2H_5\diagdown \overset{}{\underset{H}{N}} \diagup C_2H_5$

d. $C_2H_5\diagdown \overset{}{\underset{C_3H_7}{N}} \diagup CH_3$

e. structure with NH_2 groups: $-C-C-C-C-$ with NH_2

f. $\overset{Br}{\underset{Cl}{C}}=\overset{Br}{\underset{Cl}{C}}$

g. $Br-\overset{}{C}-C=C\overset{Br}{\diagdown}$

46. a. methyl propionate
b. dimethylamine

47.

$H-\overset{H}{\underset{H}{C}}-\overset{H}{\underset{H}{C}}-OH$ — Alcohol with OH group

$H-\overset{H}{\underset{H}{C}}-O-\overset{H}{\underset{H}{C}}-H$ — Ether with O atom

The ether has a relatively low boiling point and a relatively low solubility in water compared to the alcohol. The central location of the oxygen atom in the ether gives the molecule weak polarity. In the alcohol, the terminal location of the hydroxyl group leads to strong polarity in the molecule and the opportunity for hydrogen bonding, which increases the boiling point of alcohol and solubility in water.

48. a. ethanoic (acetic) acid
b. 2-butanone
c. methanal (formaldehyde)
d. 2-propanol
e. methoxybutane
f. aminoethane (ethylamine)
g. 3-pentone
h. 1-butanol
i. 1,3-diaminopropane
j. butanoic acid

49. a. condensation polymerization
b. addition polymerization
c. substitution
d. esterification
e. oxidation

50. by the substitution of chlorine atoms for each of methane's hydrogen atoms

51. the length and/or shape of the carbon chain and the presence of functional groups

52. a large molecule composed of a repeating sequence of smaller molecular units (monomers)

53.

$-C-C-C\overset{O}{\underset{OH}{\diagdown}} + HO-C-C- \rightarrow$

$-C-C-C\overset{O}{\underset{\diagdown O-C-C-}{\diagdown}} + H_2O$

54.

$-\overset{Cl}{C}-\overset{}{C}-$ $\quad -\overset{Cl}{C}-\overset{}{\underset{Cl}{C}}-$ $\quad -\overset{Cl}{C}-\overset{}{\underset{Cl}{C}}-$

$-\overset{Cl}{\underset{Cl}{C}}-\overset{Cl}{\underset{Cl}{C}}-$ $\quad Cl-\overset{}{\underset{Cl}{C}}-\overset{Cl}{\underset{Cl}{C}}-$

$Cl-\overset{Cl}{\underset{Cl}{C}}-\overset{Cl}{\underset{Cl}{C}}-Cl$

55.

$-CH_2-\overset{CH_3}{\underset{\underset{OCH_3}{\overset{|}{C}=O}}{C}}-CH_2-\overset{CH_3}{\underset{\underset{OCH_3}{\overset{|}{C}=O}}{C}}-CH_2-\overset{CH_3}{\underset{\underset{OCH_3}{\overset{|}{C}=O}}{C}}-$

56. They are opposite. In oxidation, the oxidation number is increased and oxygen is added or hydrogen is removed. In reduction, the oxidation number is decreased when hydrogen is added or oxygen is removed.

57. The oxygen in the air would cause the oxidation of the organic compounds.

58. Mixtures of related compounds with similar properties may be separated by the repeated vaporization and condensation (fractional distillation) of increasingly purer fractions.

59. Since the silicon and carbon atoms possess identical outer electron configuration, they demonstrate similar patterns of chemical behavior, including the ability to form long, intricate molecular chains and to react in similar proportions with other substances.

60. a. $S + O_2 \rightarrow SO_2$;
$2SO_2 + O_2 \rightarrow 2SO_3$;
$SO_3 + H_2O \rightarrow H_2SO_4$
b. Emissions of sulfur dioxide can be reduced by limiting the burning of high-sulfur content fossil fuels or by removing the SO_2 components of the waste gases before they are released into the atmosphere.

61. Molecules with larger molar masses require greater amounts of energy to obtain velocities sufficient to exit the gas phase.

62. Add additional methyl alcohol or acetic acid, or remove methyl acetate or water as it is formed.

The Chemistry of Life

Investigations	Demonstrations	Texas Essential Elements★
In-text Investigation, page T798 Laboratory Manual 23–1 S	Nucleic Acids, page T782	**Process:** 4.1, 10.1, 10.2, 10.4
		Content: 2.6 **Process:** 3.2, 10.2
Laboratory Manual 23–2 IM		**Content:** 9.7, 11.5, 11.6 **Process:** 10.1, 10.2
		Process: 1.1, 1.2, 1.3, 2.1, 3.1, 4.3, 5.1, 6.1, 7.1, 8.1, 8.2, 9.1, 9.2, 10.2
		Process: 3.2, 4.2, 6.3, 7.1, 10.1, 10.2, 10.4
		Process: 10.2, 10.3

KEY:
M–Microscale **S**–Structured
I–Inquiry **IM**–Inquiry Microscale

★*See pages T8–T11 for complete
listing of Texas Essential Elements.*

23

The Chemistry of Life

Chapter Rationale

All preceding chapters can be considered as background for an understanding of the chemistry of living things. If students understand the concepts of atoms and molecules, the importance of structure, rates of chemical reactions, catalysts, acids, bases, thermodynamics, and the effects of temperature and pressure, they are on the road to understanding the chemistry of life.

This chapter focuses on aspects of biochemistry of interest, such as diet, energy conversion, and the ability to respond to changes.

About the Photograph

The fern shown is a Japanese Painted Fern, *Arthyrium goeringianum*. The Japanese are noted for their unique indoor and outdoor gardens. Part of their philosophy is respect for and devotion to nature.

Ferns were the dominant plants on land at one time. Tree ferns were able to successfully compete with giant club mosses and horsetails because their feathery leaves trapped sunlight more efficiently than the small branches and projections of these other early forest plants.

Even today, organisms at the base of the food chain harness energy from the sun via photosynthesis. Other organisms indirectly obtain energy from the sun by ingesting plants or other animals that ingest plants.

Chapter Planning Hints

Plan to complete the chapter, Laboratory Investigation, and Chapter Review in three to five classes. You may wish to obtain The World of Chemistry videotape *Biochemistry: Proteins in Chemistry* to use with Part 1. One optional demonstration is suggested for this chapter on page T782.

Biochemistry is the study of chemistry in living things. It includes looking at how plants absorb energy from the sun and how you are ultimately able to use stored energy in plants to fuel your body.

PART **1** The Chemicals of Life

How is biochemistry different from the chemistry you have been studying all year? Biochemistry consists of the study of chemistry in living things. The compounds of living things are made up of organic molecules, which are composed of a few major elements—mainly carbon, hydrogen, oxygen, and nitrogen. These few elements can be combined, along with another 20 or so minor elements, into a very large number of specialized molecules that make up your body.

Some biochemicals—such as those in bones, muscles, and blood—are present in large amounts and form the structure of the organism. Others—such as hormones, enzymes (biological catalysts), and vitamins—are present in tiny amounts but have a great effect on controlling and regulating body functions. Every move you make, everything you eat and digest, the way you adjust to a hot or cold day, even the mood you are in—all of these things can be explained by a series of reactions that biochemicals undergo. In this chapter, you will take a close look at the molecules that make up your body and the reactions occurring in it.

23.1 Carbohydrates

When you eat pasta or bread, you are consuming foods that are high in carbohydrates. Carbohydrates are organic molecules, and many have the empirical formula CH_2O. Notice that they have twice as many hydrogen atoms as either carbon or oxygen.

The smallest carbohydrates are simple sugars, or **monosaccharides** (*mono-* for "one," *saccharide* for "sugar"). Glucose, $C_6H_{12}O_6$, is the sugar in your blood—the simple sugar into which larger carbohydrates are broken down or metabolized. This formula can have many isomers, compounds that have the same formula but a different structure, as you learned in Chapter 22. Fructose, also $C_6H_{12}O_6$, is one isomer of glucose. It gives fresh fruit a sweet taste. Carbohydrates built of two monosaccharides are called **disaccharides**. Table sugar, or sucrose, $C_{12}H_{22}O_{11}$, is a disaccharide consisting of one molecule of glucose and one of fructose, joined by the release of water, as shown in Figure 23-1 on the next page.

Polysaccharides, or complex carbohydrates, are chains of glucose molecules bonded together that are hundreds of molecules long. Different types of **polysaccharides** are distinguished by their degree

Objectives

Part 1

A. **Compare and contrast** the structures and functions of familiar sugars and starches.

B. **Describe** the chemical properties that lipids share and **distinguish** them from carbohydrates, proteins, and nucleic acids.

C. **Relate** the chemical structures of proteins and nucleic acids to their ability to encode information.

D. **Discuss** the chemical attractions that provide a molecule's three-dimensional shape and **explain** why maintaining this shape is important to the molecule's function.

Developing Skills

Students may apply these skills in their study of Part 1.

Comparing/Contrasting: Have students compare the size, shape, and polarity of the molecules in Figure 23–2 and contrast them with molecules in Figure 23–3.

Predicting: Have students use the information given in Section 23.5 to predict the order of bases that will pair with TAC TAG CAT. Determine which, if any, of the triplets code for an amino acid.

≡ FOCUS

Display several samples of food including a hard-boiled egg, bread or crackers, and an avocado. Match the food sample with the appropriate label: protein, carbohydrates, and lipids (egg—protein, bread—carbohydrates, avocado—lipids).

⚠ **CAUTION: Remind students that nothing in the chemistry lab or classroom is eaten.**

≡ TEACH

Teaching Strategy

These sections cover the structure and function of different types of molecules. For example, all protein molecules have a similar structure, as do lipids and carbohydrates. However, protein structure is different from lipid structure or carbohydrate structure.

Science Background

Carbohydrates

Most monosaccharides important in the diet are hexoses (containing six C atoms). Glucose, also known as dextrose, and fructose are found in nature in fruits and honey. Honey is particularly rich in fructose. In addition to sucrose, disaccharides also include lactose, found in milk and products made from milk, and maltose, consisting of two units of glucose, which is broken down from starch. Maltose, also called dextrin, is what makes toast brown and taste sweeter than bread.

Cellulose and starch are alike except for the way the glucose units bond together. Ruminants can gain nutrition from cellulose because the bacteria in their stomachs produce an enzyme that splits these bonds.

Polysaccharides also include colloidal substances such as pectin, algin, and carrageenan, which are nondigestible. However, their ability to bind water makes them useful in jellies, thickeners for salad dressings, and ice cream, as well as over-the-counter drugs (for example, Kaopectate).

Figure 23-1 *Two monosaccharides join to form a disaccharide plus water. A hydrogen is lost from one molecule, and a hydroxyl group is lost from the other.*

DO YOU KNOW?

Many people lose their ability to digest lactose as they grow older and experience gas and bloating after drinking milk. Such lactose intolerance may be avoided by eating cheese and yogurt instead of milk, using low-lactose milk, or adding tablets of lactase, the enzyme that breaks down lactose, to milk.

of branching, as shown in Figure 23-2. Plants have two major polysaccharides, cellulose and starch. Cellulose, or fiber, forms part of cell walls and wood. Although you eat a lot of cellulose in crunchy vegetables, you lack the enzymes to digest this fiber.

Did you realize that in chewing a stalk of celery, which is mostly cellulose, you lose about ten kilocalories of energy? The energy needed to process the unusable cellulose in celery is greater than the calories in the food. In contrast, you can digest starch, which forms 70 percent of grains and 40 percent of beans and peas.

Another polysaccharide shown in Figure 23-2 is **glycogen,** or animal starch, which is more highly branched than plant starch, and is stored in your liver and muscles. An abundant polysaccharide is

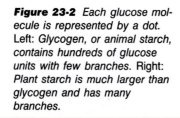

Figure 23-2 *Each glucose molecule is represented by a dot. Left: Glycogen, or animal starch, contains hundreds of glucose units with few branches. Right: Plant starch is much larger than glycogen and has many branches.*

CHEMICAL UPDATE

Only a few elements—hydrogen, carbon, oxygen, nitrogen, sulfur, and phosphorus—make up more than 95 percent of all living organisms. All are nonmetals. Around thirty other elements are presently known to be required in small amounts (trace elements) or very small amounts (microtrace elements). The September 1991 issue of *The Journal of Chemical Education* contains an article titled "Important Elements," by P.G. Nelson. One of the criteria used in determining the importance of an element is whether the element is required for life.

chitin, which forms the exoskeletons of insects and is shown in Figure 23-3. It is built of monosaccharides containing nitrogen.

While chitin and cellulose provide support and structure for living organisms, starch and glycogen provide fuel. When you digest disaccharides and polysaccharides, they break apart into glucose molecules. As you will learn in Part 2, glucose molecules are oxidized in a complex series of chemical reactions to produce carbon dioxide and water. One gram of glucose will provide you with 17 kilojoules (4 kilocalories) of energy to fuel the processes of life.

chitin

cellulose

Figure 23-3 *Chitin,* left, *is the second most abundant polymer in nature. It forms the exoskeleton of this insect, which clings to plant cellulose,* right, *the most abundant polymer in nature.*

23.2 Lipids

The class of biochemicals that includes fats and oils is called lipids. Recently lipids have developed a bad reputation. Too much lipid from the diet can accumulate in your arteries, blocking circulation, as shown in Figure 23-4. This can cause heart disease. Storing too much lipid in your body results in obesity. But lipids are essential to life, providing energy between meals, making furs and feathers water-repellent, cushioning vital organs, insulating nerves, forming cell membranes, and carrying vitamins. Fat adds flavor to foods and delays hunger. Every time you skip a meal, you need to draw on fat stores for energy. A male marathon runner starts drawing on fat stores when he "hits the wall," about 20 miles along in a 26-mile race.

Lipids dissolve in the nonpolar organic solvents ether, benzene, and chloroform. Percentage-wise they have fewer oxygens than proteins and carbohydrates. Most of the fats and oils you eat are esters of glycerol, a triple alcohol. Typically, three long carboxylic or fatty acids are attached to one molecule of glycerol to form a **triglyceride.** For example, in Figure 23-5 on the next page, three stearic acid molecules attach to one glycerol to form the triglyceride called tristearin.

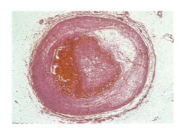

Figure 23-4 *This human artery is clogged by fat, blocking the flow of blood to the heart.*

PART 1

Section 23.1 *continued*

Science Background

Lipids

Most triglycerides are mixtures of several fatty acids. The term "tropical oils" refers to coconut, palm, or palm kernel oils, which are highly saturated. If you pour boiling water over freshly shredded coconut, strain it, and let it stand, the semisolid coconut fat will rise to the top of the liquid. Hydrogenated fat is formed from liquid unsaturated fatty acids by adding hydrogen to the double bond. The resulting fat is a solid.

Rancidity is a term associated with an "off" odor and taste of foods that have a high fat content (for example, crackers, chips, mayonnaise, butter). This is caused by the addition of oxygen to the fat molecule at the double bonds. Exposure to light and heat hastens the reaction, hence opened products should be kept covered, out of the light, and in a cool place.

Have students look for the terms *antioxidant* or *alpha-tocopherol* on a label for crackers, cookies, or similar foods. The substance used as an antioxidant reacts more readily with oxygen than the fatty acids, thereby helping lengthen the shelf life of the product.

$$CH_2-OH + H-O-\overset{\overset{\displaystyle O}{\|}}{C}-(CH_2)_{16}-CH_3$$

$$CH-OH + H-O-\overset{\overset{\displaystyle O}{\|}}{C}-(CH_2)_{16}-CH_3 \longrightarrow$$

$$CH_2-OH + H-O-\overset{\overset{\displaystyle O}{\|}}{C}-(CH_2)_{16}-CH_3$$

Glycerol   Three stearic acid molecules

$$CH_2-O-\overset{\overset{\displaystyle O}{\|}}{C}-(CH_2)_{16}-CH_3$$

$$CH-O-\overset{\overset{\displaystyle O}{\|}}{C}-(CH_2)_{16}-CH_3 + 3H_2O$$

$$CH_2-O-\overset{\overset{\displaystyle O}{\|}}{C}-(CH_2)_{16}-CH_3$$

Tristearin

Figure 23-5 *The formation of fat. One molecule of glycerol combines with three molecules of fatty acids to form one molecule of fat.*

Fatty acids are long chains of carbon atoms with a carboxylic acid group, —COOH, at one end. If the carbons of a fatty acid have no double bonds, the fatty acid is **saturated** with hydrogen. If the fatty acid has one carbon-carbon double bond, it is **monounsaturated.** Figure 23-6 shows the large change that one double bond introduces to a molecule. A fatty acid with two or more double bonds is **polyunsaturated.** Most animal fats are saturated, and are solids at room temperature. Most vegetable oils are polyunsaturated and are usually liquids. Olive oil is monounsaturated.

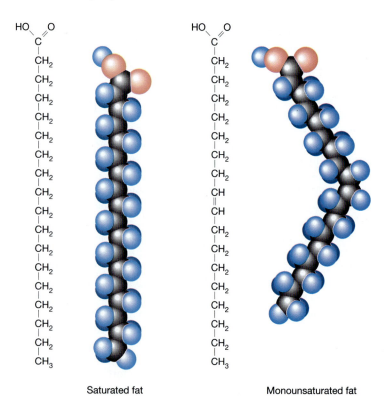

Figure 23-6 Left: *This saturated fat is 18 carbons long, and every bond is saturated with hydrogen. It is a solid at room temperature.* Right: *This monounsaturated fat is 18 carbons long, with one double bond that introduces a bend. It is a liquid at room temperature.*

Saturated fat   Monounsaturated fat

Teaching Strategy

Lipids

The National Cholesterol Education Program has recommended that Americans decrease the total percentage of calories consumed as fat to 30 percent or less. Changing from whole milk to milk with a lower fat content constitutes a considerable reduction, yet probably not a big sacrifice of eating pleasure for most individuals. Have students use the information found on milk cartons to record the type of milk, the amount of fat in one cup, and the percentage of Calories from fat. Then have them calculate the decrease in fat consumption if one changed to a lower-fat milk.

Example: 2 cups whole milk per day = 16 g fat/day. 16 g × 365 days = 5840 g fat/year

Have students calculate what 5840 g of fat is equivalent to in Calories, and compare to the fat content of other common foods. If 3500 kcal = 1 pound of body fat, how much does the milk equal?

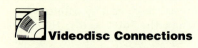

Videodisc Connections

28741 to 30417, side 2
Soap (movie)

Myths and Misconceptions

Many individuals think that cholesterol is a harmful body substance that is obtained solely from the diet. Explain that although high blood cholesterol levels are associated with an increased risk for cardiovascular disease, a certain amount of cholesterol is needed by the body. Normally synthesized by the liver, cholesterol is a component of various steroid hormones and is essential to cell membrane structure.

One of the most common misconceptions about cholesterol is that it is contained in all fatty foods, hence the advertising claim "No cholesterol." Point out that some fats, such as margarine, contain no cholesterol. However, they do contain saturated fats, which can lead to increased cholesterol production in the body.

Saturated fats are associated with heart disease, although the exact role they play is not known. In unsaturated fats, the site of the carbon-carbon double bond plays a role in how the fat affects the blood vessels.

One gram of fat produces 38 kilojoules of energy (9 kilocalories), whereas 1 gram of protein or carbohydrate produces 17 kilojoules of energy (4 kilocalories). Stored fats in body tissues are an energy reserve. About 10 to 25 percent of your body weight comes from fat. It can provide a month's worth of energy. In contrast, your supplies of glucose and glycogen are gone in 24 hours!

Sterols are lipids with four carbon rings. Sterols include vitamin D, cholesterol, sex hormones, and cortisone. Cholesterol, shown below, is found naturally in animal tissues, especially in the brain and spinal cord. Most cell membranes contain cholesterol.

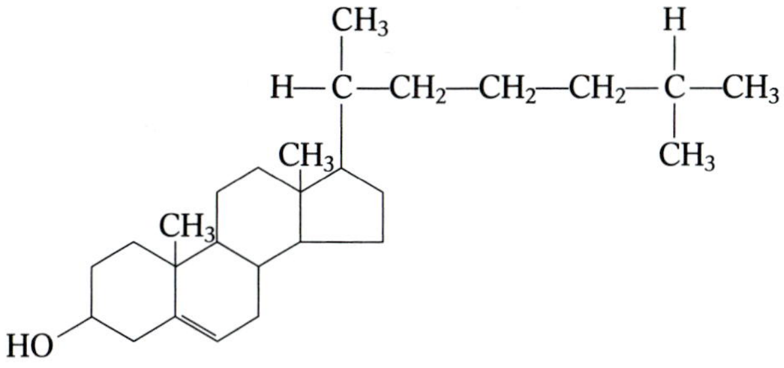

Cholesterol is essential, but you don't need to eat it because your body can make it from simpler compounds. Blood cholesterol levels may go up to dangerous levels when you eat a diet high in saturated fats, whether or not you eat a lot of cholesterol.

23.3 Proteins

You consume about 30 percent of your calories as protein-rich foods such as beef, chicken, and milk. Your body converts these into amino acids, from which it makes new proteins.

TABLE 23-1

Protein Diversity		
Name	**Location**	**Function**
ferritin	blood	transport (Fe)
hemoglobin	blood	transport (O_2)
myoglobin	muscle	transport (O_2)
antibodies	blood, lymph	protection
tubulin	growing tissue	cell division
insulin, glucagon	blood	blood-sugar control
salivary amylase, pepsin, carbohydrases	digestive tract	digestion

DO YOU KNOW?

Many foods such as salad dressing and pastries are now labeled as "no cholesterol." This is accurate, but misleading since they contain only vegetable oil, and never had cholesterol in the first place.

Science Background

Lipids

Blood cholesterol levels above 200 mg/dL are considered a risk factor for heart disease. Factors such as heredity and life style, as well as diet, may affect your cholesterol level. Cholesterol is transported through the blood by a lipid-protein complex called a lipoprotein. HDL and LDL are forms of this lipoprotein. (HDL is beneficial; it removes cholesterol from the cells and brings it back to the liver and intestines. LDL deposits cholesterol along the arterial walls.)

Teaching Strategy

Protein Structure

After reading the labels on a home-permanent package, have students write the formula and draw the structure of the ingredients. A Merck Index can be used to find formulas. Examples are waving agents ethanolamine (CH_3CONH_2), thioglycolate ($HSCH_2COONa$), and isopropyl myristate [$(CH_3)_2COH\ (CH_2)_{13}COONa$].

PART 1
Section 23.3 *continued*

Science Background

Proteins

PKU (phenylketonuria) is an inherited metabolic disease characterized by the inability to process the amino acid phenylalanine. It accumulates in the body tissues and acts as a toxin, causing mental retardation if not diagnosed early. Infants should be tested shortly after birth. If positive for PKU, the infant is put on a special diet that eliminates phenylalanine (present in milk, meat, and many other foods). The first five years are crucial because the brain is developing most rapidly during this time. As children get older, they can often tolerate small amounts of food with phenylalanine, but they must always be careful of their diet. Soft drinks and foods containing aspartame have a warning on the label regarding phenylalanine.

DO YOU KNOW?

The protein collagen is added to many cosmetics—but it is useless. The molecule is too large to enter the skin.

CONNECTING CONCEPTS

Protein Shape The highly specific shapes of proteins are determined by a variety of chemical attractions—covalent bonds linking amino acids, polar and nonpolar tendencies, disulfide bonds, hydrogen bonds, dispersion forces, and shape and size constraints.

Protein molecules are polymers consisting of amino acids. Amino acids all have a common structure.

$$H_2N-\underset{\underset{R}{|}}{\overset{\overset{H}{|}}{C}}-\underset{\underset{OH}{}}{\overset{\overset{O}{\|}}{C}}$$

Each amino acid has a central carbon atom to which is bonded a hydrogen atom (H), a carboxylic acid group (COOH), an amino group (NH_2), and a side chain (R). It is the side chains that distinguish amino acids from one another. Twenty amino acids occur in the proteins of organisms, although more than 2000 natural and synthetic amino acids actually exist.

There are ten amino acids that cannot be manufactured by the human body and must be obtained in your diet. When the body makes proteins, it needs all the amino acid building blocks to be present at the same time. If even one essential amino acid is absent when the protein is being made, the manufacturing process stops. You probably know that vegetarians are people who do not eat meat. Some vegetarians also do not eat cheese, milk, and eggs. These people have to choose their meals carefully so that they eat a diet containing all of the essential amino acids. This is particularly important for young people who are still growing.

A protein molecule is built by linking the amino group of one amino acid to the carboxylic acid group of another. You will recall from Chapter 22 that this is accomplished by removing a molecule of water. The resulting carbon-nitrogen linkage is called a peptide bond.

Concept ✔ Check

Why do you think that some functional groups are common to all amino acids while others are unique to each one?

Protein structure Several terms are used to describe the lengths of amino acid chains. A dipeptide has two amino acids. Aspartame, a nonsugar sweetener known as NutraSweet, is a dipeptide, consisting of aspartic acid bonded to phenylalanine. A long amino acid chain is called a polypeptide. A protein is built of one or more polypeptides. Each protein consists of hundreds or even thousands of amino acids. A protein of 100 amino acids, for example, could have any of 20^{100} possible sequences of amino acids. The amino acid sequence of the protein determines the way the chain folds in three-dimensional space.

The amino acid sequence of a protein is called its primary (1°) structure. The protein folds into a secondary (2°) structure, dictated by the way that amino acids near each other in the sequence interact. Its larger, tertiary (3°) structure is determined by interactions be-

PART **1**

Section 23.3 *continued*

Resources

The World of Chemistry videotape *Biochemistry* contains an explanation of the chemical process of curling hair.

Primary structure
amino acid sequence
of polypeptides

Secondary structure
folded polypeptides

Quaternary structure
clustering of polypeptides

Tertiary structure
3-dimensional shape
that determines function

tween amino acids that are far apart in the chain. If a protein has more than one polypeptide chain, it is said to have a quaternary (4°) structure. All of these structures are seen in Figure 23-7.

As you learned in Chapter 14, hydrogen bonds help to stabilize the molecule. If the protein is heated, the hydrogen bonds break, the three-dimensional structure of the protein changes, and the protein is said to be denatured. The solid white of a cooked egg is a denatured form of the protein called albumin.

The protein in human hair, called keratin, contains a large amount of the amino acid cysteine. In a process called cross-linking, sulfur atoms in two cysteine molecules form disulfide (S—S) bonds, as shown in Figure 23-8. These are covalent bonds and thus are much stronger than hydrogen bonds. The extensive cross-linking gives hair its shape and strength. If you have ever had a permanent wave, a reducing agent was used to break the disulfide bonds. As your hair was set and oxidized with the neutralizing agent, new cross-links were formed, holding the new shape.

Figure 23-7 *This diagram shows primary, secondary, tertiary, and quaternary structures of proteins.*

Figure 23-8 *Permanent waves can be made by treating hair with a reducing agent, setting, and adding an oxidizing agent that reintroduces disulfide bonds in a new location.*

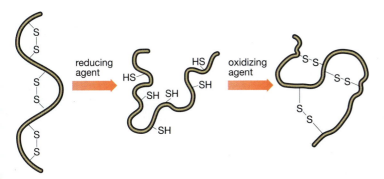

reducing agent

oxidizing agent

C O N S U M E R   C H E M I S T R Y

How Sweet It Is!

When it comes to sweetness, not all sugars are created equal. The sugar whose taste is most familiar—sucrose or table sugar—is somewhat sweeter than the glucose that courses through your blood, but not as sweet as the fructose in a ripe apple. Substitute sweeteners are many times sweeter than natural sugars, and this is why smaller amounts of them are needed to sweeten foods (see chart).

Natural sugars The sugars in foods contain characteristic proportions of simple sugars. Table sugar is 100 percent sucrose, and molasses is 50 percent sucrose, with smaller amounts of glucose and fructose. Brown sugar is table sugar plus a little molasses. Honey is plant nectar treated with bee enzymes, which produces fructose and glucose. High-fructose corn syrup, found in many desserts, begins as cornstarch. Enzymes and acids are added, which change starch first to glucose and then glucose to fructose. This product is less costly and freezes better than sucrose.

Artificial sweeteners Artificial sweeteners are organic compounds, other than sugars, that taste sweet. Saccharine is probably the best-known artificial sweetener. It was discovered over 100 years ago and has been determined to be about 400 times sweeter than a comparable amount of sugar.

Sugar substitutes are chemically not sugars, but they resemble fructose in shape. Receptor molecules in the tongue's taste buds recognize the sugar substitutes saccharin, aspartame, and acesulfame as if they were fructose.

The shape of sweetness So far a precise correlation has not been established between the specific structure of a compound and its degree of sweetness. For instance, you have learned that aspartame is made up of two amino acids—aspartic acid and phenylalanine. Aspartic acid has a flat taste, and phenylalanine is bitter. Yet when these two amino acids

are linked together, they have a distinctly sweet taste that is about 200 times sweeter than sucrose.

Because these synthetic compounds are food additives, the Food and Drug Administration is constantly monitoring the effects these compounds have on laboratory animals. In massive doses, some have caused tumors in rats, and their availability has been curtailed. Thus saccharine was partially banned in 1978. Others, in smaller doses, have caused headaches, dizziness, and nausea.

How sweet is it? If sucrose is given an arbitrary sweetness value of 100, the other sugars and sugar substitutes compare as follows.

glucose	70
fructose	170
maltose	30
lactose	16
saccharin	40,000
aspartame	20,000
acesulfame	20,000

Natural sugars and synthetic sweeteners may be in the foods you choose to eat daily.

23.4 The Importance of Shape

A type of protein in your immune system called an antibody has a 4° structure, resulting in the shape of an upright lobster. This shape is necessary for the molecule to function in its own unique way. The three-dimensional shape of a protein, called its conformation, is vital to its function in the same way that the shape of each puzzle piece is vital to an entire jigsaw puzzle.

In the case of the antibody, the claws of the lobster have a particular shape that fits the shape of a molecule on a specific germ. When that germ appears, the matching antibody locks onto it, attracting other immune system compounds that destroy the invader. Thus the immune system protects your body from infection. Conformation underlies another immune system response—hay fever, as shown in Figure 23-9.

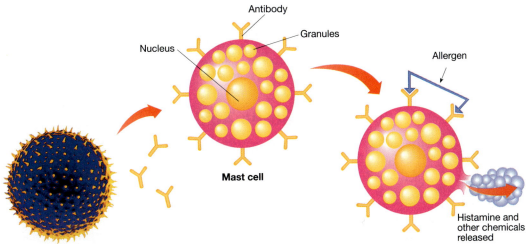

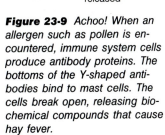

Figure 23-9 *Achoo! When an allergen such as pollen is encountered, immune system cells produce antibody proteins. The bottoms of the Y-shaped antibodies bind to mast cells. The cells break open, releasing biochemical compounds that cause hay fever.*

Insulin Insulin is a small protein hormone made of two polypeptide chains held together by two disulfide links similar to those in your hair. When the concentration of glucose in the blood rises after you have eaten your lunch, your brain sends a message to the pancreas to produce more insulin. The insulin fits onto a specific site on the membrane of your liver and muscle cells, called a receptor. When this happens, glucose can enter the cells, where it is converted to glycogen and stored. This allows the blood glucose to fall back to normal levels, which in turn allows insulin to fall to its normal level. No other hormone can fit on the insulin receptor.

Enzymes Biochemical reactions could not occur fast enough at the body temperature of 37°C were it not for proteins called enzymes, which you learned about in Chapter 17. You may wish to review Section 17.8 and Figure 17-13 at this time. Enzymes, too,

PART **1**
Section 23.4

Cooperative Learning

The Importance of Shape

Teams of 4; **Time:** 30 minutes
Objective: Students will relate the structure of a molecule to its function.
Task: Use colored marshmallows and toothpicks to construct models of glucose, starch, chitin, saturated and unsaturated fatty acid, a triglyceride, an amino acid, and a dipeptide. For smaller molecules such as glucose, use a different color marshmallow for each type of atom. For larger molecules such as starch or triglyceride, use a marshmallow to indicate a glucose unit or a CH_2 group.
CAUTION: Remind students that nothing in the chemistry lab or classroom is eaten.
Team responsibility: Have students check and compare the structures, identify the functional groups, and compare functions.
Evaluation: Have teams show their models and share insights in a class discussion.

Teaching Strategy

Enzymes

To enable students to see how enzymes function, obtain some gelatin, a fresh pineapple or frozen pineapple juice, and canned pineapple juice. Dissolve one sample of gelatin in the fresh or frozen juice; dissolve another sample in the canned juice. Label the containers as to their contents and that they are not to be eaten. Observe the two samples the next day. Fresh pineapple contains the enzyme bromelin, which breaks down protein, so the gel will not form. Heating destroys the enzyme, so the canned juice should gel. Meat tenderizer works in the same way. The enzyme in meat tenderizer is papain, which is extracted from the papaya plant.

Videodisc Connections

12403-12405, side 6
DNA: computer generated images (3-frame seq.)

12402, side 6
DNA: scanning tunneling microscope image (1 frame)

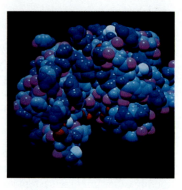

R Reactant E•R Products P P

Attracting charges

Enzyme – reactant complex

E Enzyme E

Figure 23-10 Left: *In this lock-and-key model of an enzyme-catalyzed reaction, R is the reactant, and P is the product. The enzyme finishes the reaction in the same form as it started and is ready to be used again.* Right: *The three-dimensional shape of an enzyme. The reactant fits exactly in the specific area of the enzyme's active site.*

work like puzzle pieces, physically fitting reactants like a lock fits a key and thereby lowering the activation energy needed for the reaction to proceed. The speeding of a chemical reaction by an enzyme is called catalysis, shown in Figure 23-10.

23.5 Nucleic Acids

As with any molecule, the conformation of a biochemical compound is a consequence of its chemical attractions and repulsions. A protein's shape is molded by attractions between oppositely charged amino acid building blocks and repulsions between like-charged residues. As you will learn in this section, hydrogen bonds hold together the spiral staircase of the molecule of heredity, deoxyribonucleic acid. All of these forces give this compound its characteristic conformation under physiological conditions.

Nucleic acids If proteins are the building materials of life, then nucleic acids are the blueprints. Included in this class of molecules is the genetic material **deoxyribonucleic acid** (DNA) and its less celebrated partner **ribonucleic acid** (RNA). These molecules direct the functioning of cells and the synthesis of proteins and transfer genetic information from parents to offspring.

Nucleic acids are polymers of **nucleotide** building blocks, shown in Figure 23-11. Each nucleotide consists of a five-carbon sugar bonded to a phosphate group and a nitrogen-containing, or nitrogenous base. The sugar is either ribose (in RNA) or deoxyribose (in DNA). Each nucleic acid chain has a backbone of alternating phosphates and sugars, forming a covalently linked polymer. In DNA, attached to the sugar of each nucleotide is one of four nitrogenous bases: **adenine (A)**, **guanine (G)**, **thymine (T)**, or **cytosine (C)**. Adenine and guanine have a double-ring structure and are called **pur**

Nucleotide

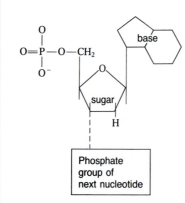

base

sugar

Phosphate group of next nucleotide

Figure 23-11 *Each DNA nucleotide consists of a phosphate group linked to either a ribose sugar (in RNA) or a 2-deoxyribose sugar (in DNA) that is in turn bonded to one of five nitrogenous bases.*

DEMONSTRATION

Nucleic Acids

Break an egg and separate the white from the yolk. Add 50 mL of distilled water to the white, and gently stir until the solution is uniform. Label seven test tubes 1 through 7. Pour 10 mL of egg solution into each test tube. Add 5 mL of 3M HCl to #1, 5 mL of 3M NaOH to #2, 5 mL of methanol or isopropyl alcohol to #3, 5 mL of 3M NaCl to #4, and 5 mL of 3M acetic acid to #5. Heat

#6 in a boiling bath on a hot plate. #7 is the control. Add 5 mL of 0.1M AgNO$_3$ to #1 to show the effect of a heavy metal on protein.

⚠ **CAUTION: When handling these acids, wear safety goggles, face shield, lab apron, and rubber gloves. The alcohols are flammable; be sure there are no flames or other sources of**

(continued on page T783)

ines. Thymine and cytosine have a single organic ring and are called **pyrimidines.** These are shown in Figure 23-12. RNA has the pyrimidine **uracil** in place of thymine.

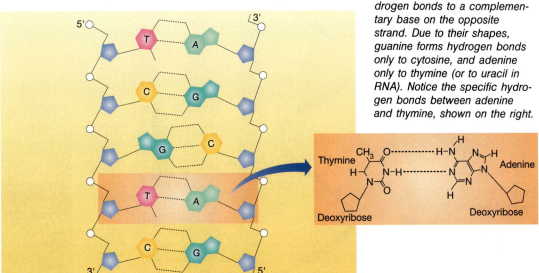

adenine   guanine

thymine   cytosine   uracil (in RNA)

Figure 23-12 Top: *The purines are the double-ringed structures adenine and guanine. Bottom: The pyrimidines are the single-ringed structures thymine, cytosine (for DNA), and uracil (for RNA).*

DNA structure The DNA structure in Figure 23-13 shows how the two chains of nucleotides twist about each other to form a right-handed double helix. The bases from the two intertwined chains form pairs that are held together by hydrogen bonds. Although a single hydrogen bond is not very strong, the overall effect of hundreds of them in a typical DNA molecule is very powerful.

DNA is a sleek, symmetrical molecule because the hydrogen bonding between the base pairs holds the helix together in very

Figure 23-13 *In a double strand of DNA, each base hydrogen bonds to a complementary base on the opposite strand. Due to their shapes, guanine forms hydrogen bonds only to cytosine, and adenine only to thymine (or to uracil in RNA). Notice the specific hydrogen bonds between adenine and thymine, shown on the right.*

Science Background

DNA Structure

Just as each individual has a unique set of fingerprints, each individual (except identical twins) has a unique set of DNA. Scientists can use blood, hair, and other biological materials to test for an individual's DNA fingerprint. Since 1987, DNA fingerprints have been allowed into courtrooms as proof of innocence or guilt. In July 1988 in Arlington, VA, DNA fingerprinting was used to convict a suspect of raping and murdering four women in spite of limited evidence, no witnesses, and no confession. The Department of Defense is in the process of creating a repository of tissue samples placed on identification cards of all military personnel. Samples of cells will be sealed and frozen to be used only to identify remains of casualties. Because of the lack of standards for testing, the use of DNA fingerprinting is controversial, and neither the states nor the federal government regulates these laboratory tests. There is also concern about the individual's right to privacy, since DNA testing also provides information about hereditary disorders or predisposition to disease.

DEMONSTRATION

(continued from page T782)
ignition, such as a plugged-in hot plate, in the room. Before plugging in the hot plate to heat #6 in a boiling bath, be sure all test tubes with alcohol and all alcohol containers are stoppered or capped. Plug the hot plate only into a socket protected by a ground fault interrupter.

Conduct the demonstration behind a shield or shields.
The chemicals added to the egg white changed the secondary, tertiary, and quaternary structure. This change in shape robs the protein of its natural function. The protein is then said to be denatured, or coagulated.

Guided Practice

Review the Concept Check question on page 778 with students. Answers can be found in Appendix E on page 808.

Reteaching Idea

Have students keep track of everything they eat for one day (24 hours). Using food labels, fast-food restaurant information, and dietary tables, ask students to calculate the number of Calories, grams of protein, grams of fat, and grams of carbohydrate they consumed. (Note: A home economics or nutrition teacher in your school may have a nutrient database on a computer that your students can use.) Calculate the percentage of Calories obtained from protein, carbohydrate, and fat. Use the conversion factors of 4 Cal/g for protein and carbohydrate and 9 Cal/g for fat. Then have students compare their total caloric intake to the total caloric requirements for their age, height, weight, sex, and activity level. (A biology or health teacher should have this information.) Generate a discussion of weight control and a balanced diet.

CONNECTING CONCEPTS

Models A lock-and-key fit between two specific compounds maintains proper signals in organisms. A hormone or nervous system neurotransmitter fits a specific receptor; an antibody fits a particular molecule on a cell's surface; an enzyme fits its reactant.

specific ways. Due to the structures of the bases, A and T always pair, as do G and C. RNA can bond with a single strand of DNA, its A pairing with T in DNA, G with C, C with G, and U with A. Note that each base pair consists of one purine and one pyrimidine. These base-pairing rules helped James Watson and Francis Crick decode the structure of DNA in 1953.

The base-pairing rules enable DNA to carry the information for a cell to build a protein. A gene is a stretch of DNA coding for a protein. A chromosome is a rod-shaped structure containing an unbroken DNA molecule long enough to encode hundreds of proteins.

DNA and cell division DNA must replicate each time a cell divides. To do this, the DNA double helix unwinds, and nucleotides that are free floating in the cell match up against the exposed bases to build two new molecules. A stretch of DNA of sequence ACTGGA, for example, would be matched by a strand of sequence TGACCT.

Figure 23-14 shows how a specific protein is made. First a strand of RNA is built against one side of the DNA double helix. This RNA leaves the nucleus, the part of the cell housing DNA. In the cytoplasm, the part of the cell outside the nucleus, RNA anchors itself against a support called a ribosome, and attracts the amino acids in the correct order for the protein being synthesized. One at

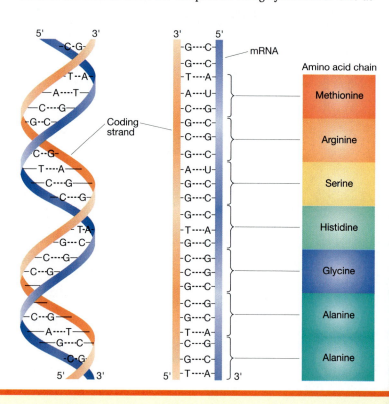

Figure 23-14 *DNA is transcribed into messenger RNA, and messenger RNA is translated into a sequence of amino acids. The end product is a functional protein.*

a time, the amino acids add to the growing peptide chain, and a protein is built. RNA has a code that determines the sequence of amino acids in a protein molecule. The code consists of 3 consecutive bases on the RNA, called the RNA triplet. The triplet of G-C-A, for example, is the code for the amino acid alanine. This correspondence between gene and protein is called the genetic code.

PART 1 REVIEW

1. How are carbohydrates classified, and what are two of their general functions in organisms?

2. A consumer buys a food high in saturated fat, thinking it is healthful because it lacks cholesterol. Is he correct? Why?

3. Why is a diet high in fat more likely to lead to obesity than a diet high in protein or carbohydrate?

4. How is a protein's function determined by its amino acid sequence and its three-dimensional structure?

5. How do nucleic acids specify protein structures and oversee the synthesis of proteins?

6. What chemical reaction is undergone in
   a. a disaccharide such as sucrose forming from monosaccharides?
   b. a dipeptide forming from two amino acids?
   c. attaching a nitrogenous base to a sugar in DNA?

CONNECTING CONCEPTS

Generating information Polysaccharides, proteins, and nucleic acids are all polymers, but only proteins and nucleic acids impart information. The reason is that proteins and nucleic acids are composed of differing building blocks, and polysaccharides are not.

Boxed numbers indicate questions that involve skills in interpretation, application, and analysis.

PART 1
Section 23.5 *continued*

☰CLOSE

Summing Up Main Ideas

Make a chart of carbohydrates, lipids, proteins, and nucleic acids. Include their molecular and three-dimensional structure, examples commonly found in nature, chemical properties, and ability to encode information.

PART 1 REVIEW

Assign the Part Review questions.

Evaluating Skills

These skills are evaluated in the Part Review questions indicated. **Classifying:** 1, 6; **Determining main ideas:** 1, 2, 3, 4, 5, 6; **Determining cause and effect:** 3, 4, 5

Videodisc Connections

23661 to 25170, side 6
Computer modeling (movie)

RESEARCH & TECHNOLOGY

Building Molecules by Computer

You have seen the importance of thinking about molecules in three dimensions. To help scientists visualize complex molecules, computer graphics can be used.

In 1985, a procedure was developed by Michael Rossmann and his research team at Purdue University for viewing rhinovirus 14 (one of about 100 common cold viruses) in three dimensions. An analytical method called X-ray crystallography was used to generate images of slices of the pure virus. X-ray crystallography produces a series of dots on film. Since the film is two-dimensional, and the virus is three-dimensional, the research team needed to take many shots of the virus from different angles and put them together later in

a three-dimensional picture. By using the Cyber 205, a supercomputer at Purdue, the data was processed in only a month. The result was a model of the rhinovirus.

With the information now being learned about the geometry of cold viruses, the synthesis of drugs to help people fight the viral attacks becomes more likely.

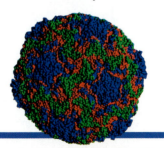

PART 1 REVIEW

ANSWERS

■ Keyed to Objectives

A 1. Carbohydrates are classified into two groups: monosaccharides, which are energy sources; and polysaccharides, which provide fuel as well as structural materials in plants and insects.

B 2. No. Saturated fats are more likely

to increase cholesterol levels in the blood, which increases the risk of heart disease.

B 3. Fats contain more than twice as many calories per gram as proteins or carbohydrates.

D 4. The shape of a protein determines its function, and the shape is controlled by the amino acid sequence.

C 5. DNA is transcribed into messenger RNA, and messenger RNA is trans-

lated into a sequence of amino acids for the protein being synthesized. RNA has a code that determines the amino acid sequence. The code consists of three consecutive nitrogenous bases, which code for a specific amino acid.

A 6. a. dehydration
      b. hydrolysis
      c. dehydration

PART
2 The Energy of Life

Developing Skills

Students may apply this skill in their study of Part 2.

Comparing/Contrasting: Have students compare the amount of energy obtained from anaerobic and aerobic respiration.

≡FOCUS

Activate Prior Knowledge

This activity will show students how plants use CO_2 and H_2O to store energy in $C_6H_{12}O_6$. Review the information about energy changes associated with making and breaking bonds in Chapter 16, Part 2. Using dry ice (CO_2), a glass of H_2O, and a wooden splint ($C_6H_{12}O_6$), demonstrate that CO_2 and H_2O will not burn, but that glucose, which is made of CO_2 and H_2O, does burn.

⚠️ **CAUTION: Wear safety goggles and a lab apron. Wear leather or cloth gloves when handling dry ice.**

Explain that plants use photosynthesis to combine low-energy CO_2 and H_2O into high-energy $C_6H_{12}O_6$. The energy released when glucose is oxidized comes from chemical bonds being broken.

≡TEACH

Teaching Strategy

Plants Harness Energy

All of our food and, with the exception of nuclear power, all of our energy is derived from the sun. Plants have the ability to store energy from sunlight as glucose. Animals depend on this glucose for food. The material in this section is often included in biology texts. Consider team teaching with a biology teacher as these concepts are reviewed.

Objectives

Part 2

E. *Explain* how plants receive solar energy and convert it into chemical energy.

F. *Describe* the chemical reactions that extract energy from the bonds of glucose.

It is the middle of the morning, and you feel as if your body has run out of fuel. You forego the urge to sneak a candy bar and wait for the lunch bell. As you finally eat your lunch, you experience a surge of biological energy. What is the source of this energy? As you have just learned, it is the strong covalent bonds that hold together sugar molecules in your lunch. The simple sugars in the food quickly enter your bloodstream, triggering your pancreas to release insulin, which stimulates cells throughout the body to take up the glucose. As energy is released from breaking chemical bonds, it is recaptured and stored in special high-energy molecules called **adenosine triphosphate** (ATP).

In this part of the chapter, you will learn about this high-energy molecule and the energy reactions of life.

23.6 Plants Harness Energy

The energy needed to fuel your body ultimately comes from the sun. Energy from the sun is captured in the bonds of the products of photosynthesis. By eating plants or by eating animals that eat plants, you are able to use that stored energy.

You may recall from biology class that biological energy transfer begins when sunlight hits green, disk-shaped structures in plant cells, called chloroplasts. Within chloroplasts are molecules of the pigment chlorophyll, which form two types of photosystems. In photosystem II—which acts first but was discovered second—light energy is absorbed by many chlorophyll molecules and is passed to partic-

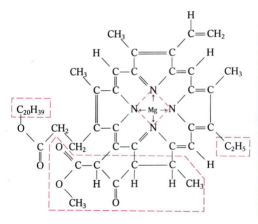 

Figure 23-15 *Chlorophyll a has a central magnesium atom and a series of alternating single and double bonds that allow it to capture light energy.*

Myths and Misconceptions

Both students and adults alike may have the misconception that the food of plants is contained in soil itself, or artificially in fertilizer. Examine the photosynthetic reaction in Section 23.6. Emphasize that carbon dioxide and water are the raw materials plants need to form glucose. Phosphorus and nitrogen are elements common in commercial fertilizers.

These elements are incorporated into molecules such as chlorophyll, plant hormones, and proteins. However, they are neither "foods" for plants nor the raw materials that plants need to form glucose.

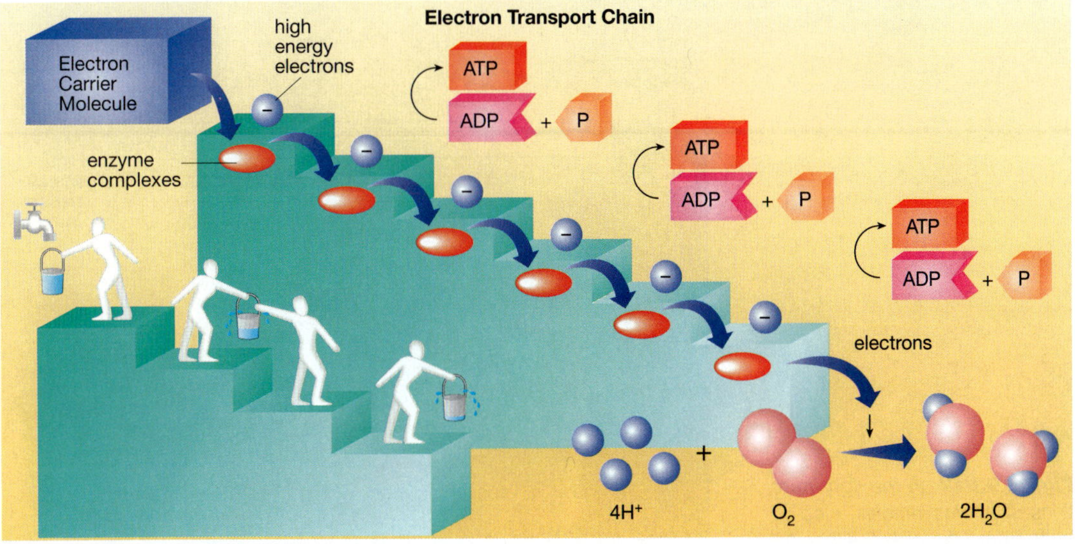

Electron Transport Chain

Electron Carrier Molecule

high energy electrons

enzyme complexes

ATP
ADP + P

ATP
ADP + P

ATP
ADP + P

electrons

$4H^+$ O_2 $2H_2O$

Figure 23-16 *Electron transport chains extract useful energy from electrons that are passed along it. Just as water spills out of the bucket along the way, electrons in the chain lose some of their energy. Electron transport chains are key parts of photosynthesis and aerobic respiration.*

ularly reactive molecules, called chlorophyll *a*. This is shown in Figure 23-15. An electron of chlorophyll *a* becomes excited and is transferred to the first of a series of molecules that form an **electron transport chain,** as shown in Figure 23-16. As electrons pass like a bucket brigade down the electron transport chain, they go to a lower energy level. This lost energy is used to form ATP. You will learn how ATP is formed in the next section. Meanwhile the electron lost from chlorophyll *a* is replaced by splitting water to yield protons (H^+) and oxygen gas. The oxygen produced by plants is the oxygen all animals breathe.

$$2H_2O \rightarrow 4H^+ + O_2 + 4e^-$$

Electrons in the chlorophyll of photosystem I are excited by light energy and send electrons through another electron transport chain. The released electron of photosystem I is replaced by the electron sent through photosystem II. As energy is dissipated down this second electron transport chain, a molecule called $NADP^+$ is reduced to form NADPH, which is another energy-containing compound. The reactions of the two photosystems are called the light reactions of photosynthesis because they require light, and their products are ATP, NADPH, and oxygen. These are shown in Figure 23-17 on the next page. These products then participate in the dark reactions, which do not require light. In the dark reactions, ATP and NADPH drive the formation of simple organic compounds from carbon dioxide and water. One of these products is glucose, a nutrient for all organisms. The overall reaction of photosynthesis is this.

$$6CO_2 + 6H_2O \xrightarrow[\text{chlorophyll}]{\text{light}} C_6H_{12}O_6 + 6O_2$$
$$\text{glucose}$$

PART 2
Section 23.6 *continued*

Science Background

Chlorophyll

Chlorophyll is green because the pigments absorb light most effectively in wavelengths of 400–500 nm (blue/violet) and 600–700 nm (yellow-red). Variations in the proportions of different pigments in different species are what cause the characteristic colors such as the deep blue-green of spruce needles, the greener greens of maple leaves, or the purple-green of cabbages and coleus. The structure of heme, the iron-containing complex in hemoglobin, is very similar to that of chlorophyll, as shown in Figure 23–15, except that the central atom in heme is iron.

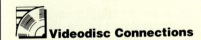

Videodisc Connections

823-829, side 6
Photosynthesis, respiration, O_3 cycles (7-frame seq.)

DO YOU KNOW?

All forests, including rain forests, are huge biological manufacturing plants. They take carbon dioxide out of the air, thus reducing the greenhouse effect and global warming, and produce glucose and oxygen. You use the glucose for food, and you breathe the oxygen. Can you think of a better reason to save the rain forests?

PART **2**
Section 23.7

Teaching Strategy

Using the Energy from Photosynthesis

To review the relationship between photosynthesis and respiration, you may wish to obtain a copy of the "Carbon Cycle Game" (available from the Massachusetts Audubon Society, South Great Road, Lincoln, MA 01773.) This is a board game that traces a carbon atom for 500 million years as it went through successive processes of photosynthesis and respiration by a series of organisms. Although simple in its approach, it is a useful representation of the relationships of photosynthesis, respiration, and conservation of matter.

Science Background

Aerobic Respiration

In the mitochondria of the cell, the series of reactions that convey pyruvic acid to acetyl CoA requires four B-vitamins— thiamin (B_1), riboflavin (B_2), niacin, and pantothenic acid, which is part of coenzyme A— as well as the mineral magnesium. Fatty acids can be converted to acetyl CoA through a different series of reactions. Some amino acids are also converted to acetyl CoA through a series of reactions that uses pyridoxine (B_6) as a coenzyme. Other amino acids are converted to acetyl CoA in a manner similar to the fatty acids.

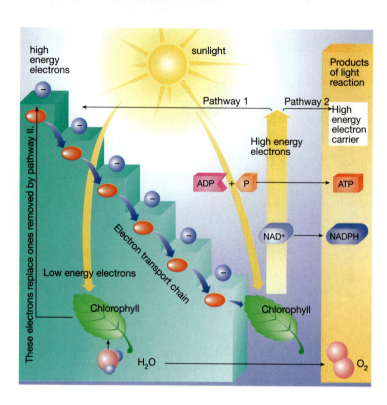

Figure 23-17 *In the light reactions of photosynthesis, electrons from chlorophyll either pass through the electron transport chain or are removed by the electron carriers. ATP, NADPH, oxygen, and high-energy electrons are the products.*

23.7 Using the Energy from Photosynthesis

When you burn gasoline in a car engine, the gasoline is converted to carbon dioxide, water, and energy in two forms—heat and mechanical energy to drive the engine. Most of the energy is lost as heat. When your body burns its fuel, glucose, the glucose is converted to carbon dioxide, water, and energy in two forms—high energy compounds such as ATP and heat. But the body is more efficient than a car engine; energy is captured in small steps, so more of it is conserved and less is lost to heat.

ATP and glucose have been produced by photosynthesis. The first step in tapping the energy from glucose is a reaction pathway called **glycolysis** (sugar-splitting). Glycolysis occurs in all cells in all organisms. In 9 enzyme-catalyzed steps, a glucose molecule is broken down into 2 molecules of pyruvic acid, a 3-carbon compound. Two ATP's are used to power glycolysis, but the reactions yield 4 ATP's, for a net gain of 2 ATP's. In addition, two molecules of a compound called NAD^+ are reduced to form NADH. Each NADH will eventually form 3 ATP's, as you saw in Figure 23-16.

Anaerobic respiration Sometimes when you run hard, your leg muscles cramp. Cells in exhausted muscles undergo a type of anaerobic respiration shown below called **lactic acid fermentation.** Lactic acid accumulating in muscles produces cramps.

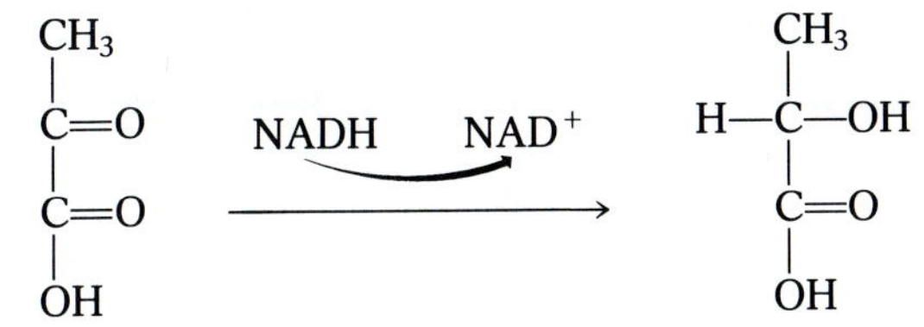

pyruvic acid   lactic acid

Aerobic respiration Anaerobic respiration is inefficient—it yields only the two ATP's from glycolysis. Several billion years ago, as oxygen built up in Earth's atmosphere, biochemical pathways evolved that allowed organisms to extract far more energy from the bonds of glucose. These are the reactions of **aerobic respiration.** In the presence of oxygen, aerobic respiration begins as pyruvic acid enters a part of the cell called a mitochondrion. Here each pyruvic acid loses CO_2 and bonds to a molecule called coenzyme A, forming **acetyl CoA.** In the process, NAD^+ is reduced to NADH, as shown below.

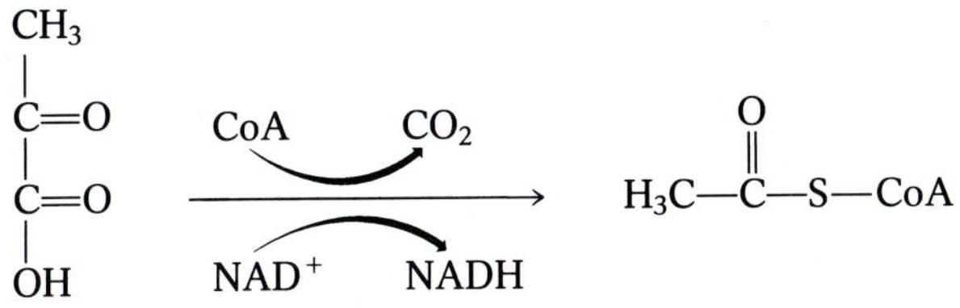

pyruvic acid   acetyl CoA

Acetyl CoA is an important enzyme in the body's extraction of energy from nutrients. It is a bridge to further respiration of glucose. Its formation is also an entry point for fats and proteins to join the remaining reactions that release the energy in their bonds.

Citric acid cycle Acetyl CoA enters a cycle of 7 reactions, called the citric acid cycle, which is shown in Figure 23-18 on the next page. The 2-carbon acetyl group from acetyl CoA combines with a 4-carbon compound to yield a 6-carbon intermediate, which loses carbon dioxide in consecutive steps to form a 4-carbon compound. After 2 rearrangements, the cycle begins again. In 1 turn of the cycle, 1 ATP is produced, 3 NAD^+'s are reduced to NADH, and 1 molecule of a compound called FAD is reduced to $FADH_2$. Remember that each glucose molecule undergoing glycolysis forms 2 molecules of pyruvic acid, so it fuels 2 turns of the citric acid cycle.

In the next and final step of aerobic respiration, the electrons from the $FADH_2$ and NADH formed in glycolysis and the citric acid cycle are passed along a series of molecules that form an electron transport chain, similar to the bucket brigade of photosynthesis. The

Science Background

Citric Acid Cycle

The electron transport chain, which is the final step of aerobic respiration, contains cytochromes, which are several iron-containing proteins that act in sequence to carry electrons from hydrogen atoms. ATP is released at each transfer reaction. Copper atoms are also involved in part of the process. At the end of the series, the hydrogen combines with molecular oxygen to form water. As the final product, water has the lowest energy content of all.

PART **2**

Section 23.7 continued

Guided Practice

Human red blood cells are unusual in that they derive all their energy from glycolysis. The concentration of glucose in an erythrocyte is 0.0050 mol/L. If all the glucose in a 1.0 L volume of red blood cells was broken down to CO_2, how much energy would be stored when ADP is converted to ATP?

$$\left(\frac{0.0050 \text{ mol}}{\text{L glucose}}\right)(1.0 \text{ L})\left(\frac{2 \text{ mol ATP}}{\text{mol glucose}}\right)$$

$= 0.010$ mol ATP

$(0.01 \text{ mol ATP})\left(\frac{29 \text{ kJ}}{\text{mol ATP}}\right)$

$= 0.29$ kJ

Reteaching Idea

To reinforce the concepts of a balanced diet and the interrelationship of nutrients in the formation and release of energy, work with students to draw a large concept map for *cell metabolism, photosynthesis,* or *cellular respiration.* Use an overhead projector, and if needed, obtain some background information from a biology or nutrition teacher. As you fill in the map with students you will be able to discuss with them the role of vitamins in the process (as coenzymes), and why eating a balanced diet and not skipping meals or eliminating a class of foods is so important.

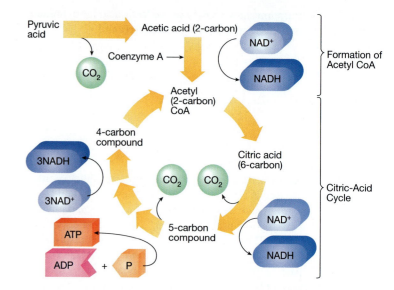

Figure 23-18 In the presence of oxygen, carbon atoms of pyruvic acid ultimately enter the citric acid cycle.

energy released is used to generate ATP. Each NADH yields three ATP's, and each $FADH_2$ yields two ATP's.

Add up the energy Now, finally, you—and the cell—can appreciate how much energy is packed into a glucose molecule. In Table 23-2, you can add the ATP's from glycolysis, acetyl CoA formation, and the citric acid cycle. Remember that each NADH yields three ATP's, and each $FADH_2$ yields two ATP's.

Therefore, the breakdown of 1 glucose molecule produces 36 molecules of ATP.

TABLE 23-2

Energy Production from Glucose		
Pathway	**Energy Source**	**ATP**
glycolysis	2 ATP directly	+ 2 ATP
	2 NADH × 3 ATP/NADH	+ 6 ATP
acetyl CoA formation (2 times)	2 NADH × 3 ATP/NADH	+ 6 ATP
citric acid cycle (2 turns)	2 ATP directly	+ 2 ATP
	6 NADH × 3 ATP/NADH	+18 ATP
	2 $FADH_2$ × 2 ATP/$FADH_2$	+ 4 ATP
		38 ATP
	−2 ATP used to conduct pyruvic acid into mitochondrion	− 2 ATP
Total		36 ATP

ATP, as seen in Figure 23-19, is a nucleotide built of adenine, deoxyribose, and three phosphate groups. When one phosphate group is split off, the molecule becomes adenosine diphosphate (ADP); and when a second phosphate is split off, it becomes adenosine monophosphate (AMP). Each release of a phosphate yields 29 kilojoules or 7 kilocalories of energy.

energy releasing →

ATP ⟷ ADP ⟷ AMP

← energy requiring

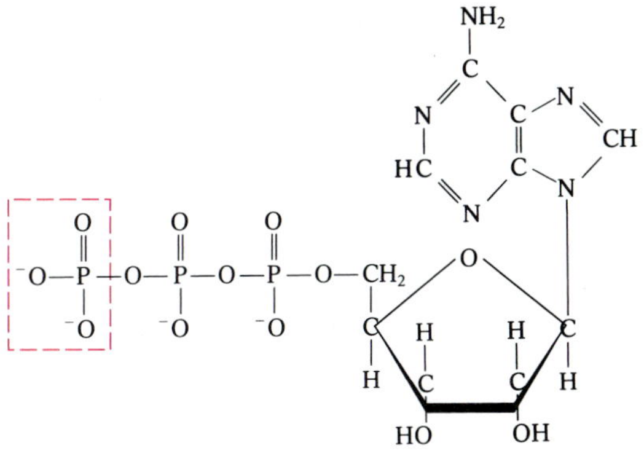

Figure 23-19 *Adenosine triphosphate—the biological energy molecule. When it splits off the end phosphate group, it becomes adenosine diphosphate and releases seven kilocalories of energy.*

The biological energy production line is very efficient. Nearly 40 percent of the energy stored in the covalent bonds of glucose is captured.

The human body requires two billion ATP-splitting reactions per minute just to remain alive. ATP enables muscles to contract, nerves and hormones to transmit messages, and cells to divide. Each cell is in a constant state of biochemical flux, with thousands of reactions either building large molecules from small ones or breaking down large molecules into small ones, constantly recycling ATP. These reactions constitute metabolism, the energy reactions of life.

PART 2 REVIEW

7. Identify the part of the ATP molecule that directly provides its energy-storing function.

8. Explain how sunlight begins the process of acquiring biological energy.

9. Outline the steps of glucose breakdown.

10. State why plant cells undergo glycolysis, even though they can manufacture glucose in photosynthesis.

11. Explain why aerobic respiration is more efficient than anaerobic respiration.

12. Identify an electron transport chain found only in plants and one found in both plants and animals.

Boxed numbers indicate questions that involve skills in interpretation, application, and analysis.

PART 2
Section 23.7 continued

☰CLOSE

Summing Up Main Ideas

Outline the steps of energy transformation from photosynthesis to the aerobic breakdown of glucose in the human body.

PART 2 REVIEW

Assign the Part Review questions.

Evaluating Skills

These skills are evaluated in the Part Review questions indicated. **Determining main ideas:** 7, 8, 11, 12; **Determining cause and effect:** 8; **Summarizing:** 8, 9, 10

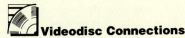

Videodisc Connections

12408-12409, side 6
ATP: computer generated images (2-frame seq.)

PART 2 REVIEW

ANSWERS

■ Keyed to Objectives

F **7.** the phosphate group

E **8.** Sunlight is absorbed by chlorophyll; an electron is excited and starts an electron transport chain.

F **9.** glycolysis, acetyl Co A formation (twice), citric acid cycle (twice)

E **10.** Glycolysis can occur without light; photosynthesis cannot.

F **11.** Anaerobic respiration yields only 2 ATPs of energy, whereas aerobic respiration is a more complete reaction and yields 36 ATPs of energy.

E **12.** plants: NADPH
plants and animals: NADH

Developing Skills

Students may apply these skills in their study of Part 3.
Predicting: Have students predict the change in blood pH resulting from rapid, nervous breathing.
Classifying: Have students classify two common food items as likely to increase or decrease the pH of body fluids.

≣ FOCUS

Activate Prior Knowledge

Discuss different weight-reduction programs that students are aware of. Examples might include low-calorie, low-carbohydrate, or liquid diets. Discuss the mechanism by which each diet plan is purported to work and whether it is actually safe and/or effective. Discuss other measures that alter the body's balance. Examples might include diuretics, appetite suppressants, antacids, beverages containing electrolytes, and steroids.

≣ TEACH

Science Background

Sugar in urine, a symptom of diabetes, was detected centuries ago by throwing the urine on the ground to see it if would attract insects. Now very sensitive test papers that detect sugar in urine can be used at home.

O b j e c t i v e s

Part 3

G. Explain the importance of maintaining characteristic concentrations of specific biochemical compounds in body compartments.

H. Identify ways that the human body maintains the pH of body fluids and **explain** why this is important.

I. Describe the effects on health of rapid changes of pressure.

PART

3 Biochemical Balance

The chemicals in living things must also be present in particular concentrations and distributed in specific ways. Bone, for example, is built largely of collagen, a protein, and minerals containing calcium and phosphorus. Children who are born with too little collagen have an inherited condition called osteogenesis imperfecta. They easily break their bones in routine activities, and may even do so before birth. Older people with a condition called osteoporosis lose bone mass. Their bones easily compress, and the people grow shorter. In this chapter, you will learn how the body fine-tunes itself to stay alive and function properly.

23.8 Concentrations of Biochemical Compounds

When Mindy K., a popular high school junior died suddenly, those who knew her were stunned—especially when they learned how she died. Mindy's heart had lost its normal rhythm, causing her sudden death. What could trigger such a malfunction in a seemingly healthy teenager?

During an autopsy, doctors discovered that Mindy's blood level of potassium ion, K^+, was very low and this had directly affected her heart. When the indirect clues were considered—rotted teeth, bite marks on the backs of her hands, evasive behavior, intense exercising, and laxatives found in her purse—a diagnosis emerged. Mindy, like millions of other teens, suffered from bulimia, an eating disorder. She would routinely eat enormous amounts of food and then make herself vomit by sticking her hand down her throat (hence the decayed teeth and bite marks), exercise frantically, or take laxatives. The vomiting depleted her body of potassium. Because Mindy's weight was normal, nobody suspected her problem until it was too late and her behavior had already altered the blood concentration of a key electrolyte, potassium.

Electrolytes in body fluids An organism can be viewed as being built of compartments, each of which has characteristic concentrations of biochemical species. As seen in Figure 23-20, intracellular ("within cells") fluids have high concentrations of K^+, monohydrogen phosphate (HPO_4^{2-}), magnesium (Mg^{2+}), and sulfate (SO_4^{2-}), and low concentrations of sodium (Na^+), chloride (Cl^-) and bicarbonate (HCO_3^-). The situation is different in extracellular compartments. These areas include tissue spaces, secretions, plasma, lymph, and pockets of fluid in the brain, spinal cord, and eyes. Here Na^+, Cl^-, and HCO_3^- are the predominant ions.

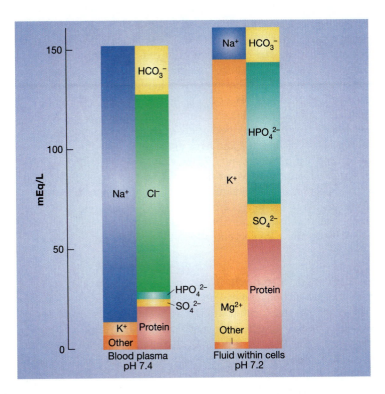

Figure 23-20 *Blood plasma has a different distribution of electrolytes from intracellular (within the cell) fluid. The major cation of blood is sodium. The major cation of intracellular fluid is potassium.*

Teaching Stategy

Balancing Acids and Bases in the Body

To tie together the concepts of normal blood pH, acid-base balance, and blood buffers, refer students to the equation on page 794 of the carbonic acid/sodium bicarbonate buffer system. Point out that, once formed, carbonic acid is broken down to CO_2 and H_2O, which can be expelled by the lungs. Ask students why hyperventilation can cause alkalosis, and why hypoventilation can lead to acidosis.

Sometimes you are very much aware of how alterations in concentrations of particular chemicals make you feel. For example, ups and downs in your energy throughout the day reflect your blood sugar level. The amount of glucose in blood can vary widely, shooting up when you eat a food rich in carbohydrates and plummeting as your cells use the glucose. Blood glucose level is normally between 70 and 120 mg/100 mL of blood. If the level drops below a value of 50, symptoms of hypoglycemia (low blood sugar) appear—confusion, nervousness, perspiration, headache, and hunger.

A blood sugar level above 140 indicates hyperglycemia, a sign of the disorder diabetes mellitus. When the blood sugar level exceeds 170 mg/100 mL blood, the sugar spills over into the urine. For healthy people, a diet of three meals a day that has a good balance of fat, protein, and soluble fiber can help to keep your blood sugar level steady.

23.9 Balancing Acids and Bases in the Body

The fluids that make up much of the bodies and cells of living things must have a particular acidity or basicity (alkalinity). Recall from Chapter 19 that an acid is an electrolyte that releases H^+ in water and that a base is a species that increases the OH^- concentration.

Acidity and alkalinity are measured using the pH scale. If the pH of a body fluid changes much from its normal value, results can be drastic. If the H^+ concentration in cells rises or falls, rates of biochemical reactions change, and chemicals involved in biological communication, such as hormones and nervous-system messengers, can malfunction. The pH of blood in the arteries is normally 7.4 and must fall within a range of 7.0 to 7.8 for survival. A blood pH between 7.0 and 7.3 is called acidosis, which causes the person to feel tired and disoriented and have difficulty in breathing. This may be caused by a brain injury, a blocked airway, lung or kidney disease, diabetes mellitus, or prolonged vomiting that depletes the small intestine of its alkaline contents. In the opposite situation, alkalosis, blood pH ranges from 7.5 to 7.8 and the person is dizzy and agitated. Alkalosis may be caused by fever, anxiety, or breathing very rapidly (hyperventilation), or by too many aspirin or antacids.

Buffers in the body Organisms have several ways to maintain the pH of body fluids. All body fluids carry conjugate acid-base pairs that react with a strong acid or base to neutralize it. One acid-base buffer system is carbonic acid, H_2CO_3, and sodium bicarbonate, $NaHCO_3$. If a body fluid contains excess hydrochloric acid, HCl, sodium bicarbonate reacts with it to yield the weaker carbonic acid as follows.

$$HCl(aq) + NaHCO_3(aq) \rightarrow H_2CO_3(aq) + NaCl(aq)$$
(strong acid) (weak acid)

If too much of the strong base sodium hydroxide (NaOH) builds up, H_2CO_3 lowers the pH as follows.

$$NaOH(aq) + H_2CO_3(aq) \rightarrow NaHCO_3(aq) + H_2O(l)$$
(strong base) (weak base)

A **phosphate buffer system** consists of the weak acid sodium dihydrogen phosphate, NaH_2PO_4, and the weak base sodium monohydrogen phosphate, Na_2HPO_4. They react with strong acids and bases much as the components of the bicarbonate buffer system do, preventing the pH of a body fluid from deviating too much from normal.

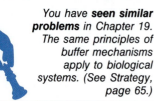

PROBLEM·SOLVING
S T R A T E G Y

*You have **seen similar** **problems** in Chapter 19. The same principles of buffer mechanisms apply to biological systems. (See Strategy, page 65.)*

Concept ✓ Check

Explain how a buffer system can deal with solutions that can be at some times too acidic and at other times too basic.

23.10 Extreme Pressure Changes Affect Health

Standing in one place, you may not be aware of air pressure. In a rapidly ascending or descending airplane, however, you may be-

Myths and Misconceptions

Students often interpret the terms *acidosis* and *alkalosis* incorrectly. Recall that the normal pH of the blood is between the range of 7.35 and 7.45. Acidosis is characterized by a blood pH between 7.0 and 7.3. Point out that, although this pH range is actually alkaline, it is still far too acidic for the normal functioning of the blood. When the blood pH rises above 7.45, the resulting condition is alkalosis. Explain that even small deviations in blood pH can be fatal, and stress the importance of the body's blood buffer systems.

come very aware of changing air pressure as your ears pop. Deep-sea divers and mountain climbers are familiar with the effects of changing air pressure on the human body.

You know that at sea level, the pressure of air is sufficient to support a column of mercury 760 millimeters high. This pressure is called 1 atmosphere. Under water, though, pressure increases by 1 atmosphere for every 10 meters. You can see how a deep-sea diver, pictured in Figure 23-21, can face some very high pressures. The real danger to a diver's breathing compressed air, however, arises upon resurfacing. If the return trip is rapid, a painful and possibly fatal condition called decompression sickness, or the bends, develops.

Figure 23-21 *Divers must ascend gradually to avoid the bends.*

With increasing depth, gas in the lungs, which is 80 percent nitrogen, becomes compressed and becomes more soluble in the blood. If resurfacing is too rapid, nitrogen dissolved in the blood comes out of solution as bubbles. (The same effect is seen when you rapidly decompress, or open, a can of soda.) The bubbles block blood flow, causing pain so severe that the sufferer bends over to relieve it. This is why the condition is called the bends. It was officially named caissons disease when divers installing underwater bridge supports called caissons in the late 1800's were affected by the disorder.

Divers have come up with a solution to this problem. They use a mixture of helium and oxygen as a breathing gas. Helium is substituted for nitrogen because the helium is less soluble in blood. In this way, gas does not dissolve into the bloodstream in the first place.

DO YOU KNOW?

Children sometimes survive near-drowning incidents in icy water for more than an hour because of a mammalian diving reflex. Cold water on the face lowers heart rate and shunts blood to vital organs. Children exhibit the reflex because their high surface area to mass ratio allows them to dissipate heat rapidly. Adults do not benefit from this evolutionary holdover.

PART **3**

Section 23.10 continued

Guided Practice

Review the Concept Check question on page 794 with students. Answers can be found in Appendix E on page 808.

Reteaching Idea

Plan ahead with students and assign a research project on a topic related to Part 3 that particularly interests them. The project can be written, oral, or visual. Examples could include such conditions as diabetes, osteoporosis, anorexia, bulimia, the use of antacids or electrolyte-containing beverages. Students could compare the win-loss records of professional sports teams that play games "on the road" in high-altitude areas (for example, Denver, CO). They could look up the training programs of Olympic and other athletes that train for marathons or bicycle competitions such as the Tour de France. Note how many train in high-altitude areas.

CLOSE

Summing Up Main Ideas

Discuss how the following factors can result in biochemical imbalance in the human body: excessive sodium, deficient potassium, excessive or low blood glucose, alkalosis, acidosis, oxygen levels too high or too low, deficient calcium. What are some consequences of these situations, and how would the body counteract them?

PART 3 REVIEW

Assign the Part Review questions.

Evaluating Skills

These skills are evaluated in the Part Review questions indicated. **Determining main ideas:** 13, 15, 16, 17; **Comparing/Contrasting:** 14, 16; **Stating a conclusion:** 16, 17

Learning from animals Divers avoid the bends by resurfacing gradually, stopping on the way up so that the nitrogen can diffuse out of the blood slowly. This preventive measure was learned by observing how diving mammals cope with great depths. Although you might expect that a sperm whale or Weddell seal could fill its lungs before submerging for an hour, exactly the opposite occurs. Whales have very small lungs, and seals actually exhale as they dive. The air in the respiratory system is forced into the bronchial passages leading to the lungs, so trapped air cannot enter the blood. The animals gradually ascend, and the excess nitrogen gas goes into the lungs rather than blocking vital blood vessels.

Getting used to high altitudes Air pressure decreases as one ascends above sea level, causing other symptoms as the partial pressure of oxygen in the arteries falls from 95 mm of mercury to 50 mm. At an altitude of 3000 meters (10 000 feet), such as in parts of Colorado and California, there are one-third fewer air molecules than there are at sea level. Therefore, each breath contains one-third less oxygen than a breath taken at sea level. Both breathing and heart rate increase to compensate, and the body steps up production of red blood cells and their oxygen-carrying protein, hemoglobin.

These adaptations are not sufficient to prevent symptoms of acute mountain sickness. If you normally live in a low elevation area and travel to the mountains, exercising may induce fatigue, headache, shortness of breath, nausea, and dizziness as oxygen delivery to tissues decreases. At still higher elevations, symptoms progress to a cough and a gurgling from the chest as fluid accumulates in the lungs. Stupor follows. Above 4000 meters (13 000 feet), the brain swells with fluid, causing a bad headache, vomiting, and loss of coordination. Hallucinations, coma, and even death may follow. However, natives living at high altitudes normally have higher concentrations of hemoglobin in their blood to allow them to adapt to the lower pressure of oxygen gas.

PART 3 REVIEW

13. What are some examples of how alterations in the concentrations of biochemicals can affect health?

14. Distinguish between the electrolyte concentrations within cells and outside cells.

15. How does an organism maintain the pH of body fluids within specific ranges?

16. State two fates of glucose after it is admitted inside a cell.

17. How do chemical and physical changes at great depths and high altitudes cause health problems?

Boxed numbers indicate questions that involve skills in interpretation, application, and analysis.

PART 3 REVIEW

ANSWERS

■ Keyed to Objectives

G 13. Answers may vary and may include: depletion of potassium ions causes muscle weakness and cramps; acidosis causes tiredness.

H 14. The concentration of the K^+, HPO_4^{2-}, Mg^{2+}, and SO_4^{2-} electrolytes within cells (heart, muscle, liver, and skin) is higher than Na^+, Cl^-, and HCO_3^-. The concentrations of K^+, HPO_4^{2-}, Mg^{2+}, and SO_4^{2-} in blood and other body fluids is lower than Na^+, Cl^-, and HCO_3^-.

H 15. Several ions such as bicarbonate (HCO_3^-) and hydrogen phosphate (HPO_4^{2-}) serve as buffers.

G 16. Glucose can be used as an energy source or converted to fat.

G,I 17. High altitudes lead to an oxygen

CAREERS IN CHEMISTRY

Electrical Engineer

At an early age, Miriam Santana was already helping her father, an electronics technician, fix radios and TV's. As she found parts for him and cut wires, she was introduced to the wonders of electricity.

Following early interests In school, science and math were her favorite subjects. She took all the advanced math, physics, and chemistry courses she could. It didn't surprise her father when she majored in electrical engineering in college. Later she earned her master's degree in electrical engineering.

Helper as a child, designer as an adult Miriam now works for a high tech company, designing antennas and evaluating their performance. She first writes a computer program that models the operation of an antenna. New designs for antennas can then be entered into the computer and analyzed for performance. Computer simulation such as this eliminates the cost of building antennas for testing purposes.

> *The most important part of science is that you will find it fun to learn and discover . . .*

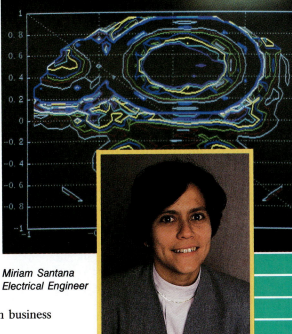

Miriam Santana
Electrical Engineer

Technology and economics Miriam is very much aware of the cost side of her job. Third World countries are making an effective bid for a share of world markets. Their lower production costs could cause the United States to lose markets. This possible loss, coupled with aggressive marketing by Japan and the economic unification of Europe, makes it absolutely necessary that high tech companies in the United States reduce production costs. In order to learn to deal with these issues in her job, Miriam went back to school to earn a master's degree in business administration.

Future discoverers Miriam believes that future engineers must be trained broadly to develop the high-level thinking skills that will allow them to take advantage of the computer's capability and efficiency. Begin with a solid education in math and science, Miriam advises. That will not only give you an edge in the job market, but it will also change your perspective of the world. Miriam also strongly believes that "the most important part is that you will find it is fun to learn and discover . . ."

deficiency, whereas the pressure at great depths increases the dissolved nitrogen in the blood. During decompression, bubbles of nitrogen emerge and block the blood vessels.

CAREERS IN CHEMISTRY

Teaching Strategies

1. Have students think about the concept of professional responsibility, that is, the notion that society expects that individuals in a given profession have responsibilities associated with that profession, e.g., doctors, lawyers, judges, teachers. Then have them discuss the professional responsibilities of engineers, including the development of effective, safe, and economical products. These factors are not always compatible, such as a product being both safe and economical.

2. Have students consider the different work environments of engineers in different specialties, e.g., civil engineers who may build bridges and dams, automotive engineers, aerospace engineers, and electrical engineers.

3. Have students research computer simulation. Consider the role of computer modeling and its potential limitations in the development of products.

Related Careers

Have students identify other careers in engineering including computing, nuclear engineering, aeronautics, and astronautics. In addition, discuss other careers involving electricity, such as electronics and electrochemistry. For more information on related careers, contact the Institute of Electrical and Electronic Engineers, 345 East 47th St., New York, NY 10017; the U.S. Army Corps of Engineers, 20 Massachusetts Ave., NW, Casimir Pulaski Building, Washington, DC 20314; and the Computer Music Association, P.O. Box 1634, San Francisco, CA 94101.

Using Chemical Tests to Identify Carbohydrates

Estimated time: (50 minutes)

Measuring
Comparing/Contrasting
Designing and performing
  experiments
Classifying
Analyzing data
Stating a conclusion

Preparation

■ Materials

(for a class of 24, working in groups of 4)
Apparatus
400-mL beakers (6), test tubes (60–80), 10-mL graduates (6), eye droppers (25) or Beral pipettes, marking pencils, test tube holders, Tes-Tape strips, hot plates or Bunsen burners (6)
Reagents
■ 1% solutions of: glucose, sucrose, lactose, and soluble starch, freshly prepared
■ Unknown carbohydrate solutions (the above solutions, labeled A, B, C, D)
■ Barfoed's reagent
■ Benedict's reagent
■ I_2-KI solution

■ Preparation Hints

Barfoed's reagent: Dissolve 13.3 g of copper acetate in 200 mL water; filter if necessary; then add 5 mL $6M$ acetic acid.
Benedict's reagent: Order or prepare your own: Dissolve 173 g of sodium citrate and 100 g of anhydrous sodium carbonate in 800 mL water, while heating; filter if necessary. Prepare 17.3 g of copper sulfate ($CuSO_4\cdot5H_2O$) in 100 mL water. Combine the solutions and dilute to 1 liter.
I_2-KI solution: Dissolve 10 g of iodine and 20 g of potassium iodide in 400 mL water; then dilute the solution to 1 liter.

Laboratory

Investigation

Using Chemical Tests to Identify Carbohydrates

In this lab, you will observe the chemical reactions of four carbohydrates found in food: glucose, sucrose, lactose, and starch. Using the test reactions, you will be able to identify the carbohydrates in "unknown" samples.

Objectives

Distinguish the different reactions of four carbohydrate solutions.

Summarize the chemistry involved in the tests and **describe** how the chemistry of the tests relates to the structure of the compounds.

Design a strategy to identify the unknown samples.

■ Materials

Apparatus	Reagents
□ droppers	□ 1-percent solutions of:
□ test tubes	glucose
□ 10-mL graduated cylinders	sucrose
□ Tes-Tape strips	lactose
□ 400-mL beaker	soluble starch
□ hot plate or Bunsen burner	□ Barfoed's reagent
□ marker pencil	□ Benedict's reagent
	□ iodine-KI solution
	□ unknown samples

■ The Reagents

Barfoed's reagent distinguishes between reducing monosaccharides and reducing disaccharides. The red color indicates the presence of a reducing monosaccharide. Barfoed's reagent and Benedict's reagent both involve the oxidation of the carbohydrate and the reduction of the Cu^{2+} ion.

Benedict's reagent will distinguish reducing from nonreducing sugars (either monosaccharides or disaccharides) with the formation of a red precipitate of copper(I) from the original copper(II) solution. The sugar is oxidized and Cu^{2+} is reduced to Cu^+.

Tes-Tape strip uses enzymes, and is specific for glucose, even in the presence of other sugars. The strip will turn green within 60 seconds if glucose is present.

Iodine-KI solution is used to test for starch. A dark blue-black color is positive for starch; a red-brown color is negative.

■ Procedure

1. Put on your safety goggles and lab apron.

2. Set up a boiling-water bath, using a 400-mL beaker about half full of tap water. The water *must* be boiling before tests are done.

3. Obtain and label 10-mL samples of each of the carbohydrates to be tested.

4. **Barfoed's test** Put 20 drops (1 mL) of each sample in a clean, labeled test tube and add 5 mL of Barfoed's reagent to each. Use a control of 20 drops of water and 5 mL of Barfoed's reagent. Place all test tubes in the boiling-water bath for exactly 10 minutes. A red-orange precipitate of Cu_2O is considered a positive test for monosaccharides. Record your results in your data table.

Data Table

| Carbohydrates | Tests | | | | |
	Barfoed	Benedict	Tes-Tape	I_2-KI	Control
Glucose	red	red	green	NR	NR
Sucrose	NR	NR	NR	NR	NR
Lactose	NR	red	NR	NR	NR
Starch	NR	NR	NR	blue-black	NR
Unknown(s)	Depends on identity of unknown				NR

5. **Benedict's test** Put 20 drops of each sample into a clean, labeled test tube and add 5 mL of Benedict's reagent. Use a control of 20 drops of water and 5 mL of Benedict's reagent. Place all test tubes in a boiling-water bath for three or four minutes. Note the color and presence or absence of a precipitate. A red-orange precipitate is considered positive. Record your results in the data table.

6. **Tes-Tape test**

   ☠ **CAUTION: Keep test papers out of your mouth. Some are poisonous.**

   Dip strips of the tape into your samples and observe for 1 minute. Use a control tube of 20 drops of water and the Tes-Tape. Any green color is a positive test for glucose. Record your results.

7. **Iodine-KI** Use 20-drop samples of each carbohydrate and add three drops of the iodine-KI solution to each. Set up your control and record your observations as before. A dark blue-black color is positive; a red-brown color is negative.

8. After your results are completely recorded in the data table, design a test to identify the carbohydrate(s) in your unknown sample or samples. Obtain approval from your teacher. Then perform the tests and record the results in the data table.

■ Data Analysis

Data Table

Carbohydrate	Tests				
	Barfoed	Benedict	Tes-Tape	I₂-KI	Control Tube
Glucose					
Sucrose					
Lactose					
Starch					
Unknown(s)					

1. Identify each of your carbohydrate samples as a monosaccharide, disaccharide, or polysaccharide.

2. Write the structural formulas for each carbohydrate you tested. Circle the aldehyde and ketone groups in each structure.

3. What two monosaccharides make up lactose? Circle the potential aldehyde or ketone group in lactose.

4. What two monosaccharides make up sucrose? How does the structure of sucrose differ from that of lactose?

■ Conclusions

1. If your unknown carbohydrate was negative for all four tests, what was it?

2. What group or groups are necessary for a positive Benedict's or Barfoed's test?

3. List a food source for each of the carbohydrates used in this activity.

Guiding the Investigation

■ Procedural Hints

Have all solutions ready ahead of time. Make the reagent solutions available in convenient locations in the lab. Start heating water baths immediately at the beginning of the lab period. Mark the test tubes with a marking pencil. Timing is not critical in Barfoed's and Benedict's tests, but is critical in Tes-Tape tests.

Disposal

All solutions except those containing elemental iodine may be poured down the drain. Treat the iodine-containing solutions with 0.1M sodium thiosulfate solution until colorless, then pour down the drain.

Data Analysis

■ Sample Data
(See table below.)

■ Analysis

1. Monosaccharides: glucose and fructose

   Disaccharides: sucrose and lactose

   Polysaccharide: starch

2. (See diagrams below.)

3. Lactose is made up of glucose and galactose. Lactose rings can open up, thus freeing an aldehyde group. (See diagram below.)

4. Sucrose is made of glucose and fructose. Sucrose does not have a potential aldehyde or ketone group.

Conclusions

1. If the carbohydrate sample was negative for all four tests, it would have to be sucrose.

2. An aldehyde or ketone group is necessary for a positive Barfoed's or Benedict's test.

3. The main food sources of the carbohydrates used in this lab are glucose (fruits and honey), sucrose (sugar), lactose (milk), and starch (corn, rice, potatoes, grains).

glucose   fructose   sucrose   lactose   starch

Chapter 23 Review ANSWERS begin on page T803a.

Summary

The Chemicals of Life

- Carbohydrates are sugars, or polymers of sugars, containing primarily hydrogen, carbon, and oxygen. Some carbohydrates supply energy, and some are used for support.

- The functionally diverse lipids dissolve in ether, benzene, and chloroform, and have fewer oxygens than carbohydrates and proteins. They include triglycerides, sterols, and phospholipids.

- Proteins are polymers made of different combinations of some or all of the 20 amino acids.

- Nucleic acids are polymers of nucleotides distinguished by five types of nitrogenous bases. The base sequence of a nucleic acid specifies the primary sequence of amino acids of a particular protein.

- A molecule's three-dimensional shape is usually essential to its biochemical function.

The Energy of Life

- The source of biological energy is light, which excites chlorophyll *a* in plant cells, sending electrons through electron transport chains in two photosystems, yielding ATP, NADPH, and oxygen. In photosynthesis, the products of the light reactions are used to synthesize simple organic compounds from CO_2 and H_2O.

- Extracting energy from glucose begins with glycolysis, in which the molecule is split into two molecules of pyruvic acid. If oxygen is absent, lactic acid fermentation follows. In the presence of oxygen, pyruvic acid loses carbon dioxide and forms acetyl CoA; then it enters the citric acid cycle. Finally an electron transport chain uses the energy released from the products of the preceding reactions to form ATP. Overall aerobic metabolism of one glucose molecule yields 36 ATP's.

Biochemical Balance

- Ion distribution, biochemical reaction rates, and the functioning of communication molecules depend upon maintenance of specific pH values of body fluids. This is accomplished with chemical and physiological buffer systems.

- Specific concentrations of electrolytes and nutrients must be maintained in different body compartments.

- Decreased oxygen at high altitudes produces acute mountain sickness. Divers ascending rapidly experience decompression sickness when nitrogen forms bubbles in the blood.

Chemically Speaking

acetyl CoA 23.7
adenine 23.5
adenosine triphosphate 23.5
aerobic respiration 23.7
anaerobic respiration 23.7
citric acid cycle 23.7
cytosine 23.5
deoxyribonucleic acid (DNA) 23.5
disaccharide 23.1
electron transport chain 23.6
glycolysis 23.7
guanine 23.5
insulin 23.4

monosaccharide 23.1
monounsaturated fat 23.2
nucleic acid 23.5
nucleotide 23.5
polysaccharide 23.1
polyunsaturated fat 23.2
protein 23.3
purine 23.5
pyrimidine 23.5
ribonucleic acid (RNA) 23.5
saturated fat 23.2
sterol 23.2
thymine 23.5
triglyceride 23.2
uracil 23.5

Concept Mapping

Using the method of concept mapping described at the front of this book, make a concept map for *energy,* using the terms *photosynthesis, con-*

PROBLEM-SOLVING STRATEGIES

Students apply these strategies in the following questions.

- Factor-label method: 52
- Using what you know: 7, 11, 13, 15, 22, 23, 25, 26, 30, 31, 34, 37, 38, 39, 40, 43, 45, 53, 54, 55, 56, 57, 58, 59, 60
- Using patterns: 19, 51
- Using calculators: 52
- Verifying your answer: 52

trol, ATP, glucose, proteins, nucleic acids, and *pH.* Using what you have learned, add more key words and draw the map. Pay particular attention to the interconnections, as they are numerous in this chapter.

Questions and Problems

THE CHEMICALS OF LIFE

A. Objective: **Compare and contrast** *the structures and functions of familiar sugars and starches.*

1. Arrange these carbohydrates from smallest to largest.
   glycogen   glucose   sucrose   deoxyribose
2. State the two monosaccharides that are linked to form sucrose.
3. Distinguish between the plant polysaccharides cellulose and starch.
4. State the empirical formula for carbohydrates.
5. How does chitin differ in chemical structure from other carbohydrates?
6. Distinguish between glycogen and starch.
7. Explain how energy is obtained from polysaccharides.

B. Objective: **Describe** *the chemical properties that lipids share and* **distinguish** *them from carbohydrates, proteins, and nucleic acids.*

8. State how the number and location of double bonds in the fatty acid chains of triglycerides affect human health.
9. Cite five ways that lipids are useful.
10. A label on a plant-based food reads "no cholesterol." How is this an attempt to deceive a consumer?
11. Distinguish between a monounsaturated fat and a polyunsaturated fat.
12. Cite a chemical reason why a diet containing lots of fatty foods leads to weight gain.

C. Objective: **Relate** *the chemical structures of proteins and nucleic acids to their ability to encode information.*

13. Identify which part of an amino acid distinguishes the 20 types and which part of a nucleotide distinguishes the 4 types.
14. Cite a reason for making an RNA copy of a gene.
15. Explain how organisms can contain millions of different proteins, if there are only 20 types of amino-acid building blocks.
16. How are hydrogen bonds important to the shapes of proteins and nucleic acids?
17. Name the parts of two adjacent amino acids that are bonded to form a part of a protein.
18. Hypothesize what might happen to a DNA molecule if bases paired at random.
19. A section of a gene has the sequence ATCGCGTACGGA. What is the sequence of RNA made from this DNA? How many amino acids does that RNA encode?
20. Arrange the following from smallest to largest. polypeptide   dipeptide   amino acid

D. Objective: **Discuss** *the chemical attractions that provide a molecule's three-dimensional shape, and* **explain** *why maintaining this shape is important to the molecule's function.*

21. How does a hormone transmit information to its target cell?
22. Explain how a protein's amino acid sequence determines its conformation.
23. Cite two ways that conformation is important in immune-system function.
24. How would abnormally shaped insulin receptors on a muscle or liver cell cause diabetes mellitus?
25. A pregnancy test consists of an antibody molecule bonded to a detectable dye molecule. The antibody is specific for human chorionic gonadotropin, a hormone made by the embryo that appears in a pregnant woman's urine and blood. Explain how the test works.

THE CHEMISTRY OF LIFE **801**

■ Writing chemical equations: 43

Boxed numbers indicate questions that involve skills in interpretation, application, and analysis.

26. Identify a common chemical phenomenon in the mechanisms of action of the following.
    a. enzymes
    b. antibodies

THE ENERGY OF LIFE

E. Objective: **Explain** *how plants receive solar energy and convert it into chemical energy.*

27. What is the source of the carbon in the products of photosynthesis?
28. Describe the events in photosystems I and II.
29. Why do potatoes, which grow underground, stop accumulating starch when potato beetles chew off the plant's leaves?
30. Identify the source of the oxygen emitted in photosynthesis.
31. In photosynthesis, how is the electron that is excited in photosystem II replaced?
32. List the products of the light reactions of photosynthesis.

F. Objective: **Describe** *the chemical reactions that extract energy from the bonds of glucose.*

33. Describe a situation in which your muscle cells might undergo anaerobic respiration.
34. Account for the 36 ATP molecules formed by breaking down one glucose molecule.
35. Name a chemical event that occurred several billion years ago and was necessary for aerobic respiration to evolve.
36. Explain why extracting energy from one glucose molecule requires two turns of the citric acid cycle.
37. At what point in the reactions of metabolism is the energy in NADH used to form ATP?

BIOCHEMICAL BALANCE

G. Objective: **Explain** *the importance of maintaining characteristic concentrations of specific biochemicals in body compartments.*

38. How can an eating disorder such as bulimia have such a drastic effect as stopping the heart?
39. Distinguish between concentrations of K^+, HPO_4^{2-}, and Na^+ inside and outside cells.
40. Is it healthier to eat one big carbohydrate-rich meal a day or to have small portions of carbohydrates several times a day? Cite a reason for your answer.
41. Why do some people with diabetes mellitus need to inject insulin? What can happen if they inject too much?
42. A biker nears the end of a race. He has long since used up the sugar supplied by a fruit drink shortly before the start of the race. His leg muscles call on stored energy by breaking down glycogen. What biochemical compound assists in this process?

H. Objective: **Identify** *ways that the human body maintains the pH of body fluids and* **explain** *why this is important.*

43. Excess stomach acid causes the sharp pain of a sour stomach. Describe how an acid-base buffer system might prevent this problem.
44. Name two types of biological molecules that can only function within a narrow pH range.
45. After a two-day stomach virus that caused frequent vomiting, a person feels exhausted and isn't sure where he is. His breathing becomes labored. His doctor orders a blood test. What is the doctor looking for?
46. Distinguish between the blood pH associated with acidosis and alkalosis.
47. Why is the enzyme carbonic anhydrase essential to life?

I. Objective: **Describe** *the effects on health of rapid changes in pressure.*

48. Explain how resurfacing rapidly causes decompression sickness.
49. A runner accustomed to exercising at sea level vacations in Denver, Colorado, an area

considerably above sea level. Why is she un-characteristically exhausted while exercising?

50. Explain why heart rate and breathing speed up as one ascends above 3000 meters.

Critical Thinking

SYNTHESIS WITHIN THE CHAPTER

51. What type of monosaccharide is blood sugar? Draw its structure.

52. A serving of vegetable soup has 2 grams of protein, 14 grams of carbohydrate, and 2 grams of fat. How many kilocalories does it contain?

53. Would you expect an inherited disease to involve an altered structure of a carbohydrate, protein, or lipid directly? Cite a reason for your answer.

54. On the first day of track practice, a young athlete runs 400 meters in a very fast time. Afterward his muscles ache because of lactic acid accumulation. Describe two ways that the body can raise the pH in the muscle cells to its normal level.

55. Discuss how each disorder listed reflects a biochemical imbalance.
    a. bulimia
    b. diabetes mellitus
    c. hypoglycemia

56. Compare and contrast insulin and glucagon.

SYNTHESIS ACROSS CHAPTERS

57. What types of chemical bonds are important in maintaining the three-dimensional structure of DNA?

58. Explain how electrons are involved in biological energy transfers.

59. Suggest a reason why the frequency of light flashes of a firefly decreases on an unusually cold summer evening.

60. Describe some ways that changing temperature and pressure can affect biochemical molecules and their roles in an organism.

Projects

61. Eat a meal in which you can easily identify how many grams of fat, protein, and carbohydrate are present. Then calculate the number of kilocalories in the meal.

62. Look up the times recorded for specific events of interest to you at several Olympics. Record the elevations of the cities in which the Olympics were held. Is there a trend between athletic performance and elevation? Try to include the 1968 Olympics, which were held in Mexico City.

Research and Writing

63. How are the proportions of compounds in bone altered in the diseases rickets, osteoporosis, and osteogenesis imperfecta?

64. How does the body maintain a very low pH in the stomach without damaging other digestive organs?

65. Discuss the reasoning behind carbohydrate loading, the practice of eating lots of carbohydrates the day before a strenuous athletic event.

66. For the following common inherited diseases, indicate the protein involved, state how it is abnormal, and suggest how this problem leads to the symptoms of the particular illness.
    a. Duchenne's muscular dystrophy
    b. hemophilia
    c. cystic fibrosis
    d. phenylketonuria
    e. Tay-Sachs disease
    f. sickle-cell anemia

67. One theory of how the dinosaurs died out is that a meteorite impact caused a great dust cloud to block the sun for many years. How might this have caused mass extinctions?

68. Find out how luciferase has been used in genetic engineering.

Review ANSWERS

☐ Boxed numbers indicate questions that involve skills in interpretation, application, and analysis.

1. deoxyribose, glucose, sucrose, glycogen

2. glucose and fructose

3. Both are made of long chains of glucose, but the glucose molecules are linked in different ways.
   Our enzymes can digest starch but not cellulose.

4. CH_2O

5. chitin contains nitrogen

6. Glycogen, or animal starch, is more highly branched than plant starch and is stored in muscles and in the liver.

7. Energy is obtained from the breaking apart of polysaccharides to form glucose, and the oxidation of glucose to produce carbon dioxide and water.

8. Fatty acid chains containing more than one double bond are called polyunsaturated. Unsaturated fats are less likely to cause high blood cholesterol.

9. Lipids are useful for energy, insulation, cushioning, constructing cell membranes, and carrying vitamins.

10. No plant-based foods contain cholesterol. The label implies the food was specially prepared to contain no cholesterol.

11. A monounsaturated fat has one double bond, while a polyunsaturated fat has two or more double bonds.

12. Compared to proteins, fats contain more than twice as many calories per gram so the extra energy available, if not used, will be stored as fat.

13. The nitrogen-containing base distinguishes nucleotides. The side chain (R) distinguishes amino acids.

distinguishing part

DNA Molecule

14. The RNA carries the code for making a protein molecule.

15. The 20 amino acids can be arranged in billions of different sequences.

16. Hydrogen bonding determines the ways the parts bond together and thus determines their shape.

17. The amino group links to the carboxylic acid group, and the resulting C—N linkage is a peptide bond.

18. DNA would not be replicated and genetic information in DNA would not be transmitted.

19. UAG CGC AUG CCU; 4 amino acids

20. amino acid, dipeptide, polypeptide

21. Hormones act on receptor sites in proteins.

22. The conformation of proteins is determined by interactions, such as hydrogen bonding, between the amino acids. The sequence of amino acids determines which interactions are possible.

23. Conformation allows for the recognition of a foreign substance and helps trap and destroy it.

24. The misshapen insulin would not fit on the receptor so glucose could not enter the cells. Blood glucose remains high.

25. If the woman is pregnant, her urine contains gonadotropin, which fits the shape of an antibody molecule. An attached dye molecule changes color to indicate pregnancy.

26. A specific conformation correct for the needed function

27. carbon dioxide

28. In photosystem II, light energy is transmitted to chlorophyll a. An electron from chlorophyll a is passed down an electron transport chain and ends up at a lower energy. The energy evolved is used to form ATP. A similar sequence of events occurs in photosystem I, except this time energy is stored as NADPH.

29. Without the leaves, chlorophyll is not available for photosynthesis I and II.

30. water

31. by splitting water
    $2H_2O \rightarrow 4H^+ + O_2 + 4e^-$

32. ATP, NADPH, oxygen, and high energy electrons

33. Strenuous exercise uses oxygen faster than it can be transported to the cells.

34. See Table 23–2.

35. production of oxygen in the atmosphere

36. Each glucose molecule forms two molecules of pyruvic acid.

37. at the end of the electron transport chain, the final step

38. The delicate balance of pH and electrolytes can be upset and cause the heart to stop.

39. Concentrations of K^+ and HPO_4^{2-} are high within cells; the concentration of Na^+ is high in extracellular spaces.

40. Eating several small portions is preferable since it decreases the wide swings of sugar and insulin levels.

41. Their pancreas produces too little insulin. Too much insulin can cause insulin shock, resulting in dizziness, loss of consciousness and death.

42. The hormone glucagon stimulates the breakdown of glycogen.

43. Bicarbonate ions combine with the excess acid to form carbonic acid, which decomposes to carbon dioxide and water.

44. hormones and nervous system messengers

45. Symptoms suggest that the blood pH is low (acidosis).

46. Acidosis is between 7.0 and 7.3; alkalosis is between 7.5 and 7.8.

47. This enzyme catalyzes the conversion of CO_2, from tissues, into H_2CO_3.

48. At high pressures, nitrogen gas dissolves in the blood. As the pressure decreases during resurfacing, the nitrogen gas comes out of solution. If this happens too rapidly, the bubbles of gas block arteries, causing dizziness, fainting, or death.

49. The concentration of oxygen is much lower so she exhausts the available oxygen quickly. Anaerobic respiration occurs, producing lactic acid. This causes fatigue.

50. The lower concentration of oxygen results in increased heart and breathing rates to compensate.

51. glucose

52. 2 g protein at 4 kcal/g + 14 g carbohydrate at 4 kcal/g + 2 g fat at 9 kcal/g = 82 kcal.

53. protein; DNA is the genetic material, and it carries the code for making protein molecules.

54. buffering with phosphate or carbonate ions

55. **a.** Poor diet and vomiting cause an imbalance in electrolyte concentrations.

b. Insufficient insulin is produced, resulting in inadequate metabolism of glucose.

c. Overproduction of insulin causes low blood sugar.

56. Insulin and glucagon have opposite effects. Insulin triggers the lowering of the blood glucose level. Glucagon signals liver cells to break down glycogen, releasing glucose into the blood.

57. hydrogen bonds

58. Electrons are transported through the energy cycle like water in a "bucket brigade."

59. Lower temperature decreases the reaction rate.

60. A great change in pressure or temperature affects many metabolic reactions and may cause fatigue, shortness of breath, nausea, dizziness, headaches, vomiting, and hallucinations. Changes in body temperature (for example, hypo- or hyperthermia) can affect the activity of enzymes and, therefore, alter the rate of the body's metabolic reactions.

Science
Technology &
Society

CHEMICAL PERSPECTIVES

Critical Thinking Skills

These skills are applied in the feature.

- Evaluating an opinion or point of view
- Using library sources
- Distinguishing between fact and opinion
- Identifying valid/invalid interpretations
- Devising multiple solutions/interpretations
- Making an informed decision

FOCUS

Activate Prior Knowledge

Ask students to compare what they have learned in school health or biology classes about drugs and alcohol with what they have heard or seen from SADD (Students Against Drunk Driving) or MADD (Mothers Against Drunk Driving). If possible, have students bring in materials from these sources.

TEACH

Science Background

The amount of alcohol a person drinks is usually represented as a percentage of blood, or blood alcohol content (BAC).

BAC	Effect
.01–.04%	mild judgment/memory impairment
.05–.08%	clumsy movement, slowed reaction time
.08–.10%	poor judgment and balance, blurred vision; considered intoxicated (DWI) in most states
.10–.15%	poorer judgment; speech, hearing, balance altered; decrease in sense of pain
.15–.20%	mental confusion, lack of motor control
.20–.30%	confused or dazed, may be unconscious, severely impaired
.30+%	unconscious, possible coma or death
.40–.50%	death likely from respiratory arrest

A Test You Cannot Afford to Fail

A man gets up, gets dressed, eats breakfast, and takes the morning commuter train to work—the same train he takes to work every day. While he is reading his morning paper and thinking about the day's activities, the train suddenly misses a track connection, jumps the track, and crashes into an oncoming train. Forty people are killed, and hundreds, including this man, are seriously injured. Upon examination, substantial amounts of cocaine and alcohol are found to have been recently ingested by the train operator.

Cocaine, an organic molecule that affects the biochemistry of the brain, is a stimulant to the central nervous system. The effects from cocaine vary from feelings of euphoria to death. Excessive doses may cause seizures and death from respiratory failure, heart failure, a cerebral hemorrhage, or a stroke. No dose of cocaine is safe. Even a small dose causes the heart to beat too fast and too powerfully, and eventually to tire. In addition, prolonged use of this drug can produce disrupted eating and sleeping habits, irritability, disturbed concentration, and drug addiction.

One way to determine if an accident may be drug related is to test for the presence of particular drugs. Enzymes in the blood and liver metabolize, or break down, cocaine molecules and yield products called metabolites. While the body seems to rid itself of cocaine molecules within a few hours, the metabolites remain in the urine for many hours or even days. Occasionally, these tests are not accurate. Using gas

Chemical Update

A portable, consumer BAC breath-tester is being marketed to individuals already convicted of DUI or DWI. Some groups are concerned that the device will allow people to drink up to the limit instead of avoiding drinking and driving.

The issue of mandatory drug testing remains controversial, since it pits concerns for public safety against the rights of an individual.

chromatography/mass spectrometry for testing is more reliable, but more expensive.

What about alcohol use on the job? It is not possible to test for excessive alcohol use prior to employment because alcohol disappears from the bloodstream by the following day. Yet alcoholism can be a cause of poor job performance and has been implicated in many accidents involving losses of lives, injuries, and environmental damage.

How can tragic, drug-related accidents be avoided? One way is to require *mandatory* drug testing of people who are involved with public safety. If this requirement was implemented, applicants for these jobs would be tested before they were hired as well as periodically on the job.

Some say that drug testing is a violation of a worker's civil rights. Freedom from unreasonable search and seizure is guaranteed by the United States Constitution's Fourth Amendment, which is part of the Bill of Rights. People also claim that a worker's right to privacy is violated. Others say that a company shouldn't have to hire anyone who has drug

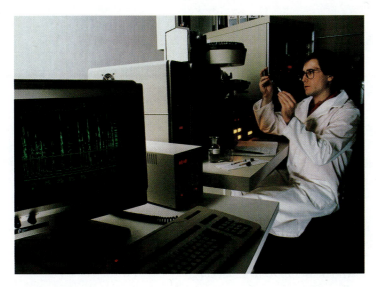

The gas chromatography/mass spectrometry test results are reliable, but expensive.

problems, because studies indicate that those people tend to make more mistakes and are absent more frequently than the average worker.

The courts have upheld mandatory drug testing in many cases, particularly where public safety is involved. The question of civil rights remains sensitive for many people. At the same time, there is also deep concern for the public's right to safety.

Discussing the Issues

1. Do you think there should be random testing for drug or alcohol use on the job? What occupations should be involved in mandatory testing? What about errors in test results?
2. Is an individual's civil rights a greater or lesser need than the public's right to safety? Will relinquishing an individual's rights on this issue jeopardize individual rights in the future?

Take Action

1. Find out which jobs in your community require drug and alcohol testing as a condition of employment. Write a letter to a local paper either supporting or rejecting this program.
2. Take a poll on this issue in your school. Then help organize a campaign that represents the school's position to present to the community. You may want to write to state officials also.

Teaching Strategy

Contact a personnel director of a business or government agency where mandatory drug testing is a condition of employment. Find out and share with students: 1) why the policy was necessary, 2) what happens when an employee fails a drug test, 3) how employees reacted to the policy, and 4) how much drug testing costs the company.

Demonstration

Have a law enforcement officer demonstrate a Breathalyzer. Include a discussion of what BAC constitutes DUI and DWI and possible penalties for being convicted of either. Find out how other possible intoxicants are tested for.

*C*lose

Discussing the Issues

These questions enable students to practice their research skills. Students should read the entire Bill of Rights, not just the 4th Amendment.

1. Answers will vary. Students should consider dangers, risks, and costs of drug-impaired employees; the cost of drug testing; and potential damage to employees from false-positive tests.
2. Answers will vary. Students should consider best- and worst-case scenarios of a) accidents or damage due to drugs and alcohol and b) enforcement of drug testing and violation of medical privacy.

Take Action

1. Assist students in obtaining information from local employers. Review students' letters before they are submitted to the paper.
2. Help students to focus their poll on only a few issues and to design an unbiased questionnaire for the poll. Obtain clearance from the school administration on any positions to be taken on these issues in the community.

Appendices

Appendix A

SCIENTIFIC NOTATION

Scientists use scientific notation as a convenient and efficient way to express very large and very small values.

For example,
1000 in scientific notation is 1.0×10^3,
which is actually shorthand for
$1 \times 10 \times 10 \times 10$.
The value .001 is written as 1.0×10^{-3}, meaning
$1 \div 10 \div 10 \div 10$.
As you can see from these examples, positive exponents are used for numbers larger than 1, and negative exponents are used for numbers less than 1.

To convert a number to scientific notation, move the decimal point until there is only one nonzero digit to the left of it. Each place the decimal point is moved involves a power of 10, which is represented by the exponent. For each place the decimal point is moved to the *left*, the exponent is *increased* by one; for each place the decimal point is moved to the *right*, the exponent is *decreased* by one.

$$5280 = 5.280 \times 10^3$$
$$0.0899 = 8.99 \times 10^{-2}$$

Mathematical operations involving numbers expressed in scientific notation are carried out as follows.

Multiplication The base numbers are multiplied and the exponents are added algebraically. Convert the answer to correct scientific notation if necessary.

$(4.0 \times 10^3)(2.0 \times 10^5)$
$$= (4.0 \times 2.0) \times 10^{3+5}$$
$$= 8.0 \times 10^8$$

$(6.0 \times 10^6)(2.0 \times 10^{-2})$
$$= (6.0 \times 2.0) \times 10^{6+(-2)}$$
$$= 12 \times 10^4$$
$$= 1.2 \times 10^5$$

Division The base numbers are divided and the exponents are subtracted algebraically. Make sure that the answer is in correct scientific notation.

$$\frac{1.06 \times 10^4}{2.0 \times 10^{-2}} = \frac{1.06 \times 10^{4-(-2)}}{2.0}$$
$$= 5.3 \times 10^5$$

Addition or Subtraction Express all numbers with exponents as the same power of 10. Perform the addition or subtraction on the base numbers and then, if necessary, convert the answer to correct scientific notation.

$(7.11 \times 10^4) + (4.0 \times 10^4)$
$$= (7.11 \times 10^4) + (0.40 \times 10^3)$$
$$= 7.51 \times 10^3$$

Appendix B   Table of SI Derived Quantities

Quantity	Name	Symbol	Derivation	Expressed in Terms of SI Base Units
area	square meter	m^2	$length \times width$	m^2
volume	cubic meter	m^3	$length \times width \times height$	m^3
speed, velocity	meter per second	m/s	$\dfrac{length}{time}$	m/s
wave number	1 per meter	m^{-1}	$\dfrac{number}{length}$	m^{-1}
density	kilogram per cubic meter	kg/m^3	$\dfrac{mass}{volume}$	kg/m^3
force	newton	N	$\dfrac{length \times mass}{time \times time}$	$kg \cdot m \cdot s^{-2}$
pressure	pascal	Pa	$\dfrac{force}{area}$	$kg \cdot m^{-1} \cdot s^{-2}$ or N/m^2
energy	joule	J	$force \times length$	$kg \cdot m^2 \cdot s^{-2}$ or $N \cdot m$

Appendix C

$$m = \frac{\text{moles of solute}}{\text{kilogram of solvent}}$$

CONCENTRATION OF SOLUTIONS

The following is a summary of several of the different ways that the concentration of a solution may be quantitatively expressed.

Molarity (M)—the number of moles of solute per liter of solution

$$M = \frac{\text{moles of solute}}{\text{liter of solution}}$$

For example, to prepare a 1M solution of sodium hydroxide, place 1 mole (40.0 g) of sodium hydroxide in a flask; then add enough water to bring the volume to 1.00 L. The amount of water added is not a known quantity.

Molality (m)—the number of moles of solute per kilogram of solvent

To prepare a 1m solution of sodium hydroxide, place 1 mole (40.0 g) of sodium hydroxide in a flask; then add *exactly* 1.000 kg (1000 g) of water. The total volume of the solution is not a known quantity.

Normality (N)—the number of equivalents of solute per liter of solution

$$N = \frac{\text{equivalents of solute}}{\text{liter of solution}}$$

One *equivalent* is the amount of acid or base in grams that will supply 1 mole of hydrogen (or hydroxide) ions. To prepare a 1N solution of sulfuric acid, the mass of 1 mole of H_2SO_4, which is 98.0 g, must be divided by 2 because H_2SO_4 provides 2 equivalents per mole. Place 49.0 g of sulfuric acid in a flask and add enough water to bring the volume to 1.00 L. The amount of water added is not a known quantity.

Appendix D   Table of Solubilities of Some Ionic Compounds in Water

Negative Ion	Plus	Positive Ion	Form a Compound Which is
Any negative ion	+	Alkali metal ions (Li^+, Na^+, K^+, Rb^+, or Cs^+)	Soluble, i.e., >0.1 mol/L
Any negative ion	+	Ammonium ion, NH_4^+	Soluble
Nitrate, NO_3^-	+	Any positive ion	Soluble
Acetate, CH_3COO^-	+	Any positive ion except Ag^+ or Hg^+	Soluble
Chlorine, Cl^-, or Bromide, Br^-, or Iodide, I^-	+ +	Ag^+, Pb^{2+}, Hg^{2+}, or Cu^+ Any other positive ion	Not soluble Soluble
Sulfate, SO_4^{2-}	+ +	Ca^{2+}, Sr^{2+}, Ba^{2+}, Ra^{2+}, Ag^+, or Pb^{2+} Any other positive ion	Not Soluble Soluble
Sulfide, S^{2-}	+ + +	Alkali ions or NH_4^+, Be^{2+}, Mg^{2+}, Ca^{2+}, Sr^{2+}, Ba^{2+}, or Ra^{2+} Any other positive ion	Soluble Soluble Not soluble
Hydroxide, OH^-	+ +	Alkali ions or NH_4^+ Any other positive ion	Soluble Not soluble
Phosphate, PO_4^{3-}, or Carbonate, CO_3^{2-}, or Sulfite, SO_3^{2-}	+ +	Alkali ions or NH_4^+ Any other positive ion	Soluble Not soluble

Appendix E
Answers to Concept Checks and Solutions to Practice Problems

Concept Checks — Chapter 1

p.19 Construct a graph of each set of data. If all data points fall exactly on the line or curve, the data would have no uncertainty. Data from measurements would have uncertainties and would not fall exactly along a line.

p.21 A zero amount of pennies would have no mass.

p.26 Chemical changes produce a new kind of matter with different properties. Physical changes often can be reversed to get back the original material. A new kind of matter is not produced.

Practice Problems

6. $? \text{mm} = 2 \cancel{\text{m}} \times \dfrac{1000 \text{ mm}}{1 \cancel{\text{m}}} = 2000 \text{ mm}$

7. $? \text{cm} = 1.3 \cancel{\text{m}} \times \dfrac{100 \text{ cm}}{1 \cancel{\text{m}}} = 130 \text{ cm}$

$\dfrac{130 \cancel{\text{cm}}}{10 \cancel{\text{cm}}} = 13 \text{ sections}$

15. $D = m/V$; $0.8787 \text{ g/cm}^3 = \dfrac{760.0 \text{ g}}{V}$

$V = 864.9 \text{ cm}^3$

16. No. The samples have different densities.

Concept Checks — Chapter 2

p.43 The temperature of a pure substance will remain constant from the time it starts to boil. The temperature of a mixture will gradually rise as some of the liquid boils away. One exception is a mixture of 95.6 percent ethanol and 4.4 percent water, which has a constant boiling point of 78.2°C.

p.46 Since matter is something that has mass and volume, any substance that has a definite composition could be described in terms of a definite mass or volume of the elements of which it is composed. An example is water: the volume of hydrogen gas in water is always twice the volume of oxygen gas; every nine grams of water contains eight grams of oxygen and one gram of hydrogen.

p.57 A systematic method of naming compounds enables you to know exactly the number and kind of elements present in a compound in order to distinguish one substance from another.

Practice Problems

10. silicon carbide
11. carbon disulfide
12. sulfur hexafluoride
19. MgO
20. $AlBr_3$
21. Na_2S
22. K_3N
23. KBr
24. CaO
25. Mg_3N_2
26. $Ca(C_2H_3O_2)_2$
27. Na_3PO_4
28. $Al(OH)_3$
29. $(NH_4)_3PO_4$
30. sodium oxide
31. magnesium hydroxide
32. aluminum nitrate
33. ammonium chloride
34. tin(II) nitrate
35. copper(II) carbonate
36. nickel(II) oxalate
37. chromium(III) oxide

Concept Checks — Chapter 3

p.84 Energy is neither created nor destroyed, although it can be transformed. Kinetic energy is the energy of motion; potential energy is the energy stored in an object. Examples of kinetic energy converted into potential energy include photosynthesis, where through a series of transformations, the energy of sunlight is stored as starch in various parts of plants; the mechanical energy used to wind a spring is stored until released to run a watch or clock; and the energy of water running down a mountainside is stored in a lake behind a dam.

p.87 $2Zn(s) + O_2(g) \rightarrow 2ZnO(s)$

p.91 There must be the same number and kind of product atoms as there are reactant atoms.

p.103 Decomposition: $2LiCl(l) \rightarrow 2Li(l) + Cl_2(g)$

Dissociation: $LiCl(s) \rightarrow Li^+ + Cl^-(aq)$

p.109 Yes. $AgNO_3(aq) + NaBr(aq) \rightarrow AgBr(s) + NaNO_3(aq)$

Practice Problems

1. $Na(s) + H_2O(l) \rightarrow NaOH(aq) + H_2(g)$
   $Na(s) + 2H_2O(l) \rightarrow NaOH(aq) + H_2(g)$
   $2Na(s) + 2H_2O(l) \rightarrow 2NaOH(aq) + H_2(g)$

2. $Mg(s) + N_2(g) \rightarrow Mg_3N_2(s)$
   $3Mg(s) + N_2(g) \rightarrow Mg_3N_2(s)$

11. Yes. $Cu(s) + 2AgNO_3(aq) \rightarrow$
    $Cu(NO_3)_2(aq) + 2Ag(s)$

12. $Ni(s) + MgCl_2(aq) \rightarrow$ N.R.

13. $4Na(s) + O_2(g) \rightarrow 2Na_2O(s)$

14. The container should have a number of tightly packed units consisting of one smaller sphere representing sodium attached to two larger spheres representing oxygen.

Concept Checks   *Chapter 4*

p.127 $? \text{ atoms Cl} = 0.20 \text{ mol PCl}_3 \times \dfrac{3 \text{ mol Cl}}{1 \text{ mol PCl}_3}$

$\times \dfrac{6.02 \times 10^{23} \text{ atoms Cl}}{1 \text{ mol Cl}} = 3.6 \times 10^{23} \text{ atoms Cl}$

Practice Problems

1. $25 \text{ g Ni} \times \dfrac{1 \text{ mol Ni}}{58.7 \text{ g Ni}} = 0.43 \text{ mol Ni}$

2. $2.50 \text{ mol Cu} \times \dfrac{63.6 \text{ g Cu}}{1 \text{ mol Cu}} = 159 \text{ g Cu}$

3.   Na   C   O
   $2(23.0 \text{ g}) + 12.0 \text{ g} + 3(16.0 \text{ g}) = 106.0 \text{ g/mol Na}_2\text{CO}_3$

4.   Al   S   O
   $2(27.0) + 3[32.0 + 12(16.0)]$
   $= 342.0 \text{ g/mol Al}_2(\text{SO}_4)_3$

5.   S   O
   molar mass $SO_3 = 32.0 \text{ g} + 3(16.00 \text{ g}) = 80.0 \text{ g/mol}$

   $1.25 \text{ mol SO}_3 \times \dfrac{80.0 \text{ g SO}_3}{1 \text{ mol SO}_3} = 100.0 \text{ g SO}_3$

6. $350 \text{ g CaCO}_3 \times \dfrac{1 \text{ mol CaCO}_3}{100.1 \text{ g CaCO}_3} = 3.5 \text{ mol CaCO}_3$

7. $700.0 \text{ g C}_{12}\text{H}_4\text{Cl}_4\text{O}_2 \times \dfrac{1 \text{ mol C}_{12}\text{H}_4\text{Cl}_4\text{O}_2}{322.0 \text{ g C}_{12}\text{H}_4\text{Cl}_4\text{O}_2}$
   $= 2.17 \text{ mol C}_{12}\text{H}_4\text{Cl}_4\text{O}_2$

   $2.17 \text{ mol C}_{12}\text{H}_4\text{Cl}_4\text{O}_2$
   $\times \dfrac{6.02 \times 10^{23} \text{ molecules C}_{12}\text{H}_4\text{Cl}_4\text{O}_2}{1 \text{ mol C}_{12}\text{H}_4\text{Cl}_4\text{O}_2}$
   $= 1.31 \times 10^{24} \text{ molecules C}_{12}\text{H}_4\text{Cl}_4\text{O}_2$

8. mass of 1 mole $C_{14}H_{20}N_2SO_4 = 312.1 \text{ g}$
   $250 \text{ mg} = 0.250 \text{ g}$

   $0.250 \text{ g C}_{14}\text{H}_{20}\text{N}_2\text{SO}_4 \times \dfrac{1 \text{ mol C}_{14}\text{H}_{20}\text{N}_2\text{SO}_4}{312.1 \text{ g C}_{14}\text{H}_{20}\text{N}_2\text{SO}_4}$

   $\times \dfrac{6.02 \times 10^{23} \text{ molecules C}_{14}\text{H}_{20}\text{N}_2\text{SO}_4}{1 \text{ mol C}_{14}\text{H}_{20}\text{N}_2\text{SO}_4}$
   $= 4.82 \times 10^{20} \text{ molecules C}_{14}\text{H}_{20}\text{N}_2\text{SO}_4$

24. $? \text{ mol} = 3.5 \text{ L} \times \dfrac{6.5 \text{ mol H}_2\text{SO}_4}{1 \text{ L}} = 23 \text{ mol H}_2\text{SO}_4$

25. $? \text{ mol} = 2.5 \text{ L} \times \dfrac{1.5 \text{ mol NaCl}}{1 \text{ L}} = 3.8 \text{ mol NaCl}$

26. $? \text{ mol} = 3.00 \text{ L} \times \dfrac{1.50 \text{ mol CuSO}_4}{1 \text{ L}}$
    $= 4.50 \text{ mol CuSO}_4$

    $4.50 \text{ mol CuSO}_4 \times \dfrac{159.6 \text{ g CuSO}_4}{1 \text{ mol CuSO}_4}$
    $= 718 \text{ g CuSO}_4$

    718 g $CuSO_4$ needed in a volume of 3.0 L

27. $? \text{ mol} = 2.0 \text{ L} \times \dfrac{1.0 \text{ mol NaOH}}{1 \text{ L}}$
    $= 2.0 \text{ mol NaOH}$

    $2.0 \text{ mol NaOH} \times \dfrac{40.0 \text{ g NaOH}}{1 \text{ mol NaOH}} = 80 \text{ g NaOH}$

    80 g NaOH needed in a volume of 2.0 L

32. $\% \text{Fe} = \dfrac{35.1 \text{ g Fe}}{45.0 \text{ g sample}} \times 100 = 78\% \text{ Fe}$

    $\% \text{Fe} = \dfrac{167.7 \text{ g Fe}}{215.0 \text{ g sample}} \times 100 = 78.0\% \text{ Fe}$

    Same compounds, 78% Fe in each.

33. $\% \text{C} = \dfrac{20.5 \text{ g C}}{75.0 \text{ g sample}} \times 100 = 27.3\% \text{ C}$

    $\% \text{C} = \dfrac{67.5 \text{ g C}}{135.0 \text{ g sample}} \times 100 = 50.0\%$

    Different compounds because % C is different in each.

34. In a 27.0 gram sample, 50% sulfur would be 13.5 g S.

    $27.0 \text{ g} - 13.5 \text{ g S} = 13.5 \text{ g O}$

    $13.5 \text{ g S} \times \dfrac{1 \text{ mol S}}{32.1 \text{ g S}} = 0.420 \text{ mol S}$

    $\dfrac{\text{S}}{\text{O}} = \dfrac{0.420}{0.843} = \dfrac{1}{2} = \text{SO}_2$

    $13.5 \text{ g O} \times \dfrac{1 \text{ mol O}}{16.00 \text{ g O}} = 0.843 \text{ mol O}$

35. In a 78.0 g sample, 60% oxygen would be 46.8 g O.

78.0 − 46.8 g O = 31.2 g S

$$31.2 \text{ g S} \times \frac{1 \text{ mol S}}{32.1 \text{ g S}} = 0.972 \text{ mol S}$$

$$\frac{S}{O} = \frac{0.972}{2.93} = \frac{1}{3.01} = SO_3$$

$$46.8 \text{ g O} \times \frac{1 \text{ mol O}}{16.0 \text{ g O}} = 2.93 \text{ mol O}$$

36. 35.74 g aluminum oxide − 18.94 g aluminum
= 16.80 g oxygen

$$18.94 \text{ g Al} \times \frac{1 \text{ mol Al}}{27.0 \text{ g Al}} = 0.701 \text{ mol Al}$$

$$16.80 \text{ g O} \times \frac{1 \text{ mol O}}{16.0 \text{ g O}} = 1.05 \text{ mol O}$$

$$\frac{Al}{O} = \frac{0.701}{1.05} = \frac{(1)}{(1.5)} \times 2 = \frac{2}{3} \neq Al_2O_3$$

37. 88.06 g propane − 72.06 g carbon = 16.00 g hydrogen

$$72.06 \text{ g C} \times \frac{1 \text{ mol C}}{12.0 \text{ g C}} = 6.01 \text{ mol C}$$

$$16.00 \text{ g H} \times \frac{1 \text{ mol H}}{1.0 \text{ g H}} = 16 \text{ mol H}$$

$$\frac{C}{H} = \frac{6.01}{16.0} = \frac{6}{16} = \frac{3}{8} = C_3H_8$$

38. molar mass P_2O_5 = 142.0 g

$$\frac{283.88 \text{ g/mol}}{142.0 \text{ g/mol}} = 2 = (P_2O_5)_2 = P_4O_{10}$$

39. $28.0 \text{ g N} \times \dfrac{1 \text{ mol N}}{14.0 \text{ g N}} = 2.00 \text{ mol N}$

$$4.0 \text{ g H} \times \frac{1 \text{ mol H}}{1.0 \text{ g H}} = 4.0 \text{ mol H}$$

$$\frac{N}{H} = \frac{2}{4} = \frac{1}{2} = NH_2 \text{ empirical formula}$$

$$\frac{32.0 \text{ g}}{16 \text{ g}} = 2 = (NH_2)_2 = N_2H_4 \text{ molecular formula}$$

Concept Checks   Chapter 5

p.165 See Table 4-1, page 133.

Practice Problems

1. $4Na(s) + O_2(g) \rightarrow 2Na_2O(s)$

$$? \text{ mol } Na_2O = 5.00 \text{ mol Na} \times \frac{2 \text{ mol } Na_2O}{4 \text{ mol Na}}$$

$$= 2.50 \text{ mol } Na_2O$$

2. $4NH_3(g) + 7O_2(g) \rightarrow 4NO_2(g) + 6H_2O(g)$

$$? \text{ mol } O_2 = 1.22 \text{ mol } NH_3 \times \frac{7 \text{ mol } O_2}{4 \text{ mol } NH_3}$$

$$= 2.14 \text{ mol } O_2$$

$$? \text{ mol } NO_2 = 1.22 \text{ mol } NH_3 \times \frac{4 \text{ mol } NO_2}{4 \text{ mol } NH_3}$$

$$= 1.22 \text{ mol } NO_2$$

$$? \text{ mol } H_2O = 1.22 \text{ mol } NH_3 \times \frac{6 \text{ mol } H_2O}{4 \text{ mol } NH_3}$$

$$= 1.83 \text{ mol } H_2O$$

3. $2KClO_3(s) \rightarrow 2KCl(s) + 3O_2(g)$

$$? \text{ } KClO_3 = 1.45 \text{ mol } O_2 \times \frac{2 \text{ mol } KClO_3}{3 \text{ mol } O_2}$$

$$\times \frac{122.6 \text{ g } KClO_3}{1 \text{ mol } KClO_3} = 119 \text{ g } KClO_3$$

4. $Cu(s) + 2AgNO_3(aq) \rightarrow 2Ag(s) + Cu(NO_3)_2(aq)$

$$? \text{ mol } Cu = 5.5 \text{ g Ag} \times \frac{1 \text{ mol Ag}}{107.9 \text{ g Ag}}$$

$$\times \frac{1 \text{ mol Cu}}{2 \text{ mol Ag}} = 0.025 \text{ mol Cu}$$

5. $2Na(s) + Cl_2(g) \rightarrow 2NaCl(s)$

$$? \text{ g } NaCl = 20.4 \text{ g Na} \times \frac{1 \text{ mol Na}}{23.0 \text{ g Na}}$$

$$\times \frac{2 \text{ mol } NaCl}{2 \text{ mol Na}} \times \frac{58.5 \text{ g } NaCl}{1 \text{ mol } NaCl} = 51.9 \text{ g } NaCl$$

6. $CaCO_3(s) \rightarrow CaO(s) + CO_2(g)$

$$10 \text{ kg } CaO \times \frac{1000 \text{ g}}{1 \text{ kg}} = 10\,000 \text{ g } CaO$$

$$? \text{ kg } CaCO_3 = 10\,000 \text{ g } CaO \times \frac{1 \text{ mol } CaO}{56.1 \text{ g } CaO}$$

$$\times \frac{1 \text{ mol } CaCO_3}{1 \text{ mol } CaO} \times \frac{100.1 \text{ g } CaCO_3}{1 \text{ mol } CaCO_3} \times \frac{1 \text{ kg}}{1000 \text{ g}}$$

$$= 17.8 \text{ kg } CaCO_3$$

7. $Cu(s) + 2AgNO_3(aq) \rightarrow Cu(NO_3)_2(aq) + 2Ag(s)$

$$0.208 \text{ L } AgNO_3 \times \frac{0.100 \text{ mol } AgNO_3}{1 \text{ L } AgNO_3}$$

$$\times \frac{2 \text{ mol Ag}}{2 \text{ mol } AgNO_3} \times \frac{107.9 \text{ g Ag}}{1 \text{ mol Ag}} = 2.24 \text{ g Ag}$$

8. $PbCO_3(s) + 2HNO_3(aq) \rightarrow$
$Pb(NO_3)_2(aq) + H_2O(l) + CO_2(g)$

$$0.0275 \text{ L } HNO_3 \times \frac{3.00 \text{ mol } HNO_3}{1 \text{ L } HNO_3}$$

$$\times \frac{1 \text{ mol } Pb(NO_3)_2}{2 \text{ mol } HNO_3} \times \frac{331.2 \text{ g } Pb(NO_3)_2}{1 \text{ mol } Pb(NO_3)_2} = 13.7 \text{ g } Pb(NO_3)_2$$

15. $2Mg(s) + O_2(g) \rightarrow 2MgO(s)$

$$\frac{7.24 \text{ mol Mg}}{3.86 \text{ mol } O_2} = \frac{1.88}{1} \text{ vs } \frac{2}{1}$$

O_2 is in excess.

$$? \text{ mol } O_2 = 7.24 \text{ mol Mg} \times \frac{1 \text{ mol } O_2}{2 \text{ mol Mg}}$$

$$= 3.62 \text{ mol } O_2$$

$3.86 \text{ mol } O_2 - 3.62 \text{ mol } O_2 = 0.24 \text{ mol } O_2$ in excess

16. $2Al(s) + 3I_2(s) \rightarrow 2AlI_3(s)$

$$\frac{0.50 \text{ mol Al}}{0.72 \text{ mol } I_2} = \frac{2 \text{ mol Al}}{2.9 \text{ mol I}}$$

$$? \text{ mol Al} = 0.72 \text{ mol } I_2 \times \frac{2 \text{ mol Al}}{3 \text{ mol } I_2}$$

$$= 0.48 \text{ mol Al}$$

$0.50 \text{ mol Al} - 0.48 \text{ mol Al}$
$= 0.02 \text{ mol Al remaining}$

17. $Zn(s) + Pb(NO_3)_2(aq) \rightarrow Pb(s) + Zn(NO_3)_2(aq)$

$$1.00 \text{ g Zn} \times \frac{1 \text{ mol Zn}}{65.39 \text{ g Zn}} = 0.0153 \text{ mol Zn}$$

$$25 \text{ mL} \times \frac{1 \text{ L}}{1000 \text{ mL}} \times \frac{0.250 \text{ mol Pb(NO}_3)_2}{1 \text{ L}}$$

$$= 0.00625 \text{ mol Pb(NO}_3)_2$$

Zn is in excess, since the molar ratio in the equation is 1:1.

$$0.00625 \text{ mol Pb(NO}_3)_2 \times \frac{1 \text{ mol Pb}}{1 \text{ mol Pb(NO}_3)_2}$$

$$\times \frac{207.2 \text{ g Pb}}{1 \text{ mol Pb}} = 1.3 \text{ g Pb formed}$$

18. $Fe(s) + 2HCl(aq) \rightarrow H_2(g) + FeCl_2(aq)$

$$7.56 \text{ g Fe} \times \frac{1 \text{ mol Fe}}{55.85 \text{ g Fe}} = 0.135 \text{ mol Fe}$$

$$\frac{Fe}{HCl} = \frac{.135 \text{ mol}}{.100 \text{ mol}} = \frac{1 \text{ mol}}{.74 \text{ mol}} \text{ vs } \frac{1}{2}$$

$$.100 \text{ L HCl} \times \frac{1 \text{ mol HCl}}{1 \text{ L HCl}}$$

$$= 0.100 \text{ mol HCl; Fe excess}$$

$$0.100 \text{ mol HCl} \times \frac{1 \text{ mol Fe}}{2 \text{ mol HCl}}$$

$$= 0.050 \text{ mol Fe needed}$$

$0.135 \text{ mol Fe} - 0.050 \text{ mol Fe}$
$= 0.085 \text{ mol Fe in excess}$

$$0.100 \text{ mol HCl} \times \frac{1 \text{ mol H}_2}{2 \text{ mol HCl}} \times \frac{2.0 \text{ g H}_2}{1 \text{ mol H}_2} = 0.100 \text{ g H}_2$$

$$0.100 \text{ mol HCl} \times \frac{1 \text{ mol FeCl}_2}{2 \text{ mol HCl}} \times \frac{126.8 \text{ g FeCl}_2}{1 \text{ mol FeCl}_2}$$

$$= 6.34 \text{ g FeCl}_2$$

19. $Cu(s) + Cl_2(g) \rightarrow CuCl_2(s)$

$$12.5 \text{ g Cu} \times \frac{1 \text{ mol Cu}}{63.5 \text{ g Cu}} \times \frac{1 \text{ mol CuCl}_2}{1 \text{ mol Cu}}$$

$$\times \frac{134.5 \text{ g CuCl}_2}{1 \text{ mol CuCl}_2} = 26.5 \text{ g CuCl}_2$$

$$\text{percent yield} = \frac{25.4 \text{ g CuCl}_2}{26.5 \text{ g CuCl}_2} \times 100 = 95.8\%$$

20. $\dfrac{140.15 \text{ g ZnCl}_2}{143 \text{ g ZnCl}_2} \times 100 = 98.0\%$

Concept Checks   *Chapter 6*

p.197 Ping-Pong balls are analogous to individual gas molecules. The box represents a closed volume. The Ping-Pong balls are free to move randomly around in the box, much as gas molecules behave.

p.215 As the pressure increases, the gas molecules are closer together, and the volume of the syringe containing gas molecules decreases. As one factor increases, the other factor decreases.

Practice Problems

1. $74.5 \text{ cm Hg} \times \dfrac{10 \text{ mm Hg}}{1 \text{ cm Hg}} \times \dfrac{1 \text{ atm}}{760 \text{ mm Hg}}$

$\quad = 0.980 \text{ atm}$

2. $97.5 \text{ kPa} \times \dfrac{0.009869 \text{ atm}}{\text{kPa}} = 0.962 \text{ atm}$

3. $99.4 \text{ kPa} - 4.5 \text{ kPa} = 94.9 \text{ kPa}$

4. $101 \text{ kPa} - 93 \text{ kPa} = 8 \text{ kPa}$

14. $k = \dfrac{V}{T} = \dfrac{2.25 \text{ dm}^3}{298 \text{ K}} = 0.00755 \text{ dm}^3/\text{K}$

$\quad 373 \text{ K} \times \dfrac{0.00755 \text{ dm}^3}{\text{K}} = 2.82 \text{ dm}^3$

15. $k = \dfrac{V}{T} = \dfrac{275 \text{ cm}^3}{273 \text{ K}} = 1.007 \text{ cm}^3/\text{K}$

$\quad 325.0 \text{ cm}^3 \times \dfrac{1 \text{ K}}{1.007 \text{ cm}^3} = 323.0 \text{ K (or 50°C)}$

16. The line on the graph should slope upward, passing through the origin in a straight line, to illustrate a direct relationship between temperature and volume. At 367 K, $V = 560 \text{ cm}^3$.

17. $T_1 = 27°C + 273 = 300$ K

$T_2 = -48°C + 273 = 225$ K

$$\frac{V_1}{T_1} = \frac{V_2}{T_2}$$

$$V_2 = \frac{T_2 \times V_1}{T_1} = 225\,K \times \frac{500 \text{ cm}^3}{300\,K} = 375 \text{ cm}^3$$

18. $P_1V_1 = P_2V_2$

$$V_2 = \frac{P_1V_1}{P_2} = \frac{(1.00 \text{ kPa})(25 \text{ dm}^3)}{(75.0 \text{ kPa})} = 33 \text{ dm}^3$$

19. $P_1V_1 = P_2V_2$

$$P_2 = \frac{P_1V_1}{V_2} = \frac{(98.0 \text{ kPa})(1.00\,L)}{(0.250\,L)} = 392 \text{ kPa}$$

Concept Checks — Chapter 7

p.233 The equation should be rearranged according to which variable is being solved for. If some variables are held constant, they do not have to be used in the calculations. Therefore, rearranging the equation simplifies the work.

p.249 No, before 0 K is approached, the substance as it was cooled would have turned to a liquid or even possibly a solid and therefore, the ideal gas law does not apply.

p.251 Increasing the temperature of a gas increases the speed of the gas molecules, thereby increasing the force. Since pressure is force over a given area, increasing the force increases the pressure.

Practice Problems

1. $n = 0.412$ mol

$T = 289$ K

$V = 3.25$ L

$$P = \frac{nRT}{V}$$

$$= \frac{(0.412 \text{ mol})(0.08206\,L \cdot \text{atm/mol} \cdot K)(289\,K)}{(3.25\,L)}$$

$$= 3.01 \text{ atm} \times \frac{101.325 \text{ kPa}}{\text{atm}}$$

$$= 305 \text{ kPa}$$

2. $V = \dfrac{nRT}{P}$

$$= \frac{(2.5 \text{ mol})(8.315 \text{ dm}^3 \cdot \text{kPa/mol} \cdot K) \times 298\,K}{104.5 \text{ kPa}}$$

$$= 59 \text{ dm}^3 \text{ oxygen}$$

3. $T = \dfrac{PV}{nR} = \dfrac{(100 \text{ kPa})(0.275 \text{ dm}^3)}{(0.0100 \text{ mol})\left(8.315 \dfrac{\text{dm}^3 \cdot \text{kPa}}{\text{mol} \cdot K}\right)}$

$$= 331 \text{ K} - 273 = 58°C$$

4. a. $\dfrac{P_1}{T_1} = \dfrac{nR}{V} = \dfrac{P_2}{T_2}$

constant

$$\frac{P_1}{T_1} = \frac{P_2}{T_2}$$

$$T_2 = \frac{P_2T_1}{P_1} = \frac{(4.0 \text{ atm})(25 + 273) \text{ K}}{(2.5 \text{ atm})} = 477 \text{ K}$$

$477 \text{ K} - 273 = 204°C$

b. $\dfrac{P_1}{n_1} = \dfrac{RT}{V} = \dfrac{P_2}{n_2}$

constant

$$P_2 = \frac{n_2P_1}{n_1} = \frac{(0.75 \text{ mol})(98.0 \text{ kPa})}{(0.50 \text{ mol})} = 147 \text{ kPa}$$

5. a. $NaHCO_3 + HCl \rightarrow CO_2 + H_2O + NaCl$

$$0.50 \text{ g NaHCO}_3 \times \frac{1 \text{ mol NaHCO}_3}{84 \text{ g NaHCO}_3}$$

$$\times \frac{1 \text{ mol CO}_2}{1 \text{ mol NaHCO}_3} = 0.0059 \text{ mol CO}_2$$

$$V = \frac{0.0060 \text{ mol} \times 8.314 \text{ L} \cdot \text{kPa/mol} \cdot K \times 283\,K}{99 \text{ kPa}}$$

$$= 0.14 \text{ L CO}_2$$

b. $3Mg + N_2 \rightarrow Mg_3N_2$

$$5.0 \text{ g Mg} \times \frac{1 \text{ mol Mg}}{24 \text{ g Mg}} \times \frac{1 \text{ mol N}}{3 \text{ mol Mg}}$$

$$= 0.07 \text{ mol N}$$

$V =$

$$\frac{0.07 \text{ mol} \times 8.314 \text{ L} \cdot \text{kPa/mol} \cdot K \times 300\,K}{102 \text{ kPa}}$$

$$= 1.7 \text{ L N}$$

11. $50 \text{ dm}^3 \times \dfrac{1 \text{ mol}}{22.4 \text{ dm}^3} = 2.2$ mol ammonia gas

12. $1.0 \text{ dm}^3 \times \dfrac{1 \text{ mol}}{22.4 \text{ dm}^3} \times \dfrac{28.0 \text{ g}}{1 \text{ mol}}$

$$= 1.25 \text{ g nitrogen}$$

13. $350 \text{ cm}^3 \text{ CH}_4 \times \dfrac{1 \text{ cm}^3 \text{ CO}_2}{1 \text{ cm}^3 \text{ CH}_4} = 350 \text{ cm}^3 \text{ CO}_2$

14. $C_3H_8(g) + 5O_2(g) \rightarrow 3CO_2(g) + 4H_2O(g)$

$$22.5 \text{ dm}^3 \text{ C}_3\text{H}_8 \times \frac{3 \text{ dm}^3 \text{ CO}_2}{1 \text{ dm}^3 \text{ C}_3\text{H}_8}$$

$$= 67.5 \text{ dm}^3 \text{ CO}_2$$

15. $250 \text{ cm}^3 \text{ CO}_2 \times \dfrac{1 \text{ dm}^3 \text{ CO}_2}{1000 \text{ cm}^3 \text{ CO}_2}$

$\times \dfrac{1 \text{ mol CO}_2}{22.4 \text{ dm}^3 \text{ CO}_2} \times \dfrac{1 \text{ mol CaCO}_3}{1 \text{ mol CO}_2}$

$\times \dfrac{100.1 \text{ g CaCO}_3}{1 \text{ mol CaCO}_3} = 1.1 \text{ g CaCO}_3$

16. $2HgO(s) \rightarrow 2Hg(l) + O_2(g)$

$2.00 \text{ dm}^3 \text{ O}_2 \times \dfrac{1 \text{ mol O}_2}{22.4 \text{ dm}^3 \text{ O}_2} \times \dfrac{2 \text{ mol HgO}}{1 \text{ mol O}_2}$

$= 0.179 \text{ mol HgO}$

23. $\dfrac{V_A}{V_B} = \sqrt{\dfrac{m_B}{m_A}}$

$\dfrac{1}{0.71} = \sqrt{\dfrac{m_B}{32.0 \text{ g/mol}}}$

$m_B = 63 \text{ g/mol}$

24. $\dfrac{1}{0.34} = \sqrt{\dfrac{m_B}{2.0 \text{ g/mol}}}$

$m_B = 17 \text{ g/mol}$

Concept Checks *Chapter 8*

p.268 In Thomson's experiments, the cathode-ray beam was always deflected upward towards the positively charged plates. Therefore, he concluded that the particles in the beam must be negative.

p.272 Because of cloudy weather, Becquerel put his uranium-containing photographic plates away in a drawer. Several days later, the plates had images of uranium without having been exposed to sunlight. He concluded that radiation was coming from the uranium itself.

p.279 Silver must lose a proton; it will then have only 46 protons and will become palladium. For the atom to be neutral, an electron must be removed as well so that the number of protons and electrons are the same.

p.281 The atomic number is the number of protons; it determines the identity of the element. The mass number varies because isotopes can have different numbers of neutrons.

Concept Checks *Chapter 9*

p.294 Alpha radiation consists of 2 protons and 2 neutrons. Beta radiation consists of just an electron. Gamma radiation has no mass and no electrical charge.

p.298 No.

p.302 The radioactive daughter nuclide from one decay becomes the parent nuclide of the next decay.

p.307 A transuranium element does not exist in nature, it has been synthesized by scientists and is radioactive. Example: U-238 is changed into Pu-242.

p.313 Adding a neutron makes the nucleus unstable, causing the nucleus to split apart and form two nuclei. This releases energy. The neutrons emitted may be absorbed by other nuclei, causing them to become unstable and emit more neutrons and release more energy. This process repeats itself, releasing a tremendous amount of energy.

Practice Problems

1. $^{226}_{88}\text{Ra} \rightarrow {}^{4}_{2}\text{He} + {}^{222}_{86}\text{Rn}$

2. $^{240}_{94}\text{Pu} \rightarrow {}^{4}_{2}\text{He} + {}^{236}_{92}\text{U}$

3. $^{222}_{86}\text{Rn} \rightarrow {}^{4}_{2}\text{He} + {}^{218}_{84}\text{Po}$

4. $^{222}_{86}\text{Rn} \rightarrow {}^{4}_{2}\text{He} + {}^{218}_{84}\text{Po}$

$E = 5.4 \times 10^8 \text{ kJ} = 5.4 \times 10^{11} \text{ kg m}^2/\text{s}^2$

$E = mc^2$

$5.4 \times 10^{11} \text{ kg m}^2/\text{s}^2 = (3.00 \times 10^8 \text{ m/s})^2(m)$

$m = \dfrac{5.4 \times 10^{11} \text{ kg m}^2/\text{s}^2}{9 \times 10^{16} \text{ m}^2/\text{s}^2} = 0.6 \times 10^{-5} \text{ kg}$

$= 6.0 \times 10^{-6} \text{ kg}$

$6.0 \times 10^{-6} \text{ kg} \times \dfrac{1 \times 10^3 \text{ g}}{1 \text{ kg}} = 6.0 \times 10^{-3} \text{ g}$

$= 0.0060 \text{ g}$

5. $^{14}_{8}\text{O} \rightarrow {}^{0}_{+1}\text{e} + {}^{14}_{7}\text{N}$

mass $^{14}_{8}\text{O} - $ (mass $^{14}_{7}\text{N} + $ mass B^+) = mass loss

$14.0086 \text{ g} - (14.0031 \text{ g} + 0.0005 \text{ g}) = 0.005 \text{ g}$

$0.005 \text{ g} \times \dfrac{1 \text{ kg}}{1000 \text{ g}} = 5.0 \times 10^{-6} \text{ kg}$

$E = mc^2$

$E = (5.0 \times 10^{-6} \text{ kg})(3.00 \times 10^8 \text{ m/s})^2$

$E = 4.5 \times 10^{11} \text{ kg m}^2/\text{s}^2$

$E = 4.5 \times 10^8 \text{ kJ}$

6. 32 days/8 days = 4 $(1/2)^4 = 1/16$

7. 56 days/28 days = 2 $(1/2)^2 = 1/4$

$510 \text{ g} \times \dfrac{1}{4} = 127.5 = 130 \text{ g}$

365 days/28 days = 13 $(1/2)^{13} = \dfrac{1}{8192}$

$510 \text{ g} \times \dfrac{1}{8192} = 0.062 \text{ g}$

Concept Checks — Chapter 10

p.332 Blue light can be described as having a frequency, v, of 6.4×10^{14} hertz or as having a wavelength of 4.7×10^{-7} meters.

p.341 Ionization energy is the amount of energy required to remove a mole of electrons from a mole of gaseous atoms. Hydrogen can absorb definite quantities of energy to move an electron from its ground state to higher energy levels. The maximum quantity of energy is that needed to completely remove an electron from the atom and create a separate ion and electron.

p.349 The symbol n designates the size of the orbital; l designates the shape of the orbital, and m designates the orientation of the orbital around the x, y, and z axes.

Practice Problems

18.

$_{11}$Na

1s	2s	2p	3s
(⇅)	(⇅)	(⇅)(⇅)(⇅)	(↑)

$_{18}$Ar

1s	2s	2p	3s	3p
(⇅)	(⇅)	(⇅)(⇅)(⇅)	(⇅)	(⇅)(⇅)(⇅)

19.

$_{38}$Sr

1s	2s	2p	3s	3p
(⇅)	(⇅)	(⇅)(⇅)(⇅)	(⇅)	(⇅)(⇅)(⇅)

3d	4s	4p	5s
(⇅)(⇅)(⇅)(⇅)(⇅)	(⇅)	(⇅)(⇅)(⇅)	(⇅)

$_{36}$Kr

1s	2s	2p	3s	3p
(⇅)	(⇅)	(⇅)(⇅)(⇅)	(⇅)	(⇅)(⇅)(⇅)

3d	4s	4p
(⇅)(⇅)(⇅)(⇅)(⇅)	(⇅)	(⇅)(⇅)(⇅)

Concept Checks — Chapter 11

p.362 Mendeleev arranged the elements in rows according to increasing atomic mass *and* chemical and physical properties. He saw that in placing the known elements, blank spaces occurred in his arrangement. He was thus able to predict the existence of elements that would fill those spaces.

p.374 $1s^2 2s^2 2p^6 3s^2 3p^6$; Argon

p.380 As you move across a period, the charge on the nucleus increases, thereby increasing the attraction of the nucleus for the valence electrons. This pulls the electrons in closer and reduces the radius of the atom. As you move down a group, the valence electrons are further from the nucleus because they are in orbitals that have increasingly higher principal quantum numbers.

Practice Problems

7. The atomic number of calcium is 20. Calcium has 20 electrons and it has an electron configuration of $1s^2 2s^2 2p^6 3s^2 3p^6 4s^2$. Calcium is a metal, so it is predicted to lose its 2 valence electrons (from the 4s orbital electrons) to give the calcium ion. The charge will be 2^+, and the electron configuration is isoelectronic with argon.

8. Chlorine is element 17. Its electron configuration is $1s^2 2s^2 2p^6 3s^2 3p^5$. It is a nonmetal and will form a chloride ion by gaining one more electron. With one more electron, the chloride ion will have a $1-$ charge and be isoelectronic with argon. Note that it is also isoelectronic with the sulfide ion.

Concept Checks — Chapter 12

p.397 Having low ionization energy, alkali metals readily donate their valence electrons to other atoms. They are so reactive, they are rarely found in an uncombined state.

p.404 Silicon, boron, and arsenic have a nonmetallic crystalline structure. Therefore, electrons are not as free to move around as they are in a metal.

p.408 In order to increase the conductivity of a metalloid such as silicon, impurities such as arsenic are added, providing mobile electrons.

p.409 The equation for photosynthesis is the reverse of the equation for respiration.

p.416 Fluorine is used in the purification of uranium-235. Chlorine is used in the production of chlorinated hydrocarbons, in water purification, and the production of bleaches. Bromine is used in photographic film and pesticides. Iodine is used in photographic film and in a food additive.

Concept Checks — Chapter 13

p.440 A molecule composed of two different elements forming a covalent bond could have a partial positive charge on one end of the molecule and a partial negative charge on the other end as in HCl.

p.447 Electron dot structure shows a bond between atoms as a pair of dots. Structural formulas represent a pair of dots between atoms as a straight line. Double and triple bonds are shown by two and three lines. In a structural formula nonbonded electrons are still shown as dots. Structural formulas are quicker and more convenient to write.

p.455 The lone pair of electrons occupies a larger orbital.

Practice Problems

1. $:\overset{\cdot\cdot}{\underset{\cdot}{I}}\cdot$

2. $:\overset{\cdot\cdot}{\underset{\cdot\cdot}{S}}:$

3. $:\overset{\cdot\cdot}{\underset{\cdot\cdot}{Kr}}:$

4. $Sr + \cdot\overset{\cdot\cdot}{\underset{\cdot\cdot}{O}}\cdot \rightarrow [Sr]^{2+} + [:\overset{\cdot\cdot}{\underset{\cdot\cdot}{O}}:]^{2-} \rightarrow SrO$

5. $\cdot Al + 3:\overset{\cdot\cdot}{\underset{\cdot\cdot}{Cl}}: \rightarrow [Al]^{3+} + 3[:\overset{\cdot\cdot}{\underset{\cdot\cdot}{Cl}}:]^{-} \rightarrow AlCl_3$

6. polar covalent

7. ionic

8. nonpolar covalent

18. $H:\overset{\cdot\cdot}{\underset{\cdot\cdot}{S}}:H$

19. $:\overset{\cdot\cdot}{\underset{\cdot\cdot}{F}}:\overset{}{\underset{:\overset{\cdot\cdot}{\underset{\cdot\cdot}{F}}:}{\overset{:\overset{\cdot\cdot}{F}:}{Si}}}:\overset{\cdot\cdot}{\underset{\cdot\cdot}{F}}:$

20. $H:\overset{\overset{\textstyle H}{\cdot\cdot}}{C}::\overset{\overset{\textstyle H}{\cdot\cdot}}{C}:H$

21. $:C:::O:$

22. $\left[H:\overset{\overset{\textstyle H}{\displaystyle}}{\underset{\underset{\textstyle H}{\displaystyle}}{N}}:H \right]^{+}$

23. $\left[:\overset{\overset{\textstyle :\overset{\cdot\cdot}{O}:}{}}{\underset{\underset{\textstyle :\overset{\cdot\cdot}{O}:}{}}{\overset{\cdot\cdot}{\underset{\cdot\cdot}{O}}:\overset{\cdot\cdot}{\underset{\cdot\cdot}{S}}:\overset{\cdot\cdot}{\underset{\cdot\cdot}{O}}}}: \right]^{2-}$

33. $H-\overset{\cdot\cdot}{\underset{\cdot\cdot}{O}}-\overset{\cdot\cdot}{\underset{\cdot\cdot}{Cl}}:$ bent

34. $:\overset{\cdot\cdot}{\underset{\cdot\cdot}{Cl}}:\overset{\overset{\textstyle :\overset{\cdot\cdot}{Cl}:}{}}{\underset{\underset{\textstyle :\overset{\cdot\cdot}{Cl}:}{}}{C}}:\overset{\cdot\cdot}{\underset{\cdot\cdot}{Cl}}:$ tetrahedral

35. $H-\overset{\cdot\cdot}{\underset{\cdot\cdot}{S}}-H$ polar

36. nonpolar

37. $H:\overset{\cdot\cdot}{\underset{\cdot\cdot}{F}}:$ polar

Concept Checks   *Chapter 14*

p.473 As the strength of the intermolecular forces between molecules increases, the boiling point increases.

p.474 Dipole-dipole forces such as hydrogen bonds must be overcome in polar molecules. Nonpolar molecules lack dipole-dipole forces.

p.479 A liquid will boil when the vapor pressure equals the atmospheric pressure. When the atmospheric pressure

is increased, the vapor pressure must be increased as well. Therefore, a higher temperature is required to reach the boiling point.

p.481 All of the added heat is used to overcome the hydrogen bonds holding the water molecules together.

Concept Checks   *Chapter 15*

p.502 The negatively charged oxygen end of the water molecule is attracted by the positive ion of the solid. Simultaneously, the positively charged hydrogen ends of the water molecule attract the negative ions. This enables water molecules to surround and isolate the ions of the solute.

p.504 Both parts of the solution are compatible. Polar molecules are soluble in polar solvents; nonpolar molecules are soluble in nonpolar solvents.

p.516 Yes, according to the data in Table 15-3 and because $CaCl_2$ produces 3 ions when it dissociates in water, as opposed to NaCl, which produces only 2 ions.

Practice Problems

8. $Pb^{2+}(aq) + 2NO_3^{-}(aq) + 2NH_4^{+}(aq)$
   $+ SO_4^{2-}(aq) \rightarrow PbSO_4(s) + 2NH_4^{+}(aq)$
   $+ 2NO_3^{-}(aq)$
   $Pb^{2+}(aq) + SO_4^{2-}(aq) \rightarrow PbSO_4(s)$

   The spectator ions are NO_3^{-} and NH_4^{+}.

9. $Ba^{2+}(aq) + S^{2-}(aq) + Fe^{2+}(aq)$
   $x + SO_4^{2-}(aq) \rightarrow BaSO_4(s) + FeS(s)$

20. $0.77\,m = \dfrac{0.77\ \text{mol}\ C_6H_{12}O_6}{1\ \text{kg water}}$

   $450\ \cancel{g} \times \dfrac{1\ \text{kg}}{1000\ \cancel{g}} = 0.450\ \text{kg}$

   $0.450\ \cancel{\text{kg } H_2O} \times \dfrac{0.77\ \text{mol}\ C_6H_{12}O_6}{1\ \cancel{\text{kg water}}}$
   $= 0.347\ \text{mol}\ C_6H_{12}O_6$

   $0.347\ \cancel{\text{mol } C_6H_{12}O_6} \times \dfrac{180.0\ \text{g}\ C_6H_{12}O_6}{\cancel{\text{mol } C_6H_{12}O_6}}$
   $= 62.5\ \text{g}\ C_6H_{12}O_6$

21. $0.0050\,m = \dfrac{0.0050\ \text{mol NaCl}}{1\ \text{kg water}}$

   $2.0\ \cancel{\text{kg } H_2O} \times \dfrac{0.0050\ \text{mol NaCl}}{1\ \cancel{\text{kg water}}} = 0.010\ \text{mol NaCl}$

   $0.010\ \cancel{\text{mol NaCl}} \times \dfrac{58.5\ \text{g NaCl}}{1\ \cancel{\text{mol NaCl}}} = 0.58\ \text{g NaCl}$

22. $0.40\ m = \dfrac{0.40\text{ mol BaCl}_2}{1\text{ kg water}}$

$100.0\ \cancel{g} \times \dfrac{1\text{ kg}}{1000\ \cancel{g}} = 0.1000\text{ kg}$

$0.1000\ \cancel{\text{kg H}_2\text{O}} \times \dfrac{0.40\text{ mol BaCl}_2}{1\ \cancel{\text{kg water}}}$

$= 0.04\text{ mol BaCl}_2$

$0.040\ \cancel{\text{mol BaCl}_2} \times \dfrac{208.3\text{ g BaCl}_2}{1\ \cancel{\text{mol BaCl}_2}} = 8.3\text{ g BaCl}_2$

23. $?\text{ kg} = 600.0\ \cancel{\text{mL}} \times \dfrac{1\ \cancel{g}}{1\ \cancel{\text{mL}}} \times \dfrac{1\text{ kg}}{1000\ \cancel{g}}$

$= 0.6000\text{ kg H}_2\text{O}$

$\text{molality} = \dfrac{\text{mol}_{\text{solute}}}{\text{kg}_{\text{solvent}}} = \dfrac{1.55\text{ mol sucrose}}{0.6000\text{ kg H}_2\text{O}}$

$= 2.58\ m$

$\Delta T_b = 0.51\ \dfrac{°C \times \cancel{\text{kg H}_2\text{O}}}{\cancel{\text{mol}_{\text{sucrose}}}} \times \dfrac{2.58\ \cancel{\text{mol sucrose}}}{\cancel{\text{kg H}_2\text{O}}}$

$= 1.3°C$

$100.0°C + 1.3°C = 101.3°C$

24. $120\ \cancel{g} \times \dfrac{1\text{ mol}}{62.1\ \cancel{g}} = 1.9\text{ mol}$

$?\text{ kg} = 500.0\ \cancel{\text{mL}} \times \dfrac{1\ \cancel{g}}{1\ \cancel{\text{mL}}} \times \dfrac{1\text{ kg}}{1000\ \cancel{g}}$

$= 0.5000\text{ kg H}_2\text{O}$

$\text{molality} = \dfrac{\text{mol}_{\text{solute}}}{\text{kg}_{\text{solvent}}} = \dfrac{1.9\text{ mol}}{0.500\text{ kg H}_2\text{O}} = 3.8\ m$

$\Delta T_f = k_f \times m = \dfrac{1.86°C \times \cancel{\text{kg H}_2\text{O}}}{\cancel{\text{mol}_{\text{solute}}}}$

$\times \dfrac{3.8\ \cancel{\text{mol}}}{\cancel{\text{kg H}_2\text{O}}} = 7.1°C$

$0.0°C - 7.1°C = -7.1°C$

25. $120\ \cancel{\text{g NaCl}} \times \dfrac{1\text{ mol NaCl}}{58.5\ \cancel{\text{g NaCl}}} \times \dfrac{1}{1\text{ kg water}} = 2.1\ m$

$2.1\ m \times 2 = 4.2\ m$

$\Delta T_b = k_b \times m$

$= 0.51\ \dfrac{°C \times \cancel{\text{kg H}_2\text{O}}}{\cancel{\text{mol}_{\text{solute}}}} \times \dfrac{4.2\ \cancel{\text{mol}}}{\cancel{\text{kg H}_2\text{O}}} = 2.1°C$

$100.0°C + 2.1°C = 102.1°C$

26. $850.0\ \cancel{\text{mL}} \times \dfrac{1\ \cancel{g}}{1\ \cancel{\text{mL}}} \times \dfrac{1\text{ kg}}{1000\ \cancel{g}} = 0.8500\text{ kg}$

$200.0\ \cancel{\text{g CaCl}_2} \times \dfrac{1\text{ mol CaCl}_2}{111.1\ \cancel{\text{g CaCl}_2}} \times \dfrac{1}{0.8500\text{ kg}}$

$= 2.118\ m$

$2.118\ m \times 3 = 6.354\ m$

$\Delta T_f = 1.86\ \dfrac{°C \times \cancel{\text{kg H}_2\text{O}}}{\cancel{\text{mol}_{\text{solute}}}} \times \dfrac{6.354\ \cancel{\text{mol}_{\text{solute}}}}{\cancel{\text{kg H}_2\text{O}}}$

$= 11.8°C$

$0.0°C - 11.8°C = -11.8°C$

27. $m = \dfrac{\Delta T_f}{k_f}$

$m = \dfrac{.49°C}{1.86°C \times \text{kg/mol}} = 0.26\ m$

$\text{mol}_{\text{solute}} = \dfrac{0.26\text{ mol}_{\text{solute}}}{\cancel{\text{kg water}}} \times \dfrac{0.300\ \cancel{\text{kg water}}}{1}$

$= 0.078\text{ mol}_{\text{solute}}$

$\text{molar mass} = \dfrac{27.3\text{ g}}{0.078\text{ mol}} = 350\text{ g/mol}$

28. CS_2; $\Delta k_b = 2.34$; boiling point = $46.2°C$

$m = \dfrac{\Delta T_b}{k_b} = 47.8°C - 46.2°C$

$= \dfrac{1.6°\cancel{C}}{2.34°\cancel{C} \times \text{kg}_{\text{solvent}}/\text{mol}_{\text{solute}}} = 0.68\ m$

$\text{mol}_{\text{solute}} = \dfrac{0.68\text{ mol}_{\text{solute}}}{\cancel{\text{kg water}}} \times \dfrac{0.100\ \cancel{\text{kg water}}}{1}$

$= 0.068\text{ mol}$

$\text{molar mass} = \dfrac{10.0\text{ g}}{0.068\text{ mol}} = 150\text{ g/mol}$

Concept Checks *Chapter 16*

p.540 As the line slants upward, heat is being absorbed and the temperature of the water increases. When the line is horizontal, the water is changing from a liquid to a gas and the temperature remains constant.

p.547 In an exothermic reaction, the temperature of the system decreases as heat energy is transferred to the surroundings. In an endothermic reaction, the temperature of the surroundings decreases as heat is transferred to the system.

p.557 ΔH is $+$; ΔS is $-$.

Practice Problems

1. heat transferred $= 0.448\ \dfrac{J}{g°C}(7.0\text{ g})(725°C)$

$= 2273.6\text{ J} = 2.3\text{ kJ}$

2. ΔT in $°C = \dfrac{1\text{ g°C }(5750\text{ J})(1)}{0.803\text{ J }455\text{ g}} = 15.7°C$

final temperature $= 24.0°C + 15.7°C$

$= 39.7°C$

3. $1000 \text{ J} = s \times 30 \text{ g} \times 37.2°\text{C}$

$s = \dfrac{1000 \text{ J}}{30 \text{ g} \times 37.2°\text{C}} = 0.896 \dfrac{\text{J}}{\text{g}°\text{C}} = \text{aluminum}$

4. heat transferred $= 15 \text{ g} \times \dfrac{334 \text{ J}}{\text{g}} = 5010 \text{ J} = 5.0 \text{ kJ}$

5. heat transferred $= 15 \text{ g} \times \dfrac{2260 \text{ J}}{\text{g}} = 33\,900 \text{ J}$

$= 34 \text{ kJ}$

6. heat gained water $=$ heat loss metal

$4.18 \dfrac{\text{J}}{\text{g}°\text{C}} \times 25 \text{ g} \times 9.4°\text{C} = 980 \text{ J } H_2O$

$= s_{(metal)}(25 \text{ g})(44.1°\text{C})$

$s_{(metal)} = \dfrac{980 \text{ J}}{(25 \text{ g})(44.1°\text{C})} = \dfrac{0.89 \text{ J}}{\text{g}°\text{C}}$

12. a. $H_2(g) + O_2(g)\ H_2O_2(l) = \Delta H°_f$

$= -187.6 \text{ kJ}$

$H_2(g) + \dfrac{1}{2}O_2(g) \rightarrow H_2O(l)\ \Delta H°_f$

$= -285.8 \text{ kJ}$

$H_2(g) + 2H_2O_2(l) \rightarrow 2H_2O(l)$

$\Delta H° = 2(+187.6) \text{ kJ} + 2(-285.8) \text{ kJ}$

$= -196.4 \text{ kJ}$

b. $C(s) + \dfrac{1}{2}O_2(g) \rightarrow CO(g)\ \Delta H°_f = -110.5 \text{ kJ}$

$CO(g) + \dfrac{1}{2}O_2(g) \rightarrow CO_2(g)\Delta H°_f$

$= -393.5 \text{ kJ}$

$2C(s) + 2O_2(g) \rightarrow 2CO_2(g)$

$\Delta H° = 2(+110.5) \text{ kJ} + 2(-393.5) \text{ kJ}$

$= -566.0 \text{ kJ}$

Concept Checks   *Chapter 17*

p.573 On a reaction-rate graph, an increase in the slope of the line indicates an increase in the reaction rate.

p.574 One can measure changes in the amount of any substance in the reaction mixture and any changes in temperatures. One can also observe any odors being produced. Another method is to take a sample periodically during the reaction and add a chemical that reacts with the product of the reaction. This will give an indication of how much product has been formed at a given time.

p.579 As the temperature increases, the average kinetic energy of the molecules increases. However, not all of the molecules will have the same kinetic energy.

Practice Problems

1. $25 \text{ m} - 0 \text{ m} = 25 \text{ m}$

$\dfrac{25 \text{ m}}{4.0 \text{ s}} = 6.3 \text{ m/s}$ **2.** $\dfrac{150 \text{ m}}{10.0 \text{ s}} = 15.0 \text{ m/s}$

Concept Checks   *Chapter 18*

p.603 The rate at which reactant particles are produced is equal to the rate at which product particles are produced.

p.614 $K_{eq} = [CO_2]$

p.617 $AgBr(s) = Ag^+(aq) + Br^-(aq)$

$K_{sp} = [Ag^+] + [Br^-]$

p.620 The concentration of Fe^{3+} decreases as more $FeSCN^{2+}$ is formed. The concentration of SCN^- increases. The equilibrium constant does not change.

Practice Problems

5. $K_{eq} = 0.018$

6. $\dfrac{[H_2][I_2]}{[HI]^2} = \dfrac{(0.00078)(0.00078)}{(0.0035)^2} = 0.050$

7. $[Ca^{2+}][Co_3^{2-}] = 3.9 \times 10^{-9}$

$[Ca^{2+}](0.50) = 3.9 \times 10^{-9}$

$[Ca^{2+}] = 7.8 \times 10^{-9}$

8. $[Ag^+][Br^-] = 5.0 \times 10^{-13}$ $s = \text{solubility}$

$s^2 = 5.0 \times 10^{-13}$

$s = 7.1 \times 10^{-7} = \text{solubility}$

9. $[Pb^{2+}][SO_4^{2-}] = 1.3 \times 10^{-8}$

$s^2 = 1.3 \times 10^{-8}$

$s = 1.1 \times 10^{-4} \text{ mol/L}$

Concept Checks   *Chapter 19*

p.641 The Brønsted definition of an acid is a substance that donates a H^+ ion (proton). A base accepts an H^+ ion. The Arrhenius definition states that in water solutions acids form hydronium ions (H_3O^+) and bases form hydroxide ions.

p.643 Yes. An acid can be concentrated in terms of molar concentration, yet be weak because it does not ionize completely.

p.644 Two substances that are related to each other by the donating and accepting of a single proton are a conjugate acid-base pair.

p.661 Indicators are one color in the acid form when hydrogen ions are attached. When the indicator molecules donate a proton to a more basic substance, the indicator changes color.

p.663 The relationship is pH + pOH = 14

Practice Problems

13. $CH_3COOH + NaOH \rightarrow CH_3COONa + H_2O$

$11.10 \text{ mL NaOH} \times \dfrac{1 \text{ L}}{1000 \text{ mL}}$

$\times \dfrac{0.748 \text{ mol NaOH}}{1 \text{ L NaOH}} \times \dfrac{1 \text{ mol } CH_3COOH}{1 \text{ mol NaOH}}$

$= 0.008303 \text{ mol } CH_3COOH$

$\dfrac{0.008303 \text{ mol } CH_3COOH}{0.0100 \text{ L}} = 0.830 M$

14. $HA + NaOH \rightarrow NaA + H_2O$

$25.12 \text{ mL NaOH} \times \dfrac{1 \text{ L}}{1000 \text{ mL}}$

$\times \dfrac{0.00105 \text{ mol NaOH}}{1 \text{ L NaOH}} \times \dfrac{1 \text{ mol } HA}{1 \text{ mol NaOH}}$

$= 2.64 \times 10^{-5} \text{ mol } HA$

$\dfrac{2.64 \times 10^{-5} \text{ mol } CH_3COOH}{0.100 \text{ L}}$

$= 2.64 \times 10^{-4} M$

25. $pH = -\log[H_3O^+]$
$= -\log(0.05) = 1.3$

26. a. $pH = -\log(0.1) = 1$
b. $pH = -\log(1.00 \times 10^{-7}) = 7.000$
c. $pH = -\log(2.55 \times 10^{-3}) = 2.593$

27. $[H_3O^+] = \text{antilog}(-pH)$
$= \text{antilog}(-12)$
$= 0.01 M$
$= 1 \times 10^{-2} M$

28. $[H_3O^+] = \text{antilog}(-pH)$
$= \text{antilog}(-13)$
$= 1 \times 10^{-13} M$

Concept Checks — *Chapter 20*

p.683 Mg(s) is the reducing agent; Fe^{2+}(aq) is the oxidizing agent.

p.690 Iron is more easily oxidized than cobalt. In a voltaic cell, iron would be the anode.

p.693 The zinc anode loses mass as the zinc is oxidized because the hydrogen ion is more easily reduced. No, the copper is more easily reduced than hydrogen and will gain electrons.

p.702 Electrolytic cells need an outside source of electricity for the reaction to occur.

Practice Problems

1. $Cr^{3+}(aq) + 3e^- \rightarrow Cr(s)$
$Zn(s) \rightarrow Zn^{2+}(aq) + 2e^-$
$2Cr^{3+}(aq) + 6e^- \rightarrow 2Cr(s)$
$3Zn(s) \rightarrow 3Zn^{2+}(aq) + 6e^-$
$2Cr^{3+}(aq) + 3Zn(s) \rightarrow 2Cr(s) + Zn^{2+}(aq)$

2. $2Fe^{3+}(aq) + 2e^- \rightarrow 2Fe^{2+}(aq)$
$Ni(s) \rightarrow Ni^{2+}(aq) + 2e^-$
$2Fe^{3+}(aq) + Ni(s) \rightarrow 2Fe^{2+} + Ni^{2+}$

3.

Atoms	Total oxidation number	
N	1(?) =	?
3 O	3(−2) =	−6
NO₃	=	−1
(−1) − (−6)	=	+5 N = +5; O = −2

4. Both atoms of hydrogen are neutral with an oxidation number of zero.

5.

Atoms	Total oxidation number	
Mg	1(+2) =	+2
2 Br	2(?) =	?
MgBr₂	=	0
0 − (+2)	= −2	Mg = +2
2(−1)	= −2	Br = −1

12. Yes.

$2Ag^+(aq) + 2e^- \rightarrow 2Ag(s)$ $E° = +0.80$ volts
$Zn(s) \rightarrow Zn^{2+}(aq) + 2e^-$ $E° = +0.76$ volts
$2Ag^+(aq) + Zn(s) \rightarrow 2Ag(s) + Zn^{2+}(aq)$
$E° = +1.56$ volts

13. Yes.

$Zn(s) \rightarrow Zn^{2+}(aq) + 2e^-$ $E° = +0.76$ volts
$Ni^{2+}(aq) + 2e^- \rightarrow Ni$ $E° = -0.25$ volts
$Zn(s) + Ni^{2+}(aq) \rightarrow Zn^{2+} + Ni(s)$
$E° = +0.51$ volts

Concept Checks — *Chapter 21*

p.718 It is often necessary to determine which compounds are soluble and which compounds form precipitates.

p.726 A flowchart helps you form an organized strategy for doing a chemical analysis and also helps you interpret your results.

Practice Problems

1. $Sr^{2+}(aq) + 2 Cl^-(aq) + 2 Li^+(aq) + CO_3^{2-}(aq) \rightarrow SrCO_3(s) + 2 Li^+(aq) + 2 Cl^-(aq)$

   $Sr^{2+}(aq) + CO_3^{2-}(aq) \rightarrow SrCO_3(s)$

2. $Fe^{3+}(aq), NO_3^-(aq), Ca^{3+}(aq), Cl^-(aq)$

   All combinations of these ions are soluble.

3. $Ba^{2+} + 2 Cl^- + Co^{2+} + SO_4^{2-} \rightarrow BaSO_4(s) + Co^{2+} + 2 Cl^-$

$BaSO_4$ is the white precipitate. The product $CoCl_2$ does not form since NH_4Cl and $CoCO_3$ do not react and $NiCl_2$ and $CoCO_3$ also do not react.

4. No, there is not enough information about possible products.

5.

Unknowns	Test Solution	
	NaOH	NH₄I
1	green ppt.	N.R.
2	white ppt.	N.R.
3	white ppt.	yellow ppt.

From Table 21-2, lead nitrate forms both precipitates with unknown 3; barium chloride forms a white precipitate with NaOH and does not react with NH_4I; $NiCl_2$ forms a green precipitate with NaOH and does not react with NH_4I. The solubility table in Appendix D confirms these conclusions.

6. Test the unknown with each of the solutions in Table 21-2. Set up a data table of the results. Safety procedures include wearing safety goggles, gloves and lab apron. Do not inhale any fumes. Dispose of wastes properly and wash hands thoroughly.

7. Test both samples with lead nitrate solution. NH_4I will form a yellow precipitate. Test both samples with HCl. KCO_3 will form bubbles.

19. Add sulfuric acid, H_2SO_4, which precipitates, Ba^{2+}, but not Cu^{2+}. Separate the Cu^{2+} from $BaSO_4(s)$ by centrifuge. Add $NaCO_3(aq)$ to the liquid to precipitate the $CuCO_3(s)$ which is blue.

20.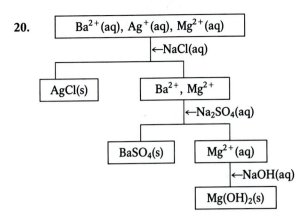

Concept Checks   Chapter 22

p.743 Yes. A saturated hydrocarbon is one that has all single bonds. An unsaturated hydrocarbon contains one or more double bonds. Straight-chain hydrocarbons have all carbons in the backbone along a single chain. Branched-chain hydrocarbons have chains of carbon atoms linked to the backbone chain.

p.751

$$H-C\equiv C-C-C-H \quad \text{1-butyne}$$

2-methyl 1-butyne is not possible.

3-methyl-1-butyne

Isomers for 3-methyl-1-butyne include 1-pentyne and 2-pentyne.

p.758

alcohol   ether   aldehyde

ketone

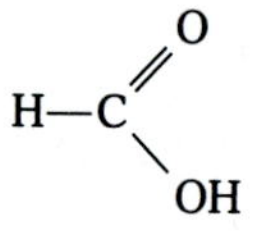

H—C \overset{O}{\underset{OH}{\big|}}

organic acid

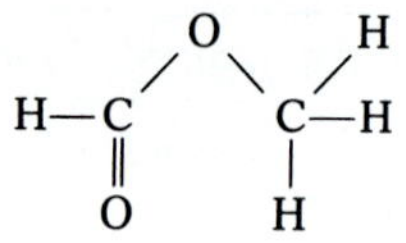

H—C \overset{O}{\underset{O}{\big|}}—C—H (ester)

ester

H—C—N (amine)

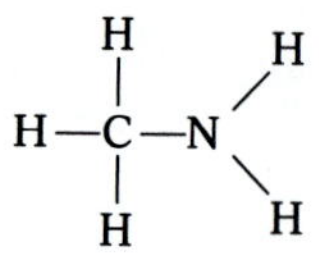

amine

No. Only methanol, methylamine and propanone are the simplest.

p.761 $CH_3CH_2OH \xrightarrow{[O]} CH_3-C\overset{O}{\underset{H}{\big\|}} + H_2O$

$CH_3-C\overset{O}{\underset{H}{\big\|}} \xrightarrow{[O]} CH_3-C\overset{O}{\underset{OH}{\big\|}}$

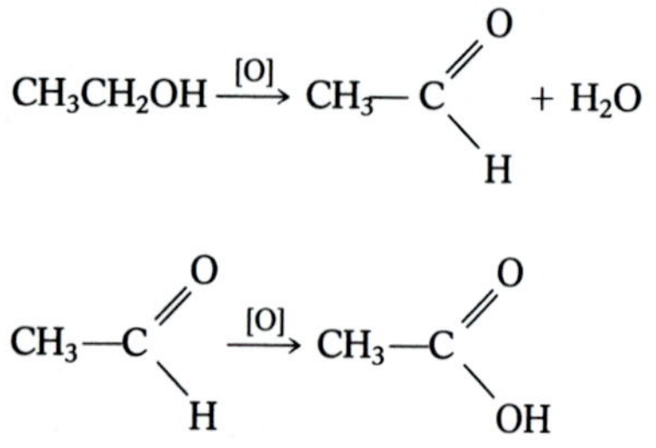

Practice Problems

1. 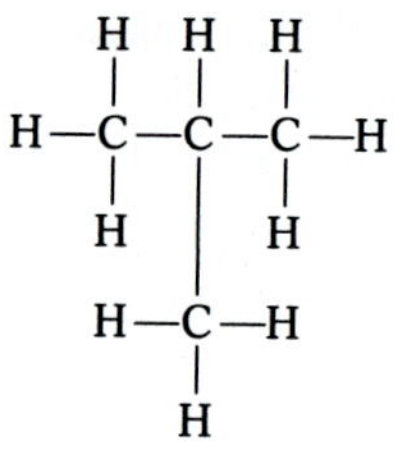 H—C—C—C—H 2-methyl propane 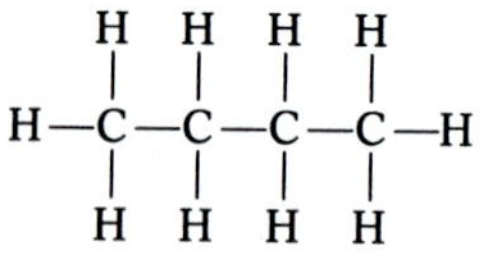
   with H—C—H branch

   H—C—C—C—C—H butane

2. 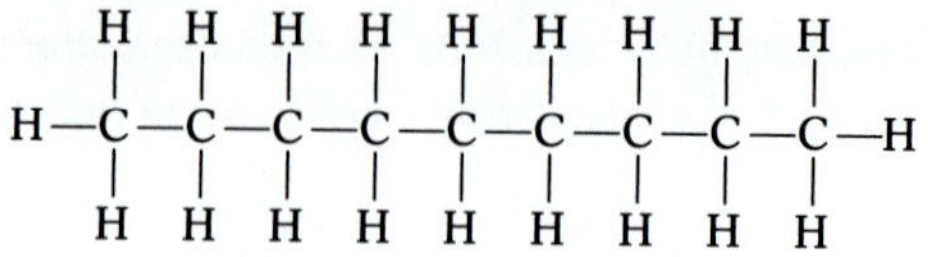 H—C—C—C—C—C—C—C—C—C—H nonane

H—C—C—C—C—C—C—C—C—C—C—H decane

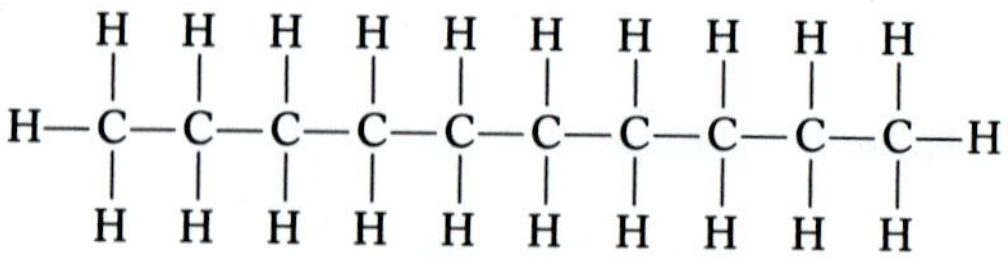

3. **a.** f   **c.** g
       b. h   **d.** e

4. **a.** 2-methyl propane
       b. 2,2-dimethylbutane
       c. 3-ethyl-2 methyl pentane

5. C_nH_{2n+2}; $C_{15} = H_{32}$; $C_{50} = H_{102}$

Concept Checks   *Chapter 23*

p.778 Common functional groups on amino acids allow all types of amino acids to be strung together in any order to form a protein. Functional groups unique to different amino acids allow proteins to be formed with unique and different properties.

p.779 They contain conjugate acid-base pairs. The acid would help neutralize a solution that was too basic, the base would neutralize a solution that was too acidic.

Glossary

A

accuracy agreement between a measured value and a true value; from the Latin *accurare,* meaning "to take care of" (p. 150).

acetyl CoA product formed through aerobic respiration (p. 789).

acid compound capable of donating a H+ ion to a water molecule, a reaction called proton donor; from the Latin *acere* meaning, "to be sour" (p. 638).

acid-base equilibrium condition in which acidic and basic ions in a solution neutralize each other; from the Latin *acere* and *aequi-* + *libra,* meaning "to be sour" and "equal + weight, balance" (p. 607).

acid-dissociation constant constant whose numerical value depends on the equilibrium between the undissociated and dissociated forms of a molecule; from the Latin *acere* + *dis* + *sociare* and *constare,* meaning "to taste sour + apart + to join" and "to stand firm" (p. 663).

activated complex high-energy arrangement of reactant molecules; from the Latin *agere* and *complectere,* meaning "to drive" and "to embrace, comprise" (p. 584).

activation energy minimum amount of energy required for a reaction to occur, also called "threshold energy;" from the Latin *agere* and Greek *energeia,* meaning "to drive" and "activity" (p. 580).

activity series list of elements (e.g. metals) in which each will replace all below it but none above it; from the Latin *agere* and Greek *eirein,* meaning "to drive" and "to string together" (p. 104).

actual yield amount of product obtained in a chemical reaction; from the Latin *agere,* meaning "to drive" (p. 180).

adenine nitrogenous base having a double-ring structure attached to the sugar of each nucelotide in DNA (p. 782).

adenosine triphosphate (ATP) high-energy molecule that recaptures and stores energy (p. 786)

addition reaction in which a carbon compound containing one or more double (or triple) bonds is reacted with another substance in order to open the double bond and add new constituents to the carbon atoms involved; from the Latin *addere,* meaning "to add to" (p. 759).

addition polymerization process in which a polymer is formed by the chain addition of unsaturated monomer molecules with one another without the formation of a byproduct; from the Latin *addere,* meaning "to add to" (p. 761).

aerobic respiration process of organisms extracting energy from the bonds of glucose in the presence of oxygen; from the Greek *bios* and Latin *respirare,* meaning "life" and "to breathe" (p. 789).

alcohol any organic compound containing the OH (hydroxyl) group (p. 756).

aldehyde organic compound in which the carbonyl group is attached to a carbon atom that has at least one hydrogen atom attached to it (p. 756).

alkali metal metal that reacts with water to form an alkaline, or basic solution, listed in Group 1 of the periodic table; from the Latin *metallum,* meaning "mine, metal" (pp. 364, 395).

alkaline earth metal any of the elements in Group 2A of the periodic table; from the Latin *metallum,* meaning "mine, metal" (pp. 365, 397).

alkane one of straight- or unbranched-chain saturated compounds containing only single bonds (p. 743).

alkene hydrocarbons containing at least one double carbon-carbon bond (p. 749).

alkyne hydrocarbon compound that contains a triple carbon-carbon bond (p. 750).

alloy mixture of metals that are melted together and cooled to form a solid; from the Latin *alligare,* "to bind" (p. 404).

alpha emission in nuclear decay, the emission by parent nuclide of an alpha particle; from *alpha,* first letter in Greek alphabet (p. 297).

alpha radiation rapidly moving ions that are positively charged; from *alpha,* first letter in Greek alphabet (p. 272).

anaerobic respiration condition of cells in exhausted muscles, also called lactic acid fermentation; from the Greek *bios* and Latin *respirare,* meaning "life" and "to breathe" (pp. 778–779).

amide organic compound produced from heating an amine with an organic acid (p. 758).

amine organic compound derived from ammonia by replacement of hydrogen by one or more univalent hydrocarbon radicals (p. 758).

amino acid building blocks of all protein, containing both an amine group and an organic acid group; from the Latin *acere,* meaning "to be sour" (p. 762).

ampere SI unit to measure rate of flow of electricity; named after French scientist, André-Marie Ampère (p. 691).

amphiprotic having both acid and base characteristics; from the Greek *amphoteros,* meaning "each of two" (p. 641).

amplitude distance from the crest (or trough) of a wave to an imaginary line between trough and crest; from the Latin *amplificare,* meaning "to enlarge" (p. 331).

anion negative ion; from the Greek *anienai,* meaning "to go up" (p. 269).

anode positive electrode and site of oxidation in voltaic cell; from the Greek *anodos,* meaning "way up" (pp. 260, 690).

area number of squares of a given size needed to cover a surface; from the Latin *arēre,* meaning "piece of level ground" (p. 14).

atmosphere measurement of pressure equivalent to 101.325 kilopascals; from the Greek *atmos* and Latin *sphaera,* meaning "vapor" and "to blow" (pp. 198–199).

atom smallest unit of matter; from the Greek *atomos,* meaning "indivisible" (p. 47).

atomic mass mass of an atom of an element in atomic mass units (amu's) (p. 51).

atomic number   number of protons in an atom of that element (pp. 47, 278).

atomic radius   half of the distance between the nuclei of atoms in a solid crystal; from the Greek *atomos* and Latin *radius,* meaning "indivisible" and "ray" (p. 378).

Avogadro's number   unit used for counting atoms (6.02×10^{23}) named after Italian scientist Amadeo Avogadro (p. 121).

Avogadro's principle   principle that equal volumes of gases at same temperature and pressure contain equal numbers of particles; named after Italian scientist, Amadeo Avogadro (p. 219).

B

background radiation   natural radiation (from Earth, food, etc.); from the Latin *radius,* meaning "ray" (p. 295).

barometer   used to measure atmospheric pressure (p. 197).

base   compound that is a proton acceptor; from the Latin *basis,* meaning "step" (p. 638).

beta emission   in nuclear decay, the emission by parent nuclide of an electron or positron; from *beta,* second letter in Greek alphabet (p. 298).

beta radiation   electrons emitted at very high speed, often approaching the speed of light; from *beta,* second letter in Greek alphabet (p. 272).

binary compound   compound that contains two elements; from the Latin *bini* and *componere,* meaning "by two" and "to put together" (p. 56).

boiling point elevation   property of solutions that describes temperature difference between boiling point of a pure solvent and temperature at which solution begins to boil (p. 515).

bond angle   angle between the bonds connecting the atoms in the molecule (p. 453).

bond energy   energy involved in forming or breaking a bond; from the Greek *energeia,* meaning "activity" (p. 432).

bond length   distance between nuclei of two atoms in formation of a covalent bond (p. 437).

Boyle's law   system used to measure the volume of gas as the pressure on the gas changes; named after Robert Boyle, British scientist (p. 213).

branched   complex hydrocarbons, composed of several carbon chains that cross (p. 742).

bright-line spectrum   several distinct (separate) lines of color present in a gas, each with its own frequency; from the Latin *spectrum,* meaning "appearance" (p. 337).

buffer   solution that resists changes in pH even when acids or bases are added (p. 665).

C

calorie   amount of energy needed to increase the temperature of water one degree Celsius; from the Latin *calor,* meaning "heat" (p. 534).

calorimeter   apparatus used for measuring heat quantities; from the Latin *calor,* meaning "heat" (p. 540).

carbon backbone   longest carbon chain in a hydrocarbon molecule; from the Latin *carbo,* "ember, charcoal" (p. 741).

carboxyl   univalent radical COOH typical of organic acids; from the Latin *carbo* and Greek *oxys,* meaning "ember, charcoal" and "acid" (p. 757).

catalyst   material that speeds up a chemical reaction; from the Greek *katalyein,* meaning "to dissolve" (p. 580).

cathode   negative electrode and site of reduction in a voltaic cell; from the Greek *kathados,* "way down" (pp. 266, 690).

cathode-ray tube (CRT)   vacuum tube used to direct cathode rays on a fluorescent screen; from the Greek *kathados,* meaning "way down" (p. 266).

cation   positive ion; from the Greek katienai, meaning "to go down" (p. 269).

centrifuge   machine used for separating substances by spinning them at high speeds (p. 724).

chain reaction   self-propagating fission reaction (p. 313).

Charles's law   relationship between volume of a gas and its temperature; described by French chemist, Jacques Charles (p. 206).

chemical bond   strong attractive force between atoms or ions in a compound; from the Latin *alchymia,* "alchemy" (p. 431).

chemical change   change that produces a new kind of matter with different properties; from the Latin *alchymia,* meaning "alchemy" (p. 25).

chemical equation   symbolic method of indicating a chemical reaction; from the Latin *alchymia* and *aequare,* meaning "alchemy" and "to equate" (p. 84).

chemical family   term for a group of elements on the periodic table; from the Latin *alchymia,* meaning "alchemy" (p. 364).

chemical reaction   movement of atoms in matter, combining or breaking apart to produce new kinds of matter; from the Latin *alchymia* and *re-* + *agere,* meaning "alchemy and "back + to drive" (p. 80).

citric acid cycle   phase of aerobic respiration consisting of seven reactions beginning with acetyl CoA combining with a 4-carbon compound (p. 789).

classification   system of organizing similar things according to common characteristics; from the Latin *classis,* meaning "class division" (p. 7).

closed system   sealed reaction vessel, not allowing matter to enter or leave after a reaction is started (p. 88).

coal   hard substance produced by pressure and heat on vegetative matter (p. 539).

coefficient   indicator of the number of molecules or formula units that are involved in a reaction; from the Latin *co-* + *efficiens,* meaning "with + efficient" (p. 89).

colligative property   characteristic of a solution that does not depend on size or type of particles present as a solute but only on concentration of the particles, e. g., boiling point elevation and freezing point depression; from the Latin *colligare,* meaning "to tie together" (p. 516).

collision theory   theory stating that the rates of chemical reactions depend upon the collision between reacting particles; from the Latin *collidere* and Greek *thēorein,* meaning "to collide" and "to look at" (p. 576).

combined gas law   derived from the ideal gas law, a convenient equation to solve gas problems; from the Latin *com-* + *binare* and *chaos,* meaning "with + by twos" and "space" (p. 235).

combustion   exothermic reaction (burning) when a substance combines with oxygen; from the Latin *comburere,* meaning "to burn up" (p. 96).

compound   matter that has been broken down by chemical means into more than one element; from the Latin *componere,* meaning "to put with" (p. 45).

concentration   how much (measure) of a substance a solution contains; from the Latin *con-* + *centrum,* meaning "with + center" (p. 136).

condensation   conversion of a gas to a liquid; from the Latin *condensare,* meaning "to make dense" (p. 480).

condensation polymerization   the formation of a polymer accompanied by the elimination of atoms; from the Latin *condensare,* meaning "to condense" (p. 762)

conjugate acid-base pair two substances that are related to each other by donating and accepting a single proton; from the Latin *conjugare* and *acere*, meaning "to unite" and "to be sour" (p. 644).

constant quantity that always has the same value as the slope of a graph line representing the ratio of mass to volume; from the Latin *constare*, meaning "to stand firm" (p. 38).

continuous spectrum rainbow of colors created by white light passing through a narrow slit and prism; from the Latin *continuous*, meaning "continuous" (p. 332).

control rods devices to control the rate of reaction in nuclear reactors (p. 313).

core electrons electrons within an atom except the valence electrons (p. 371).

coulomb SI unit to measure amount of electricity flowing through a wire; named after the French physicist, Charles de Coulomb (p. 690).

covalent bond nonionic chemical bond formed by shared electrons; from the Latin *valēre*, meaning "to be strong" (p. 437).

cracking process used to produce organic molecules containing double-bonded carbon atoms (p. 749).

critical mass minimal amount of material to sustain a chain reaction; from the Greek *kritikos*, meaning "able to judge" (p. 313).

crystal lattice three-dimensional arrangements of cations and anions; from the Greek *krystallos*, meaning "ice" (p. 433).

cytosine nitrogenous base having a single organic ring structure attached to the sugar of each nucleotide in DNA (pp. 782–783).

D

data plural term (sing.—datum) used for the observations and facts collected in science; from the Latin *datum*, meaning "something given" (p. 17).

daughter nuclide new nucleus formed in nuclear decay; from the Latin *nux* + Greek *eidos*, meaning "kernel, nut + form, species" (p. 296).

decay series radioactive decay in which a radioactive daughter nuclide becomes the parent nuclide in the next decay (p. 302).

decomposition chemical change in which a compound breaks down to form two or more simpler substances; from the Latin *de-* + *componere*, meaning "down + put together" (p. 101).

density ratio between the mass and the volume of a substance; from the Latin *densus*, meaning "dense" (p. 21).

deoxyribonucleic acid (DNA) genetic material that directs the functioning of cells and the synthesis of proteins (p. 782).

derivative organic compound in which some or all hydrogen atoms have been replaced by other atoms; from the Latin *derivare*, meaning "to draw off water" (p. 741).

destructive distillation process in which coal is heated in the absence of air producing coke; from the Latin *distillare*, meaning "to drip" (p. 739).

diatomic element element with molecules made of two atoms; from the Latin *elementum*, meaning "element" (p. 47).

diffusion ability of a gas to move from one place to another; from the Latin *diffusus*, meaning "spread out" (p. 252).

dipole bond in which there are two separated, equal but opposite, charges (p. 439).

dipole-dipole force force arising from the electrostatic attraction between the positive end of one dipole and the negative end of an adjacent dipole (p. 473).

disaccharide carbohydrates built of two monosaccharides; from the Greek *di-*, meaning "twice" (p. 773).

dispersion force intermolecular force—when positive end of one momentary molecule is attracted to the negative end of another momentary dipole; from the Latin *dispergere*, meaning "to scatter" (p. 471).

dissociate process of ionic compounds separating from the ionic network; from the Latin *dis-* + *sociare*, meaning "apart + to join" (p. 63).

dissociation separation of a molecule into two or more fragments, producing no new substances; from the Latin *dis-* + *sociare*, meaning "apart + to join" (p. 102).

distillation process used to drive vapor from liquid by heating, from the Latin *distillare*, meaning "to drip" (p. 41).

doped crystal crystal of silicon containing added impurities; from the Greek *krystallos*, meaning "ice" (p. 409).

double bond covalent bond in which four electrons (two pairs) are shared by the bonding atoms (p. 446).

double replacement a reaction in which two compounds react to form two different compounds (p. 106).

dry cell electrochemical cell in which the electrolytes are present as solids or as a paste; from the Latin *cella*, meaning "small room" (p. 699).

E

electrochemical cell chemical system in which oxidation-reduction reaction can occur; from the Greek *elektron* + Latin *alchymia* and *cella*, meaning "amber + alchemy" and "small room" (p. 688).

electrode nonmetalic conductor used to establish electrical contact in a circuit; from the Greek *elektron*, meaning "amber" (p. 265).

electrolysis process whereby an external source of electricity causes nonspontaneous redox reaction to occur and causes a substance to decompose into new matter; from the Greek *elektron*, meaning "amber" (p. 44, 701).

electrolyte chemical compound that when dissolved in certain solutions (usually water) will conduct an electric current; from the Greek *elektron*, meaning "amber" (p. 516).

electromagnetic waves product of a combination of electrical and magnetic fields traveling at the speed of light; from the Greek *elektron*, meaning "amber" (p. 335).

electron elementary particle with negative electric charge; name coined by British physicist, G. J. Stoney, from Greek *elektron*, meaning "amber" (p. 268).

electron configuration procedure for organizing electrons in atoms from orbital with lowest energy to orbital with highest; from the Greek *elektron* and Latin *configuare*, meaning "amber" and "to form from or after" (p. 350).

electron dot symbol system of arranging dots (representing valence electrons) around the symbols of elements; from the Greek *elektron* and *symbolon*, meaning "amber" and "sign" (p. 434).

electron transport chain electrons of chlorophyll a passing to lower energy levels; from the Greek *elektron* and Latin *transportare*, meaning "amber" and "to transport" (p. 787).

electronegativity measure of attraction an atom has for a shared pair of electrons; from the Greek *elektron* + Latin *negare*, meaning "amber + to deny" (p. 439).

electrostatic attraction the attraction between particles of opposite charge; from the Greek *elektron* and the Latin *attrahere*, meaning "amber" and "to draw" (p. 433).

element substances composed of a single type of atom; from the Latin *elementum*, meaning "element" (p. 45).

empirical formula formula that represents the smallest whole-number ratio of types of atoms in a compound; from the Greek *empeiria* and Latin *forma*, meaning "experience" and "form" (p. 144).

endothermic term that indicates heat is absorbed in a chemical reaction; from the Greek *endon + therma*, meaning "within" and "heat" (p. 87).

energy levels the energy state of an atom; from the Greek *energeia*, meaning "activity" (p. 339).

enthalpy change measure of the heat change in a process occurring at constant pressure; from the Greek *en + thalpein*, meaning "in + heat" (p. 545).

entropy measure of disorder; from the Greek *en + trepein*, meaning "in + to turn" (p. 555).

enzymes kind of protein that controls the rate of chemical reactions; from the Greek *enzymos*, meaning "leavened" (p. 582).

equilibrium state in a chemical reaction when velocities in both directions are equal; from the Latin *aequi- + libra*, meaning "equal + weight, balance" (p. 599).

equilibrium concentration state when the concentrations of all reactants in a mixture are constant; from the Latin *aequi- + libra* and *con- + centrum*, meaning "equal + balance" and "with + center" (p. 609).

equilibrium constant constant number used when substituting equilibrium concentrations of the reactants and products of a given reaction into equilibrium expressions; from the Latin *aequi- + libra* and *constare*, meaning "equal + weight, balance" and "to stand" (p. 611).

equilibrium constant expression rule expressed by dividing the product of the equilibrium concentrations of the reactants; from the Latin *aequi- + libra* and *constare* and *exprimere*, meaning "equal + balance" and "to stand" and "to press out" (p. 611).

equilibrium constant for water, K_w constant at a given temperature such as that when a reversible chemical reaction has reached equilibrium, e.g., for water, $K_w = [H_3O^+][OH^-]$; from the Latin *aequi- + libra* and *constare*, meaning "equal + weight, balance" and "to stand firm" (p. 662).

equivalence point point in titration where the amounts of titrant and material being titrated are equivalent chemically; from the Latin *aequi- + valēr*, meaning "equal + to be strong" (p. 648).

ester organic compound produced from a reaction between organic acid and alcohol (p. 758).

esterification process of forming esters from a reaction between organic acids and alcohols (p. 758).

ether highly volatile organic compound; from the Greek *aithein*, meaning "to ignite" (p. 756).

evaporation change from liquid to vapor state; from the Latin *e- + vapor*, meaning "from + vapor, steam" (p. 476).

exothermic term that indicates heat is released in a chemical reaction; from the Greek *exōterikos + thermē*, meaning "external + heat" (p. 87).

F

fission nuclear reaction in which nucleus is broken into two or more smaller nuclei; from the Latin *findere*, meaning "to split" (p. 312).

flame test identification of substances by heating (p. 724).

fluid any substance that flows; from the Latin *fluere*, meaning "to flow" (p. 23).

fluorescent material that glows when it absorbs certain kinds of energy, such as electrons (p. 266).

formula unit smallest whole-number ratio of each element in a compound; from the Latin *forma* and *unus*, meaning "form" and "one" (p. 54).

free energy quantity of relative contributions of enthalpy and entropy in predicting whether or not a reaction will occur under given conditions; from the Greek *energeia*, meaning "activity" (p. 557).

freezing point depression property of solution that describes the temperature difference between the freezing point of a pure solvent and temperature at which a solution begins to freeze (p. 515).

frequency number of waves that pass a point per unit of time; from the Latin *frequens*, meaning "frequent" (p. 329).

functional group organization of bonds that determines specific properties of a molecule; from the Latin *functio*, meaning "performance" (p. 754).

fusion nuclear reaction in which small nuclei join to form larger nuclei; from the Latin *fundere*, meaning "to pour, melt" (p. 314).

G

gamma radiation electomagnetic (nonparticle) energy waves similar to, but more energetic than, X rays; from *gamma*, third letter in Greek alphabet (p. 272).

gas substance that takes the shape of and fills its container; from the Latin *chaos*, meaning "space" (p. 23).

gas phase equilibrium equilibrium relationship between phase (such as vapor, liquid, solid) of a chemical compound; from the Latin *chaos* and Greek *phanein* and Latin *aequi + libra*, meaning "space" and "to show" and "equal + balance" (p. 606).

Gay-Lussac's law principle stating that for all compounds formed, the ratios of the volumes of gases are simple whole numbers; named after French chemist, Louis Gay-Lussac (p. 219).

glycolysis also called sugar splitting, first step in tapping energy from glucose in photosynthesis (p. 788).

Graham's law principle stating that the rate of diffusion of a gas is inversely proportional to the square root of its density; named after Scottish scientist, Thomas Graham (p. 253).

ground state energy level of an atomic nucleus having the least amount of energy (p. 344).

group vertical column on the periodic table identifying a chemical family (p. 364).

guanine nitrogenous base having a double-ring structure attached to the sugar of each nucleotide in DNA (p. 782).

H

half-cell potential contribution to cell voltage made by each half-reaction; from the Latin *cella* and *potens*, meaning "small room" and "power" (p. 693).

half-life time it takes for one half of parent nuclide to decay (p. 300).

half-reaction reaction showing half of a process; from the Latin *re + agere*, meaning "again + to drive" (p. 680).

halogens Group 7A of the periodic table (p. 365).

heat energy that is transferred from one object to another (p. 533).

heat capacity thermal energy required to raise the temperature of one kilogram of a substance one kelvin (p. 487).

heat of fusion quantity of heat needed to cause one gram of a solid to melt into its liquid phase, from the Latin *fundere*, meaning "to pour, melt" (p. 538).

heat of vaporization quantity of heat that must be absorbed to vaporize one gram of a liquid; from the Latin *vapor*, meaning "steam, vapor" (p. 538).

hertz measure of frequency, equal to one cycle per second; named after German physicist, Heinrich Hertz (p. 332).

Hess's Law principle stating that when reactants are converted to products, the enthalpy change is the same, regardless of the number of steps in conversion; named after Swiss chemist, Germaine Henri Hess (p. 551).

heterogeneous mixture mixture in which the parts are still visible; from the Greek *heteros* + *genos*, meaning "another + kind" (p. 500).

homogeneous mixture one in which the components are uniformly mixed and cannot be visually distinguished; from the Greek *homos* + *genos*, meaning "same + kind" (p. 499).

homologous series series of compounds whose members differ by the addition of the same structural unit; from the Greek *homologos*, meaning "agreeing" (p. 744).

hydrated condition in which a charged ion is surrounded by water molecules; from the Greek *hydōr*, meaning "water" (p. 501).

hydrocarbon compound containing only carbon and hydrogen atoms; from the Greek *hydōr* and Latin *carbo*, meaning "water" and "ember, charcoal" (pp. 84, 741).

hydrogen bonding relatively strong intermolecular dipole-dipole force; from the Greek *hydōr*, meaning "water" (p. 474).

hydronium ion result of a hydrogen ion, H^+, donated by an acid combining with water; from the Greek *hydōr* and *ienai*, meaning "water" and "to go" (p. 639).

hydroxyl group functional group -OH, containing one atom of oxygen and one atom of hydrogen and is neutrally or positively charged; from the Greek *hydōr* and *oxys*, meaning "water" and "acid" (p. 756).

hypothesis information assumed to be true (a temporary explanation) when solving a problem; from the Greek *hypotithenai*, meaning "to put under" (p. 7).

I

ideal gas law principle in which four properties are related: amount of gas, volume, temperature, and pressure; from the Greek *idein* and Latin *chaos*, meaning "to see" and "space" (p. 230).

immiscible not capable of being mixed; from the Latin *im-* + *miscere*, meaning "not- + to mix" (p. 504).

indicator substance that is one color in an acid solution and another color in a basic solution; from the Latin *indicare*, meaning "to proclaim" (p. 637).

inference interpretation of an observation; from the Latin *inferre*, meaning "to conclude" (p. 5).

inner transition element any of the lanthanide or actinide subsets of transition metals; from the Latin *transire* and *elementum*, meaning "to go across" and "element" (p. 401).

inner-transition metals lanthanide and actinide elements on periodic table; from the Latin *transire* and *metallum*, meaning "to go across" and "mine, metal" (p. 365).

insulin small protein hormone made of two polypeptide chains held together by disulfide links; from the Latin *insula*, meaning "island" (p. 781).

intermolecular force force of attraction between two or more molecules; from the Latin *inter-* + *moles*, meaning "between + mass" (p. 470).

ion particle that has electrical charge; from the Greek *ienai*, meaning "to go" (p. 48).

ionic bond chemical bond formed by electrostatic attraction between a cation and an anion; from the Greek *ienai*, meaning "to go" (p. 433).

ionic equation representation listing reactants and products as hydrated ions rather than in molecular form; from the Greek *ienai* and Latin *aequus*, meaning "to go" and "equal" (p. 510).

ionization energy amount of energy needed to remove an electron from the gaseous atom; from the Greek *ienai* and *energeia*, meaning "to go" and "activity" (p. 341).

ionizing radiation radiation sufficient to change atoms and molecules into ions; from the Greek *ienai* and Latin *radius*, meaning "to go" and "ray" (p. 294).

isoelectronic having the same electron configuration; from the Greek *isos* and *elektron*, meaning "equal" and "amber" (p. 373).

isotope atoms of the same element that contain different numbers of neutrons, consequently having different atomic masses; from the Greek *isos* and *topos*, meaning "equal" and "place" (p. 280).

J

joule measure of work: force of one newton to move an object one meter requires one joule (of work); named after British physicist James Prescott Joule (p. 83).

junction contact of a p-type semiconductor and an n-type semiconductor, causing current to flow in only one direction; from the Latin *jungere*, meaning "to join" (p. 410)

K

kelvin unit of measurement in the kelvin scale; named after British scientist, William Thomson, Lord Kelvin (p. 208).

kelvin scale temperature scale with zero temperature different from Celsius scale; named after British scientist, William Thomson, Lord Kelvin (p. 208).

ketone organic compound in which the carbonyl group is attached to a carbon atom that is attached to two other carbon atoms (p. 756).

kinetic energy energy of an object because of its motion; from the Greek *kinētos* and *energeia*, meaning "moving" and "activity" (p. 82).

kinetic molecular theory conditions that describe behavior of gas molecules: dimensionless points, characteristic motion, proportionate to temperature of molecules, endure elastic collisions, neither attractive nor repulsive forces; from the Greek *kinētos* and Latin *moles* and Greek *theorein*, meaning "moving" and "mass" and "to look at" (p. 250).

L

law of combining volumes principle stating that whenever gases react under the same conditions of temperature and pressure, the volume ratios of the reactants can be expressed as simple whole numbers (p. 219).

law of conservation of energy principle stating that energy cannot be created or destroyed, but it can change form; from the Latin *conservare* and Greek *energeia*, meaning "to preserve" and "activity" (p. 84).

law of conservation of mass principle stating that mass is neither created nor destroyed in chemical reactions; from the Latin *conservare*, meaning "to preserve" (p. 88).

law of definite composition regularity of makeup of a compound; from the Latin *compositus*, meaning "something put together" (p. 46).

law of multiple proportions fact that explains why two or more compounds can be made with different proportions of the same element (p. 46).

law of partial pressures principle stating that the total pressure of a mixture of gases is equal to the sum of the partial pressures of the individual gases in the mixture (p. 202).

Le Châtelier's principle principle stating that if you do something to disturb a system at equilibrium, the system responds in a way that partially undoes what you have just done; named after French scientist, Henri Louis Le Châtelier (p. 621).

limiting reactant the agent (substance) that controls the quantity of product that can be formed in a chemical reaction; from the Latin *re-* and *agere*, meaning "again" and "to drive" (p. 175).

liquid substance that flows and takes the shape of its container; from the Latin *liquidus*, meaning "fluid" (p. 23).

logarithm power of a number to which ten must be raised to equal that number; from the Greek *log-* + *arithmos*, meaning "word + number" (p. 655).

M

macroscopic observation large views (common observations) of matter; from the Greek *makro* + *skopos*, meaning "long + watcher (view)" (p. 24).

manometer device used to measure the pressure of gases other than the atmosphere; from the Greek *manos*, meaning "sphere" (p. 200).

mass number total number of protons and neutrons in an atom's nucleus (p. 279).

melting term used to describe the change of a solid to a liquid (p. 22).

metal solid, opaque substance, good conductor of heat and electricity; from the Latin *metallum*, meaning "mine, metal" (p. 51).

metallic bonding chemical bonding (holding together) in all metals, the result of loss of valence electrons in metal atoms; from the Latin *metallum*, meaning "mine, metal" (p. 393).

metalloid nonmetallic element (e. g., carbon) that can combine with a metal to form an alloy, often called semiconductors; from the Latin *metallum*, meaning "mine" (p. 53).

miscible capable of being mixed; from the Latin *miscere*, meaning "to mix" (p. 503).

mixture matter that can be separated into component parts; from the Latin *mixtura*, meaning "mixture" (p. 39).

model representation (picture, diagram, idea) intended to convey information about another object or event; from the Latin *modulus*, meaning "small measure of" (p. 7).

moderator substance, such as water, used to slow down movement of neutrons in nuclear reactors; from the Latin *moderare*, meaning "to moderate" (p. 313).

molality number of moles of solute per kilogram of solvent; from the Latin *moles*, meaning "mass" (p. 516).

molar heat of evaporation amount of energy required to change one mole of water from the liquid to gaseous state; from the Latin *moles* and *e-* + *vapor*, meaning "mass" and "from + vapor, steam" (p. 482).

molar heat of fusion energy required to change one mole of ice into one mole of water at 0°C; from the Latin *moles* + *fundere*, meaning "mass" and "to pour, melt" (p. 481).

molar mass mass of one mole of any element; from the Latin *moles*, meaning "mass" (p. 123).

molar volume volume of one mole of gas; from the Latin *moles* and *volumen*, meaning "mass" and "roll, or scroll" (p. 240).

molarity concentration of a solution in moles per liter; from the Latin *moles*, meaning "mass" (p. 139).

mole amount of a substance that contains 6.02×10^{23} particles (Avogadro's number); from the Latin *moles*, meaning "mass" (p. 121).

mole ratio ratio obtained from the coefficients of the combined substances in a balanced equation; from the Latin *moles* and *ratio*, meaning "mass" and "reason" (p. 163).

molecular formula formula for molecular compound, indicating total atoms of each element in a compound; from the Latin *moles* and *forma*, meaning "mass" and "form" (p. 148).

molecule particles made up of more than one atom; from the Latin *moles*, meaning "mass" (p. 47).

monomer simple molecule capable of combining with other molecules and undergoing polymerization; from the Greek *monos*, meaning "single, alone" (p. 761).

monosaccharide smallest carbohydrate, simple sugar; from the Greek *monos*, meaning "single, alone" (p. 773).

monounsaturated fat fatty acid with one carbon-carbon double bond; from the Greek *monos* and Latin *saturare*, meaning "single, alone" and "to saturate" (p. 776).

N

net ionic equation ionic equation without representation of spectator ions; from the Greek *ienai* and Latin *aequus*, meaning "to go" and "equal" (p. 510).

neutralization reactions between an acid and a base; from the Latin *neuter*, meaning "neuter" (p. 647).

neutron particle of the atom with no charge; from the Latin *neuter*, meaning "neuter" (p. 277).

noble gas nonmetal element not generally combinable with other elements; from the Latin *chaos*, "space" (p. 53).

node location on the wave that has an amplitude of zero; from the Latin *nodus*, meaning "knot" (p. 334).

nonionizing radiation radiation not capable of ionizing matter; from the Latin *non-* + Greek *ienai* and Latin *radius*, meaning "not + to go" and "ray" (p. 294).

nonpolar covalent bond bond in which electrons are equally shared by two nuclei; from the Latin *non-* + *polus* and *co-* + *valere*, meaning "not + pole" and "with + to be strong" (p. 439).

nonmetal elements that do not reflect light and are poor conductors of heat and electricity; from the Latin *non-* + *metallus*, meaning "not + mine, metal" (p. 52).

n-type semiconductor semiconductor containing impurities that produce mobile electrons; from the Latin *semi-* and *conducere*, meaning "half + to lead with" (p. 409).

nucleic acid any of various acids (as RNA or DNA) that control the activities of a cell; from the Latin *nux* and *acere*, meaning "kernel, nut" and "to be sour" (p. 782).

nucleotide building block consisting of five-carbon sugar bonded to a phosphate group and nitrogenous base; from the Latin *nux*, meaning "kernel, nut" (p. 782).

nucleus dense, positively charged center of the atom; from the Latin *nux*, meaning "kernel, nut" (p. 273).

nuclide term given to the nucleus of an atom; from the Latin *nux* + Greek *eidos*, meaning "kernel, nut + form, species" (p. 294).

O

octet rule rule based on assumption that atoms form bonds to achieve a noble gas electron configuration; from the Latin, *octo*, meaning "eight" (p. 443).

orbital region in space where there is a high probability of finding an electron; from the Latin *orbita*, meaning "path" (p. 343).

orbital diagrams diagrams that represent electron configurations; from the Latin *orbita*, meaning "path" (p. 352).

organic acid chemical compound with one or more carboxyl radicals; from the Greek *organon* and Latin *acere*, meaning "tool, instrument" and "to be sour" (p. 757).

organic chemistry chemistry of carbon; from the Greek *organon* and Latin *alchymia*, meaning "tool, instrument" and "alchemy" (p. 740).

outermost orbital orbital with highest principal quantum number that is occupied by electrons when writing ground state electron configuration; from the Latin *orbita*, meaning "path" (p. 371).

oxidation process wherein an ion becomes more positively charged (p. 680).

oxidation number real or apparent change an ion has when all bonds are assumed to be ionic (p. 683).

oxidizing agent substance that causes oxidation; from the Latin *agere*, meaning "to drive" (p. 682).

P

parent nuclide initial nucleus in nuclear decay; from the Latin *parens* and *nux* and the Greek *eidos*, meaning "parent" and "kernel, nut" + "form, species" (p. 296).

partial pressure pressure exerted by a gas if it were the only gas in a container; from the Latin *pars* and *pressare*, meaning "part" and "to press" (p. 202).

pascal SI unit to measure pressure; named after Blaise Pascal, French physicist (p. 198).

Pauli exclusion principle principle that states no two electrons can have the same set of four identical quantum numbers; named after Austro-American physicist, Wolfgang Pauli (p. 349).

peptide bond bond linking two amino acids in a molecule (p. 762).

percent composition measure (per one hundred parts) of an element in a compound; from the Latin *per* + *centum* and *componere*, meaning "through + hundred" and "to put together" (p. 143).

percent yield the ratio between the actual yield and the theoretical yield; from the Latin *per* + *centum*, meaning "through + hundred" (p. 180).

period family of elements on the periodic table with closely related properties; from the Greek *periodus*, meaning "period of time" (p. 365).

periodic law principle that the properties of the elements are arranged in increasing order of their atomic numbers; from the Greek *periodus*, meaning "period of time" (p. 362).

periodic trends repetitive nature of properties of elements on the periodic table, e. g., increase or decrease of radii; from the Greek *periodus*, meaning "period of time" (p. 379).

pH log of the hydronium ion concentration (p. 657).

phase changes changes from one state (gas, liquid, solid) to another; from the Greek *phanein*, meaning "to show" (p. 469).

photon packet of light energy (p. 333).

polar covalent bond covalent bond that has a dipole; from the Latin *polus* and *co-* + *valere*, meaning "pole" and "with + to be strong" (p. 439).

polyatomic ion ions composed of several atoms joined with 1-charge; from the Greek *polys* + *atomos* and *ienai*, meaning "full (many) + indivisible" and "to go" (p. 66).

polymer molecule composed of a regularly repeating sequence of molecules (p. 761).

polyprotic acids that can donate more than one proton in a reaction; from the Greek *polys* + *protos*, meaning "full (many) + first" (p. 648).

polysaccharide chains of glucose molecules bonded together; a complex carbohydrate; from the Greek *polys*, meaning "full" (p. 773).

polyunsaturated fat fatty acid with two or more carbon-carbon double bonds; from the Greek *polys* and the Latin *saturare*, meaning "full" and "to saturate" (p. 776).

positron particle with same mass as an electron but with positive charge; from the Latin *positus*, meaning "laid down" (p. 294).

potential energy energy an object has because of its position; from the Latin *potens* and the Greek *energeia*, meaning "power" and "activity" (p. 82).

ppm precision parts-per-million indicating the degree of concentration of a substance in a solution as compared among several measurements of the same quantity (pp. 136, 150).

precipitate insoluble substance formed through a chemical reaction in a solution; from the Latin *praecipitare*, meaning "to throw down" (p. 509).

pressure force exerted over a given area; from the Latin *pressare*, meaning "to press" (p. 195).

principal quantum number number used to describe an electron in an orbital; from the Latin *quantum*, meaning "how much" (p. 344).

probability likelihood of an occurrence; from the Latin *probabilis*, meaning "probable" (p. 343).

product new substance formed as a result of a chemical reaction; from the Latin *producere*, meaning "to lead forward (produce)" (p. 84).

protein polymer molecule consisting of amino acids; from the Greek *prōtos*, meaning "first" (p. 778).

proton positively charged particle found in all atoms; from the Greek *prōtos*, meaning "first" (p. 269).

p-type semiconductor semiconductor with a deficiency of electrons that cause movement of an electron from one atom to another "to fill the hole" of that atom; from the Latin *semi-* + *conducere*, meaning "half + to lead with" (p. 410).

purine double-ring structured nitrogenous base, such as adenine and guanine; from the Latin *purus*, meaning "pure" (p. 782).

pyrimidine nitrogenous base having a single-ring structure, such as thymine and cytosine (p. 783).

Q

quantum mechanics branch of physics that describes the behavior of electrons in terms of energy; from the Latin *quantus*, meaning "how much" (p. 343).

quantity property that can be measured and described by a number and a unit that names the standard used; from the Latin *quantus*, meaning "how much" (p. 9).

R

radiation term used for energy emitted from a source and traveling through space; from the Latin *radius*, meaning "ray" (p. 271).

radioactivity spontaneous emission of radiation from the nucleus of an atom; from the Latin *radius* + *agere*, meaning "ray + to drive" (p. 272).

rate-determining step slowest reaction in a reaction mechanism (p. 587).

reactant substance that is a starting material before a chemical change; from the Latin *re* + *agere*, meaning "again + to drive" (p. 84).

reaction mechanism sequence of steps in chemical reaction; from the Latin *re* + *agere* and the Greek *mēchanē* (p. 587).

reagent test solution used to identify positive and negative ions in a solution; from the Latin *re-* + *agere*, meaning "again + to drive" (p. 725).

redox reaction reaction made up of two half-reactions (one for oxidation and one for reduction); combined word for reduction and oxidation; from the Latin *reducere* and *re-* + *agere*, meaning "to reduce" and "again + to drive" (p. 681).

reducing agent substance that causes reduction; from the Latin *reducere* and *agere*, meaning "to reduce" and "to drive" (p. 682).

reduction process in which an ion becomes less positively charged; from the Latin *reducere*, meaning "to reduce" (p. 680).

rem unit used to measure amount of radiation (p. 295).

representative element element in Groups 1A–8A, known as main groups of periodic table; from the Latin *repraesentare* and *elementum*, "to present again" and "element" (p. 365).

resonance phenomenon in bonding contrary to the octet rule in multiple electron dot structures; from the Latin *resonare*, meaning "to resound" (p. 450).

ribonucleic acid (RNA) genetic material that directs the functioning of cells and the synthesis of proteins (p. 782).

S

salt ionic product resulting from a neutralization reaction; from the Latin *sal*, meaning "salt" (p. 648).

salt bridge concentrated solution of a strong electrolyte, used to prevent buildup of excess positive or negative charges; from the Latin *sal*, meaning "salt" (p. 688).

saturated condition that exists when a solution cannot dissolve any more solute at a given temperature; from the Latin *saturare*, meaning "to saturate" (pp. 504, 742).

saturated fat fatty acid with as many hydrogen atoms as possible and no double bonds; from the Latin *saturare*, meaning "to saturate" (p. 776).

shielding core electrons effect of shielding valence electrons from full charge of the nucleus (p. 380).

SI base units system of measurement used in science based on decimal numbers (pp. 10–11).

significant digits those digits that are certain in a measurement plus the last digit, which is presumed to be uncertain; from the Latin *significare*, meaning "to signify" (p. 151).

single replacement reaction where one element takes the place of another as part of a compound (p. 102).

slope the direction of a line plotted on two axes of a graph (p. 21).

solid substance with a definite volume and shape (rigid); from the Latin *solidus*, meaning "solid or dense" (p. 23).

solubility maximum quantity of a substance that will dissolve in a solvent; from the Latin *solvere*, meaning "to loosen, dissolve" (p. 504).

solubility equilibrium equilibrium that exists between an ionic solid and ions in solution; from the Latin *solvere* and *aequi-* + *libra*, meaning "to loosen, dissolve" and "equal + balance" (p. 616).

solubility product constant equilibrium constant useful for solids and their respective ions in solution; from the Latin *solvere* and *constare*, meaning "to loosen, dissolve" and "to stand" (p. 616).

solute component of a solution in the lesser amount; from the Latin *solvere*, meaning "to loosen, dissolve" (p. 500).

solution mixture that looks uniform throughout and does not scatter light; from the Latin *solvere*, meaning "to loosen" (pp. 40, 499).

solvation process of dissolving a solute in a solvent; from the Latin *solvere*, meaning "to loosen, dissolve" (p. 501).

solvent component of a solution that is in the greater quantity; from the Latin *solvere*, which means "to loosen, dissolve" (p. 500).

specific heat quantity of heat needed to raise one gram of a substance one degree Celsius; from the Latin *species*, meaning "species" (p. 535).

spectator ion ion that is present but does not participate in a reaction; from the Latin *spectare* and the Greek *ienai*, meaning "to watch" and "to go" (p. 510).

spontaneous quality of reactions that occur under specific conditions without assistance; from the Latin *sponte*, meaning "freely" (p. 554).

spontaneous decay condition in which alpha and beta emissions occur naturally; from the Latin *sponte*, "freely" (p. 303).

standard enthalpy of formation amount of energy involved in the change of each substance in the formation of a compound; from the Greek *en-* + *thalpein*, meaning "in + to heat" (p. 548).

standard pressure average pressure of air at sea level; from the Latin *pressare*, meaning "to press" (p. 199).

sterol lipid with four carbon rings (p. 777).

stoichiometry study of the amount of substances produced and consumed in chemical reactions; from the Greek *stoicheion* and *metrein*, meaning "element" and "to measure" (p. 165).

STP abbreviation for standard temperature and pressure (p. 231).

straight-chain simplest hydrocarbon molecule, consisting of single linear chain of carbon atoms with hydrogens bonded (pp. 741–752).

strong acid acid that has high concentration of hydronium ions; from the Latin *acere*, meaning "to be sour" (p. 642).

structural isomer one of the compounds that have the same molecular formula but a different structure; from the Latin *struere*, meaning "to build" (p. 746).

sublimation process by which a solid changes into a gas; from the Latin *sub-* + *limen*, meaning "under + threshold" (p. 480).

submicroscopic on an invisible level; term used to describe properties of matter; from the Latin *sub-* + Greek *mikro-* + *skopos,* meaning "under + small + watcher, review" (p. 23).

subscript number used in chemical formula to represent a ratio of two or more parts of the same element; from the Latin *subscribere,* meaning "to write beneath" (p. 55).

substitution organic chemistry reaction in which a hydrogen atom is replaced by another atom or group of atoms; from the Latin *substituere,* meaning "to put in place of" (p. 759).

supersaturated condition that exists when a solution contains more solute than usual at a given temperature; from the Latin *super-* + *saturare,* meaning "over, above + to saturate" (p. 506).

surface tension property of a liquid's surface to act like a weak, elastic skin (p. 484).

surroundings everything outside the system, as in thermochemistry (p. 544).

synthesis combination of two or more substances to form a compound; from the Greek *syntithenai,* meaning "to put together" (p. 97).

system specific part of the universe, as contrasted to surroundings; from the Greek *synistanai,* meaning "to combine" (p. 544).

T

temperature measure of heat, the average kinetic energy of particles; from the Latin *temperatura,* meaning "mixture" (p. 533).

tetrahedral molecule four-faced molecule; from the Greek *tetra-* + *hedra* and Latin *moles,* meaning "four- + faces" and "mass" (p. 454).

theoretical yield amount of product predicted to be formed on the basis of a balanced equation; from the Greek *theōrein,* meaning "to look at" (p. 180).

theory explanation based on hypothesis that has been tested many times and predicts future events; from the Greek *theōrein,* meaning "to look at" (p. 7).

thermochemistry study of heat transfers that accompany chemical reactions, from the Greek *thermē* + Latin *alchymia,* meaning "hot" + "alchemy" (p. 544).

thymine nitrogenous base having a single organic ring structure attached to the sugar of each nucleotide in DNA (pp. 782–783).

titration process to determine equivalent amounts of reactants in a solution (p. 649).

tracer radioisotope used for tracking (p. 308).

transition metal any of the elements in Groups 3B to 2B on the periodic table that has valence electrons in two shells instead of only one; from the Latin *transire* and *metallum,* meaning "to go across" and "mine, metal" (pp. 365, 401).

transmutation transformation of one element into another; from the Latin *transmutare,* meaning "to change" (p. 305).

transuranium element synthesized element, that is, one that does not exist in nature; from the Latin *trans-* and *elementum,* meaning "across" and "element" (p. 306).

triglyceride a lipid formed by the attachment of three carboxylic or fatty acids to one molecule of glycerol; from the Latin *tri-,* meaning "three" (p. 775).

trigonal planar molecule planar molecule with three atoms at the corners of a triangle and the central atom in the middle; from the Greek *trigonos* and Latin *planum* and *moles,* meaning "triangle" and "plane" and "mass" (p. 453).

trigonal pyramidal molecule three-sided, pyramid-shaped molecule; from the Greek *trigonos* and Latin *moles,* meaning "triangle" and "mass" (p. 454).

triple bond bond in which two atoms share three pairs of electrons (p. 446).

U

unbranched *See* straight-chain.

unsaturated condition that exists when a solution is able to dissolve more solute; from the Latin *un-* + *saturare,* meaning "not + to saturate" (pp. 504, 742).

unit cell smallest blocklike unit from which a larger crystal can be built; from the Latin *unus* and *cella,* meaning "one" and "small room" (p. 488).

universal gas constant constant of proportionality in the equation of state of an ideal gas; from the Latin *universum* and *chaos* and *constare,* meaning "universe" and "space" and "to stand firm" (p. 230).

uracil pyrimidine found in RNA (p. 783).

V

vacuum a space devoid (empty) of matter; from the Latin *vacare,* meaning "to be empty" (p. 198).

valence electrons electrons in the outermost orbitals, often involved in chemical bonding; from the Latin *valēre,* meaning "to be strong" (p. 371).

valence shell electron pair repulsion (VSEPR) model used to predict the shape, or geometry, of simple molecules; from the Latin *valēre* and the Greek *elektron* and Latin *repellere,* meaning "to be strong" and "amber" and "to drive back" (p. 452).

vapor gaseous form of a substance that exists as a liquid or a solid under normal conditions of temperature and pressure; from the Latin *vapor,* meaning "vapor, steam" (p. 476).

vapor pressure partial pressure of vapor above a liquid; from the Latin *vapor* and *pressare,* meaning "vapor, steam" and "to press" (p. 478).

vapor-liquid equilibrium relationship between a liquid and its vapor phase for a partially vaporized compound or mixture at specified conditions of pressure and temperature; from the Latin *vapor* and *liquēre* and *aequi-* + *libra,* meaning "steam, vapor" and "to be fluid" and "equal + weight, balance" (p. 606).

volatile description of liquids that readily evaporate at room temperature; from the Latin *volare,* meaning "to fly" (p. 478).

voltaic cell electrochemical cells in which the redox reaction occurs simultaneously; named after the Italian physicist, Alessandro Volta (p. 688).

voltage measure of the tendency of electrons to flow; named after the Italian physicist, Alessandro Volta (p. 691).

volume property that indicates space an object occupies and determined by multiplying area by height; from the Latin *volumen,* meaning "roll or scroll" (p. 15).

W

wavelength distance between similar points in a set of waves, e.g., crest to crest or trough to trough (p. 330).

weak acid acid that has low concentration of hydronium ions; from the Latin *acere,* meaning "to be sour" (p. 643).

Index

Credits

Illustrations by Morgan Cain:

iii, iv, vi, vii, viii, xiii, xiv, xvi, xvii, xxii, xxiii, 15, 18, 20, 21, 28, 29, 41, 42, 44, 47, 48, 49, 54, 88, 90, 92, 94, 95, 103, 111, 112, 116, 119, 133, 138, 144, 159, 162, 175, 195, 196, 198, 200, 202, 203, 206, 207, 208, 209, 213, 214, 215, 221, 230, 242, 248, 252, 253, 264, 265, 266, 267, 269, 270, 273, 274, 277, 278, 279, 282, 283, 303, 312, 314, 315, 318, 323, 330, 331, 335, 341, 344, 345, 346, 351, 352, 362, 371, 379, 380, 381, 383, 394, 396, 403, 405, 406, 407, 409, 411, 414, 415, 416, 417, 418, 429, 433, 436, 437, 439, 441, 452, 453, 454, 455, 456, 459, 460, 472, 474, 475, 477, 478, 479, 481, 486, 487, 489, 490, 497, 501, 502, 503, 506, 510, 539, 540, 546, 551, 555, 556, 559, 568, 569, 571, 572, 576, 580, 584, 585, 586, 604, 606, 623, 624, 639, 643, 654, 655, 656, 661, 662, 681, 689, 691, 692, 697, 700, 742, 743, 755, 774, 776, 779, 781, 782, 783, 784, 787, 788, 790, 793.

Photo Research by Sue McDermott

Photo Credits

Front Matter and Table of Contents:
Title page: Francisco Chanes (Custom Medical Stock Photo). P. iii: Ken O'Donoghue/C. D.C. Heath. P. iv: t, Gary Milburn (Tom Stack & Associates); b, E. R. Degginger. P. v: l, Ken O'Donoghue/C. D.C. Heath.; tr, Michal Heron; br, Ken O'Donoghue/C. D.C. Heath. P. vi: l & r, Ed Braverman. P. vii: Lawrence Berkeley Laboratory (Photo Researchers, Inc.). P. viii: t, Alfred Pasieka (Photo Researchers, Inc.); b, Mike & Carol Wemer (Comstock, Inc.). P,. ix: t, Dr. Joel M. Hawkins/University of California, Berkeley; mr, Ned McCormick/C. D.C. Heath; bl, Smithsonian Institution, Photo #77-14194; br, Michael Manheim (The Stock Market). P. x: t, Dr. Paul Fagan, Dupont; m, Science Source (Photo Researchers, Inc.), b, Jan Halaska (Photo Researchers, Inc.). P. xi: t, Runk/Schoenberger (Grant Heilman Photography); m, E. R. Degginger; b, NASA (Photo Researchers, Inc.). P. xii: t, Richard Megna (Fundamental Photographs); m, Bjorn Bolstad (Peter Arnold, Inc.); b, Peter Menzel. P. xiii: t, Ned McCormick/C. D.C. Heath; b, Ken O'Donoghue/C. D.C. Heath. P. xiv: t & b, Comstock, Inc. P. xv: tl, Dave Umberger, University News Service, Perdue University; tr, Myron Wood (Photo Researchers, Inc.); mr, Runk/Schoenberger (Grant Heilman Photography): b, Dr. Jeremy Burgess (Photo Researchers, Inc.). P. xvi: t, Francisco Chanes (Custom Medical Stock Photo); m, Comstock, Inc.; b, NASA-Goddard SFC (Peter Arnold, Inc); P. xvii: Comstock, Inc. P. xviii: Comstock, Inc.. P. xix: Ken O'Donoghue/C. D.C. Heath. P. xx: Ken O'Donoghue/C. D.C. Heath. P. xxi: Nancy Sheehan/C. D.C. Heath. xxiv: Francisco Chanes (Custom Medical Stock Photo).

Chapter 1: P. 2: Steve Weber (Stock Imagery). P. 4: l, Junebug Clark (Photo Researchers, Inc.); r, Bill Leatherman/C. D.C. Heath. P 5: t, Comstock; b, Standard Scholarship. P. 6: tl, Chemical Design Ltd. (Photo Researchers, Inc.); bl, Richard Megna (Fundamental Photographs); tr & br, Comstock, Inc. P. 8: l, Ken O'Donoghue/C. D.C. Heath; r, NIH (Photo Researchers, Inc.). P. 9: l & r, National Bureau of Standards. P. 11: l, Ken O'Donoghue/C. D.C. Heath; r, David Madison. P. 14: l, John Bird; r, Ken O'Donoghue/C. D.C. Heath; P. 16: t, Mike & Carol Wemer (Comstock); b, Leroy Sanchez/C. D.C. Heath. PP. 19–26: Ken O'Donoghue/C. D.C. Heath. P. 28: E. R. Degginger.

Chapter 2: P. 38: Gary Milburn (Tom Stack & Associates). PP. 40–43: Ken O'Donoghue/C. D.C. Heath. P. 49: Charles Falco (Photo Researchers, Inc.). PP. 51–52: c, E. R. Degginger; b, E. R. Degginger (Bruce Coleman, Inc.). P. 53: t, Day Williams (Photo Researchers, Inc.); b, Ron Watts (First Light Associated Photographers). P 59: Ken O'Donoghue/C. D.C. Heath. P. 68: l & r, Philippe Plailly (Photo Researchers, Inc.). P. 78: Ned McCormick/C. D.C. Heath. P. 79: Nancy Sheehan/C. D.C. Heath. P. 80: Richard Megna (Fundamental Photographs).

Chapter 3: P. 82: l, Frank P. Rossotto (The Stock Market); m & r, Charles D. Winters. P. 83: Ken Levine (Allsport). P. 84: Jim Gund (Allsport). P. 85: Nancy Sheehan/C. D.C. Heath. P. 87: NASA. P. 89: Ken O'Donoghue/C. D.C. Heath. P. 97: Blair Seitz (Photo Researchers, Inc.). P. 98: l & r, Ken O'Donoghue/C. D.C. Heath. P. 99: tl & tr, Ken O'Donoghue/C. D.C. Heath; tm & b, E. R. Degginger. P. 101: Tom Myers (Photo Researchers, Inc.). P. 102: Charles D. Winters. P. 104: t & b: National Draeger, Inc. PP. 105–107: Ken O'Donoghue/C. D.C. Heath. P. 108: l & r, Charles D. Winters.

Chapter 4: P. 120: Michal Heron. p. 122: Alex MacLean (Landslides). P. 123: t, Roy Morsch (The Stock Market); r, Steve Elmore (The Stock Market). PP. 124–129: Ken O'Donoghue/C. D.C. Heath. P. 132: l, Phil Degginger; r, Fred Ward (First Light Associated Photographers). P. 137: Michael Gross (Allsport). P. 140: Ken O'Donoghue/C. D.C. Heath. P. 142: t & b, Courtesy of Dow Chemical Company. P. 150: t & b, E. R. Degginger. P. 151: Ken O'Donoghue/C. D.C. Heath.

Chapter 5: P. 160: Ned McCormick/C. D.C. Heath. P. 163: Ken O'Donoghue/C. D.C. Heath. P. 167: Coleman Outdoor Products. PP. 171–177: Ken O'Donoghue/C. D.C. Heath. P. 180: Courtesy of Binney & Smith. P. 183: t & b, Susan Doheny/C. D.C. Heath. P. 190: Gordon Wiltsie (Peter Arnold, Inc.). P. 191: Ben Barnhart.

Chapter 6: Dick Davis (Photo Researchers, Inc.). P. 194: Larry White (LGI). P. 197: Ken O'Donoghue/C. D.C. Heath. P. 200: Bob Daemmrich (The Image Works). P. 205: Ruth Dixon.

Chapter 7: P. 228: Ed Braverman. PP. 235–237: Ken O'Donoghue/C. D.C. Heath. P. 239: t, Larry LeFever (Grant Heilman Photography); b, Gary Truman/C. D.C. Heath. P. 240: Philippe Plailly (Photo Researchers, Inc.). P. 247: Ed Braverman. P. 252: Ken O'Donoghue/C. D.C. Heath.

Chapter 8: P. 262: Lawrence Berkeley Laboratory (Photo Researchers, Inc.). P. 265: David Kukla. P. 276: The Bettmann Archive. P. 283: t, Ken Straiton (First Light Associated Photographers); b, James Prince (Photo Researchers, Inc.).

839

Chapter 9: P. 292: Founders Society Detroit Institute of Arts. P. 295: l, Virginia Carleton (Photo Researchers, Inc.); r, Pastner (FPG). P. 296: Bob Abraham (The Stock Market). P. 305: l, Ken O'Donoghue/C. D.C. Heath; r, Derby Art Gallery. P. 306: Courtesy of Lawrence Berkeley Laboratory. P. 309: Peticolas/Megna (Fundamental Photographs). P. 310: SIU (Custom Medical Stock Photos). P. 311: l, Brookhaven National Laboratory; r, Larry Mulvehill (Photo Researchers, Inc.). P. 313: FPG. P. 315: Princeton University, Plasma Physics Laboratory. P. 316: Ken Sherman (Phototake). P. 317: Battelle, Pacific Northwest Laboratories. P. 326: Ed Wheeler (The Stock Market). P. 327:David Joel (Tony Stone Worldwide).

Chapter 10: P. 328: Richard Megna (Fundamental Photographs). P. 332: David Parker (Photo Researchers, Inc.). P. 334: l & r: Ken O'Donoghue/C. D.C. Heath. P. 337: Education Development Center. P. 338: l, Tom Pantages; r, adapted by permission from C. W. Keenan, D.C. Kleinfelder, and J.H. Wood, *General College Chemistry*, Sixth Edition, Harper and Row Publishers, Inc. P. 342: Alfred Pasieka (Photo Researchers, Inc.). P. 344: NASA (Peter Arnold, Inc.).

Chapter 11: P. 360: Lee Boltin Picture Library. P. 365: Ken O'Donoghue/C. D.C. Heath. P. 369: t & bottom: Susan Doheny/C. D.C. Heath. P. 373: t, Chuck O'Rear (West Light); b, Ronald Sheridan (Ancient Art & Architecture). P. 374: Ken O'Donoghue/C. D.C. Heath. P. 382: Ned McCormick/C. D.C. Heath.

Chapter 12: P. 392: Lee Boltin Picture Library. P. 395: Richard Megna (Fundamental Photographs). P. 398: Ken O'Donoghue/C. D.C. Heath. P. 399: l, Sutton (FPG); r, Gerard Photography. P. 402: Richard Megna (Fundamental Photographs). P.403: Ken O'Donoghue/C. D.C Heath. P. 406: Frank Wing (Stock Boston). P. 407: t, Grant Heilman (Grant Heilman Photography; b, Carl Frank (Photo Researchers, Inc.). P. 408: Lester V. Bergman. P. 409: Michael Manheim (The Stock Market). P. 411: Paul Silverman (Fundamental Photographs). 412: Photri. P. 414: l & r, E. R. Degginger. P. 415–417: Runk/Schoenberger (Grant Heilman Photography). P. 420: t, E. R. Degginger;, m, Richard Megna (Fundamental Photographs); r, E. R. Degginger. P. 421: Smithsonian Institution, Photo # 77-14194. P. 428: Joe Towers (George Hall/Check Six).

Chapter 13: P. 430: Science Source (Photo Researchers, Inc.). P. 451–454: Ken O'Donoghue/C. D.C. Heath. P. 458: m, Dr. Paul Fagan/Dupont, r, Dr. Joel M. Hawkins/University of California, Berkeley

Chapter 14: P. 468: Jan Halaska (Photo Researchers, Inc.). P. 471: t, Larry Lee (West Light); r, Len Rue Jr. (Photo Researchers, Inc.). P. 480: Ken O'Donoghue/C. D.C. Heath. P. 483: l, The Bettmann Archive, ml, the Bettmann Archive; mr, Black Pioneers of Science and Invention by Louis Haber, New York Harcourt, Brace and World, 1970 r, Historical Pictures Service. P. 484: Herman Eisenbeiss (Photo Researchers, Inc.). PP. 485–488: Ken O'Donoghue/C. D.C. Heath. P. 489: l & r, Brian Parker (Tom Stack & Associates). P. 491: Stan Ries (Leo de Wys, Inc.).

Chapter 15: P. 498: Runk Schoenberger (Grant Heilman Photography). P. 500–507: Ken O'Donoghue/C. D.C. Heath. P. 508: Excavation of the Metropolitan Museum of Art 1919–20; Rogers Fund supplemented by contribution of Edward S. Harkness (20.3.6) C. 1976/79 By The Metropolitan Museum of Art. P. 509: Ken O'Donoghue/C. D C. Heath. P. 514: Julie Habel (West Light). P. 530: Dan McCoy (Rainbow). P. 531: Hank Andrews (Visuals Unlimited).

Chapter 16: P. 532: Yoav Levy (Phototake). P. 534: t, Nancy Sheehan/C. D.C. Heath; b, Erik Anderson. P. 535: t, Ken O'Donoghue/C. D.C. Heath; b, NASA (Photo Researchers, Inc.). P. 537: Gabe Palmer (The Stock Market). P. 543: Susan Doheny/C. D.C. Heath. P. 544: E. R. Degginger. PP 545–546: Ken O'Donoghue/C. D.C. Heath. P. 552: Maratea (International Stock Photo). P. 554: David Woods (The Stock Market). P. 555: Ken O'Donoghue/C. D.C. Heath.

Chapter 17: P. 566: A. Copley (Visuals Unlimited). PP. 572–581: Ken O'Donoghue/C. D.C. Heath. P. 583: Richard Pasley (Stock Boston). PP.: 596–597: Ned McCormick/C. D.C. Heath.

Chapter 18: P. 598: Treat Davidson (Photo Researchers, Inc.). P. 600: Ken O'Donoghue/C. D.C. Heath. P. 602: t, Zig Leszczynski (Animals, Animals); b, Peter Menzel. P. 603: Ken O'Donoghue/C. D.C. Heath. P. 608: l & r, Susan Doheny/C. D.C. Heath. p. 611: Joseph A. Dichello. P. 616: Bjorn Borstad (Peter Arnold, Inc.). PP. 619–622: Ken O'Donoghue/C. D.C. Heath. P. 632: Vince Streano (The Stock Market). P. 633: t & b, NASA-Goddard CFS (Peter Arnold, Inc.).

Chapter 19: P. 634: Ned McCormick/C. D.C. Heath. PP. 636–649: Ken O'Donoghue/C. D.C. Heath. P. 653: l, Jim Strawser (Grant Heilman Photography); r, Ken O'Donoghue/C. D.C. Heath. PP: 660–666: Ken O'Donoghue/C. D.C. Heath. P. 676: Maurice & Sally Landre (Photo Researchers, Inc.). P. 677: Will McIntyre (Photo Researchers, Inc.).

Chapter 20: P. 678: Bill Gallery (Stock Boston). P. 680: l & r, Ken O'Donoghue/C. D.C. Heath. P. 687: T. J. Florian (Rainbow). P. 688: Richard B. Levine. PP. 694–701: Ken O'Donoghue/C. D.C. Heath. P. 703: Karen Preuss (The Image Works).

Chapter 21: P.P. 710–718: Ken O'Donoghue/C. D.C. Heath. P. 719: Nancy Sheehan/C. D.C. Heath. P. 721: l, Nancy Sheehan/C. D.C. Heath; r, Courtesy of the Hach Company. P. 722: Susan Doheny/C. D.C. Heath. PP. 723–725: Ken O'Donoghue/C. D.C. Heath. P. 731: t, Bob Daemmrich (The Image Works); b, Larry LeFever (Grant Heilman Photography).

Chapter 22: P. 738: Bruce Roberts (Photo Researchers, Inc.). P. 740: Courtesy of Department of Library Services, American Museum of Natural History. P 744: Adrian Atwater (Shostal Associates). P. 748: Donald Clegg. P. 751: David Halpern (Photo Researchers, Inc.). P. 757: Ken O'Donoghue/C. D.C. Heath. P. 761: Phil Degginger. P. 763: John Henebry/C. D.C. Heath.

Chapter 23: P. 772: LeFever/Grushow (Grant Heilman Photography). P. 775: t, Runk/Schoenberger (Grant Heilman Photography; b, Biophoto Associates (Photo Researchers, Inc.). P. 779: Richard Price (West Light). P. 780: Ned McCormick/C. D.C. Heath. P. 781: Dr. Jeremy Burgess (Photo Researchers, Inc.). P. 782: Richard Feldman, National Institutes of Health. P. 785: Dave Umberger, University News Service, Perdue University. P. 786: Myron Wood (Photo Researchers, Inc.). P. 795: Dave B. Fleetham (Visuals Unlimited). P. 797: Susan Doheny/C. D.C. Heath. P. 804: Ken O'Donoghue/C. D.C. Heath. P. 805: Julie Houck (Tony Stone Worldwide).

Laboratory Investigations: Francisco Chanes (Custom Medical Stock Photo).

Problem Solving Strategies: Comstock, Inc.

840

(continued from Chapter 4, Part 1 Review, on page T135)

   c. $2(1.0 \text{ g}) + 32.1 \text{ g} + 4(16.0 \text{ g})$
     $= 98.1 \text{ g}$

   d. $12.0 \text{ g} + 2(32.1 \text{ g}) = 76.2 \text{ g}$

B 21. a. $39.1 \text{ g} + 54.9 \text{ g} + 4(16.0 \text{ g})$
     $= 158.0 \text{ g}$

   b. $54.9 \text{ g} + 2(16.0 \text{ g}) = 86.9 \text{ g}$

   c. $3(40.1 \text{ g}) + 2(31.0 \text{ g}) + 8(16.0 \text{ g})$
     $= 310.3 \text{ g}$

C 22. $\dfrac{56 \text{ g}}{76.2 \text{ g}}$ of CS_2 per mol $= 0.73$ mol

B 23. A mole is defined as the number of atoms in exactly 12 grams of carbon-12. Titanium atoms have a mass nearly four times greater than carbon atoms. It would take four times as much mass of titanium (48 grams) to contain Avogadro's number of atoms. The molar mass of titanium is 48 grams.

(continued from Chapter 5, Part 2 Review, on page T183)

D 25. $Pb(NO_3)_2 + 2NaCl \rightarrow$
                  $2NaNO_3 + PbCl_2$

   a. $15.50 \text{ g } Pb(NO_3)_2$

    $\times \dfrac{1 \text{ mol } Pb(NO_3)_2}{331 \text{ g } Pb(NO_3)_2} \times \dfrac{2 \text{ mol NaCl}}{1 \text{ mol } Pb(NO_3)_2}$

    $\times \dfrac{58.44 \text{ g NaCl}}{1 \text{ mol NaCl}}$

    $= 5.47 \text{ g NaCl required}$

   Only 3.81 g NaCl are present. Therefore $Pb(NO_3)_2$ is in excess and the limiting reactant is NaCl.

   b. $3.81 \text{ g NaCl} \times \dfrac{1 \text{ mol NaCl}}{58.44 \text{ g NaCl}}$

    $\times \dfrac{1 \text{ mol } Pb(NO_3)_2}{2 \text{ mol NaCl}} \times \dfrac{331.2 \text{ g } Pb(NO_3)_2}{1 \text{ mol } Pb(NO_3)_2}$

    $= 10.80 \text{ g } Pb(NO_3)_2$

   The amount of $Pb(NO_3)_2$ in excess is $15.50 - 10.80 = 4.70 \text{ g}$ $Pb(NO_3)_2$.

   c. $3.81 \text{ g NaCl} \times \dfrac{1 \text{ mol NaCl}}{58.44 \text{ g NaCl}}$

    $\times \dfrac{1 \text{ mol } PbCl_2}{2 \text{ mol NaCl}} \times \dfrac{278.1 \text{ g } PbCl_2}{1 \text{ mol } PbCl_2}$

    $= 9.06 \text{ g } PbCl_2$

   The limiting reactant, NaCl, is used to calculate the mass of $PbCl_2$.

E 26. $Fe + 2HCl \rightarrow H_2 + FeCl_2$

   $6.57 \text{ g Fe} \times \dfrac{1 \text{ mol Fe}}{55.85 \text{ g Fe}}$

   $\times \dfrac{1 \text{ mol } FeCl_2}{1 \text{ mol Fe}} \times \dfrac{126.8 \text{ g } FeCl_2}{1 \text{ mol } FeCl_2}$

   $= 14.93 \text{ g } FeCl_2$

   theoretical yield

   % yield $= \dfrac{14.63 \text{ g}}{14.93 \text{ g}} \times 100 = 98.0\%$

(continued from Chapter 5 Review, on page T189b)

   b.

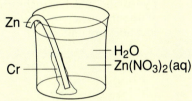

   c. $425 \text{ cm}^3 \text{ } Cr(NO_3)_3$

    $\times \dfrac{0.25 \text{ mol } Cr(NO_3)_3}{1000 \text{ cm}^3 \text{ } Cr(NO_3)_3}$

    $\times \dfrac{2 \text{ mol Cr}}{2 \text{ mol } Cr(NO_3)_3} \times \dfrac{52 \text{ g Cr}}{1 \text{ mol Cr}}$

    $= 5.5 \text{ g Cr}$

(continued from Chapter 14, Part 3 Review, page T487)

H 17. When ice freezes, it expands. If water seeps into a crack in the roadway, it will push the paving material apart when it freezes. When the ice thaws, the loosened paving material is no longer bonded to the adjacent pavement.

(continued from Chapter 19, Part 3 Review, on page T667)

This buffer works because CH_3COOH can react with any added base, whereas CH_3COO^- can react with any added acid.

I 42. a. $HCl + HPO_4^{2-} \rightarrow$
                $Cl^- + H_2PO_4^-$

   b. $OH^- + H_2PO_4^- \rightarrow$
                $H_2O + HPO_4^{2-}$

(continued from Chapter 20, Part 2 Review, on page T699)

E 20. a. ampere $=$ coulomb/second

   b. Since one coulomb is 1.04×10^{-5} mol e^-, then one coulomb is $6.26 \times 10^{18} \text{ } e^-$. Then, for a one amp current there are $6.26 \times 10^{18} \text{ } e^-$ per second

   c.

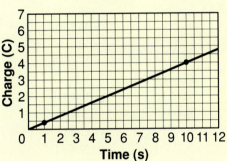

   d. $0.40 \text{ amp} \times 10 \text{ sec} = 4.0$ Coulombs

   e. $4C \times 6.26 \times 10^{18} \text{ } e^-/C = 2.50 \times 10^{19} \text{ } e^-$.

   f. From current and time you can calculate coulombs, and coulombs can be easily converted to electrons as seen in answer 20b.

D 21. The aluminum spoon will be oxidized and the Fe^{2+} ions will be reduced to iron metal.

D 22. There will be no spontaneous reaction.

D 23. No, the container will dissolve. The cell potential for the oxidation of nickel metal and the reduction of Fe^{3+} ions to Fe^{2+} ions is positive.

E 24. $E° = 0.30$ volts

(continued from Chapter 21, Part 1 Review, on page T721)

$$2K^+(aq) + CO_3{}^{2-}(aq) + Co^{2+}(aq)$$
$$+ SO_4{}^{2-}(aq) \rightarrow CoCO_3(s)$$
$$+ 2K^+(aq) + SO_4{}^{2-}(aq)$$
$$Ba^{2+}(aq) + 2Cl^-(aq) + Co^{2+}(aq)$$
$$+ SO_4{}^{2-}(aq) \rightarrow BaSO_4(s) +$$
$$Co^{2+}(aq) + 2Cl^-(aq)$$

A 11. $Pb^{2+}(aq) + 2Cl^-(aq) \rightarrow PbCl_2(s)$
$Pb^{2+}(aq) + 2I^-(aq) \rightarrow PbI_2(s)$
$Pb^{2+}(aq) + 2Cl^-(aq) \rightarrow PbCl_2(s)$
$Pb^{2+}(aq) + SO_4{}^{-2}(aq) \rightarrow PbSO_4(s)$
$Pb^{2+}(aq) + CO_3{}^{2-}(aq) \rightarrow PbCO_3(s)$
$Pb^{2+}(aq) + 2OH^-(aq) \rightarrow Pb(OH)_2(s)$
$Pb^{2+}(aq) + 2Cl^-(aq) \rightarrow PbCl_2(s)$
$Pb^{2+}(aq) + SO_4{}^{2-}(aq) \rightarrow PbSO_4(s)$
$Ba^{2+}(aq) + SO_4{}^{2-}(aq) \rightarrow BaSO_4(s)$
$Cu^{2+}(aq) + CO_3{}^{2-}(aq) \rightarrow CuCO_3(s)$
$Cu^{2+}(aq) + 2OH^-(aq) \rightarrow Cu(OH)_2(s)$
$Ni^{2+}(aq) + 2OH^-(aq) \rightarrow Ni(OH)_2(s)$
$Ba^{2+}(aq) + 2OH^-(aq) \rightarrow Ba(OH)_2(s)$
$Co^{2+}(aq) + 2OH^-(aq) \rightarrow Co(OH)_2(s)$
$Ni^{2+}(aq) + CO_3{}^{2-}(aq) \rightarrow NiCO_3(s)$
$Ba^{2+}(aq) + CO_3{}^{2-}(aq) \rightarrow BaCO_3(s)$
$Co^{2+}(aq) + CO_3{}^{2-}(aq) \rightarrow CoCO_3(s)$
$Ba^{2+}(aq) + SO_4{}^{2-}(aq) \rightarrow BaSO_4(s)$

B 12. Yes. All other combinations of ions form soluble substances.

B 13.

insoluble	soluble
$NiCO_3$	BaI_2
$PbCl_2$	KI
PbI_2	Na_2SO_4
$PbSO_4$	HI
$PbCO_3$	K_2CO_3
$Pb(OH)_2$	NH_4I
$Ba(OH)_2$	$CuSO_4$
$Ni(OH)_2$	$NaOH$
$CuCO_3$	HCl
$Co(OH)_2$	$BaCl_2$
$Cu(OH)_2$	$Pb(NO_3)_2$
$CoCO_3$	NiI_2
	CoI_2
	$NaCl$
	KNO_3
	$CoSO_4$
	K_2SO_4
	H_2SO_4

B 14. Most lead compounds are insoluble. Hydroxides are usually insoluble. Most ammonium compounds are soluble.

C 15. Step 1. Add $HCl(aq)$—bubbles given off, x = K_2CO_3, white ppt, x = $Pb(NO_3)_2$, hot reaction, x = NaOH.
Step 2. Add NaOH—hot reaction, x = HCl,
ammonia odor, x = NH_4I,
green ppt, x = $NiCl_2$,
red ppt, x = $CoSO_4$,
blue ppt, x = $CuSO_4$,
white ppt, x = $Pb(NO_3)_2$.
Step 3. Add $CoSO_4$—
white ppt, x = $Pb(NO_3)_2$, or $BaCl_2$
Step 4. Add HCl—
white ppt, x = $Pb(NO_3)_2$,
no reaction, x = $BaCl_2$.
If no reaction with HCl, NaOH, or $CoSO_4$, x = KNO_3.

C 16. Carbon dioxide is produced. $2K^+(aq)$
$+ CO_3{}^{2-}(aq) + 2H^+(aq)$
$+ 2Cl^-(aq) \rightarrow H_2O + CO_2(g)$
$+ 2K^+(aq) + 2Cl^-(aq)$

B 17. Solution A must be lead(II) nitrate. No other reagent forms a precipitate with HCl, which is solution B or C.

B 18. Solutions B and C must be sodium hydroxide and hydrochloric acid. Without further tests, their exact identities are unknown.

T843